PSYCHOPATHOLOGICAL DISORDERS OF CHILDHOOD

3
EDITION

PSYCHOPATHOLOGICAL DISORDERS OF CHILDHOOD

EDITED BY
HERBERT C. QUAY
University of Miami

JOHN S. WERRY
University of Auckland School of Medicine

JOHN WILEY & SONS

New York   Chichester   Brisbane   Toronto   Singapore

Copyright © 1972, 1979, 1986, by John Wiley & Sons, Inc.

All rights reserved. Published simultaneously in Canada.

Reproduction or translation of any part of
this work beyond that permitted by Sections
107 and 108 of the 1976 United States Copyright
Act without the permission of the copyright
owner is unlawful. Requests for permission
or further information should be addressed to
the Permissions Department, John Wiley & Sons.

Library of Congress Cataloging in Publication Data:

Psychopathological disorders of childhood.

    Includes bibliographies and indexes.
      1. Child psychopathology.   2. Child psychotherapy.
I. Quay, Herbert C. (Herbert Callister), 1927–
II. Werry, John S.   [DNLM: 1. Psychopathology—in
infancy & childhood.   WS 350 P97]
RJ499.Q32   1986   618.92′89   86–11105
ISBN 0–471-88974-1

Printed in the United States of America

10 9 8 7 6 5 4 3 2 1

PREFACE
TO THE THIRD EDITION

The considerable difference in the organization of this third edition as compared to earlier editions is a function of the continuing expansion of knowledge in the field of child psychopathology. Accumulated information as to the characteristics, correlates, and consequences of the major "broad-band" disorders necessitated that these disorders be discussed in separate chapters. Thus, data from epidemiological and follow-up studies previously considered in separate chapters have been incorporated into these chapters.

While efficacy data remain scarce, a chapter in psychotherapies has been added which reviews the extant literature and highlights research problems in the area as well. The chapter on community interventions is entirely new and has been expanded to deal with prevention as well. A new chapter on social and ecological factors in childhood disorders has also been added. Only the chapter on residential treatment remains much as it was in the second edition; very little has happened in this area in recent years.

Our original focus on critical review of the research literature continues. Fortunately, the quality of research, as well as its quantity, continues to improve. Case descriptions and uncontrolled "research" are fading from the scientific scene as well they should.

Finally, research into the role which biological factors may play in all disorders is clearly on the upswing and is likely to come even more to the fore in the late 1980s.

Herbert C. Quay

John S. Werry

CONTRIBUTORS

Herbert C. Quay, Ph.D., Department of Psychology, University of Miami

John S. Werry, M.D., Department of Psychiatry, Auckland University School of Medicine

Susan B. Campbell, Ph.D., Department of Psychology, University of Pittsburgh

Jeanne M. Devany, Ph.D., Department of Psychology, Auburn University

David P. Farrington, Ph.D., Institute of Criminology, Cambridge University

Rachel Gittelman, Ph.D., New York State Psychiatric Institute and Columbia University

E. Mavis Hetherington, Ph.D., Department of Psychology, University of Virginia

Suzanne B. Johnson, Ph.D., Department of Psychiatry, University of Florida

Andres Kanner, M.D., College of Physicians and Surgeons, Columbia University

Kenneth A. Kavale, Ph.D., Division of Special Education, University of Iowa

Maria Kovacs, Ph.D., Department of Psychiatry, University of Pittsburgh

Annette M. La Greca, Ph.D., Department of Psychology, University of Iowa

Donald L. MacMillan, School of Education, University of California, Riverside

Barclay Martin, Ph.D., Department of Psychology, University of North Carolina, Chapel Hill

Rosemery O. Nelson, Ph.D., Department of Psychology, University of North Carolina, Greensboro

K. Daniel O'Leary, Ph.D., Department of Psychology, State University of New York, Stony Brook

Stana Paulauskas, Ph.D., Western Psychiatric Institute and Clinic, University of Pittsburgh

Lizette Peterson, Ph.D., Department of Psychology, University of Missouri-Columbia

Margot Prior, Ph.D., Department of Psychology, La Trobe University

Michael C. Roberts, Ph.D., Department of Psychology, University of Alabama

TABLE OF CONTENTS

CHAPTER 1   Classification   HERBERT C. QUAY   1

CHAPTER 2   Conduct Disorders   HERBERT C. QUAY   35

CHAPTER 3   Disorders of Anxiety, Withdrawal, and Dysphoria   HERBERT C. QUAY and
              ANNETTE M. La GRECA   73

CHAPTER 4   Attention Deficit Disorder (Hyperactivity)   SUSAN B. CAMPBELL and
              JOHN S. WERRY   111

CHAPTER 5   Autism, Schizophrenia and Allied Disorders   MARGOT PRIOR and
              JOHN S. WERRY   156

CHAPTER 6   Organic and Substance Use Disorders   JOHN S. WERRY   211

CHAPTER 7   Physical Illness, Symptoms and Allied Disorders   JOHN S. WERRY   232

CHAPTER 8   Biological Factors   JOHN S. WERRY   294

CHAPTER 9   Family Factors and Psychopathology in Children   E. MAVIS HETHERINGTON
              and BARCLAY MARTIN   332

CHAPTER 10   The Sociocultural Context of Childhood Disorders   DAVID P. FARRINGTON   391

CHAPTER 11   Assessment and Assessment of Change   K. DANIEL O'LEARY and
              SUZANNE B. JOHNSON   423

CHAPTER 12   Psychopharmacotherapy   RACHEL GITTELMAN and ANDRES KANNER   455

CHAPTER 13   The Traditional Psychotherapies   MARIA KOVACS and STANA PAULAUSKAS   496

CHAPTER 14   Behavioral Approaches to Treatment   JEANNE M. DEVANY and
              ROSEMERY O. NELSON   523

CHAPTER 15   Residential Treatment   HERBERT C. QUAY   558

CHAPTER 16   Educational Intervention   DONALD L. MACMILLAN and KENNETH A. KAVALE   583

CHAPTER 17   Community Intervention and Prevention   LIZETTE PETERSON and
              MICHAEL C. ROBERTS   622

              Author Index   661

              Subject Index   681

1 CLASSIFICATION

HERBERT C. QUAY

INTRODUCTION

Scientific understanding is, in large measure, the ability to describe precisely the functional relations between entities or events. The ability to set apart such entities or events from one another and to describe their properties in terms of observable phenomena is a precursor to understanding the relations between them. In abnormal psychology, the entities (disorders) that need to be understood in terms of their etiologies, responses to differing forms of treatment, and prognoses have not been easy to describe. The complexities and dynamic nature (especially in children) of human behavior and the crude state of our observational techniques have all contributed to the difficulty of describing (and measuring) those disorders that must form the essential elements of a science of childhood psychopathology.

Furthermore, the need for a classification of disorders as well as the process of classification of children has often come under attack. Since there has historically been little agreement as to what disorders in fact exist and perhaps even less agreement on the utility of diagnosis, the whole enterprise has sometimes been considered to be of doubtful utility if not actually damaging to children. There has, however, been a marked resurgence of interest in the classification of psychopathological disorders in both adults and children in the last decade and an increasing recognition of the need for a taxonomy of disorders.

Blashfield (1984) has enumerated the following purposes that can be served by a good classification system: (1) It may provide a *nomenclature* necessary for communication among people working in the field—a basic set of terms is needed to describe the various disorders of concern. (2) It may also furnish a basis for *description and information retrieval*. Knowing that a child has a certain disorder should tell one about the likely symptoms, prognosis, and best treatment. We must note, however, that the descriptions and the information retrieved are almost always less than ideal in both quantity and quality as regards psychopathological disorders. (3) A good

1

classification system may also provide a basis for making *predictions*. Knowing that a child has a particular disorder should enable us to predict that he or she should have other concomitant behavioral features, perhaps as yet unobserved, and is likely to manifest certain forms of behavior in the future. Again, we note that our predictive ability falls far short of perfection in the case of most disorders of childhood and adolescence. (4) Finally, and in our view most importantly, a system of classification can provide the basic concepts for *theory formation* about etiology, pathology, prognosis, and response to treatment. We cannot research disorders that we cannot describe and set apart from other disorders. As we noted above, we can never arrive at a scientific understanding of any specific disorder until we can describe it accurately and determine how it is different from other disorders.

Historically, there have been two competing points of view in regard to the classification of psychopathological disorders. The "class or categorical model" common in pathology holds that the disorder is either present or absent; it cannot vary in amount, and all, or nearly all, symptoms must be present before the disorder itself can be considered to be present. This view also holds that disorders are mutually exclusive; a person cannot be both psychotic and neurotic at the same time. On the other hand, the "quantitative model" conceives of a disorder as a group of symptoms with the number of symptoms present being the measure of the intensity of the disorder. This model assumes that symptoms form a dimension or continuum of disorder and that all individuals have a place on this dimension; that is, all persons possess the disorder to a lesser or greater degree. This quantitative or dimensions model also recognizes that, since the basic dimensions are independent, an individual can have, at the same time, features, to a greater or lesser degree, of more than one disorder. (See Blashfield, 1984; Lorr, 1961.)

CRITERIA FOR EVALUATING A CLASSIFICATION SYSTEM

The degree to which a classification, or taxonomic, system of behavioral abnormality will serve those purposes just described is a function of the extent to which it satisfies the criteria by which any system for the classification of behavior must be evaluated. First and foremost, those features said to constitute the category or the continuum must be clearly described and operationally defined. Then it must be demonstrated that those features exist as a cluster of covarying characteristics, observable with regularity in one or more situations by one or more methods of observation. Without the reasonably objective definition of those characteristics delimiting the patterns and without empirical demonstration that they generally occur in company with one another, the stage is set for the system to fail on most of the remaining criteria.

Another critical requisite is reliability. The assignment of an individual to a discrete category or to a place on a continuous dimension must be reasonably consistent. Agreement should occur between different ways of measuring the disorder or between clinicians viewing the individual at the same time. Assignment of the individual to a category or a relative position on a dimension should also be stable over reasonable time intervals. Since reliability sets a ceiling on validity, questions about reliability are extremely critical for any classification system.

An additional important criterion is validity. This is a complex concept and can be assessed in different ways. At the very least, however, the patterns should be discriminable from one another and should demonstrate coherent relationships with variables other than those initially used to define them. Validity will finally determine the extent to which the system can adequately serve those functions of nomenclature, information retrieval, description, prediction, and theory building.

There are three other criteria that, while not so crucial, are nevertheless of concern. Completeness is a factor to be considered. A system of describing child psychopathology should not consistently be embarrassed by the occurrence of clearly pathological children who do not fit any of the existing patterns. At the same time, parsimony is equally desirable. Whereas the ultimate in completeness may be a system in which a multitude of subgroups are defined by a single symptom or characteristic, the best classification system should have no more subcategories than are necessary to produce maximum reliability and validity.

Finally, as nearly as possible, the patterns should be mutually exclusive. Ideally, cases should be assignable to one category only. While the complex nature of human behavior sometimes may make one wonder about the feasibility of assigning an individual to one and only one subgroup, multiple assignments obviously lessen the degree of orderliness that classification initially seeks to enhance.

CLINICALLY DERIVED CLASSIFICATION SYSTEMS

Historically, diagnostic categories have evolved out of the observations of clinicians working with disordered individuals on a day-to-day basis where the immediate requirements have seldom permitted systematic investigation. The clinician notices the regularity with which certain characteristics apparently occur together and conceptually "abstracts these out" as comprising a diagnostic entity. These various entities then gain some degree of consensual validation, again in the clinical setting, and subsequently become codified into a classification system. One of the more persistent difficulties is that the development of these clinically derived systems is essentially hypothesis formation, and few such systems have escaped the direct transmutation of hypothesis into accepted dogma. Usually it is authority, not proof, that is the benchmark.

DSM-III

The most widely used classification system for psychopathological disorders in North America is set forth in the *Diagnostic and Statistical Manual,* third edition (DSM-III), published by the American Psychiatric Association in

1982. This system is the "official" one in the United States and its categories are used for reporting of disorders to government health agencies, for categorizing the mentally ill in various official reports, for other administrative purposes, as well as for treatment and research. In addition to providing descriptions and diagnostic criteria for major syndromes (Axis I) and minor (Personality and Specific Developmental) disorders (Axis II), the system also provides for listing of information as to concomitant physical disorders (Axis III), associated stresses (Axis IV), and premorbid level of functioning (Axis V).

As a classification system for psychopathological disorders of childhood, we are most concerned with the categories of Axis I of that section of DSM-III devoted to "Disorders usually first evident in infancy, childhood, or adolescence" (pp. 35–99).

We note here that criticism of this section of DSM-III is not new; there was considerable published criticism even before the final version appeared in print (e.g., Garmezy, 1978; Schact & Nathan, 1977; Zubin, 1978). These early critiques dealt with a variety of issues including whether or not the various syndromes constituted mental disorders and/or medical conditions, the issue of medical control of diagnosis and treatment, and the effects of labeling. Most of these concerns were subsequently discussed by Rutter and Shaffer (1980) in the context of a much broader critique of the published version (see also Achenbach, 1980). Millon (1983) has responded to many of the criticisms raised. While these issues may be relevant to both the clinical and administrative uses of DSM-III, as may a host of problems associated with Axes II, III, IV, and V (see Garmezy, 1978; Rutter & Shaffer, 1980), the critical scientific question, and our major concern, has to do with the adequacy of Axis I DSM-III as a taxonomy of psychopathology in childhood and adolescence.

An analysis of the childhood and adolescence section of DSM-III as a classification system for childhood disorder is complicated by the fact that any of the adult disorders may also be used to diagnose children and adolescents. Thus, while no disorder of depression appears in this section, depression in children may be diagnosed using any one of the adult depressive disorders.

Table 1.1 sets out the major disorders (disorders with physical manifestations excluded) and provides a very brief listing of major characteristics associated with each. A more detailed description of many of the disorders will be found in later chapters. We will return to a detailed evaluation of DSM-III after a brief discussion of two other clinically derived systems.

WHO Multiaxial Classification

Another clinical approach to classification has been developed for the World Health Organization (Rutter et al., 1969; Rutter, Shaffer, & Shepherd, 1975). This system also looks upon the process of diagnosis as involving not only classification with regard to the nature of the disorder itself but

TABLE 1.1 *Major Diagnostic Categories of Axis I of DSM-III (Descriptions Abridged)*

Attention Deficit Disorder

Attention Deficit Disorder with Hyperactivity

Developmentally inappropriate inattention, impulsivity, hyperactivity

Attention Deficit Disorder without Hyperactivity

Developmentally inappropriate inattention, impulsivity but without gross motor overactivity

Conduct Disorder

Conduct Disorder, Undersocialized, Aggressive

Physical violence, thefts outside the home, failure to establish normal affective bonds

Conduct Disorder, Undersocialized, Nonaggressive

Chronic violation of rules, running away, lying, stealing, failure to establish normal affective bonds

Conduct Disorder, Socialized, Aggressive

Physical violence, thefts outside the home, evidence of social attachment

Conduct Disorder, Socialized, Nonaggressive

Chronic rule violations, running away, lying, stealing, evidence of social attachment

Anxiety Disorders of Childhood

Separation Anxiety Disorder

Excessive anxiety on separation from major attachment figures or familiar surroundings

Avoidant Disorder of Childhood or Adolescence

Persistent and excessive shrinking from social contact with strangers interfering with social functioning

Overanxious Disorder

Excessive worrying and fearful behavior not focused on a specific situation or objection

Other Disorders of Infancy, Childhood, or Adolescence

Reactive Attachment Disorder of Infancy

Poor emotional and physical development due to inadequate caretaking

Schizoid Disorder of Childhood or Adolescence

Defect in capacity to form social relationships, very limited peer relations

Elective Mutism

Continuous refusal to speak despite ability to speak and comprehend

Oppositional Disorder

Disobedient, negative, and provocative opposition to authority figures

Identity Disorders

Uncertainty about goals, career, friendships, sexual orientation and behavior

Pervasive Developmental Disorder

Infantile Autism

Lack of responsiveness to others, gross impairment in communication skills, bizarre responses to environment, developing before 30 months of age

Childhood Onset Pervasive Developmental Disorder

Profound disturbance in social relations and multiple oddities of behavior developing after 30 months but before 12 years with regard to the associated intellectual level, biological factors, and associated or etiological psychosocial influences.

Excluding psychotic disorders, this system recognizes eight major categories and eight subcategories of specific developmental disorders that are seen as true psychopathological disorders rather than deviations from normal development as in DSM-III; this system also recognizes categories of psychosomatic disorder and personality disorder and a set of other clinical syndromes that include confusional states, tics, and anorexia nervosa. Here the three categories of greatest interest are Hyperkinetic Syndrome (a subcategory of Specific Developmental Disorders), Conduct Disorder, and Neurotic Disorder; brief descriptions of these are also provided in Table 1.2.

It is interesting to note that this system recognizes that legally delinquent behavior may arise "naturally" out of a cultural milieu and, thus, may not necessarily be abnormal; in fact, there is no equivalent category to the two socialized conduct disorders of DSM-III.

The WHO system is also the only approach that does not try to differentiate disorders of anxiety, dysphoria, and social withdrawal into subcategories with the recognition that: "Most neurotic disorders in children are less differentiated than are neuroses in adults, and even when disorders could be specified as some particular subvariety of neurosis, it was uncertain whether this subdivision had much clinical meaning or much predictive value" (Rutter et al., 1969, p. 47).

International Classification of Diseases (ICD-9)

Although this system does not, on principle, provide for different classifications for different age-groups, there are provisions for disorders that occur only at particular age periods. The ICD-9 provides for five categories (excluding a category of psychosis with origin specific to childhood, which is found in the adult section) of disorders relevant to children and adolescents. There are nine subtypes of neurotic disorders that are described similarly for adults, children, and adolescents, eight special symptoms or syndromes including most of the disorders listed under the specific developmental disor-

TABLE 1.2 *Major Diagnostic Categories of the World Health Organization Classification System (Descriptions Abridged)*

Hyperkinetic Syndrome
Poorly organized and poorly regulated extreme overactivity, distractibility, short attention span and impulsiveness, mood fluctuations and aggression

Neurotic Disorder
Includes states of disproportionate anxiety and depression, obsessions, compulsions, phobias, hypochondriasis, and "conversion hysteria"

Conduct Disorder
Includes some types of legally disturbed delinquency and nondelinquent disorders of conduct (e.g., fighting, bullying, destructive behavior, cruelty to animals). The behavior must be abnormal in its sociocultural context.

ders (Axis II) of DSM-III, and nine adjustment reactions of a transient nature. There are also three categories, Disturbance of Conduct, Disturbance of Emotions Specific to Childhood and Adolescence, and Hyperkinetic Syndrome of Childhood, that are of greater interest here and are listed and briefly described in Table 1.3.

The Common Elements   By and large, all of the major clinical approaches provide for separate categories covering attention-deficit (or hyperkinetic), undersocialized aggressive, socialized aggressive, and anxiety-withdrawal-dysphoria disorders.

TABLE 1.3   *Major Diagnostic Categories of ICD-9 (Descriptions Abridged)*

Hyperkinetic Syndrome of Childhood

Simple Disturbance of Activity and Attention

Short attention span, distractibility, overactivity without conduct disturbance

Hyperkinesis with Developmental Delay

Hyperkinesis associated with speech delay, clumsiness, delay in academic skills

Hyperkinetic-conduct Disorder

Hyperkinesis associated with conduct disturbance but not developmental delay

Disturbance of Emotions Specific to Childhood and Adolescence

With Anxiety and Fearfulness

May include school refusal, elective mutism

With Misery and Unhappiness

May include eating and sleep disturbance

With Sensitivity, Shyness, and Social Withdrawal

Relationship Problems

May include sibling jealousy

Other or Mixed

Unspecified

Disturbance of Conduct Not Elsewhere Classified

Unsocialized Disturbance of Conduct

Defiance, disobedience, quarrelsomeness, aggression, destructive behavior, tantrums, solitary stealing, lying, teasing sibling

Socialized Disturbance of Conduct

Holds values of delinquent peer groups to whom they are loyal; stealing, truancy, staying out late at night

Compulsive-conduct Disorder

Disorders specifically compulsive in nature, kleptomania

Mixed Disturbance of Conduct and Emotions

Behaviors of either unsocialized or socialized conduct disorders but with considerable emotional disturbance, anxiety, misery, or obsessive neurotic delinquency

With regard to "hyperactivity," DSM-III places emphasis on the attention deficit and subdivides according to whether or not hyperactivity is an accompanying feature. The WHO system considers hyperkinesis as a separate subcategory of developmental disorders, whereas ICD-9 recognizes three separate hyperkinetic syndromes. There is clearly little agreement among these approaches as to the categorization of attentional deficits and motor overactivity.

There is some agreement in regard to the separateness of undersocialized and socialized conduct disorder, though DSM-III recognizes unaggressive subtypes of both, and ICD-9 provides for both compulsive and neurotic forms of conduct disturbance.

With respect to anxiety, dysphoria, and social withdrawal, DSM-III provides for two subcategories involving anxiety and one involving shyness, while ICD-9 differentiates between disorders involving anxiety and fear, misery and unhappiness, and shyness and social withdrawal. The success with which a syndrome involving anxiety, social withdrawal, and dysphoric mood can be empirically differentiated into three, or even two, subcategories is not at all certain, as will be indicated later in this chapter.

An additional comparison of the various features of DSM-III and ICD-9 may be found in Werry (1985). Finally, mention may be made of two other clinically derived approaches, that of the Group for the Advancement of Psychiatry (1966), which has been superseded by DSM-III, and the California I-level System (see Sullivan, Grant, & Grant, 1957; Warren, 1969), which has been limited in its applicability to juvenile delinquents (see Chapter 15).

MULTIVARIATE STATISTICAL APPROACHES TO CLASSIFICATION

Those espousing a quantitative view of behavior disorders have approached the problem of classification in a way that has obviated many of the difficulties associated with the clinical method. This approach utilizes statistical techniques that isolate interrelated patterns of behavior; it was first used by Ackerson (1942) and Hewitt and Jenkins (1946), who analyzed case histories of problem children for the conjoint appearance of certain behavioral characteristics. Although their methodology was unsophisticated by today's standards, the findings of Hewitt and Jenkins (1946), the more definitive of the two early investigations, have been generally supported by later research.

These investigators began with a pool of 500 case records of children who had been referred to a Chicago child guidance clinic for some behavioral problem. They noted the presence or absence of 45 behaviors in each of the case records and then calculated the joint occurrence of each. A further analysis of the intercorrelations among the behavior traits was then performed by visual inspection. The purpose of this analysis was to determine those traits that occurred together, thus forming clusters or syndromes of deviant behavior. Three primary behavioral syndromes were identified and were labeled the unsocialized aggressive, the socialized delinquent, and the overinhibited child.

Fifty-two children were classified as unsocialized aggressive, 70 as socialized delinquent, and 73 as overinhibited. The number of multiple classifications was small but, as these figures reveal, only about two-fifths of the 500 children could be designated as representative of any of the three major syndromes. This failure to be able to classify over three-fifths of the sample illustrates a problem that arises when one uses behavior dimensions as if they were discrete categories—a problem that will be discussed in greater detail later in this chapter. Nonetheless, Hewitt and Jenkins (1946) were successful in establishing that a variety of problem behaviors were subsumable by only three patterns—one of behavioral inhibition, anxiety, and withdrawal, and two of differing forms of aggression.

A much later study by Peterson (1961), which has served as a model for much additional work, is an excellent illustration of the use of a more sophisticated methodology. Peterson began by carefully considering the need for an adequate sampling of the many behaviors of children that could be considered deviant. This sampling was an important step, since behavior traits not included obviously could not appear in any patterns that might be isolated. Over 400 representatively selected case folders from the files of a child guidance clinic were inspected, and the referral problems of each child were noted. Eliminating overlap and selecting on the basis of relatively frequent occurrence, 58 items descriptive of deviant behavior were chosen and compiled into a checklist. A sample of 831 grammar school students in kindergarten through sixth grade were then rated by their teachers on this problem checklist.

The intercorrelations among all the items were obtained and this matrix of intercorrelations was subjected to further study by means of factor analysis. This statistical technique enables one to isolate clusters of behaviors (or other variables) that are interrelated and thus form a coherent behavioral dimension. A factor loading, which is a numerical expression equivalent to a correlation, reveals the extent to which a particular behavior is related to the dimension.

Peterson's (1961) results indicated that the interrelations among the 58 items could be resolved into two independent clusters, which he called "conduct" problem and "personality" problem. Thus, Peterson demonstrated that the vast majority of problem behaviors in public school students could be accounted for by two major dimensions: essentially one of aggression and one of withdrawal. Furthermore, each child could be placed somewhere on these two dimensions according to the number of problem behaviors related to the dimension that the child manifested. It is important to note that in this instance children differ in quantity but not in quality; the normal and abnormal differ only in degree.

Advantages and Disadvantages of Statistical Approaches

In the building of a classification system, the statistical approach clearly obviates two of the basic weaknesses characteristic of the clinical approach. First, empirical evidence is obtained showing that the dimension in fact exists as an observable constellation of behavior. Second, as will be discussed later in this chapter, the relatively objective nature of most of the constituent behaviors utilized in the statistical analyses permits reliable measurement of the degree to which a child manifests the dimension.

This approach is not, however, without pitfalls of its own. One criticism, which has been applied to the technique of factor analysis in general, is that "If something does not go into the analysis, it cannot come out." This simply means that a dimension not represented by its constituent behavior traits in the analysis cannot possibly emerge from the analysis. Neither can a dimension be identified unless there is an intercorrelation of *some* subset of behaviors, since this intercorrelated subset, in fact, constitutes the dimension. Such intercorrelation depends, at least in part, on the sample in which the behaviors are observed. In the Peterson (1961) study, for example, a dimension of behavior that might have been labeled "psychoticism" was not found. There clearly is such a syndrome (see Chapter 5), and its failure to emerge was a function of the fact that there were no behaviors related to it in Peterson's checklist, and there were no children manifesting the syndrome in the samples studied. Clearly, Peterson's method did not permit a dimension of psychoticism to emerge in his analysis. But such problems are by no means fatal to the development of a classification system; those deviant behaviors to be studied can be selected carefully for inclusiveness, and different samples of children can be systematically studied.

An additional criticism of the factor-analytic technique that is sometimes voiced is that the factors that emerge are dimensions of behavior—not types of individuals. This is true and, as we have already pointed out, Peterson's two dimensions are sets of behaviors that all children possess to varying degrees: a child is rarely "all problem" or "no problem."

A somewhat more serious and more complex problem for the establishment of descriptive systems based on multivariate statistical analyses has been the degree to which the methods of data collection and the settings in which the data are collected influence the results. Are the dimensions that result from different methods really the same? Categories arising from the analysis of behavior ratings may or may not be the same as those arising from the analysis of life history data even though they look the same. There is always some possibility that the method may produce the result. Peterson (1965a), for example, has suggested that the interpretive biases of those doing the ratings may be more reflected in the factors arising from behavior ratings than is the actual behavior of those being rated. It is also clear that the situation in which the behavior is observed influences whether the behavior does, in fact, occur. Yet, as Achenbach and Edelbrock (1978) have suggested, determining which ratings are predictive of other important variables is more important than trying to obtain high levels of agreement between raters.

Although it may be necessary to develop a particular method to assess a given behavior dimension as it may be observed in a particular setting (e.g., classroom), this complicates, but in no way invalidates, the meaningfulness of the dimension. It is the relationship of factorially derived dimensions of behavior, however measured, to etiological and treatment variables that give the dimensions psychological relevance. Clearly multivariate statistical approaches, although not without some associated difficulties, are the methods of choice for the construction of a descriptive behavioral taxonomy for disorders of childhood and adolescence. The techniques and results of multivariate studies have been reviewed earlier from somewhat different perspectives by Achenbach and Edelbrock (1978), by Dreger (1982), and by Quay (1979).

The analysis presented here is based on 61 studies spanning almost 40 years in which descriptors of behavior have been analyzed and factor loadings reported. Data have been obtained by behavior ratings, behavior observations, analyses of case histories, peer ratings, and self-reports. Informants have included parents, peers, teachers, child-care workers, corrections personnel, and mental health professionals. Samples have ranged in age from 3 to 18 years, both sexes have been included, and sample sizes in some studies have gone well into the thousands. Subjects have come from normal public school classes, special classes for the behaviorally disordered and learning disabled, retarded, and deaf, and institutions for delinquents, as well as hospitals and clinics.

It is important to recognize that matching the results of the different studies is not, by any means, perfectly straightforward. To determine whether or not one investigator's conduct disorder factor is the same as another's undersocialized aggressive factor, especially when the two contain few of the same variables in common, requires judgment on the part of the reviewer. Such judgment can, of course, be influenced by preconceptions of what ought to be. Since labels vary, the matching of factors from the various studies has been done on the basis of the actual behavior subsumed by the factors and only secondarily on the basis of the factor titles assigned in the original study.

A dimension most reasonably labeled Undersocialized Aggressive Conduct Disorder has emerged almost without exception. As can be seen from Table 1.4, the most frequently (those appearing in one-third or more of studies reviewed) associated behaviors are those generally considered as aggressive, disruptive, and noncompliant. It is of interest to note that both hyperactivity and restlessness frequently appear in this pattern. The association of the *behavior* of "hyperactivity" (not the putative *syndrome*) with this undersocialized aggressive conduct disorder dimension provided some of the evidence against the notion of the independent existence of a syndrome with motor overactivity (rather than attentional problems) as the central characteristic (see Chapter 4). It is also noteworthy that stealing has not been found at all central to this dimension, a finding which stands in contrast to the fact that "theft outside the home involving confrontation with

TABLE 1.4 *Principal Characteristics of Undersocialized Aggressive Conduct Disorder as Derived from Multivariate Statistical Studies*

Characteristics	Studies
Fighting, hitting, assaultive	1,[a] 2, 3, 5, 6, 7, 8, 11, 12, 13, 14, 15, 16, 19, 20, 21, 22, 23, 25, 26, 27, 30, 31, 33, 34, 36, 39, 40, 41, 42, 46, 47, 48, 49, 50, 53, 54, 55, 56, 57, 59, 60 (42)[b]
Disobedient, defiant	1, 2, 3, 5, 7, 8, 9, 10, 13, 16, 17, 18, 19, 20, 21, 22, 23, 25, 26, 27, 29, 30, 31, 33, 34, 37, 38, 41, 42, 45, 47, 48, 49, 50, 51, 52, 53, 54, 57, 61 (40)
Temper tantrums	1, 2, 3, 5, 7, 8, 10, 11, 13, 14, 16, 17, 18, 19, 20, 22, 23, 24, 25, 26, 27, 28, 30, 33, 34, 36, 37, 38, 41, 42, 45, 47, 49, 50, 51, 53, 57, 59, 61 (39)
Destructiveness	1, 3, 4, 6, 7, 8, 10, 12, 13, 14, 17, 19, 23, 25, 26, 27, 30, 31, 33, 34, 36, 37, 38, 39, 40, 41, 42, 47, 49, 50, 51, 55, 57, 59, 61 (35)
Impertinent, "smart," impudent	5, 7, 10, 13, 14, 16, 17, 18, 19, 22, 23, 25, 26, 27, 29, 30, 35, 40, 41, 42, 45, 47, 48, 49, 50, 51, 52, 53, 54, 57, 61 (31)
Uncooperative, resistant, inconsiderate, stubborn	2, 3, 4, 6, 7, 8, 9, 10, 14, 17, 18, 19, 22, 25, 30, 34, 41, 42, 45, 47, 49, 50, 51, 52, 53, 57, 59, 61 (28)
Attention seeking, "show-off"	1, 2, 3, 7, 9, 14, 19, 20, 22, 23, 25, 27, 30, 34, 37, 38, 41, 42, 47, 49, 50, 51, 52, 53, 55, 57 (26)
Dominates, bullies, threatens	2, 3, 4, 5, 6, 8, 11, 12, 13, 16, 20, 24, 25, 26, 31, 34, 36, 37, 38, 39, 45, 52, 54, 55, 58, 60 (26)
Disruptive, interrupts, disturbs others	7, 8, 10, 14, 16, 17, 19, 20, 22, 25, 27, 30, 33, 34, 37, 38, 41, 42, 47, 49, 50, 52, 53, 55, 57, 61 (26)
Boisterous, noisy	2, 3, 7, 12, 14, 19, 20, 22, 25, 26, 30, 36, 37, 38, 41, 42, 45, 47, 49, 50, 51, 52, 53, 55, 57 (25)
Irritability, "blows up" easily	5, 7, 9, 14, 16, 19, 20, 22, 25, 27, 28, 30, 40, 41, 42, 47, 48, 49, 50, 51, 53, 56, 57 (23)
Negative, refuses directions	1, 7, 12, 14, 19, 22, 23, 24, 25, 28, 30, 40, 41, 42, 45, 47, 49, 50, 51, 53, 57, 59 (22)
Restless	7, 11, 19, 20, 22, 23, 26, 30, 34, 40, 41, 42, 47, 49, 50, 51, 52, 53, 54, 55, 57 (21)
Untrustworthy, dishonest, lies	1, 2, 5, 10, 12, 13, 17, 20, 23, 25, 26, 27, 28, 31, 36, 37, 38, 46, 56, 61 (20)
Hyperactivity	1, 3, 7, 19, 20, 22, 23, 25, 30, 36, 40, 41, 42, 49, 50, 51, 53, 57 (18)

[a]Numbers refer to references listed for Tables 1.2–1.11 at the end of the chapter.

[b]Total number of studies in which characteristic was found associated with this dimension is in parentheses.

the victim" is one of the diagnostic criteria for Undersocialized Conduct Disorder in DSM-III (p. 48). As we will see later, stealing is more commonly associated with the Socialized Aggressive Conduct Disorder pattern, which, since that pattern is more likely to be found in older children and adolescents, makes sense from a developmental perspective. This pattern of Undersocialized Aggressive Conduct Disorder has a very firm empirical basis by virtue of its ubiquitous appearance and its well-validated, easily observable characteristics. It will be discussed in detail in Chapter 2.

A second pattern involving "externalizing" (Achenbach, 1966) deviant behavior has less frequently emerged but has been clearly empirically established (see also Loeber & Schmaling, 1985). In this pattern involvement with peers in illegal or at least norm-violating behavior is central. Its characteristics (see Table 1.5), considered from a developmental perspective, suggest that it is mainly a phenomenon of older childhood and adolescence. A label of Socialized Conduct Disorder seems most appropriate. A number of the characteristics found here do reflect evidence of the social attachment that is a part of the DSM-III diagnostic criteria (p. 49) for Conduct Disorder, Socialized, Aggressive but also subsumes a number of the criteria (truancy from home, lying) for Conduct Disorder, Socialized, Nonaggressive. Again, this disorder is discussed in more detail in Chapter 2.

A third syndrome, principally defined by problems in concentration and attention, impulsivity, lack of perseverance, clumsiness, and passivity, has also made a very frequent appearance (see Table 1.6). While "hyperactivity" as a behavior trait has appeared on this dimension, it is by no means central, and behaviors reflective of motor *underactivity* are more frequently associated. While the writer (Quay, 1979) earlier labeled this dimension as Immaturity, Attention Deficit Disorder now seems the most appropriate designation. This disorder is covered in depth in Chapter 4.

TABLE 1.5 *Principal Characteristics of Socialized Aggressive Conduct Disorder as Derived from Multivariate Statistical Studies*

Characteristics	Studies
Has "bad" companions	2,[a] 3, 7, 14, 21, 22, 35, 39, 48, 49 (10)[b]
Truant from school	2, 3, 7, 14, 21, 31, 33, 39 (8)
Truant from home	2, 3, 21, 31, 33, 40 (6)
Steals in company with others	7, 21, 22, 33, 39, 49 (6)
Belongs to a gang	7, 14, 21, 22, 35, 48 (6)
Is loyal to delinquent friends	7, 14, 21, 22, 48 (5)
Stays out late at night	7, 14, 21, 31, 48 (5)
Steals at home	2, 3 (2)
Lies, cheats	2, 3 (2)

[a]Numbers refer to references listed for Tables 1.2–1.11 at the end of the chapter.
[b]Total number of studies in which characteristic was found associated with this dimension is in parentheses.

TABLE 1.6 *Principal Characteristics of Attention Deficit Disorder as Derived from Multivariate Statistical Studies*

Characteristics	Studies
Poor concentration, short attention span, inattentive, distractible	1,[a] 2, 3, 6, 10, 13, 14, 15, 16, 17, 18, 19, 20, 22, 23, 26, 27, 29, 30, 31, 32, 34, 35, 42, 45, 49, 51, 53, 57, 61 (31)[b]
Daydreaming	2, 3, 5, 7, 10, 14, 16, 18, 19, 22, 23, 30, 33, 34, 42, 45, 49, 51, 54, 61 (20)
Clumsy, poor coordination	2, 3, 7, 10, 13, 27, 30, 31, 34, 37, 38, 42, 46, 47, 53, 59, 61 (17)
Preoccupied, stares into space	2, 3, 13, 14, 16, 20, 22, 29, 30, 33, 42, 45, 49, 51, 52, 53 (16)
Passive; lacks initiative, easily led	10, 18, 20, 22, 27, 33, 34, 40, 42, 47, 52, 53, 61 (13)
Fidgety, restless	14, 16, 17, 18, 20, 26, 27, 31, 34, 35, 57, 61 (12)
Fails to finish tasks, lack of perseverance	5, 13, 16, 17, 18, 20, 23, 29, 35, 46, 54 (11)
Sluggish, lazy	7, 22, 26, 30, 33, 42, 45, 49, 53, 57 (10)
Impulsive	2, 3, 17, 18, 23, 27, 29, 31, 32 (9)
Lacks interest, bored	5, 16, 18, 23, 26, 30, 37, 38, 49, 51, 52 (11)
Hyperactive	1, 2, 3, 14, 17, 18, 31, 32 (8)
Drowsy	7, 22, 30, 42, 49, 51, 53 (7)

[a]Numbers refer to references listed for Tables 1.2–1.11 at the end of the chapter.
[b]Total number of studies in which characteristic was found associated with this dimension is in parentheses.

The dimension we have now labeled anxiety-withdrawal-dysphoria is actually the second most frequently appearing cluster. It is defined by internalizing (Achenbach, 1966) types of behavior: anxiety, fearfulness, shyness, sadness, social withdrawal, self-consciousness, and crying (see Table 1.7). This broad-band dimension subsumes the three subtypes of Anxiety Disorder found in DSM-III (see Table 1.1) as well as "childhood depression" and the subtypes of Disturbance of Emotion in ICD-9 (see Table 1.3). More on this disorder will be found in Chapter 3.

There are two additional dimensions whose empirical foundations are not nearly so firm. A dimension we have labeled schizoid-unresponsive has emerged in eight separate analyses in the six different studies noted in Table 1.8. The unresponsiveness in this pattern is *not* limited to peer relations, and it could well represent the extreme of the personality dimension of introversion. As we will suggest later, it may also be the counterpart of the DSM-III category of Schizoid Disorder (see Table 1.1).

In 12 analyses there has appeared a dimension reflecting poor peer relations but *without* accompanying anxiety, depression, or generalized underresponsiveness. This pattern, labeled Social Ineptness in Table 1.9, may simply reflect a limited repertoire of social skills and may not, in fact, need to be considered a psychopathological disorder.

TABLE 1.7 *Principal Characteristics of Anxiety-withdrawal-dysphoria as Derived from Multivariate Studies*

Characteristics	Studies
Anxious, fearful, tense	1,[a] 2, 3, 4, 6, 7, 9, 10, 11, 14, 16, 19, 20, 21, 25, 27, 31, 34, 37, 38, 40, 41, 42, 45, 47, 48, 49, 50, 51, 53, 54, 55, 56, 57, 61 (35)[b]
Shy, timid, bashful	1, 2, 4, 7, 10, 11, 12, 14, 16, 19, 20, 21, 22, 41, 42, 45, 47, 48, 49, 50, 51, 52, 53, 56, 57, 58, 61 (27)
Depressed, sad, disturbed	1, 2, 3, 5, 6, 9, 10, 12, 14, 16, 19, 20, 23, 24, 25, 27, 28, 30, 33, 34, 41, 42, 45, 47, 49, 51, 57 (27)
Hypersensitive, easily hurt	5, 7, 9, 10, 14, 16, 19, 20, 21, 22, 25, 30, 33, 41, 42, 45, 47, 48, 49, 50, 51, 58, 61 (23)
Feels inferior, worthless	2, 3, 7, 14, 19, 22, 25, 30, 33, 41, 42, 47, 49, 50, 51, 52, 53, 55, 57, 58 (20)
Self-conscious, easily embarrassed	1, 2, 3, 7, 14, 19, 22, 23, 30, 41, 42, 45, 47, 49, 50, 51, 52, 53, 55, 57, 58 (21)
Lacks self-confidence	7, 14, 19, 22, 23, 37, 38, 41, 42, 45, 47, 49, 50, 51, 53, 57, 58 (17)
Easily flustered and confused	5, 7, 14, 19, 20, 22, 23, 25, 41, 42, 47, 49, 50, 51, 53, 54 (16)
Cries frequently	1, 2, 3, 6, 11, 22, 23, 30, 31, 35, 41, 49, 57, 58, 61 (15)
Aloof	5, 19, 24, 26, 28, 41, 42, 53, 57 (9)
Worries	2, 3, 25, 31, 34, 54 (6)

[a]Numbers refer to references listed for Tables 1.2–1.11 at the end of the chapter.

[b]Total number of studies in which characteristic was found associated with this dimension is in parentheses.

TABLE 1.8 *Principal Characteristics of Schizoid-unresponsive as Derived from Multivariate Statistical Studies*

Characteristics	Studies
Won't talk	2,[a] 3, 31, 35 (4)[b]
Withdrawn	3, 15, 31, 39 (4)
Shy, timid, bashful	2, 3, 31 (3)
Cold and unresponsive	15, 31, 35 (3)
Lack of interest	15, 31, 35, 39 (4)
Sad	2, 3 (2)
Stares blankly	2, 3 (2)
Confused	2, 3 (2)
Secretive	2, 3 (2)
Likes to be alone	3, 39 (2)

[a]See footnote *a*, Table 1.7.

[b]See footnote *b*, Table 1.7.

TABLE 1.9 *Principal Characteristics of Social Ineptness as Derived from Multivariate Statistical Studies*

Characteristics	Studies
Poor peer relations	2,[a] 3, 13, 16, 17, 20, 28, 31, 39, 55 (10)[b]
Likes to be alone	2, 3, 17, 20, 28, 35, 37, 38 (8)
Is teased, picked on	2, 3, 13, 16, 31, 35 (6)
Prefers younger companions	2, 3, 13, 31, 37, 38, 39 (7)
Shy, timid	3, 16, 31, 37, 38, 39 (6)
Stays with adults, ignored by peers	16, 31, 58 (3)

[a]Numbers refer to references listed for Tables 1.2–1.11 at the end of the chapter.

[b]Total number of studies in which characteristic was found associated with this dimension is in parentheses.

The problems associated with describing childhood psychosis have not readily yielded to clarification by multivariate statistical analysis. Few of the 61 studies reviewed here used descriptors related to thought disorder, delusions, hallucinations, or other psychotic manifestations. As will be pointed out in Chapter 5, psychotic children are rare, and it has been difficult to find them in sufficient quantity for multivariate statistical study. However, 11 studies have identified a dimension in which apparently psychotic forms of behavior were present (see Table 1.10).

Only one study has focused on multivariate analysis of the characteristics of psychotic children (Prior, Boulton, Gajzago, & Perry, 1975); some evidence was found for two separate syndromes distinguishable mainly by age of onset and severity of impairment.

Finally, a very limited number of studies have isolated a dimension wherein behaviors reflecting excess motor activity have appeared unaccompanied by attentional or conduct problems (see Table 1.11). The appearance of this pattern does, as we will see, suggest some utility in distinguishing between Attention Deficit Disorder with and without Hyperactivity (see also Chapter 4 and Lahey, Schaughency, Strauss, & Frame, 1984).

TABLE 1.10 *Principal Characteristics of Psychotic Disorder as Derived from Multivariate Statistical Studies*

Characteristics	Studies
Incoherent	13,[a] 31, 39, 50, 59 (5)[b]
Repetitive speech	13, 31, 50, 59 (4)
Bizarre, odd, peculiar	1, 13, 50, 59 (4)
Visual hallucinations	2, 3, 13, 31 (4)
Auditory hallucinations	2, 3, 31 (3)
Strange ideas, behavior	1, 3 (2)

[a]See footnote *a*, Table 1.9.

[b]See footnote *b*, Table 1.9.

TABLE 1.11 *Principal Characteristics of Motor Overactivity as Derived from Multivariate Statistical Studies*

Characteristics	Studies
Restless, overactive	10,[a] 13, 18, 37, 38, 45 (6)[b]
Excitable, impulsive, can't wait	5, 10, 18, 37, 38 (5)
Squirmy, jittery	18, 37, 38, 45 (4)
Overtalkative	13, 37, 38, 45 (4)
Hums and makes other odd noises	10, 18 (2)

[a]Numbers refer to references listed for Tables 1.2–1.11 at the end of the chapter.

[b]Total number of studies in which characteristic was found associated with this dimension is in parentheses.

It is clear from the ages and sexes of the thousands of children and adolescents that have now been studied that the major broad-band disorders are common to both sexes and, with the possible exception of Socialized Conduct Disorder in very young children, to all ages. This is not to say that separate analyses by age and sex may not reveal—at least in the particular samples studied, with the particular items used, and with particular analytic methods—more narrow-band dimensions that may be age and sex specific (e.g., Achenbach & Edelbrock, 1983). What is certain, however, is that the prevalence of most childhood and adolescent disorders (see Eme, 1979, and Links, 1983, as well as Chapters 2–4), defined either categorically or quantitatively, varies with sex.

CROSS-CULTURAL GENERALITY

The majority of the multivariate studies just reviewed have been carried out with children (both white and black) in the cultural mainstream of the United States and in the United Kingdom. The question naturally arises as to whether these dimensions are culturally bound or may be found in diverse cultures.

There is now considerable evidence for the generality of both the Undersocialized Conduct Disorder and the Anxiety-Withdrawal-Dysphoria pattern both in culturally distinct groups in the United States and in other countries of the world. Within the United States these two dimensions have emerged very clearly in studies of Hawaiian-American adolescents (Gordon & Gallimore, 1972), American Indian adolescents (O'Donnell & Cress, 1975), and Mexican-American elementary (Touliatos & Lindholm, 1976) and preschool (O'Donnell, Stein, Machabanski, & Cress, 1982) aged children.

In other English-speaking countries both patterns have been found, often in more than one study in England (Collins, Maxwell, & Cameron, 1962; Herbert, 1974), Australia (Glow, 1978a, 1978b), and New Zealand (Aman, Werry, Fitzpatrick, Lowe, & Waters, 1983). Both have also emerged in studies in Sicily (Peterson, 1965b), Greece, Iran, and Finland (Quay & Paraskevopoulos, 1972), Japan (Hayashi, Toyama, & Quay, 1976; Kobayashi, Mizu-shima, & Shinohara, 1967), Taiwan (Yang, 1981), Mauritius (Venables et al., 1983), and Sweden (Bergman & Magnusson, 1984a, 1984b).

The Socialized Aggressive dimension has appeared much less often, perhaps due in part to the failure of investigators to use relevant groups and/or items tapping this syndrome. It has, however, appeared in studies of delinquent and problem children in Japan (Hayashi et al., 1976; Kobayashi et al., 1967) and New Zealand (Aman et al., 1983).

The emergence of a clear-cut Attention Deficit dimension has occurred in studies in Australia (Glow, 1978a, 1978b, 1980), in New Zealand (Aman et al., 1983; McGee, Williams, & Silva, 1985), and in five of nine samples analyzed by Quay and Paraskevopoulos (1972), in Italy (O'Leary, Vivian, & Nisi, 1985), in Mexican-American preschoolers (O'Donnell et al., 1982), and in Sweden (Bergman & Magnusson, 1984a, 1984b).

The generality of the four major patterns across widely varying cultures is striking, suggesting that the biological and environmental factors giving rise to these disorders are in no way limited to Anglo or even Western cultures.

CLINICAL AND STATISTICAL APPROACHES COMPARED

In order to match the disorders of the DSM-III, WHO, and ICD-9 taxonomic systems with dimensions arising out of multivariate statistical studies, the best that can be done is to compare the principal behavioral characteristics of the dimensions to the descriptions and/or diagnostic criteria of the clinically derived systems. We must recognize that any such comparisons are approximate at best.

Empirical comparisons, wherein categorical diagnoses are compared to dimensional scores, are only beginning to appear (e.g., Stein & O'Donnell, 1985). Another approach—to independently select different cases on the basis of clinical diagnosis and on cutoff scores on the relevant dimension and then to compare the two groups on variables of etiologic or prognostic significance—has yet to be tried.

Table 1.12 provides a matching of disorders from the WHO and ICD-9 systems to the major multivariate syndromes we have just considered. Obviously, the three major disorders of the WHO system have been well substantiated by a host of multivariate investigations and we need say no more about them. The major disorders (Hyperkinetic, Disturbance of Emotions, Conduct Disturbance) of ICD-9 are well matched to the empirically derived patterns, but of the narrower categories (see Table 1.3) only the Simple Disturbance of Activity and Attention form of the Hyperkinetic syndrome and the Unsocialized and Socialized subtypes of Disturbance of Conduct have empirical counterparts.

Of greatest interest, of course, is comparison of DSM-III to the replicated dimensions of the multivariate statistical studies (see Table 1.13). It is immediately apparent that there are many more DSM-III *disorders* than there are empirically derived *dimensions*.

TABLE 1.12 *Comparison of Major Categories of WHO and ICD-9 with the Principal Dimensions Emerging from Multivariate Statistical Studies*

WHO	ICD-9	Multivariate
Hyperkinetic Syndrome	Hyperkinetic Syndrome	Attention Deficit Disorder (motor overactivity)
Neurotic Disorder	Disturbance of Emotions specific to childhood and adolescence	Anxiety-Withdrawal-Dysphoria
Conduct Disorder	Disturbance of Conduct not elsewhere classified	
	Undersocialized	Undersocialized Aggressive Conduct Disorder
	Socialized	Socialized Aggressive Conduct Disorder

TABLE 1.13 *Comparison of the Major Categories of DSM-III with the Principal Dimensions Emerging from Multivariate Statistical Studies*

DSM-III	Multivariate
Attention Deficit Disorder	Attention Deficit Disorder
with Hyperactivity	(motor overactivity)
without Hyperactivity	Attention Deficit Disorder
Conduct Disorder	Conduct Disorder(s)
Undersocialized, Aggressive	Undersocialized Aggressive
Undersocialized, Nonaggressive	—
Socialized, Aggressive	Socialized Aggressive
Socialized, Nonaggressive	—
Anxiety Disorder	Anxiety-Withdrawal-Dysphoria
Separation Anxiety Disorder	—
Avoidance Disorder	—
Overanxious Disorder	—
Other Disorders	
Reactive Attachment Disorder	—
Schizoid Disorder	Schizoid-Unresponsive
Elective Mutism	—
Oppositional Disorder	—
Identity Disorder	—
Pervasive Developmental Disorder	Psychotic Disorders
Infantile Autism	(not adequately studied)
Pervasive Developmental Disorder	(not adequately studied)

The major category of Attention Deficit Disorder has a clear counterpart and the differentiation between the subtypes could possibly be made on the basis of the Motor Overactivity dimension. There is ample empirical evidence for the Undersocialized Aggressive and the Socialized Aggressive Conduct Disorders but none for the two Nonaggressive subtypes. The major category of Anxiety Disorder is well substantiated, but the subtypes have not been confirmed. With respect to the other Disorders, only one, Schizoid Disorder, seems to have an empirical counterpart. Pervasive Developmental Disorder as a major category has an empirically derived counterpart, but the separate subtypes as yet do not.

We cannot say, of course, that additional research may not provide support for those DSM-III disorders with no current empirical counterparts. Yet the depth and breadth of the multivariate research currently available makes such a possibility remote at best unless new variables, especially biological ones, can be entered into the basic defining symptomatology.

We will return to the problem of empirical substantiation of the DSM-III and ICD after a consideration of the reliability of these two clinical systems and the multivariate dimensions.

RELIABILITY

As noted earlier, reliability is the *sine qua non* of a classification system. Different clinicians using the categorical system and informants providing the basic data for instruments measuring the dimensions must show reasonable levels of agreement as regards diagnosis in the former case and relative position on a dimension in the latter. Furthermore, there should be reasonable stability of diagnosis and score at least over short-term intervals.

RELIABILITY OF DSM-III AND ICD-9

DSM-III

To their considerable credit, the developers of DSM-III were concerned with interrater reliability and began assessing it even prior to release of the final version of the taxonomy. These efforts were referred to as field trials, and the data may be found in Appendix F of DSM-III (see also Spitzer & Forman, 1979; and Spitzer, Forman, & Nee, 1979).

In these field trials the participating clinicians were volunteers who were asked to evaluate jointly from one to four patients after having had the experience of evaluating at least 15 patients of their own using a draft version of DSM-III. The reliability interviews were generally initial diagnostic evaluations. There were two phases of field trials; in Phase One approximately 60 percent of the assessments were done in separate evaluations, while in Phase Two about 66 percent were done separately. Overall, 84 clinicians participated.

In both phases, degree of agreement was assessed using the Kappa Statistic (Cohen, 1960), which corrects for chance agreement as calculated from the frequency with which a given diagnosis is used by both judges. This correction is important since the frequent use of a particular diagnosis (irrespective of its validity) by two clinicians will increase their degree of agreement over all the cases by a factor related to that frequency. The extreme case would be that in which two clinicians each diagnosed *all* cases as Conduct Disorder, Undersocialized Aggressive, irrespective of the true state of affairs. In this instance agreement would be perfect due to the fact that neither clinician *used* any other category.

The results of both Phase One and Phase Two are given in Table 1.14, which provides both the Kappa value and the percentage of cases in each diagnostic category. A problem that is immediately apparent is that relatively few of the major categories were assessed; no reliabilities were obtained for any of the subtypes of Attention Deficit Disorder, Conduct Disorder, or Anxiety Disorder. An additional difficulty in interpreting the results of the field trials arises from the widely varying number of cases upon which the reliabilities were based. For example, the very dramatic difference (.84 vs. − .01) in the reliability of pervasive Developmental Disorder is quite possibly the result of a *very* few disagreements in Phase One (4 cases rated) vs. very few agreements in Phase Two (only 1 case rated). Only for the broad categories of Conduct Disorder and Attention Deficit Disorder are the actual number of cases likely to provide stable estimates of reliability.

Two subsequent studies (Cantwell, Russell, Mattison, & Will, 1979; Mattison, Cantwell, Russell, & Will, 1979) utilized a different approach. These investigators prepared 24 case histories upon which 20 psychiatrists completed standardized diagnostic questionnaires. Reliability was assessed both by the extent to which the raters agreed with the "expected" diagnosis (the diagnosis considered most appropriate by the researchers) and the extent of agreement among the raters.

Again, many of the diagnostic categories were not represented (see Table 1.14), but the reliability of some of the subtype diagnoses were assessed. The measure of reliability was percentage of agreement, which does not correct for chance agreement and is thus more "liberal" than Kappa. Again, there is wide variation in the obtained reliabilities. Autism was obviously reliably diagnosed by all clinicians, while Conduct Disorder, Undersocialized, Nonaggressive clearly was not. We will return to the problem of such different reliabilities later in this chapter.

Strober, Green, and Carlson (1981) assessed reliability on a series of 95 adolescents consecutively admitted to a hospital. Diagnoses were based on a joint interview using a structured mental-status examination, nursing observation, and referral materials. Kappa was used to calculate degree of agreement. In this study, somewhat more of the subtype categories were used, but the number of patients falling into many of them was very limited (see Table 1.14). Only in the case of the diagnosis of some form of conduct disorder was the sample size sufficient to provide a stable estimate. The Kappa of 1.00 obtained for "other disorders" is based on two cases.

TABLE 1.14 *Interrater Reliabilities of the Major DSM-III Diagnostic Categories*

	Study Field Trials				Cantwell/Mattison		Strober		Werry		From Werry
	Phase One		Phase Two		"Expected" % Agreement	Interrater % Agreement					Mean Weighted Kappa
	K	%	K	%			K	% cases	K	% cases	
Attention Deficit Disorder	.58	15.5	.50	14.6	75	75	-	1	.76	9.2	.68
With hyperactivity									.73	8.2	
Without hyperactivity									.05	1.0	
Conduct Disorder	.61	26.8	.61	38.2			.75	22.1	.53	30.1	.60
Undersocialized, aggressive							.86		.59	8.2	.67
Undersocialized, nonaggressive					30	30	.60		.18	9.2	.32
Socialized, aggressive					70	70			−.04	3.1	
Socialized, nonaggressive									.32	6.2	
Anxiety Disorders	.25	8.5	.44	16.4	15	55	.47	6.3	.67	21.0	.52
Separation									.72	14.4	
Avoidant									.05	2.1	
Overanxious									.65	4.6	
Other Disorders	.79	8.5	.73	9.1			1.00	2.1	.39	24.6	.64
Reactive attachment											
Schizoid									.37	3.6	
Mutism											
Oppositional									.39	20.0	
Identity									.28	1.0	
Pervasive Developmental Disorder	.85	5.6	−.01	1.8	100	100					
Infantile Autism											
Childhood onset											

A much larger number of cases was utilized by Werry, Methven, Fitzpatrick, and Dixon (1983). In their research 195 successive admissions to an inpatient unit in New Zealand were assigned a diagnosis by one or more of six participating clinicians. Diagnoses were made on the basis of a case presentation in the week of the patient's admission to the unit. The presentation was made by a person not involved in assigning the diagnosis, and this person was instructed not to use diagnostic terms during the discussion of the case. Only a single diagnosis, that which was the focus of the admission, was allowed. These investigators utilized many more of the available diagnostic categories, and the obtained reliabilities were usually based on more cases than in the earlier studies (see Table 1.14).

It is of interest that all of these studies have utilized differing methodologies, each of which had facets that might have tended to either increase or decrease the degree of agreement among raters. However, except in a very few instances, degree of agreement in categories common to two or more studies does not differ appreciably.

Werry et al. (1983) also calculated a mean weighted Kappa for the studies reviewed here; these values may also be found in Table 1.14. The reliabilities from all of the studies can be interpreted in a number of ways. For example, Werry et al. concluded that "overall, the system (DSM-III) is of satisfactory reliability and the value of (overall) Kappa obtained (.71) approximates that of other studies which have used this statistic" (p. 345). There is very little meaning to this particular Kappa, however, as no patient was diagnosed as "overall."

An inspection of Table 1.14 leads to a number of conclusions. First of all, despite the efforts of various researchers to date, the reliability of many of the major Axis I diagnostic categories of DSM-III remains insufficiently examined, either because there are no data or because the data came from a single study where sample sizes in many of the diagnostic categories were very small. Thus, nothing can be said about Reactive Attachment Disorder, Elective Mutism, and Childhood Onset Pervasive Developmental Disorder except that these disorders must occur with extremely low prevalence rates.

There is also relatively little to be said about the reliability of Attention Deficit Disorder without Hyperactivity, Socialized Nonaggressive Conduct Disorder, Avoidant Disorder, Schizoid Disorder, Oppositional Disorder, and Identity Disorder except that in the series where these disorders were diagnosed (Werry et al., 1983), the interrater reliability was extremely unsatisfactory.

With respect to categories appearing with greater frequency, the picture is somewhat brighter. The major category of Attention Deficit Disorder, while showing rather poor interrater reliability in both phases of the field trials, was found to be quite reliable in later studies. The subtype with Hyperactivity seems equally reliable. The major category of Conduct Disorder fares reasonably well, as do the Undersocialized, Aggressive and Socialized, Aggressive subtypes. The Undersocialized, Nonaggressive subtype is not diagnosed at all reliably, nor is the Socialized, Nonaggressive, as noted previously.

The major category of Anxiety Disorder is slightly below the level of .60 for the Conduct Disorder. For the subtypes there are few data, but what data are available indicate that only Overanxious Disorder is acceptably reliable. The Other Disorders as a group seem diagnosed with reasonable reliability (overall Kappa of .64). However, data on the subtypes either are lacking or, as noted, reflect serious unreliability.

As a group, the Pervasive Developmental Disorders were, as noted, highly reliable in Phase One of the field trials but totally unreliable in Phase Two. The one case history of Infantile Autism was rated with perfect agreement in both the Cantwell et al. (1979) and Mattison et al. (1979) studies. More work clearly needs to be done in assessing the reliability of the Pervasive Developmental Disorders.

Taking what data are available, it is of interest to compare the reliabilities of those categories for which there was strong confirmation, weaker confirmation, or no confirmation for the multivariate statistical research (see Tables 1.4–1.11).

Attention Deficit Disorder and Conduct Disorder Undersocialized, Aggressive are well established and have satisfactory reliability. The strongly supported Conduct Disorder Socialized, Aggressive fares less well, particularly in the Werry et al. (1983) study, although its prevalence in their series was very low.

Overanxious Disorder, also well documented empirically, was assessed only by Werry et al. (1983), where it was found to be reasonably reliable. While there is good evidence in the empirical literature for at least one, if not two, forms of Psychotic Disorder, the reliability data are too limited to draw any conclusions.

The two disorders that were judged to have much less firm empirical confirmation, Avoidant Disorder and Schizoid Disorder, were reported upon only by Werry et al. (1983), where they were infrequent and unreliable. For those many disorders for which there is an absence of empirical confirmation, there is generally an accompanying absence of reliability. Notable examples here are Conduct Disorder, Undersocialized, Nonaggressive; Oppositional Disorder; and Identity Disorder.

All in all there is, as might be expected, considerable correspondence between empirical confirmation (or lack thereof) of a disorder and its reliability. Thus, the data from those reliability studies reinforce the conclusions drawn from the review of the multivariate studies that DSM-III has far too many unvalidated and unreliable diagnostic categories. Among those categories considered here, there seems little reason to include Undersocialized, Nonaggressive and Socialized, Nonaggressive Conduct Disorder; Avoidant Disorder; Schizoid Disorder; Oppositional Disorder; and Identity Disorder in taxonomy of child and adolescent psychopathology. Other ''lesser'' disorders such as Reactive Attachment Disorder, Separation Anxiety Disorder, and Childhood Onset Pervasive Developmental Disorder are also good candidates for exclusion.

ICD-9

As ICD-9 is the principal "competitor" of DSM-III as a clinically derived taxonomy, its reliability is also of interest. Two recent reports (Gould, Shaffer, & Rutter, 1984; Remschmidt, 1984) are relevant. The British study (Gould et al., 1984) utilized the standardized case history method in which 28 case histories were abstracted from actual case records. Four different groups composed of 13 psychiatrists in each group rated 14 of the cases during a single day's meeting. The authors reported interrater reliabilities (Kappas) on both broad and narrow groupings of disorders. The reliabilities for the broader groupings were as follows: Psychoses Specific to Childhood ($K = .66$), Hyperkinetic Syndrome of Childhood ($K = .63$), Disturbances of Conduct ($K = .48$), Disturbances of Emotions Specific to Childhood and Adolescence ($K = .17$), and Neurotic Disorders ($K = .37$).

The reliabilities for the more narrowly defined disorders were Socialized Conduct Disorders ($K = .49$), Undersocialized ($K = .27$); Disturbance of Emotions with Anxiety and Fearfulness ($K = .06$), with Misery and Unhappiness ($K = .05$), with Sensitivity, Shyness, and Social Withdrawal ($K = .26$), and with Relationship Problems ($K = .09$).

In the German study (Remschmidt, 1984), the same 28 cases were classified by 21 psychiatrists. The measure of agreement R was "based on the measures derived from information theory, redundancy and entropy" (Remschmidt, 1984, p. 12), which has a value of 0 in the case of total nonagreement and 1 in the case of complete agreement of all judges. As reported by Remschmidt (personal communication, September 2, 1984), the reliabilities were Psychoses, .70; Hyperkinetic Syndrome, .77; Disturbances of Conduct, .87; Disturbance of Emotions, .62; and Neurotic Disorders, .79. These figures are, unlike the British study, not corrected for chance agreement and can thus be inflated by the tendency for raters simply to use certain diagnoses more frequently than others (higher base rate).

The results of both studies suggest that, at the broad category level, ICD-9 is no more or less reliable than DSM-III and that the narrower categories, reported only in the British study, are equally unreliable. It is with chagrin that we observe that the very existence of two competing clinically derived classification systems, whose major proponents share a common language and a not terribly dissimilar culture, suggests that the means by which these systems are developed and promulgated permits empirical data to be less influential than it should be.

Finally, we do not know of any research on the stability of DSM-III diagnoses over time. The notion of stability reliability of psychopathological disorders presents some conceptual problems, as will be noted subsequently.

RELIABILITY OF THE DIMENSIONS DERIVED FROM MULTIVARIATE STUDIES

Interrater Reliability

A number of researchers whose interest has primarily been in the investigation of the dimensionality of child and adolescent psychopathology have also developed rating scales for the measurement of the various dimensions as observed by parents, teachers, and others. (See Chapter 11 for more detail on these instruments.)

The Child Behavior Checklist (Achenbach & Edelbrock, 1983) is one of the most thoroughly studied of these rating scales and permits ratings on subscales corresponding to the major dimensions discussed before as well as some more "narrow-band" dimensions. Achenbach and Edelbrock have reported interparent reliabilities on scales apparently measuring Undersocialized and Socialized Conduct Disorder of .72 and .78 on a combined sample of both sexes with ages ranging from 4 to 16 years. Reported reliabilities for Hyperactive were .65; Immature, .69; Social Withdrawal, .58; and Depressed, .54.

The Revised Behavior Problem Checklist, also a factor analytically derived instrument (see Quay, 1983; Quay & Peterson, 1983), contains broadband scales measuring Undersocialized and Socialized Conduct Disorder, Attention Problems, Anxiety-Withdrawal, Psychotic Disorder, and Motor Excess. Interrater reliabilities for teachers of .85, .75, .53, .52, .58, and .58 for these scales have been reported.

The reliabilities reported for scales of these two instruments are comparable and within the range generally reported for behavioral dimensions, normal and abnormal, in children. Unfortunately, one cannot statistically compare the interobserver scale correlations (often artificially lowered by the restricted range of obtained scores) with those obtained on categorical diagnoses. However, the reliabilities for the broader-band scales are all satisfactory, while reliabilities for many subtype diagnoses are clearly not.

Stability

The assessment of stability over time presents a bit of a paradox. As Achenbach and Edelbrock (1983) have noted: "If there were no consistency from one rating period to another, this would cast doubt on the ability of the ratings to capture enduring individual differences. Yet if there were no long term change in ratings of treated children, this would cast doubt on the sensitivity of the ratings to changes that might actually occur" (p. 46).

These authors have reported correlations of ratings by both parents and child care workers on a small ($n = 14$) sample of boys aged 6 to 11 years over a three-week period. The obtained values for the two sets of raters were: Depressed, .69 and .80; Hyperactive, .47 and .78; Aggressive (Undersocialized Conduct Disorder), .69 and .84; Delinquent (Socialized Conduct Disorder), .83 and .51; Schizoid or Anxious, .86 and .51.

Quay and Peterson (1983) have reported two-month stability correlations for teacher ratings of a sample of 149 children. The values were .63 for Undersocialized Conduct Disorder, .49 for Socialized Conduct Disorder, .83 for Attention Problems, .79 for Anxiety-Withdrawal, .61 for Psychotic Behavior, and .63 for Motor Excess. As they noted, (p. 4) the reliabilities for Socialized Aggression and Psychotic Behavior were attenuated by restriction of range. For example, 84 percent of the sample received exactly the same (zero) scores on the Socialized Aggression scale at both ratings.

Thus, data obtained on both scales suggests considerable short-term stability of the major dimensions derived from multivariate statistical analyses.

As we noted early in this chapter, factor analysis, by far the most frequently used statistical technique, results in dimensions, not categories, of disorder. However, there are methods for converting dimensional scores to categorical form. The simplest and most often used approach is to treat cases falling below or above a certain score (usually defined in terms of the mean plus or minus one or more standard deviations) *as if* they represented categories of "disorder absent" or "disorder present." As we will see in later chapters, this is most often done when the researcher wishes to study differences that may characterize groups extreme on one or more dimensions. The obvious problem with this dimension-to-category conversion technique is that the cutoff score is arbitrary, just as when a particular IQ score is used to define mental retardation.

Profile analyses may also be used to categorize individuals based on their score on multiple dimensions. These techniques look for similarities among individuals in the patterns (profiles) of their scores and group persons together who are like each other but different from those with other patterns of scores. The problem here is that the profiles may themselves be defined differently, and arbitrarily, by different techniques and not all cases will clearly fit any profile type.

Thus, while it is easy to think categorically and we can arbitrarily create categories out of dimensions, it seems very likely that with very few possible exceptions (Early Infantile Autism the most likely), the quantitative view of childhood psychopathology is the correct one. The vast majority of disorders are sets of interrcorrelated characteristics, forming statistically homogeneous dimensions upon which every child has some place.

SUMMARY

There are clearly some major areas of agreement among the clinical and statistical approaches to taxonomy. The broader the category of the clinical system, the more likely there is to be a clear statistically derived counterpart. Some clinically derived disorders remain unstudied due to their very low prevalence in children (e.g., Psychotic and Pervasive Developmental Disorders) or to their very circumscribed nature (e.g., Eating Disorders, Obsessive Compulsive Disorders, Stereotyped Movement Disorders).

The evidence is very strong for the existence of the two forms of Conduct Disorder (Undersocialized and Socialized), Attention Deficit Disorder with and without accompanying motor overactivity, and a broad syndrome of

Anxiety-Withdrawal-Dysphoria. These major disorders, considered either categorically or dimensionally, have also proven to have satisfactory reliability.

This chapter has been concerned with the empirical proof and reliability of childhood and adolescent disorders. In later chapters (2 through 7), the correlates, epidemiology, and prognoses for these major, as well as some of the more circumscribed, disorders will be considered in detail.

REFERENCES

Achenbach, T. M. (1966). The classification of children's psychiatric symptoms: A factor analytic study. *Psychological Monographs, 80*, 1–37.

Achenbach, T. M. (1980). DSM-III in light of empirical research on the classification of child psychopathology. *Journal of the American Academy of Child Psychiatry, 3*, 395–412.

Achenbach, T. M., & Edelbrock, C. S. (1978). The classification of child psychopathology: A review and analysis of empirical efforts. *Psychological Bulletin, 85*, 1275–1301.

Achenbach, T. M., and & Edelbrock, C. S. (1983). *Manual for the Child Behavior Checklist and Revised Child Behavior Profile*. Burlington, VT: Queen City Printers.

Ackerson, L. (1942). *Children's behavior problems*. Chicago: University of Chicago Press.

Aman, M. G., Werry, J. S., Fitzpatrick, J., Lowe, M., & Waters, J. (1983). Factor structure and norms for the Revised Behavior Problem Checklist in New Zealand children. *Australian and New Zealand Journal of Psychiatry, 17*, 354–360.

American Psychiatric Association. (1980). *Diagnostic and Statistical Manual of Mental Disorders* (3rd ed). DSM-III. Washington, DC: Authors.

Bergman, L. R., & Magnusson, D. (March 1984a). Patterns of adjustment problems at age 10. An empirical and methodological study. Reports from the Department of Psychology, University of Stockholm. No. 615.

Bergman, L. R., & Magnusson, D. (June 1984b). Patterns of adjustment problems at age 13. An empirical and methodological study. Reports from the Department of Psychology, University of Stockholm. No. 620.

Blashfield, R. K. (1984). *The classification of psychopathology. Neo-Kraepelinian and quantitative approaches*. New York: Plenum.

Cantwell, D. P., Russell, A. T., Mattison, R., & Will, L. (1979). A comparison of DSM-II and DSM-III in the diagnosis of childhood psychiatric disorders. I. Agreement with expected diagnosis. *Archives of General Psychiatry, 36*, 1208–1213.

Cohen, J. (1960). A coefficient of agreement for nominal scales. *Educational and Psychological Measurement, 20*, 37–46.

Collins, L. F., Maxwell, A. E., & Cameron, C. (1962). A factor analysis of some child psychiatric clinic data. *Journal of Mental Science, 108*, 274–285.

Dreger, R. M. (1982). The classification of children and their emotional problems: An overview—II. *Clinical Psychology Review, 2*, 349–385.

Eme, R. F. (1979). Sex differences in childhood psychopathology: A review. *Psychological Bulletin, 86*, 574–595.

Garmezy, N. (1978). Never mind the psychologists: Is it good for the children? *Clinical Psychologist, 31*, 1–6.

Glow, R. A. (1978a). Children's behavior problems: A normative study of a parent rating scale. Unpublished monograph.

Glow, R. A. (1978b). Classroom behavior problems: An Australian normative study of the Conners' Teacher Rating Scale. Unpublished monograph.

Glow, R. A. (1980). A validation of Conners TQ and a cross-cultural comparison of prevalence of hyperactivity in children. In G. D. Burrows & J. S. Werry (Eds.), *Advances in human psychopharmacology* (pp. 303–330), Greenwich, CT: JAI Press.

Gordon, G. P., & Gallimore, R. (1972). Teacher ratings of behavior problems in Hawaiian-American adolescents. *Journal of Cross-Cultural Psychology, 3*, 209–213.

Gould, M. S., Shaffer, D., & Rutter, M. (Sept. 1984). UK/WHO Study of ICD-9. Working paper for NIMH Conference on the definition and measurement of psychopathology in children and adolescents. Washington, DC: NIMH.

Group for the Advancement of Psychiatry. (1966). *Psychopathological disorders in childhood. Theoretical considerations and a proposed classification.* New York: Author.

Hayashi, K., Toyama, B., & Quay, H. C. (1976). A cross cultural study concerned with differential behavioral classification. I. The Behavior Checklist. *Japanese Journal of Criminal Psychology, 2*, 21–28.

Herbert, G. W. (1974). Teachers' ratings of classroom behaviour: Factorial structure. *British Journal of Educational Psychology, 44*, 233–240.

Hewitt, L. E., & Jenkins, R. L. (1946). *Fundamental patterns of maladjustment, the dynamics of their origin.* Springfield, IL: State of Illinois.

Kobayashi, S., Mizushima, K., & Shinohara, M. (1967). Clinical groupings of problem children based on symptoms of behavior. *International Journal of Social Psychiatry, 13*, 206–215.

Lahey, B. B., Shaughency, B. S., Strauss, C. C., & Frame, C. L. (1984). Are attention deficit disorders with and without hyperactivity similar or dissimilar disorders? *Journal of the American Academy of Child Psychiatry, 23*, 302–309.

Links, P. S. (1983). Community surveys of the prevalence of psychiatric disorders: A review. *Child Development, 54*, 531–548.

Loeber, R., & Schmaling, K. B. (1985). Empirical evidence and covert patterns of antisocial conduct problems. *Journal of Abnormal Child Psychology, 12*, 337–352.

Lorr, M. (1961). Classification of the behavior disorders. In P. R. Farnsworth, O. McNemar, & Q. McNemar (Eds.), *Annual Review of Psychology* (pp. 195–216). Palo Alto, CA: Annual Reviews.

Mattison, R., Cantwell, D. P., Russell, A. T., & Will, L. (1979). A comparison of DSM-II and DSM-III in the diagnosis of childhood psychiatric disorders. II. Interrater agreement. *Archives of General Psychiatry, 36*, 1217–1222.

McGee, R., Williams, S., & Silva, P. (1985). Factor structure and correlates of ratings of inattention, hyperactivity, and antisocial behavior in a large sample of 9-

year old children from the general population. *Journal of Clinical and Consulting Psychology, 53*, 480–490.

Millon, T. (1983). The DSM-III: An insider's perspective. *American Psychologist, 38*, 804–814.

O'Donnell, J. P., & Cress, J. N. (1975). Dimensions of behavior problems among Oglala Sioux adolescents. *Journal of Abnormal Psychology, 3*, 163–169.

O'Donnell, J. P., Stein, M. A., Machabanski, H., & Cress, J. N. (1982). Dimensions of problem behavior in Anglo-American and Mexican-American preschool children: A comparative study. *Journal of Consulting and Clinical Psychology, 50*, 643–651.

O'Leary, K. D., Vivian, D., & Nisi, A. (1985). Hyperactivity in Italy. *Journal of Abnormal Child Psychology, 12*, 485–500.

Peterson, D. R. (1961). Behavior problems of middle childhood. *Journal of Consulting Psychology, 25*, 205–209.

Peterson, D. R. (1965a). The scope and generality of verbally defined personality factors. *Psychological Review, 72*, 48–59.

Peterson, D. R. (1965b). Structural congruence and metric variability in a cross-cultural study of children's behavior problems. *Archivo di Psychologia, Neurologia, e Psichiatria, 2*, 174–187.

Prior, M., Boulton, D., Gajzago, C., & Perry, D. (1975). A classification of childhood psychoses by numerical taxonomy. *Journal of Child Psychiatry and Psychology, 16*, 321–330.

Quay, H. C. (1979). Classification. In H. C. Quay & J. S. Werry (Eds.), *Psychopathological disorders of childhood* (2nd ed., pp. 1–42). New York: Wiley.

Quay, H. C. (1983). A dimensional approach to children's behavior disorder: The Revised Behavior Problem Checklist. *School Psychology Review, 12*, 244–249.

Quay, H. C., & Paraskevopoulos, I. N. (1972). *Dimensions of problem behavior in elementary school children in Greece, Iran and Finland*. Paper presented at the XXth International Congress of Psychology, Tokyo, Japan.

Quay, H. C., & Peterson, D. R. (1983). *Interim manual for the revised behavior problem checklist*. Miami, FL: Authors.

Remschmidt, H. (Sept. 1984). UK/WHO study of ICD-9. Working paper for NIMH conference on the definition and measurement of psychopathology in children and adolescents. Washington, DC: NIMH.

Rutter, M., Lebovici, S., Eisenberg, L., Sneznevskij, A. V., Sadoun, R., Brooke, E., & Lin, T.-Y. (1969). A tri-axial classification of mental disorder in childhood. *Journal of Child Psychology and Psychiatry, 10*, 41–61.

Rutter, M., & Shaffer, D. (1980). A step forward or a step backward in terms of the classification of child psychiatric disorders. *Journal of the American Academy of Child Psychiatry, 19*, 371–394.

Rutter, M., Shaffer, D., & Shepherd, M. (1975). *A multi-axial classification of child psychiatric disorders*. Geneva: World Health Organization.

Schact, T., & Nathan, P. E. (1977). But is it good for the psychologists? Appraisal and status of DSM-III. *American Psychologist, 32*, 1015–1025.

Spitzer, R. L., & Forman, J. B. W. (1979). DSM-III field trials: II. Initial experiences with the multiaxial system. *American Journal of Psychiatry, 136*, 818–820.

Spitzer, R. L., Forman, J. B. W., & Nee, J. (1979). DSM-III field trials: I. Initial diagnostic reliability. *American Journal of Psychiatry, 135*, 815–817.

Stein, M. A., & O'Donnell, J. P. (1985). Classification of children's behavior problems: Clinical and quantitative approaches. *Journal of Abnormal Child Psychology, 13*, 269–299.

Strober, M., Green, J., & Carlson, G. (1981). Reliability of psychiatric diagnoses in hospitalized adolescents. Interrater agreement using DSM-III. *Archives of General Psychiatry, 38*, 141–145.

Sullivan, C., Grant, M. Q., & Grant, J. D. (1957). The development of interpersonal maturity: Applications to delinquency. *Psychiatry, 20*, 373–385.

Touliatos, J., & Lindholm, B. W. (1976). Behavior problems of Anglo and Mexican-American children. *Journal of Abnormal Child Psychology, 4*, 299–304.

Venables, P. H., Fletcher, R. P., Dalais, J. C., Mitchell, D. A., Schulsinger, F., & Mednick, S. A. (1983). Factor structure of Rutter's 'Children's Behavior Questionnaire' in a primary school population in a developing country. *Journal of Child Psychology and Psychiatry, 24*, 213–222.

Warren, M. Q. (1969). The case for differential treatment of delinquents. *Annals of the American Academy of Political and Social Science, 381*, 47–59.

Werry, J. S. (1985). ICD-9 and DSM-III classification for the clinician. *Journal of Child Psychology and Psychiatry, 26*, 1–6.

Werry, J. S., Methven, R. J., Fitzpatrick, J., & Dixon, H. (1983). The inter-rater reliability of DSM-III in children. *Journal of Abnormal Child Psychology, 11*, 341–354.

Yang, K.-S. (1981). Problem behavior in Chinese adolescents in Taiwan: A classification-factorial study. *Journal of Cross-Cultural Psychology, 12*, 179–193.

Zubin, J. (1978). But is it good for science? *Clinical Psychologist, 31*, 1–7.

REFERENCES FOR TABLES 1.4–1.11

1. Achenbach, T. M. (1966). The classification of children's psychiatric symptoms: A factor analytic study. *Psychological Monographs, 80*, 1–37.

2. Achenbach, T. M. (1978). The child behavior profile: I. Boys aged 6–11. *Journal of Consulting and Clinical Psychology, 46*, 478–488.

3. Achenbach, T. M., & Edelbrock, C. S. (1979). The child behavior profile: II. Boys aged 12–16 and girls aged 6–11 and 12–16. *Journal of Consulting and Clinical Psychology, 47*, 223–233.

4. Alderton, H. R., & Hoddinott, B. A. (1968). The children's pathology index. *Canadian Psychiatric Association Journal, 13*, 353–361.

5. Arnold, L. E., & Smeltzer, D. J. (1974). Behavior checklist factor analysis for children and adolescents. *Archives of General Psychiatry, 30*, 1199–1804.

6. Behar, L., & Stringfield, S. A. (1974). A behavior rating scale for the preschool child. *Developmental Psychology, 10*, 601–610.

7. Brady, R. C. (1970). Effects of success and failure on impulsivity and distractibility of three types of educationally handicapped children (Doctoral dissertation, University of Southern California, 1970). *Dissertation Abstracts International, 31*, 2167A. (University Microfilms No. 70-23148.)

8. Bullock, L. M., & Brown, R. K. (1972). Behavioral dimensions of emotionally disturbed children. *Exceptional Children, 38*, 740–741.

9. Clough, F. (1978). Staff ratings of children's behavior in hospital: Comparability of factor structures. *British Journal of Psychology, 69*, 59–68.

10. Conners, C. K. (1969). A teacher rating scale for use in drug studies with children. *American Journal of Psychiatry, 126*, 884–888.

11. Conners, C. K. (1970). Symptom patterns in hyperkinetic, neurotic and normal children. *Child Development, 41*, 667–682.

12. Digman, J. M. (1963). Principal dimensions of child personality as inferred from teacher judgements. *Child Development, 34*, 43–60.

13. Dreger, R. M., Reid, M. P., Lewis, P. M., Overlade, D. C., Rich, T. A., Miller, K. J., & Flemming, E. L. (1964). Behavioral classification project. *Journal of Consulting Psychology, 28*, 1–13.

14. Epstein, M. H., Cullinan, D., & Rosemier, R. (1983). Behavior problem patterns among the learning disabled: Boy aged 6–11. *Learning Disability Quarterly, 6*, 305–311.

15. Fanshel, D., Hylton, L., & Borgatta, E. F. (1963). A study of behavior disorders of children in residential treatment centers. *Journal of Psychological Studies, 14*, 1–23.

16. Glow, R. A. (1978). *Children's behavior problems: A normative study of a parent rating scale.* Unpublished monograph.

17. Glow, R. A. (1978). *Classroom behavior problems: An Australian normative study of the Conners' Teacher Rating Scale.* Unpublished monograph.

18. Goyette, C. H., Conners, C. K., & Ulrich, R. F. (1978). Normative data on revised Conners' Parent and Teacher Rating Scales. *Journal of Abnormal Child Psychology, 6*, 221–236.

19. Grieger, R. M., & Richards, H. C. (1976). Prevalence and structure of behavior symptoms among children in special education and regular classroom settings. *Journal of School Psychology, 14*, 27–38.

20. Herbert, G. W. (1974). Teachers' ratings of classroom behaviour: Factorial structure. *British Journal of Educational Psychology, 44*, 233–240.

21. Hewett, L. E., & Jenkins, R. L. (1946). *Fundamental patterns of maladjustment, the dynamics of their origin.* Springfield, IL.: State of Illinois.

22. Hirshoren, A., & Schnittjer, C. J. (1979). Dimensions of problem behavior in deaf children. *Journal of Abnormal Child Psychology, 7*, 221–228.

23. Kaufman, A. S., Swan, W. W., & Wood, M. M. (1979). Dimensions of problem behaviors of emotionally disturbed children as seen by their parents and teachers. *Psychology in the Schools, 6*, 207–217.

24. Kohn, M., & Rosman, L. (1972). A Social Competence Scale and Symptom Checklist for the preschool child: Factor dimensions, their cross instrument generality, and longitudinal persistence. *Developmental Psychology, 6*, 430–444.

25. Kohn, M., Koretzky, M. B., & Haft, M. (1979). An adolescent symptom checklist for juvenile delinquents. *Journal of Abnormal Child Psychology, 7*, 15–29.

26. Kanfer, D. J., Detre, T., & Koral, J. (1974). ''Deviant'' behavior patterns in

school children, application of KDSTM-14. *Psychological Reports, 35*, 183–191.

27. Lahey, B. B., Stempniak, M., Robinson, E. J., & Tyroler, M. J. (1978). Hyperactivity and learning disabilities as independent dimensions of child behavior problems. *Journal of Abnormal Psychology, 87*, 333–340.

28. Langner, T. S., Gersten, J. C., McCarthy, E. D., Eisenberg, J. C., Green, E. L., Herson, J. H., & Jameson, J. D. (1976). A screening inventory for assessing psychiatric impairment in children 6 to 18. *Journal of Consulting and Clinical Psychology, 44*, 286–296.

29. Larrivee, B., & Borque, M. L. (1981). Factor structure of classroom behavior symptoms for mainstreamed and regular students. *Journal of Abnormal Child Psychology, 9*, 399–406.

30. Lessing, E. E., & Zagorin, S. W. (1971). Dimensions of psychopathology in middle childhood as evaluated by three symptom checklists. *Educational and Psychological Measurement, 31*, 175–197.

31. Lessing, E. E., Williams, V., & Revelle, W. (1982). Parallel forms of the IJR Behavior Checklist for parents, teachers, and clinicans. *Journal of Clinical and Consulting Psychology, 10*, 337–362.

32. Loney, J., Longhorne, J. E., & Paternite, C. E. (1978). An empirical basis for subgrouping the hyperkinetic/minimal brain dysfunction syndrome. *Journal of Abnormal Psychology, 87*, 431–441.

33. Lorr, M., & Jenkins, R. L. (1953). Patterns of maladjustment in children. *Journal of Clinical Psychology, 9*, 16–19.

34. Mattison, R. E., Cantwell, D. P., & Baker, L. (1980). Dimensions of behavior in children with speech and language disorders. *Journal of Abnormal Child Psychology, 8*, 323–338.

35. McDermott, P. A. (1984). Child behavior disorders by age and sex based on item factoring of the Revised Bristol Guides. *Journal of Abnormal Child Psychology, 12*, 15–35.

36. McMahon, R. C., Kunce, J. T., & Salamak, M. (1979). Diagnostic implications of parental ratings of children. *Journal of Clinical Psychology, 35*, 757–762.

37. Miller, L. C. (1967a). Louisville Behavior Checklist for males, 6–12 years of age. *Psychological Reports, 21*, 885–896.

38. Miller, L. C. (1967b). Dimensions of psychopathology in middle childhood. *Psychological Reports, 21*, 897–903.

39. Miller, L. C. (1980). Dimensions of adolescent psychopathology. *Journal of Abnormal Child Psychology, 8*, 161–173.

40. Patterson, G. R. (1964). An empirical approach to the classification of disturbed children. *Journal of Clinical Psychology, 20*, 326–337.

41. Peterson, D. R. (1961). Behavior problems of middle childhood. *Journal of Consulting Psychology, 25*, 205–209.

42. Peterson, D. R., Becker, W. C., Schoemaker, D. J., Luria, Z., & Hellmer, L. A. (1961). Child behavior problems and parental attitudes. *Child Development, 32*, 151–162.

43. Peterson, D. R., Quay, H. C., Cameron, G. R. (1959). Personality and background factors in juvenile delinquency as inferred from questionnaire responses. *Journal of Consulting Psychology, 23*, 395–299.

44. Peterson, D. R., Quay, H. C., & Tiffany, T. L. (1961). Personality factors related to juvenile delinquency. *Child Development, 32*, 355–372.

45. Phillips, B. N. (1968). Problem behavior in the elementary school. *Child Development, 39*, 887–894.

46. Pimm, J. B., Quay, H. C., & Werry, J. S. (1967). Dimensions of problem behavior in first grade children. *Psychology in the Schools, 4*, 155–157.

47. Quay, H. C. (1964a). Personality dimensions in delinquent males as inferred from the factor analysis of behavior ratings. *Journal of Research in Crime and Delinquency, 1*, 33–37.

48. Quay, H. C. (1964b). Dimensions of personality in delinquent boys as inferred from the factor analysis of case history data. *Child Development, 35*, 479–484.

49. Quay, H. C. (1966). Personality patterns in preadolescent delinquent boys. *Educational and Psychological Measurement, 16*, 99–110.

50. Quay, H. C., & Gredler, Y. (1981). Dimensions of problem behavior among institutionalized retardates. *Journal of Abnormal Child Psychology, 9*, 523–528.

51. Quay, H. C., Morse, W. C., & Cutler, R. L. (1966). Personality patterns of pupils in special classes for emotionally disturbed. *Exceptional Children, 32*, 297–301.

52. Quay, H. C., & Quay, L. C. (1965). Behavior problems in early adolescence. *Child Development, 36*, 215–220.

53. Reivich, R. S., & Rothrock, I. A. (1972). Behavior problems of deaf children and adolescents: A factor analytic study. *Journal of Speech and Hearing Research, 15*, 93–104.

54. Roper, R., & Hinde, R. A. (1979). A teacher's questionnaire for individual differences in social behavior. *Journal of Child Psychology and Psychiatry, 20*, 287–298.

55. Ross, A. O., Lacey, H. M., & Parton, D. A. (1965). The development of a behavior checklist for boys. *Child Development, 36*, 1013–1027.

56. Schaefer, C. E., & Millman, H. L. (1973). A factor analytic and reliability study of the Devereux Child Behavior Rating Scale. *Journal of Abnormal Child Psychology, 1*, 241–247.

57. Schnittjer, C. J., & Hirshoren, A. (1981). Factors of problem behavior in visually impaired children. *Journal of Abnormal Child Psychology, 9*, 517–522.

58. Siegelman, M. (1964). Psychometric properties of the Wiggins and Winder Peer Nomination Inventory. *The Journal of Psychology, 64*, 143–149.

59. Spivack, G., & Levine, M. (1964). The Devereux Child Behavior Rating Scale: A study of symptom care behaviors in latency age atypical children. *American Journal of Mental Deficiency, 68*, 700–717.

60. Spivack, G., & Spotts, J. (1965). The Devereux Child Behavior Scale: Symptom Behaviors in latency age children. *American Journal of Mental Deficiency, 69*, 839–853.

61. Werry, J. S., Sprague, R. L., & Cohen, M. N. (1975). Conners' Teacher Rating Scale for use in drug studies with children—An empirical study. *Journal of Abnormal Child Psychology, 3*, 217–229.

2 CONDUCT DISORDERS

HERBERT C. QUAY

INTRODUCTION

As we saw in Chapter 1, the undersocialized aggressive pattern of conduct disorder is ubiquitous and well defined empirically. The socialized syndrome, while less common and occurring much more often in later childhood and adolescence, is also firmly established as a major dimension of disorder. As we shall see, however, much of the research on conduct disorder has failed to consider the differences between the two disorders even though there is now considerable evidence for basic differences in their causes, correlates, and consequences (as discussed later as well as in Loeber & Schmaling, 1985). The frequent failure of researchers to distinguish between the two disorders often makes it difficult to know to which group, if either, the findings pertain.

Furthermore, as was evident in Chapter 1, aggressive behavior, defined in a wide variety of different ways, is associated with both disorders. Thus, in reviewing the research literature, particularly as it relates to the undersocialized pattern, we must frequently draw upon studies of children and adolescents labeled "aggressive" rather than on studies of cases formally diagnosed as conduct disorder. In general, the more extreme and pervasive the aggression, the more likely the aggressive group approximates those with a diagnosable disorder.

There is also the problem presented by the intertwined nature of undersocialized conduct disorder and motor overactivity. As was noted in Chapter 1, hyperactivity, as a behavioral characteristic, is frequently found to be associated with the undersocialized conduct disorder dimension. In addition, studies of children with diagnoses of conduct disorder often have found large (up to 75%) subgroups who are motorically overactive as well as aggressive (e.g., Stewart & Behar, 1983; Stewart, Cummings, Singer, & de Blois, 1981), and studies of nonclinic populations have frequently found high correlations between conduct disordered behavior and hyperactivity (e.g., Prinz, Connor, & Wilson, 1981; Sandberg, Wieselberg, & Shaffer,

1980). There is also evidence that those cases of conduct disorder who also manifest hyperactivity and attentional problems are more likely to show deficits in cognitive, linguistic, and academic functioning (see Stewart & Behar, 1983, the section on academic skills later in this chapter, and Chapter 4). It is often difficult, then, to determine whether the correlates of conduct disorder that may be found in any particular study are related to aggressive component conduct disorder or to the attentional problems likely to be present in many of the subjects.

PRINCIPAL CHARACTERISTICS OF THE TWO DISORDERS

In contrast to many other childhood disorders, the central features of both types of conduct disorder are well established. As we saw in Chapter 1, the behavioral symptoms of the undersocialized pattern relate to physical and verbal aggression (e.g., fighting, hitting others, bullying, impertinent, impudent), noncompliance (e.g., disobedient, defiant, negative, uncooperative), intrusiveness (e.g., attention-seeking, boisterous, disruptive), lack of self-control (e.g., temper tantrums, irritable, irresponsible), and impaired interpersonal relations (e.g., dishonest, lying, callous). The more specific empirically derived characteristics are reasonably well reflected in the more global inclusionary and exclusionary criteria for Conduct Disorder, Undersocialized Aggressive, in DSM-III (American Psychiatric Association, 1980), although, as was noted in Chapter 1, there are some discrepancies such as stealing, which is associated with the socialized dimension.

The socialized syndrome primarily involves delinquent activities (e.g., group stealing, truancy from home and school, staying out at night), carried out in a peer group context (e.g., gang membership, group loyalty). Again, the diagnostic criteria of DSM-III fairly well reflect these empirically established characteristics.

It is important to recognize that delinquency (a legal term) cannot be exactly equated to either form of conduct disorder. Multivariate statistical studies have clearly shown (e.g., Quay, 1964a, 1964b, 1966), however, that most of the major dimensions of disorder may be found among juvenile delinquents.

ASSESSMENT

Because assessment is discussed in depth in Chapter 11, we need only note here that there are a variety of observation schedules, rating scales, and standardized clinical interviews that can be used to assess conduct disorder, especially the undersocialized form, usually somewhat more reliably than most other disorders. Diagnosis of the socialized pattern does require a knowledge about peer relations and group-related activities, but as noted in Chapter 1, this disorder can also be reliably assessed in dimensional form as well as clinically diagnosed.

CORRELATES: PERSONAL, SOCIAL, AND BIOLOGICAL

To develop a scientific understanding of the disorder, it is necessary to go beyond those characteristics that are used to define the disorder in the first place. A disorder is empirically validated by determining its relationship to other variables. Of particular concern is *differential* validity; two putatively separate disorders ought not to be related in the same way to the same variable. As we shall see below, and in subsequent chapters concerned with etiology and treatment, there is accumulating evidence for the differential validity of the undersocialized and socialized patterns since these two disorders do not have the same personal, social, and biological correlates.

Cognitive Functioning

GENERAL INTELLIGENCE (IQ)

At the outset it must be emphasized that studies seeking to demonstrate differences in IQ among groups of deviant children must carefully control for race and socioeconomic status as these factors are related to performance on the most widely used individually administered measure (the WISC-R) as well as other tests (Sattler, 1982).

On the basis of the results of a number of studies (e.g., Beitchman, Patterson, Gelfand, & Minty, 1982; Quay & Levinson, 1967; Rutter, 1964) there is little reason to believe that general intelligence as measured by IQ tests is significantly lower than SES-comparable groups with and without other disorders for either undersocialized or socialized groups. Parenthetically, we may note that the same conclusion is also warranted about unselected juvenile delinquents who may or may not qualify as conduct disordered by either DSM-III or statistical criteria (see Hogan & Quay, 1984, for a review).

In addition to overall IQ, there has been considerable interest in discrepancies between performance and verbal scores. What is often not recognized in this body of research is that subtest differences of considerable magnitude (10–15 points) may occur in samples of ostensibly normal children (Kaufman, 1976). Overall, when adequate controls are utilized, performance–verbal discrepancies of a magnitude to be diagnostically useful or to be revealing of meaningful differences in cognitive abilities have not been demonstrated in either heterogeneous groups of delinquents or more strictly diagnosed subgroups (see Hecht & Jurkovic, 1978; Hogan & Quay, 1984).

Differences among the subtest scores usually found in most individually administered IQ tests have also been studied. Hale and Landino (1981) attempted to use WISC-R subtest scores to differentiate among subgroups of conduct-disorder, anxious-withdrawn, mixed, and nonproblem groups but were unable to classify their groups correctly at higher than chance rate. Neither is the internal (factor) structure of the WISC-R different for conduct-disordered groups when compared to normals (Hubble & Groff, 1981).

A study by McGee, Williams, and Silva (1984) serves to point up the need for diagnostic specificity. Their investigation compared children from a birth cohort ($n = 900$) who were selected on the basis of either parent or teacher rating as either aggressive (conduct disordered), hyperactive, hyperactive *and* aggressive (20.3% prevalence for all three groups combined), or neither. They compared the groups (at age 7) on a number of cognitive (as well as other) variables; in almost all instances the group that was both hyperactive and aggressive was at the greatest disadvantage. The pure aggressives did not differ from the normals on WISC PIQ, ITPA comprehension, and ITPA expression. They were significantly lower (101.90 vs. 107.05) on WISC VIQ—but the mean for the hyperactive-aggressive group was 95.67; a difference twice as large as between the normal and pure aggressive.

In a later study, McGee, Williams, & Silva (1985) found that both verbal and performance IQ deficits were related to parent and teacher ratings of inattention but not aggression. Thus as we noted in the Introduction to this chapter, if cases of undersocialized conduct disorder who are concomitantly hyperactive (with the usual accompanying attentional problems) are utilized, the results are likely to make it appear that undersocialized conduct disorder is associated with more cognitive deficits than is the case when subjects do not have attentional problems as well (see subsequent section on academic skills).

Richman and Lindgren (1981) have taken a more sophisticated approach. They began with a sample who had a WISC-R Performance IQ at least 15 points higher than their Verbal IQ and separated them into three groups based on factor scores derived from the same sample. The groups were labeled abstract reasoning, sequential memory, and language disability. The language-disability group was the highest in conduct problems and lowest in behavioral inhibition and academic achievement in both reading and arithmetic. This study suggests that undersocialized conduct disorder is related to verbal mediation deficiencies; a finding in keeping with some studies of cognitive processing to be discussed later.

HIGHER-ORDER COGNITIVE FUNCTIONING

While most inquiries into cognitive functioning in deviant children have relied on psychometric tests, other, generally more recent, studies have focused on particular aspects of cognitive performance. The cognitive tasks chosen have usually followed from some theory of cognitive development and are age-specific. Variables studied have included attribution, self-regulation, moral development, empathy, and impulsivity. It is critical to note that in this type of research, controls must be matched for mental age to assure that obtained differences are not simply due to differences in global intellectual functioning. (See Hogan & Quay, 1984, for a discussion of the pros and cons of this approach.) Studies of these higher-order functions have found aggressive or undersocialized children more likely to infer hostility on the part of others (Nasby, Hayden, & De Paulo, 1980) and for this type of attribution to be accompanied by relatively quick responding and relatively poor selective recall (Dodge & Frame, 1982; Dodge & Newman, 1981). Diminished capacity to inhibit responding and verbally self-regulate behavior has also been reported (Camp, 1977), as has a tendency to verbalize aggressive responses, as solutions to conflict situations (Deluty, 1981).

Moral judgment has also been the focus of considerable research. This is a complex area of study because the tasks used are heavily dependent upon verbal intelligence and the relation between performance on these tasks and actual moral (or immoral) behavior is problematic. Some studies (e.g., Bear & Richard, 1981; Nucci & Herman, 1982) have found that children with undersocialized conduct problems reason at a somewhat lower level of moral development. Similar findings of lower levels of moral reasoning among undersocialized adolescent delinquents have also been reported (Campagna & Harter, 1975; Jurkovic & Prentice, 1977).

Empathy and the ability to take the perspective of the other have also been studied in delinquent adolescents. Jurkovic and Prentice (1977) found that those classified as undersocialized were less skilled in perspective taking (and poorer in abstract reasoning ability) than were the socialized, who were no different from normals. Ellis (1982) found less empathic ability in undersocialized as compared to socialized delinquents but, surprisingly, found the anxious group less empathic than the undersocialized. When his subjects were rated for overall aggression, those in the more aggressive group were less empathic. Type of disorder and rated aggression jointly accounted for 41 percent of the variance of empathy scores.

As Hogan and Quay (1984) have pointed out, the overall picture suggests that deficits in language development and language use are associated with undersocialized conduct disorder. As they noted, ''The deficits could play a causative role in mislabeling environmental stimuli, in limiting available response alternatives, in constraining search strategies for appropriate responses already in the repertoire, and in generating frustration as a function of decreased ability to meet academic and social-behavior demands'' (p. 28).

While there are conceptual and measurement problems associated with the notion of cognitive and motor impulsivity as unitary constructs (e.g., Paulsen & Johnson, 1980), undersocialized subjects have been shown to perform poorly on a number of measures of impulsivity such as the Matching Familiar Figures Test of Kagan, Rosman, Day, Albert, and Phillips (1964) (see Paulsen, 1978; Weinstein, 1974), the Q-Score of the Porteus Maze Test (Docter & Winder, 1954; Roberts & Erikson, 1968), and measures of persistence (Kendall, Zupan, & Braswell, 1981).

It is likely, of course, that owing to the diagnostic confusion already noted between undersocialized conduct disorder and hyperactivity, subjects for many of these studies had attentional problems as well, so that the greater impulsivity may be more related to the attentional deficits than to aggression (see later and Chapter 4).

**Academic
Performance**

The real relationship between academic achievement and conduct disorder is not nearly as obvious as it might seem. Surveys of delinquent and anti-social children have almost always revealed lower levels of academic achievement in these groups (e.g., Glueck & Glueck, 1950; Gold & Mann, 1972) even though their intelligence may be well within the normal range (see Offord, Poushinsky, & Sullivan, 1978).

Without considering, at least for the moment, the question of cause and effect, the findings, as they stand, may be attributable to a variety of factors. Included among these are failure to have attended school, poor motivation for test-taking, teacher bias in assigning grades, and lack of parental interest in school performance. It would seem likely that the deficits in the ability pointed out earlier to mediate one's behavior verbally could also serve to depress academic achievement, but this linkage has yet to be demonstrated.

Cause and effect have been argued in both directions, often on the bases of limited, if any, evidence as to the time of onset of either the conduct-disordered behavior or the academic underachievement. Clearly, conduct disorder, involving continued noncompliance to school routine (undersocialized) or frequent truancy (socialized), could easily lead to underachievement even in the presence of normal or superior intelligence. It has also been suggested that poor school achievement leads to feelings of poor self-esteem, which then result in aggressive behavior (see Rutter, Tizard, & Whitmore, 1970) although others have argued to the contrary (Offord & Poushinsky, 1981; Offord et al., 1978).

In any case, as we have noted earlier, all major disorders may be found among the legally delinquent. Surveys of academic achievement in delinquents tell us little about the relationship between academic skills and conduct disorder. To address this question, even in a purely correlational form, carefully selected cases of conduct disorder (of both or either subtype) must be compared to controls as well as to cases with other types of disorder. Since it is clear that poor academic performance is associated with Attention Deficit Disorder (see Chapter 4) (where it is also clear that the disorder antedates the academic problems), special care must be taken not to confound these two groups, as is often the case.

Studies meeting these criteria are few in number and of recent origin. Ledingham and Schwartzman (1984) found that, three years following their identification based on peer nominations, aggressive children were more likely to have failed a grade than were either normal controls or withdrawn children. Fewer aggressive children were in regular classes at the expected grade level than were either withdrawn or control cases. Another finding of interest, not unexpected, was that in all groups boys fared worse; fewer were in regular classes at expected grade level than were girls. Unfortunately, a problem with this study is that the peer nomination method of subject selection did not preclude the confounding of aggression and attentional problems.

This deficiency has been remedied in studies by McGee and his colleagues of a large birth cohort in New Zealand. When the children were aged 7, McGee et al. (1984) used behavior ratings from parents and teachers to select groups of boys who were aggressive, hyperactive, and both aggressive and hyperactive and then compared them to each other and to normal controls. With regard to their academic measure, reading retardation, only the group rated both aggressive and hyperactive was significantly more retarded than the controls. In a later study when the children were 9, McGee, Williams, Share, Andersen, and Silva (unpublished) found that both parent and teacher ratings of inattentiveness, but not antisocial behavior, were (negatively) related to reading and spelling performance. Subsequently, at age 11 (McGee et al., unpublished) the teacher but not the parent ratings were related to reading retardation; both hyperactivity and aggressiveness were negatively associated with reading performance.

Somewhat similar data were reported by Quay and Peterson (1983). Teacher ratings of normal children in grades 4, 5, and 6 on the Attention Problems Subscale of the Revised Behavior Problem Checklist were significantly negatively correlated with standardized test scores in reading, language, and arithmetic ($-.19$, $-.35$, and $-.20$, respectively) even when the effects of intellectual ability were partialed out. There were no significant relationships between the Socialized Aggression subscale and achievement and only one significant relationship ($-.19$ with reading) with the Conduct Disorder subscale.

Taken together, these studies suggest that deficient academic achievement is more likely to be associated with the attentional problems than with either undersocialized or socialized aggression. Problems in attention and concentration are clearly more inimical to the acquisition of academic learning than are aggressive behaviors, although when the two occur in conjunction, the academic problems may be even more severe for all of the reasons discussed earlier.

Instrumental Learning

Stimulated on the one hand by theory about the nature of adult psychopathic personality (now Antisocial Personality Disorder in DSM-III) and on the other by research concerning individual differences in sensitivity to social reward, a number of studies have investigated the responsivity of psychopathic and other deviant subgroups to social reinforcement. The basic hypothesis underlying these studies was that psychopaths are less sensitive to verbal or social reinforcement than are normals or other clinical groups. The majority of these studies have used verbal conditioning procedures and have most often used adult offenders classified into subgroups by a variety of clinical and psychometric techniques. As regards the insensitivity of psychopaths to verbal reward, the results have been contradictory and not at all convincing (see Bryan & Kapche, 1967; Johns & Quay, 1962, as examples).

Only three studies of the differential responsiveness to social reward have been reported in which children and adolescents were used as subjects. Levin and Simmons (1962a) reported that for a sample of 15 severely emotionally disturbed boys in a residential setting, "praise did not function as a reinforcer for the group as a whole or for the majority of the Ss" (p. 10). No information was given in the original paper as to the nature of the emotional disturbance, but the subjects were later described (Levin & Simmons, 1962b) as unusually hyperactive and aggressive.

In the second study (Levin & Simmons, 1962b), six of the hyperactive and aggressive boys who had participated in the first study were reinforced either by food alone or by food plus praise. The boys who received food performed significantly better than they had in the earlier study when praise was the sole reinforcer. Comparison of the subjects who received food and praise with with those who received food alone "suggested that praise suppressed the response rate" (p. 546). Obviously, the very small number of subjects in this study limited the experimenters' ability to use inferential statistics and, hence, the confidence that can be placed in the results.

A much more searching look at the relationship between patterns of adolescent psychopathology and response to social reinforcement was taken by Stewart (1972). His subjects were institutionalized delinquents who had been classified as undersocialized, socialized, or anxious-withdrawn (see Chapter 3) by a combination of psychometric measures. Subjects were given a sentence-building, verbal-conditioning task preceded by a frustrating condition (working on an insoluble puzzle) or by a neutral condition. The conditioning tasks used three kinds of verbs: aggressive, dependent, and neutral; the use of aggressive, independent verbs were socially reinforced by the experimenter.

Under the frustration condition, the anxious and socialized groups significantly increased, while the undersocialized group significantly decreased, the use of the reinforced verbs. When conditioning was preceded by the neutral condition, the anxious and the socialized aggressives did not significantly increase their use of reinforced verbs but the undersocialized groups significantly decreased. The most interesting analysis revealed that the anxious group increased in the use of dependency verbs and decreased in the use of aggressive verbs over trials, whereas the socialized group increased in the use of the aggressive verbs. In addition to measures of conditionability, Stewart (1972) also measured "frustration-induced" behavior (e.g., requests for help, complaining, fidgeting). The anxious group gave the highest number of such behavior followed by the socialized group and the undersocialized group, respectively.

Two studies have dealt with the issue of reinforcement responsiveness in much more complex experimental designs. Moses (1974) used no less than seven reward conditions, while Dietrich (1976) varied task structure and reward conditions. Both of these studies demonstrated differential response tendencies among the various subgroups but the relationships were not nearly so straightforward as had been predicted—nor were they easily interpretable without recourse to a host of additional explanatory theories and constructs (e.g., expectancy, practice, consolidation).

Akamatsu and Farudi (1978) studied the imitative behavior of a group of socialized conduct disordered and a group characterized as immature. As predicted, the socialized group was more likely to imitate peer models while the immature group was more likely to imitate staff models. This finding is, of course, in accord with the notion that the socialized are highly responsive to, and influenced by, their peers.

Despite an early flurry of activity in the 1970s, there has been little additional research in this area. The issue of differential responsiveness to various kinds of reinforcing events among deviant subgroups is obviously a complex one. There is apparently no straightforward relationship between undersocialized conduct disorder and lowered responsiveness to social reward that transcends the nature of the task and response being reinforced, among other possible influencing variables. As is apparently the case with adult psychopaths (see Hare, 1978), there does not seem to be anything seriously amiss with the reward-learning ability of either the undersocialized or socialized groups. Later in this chapter we will consider the possibility that the undersocialized group is, in fact, hypersensitive to the possibility of reward and underresponsive to the possibility of punishment.

Sustained Attention and Stimulation Seeking

A number of investigators have sought to test the theoretical proposition that the extreme of the undersocialized syndrome (psychopathy) is related to an underlying pathological need for stimulation (see Quay, 1965, 1977) and that deficits in sustained attention might reflect stimulation-seeking tendencies.

Orris (1969) was the first to test this hypothesis experimentally. He predicted that undersocialized delinquents would show poorer performance on a task requiring continuous attention than would socialized and anxious groups. His hypothesis was confirmed with the added observation that the undersocialized engaged to a greater degree in boredom-relieving activity, such as singing and talking to themselves, in lieu of attending to the experimental stimuli.

A much more complex inquiry was undertaken by Skrzypek (1969). He compared undersocialized and anxious-withdrawn delinquents as to their preference for novelty and complexity of stimuli under conditions of both perceptual arousal and perceptual isolation. On initial testing, the undersocialized group indicated greater preference for the complex and the novel; in contrast, the anxious group preferred the less complex and the more mundane. Skrzypek (1969) also found that the effect of a brief period of perceptual isolation was to increase preference for novelty and complexity in the undersocialized group. The arousal experience served to increase the anxiety of the anxious subjects and to decrease their preference for complexity. The results of this extremely complex experiment served further to demonstrate differences in psychological processes between the undersocialized group and the anxious group. The results also supported the stimulation-seeking hypothesis of psychopathic behavior.

Two subsequent studies investigated the stimulation-seeking hypothesis in groups of younger children. Whitehill, DeMyer-Gapin, and Scott (1976) studied two samples of male residents (mean age 11.6) of a treatment center described as undersocialized and anxious. The experimental procedure permitted the subject to watch a slide for as long as he cared to before pushing a button to move on to the next one. Both the normal and undersocialized groups showed a significant decrement in their viewing time across trials while the anxious group did not. Furthermore, the undersocialized group showed a decrement in viewing time earlier than either of the other groups; this group was significantly different from the normals on 7 of the 11 trial blocks.

In a study with boys of approximately the same age, DeMyer-Gapin and Scott (1977) employed essentially the same methodology but varied the content of the slides with one set being relatively novel, while the other was highly repetitive. Although the undersocialized group showed a decrement as compared to the anxious group in viewing time for the novel slides, there was no difference between the groups for the repetitive set. However, as the authors pointed out, there was an immediate decrement in viewing time exhibited by both groups to what was apparently a boring set of slides. In an observation similar to that made by Orris (1969), the authors noted that four of their nine undersocialized children grew restless, became talkative, and fidgeted excessively with the projector switch.

While these studies are all unequivocal in their findings of shifting attention, apparent boredom susceptibility, and stimulation-seeking behavior in undersocialized children and adolescents, there is the possibility that the undersocialized groups were confounded by cases of attention deficit disorder. However, these findings not only provide support for a theory relating undersocialized conduct disorder to stimulation-seeking but can also be incorporated into a more general theory related to reward seeking and lack of inhibition mentioned before and to be discussed later in this chapter.

Peer Relations

Poor interpersonal relations are, as we have seen in Chapter 1, one of the principal characteristics of the undersocialized pattern. In contrast, strong peer loyalties are part and parcel of the socialized pattern. However, very little actual study has been done of the *specific* ways in which either group interacts with others in interpersonal situations.

Panella and Henggeler (1986) studied the social interaction patterns of black male adolescents classified as conduct disordered (undersocialized), anxious-withdrawn, and well adjusted using a number of measures. Compared to the well-adjusted controls, the undersocialized group was less socially appropriate and showed a lower degree of positive affect and social competence when interacting with both strangers and friends of their own age-group. These researchers concluded that undersocialized adolescents have difficulty exchanging the sensitive, responsive, and positive behaviors that are characteristic of friendship relations.

With respect to the socialized pattern, empirical research on the personal characteristics of group-oriented delinquents is exceedingly sparse and not revealing of serious psychopathology (e.g., Cartwright, Howard, & Reuterman, 1980). The vast majority of studies of delinquent gangs, theoretically at least, including many with Socialized Conduct Disorder, have been done from a sociological perspective (see Moore, Vigil, & Garcia, 1983, for a recent example).

Konstantareas and Homatidis (1985) found that conduct-disordered children (presumably undersocialized) established dominance hierarchies among themselves, but that, compared to normal children, their hierarchies were less stable and their social relationships more unpredictable and poorly ordered.

These studies, limited as they are in number, shed some light on the specifics (beyond aggression and noncompliance) of the interpersonal difficulties of the undersocialized group. They suggest that it is a lack of interpersonal sensitivity, responsiveness, competence, and order that, when coupled with aggression, make the undersocialized individual aversive to other people—peers and adults alike.

Behavior in Intervention Programs

Because of the high degree of social relevance of juvenile delinquency, there have been a number of studies that have looked at the relationship between conduct disorder and delinquency. The tendency for undersocialized boys to have been more frequently institutionalized for delinquency has been demonstrated in two studies (Mack, 1969; Quay, Peterson, & Consalvi, 1960).

Within a juvenile correctional institution, the undersocialized pattern has been found both concurrently related to disciplinary problems (Quay et al., 1960; Schuck, Dubek, Cymbalisty, & Green, 1972) and predictive of them (Quay & Levinson, 1967). In the latter study, a sample of incoming delinquents were assigned, for research purposes only, and without the knowledge of the institution staff, to one of four categories of disorder. In addition to evidencing a wider variety of disciplinary problems during their stay in the institution, the undersocialized group was significantly less successful in a program involving working outside the institution during the day. Their success rate in this "work release" program was only 25 percent compared to a success rate of 75 percent for an anxious group. The socialized group was close to the base rate for the program as a whole (50%).

Smyth and Ingram (1970) studied institutional sick call visits that were classified by medical staff as being primarily medical, emotional, or malingering. The undersocialized group accounted for 39 percent of the visits judged to be malingering while constituting only 16 percent of the sample.

Devies (1975) found undersocialized boys to be less likely to succeed on probation. Similarly, a measure of undersocialized conduct disorder entered into an equation that predicted the rearrest of a group of juveniles participating in a diversion project (Quay & Love, 1977; see also Chapter 17).

All of these studies indicate, as might be expected, that undersocialized delinquent groups uniformly perform more poorly in programs designed to alter their behavior. Their relative refractoriness to traditional correctional programs has led to attempts to conceptualize and implement more specialized programs to remediate their aggressive and recidivistic tendencies (see Chapter 15).

Psychophysiological Correlates

Psychophysiological responsiveness with respect to both tonic (basal) and phasic (response to stimuli) levels have been extensively studied in children with Attention Deficit Disorders as both their attentional and activity problems have been theorized to relate to both over- and underarousal (see Chapter 4).

HEART RATE

Raine and Venables (1984a) have reviewed studies relating heart rate to antisocial behavior in adolescents and have themselves researched the question. Although studies of adults have failed to find evidence for lower resting levels, studies of antisocial/delinquent/high-risk adolescents have obtained results in the direction of lower tonic levels. In their own study Raine and Venables found lower tonic heart rates related to teacher ratings of conduct disorder but only for children of higher SES. Since lower pulse rates may be associated with physical fitness and larger body size, these findings are, as indicated by Raine and Venables, difficult to interpret.

ELECTRODERMAL (GSR) RESPONDING

Borkovec (1970) was the first to find evidence for reduced phasic GSR responding in undersocialized, as compared with socialized and anxious, delinquents. Subsequently, Siddle, Nicol, and Foggitt (1973) reported lower GSR reactivity in aggressive adolescents. Raine and Venables (1984b) have reported significant negative correlations between both teacher and self-report measures of undersocialized conduct disorder and GSR amplitudes (r's of $-.21$ to $-.36$). However, Dwivedi, Beaumont, and Brandon (1984) found *greater* response amplitudes to a stimulus in an undersocialized group selected on the basis of staff ratings on the same measure used by Raine and Venables (1984b).

Delameter and Lahey (1983) studied children in the 10 to 12 year range whose primary diagnosis was learning disability. Within this group, however, those selected for high scores on a rating scale measure of undersocialized conduct disorder showed significantly lower levels of skin conductance during a continuous performance task. In an attempted replication, Zweben, Quay, and Hammer (1985) did not find the same differential responsiveness (although the task involved was of much shorter duration) but did find a significant negative correlation across all subjects between errors of commission on a continuous performance task and magnitude of GSR response, suggesting a negative relationship between GSR response and the ability to withhold responding. Most recently Schmidt, Solanto, and Bridger (1985) studied younger children (mean age 9.0) who met the DSM-III criteria for Undersocialized Aggressive Conduct Disorder. Again, they found significant phasic, but not tonic, differences; the undersocialized children were less responsive than controls.

It is of interest that underresponsiveness of the GSR is also the most stable psychophysiological finding in adult psychopaths (Hare, 1978). While lower electrodermal responsivity can certainly be interpreted as reflecting a lower level of general arousability, a more specific hypothesis is available.

Fowles (1980) has suggested that the GSR responsivity indexes activity in Gray's behavioral inhibition system while increases in heart rate reflect activity in the reward system (Gray, 1979, 1982). Since, according to Gray (1979, 1982), the behavioral inhibition system reacts to signals of pain, punishment, and novelty to stop ongoing behavior, the strong "approach" reaction to novelty among the undersocialized discussed earlier suggests the possibility of an underfunctional inhibitory system. Additionally, passive avoidance (withholding responding to signals of punishment) is controlled by this behavioral inhibition system and passive avoidance behavior is clearly impaired in psychopaths (Hare, 1978). Furthermore, the negative relationship between errors of commission and GSR response found by Zweben et al. (1985) fits this model.

The reward system responds to signals of both reward and relief from punishment. As already noted in the earlier discussion of instrumental learning, there is little evidence of a consistent deficit in reward, escape, or active avoidance learning in the undersocialized. Thus, lowered phasic GSR responsivity, a reasonably consistent finding, can be incorporated into a broader theory of response to potentially appetitive and aversive events. As we have suggested elsewhere (Quay, 1986), an overactive reward system very likely coupled with an underactive behavioral inhibition system may be implicated in the genesis of undersocialized conduct disorder.

ELECTROENCEPHALOGRAM (EEG)

As Ferguson (1984) has noted, most EEG studies have used heterogeneous groups of subjects with "behavior problems." These studies have generally reported a higher than normal frequency of abnormalities, primarily excessive slow activity with poor background organization and the frequent occurrence of paroxysmal or epileptic forms of activity.

We know of only one study that contrasted undersocialized and socialized (and anxious) subgroups. Mueller and Shamsie (1967) studied the EEG records of 78 girls admitted to the adolescent unit of a psychiatric hospital. The anxious group manifested more fast activity in the temporal region, a finding that, according to the authors, might be expected in anxious and sensitive individuals and that might also contribute to the inhibition of impulses originating in lower parts of the central nervous system. The undersocialized group exhibited more generalized slow waves, interpreted by the authors as related to a lack of inhibition. The socialized group provided EEG tracings more regular and more normal than either of the other two groups. Although these results were consonant with expectations based on the behavior of the three groups, as the authors pointed out, the study did not include a nonproblem control group and results could have been influenced by medication being taken by some, though not all, of the subjects. Basically, EEG studies have been unrevealing with respect to the role of disturbed electrical activity in the brain in conduct disorder except to suggest a lack of involvement in the socialized subtype.

BIOLOGICAL FACTORS

The role of brain damage and the effect of toxins in the etiology of all psychopathological disorders are discussed in detail in Chapter 8. The factors to be discussed herein do not involve expressed (or implied) structural damage but reflect recent interest in possible genetic influences, the potential role of temperament (usually presumed to be genetic) and, perhaps most promising of all, findings from biochemical studies.

Genetic Factors

There have been a number of studies involving parents and offspring (see Bohman, Cloninger, Sigvardsson, & Von Knorring, 1982; Gabrielli & Mednick, 1983; Mednick & Christiansen, 1977) suggesting some genetic contribution to adult criminality. However, these studies are not yet conclusive, especially with regard to the mechanisms involved, and do not bear directly on the issue of a genetic component in childhood and adolescent conduct disorder, since as we have already noted criminality per se cannot be equated to conduct disorder for either adolescents or adults.

At least tangentially relevant, however, are studies conducted in Sweden by Bohman (cited by DeFries & Plomin, 1978), who was interested in the adjustment of adopted children. About one-third of his sample of 168 adoptees had criminal biological fathers. When the adopted children were 10 to 11 years old, he did not find more *maladjustment* (italics ours) in those with criminal fathers.

We know of no study that has carefully investigated possible genetic contributions to childhood conduct disorder by the use of the most relevant method: the study of differences among carefully diagnosed monozygotic and dizygotic twins reared apart. Thus, what evidence there is for a genetic contribution to the etiology of conduct disorder is indirect at best.

TEMPERAMENT

Since the majority of studies on infant and early childhood temperament have isolated a pattern of behavior often labeled "fussy-difficult" (see Rutter, 1982), it is tempting to think of this temperamental variable as a precursor to childhood psychopathology, especially conduct disorder. If this "difficultness" has a significant hereditary component, which most believe it does, then it could provide one source of a genetic contribution to conduct disorder.

While there are a number of studies that have suggested that some temperamental factors do have a significant heretability component, for example, activity level (see Plomin, 1983, for a review), there is the problem that, according to Plomin (1983, p. 83), "So far, it appears that temperament in infancy is not significantly associated with later problems. Childhood temperament, particularly the 'difficult' cluster of temperament dimension, does predict behavioral outcomes at statistically significant levels, but it remains to be seen whether the association will be strong enough to be useful clinically."

BEHAVIOR "PROBLEMS"

If specific behavior problems or clusters of behavior problems related to conduct disorder can be shown to be genetically influenced, then one might generalize these findings to carefully selected children manifesting high levels of conduct-disordered behavior. O'Conner, Foch, Sherry, and Plomin (1980) compared parent ratings of problem behavior on normal identical versus same-sex fraternal twins, who averaged about eight years of age. On eight factor analytically derived scales, the intraclass correlations for the identicals were higher than for the fraternals. On their scales seemingly related to conduct disorder (Bullying, Restless, School Problems), the identical pair correlations were .72, .70, and .91 as compared to .42, .26, and .56 for the fraternals. Even given a possible predilection of the parents of identicals to view their children as more similar and the possibility that parents create a more homogeneous environment for identicals, the possibility of a genetic component in the conduct disorder type behavior studied must be taken seriously.

Given the evidence for psychophysiological correlates already presented, and evidence for neurochemical correlates in severe undersocialized conduct disorder and aggression to be discussed later, more research into the genetics of conduct disorder is clearly necessary. Future genetic inquiries might first and most profitably be directed toward cases of severe undersocialized conduct disorder (carefully differentiated from the socialized subtype and from attention deficit disorder) that have persisted at least into late childhood or adolescence, for which there is concurrent evidence for some biochemical and/or psychophysiological abnormality. The prevalence of such cases among twins will, of course, be very few in number, but there would seem to be little to be gained by studying larger normal cohorts of twins where there is likely to be a high degree of transience of any disturbances, few severe cases, and likely little evidence for neurochemical abnormalities.

BIOCHEMICAL FACTORS

Genes operate primarily through specific enzymes or biochemical catalysts. While there have been frequent biochemical studies of children with attention deficit disorder (see Chapter 4), there has been much less study of children with conduct disorders, though the diagnostic confusion already mentioned suggests that some of the findings may well apply to children with undersocialized conduct disorder.

Rogeness, Hernandez, Macedo, and Mitchell (1982) have contrasted socialized ($n = 9$), undersocialized ($n = 16$), and normal control children ($n = 20$) on four biochemical factors measured in blood plasma: dopamine-beta-hydroxylase (DBH) [converts dopamine (DA) to noradrenaline (NA)] catechol-O-methyl transferase (COMT) (inactivates DA and NA), monoamine-oxidase (MAO) (the primary inactivator of DA and NA), and serotonin (5HT). Results indicated that the undersocialized group had significantly lower DBH activity than either the controls or the socialized group; the latter had significantly higher activity than the controls. As regards COMT, activity was higher in the socialized group compared with both the undersocialized and the controls; the latter two did not differ. There were no differences in MAO or 5HT.

Two later studies with larger sample sizes confirmed the relationship between low levels of plasma DBH activity and undersocialized conduct disorder. Rogeness, Hernandez, Macedo, Mitchell, Amrung, and Harris (1984) compared 20 cases with low DBH levels to 20 cases with normal levels and found hyperaggressive behavior and a formal diagnosis of Undersocialized Aggressive Conduct Disorder significantly more frequent in the low DBH group. Further confirmation was provided by Rogeness, Hernandez, Macedo, Amrung, and Hoppe (1984) when 44 low-DBH cases were compared to 200 cases with higher levels. Again, symptoms of undersocialized conduct disorder were greater in the low DBH group.

One can also infer possible neurochemical involvement in severe conduct disorder from studies of highly selected groups of young adults. Brown, Ballanger, Minichiello, and Goodwin (1979) studied young adult volunteers (mean age 22) who had a "personality disorder" as a primary diagnosis and a group of same-age volunteer normal controls. The experimental group had been admitted to a government hospital for evaluation of suitability for further military service; extensive historical material was present to permit an overall reliable rating of aggressive behavior. Determination of three metabolites [5-hydroxyindoleactic acid (5HIAA), 3-methoxy-4-hydroxyphenylglycol (MHPG), and homovanillic acid (HVA)] was made from cerebrospinal fluid (CSF) and hence, unlike blood and urine studies, was brain derived. Within the personality-disorder group, aggression scores were significantly negatively correlated with 5-HIAA ($r = -.78$; $n = 24$), the principal metabolite of 5HT (an inhibitory neurotransmitter); significantly positively correlated with MHPG ($r = .64$; $n = 12$), the principal metabolite of NA; and uncorrelated with HVA, a metabolite of DA. The authors interpreted their findings as in accord with animal studies indicating aggression to be a function of serotonergic-catecholaminergic balance.

In a later study Brown et al. (1982) studied 12 additional patients (mean age 22) who had primary DSM-III diagnoses of borderline personality disorder and who were also being studied as to suitability for further military service. An aggression score similar to that used in the earlier study was calculated. Additionally, the MMPI and Buss-Durkee inventory for aggression were obtained. The global aggression score was negatively correlated ($-.53$) with CSF 5HIAA, as was the MMPI Pd scale ($r = -.77$). There were no significant relationships between the Buss-Durkee and 5HIAA. None of the behavioral measures was related to MHPG or HVA. The failure to replicate the correlation between aggression and MHPG was attributed to that fact that MHPG scores had clustered at the high and low ends in the earlier study.

In particular, the consistent findings with respect to the relationship between low DBH levels and undersocialized conduct disorder can be interpreted as concordant with the behavioral reward and inhibition framework presented earlier in this chapter. As noted above, we have proposed (Quay, 1985) that undersocialized conduct disorder reflects an overactive reward system and an underfunctioning behavioral inhibition system resulting in impulsive, disinhibited, and reward-seeking behavior. According to Gray (1979, 1982), the principal neurotransmitter of the behavioral inhibition system is NA, while DA is apparently the principal transmitter for reward pathways (see also Olds & Fobes, 1981). Thus, if very low levels of DBH can be interpreted to mean the availability of an excess of DA but a diminished amount of NA (due to lack of conversion of the former to the latter), then the reward system might be overenergized while the inhibition system is transmitter-deficient.

It is of interest that Rogeness et al. (1982) reported that a combination of methylphenidate and a phenothiazine (thorazine) (see Chapter 12) seemed to be the most effective form of pharmacotherapy for their undersocialized patients. This would make sense because methylphenidate releases stored DA and NA while the phenothiazines are DA blockers. Thus, the effect of the combination of drugs might well be to agonize the behavioral inhibition (NA) system while antagonizing the reward system (DA), thus establishing a normal level of dynamic equilibrium.

While biochemical theorizing of this nature is fraught with problems derived from measurement difficulties and multiple sources of any neurotransmitter and its metabolites, there is a developing attractive coherence between empirical fact and theory with respect to biochemical involvement in undersocialized conduct disorder.

EPIDEMIOLOGY

Establishing the prevalence of behavior disorders presents a number of methodological problems. Decisions must be made as to what constitutes a disorder, how it is to be determined when a disorder is present, and who is going to be surveyed to determine prevalence. A discussion of the many problems associated with the epidemiology of behavior disorder is far beyond the scope of this chapter and the interested reader is referred to Graham (1979), Gould, Wunsch-Hitzig, and Dohrenwend (1981), and Links (1983) for fuller discussions. Suffice it to say that how broadly or narrowly a disorder is defined, how reliable and valid the methods are for assessing the presence of the disorder, and what segment of the population is assessed will drastically influence the number of cases reported. The influence of these factors is best illustrated in the widely varying prevalence rates for Attention Deficit Disorder, for which there has been much less agreement on diagnostic criteria (see Chapter 4). Furthermore, as will be seen in Chapter 10, the frequency of disorder varies with ecological factors.

To date no study has obtained separate prevalence estimates for undersocialized and socialized conduct disorder. One can only assume that if urban adolescents are studied and conduct disorder is defined so as to include the characteristics of the socialized pattern, then the obtained prevalence estimate for "conduct disorder" no doubt includes both subgroups.

The better studies, using more representative samples of the general population of children, have been carried out in Britain, Australia, and New Zealand. In 10- and 11-year-olds in Britain, population prevalence rates for conduct disorder for both sexes have been reported to be 4 percent in a rural area (Rutter, Cox, Tupling, Berger, & Yule, 1975; Rutter et al., 1970), and 8 percent in an urban area (see Graham, 1979, p. 205). In the Rutter et al. (1975) study, the rate for all disorders was 6.8 percent, so it can be seen that conduct disorder was by far the most prevalent. In both studies the rates for boys was about three times that for girls. In Australia, Glow (1978a, 1978b), using data from parent and teacher ratings, has reported rates for "severe" conduct disorder for both sexes, ages 5 to 12, in urban and suburban area combined to be about 4 percent for both sexes against a rate for all disorders of about 12 percent, with the rate for boys about twice that for girls.

It is unlikely that any of these three studies counted many cases of the socialized type. It is clear that conduct disorder is the most prevalent form of specific childhood disorder, accounting for one-third to one-half or more of all cases, and that boys predominate at a rate of two or three to one.

When hospital admissions and clinic-attenders have been studied, conduct disorder is also the most prevalent form of specific disorder (e.g., Cerreto & Tuma, 1977; Kotsopoulos & Nandy, 1981; Stewart, Gath, & Hierowski, 1981; Werry, Methven, Fitzpatrick, & Dixon, 1983), and boys outnumber girls about three to one.

In addition to studies of diagnosed or diagnosable disorders, there have been a number of inquiries into the prevalence of specific characteristics of both undersocialized and socialized conduct disorder. Among three-year-olds in a suburb of London, Richman, Stevenson, and Graham (1982) found that 12.4 percent of boys were considered by their parents to have definite problems in regard to difficultness to control, 10.8 percent to have problems with siblings, and 16.9 percent to be overactive. However, lower frequencies were reported for rural three-years-olds in the United States by Earls (1980), who found rates (for boys) of 3.7 percent for overactivity, 7.5 percent for problems with siblings or peers, and 7.5 percent for difficultness to manage. In both the British and U.S. studies, the rates for girls were somewhat lower but only in the case of overactivity in Britain (16.9% and 10.5%) were the differences statistically significant.

In an early study, Lapouse and Monk (1964) interviewed parents of a representative sample of 6- to 12-year-olds with regard to problem behaviors and found 31 percent of boys and 21 percent of girls to be considered by their mothers to be behavior control problems. Utilizing teacher ratings, Werry and Quay (1971) studied a group of over 1,700 children in kindergarten, first, and second grades. Although the sample was very predominantly middle-class white, they reported high rates (for boys and girls, respectively) for restlessness (49.7% vs. 27.8%); attention seeking (36.7% vs. 20.6%); disruptiveness (46.3% vs. 22.3%); boisterousness (33.8% vs. 11.2%); fighting (31.3% vs. 6.2%); disobedience (26.1% vs. 10.6%); and hyperactivity (30.3% vs. 13.8%). All of the sex differences were highly significant. As might be expected given the ages of the children, behaviors associated with socialized conduct disorder were infrequent [e.g., steals in company with others (5.7% vs. 3.0%), truancy (3.7% vs. 2.3%)].

These studies as well as others (see Links, 1983, for a review) demonstrate that many of the specific behaviors related to the undersocialized pattern are relatively common, especially in boys. Thus, the use of any single symptom to infer the presence of a disorder is unjustified.

OUTCOME

There are three principal ways in which we may pose questions relevant to the outcome of both forms of conduct disorder. We may first ask whether any or all of the *behavioral characteristics* of these disorders persist over time in the childhood and adolescent years. Second, we may look at the relationship of these characteristics to legally defined behavioral dysfunction (e.g., delinquency, crime) occurring in adolescence or childhood. Finally, we may study social dysfunction in adulthood among those who have actually been *diagnosed* as having one or the other (or possibly both) form of disorder in childhood or adolescence.

Stability of Aggressive Behavior

As we have seen, aggression, both physical and verbal, against people and property is characteristic of both forms of disorder, but especially the undersocialized subtype. Olweus (1979) has reviewed the stability of aggression in boys from the results of studies appearing from 1935 to 1978. In these studies, the average number of subjects was 116; the age at first measurement of aggression varied from 2 to 18 years and the subjects had been followed for intervals of from 6 months to 21 years (the average interval was 5.7 years). The methods of assessment included direct observation, teacher ratings, clinical ratings, peer ratings, and peer nominations. In order to correct for unreliability of measurement, Olweus (1979) recalculated the original stability correlations. He drew a number of conclusions from his analyses: (1) The size of the stability coefficients tended to decrease as the time interval covered increased. (2) The difference in stability between aggression over time and intelligence over time is not great; over a 10-year period, Olweus calculated the extrapolated stability values to be .70 for intelligence and .60 for aggression. (3) The younger the child at first measurement, the less stability. (4) No particular method of measuring aggression produced greater stability.

Olweus (1979) also concluded that: (1) Aggression at age 8 or 9 is correlated with aggression observed 10 to 14 years later, with about 25 percent of the variance accounted for. (2) Aggressive behavior at age 12 and 13 may show a high to very high degree of stability (50–90% of the variance accounted for) and that for periods as long as 10 years, stability is high (45% of the variance accounted for). He also noted in passing (p. 866) that stability for females, not the focus of his analysis, was also substantial. (See also Eron, Huesmann, Lefkowitz, & Walder, 1972.)

A number of recent studies have looked at both preschool and school-aged children over time spans ranging from one to five years. Jenkins, Owen, Bax, and Hart (1984) reported that 45 percent of children having frequent temper tantrums at two years (20% of the study sample) were found to be still having frequent tantrums at age three, while of the 17 percent of the sample having tantrums at age three, 34 percent were still having frequent tantrums at age 4.5. However, the converse was much more certain, over 90 percent *not* having tantrums at one age (either 2 or 3) were found not to have them at the next age (either 3 or 4.5).

Fagot (1984) studied both boys and girls whose ages ranged from 18 to 27 months; each child was observed between 480 and 720 times during a preschool term. One category of behavior represented conduct problems with aggression and included hitting, taking of objects, and verbal assaults. Over a period of one year, the 137 boys showed high stability ($r = .78$); the girls

($n = 121$) were much less stable ($r = .23$). For those 75 boys who attended over a two-year period, there was also high stability ($r = .68$) while for girls ($n = 65$) there was little continuity ($r = .15$).

Fagot's (1984) findings about stability in girls clearly run counter to Olweus' (1979) conclusions from his review. In her study of normal children, it is possible that there was a restriction of range in the conduct problem scores for the girls as well as the possibility that the initially more aggressive girls might have been extinguished due to the ignoring of their aggression; Fagot's data indicated that while boys' aggression was somehow responded to 81 percent of the time, girls received responses only 21 percent of the time—an interesting sidelight on both differential teacher and peer responses according to the sex of the aggressor.

Glow, Glow, and Rump (1982) have reported on the one-year stability of (different) teacher ($n = 169$) and (same) parent ratings ($n = 155$) of problem behavior in children ages 5 to 11 years. Their scales yield scores on factor-analytically derived dimensions of behavior and are thus less specific than individual variables such as "temper tantrums" but less global than clinical ratings. Scores can also be considered as a measure of severity. Overall, there were few significant differences in stability as a function of age at first rating so that the results for the entire sample are presented here. For the teacher ratings, the stability correlations were .53 for the conduct problems and .37 for the antisocial scales, respectively. For parents, the stabilities were .56 for conduct problems, .61 for self-gratification-hostility, and .06 for antisocial. The low stability value for the antisocial scale was attributed to the high frequency of very low scores on that scale; a factor that restricts the range and attenuates the value of the correlation was noted in Chapter 1.

Richman et al. (1982) studied a sample of children living in a working-class suburb of London who had been born over a 12-month period. From a sample of 705, 94 were identified for further study as disturbed on the basis of a questionnaire administered to parents. After initial identification, each child was given a clinical rating of no-problem, dubious, mild, or severe; the reported reliability of this ranking in a subsample of 50 was .88 (p. 18). While Richman et al. (1982) also studied 91 randomly selected controls and a representative sample of disturbed plus controls, the findings reported here focus on the disturbed group.

With respect to the stability of conduct-disorder-related behavior, the percentage of children (sexes combined) showing the behavior at age three and at age four was 54 percent for difficult to control, 48 percent for temper tantrums, 57 percent for poor sib relations, 22 percent for poor peer relations, and 34 percent for attention-seeking. Stability from age four to age eight was 27 percent for difficult to control, 35 percent for temper, 66 percent for sib relations, 40 percent for peer relations, and 38 percent for attention-seeking. Finally, from ages three to eight, stability was 28 percent for difficultness, 43 percent for temper, 46 percent for sib relations, 30 percent for peer relations, and 24 percent for attention-seeking.

With respect to these figures it must be noted that even within the problem group, many children did not manifest conduct-type problems at age three (e.g., difficult to control, 34.4%; attention-seeking, 30.4%; temper, 19.4%) so that the pool of those "eligible" to show consistency over time was quite limited. Nevertheless, among those who did manifest the behavior, there is about a one-third continuity from ages three to eight.

As noted, Richman et al. (1982) also made clinical ratings of severity of disturbance at the three ages. Of those having ratings of moderate or severe disturbance at age three, 74 percent were still so rated at age eight; of the cases of mild disturbance at age three, 47 percent were so rated at age eight. Of those rated moderate or severe at age four, 84 percent were still in that category at age eight, while 56 percent of the "milds" at age four were still "milds" at age eight. Thus, among those judged to be moderately to severely disturbed, there was a high degree of continuity between preschool years three and four and school age eight.

At age eight, the investigators made clinical diagnoses of antisocial disorder (presumably undersocialized plus socialized conduct disorder) versus neurotic disorder (anxiety and depression). Among boys (27 of 52) who were diagnosed as antisocial at age eight, significantly more than those found to be without disorder had earlier been rated as difficult to control (63% vs. 29%) or overactive (78% vs. 29%) at three years, as having poor relations with siblings (52% vs. 8%), and as having had a clinical rating of marked problem (71% vs. 29%).

Only eight girls were diagnosed as antisocial at age eight and the only factor at age three that was significantly different was that the girls with *no disorder* at age eight had been more often rated as having a marked problem at age three (100% vs. 63%). (This unexpected finding is presented in Table 11.5, p. 154, but is not commented upon in the text.) For the 10 boys and 11 girls diagnosed as having a neurotic disorder at age eight versus those not, there were no significant differences with respect to any behavior problems at age three.

Thus, it appears that for boys, the behavioral characteristics of conduct disorder at age three are associated with diagnosed disorder at age eight, while such associations for girls are much weaker.

Fischer, Rolf, Hasazi, and Cummings (1984) have reported on the stability of parent ratings of externalizing behavior assessed at ages 2 to 6 and at ages 9 to 15. The stability correlation for all subjects combined was .36; for boys it was .40 and for girls .32 (a nonsignificant difference). The overall stability for internalizing behavior was only .10 (see Chapter 3). There was also a small negative correlation (− .12) between earlier externalization and later social competence. Subjects were classified as disturbed on the basis of a 90th percentile cutoff score for either scale. While there was no predictability for internalization, the chances of a child's being categorized as significantly externalizing at follow-up was about three times greater if he had been so categorized in preschool.

The stability values obtained in this study are lower than many of those reported for aggressives. This may be due, at least in part, to the fact that the externalizing dimension at follow-up encompasses more than just aggressive (or even conduct disorder) behavior and includes scales related to attention problems as well (see Achenbach & Edelbrock, 1981).

Overall, it is clear that aggressive behavior persists from the preschool into the school years and later and that early aggressive behavior presages later conduct disorder (probably of the undersocialized type). It is important to note that aggressive behavior is also the most important variable in the prediction of later aggression and antisocial behavior even when conduct problems are not the principal cause for complaint (e.g., August, Stewart, & Holmes, 1983; Loney, Whaley-Klahn, Kosier, & Conboy, 1981; see also Chapter 4).

Prediction of Later Delinquency and Crime from Childhood Behavior

In evaluating studies in which delinquency is related, either prospectively or retrospectively, to earlier behavior, it is necessary to be cognizant of two important facts. First, many youths commit delinquent acts who are either never apprehended or, if they are, are for various reasons not officially adjudicated delinquent. While it is likely that serious and persistent offenders are caught and adjudicated, there is always some risk of false negatives in the nondelinquent group, so that the relationship of earlier deviance and later delinquency may be understated.

Second, while the majority of persistent delinquents, especially those institutionalized, *could* most probably be diagnosed as either undersocialized or socialized conduct disorder, there is a group, perhaps up to 25 percent, who are primarily anxious, withdrawn, and depressed or who have problems of attention and behavioral immaturity (see Chapter 1). Thus, the delinquency of this group is unlikely to be foreshadowed by the characteristics of either type of conduct disorder. Since these more internalizing characteristics do not generally relate to later delinquency, delinquents of this type may be very difficult, if not impossible, to predict.

A number of recent studies have looked at the childhood precursors of juvenile delinquency. Farrington (1978) has reported research on a sample of boys in inner-city London who were first contacted at age 8 and who were followed until they were about 22. A multitude of data were collected, including measures of aggressiveness at ages 8, 10, 12, and 14 based on information obtained from their teachers. At ages 16 and 18, aggressiveness was determined on the basis of the boys' responses to a questionnaire. A group of 27 violent delinquents was identified using conviction records up to age 21. Ninety-eight others who had been convicted of other types of crime were classified as nonviolent delinquents.

Measures of aggressiveness were combined for ages 8 and 10, 12 and 14, and 16 and 18, and stability was then assessed. Considerable continuity was evident in that of the 93 boys rated most aggressive at age 8 to 10, 59 percent were still among those rated most aggressive at 12 to 14 and 40 percent at 16 to 18. Fourteen percent were later found in the violent delinquent group. In contrast, of the 317 boys *not* rated among the most aggressive at ages 8 to 10, 25 percent and 27 percent were among the most aggressive at ages 12 to 14 and 16 to 18, respectively; only 4.5 percent became violent delinquents. Of those teacher-rated most aggressive at 12 to 14, 46 percent were so self-rated at 16 to 18 as compared to 22 percent not so rated earlier; 14 percent became violent delinquents. Finally, of those who rated themselves most aggressive at 16 to 18, 15 percent became violent delinquents.

Farrington (1978) also reported that if a boy had been rated high in aggression at age 12 to 14 whether or not he had been high at 8 to 10 did not help in predicting a high rating at 16 to 18. Of the boys high at 12 to 14 and at 8 to 10, 45 percent were high at 16 to 18 in comparison with 47 percent of those high at 12 to 14 but low at 8 to 10. However, if a boy had been high at 8 to 10 but low at 12 to 14 he was more likely to be high at 16 to 18 (33%) than those low at both prior periods (20%). Thus, while as usual, ratings closer in time to the criterion were more predictive, there was some predictability even for those who fell out of the aggressive group at the second rating.

Returning to the prediction of violent delinquency, nearly half the violent delinquents (48%) had been rated aggressive at 8 to 10 and 70 percent of the violent delinquents had been among the most aggressive at age 12 to 14 (as were 49% of the nonviolent delinquents and 23% of the nondelinquents). It is also of interest that a measure of "daring" at 8 to 10 was related to violent delinquency; 13.2 percent of the "daring" boys became violent delinquents while only 3.9 percent of those rated as not daring did so. (While not statistically significant, children rated as highly nervous and withdrawn at 8 to 10 were *less* likely to be violent delinquents than those not so rated: 5.4% vs. 6.8%).

Of interest with respect to socialized conduct was the finding that having a parent convicted of a crime before the child reached age 10 was significantly related to violent delinquency; 14.4 percent of those with a criminal parent (97 of 314) were among the violent delinquents, while only 4.2 percent of those who did not have a criminal parent (217 of 314) became violent. Thus, even though only about 31 percent of the sample had a convicted parent, this 31 percent contributed more actual cases to violent groups than did the remaining 69 percent.

Roff and Wirt (1984) studied samples of over 1000 boys and girls in third through sixth grades who were first classified as low, middle, and high peer status on the basis of sociometric ratings. Teacher interviews were then conducted about the most and least popular boy and girl in each classroom and a middle status peer of the opposite sex for the most popular child. Delinquency and adult criminality (boys only) defined by official records were the outcomes of interest.

For the low-status children, the teacher interviews were analyzed to identify problems apparently associated with peer rejection. The resultant list of problems was factor analyzed and yielded, among others, a rebellious-aggressive factor for both sexes. A scale labeled "predelinquent" was also constructed from low-frequency items not included in the factor analysis and included stealing in school, stealing in the community, trouble with the law, running away from home, plus lying and truancy, which did not have high loadings on any of the factors. Additionally, data on SES and a rating of family disturbance were obtained.

For all boys with teacher interviews, the delinquency rate was 26.3 percent, with low-status boys in the lowest social class having the highest rate (46.3%); the R for peer status and social class as predictors was significant, but quite low (.28). For girls the overall rate was 8.2 percent with a similar pattern but an R of only .19.

Of particular interest was the finding that within the low-status group, boys' aggressive behavior was significantly correlated with delinquency ($r = .30$) as was the predelinquent scale ($r = .25$). For girls, aggression was significantly, but only weakly ($r = .13$), related to delinquency. It is worth noting here that the scale measuring anxiety and tension was not at all related to delinquency for either sex (see also Chapter 3). For the boys adult criminality was significantly related to aggression ($r = .24$) and more so to delinquency ($r = .41$). Of those delinquent, 34.2 percent had adult criminal records while among nondelinquents only 3.2 percent had adult offenses. Finally, as might be expected, behavior closer in time to the criterion was more highly correlated; for third- and fourth-grade males the aggression-delinquency correlation was .23 while for fifth and sixth graders it was .35.

Huesmann, Eron, Lefkowitz, and Walder (1984) have provided a long-term follow-up of 198 males and 211 females first assessed (peer nomination) at age 8 and last assessed at age 30. Subjects' self-ratings and ratings by the spouse were supplemented by data on criminal activity and traffic violations.

The stability correlations (all significant) for males were .30 and .29 for two measures of self-reported aggression, .27 for spouse-reported abuse, .24 for criminal convictions, .21 for seriousness of criminal act, .21 for moving traffic violations, and .29 for driving while intoxicated. For females the significant correlations were .20 for aggression and .17 for seriousness of criminal acts. Of those males highest in peer-nominated aggression at age eight, 23 percent had been convicted of a crime in their home state versus 15 percent in the medium group, and 9 percent in the low aggressive group. For females, the percentages were 6.3, 1.8, and 0.

Additional data analyses led Huesmann et al. (1984) to conclude that stability of aggression increases with age, is higher for males than females, and is no less stable over time when the effects of intelligence are partialed out, and that the stability of aggression measured with perfect reliability would be about .50 for males and .34 for females.

Mitchell and Rosa (1981) studied large random samples (3258 boys and 3046 girls) between 5 and 15 years old who had been rated by their teachers as to behavior and health. They selected the 10 percent of boys who were most deviant and compared them to a nondeviant group matched boy-for-boy for ages and school. Data on criminality were collected from official records and offenses were classified as theft, damage to property, and interpersonal violence.

Of the 321 matched pairs, 19.6 percent of the deviant group had ben convicted of one offense as compared to 9 percent of the controls. Theft was twice as frequent (15.6% vs. 6.9%) as was damage to property (5.0% vs. 1.6%). Interpersonal violence was low in both groups (3.4% vs. 1.2%) and was not significantly different. In terms of court appearances, 17 of the deviators (5.3%) versus only 1 of the controls (0.3%) had had five court appearances.

At the behavioral level, only six parent-related items were associated with criminality or recidivism: stealing, destructiveness, wandering from home, and lying (generally characteristics of socialized aggression) were positively associated while excessive worrying and food fads were negatively related. Two out of three boys reported by parents as having stolen things on several occasions had subsequently appeared in court, compared to one in five of the total group of deviants. Most of them had been convicted of theft, but they were also five times as likely to be convicted of damage to property and seven times as likely to be convicted of interpersonal violence than the total group (only one boy had had a court appearance *prior* to the parental rating). Boys parent rated as destructive were also five times as likely to be convicted than those not destructive. The truants from home, however, were more likely to be convicted of theft only.

When teacher scores were combined with parent scores, those with the high combined scores were twice as likely to be offenders as those with low combined scores; recidivism was three times as likely. It is important to note, however, that 71 percent of all those with high combined scores were *not* convicted. Of further interest was the finding that *if* the child had been rated by the parent as markedly deviant, the addition of the teachers' information adds nothing to the predictability of delinquency. Teachers' information on thievery or lying was, however, predictive of court appearance (42.9% vs. 7.1% and 40.9% vs. 6.3% for thieves and liars, respectively, as compared to the rest of the deviant group).

There was, however, considerable divergence as regards those boys identified by parents and teachers. Sixty-one percent of boys said by their parents to have stolen were not so labeled by teachers; of those seen as thieves by teachers, 58 percent were not so categorized by parents. Of the seven boys labeled thieves by both informants, five became persistent offenders. In the case of lying, of those 14 boys jointly labeled by both, 9 were in court, of whom 7 appeared two times or more. Those labeled by *both* informants as either liars or thieves have about twice the chance of a court appearance as those labeled by *either* informant alone.

This study would suggest that while general behavioral deviance is related to delinquency, those behaviors most predictive (truancy from home, stealing, and lying) are those related to socialized conduct disorder. This deviant sample, however, had a low rate (3.2%) for conviction of a violent offense, the theft conviction rate (15.8%) being three times as great.

Research by Moore, Chamberlain, and Mukai (1979) is relevant to the undersocialized-socialized distinction. They obtained data on court-recorded offenses for three groups of children seen two to nine years earlier for primarily aggression in the home ($n = 21$) or stealing ($n = 25$) or as normal comparison cases ($n = 14$). The aggressives averaged 8 years in age, the controls 8.9, and the stealers 11.1. They found that 21 of 25 of the stealers, 5 of 21 of the aggressives, and 3 of 14 normals had had court appearances for nonstealing offenses. Among those for whom both stealing and aggression were noted at referral, 11 of 14 had a court-recorded offense; of those who *only* stole, 11 of 13 were offenders while of those who were *only* aggressive or normals, the number of offenders were 2 of 13 and 3 of 15, respectively.

It should be noted, however, that 13 of the 31 stealers had court contact prior to being referred. Nevertheless, of the 18 who had not had prior contact, 10 did have subsequent contact. Only two of the aggressives and three of the controls had had prior contact. For the stealers the probability of a second offense given a first was .92, the probability of a third given a second was .91, the probability of a fourth given a third was .80, and the probability of a fifth given a fourth was .88. Fifty-two percent of the stealers had four or more offenses.

As in the study of Mitchell and Rosa (1981), stealing was highly related to court contact. It is, of course, the case that stealing is considered as clearly illegal while even persistent initiation of fights may not often come to the attention of police. Thus, while undersocialized aggressive behavior persists into late childhood and adolescence, it does not seem to foretell legally defined delinquency, especially property offenses, as well as does behavior related to socialized conduct disorder. This finding is also in accord with recent work by Hanson, Henggeler, Haefele, and Rodick (1984), who found that parent-rated socialized aggressive behavior was most closely related to official delinquency on a concurrent basis.

Robins and her colleagues have contributed a number of follow-up studies linking childhood behavior to various types of adult outcomes. The earliest and most widely cited study (see Robins, 1966) compared more than 500 child guidance clinic patients (age 18 years and under; median of 13) with 100 nonpatient school children of the same age, sex (70% male), and race, of similar intelligence, living in the same neighborhoods as the patients. Seventy-three percent of the patients had been referred for antisocial behavior, many from the juvenile court. Interviews in their adult years were completed on 82 percent of the subjects while official records were obtained on 98 percent. The results of this study clearly indicated that the antisocial children were more deviant as adults than were the controls or children with other diagnoses. Among males 71 percent of the antisocials, 30 percent of those with other diagnoses, and 22 percent of the controls had been arrested as an adult for a nontraffic offense; the same percentages for females were 40, 10, and 0. Half of the antisocial males had been arrested three or more times versus 18 percent for the other patients and only 4 percent for the controls; 44 percent had been arrested for a major crime versus 12 percent and 3 percent for the other two groups. Of the male antisocial group, only 70 percent had full-time jobs at follow-up compared with 87 percent of those referred for other problems and 95 percent of the controls. Additionally, the antisocial groups were significantly more socially alienated, more often hospitalized, reported more subjective feelings of ill health, and had more problems with alcohol.

Psychiatric diagnosis (consensus of two psychiatrists) was also obtained for most of the adults. Among all the patients, 22 percent were diagnosed as without disorder as compared to 52 percent of the controls; 25 percent of male and 12 percent of female patients were diagnosed as sociopathic personality as against 3 percent for male controls and 0 percent for female controls. Among those of both sexes referred for antisocial behavior (73% of the total sample), 28 percent were later diagnosed as sociopathic versus 4 percent of those referred for other reasons and 2 percent of controls. The number, seriousness, and frequency of antisocial symptoms present in childhood were also significantly related to an adult diagnosis of sociopathy.

In later research Robins and her associates have studied young black men and Vietnam veterans (see Robins, 1974; Robins, West, & Herjanic, 1975). In summarizing her work, Robins (1979) concluded,

> *Antisocial personality seems to be a real syndrome in American males, one that rarely occurs in the absence of serious antisocial behavior in childhood. It is better predicted by the variety of childhood antisocial behaviors than any particular behavior, and childhood behaviors are better predictors than are family variables. Social class is not a family characteristic that helps in the prediction. Despite the important role that childhood antisocial behavior plays in forecasting adult antisocial behavior, most antisocial children do not grow into severely antisocial adults (although very few of them are completely free of antisocial behavior as adults). (p. 232)*

While these are extremely valuable studies, it is unfortunate that they did not differentiate among childhood behaviors related to undersocialized versus socialized conduct disorder so as to determine which pattern is more closely related to adult dysfunction.

A recent study, however, has compared the adult outcomes of the two different forms of conduct disorder (Henn, Bardwell, & Jenkins, 1980). These investigators used the case files in a state institution for delinquent boys to classify subjects as undersocialized conduct disorder—aggressive ($n = 51$), socialized conduct disorder ($n = 107$), and undersocialized conduct disorder—unaggressive ($n = 49$). The defining criteria for the last group (see Henn et al., 1980, p. 1161) were a mixture of both internalizing (e.g., fearfulness and timidity, lonesomeness) and externalizing (e.g., chronic disobedience, stealing in the home) behaviors. The adult criminal records of the subjects were obtained from official sources including arrests, convictions, prison terms, and types of crimes.

Initial data analyses revealed that the groups were comparable as to age at admission to the training school, ethnicity, number of children in the home, and urban–rural residence. Analyses of the training school's records found that the socialized group had done better while incarcerated than the undersocialized groups combined; they had spent less time in the institution, had been discharged at a younger age, and had had fewer returns to the school.

The data on adult criminal activity revealed that the likelihood of conviction on an adult charge was significantly greater for the two undersocialized groups than for the socialized group (62.7% for aggressives, 57.1% for nonaggressive, and 42.1% for the socialized group), as was the likelihood of incarceration (52.9% and 46.9% vs. 33.6%), and arrest for a violent crime (31.4% and 12.2% vs. 16.8%). With regard to adult violent crimes, the nonaggressive group differed significantly from the aggressive but not the socialized group.

Thus, while we have already seen that behavior of a socialized aggressive nature occurring in childhood and adolescence presages later official delinquency (apparently even more so than does undersocialized conduct disorder behavior), those among the undersocialized who *do* become involved in illegal behavior as adolescents are at greater risk for serious adult criminality.

Why this should be so, especially the "reversal" in prognosis, may be due to a number of factors. As we suggested, socialized aggressive behavior in later childhood and adolescence is more apt to attract official attention as it very often involves misappropriation of other people's property, school truancy, and curfew violation. Fighting, verbal aggression, and noncompliance are troublesome to parents and schools but do not necessarily come to the attention of the criminal justice system. However, as the years go by the undersocialized conduct disorder pattern does bring more conflict with the law as verbal aggression and fighting may become criminal assault, strong-arm robbery, resisting arrest, or worse. As Henn et al. (1980) found, and as we have noted, the undersocialized group does not adjust well in institutional settings and their behavior is very resistant to change. Now as older adolescents and adults, they are prone to behavior that does, often dramatically, come to the attention of the police.

The better adult outcomes for the socialized group may be due to their ability to change—to learn that at least *petty* crime does not pay. As has been pointed out earlier in this chapter, the socialized group generally has unimpaired cognitive skills, good social skills, learning ability, and affiliative needs, all of these factors being on the plus side for making an adequate social adjustment in adulthood.

Overall, it is clear that there is considerable persistence throughout childhood, into adolescence, and even into adulthood, particularly of undersocialized behavior. However, most aggressive children do not become juvenile delinquents or adult criminals, as is clearly shown by the results of Farrington (1978) and Robins (1966). At the same time adult antisocial behavior and criminality rarely arise de novo, and the ranks of adult offenders are filled by those who were conduct disordered children and adolescents.

SUMMARY

The two patterns of conduct disorder combined are the most prevalent form of childhood and adolescent disorder, with a preponderance of males at a ratio of at least three to one. The correlates of the undersocialized pattern include deficient verbal mediational skills, poor social skills, persistent failure in social intervention programs, and a generally poorer prognosis for successful adult living than, as will be noted in subsequent chapters, any other disorder except psychosis. While environmental factors play a major etiological role (see Chapters 9 and 10), recent research has implicated psychophysiological and biochemical factors.

The socialized form is not associated with cognitive deficits or demonstrably poor social relations. Neither are there any intimations of a biological component in its etiology. While childhood behavior related to this pattern is clearly related to delinquency in adolescence, adjustment in adult life appears to be superior to that of the undersocialized form.

The social cost of the conduct disorders is high and, as will be seen in Chapters 13 to 17, these two disorders have been the primary focus of intervention and prevention efforts coming from the entire spectrum of social agencies. Clearly, no other disorder of childhood and adolescence is so widespread and disruptive of the lives of those who suffer it and of the lives of others, and thus it deserves continued research investigation.

REFERENCES

Achenbach, T. M., & Edelbrock, C. S. (1981). Behavioral problems and competencies reported by parents of normal and disturbed children aged four through sixteen. *Monographs of the Society for Research in Child Development, 46*, 1 (No. 188).

Akamatsu, T. J., & Farudi, P. A. (1978). Effects of model status and juvenile offender type on the imitation of self-reward criteria. *Journal of Consulting and Clinical Psychology, 46*, 187–188.

American Psychiatric Association. (1980). *Diagnostic and statistical manual of mental disorders* (3rd ed.). Washington, DC: American Psychiatric Association.

August, G. J., Stewart, M. A., & Holmes, C. S. (1983). A four-year follow-up of hyperactive boys with and without conduct disorder. *British Journal of Psychiatry, 143*, 192–198.

Bear, G. C., & Richard, H. C. (1981). Moral reasoning and conduct problems in the classroom. *Journal of Educational Psychology, 73*, 644–670.

Beitchman, J. H., Patterson, P., Gelfand, B., & Minty, G. (1982). IQ and child psychiatric disorder. *Canadian Journal of Psychiatry, 27*, 23–28.

Bohman, M., Cloninger, C. R., Sigvardsson, S., & von Knorring, A.-L. (1982). Predisposition to petty criminality in Swedish adoptees. I. Genetic and environmental heterogeneity. *Archives of General Psychiatry, 39*, 1233–1241.

Borkovec, T. D. (1970). Autonomic reactivity to sensory stimulation in psychopathic, neurotic and normal delinquents. *Journal of Consulting and Clinical Psychology, 35*, 217–222.

Brown, G. L., Ballanger, J. C., Minichiello, M.D., & Goodwin, F. K. (1979). Human aggression and its relationship to cerebrospinal fluid 5-hydroxyindoleacetic acid, 3-methoxy-4-hydroxyphenylglycol, and homovanillic acid. In M. Sandler (Ed.), *Psychopharmacology of aggression* (pp. 131–148). New York: Raven Press.

Brown, G. L., Ebert, M. H., Goyer, P. F., Jimerson, D. C., Klein, W. J., Bunney, W. E., & Goodwin, F. K. (1982). Aggression, suicide, and serotonin: Relationships to CSF amine metabolites. *American Journal of Psychiatry, 139*, 741–746.

Bryan, J. H., & Kapche, R. (1967). Psychopathy and verbal conditioning. *Journal of Abnormal Psychology, 72*, 71–73.

Camp, B. W. (1977). Verbal mediation in young aggressive boys. *Journal of Abnormal Psychology, 86*, 145–153.

Campagna, A. F., & Harter, S. (1975). Moral judgment in sociopathic and normal children. *Journal of Personality and Social Psychology, 31*, 199–205.

Cartwright, D. S., Howard, K. I., & Reuterman, N. A. (1980). Multivariate analysis of gang delinquency: IV. Personality factors in gangs and clubs. *Multivariate Behavioral Research, 15*, 3–22.

Cerreto, M. C., & Tuma, J. M. (1977). Distribution of DSM-II diagnoses in a child psychiatric setting. *Journal of Abnormal Child Psychology, 5*, 147–155.

DeFries, J. C., & Plomin, R. (1978). Behavioral genetics. In M. R. Rosenzweig & L. W. Porter (Eds.), *Annual review of psychology* (Vol. 29, pp. 473–515). Palo Alto, CA: Annual Review.

Delamater, A. M., & Lahey, B. B. (1983). Physiological correlates of conduct problems and anxiety in hyperactive and learning-disabled children. *Journal of Abnormal Child Psychology, 11*, 85–100.

Deluty, R. H. (1981). Alternative-thinking ability of aggressive, assertive and submissive children. *Cognitive Therapy and Research, 5*, 309–312.

DeMyer-Gapin, S., & Scott, T. J. (1977). Effects of stimulus novelty on stimulation seeking in antisocial and neurotic children. *Journal of Abnormal Psychology, 86*, 96–98.

Devies, R. K. (1975). The use of the differential behavioral classification system of the juvenile offender to distinguish probation successes from probation failures. (Doctoral dissertation, Kent State University, 1975). *Dissertation Abstracts International, 36*, 5819A. (University Microfilm No. 75-4921.)

Dietrich, C. (1976). Differential effects of task and reinforcement variables on the performance of three groups of behavior problem children. *Journal of Abnormal Child Psychology, 4*, 155–171.

Docter, R. F., & Winder, C. L. (1954). Delinquent *vs.* nondelinquent behavior in the Porteus Qualitative Maze Test. *Journal of Consulting Psychology, 18*, 71–73.

Dodge, K. A., & Frame, C. L. (1982). Social cognitive biases and deficits in aggressive boys. *Child Development, 53*, 620–635.

Dodge, K. A., & Newman, J. P. (1981). Biased decision-making processes in aggressive boys. *Journal of Abnormal Psychology, 90,* 375–450.

Dwivedi, K. N., Beaumont, G., & Brandon, S. (1984). Electrophysiological responses in high and low aggressive young adolescent boys. *Acta Paedopsychiatrica, 50,* 179–190.

Earls, F. (1980). Prevalence of behavior problems in 3-year-old children. *Archives of General Psychiatry, 37,* 1153–1157.

Ellis, P. L. (1982). Empathy: A factor in antisocial behavior. *Journal of Abnormal Child Psychology, 10,* 123–134.

Eron, L. D., Huesmann, L. R., Lefkowitz, M. M., & Walder, L. O. (1972). Does television cause aggression? *American Psychologist, 27,* 253–263.

Fagot, B. I. (1984). The consequences of problem behavior in toddler children. *Journal of Abnormal Child Psychology, 12,* 385–395.

Farrington, D. P. (1978). The family backgrounds of aggressive youths. In L. A. Hersov, A. L. Berger, & D. Shaffer (Eds.), *Aggression and anti-social behavior in childhood and adolescence* (pp. 73–93). London: Pergamon.

Ferguson, B. (Sept. 1984). *Review of psychobiological assessment procedures in research on child and adolescent psychopathology.* Paper prepared for NIMH Conference on the Definition and Measurement of Psychopathology in Children and Adults, Washington, DC.

Fischer, M., Rolf, J. E., Hasazi, J. E., & Cummings, L. (1984). Follow-up of a preschool epidemiological sample: Cross-age continuities and predictions of later adjustments with internalizing and externalizing dimensions of behavior. *Child Development, 55,* 137–150.

Fowles, D. C. (1980). The Three Arousal Model: Implications of Gray's two-factor learning theory for heart rate, electrodermal activity, and psychopathy. *Psychophysiology, 17,* 87–104.

Gabrielli, W. F., & Mednick, S. A. (1983). Genetic correlates of criminal behavior. *American Behavioral Scientist, 27,* 59–74.

Glow, R. A. (1978a). *Children's behaviour problems. A normative study of a parent rating scale.* Unpublished monograph.

Glow, R. A. (1978b). *Classroom behaviour problems. An Australian normative study of the Conners' Teachers' Rating Scale.* Unpublished monograph.

Glow, R. A., Glow, P. H., & Rump, E. E. (1982). The stability of child behavior disorders: A one year test-retest study of Adelaide versions of the Conners' Teacher and Parent Rating Scales. *Journal of Abnormal Child Psychology, 10,* 33–60.

Glueck, S., & Glueck, E. (1950). *Unraveling juvenile delinquency.* Cambridge: Harvard University Press.

Gold, M., & Mann, D. (1972). Delinquency as a defense. *American Journal of Orthopsychiatry, 42,* 463–479.

Gould, M. S., Wunsch-Hitzig, R., & Dohrenwend, B. (1981). Estimating the prevalence of childhood psychopathology. *Journal of the American Academy of Child Psychiatry, 20,* 462–476.

Graham, P. (1979). Epidemiological studies. In H. C. Quay & J. S. Werry (Eds.), *Psychopathological disorders of childhood* (2nd ed., pp. 185–209). New York: Wiley.

Gray, J. A. (1979). A neuro-psychological theory of anxiety. In C. E. Izard (Ed.), *Emotions in personality and psychopathology* (pp. 303–335). New York: Plenum.

Gray, J. A. (1982). *The neuropsychology of anxiety: An enquiry into the functions of the Septo-Hippocampal System.* New York: Oxford University Press.

Hale, R. L., & Landino, S. A. (1981). Utility of WISC-R subtest analysis in discriminating among groups of conduct-problem, withdrawn, mixed and nonproblem boys. *Journal of Consulting and Clinical Psychology, 49,* 91–95.

Hanson, C. L., Henggeler, S. W., Haefele, W. F., & Rodick, J. D. (1984). Demographic, individual, and family relationship correlates of serious and repeated crime among adolescents and their siblings. *Journal of Consulting and Clinical Psychology, 52,* 528–538.

Hare, R. D. (1978). Electrodermal and cardiac correlates of psychopathy. In R. D. Hare & D. Schalling (Eds.), *Psychopathic behavior: Approaches to research* (pp. 107–144). New York: Wiley.

Hecht, I. H., & Jurkovic, G. J. (1978). The performance-verbal discrepancy in differentiated subgroups of delinquent boys. *Journal of Youth and Adolescence, 7,* 197–201.

Henn, F. A., Bardwell, R., & Jenkins, R. L. (1980). Juvenile delinquents revisited. *Archives of General Psychiatry, 37,* 1160–1163.

Hogan, A. E., & Quay, H. C. (1984). Cognition in child and adolescent behavior disorders. In B. B. Lahey & A. E. Kazdin (Eds.), *Advances in clinical child psychology* (pp. 1–34). New York: Plenum.

Hubble, L. M., & Groff, M. (1981). Factor analysis of WISC-R scores of male delinquents referred for evaluation. *Journal of Consulting and Clinical Psychology, 49,* 738–739.

Huesmann, L. R., Eron, L. D., Lefkowitz, M. M., & Walder, L. O. (1984). The stability of aggression over time and generations. *Developmental Psychology, 20,* 1120–1134.

Jenkins, S., Owen, C., Bax, M., & Hart, H. (1984). Continuities of common behaviour problems in preschool children. *Journal of Child Psychology and Psychiatry, 25,* 75–89.

Johns, J. H., & Quay, H. C. (1962). The effect of social reward on verbal conditioning in psychopathic and neurotic military offenses. *Journal of Consulting Psychology, 26,* 217–220.

Jurkovic, G. J., & Prentice, N. M. (1977). Relation of moral and cognitive development to dimensions of juvenile delinquency. *Journal of Abnormal Psychology, 86,* 414–420.

Kagan, J., Rosman, B. L., Day, D., Albert, J., & Phillips, W. (1964). Information processing in the child: Significance of analytic and reflective attitudes. *Psychological Monographs, 78* (Whole No. 578).

Kaufman, A. S. (1976). Verbal-Performance IQ discrepancies on the WISC-R. *Journal of Consulting and Clinical Psychology, 44,* 739–744.

Kendall, P. C., Zupan, B. A. & Braswell, L. (1981). Self-control in children: Further analyses of the Self-Control Rating Scale. *Behavior Therapy, 12,* 667–681.

Konstantareas, M. M., & Homatidis, S. (1985). Dominance hierarchies in normal and conduct-disordered children. *Journal of Abnormal Psychology, 13,* 259–267.

Kotsopoulos, S., & Nandy, S. (1981). A profile of the child psychiatric population of Newfoundland. *Canadian Journal of Psychiatry, 26*, 189–191.

Lapouse, R., & Monk, M. A. (1964). Behavior deviations in a representative sample of children. Variations by sex, age, social class, and family size. *American Journal of Orthopsychiatry, 34*, 436–446.

Ledingham, J. E., & Schwartzman, A. E. (1984). A 3-year follow-up of aggressive and withdrawn behavior in childhood: Preliminary findings. *Journal of Abnormal Child Psychology, 12*, 157–168.

Levin, G. R., & Simmons, J. J. (1962a). Response to food and praise by emotionally disturbed boys. *Psychological Reports, 11*, 10.

Levin, G. R., & Simmons, J. J. (1962b). Response to food and praise by emotionally disturbed boys. *Psychological Reports, 11*, 539–546.

Links, P. S. (1983). Community surveys of the prevalence of childhood psychiatric disorders: A review. *Child Development, 54*, 531–548.

Loeber, R., & Schmaling, K. B. (1985). The utility of differentiating between mixed and pure forms of antisocial child behavior. *Journal of Abnormal Child Psychology, 13*, 315–335.

Loney, J., Whaley-Klahn, M. A., Kosier, T., & Conboy, J. (Nov. 1981). *Hyperactive boys and their brothers at 21: Predictors of aggressive and antisocial outcomes.* Paper presented at the meeting of the Society for Life History Research, Monterey, CA.

Mack, J. L. (1969). Behavior ratings of recidivist and nonrecidivist delinquent males. *Psychological Reports, 25*, 260.

McGee, R., Williams, S., Share, D., Anderson, J., & Silva, P. A. *The relationship between specific reading retardation, general reading backwardness and behavioural disorders in a large sample of Dunedin boys: A longitudinal study for five to eleven years.* Unpublished paper.

McGee, R., Williams, S., & Silva, P. A. (1984). Behavioral and developmental characteristics of aggressive, hyperactive and hyperactive-aggressive boys. *Journal of the American Academy of Child Psychiatry, 23*, 270–290.

McGee, R., Williams, S., & Silva, P. A. (1985). Factor structures and correlates of ratings of inattention, hyperactivity and antisocial behavior in a large sample of 9 year old children from the general population. *Journal of Consulting and Clinical Psychology, 53*, 480–490.

Mednick, S. A., & Cristiansen, K. O. (Eds.) (1977). *Biosocial bases of criminal behavior.* New York: Gardner Press.

Mitchell, S., & Rosa, P. (1981). Boyhood behaviour problems as precursors of criminality: A fifteen-year follow-up study. *Journal of Child Psychiatry, 22*, 19–23.

Moore, D. R., Chamberlain, P., & Mukai, L. H. (1979). Children at risk for delinquency: A follow-up comparison of aggressive children and children who steal. *Journal of Abnormal Child Psychology, 7*, 345–355.

Moore, J., Vigil, D., & Garcia, R. (1983). Residence and territoriality in Chicano gangs. *Social Problems, 31*, 182–194.

Moses, J. A. (1974). Two choice discrimination learning of delinquent boys as a joint function of reinforcement contingency and delinquent subtype (Doctoral dissertation, University of Colorado). *Dissertation Abstracts International, 35*, 1922B. (University Microfilm No. 74-22, 375.)

Mueller, H. F., & Shamsie, S. J. (June 1967). *Classification of behavior disorders in adolescents and EEG findings.* Paper presented at the 17th Annual Meeting of the Canadian Psychiatric Association, Quebec City.

Nasby, W., Hayden, B., & De Paulo, B. M. (1980). Attributional bias among aggressive boys to interpret unambiguous social stimulus as displays of hostility. *Journal of Abnormal Psychology, 89*, 459–468.

Nucci, L. P., & Herman, S. (1982). Behavioral disordered children's conceptions of moral, conventional, and personal issues. *Journal of Abnormal Child Psychology, 10*, 411–426.

O'Connor, M., Foch, T., Sherry, T., & Plomin, R. (1980). A twin study of specific behavioral problems of socialization as viewed by parents. *Journal of Abnormal Child Psychology, 8*, 189–199.

Offord, D. R., & Poushinsky, M. F. (1981). School performance, IQ, and female delinquency. *International Journal of Social Psychiatry, 27*, 53–62.

Offord, D. R., Poushinsky, M. F., & Sullivan, K. (1978). School performance, IQ and delinquency. *British Journal of Criminology, 18*, 110–127.

Olds, M. E., & Fobes, J. C. (1981). The central basis of motivation: Intracranial self-stimulation studies. In M. R. Rosenzweig & C. W. Porter (Eds.), *Annual review of psychology* (pp. 523–574). Palo Alto, CA: Annual Reviews.

Olweus, D. (1979). Stability of aggressive reaction patterns in males: A review. *Psychological Bulletin, 86*, 852–875.

Orris, J. B. (1969). Visual monitoring performance in three subgroups of male delinquents. *Journal of Abnormal Psychology, 74*, 227–229.

Panella, D., & Henggeler, S. W. (1986). Peer interactions of conduct disordered, anxious-withdrawn, and well-adjusted black adolescents. *Journal of Abnormal Child Psychology, 14*, 1–11.

Paulsen, K. A. (1978). Organismic characteristics as predictions of problem behavior for boys in residential treatment (Doctoral dissertation, Southern Illinois University, 1977). *Dissertation Abstracts International, 38*, 4992B. (University Microfilm No. 7804295.)

Paulsen, K., & Johnson, M. (1980). Impulsivity: A multidimensional concept with developmental aspects. *Journal of Abnormal Child Psychology, 8*, 269–277.

Plomin, R. (1983). Childhood temperament. In B. B. Lahey & A. E. Kazdin (Eds.), *Advances in clinical child psychology* (Vol. 6, pp. 45–92). New York: Plenum.

Prinz, R. J., Connor, P. A., & Wilson, C. C. (1981). Hyperactive and aggressive behaviors in childhood: Intertwined dimensions. *Journal of Abnormal Child Psychology, 9*, 191–202.

Quay, H. C. (1964a). Personality dimensions in delinquent males as inferred from the factor analysis of behavior ratings. *Journal of Research in Crime and Delinquency, 1*, 33–37.

Quay, H. C. (1964b). Dimensions of personality in delinquent boys as inferred from the factor analysis of case history data. *Child Development, 35*, 479–484.

Quay, H. C. (1965). Psychopathic personality as pathological stimulation-seeking. *American Journal of Psychiatry, 122*, 180–183.

Quay, H. C. (1966). Personality patterns in preadolescent delinquent boys. *Educational Psychological Measurement, 16*, 99–110.

Quay, H. C. (1977). Psychopathic behavior: Reflections on its nature, origins and treatment. In F. Weizmann & I. Uzgiris (Eds.), *The structuring of experience* (pp. 371–382). New York: Plenum.

Quay, H. C. (1986). The behavioral reward and inhibition systems in childhood behavior disorder. In L. M. Bloomingdale (Ed.), *Attention deficit disorder 3*. New York: Spectrum.

Quay, H. C., & Levinson, R. B. (1967). *The prediction of the institutional adjustment of four subgroups of delinquent boys*. Unpublished manuscript.

Quay, H. C., & Love, C. T. (1977). The effects of a juvenile diversion program on rearrests. *Criminal Justice and Behavior, 4*, 377–396.

Quay, H. C., & Peterson, D. R. (1983). *Interim manual of the revised behavior problem checklist*. Miami, FL: Authors.

Quay, H. C., Peterson, D. R., & Consalvi, C. (1960). The interpretation of three personality factors in juvenile delinquency. *Journal of Consulting Psychology, 24*, 555.

Raine, A., & Venables, P. H. (1984b). Tonic heart rate level, social class and antisocial behaviour in adolescents. *Biological Psychology, 18*, 123–132.

Raine, A., & Venables, P. H. (1984b). Electrodermal nonresponding, antisocial behavior, and schizoid tendencies in adolescents. *Psychophysiology, 21*, 424–433.

Richman, L. C., & Lindgren, S. D. (1981). Verbal mediation deficits: Relation to behavior and achievement in children. *Journal of Abnormal Psychology, 90*, 99–104.

Richman, N., Stevenson, J., & Graham, P. J. (1982). *Pre-school to school: A behavioural study*. London: Academic Press.

Roberts, A. H., & Erikson, R. V. (1968). Delay of gratification, Porteus Maze Test performance, and behavioral adjustment in a delinquent group. *Journal of Abnormal Psychology, 73*, 449–453.

Robins, C. N. (1966). *Deviant children grown up*. Baltimore: Williams & Wilkins.

Robins, C. N. (1974). *The Vietnam drug user returns*. Special Action Office monograph, Series A. No. 2. Washington, DC: Government Printing Office.

Robins, C. N. (1979). Sturdy childhood predictors of adult outcome replication from longitudinal studies. In J. E. Barrett, R. M. Rose, & G. L. Klerman (Eds.), *Stress and mental disorder*. New York: Raven Press.

Robins, C. N., West, P. A., & Herjanic, B. (1975). Arrests and delinquency in two generations: A study of black urban families and their children. *Journal of Child Psychology and Psychiatry, 16*, 125–140.

Roff, J. D., & Wirt, R. D. (1984). Childhood aggression and social adjustments as antecedents of delinquency. *Journal of Abnormal Child Psychology, 12*, 111–126.

Rogeness, G. A., Hernandez, J. M., Macedo, C. A., Amrung, S. A., & Hoppe, S. K. (1984). *Dopamine-beta-hydroxylase and conduct disorder in emotionally disturbed boys*. Unpublished manuscript, University of Texas Health Science Center, Department of Psychiatry, San Antonio.

Rogeness, G. A., Hernandez, J. M., Macedo, C. A., & Mitchell, E. L. (1982). Biochemical differences in children with conduct disorder socialized and undersocialized. *American Journal of Psychiatry, 139*, 307–311.

Rogeness, G. A., Hernandez, J. M., Macedo, C. A., Mitchell, E. L., Amrung, S. A., & Harris, W. R. (1984). Clinical characteristics of emotionally disturbed boys with very low activities of dopamine-beta-hydroxylase. *Journal of the American Academy of Child Psychiatry, 23*, 203–208.

Rutter, M. (1964). Intelligence and childhood psychiatric disorder. *British Journal of Social and Clinical Psychology, 3*, 120–129.

Rutter, M. (1982). Temperament: Concepts, issues and problems. In R. Parker & G. Lawrenson (Eds.), *Temperamental differences in young children*. London: Pitman.

Rutter, M., Cox, A., Tupling, C., Berger, M., & Yule, W. (1975). Attainment and adjustment in two geographical areas. I. Prevalence of psychiatric disorder. *British Journal of Psychiatry, 126*, 493–509.

Rutter, M., Tizard, J., & Whitmore, K. (1970). *Education, health and behavior*. London: Longmans.

Sandberg, S. T., Wieselberg, M., & Shaffer, D. (1980). Hyperkinetic and conduct problem children in a primary school population: Some epidemiological considerations. *Journal of Child Psychology and Psychiatry, 21*, 293–311.

Sattler, J. M. (1982). *Assessment of children's intelligence and special abilities* (2nd ed.). Boston: Allyn & Bacon.

Schmidt, K., Solanto, M. V., & Bridger, W. H. (1985). Electrodermal activity of undersocialized aggressive children: A pilot study. *Journal of Child Psychology and Psychiatry, 26*, 653–660.

Schuck, S., Dubeck, J. A., Cymbalisty, B. Y., & Green, C. (1972). Delinquency, personality tests and relationships to measures of guilt and adjustment. *Psychological Reports, 31*, 219–226.

Siddle, D. A. T., Nicol, A. R., & Foggitt, R. H. (1973). Habituation and over-extinction of the GSR component of the orienting response in anti-social adolescents. *British Journal of Social and Clinical Psychology, 12*, 303–308.

Skrzypek, G. J. (1969). Effect of perceptual isolation and arousal on anxiety, complexity preference, and novelty preference in psychopathic and neurotic delinquents. *Journal of Abnormal Psychology, 74*, 321–329.

Smyth, R. A., & Ingram, G. (1970). Relationship between type of offender and for seeking medical care in a correctional setting. *Nursing Research, 9*, 456–458.

Stewart, D. J. (1972). Effects of social reinforcement on dependency and aggressive responses of psychopathic, neurotic and subcultural delinquents. *Journal of Abnormal Psychology, 79*, 76–83.

Stewart, M. A., & Behar, D. (1983). Subtypes of aggressive conduct disorder. *Acta Psychiatrica Scandinavica, 68*, 178–185.

Stewart, M. A., Cummings, C., Singer, S., & de Blois, C. S. (1981). The overlap between hyperactive and unsocialized aggressive children. *Journal of Child Psychology and Psychiatry, 22*, 35–45.

Stewart, M. A., Gath, A., & Hierowski, E. (1981). Differences between girls and boys admitted to a child psychiatry ward. *Journal of Clinical Psychiatry, 42*, 386–388.

Weinstein, L. (Dec. 1974). *Evaluation of a program for re-educating disturbed children: A follow-up comparison with untreated children*. Final report to the Bureau for the Education of the Handicapped, OE, USDHEW. Project Nos. 6-2974 and 552028.

Werry, J. S., Methven, R. J., Fitzpatrick, J., & Dixon, H. (1983). The interrater reliability of DSM-III in children. *Journal of Abnormal Child Psychology, 11*, 341–354.

Werry, J. S., & Quay, H. C. (1971). The prevalence of behavior symptoms in younger elementary school children. *American Journal of Orthopsychiatry, 41*, 136–143.

Whitehill, M., DeMyer-Gapin, S., & Scott, T. J. (1976). Stimulation-seeking in antisocial preadolescent children. *Journal of Abnormal Psychology, 85*, 101–104.

Zweben, R. B., Quay, H. C., & Hammer, D. (April 1985). *Physiological and behavioral correlates of attention problems, conduct problems and anxiety in children.* Paper presented at the Annual Meeting of the Southeastern Psychological Association, Atlanta, GA.

3

DISORDERS OF ANXIETY, WITHDRAWAL, AND DYSPHORIA

HERBERT C. QUAY
ANNETTE M. LA GRECA

INTRODUCTION

As was pointed out in Chapter 1, evidence from multivariate statistical studies most clearly supports the existence of a single broad-band "internalizing" dimension that encompasses indicators of anxiety, depression, and social withdrawal (AW). Furthermore, as was also noted, when this dimension is categorically subdivided as in DSM-III and ICD-9, many of the resultant subcategories have been found to have highly questionable diagnostic reliability. Finally, there is research demonstrating that supposedly separate subtype internalizing disorders coexist. For example, Kovacs, Feinberg, Crouse-Novak, Paulauskas, and Finkelstein (1984) found that a diagnosis of anxiety disorder was also made in about 35 percent of their sample diagnosed as some form of depression. Nevertheless, there is a considerable literature related to the more narrowly defined subtypes on which we will draw in succeeding sections of this chapter.

SUBTYPES OF INTERNALIZING DISORDERS

Childhood Depressive Disorder

Considerable recent interest has centered on whether or not there is a childhood disorder corresponding to major depressive disorder in adults. There is little doubt that both children and adolescents can suffer from depressed mood or from a number of symptoms associated with adult depressive disorder. The question as to the existence, especially in prepubertal children, of major depressive *disorder* is not so easily answered.

Graham (1974) was one of the earlier critics, and while apparently not questioning the existence of depression in children, he did point out the rarity of the disorder and the relative frequency which which dysphoria was associated with stress reactions and with other forms of childhood disorders; he also cautioned against the notion of accepting so-called depressive equivalents (e.g., externalizing symptoms) as indications of depression in children.

Lefkowitz and Burton (1978) criticized the concept of depressive disorders on a number of grounds. They noted that the literature on childhood depression was primarily clinical and case-descriptive, that the clinical criteria for depression varied widely and included such diverse symptoms as crying, school failure, and aggression, and that *symptoms* of depression occur with a relatively high frequency in the general population of children. They also pointed out the problems associated with the concept of "masked" depression—the assumption that externalizing symptoms are actually reflective of an underlying depression. Considering such behavior, clearly related to Conduct Disorder, as symptomatic of depression widens the category of depression to the point that it can encompass almost any observable form of psychopathology except psychosis. Furthermore, the "masked" (externalizing) symptoms are not to be found among the diagnostic criteria for depressive disorder in adults in DSM-III (American Psychiatric Association, 1980).

Werry (in press) has also criticized the concept of depressive disorder in prepubertal children, noting that (1) the prevalence of major depressive disorder is unknown but certainly low (see later text), (2) most *adults* with the disorder do not have their first clinical episode until after age 20 (bipolar) or 30 (unipolar) so that the frequency of disorder is likely to be inversely proportional to age, (3) techniques for assessing depression in children are inadequately validated, (4) suicide, an important indicator of depression in adults, is very rare in children, and (5) adequate controlled studies of the response of depressive children to antidepressant medication to which adult depressives respond are lacking. Thus, Werry concluded that the hypothesis that major depressive disorder exists in children awaits confirmation.

At this juncture it seems most prudent to remain skeptical about the existence of adult-type major depressive disorder in children. This is not to say that children may not manifest some of the symptoms of depression, especially dysphoric mood, and that the examination of the prevalence, etiology, correlates and outcomes of these *symptoms*, as we will do later in this chapter, is not of value.

Anxiety Disorder

While DSM-III (American Psychiatric Association, 1980) lists separation anxiety disorder, avoidant disorder, and overanxious disorders as subtypes of anxiety disorder, there is, as was discussed in Chapter 1, little empirical evidence for the independence (and diagnostic reliability) of separation anxiety disorder and overanxious disorder from the broad-band AW dimension. As we also noted, avoidant disorder may well be an extreme of the personality dimension of introversion. In fact, as pointed out by Werry and Aman (1980), DSM-III suggests that the adult parallel of avoidant disorder is avoidant *personality* disorder.

As in the case of depression, it seems most prudent to consider anxiety a symptom, albeit a rather global one, that may encompass fears of people, objects, and events as well as "fear" of unfamiliar persons or situations, all of which, in fact, may reflect a generalized tendency to react to a wide variety of environmental stimuli as signals of impending pain or punishment or as novel events giving rise to the inhibition of behavior (see Gray, 1982, and subsequent text). While, as we have seen, anxiety in children generally occurs in company with symptoms of social withdrawal and dysphoria, in a particular child at a particular time indicators of anxiety may predominate. In fact, from one perspective (Gray, 1982; see later), the accompanying social withdrawal may be a manifestation of a more general behavioral inhibition, while the dysphoria may be a later-stage symptom (Gray, 1982). As with depression it is useful to look at the antecedents, correlates, and consequences of anxiety *qua* anxiety, as we will do later in this chapter.

Obsessive-compulsive Disorder

The empirical evidence for the separateness of this disorder from the general AW syndrome is extremely limited (see Achenbach, 1978, and Achenbach & Edelbrock, 1979, for two reports of the occurrence of obsessive-like factor-analytically derived syndromes). However, this disorder may be an example of a very narrow and *very* infrequent disorder that usually escapes detection by multivariate statistical inquiry.

The rarity of this disorder is attested to by a prevalence in *clinical* samples of between 1 percent and .2 percent (Hollingsworth, Tanguay, Grossman, & Pabst, 1980; Judd, 1965). Rapoport and her colleagues (Elkins, Rapoport, & Lipsky, 1980; Rapoport et al., 1981) have intensively studied small numbers of cases recruited into the U.S. National Institutes of Health for research purposes. They have asserted that childhood obsessive-compulsive disorder is unique among childhood disorders in that the symptoms and clinical picture are "virtually identical to those of adult patients" (Rapoport et al., 1981, p. 1545).

Summary

The diagnostic reliability and empirical validity of narrowly defined disorders separable from the broad syndrome of AW remains questionable. In the review that follows we will, owing to the nature of the literature, sometimes be discussing findings based on the study of symptoms, sometimes on the study of broadly defined "disorder," and sometimes also on the study of a more circumscribed disorder.

ASSESSMENT

General Considerations

Assessment of internalizing disorder in children poses some difficulties that are not apparent for disorders with more obvious behavioral characteristics (e.g., autism, conduct problems, hyperactivity). Emotional discomfort and subjective feelings of distress, which are central aspects of internalizing problems, may be more difficult for adult observers, such as parents and teachers, to identify accurately and reliably. Other than for fears and phobias, which usually are accompanied by specific avoidance behaviors, parent and teacher reports of internalizing problems in children have not been found to correspond well with children's self-reports (see Chapter 11).

Children, on the other hand, while often aware of emotional discomfort, may experience considerable difficulty in labeling, defining, or verbally communicating their subjective state. Systematic input from children and adolescents appears to be critical in the assessment of internalizing disorders, but this input must be obtained in a manner that minimizes demands for verbal expression and is sensitive to the capabilities of the child and his/her level of development. In this regard, several recently developed structured diagnostic interviews for children and adolescents, such as the Child Assessment Schedule (Hodges, Kline, Stern, Cytryn, & McKnew, 1982; Hodges, McKnew, Cytryn, Stern, & Kline, 1982), the Diagnostic Interview for Children and Adolescents (Herjanic & Campbell, 1977; Herjanic & Reich, 1982), and the Diagnostic Interview Schedule for Children (Costello, Edelbrock, Kalas, Kessler, & Klario, 1982; Costello, Edelbrock, Dulcan, Kalas, & Klario, 1984) all may be useful tools for assessing internalizing disorders of childhood. Specific, problem-oriented, self-report instruments also have been valuable and will be discussed shortly. Despite the importance of soliciting input from children and adolescents, most authors agree that additional sources of information, such as parent and teacher reports, should be utilized (Kazdin & Petti, 1982).

Another assessment-related issue pertains to the focus on broad-band versus narrow-band dimensions of internalizing behavior as noted earlier in this chapter. As will be discussed in Chapter 11, several well-validated parent and teacher checklists provide information on both the broad internalizing behavior dimension and specific problems that fall within the internalizing realm (e.g., depression, social withdrawal). As noted in Chapters 1 and 11, the broad-band factors appear to have much greater reliability than the specific subdisorders. Moreover, substantial overlap between behavioral symptoms of anxiety, social withdrawal, and depression (e.g., Achenbach, 1978, 1979) often precludes differential diagnoses.

Given these difficulties, assessments that combine the use of well-validated behavioral instruments with other problem-focused measures may be most desirable.

Anxiety Disorders

Several self-report instruments have been designed to assess anxiety-related symptoms in children and adolescents. These are discussed in detail in Chapter 11. Observational measures of anxiety also have been commonly employed with children and adolescents (see Barrios, Hartmann, & Shigetomi, 1981; Ollendick, 1983). One recently developed observational system for assessing anxiety-related behaviors in young children shows some promise (Glennon & Weisz, 1978), though further validation of the scale would be desirable.

Finally, physiological measures of arousal, such as blood pressure and heart rate, have been considered in the assessment of children's anxiety, although such measures have received far less attention than other methods. (See Chapter 11.)

Social Withdrawal

In the case of social withdrawal or extreme shyness in children, specific self-report instruments have not been developed, although many of the fear- or anxiety-related measures contain some items that focus on social areas. In addition, there are several self-report measures of assertiveness that have been designed for children, most notably the Children's Assertive Behavior Scale (Wood, Michelson, & Flynn, 1978) and the Children's Action Tendency Scale (Deluty, 1979). (See Michelson, Foster, & Ritchey, 1981, for a review.)

Most often, social withdrawal is assessed through observations of children's social interactions (see Foster & Ritchey, 1979; La Greca & Stark, 1986; Wanlass & Prinz, 1982). Socially withdrawn children are believed to engage in low levels of positive peer interactions, relative to their more socially active peers. However, low interaction rates alone are not indicative of emotional problems (see Asher, Markell, & Hymel, 1981). As a consequence, sociometric measures (i.e., peer ratings of acceptance and rejection) are commonly used adjuncts (Asher & Hymel, 1981). Children who display low levels of social interaction and who are disliked or not well accepted by peers may warrant clinical attention as social isolates.

Depression

Of all the internalizing disorders, childhood depression may be the most difficult for adults to identify. Many of the cognitive and affective components of clinical depression are difficult to observe, such as guilt, self-blame, feelings of rejection, lethargy, low self-esteem, and negative self-image (Poznanski & Zrull, 1970; Rutter & Garmezy, 1983; Sandler & Joffe, 1965). Rutter and Graham (1968) found it more difficult to obtain agreement from psychiatrists on ratings of depression than anxiety, and this difficulty was exacerbated when the children were uncommunicative, unresponsive, or cognitively delayed. Others have noted that adolescents' reports of severe depression may go undetected by parents and teachers (Rutter, 1979; Rutter & Garmezy, 1983).

In view of the difficulties in assessing childhood depression through adult report alone, and concomitant with the growing empirical interest in this disorder, a variety of self-report instruments recently have been developed to assess depressive symptomatology in children and adolescents. These are discussed in Chapter 11.

Peer nomination measures have also begun to receive attention. The Peer Nomination Inventory for Depression (PNID) (Lefkowitz & Tesiny, 1980) has been employed in several recent studies of depression in children, with promising results (Jacobsen, Lahey, & Strauss, 1983; Lefkowitz & Tesiny, 1980; Tesiny, Lefkowitz, & Gordon, 1980).

In some cases, a favorable response to antidepressant medication has been used to confirm the diagnosis of depression. However, this is certainly a less than satisfactory means of assessing childhood depression (see Rutter & Garmezy, 1983).

CORRELATES: PERSONAL, SOCIAL, AND BIOLOGICAL

Cognitive Functioning

GENERAL INTELLIGENCE

The major portion of research related to intellectual functioning and internalizing disorder has focused mainly on the role of anxiety as it affects performance on intellectual tasks. While high levels of both anxiety and dysphoria may adversely affect test performance (discussed later), there is almost no evidence linking lowered general intelligence to disorders involving anxiety, dysphoria, and social withdrawal (see Hogan & Quay, 1984, for a review and discussion of the methodological problems).

HIGHER-ORDER COGNITIVE FUNCTIONING

Anxiety   As with academic achievement (see later), empirical work on the effects of anxiety has been largely conducted with test-anxious children. The extent to which performance anxiety is typical of other anxiety-related problems is not known.

With this caveat in mind, some investigators have examined children's performance on various types of tasks. Highly anxious children have been found to perform more poorly than less anxious classmates on complex tasks, such as solving an anagram or Block Design, and tasks requiring new learning (Hill & Sarason, 1966; Nottelmann & Hill, 1977; Zatz & Chassin, 1983). However, these findings must be qualified by the extent to which evaluative cues are present. Under conditions that minimize such cues, the performance of anxious children has been noted to be much less impaired (Hill, 1972; Wine, 1971, 1982). (Processes that may underlie the poorer task performance of anxious children are discussed in the next section.)

Social Withdrawal   The cognitive task performance of children considered to be socially withdrawn has not been a subject of systematic inquiry. Certainly, social withdrawal can coexist with anxiety and/or depression in children; these latter behavioral dimensions have been implicated in children's cognitive functioning. However, in the absence of further defining information regarding the nature of social withdrawal, it is unclear how this behavioral dimension alone would be predictive of functioning on cognitive tasks.

Although the evidence is scanty at this point, some work has been conducted on shyness in children and its relationship to cognitive style (Ludwig

& Lazarus, 1983). In this study, shyness was conceptualized as a personality style that incorporates features such as social withdrawal and social anxiety, accompanied by a behaviorally unassertive interpersonal style (poor eye contact, speaking in a low voice etc.) (Lazarus, 1980, 1982; Ludwig & Lazarus, 1983). Shy individuals are thought to overly utilize the cognitive processes of self-monitoring and social evaluation (Zimbardo, Pilkonis, & Norwood, 1975) and, as a consequence, exhibit a constricted (versus flexible) style of cognitive control.

To test this hypothesis, Ludwig and Lazarus (1983) selected shy and nonshy fourth and fifth graders from a large school population, based on teacher rankings of the five most and five least shy children in their classes. The children were administered the Stroop Color-Word Test (Golden, 1978) as a measure of cognitive control. Shy children were found to perform in a more constricted manner on the task than the nonshy children. Achievement test data on a subset of the sample suggested that these differences could not be attributed to poorer academic skills for the shy group; both shy and nonshy children were found to score comparably on measures of language achievement and grade point average.

These findings suggest that the cognitive style of socially withdrawn or shy children may be a fruitful avenue for further inquiry. However, careful delineation of the defining characteristics of the children under study and the type of social withdrawal they represent will be essential.

Depression   An emerging area of interest has been the cognitive correlates of depressed states in children. Although the results have not been entirely consistent (e.g., Gotlib & Asarnow, 1979), among adults depression appears to affect cognitive functioning in a selective manner. Depression has been associated with impaired performance on tasks that involve complex problem solving (such as anagrams or Block Design) or speed and accuracy (such as copying abstract symbols), whereas performance on well-learned verbal tasks (such as a vocabulary test) appears to be unaffected (Kaslow, Rehm, & Siegel, 1984; Klein, Fencil-Morse, & Seligman, 1976; Klein & Seligman, 1976; Price, Tryon, & Raps, 1978).

Recent work with children has begun to confirm a similar pattern. In one study (Kaslow, Tanenbaum, Abramson, Peterson, & Seligman, 1983), it was found that fifth and sixth graders who scored high on depressive symptomatology, as assessed by the Children's Depression Inventory (CDI), performed more poorly on two problem-solving tasks (Block Design and anagrams), but obtained comparable scores on a measure of receptive vocabulary (Peabody Picture Vocabulary Test). In another study that employed the CDI, Mullins, Siegel, and Hodges (1985) found that depression in fourth through sixth graders was related to poorer problem-solving scores on an anagram task.

More recently, Kaslow and associates (Kaslow et al., 1984) administered a comprehensive battery of measures to first, fourth, and eighth graders who were classified as depressed or not depressed based on the CDI. The cognitive measures included several subtests of the WISC-R (Vocabulary, Block Design, Digit Span, and Coding), as well as two trailmaking tasks from a neuropsychological battery. Correlational analyses disclosed a mild relationship between depression and poorer performance on the Block Design, Coding, and Digit Span tests, though not for the other measures. While supporting the pattern of relatively poor performance for depressed individuals on complex problem-solving tasks, but not on verbal ones, the findings pertaining to speed and memory tasks were less clear. This may have been due to the relatively mild level of depression apparent in the children; replication of this study with a more clinically depressed group of youngsters may help to clarify these findings.

Using more stringent criteria for a depression classification (i.e., deviant scores on a battery of tests that included the CDI and measures of self-esteem, locus of control, and stimulus appraisal), Schwartz and associates obtained support for slower and less efficient cognitive functioning in depressed children (Schwartz, Friedman, Lindsay, & Narrol, 1982). Fifth and sixth graders were administered the matching Familiar Figures Tests; the depressed group had longer response latencies, made more errors, and were less efficient in their approach to the task.

Along different lines, some very interesting analogue studies of induced affective states in children also are supportive of a relationship between sad affect, one aspect of depression, and slower cognitive processing. Barden and colleagues (Barden, Garber, Duncan, & Masters, 1981) experimentally induced happy, sad, or neutral states in preschool children, and then examined the children's behavior on a memory recall task. Children who were in a sad affective state recalled memories (of any valence) at a slower rate than children who were happy. Sad memories also were recalled more slowly than happy ones. Other work by Masters (Masters, Barden, & Ford, 1979; Masters, Felleman, & Barden, 1981) additionally supports a relationship between affective state and speed of cognitive processing.

In summary, there appears to be growing evidence supporting greater difficulties in speed of cognitive processing and in problem-solving skills among depressed versus nondepressed children. Although the specific processes underlying such difficulties have yet to be delineated, preliminary evidence suggests that self-defeating metacognitive processes may come into play. Depressed children have been found to display lower expectancies for performance, evaluate their performance more negatively, and set overly stringent standards for success relative to nondepressed controls (Kaslow et al., 1984). These metacognitive processes are strikingly similar to those of children who exhibit achievement-inhibiting patterns of behavior, such as highly anxious children or learned helpless children (see Dweck & Elliot, 1983), suggesting that the findings are likely related to the broad AW pattern rather than to depression per se. Lower expectancies and negative self-evaluations also are more typically found among girls (Dweck & Elliot, 1983), a factor that must be considered or controlled for in future research on cognitive processes in childhood depression. The likely presence of anxiety and/or a learned helpless orientation toward academic tasks in depressed children are topics that merit further inquiry.

Academic Performance

ANXIETY DISORDERS

Although specific anxiety disorders have not been associated in any special ways with academic achievement (Graham, 1979), highly anxious students have been found to perform more poorly than less anxious peers on a variety of achievement measures, such as scores on standardized tests, grades in school, and number of grades repeated (Hill, 1972; Hill & Sarason, 1966; Spielberger, 1972). The debilitating effects of anxiety appear to be most apparent for those children who are test-anxious, that is, those who are extremely concerned about their performance and perceive their abilities to be low (Nicholls, 1976). For these children, impaired academic performance is most likely to occur in situations that emphasize evaluation; under less pressured conditions, highly anxious children generally perform more adequately (Hill, 1972; Wine, 1971, 1982). Moreover, the adverse effects of anxiety on performance appear to be cumulative. In one longitudinal study (Hill & Sarason, 1966), anxiety was found to interfere with children's academic performance to a greater degree as they progressed from first to fifth grade.

Several cognitive, attentional, and motivational mechanisms have been posited to explain the poor academic performance of highly anxious children. Most likely, a constellation of such factors comes into play. In the cognitive realm, Dweck and Elliot (1983) maintain that highly anxious children focus on avoiding negative judgments but also have low expectancies of avoiding those judgments through task performance; these children have chronically low expectancies for success in the presence of evaluative cues. Consequently, under such conditions, their performance is impaired.

Consistent with this view is the recent work of Zatz and Chassin (1983). These authors examined the cognitions endorsed by low, moderate, and high test-anxious children during anagram and coding tasks. Relative to the low-anxious children, the high-anxious group reported significantly more negative self-evaluations and social comparisons (e.g., "I have a bad memory." "Everyone usually does better than me."), more off-task thoughts (e.g., "I can't seem to sit still."), and fewer positive evaluations (e.g., "I do well on tests like this.").

Others have stressed attentional factors, such as poor concentration and high distractibility in evaluative situations (Dusek, Mergler, & Kermis, 1976; Nottelmann & Hill, 1977). Along these lines, Nottelmann and Hill (1977) found that highly test-anxious children performed more poorly on an anagram task that was administered under highly evaluative conditions. During the task, anxious children exhibited more off-task behavior and were overly attentive to feedback cues from adult-evaluators; the children's extreme concern about adequacy of performance was thought to result in greater task distraction and difficulty in concentrating. Others (Dusek et al., 1976) have shown highly anxious students to be more distracted by irrelevant stimuli. Together, these studies implicate attentional factors in the poor performance of highly (test) anxious children.

Attributional style and motivational set also have been considered as factors contributing to the poor performance of anxious children. Such children's attributions for failure in test-taking situations tend to be internal, stable, and global (Weiner & Kukla, 1970). This type of attributional style may potentially undermine task effort and persistence. (See Dweck & Elliot, 1983, for a detailed discussion of factors relating to achievement motivation in children.)

One major limitation of research on test-anxious children bears consideration. Little is known about the relationship between test anxiety in children and other forms of anxiety (Campbell, 1986). Whether test anxiety is symptomatic of a more global anxiety disorder, is a common component of other types of anxiety disturbance, or is a specific disorder itself are questions that have not been adequately addressed. Certainly, in at least some cases of school phobia or school avoidance, performance anxiety may play a role as a precipitating factor (Graham, 1979; Ollendick, in press). (It is also likely that academic problems result from frequent or prolonged absences associated with school avoidance.) Further investigation of test anxiety in children should illuminate these issues.

SOCIAL WITHDRAWAL

Considerably less is known about the achievement status of children who are socially withdrawn. Varying definitions of social withdrawal undoubtedly contribute to some of the confusion in this area. Moreover, it is quite possible that the academic implications of this behavioral dimension are not consistent, but instead may vary depending upon the age or development level of the child or presence of other associated behaviors (e.g., anxiety, depression, aggression).

Some evidence suggests that socially withdrawn youngsters are at risk for academic underachievement and educational problems (Havighurst, Bowman, Liddle, Matthews, & Pierce, 1962; Kohn & Rosman, 1972a). Support for this position is derived largely from studies of normal children. Kohn and Rosman (1972a) found that preschoolers who were rated by teachers as high on apathy-withdrawal (as opposed to interest-participation) received lower academic ratings in the first and second grade. A recent study of third graders (Green, Forehand, Beck, & Vosk, 1980) found that teacher ratings of social withdrawal correlated negatively with scores on standardized achievement tests. In an investigation of high school students, Havighurst et al. (1962) reported that those rated in the top 10 percent on withdrawal had a much higher rate of school failure than average and were more likely to drop out of school before graduation.

In contrast with these findings, Ludwig and Lazarus (1983) found no dif- ferences between shy and nonshy fourth and fifth graders on measures of academic achievement and grade point average. Moreover, recent work by Ledingham and Schwartzman (1984) suggests that withdrawn children are comparable to no-problem control children in terms of educational attain- ment; however, children who are both withdrawn and aggressive have a much poorer academic prognosis. These authors followed over 600 children for a three-year period; the children had previously been identified by peer ratings as either withdrawn, aggressive, withdrawn and aggressive, or no problem. Although the academic adjustment of the withdrawn-only group was not distinguishable from the no-problem controls, children in the com- bined withdrawn and aggressive group were more likely to have failed a grade or be in a special class.

This work suggests that social withdrawal, in combination with other risk factors such as aggressive behavior, may be a prognostic indicator for poor academic achievement. However, it is unclear whether social withdrawal alone is associated with academic failure.

DEPRESSION

Little is known about the academic correlates of childhood depression, un- doubtedly owing to the very recent nature of empirical work in this area. Current findings present an equivocal picture. One study of elementary school students (Strauss, Lahey, & Jacobsen, 1982) obtained very few sig- nificant correlations between measures of childhood depression, such as the Children's Depression Inventory, and achievement test scores. However, us- ing the Peer Nomination Inventory for Depression, Lefkowitz and col- leagues found that depression in children was negatively correlated with ac- ademic achievement and teacher ratings of study habits and was positively related to the number of days late and days absent from school (Lefkowitz & Tesiny, 1980; Tesiny et al., 1980). Graham (1979) has suggested that poor school performance may be a precipitant of depression in some children; this hypothesis bears further investigation. Studies of academic achieve- ment in clinically depressed children have not as yet been conducted.

Motivation and Reinforcement Effects

This area of research has received very little attention. One available study (Fisher, 1973) focused primarily on the broad-band internalizing dimension of anxiety-withdrawal, rather than on specific types of internalizing prob- lems. The results suggested that differential needs motivate AW versus conduct-disordered (CD) individuals. Using projective measures, AW and CD adolescent delinquents were compared on indices of their need for power and need for affiliation. Relative to the CD group, the AW delin- quents indicated a greater need for affiliation and a lower need for power. Although these findings are limited to delinquents, the data suggest that the behavior of AW individuals may be oriented toward gaining attention, ap- proval, and acceptance from others.

Peer Relations

The peer relations of children displaying AW behavior can be characterized as problematic, though generally not as negative and rejecting as those of children with more aggressive behaviors (see Chapter 2 and Rolf, 1972; Rubin & Clark, 1983). Although less extreme, one must be careful not to discount or minimize the social difficulties encountered by children with AW problems. Successful interpersonal functioning during childhood contributes in important ways to the course of normal development and emotional adjustment (Hartup, 1983). In its extreme form, social isolation may be predictive of serious adjustment difficulties. Consonant with this view, Reese (1967) found that severe social isolation was the single most characteristic feature of children who committed suicide. These children were almost totally lacking in involvement with peers and teachers.

Describing the social behavior and peer relations of children with specific types of AW problems is a complicated task. Most studies do not adequately differentiate among subtypes of internalizing problems. To obscure matters further, socially withdrawn behavior has been utilized as a selection criterion as well as an outcome measure for social difficulties. Thus, in some cases it is very difficult to tease apart the defining characteristics of a subject sample and the associated behavioral correlates.

Another complicating factor is the paucity of observational studies of social behavior for children beyond the preschool years (Hartup, 1983; La Greca & Stark, 1986). In contrast, most of the literature on children's behavior disorders focuses on youngsters of elementary school age or older. When behavioral observations of older children have been conducted, investigators typically have used observation codes developed for preschoolers, despite developmental data suggesting that the parameters of peer interactions change substantially over time, becoming less obvious and more complex (Stone & La Greca, 1986). (Also see Asher & Hymel, 1981, and La Greca & Stark, 1986, for further discussions of this issue.)

Still another difficulty is the multiple ways in which peer relationships have been assessed. Sociometric measures (peer ratings of acceptance and/or rejection) represent the most common means of determining the quality of children's peer relations. Relative to teacher ratings or other sources of information, peer ratings have the greatest predictive validity and are viewed as stable and valid indicators of social adjustment (Asher & Hymel, 1981; Asher et al., 1981). However, diverse methods of obtaining peer ratings have been employed, and these methods often yield different correlates. It is only very recently that investigators have moved beyond the simple classification of "popular" and "unpopular" children and have more carefully delineated different sociometric subgroups (e.g., Coie, Dodge, & Coppotelli, 1982). Included among those who are not well-liked by peers (and thus may be at risk for later psychological difficulties) are children who are socially neglected and actively rejected. More likely than not, the majority of children with AW behavior problems who encounter peer difficulties fall largely within the socially neglected rather than the actively rejected group.

Yet research on the interpersonal behaviors and long-term adjustment of socially neglected children has just begun, so the precise implications of this peer status have yet to be determined.

Thus, these caveats and cautions must be kept in mind when examining the current literature on the peer status of children with internalizing problems.

ANXIETY

Little attention has been devoted to studying the relationship between anxiety per se and peer relationships in children. To date, findings in this area are scanty and equivocal.

Among preschoolers, some evidence for a relationship between anxious-fearful behavior and peer difficulties has been obtained. Rubin and Clark (1983) examined the relationship between teacher ratings of behavior problems and the classroom behavior, sociometric ratings, and social problem-solving skills of 123 preschool children. Teacher ratings of anxious-fearful behavior in the children were significantly related to lower levels of parallel play, group-dramatic play, and transitional behaviors with peers, and higher frequencies of unoccupied behavior in the classroom. More simply stated, the anxious-fearful children were more socially withdrawn than their peers (a finding consonant with the evidence for a broad-based AW syndrome noted earlier in this chapter and in Chapter 1). In addition, these children were less popular and more disliked by peers than other classmates. Ratings of anxious-fearful behavior correlated negatively with positive peer ratings and positively with negative peer ratings, although these correlations were quite modest ($-.18$, $.19$, respectively).

Beyond the preschool years, support for a relationship between anxiety and interpersonal functioning is extremely limited. In a sample of third through fifth graders, La Greca (1978) discerned no relationship between children's self-reports of anxiety, as assessed by the Children's Manifest Anxiety Scale, and peer ratings of acceptance. Although highly anxious children were rated by their teachers as less likable, the validity of teacher ratings of peer-likability has been questioned (see La Greca, 1981; La Greca & Stark, 1986). It is possible that anxiety per se may be independent of social competence in children, yet may be an important factor *in conjunction with* other social behaviors. Anxiety combined with social withdrawal or poor interpersonal skills may be predictive of peer difficulties; anxiety alone may not. This hypothesis has received very limited attention and warrants systematic investigation, although the likely difficulty in finding purely anxious children may present problems.

One recent study examined the social correlates of the broad AW dimension and obtained evidence for interpersonal difficulties in this multi-problem group. Panella and Henggeler (1986) compared anxious-withdrawn, conduct-disordered, and well-adjusted black, male adolescents on several peer relationship measures. Adolescents were videotaped interacting with a friend and with a well-adjusted stranger, and behavioral measures of dominance, conflict, affect, and social competence were subsequently obtained. Both the anxious-withdrawn and conduct-disordered groups (as noted in Chapter 2) evidenced less positive affect and lower social competence than well-adjusted adolescents. In addition, the AW adolescents displayed greater personal apprehension than those in the well-adjusted group. Although not statistically significant, there was some suggestion that the social problems of the AW adolescents were exacerbated when interacting with strangers. Anecdotally, few of these adolescents were noted to have peer friends. This study represents an indirect attempt to link anxiety *and* withdrawal to peer relations; further systematic inquiry along these lines will be important.

Another potentially productive avenue for investigation concerns the presence of social anxiety in children and its possible implications for interpersonal functioning. While measures for assessing social anxiety in children are in the early stages of development (e.g., Dandes, La Greca, Wick & Shaw, 1986), several global measures of anxiety, such as the Children's Manifest Anxiety Scale (see Chapter 13), contain items that appear to be socially oriented. Efforts to develop measures of social anxiety may eventually yield some important findings. Just as test anxiety is predictive of children's functioning on academic tasks, one would anticipate that social anxiety (and not general anxiety) will be more directly related to children's functioning in interpersonal situations.

SOCIAL WITHDRAWAL
For the most part, extant evidence suggests that social withdrawal alone is not predictive of peer interaction difficulties. Much of the impetus for investigating social isolation in children was based on retrospective studies of psychotic and schizophrenic adults that noted that these individuals were socially withdrawn as children. However, this literature has been severely criticized on methodological and conceptual grounds (Asher et al., 1981). (Also see Strain, Cooke, & Apolloni, 1976, for a detailed review and critique.) Moreover, recent studies of preschool and elementary school children provide little or no support for a relationship between behavioral measures of social withdrawal (i.e., the frequency of children's peer interactions) and children's level of social competence (Deutsch, 1974; Foster & Ritchey, 1985; Gottman, 1977a, 1977b; Gottman, Gonso, & Rasmussen, 1975; Hymel, Tinsley, Geraci, & Asher, 1981; Jennings, 1975; Krantz, 1982).

Despite these negative findings, teacher ratings of children's withdrawn behavior generally have been found to relate modestly and in a predictable manner with peer status for preschoolers (Kohn & Rosman, 1972b), elementary school children (La Greca, 1981; Vosk, Forehand, Parker, & Richard, 1982), and adolescents (Jones, 1974; Panella & Henggeler, 1985). Although this discrepancy, at least in part, may be due to difficulties inherent in observational methods for older children, a major contributing factor is that teacher ratings of withdrawal generally measure more than just social isolation. Rating scales employed with teachers, such as the Pupil Evaluation Inventory (Pekarik, Prinz, Liebert, Weintraub, & Neale, 1976), contain items on the withdrawal scale that reflect shyness or social anxiety (e.g., "*never* seems to be having a good time"), interpersonal sensitivity ("feelings are hurt too easily"), depressed affect ("is unhappy or sad"), and peer rejection ("usually chosen last to join in group activities"). Thus, it is some (unspecified) combination of these internalizing behaviors that predicts peer difficulties.

In contrast to these confusing and equivocal findings for social withdrawal, a very different picture emerges when one additionally considers the *qualitative* aspects of the individual's peer interactions. Children who are both withdrawn *and* aggressive appear to be more actively rejected and less accepted by their peers than those who are primarily aggressive or primarily socially withdrawn (Ledingham, 1981; Milich & Landau, 1984). Moreover, these relationships become more pronounced as children reach the later elementary school years, and these aggressive-withdrawn children become more atypical as compared with the increasing numbers of withdrawn or aggressive youngsters (Ledingham, 1981). Of further interest is an accumulating body of evidence suggesting that children who are extremely withdrawn and aggressive at the same time may potentially be at risk for developing schizophrenia (Ledingham, 1981; Ledingham & Schwartzman, 1984; Ledingham, Schwartzman, & Serbin, 1984; Michael, Morris, & Soroker, 1957; Robins, 1979).

In summary, social withdrawal alone does not appear to be predictive of poor peer relations; however, in conjunction with other AW behaviors (anxiety, sadness, etc.), it may be associated with moderately poor status among peers. To date, the only evidence for active peer rejection associated with social withdrawal is based on a very small group of children who are both withdrawn and aggressive in their social interactions. This particular group, however, warrants much closer examination, as the risks for later psychological difficulties may be especially pronounced.

DEPRESSION

Using self-report and peer-nomination measures of depression, several studies have found that depressed children are less well liked by peers than their nondepressed classmates (Jacobsen et al., 1983; Lefkowitz & Tesiny, 1980; Vosk et al., 1982). All the investigations were conducted with normal elementary school children; low to moderate negative correlations between peer acceptance and depression ratings were obtained.

One critical area that remains to be explored concerns the actual social behavior displayed by depressed children and adolescents. Information regarding the interaction styles of depressed youngsters would be tremendously useful for discerning factors contributing to the lower peer status of these children.

It is also imperative to consider the possibility that peer rejection and poor social relationships may play a causative role in the development of depression in children. Given the tremendous importance of peer relationships throughout the life span, efforts to examine peers' impact on children's affective functioning will be of utmost interest. Moreover, longitudinal efforts that examine the likely interactive effects of peer difficulties and depression will be very informative.

Social Cognitive Abilities

Intimately related to children's interpersonal functioning is their ability to perceive, evaluate, and generally comprehend their social world. During the past 20 years we have witnessed tremendous growth in our understanding of how children conceptualize others and interpret social behaviors and situations. This general area of investigation, referred to as social cognition, has been carefully reviewed by Shantz (1975). More specifically, she has stated:

> the area of social cognition refers to the child's intuitive or logical representation of others, that is how he characterizes others and makes inferences about their covert, inner psychological processes. . . . If one's conceptual system is not sufficiently accurate, one's interrelationships are drastically affected, as when . . . a child views an accidental act by another to be an aggressive provocation. (1975, p. 1)

Most of the research in this area has focused on delineating developmental parameters and correlates of social cognitive functioning. Recently, however, evidence has been accumulating on the social cognitive deficits of children with behavior problems and emotional difficulties.

For the most part, studies examining the social cognitive abilities of "emotionally disturbed" children have failed to identify the specific behavioral characteristics of their subject samples (e.g., Chandler, Greenspan, & Barenboim, 1974). Consequently, findings of poorer social-perspective taking (i.e., the ability to take another's perspective in a social situation) in deviant versus normal groups are not clearly associated with internalizing behavior problems.

The following discussion is limited to studies that attempted to link internalizing behavioral characteristics with social cognitive abilities.

ANXIETY

Almost no information is available on the relationship between anxiety per se and social cognitive functioning. One previously mentioned study of preschool children (Rubin & Clark, 1983) found that teacher ratings of anxious-fearful behavior were unrelated to the scores children obtained on a social-problem-solving test.

One might speculate that, in part, children's anxiety in social situations may be a function of their ability or inability to read social situations accurately, and their oversensitivity to and perhaps misperception of negative feedback from others. Extrapolating from the data on test anxiety, one might further speculate that socially anxious children might display difficulties processing social information in complex (i.e., subtle and ambiguous) social situations, novel situations, and situations where social-evaluative cues are prominent.

The interface between anxiety and social cognitive functioning may be a fertile area for investigation. In fact, the paucity of studies in this area is surprising.

SOCIAL WITHDRAWAL

Socially withdrawn or isolated children have been found to evidence some social cognitive difficulties, although studies in this area have also been lacking. In a study by Richard and Dodge (1982), popular, aggressive, and isolated males were presented with hypothetical problem situations and asked to generate alternative solutions. In addition, subjects evaluated a standard set of solutions presented by the experimenter. Relative to the popular boys, aggressive and isolated males generated fewer solutions and, after their initial response, were more likely to generate ineffective and aggressive solutions. Interestingly, no differences among the groups were obtained for the youngsters' ability to evaluate the presented set of solutions. These findings suggest that isolated children's difficulties may lie more in the area of generating, rather than recognizing, appropriate social strategies.

In one well-controlled investigation, Waterman and colleagues (Waterman, Sobesky, Silvern, Aoki, & McCaulay, 1981) compared the social-perspective-taking skills of normal, learning disabled, and "emotionally disturbed" children. Across the total sample, teacher ratings of withdrawn behavior were significantly related to poorer cognitive perspective-taking skills, even with mental age controlled. However, when the relationship between withdrawal and social cognitive skills was examined separately for each group, it held only for the emotionally disturbed youngsters, although the correlations for the other two groups were in the same direction.

DEPRESSION

Given the relatively recent status of research on childhood depression, very limited evidence is available regarding the social cognitive functioning of depressed children. Although a relationship between clinical depression and deficient interpersonal problem-solving skills has been obtained with college students (Gotlib & Asarnow, 1979), Mullins et al. (1985) failed to replicate these findings with children of elementary school age.

Psychophysiological Correlates

Much of the work attempting to establish psychophysiological correlates of childhood psychopathology has been undertaken with regard to either conduct disorder (see Chapter 2) or attention deficit disorder (see Chapter 4). What little work that has been reported with AW children has attempted to relate level of anxiety or degree of behavioral inhibition to physiological responsivity.

ELECTRODERMAL (GSR) RESPONDING

Among groups of children diagnosed as hyperactive, Conners (1975) reported that children with higher skin conductance levels had higher levels of rated anxiety. Delamater and Lahey (1983) found that higher ratings on anxiety did not produce main effects on GSR measures but did serve to moderate the effects of ratings of conduct disorder in producing lower levels of GSR responding. These tentative findings of increased electrodermal responding related to anxiety is in accord with the hypothesis advanced by Fowles (1980, 1983) that the GSR indexes Gray's (1979, 1982) behavioral inhibition system (see Chapter 2; Quay, 1986). According to Gray, activity in this system, cued off by signals of impending pain, punishment, and novelty, is subjectively experienced as anxiety. Thus, higher levels of anxiety would be reflected in higher levels of GSR responsivity.

HEART RATE (HR)

Heart rate is subject to the influence of a variety of variables including somatic activity, active coping, and the incentive value attached to the task, and Fowles (1983) has questioned the presumed correlation between anxiety and increased HR. There has been very little study of the relation of either tonic or phasic HR to childhood disorder. As pointed out in Chapter 2, the occasional finding of lower tonic HR levels as related to conduct disorder are difficult to interpret.

Delamater and Lahey (1983) found increased tonic HR in their higher anxiety group during one baseline period and not another, and reported that there were no significant phasic HR changes throughout the experiment related to anxiety ratings.

On the other hand, Garcia-Coll, Kagan, and Reznick (1984) have argued that behaviorally inhibited children might invest more effort in attempting to assimilate unfamiliar information, and thus exhibit higher and more stable HR while processing unfamiliar visual and auditory information than uninhibited children. They found, among 21- to 22-month-olds, that while there were no tonic differences, the most inhibited quartiles of both boys and girls had significantly higher phasic HR during stimulus presentations—about 131 beats per minute as compared to 125 beats per minute. In a subsequent study, when the children were 31 to 32 months of age, these investigators failed to find any significant correlation between absolute HR and HR variability and behavioral inhibition. Furthermore, they did not find consistent relations between these HR measures at 21 and at 31 months. Additional work by Kagan and Reznick (1984) indicated that 3-year-old children with high and stable HR were described by their mothers as motivated for intellectual mastery and obedient and behaved in this manner on experimental tasks and during home observations. In this study, these authors report that "the Group H (high HR) seemed to play the adult role with the peer, offering toys and giving orders while Group L (low HR) just tended to be passive and quiet" (Kagan & Reznick, 1984, p. 144). Thus it appears that the relationship of behavioral inhibition and higher HR may be a function of inhibited children investing more effort in cognitive tasks.

In a later study (Kagan, Reznick, Clarke, Snidman, & Garcia-Coll, 1984), higher HR during tasks requiring mental effort was again correlated with behavioral inhibition (.33 to .39) in the same children initially seen at age 11 to 21 months. Furthermore, the inhibition index at 21 months was correlated with HR measures at age 4 years at values around .45.

It is difficult, however, to draw conclusions about the relation between HR and behavioral inhibition per se from these studies. At first blush it would appear that the apparent positive relationship runs counter to Fowles' (1980, 1983) review and theory that HR indexes the appetitive rather than the inhibitory system. HR does increase with mental effort (and metabolic demand), however, and since the increases are obtained during tasks involving such efforts, the increased HR may be related to a greater involvement of inhibited children with intellectual tasks (and mothers of three-year-olds report such according to Kagan & Reznick, 1984) rather than to behavioral inhibition per se. One can even speculate that inhibited children learn to find intellectual tasks more rewarding than social encounters and the increased HR actually reflects activity in the reward system.

Further research on inhibited children involving manipulations of appetitive and avoidant motivation with concomitant measurement of both HR and GSR would seem worthwhile.

Biological Factors

The evidence for the involvement of genetic influences (including temperament) and behavioral factors in anxiety, withdrawal, and dysphoria is even sketchier than was the case for undersocialized conduct disorder, discussed in Chapter 2.

TEMPERAMENT

Temperament studies have often isolated a dimension related to approach-withdrawal or sociability, and there is some evidence for the heritability of sociability toward strangers (see Plomin, 1983, for a review). In the Fels longitudinal study, Kagan and Moss (1962) reported that "inhibition to the unfamiliar" during the first three years of life predicted social timidity at ages 6 to 10. However, there is, at least as yet, no evidence linking this temperament dimension to later internalizing *disorder*.

"BEHAVIOR PROBLEMS"

As was noted in Chapter 2, if clusters of behavior problems that are empirically related to a disorder are genetically influenced, then one might presume a genetic component to the full-blown disorder. The O'Connor, Foch, Sherry, and Plomin (1980) study of twins found that for a cluster of behaviors labeled "shyness," the intraclass correlations for identicals (.69) was significantly higher than that for same-sex fraternals (.27), suggesting a genetic component to social withdrawal. In a much earlier study, Eysenck and Prell (1951) reported that an index of "neuroticism" was much more highly correlated in identical (.85) as opposed to fraternal (.22) twins ages 11 to 13.

AW DISORDER

We can only note here that adoptive and family history studies of children, adolescents, and adults have suggested that children of parents with psychiatric disorder are at greater risk for AW disorder than children of unimpaired parents (see Beardslee, Bemporad, Keller, & Klerman, 1983; von Knorring, Cloninger, Bohman, & Sigvardsson, 1983; Weissman, Gershon, Kidd, Prusoff, Leckman, Dibble, Hamovit, Thompson, Pauls, & Guroff, 1984; Weissman, Leckman, Merikangas, Gammon, & Prusoff, 1984). These studies suggest, but certainly do not prove, genetic influences. In fact, in the adoptive study (von Knorring et al., 1983), there were no significant concordance rates between specific diagnoses in biological parents and their adopted-away children.

The evidence, limited as it is, does suggest that, as was the case with conduct disorder, additional study of genetic influences in internalizing disorders is warranted.

Biochemical Factors

The recent interest in biochemical correlates of Attention Deficit Disorder and Conduct Disorder (see Chapters 2 and 4) has not been paralleled by similar interest in internalizing disorders, and data are very limited.

Tennes, Downey, and Vernadakis (1977) found that, in one-year-olds, level of urinary cortisol excretion after imposed stress was significantly related (.46) to observers' rating of manifest anxiety when the children were separated from their mothers. However, among children between three and six years of age, Lundberg (1983) did not find relationships between behavioral characteristics and cortisol (or catecholamine) excretion, although AW behavior was not directly assessed in this study.

Similarly, Cederblad and Hook (1984) studied 84 children between three and nine years of age and did not find relationships between either ratings of internalizing (or externalizing behavior) deviance and urinary catecholamines.

What are needed are studies of children reliably diagnosed as having AW disorder to parallel those with CD children described in Chapter 2.

EPIDEMIOLOGY

AW or "Neurotic" Disorder in Normal Samples

There have been a number of studies that have provided estimates of the prevalence of AW (in these studies generally called neurotic disorder). Rutter, Tizard, and Whitmore (1970) in their study of 10- and 11-year-olds on the rural Isle of Wight reported a rate of 2.5 percent for both males and females combined using a joint rating and interview procedure. In a subsequent study of similar aged children in inner London, Rutter, Cox, Tupling, Berger, and Yule (1975) found a rate of 5 percent for both sexes combined.

In a representative sample of Australian school children, ages 5 to 12 years, Glow (1978a, 1978b) found rates for her large (2,000+) urban and suburban sample for both sexes to range from 3.0 to 8.7 percent for severe disorder depending on whether the ratings were done by teachers or parents, respectively. As noted in Chapter 2, McGee, Silva, and Williams (1984) have studied a cohort of 951 seven-year-olds in New Zealand. Using a parent and a teacher rating scale, they found that 8.3 percent of boys and 11.1 percent of girls (a nonsignificant difference) were identified as "neurotic" by either parent *or* teacher. Most of these children had also been rated as five-year-olds. Among boys, 1.8 percent were identified as "neurotic" at both ages (the "stable problem" group), as were 2.4 percent of girls.

Anderson, Williams, McGee, and Silva (1985) studied 792 children from this cohort when they were age 11 using a structured interview, parent and teacher ratings, and observations made during psychological testing to arrive at DSM-III diagnoses. These diagnoses were made at different "levels" depending on the degree of agreement between sources of information as to symptomatology and the meeting of DSM-III operational criteria. Thus, four different prevalence estimates were obtained depending upon these levels. Combining all levels, 94 cases (12%) were diagnosed as having either separation anxiety disorder, overanxious disorder, simple phobia, depression/dysthymia, or social phobia. However, if prevalence figures were based only on those cases in which diagnostic criteria were met by more than one source independently (most conservative approach), only two cases received AW-type diagnoses. Using cases where the diagnostic criteria were met by one source and symptoms confirmed by one or both of the other sources (next most conservative), 19 cases (2%) were of the AW type. A more liberal level wherein diagnostic criteria were met by one source without confirming symptoms from one or both of the other sources produced 34 AW cases for a prevalence of about 4 percent.

This study very well illustrates one of the problems of psychiatric epidemiology mentioned in Chapter 2: The criteria by which the presence of a disorder is determined greatly influences the prevalence figures. Clearly, the estimate of 12 percent obtained by combining all levels is far too high, particularly for a population cohort of this homogeneous ethnicity and middle-class socioeconomic status. The 4 percent estimate is much closer to those derived from other studies.

While Anderson et al. (1985) reported on sex differences, they did so only for the diagnoses derived from all the levels combined. For these clearly overgenerous estimates, AW disorders were diagnosed in 44 boys (11%) and 47 (13%) girls, providing almost equal ratios, a quite different state of affairs from that for conduct disorder, as noted in Chapter 2.

It is unfortunate that there as yet are no population prevalence studies in the United States since extrapolation from Britain, Australia, and New Zealand to the United States may or may not be appropriate. It is clear, however, that the population prevalence of *persistent* AW or neurotic disorder is quite low, around 2 percent for both sexes, while a point prevalence of 5 percent is probably a liberal, but reasonable, estimate. Sex differences seem minimal.

AW or Neurotic Disorder in Clinical Sampies

In the Cerreto and Tuma (1977) study discussed in Chapter 2, AW-type diagnoses were made in about 22 percent of the cases. In their series of 195 cases, Werry, Methven, Fitzpatrick, and Dixon (1983) made AW-type diagnoses in about 34 percent of the cases. Of 202 children referred to a clinic in Newfoundland, 15.8 percent of boys and 10.4 percent of girls received a diagnosis of neurotic disorder (Kotsopoulos & Nandy, 1981). In a series of 95 adolescents who were consecutive admissions to an inpatient unit, Strober, Green, and Carlson (1981) made diagnoses involving anxiety and depression in just over 25 percent of their cases.

In clinical samples, AW-type disorders seem to account for 20 to 30 percent of the cases. Again, estimates vary but the range seems not nearly so wide as for more specific disorders (see Depression, later), suggesting, as might be expected, more reliability in diagnostic practice for the more broadly defined grouping.

Depressive Disorder in Normal Samples

Kashani and Simonds (1979) studied 102 children (51 boys; 51 girls; aged 7–12), who were selected randomly from families who attended a family practice clinic and from children born at a University Medical Center. Based on a psychiatric interview, only two boys (1.9%) met the DSM-III criteria for depression.

Kashani et al. (1983) studied the New Zealand cohort discussed previously when they were near their ninth birthdays. A two-stage process was used in which a child's questionnaire, based on DSM-III criteria, and a parent questionnaire were used to select cases for a structured interview. Using all sources of data, children were diagnosed as having either major (2.5%) or minor (1.8%) depression.

Anderson et al. (1985) diagnosed 17 cases (2%) as depression/dysthymic using their most liberal level. Using the level that produced a prevalence of 4 percent for all AW disorders, four cases of depressive disorder (.5%) were diagnosed. Based on self-reports of symptoms of depression and using a cutoff score, Kaplan, Hong, and Weinhold (1984) reported a prevalence of

13.5 percent for mild depression, 7.3 percent for moderate depression, and 1.3 percent for severe depression among junior and senior high school students.

It is obvious from these studies that cases of diagnosable depressive disorder in the general child *and adolescent* population are infrequent—likely less than 2 percent, if that high.

Depressive Disorder in Clinical Samples

Among preschoolers referred for developmental, behavioral, or emotional problems, Kashani, Ray, and Carlson (1984) found 4 of 100 children to meet DSM-III criteria for depressive disorder. In their series, Werry et al. (1983) did not report *any* cases of depressive disorder. Among their clinic sample of wide age range, Cerreto and Tuma (1977) reported that 4.5 percent of cases were diagnosed as depressive neurosis.

Lobovits and Handol (1985) studied 50 8- to 12-year-olds consecutively referred to an outpatient psychology service center. Interviews with each child resulted in 35 percent of boys and 31 percent of girls being diagnosed as having a major depressive episode, while interviews with parents (considered independently) produced a rate of 22 percent for boys and 23 percent for girls. In their series of adolescent inpatients, Strober et al. (1981) made a diagnosis of major affective disorder (episodic) in 17.8 percent of the cases.

While rates vary from zero to 35 percent in these studies, diagnosable depressive disorder is rare in younger children, but more frequent among 10- to 12-year-olds and adolescents. The varying estimates again illustrate problems of definition and diagnostic practice, especially for more narrowly defined subdisorders.

Depressive Symptoms in Clinical Samples

A number of investigators have chosen to look at the extent to which *symptoms* of depression may be found in clinical samples. Carlson and Cantwell (1979) found that among a random sample of outpatients and inpatients, ages 7 to 17, 60 percent of the cases self-reported symptoms of either depression, withdrawal, low self-esteem, or suicidal ideation.

Feinstein, Blouin, Egan, and Connors (1984) assessed depressive symptomatology in a consecutive series of 224 patients in a child psychiatry clinic by means of the Bellevue Index of Depression (child). The dysphoric mood cluster of symptoms was present in 82.3 percent of the entire sample, in 90.5 percent of the sample diagnosed as having some type of depressive disorder, and in 86.6 percent of the sample with some form of CD. This symptom cluster clearly did not discriminate those diagnosed as depressed from those diagnosed as CD even though the diagnosis of depression was not totally independent of this dysphoric cluster of depression. On the other hand, self-deprecating ideation, while present in 47.4 percent of the entire sample, was found in 63.5 percent of those with depressive disorder and in 42.6 percent of those with CD, a statistically significant difference. These authors also factor analyzed the Bellevue Index independently on parent and clinician ratings. On only one factor (derived from clinician ratings) did the depressive cases obtain scores significantly different from those with CD. This factor was comprised of seven items: sad/unhappy, mood swings, unstable, hypersensitive, feelings of worthlessness, feelings of persecution, and anorexia.

The results of both of these studies indicate that symptoms of dysphoric mood are widespread in clinical cases, irrespective of diagnosis. However, self-deprecatory ideation, while not really uncommon, is *less* common among cases with CD. With the prevalence of depressive symptoms as high as it apparently is in clinic cases irrespective of diagnosis, the diagnosis of depressive disorder would apparently have to be made by the process of the exclusion of at least the major symptoms of other disorders, unless one is content with a majority of cases carrying multiple diagnoses.

Depressive Symptoms in Normal Samples

There have been a number of studies in which the prevalence of various symptoms of depression have been assessed in samples of ostensibly normal children and adolescents by means of parent and teacher ratings and self-reports. In a study of behavior symptoms in a large sample of elementary school-age children, as assessed by teacher ratings, Werry and Quay (1971) found that the item "depression, chronic sadness" was endorsed for 7.2 percent of boys and 7.6 percent of girls. However, social withdrawal was present in 16.7 percent of boys and 15.5 percent of girls, feelings of inferiority in 28.8 percent of boys and 23.7 percent of girls, and lethargy in 13.5 percent of boys and 10.6 percent of girls. Glow (1978a) found 9 percent of her teacher-rated sample to be considered as "pretty much" or "very much" serious or sad. In her parent-rating study, she (Glow, 1978b) found unhappiness as a moderate or extreme problem in 2.1 percent of her sample. Kashani et al. (1984) found that parents reported sadness in only .4 percent of a rather select sample of normal preschoolers. However, appetite disturbance (7.4%) and sleep disturbance (12.8%) were relatively more frequent.

These studies suggest that dysphoria is, in fact, rather uncommon and more often reported by teachers than by parents. Other putative symptoms of depression are more prevalent but still much less frequent than symptoms of conduct disorder.

Anxiety Disorder in Normal Samples

In the Isle of Wight study, Rutter et al. (1970) reported a prevalence of 2.5 percent, while Graham (1979) has suggested a rate of 5 percent for inner London.

Anderson et al. (1985) diagnosed 51 cases (7%) as either separation anxiety disorder or overanxious disorder using data from all their levels combined. Using the level that produced the most reasonable overall prevalence for all AW disorders, they found 18 cases of anxiety disorder (2.4%). When these figures are compared to those for depression, it appears that prevalence of anxiety in population studies exceeds the prevalence of depression.

Anxiety Disorder in Clinical Samples

Cerreto and Tuma (1977) found that only .3 percent of their clinic cases were diagnosed as anxiety neurosis but 10.6 percent were diagnosed as overanxious reaction of childhood. Werry et al. (1983) diagnosed 21 percent of their cases as anxiety disorder with separate anxiety disorder accounting for 14.4 percent, overanxious disorder, 4.6 percent, and avoidant disorder, 2.1 percent. Strober et al. (1981) diagnosed 8 percent of their cases as having some form of anxiety disorder.

The limited data available on clinical samples suggest that anxiety disorder is certainly diagnosed more frequently in children than is depression, perhaps three to four times more frequently. Although there is only one study on adolescents, the rates are reversed, and depressive diagnoses predominate by two or three to one.

Anxiety Symptoms in Normal Samples

While anxiety *disorder* is infrequent in unselected children, there is considerable evidence that symptoms of anxiety (and fear) are quite often found in normal children. Lapouse and Monk (1959) were the first to study anxiety-type symptoms in a representative sample of children. They reported that seven or more fears and worries were present in 43 percent of 482 children age 6 to 12 as reported by mothers. Most frequent fears and worries included snakes (44%), family illness or death (41%), and school marks (38%). Werry and Quay (1971) found teacher-rated anxiety or chronic fearfulness to be present in 16 percent of boys and 17 percent of girls, while tension and inability to relax were rated as present in 23.1 percent of boys but only 12.3 percent of girls.

Summary

While, as we have emphasized earlier, prevalence figures are very much influenced by how disorders are defined and diagnosed, a reasonable population prevalence for AW disorder is about 4 to 5 percent. AW type diagnoses account for about 20 to 30 percent of clinic cases. At the subtype level, depressive disorder is clearly rare in the population of children, likely less than 2 percent. Clinic rates are much higher but also much more variable and clearly reflect different diagnostic practice. The population prevalence of anxiety disorder is greater than that of depression, with 2 to 3 percent seeming to be a reasonable estimate. Among clinical cases there is, as with depression, great variability, with rates ranging from 8 to 21 percent.

OUTCOME

Despite the historical clinical concerns about the progression of childhood "neurotic" disorder into full-blown adult neuroses, or even psychoses, there has been much less research on the persistence of actual AW than CD. Since there are very few studies of the persistence of formally diagnosed AW disorder, we must again rely heavily on research on the persistence of symptoms. As was the case in our review of the persistence of CD in Chapter 2, the time intervals between assessments vary considerably across studies, as do the ages of children studied and the methods of assessment.

AW Symptoms

As previously mentioned in the discussion of biological factors, Kagan and his colleagues (Garcia-Coll et al., 1984; Kagan et al., 1984) have followed children initially identified at 21 months as behaviorally inhibited. Across a one-month interval a composite measure of inhibition had a stability coefficient of .63, and 68 percent of children classified as consistently inhibited at the initial assessment retained that classification at the second testing (Garcia-Coll et al., 1984).

Both the inhibited and uninhibited groups were seen again when they were 31 to 32 months old. At that time the stability of the inhibition index dropped to .39. There was a greater probability that an inhibited child would become less inhibited than the reverse type of change.

Additional assessments were made when the children were four years old (Kagan et al., 1984). The inhibition index taken from both experimental sessions at age 21 months was significantly related to a number of variables at age four including inhibited peer play (.46), number of fears derived from an interview with the mothers (.41), and a measure of inhibition based on the mothers Q-sort (.56). As the authors noted, the data reflect moderate stability of behavioral inhibition over the years two to four.

In a study of children followed from age one to age six, Lewis, Feiring, McGuffog, and Jaskir (1984) related earlier assessments of the attachment relationship with the mother to ratings on the Child Behavior Profile (Achenbach & Edelbrock, 1981). This latter instrument permits the calculation of a total "internalizing" score from intercorrelated subscales. Lewis et al. (1984) reported that attachment category produced significantly different internalizing scores only for males where the securely attached scored lowest and the ambivalently attached scored highest. Avoidant males scored higher than secure males on the Schizoid subscale; the ambivalent group scored higher than the secure group on both Depression and Social Withdrawal.

As noted in the discussion of academic skills, Ledingham and Schwartzman (1984) identified a group of withdrawn children in grades 1, 4, and 7 by means of a sociometric technique. Of 219 originally identified (out of 1537), 150 (68%) were found three years later and school placement data obtained. Seventy-five percent of the withdrawn group were in regular classes at the expected grade level as compared to 83 percent of controls, a nonsignificant difference.

To test the results of earlier studies (e.g., Kellam, Branch, Agrawal, & Ensminger, 1975; Kohn, 1977) that had suggested both stability and prognostic significance for internalizing symptoms, Fischer, Rolf, Hasazi, and Cummings (1984) studied the continuity of behavioral adjustments from preschool through elementary and junior high school. Internalizing checklist scores obtained at preschool were significantly but very weakly (.16) related for girls but not for boys. Moreover, as the authors noted, ''The results for the internalizing dimension indicate that the probability of detecting 'healthy' and 'disturbed' children at follow-up on the bases of their level of preschool functioning was not basically different than chance'' (p. 145).

Glow, Glow, and Rump (1982) have reported on the one-year stability of teacher and parent behavior ratings on children ages 5 to 11. For the teacher ratings, scales measuring shyness and depressed mood had stabilities of .50 and .33 with nonsignificant age differences. Parent ratings of shyness, perfectionistic-compulsive, and tearful-dependent had stabilities of .65, .49, and .63, respectively, with no significant age differences. Tesiny and Lefkowitz (1982) studied the six-month stability of depressive symptoms in over 400 normal children in fourth and fifth grades as measured by peer, self, and teacher ratings. They reported stability correlations of .70 for peer nominations, .60 for teacher ratings, and .40 for self-ratings.

As might be expected, the six-month and one-year intervals for elementary age children produced greater stability than that found for much younger children and/or longer time intervals.

Taken together, the studies of the persistence of various types of AW symptoms suggest, as was the case for CD symptoms, that stability is reasonably good over short intervals, and better for older (elementary age) than younger (preschoolers) children. However, longer term predictability especially as found by Fischer et al. (1984) is poor, and preschool ''symptoms'' do not predict later problem status.

AW Disorders

There is very little research on the persistence of diagnosed AW type disorders in childhood. Hollingsworth et al. (1980) followed up 10 of 17 patients (.2% of a clinical sample) who ranged in age from 3 to 15 years at admission and who met criteria for the diagnosis of obsessive-compulsive disorder. At follow-up (1½ to 14 years post-admission), the patients ranged from 12 to 30 years of age. Of the 10, 7 still reported obsessive-compulsive behavior to some degree; only 3 denied any such symptoms. As we have already noted, obsessive-compulsive disorder in children is very rare, but as these data show, apparently very persistent.

While there are follow-up studies of childhood and adolescent depression using very small sample sizes (e.g., Chess, Thomas, & Hassibi, 1983; Poznanski, Krakenbuhl, & Zrull, 1976), the best data have been provided by Kovacs and her colleagues (Kovacs, Feinberg, Crouse-Novak, Paulauskas, & Finkelstein, 1984; Kovacs, Feinberg, Crouse-Novak, Paulaskas, Pollock, & Finkelstein, 1984), who have intensively studied a group of 64 children (49% males; mean age 11.2 years) diagnosed as major depressive disorder, dysthymic disorder, adjustment disorder with depressed mood, or a combination of one or more of these disorders. They have reported a 92 percent recovery rate for major depressive disorder within 1½ years of onset, a recovery rate for adjustment disorder with depressed mood of 90 percent within nine months, and a recovery rate for dysthymic disorder of 89 percent, but only after six years beyond onset. For both major depression and dysthymia, earlier onset predicted a more protracted recovery period.

Even though recovery rates were high, there was considerable likelihood of additional episodes of some form of depression. Within three years and four months of the onset of dysthymic disorder, 50 percent of these patients would have an episode of major depressive disorder, with this rate uninfluenced by either sex or age of onset of the dysthymia. Among those with major depressive disorder, there was a cumulative risk of 72 percent for a new episode within about five years. Neither sex nor age at initial onset was related to likelihood of recurrence, nor was duration of the initial episode related to time between episodes. The presence of depressive mood, however, did not predict major depression; none of these 11 children developed major depression (only 1 patient of 30 in a nondepressed control group with other disorders subsequently developed major depression).

These studies by Kovacs et al. (1984) certainly suggest that diagnosable depressive disorder, at least when the severity of such disorder results in referral, persists over time to a very high degree, but with periods of remission. On the other hand, dysphoric mood is short-lived and not at all predictive of either later dysthymia or major depression, suggesting that, as seems to be the case with AW symptoms, there is a real difference between the persistence of isolated symptoms, or even clusters of symptoms (e.g., internalizing dimensions on rating scales), and the persistence of a carefully diagnosed disorder.

Adult Social Functioning

As we saw in Chapter 2, undersocialized CD in childhood and adolescence is predictive of social dysfunction in adulthood. However, Robins' (1966) report on the later adjustment of children diagnosed as neurotic stands in contrast to the findings with regard to CD. For example, she has reported that "few differences were found between the childhood histories of ex-patients diagnosed neurotic (excluding hysteria) and those well as adults" (p. 254). "Furthermore, those later found to be well as adults were more often referred for neurotic behavior than for theft," and "shy withdrawn personality sometimes thought to be predictive of schizophrenia did not predict it in these children" (p. 258). Robins' (1966) data certainly indicate that internalizing symptomatology in childhood does not predict adult dysfunction, even of an internalizing type.

While more study is clearly warranted, the extant data indicate that AW-type symptoms may persist in school-aged, and even younger, children over the short term but there is little evidence for persistence over periods of more than a year or two. There is clearly no evidence to date that one, or even a few, early symptoms are predictive of later disorder or that childhood "neurotic" disorder portends adult dysfunction. Clearly, AW symptoms do not have the rather foreboding prognosis that is associated with undersocialized CD. What data there are on the persistence of disorder is limited to diagnosed obsessive-compulsive disorder and depression in clinical samples and does suggest considerable persistence but with intermitted remission.

SUMMARY

Broad-band AW disorder is less prevalent than is CD and such subtypes as major depressive disorder and obsessive-compulsive disorder are rare. Sex differences are much less well documented (and researched). The personal and social correlates of AW, beyond those characteristics defining the disorder, are also less well established. Very few stable cognitive correlates have been found. The role of physiological factors in the development of AW disorder has only recently been the focus of research, and the findings are not, at least as yet, as consistent and intriguing as in the case of CD. Outcome studies suggest considerable short-term stability of AW symptomatology but longer term stability does not permit accurate prediction from early symptoms to later disorder over the school years. What data there are indicate that childhood AW does not portend adult dysfunction. However, limited research has suggested considerable persistence of clinically diagnosed dysphoric and major depressive disorder as well as obsessive-compulsive disorder.

REFERENCES

Achenbach, T. M. (1978). The child behavior profile, I. Boys aged 6–11. *Journal of Consulting and Clinical Psychology, 46*, 478–488.

Achenbach, T. M. (1979). The child behavior profile: An empirically based system for assessing children behavioral problems and competences. *International Journal of Mental Health, 7*, 24–42.

Achenbach, T. M., & Edelbrock, C. S. (1979). The child behavior profile, II. Boys aged 12–16 and girls aged 6–11 and 12–16. *Journal of Consulting and Clinical Psychology, 47*, 223–233.

Achenbach, T. M., & Edelbrock, C. S. (1981). Behavioral problems and competencies reported by parents of normal and disturbed children aged four through sixteen. *Monograph of the Society for Research in Child Development, 46*, 1 (No. 188).

American Psychiatric Association (1980). *Diagnostic and statistical manual of mental disorders* (3rd ed.). Washington, DC: Authors.

Anderson, J. C., Williams, S., McGee, R., & Silva, P. A. (1985). *The prevalence of DSM III disorders in a large sample of pre-adolescent children from the general population.* Unpublished manuscript. University of Otago Medical School, Dunedin, New Zealand.

Asher, S. R., & Hymel, S. (1981). Children's social competence in peer relations: Sociometric and behavioral assessment. In J. D. Wine & M. D. Smye (Eds.), *Social competence* (pp. 126–157). New York: Guilford.

Asher, S. R., Markell, R. A., & Hymel, S. (1981). Identifying children at risk in peer relations: A critique of the rate-of-interaction approach to assessment. *Child Development, 52*, 1239–1245.

Barden, R. C., Garber, J., Duncan, S. W., & Masters, J. C. (1981). Cumulative effects of induced affective states in children: Accentuation, innoculation, and remediation. *Journal of Personality and Social Psychology, 40*, 750–760.

Barrios, B. A., Hartmann, D. B., & Shigetomi, C. (1981). Fears and anxieties in children. In E. J. Mash & L. G. Terdal (Eds.), *Behavioral assessment of childhood disorders* (pp. 259–304). New York: Guilford.

Beardslee, W. R., Bemporad, J., Keller, M. B., & Klerman, G. L. (1983). Children of parents with major affective disorder: A review. *American Journal of Psychiatry, 140*, 825–832.

Campbell, S. B. (1986). Developmental issues. In R. Gittelman (Ed.), *Anxiety disorders of childhood*. New York: Guilford.

Carlson, G. A., & Cantwell, D. P. (1979). A survey of depressive symptoms in a child and adolescent psychiatric population: Interview data. *Journal of the American Academy of Child Psychiatry, 18*, 587–599.

Cederblad, M., & Hook, B. (1984). Catecholamine excretion in children in relation to behaviour deviances and psychosocial background factors: A longitudinal study. *Acta Paedopsychiatrica, 50*, 191–200.

Cerreto, M. C., & Tuma, J. M. (1977). Distribution of DSM-III diagnoses in a child psychiatric setting. *Journal of Abnormal Child Psychology, 5*, 147–155.

Chandler, M. J., Greenspan, S., & Barenboim, C. (1974). Assessment and training of role-taking and referential communication skills in institutionalized emotionally disturbed children. *Developmental Psychology, 10*, 546–553.

Chess, S., Thomas, A., & Hassibi, M. (1983). Depression in childhood and adolescence: A prospective study of sex cases. *Journal of Nervous and Mental Diseases, 171*, 411–420.

Coie, J. D., Dodge, K. A., & Coppotelli, H. (1982). Dimensions and types of social status: A cross-age perspective. *Developmental Psychology, 18*, 557–570.

Costello, A. J., Edelbrock, C., Dulcan, M. K., Kalas, R., & Klario, S. H. (1984). *Development and testing of the NIMH Diagnostic Interview Schedule for children in a clinic population*. Final report (Contract #RFP-DB-81-0027). Rockville, MD: Center for Epidemiologic Studies, NIMH.

Costello, A. J., Edelbrock, C., Kalas, R., Kessler, M. D., & Klario, S. H. (1982). *The NIMH Diagnostic Interview Schedule for Children* (DISC). Unpublished interview schedule, Department of Psychiatry, University of Pittsburgh.

Dandes, S. K., La Greca, A. M., Wick, P., & Shaw, K. (March, 1986). The development of the Social Anxiety Scale for Children (SASC) II: Relationship to teacher and peer ratings. Paper presented at the annual meeting of the Southeastern Psychological Association, Orlando, FL.

Delameter, A. H., & Lahey, B. B. (1983). Physiological correlates of conduct problems and anxiety in hyperactive and learning-disabled children. *Journal of Abnormal Child Psychology, 11*, 85–100.

Deluty, R. H. (1979). Children's Action Tendency Scale: A self-report measure of aggressiveness, assertiveness, and submissiveness in children. *Journal of Consulting and Clinical Psychology, 47*, 1061–1071.

Deutsch, F. (1974). Observational and sociometric measures of peer popularity and their relationship to egocentric communication in female pre-schoolers. *Developmental Psychology, 10*, 745–747.

Dusek, J. B., Mergler, N. L., & Kermis, M. D. (1976). Attention, encoding, and information processing in low and high test anxious children. *Child Development, 47*, 201–207.

Dweck, C. S., & Elliot, E. S. (1983). Achievement motivation. In E. Mavis Hetherington (Ed.), *Socialization, personality, and social development, Handbook of child psychology* (Vol. IV, pp. 643–691). New York: Wiley.

Eysenck, H. J., & Prell, D. B. (1951). The inheritance of neuroticism: An experimental study. *The Journal of Mental Science, XCVII*, 441–465.

Elkins, R., Rapoport, J. L., & Lipsky, A. (1980). Obsessive-compulsive disorder of childhood and adolescence: A neurobiological viewpoint. *Journal of the American Academy of Child Psychiatry, 19*, 511–524.

Feinstein, C., Blouin, A. G., Egan, J., & Conners, C. K. (1984). Depressive symptomatology in a child psychiatric outpatient population: Correlations with diagnosis. *Comprehensive Psychiatry, 25*, 379–391.

Fischer, M., Rolf, J. E., Hasazi, J. E., & Cummings, L. (1984). Follow-up of a preschool epidemiological sample: Cross-age continuities and predictions of later adjustment with internalizing and externalizing dimensions of behavior. *Child Development, 55*, 137–150.

Fisher, B. (1973). *Differences in motivational factors among two classifications of delinquents.* Unpublished master's thesis, Southern Illinois University.

Foster, S. L., & Ritchey, W. L. (1979). Issues in the assessment of social competence in children. *Journal of Applied Behavior Analysis, 12*, 625–638.

Foster, S. L., & Ritchey, W. L. (1985). Behavioral correlates of sociometric status of fourth-, fifth-, and sixth-grade children in two classroom situations. *Behavioral Assessment, 7*, 79–93.

Fowles, D. C. (1980). The Three Arousal Model: Implications of Gray's two-factor learning theory for heart rate, electrodermal activity and psychopathy. *Psychophysiology, 17*, 87–104.

Fowles, D. C. (1983). Motivational effects on heart rate and electrodermal activity: Implications for research in personality and psychopathology. *Journal of Research in Personality, 17*, 48–71.

Garcia-Coll, C., Kagan, J., & Reznick, J. S. (1984). Behavioral inhibition in young children. *Child Development, 55*, 1005–1019.

Glennon, B., & Weisz, J. R. (1978). An observational approach to the assessment of anxiety in young children. *Journal of Consulting and Clinical Psychology, 46*, 1246–1257.

Glow, R. A. (1978a). *Children's behaviour problems: A normative study of a parent rating scale.* Unpublished monograph.

Glow, R. A. (1978b). *Classroom behaviour problems: An Australian normative study of the Conners' Teachers' Rating Scale.* Unpublished monograph.

Glow, R. A., Glow, P. H., & Rump, E. E. (1982). The stability of child behavior disorders: A one year test-retest study of Adelaide versions of the Conners Teacher and Parent Rating Scales. *Journal of Abnormal Child Psychology, 10*, 33–60.

Golden, C. J. (1978). *The Stroop Color and Word Test: A manual for clinical and experimental uses.* Chicago: Stoelting.

Gotlib, I. H., & Asarnow, R. G. (1979). Interpersonal and impersonal problem-solving skills in mildly and clinically depressed university students. *Journal of Consulting and Clinical Psychology, 1*, 86–95.

Gottman, J. M. (1977a). The effects of a modeling film on social isolation in preschool children: A methodological investigation. *Journal of Abnormal Child Psychology, 5*, 69–78.

Gottman, J. M. (1977b). Toward a definition of social isolation in children. *Child Development, 48*, 513–517.

Gottman, J. M., Gonso, J., & Rasmussen, B. (1975). Social interaction, social competence, and friendship in children. *Child Development, 46*, 709–718.

Graham, P. (1974). Depression in prepubertal children. *Developmental Medicine and Child Neurology, 16*, 340–349.

Graham, P. J. (1979). Epidemiological studies. In H. C. Quay & J. S. Werry (Eds.), *Psychopathological disorders of childhood* (2nd ed., pp. 185–209). New York: Wiley.

Gray, J. A. (1979). A neuro-psychological theory of anxiety. In C. E. Izard (Ed.), *Emotions in personality and psychopathology* (pp. 303–335). New York: Plenum.

Gray, J. A. (1982). *The neuropsychology of anxiety: An enquiry into the Septo-Hippocampal System.* New York: Oxford University Press.

Green, K. D., Forehand, R., Beck, S. J., & Vosk, B. (1980). An assessment of the relationship among measures of children's social competence and children's academic achievement. *Child Development, 51*, 1149–1156.

Hartup, W. W. (1983). Peer relations. In P. H. Mussen (Ed.), *Handbook of child psychology* (Vol. 4, pp. 103–196). New York: Wiley.

Havighurst, R. J., Bowman, P. H., Liddle, G. P., Matthews, C. V., & Pierce, J. V. (1962). *Growing up in River City.* New York: Wiley.

Herjanic, B., & Campbell, W. (1977). Differentiating psychiatrically disturbed children on the basis of a structured interview. *Journal of Abnormal Child Psychology, 5*, 127–134.

Herjanic, B., & Reich, W. (1982). Development of a structured psychiatric interview for children: Agreement between child and parent on individual symptoms. *Journal of Abnormal Child Psychology, 10*, 307–324.

Hill, K. T. (1972). Anxiety in the evaluative context. In W. W. Hartup (Ed.), *The young child: Reviews of research*, (Vol. 2 pp. 255–263). Washington, DC: National Association for the Education of Young Children.

Hill, K. T., & Sarason, S. B. (1966). The relation of test anxiety and defensiveness to test and school performance over the elementary school years. *Monographs of the Society for Research in Child Development, 31* (2, Serial No. 104).

Hodges, K., Kline, J., Stern, L., Cytryn, L., & McKnew, D. (1982). The development of the child assessment schedule for research and clinical purposes. *Journal of Abnormal Child Psychology, 10*, 173–189.

Hodges, K., McKnew, D., Cytryn, L., Stern, L., & Kline, J. (1982). The Child Assessment Schedule (CAS) Diagnostic Interview: A report on reliability and validity. *Journal of American Academy of Child Psychiatry, 21*, 468–473.

Hogan, A. E., & Quay, H. C. (1984). Cognition and adolescent behavior disorders. In B. B. Lahey, & A. E. Kazdin (Eds.), *Advances in clinical child psychology* (Vol. 7, pp. 1–34). New York: Plenum.

Hollingsworth, C. E., Tanguay, P. E., Grossman, L., & Pabst, P. (1980). Long-term outcome of obsessive-compulsive disorder in childhood. *Journal of the American Academy of Child Psychiatry, 19*, 134–144.

Hymel, S., Tinsley, B. R., Geraci, R., & Asher, S. R. (1981). *Sociometric status and social skills: The initiating style of preschool children.* Unpublished manuscript, University of Illinois.

Jacobsen, R., Lahey, B., & Strauss, C. (1983). Correlates of depressed mood in normal children. *Journal of Abnormal Child Psychology, 11*, 29–40.

Jennings, K. D. (1975). People versus object orientation, social behavior, and intellectual abilities in children. *Developmental Psychology, 11*, 511–519.

Jones, F. H. (1974). A 4-year follow-up of vulnerable adolescents. *Journal of Nervous and Mental Disease, 159*, 20–39.

Judd, L. J. (1965). Obsessive-compulsive neurosis in children. *Archives of General Psychiatry, 12*, 136–143.

Kagan, J., & Moss, H. A. (1962). *Birth to maturity.* New York: Wiley.

Kagan, J., & Reznick, J. S. (1984). Task involvement and cardiac response in young children. *Australian Journal of Psychology, 36*, 135–147.

Kagan, J., Reznick, J. S., Clarke, C., Snidman, N., & Garcia-Coll, C. (1984). Behavioral inhibition to the unfamiliar. *Child Development, 55*, 2212–2225.

Kaplan, S. L., Hong, G. K., & Weinhold, C. (1984). Epidemiology of depressive symptomatology in adolescents. *Journal of the American Academy of Child Psychiatry, 23*, 91–98.

Kashani, J. H., McGee, R. O., Clarkson, S. E., Anderson, J. C., Walton, L. A., Williams, S., Silva, P. A., Robins, A. J., Cytryn, L., & McKnew, D. H. (1983). Depression in a sample of 9-year-old children. *Archives of General Psychiatry, 40*, 1217–1223.

Kashani, J. H., Ray, J. S., & Carlson, G. A. (1984). Depression and depressive-like states in preschool-age children in a child development unit. *American Journal of Psychiatry, 141*, 1397–1402.

Kashani, J. H., & Simonds, J. F. (1979). The incidence of depression in children. *American Journal of Psychiatry*, 136, 1203–1204.

Kaslow, N. J., Rehm, L. P., & Siegel, A. W. (1984). Social-cognitive correlates of depression in children. *Journal of Abnormal Child Psychology, 12*, 605–620.

Kaslow, N. J., Tanenbaum, R. L., Abramson, L. Y., Peterson, C., & Seligman, M. E. P. (1983). Problem-solving deficits and depressive symptoms among children. *Journal of Abnormal Child Psychology, 11*, 497–502.

Kazdin, A. E., & Petti, T. A. (1982). Self-report and interview measures of childhood and adolescent depression. *Journal of Child Psychology and Psychiatry, 23*, 437–457.

Kellam, S. G., Branch, J. D., Agrawal, K. C., & Ensminger, M.E. (1975). *Mental health and going to school.* Chicago: University of Chicago Press.

Klein, D. C., Fencil-Morse, E., & Seligman, M. E. P. (1976). Learned helplessness, depression, and the attribution of failure. *Journal of Personality and Social Psychology, 33*, 508–516.

Klein, D. C., & Seligman, M. E. P. (1976). Reversal of performance deficits in learned helplessness and depression. *Journal of Abnormal Psychology, 85*, 11–26.

Kohn, M. (1977). *Social competence, symptoms, and underachievement in childhood: A longitudinal perspective.* Washington, DC: Winston.

Kohn, M., & Rosman, B. (1972a). Relationship of preschool social-emotional functioning to later intellectual achievement. *Developmental Psychology, 6*, 445–452.

Kohn, M., & Rosman, B. L. (1972b). A social competence scale and symptom checklist for the preschool child: Factor dimensions, their cross-instrument generality, and longitudinal persistence. *Developmental Psychology, 6*, 430–444.

Kotsopoulos, S., & Nandy, S. (1981). A profile of the child psychiatric population of Newfoundland. *Canadian Journal of Psychiatry, 26*, 189–191.

Kovacs, M., Feinberg, T. L., Crouse-Novak, M. A., Paulauskas, S. L., & Finkelstein, R. (1984). Depressive disorders in childhood. I. A longitudinal prospective study of characteristics and recovery. *Archives of General Psychiatry, 41*, 229–237.

Kovacs, M., Feinberg, T. L., Crouse-Novak, M., Paulauskas, S. L., Pollock, M., & Finkelstein, R. (1984). Depressive disorders in childhood. II. A longitudinal study of the risk for a subsequent major depression. *Archives of General Psychiatry, 41*, 643–649.

Krantz, M. (1982). Sociometric awareness, social participation, and perceived popularity in preschool children. *Child Development, 53*, 376–379.

La Greca, A. M. (1978). *Teaching children how to interact with peers: Evaluating the effectiveness of social-skills training with low accepted elementary school children.* Doctoral dissertation. Purdue University, West Lafayette, IN.

La Greca, A. M. (1981). Peer acceptance: The correspondence between children's sociometric scores and teachers' ratings of peer interaction. *Journal of Abnormal Child Psychology, 9*, 167–178.

La Greca, A. M., & Stark, P. (1986). Naturalistic observations of children's social behavior. In P. Strain, M. Guralnick, & H. Walker (Eds.), *Children's social behavior: Development, assessment, and modification* (pp. 181–213). New York: Academic Press.

Lapouse, R., & Monk, M. A. (1959). Fears and worries in a representative sample of children. *American Journal of Orthopsychiatry, 29*, 803–818.

Lazarus, P. J. (1980). *The assessment of shyness in children.* Paper presented at the meeting of the American Personnel and Guidance Association, Atlanta. (ERIC Document Reproduction Service No. 198 441.)

Lazarus, P. J. (1982). Correlation of shyness and self-esteem for elementary school children. *Perceptual and Motor Skills, 55*, 8–10.

Ledingham, J. (1981). Developmental patterns of aggressive and withdrawn behavior in childhood: A possible method for identifying preschizophrenics. *Journal of Abnormal Child Psychology, 9*, 1–22.

Ledingham, J., & Schwartzman, A. (1984). A 3-year follow-up of aggressive and withdrawn behavior in childhood: Preliminary findings. *Journal of Abnormal Child Psychology, 12*, 157–168.

Ledingham, J. E., Schwartzman, A. E., & Serbin, L. (1984). Current adjustment and family functioning of children behaviorally at risk for schizophrenia. In A. B. Doyle, D. Gold, & D. Moskowitz (Eds.), *Children in families under stress: Research strategies* (pp. 99–112). San Francisco: Jossey-Bass.

Lefkowitz, M. M., & Burton, N. (1978). Childhood depression: A critique of the concept. *Psychological Bulletin, 85*, 716–726.

Lefkowitz, M., & Tesiny, E. (1980). Assessment of childhood depression. *Journal of Consulting and Clinical Psychology, 48*, 43–50.

Lewis, M., Feiring, C., McGuffog, C., & Jaskir, J. (1984). Predicting psychopathology in six-year-olds from early social relations. *Child Development, 55*, 123–136.

Lobovits, D. A., & Handol, P. J. (1985). Childhood depression: Prevalence using DSM-III criteria and validity of parent and child depression scales. *Journal of Pediatric Psychology, 10*, 45–54.

Ludwig, R. P., & Lazarus, P. J. (1983). Relationship between shyness in children and constricted cognitive control as measured by the Stroop Color-Word Test. *Journal of Consulting and Clinical Psychology, 51*, 386–389.

Lundberg, U. (1983). Sex differences in behaviour pattern and catecholamine and cortisol excretion in 3–6 year old day-care children. *Biological Psychology, 16*, 109–117.

Masters, J. C., Barden, R. C., & Ford, M. E. (1979). Affective states, expressive behavior and learning in children. *Journal of Personality and Social Psychology, 37*, 380–390.

Masters, J. C., Felleman, E. S., & Barden, R. C. (1981). Experimental studies of affective states in children. In B. B. Lahey & A. E. Kazdin (Eds.), *Advances in clinical child psychology* (Vol. 4, pp. 91–118). New York: Plenum.

McGee, R., Silva, P. A., & Williams, S. (1984). Behaviour problems in a population of seven-year-old children: Prevalence, stability, and types of disorder—A research report. *Journal of Child Psychology and Psychiatry, 25*, 251–259.

Michael, C. M., Morris, D. P., & Soroker, E. (1957). Follow-up studies of shy, withdrawn children: II. Relative incidence of schizophrenia. *American Journal of Orthopsychiatry, 27*, 331–337.

Michelson, L., Foster, S. L., & Ritchey, W. L. (1981). Social-skills assessment of children. In B. B. Lahey & A. E. Kazdin (Eds.), *Advances in clinical child psychology* (Vol. 4, pp. 119–165). New York: Plenum.

Milich, R., & Landau, S. (1984). A comparison of the social status and social behavior of aggressive and aggressive/withdrawn boys. *Journal of Abnormal Child Psychology, 12*, 277–288.

Mullins, L. L., Siegel, L. J., & Hodges, K. (1985). Cognitive problem-solving and life event correlates of depressive symptoms in children. *Journal of Abnormal Child Psychology, 13*, 305–314.

Nicholls, J. G. (1976). When a scale measures more than its name denotes: The case of the Test Anxiety Scale for Children. *Journal of Consulting and Clinical Psychology, 44*, 976–985.

Nottelmann, E. D., & Hill, K. T. (1977). Test anxiety and off-task behavior in evaluative situations. *Child Development, 48*, 225–231.

O'Connor, M., Foch, T., Sherry, T., & Plomin, R. (1980). A twin study of specific behavioral problems of socialization as viewed by parents. *Journal of Abnormal Child Psychology, 8,* 189–199.

Ollendick, T. H. (1983). Anxiety disorders in children. In M. Hersen (Ed.), *Practice of outpatient behavior therapy; A clinician's handbook* (pp. 273–305). New York: Grune & Stratton.

Panella, D., & Henggeler, S. W. (1986). Peer interactions of conduct problem, anxious-withdrawn, and well-adjusted black adolescents. *Journal of Abnormal Child Psychology, 14,* 1–12.

Pekarik, E. G., Prinz, R. J., Liebert, D. E., Weintraub, S., & Neale, J. M. (1976). The pupil evaluation inventory: A sociometric technique for assessing children's social behavior. *Journal of Abnormal Child Psychology, 4,* 83–97.

Poznanski, E. O., Krakenbuhl, V., & Zrull, J. P. (1976). Childhood depression: A longitudinal perspective. *Journal of the American Academy of Child Psychiatry, 25,* 491–501.

Poznanski, E. O., & Zrull, J. P. (1970). Childhood depression: Clinical characteristics of overtly depressed children. *Archives of General Psychiatry, 23,* 8–15.

Plomin, R. (1983). Childhood temperament. In B. B. Lahey & A. E. Kazdin (Eds.), *Advances in clinical child psychology* (Vol. 6, pp. 45–92). New York: Plenum.

Price, K. P., Tryon, W. W., & Raps, C. S. (1978). Learned helplessness and depression in a clinical population: A test of two behavioral hypotheses. *Journal of Abnormal Psychology, 87,* 113–121.

Quay, H. C. (1986). The behavioral reward and inhibition systems in childhood behavior disorder. In L. M. Bloomingdale (Ed.), *Attention deficit disorder 3.* New York: Spectrum.

Rapoport, J., Elkins, R., Langer, D. H., Sceery, W., Buchsbaum, M. S., Gillin, J. C., Murphy, D. L., Zahn, T. P., Lake, R., Ludlow, C., & Mendelson, W. (1981). Childhood obsessive-compulsive disorder. *American Journal of Psychiatry, 138,* 1545–1554.

Reese, R. D. (1967). School-age suicide: The educational parameters. *Dissertation Abstracts International, 27*(9-A), 2895–2896.

Richard, B. A., & Dodge, K. A. (1982). Social maladjustment and problem solving in school-aged children. *Journal of Consulting and Clinical Psychology, 50,* 226–233.

Robins, C. N. (1966). *Deviant children grown up.* Baltimore: Williams & Wilkins.

Robins, L. (1979). Follow-up studies of behavior disorders in children. In H. C. Quay & J. S. Werry (Eds.), *Psychopathological disorders of childhood* (2nd ed., pp. 483–513). New York: Wiley.

Rolf, J. E. (1972). The social and academic competence of children vulnerable to schizophrenia and other behavior pathologies. *Journal of Abnormal Psychology, 80,* 225–243.

Rubin, K. H., & Clark, M. L. (1983). Preschool teachers' ratings of behavioral problems: Observational, sociometric, and social-cognitive correlates. *Journal of Abnormal Child Psychology, 11,* 273–286.

Rutter, M. (1979). *Changing youth in a changing society.* London: Nuffield Provincial Hospitals Trust.

Rutter, M., Cox, A., Tupling, C., Berger, M., & Yule, W. (1975). Attainment and adjustment in two geographical areas. I. Prevalence of psychiatric disorder. *British Journal of Psychiatry, 126*, 493–509.

Rutter, M., & Garmezy, N. (1983). Developmental psychopathology. In E. M. Hetherington (Ed.), *Socialization, personality, and social development. Handbook of child psychology* (Vol. IV, pp. 775–911). New York: Wiley.

Rutter, M., & Graham, P. (1968). The reliability and validity of the psychiatric assessment of the child. I. Interview with the child. *British Journal of Psychiatry, 114*, 563–579.

Rutter, M., Tizard, J., & Whitmore, K. (1970). *Education, health, and behavior.* London: Longmans.

Sandler, J., & Joffe, W. (1965). Notes on childhood depression. *International Journal of Psychoanalysis, 46*, 88–96.

Schwartz, M., Friedman, R., Lindsay, R., & Narrol, H. (1983). The relationship between conceptual tempo and depression in children. *Journal of Consulting and Clinical Psychology, 50*, 488–490.

Shantz, C. U. (1975). *The development of social cognition.* Chicago: The University of Chicago Press.

Spielberger, C. D. (1972). Current trends in theory and research on anxiety. In C. D. Spielberger (Ed.), *Anxiety: Current trends in theory and research* (Vol. 1, pp. 3–19). New York: Academic Press.

Stone, W. L., & La Greca, A. M. (1986). The development of social skills in children. In E. Schopler & G. Mesibov (Eds.), *Social behavior in autism* (pp. 35–60). New York: Plenum.

Strain, P. S., Cooke, T. P., & Apolloni, T. (1976). *Teaching exceptional children: Assessing and modifying social behavior.* New York: Academic Press.

Strauss, C. C., Lahey, B. B., & Jacobsen, R. H. (1982). The relationship of three measures of childhood depression to academic underachievement. *Journal of Applied Developmental Psychology, 3*, 375–380.

Strober, M., Green, J., & Carlson, G. (1981). Reliability of psychiatric diagnoses in hospitalized adolescents. Interrater agreement using DSM-III. *Archives of General Psychiatry, 38*, 141–145.

Te.nes, K., Downey, K., & Vernadakis, A. (1977). Urinary cortisol excretion rates and anxiety in normal 1-year-old infants. *Psychosomatic Medicine, 39*, 178–186.

Tesiny, E. P., & Lefkowitz, M. M. (1982). Childhood depression: A 6-month follow-up study. *Journal of Consulting and Clinical Psychology, 50*, 778–780.

Tesiny, E. P., Lefkowitz, M. M., & Gordon, N. H. (1980). Childhood depression, locus of control and school achievement. *Journal of Educational Psychology, 72*, 506–510.

von Knorring, A.-L., Cloninger, C. R., Bohman, M., & Sigvardsson, S. (1983). An adoption study of depressive disorders and substance abuse. *Archives of General Psychiatry, 40*, 943–950.

Vosk, B., Forehand, R., Parker, J. B., & Richard, K. (1982). A multimethod comparison of popular and unpopular children. *Developmental Psychology, 18*, 571–575.

Wanlass, R. L., & Prinz, R. J. (1982). Methodological issues in conceptualizing and treating childhood social isolation. *Psychological Review, 91*, 39–55.

Waterman, J., Sobesky, W., Silvern, L., Aoki, B., & McCaulay, M. (1981). Social perspective-taking and adjustment in emotionally disturbed, learning-disabled, and normal children. *Journal of Abnormal Child Psychology, 9*, 133–148.

Weiner, B., & Kukla, A. (1970). An attributional analysis of achievement motivation. *Journal of Personality and Social Psychology, 15*, 1–20.

Weissmann, M. M., Gershon, E. S., Kidd, K. K., Prusoff, B. A., Leckman, J. F., Dibble, E., Hamovit, J., Thompson, W. D., Pauls, D. L., & Guroff, J. J. (1984). Psychiatric disorders in the relatives of probands with affective disorders. *Archives of General Psychiatry, 43*, 13–21.

Weissman, M. M., Leckman, J. F., Merikangas, K. R., Gammon, G. D., & Prusoff, B. A. (1984). Depression and anxiety disorders in parents and children. *Archives of General Psychiatry, 41*, 845–852.

Werry, J. S. (In press). Major depressive disorder in prepubertal children: A critique. In G. Andrews (Ed.), *Depression: A festschrift for L. G. Kiloh*. Sydney: University of New South Wales Press.

Werry, J. S., & Aman, M. G. (1980). Anxiety in children. In G. D. Burrows & B. M. Davies (Eds.), *Handbook of studies on anxiety* (pp. 165–192). Amsterdam: ASP Biological and Medical Press.

Werry, J. S., Methven, R. J., Fitzpatrick, J., & Dixon, H. (1983). The inter-rater reliability of DSM-III in children. *Journal of Abnormal Child Psychology, 11*, 341–354.

Werry, J. S., & Quay, H. C. (1971). The prevalence of behavior symptoms in younger elementary school children. *American Journal of Orthopsychiatry, 41*, 136–143.

Wine, J. (1971). Test anxiety and direction of attention. *Psychological Bulletin, 76*, 92–104.

Wine, J. D. (1982). Evaluation anxiety: A cognitive-attentional construct. In H. W. Krohne & L. Laux (Eds.), *Achievement, stress, and anxiety* (pp. 207–222). Washington, DC: Hemisphere.

Wood, R., Michelson, L., & Flynn, S. (1978). *Assessment of assertive behavior in elementary school children*. Paper presented at the Annual Meeting of the Association for Advancement of Behavior Therapy, Chicago.

Zatz, S., & Chassin, L. (1983). Cognitions of test-anxious children. *Journal of Consulting and Clinical Psychology, 51*, 526–534.

Zimbardo, P. G., Pilkonis, P., & Norwood, R. (1975). The social disease called shyness. *Psychology Today*, 69–72.

4 ATTENTION DEFICIT DISORDER (HYPERACTIVITY)

SUSAN B. CAMPBELL and JOHN S. WERRY

INTRODUCTION

Few childhood behavior disorders have generated so much interest or controversy as that which has been variously known as hyperkinesis, minimal brain dysfunction, hyperactivity, and, most recently, Attention Deficit Disorder (ADD). A wide array of papers, reviews, and monographs has appeared in the past decade and it is a daunting task to try to pull all the threads together into a short review. As a result, this chapter is based in part on authoritative reviews and monographs and in part on particularly representative studies. The details of original studies will not be discussed unless it is felt that they are critical to the understanding or resolution of controversial points.

HISTORY

The history of hyperactivity has been reviewed in some detail by Ross and Ross (1982), among others. Suffice it to say that the idea has been around for almost a century. Early writings through World War II were dominated largely by the neurological view that hyperactivity (or "organic driveness") was an organic brain syndrome. The most influential work of this period was that of the neurologist Strauss (Strauss & Lehtinen, 1947). Perhaps as a consequence, much of the thinking about and research on the condition since has been inextricably interwoven with that of brain damage–behavior relationships that are reviewed in Chapter 8. While the rise in popularity of psychoanalytic theory and practice after World War II temporarily eclipsed organic syndromal views of hyperactivity, the idea persisted and seems to have been rejuvenated around the mid 1960s.

Two papers from this period are heralds of the dawning of the "Golden Age" of hyperactivity, the first by Laufer and Denhoff (1957) and the second by Clements and Peters (1962). Both embraced organic and syndromal views of hyperactivity. The latter introduced the term *minimal brain dysfunction* (MBD) and, continuing the pattern set by Strauss, placed heavy emphasis on associated neuropsychological and cognitive symptomatology. They also opened a Pandora's box, because the description of symptomatology was so vague that almost anything could be encompassed under the rubric of MBD. Clements (1966) then nominated overactivity as the core symptom of MBD, and the notion of "hyperactivity" became an ideological epidemic.

Also highly influential was the book by Wender (1971). While largely speculative, it is still cited as if it described established fact about brain–behavior relationships.

Reaction to the hyperactivity epidemic was not long in coming. English psychiatry, dominated by Rutter and his colleagues (e.g., Rutter & Shaffer, 1980; Schachar, Rutter, & Smith, 1981), claimed that hyperactivity was a rare disorder that might be related to brain damage but was, in fact, an unusual, not an inevitable, consequence of it. Along with a few American psychologists such as Quay (1979), they insisted that most cases of hyperactivity were indistinguishable from Conduct Disorder.

Serious researchers were then joined by social and educational critics who attacked the idea as dangerous since it led to labeling different but normal children as "sick" and to an epidemic of "chemical straitjacketing" with stimulant drugs (Grinspoon & Singer, 1973; Schrag & Divoky, 1975).

Increasingly high-quality research and thinking about hyperactivity have emerged over the last decade along with a better integration of research and practice. This is reflected in the shift of focus from "hyperactivity" to attentional problems in the new DSM-III classification (1980) of "Attention Deficit Disorder" (ADD). (See Chapter 1.) Throughout the remainder of this chapter we will refer to the disorder as ADD even though this term is of recent origin.

Despite the problems associated with hyperactivity as a diagnosis and as a prescription for action, its domination of childhood psychopathology research and theory in the 1970s had a dramatically beneficial effect upon the quality of empirical work in the field.

At the moment, high-quality research is basically focused on issues of differential diagnosis and descriptive psychopathology, as well as social behavior. New directions in research on etiology appear to be awaiting some kind of conceptual breakthrough. If the concept of ADD as a distinct disorder is to survive, this breakthrough will most likely come at the level of brain function or biochemistry since the principal stumbling block to research, diagnosis, and treatment seems to be the remoteness of much of the clinical symptomatology from the posited causes of the syndrome, which are held by many to reflect, at least in part, constitutional factors (Douglas, 1983; Loney, 1980; Quay, 1985; Ross & Ross, 1982).

PRINCIPAL CHARACTERISTICS

Diagnostic Criteria and Subclassifications

Almost every symptom of psychopathology has at one time or another been included under the rubric of "hyperactivity," although overactivity, inattention, poor impulse control, noncompliance, specific cognitive deficits, and neurological symptoms have usually figured prominently (Aman, 1984).

Barkley (1982) surveyed 210 studies and found that in 64 percent no diagnostic criteria at all were specified, while the majority failed to meet what were considered to be a minimally acceptable set of subject selection criteria. Recently several sets of research diagnostic criteria have been proposed to end this chaos (e.g., American Psychiatric Association, 1980; Barkley, 1982; Loney, 1982). However, the DSM-III criteria are likely to dominate clinical thinking for the foreseeable future.

The DSM-III category of ADD with hyperactivity is narrower than that used formerly since it is restricted to three areas: Attention, Impulsivity, and Hyperactivity. In addition, there are chronological and exclusionary criteria. The criteria, all of which must be present, are (American Psychiatric Association, 1980, pp. 27–30):

A. *Inattention.* At least three of the following:
1. often fails to finish things he or she starts
2. often doesn't seem to listen
3. easily distracted
4. has difficulty concentrating on schoolwork or other tasks
5. has difficulty sticking to a play activity

B. *Impulsivity.* At least three of the following:
1. often acts before thinking
2. shifts excessively from one activity to another
3. has difficulty organizing work (this not being due to cognitive impairment)
4. needs a lot of supervision
5. frequently calls out in class
6. has difficulty awaiting turn in games or group situations

C. *Hyperactivity.* At least two of the following:
1. runs about or climbs on things excessively
2. has difficulty sitting still or fidgets excessively
3. has difficulty staying seated
4. moves about excessively during sleep
5. is always "on the go" or acts as if "driven by a motor"

D. *Onset.* Before the age of seven.
E. *Duration.* Of at least six months.
F. Not due to Schizophrenia, Affective Disorder, or Severe or Profound Mental Retardation.

Barkley (1982) has reviewed these criteria and, while generally applauding the effort, has drawn attention to some problems: lack of norms for determining abnormality of symptoms; no specified way of operationalizing or measuring symptoms; not clarifying whether or not the disorder must be situationally pervasive; a maximum age of onset at seven rather than five or younger; and duration of component symptoms of only six months. He has proposed a working definition and, most importantly, seven truly operational criteria for diagnosis that follow from his definition:

> *Hyperactivity or ADD is a significant deficiency in age-appropriate attention, impulse control and rule-governed behavior (compliance, self-control and problem-solving) that arises in infancy or early childhood, is significantly pervasive in nature and is not the direct result of general intellectual retardation, severe language delay or emotional disturbance or gross sensory or motor impairment. (p. 153)*

However, Barkley's "rule-governed behavior" and the descriptive items relating to behavioral control could perpetuate current confusion between Conduct Disorder and ADD, unless they can be more specifically defined.

The DSM-III lists two other subcategories of ADD—ADD without hyperactivity (same criteria as ADD with hyperactivity omitting only criterion C) and a Residual State. The utility of these two categories awaits the kind of research that has been done for ADD with hyperactivity and is only just beginning to appear for ADD without hyperactivity (e.g., King & Young, 1982; Lahey, Schaughency, Strauss, & Frame, 1984). Psychometric, epidemiological, or validating data merit little comment so far.

The ICD-9 is detailed in Chapter 1. In passing it may be noted that the main category (Hyperkinetic Syndrome) differs from the DSM-III by retaining the *motor* rather than attentional symptomatology as primary. Also, there is a mixed Hyperkinetic Conduct Disorder rather than two distinct disorders that may coexist.

Amplification and description of the core and commonly associated symptomatology may be found in Weiss and Hechtman (1979), Loney (1978, 1980), and in monographs on ADD such as those by Barkley (1981a), Cantwell (1975), and Ross and Ross (1982).

Assessment

Assessment is reviewed in more detail in Chapter 12 and comprehensive discussions can be found in Barkley (1981a, 1981b, 1982), Loney (1978, 1980), and Ross and Ross (1982).

Rating scales for teachers and parents have dominated research on ADD (see Barkley, 1981b; Loney, 1978; Ross & Ross, 1982). By far the best known are the various Conners scales (see Goyette, Conners, & Ulrich, 1978), which have served as diagnostic, assessment, and change measures and are being used normatively as diagnostic criteria for ADD, a move endorsed by Barkley (1982). Their use as *sole* criteria is to be deplored, since they meet no current DSM-III or research diagnostic criteria in entirety (see Barkley, 1982) and there is evidence that, used alone, they are less valid than comprehensive data bases (e.g., Milich, Loney, & Landau, 1982; see also subsequent discussion).

As in much of childhood psychopathology, the best results will come from the use of a variety of methods of assessment and a variety of assessors across all of the child's typical environments (e.g., Aman, 1984; Barkley, 1981a, 1981b, 1982; S.B. Campbell, Szumowski, Ewing, Gluck, & Breaux, 1982; Loney, 1978; Whalen & Henker, 1980).

Empirical Validation of ADD as a Distinct Disorder

The principal bugbear is the continuing debate about whether ADD is distinct from Conduct Disorder. It is possible to argue the case at different levels. At the statistical level (see Chapter 1), the case is now clearly in favor of separate dimensions of motor overactivity and inattention (Edelbrock, Costello, & Kessler, 1984; Quay, 1985; Trites & Laprade, 1983). However, both dimensions and disorders can, in the end, be validated only externally.

At the level of correlates (see later text), there are some studies that have clearly separated ADD from other disorders and then attempted comparative validation studies (Firestone & Martin, 1979; Loney, Langhorne, & Paternite, 1978; McGee, Williams, & Silva, 1984a, 1984b; Milich, Loney, & Landau, 1982; Rutter, 1982; Sandberg, Rutter, & Taylor, 1978; Sandberg, Wieselberg, & Shaffer, 1980; Schachar et al., 1981; Stewart, deBlois, & Cummings, 1980). The evidence from these is largely, but not entirely, negative. The study by Milich, Loney, and Landau suggests that ADD and Conduct Disorder can be distinguished when the diagnosis is based on comprehensive clinical interviews, not merely parent or teacher rating scales. Further, when ADD is narrowly defined (Schachar et al., 1981), the disorder may be distinctive (see Aman, 1984; Loney & Milich, 1981; McGee et al., 1984a; Milich, Loney, & Landau, 1982). This issue is discussed in more detail under various aspects of the correlates section later.

The lack of clear evidence on etiology further complicates syndrome validation. Similarly, data on treatment efficacy has not resolved the debate. So far, despite claims that stimulants are specific for ADD, pharmacotherapy has not contributed to validation of the syndrome either. Problems such as lack of diagnostic precision and of comparative studies apply there too (see M. Campbell, Cohen, & Small, 1982). Further, recent studies demonstrate that stimulant medication has similar effects on normal children (Rapoport et al., 1978) and on enuretic but otherwise normal children (Werry & Aman, 1984).

The entrenched belief that ADD and Conduct Disorder are distinct cannot be taken as evidence of validity. Rather, one is forced into the defensive position of concluding that the possibility is still there, but that much of what has been shown to characterize the ADD child may yet prove to be just as characteristic of children with Conduct Disorder. The idea remains, however, scientifically heuristic, as well as tenable from an etiological point of view, since aggressive antisocial behavior *may* be learned and problems of attention and overactivity *may* be organismic. Further, as suggested by Schachar et al. (1981), the presence of ADD may facilitate the learning of aggressive and noncompliant behaviors. One major problem with existing studies, however, is that sample composition has been based primarily on "nuisance value"—that is, some adult had to declare the child's behavior a problem and then label the behavior "hyperactive." This process alone seems calculated to confound Conduct Disorder and ADD hopelessly (see Loney & Milich, 1981). It thus seems obvious that detection of "pure" forms of ADD will require that criteria other than social behavior be used, including selection of children on objective, attentional measures (Levy & Hobbes, 1981); extending the range and sophistication of biological measures including pharmacotherapy; narrowing the behavioral criteria to exclude aggression (Prinz, Connor, & Wilson, 1981); obtaining large enough samples to permit identification and comparison of children with "pure" forms of ADD and Conduct Disorder; and/or the use of multimodal diagnostic methods that assess symptoms of both ADD and Conduct Disorder (Milich, Loney, & Landau, 1982).

The question cannot be resolved on the basis of existing evidence, but it does seem premature to conclude that ADD is not a viable construct. Empirical work and clinical wisdom suggest that, despite some uncertainty, the ADD construct has both research and clinical utility. New research strategies will be needed to resolve these differential diagnostic/definitional issues and the related questions of correlates, course, and outcome.

The Etiology of ADD

Speculation on the etiology of ADD has focused on neurological, genetic, constitutional, and environmental factors. Despite the early emphasis on neurological dysfunction and the assumption that neurological mechanisms are implicated, there are few hard data to support the many competing hypotheses about the presence or site of possible structural damage, neurological immaturity, faulty arousal mechanisms, or the specifics of neurotransmitter imbalances (e.g., Douglas, 1983; Ferguson & Pappas, 1979; Gorenstein & Newman, 1980; Kinsbourne & Swanson, 1979; Rosenthal & Allen, 1978; Routh, 1980; Wender, 1971; Zentall & Zentall, 1983). Since data on neurological dysfunction is at best indirect (Gorenstein & Newman, 1980; Porges & Smith, 1980) and the relationships between specific aspects of neurophysiological functioning and overt behavior are highly complex, these remain fertile areas for hypothesis generating, but specific conclusions remain elusive.

Genetic-familial hypotheses have received modest support, but the methodological limitations of extant studies and differential diagnostic problems make these data difficult to interpret (McMahon, 1980). While it has been suggested that alcoholism, hysteria, antisocial personality, and hyperactivity run in families and form a spectrum of disorders characterized by a primary deficit in impulse control (Gorenstein & Newman, 1980), the studies in support of this position have failed to adequately differentiate between Conduct Disorder and hyperactivity, with the possible exception of the study by Stewart et al. (1980). Studies examining family pathology in cases clearly diagnosed as ADD remain to be conducted. Others have speculated on the role of difficult temperament in the development of hyperactivity (Kinsbourne & Swanson, 1979) and on environmental factors such as family stress and poor parenting (Battle & Lacey, 1972). While all these notions have some inherent appeal, only limited data exist to support them and alternative interpretations of findings are equally plausible.

Despite the lack of definitive empirical findings on etiology, research on ADD has proceeded at a rapid pace. Many workers in the field have argued that ADD results from multiple etiologies (Barkley, 1982; Ross & Ross, 1982; Whalen & Henker, 1980) or have adopted interactionist positions (Gorenstein & Newman, 1980; Porges & Smith, 1980). An excellent review of these issues may be found in Ross and Ross (1982).

An alternative approach to this problem has been taken by Douglas (1980, 1983). She assumes that the cause of ADD is "constitutional," although the basic problem is not specified further. She then proceeds to develop a comprehensive model to account for the behavioral and cognitive difficulties, positing four interrelated constitutional deficits which include: "1) the investment, organization and maintenance of attention and effort; 2) the inhibition of impulsive responding; 3) the modulation of arousal levels to meet situational demands; and 4) an usually strong inclination to seek immediate reinforcement" (p. 280). Douglas argues that, taken together, these deficits can account for much of the data on ADD–normal differences in attentional, cognitive, and physiological functioning as well as treatment effects, although the specific mechanisms that lead to these defective processes and their interactions remain to be determined. Various aspects of this model have been discussed by others (e.g., Rosenthal & Allen, 1978; Zentall & Zentall, 1983), although Douglas (1983) stresses the importance of conceptualizing ADD as reflecting the interactions among these several pervasive information-processing deficits and personality characteristics. These notions will be touched on again throughout the sections on core features and correlates.

Core Features

INATTENTION

A large body of data has documented attentional problems in children previously labeled "hyperactive." Attention is not a unitary construct, however, and the specific nature of the ADD child's attentional deficit has been the subject of both empirical research and theoretical debate. The complexity inherent in studying attention is highlighted by reviews of research on attention and ADD (Douglas, 1983; Douglas & Peters, 1979; Rosenthal & Allen, 1978). Douglas stresses the ADD child's difficulty organizing and maintaining attention (Douglas, 1983; Douglas & Peters, 1979). Rosenthal and Allen (1978) argue that conclusions about the specific nature of the attention deficit are premature and stress the need to operationalize aspects of attention deficit more precisely, particularly distractibility. Cunningham and Barkley (1978) suggest that the attentional problems of ADD children are a response to school failure rather than a cause of impaired performance on academic tasks, an argument that might be interpreted to mean that studies of information-processing deficits are more germane than studies of attention per se.

A number of studies have examined the performance of school-age ADD children and controls of comparable age and IQ on a variety of measures that tap different facets of attention. These studies are generally consistent in demonstrating that ADD children perform more poorly than controls when they must respond rapidly to stimulus onset with (delayed reaction time) or without (simple reaction time) a warning signal (Douglas & Peters, 1979; Rosenthal & Allen, 1978; Ross & Ross, 1982). Responses are slower and performance is more variable. Furthermore, their performance tends to deteriorate over time. These findings suggest that such youngsters are less alert to incoming stimuli and less able to sustain attention. Similar conclusions have been drawn from their performance on vigilance tasks such as the Continuous Performance Test (CPT) (Douglas & Peters, 1979). ADD children respond less often to signal stimuli and more often to incorrect stimuli and their performance deteriorates more rapidly with repeated trials relative to controls. More recently, Sergeant and Scholten (1985a, 1985b) have questioned the extent to which the deterioration in performance is greater for hyperactive children than for normals. Regardless, however, performance on both reaction time tasks and vigilance tasks has been found to improve when hyperactive children are administered stimulant medication (see Chapter 12) or when response contingent reward is introduced (Douglas & Peters, 1979). These findings will be discussed later in the context of arousal and reinforcement effects.

Several studies also suggest that ADD children are particularly sensitive to the pacing of the task. Both vigilance tasks and reaction-time tasks are characterized by either a fixed or unpredictable onset of a stimulus to which the child must respond. These tasks have been termed experimenter-paced (Sykes, Douglas, & Morgenstern, 1972), since the experimenter controls the rate and timing of stimulus presentation. There is some evidence that ADD children perform as well as normal controls on reaction-time tasks that are self-paced with target stimuli appearing contingent on the child's previous response. Such tasks would permit the child to show lapses in attention and still perform optimally, while lapses in attention would be reflected in poorer performance on experimenter-paced tasks. This is consistent with the argument that ADD children have a deficit in sustained attention (Douglas & Peters, 1979).

A number of studies have examined the effects of irrelevant and competing stimuli on the performance of ADD children in an attempt to operationalize distractibility. Several studies have found the ADD children are no more disrupted by distracting stimuli than controls, although results are less clear-cut than the studies noted previously that indicate a deficit in sustained attention. The introduction of task-irrelevant stimuli such as flashing lights, white noise, and peripheral drawings do not consistently produce more deterioration in performance (i.e., relative to initial levels) among ADD children than among controls on a variety of tasks (Douglas & Peters, 1979; Radosh & Gittelman, 1981; Rosenthal & Allen, 1978, 1980). Similarly, introduction of competing stimuli designed specifically to interfere with the central task does not differentially impair the performance of ADD children.

Using an incidental learning paradigm (Hallahan, Kauffman, & Ball, 1974), Peters (1977) examined the performance of ADD and control children on several central tasks and also assessed memory for nontarget visual and auditory stimuli. While the ADD group performed more poorly than controls on the central task, they were not differentially influenced by distracting stimuli and did not recall more incidental stimuli than controls. Based on these findings, as well as those cited previously, Douglas and Peters (1979) have concluded that ADD children are not necessarily more distractible than their normal peers.

Others have argued that ADD children should not necessarily be distracted by any and all irrelevant or competing stimuli, but that very interesting or highly salient stimuli presented within the task context would be more likely to serve as distractors and to differentially affect task performance (Radosh & Gittelman, 1981; Rosenthal & Allen, 1980). Rosenthal and Allen (1980) found, consistent with their predictions, that the performance of ADD and control children did not differ when the distractor was of low salience, but that ADD children made more errors on a speeded classification task when confronted with highly salient distractors embedded within the target stimuli. Radosh and Gittelman (1981) found that both groups made more errors when faced with appealing distractors relative to their performance in a no-distractor condition, but the performance of ADD children was also impaired by the presence of distractors of apparently low appeal. While these results appear contradictory, investigators have used a wide variety of tasks differing in difficulty level, content, and novelty; distractors likewise have varied along numerous dimensions including task relevance, modality, and interest value. Overall, however, it seems safe to conclude that distracting stimuli have a less deleterious effect on the performance of ADD children on laboratory tasks than would be predicted from clinical descriptions of their distractibility. Taken together, findings from laboratory measures of attention indicate that ADD children have difficulty deploying and sustaining attention in response to externally controlled demands. While they are not necessarily more distracted than normal children by irrelevant stimuli, it appears that on some tasks requiring organization and effort, they may be more susceptible to the influence of interesting alternative stimuli. Observational measures of behavior during problem solving indicate, however, that, consistent with clinical descriptions, ADD children spend more time than controls "off-task" and engage in task-irrelevant activities both during experimenter-administered structured cognitive tasks and teacher-directed classroom activities (e.g., S. B. Campbell et al., 1982; Henker & Whalen, 1980; Klein & Young, 1979). Thus, differing results reflect variations in situational context, the definition and interpretation of distractibility, and whether behavioral or task performance indices of "distractibility" are employed. Furthermore, Douglas (1983) has pointed out the difficulties in separating attentional control from failure to inhibit impulsive responding. When ADD children are pulled by salient but irrelevant stimulus attributes, this may reflect avoidance of a boring or difficult task or poor inhibitory control, rather than a failure to discriminate and filter relevant from irrelevant stimuli.

IMPULSIVITY

Although impulsivity has been considered one of the defining features of ADD (Douglas, 1972) and is included as a core symptom of ADD in DSM-III, the construct of impulsivity is even more poorly defined than that of attention, and there is little evidence that it is a unitary construct. In a recent review, Milich and Kramer (1985) noted the diversity of behaviors encompassed under the rubric of impulsivity and its correlation with a wide range of antisocial and externalizing disorders of both childhood and adulthood (see also Gorenstein & Newman, 1980). Thus, problems of impulse control are hardly specific to ADD, although the behavioral manifestations of impulsivity may vary considerably, given the elasticity of the concept.

While the attention deficits of ADD children have been the subject of considerable research, surprisingly few studies have examined their deficiencies in impulse control. This lack partly reflects problems defining and operationalizing impulsivity. Furthermore, there is only limited empirical support for a construct of impulsivity, since numerous measures purported to assess impulsivity fail to co-vary. These studies are reviewed in some detail by Milich and Kramer (1985).

The clinical observation that ADD children demonstrate erratic and poorly controlled behavior has made impulse-control problems central to various formulations of their impaired cognitive (Douglas, 1983; Douglas & Peters, 1979) and social (Campbell & Paulauskas, 1979; Milich & Landau, 1982) functioning. Douglas (1983) has noted that impulsive responding can influence performance on a wide range of cognitive tasks. On simple tasks, impulsivity may be manifest by failure to inhibit responding in the absence of target stimuli while on complex tasks, ADD children may respond prematurely before they have understood the problem or assessed possible solutions. Similarly, others have attributed ADD children's peer problems to the tendency to fail to inhibit impulsive responses in game and group situations requiring sharing and turn-taking (Campbell & Cluss, 1982; Milich & Landau, 1982).

The most widely used measure of cognitive impulsivity has been the Matching Familiar Figures Test (MFF) (Kagan, Rosman, Day, Albert, & Phillips, 1964), despite numerous criticisms of its psychometric properties and construct validity (Ault, Mitchell, & Hartmann, 1976; Block, Block, & Harrington, 1974; Milich & Kramer, 1985). The MFF is a matching-to-sample task that requires children to select from an array the one picture that is identical to a standard. Children who respond rapidly prior to evaluating each stimulus picture and therefore make many errors are considered impulsive. Several studies have indicated that ADD children from preschool age through adolescence (e.g., Campbell, Douglas, & Morgenstern, 1971; Cohen, Weiss, & Minde, 1972; Schleifer et al., 1975) have shorter response latencies and make more errors on this measure than matched controls and that their performance improves with stimulant medication. (See Chapter 11.) It does not appear, however, that these differences are specific to ADD since conduct problem (Firestone & Martin, 1979) and learning-disabled (LD) children (Campbell, 1974) sometimes show similar response patterns.

Maze tests have also been considered measures of impulsivity since they require both planning ability and inhibition of motor behavior. Studies comparing ADD children with controls indicate that they make more careless errors (as do Conduct Disordered children, see Chapter 1) on both paper and pencil mazes such as the Porteus (see Milich & Kramer, 1985) and on mechanical mazes (Firestone & Martin, 1979).

A consistent finding from studies of reaction time and vigilance tasks is that ADD children make more responses between trials and more errors of commission to nonsignal stimuli (Douglas & Peters, 1979; Dykman, Ackerman, & McCray, 1980). In addition, on tasks assessing distractibility, ADD children tend to make more intrusive errors and to attend to irrelevant stimuli even when performance on the central task is not impaired relative to baseline performance or relative to controls (Douglas & Peters, 1979). Douglas and Peters (1979) have interpreted these findings to indicate a deficit in inhibitory control. Similarly, on a range of complex problem-solving tasks, ADD youngsters have been noted to make irrelevant and inappropriate responses as well as very rapid responses, suggesting that their tendency to respond impulsively and carelessly is influencing both the style and the accuracy of performance on numerous measures of information processing (Douglas, 1983).

Although measures of delay of gratification and resistance to temptation (Hartig & Kanfer, 1973; Mischel & Mischel, 1983; Schwarz, Schrager, & Lyons, 1983) are often considered under the rubric of impulse-control deficits (Gorenstein & Newman, 1980; Milich & Kramer, 1985) and would be expected to differentiate ADD children from controls, few systematic studies have examined this issue. In a study of parent-referred "hyperactive" toddlers and preschoolers, however, S. B. Campbell et al. (1982) found that problem youngsters made more impulsive responses than controls when required to wait for a signal from the experimenter before finding and eating an animal cracker hidden under one of three cups; furthermore, this difference persisted at a follow-up assessment one year later. In a similar vein, Gordon (1979) found that ADD school-aged boys had more difficulty delaying responding than controls on a simple task requiring short delays between operant responses for which they earned M & M's. In a comparative study of parent-rated ADD preschoolers and controls, however, no differences were found on either resistance to temptation or delay of gratification tasks (Breaux, 1982).

Observational studies of classroom behavior consistently reveal that ADD children engage in more disruptive and inappropriate behavior such as interrupting, calling out, and "clowning" (e.g., Abikoff, Gittelman-Klein, & Klein, 1977; Henker & Whalen, 1980), behaviors also observed in play groups (Pelham & Bender, 1982). While these behaviors may be considered as a failure to follow rules (Barkley, 1982), they are also likely to reflect lack of inhibition and are considered indices of impulsivity in DSM-III. Thus, the main research issue to be addressed is the specificity of particular impulse-control problems to ADD, assuming that the construct can be operationally defined and adequately measured.

ACTIVITY LEVEL

Clinical descriptions of increased motor activity and restlessness have been objectified in parent and teacher behavior rating scales described in Chapters 1 and 11. Because these scales are usually used as criterion measures, they are themselves of little real use in validating the underlying assumption of an elevated level of activity. It is clear, however, that motor overactivity is considerably less robust as an independent dimension of psychopathology than is inattention. (See Chapter 1.)

Objective measures of activity level have been reviewed in a number of recent publications (e.g., Barkley, 1981b; Pfadt & Tyron, 1983; Ross & Ross, 1982; Werry, 1978). Measurement techniques can be subdivided into technological and behavioral approaches. Barkley (1981b), in summarizing these findings, concludes that ADD children consistently show greater "restlessness" (seat movements, task irrelevant movement, being out-of-seat, wrist and ankle movements, and grid crossings) than normal children. Findings vary, however, as a function of sample characteristics, measurement techniques, and situational factors. Further, these differences are most marked in younger children. As with normal children, their magnitude decreases with age. Finally, while amount of activity does differentiate clinical from nonclinical samples, qualitative features such as the inappropriateness of the activity within a particular context (e.g., playground vs. classroom) appears more germane to the clinical picture (Henker & Whalen, 1980; Ross & Ross, 1982).

Evidence for higher activity level on a 24-hour basis is hard to find. One recent study (Porrino et al., 1983) did indicate that ADD children were more active overall (including during sleep) than neighborhood controls.

On the other hand, correlations between these objective measures and rating scale measures of "hyperactivity" are low to moderate (e.g., Barkley & Ullman, 1975). Although group trends are significant, many individual children clinically diagnosed as ADD do not score higher than normals. Finally, the few studies comparing ADD and conduct-problem children (Firestone & Martin, 1979; Milich, Loney, & Landau, 1982; Sandberg et al., 1978, 1980) are inconsistent, suggesting that a heightened activity level may not be specific to ADD.

Barkley (1981b) has emphasized the fact that most of these mechanical measures fail to capture the situational or social inappropriateness of the movement. In fact, observational measures of out-of-seat behavior and gross motor movement that take into account social and ecological factors are particularly robust and do consistently differentiate clinical samples from controls (e.g., Abikoff et al., 1977; Henker & Whalen, 1980).

CORRELATES OF ATTENTION DEFICIT DISORDER

Cognitive Functioning

Although "hyperkinetic disorder" and "minimal brain dysfunction" included cognitive and perceptual deficits along with attentional problems as defining features (e.g., Clements, 1966), there is general agreement that this approach has led to a marked confusion between LD and ADD (e.g., Douglas & Peters, 1979; Dykman, Ackerman, & McCray, 1980; Rie & Rie, 1980). Recent studies have indicated that attentional and cognitive impairments can be separated (Lahey, Stempniak, Robinson, & Tyroler, 1978). Research that has employed specific selection criteria for ADD and for LD has confirmed that, despite some overlap, many children who show symptoms of ADD are achieving adequately; conversely, not all LD children are ADD (Delameter, Lahey, & Drake, 1981; Dykman, Ackerman, & Oglesby, 1980; Lambert & Sandoval, 1980). These findings have led several workers in the field to propose different models for the development of these distinct disorders (Ackerman, Elardo, & Dykman, 1979; Douglas & Peters, 1979) and to recommend different approaches to treatment (Lambert & Sandoval, 1980).

In an attempt to clarify this confusing issue, researchers have also begun to compare subgroups of LD, ADD, and LD-ADD children (e.g., Ackerman et al., 1979; Delameter et al., 1981; Dykman, Ackerman, & Oglesby, 1980; Tant & Douglas, 1982). While this approach holds promise, most studies have yielded few differences among subgroups on measures of attention, impulse control, social cognition, or orienting. Tant and Douglas (1982) found, however, that ADD children performed more poorly than reading-disabled children on complex problem-solving tasks and Dykman, Ackerman, and Oglesby (1980) found that ADD children made more impulsive responses. These findings may reflect differences in the nature of the task and/or variations in sample selection criteria. In any event, this issue is important in evaluating the early work on cognitive functioning in hyperactive children, since samples invariably contain some proportion of ADD children who are also LD. The relative contributions of attentional/impulse-control problems and specific cognitive deficits to performance on measures of cognitive functioning remain to be determined (see Douglas & Peters, 1979).

INTELLIGENCE

Assessment of intelligence in ADD youngsters is a complex issue. Most investigators have attempted to match ADD and control groups on IQ in order to rule out intelligence as an explanation for group differences. This approach, by necessity, selects nonrepresentative control groups that are biased in unknown ways, since many unmeasured variables will be correlated with IQ. When ADD youngsters have been compared to controls of similar age, sex, and social status on standard measures of intelligence, results have varied considerably. Douglas (1972) reported that a clinical sample of ADD children performed more poorly than controls on group-administered but not individually administered tests. She also noted more subtest variability on the Wechsler Intelligence Scale for Children (WISC; Wechsler, 1949), while Lambert and Sandoval (1980) found more verbal-performance discrepancies among hyperactives than controls. Palkes and Stewart (1972) reported that clinically diagnosed ADD children performed more poorly than controls on all WISC subtests. Loney (1974) studied the performance of teacher-rated ADD children and classroom controls on a group-administered test; the second-grade ADDs did not differ from each other, but by fifth grade a deficit was apparent in the ADD group. Other studies confirm that adolescent ADD children do more poorly than controls on IQ tests (Minde et al., 1971). In a recent prospective epidemiological study in New Zealand, McGee et al. (1984b) found that ADD children performed more poorly than controls as preschoolers and continued to show cognitive deficits at age seven. Thus, findings suggest that ADD children perform more poorly than controls on standard measures of intelligence, but the specific nature of their deficit is unclear. Differences across studies undoubtedly reflect variations in selection criteria, sources of subjects, referral policies, and measurement instruments. It is clear, however, that youngsters vary widely in intelligence as measured by standardized tests. Further, the interpretation of group differences is complicated by attentional and impulse-control problems, which obviously influence performance on intelligence tests as they do any measure of cognitive functioning.

ACADEMIC ACHIEVEMENT

There is little doubt that ADD children perform more poorly than controls in school, as evidenced by more grade repetitions (e.g., Douglas, 1972; Hechtman, Weiss, Finkelstein, Wener, & Benn, 1976; Hoy, Weiss, Minde, & Cohen, 1978) and poorer grades in academic subjects (Hoy et al., 1978; Minde et al., 1971; Riddle & Rapoport, 1976). ADD youngsters also do more poorly on standard measures of academic achievement that assess reading, spelling, word knowledge, and mathematics (e.g., Cantwell & Satterfield, 1978; Hoy et al., 1978; McGee et al., 1984b; Riddle & Rapoport, 1976; Worland, 1976). As Ross and Ross (1982) have pointed out, however, active and impulsive children who achieve at grade level or above may be perceived as less problematic by parents and teachers and, therefore, may be less often referred for treatment. Likewise, reliance on parent or teacher ratings (e.g., McGee et al., 1984b) in epidemiological studies may mean that negative halo effects inflate the association between poor academic achievement and behavior problems. McGee et al. (1984b) found, however, that, in a representative sample, ADD and ADD-aggressive children had more academic problems and more cognitive deficits that persisted over time than aggressive youngsters and normal controls, suggesting that something more basic to the ADD child's cognitive functioning is impeding school achievement.

Douglas (1983) has suggested that the core features of impaired attention, impulse control, and arousal regulation result in the development of impoverished cognitive schemas and problem-solving strategies, which in turn lead to worsening academic performance over time. Loney (1974) has suggested that secondary symptoms such as low self-esteem and frequent failure experiences result in lowered motivation and poorer academic functioning with increasing age. Finally, Cunningham and Barkley (1978) have noted that symptoms of ADD may result from academic failure initially caused by learning disabilities, CNS dysfunction, or environmental disadvantage. Thus, while the specific mechanism that underlies the academic underachievement of ADD children remains to be determined, it is clear that they do perform more poorly than controls of equivalent IQ, and it appears that performance relative to normal peers may deteriorate with age. Furthermore, stimulant medication, despite its positive effects on attention and impulse control, does not seem to improve academic achievement or performance on achievement tests (Aman, 1980; Cunningham & Barkley, 1978; see also Chapter 11).

MEMORY

Studies of memory ability have been reviewed in detail by Douglas (Douglas, 1983; Douglas & Peters, 1979) and will be noted only briefly here. There are clearly problems inherent in an attempt to study memory independent of attention, and any deficit in memory can be interpreted as a failure to focus on the to-be-remembered stimuli and to concentrate adequately on the task at hand. In a recent analysis of memory studies, however, Douglas (1983) notes the variability in research findings. ADD children appear to do poorly on some tasks and not others. Interpretations are complicated further by the probable inclusion of LD children in some samples.

In general, it appears that ADD children are not impaired relative to controls on a variety of recall and recognition tasks, with or without delay intervals, in which relatively short strings of stimuli were employed or stimuli could be grouped together in meaningful ways (Douglas, 1972; Douglas & Peters, 1979). The performance of ADD youngsters appears to deteriorate, however, as the number of stimuli to be remembered increases and to get worse with repeated trials (Douglas, 1983; Peters, 1977). Douglas (1983) has suggested that as the demands on memory increase, ADD children expend less effort, process information at a more superficial and obvious level, and use less efficient strategies to facilitate recall. Support for the depth-of-processing interpretation comes from a study by Weingartner and colleagues (1980), who found that on a free-recall task, ADD children reported fewer semantically though not acoustically related words than controls, suggesting that ADD children were attending more to surface features of the stimuli. Using a multiple-choice format and a paired associate recall task, Benezra (1980) found that ADD children made more acoustic errors than normal and reading-disabled controls, presumably because they responded impulsively and failed to attend to or adequately process all stimulus features. Studies using visual stimuli likewise suggest that ADD youngsters expend less effort and employ less efficient memory strategies on tedious and uninteresting memory tasks (e.g., Dalby, Kinsbourne, Swanson, & Sobel, 1977). Taken together, then, data are consistent with the position that attentional and problem-solving strategies may account for the impaired performance of ADD children on some memory tasks, an interpretation that is strengthened by studies indicating improved performance with stimulant medication (Dalby et al., 1977; Douglas, 1983; Weingartner et al., 1980; see also Chapter 11).

COMPLEX LEARNING AND PROBLEM SOLVING
Early research on abstract-conceptual abilities and language skills revealed few differences between ADD youngsters and controls (see Douglas, 1972). In a recent study, Parry and Douglas (1983) replicated some of these earlier findings. They found that on a two-choice concept identification task, ADD children discovered the relevant dimension as efficiently as controls provided they were given reinforcement for every correct response. Similarly, Hoy et al. (1978) found that on a verbal concept-identification task, adolescent ADDs and controls did not differ when generating their own responses. On another task assessing word knowledge, they performed as well as controls when choosing between two alternatives, but more poorly than controls when confronted with five.

In line with Hoy et al. (1978), research has also suggested that ADD children may perform more poorly when they must search large stimulus arrays for relevant dimensions and categorize stimuli accordingly (e.g., Parry, 1973; Tant & Douglas, 1982). Furthermore, Dykman, Ackerman, and Oglesby (1980) found that performance deteriorated as the number of stimuli to be processed increased. Similarly, Tant and Douglas (1982) examined the performance of ADD, reading-disabled, and control children on matrix-solution tasks requiring them to find the "correct" stimulus from an array of 16 varying on four dimensions. ADD children asked less efficient questions than either control group, identified fewer relevant dimensions, and made less efficient use of the dimensions they did identify. Other research by Douglas and her students (see Douglas, 1983) likewise suggests that ADD children perform poorly on complex rule-learning and concept-formation tasks that require careful and effortful processing of relatively large amounts of information. Consistent with the findings of others (e.g., Juliano, 1974; Henker & Whalen, 1980), Douglas noted that on the more interesting and challenging tasks, ADD children show some improvement with practice, although in line with the observations of Dykman, Ackerman, and Oglesby (1980), they tend to be less invested in task solution and to persist in their use of less efficient strategies. Douglas (1983) suggested that these poor strategies account for some of the deficits shown by ADD children on complex tasks. These will be discussed next.

PROBLEM-SOLVING STRATEGIES AND METACOGNITION

Interest in the problem-solving strategies of ADD children is not new. Early research documenting an impulsive response style led to a focus on cognitive impulsivity as one explanation of their difficulties (e.g., S.B. Campbell et al., 1971; Douglas, 1972). More recently, there have been attempts to alter this maladaptive approach to problem solving through the use of cognitive training in impulse-control strategies, a technique that has met with mixed reviews (see Douglas, 1980; Urbain & Kendall, 1980).

Studies clearly indicate, however, that ADD children approach problems in a less organized and less thoughtful manner; that is, their spontaneous strategies tend to be less efficient or well-planned. Recently, interest in problem solving has been expanded to include the study of children's awareness of their own strategies and approaches to cognitive tasks, what has been termed metacognition (see, for example, Brown, 1975). There is some evidence that ADD children not only utilize less efficient strategies in a range of problem-solving situations but that they demonstrate less cognizance of their own typical approaches (Douglas, 1983; Douglas & Peters, 1979). Although relatively little systematic research has appeared on the metacognitive skills of ADD children, anecdotal and other evidence led Douglas (1983) to suggest that impaired metacognitive skills, as reflected in less efficient, effortful, and self-conscious approaches to cognitive tasks, can account for many of the problems ADD youngsters encounter in academic and social situations.

For example, on tasks requiring careful visual scanning of complex stimulus arrays, as in visual-search, reading, and matching-to-sample tasks, ADD children appear to process fewer stimuli, skipping over some relevant stimuli, examining the display less thoroughly, and making extraneous and/or overly hasty responses (Bremer & Stern, 1976; Douglas & Peters, 1979; Dykman, Ackerman, and Oglesby, 1979). Douglas and Peters (1979) suggested that this reflects a deficiency in visual-search strategies. They argue that ADDs are more likely to use an exploratory approach focusing on salient, novel, or obvious stimulus features rather than the organized, goal-directed, and logical approach required by such tasks (Douglas & Peters, 1979, p. 225; see also Wright & Vliestra, 1975).

That ADD youngsters also make less efficient use of the time available for problem solutions is consistent with clinical impressions as well as systematic observations in classrooms (e.g., Klein & Young, 1979) and during laboratory tasks (e.g., Barkley, 1977; Dalby et al., 1977; Parry, 1973): for example, the tendency to shift attention back and forth from the task at hand, to be impatient, and to rush through a task with little concern for the final product. Dalby et al. (1977) systematically examined ADD children's use of learning time. On a paired associate-learning task, ADD children on placebo made more errors as the time between stimulus presentations increased. Further, they made fewer errors when given several short exposures to the stimulus pairs rather than one long one, presumably because during long trials their attention was more likely to wander.

Dalby et al. (1977) suggested that ADD children tend to stop processing available information prematurely and, therefore, make incorrect decisions. Others have noted more superficial processing and a failure to identify all relevant stimulus dimensions (Douglas, 1983; Parry & Douglas, 1983; Tant & Douglas, 1982), as well as a failure to utilize all the dimensions they have labeled. This suggests a lack of strategic planning and organized effort, despite the ability to perform better. Data from the Tant and Douglas study also suggest, however, a more basic deficit in identifying efficient problem-solving strategies on certain types of complex tasks. On a series of matrix-solution tasks, ADD children formulated less efficient questions, thereby obtaining less information on each trial. They were also less able to recognize strategically good questions presented to them by the experimenter. Thus, while spontaneously produced but inefficient strategies were part of the problem, a more basic deficit was implicated as well, suggesting less ability to think about the demands of the task and plan accordingly.

Other findings also suggest that ADD children are less self-conscious or aware of their problem-solving strategies and that they spontaneously rely on less useful approaches. For example, on a delay task, Gordon (1979) found that ADD youngsters used more motor activity to bridge the delay while controls used cognitive strategies. In fact, only 30 percent of the hyperactive sample reported using a cognitive mediator, as compared to 80 percent of controls. The use of cognitive mediators was strongly associated with successful delay. Studies of memory likewise suggest that grouping or other complex rehearsal strategies are not used spontaneously (Benezra, 1980; Weingartner et al., 1980). Tant also reported that her ADD subjects were less likely to verbalize strategies spontaneously. Taken together, these findings of deficient problem-solving approaches and a relative lack of awareness of their own problem-solving styles suggest a fertile area for continued research, which may clarify the basic mechanisms of ADD children's difficulties and suggest appropriate directions for intervention.

Motivation and Reinforcement Effects

It has been suggested that ADD children have a lowered level of motivation, especially when performing on cognitive and school-related tasks (Douglas, 1983; Dykman, Ackerman, & Oglesby, 1980; Worland, North-Jones, & Stern, 1973). As noted previously, ADD children invest less effort and make less efficient use of stimulus information and available cognitive strategies. Performance also tends to be more variable and haphazard, making them seem less interested in success on a range of tasks requiring concentration, reasoning, effort, and persistence (see Douglas, 1983). Parent and teacher complaints often focus on this careless and diffident approach as well as their apparent need for structure and direction. Further, their general tendency not to work independently or to gain much satisfaction from success on cognitive tasks may be interpreted as lowered motivation. A motivational deficit is difficult to pinpoint, although these behaviors may reflect, in part, a lower than optimal level of mastery motivation. On the other hand, clinical observation also indicates that some ADD children can persist and derive satisfaction from tasks they find very appealing. Thus, the question becomes, motivation for what? Research needs to examine individual differences in mastery motivation as a function of task demands and child characteristics; the relative contributions of task demands and child competencies, as well as the role of self-esteem deficits (Loney, 1980) and failure avoidance (Cunningham & Barkley, 1978) must also be considered before the question of an apparent motivational deficit can be resolved.

Research on the effect of reinforcement has some bearing on this issue. If ADD children perform poorly or erratically on a task in the absence of reinforcement, but show marked improvement when response contingent reinforcement is introduced, this may indicate a lowered motivational level, since it distinguishes competence from performance deficits and highlights the need for external incentives. Therefore, several studies have examined the effects of reinforcement on the behavior, attention, and problem solving of hyperactive children. These few studies vary widely in terms of task demands and type and schedule of reinforcement; consequently, results provide a confusing picture (see reviews by Douglas, 1983; Parry & Douglas, 1983). Data indicate that ADD children perform as well as nonclinical controls on concept learning tasks when provided with positive reinforcement for every correct response, but their performance deteriorates when reinforcement only appears after every second correct response, even when information feedback is provided consistently (Freibergs & Douglas, 1969; Parry & Douglas, 1983). Other studies indicate that contingent rewards can decrease fidgety and off-task behavior (Worland et al., 1973), although results are inconsistent (Gittelman et al., 1980). However, Dykman, Ackerman, and McCray (1980) noted that ADD children are less persistent than LD and control children on complex tasks even when offered monetary rewards and suggested that ADD children are often able but unwilling to perform even for desired rewards when effortful processing is required.

Studies have also examined the effects of social reinforcement on reaction time and autonomic arousal. Praise appears to speed up performance and increase arousal when it is delivered contingently (Cohen & Douglas, 1972; Douglas & Parry, 1983; Firestone & Douglas, 1975), although it may also lead to more variable performance and more impulsive errors. Noncontingent praise can disrupt performance, increasing reaction time above baseline levels. Praise for fast reaction times paired with negative feedback for slow responses does not appear to result in greater response variability or marked increases in arousal. Similar results have been obtained with negative feedback alone. However, the effects of negative reinforcement have also been inconsistent. Worland (1976) found that an aversive stimulus, contingent on off-task behavior, was associated with increased errors on a cognitive task, although time on task increased. Finally, several studies have indicated that reinforcement withdrawal leads to slower performance on reaction time measures (Firestone & Douglas, 1975) and to an increase in off-task behavior (Worland, 1976), but that withdrawal of noncontingent reward is associated with increases in reaction time (Douglas & Parry, 1983).

Taken together, these few studies suggest that partial and noncontingent rewards can disrupt the performance of ADD children on some attentional and problem-solving tasks. The introduction of rewards appears to increase arousal level, while both rewards and punishments have been associated with more careless responses as well as improvements in performance. Finally, the withdrawal of expected rewards or the appearance of unpredictable rewards can interfere with performance even on simple tasks and increase task-irrelevant behavior. These findings may, in part, account for the relatively poor response of ADD children to behavior modification programs, since in the natural environment rewards cannot possibly be dispensed for every correct response and, even in the best designed program, an expected reinforcer may not appear. (See also Chapter 14.) These data also may help to explain the lack of generalization and maintenance when reinforcers are faded or withdrawn (Parry & Douglas, 1983; Ross & Ross, 1982).

Douglas (1983; Parry & Douglas, 1983) has suggested that ADD children "may be overly sensitive to rewards, to the loss of rewards, and to the failure of expected rewards to appear" (Parry & Douglas, 1983, p. 327). She has noted that they may require especially explicit and clear guidelines that provide structure and increase the predictability of reinforcement. Douglas has also hypothesized that ADD children may be characterized by a particularly strong need to seek immediate gratification, a suggestion also made by Gorenstein and Newman (1980). This focus on immediate reward is reflected in their tendency to invest more energy and interest in obtaining external rewards than in solving complex problems or meeting intellectual challenges. Douglas and Parry have noted that ADD youngsters shift attention from the task to the source of reward and may become particularly frustrated and upset by reward withdrawal. Douglas (1983) also has proposed that both the introduction and withdrawal of rewards may increase the arousal level of ADD children beyond an optimal level necessary for efficient problem solving and organized responding. These ideas are certainly consistent with clinical observations, parent complaints, and the limited evidence available. They are also relevant to the ADD–Conduct Disorder debate, given the similarity of these hypotheses to those put forth to account for the behavior of antisocial and psychopathic adults (see Gorenstein & Newman, 1980). Additional research on the relationship between autonomic arousal and reinforcer effectiveness as a function of child characteristics (ADD vs. aggressive), the nature of the reinforcer (tangible vs. intangible; social vs. nonsocial; positive vs. negative), and the reinforcement schedule will be needed to test these intriguing theoretical notions further. Given the popularity of behavioral approaches along with the potential theoretical importance of responses to reinforcement, such research is clearly needed.

Psychophysiological Measures and Arousal

In view of the oftimes frenetic and "driven" quality of ADD children's behavior, the notion of a defect in the arousal system is inherently attractive and consistent with clinical impression. Thus, it is not surprising that numerous variations on this theme have been proposed over the past 30 years, with impaired arousal viewed as either a cause or a correlate of purported central nervous system dysfunction (e.g., Laufer, Denhoff & Solomons, 1957; Wender, 1971; Zentall & Zentall, 1983). For example, Laufer et al. (1957) postulated a defect in subcortical arousal mechanisms, which in turn decreased central inhibitory processes leading the organism to be easily bombarded by external stimuli. Early theories focused on overarousal, which was reduced to normal levels by the "paradoxical" effect of stimulant drugs. More recent formulations emphasize problems of underarousal (e.g., Satterfield, Cantwell, & Satterfield, 1974; Zentall & Zentall, 1983) or problems of arousal regulation (Douglas, 1983).

Numerous studies have examined various aspects of peripheral (autonomic) and central arousal in order to delineate differences between hyperactive and normal children and to explore the effects of stimulants on the psychophysiological functioning of hyperactives. This is a very complex and contradictory body of data in which technical problems and variations in measurement techniques compound the methodological problems noted in the more purely behavioral studies. These studies have been reviewed in depth and their methodological and conceptual limitations cogently discussed in several recent papers (Ferguson & Pappas, 1979; Ferguson & Rapoport, 1983; Hastings & Barkley, 1978; Porges & Smith, 1980; Rosenthal & Allen, 1978).

Studies have compared hyperactive children with controls on peripheral measures of arousal such as skin conductance and heart rate during both resting periods (tonic arousal) and in response to stimulation (phasic arousal). Despite differences in subject characteristics and measurement techniques, few studies find differences between hyperactive children and nonclinical controls on indices of basal autonomic arousal. Studies examining hyperactives and controls in response to target stimuli or task demands suggest some differences. Hyperactive children appear somewhat less responsive than controls as evidenced by smaller phasic responses to signal stimuli on measures of heart rate deceleration and by slower and smaller electrodermal responses. Further, when drug effects have been found, they reflect an increase in indices of autonomic arousal that appear to be associated with improved attention. Such findings are obviously not supportive of an overarousal model, which would predict both higher basal arousal levels and faster, higher amplitude changes in response to stimulation. Findings of decreased reactivity to stimulus onset may be interpreted as consistent with variants of underarousal and arousal regulation notions.

Studies have also examined central measures of arousal, primarily EEG responses and cortical evoked potentials. Results of these studies are less consistent than those focusing on peripheral measures, and variations in methodology make interpretations across studies hazardous. Hastings and Barkley (1978) cautiously conclude, however, that these studies may be viewed as consistent with underarousal in a subgroup of hyperactive children since whatever common findings emerge suggest a slight excess of slow wave EEG activity and somewhat lowered cortical evoked responses to both auditory and visual stimuli. Further, stimulant drugs tend to modify slow wave activity and increase arousal as measured by cortical evoked responses. Ferguson and Pappas (1979) likewise lament the inconsistencies across studies but conclude that the data are more supportive of an underarousal formulation.

Taken together, then, knowledgeable reviewers of the psychophysiological literature conclude that overarousal theories are no longer tenable. When convergent and interpretable findings do emerge, they are consistent with an underarousal view. However, interpretations of psychophysiological studies are difficult since measures of arousal, activity, and attention are difficult to disentangle and assess independent of one another (Ferguson & Pappas, 1979; Porges & Smith, 1980; Rosenthal & Allen, 1978). As Porges and Smith (1980) note, psychophysiological measures do not reflect a "pure" biological substrate independent of situational factors, and wide individual differences exist in these measures that may override diagnostic differences. Further, more consistent hyperactive–control differences have been found on peripheral rather than central measures, that is, on more indirect measures of the construct in question. The lack of direct correspondence among autonomic, central, and behavioral indices and contamination of arousal and attention make specific etiological hypotheses impossible to test. Hyperactive–control differences may reflect a poorly understood and vaguely formulated causal mechanism implicating lowered arousal or the lowered arousal may reflect attentional or other problems.

Hastings and Barkley (1978) suggest that arousability (i.e., to stimuli) rather than arousal level is more likely to be the problem. Douglas (1983) has proposed that neither under- nor overarousal per se may be as important as arousal regulation in the face of environmental and internal stimuli. She suggests that the erratic behavior of these youngsters reflected in their lowered responsiveness to boring, repetitive tasks and their overexcitability when placed in some highly arousing situations (e.g., when frustrated, when praised, in some social situations) results from an inability to modulate arousal to the optimal level necessary to cope with particular types of events. While inadequate data exist to permit one to choose among these competing hypotheses, it does appear that studies of arousal level, arousability, and arousal regulation continue to be fruitful areas to pursue. As Ferguson and Pappas (1979) note, both behavioral and pharmacological data are logically compatible with formulations of hyperactivity that implicate arousal mechanisms. To date, however, the description of supposed faulty arousal mechanisms have been either vague and poorly defined or highly specific, in the absence of adequate supporting data. Thus, while these ideas are intriguing, they require more work, both conceptual and empirical.

Social Behavior and Social Cognition

Research on social functioning reflects the recent emphasis on contextual influences on child behavior and the awareness that ADD children do poorly in interpersonal as well as academic situations. These studies can be grouped in terms of social behavior with peers and family members, social cognition, and peer perceptions. Some of this work has been reviewed in previous publications (Barkley, 1981a; Campbell & Cluss, 1982; Campbell & Paulauskas, 1979; Henker & Whalen, 1980; Milich & Landau, 1982; Pelham & Bender, 1982; Ross & Ross, 1982). As the list of recent reviews suggests, this has been an area of burgeoning research interest, and recent findings on social behavior complement the large body of research on cognitive and attentional processes.

PARENT–CHILD RELATIONS

Research on the social behavior of school-aged ADD children initially focused on patterns of mother–child interaction. (See also Chapter 9.) Several investigators have used observational methodologies to examine mother–child interaction as a function of situational demands and task difficulty (e.g., Barkley & Cunningham, 1980; S. B. Campbell, 1973; Cunningham & Barkley, 1979; Humphries, Kinsbourne, & Swanson, 1978; Mash & Johnston, 1982). In general, these studies find that ADD children are more talkative, seek more help and attention, and are more negative and noncompliant, especially when the situation requires them to focus attention and become involved in relatively difficult tasks. Mothers of ADD boys are more directive and controlling, providing more help and encouragement as well as more commands and fewer rewards for compliance than mothers of controls. Furthermore, during free play, mothers of ADD boys are less likely to respond positively to their social initiations or to reward independent play (Cunningham & Barkley, 1979).

Mash and Johnston (1982) reported that the interactions of younger (3–7) ADD children and their mothers are more negative than those of older (7–10) dyads. Younger children are less compliant and less responsive to maternal praise, a finding that may partly reflect the ADD–Conduct Disorder overlap in this age range. Mothers of these young children are more directive and less responsive to child initiations or independent play. These differences are less dramatic, however, when children are confronted with easy tasks, clearly within their range of competence, or when demands for focused attention are less, as in free play, underlining the important role of situational factors (Mash & Johnston, 1983; Whalen & Henker, 1980). In addition, several studies (Barkley & Cunningham, 1980; Humphries et al., 1978) have indicated that these negative patterns of mother–child interaction decrease dramatically when children are on stimulant medication. This finding suggests that this negative and controlling behavior is, at least in part, a response to the high intensity, inappropriate, and often exasperating behavior of these youngsters and represents a cycle of escalating and mutually maintained negative interaction (Barkley, 1981a; Mash & Johnston, 1982).

Only one study has examined the interactions of ADD children with both mothers and fathers. Tallmadge and Barkley (1983) found that fathers, like mothers, were more directive, but consistent with parental reports, ADD children were more likely to comply with fathers' commands than with mothers'.

In two studies, the mother–child interactions of younger samples have been explored. S. B. Campbell and her colleagues studied a sample of parent-referred behavior problem two- and three-year-olds whose parents' complaints were suggestive of ADD (S. B. Campbell et al., 1982). During a structured play interaction, referred children played more aggressively than controls and their mothers were more likely to reprimand them and to redirect their activities (Campbell, Breaux, Ewing, Szumowski & Pierce, in press). Similarly, Cohen and Minde (1983) found that mothers of kindergarten-aged "situational" but not "pervasive" ADDs were more disapproving than mothers of controls during structured tasks. Thus, there is some evidence that this pattern of negative and controlling interaction begins quite early. Implications of these findings for development and symptom course as well as family intervention appear fruitful areas for research.

A small body of research also suggests that the presence of an ADD child in the home is associated with other aspects of family stress and dysfunction, although cause–effect relationships cannot be disentangled. For example, Delameter et al. (1981) found that LD children who were also ADD came from families characterized by more psychosocial stress including marital separation, illness, alcoholism, and child abuse. Other studies have likewise noted associations between family disorganization and hyperactivity (e.g., Ackerman et al., 1979; Campbell, in press; Cohen & Minde, 1983;

McGee et al., 1984b). Child characteristics may contribute to these family stressors or these family problems may exacerbate symptoms in children with cognitive deficits.

Parents' perceptions of their parenting skills were assessed in one study. Mash and Johnston (1983) found that parents of ADD children reported less confidence in their parenting knowledge and mothers reported more stress associated with the mother–child relationship, more role restriction, and more social isolation. These findings may indicate, consistent with clinical reports, that mothers feel drained by the demands of an ADD child and isolated because of their reluctance to take their child visiting or on outings. Mothers of younger ADD children in this sample also reported more self-blame and depression. These findings agree with other studies documenting more maternal depression and distress in families with a range of behavior-disordered children (e.g., Greist, Forehand, Wells, & McMahon, 1980; McGee et al., 1984a; Richman, Stevenson, & Graham, 1982; Sandberg et al., 1980). General family distress would not be expected to be specific to ADD but to be associated with child psychopathology in general. However, data such as these underscore the need for more systematic studies on the family environment of ADD children since there is accumulating evidence that family factors influence both the nature of symptomatology and outcome (e.g., Paternite & Loney, 1980) and have obvious implications for intervention (Mash & Johnston, 1983).

PEER RELATIONS

Observational studies of peer interaction have indicated that ADD youngsters have more difficulty with peers, suggesting that their impulsivity and lack of attention to social cues interfere with reciprocity, sharing, and turn-taking, as well as other rules of social exchange (Campbell & Cluss, 1982; Campbell & Paulauskas, 1979; Milich & Landau, 1982). Results have consistently indicated that young ADD children are more aggressive than controls during free play (Campbell & Cluss, 1982; Cohen & Minde, 1983; Schleifer et al., 1975). Cohen and Minde (1983) also found that "pervasively" hyperactive kindergarteners were more disruptive of peers' play and engaged in more solitary and less parallel play than comparison groups of normal controls and less severely impaired ADD children. Results were consistent across studies in indicating no differences in the frequency of social approach behaviors. Follow-up of the Campbell et al. sample to age six indicates that mothers continue to report peer problems (Campbell, in press). This may suggest that early patterns of coercive and negative interactions with peers persist and that ADD children develop a style of relating to others that is relatively resistant to change without specific intervention.

These findings are in accord with observational studies in elementary school classrooms that also demonstrate more disruptive and negative peer interactions (e.g., Abikoff et al., 1977; Henker & Whalen, 1980; Klein & Young, 1979). Medication appears to control some of this negative and inappropriate behavior (Gittelman et al., 1980; Henker & Whalen, 1980). Particularly intriguing is the finding that disruptive and negative peer interactions vary as a function of both drug or placebo condition and nature of classroom activity (Whalen et al., 1978). That is, ADD boys on placebo were more disruptive and inappropriate and initiated more interaction with peers than ADD boys on medication or control boys. These differences were more pronounced, however, when children were confronted with demanding tasks that were not self-paced.

Although situational factors may interact with child characteristics to facilitate or inhibit aggressive and annoying behaviors directed toward peers, data obtained from observations in small, minimally supervised play groups indicate that these difficulties cut across both school and social situations. Pelham and Bender (1982) observed five- to nine-year-olds with normal peers during both a free play and cooperative, structured task over five sessions. ADD children were more talkative, aggressive, disruptive, and noncompliant and engaged in more negative verbal interactions such as teasing and name-calling. Furthermore, aggressive and noncompliant behavior was particularly pronounced during free play. Contrary to findings from other studies, however, stimulant medication had only a limited effect on peer interactions with only the most aggressive children showing a decrease in negative interactions. Similarly, behavior management in the absence of social skills training was ineffective, leading Pelham to suggest that ADD children are deficient in social skills. Possibly their history of impulsive and poorly regulated behaviors has impeded the acquisition of a repertoire of appropriate social behaviors.

Taken together, these observational studies indicate that ADD children are particularly prone to engage in physically and verbally aggressive behaviors and to disrupt the behavior of others in a range of settings, though the intensity and/or frequency of these behaviors may vary as a function of specific characteristics of the setting. While these findings may be interpreted as reflecting the influence of attentional problems, poor impulse control, and poorly regulated arousal level on social behavior, the prominence of aggressive and noncompliant behavior raises the issue of the ADD–Conduct Disorder overlap noted earlier. None of these observational studies differentiated between children meeting criteria for ADD only from those who were also aggressive (Milich, Loney, & Landau, 1982; Prinz, Connor & Wilson, 1981). Studies of this nature will need to be conducted before we can clearly interpret these findings.

SOCIAL COGNITION

Research on ADD children's understanding of their social world and their reasoning about interpersonal relations is just beginning to appear. Studies of social problem solving and social cognition suggest that when they are interacting with peers in referential communication tasks or tasks requiring group decision making, they are less responsive to communications from peers and more likely to ignore them or behave inappropriately. They also provide fewer task-relevant communications and less helpful information to their partners (Henker & Whalen, 1980). Studies of social cognition requiring communication with a hypothetical peer via the experimenter suggest, however, that in a one-to-one structured situation, ADD children can reason about the perspective of another. as well as controls (e.g., Ackerman et al., 1979; Paulauskas & Campbell, 1979). Rather, the presence of a peer seems to increase arousal to a more than optimal level and disinhibit inappropriate and impulsive behavior. More recent research by Dodge and his co-workers suggests, however, that the nature of the task may interact with symptoms (Dodge & Frame, 1982), since aggressive boys attributed aggressive intent to peers when confronted with hypothetical situations involving harm.

Several studies have examined ADD children's self-perceptions of their symptomatology and attributions about their control over their own behavior, particularly in the context of drug treatment. Bugenthal, Whalen, and Henker (1977) reported that those with internal attributions about causality and their own ability to control their symptoms responded better to self-control training than those with external attributions, who responded better to stimulant medication. Whalen and Henker (1980) have suggested that prior assessment of causal attributions might influence treatment choices and have noted that reliance on stimulant drugs may reinforce children's feelings of lack of control. Two interview studies of children's attributions reveal that ADD children on stimulant medication tend to perceive both good and bad behavior as being out of their own control, but dependent upon whether they have taken their medication (Baxley, Turner, & Greenwald, 1978; Whalen & Henker, 1980). Thus, as Whalen and Henker (1980) stress, children's attitudes and expectations may have an important influence on treatment outcome. These data and clinical experience also indicate that school-aged ADD children have some awareness of their problems as well as the effect of their impulsive, inattentive, disruptive, and noncompliant behavior on others. Self-perceptions clearly merit further research.

PEER PERCEPTIONS

ADD children perceive themselves as less popular with peers than controls (Campbell & Paulauskas, 1979), a finding consistent with several studies of the peer perceptions of preschool (Milich, Landau, Kilby, & Whitten, 1982) and school-aged classmates of ADD children (King & Young, 1981; Klein & Young, 1979; Pelham & Bender, 1982). ADD children are also more actively rejected by peers on peer-nomination measures, less likely to be chosen as popular or as a "true friend," and more likely to be described in negative terms reflective of their aggressive, disruptive, and noncompliant behavior. For example, Pelham and Bender reported that ADD children were described most frequently as getting mad, trying to get others into trouble, being mean, telling others what to do, getting into trouble, and bothering others who are trying to work. As Pelham and Bender noted, these differences reflect the same kinds of behaviors about which adults complain. Furthermore, in the play-group study described earlier, ADD children were rejected by peers after only the first session, suggesting that in new situations with new peers, their inappropriate and provocative behavior is immediately apparent, contrary to common observations in clinical settings.

While research on social behavior has been only descriptive, we have a clearer picture of the nature of the ADD child's relationships with family members and peers. However, their reasoning about social interactions and the mechanisms underlying their impaired social relationships remain to be considered, particularly since disturbed relationships with parents and peers have been associated with poor outcome in a variety of clinical groups (Milich & Landau, 1982; Paternite & Loney, 1980; Richman et al., 1982; Rutter, 1971). Since these findings parallel follow-up studies of conduct disordered children and since aggressive and noncompliant behaviors figure prominently in descriptions of ADD children's social problems, future studies of social behavior must assess both ADD and aggression before the prognostic significance of impaired social functioning in ADD children can be evaluated.

Neurological and Pathological Findings

Neurological findings associated with general child psychopathology are discussed in more detail in Chapter 7. Here those relative to ADD will be summarized briefly. For more exhaustive reviews see Ferguson and Pappas (1979) and Ferguson and Rapoport (1983).

A number of studies have looked at neurological status (see Reeves & Werry, in press). While most have failed to find an increased incidence of major neurological signs in samples of ADD youngsters, they have sometimes, though not always (Sandberg et al., 1980), revealed an increased rate of so-called soft neurological signs in comparison to normal children. Most of these signs can be subsumed under the rubric of delayed sensorimotor coordination (see also Werry & Aman, 1976). Studies comparing ADD children with other diagnostic groups are infrequent, and in those, diagnosis is often less than precise; but there is some evidence that the signs may be more frequent in ADD children than in children with Anxiety Withdrawal (Werry et al., 1972), the same as in Conduct Disorder (Sandberg et al., 1978), and lower than in psychosis (Kennard, 1960). Unfortunately, the association of these "neurological" signs with ADD may only reflect their correlation with disturbance in general and with impaired intelligence (Gillberg, Carlstrom, & Rasmussen, 1983; Schachar et al., 1981; see also Chapter 8).

Minor Physical Anomalies (see Chapter 8), which are thought to indicate prenatal (including genetic) factors operative before the twelfth week of pregnancy, are similarly raised in frequency in ADD children but, again, are nondiscriminatory with respect to several other diagnostic groups including Conduct Disorder (see Gualtieri, Adams, Shen, & Loiselle, 1982; Gillberg et al., 1983), autism (Steg & Rapoport, 1975; Walker, 1977), LD (Steg & Rapoport, 1975), and retardation (Firestone, Peters, Rivier, & Knights, 1978). Firestone et al. also found higher rates of physical anomalies in the parents and sibs of ADD children and retardates, but not controls. Firestone and Prabhu (1983) suggested a relationship among obstetrical complications, minor physical anomalies, and ADD. However, the lack of methodological rigor inherent in most physical anomaly research including lack of "blind" assessments (see Krouse & Kauffman, 1982) makes these findings questionable.

The EEG (Gillberg et al., 1983; Hastings & Barkley, 1978) has produced conflicting results with most studies, but not all, showing an increase in nonspecific minor abnormalities of the type commonly seen in children attending psychiatric clinics. The significance of these is unclear, but these children are often described as immature rather than abnormal and become normal by puberty (Weiss & Hechtman, 1979). These crude EEG techniques are likely to be superseded by newer organ-imaging techniques. (See Chapter 8.)

Rapoport and Ismond (1982) have reviewed the use of CT scans in ADD in three studies. Two reported cerebral atrophy, asymmetry, or abnormal ventricular dilation in about one quarter of the subjects, while the third revealed major abnormalities in only 5 percent of the sample. In general, these studies were poorly described and inadequately controlled so it is difficult to interpret these findings. They should encourage properly controlled studies in the future.

Recently, as in other areas of childhood psychopathology, there has been an increased interest in biochemical measures. Although there have been one or two promising leads with respect to biogenic monoamines like catecholamines and serotonin (Coleman, 1973; Greenberg & Coleman, 1976; Rapoport, Quinn, & Lamprecht, 1974; Shaywitz, Cohen, & Shaywitz, 1978; Shekim, Dekirmenjian, & Chapel, 1979), none of these has as yet been adequately replicated or shown distinctive biochemical differences related to ADD or to any other disorder (see Ferguson & Pappas, 1979; Ferguson & Rapoport, 1983; Rutter, 1982). The area is one of great complexity and one in which developments may be expected in the future.

Sensory handicaps such as undetected partial deafness have been shown to have some association with ADD in one study of a cohort of nine-year-olds (Silva, Kirkland, Simpson, Stewart, & Williams, 1982), but this too is unreplicated and likely to be associated only in a minority of cases.

Large-scale studies have nearly all revealed a small but significant association between pre- and perinatal events and ADD (Gillberg et al., 1983; Nichols & Chen, 1981; Towbin, 1978), the most convincing of which come from the huge Perinatal Collaborative Study of 30,000 children conducted by the National Institutes of Health (Nichols, 1980; Nichols & Chen, 1981). Although certain pre- and perinatal factors did "survive" an unusually competent multivariate analysis, Nichols and Chen concluded that they were weak and inefficient predictors of ADD. Towbin (1978) has suggested the ultimate factor involved in most of these perinatal events is anoxia, although prospective studies of anoxic infants are not entirely consistent with this view (see Sameroff & Chandler, 1975; Chapter 8). Furthermore, these studies still give cause for concern at the diagnostic level, leaving the question unresolved.

Various toxic environmental factors such as lead, food additives, X rays and other radiations, and maternal alcohol intake during pregnancy have occasionally been shown to be correlated with ADD but none has so far either survived further critical scrutiny or been replicated (see Barkley, 1982; Ferguson & Rapoport, 1983; Ross & Ross, 1982). One possible exception is lead (see Chapter 8), but even if it remains significant in future research, it can be a factor in only a small proportion of cases.

In summary, while there are a variety of neurological, pathological, and other physical correlates of ADD, these are often developmental in nature and occur only in a minority of children with the disorder. There is some evidence that the more severe the ADD, the greater the likelihood of this association (e.g., Gillberg et al., 1983; Schachar et al., 1981). However, they are no more frequent than in certain other psychiatric disorders, notably Conduct Disorder or the Psychoses (Ferguson & Rapoport, 1983; Rutter, 1981, 1982).

Motor Functioning

A wide range of studies, some laboratory, some psychometric using such scales as the Lincoln-Oseretsky Motor Development Scale and some using wide-range neurological examinations (see Reeves & Werry, in press; Werry & Aman, 1976), have shown that there is some, but by no means an inexorable, association between ADD and impaired motor performance; however, it is not specific to ADD. These findings are usually interpreted as "soft" or developmental neurological signs of uncertain significance (see Chapter 8) so the conclusions drawn above about neurological correlates apply here as well.

EPIDEMIOLOGY

The specific symptoms of ADD are extremely common in large samples of children of preschool (Crowther, Bond, & Rolf, 1981; Richman et al., 1982) and school age (Rutter, Tizard, & Whitmore, 1970; Trites, Dugas, Lynch, & Ferguson, 1979; Werry & Quay, 1971) with studies consistently finding both sex and age differences in the prevalence of annoying rates of restlessness, inattention, and distractibility. (See also Chapter 9.) Adults rate these behaviors as more common in boys and as showing a decrease in prevalence with increasing age. However, the prevalence of a cluster of symptoms indicative of a potentially diagnosable disorder is, of course, much lower (Rutter et al., 1970).

The frequency of hyperactivity in population studies ranges from a low of 1.6 percent in U.K. 10-year-olds in the Isle of Wight Study to a high of 20 percent in some U.S. studies (see Barkley, 1981a; LaGreca & Quay, 1984). Considering the variability of diagnostic criteria and methods, this is no surprise. There are two radically different approaches to the problem. The first, embodied in the Isle of Wight approach (Rutter et al., 1970) and Gillberg et al.'s (1983) Swedish study, is the traditional medical approach in which the diagnosis is made on an all-or-nothing, present-absent basis by professional (usually psychiatric) judgment. Figures here range from 1.6 percent at age 10 in the former study to 3 percent at age seven in the latter. The other is the quantitative or statistical approach (see Chapter 1), which surveys a whole population and then selects a cutoff point on the basis of some parametric statistic or other criterion (e.g., Glow, 1980; Trites et al., 1979; Werry, Sprague, & Cohen, 1975). Glow (1980) in Australia, using a modified Conners TQ, addressed the issue of the discrepancies between British and U.S. figures and was able to show that some of these are rooted in the categorical approach as well as in the British belief that a Conduct Disorder takes precedence and excludes a diagnosis of ADD. When the British approaches were applied in her studies, the frequency of ADD fell dramatically, approximating British figures. Similarly, when criteria such as seeking treatment are considered or when agreement among teachers, parents, and physicians is required, U.S. rates are consistent with those in Britain (Bosco & Robin, 1980; Lambert, Sandoval, & Sassone, 1978).

Using the statistical approach, however, Trites et al. (1979) showed that on the Conners TQ, there was still considerable variation across four countries with, somewhat surprisingly, Canada and New Zealand yielding the highest figures and the United States and Germany the lowest! This study has been widely misinterpreted as giving prevalence rates, whereas Trites et al. simply applied a two SD cutoff derived in one of the first studies in a highly atypical Midwestern town (Werry et al., 1975). There is no reason a priori to assume that ADD conveniently conforms to a normal distribution on a teacher rating scale or that norms from one small city are universal. Furthermore, this method ignores the problem of pure and mixed cases so elegantly studied by Trites and Laprade (1983).

While there is some disagreement as to the exact prevalence of ADD, later, better studies are showing some convergence on about 2 percent in elementary school children for pure ADD rising to twice that for mixed ADD and Conduct Disorder cases (e.g., McGee et al., 1984a; Trites and Laprade, 1983).

One epidemiological finding is, however, consistent—whether in the general population or clinic attenders—boys outnumber girls in a ratio of at least 3:1 (Barkley, 1982; Gillberg et al., 1983; LaGreca & Quay, 1984; McGee et al., 1984a), which, in the clinic cases, exceeds that of the ratio of male:female referrals in general.

Trites et al. (1979) showed that the prevalence of hyperactivity and the severity of symptoms increased inversely with socioeconomic class, a finding not supported by McGee et al. (1984a). It is difficult to interpret these findings since associations between social class and disorder have been found for a number of diagnostic groups (i.e., Paternite & Loney, 1980; Richman et al., 1982; Schachar et al., 1981; see also Chapter 10), and if valid, the explanations could be medical, cultural, economic, or some combination of these.

Most of the studies of ADD have been confined to children of elementary school age. Outcome studies suggest that there is a decline in the prevalence or, perhaps better stated, clinical visibility of the disorder as childhood proceeds. Some cases, however, are still active in adolescence and a few studies (see Wood, Wender, & Reimherr, 1983) show that the syndrome can still be detected in adulthood in "residual forms," which are in fact less residual than one would expect given maturational and developmental changes.

Diagnosis and identification of the syndrome in preschoolers seems to present particular difficulties in distinguishing normal from abnormal behavior, defining symptomatology, and hence assessing prevalence (see Campbell, 1985). As a general rule, psychopathology is less clearly differentiated. While extreme forms of disorder such as autism can be readily distinguished at an early age, others such as ADD are more difficult, perhaps as a consequence of the prominence of gross motor behavior in the repertoire of very young children. There is evidence from a few studies (see S. B. Campbell et al., 1982) that whatever the contamination of the diagnoses of ADD and Conduct Disorder in older children, it is much more marked in the preschool group. In addition, the picture is complicated even more because some children identified as problems in the early preschool years may be going through a turbulent developmental phase (S. B. Campbell et al., 1982) and will settle into elementary school without apparent difficulty (Campbell, in press; McGee et al., 1984a). This suggests that some children identified as problems in early childhood are essentially a normal group of somewhat difficult children, devoid of the durable or pervasive psychopathology that characterizes the Conduct Problem or ADD child, but which overinflate preschool prevalence figures even further.

In summary, then, the epidemiology of ADD, which could contribute considerably to hypotheses about etiology, is hampered by the problem of valid criteria for diagnosis. The most robust finding seems to be the predominance of males, a finding that is open to a variety of interpretations.

FOLLOW-UP AND OUTCOME

At least 20 follow-up studies (see Aman, 1984; Milich & Loney, 1979; Ross & Ross, 1982; Satterfield, Hoppe, & Schell, 1982; Weiss, 1983) have been reported, varying in age at intake and length of follow-up. These studies are also subject to the diagnostic problems identified earlier. In addition, they are prone to subject attrition and, regrettably, often ill-defined or ad hoc outcome measures and inadequate control groups, if any. Despite these methodological shortcomings, some tentative generalizations can be made about the developmental course and adult outcome of ADD.

Consistent with parental reports and clinical formulations (Barkley, 1982; Campbell, 1983; Ross & Ross, 1982), ADD appears to have its onset in infancy or early childhood, and attempts at early identification have been reasonably successful in targeting samples of preschoolers (Campbell et al., 1982; Schleifer et al., 1975) who differ from controls on objective measures of core features. Further, there is evidence that some children identified as extremely inattentive, impulsive, and overactive in preschool are at risk for continued difficulties in early elementary school (Campbell, in press; Campbell, Endman, & Bernfeld, 1977; Richman et al., 1982).

The majority of follow-up studies have assessed the course of ADD from middle childhood to adolescence. In general, school-aged boys continue to have academic, behavioral, and social problems in adolescence, and a somewhat higher proportion of ADD children than controls demonstrate antisocial behavior and/or delinquency (Weiss, 1983). In summarizing these studies, Aman (1984) concludes that while manifestations of the disorder change over time, problems in general remain. Symptoms of ADD seem to subside during childhood into more fidgetiness; inattention increasingly presents as academic failure; and poor self-image and social incompetence become more prominent. Further, in spite of clear short-term benefits, drug treatment seems not to influence long-term prognosis (Aman, 1984; Weiss, 1983). Further, family stability, favorable parent–child relations, and child IQ appear to be predictors of good outcome in adolescence, whereas family discord and punitive child-rearing techniques are associated with antisocial outcome (Milich & Loney, 1979; Weiss, 1983).

The largest and most continuous follow-up study (childhood, adolescence, adulthood) has been conducted by Weiss and her colleagues (see Weiss, 1983; Weiss et al., 1979). She has reported that ADD children continue to have some social, academic, and achievement problems in young adulthood and to manifest more problems with concentration, impulsivity, restlessness, and poor self-esteem than normal controls. By adulthood, however, a majority have managed to settle well into work, although often below their intellectual potential. Finally, Weiss did not find marked or severe psychopathology in her sample and less antisocial behavior was evident than in adolescence. These findings now require replication in other samples in which both ADD children and controls are followed longitudinally.

Studies have also suggested that different problems at follow-up appear to have different predictors. In particular, serious antisocial behavior at follow-up is associated with early predictors of Conduct Disorder, particularly family discord and other social correlates (Milich & Loney, 1979; Weiss, 1983). This suggests that the core symptomatology of ADD or, in Cantwell's (1975) terms, the primary symptoms, may well be biogenic or developmental in nature and independent of antisocial or conduct problems as Loney and her colleagues suggest (Loney & Milich, 1981; Milich & Loney,

1979; Milich, Loney, & Landau, 1982). This is also one more illustration of the importance of trying to distinguish ADD from Conduct Disorder at the initial diagnosis. Because it is unusual for any of these outcome studies to have eliminated all contamination with Conduct Disorder, and because the contrast groups are commonly normal controls (e.g., Satterfield et al., 1982; Weiss, 1983), it is difficult to know the extent to which the outcome, particularly the poor outcome, is a function of ADD or Conduct Disorder. Studies comparing outcome in groups of ADD, Conduct Disorder, and ADD–Conduct Disorder children will be needed before this question can be resolved. Obviously, studies on the predictive validity of initial symptomatology are critical to the debate over whether or not these disorders are distinct.

SUMMARY

Research on Attention Deficit Disorder has burgeoned during the last two decades. In particular a wealth of data has provided important insights into the attentional, cognitive, and social functioning of ADD children. Research has also begun to delineate demographic and family correlates of this disorder and to provide information on its course and outcome. Despite the gains made at a descriptive level, the question of diagnostic specificity continues to cloud the interpretation of results. In addition, the mechanism or mechanisms that underlie hyperactivity still elude investigators. Research must continue to address questions of syndrome definition and to assess the biological, family, and cognitive characteristics of ADD children. The search for possible causal mechanisms must likewise be pursued with increased vigor. Research in which ADD children are compared to children with other carefully defined disorders will be necessary, if we are to begin to disentangle correlates of disorder in general from correlates of ADD in particular. Both multidimensional and multidisciplinary studies will be needed to identify risk factors, possible causal mechanisms, and their interactions.

REFERENCES

Abikoff, H., Gittelman-Klein, R., & Klein, D. F. (1977). Validation of a classroom observation code for hyperactive children. *Journal of Consulting and Clinical Psychology, 45*, 772–783.

Ackerman, P. T., Elardo, P. T., & Dykman, R. A. (1979). A psychosocial study of hyperactive and learning disabled boys. *Journal of Abnormal Child Psychology, 7*, 91–100.

Aman, M. G. (1980). Psychotropic drugs and learning problems—A selective review. *Journal of Learning Disabilities, 13*, 87–97.

Aman, M. G. (1984). Hyperactivity—the nature of the syndrome and its natural course. *Journal of Autism and Developmental Disorders, 14*, 35–56.

American Psychiatric Association. (1980). *Diagnostic and statistical manual of mental disorders*. Washington, DC: Author.

Ault, R., Mitchell, C., & Hartmann, D. (1976). Some methodological problems in reflection-impulsivity research. *Child Development, 47*, 227–231.

Barkley, R. A. (1977). The effects of methylphenidate on various types of activity level and attention in hyperkinetic children. *Journal of Abnormal Child Psychology, 5*, 351–370.

Barkley, R. A. (1981a). *Hyperactive children: A handbook for diagnosis and treatment*. New York: Guilford.

Barkley, R. A. (1981b). Hyperactivity. In E. J. Mash & L. G. Terdal (Eds.), *Behavioral assessment of childhood disorders*. New York: Guilford.

Barkley, R. A. (1982). Guidelines for defining Hyperactivity in children. In B. B. Lahey & A. E. Kazdin (Eds.), *Advances in clinical child psychology* (Vol. 5). New York: Plenum.

Barkley, R. A., & Cunningham, C. E. (1980). The parent-child interactions of hyperactive children and their modification by stimulant drugs. In R. M. Knights & D. J. Bakker (Eds.), *Treatment of hyperactive and learning disordered children*. Baltimore: University Park Press.

Barkley, R., & Ullman, D. G. (1975). A comparison of objective measures of activity and distractibility in hyperactive and non-hyperactive children. *Journal of Abnormal Child Psychology, 3*, 231–244.

Battle, E. S., & Lacey, B. (1972). A context for hyperactivity in children over time. *Child Development, 43*, 757–773.

Baxley, G. B., Turner, P. F., & Greenwald, W. E. (1978). Hyperactive children's knowledge and attitudes concerning drug treatment. *Journal of Pediatric Psychology, 3*, 172–176.

Benezra, E. (1980). *Verbal and nonverbal memory in hyperactive, reading disabled, and normal children*. Unpublished doctoral dissertation, McGill University.

Block, J., Block, H. J., & Harrington, D. M. (1974). Some misgivings about the Matching Familiar Figures Test as a measure of reflection-impulsivity. *Developmental Psychology, 10*, 611–632.

Bosco, J. J., & Robin, S. S. (1980). Hyperkinesis: Prevalence and treatment. In C. K. Whalen & B. Henker (Eds.), *Hyperactive children: The social ecology of identification and treatment*. New York: Academic Press.

Breaux, A. M. (1982). *Self-control in "hyperactive" preschool boys*. Unpublished master's thesis, University of Pittsburgh.

Bremer, D. A., & Stern, J. A. (1976). Attention and distractibility during reading in hyperactive boys. *Journal of Abnormal Child Psychology, 4*, 381–388.

Brown, A. L. (1975). The development of memory, knowing, knowing about knowing and knowing how to know. In H. W. Reese (Ed.), *Advances in child development and behavior* (Vol. 10). New York: Academic Press.

Bugenthal, D. B., Whalen, C. K., & Henker, B. (1977). Causal attributions of hyperactive children and motivational assumptions of two behavior change approaches: Evidence for an interactionist position. *Child Development, 48*, 874–884.

Campbell, M., Cohen, I. L., & Small, A. M. (1982). Drugs in aggressive behavior. *Journal of the American Academy of Child Psychiatry, 21*, 107–117.

Campbell, S. B. (1973). Mother–child interaction in reflective, impulsive, and hyperactive children. *Developmental Psychology, 8*, 341–349.

Campbell, S. B. (1974). Cognitive styles and behavior problems of clinic boys. *Journal of Abnormal Child Psychology, 2*, 307–312.

Campbell, S. B. (1983). Developmental perspectives in child psychopathology. In T. Ollendick & M. Hersen (Eds.), *Handbook of child psychopathology*. New York: Plenum.

Campbell, S. B. (1985) Hyperactivity in preschoolers: Correlates and prognostic implications. *Clinical Psychology Review, 5*, 405–428.

Campbell, S. B. (In press). Longitudinal research on active and aggressive preschoolers: Predictors of problem severity at school entry. In L. M. Bloomingdale & J. Swanson (Eds.), *Attention deficit and conduct disorders: Emerging trends*. Jamaica, NY: Spectrum.

Campbell, S. B., Breaux, A. M., Ewing, L. J., Szumowski, E. K., & Pierce, E. W. (In press). Parent-identified problem preschoolers: Mother-child interaction at intake and one-year follow-up. *Journal of Abnormal Child Psychology*.

Campbell, S. B., & Cluss, P. (1982). Peer relationships of young children with behavior problems. In K. H. Rubin & H. S. Ross (Eds.), *Peer relationships and social skills in childhood*. New York: Springer-Verlag.

Campbell, S. B., Douglas, V. I., & Morgenstern, G. (1971). Cognitive styles in hyperactive children and the effect of methylphenidate. *Journal of Child Psychology and Psychiatry, 12*, 55–67.

Campbell, S. B., Endman, M., & Bernfeld, G. (1977). A three-year follow-up of hyperactive preschoolers into elementary school. *Journal of Child Psychology and Psychiatry, 18*, 239–249.

Campbell, S. B., & Paulauskas, S. L. (1979). Peer relations in hyperactive children. *Journal of Child Psychology and Psychiatry, 20*, 233–246.

Campbell, S. B., Szumowksi, E. K., Ewing, L. J., Gluck, D. S., & Breaux, A. M. (1982). A multidimensional assessment of parent-identified behavior problem toddlers. *Journal of Abnormal Child Psychology, 10*, 569–591.

Cantwell, D. P. (1975). *The hyperactive child*. New York: Spectrum.

Cantwell, D. P., & Satterfield, J. H. (1978). The prevalence of academic underachievement in hyperactive children. *Journal of Pediatric Psychology, 3*, 168–171.

Clements, S. D. (1966). *Minimal brain dysfunction in children*. DHEW/NINDB Monograph No. 3. Washington, DC: U.S. Government Printing Office.

Clements, S. D., & Peters, J. (1962). Minimal brain dysfunctions in the school-age child. *Archives of General Psychiatry, 6*, 185–197.

Cohen, N. J., & Douglas, V. I. (1972). Characteristics of the orienting response in hyperactive and normal children. *Psychophysiology, 9*, 238–245.

Cohen, N. J., & Minde, K. (1983). The "hyperactive syndrome" in kindergarten children: Comparison of children with pervasive and situational symptoms. *Journal of Child Psychology and Psychiatry, 24*, 443–456.

Cohen, N., Weiss, G., & Minde, K. (1972). Cognitive styles in adolescents previously diagnosed as hyperactive. *Journal of Child Psychology and Psychiatry, 13*, 203–209.

Coleman, M. (1973). Serotonin and central nervous system syndromes of childhood: A review. *Journal of Autism and Childhood Schizophrenia, 3*, 27–35.

Crowther, J. K., Bond, L. A., & Rolf, J. E. (1981). The incidence, prevalence, and severity of behavior disorders among preschool-aged children in day care. *Journal of Abnormal Child Psychology, 9*, 23–42.

Cunningham, C. E., & Barkley, R. A. (1978). The role of academic failure in hyperactive behavior. *Journal of Learning Disabilities, 11*, 274–280.

Cunningham, C. E., & Barkley, R. A. (1979). The interactions of normal and hyperactive children with their mothers in free play and structured tasks. *Child Development, 50*, 217–224.

Dalby, J. T., Kinsbourne, M., Swanson, J. M., & Sobol, M. (1977). Hyperactive children's underuse of learning time: Correction by stimulant treatment. *Child Development, 48*, 1448–1453.

Delameter, A. M., Lahey, B. B., & Drake, L. (1981). Toward an empirical subclassification of "learning disabilities": A psychophysiological comparison of "hyperactive" and "nonhyperactive" subgroups. *Journal of Abnormal Child Psychology, 9*, 65–77.

Dodge, K., & Frame, C. L. (1982). Social cognitive biases and deficits in aggressive boys. *Child Development, 53*, 620–635.

Douglas, V. I. (1972). Stop, look, and listen: The problem of sustained attention and impulse control in hyperactive and normal children. *Canadian Journal of Behavioural Science, 4*, 259–276.

Douglas, V. I. (1980). Treatment and training approaches to hyperactivity: Establishing external or internal control. In C. K. Whalen & B. Henker (Eds.), *Hyperactive children: The social ecology of identification and treatment*. New York: Academic Press.

Douglas, V. I. (1983). Attentional and cognitive problems. In M. Rutter (Ed.), *Developmental neuropsychiatry*. New York: Guilford.

Douglas, V. I., & Parry, P. (1983). Effects of reward on the delayed reaction time task performance of hyperactive children. *Journal of Abnormal Child Psychology, 11*, 313–326.

Douglas, V. I., & Peters, K. (1979). Toward a clearer definition of the attentional deficit of hyperactive children. In G. Hale & M. Lewis (Eds.), *Attention and the development of cognitive skills*. New York: Plenum.

Dykman, R. T., Ackerman, P., & McCray, D. S. (1980). Effects of methylphenidate on selective and sustained attention in hyperactive, reading-disabled, and presumably attention-disordered boys. *Journal of Nervous and Mental Disease, 168*, 745–752.

Dykman, R. A., Ackerman, P. T., & Oglesby, D. M. (1979). Selective and sustained attention in hyperactive, learning disabled, and normal boys. *Journal of Nervous and Mental Disease, 167*, 288–297.

Dykman, R. A., Ackerman, P. T., & Oglesby, D. M. (1980). Correlates of problem solving in hyperactive, learning disabled, and control boys. *Journal of Learning Disabilities, 13*, 309–318.

Edelbrock, C., Costello, A. J., & Kessler, M. (1984). Empirical corroboration of Attention Deficit Disorder. *Journal of the American Academy of Child Psychiatry, 23*, 285–290.

Ferguson, H. B., & Pappas, B. A. (1979). Evaluation of psychophysiological, neurochemical, and animal models of hyperactivity. In R. L. Trites (Ed.), *Hyperactivity in children: Etiology, measurement, and treatment implications.* Baltimore: University Park Press.

Ferguson, H. B., & Rapoport, J. L. (1983). Nosological issues and biological validation. In M. Rutter (Ed.), *Developmental Neuropsychiatry.* New York: Guilford.

Firestone, P., & Douglas, V. I. (1975). The effects of reward and punishment on reaction times and autonomic activity in hyperactive and normal children. *Journal of Abnormal Child Psychology, 3,* 201–215.

Firestone, P., & Martin, J. E. (1979). An analysis of the hyperactive syndrome: A comparison of hyperactive, behavior problem, asthmatic, and normal children. *Journal of Abnormal Child Psychology, 7,* 261–274.

Firestone, P., Peters, S., Rivier, M., & Knights, R. M. (1978). Minor physical anomalies in hyperactive, retarded, and normal children. *Journal of Child Psychology and Psychiatry, 19,* 155–160.

Firestone, P., & Prabhu, A. N. (1983). Minor physical anomalies and obstetrical complications: Their relationship to hyperactive, psychoneurotic, and normal children and their families. *Journal of Abnormal Child Psychology, 11,* 207–216.

Freibergs, V., & Douglas, V. I. (1969). Concept learning in hyperactive and normal children. *Journal of Abnormal Psychology, 74,* 388–395.

Gillberg, C., Carlstrom, G., & Rasmussen, P. (1983). Hyperkinetic disorders in seven-year-old children with perceptual, motor and attentional disorders. *Journal of Child Psychology and Psychiatry, 24,* 233–246.

Gittelman, R., Abikoff, H., Pollack, E., Klein, D. F., Katz, S., & Mattes, J. (1980). A controlled trial of methylphenidate and behavior modification in hyperactive children. In C. K. Whalen & B. Henker (Eds.), *Hyperactive children: The social ecology of identification and treatment.* New York: Academic Press.

Glow, R. A. (1980). A validation of Conners TQ and a cross-cultural comparison of prevalence of hyperactivity in children. In G. D. Burrows & J. S. Werry (Eds.), *Advances in human psychopharmacology: A research annual* (Vol. 1). Greenwich, CT: JAI.

Gordon, M. (1979). The assessment of impulsivity and mediating behaviors in hyperactive and non-hyperactive boys. *Journal of Abnormal Child Psychology, 7,* 317–326.

Gorenstein, E., & Newman, J. (1980). Disinhibitory psychopathology: A new perspective and a model for research. *Psychological Review, 87,* 301–315.

Goyette, C. H., Conners, C. K., & Ulrich, R. F. (1978). Normative data on Revised Conners Parent and Teacher Rating Scales. *Journal of Abnormal Child Psychology, 6,* 221–236.

Greenberg, A., & Coleman, M. (1976). Depressed five-hydroxyindole levels associated with hyperactive and aggressive behavior. *Archives of General Psychiatry, 33,* 331–336.

Greist, D. L, Forehand, R., Wells, K. C., & McMahon, R. J. (1980). An examination of differences between nonclinic and behavior-problem clinic-referred children and their mothers. *Journal of Abnormal Psychology, 89,* 497–500.

Grinspoon, L., & Singer, S. (1973). Amphetamine in the treatment of hyperkinetic children. *Harvard Educational Review, 43,* 515–555.

Gualtieri, C. T., Adams, A., Shen, C. D., & Loiselle, D. (1982). Minor physical anomalies in alcoholic and schizophrenic adults and hyperactive and autistic children. *American Journal of Psychiatry, 139*, 640–643.

Hallahan, D. P., Kauffman, J. M., & Ball, D. W. (1974). Developmental trends in recall of central and incidental auditory material. *Journal of Experimental Child Psychology, 17*, 409–421.

Hartig, M., & Kanfer, F. H. (1973). The role of verbal self-instruction in children's resistance to temptation. *Journal of Personality and Social Psychology, 25*, 259–267.

Hastings, J. E., & Barkley, R. A. (1978). A review of psychophysiological research with hyperkinetic children. *Journal of Abnormal Child Psychology, 6*, 413–447.

Hechtman, L., Weiss, G., Finkelstein, J., Wener, A., & Benn, R. (1976). Hyperactives as young adults: Preliminary report. *Canadian Medical Association Journal, 115*, 625–629.

Henker, B., & Whalen, C. K. (1980). The changing faces of hyperactivity: Retrospect and prospect. In C. K. Whalen & B. Henker (Eds.), *Hyperactive children: The social ecology of identification and treatment*. New York: Academic Press.

Hoy, E., Weiss, G., Minde, K., & Cohen, N. (1978). The hyperactive child at adolescence: Cognitive, emotional, and social functioning. *Journal of Abnormal Child Psychology, 6*, 311–324.

Humphries, T., Kinsbourne, M., & Swanson, J. (1978). Stimulant effects on cooperation and social interaction between hyperactive children and their mothers. *Journal of Child Psychology and Psychiatry, 19*, 13–22.

Juliano, D. (1974). Conceptual tempo, activity, and concept learning in hyperactive and normal children. *Journal of Abnormal Psychology, 83*, 629–634.

Kagan, J., Rosman, B., Day, D., Albert, J., & Phillips, W. (1964). Information processing in the child: Significance of analytic and reflective attitudes. *Psychological Monographs 78*, (1, Whole No. 578).

Kennard, M. (1960). Value of equivocal signs in neurological diagnosis. *Neurology, 10*, 753–764.

King, C. A., & Young, R. D. (1981). Peer popularity and peer communication patterns: Hyperactive vs. active but normal boys. *Journal of Abnormal Child Psychology, 9*, 465–482.

King, C., & Young, R. D. (1982). Attentional deficits with and without hyperactivity: Teacher and peer perceptions. *Journal of Abnormal Child Psychology, 10*, 483–496.

Kinsbourne, M., & Swanson, J. (1979). Models of hyperactivity. In R. L. Trites (Ed.), *Hyperactivity in children: Etiology, measurement, and treatment implications*. Baltimore: University Park Press.

Klein, A. R., & Young, R. D. (1979). Hyperactive boys in their classroom: Assessment of teacher and peer perceptions, interactions, and classroom behaviors. *Journal of Abnormal Child Psychology, 7*, 425–442.

Krouse, J. P., & Kauffman, J. M. (1982). Minor physical anomalies in exceptional children: A review and critique of research. *Journal of Abnormal Child Psychology, 10*, 247–264.

LaGreca, A. M., & Quay, H. C. (1984). Behavior disorders of children. In N. S. Endler & J. McV. Hunt (Eds.), *Personality and the behavior disorders* (2nd ed.). New York: Wiley.

Lahey, B. B., Schaughency, E. A., Strauss, C. C., & Frame, C. L. (1984). Are attention deficit disorders with and without hyperactivity similar or dissimilar disorders? *Journal of the American Academy of Child Psychiatry, 23,* 302–309.

Lahey, B. B., Stempniak, M., Robinson, E. J., & Tyroler, M. J. (1978). Hyperactivity and learning disabilities as independent dimensions of child behavior problems. *Journal of Abnormal Psychology, 87,* 333–340.

Lambert, N. M., & Sandoval, J. (1980). The prevalence of learning disabilities in a sample of children considered hyperactive. *Journal of Abnormal Child Psychology, 8,* 33–50.

Lambert, N. M., Sandoval, J., & Sassone, D. (1978). Prevalence of hyperactivity in elementary school children as a function of social system definers. *American Journal of Orthopsychiatry, 48,* 446–463.

Laufer, M. W., & Denhoff, E. (1957). Hyperkinetic behavior syndrome in children. *Journal of Pediatrics, 50,* 453–474.

Laufer, M. W., Denhoff, E., & Solomons, G. (1957). Hyperkinetic impulse disorder in children's behavior problems. *Psychosomatic Medicine, 19,* 38–49.

Levy, F., & Hobbes, G. (1981). The diagnosis of Attention Deficit Disorder (hyperkinesis) in children. *Journal of the American Academy of Child Psychiatry, 20,* 376–384.

Loney, J. (1974). The intellectual functioning of hyperactive elementary school boys: A cross-sectional investigation. *American Journal of Orthopsychiatry, 44,* 754–762.

Loney, J. (1978). Childhood hyperactivity. In R. H. Woody (Ed.), *Encyclopedia of clinical assessment*. San Francisco: Jossey-Bass.

Loney, J. (1980). Hyperkinesis comes of age: What do we know and where we should go? *American Journal of Orthopsychiatry, 50,* 28–42.

Loney, J. (1982). *Research diagnostic criteria for childhood hyperactivity*. Paper presented at the annual meeting of the American Psychopathological Association, New York.

Loney, J., Langhorne, J., & Paternite, C. (1978). An empirical basis for subgrouping the hyperkinetic/minimal brain dysfunction syndrome. *Journal of Abnormal Psychology, 87,* 431–441.

Loney, J., & Milich, R. (1981). Hyperactivity, inattention, and aggression in clinical practice. In M. Wolraich & D. K. Routh (Eds.), *Advances in behavioral pediatrics* (Vol. 2). Greenwich, CT: JAI.

Mash, E. J., & Johnston, C. (1982). Comparison of the mother–child interactions of younger and older hyperactive and normal children. *Child Development, 53,* 1371–1381.

Mash, E. J., & Johnston, C. (1983). Parental perceptions of child behavior problems, parenting self-esteem, and mothers' reported stress in younger and older hyperactive and normal children. *Journal of Consulting and Clinical Psychology, 51,* 86–99.

McGee, R., Williams, S., & Silva, P. A. (1984a). Background characteristics of aggressive, hyperactive, and aggressive-hyperactive boys. *Journal of the American Academy of Child Psychiatry, 23*, 280–284.

McGee, R., Williams, S., & Silva, P. A. (1984b). Behavioural and developmental characteristics of aggressive, hyperactive, and aggressive-hyperactive boys. *Journal of the American Academy of Child Psychiatry, 23*, 270–279.

McMahon, R. C. (1980). Genetic etiology in the hyperactive child syndrome: A critical review. *American Journal of Orthopsychiatry, 50*, 145–150.

Milich, R., & Kramer, J. (1985). Reflections on impulsivity: An empirical investigation of impulsivity as a construct. In K. Gadow & I. Bialer (Eds.), *Advances in learning and behavioral disabilities* (Vol. 3). Greenwich, CT: JAI.

Milich, R., & Landau, S. (1982). Socialization and peer relations in hyperactive children. In K. D. Gadow & I. Bialer (Eds.), *Advances in learning and behavior disabilities* (Vol. 1). Greenwich, CT: JAI.

Milich, R., Landau, S., Kilby, G., & Whitten, P. (1982). Preschool peer perceptions of the behavior of hyperactive and aggressive children. *Journal of Abnormal Child Psychology, 10*, 497–510.

Milich, R., & Loney, J. (1979). The role of hyperactive and aggressive symptomatology in predicting adolescent outcome in hyperactive children. *Journal of Pediatric Psychology, 4*, 93–112.

Milich, R., Loney, J., & Landau, S. (1982). Independent dimensions of hyperactivity and aggression: A validation with playroom observation data. *Journal of Abnormal Psychology, 91*, 183–198.

Minde, K., Lewin, D., Weiss, G., Lavigueur, H., Douglas, V., & Sykes, E. (1971). The hyperactive child in elementary school: A five-year controlled follow-up. *Exceptional Children, 38*, 215–221.

Mischel, H. N., & Mischel, W. (1983). The development of children's knowledge of self-control strategies. *Child Development, 54*, 603–619.

Nichols, P. (1980). Early antecedents of hyperactivity. *Neurology, 30*, 439–443.

Nichols, P. L., & Chen, T. C. (1981). *Minimal brain dysfunction: A prospective study*. Hillsdale, NJ: Erlbaum.

Palkes, H., & Stewart, M. A. (1972). Intellectual ability and performance of hyperactive children. *American Journal of Orthopsychiatry, 42*, 35–39.

Parry, P. (1973). *The effect of reward on the performance of hyperactive children*. Unpublished doctoral dissertation, McGill University.

Parry, P., & Douglas, V. I. (1983). Effects of reinforcement on concept identification in hyperactive children. *Journal of Abnormal Child Psychology, 11*, 327–340.

Paternite, C. E., & Loney, J. (1980). Childhood hyperkinesis: Relationships between symptomatology and home environment. In C. K. Whalen & B. Henker (Eds.), *Hyperactive children: The social ecology of identification and treatment*. New York: Academic Press.

Paulauskas, S. L., & Campbell, S. B. (1979). Social perspective-taking and teacher ratings of peer interaction in hyperactive boys. *Journal of Abnormal Child Psychology, 7*, 483–494.

Pelham, W., & Bender, M. E. (1982). Peer relationships in hyperactive children: Description and treatment. In K. D. Gadow & I. Bialer (Eds.), *Advances in learning and behavioral disabilities*, Vol. I. Greenwich, CT: JAI.

Peters, K. W. (1977). *Selective attention and distractibility in hyperactive and normal children*. Unpublished doctoral dissertation, McGill University.

Pfadt, A., & Tyron, W. (1983). Issues in the selection and use of mechanical transducers to directly measure motor activity in clinical settings. *Applied Research in Mental Retardation, 4*, 251–270.

Porges, S. W., & Smith, K. M. (1980). Defining hyperactivity: Psychophysiological and behavioral strategies. In C. K. Whalen & B. Henker (Eds.), *Hyperactive children: The social ecology of identification and treatment*. New York: Academic Press.

Porrino, C. J., Rapoport, J. L., Behar, D., Sceery, W., Ismond, D. R., & Bunney, W. E. (1983). A naturalistic assessment of the motor activity of hyperactive boys: I. Comparison with normal boys. *Archives of General Psychiatry, 40*, 681–687.

Prinz, R. J., Connor, P. A., & Wilson, C. C. (1981). Hyperactive and aggressive behavior in childhood: Intertwined dimensions. *Journal of Abnormal Child Psychology, 9*, 191–202.

Quay, H. C. (1979). Classification. In H. C. Quay & J. S. Werry (Eds.), *Psychopathological disorders of childhood* (2nd ed.) New York: Wiley.

Quay, H. C. (1985). A critical analysis of DSM III as a taxonomy of psychopathology in children and adolescents. In T. Millon & G. Klerman (Eds.), *Contemporary issues in psychopathology*. New York: Guilford.

Radosh, A., & Gittelman, R. (1981). The effect of appealing distractors on the performance of hyperactive children. *Journal of Abnormal Child Psychology, 9*, 179–189.

Rapoport, J. L., Buchsbaum, M. S., Zahn, T. P., Weingartner, H., Ludlow, C., & Mikkelson, E. J. (1978). Dextroamphetamine: Cognitive and behavioral effects in normal prepubertal boys. *Science, 199*, 560–563.

Rapoport, J. L., & Ismond, D. R. (1982). Biological research in child psychiatry. *Journal of the American Academy of Child Psychiatry, 21*, 543–548.

Rapoport, J. L., Quinn, P. O., & Lamprecht, F. (1974). Minor physical anomalies and plasma dopamine-beta-hydroxylase activity in hyperactive boys. *American Journal of Psychiatry, 131*, 386–390.

Reeves, J. C., & Werry, J. S. (In press). Soft signs in abnormality. II. Hyperactivity. In D. E. Tupper (Ed.), *Soft neurological signs: Manifestations, measurement, research, and meaning*. New York: Grune & Stratton.

Richman, N., Stevenson, J., & Graham, P. J. (1982). *Preschool to school: A behavioural study*. London: Academic Press.

Riddle, K., & Rapoport, J. L. (1976). A two-year follow-up of 72 hyperactive boys. *Journal of Nervous and Mental Disease, 162*, 126–134.

Rie, H. E., & Rie, E. C. (1980). *Handbook of minimal brain dysfunctions: A critical review*. New York: Wiley.

Rosenthal, R. H., & Allen, T. W. (1978). An examination of attention, arousal, and learning dysfunctions of hyperkinetic children. *Psychological Bulletin, 85*, 689–715.

Rosenthal, R. H., & Allen, T. W. (1980). Intratask distractibility in hyperkinetic and non-hyperkinetic children. *Journal of Abnormal Child Psychology, 8*, 175–187.

Ross, D. M., & Ross, S. A. (1982). *Hyperactivity: Theory, research, and action* (2nd ed.). New York: Wiley.

Routh, D. (1980). Developmental and social aspects of hyperactivity. In C. K. Whalen & B. Henker (Eds.), *Hyperactive children: The social ecology of identification and treatment.* New York: Academic Press.

Rutter, M. (1971). Parent-child separation: Psychological effects on the children. *Journal of Child Psychology and Psychiatry, 12,* 233–260.

Rutter, M. (1981). Psychological sequelae of brain damage in children. *American Journal of Psychiatry, 138,* 1533–1544.

Rutter, M. (1982). Syndromes attributed to "minimal brain dysfunction" in childhood. *American Journal of Psychiatry, 139,* 21–33.

Rutter, M., & Shaffer, D. (1980). DSM III: A step forward or back in terms of the classification of child psychiatric disorders? *Journal of the American Academy of Child Psychiatry, 19,* 371–394.

Rutter, M., Tizard, J., & Whitmore, K. (1970). *Education, health, and behaviour.* London: Longman.

Sameroff, A. J., & Chandler, M. J. (1975). Reproductive risk and the continuum of caretaking casualty. In F. D. Horowitz (Ed.), *Review of child development research* (Vol. 4). Chicago: University of Chicago Press.

Sandberg, S., Rutter, M., & Taylor, E. (1978). Hyperkinetic disorder in psychiatric clinic attenders. *Developmental Medicine and Child Neurology, 20,* 279–299.

Sandberg, S. T., Wieselberg, M., & Shaffer, D. (1980). Hyperkinetic and conduct problem children in a primary school population: Some epidemiological considerations. *Journal of Child Psychology and Psychiatry, 21,* 293–312.

Satterfield, J. H., Cantwell, D. P., & Satterfield, B. T. (1974). Pathophysiology of the hyperactive child syndrome. *Archives of General Psychiatry, 31,* 839–844.

Satterfield, H. H., Hoppe, C. M., & Schell, A. M. (1982). A prospective study of delinquency in 11 adolescent boys with Attention Deficit Disorder and 88 normal adolescent boys. *American Journal of Psychiatry, 139,* 795–798.

Schacher, R., Rutter, M., & Smith, A. (1981). The characteristics of situationally and pervasively hyperactive children: Implications for syndrome definition. *Journal of Child Psychology and Psychiatry, 22,* 375–392.

Schleifer, M., Weiss, G., Cohen, N. J., Elman, M., Cvejic, H., & Kruger, E. (1975). Hyperactivity in preschoolers and the effect of methylphenidate. *American Journal of Orthopsychiatry, 45,* 38–50.

Schrag, P., & Divoky, D. (1975). *The myth of the hyperactive child.* New York: Pantheon.

Schwarz, J. C., Schrager, J. B., & Lyons, A. E. (1983). Delay of gratification by preschoolers: Evidence for the validity of the choice paradigm. *Child Development, 54,* 620–625.

Sergeant, J. A., & Scholten, C. A. (1985a). On resource strategy limitations in hyperactivity: Cognitive impulsivity reconsidered. *Journal of Child Psychology and Psychiatry, 26,* 97–109.

Sergeant, J. A., & Scholten, C. A. (1985b). On data limitations in hyperactivity. *Journal of Child Psychology and Psychiatry, 26,* 111–124.

Shaywitz, S. E., Cohen, D. J., & Shaywitz, B. A. (1978). The biochemical basis of minimal brain dysfunction. *Journal of Pediatrics, 92*, 179–187.

Shekim, W. O., Dekirmenjian, H., & Chapel, J. L. (1979). Urinary MPHG excretion in minimal brain dysfunction and its modification by d-amphetamine. *American Journal of Psychiatry, 136*, 667–671.

Silva, P. A., Kirkland, C., Simpson, A., Stewart, I. A., & Williams, S. M. (1982). Some developmental and behavioral problems associated with bilateral otitis media with effusion. *Journal of Learning Disorders, 15*, 417–420.

Steg, J. P., & Rapoport, J. L. (1975). Minor physical anomalies in normal, neurotic, learning disabled, and severely disturbed children. *Journal of Autism and Childhood Schizophrenia, 5*, 299–307.

Stewart, M. A., deBlois, C. S., & Cummings, C. (1980). Psychiatric disorder in the parents of hyperactive boys and those with conduct disorder. *Journal of Child Psychology and Psychiatry, 21*, 283–292.

Strauss, A., & Lehtinen, L. W. (1947). *Psychopathology and education of the brain-injured child.* New York: Grune & Stratton.

Sykes, D. H., Douglas, V. I., & Morgenstern, G. (1972). The effect of methylphenidate (Ritalin) on sustained attention in hyperactive children. *Psychopharmacologia, 25*, 262–274.

Tallmadge, J., & Barkley, R. A. (1983). The interactions of hyperactive and normal boys with their fathers and mothers. *Journal of Abnormal Child Psychology, 11*, 565–579.

Tant, J. L., & Douglas, V. I. (1982). Problem solving in hyperactive, normal, and reading-disabled boys. *Journal of Abnormal Child Psychology, 10*, 285–306.

Towbin, A. (1978). Cerebral dysfunctions related to perinatal organic damage: Clinical-neuropathologic correlates. *Journal of Abnormal Psychology, 87*, 617–635.

Trites, R. L., Dugas, E., Lynch, G., & Ferguson, H. B. (1979). Prevalence of hyperactivity. *Journal of Pediatric Psychology, 4*, 179–188.

Trites, R. L., & Laprade, K. (1983). Evidence for an independent syndrome of hyperactivity. *Journal of Child Psychology and Psychiatry, 24*, 573–586.

Urbain, E. S., & Kendall, P. C. (1980). Review of social-cognitive problem-solving interventions with children. *Psychological Bulletin, 88*, 109–143.

Walker, H. A. (1977). Incidence of minor physical anomaly in autism. *Journal of Autism and Childhood Schizophrenia, 1*, 165–176.

Wechsler, D. (1949). *Manual for the Wechsler Intelligence Scale for Children.* New York: Psychological Corporation.

Weingartner, H., Rapoport, J. L., Buchsbaum, M. S., Bunney, W. E., Ebert, M. H., Mikkelson, E. J., & Caine, E. D. (1980). Cognitive processes in normal and hyperactive children and their response to amphetamine treatment. *Journal of Abnormal Psychology, 89*, 25–37.

Weiss, G. (1983). Long-term outcome: Findings, concepts, and practical implications. In M. Rutter (Ed.), *Developmental neuropsychiatry.* New York: Guilford.

Weiss, G., & Hechtman, L. (1979) The hyperactive child syndrome. *Science, 205*, 1348–1352.

Weiss, G., Hechtman, L., Perlman, T., Hopkins, J., & Wener, A. (1979) Hyperactive children as young adults: A controlled prospective 10-year follow-up of the psychiatric status of 75 hyperactive children. *Archives of General Psychiatry, 36*, 675–681.

Wender, P. H. (1971). *Minimal brain dysfunction in children.* New York: Wiley.

Werry, J. S. (1978) *Pediatric psychopharmacology: The use of behavior modifying drugs in children.* New York: Brunner/Mazel.

Werry, J. S., & Aman, M. (1976). The reliability and diagnostic validity of the Physical and Neurological Examination for Soft Signs (PANESS). *Journal of Autism and Childhood Schizophrenia, 6*, 253–263.

Werry, J. S., & Aman, M. G. (1984). Methylphenidate in hyperactive and enuretic children. In B. Shopsin & L. Greenhill (Eds.), *The psychobiology of childhood: Profile of current issues.* Jamaica, NY: Spectrum.

Werry, J. S., Minde, K., Guzman, D., Weiss, G., Dogan, K., & Hoy, E. (1972). Studies on the hyperactive child: VII. Neurological status compared with neurotic and normal children. *American Journal of Orthopsychiatry, 45*, 441–451.

Werry, J. S., & Quay, H. C. (1971). The prevalence of behavior symptoms in younger elementary school children. *American Journal of Orthopsychiatry, 41*, 136–143.

Werry, J. S., Sprague, R. L., & Cohen, M. N. (1975). Conners' teacher rating scale for use in drug studies with children: An empirical study. *Journal of Abnormal Child Psychology, 3*, 217–229.

Whalen, C. K., Collins, B. E., Henker, B., Alkus, S. R., Adams, D., & Stapp, J. (1978). Behavior observations of hyperactive children and methylphenidate (Ritalin) effects in systematically structured classroom environments: Now you see them, now you don't. *Journal of Pediatric Psychology, 3*, 177–187.

Whalen, C. K., & Henker, B. (1980) The social ecology of psychostimulant treatment: A model for conceptual and empirical analysis. In C. K. Whalen & B. Henker (Eds.), *Hyperactive children: The social ecology of identification and treatment.* New York: Academic Press.

Wood, D., Wender, P. H., & Reimherr, F. W. (1983). The prevalence of attention deficit disorders, residual type, or minimal brain dysfunction in a population of male alcoholic patients. *American Journal of Psychiatry, 140*, 95–98.

Worland, J. (1976). Effects of positive and negative feedback on behavior control in hyperactive and normal boys. *Journal of Abnormal Child Psychology, 4*, 315–326.

Worland, J., North-Jones, M., & Stern, J. A. (1973). Performance and activity of hyperactive and normal boys as a function of distraction and reward. *Journal of Abnormal Child Psychology, 1*, 363–377.

Wright, J. C., & Vliestra, A. G. (1975). The development of selective attention: From perceptual exploration to logical research. In H.W. Reese (Ed.), *Advances in child development and behavior* (Vol. 10). New York: Academic Press.

Zentall, S. S., & Zentall, T. R. (1983). Optimal stimulation: A model of disordered activity and performance in normal and deviant children. *Psychological Bulletin, 94*, 446–471.

5 AUTISM, SCHIZOPHRENIA, AND ALLIED DISORDERS

MARGOT PRIOR and JOHN S. WERRY

INTRODUCTION

The term *psychosis* is a generic one, implying a severe degree of psychopathology such that the interpretation of oneself, of the world, and of one's place in it, is so seriously at variance with the actual facts of the matter as to interfere with everyday adaptation and to strike the impartial observer as incomprehensible. In technical parlance, it is characterized primarily by grossly impaired reality testing. It is what the man in the street calls "insanity" and it carries with it a set of legal and social conventions including release from responsibility for many of one's actions and the need for supervision, treatment, and protection of the person and society by the health and other helping systems.

The term *psychosis* has, however, been debased in meaning. Because of this and also because thinking and research now place great emphasis on distinctiveness, the term has all but disappeared from the DSM-III (American Psychiatric Association, 1980), though it has proved more durable in the ICD-9, which still has the psychosis/neurosis subdivisions. Thus for historical reasons, it is appropriate still to refer to childhood psychosis, though most of this chapter will proceed disorder by disorder.

Although discussing the ICD-9, we will place the greatest emphasis on DSM-III where there are several disorders affecting children and younger adolescents formerly referred to as psychoses but now for the most part categorized somewhat differently. First, there are those in a subgrouping called "Pervasive Developmental Disorders," which includes Infantile Autism. The rest are scattered among disorders that ordinarily begin in adulthood but can, in some instances, occur before that. Included here are Schizophrenic, Major Affective, Reactive, certain Organic and Schizoaffective disorders. In the ICD-9, the main difference is that all psychotic disorders occur in a single section, with a subcategory "Psychoses specific to childhood."

156

With certain exceptions, each of the psychotic disorders will be discussed separately and comparison with the ICD-9 will be made, though it may be noted now that, apart from terminology and siting, there is little real difference between the two classifications—less so than for most other disorders. For historical reasons, most of the discussion will center on two conditions: Infantile Autism and Schizophrenia. Schizoaffective disorders will not be discussed since there is still considerable doubt about their existence and since the literature relating to children is sparse indeed. Major Affective Disorders, notably childhood depression, will not be discussed here because true psychotic states of an affective nature are very rare in children and younger adolescents, and depression has been considered in Chapter 3.

HISTORY

Study of the childhood psychoses has been dominated by two disorders with a third, organic psychosis, playing a minor role despite its greater frequency. The study of schizophrenia in children was only sporadic until the 1940s. In 1943 Kanner described Infantile Autism as a disorder separate from Schizophrenia and other childhood psychoses. Subsequently, a variety of other terms and purported types of psychosis peculiar to childhood have been introduced, such as the atypical child (Rank, 1949) and symbiotic psychosis (see Ornitz & Ritvo, 1976; Wing & Gould, 1979). Most recently "disintegrative psychosis" has apparently been identified (Corbett, Harris, Taylor, & Trimble, 1977) with age of onset in between that of Autism and Childhood Schizophrenia (age three to five years). In this very rare condition, severe regression in all areas of functioning occurs after apparently normal early development. Organic factors are usually identified or suspected in the etiology (see Chapter 6).

Historically, it is possible to identify two points of view about nonorganic childhood psychosis—*unitary* and *differentiated*. The first, led by the Bellevue Group of Bender and Fish, held that there was only one type of disorder, namely Schizophrenia, and that the variations in symptomatology were due primarily to development or age of onset (e.g., Fish, 1976). This unitary view was also strong in the United Kingdom during the same period, although it was less a single disease concept than that of a clinical phenotype that recognized the possibility of many differing etiologies. The famous British "nine points" for diagnosis (Creak et al., 1961) greatly reinforced the unitary view in the 1960s.

The differentiating view is essentially that of Kanner, Rutter, and Kolvin. Under the influence of psychoanalysis in the 1950s and 1960s, however, which emphasized developmental stages rather than symptomatology or behavior, categorization was so poorly defined that apart from Kanner and his pupil Eisenberg and a few others, study of childhood psychosis became debased into one of severity of disorder only, with a number of unitary factions each using its own terminology (see Anthony, 1958: Wing & Gould, 1979).

Other attempts at subclassification were those of Goldfarb (1961), who espoused an etiological (organic/nonorganic) classification, and most importantly, that of the Group for the Advancement of Psychiatry (1966), which, following suggestions by Anthony (1958), offered a developmental typology, classifying psychosis by age of onset. Following the studies of Kolvin (1971) and the eloquent championing by Rutter (1972), the differentiated view, which separates Autism from Schizophrenia and from some of the early organic disorders, has gradually gained supremacy. Kolvin (1971) assembled cases of childhood psychosis, which he grouped by age of onset (before three, three to five, and after five) and found not only that the three groups had different symptomatology (although this was already known following the work of Bender, 1953, Fish, 1976, and others) but, more importantly, differing family histories of schizophrenia, associated neurological signs, and prognosis. Though there is still some remaining dissent about the distinctiveness of Autism and Schizophrenia (e.g., Ornitz & Ritvo, 1976), such dissent is clearly now confined to a small minority.

Statistically based attempts at subclassification of childhood psychoses have been rare, possibly because of the very low frequency of the disorders. As noted in Chapter 1, Prior, Boulton, Gajzago, and Perry (1975) reported a taxonomic study of 162 cases in which two subgroups could be clearly differentiated—one having early onset and severe autistic-type behavior and the other having a later onset and less severe impairments in social relationships. The classification was very similar to that of Kolvin, Ounsted, Humphrey, and McNay (1971), although derived by different means. Multivariate studies, probably because of a very restricted data base, usually produce only a single "psychosis" dimension characterized by severity, bizarreness, impaired social interaction, and distorted reality testing. (See Chapter 1.) There is now so much in the literature that points directly or indirectly to the value of differentiating psychotic states, however, for treatment, prognosis, and probably etiology, that it seems proper to accept, tentatively at least, the validity of the broad separation between Autism, Schizophrenia, organic, and other psychotic disorders, while recognizing the need for major, large-sample, multivariate investigations.

It is most important to bear in mind that the childhood psychoses are rare and that they have received an emphasis that is out of all proportion to the numbers of children affected. It is more the load that they put on clinics, facilities, families, and communities than their numbers that highlights them. Thus, the disease model may well be most helpful for studying and treating this group of disorders when detected but, in view of their infrequency, the statistical concept of psychotic behavior may be much more useful at the screening level.

Psychotic children have held a peculiar fascination for the child mental health professions, and the literature is now voluminous (DeMyer, Hingtgen, & Jackson, 1981). Although there has been a marked improvement in the quality of work in the last decade or so, much of the early literature is methodologically poor and subject to grossly overelaborated speculation about the child's inner world and what had caused the disorder. As DeMyer et al. (1981) in their comprehensive and highly recommended review of Autism point out, not only has there been a marked shift in the quality of studies in the period 1970–1980, but there has been a clear movement away from psychogenic views to acceptance of a biogenic origin and, as a consequence, a great increase in biologically oriented studies.

THE PERVASIVE DEVELOPMENT DISORDERS (PDD) (AUTISM AND ALLIED DISORDERS)

Infantile Autism— Principal Characteristics

The DSM-III offers the following necessary and sufficient criteria for the diagnosis of Infantile Autism.

A. Onset before 30 months of age.
B. Pervasive lack of responsiveness to other people (Autism).
C. Gross deficits in language development.
D. If speech is present, peculiar speech patterns such as immediate and delayed echolalia, metaphorical language, pronomial reversal.
E. Bizarre responses to various aspects of the environment, e.g., resistance to change, peculiar interest in or attachments to animate or inaminate objects.
F. Absence of delusions, hallucinations, loosening of associations, and incoherence as in Schizophrenia. (American Psychiatric Association, 1980, p. 89–90)

These are much as Kanner originally stated them in 1943. In addition to this category, that is, the full syndrome, there is a residual one, consisting of two criteria:

A. Once had an illness that met the criteria for Infantile Autism.
B. The current clinical picture no longer meets full criteria for Infantile Autism, but signs of the illness have persisted to the present, such as oddities of communication and social awkwardness.

The ICD-9 has only a single equivalent category called ''Infantile Autism'' and, as with all ICD-9 categories, it is only loosely defined, not with a set of specific necessary and sufficient diagnostic criteria.

Other Categories of PDD

There is also a PDD–Childhood Onset, which has the following criteria:

A. Gross and sustained impairment in social relationships, e.g., lack of appropriate affect responsivity, inappropriate clinging, asociality, lack of empathy.
B. At least three of the following:
  1. Sudden excess of anxiety
  2. Constricted or inappropriate affect
  3. Resistance to change in the environment

4. Oddities of motor movement
5. Abnormalities of speech
6. Hyper- or hypo-sensitivity to sensory stimuli
7. Self mutilation

C. Onset of the full syndrome after 30 months of age and before 12 years of age.
D. Absence of delusions, hallucinations, incoherence, or marked loosening of association. (American Psychiatric Association, 1980, p. 91)

An inspection of the diagnostic criteria for Infantile Autism and PDD–Childhood Onset suggests that if one makes allowances for the older age of onset and therefore the more advanced developmental state, PDD–Childhood Onset would appear to be simply a variant of Infantile Autism. Indeed Quay (1985; see also Chapter 1) has argued that there is no empirical support for the PDD–Childhood Onset diagnostic category. As with Autism, there is also a PDD–Childhood Onset residual state, the criteria of which are identical to those for Infantile Autism residual state.

There is also a grab-bag category called "Atypical Pervasive Developmental Disorder," which may be invoked when symptomatology is incomplete. Similarly, the ICD-9 lists an "Other" category in the section of "Psychosis with Origins Specific to Childhood."

Other Views

Some hold that the term *Autism* should be reserved for a small subgroup of children who present with Kanner's classical symptomatology of severe social aloofness, all-absorbing elaborate repetitive rituals, characteristic language disturbances (pronomial reversals and idiosyncratic use of words) when language is present, evidence of islets of normal or near normal intelligence, and absence of gross neurological signs (e.g., Lotter, 1966; Rimland, 1964; Wing & Gould, 1979). Rimland introduced the term *Kanner's syndrome* and Lotter *Nuclear Autism* for this group.

A recent and thought-provoking proposal is that of Wing (Wing, 1981; Wing & Gould, 1979; Wing, Gould, Yeates, & Brierley, 1977), who has argued for grouping children on the basis of severity of impairment in the ability for reciprocal social interaction; in comprehension and use of verbal and nonverbal communication; and in imaginative or symbolic play, with the substitution of repetitive stereotyped activity. Wing's own uniquely comprehensive data support the validity of this system and its advantages over Kanner's syndrome or "classical autism" versus a more diffuse syndrome, or early versus later onset (see later discussion).

Validity of the Syndrome

Empirical studies have been sparse and hampered by certain methodological and practical problems such as the lack of a set of universally accepted criteria for its diagnosis.

A second problem is that of operationalizing the criteria used. The DSM-III criteria are, in reality, far from operationalized in that they use judgmental descriptors such as pervasive, gross, peculiar and bizarre. One attempt to be much more precise in description is the system of Ritvo and Freeman (1978), prepared for and adopted by the National Association for Autistic Children. Although it reflects some of the particular emphases of its originators (the UCLA Group), particularly the presence of "perceptual inconstancy," it is much more operationalized and could serve as a set of research diagnostic criteria.

A third problem lies in the development of reliable and valid methods to measure the symptomatology. A number of systems exist (e.g., Cohen et al., 1978; Freeman et al., 1981; Wing & Gould, 1979), but most of these are peculiar to one investigator, unproven, or in some cases invalid.

A fourth problem is that of appropriate control groups. Many studies are marred by failure to match subjects for mental age and, as a consequence, are less studies of autism than of mental retardation (see Freeman et al. 1981; Prior, 1979).

Looking first at the validity of the clustering and specificity of the clinical symptomatology, perhaps because of the rarity of the disorder and thus the small size of samples, only a few multivariate analyses, such as have typified the work with Conduct, Anxiety, and Attention Deficit Disorders, appear to have been done to date (e.g., Prior, Boulton, Gajzago, & Perry, 1975; Prior, Perry, & Gajzago, 1975). At the level of clinical diagnosis, however, most good studies have been able to achieve satisfactory reliability (e.g., Cohen et al., 1978; Wing & Gould, 1979), and this, it could be argued, is one crude validation of empirical validity of the syndrome. As several investigators have pointed out, however, (e.g., DeMyer et al., 1981; Wing & Gould, 1979), though the *clustering* may be valid, *individual symptoms* lack specificity since they are found scattered across a variety of serious developmental and organic disorders.

The validity of the syndrome in terms of a systematic relationship to external criteria is largely unproven. Wing and Gould (1979), for example, though they could diagnose autism reliably, found that the core symptoms did not discriminate autistic from other severely developmentally impaired children and that there was no relationship to a set of other correlates of etiological import. This led them to conclude that the diagnosis of autism was neither valid nor useful and to argue for an alternative classification based on degree of social impairment—a sort of reversion to the once popular severity view of psychosis, though more restricted in symptomatology. A study of mentally retarded adults confirmed the greater validity of this alternative classification (Shah, Holmes, & Wing, 1982). This is an extreme view, however, and as study of the large literature on correlates of autism shows (see later text), even if Wing is correct, the heuristic value of the concept of autism has been considerable.

Empirical proof of the validity of autism as a syndrome does seem to have some support at the level of reliability of the DSM-III core symptomatology, but as yet the unequivocal utility, validity, and distinctiveness of the disorder remains to be demonstrated. Rutter (1974) supported the predictive validity of autism on the grounds of its association with a distinctive profile on IQ tests, a characteristic pattern of language impairments (Bartak, Rutter, & Cox, 1975), the development of seizures in adolescence, and a poor prognosis. This incomplete picture is still being elaborated, and the use of Axis V (highest level of adaptive functioning past year) in DSM-III ought to assist in this regard. Differential diagnosis from Mental Retardation has always been a problem, and the use of Axis V may permit further assessment of the proposition (Bartak & Rutter, 1976; Prior, 1979) that there may be two distinct autistic groups—a minority who are relatively high functioning and a majority for whom retardation is paramount.

A number of checklists that purport to diagnose autism and sometimes to differentiate it from other related disorders have been developed by various groups of clinicians and researchers (e.g., Rimland, 1964, 1965; Ruttenberg, Dratman, Franknoi, & Wenar, 1966). Some of these were compared by De-Myer, Churchill, Pontius, and Gilkey (1971) and showed an unsatisfactory degree of agreement.

As far as the validity of Childhood Onset Pervasive Developmental Disorder and Atypical or other forms is concerned, there appears to be so little study of these to date that it is difficult to comment (although see Quay, 1985). Kolvin in his studies found no such disorders though, as noted, an occasional case of later onset has appeared in other studies (e.g., Wing & Gould, 1979). Ornitz and Ritvo (1976) feel that later detection and consequent modification of symptomatology reflect mildness of the disorder or failure of early diagnosis. This issue is thus currently insoluble, and the most parsimonious view to take is that the case for their distinctiveness from autism is unsupported.

CORRELATES OF AUTISM

Cognitive

INTELLIGENCE

Earlier concepts of autism involved a belief that intelligence in autistic children was potentially normal but was masked by the severe social and behavioral abnormalities. This belief arose from the normal physical appearance and occasional signs of islets of normal or above normal ability in certain highly specific areas (such as music) in some cases. Consistent clinical and research evidence over the last 25 years has shown this conceptualization to be false with regard to the vast majority of cases. Between one-quarter and one-fifth of autistic children have a measured IQ in the normal-to-borderline range, with the majority being moderately to severely retarded (DeMyer et al., 1973; Wing, 1981). Despite resistance to this evidence at first, time and experience have shown that:

1. Testing is reliable in that there is little change in the level of tested intelligence over time and repeated testing produces similar results.

2. Testing has predictive validity since psychosocial outcome is predicted by IQ with considerable accuracy even when the child is "untestable" (De-Myer et al., 1973, DeMyer et al., 1974; Lotter, 1978). Untestable children have a very poor prognosis.

3. Nonverbal performance tests can be used successfully to elicit cooperation and even interest in autistic children, that is, to decrease the proportion who are untestable, and yet the majority continue to achieve in the retarded range on such tests.

Thus there is reasonable confidence that IQ testing is useful and enlightening, as it is for normal children. For most autistic children performance on verbal IQ tests is considerably poorer than that on performance tests, but both verbal and/or performance IQ are valid predictors of outcome. DeMyer et al. (1974) reported a highly significant correlation between initial and follow-up IQ, with most children remaining in the retarded range intellectually despite some improvement in social areas. There are few systematic data on social and adaptive functioning that might be used as an alternative or additional assessment technique. For the mentally retarded population, it is often considered that this type of assessment has greater utility in predicting adaptive outcome than standard IQ testing, and it might be considered that the same relationship could apply to autistic children. However, although many autistic children become at least superficially more sociable and can learn elementary survival skills, prognosis remains poor and strongly related to IQ.

Some have suggested that autistic children may be subgrouped on the basis of IQ (Bartak & Rutter, 1976; DeMyer et al., 1974; Prior, 1979) and may form (at least) two different groups: those with measured IQ in the normal range and those below. There appear to be behavioral as well as intellectual differences between the two groups (Bartak & Rutter, 1976; Freeman et al., 1981). Freeman et al. (1981) have reported detailed behavioral observations that show more overlap between mentally retarded and low functioning autistic groups than between normal children and high functioning autistic children. Researchers concerned with this issue affirm, however, that the core problems relating to social behavior and communication (DSM-III criteria A through E) are universal across the IQ range (Freeman et al., 1981; Prior, 1984).

The particular pattern of performance on intelligence tests is useful in illuminating particular strengths and weaknesses. For those in the moderately retarded range and above, there seems to be a particular and idiosyncratic test profile. Autistic children are least handicapped on subtests involving perceptual-motor and visuospatial skills (DeMyer et al., 1973; Hoffmann & Prior, 1982; Lockyer & Rutter, 1970; Tymchuk, Simmons, & Neafsey, 1977). Tasks that suggest their own solution and that do not require symbolic, analytic, or sequential processing strategies are those that elicit best levels of achievement. By contrast, tests involving language, abstract thought, flexible manipulation of symbolic or sequential material, and abstract conceptual knowledge (such as in the verbal subtests of the WISC) are poorly comprehended and elicit poor performance.

Hoffman and Prior (1982) have reported the assessment of a group of relatively high functioning autistic children on a battery of neuropsychological tests that confirms the above descriptions. Dawson (1983) reported remarkably similar results, with a lower functioning autistic sample showing significantly greater left- than right-hemisphere dysfunction and similarly greater left-hemisphere dysfunction than retarded and brain-damaged control subjects. Such results suggest that this particular pattern indicates strengths in cognitive processes mediated by the right hemisphere of the brain and severe handicap in those mediated by the left hemisphere. These data suggest directions in the search for etiology, in drawing attention to relatively specific brain–behavior relationships.

There are a number of theoretical considerations, however, that presently impose caution in following such an hypothesis concerning the profile of abilities in these children (Prior, 1985). One of the more important ones of these is that the majority cannot be said to show this pattern strongly since their cognitive level is very low in a global sense. The question of left hemisphere dysfunction in autism has been considered in detail in a recent review by Fein, Humes, Kaplan, Lucci, and Waterhouse (1984). They have rejected this theory on a number of grounds, including the lack of corroborative physiological and anatomical data; the criticism made above concerning its lack of applicability to all but higher functioning autistic children (although this must be qualified by the Dawson, 1983, study); perceived undue weight placed on the primacy of the language disorder with corresponding de-emphasis of social emotional factors; and the marked individual variation across cases and almost certainly in the biological/neurological substrates of autism.

Whatever the source and pattern of cognitive disabilities, it is unquestionable that the influence of intelligence in the overall picture of autism is a very dominant one. Not only does it predict whether meaningful language will be acquired as well as the long-term adaptive outcome, but in addition it exerts powerful effects in the assessment and investigation of every aspect of behavior (Prior, 1979). The pervasive developmental nature of the disorder is nowhere better illustrated than in the data relating to the intellectual functioning of autistic children.

LANGUAGE

It is generally accepted that the language disorder (DSM-III criteria C and D) is a central and ubiquitous feature of autism (Churchill, 1972; Rutter, 1974) and that the development of communicative language is strongly predictive of prognosis. Only a minority of autistic children acquire functional language, and even then their language is usually immature, deviant, inflexible, and lacking in communicative competence. Some writers have stressed the absence of ''inner language'' or symbolic thought, which is basic to normal language development (e.g., Hermelin & O'Connor, 1970; Ricks & Wing, 1975; Wing, 1976).

Comparative studies of autistic children and other groups with severe language impairment (e.g., Bartak et al., 1975) have shown that the former group show more deviant forms of language (delayed echolalia, pronominal reversal, repetitive and stereotyped output), more severe comprehension deficits, lack of gestural communication, and deficient spontaneous and appropriate social language, by comparison with dysphasic children. Ricks and Wing (1975) have noted other facets of social/communicative impairment such as impoverished facial expression, abnormal vocalization patterns, and poor comprehension of nonverbal communication which persist even when cognitive and language skills develop in other ways. Babbling is often notably absent in autistic children, and a delay in speaking first words is almost universal. More than half of children with this disorder never speak at all.

A recent study of the use of gesture for gaining and directing attention (Loveland & Landry, 1985) showed that use of gesture for directing attention (as for example in pointing to a desired object) was strongly influenced by developmental factors, including IQ and language competence, but that autistic children were notable for their impoverished use of gestures to communicate even when such gestures were within their repertoire. This problem of apparent lack of wish or intention to communicate is a key one in the puzzle of autism and requires investigation involving conceptualization beyond the current focus on deficient or absent skills (Prior, 1984).

A number of recent detailed studies and reviews of autistic language (see the *Journal of Autism and Developmental Disorders*, Vol. 11, No. 1, 1981) suggest that although some aspects of autistic language are similar to those found in other groups with language delay, particular deficits are evident in free speech in the use of syntax (Pierce & Bartolucci, 1977), prosody, semantics, and the ability to switch linguistic codes (Baltaxe & Simmons, 1975). Recent studies of echolalic speech seem to suggest that this phenomenon is a developmental one that persists abnormally in autistic children and that echolalia is frequently a response made in situations of communicative uncertainty or incomprehension (Carr, Schriebmann, & Lovaas, 1975; Shapiro & Lucy, 1978), a notion supported by Howlin's (1982) report that echolalia diminishes as linguistic competence increases.

Speaking autistic children appear to have greatest problems with the semantics and pragmatics of language corresponding to the cognitive and social components of their overall disabilities. Pragmatic problems arise from difficulties in understanding facial expression, gesture, and intonation and in simultaneous processing of situational and linguistic information (Menyuk & Wilbur, 1981). Syntactic and morphological problems are attributed to memory and/or sequencing difficulties. Thus, autistic children appear to have deficits in language-specific systems as well as in the cognitive, conceptual development basic to normal language proficiency. Ungerer and

Sigman (1981) and Sigman and Ungerer (1984) have suggested that autistic children do have sufficient sensorimotor capacities to acquire language; it is the impairments in play, imitation, and symbolic skills that are critical factors in their language handicaps.

Despite some equivocality and inconclusiveness in the literature, Tager-Flusberg (1981) has concluded that the various aspects of linguistic functioning are differentially impaired in autism. Developmental delay characterizes the phonological and syntactic aspects, but semantic and pragmatic aspects are especially deficient even in high functioning autistic speakers, reflecting impoverished social and cognitive development. The complexity, abstractness, and subtlety of social language are never mastered.

There is quite a substantial literature reporting on attempts to teach autistic children to speak and, more recently, to use sign language. Most reports, however, are single or small N case studies. Teaching speech is usually more successful with echolalic or minimally speaking children than with those who are mute (Stevens-Long, Schwartz, & Bliss, 1976). Much of the considerable effort expended has produced limited gains though, since autistic children tend not to generalize what they have learned and rarely go on to develop spontaneous original language (Harris, 1975; Koegel & Rincover, 1974). Some success in training in the use of sign language has been reported (e.g., Carr, Binkoff, Kologinsky, & Eddy, 1978; Konstantareas, Webster, & Oxman, 1979). This approach has not, however, provided any notable breakthrough. Some children show increased spontaneous communication, decreased self-stimulatory behavior, and increased social skills but rarely move from signed to spoken language. Again, degree of retardation and existing basic verbal skills are important predictors of success. Multisensory training combining speech and signs has been recommended (Konstantareas et al., 1979). The general increase in adaptive and communicative behavior that sometimes develops out of language intervention programs supports their continuing growth. But even with extensive and intensive training, realistic assessment suggests that the cognitive deficits that are fundamental in the disorder prohibit too much optimism.

A recent report by Frith and Snowling (1983) of reading ability in autistic children is worth noting, particularly since it provides further insight into the ways in which autistic children process language (in this case in print). Despite the inclusion of some autistic subjects with IQs in the retarded range, their group of eight cases showed unexpected linguistic competence in phonological and syntactic aspects of their reading. When semantic content was critical in reading tasks, however, such as in a ''Cloze'' task, the autistic children showed specific problems with reading comprehension. This breakdown in ability to use semantic cues occurred only when complementary syntactic cues (these are normally an integrated part of semantic content) were unavailable. Frith and Snowling suggested that reading for meaning was selectively impaired while reading for sound was intact and that perhaps the ''inner lexicon'' or word store was adequate while the ''inner encyclopedia'' was not. Since this is apparently a unique study in the area and the sample was very small, the generalizability of the results is unknown, but further exploration of reading processes in autistic children may be a useful means of illuminating strengths as well as weaknesses in language and cognitive areas.

MEMORY

Early studies reported impairments in visual and auditory memory (Bryson, 1972; Hagen, Winsberg, & Wolff, 1969), although methodological problems can be seen in retrospect to have detracted from the findings. Many autistic children appear to have good short-term rote memories (Boucher, 1978; Hermelin & O'Connor, 1970), for example, in the retention of rhymes, television jingles, and lists of nonmeaningful material. While auditory memory seems to be superior to visual memory (Prior, 1977a), there are extreme individual differences as shown, for example, in digit-span tests, and these correlate with intellectual level (Fyffe & Prior, 1978; Hermelin & O'Connor, 1970; Prior, 1977a). The methodological inadequacies of early research have precluded the development of a clear picture of memory functions in autism, but in studies where acquisition of the material to be tested for recall has been properly controlled, performance is consistent with mental age (e.g., Prior & Chen, 1976).

Boucher (1978) has assessed immediate and delayed recall for lists of words in a group of relatively high functioning autistic children matched for digit span with chronological age-matched controls. She demonstrated that echoic memory was consistent with (normal) digit span but that delayed recall was inferior. This latter deficit is probably a consequence of disabilities in language and semantic coding (see also Boucher & Warrington, 1976). Autistic children appear to show good acoustic memory only for recency recall and probably also for certain kinds of material such as lists of digits. Thus there appears to be considerable support for the Hermelin & O'Connor (1970) claim that autistic children store material in a raw, untransformed state, thus limiting their capacity to make adaptive use of information.

As in so much autism research, there is little to suggest syndrome-specific problems in memory; well-designed studies find little but developmentally influenced effects. The more interesting issue is not that of memory impairment (since the retardation of the majority almost inevitably means that this exists), but rather whether there is anything specific to the disorder in any aspect of memory. Thus, much has been made of the experiment of Hermelin and O'Connor (1970) in which recall of sentences was not better than for random strings of words. Recall was not aided by semantic and syntactic cues and did not profit by redundancy. Fyffe and Prior (1978) showed, however, that this recoding ability was not impaired in high functioning autistic children and that even in lower functioning children the ability was at a lower level rather than being absent. They claimed that results on this kind of task were interpretable in developmental terms and did not show autism-specific characteristics.

Intuitively, the inability to use redundancy and meaning in language is an appealing explanation for cognitive deficits, and it is concordant with other evidence (see subsequent text). However, well-controlled replications of a number of key studies relating to memory and cognition are critical to future theory building. There is insufficient evidence to suggest particular memory problems in autism; data so far show task-specific, mental-age level (and possibly motivational level) performance. Rather, it seems that the information processing factors that mediate between perception and memory should be a prime target for investigation.

HIGHER COGNITIVE PROCESSES

There is a general consensus supportive of the notion that cognitive deficits, embracing a variety of processing problems and with language as a central handicap, are basic and universal in autism and are significant in the social and behavioral problems (Prior, 1984; Rutter, 1974; 1983). The limited biological data available also offers some support for this view of the disorder since family studies show inherited general cognitive and learning problems (e.g., August, Stewart, & Tsai, 1981; Folstein & Rutter, 1977). Many cognitive processes such as simple discrimination learning, memory, and cross-modal learning are at a retarded level but consistent with mental age and IQ, thus supporting the developmental nature of the disorder. There are, though, some specific problems in higher order processing that become evident in work with less retarded children. Hermelin (1976) has concluded that coding and organization of stimuli via rules and categories, which is the normal way of reducing information load to permit adequate integration and interpretation of material, is deficient in autistic children. Instead they are likely to use short-term rote memory (untransformed), which is ineffective for higher order processing. Language deficits are seen as one aspect of a more general inability to use signs and symbols and to process temporally sequenced material, especially in the auditory modality. Visuospatial processing seems less impaired (Hermelin, 1976; Hermelin & O'Connor, 1970).

The stereotyped and restricted behavior patterns and task responses of these children may thus represent their reaction to input that they cannot process adaptively. Areas of functioning that require complex and flexible rule extraction and application, such as language and social interaction, are severely handicapped as a consequence of these specific processing difficulties. Learning-set experiments involving a variety of discriminative stimuli and task conditions have shown that autistic children have particular difficulty with two-dimensional symbolic stimuli as compared with three-dimensional concrete stimuli (Prior, 1977b; Prior & Chen, 1975; Prior & McGillivray, 1980). Such deficits may be linked to those noted by other workers, viz., lack of symbolic "representational" ability in young autistic children (Ricks & Wing, 1975; Sigman & Ungerer, 1984; Ungerer & Sigman, 1981).

Thus, autistic children are not only developmentally delayed in cognitive areas but have syndrome-specific problems in dealing with symbolic material, in capacity for imitation, learning, flexibility, creativity, and transformation and recombination of incoming information. These deficits remain in evidence even in children with relatively good prognosis and continue to limit capacity for normal development.

ATTENTION AND PERCEPTION

Autistic children are noted for their abnormal responses to stimuli in the environment. They are most commonly reported as underresponsive, but extreme overresponsiveness is also an idiosyncratic characteristic in some children in some situations (Prior, Gajzago, & Knox, 1976). Many appear particularly unresponsive to sound and often the impetus to referral is a concern that the child may be deaf. Young autistic children show disturbed perception in auditory, visual, tactile, olfactory, vestibular, and pain modalities; these peculiarities are apparent from very early in life and thus precede or at least coincide with the beginning of other behavioral anomalies. Such early manifestations may argue for the primary nature of perceptual abnormalities in the genesis of autism, but because of the difficulties of reliable diagnosis before the age of two or three years, we know little about their origins.

There are also problems of sensory integration in autistic as in other developmentally delayed and sensorily impaired groups (Wing, 1969). Ornitz and Ritvo (1976) have argued that perceptual, nystagmatic, and neurophysiological abnormalities suggest that perceptual inconstancy is basic to autism, but others have claimed that there are no specific problems of "simple perception" (Hermelin, 1976). Certainly the more extreme perceptual peculiarities seem to diminish with age.

Selective perception—or perhaps selective attention processes—do seem to be impaired (Frith, 1971) and may be seen in tasks requiring selection and processing of specific features of material. It is difficult to know, however, whether this is due to deficits at a sensory perception level or information decoding and encoding level of processing. Lovaas and his colleagues have proposed that "stimulus overselectivity" is basic to autism (see, e.g., Stevens-Long & Lovaas, 1974), but in fact this is a general developmental phenomenon (Koegel & Lovaas, 1978) strongly influenced by intelligence level and varying task parameters. Frankel, Simmons, Fichter, and Freeman (1984) have disputed this latter criticism of overselectivity and have reported data from a carefully controlled (albeit small sample size) study that demonstrates autism-specific, particular cue preference. Prior and McGillivray (1980), however, did not find overselectivity in discrimination learning-set tasks. Because of the importance of cue discrimination and use in basic learning, further research into this controversial phenomenon may be valuable.

Perceptual discrimination and learning appear to be enhanced by the provision of haptic cues (Frith & Hermelin, 1969; Prior & McGillivray, 1980) and by provision of tasks that suggest their own solution (DeMyer, Barton, & Norton, 1972; Prior, 1979). DeMyer (1976) has also noted improved performance when visual models of the task remain available during testing. Auditory perception and discrimination seem particularly impaired in autistic children, and this auditory "agnosia" has been linked to their difficulties in language acquisition (Rutter, 1974; Student & Sohmer, 1978).

Earlier reports of greater sensitivity of proximal rather than distal receptors (Hermelin & O'Connor, 1970; Schopler, 1966) have not been confirmed. Kootz, Marinelli, and Cohen (1981) reported that autistic children show the same hierarchy of receptor response sensitivity as normal children, although the responses of autistic children are slower and influenced by level of mental age and communicative skill.

Perception of self has long been considered deficient, and in some of the early literature this was considered of prime significance in the disorder. Recent data, however, lead to the conclusion that this deficit is not syndrome specific but part of the general characteristic developmental delay (Ferrari & Matthews, 1983; Spiker & Ricks, 1984). It is difficult to interpret the obtained data, however, when the visual self-recognition measure is assessment of the child's reaction to his image in a mirror when a spot of color has been surreptitiously placed on his face. It is arguable whether any reaction necessarily implies *self*-recognition. More sophisticated methods will be needed for further exploration of the autistic child's perception of self.

The strong influence of task difficulty in assessment of perception and discrimination ability should not be forgotten (Clark & Rutter, 1979; De-Myer, 1976). Overall, experimental findings seem to be primarily influenced by developmental rather than autism-specific factors; nevertheless, disorders of perception and organization of sensory input are a significant correlate of autism and deserve further investigation.

Attentional processes are neither well defined nor adequately understood (see Chapter 4) nor is their development well mapped in the normal-child area, and there are few experimental data relating to autism. Porges (1976) has claimed that autistic children are underactive both behaviorally and neurophysiologically, although there are minimal systematic empirical data to support this proposal. It is clear, though, that some attentional processes are not normal if one observes the frequent bizarre responses to the environment. In learning environments, autistic children, like other groups with a wide variety of handicapping conditions, do not orient, focus, control, or sustain their attention effectively. The influence of motivation and interest is also salient, since many children will show extreme overfocusing of attention on specific chosen activities, albeit of a nonadaptive kind.

LEARNING

Almost all aspects of learning appear to be impaired in autistic children. Learning through imitation is notably absent, although it must be admitted that there are few research studies to support this claim (Jones & Prior,

1985; Prior, 1979). Operant conditioning has been used with success to train imitative responses including motor and verbal performance (e.g., Hewitt, 1965; Lovaas & Butcher, 1974). Such training, however, seems rarely to generalize or to develop into spontaneous learning of new responses. As noted previously, autistic children are "overselective" in learning situations (they respond to only limited cues in multiple cue situations), which severely restricts their ability to learn, just as it does for retarded children. In fact, overselectivity is a prime index of developmental delay. Other behavioral techniques that are normally effective with teaching young normal and retarded children, such as prompt fading, seem ineffective with autistic children (Rincover & Koegel, 1975; Schriebman, 1975).

Operant techniques have also been used to decrease unwanted behavior such as self-multilation, stereotypies, and antisocial behavior (Foxx & Azrin 1973; Lovaas & Butcher, 1974). Autistic children are responsive to reinforcement, although they are often idiosyncratic in their reward preferences; they can and do learn with carefully graded, systematically and consistently applied programs and appropriate reinforcers. It is the failure to generalize beyond the immediate learning situation that is so discouraging (Prior, 1979). Although this failure is shared with other handicapped groups (Harris, 1975), it seems relatively more severe in autism. Highly structured, task-oriented, well controlled individual and classroom programs are reported as most successful in aiding progress in learning and socialization (Bartak & Rutter, 1973; Schopler, Brehm, Kinsbourne, & Reichler, 1971). The normality of responses to success and failure observed among autistic children has been noted (Churchill, 1971; Davids, 1974) and the increase in noncompliant or withdrawal responses when tasks become too taxing is similar to that observed in assessment of normal children.

Despite the gains made with operant procedures and precision teaching, the symptom of "resistance to new learning" in autism is a pervasive one.

Psychophysiological Factors

These factors have been comprehensively reviewed by James and Barry (1980) and summarized by DeMyer et al. (1981). Although James and Barry suggested that "the central behavioral anomalies associated with the condition may result from abnormal neurophysiological reactivity to sensory stimulation" (1980, p. 506), their review led to the conclusion that no abnormalities could be specifically related to "early onset psychosis," and where abnormalities were found their interpretation in arousal terms could be only speculative. Importantly, their review emphasized the probable significant influence of maturational factors.

Most EEG studies suffer from methodological and technical deficiencies as well as from interpretive difficulties. (See Chapter 8.) Small (1981) has argued, however, that despite these problems the current EEG evidence supports the existence of CNS impairment as central in autism.

Evoked potential studies also have technical and interpretation problems, especially since there are idiosyncratic and often severe attentional and auditory-processing deficits in autistic subjects. Studies to date, though limited and often lacking controls for retardation factors, suggest some abnormalities in autistic children in both visual and auditory evoked responses, the interpretation of which is still obscure. James and Barry (1980) also reviewed data pertaining to cardiovascular, respiratory, and electrodermal activity without being able to derive very much pertaining to autism. Lack of normal developmental data as well as sampling and methodological problems in the psychophysiological research area preclude useful conclusions.

Motor Development and Perceptuomotor Skills

An early assumption was that autistic children exhibited normal motor development with few obvious signs of neurodevelopmental problems; in some children the grace and skill in spontaneous movement was notable. Informal clinical reports suggested that many were especially skillful in their manipulation of objects and could climb with great facility. Systematic investigation has shown, however, that motor milestones are often reported as slow (DeMyer et al., 1981; Kolvin, Ounsted, Humphrey, & McNay, 1971), and when formally tested, motor development is rarely found to be consistent with chronological age.

In a large retrospective study, Ornitz, Guthrie, and Farley (1978) reported delay in posturomotor development (as assessed via age of first walking), although it was mild to moderate for the majority of children. Delays were primarily seen after six months, although this could reflect greater ease of remembering developmental stages after this age. There was little relationship between motor retardation and severity of social and language impairments. Most of the limited data available suggest that developmental delay in motor and perceptuomotor skills is a feature of the disorder to the same extent as it is in other aspects of learning and development. DeMyer's group has investigated this area (DeMyer, 1976) and has reported that gross motor abilities involving the lower limbs, for example, in stair climbing, hopping, skipping, running, are at a retarded level but somewhat less handicapped by comparison with fine motor and ball play tasks. These latter are significantly poorer than in retarded control children. DeMyer, who described autistic children as "neurologically disabled," noted that visual–motor integration skills were very low.

Autistic children often have difficulty in carrying out organized sequential movements in conventional patterns, for example, in riding a tricycle, or in coping with more than one motor task at a time (Wing, 1976). Motor imitation skills are also very poor (DeMyer et al., 1973). Jones and Prior (1985) found imitation of gestures and body movements to be at a level lower than that of mental age matched controls and confirmed DeMyer's claim (DeMyer et al., 1981) that these children are "dyspraxic" (i.e., unable to perform developmentally appropriate integrated motor sequences). This dyspraxia may underlie the failure to use gesture that is a characteristic of autistic children.

Fulkerson and Freeman (1980) have reported a motor coordination deficit in autistic children, task matched with younger controls. Specific deficits, as opposed to developmental delay, were found only when task conditions were at a high demand level, and even then their subjects were able to improve their performance when provided with facilitating task conditions. Such difficulties with complex coordinated motor tasks suggest central nervous system dysfunction, an hypothesis supported both by DeMyer et al.'s (1973) finding that most of their autistic subjects showed "brain dysfunction" indices more than one standard deviation from the normal means and the Jones and Prior (1985) report of a marked excess of "soft signs" (see Chapter 8) of neurological dysfunction in their autistic group.

Although it might be that a proportion of reported cases show neurodevelopmental problems because the autism is associated with other primary biologically based disorders, there does seem sufficient evidence to support an overall claim for abnormalities in this area. More information on motor development in the higher functioning minority might be helpful in distinguishing between autism-related and general retardation-related problems.

Damasio and Maurer (1978) have emphasized the motor deficits of autistic children, suggesting that they particularly implicate basal ganglia structures in etiology. Vilensky, Damasio, and Maurer (1981) reported abnormalities of gait including reduced stride lengths, increased stance times, increased hip flexion, and decreased knee extension and ankle dorsiflexion. None of these, however, seemed systematically related to other developmental indices. They suggested that there were similarities between autistic and Parkinsonian patients in these gait patterns. It should be noted, however, that the *range* of measurements was the same for autistic as for normal children and the interpretation of significant *mean* differences should be considered with caution. DeMyer (1976) noted no abnormalities of gait in her group.

Stereotypies

Repetitive, stereotyped movement patterns such as rocking, finger flicking, head banging, and a variety of self-mutilating behaviors are relatively common in low functioning autistic children. This is particularly distressing and frustrating for parents and teachers and is often a barrier to the learning of adaptive behavior. It is not a particular characteristic of autism, however, but a feature of the behavior of a proportion of mentally retarded, brain-damaged, and physically and sensorily impaired children such as deaf-blind rubella cases (Werry, Carlielle, & Fitzpatrick, 1983; see also Chapter 7). It is also believed more common in institutionalized children whose daily routine may leave them with periods of time with no organized alternative activities. There are few data on the frequency, etiology, and significance of motor stereotypies in autism; however, a variety of successful treatment approaches, mostly of the behavioral variety, have emerged in the last few years and these permit some control over the stereotypies and self-destructive behavior along with training to alternative modes of behavior (Lovaas & Butcher, 1974).

Social Behavior

Perhaps because of the strong emphasis on research into cognitive deficits, detailed experimental investigation of social behavior has only recently been reported. The inability of the cognitive disability theory to satisfactorily explain the severe social impairments found in the disorder has been repeatedly noted (Hermelin, 1982; Prior, 1984; Rutter, 1983; Wing & Gould, 1979).

Lack of normal social development in early infancy is seen in the absence of attachment or bonding and comfort-seeking with parents; the failure to assume an anticipatory posture preparatory to being picked up; and the stiffening of the body against or passive rejection of physical contact. Some children may accept tickling, romping, or swinging. The most severely handicapped autistic children do not appear to differentiate between people (DeMyer, 1976), and even with higher functioning children there is deficient selective bonding. Varying features of the social impairment described by Wing and Gould (1979) include aloofness and indifference, especially toward other children; passive interaction, that is, nonresistance to approach by others; and inappropriate social approaches, mainly in pursuit of repetitive, idiosyncratic preoccupations that take no account of the feelings of those approached. The quality of social interaction is universally deviant, notably in its lack of reciprocity (Rutter, 1978) and the apparent complete lack of ability to empathize.

Socially unacceptable and difficult behavior is also common, including screaming, temper tantrums, undressing in public, amassing collections of objects that must be taken everywhere, purloining of desired objects, and embarrassing verbal, eating, and toileting behavior. Some children are abnormally quiet, passive, and hyporesponsive. While behavior problems such as these often improve, especially with systematic training, after the age of five or six years, the basic social aloofness and isolation are more difficult to modify. Some children do form relationships of a dependent and stereotyped kind with particular family members or teachers. Ethologists such as Richer (1978) and Tinbergen and Tinbergen (1972) have suggested that autistic children actively avoid social encounters, although Clark and Rutter (1981) claim that maladaptive asocial and stereotyped behavior is more common when children are left alone.

Unfortunately, the core social problems persist throughout life, are resistant to treatment, and are little affected by improvement in cognitive and language skills except at a superficial level. Even the handful of autistic adults who show some insight into their deficiencies are unable to experience empathy (Rutter, 1983). It seems that the basic foundations of social cognition that normally develop in reciprocal adult–infant interactions from the beginning of life are missing in autistic children, and this loss is never overcome.

Recent experimental work by Hobson (1983) has indicated specific impairments in the recognition and discrimination of emotional expression on human faces, in contrast with adequate discrimination of object and action. Hobson's autistic subjects also showed deficiencies in the ability to distinguish age-related features of human faces, suggesting a lack of "personal knowledge" (Hobson, 1983, p. 351).

Rutter (1983) has conceptualized the problem as a deficit in the processing of social and emotional cues. Hermelin (1982) ascribes the social impairments to basic developmental deficits in genetically preprogrammed capacities for nonverbal as well as verbal communication. Failure to develop adequate communication in either thought or feeling can thus lead to both cognitive and social impairments arising from a common source. This is perhaps the most elegant theoretical formulation of autism so far offered.

Neurological Pathological Correlates

The association of a wide assortment of genetic, neurological, biochemical, and pathological factors with autism is well established (Cohen & Shaywitz, 1982; DeMyer et al., 1981; Maurer & Damasio, 1982; Ornitz & Ritvo, 1976). These include an increased frequency of the disorder in identical twins and in families (Folstein & Rutter, 1977; Ornitz & Ritvo, 1976; Ritvo, Ritvo, & Brothers, 1982); evidence of minor physical anomalies (Gualtieri, Adams, Shen, & Loiselle, 1982); minor or complex neurological signs (DeMyer et al., 1981; Maurer & Damasio, 1982; Ornitz & Ritvo, 1976); EEG and electrophysiological abnormalities (DeMyer et al., 1981; James & Barry, 1980; Ornitz & Ritvo, 1976; Tanguay & Edwards, 1982); hematological, immunological, and biochemical abnormalities (Piggot, 1979), particularly in biogenic amines like serotonin (Geller, Ritvo, Freeman, & Yuwiler, 1982; Young, Cavanagh, Anderson, Shaywitz, & Cohen, 1982); and increased frequency of pre-, peri-, and postnatal insults.

There is a strong association with certain disorders such as phenylketonuria and tuberous sclerosis (DeMyer et al., 1981; Wing & Gould, 1979) and with antenatal rubella infection (Chess, 1971, 1977). Further, later development of frank neurological signs, most conspicuously seizures, including infantile spasm, is common (Ornitz & Ritvo, 1976). These were noted, interestingly, in about one-third of Kanner's original cases, all of whom were initially adjudged neurologically normal.

As is so often the case in psychopathological disorders of childhood (and adults), however, none of these abnormal correlates is unique to or inevitable in autism (see Chapters 6 and 8) and most are highly inversely correlated with IQ and, possibly, with degree of impairment of social interaction in general (Wing & Gould, 1979). Studies to date of autistic children, probably mostly of the nuclear or Kanner type, using advanced neuroradiological methods such as CT scans have shown no abnormalities (see Campbell, Rosenbloom, & Perry, 1982; Prior, Tress, Hoffmann, & Boldt, 1984).

In short, these correlates in general suggest some as yet undiscovered relationship between autism and brain damage or major dysfunction and the potential profitability of a more refined study of organic disorders. (See Chapter 8.) Progress so far has been severely hampered by the use of heterogeneous, ill-defined samples of autistic children; by methodological and measurement problems in biological research; by the lack of normative developmental data for comparison; and by the still relatively unsophisticated level of our knowledge of brain–behavior relationships. While there is a strong belief in the proposed organic etiology in autism, and while a close analysis of the specific dysfunctions considered central to autism *may* implicate certain areas of the brain (Dawson, 1983; Hoffmann & Prior, 1982; Maurer & Damasio, 1982), it appears that these areas can be damaged in a variety of ways by a variety of etiological agents. Thus, more precise areas remain to be positively identified and in many cases of autism, the etiological agent as well. Since it is possible to postulate that damage can occur partially or completely, in a very localized area or more diffusely, then the possibility of incomplete and of widely varying associated degrees of neurological impairment and behavior disturbance is high. A variety of etiological agents and of biological dysfunctions probably are relevant in the genesis of the disorder.

Family Correlates

The considerable methodological problems of this type of study are discussed in Chapter 9. No doubt because of these problems, opinions on the frequency of pathological attitudes and disorders in the parents and families of psychotic children vary greatly. Though it is difficult to disentangle studies of autistic from schizophrenic children, most probably were concerned with autism and so are discussed here. Earlier work (Bettelheim, 1956; Esman, Kahn, & Nyman, 1959; Kanner, 1943; Mahler, 1965; Rank, 1949; Szurek, 1956) was nearly unanimous in considering that childhood psychosis is frequently (and in some cases always, e.g., Reiser, 1963; Szurek, 1956) accompanied by significant psychopathology in one or both parents. Kanner's view (see Eisenberg & Kanner, 1956) that parents of autistic children were of the refrigerator type—highly intelligent obsessive people incapable of warmth—is probably best known, though he also emphasized the primary affection defect in the child (Kanner, 1943, 1973). Mahler (1965), Rank (1949), and Reiser (1963) expressed a point of view that is essentially similar to that enunciated earlier by Kanner, namely, that the mothers are incapable of giving their child a warm sustaining relationship because of their own severe disturbance (psychosis, depression, and immaturity). In a well-designed study, Ogdon, Bass, Thomas, and Lordi (1968) found parents of autistic children to have significantly more psychopathology along several dimensions of the Rorschach (though not of Kanner's perfectionistic kind) than a matched group of parents of normal children. With the exception of the last study, most of these views appear to have been derived largely from interviews of varying duration, some psychoanalytic, some not, and in the absence of proper control groups.

Since 1960, studies have increasingly begun to produce negative findings (Cox, Rutter, Newman, & Bartok, 1975; Creak & Ini, 1960; DeMyer et al., 1972; Klebanoff, 1959; Kolvin, 1971; Rutter & Lockyer, 1967; Schopler, 1974). These studies differ from those with positive findings in (1) using less observer error-prone measures; (2) using proper contrast groups, that is, the nonautistic severely disabled such as mentally retarded, handicapped, or aphasic children; and (3) separating out autistic and schizophrenic children. As such, they are more acceptable. They suggest the following: (1) parents of autistic children are (mostly) normal and have families free of schizophrenia (Anthony, 1958; Cox et al., 1975; Creak & Ini, 1960; DeMyer et al., 1972; Kanner, 1954; Kolvin, Garside, & Kidd, 1971; Kolvin, Ounsted, Richardson, & Garside, 1971; Lotter, 1966; Rutter & Lockyer, 1967) and are free of schizophrenic symptoms, such as abnormal thought styles common in relatives of schizophrenics (Lennox, Callias, & Rutter, 1977); (2) when parental psychopathology is present, it is either the result of having a handicapped child (Cox et al., 1975; Klebanoff, 1959; Pittfield & Oppenheim, 1965) or the result of scapegoating by mental health professionals (Schopler, 1974), or, less certain, a reflection of an etiologically distinctive subgroup (Anthony, 1958; Rimland, 1964). A recent review by DeMyer et al. (1981) refutes even more strongly the view that autism is associated with antecedent parental psychopathology but reaffirms the reactive psychopathology that both having an autistic child and, unwittingly, professionals create in parents.

A frequently attributed characteristic of parents due initially to Kanner, that parents are more intelligent and of higher social class, was initially affirmed (Cox et al., 1975; Kolvin, 1971; Lotter, 1967; Rimland, 1964, 1974; Rutter & Lockyer, 1967; Treffert, 1970), but this has increasingly been disputed and is now thought to be due to selective referral patterns and diagnostic bias favoring higher social classes (DeMyer et al., 1981; Wing, 1980).

Epidemiology

PREVALENCE

It is obvious that estimates of the frequency of autism require a reliable and valid way of detecting a "case." Since no such universally accepted diagnostic criteria or method of so doing exists, all studies must be subject to an unknown degree of error. Despite this, there is remarkable agreement in the few studies that have attempted to estimate the frequency of autism in the population as a whole, though agreement on other population parameters such as social classes is less.

Studies in England (Lotter, 1966, 1967; Wing, 1980) Denmark, (Brask, 1972), Sweden (Gillberg, 1984), and Japan (Hoshino, Kumashiro, Yashima, Tachibana, & Watanabe, 1982), using different methods of case detection ranging from teacher screening to exceptional children registers, varying ways of detecting core (usually Kanner-type) symptoms, and somewhat differing age ranges, all showed that for children under 14 prevalence is of the order of 4.5 cases per 10,000. Of these, about half at the most have a severe, nuclear, or classic disorder and half a mild degree, though still diagnosable as autism.

Children with autistic features but with the incomplete syndrome—as would be expected from the nonspecific nature of individual symptoms of autism (see previous discussion)—are considerably more numerous: four times the above rate in Wing's study (Wing & Gould, 1979). The only U.S. studies of a comparable nature appear to be two in number, the first, that by Treffert (1970) in the state of Wisconsin, which revealed a much lower figure of 0.7 per 10,000 although his methods were less reliable than those of the studies in Europe, where the maintenance of registers is particularly well developed. The second, the Prospective Perinatal Collaborative Study (Torrey, Hersh, & McCabe, 1975) found 14 psychotic children in 30,000 at age 7, a frequency of 4.5 per 10,000, which is remarkably similar to the European and Japanese figures.

For obvious reasons, figures for clinics are in general much higher, ranging from 3 to 10 percent of the caseload depending on the interest in autism, the number of child psychiatrists, and other similar detection services in the area.

SEX RATIO

This varies from Lotter's 2:1 excess of males to about 10:1 (Hoshino et al., 1982; Wing, 1981; Wing & Gould, 1979). The significance of this excess of males has to be tempered by the ordinary 2:1 male–female ratio in severely handicapped children (Wing, 1981; Wing & Gould, 1979) and by the low numbers of actual cases found in even quite large-scale studies. In spite of these problems, there seems to be a clear trend for an excess of males, but the exact size of this excess remains in doubt. It is probably similar to that seen in Developmental Language Disorders (Wing, 1981) and Attention Deficit Disorders (see Chapter 4).

AGE

Onset of the disorder in DSM-III criteria is set at under 30 months, but it does seem that occasional later cases (e.g., Lotter, 1966; Wing & Gould, 1979) that otherwise meet the criteria for Autism do occur. Ornitz and Ritvo (1976) claim that it is always present at birth and the cases of later onset are in fact missed cases because of mildness or the fact that the infant is "excessively good" and at first creates no problems. No firm conclusion can be drawn on this issue, though as has already been pointed out, in spite of the DSM-III criteria, there is some reason to believe that in exceptional cases, the disorder may present after the infancy/toddler stage. It is this that has given rise to the separate category of Childhood Onset Pervasive Developmental disorder, although its validity remains questionable.

As far as age prevalence rates are concerned, there is good evidence that the frequency of the full-blown syndrome of Autism declines to an unknown degree with age. For example, Wing and Gould (1979), Hoshino et al. (1982), Knobloch & Pasamanick (1975), Rimland (1974), and Shah et al. (1982) all found somewhat lower rates in older children or adults, though the size of this effect varied and is subject to the inherent variation in small numbers. This does agree, however, with the idea that, in some cases at least, there is some remission or more probably mitigation in symptomatology, though in others, the reduction with age may be due to mortality in very severe cases (Knobloch & Pasamanick, 1975). Reclassification of cases to one of the categories of mental retardation or other handicap is also likely to influence older age prevalence rates. This can occur for purely administrative/service reasons.

For a discussion of social class, see the foregoing section Parental Correlates and Chapter 10.

Outcome

In contrast to most other areas, there appear to be few new data in this area since 1975. Perhaps as a consequence, this area is much more affected by poor methodology, of which the most conspicuous is the failure to specify diagnostic criteria and to distinguish between autism and other kinds of childhood psychoses. For example, of 19 studies examined by Werry (1979), only eight seemed to cover autism exclusively or clearly. Even DeMyer et al. (1981) were not able to resolve this problem in their comprehensive review.

Here, the criteria for inclusion are based on prospectiveness, on use of the DSM-III symptomatology or close approximations, and on age of onset, or at least identification before age 5 years. The reason for the latter somewhat more relaxed criterion is that onset data are the least consistently given, being a recent criterion, and because the apparent rarity of psychoses of onset between 30 months and 5 years (see above) would not create too much error. Nevertheless, these criteria collectively have some inherent weaknesses. Inasmuch as few studies actually make the diagnosis early in life, prospectiveness from diagnosis will tend to overemphasize poor outcome (e.g., Knobloch & Pasamanick, 1975) in that any cases spontaneously improving will be missed. It will also minimize early mortality. Another problem is that, as would be expected, few if any of the studies were actually that of the true natural history, since to withhold "treatment" is impossible in such a severe disorder in modern societies. With the possible exception of intensively socializing treatments available only to a very few, however, there is not much evidence that treatment has any specific effect in overcoming the core symptomatology of autism (DeMyer et al., 1981; Prior, 1979).

DeMyer et al. (1981) reviewed what they considered to be the better and longer (more than 5 years) studies with a total number of 339 subjects. Overall outcome was good or better in only 5 to 19 percent with the majority around 14 to 19 percent. Rather consistently, approximately half were institutionalized, though DeMyer et al. noted that the number increases with age as parents become less able to cope. In the studies reviewed containing these data, about 50 percent had useful communicative speech, but only 10 percent of those mute at 5 had subsequently developed any language. DeMyer et al. note that, though outcome is generally poor, there is nevertheless a general improvement in symptomatology in many cases.

Campbell and Green (1984) have followed up 90 autistic children seen at Bellevue Hospital for periods ranging from 9 months to 15 years. Despite continuing therapy, in most cases an increased number were in institutions. At follow-up IQ remained relatively stable and as in other studies was a good predictor of outcome. Although some children developed attachments and there was decreased withdrawal in many, even the more intelligent cases had persisting serious impairments in social relations. These authors described most of their teenage cases as anergic and lacking in initiative. Some researchers have reported postpubertal cognitive deterioration (Coleman, 1978; Gillberg & Schaumann, 1981) after relatively steady prepubertal cognitive development (Waterhouse & Fein, 1984). The latter authors reported similar patterns of cognitive growth and decline in a subgroup of schizophrenic children (diagnosed by DSM-III criteria).

A 10-year follow-up of 93 cases in Australia, the majority of whom would meet current DSM-III criteria, showed that about 17 percent were in residential schools or institutionalized, 8 percent were in schools for moderately and severely retarded children, 8 percent were in schools for mildly mentally retarded, and 8 percent were in mainstream education, although needing considerable support in most cases (Prior & Sanson, 1979). Forty percent were still attending special centers for autistic children. Apart from the low institutionalization rate, the findings were very similar to those from other countries, especially in showing that the same predictors of outcome (IQ, speech development, and severity of autism) were clearly evident.

A study that differs from others in including a large proportion of "organic cases" and 85 percent of very early (and therefore unreliable) diagnoses (Knobloch & Pasamanick, 1975) unsurprisingly reported results at variance with most other surveys. Almost all children were still retarded while 75 percent were described as no longer autistic.

To explain these discrepancies, one must take care not to use the outcome criteria (loss of autism), since this would be tautological. The criteria for diagnosis (if not the methods of diagnosis) were apparently rigorous. Wing and Gould (1979) and Shah et al. (1982) showed that "Autism" is only one subgroup of severe abnormality of social relationships associated with severe brain damage/mental retardation. It seems more reasonable to conclude, therefore, that the younger the child, the more difficult it may be to diagnose Autism. The objection that because the group had frank neurological disease that a diagnosis of Autism is precluded is not tenable using DSM-III criteria (nor in view of the later developments in the disorder, e.g., Rutter & Lockyer, 1967).

Variables that have been found to predict prognosis (DeMyer et al., 1981; Brown, 1960, 1963) are IQ (especially the closely related factor of language development; Lotter, 1974) and a variety of variables that seem to reflect severity, such as symptomatology, social development, and neurological signs. In addition to the usual social/behavioral and cognitive aspects of prognosis, one must note the medical ones too, notably development of frank neurological disease, seizures, and death. However, with the exception of seizures, which have been reported to be as high as 25 percent (Rutter & Lockyer, 1967) and occurred in 20 percent of Kanner's original 11, other medical factors are infrequent but significant. DeMyer (1976) has claimed that her "Work/School Status" score, an attitudinal variable reflecting cooperation and accessibility in the childhood years, has very good validity as an outcome predictor.

In summary then, though there are some changes (often positive) in symptomatology and even in prevalence with time (DeMyer et al., 1981; Shah et al., 1982), autism is an often lifelong, seriously handicapping disorder, the outcome of which is best predicted by initial severity and is generally similar to that of children of comparable intellectual level. Interpersonal relationship problems continue although not necessarily at an "autistic" level. In those with higher intellectual ability, the persistent lack of "social intelligence" has been noted to result in poorer than expected levels of personal, social, and vocational adaptation (DeMyer et al., 1981; Prior, 1984). This generally poor picture is complicated even further by the development in a significant number of cases of neurological disorder, notably seizures, in a much smaller number cases who die, and as in other severe developmental handicaps, in the risk of institutionalization, increasing for family and social reasons with adulthood. The age at which diagnosis is made may influence sampling and hence prognosis estimates, thus this needs to be studied further.

SCHIZOPHRENIC AND ALLIED DISORDERS

Introduction

Bender (1953) pointed out that while schizophrenia is characteristically regarded as beginning after puberty, both Kraepelin and Bleuler stated that in about 5 percent of cases, the disorder began in childhood. According to Bleuler, this could be even in the first year of life. A good description of Kraepelin's views can be found in Green et al. (1984).

One of the first English-language papers was that of Potter (1933), who outlined a set of six diagnostic criteria derived from adult Schizophrenia but adapted somewhat to suit children. He then looked for children with such characteristics in a hospitalized mentally retarded population and found a number who could thus be diagnosed as schizophrenic. Bradley and Bowen (1941) had eight criteria, which differed from Potter's by concentrating more on observable behavior, thus omitting the classical symptoms of disturbances of thinking so emphasized by Bleuler. Bender's work, beginning in the 1940s, is described by Kanner (1971) in his excellent historical review of the childhood psychoses, as "widening the roof beyond Kraepelinian boundaries" (p. 17). For three decades, she was the strongest proponent of the continuity of all forms of infantile and childhood psychoses with adult

Schizophrenia (see Bender, 1953). While U.S. psychiatry, over Kanner's (1971) acerbic protests, was abandoning the idea of the separateness of schizophrenia from other childhood psychoses, English child psychiatry led by Anthony (1958) and subsequently Rutter (1972) argued that the ICD-8 and the DSM-II "childhood schizophrenia" category was misleading in failing to differentiate Schizophrenia, Autism, and other psychoses. Further, since Kolvin's (1971) comparative study of infantile (onset before age 3 years) and late-onset (at age 5 to 15 years) psychoses had noted symptomatology which, in the late-onset group were adult-type Schneiderian first-ranked symptoms (see DSM-III criterion A later), he claimed that Schizophrenia was apparently identical with the adult disorder, and the term "childhood" should be dropped. So successful was this argument that the ICD-9 and the DSM-III both have complied, noting that schizophrenia can occur before adolescence and dropping the separate category of Childhood Schizophrenia. It should be noted, though, that this is not a reversion to Bender's position since she denied the separateness of Autism and other psychoses reflected in the ICD-9 and DSM-III. Also, as Kanner (1971) pointed out, she also had more elastic symptomatological criteria than in present classifications.

An important issue relating to schizophrenia in childhood that appears to remain unresolved in DSM-III is that while adult psychiatric disorders are generally assumed (though often incorrectly) to exist in a relatively stable social, cognitive, and biological background, this is clearly not so for childhood disorders, where developmental influences are fluid as well as powerful.

A review dependent on an age-based diagnostic position faces problems since studies of schizophrenia using adult criteria and clearly separating it from autism and other psychoses are few indeed in children under 15. Most of the existing studies either can be seen to be concerned primarily with autism or hopelessly entangled between the two or even three types of psychoses (e.g., Annell, 1963). If one relies on adult research, however, it is unclear how much of this work is actually valid for children under 15 (most adult studies seem to begin at 15). One exception is the area of children "at risk" of developing schizophrenia in later life, and although few of the subjects in these studies are yet at the age of maximum risk, it seems important to include in any discussion of Schizophrenia in children a section on this topic (as is done subsequently).

Schizophrenic and Allied Disorders: Principal Characteristics

DIAGNOSTIC CRITERIA AND SUBCLASSIFICATIONS

The DSM-III, after several pages of discussion of symptomatology, lists for Schizophrenic Disorders the following necessary and sufficient criteria (abbreviated):

A. At least one of the following during a phase of the illness:

    1. Bizarre delusions (being controlled, thought broadcasting, thought insertion, or thought withdrawal).

2. Somatic, grandiose, religious, nihilistic or other delusions without persecutory or jealous content.
3. Delusions with persecutory or jealous content if accompanied by hallucinations.
4. Auditory hallucinations in which either a voice gives a running commentary on the individual's behavior or thoughts or two or more voices converse with each other.
5. Auditory hallucinations on several occasions.
6. Incoherent, marked loosening of associations, markedly illogical thinking or marked poverty of content of speech if associated with at least one of the following:
6.1 blunted flat or inappropriate affect;
6.2 delusions or hallucinations;
6.3 catatonic or other grossly disorganized behavior.

B. Deterioration from a previous level of functioning in such areas as work/social relations and self care.
C. Duration: continuous signs of the illness for at least six months at some time with some signs of illness at present. The six month period must include phase during which there were symptoms from A with or without a prodromal or residual phase. (Prodromal and residual are defined as deterioration in functioning either beginning or persisting before or after onset and having at least two symptoms classified as prodromal or residual—social withdrawal, impaired functioning, peculiar behavior, impairment in personal hygiene, blunt, flat or inappropriate affect, digressive, vague, over-elaborate, circumstantial or metaphorical speech, odd or bizarre indication and unusual perceptual experiences falling short of true hallucinations.)
D. The full depressive or manic syndrome, if present, developed after any psychotic symptoms or was brief in duration relative to the duration of the psychotic symptoms in A.
E. Onset of prodromal or active phase of the illness before age 45.
F. Not due to any Organic Mental Disorder or Mental Retardation (American Psychiatric Association, 1980, p. 188–190).

Subtypes described are the Disorganized (incoherence, silly affect, and no systematized delusions), which resembles the ICD-9 Hebephrenic type, Paranoid, Undifferentiated, and Residual. In addition, the course of the disorder is classified in a fifth digit of the code number as subchronic (lasting 6–24 months), chronic (more than 24 months), acute on subchronic, acute on chronic, or in remission.

When duration is less than six months but greater than two weeks, the diagnosis of Schizophreniform Disorder is made. When less than two weeks *and* a psychosocial stressor "that would evoke symptoms of distress in almost anyone" is present, Brief Reactive Psychosis is to be diagnosed.

Schizoaffective disorder lacks any diagnostic criteria and is offered reluctantly as a possibility when the symptomatology meets both Schizophrenic and Affective Disorder criteria.

Paranoid Disorders are characterized only by paranoid delusions. Their greatest interest as far as children is concerned is that this group of disorders includes Shared Paranoid Disorder (that is, folie à deux).

Other diagnostic categories relevant to this section for children are Schizoid Disorder, and Schizotypal Personality Disorder. The first is to be found in the Childhood Disorders section and, despite the unfortunate choice of name—quite misleading in view of its history (see Wolff & Chick, 1980)—is characterized primarily by absent or reduced interest in social contacts *without any schizophrenic type symptoms and without any necessary ultimate connection with Schizophrenia*. Thus, the disorder is best regarded along with those of Anxiety Dysphorical Withdrawal (see Chapter 3). For this reason, no more will be said here, except to enter a plea for a change of name in DSM-IV.

On the other hand, Schizotypal Personality Disorder is a sort of incomplete form of Schizophrenia having *some* but not sufficient of the features (four of the following: magical thinking, ideas of reference, social isolation, recurrent illusions, odd speech, inadequate rapport, suspiciousness, undue social anxiety). An important point is that though Personality Disorders are ordinarily not to be diagnosed under the age of 18, this one specifically includes children and indexes *borderline child* as a synonym. While there have been only one or two studies of Schizotypal Personality Disorder or the Borderline Child that are of sufficient quality to deserve comment here (e.g., Wolff and Chick, 1980), this category would seem to have some validity in defining a small group of odd but not psychotic children whom most mental health professionals who work with children will recognize. Wolff and Chick (1980) argue that Asperger's syndrome described in 1944 (autistic psychopathy) is in fact this diagnostic entity. By contrast, Wing (1981) argues that Asperger's syndrome is more productively considered as related to autism since the cognitive and social impairments are similar. Wolff and Chick's (1980) comparison of what they called "schizoid," autistic, and control children showed the former two groups to be similar in some aspects of cognitive performance although the "schizoid" group appeared somewhat less handicapped than the autistic group.

It should be pointed out that despite much confusion in the literature on "borderline states," the DSM-III criteria for Borderline Personality Disorder as for Schizoid Disorder show little in common with either the psychoses in general or Schizophrenia in particular. It was to try to resolve this confusion that the DSM-III chose to replace "borderline Schizophrenia" and certain erstwhile usages of "Schizoid" Personality with Schizotypal Personality Disorder (see Haier, 1980; Wolff & Chick, 1980).

The ICD-9 lists Schizophrenia under Psychoses and uses the classical subclassification of Simple, Hebephrenic, Catatonic, Paranoid, but in addition, includes an odd assortment of Acute, Latent, Residual, Schizoaffective, other, unspecified. Symptomatology covers the same domain as the DSM-III but is presented in a long discursive description before finally listing the requirement of at least two of the "characteristic" (that is in terms of their previous description) disturbances of thought, perception, mood, conduct, and personality.

The onset of Childhood Schizophrenia is highly variable and is of prognostic significance (see later section). As Kydd and Werry (1982) have described, it may be insidious, prodromal over a few days or weeks, or fulminating. In some cases, there may be what Eggers (1978) called "outpost" episodes, that is, short prodromal episodes isolated in time from the full-blown syndrome and very frequently not of a schizophrenic (e.g., affective) nature. The studies by Kolvin and the Bellevue group (see Green et al., 1984) suggest that in prepubertal schizophrenia, insidious onset predominates (about 80%). There have been a few reports, though, of schizophrenia developing after an early history of autism (see Petty, Ornitz, Michelman, & Zimmerman, 1984).

Validity of the Disorders

Good reviews of this area relating to schizophrenia and allied disorders in adults can be found in Haier (1980), Fenton, Mosher, and Matthews (1981), and Wing (1978). The level of interdiagnoser reliability achieved can be highly satisfactory when criteria are explicit, and this can be enhanced even further when a common systematized data-capture technique such as Wing's Present Status Examination is used (Haier, 1980; Wing, 1978). However, different criteria—and there are a number of competing such sets—classify the same patient in somewhat different ways (Fenton et al., 1981).

The DSM-III Kappa coefficient of agreement (American Psychiatric Association, 1980, p. 470) was 0.81 in two field studies with a total N of about 100. For those under 18, it ranged from 1.00 to 0.66 for Schizophrenia and 0.85 for other psychotic disorders, which includes the Brief Reactive Psychosis, though the N was very small (about 10). In a study of children most of whom were 15 years of age or under, Werry, Methven, Fitzpatrick, and Dixon (1983) found a Kappa of 1.00 with an N of 16 but only when the categories of Schizophrenia, Schizophreniform and Brief Reactive Psychosis were combined, suggesting that while there is little confusion about symptomatology, the duration criterion may cause difficulties when a new case is seen for the first time.

Although there is a long history of multivariate study of adult psychoses, statistical techniques are relative newcomers to the child field and the results are unclear as yet (Haier, 1980). Studies are few, confused diagnostically, and lacking in assessment of their discriminative value. Though various authors have described symptomatology (e.g., Annell, 1963; Bender, 1953; Vrono, 1974), this work is subject to the serious problem of a failure to separate schizophrenia from autism and/or other psychoses including organic ones so that its value is considerably diminished.

Some of the first studies that did attempt not only to distinguish between schizophrenia and autism but to find out what symptomatology clearly differentiates the two groups are those of Kolvin, Garside, and Kidd (1971), Kolvin, Ounsted, Humphrey, and McNay (1971), and Kolvin, Ounsted, Richardson, and Garside (1971). They found that while classical schizophrenic symptoms were present in varying mixes in all children with onset after age four, the only symptoms that clearly differentiated at a high frequency and high discrimination level in rank order were hallucinations, disorder of thought content, and blunting and incongruity of affect for schizophrenia, and abnormal preoccupations, distinterest in people, poor play, stereotypy, echolalia, and overactivity for autism. Other symptoms either did not occur frequently or did not discriminate.

A serious flaw in Kolvin's study to which he alluded but which has not been reported by any subsequent reviewers is that of circularity. Children were diagnosed as psychotic not only on the basis of age of onset, but nested within age, by the presence of classical autistic or schizophrenic symptoms. The surprise then, is not that some of these symptoms did discriminate but rather that many did not! Multivariate statistical analyses were not applied, thus limiting the discriminative power of the study.

Although Kolvin found that hallucinations did discriminate well in schizophrenia, it is important to remember that these were of the Schneiderian type (hearing one's thoughts spoken aloud, voices conversing about the patient, running commentaries, and the bodily type produced by external forces). Though Kolvin did not have a nonpsychotic or other disturbed control group, a review of hallucinations in children by Rothstein (1981) shows that such phenomena are common, especially in younger children, and thus some caution in defining the type of hallucination is necessary.

Two very recent studies (Garralda, 1983; Green et al., 1984) confirm Kolvin's (1971) work. In Green et al., using DSM-III diagnostic criteria and consensus diagnosis by two psychiatrists, 24 schizophrenic and 25 autistic children were compared on a wide set of variables. All schizophrenics had thought disorders and most had hallucinations but few delusions. Though a few schizophrenic children had psychopathological symptoms before age five, none actually developed schizophrenia before age five. Although Green et al. imposed no age-of-onset criteria in their definition, the results are remarkably similar to Kolvin's. Garralda (1983) used primarily age-of-onset criteria and, like Green et al. and Kolvin, found differences suggestive of an Autism/Schizophrenic dichotomy.

Another study of clinical symptomatology of schizophrenia in children is that by Cantor, Evans, Pearce, and Pezzott-Pearce (1982), comparing children and adolescents with "Schizophrenia," though for undiscernible reasons, the classification was on the basis of *current* not *onset* age. While there was little difference in the mean total number of schizophrenic type symptoms in the two groups, language disturbances (neologisms, echolalia, and clanging) were more common in children, while perplexity, ambivalence, paranoia, and hallucinations were more common in the adolescents. Seven of their total of 30 subjects had an age of onset before 30 months of age and the mean age of onset in the child group was 4.16 ± 1.54 years! Even for the adolescents, it was in the region of seven years. While Cantor et al. stated that none of the children was clearly autistic, in view of the average age of onset and the symptomatological differences between the children and the adolescents, there is good reason to wonder whether or not the children were mostly mild or, more probably, incomplete cases of Autism, particularly since Kolvin, Green et al., and Garralda all showed that hallucinations and language disorders such as echolalia were highly differentiating between Schizophrenia and Autism, respectively. The diagnostic imprecision of this study makes interpretation and comparison difficult.

As has been noted previously, statistical studies of children diagnosed as psychotic are few, but Quay and Peterson (1983) did find a Psychotic Disorder dimension in a series of analyses of institutionalized children and adolescents (see also Chapter 1). The seven items consistently loading on this factor were rather similar in the end to the "nuclear" syndrome of Schizophrenia (hallucinations and thought disorder, with bizarre behavior being substituted for loss of will). Achenbach's (1980) Child Behavior Checklist contains a very similar nine-item factor, which unfortunately in view of what has already been said about this term before, he termed "Schizoid." The rather greater predominance given to bizarre behavior and similar items in these statistical classifications differs from those of the DSM-III, where they are to be found largely in the prodromal or residual symptomatology and in the Schizotypal Personality Disorder. While neither of these classificatory (i.e., checklist) systems appears to have been properly validated as yet, discrimination between Autism and Schizophrenia may prove possible and perhaps validation studies will elucidate the Schizophrenic type disorder more precisely.

The status of Schizoaffective Disorder remains to be studied in children. Schizotypal Personality disorder has, however, been examined by Wolff and colleagues (Wolff & Chick, 1980). They used the classical term Schizoid Personality, though the symptomatology of solitariness, impaired empathy, sensitivity, rigidity of mental set, unusual or odd style of communication, and the occurrence of mystical or psychotic-like experiences in over 50 percent at long-term follow-up make it clear that in DSM-III terms the diagnosis was Schizotypal Personality Disorder. The validity of the disorder was tested by a retrospective 10-year follow-up study with a matched sample of other children seen at the same time. In general the diagnosis and symptomatology of "Schizoid" (i.e., Schizotypal Disorder) in childhood predicted similar symptomatology in adulthood that was quite distinctive from that of controls. However, though the old literature and the DSM-III makes it clear that there is an assumed link with later Schizophrenia [in fact, it is described as a diluted form of Schizophrenia (see Wolff & Chick, 1980)], the "Schizoid" children had only two instances of frank psychosis. While psychiatric symptoms were more common, *social adjustment* was no different from that of clinic controls.

As to the clinical validity of Schizophrenia, the limited data on correlates (see later text) and outcome suggest that there is some, if still rather low, validity to the diagnosis. A long-held idea persists, however, that present categories are still too gross and that there must be as yet undiscovered subgroupings of greater validity, with hope currently seeming to be vested in biological rather than behavioral descriptors (Haier, 1980). Fenton et al. (1981) warn that since, as yet, there is no proof of superior construct validity among six or more explicit or research diagnostic criteria, each of which defines a somewhat differing group of patients as schizophrenic, the DSM-III can have no superior claim. They express concern that because of its officialness, the DSM-III may preempt the field to the detriment of continuing investigation at the empirical diagnostic level.

In summary then, there is reason to assume that there is a clinical syndrome of Schizophrenic Disorder in children, the symptomatology of which is similar, with appropriate developmental adjustment, to that in adults. Symptomatology and syndrome have not, however, as yet been subject to the same kind of systematic study in construct validation as has characterized other childhood psychopathological disorders such as Conduct or Attention Deficit Disorders.

Correlates of Schizophrenia in Children

The literature on the cognitive and social characteristics of schizophrenic children is very limited. As noted earlier there is a growing body of data on children described as "at risk" for schizophrenia because they have at least one schizophrenic parent (e.g., Glish, Erlenmyer-Kimling, & Watt, 1982). It is scarcely legitimate to consider such children as schizophrenic, however, or even as sharing some of the characteristics of a diagnosed group, and thus although it is tempting to incorporate the literature on this group into the review of correlates, it could be misleading in examining what we know about schizophrenic children.

In the early history of the investigation of the characteristics of the childhood psychoses it was almost universal that no distinction was made between autistic and schizophrenic cases. They were considered to have similar symptomatology despite differences in age of onset and etiologically significant variables. For this reason the earlier literature relating to cognitive impairments in autism and childhood schizophrenia is difficult to interpret, and any conclusions might be considered to relate to a heterogeneous sample of psychotic children, including a proportion who would now be distinguished as Childhood Schizophrenic. Consequently, it is rarely possible to extract data relating specifically to correlates of childhood schizophrenia. Some information can be gleaned from a small number of studies that may permit some sketching of a pattern or profile of functioning in this group. If this can be extended and detailed over the next few years, a more comprehensive picture of the characteristics of these children may emerge, which in turn could permit some resolution of the existing diagnostic problems. Throughout, it should be borne in mind that since the onset of the disorder is later in schizophrenia than in autism, it is axiomatic that some differences should emerge since the schizophrenic abnormalities are presumably imposed on some previous normal or quasinormal development. Regression in functioning is often observed in these cases, whereas this is scarcely possible in autism, in which it is assumed that there has been minimal normal development from very early in life.

INTELLIGENCE AND COGNITIVE PROCESSING

Intellectual functioning as assessed via IQ tests appears to be less impaired in schizophrenic children in comparison to autistic children. Kolvin's Late Onset Psychosis Group, whose characteristics were consistent with the current DSM-III criteria for Childhood Schizophrenia included more than half with IQs in the normal range with the remainder being mildly to moderately retarded. IQ was reported as average or above in 90 percent of a German sample (Eggers, 1978); and in Kydd and Werry's New Zealand sample of 15 children for whom no psychometric assessments were available, 10 were described as functioning at an average or above level in school performance, although three had deteriorated by follow-up. Walker and Bortner (1975) and Hertzig and Walker (1975) also reported borderline intelligence in the schizophrenic children in their studies. A recent comparative study reported by Green et al. (1984) described schizophrenic children diagnosed via DSM-III criteria who had a mean IQ of 86, ranging from 65 and 125.

In one of the few reports of the pattern or profile of intellectual functioning, Walker and Birch (1974) found that performance IQ was higher than verbal IQ for a subgroup of their 10- to 15-year-old male sample with WISC IQs over 75. In children of IQ below 75, the opposite discrepancy was found. Overall, there is remarkable convergence of evidence indicating that intellectual retardation is more variable and much less prominent in childhood schizophrenia than in autism. In one of the few recent accounts of cognitive development in schizophrenic children, Waterhouse and Fein (1984) claimed that their group (selected via the Creak criteria and not DSM-III and therefore of questionable diagnostic validity) showed extremely delayed development, which, however, was not as severe as that found in autistic children. There was a decline in performance after puberty.

There have been a few studies concerned with concept formation and information processing in schizophrenic children. Developmental delay in the ability to employ class-based and function-based concepts was characteristic of Walker and Bortner's group (1975), and these authors noted a breakdown in concept organization when direct sensory cues for sorting tasks were removed. This of course echoes comments on information processing in autism (e.g., Prior & McGillivray, 1980). Caplan and Walker (1979) assessed the performance of schizophrenic children on a series of Piagetian tasks and reported developmentally immature performance in most areas. Only 7 percent of their sample achieved the preoperational and concrete operational stages and none showed formal operational thinking. They also noted impaired symbolic imagery and described their subjects as primitive transformers of the environment. Classification and seriation performance in schizophrenic children was assessed more recently by Breslow and Cowan (1984). Their subjects were described as showing deficits in imaginal ability but no differences in structure and stage of reasoning ability by comparison with controls; that is, differences between the groups were qualitative rather than quantitative.

Not surprisingly, defects in categorization and abstraction seem to be more evident in children of below average IQ. In a theoretical paper, Hertzig and Walker (1975) proposed that schizophrenic children showed impairment in information processing consequent on primary neurological abnormality (unspecified) with a dissociation of integrative processes in sensory systems. Breslow and Cowan (1984), however, did not find perceptuomotor dysfunction to be the key to cognitive disabilities. This conceptualization would seem to need considerable clarification and operationalization to be heuristically useful.

A recently reported series of studies concerned with information processing in schizophrenic children (Arsanow & Sherman, 1984) showed that these cases were poorer than mental age matched normals (and similar to adult schizophrenics) in a span of apprehension task. It appeared that schizophrenic children were using similar processing strategies to the controls, although less efficiently. The authors concluded that controlled attentional processes were poorly developed in this group while memory processes appeared relatively intact. They also drew attention to the complex mix of deficient and intact abilities in schizophrenic children.

LANGUAGE

Comprehension and use of language is also less impaired in schizophrenic as compared with autistic children. This is predictable, however, given the later onset of the disorder, which has permitted some "normal" language development, as well as the general finding of a higher level of intelligence. Nevertheless, Cantor et al. (1982) reported normal language development in only 16 percent of schizophrenic prepubertal children and in 33 percent of adolescents. It should be noted, though, that we do not have systematic data on language development or language characteristics and are obliged to rely on generally vague clinical notes. While speech and language delay and difficulties may be associated with schizophrenia, they are variable and more likely to exhibit bizarreness than impairment arising from the fundamental disabilities seen in autism. Fish (1977) has claimed that for schizophrenic children with more advanced language skills, the thought disorder is more akin to that seen in schizophrenic adults with disturbances in conceptualization and logic, in thought and association. Garralda (1983) reported language abnormalities in the associative area but provided no detailed assessment. Diagnostic and classification problems preclude satisfactory assessment of language processes in schizophrenic children, although the general impression is that language development is strongly related to intelligence level and abnormalities are akin to those seen in adult schizophrenia when language level is relatively sophisticated.

PERCEPTION AND ATTENTION

Impairments in perceptual skills have been noted by Bender (1947) and Goldfarb (1961), although they undoubtedly included a proportion of children who were autistic in this judgment. Fish (1977) suggested that child and adult schizophrenics share similar perceptuomotor integration problems, although these have never been clearly specified. Waterhouse and Fein's (1984) report, however, suggested "relative sparing of perceptual functioning" in their group of schizophrenic children (p. 245).

There are also problems with attention, with considerable intra- and interindividual variability, and it might be suggested that preoccupation with inner thoughts and perceptions of a disturbed nature underlie these problems. That is, perceptual and attentional abnormalities in schizophrenic children may be bizarre, internally generated ones, such as hallucinations; rather than specific input-processing peculiarities. The loosening of associations sometimes observed may also contribute to manifestations of disturbed perceptual and attentional processes. Attentional deficits have been noted in the "high-risk" studies and appear to predict later psychiatric disorder to some extent. The relationship, though, is nonspecific to schizophrenia, and further comparative studies such as those of Arsonow and Sherman (1984) are needed to clarify the nature and significance of attention deficits in schizophrenia. Thus far such deficits appear to be a ubiquitous symptom in a variety of handicapping conditions (Prior, 1985).

PSYCHOPHYSIOLOGICAL FACTORS

As is the case for autism, no syndrome-specific generalizations concerning psychophysiological characteristics of childhood schizophrenia are possible. The importance of maturational factors in this area and the association of schizophrenia with postpubertal onset means that reviewing the adult literature might be more appropriate. As this literature is voluminous without, however, offering any unequivocal findings, there seems little useful to be offered in this section.

SOCIAL AND EMOTIONAL CHARACTERISTICS

There has been no systematic empirical study of the social behavioral features of childhood schizophrenia. Clinical reports often refer to some or all of social withdrawal, reduced activity and interest patterns, moodiness, excessive anxiety and irrational fears, distrust, blunting of affect with sometimes the development of coldness and unkindness (Eggers, 1978), disinhibition, impaired school functioning, poor ability to initiate and sustain social relationships, disturbed motility and speech, magical thinking and loss of contact with reality. All of these are commonly observed in adolescents and adults. Some writers report ritualistic behavior, but again it is impossible to estimate how common or how characteristic this is of schizophrenic children. Garralda (1983) reported hypoactivity, bizarre behavior, social withdrawal, and inappropriate giggling in her early adolescent group of psychotic (schizophrenic) children. However, the rarity of "Schneiderian symptoms" and Bleulerian "deficits" in her group led her to challenge the view that late onset psychotics are inevitably schizophrenic. In view of the clear existence of such symptoms in the studies by Kolvin et al. (1971), Eggers (1978), Green et al. (1984), and Kydd and Werry (1982), Garralda's study requires confirmation.

LEARNING
No diagnosis-specific data are available.

MOTOR DEVELOPMENT AND PERCEPTUOMOTOR SKILLS
Although it has been suggested that schizophrenia may in some cases be associated with neurodevelopmental immaturities such as clumsiness (Rutter & Garmezy, 1983) and other "soft signs," there are in fact no real data available to allow evaluation of this claim. Since soft signs are of uncertain significance and controversial interpretation, as well as being diagnostically nondiscriminatory, this relationship is of unknown relevance (see Chapter 6). Quitkin, Rifkin, and Klein (1976) have suggested that neurodevelopmental immaturities are most commonly associated with early onset of schizophrenia, a finding that is hardly surprising and again of uncertain diagnostic implication. As noted earlier, neither Breslow and Cowan (1984) nor Waterhouse and Fein (1984) found perceptuomotor problems, although the diagnostic imprecision of these studies preclude confident conclusions.

NEUROLOGICAL AND PATHOLOGICAL FACTORS
Here again, we must rely primarily on adult studies. While it is now generally accepted that Schizophrenia has a significant, probably essential but not necessarily sufficient biological component in etiology, clear and unequivocal demonstration of necessary and specific correlates such as birth, EEG, and neurological abnormalities with Schizophrenia has not yet occurred, and the position is quite unclear (see Cooper, 1978; Rutter, 1972; Weinberger, Wagner, & Wyatt, 1983). The search for so-called biological markers of diagnoses is currently intensive and is based at the biochemical level involving dopamine primarily but also other monoamines (see Bowers, 1980). Most recently some of the newer organ-imaging techniques such as CT scans are being used (Reiss et al., 1983).

The rather persistent problem is that there is a lack of specificity of such correlates to schizophrenia and not all patients with schizophrenia have the defect (Haier, 1980). As far as children are concerned, Kolvin's (1971) find-ing of an increased frequency of organic correlates in his schizophrenic group has been suggested by Rutter (1972) as possibly due to the particular interest of his child psychiatric unit in epilepsy and other organic disorders, that is, referral bias. Cantor et al. (1982) claimed, however, that neuromus-cular dysfunction (hypotonia) and reduced power were invariable correlates of Childhood Schizophrenia. In addition, they developed a scale of Physical Characteristics that has some similarities with both Minor Physical Anoma-lies and minor neurological signs assessment. Though all children were neu-rologically normal (that is, no focal signs), the childhood group (that is, largely onset before age five) had significantly more physical signs than ad-olescents. The diagnostic anomalies of the study have already been noted and the lack of "blind" assessments and of any normative control group in an area notorious for uncertain reliability and validity makes these findings suspect (see Chapter 6). For example, differences between the children and the adolescents could in fact be age dependent. Developmental factors are of undoubted influence in this area, but their contribution in any or all of the neurological and pathological study areas has still to be defined.

FAMILY CORRELATES

This has been an area of great interest in adults, but most of the literature in children is difficult to disentangle because of the lumping together of any and all kinds of psychosis. Kolvin (1971) found that an increase in schizo-phrenia in families of late-onset psychosis (i.e., schizophrenia), while Len-nox, Callias, and Rutter (1977) found an increase of abnormal thought styles. This was in contrast to autistic children, who had no such increase. In one of the few other comparative studies, however, Green et al. (1984), though finding a raised frequency of schizophrenia in mothers of schizo-phrenics (20%), also found a 10 percent rate in mothers of autistic children (and a 15% rate in mothers of conduct-disordered children). Numbers are too small (25 in each group) to make too much of this finding, but it must be noted. The adult literature is clear: the frequency of schizophrenia is raised in families and relatives but at too low a level to support an exclusively ge-netic view of etiology (Liem, 1980). There is some evidence to support in-creased disordered role relationships and communication in families of schizophrenics, but the simplistic methods and univariate models of past re-search have given way to a much more complex picture (see Liem, 1980; Parker, 1982; Wynne, 1981).

Two distinctive areas of research have now been clearly defined: the effect of the family (1) in pathogenesis and (2) on established schizophrenia. Evi-dence in favor of family factors precipitating *relapse* is much stronger than it is in primary pathogenesis (Wynne, 1981). Perhaps as a result, emphasis in the role of family factors in etiologic research has shifted to longitudinal studies of high-risk (i.e., genetically) groups and the model is thus interac-tive with biological factors. How much of all this can validly be applied to children and younger adolescents remains to be demonstrated.

Epidemiology

The prevalence of schizophrenia is in the range of 2 to 4 per thousand for the population at large (Cooper, 1978) and 5 to 10 per 1000 in the 15 to 45 age-group. The yearly incidence at this peak risk age range (15–45) is around 1 per 1000, with a whole-life risk of around 1 percent (Najem, Lindenthal, Louria, & Thind, 1980). While it is clear that schizophrenia can begin in childhood, most incidence and prevalence data begin at 15, when there is a rapid rise to peak incidence levels over the next 10 to 15 years. Nothing is really known for sure about the frequency of schizophrenia under age 15 except that it is unusual in early adolescence and rare before puberty (Garralda, 1983). Using national health statistics, clinic figures, and some age-cohort type studies, Graham and Rutter (1976) deduced that the prevalence of psychoses of *all kinds* in mid-adolescence is probably less than 1 in a 1000 (that is, about 10% of the rate at 15 to 45). Kolvin (1971), over a 10-year period, could find only 33 cases occurring before age 15, of which about half again were before puberty. In their 10-year series, Kydd and Werry (1982) had only three cases under age 12 in a total of 15 schizophrenics under age 16, in a population in a catchment area of about one million. In the largest group by far, Eggers (1978) collected 57 cases of onset between 7 and 13 years, but these were aggregated over almost 40 years. Green et al. (1984) did find 24 over a five-year period but Bellevue Hospital has not only a catchment area of 30 million but is nationally renowned for its interest in childhood psychoses. While the DSM-III sets no minimum age, the youngest ages of onset reported so far are 5 years (one case) in Kolvin's study, 6 years in Green et al.'s, and 7 years in those of Eggers and Kydd and Werry. Bleuler (see Bender, 1953) claimed it could begin earlier than age 5 and Annell (1963) and Cantor et al. (1982), along with Bender, report onset in infancy. Their figures are all surprisingly high, however, and this in combination with their clinical reports and diagnostic criteria raise serious doubts about the accuracy of the diagnosis. Nevertheless, it would seem wise to conclude that no minimum age of onset has yet been firmly established.

Sex ratios before puberty are overwhelmingly male (Eggers, 1978; Garralda, 1983; Green et al., 1984; Kolvin 1971; Kydd & Werry, 1982), though this may be only one aspect of the generally earlier onset of the disorder in males (Cooper, 1978), and ultimately the sex ratio evens up.

In summary, epidemiological data are scanty and of poor quality in terms of true population sampling but suggest that schizophrenia rarely, if ever, begins before age five, the frequency in childhood is low, and it is not until mid or late adolescence that it becomes other than infrequent. Males have a strikingly earlier age of onset, particularly when this onset is before puberty.

Outcome

Schizophrenia (in adults) is probably the best studied of any psychiatric disorder as far as outcome is concerned. The reason is not hard to discern, since schizophrenia is one of the most disabling psychiatric disorders (J.K.

Wing, 1978). It is also responsible for much of the bed occupancy and the activity in publicly funded psychiatric facilities in most countries. Despite this, the recent review by Bland (1982) found that only between 8 to 40 percent of the variance for outcome can be predicted reliably. J.K. Wing (1978) pointed out that three sets of factors blend into each other to influence outcome: intrinsic (that is, to the disease itself), social (for example, socioeconomic class, policies on type and quality of care), and personal (that is, premorbid personality). In an obvious but often overlooked point, he stressed that so many different factors in this area and others (e.g., exactly what is called schizophrenia) are involved and interact that it is very difficult to make general statements about outcome. It should be noted, too, that by requiring a six-month history, the DSM-III will eliminate all single episode cases with complete recovery and thus affect figures in an artefactual way. Bland (1982) and J.K. Wing (1978) came to rather similar conclusions regarding outcome, though the former writer put somewhat more credence on the specific if limited predictive value of a wide group of variables from Wing's three groupings, adding the uncertain (as yet) impact of an antipsychotic drug treatment. He also concluded that while outcome may range from complete recovery to inexorable deterioration, the average outcome compares unfavorably with most other psychiatric disorders. Wing stressed that, in general, successive episodes tend to breed true to each other and that even those patients who are totally free of schizophrenic symptomatology often have other psychopathological symptoms such as "worrying a great deal." Schizophrenic children show a course rather similar to that of adults; some are nonepisodic, some are relapsing, and some have only one attack. There are problems in presenting outcome data on children, not only because studies are sparse, but additionally because it is unknown how closely adult outcome data relate to presumed outcome in childhood schizophrenia. In view of the similarity in symptomatology, genetics, and response to medication, it seems reasonable to consider outcome data as applying to both child and adult form of the same disorder, particularly where onset is close to puberty. For cases with earlier onset, the relationship is much more clouded and conclusions may have to await more follow-up data.

Kydd and Werry (1982) summarized outcome studies in children in adolescence through age 15 years and added data on 10 subjects of their own. After noting the difficulties presented by most studies because of their failure to differentiate Schizophrenia from Autism, they found only a handful that were interpretable. One of the largest, that by Annell (1963), was not usable because of her failure to separate the subjects by age of onset, many having been under five years of age then. Eggers (1978) was able to follow, at an average of a 15-year interval, 57 patients diagnosed at Marburg from the opening of the Child Psychiatric Clinic there in the 1920s, and found that 20 percent seemed to be in complete remission at the time of follow-up examination with a further 50 percent rated as "improved." One of the more interesting features of Eggers' study was that, not only was the number of acute or florid psychotic episodes highly variable (one subject had about 30 such episodes), but the number seemed to have no absolute bearing on outcome. Good predictors fell in the well-known area of acute onset, clear precipitants, good premorbid personality, and well differentiated symptomatology. These findings were generally confirmed by Kydd and Werry (1982) in their short-term (1–8 years) follow-up. Affective symptoms were found by others cited by Kydd and Werry to dictate a favorable prognosis. A 20-year follow-up of 20 childhood schizophrenics (some probably autistic cases) reported by Howells and Guirguis (1984) found little change in symptomatology with most cases similar to adult simple schizophrenics. Age of onset appeared not to influence outcome. Unfortunately, the diagnostic confusion of this study seriously limits the authority of these findings.

Age of onset has emerged consistently as a powerful predictive variable. The literature is consistent that an onset before age 14 and especially before age 11 adversely affects outcome (see Kydd & Werry, 1982), though no good review of outcome of schizophrenia in general seems to have yet noted this (e.g., Bland, 1982).

In summary, outcome and its predictors in children and younger adolescents are similar to those in adults except that the younger the onset, the worse the prognosis, though this age effect is difficult to disentangle from the highly correlated insidiousness of onset. DSM-III diagnostic criteria, by requiring a six-month history, may seem to worsen the prognosis assessment in future studies by excluding those who have had only one episode with complete recovery who would have been included previously.

CHILDREN AT RISK OF DEVELOPING SCHIZOPHRENIA IN LATER LIFE

Though schizophrenia in children is uncommon, the onset of the disorder in adolescence and early adulthood and the disabling effect in a significant minority have understandably led to an interest in trying to define those at risk of developing the disorder with a view to prevention and/or early treatment.

This area has been reviewed by Glish et al. (1982). There have been two main approaches: the follow-back and the prospective study. The follow-back studies are older, easier to pursue, and in general have utilized school records as a universally available, fairly reliable data base. These studies show that (pre) schizophrenics as a group were more often psychologically disturbed than normals, but the symptomatology varied and was nondiscriminatory as far as differentiating between future schizophrenia or other major psychiatric disorders.

The high-risk studies have a number of problems. The first is that of all long-term prospective studies—expense, delayed reward to investigators, and subject attrition. The second is that insofar as the whole-life risk of schizophrenia is no more than 1 percent, huge samples are necessary unless the usual device of increasing the risk rate is adopted by taking children of one schizophrenic parent, which raises it to a 12 percent risk rate, or children of two schizophrenic parents, which increases it to around 40 percent but presents the problem of locating such infrequent subjects. The third problem following from the second is that only about 5 percent of schizophrenics have a parent who is schizophrenic (Kessler, 1980) so this may introduce a serious bias as to the type of schizophrenia concerned. Several such studies are under way in the United States, Denmark, and Canada but none has yet got to the stage where most of the subjects have reached the age of maximum incidence of schizophrenia so that few overt cases of schizophrenia have developed thus far. The studies are in the main well designed, using normal controls and sometimes controls with huge risk for psychiatric disorder in general, with parent, teacher, and often laboratory types of cognitive and psychophysiological measures.

These studies have confirmed the findings of follow-back studies, suggesting that while disturbance is not specific, it may be somewhat more common in those at risk for schizophrenia than for other disorders and may have important attentional, emotional, and psychophysiological components (Glish et al., 1982). Interestingly, these differences are still seen in high-risk children put into foster care at an early age (McCrimmon, Cleghorn, Arsanow, & Steffy, 1980). While these findings may be interpreted to suggest a genetic or at least antenatal component to schizophrenia, the bias introduced by the method of selection and the length of the waiting period for maximum incidence (15–40 years) mean that investigation in this area has so far not been able to contribute substantially to the study of schizophrenia or its antecedents in childhood.

SUMMARY

Evidence suggests that there are at least two separate psychoses of childhood: infantile autism or early onset psychosis, and childhood schizophrenia or late onset psychosis. Apart from developmental variations in symptomatology, the latter appears identical with adult schizophrenia, both clinically and epidemiologically, and probably, therefore, of similar etiology. While etiology of schizophrenia is disputed, evidence favors a physical disorder, possibly genetic, influenced by psychosocial factors. Schizophrenia in children has not been as well studied as autism. Autism is now classified (DSM-III, 1980) as a "Pervasive Developmental Disorder" which is serious and begins very early in life. It is marked by absent or seriously impaired interaction with the social and physical environment, global language impairment, and rigid or ritualistic behavior. The cause appears related to some kind of brain damage that affects all areas of the brain concerned with language and social understanding, and which occurs pre-, peri-, or less certainly, postnatally. Since the brain damage usually extends beyond this area, defects in various other cognitive, motor, and intellectual functions are often associated with the disorder.

Although there is a strong tendency for the core symptoms of autism to disappear with age, the ultimate adjustment is usually poor, being largely dependent, though by no means exclusively, on residual intellectual capacity, which is typically in the retarded range. Outcome in schizophrenia is less certain but probably almost as unfavorable.

The role of treatment is unclear, though behaviour modification, structured education, and psychotropic drugs can produce significant and valuable symptomatic rather than elemental changes in autism. Psychotherapy appears to have little effect. While much has been made of the autistic child's "islets of normal intelligence" or special abilities, these are rare and from three-quarters to four-fifths of cases suffer from a notable degree of retardation. Research studies over the last 20 years suggest that the disorder is best understood as a cognitive developmental one rather than an emotionally based one and that autistic children not only resemble children of *comparable overall IQ* but suffer from additional handicaps that make their prognosis somewhat worse. Treatment of schizophrenia has not been well studied but seems similarly symptomatic, rather than curative, with a clearer role for medication.

The role of parents (and families) in the production of autism and schizophrenia would appear to have been grossly overemphasized. Although parents of schizophrenic children often show psychopathology this is more likely to be a manifestation of a similar genetic disorder, or, as with parents of autistic children, a reaction to having a severely handicapped child—aggravating rather than causal.

The definition of the necessary, sufficient, and excluding criteria for each condition and the operationalization of these criteria require study. Until this is accomplished, the likewise clearly needed research in etiology, treatment, and prognosis may continue to be idiosyncratic and difficult. The DSM-III classification gives promise of such possibilities, but whether the necessary validity studies will be done remains to be seen.

REFERENCES

Achenbach, T. M. (1980). DSM-III in the light of empirical research on classification of childhood psychopathology. *Journal of the American Academy of Child Psychiatry, 19*, 395–412.

American Psychiatric Association (1980). *Diagnostic and statistical manual of mental disorders* (3rd ed.) Washington, DC: Author.

Annell, L. A. (1963). The prognosis of psychotic syndromes in children: A follow-up study of one hundred and fifteen cases. *Acta Psychiatrica Scandinavica, 39*, 233–297.

Anthony, E. J. (1958). An experimental approach to the psychopathology of childhood. *British Journal of Medical Psychology, 31*, 211–223.

Arsanow, R. F., & Sherman, T. (1984). Studies of visual information processing in schizophrenic children. *Child Development, 55*, 249–261.

August, G. J., Stewart, M. A., and Tsai, L. (1981). The incidence of cognitive disabilities in the siblings of autistic chilidren. *British Journal of Psychiatry, 138*, 416–422.

Baltaxe, C. A., & Simmons, J. Q. (1975). Language in childhood psychosis: A review. *Journal of Speech and Hearing Disorders, 40*, 439–458.

Bartak, L., & Rutter, M. (1973). Special educational treatment of autistic children: A comparative study—Design of study and characteristics of units. *Journal of Child Psychology and Psychiatry, 14*, 161–179.

Bartak, L., & Rutter, M. (1976). Differences between mentally retarded and normally intelligent autistic children. *Journal of Autism and Childhood Schizophrenia, 6*, 109–120.

Bartak, L., Rutter, M., & Cox, A. (1975). A comparative study of infantile autism and specific developmental receptive language disorders: I. The children. *British Journal of Psychiatry, 126*, 127–145.

Bender, L. (1947). Childhood schizophrenia—A clinical study of 100 schizophrenic children. *American Journal of Orthopsychiatry, 17*, 40–56.

Bender, L. (1953). Childhood schizophrenia. *Psychiatric Quarterly, 27*, 663–681.

Bettelheim, B. (1956). Schizophrenia as a reaction to extreme situations. *American Journal of Orthopsychiatry, 26*, 507–518.

Bland, R. C. (1982). Predicting the outcome of schizophrenia. *Canadian Journal of Psychiatry, 27*, 52–62.

Boucher, J. (1978). Echoic memory capacity in autistic children. *Journal of Child Psychology and Psychiatry, 19*, 161–168.

Boucher, J., & Warrington, E. K. (1976). Memory deficits in early infantile autism. Some similarities to the Amnesic Syndrome. *British Journal of Psychology, 67*, 73–87.

Bowers, M. B. (1980). Biochemical processes in schizophrenia: An up-date. *Schizophrenia Bulletin, 6*, 393–403.

Bradley, C., & Bowen, M. (1941). Behavior characteristics of schizophrenic children. *Psychiatric Quarterly, 15*, 298–315.

Brask, B. H. (1972). A prevalence investigation of childhood psychosis. Cited in L. Wing & J. Gould (1979), Severe impairments of social interaction and associated abnormalities in children: Epidemiology and classification. *Journal of Autism and Developmental Disorders, 9*, 11–29.

Breslow, L., & Cowan, P. A. (1984). Structure and functional perspective on classification and seriation in psychotic and normal children. *Child Development, 55*, 226–235.

Brown, J. L. (1960). Prognosis from presenting symptoms of preschool children with atypical development. *American Journal of Orthopsychiatry, 30*, 382–390.

Brown, J. L. (1963). Follow-up of children with atypical development (infantile psychosis). *American Journal of Orthopsychiatry, 31*, 855–861.

Bryson, C. Q. (1972). Short-term memory and cross-modal information processing in autistic children. *Journal of Learning Disabilities, 5*, 81–91.

Campbell, M., & Green, W. (1984, in press). Pervasive developmental disorders of childhood. In H. I. Kaplan & B. J. Sadock (Eds.), *Comprehensive textbook of psychiatry* (Vol. IV, 4th ed.).

Campbell, M., Rosenbloom, S., & Perry, R. (1982). Computerized axial tomography in young autistic children. *American Journal of Psychiatry, 139*, 510–512.

Cantor, S., Evans, J., Pearce, J., & Pezzott-Pearce, T. (1982). Childhood schizophrenia: Present but not accounted for. *American Journal of Psychiatry, 139*, 758–762.

Caplan, J., & Walker, H. (1979). Transformal deficits in cognition of schizophrenic children. *Journal of Autism and Developmental Disorders, 9*, 161–177.

Carr, E. G., Binkoff, J. A., Kologinsky, E., and Eddy, M. (1978). Acquisition of sign language by autistic children. I: Expressive labelling. *Journal of Applied Behavior Analysis, 11*, 489–501.

Carr, E. G., Schriebmann, L., & Lovaas, O. I. (1975). Control of echolalic speech in psychotic children. *Journal of Abnormal Child Psychology, 3*, 331–351.

Chess, S. (1971) Autism in children with congenital rubella. *Journal of Autism and Childhood Schizophrenia, 1*, 33–47.

Chess, S. (1977). Follow-up report on autism in congenital rubella. *Journal of Autism and Childhood Schizophrenia, 7*, 68–81.

Churchill, D. W. (1971). Effects of success and failure in psychotic children. *Archives of General Psychiatry, 25*, 208–214.

Churchill, D. W. (1972). The relation of infantile autism and early childhood schizophrenia to developmental language disorders of childhood. *Journal of Autism and Childhood Schizophrenia, 2*, 182–197.

Clark, P., & Rutter, M. (1979). Task difficulty and task performance in autistic children. *Journal of Child Psychology and Psychiatry, 20*, 271–285.

Clark, P., & Rutter, M. (1981). Autistic children's responses to structure and to interpersonal demands. *Journal of Autism and Developmental Disorders, 11*, 201–217.

Cohen, D., & Shaywitz, C. (1982). Preface to the special issue on neurobiological research in autism. *Journal of Autism and Developmental Disorders, 12*, 103–107.

Cohen, D. J., Caparulo, B. K., Gold, J. R., Waldo, M. C., Shaywitz, B. A., Ruttenberg, B. A., & Rimland, B. (1978). Agreement and diagnosis: Clinical assessment and behavior rating scales for pervasively disturbed children. *Journal of the American Academy of Child Psychiatry, 17*, 589–603.

Coleman, M. (1978). A report on the autistic syndrome. In M. Rutter & E. Schopler (Eds.), *Autism: A reappraisal of concepts and treatment*. New York, Plenum.

Cooper, B. (1978). Epidemiology. In J. K. Wing (Ed.), *Schizophrenia: Towards a new synthesis*. London: Academic Press.

Corbett, J., Harris, R., Taylor, E., & Trimble, M. (1977). Progressive disintegrative psychoses of childhood. *Journal of Child Psychology and Psychiatry, 18*, 211–219.

Cox, A., Rutter, M., Newman, S., & Bartak, L. (1975). A comparative study of infantile autism and specific developmental receptive language disorder. II. Parental characteristics. *British Journal of Psychiatry, 126*, 146–159.

Creak, M., Cameron, K., Cowie, V., Ini, S., MacKeith, R., Mitchell, G., O'Gorman, G., Orford, F., Rogers, W. J. B., Shapiro, A., Stone, F., Stroh, G., & Yudkin, S. (1961). Schizophrenic syndrome in childhood. *British Medical Journal, 2*, 889–890.

Creak, M., & Ini, S. (1960). Families of psychotic children. *Journal of Child Psychology and Psychiatry, 1*, 156–175.

Damasio, A. R., & Maurer, R. G. (1978). A neurological model for childhood autism. *Archives of Neurology, 35*, 777–786.

Davids, A. (1974). Effects of human and non-human stimuli on attention and learning in psychotic children. *Child Psychiatry and Human Development, 5*, 108–116.

Dawson, G. (1983). Lateralized brain dysfunction in autism: Evidence from the Halstead-Reitan Neuropsychological Battery. *Journal of Autism and Developmental Disorders, 13*, 269–286.

DeMyer, M. (1976). Motor, perceptual-motor and intellectual disabilities of autistic children. In L. Wing (Ed.), *Early childhood autism* (2nd ed.). Oxford: Pergamon.

DeMyer, M. K., Barton, S., Alpern, G. D., Kimberlin, C., Allen, J., Yang, E., & Steele, R. (1974). The measured intelligence of autistic children. *Journal of Autism and Childhood Schizophrenia, 4*, 42–60.

DeMyer, M. K., Barton, S., DeMyer, W., Norton, J., Allen, J., & Steele, R. (1973). Prognosis in autism: A follow-up study. *Journal of Autism and Childhood Schizophrenia, 3* (3), 199–246.

DeMyer, M. K., Barton, S., & Norton, J. A. (1972). A comparison of adaptive, verbal and motor profiles of psychotic and non-psychotic subnormal children. *Journal of Autism and Childhood Schizophrenia, 2*, 359–377.

DeMyer, M. K., Churchill, D. W., Pontius, W., & Gilkey, K. M. (1971). A comparison of five diagnostic systems for childhood schizophrenia in infantile autism. *Journal of Autism and Childhood Schizophrenia, 1*, 175–189.

DeMyer, M. K., Hingtgen, J. N., & Jackson, R. K. (1981). Infantile autism reviewed: A decade of research. *Schizophrenia Bulletin, 7*, 388–451.

Eggers, C. (1978). Cause and prognosis of childhood schizophrenia. *Journal of Autism and Childhood Schizophrenia, 8*, 21–35.

Eisenberg, L. (1957). The course of childhood schizophrenia. *Archives of Neurology & Psychiatry, 78*, 69–83.

Eisenberg, L., & Kanner, L. (1956). Childhood schizophrenia. *American Journal of Orthopsychiatry, 26*, 556–564.

Esman, A., Kahn, M., & Nyman, L. (1959). The family of the schizophrenic child. *American Journal of Orthopsychiatry, 29*, 455–459.

Fein, D., Humes, M., Kaplan, E., Lucci, D., & Waterhouse, L. (1984). The question of left hemisphere dysfunction in infantile autism. Psychological Bulletin, *95*(2), 258–281.

Fenton, W. S., Mosher, L. R., & Matthews, S. M. (1981). Diagnosis of schizophrenia: A critical review of current diagnostic systems. *Schizophrenia Bulletin, 7*, 452–475.

Ferrari, M., & Matthews, W. (1983). Self-recognition deficits in autism and syndrome specific or general developmental delay. *Journal of Autism and Developmental Disorders, 13*, 317–324.

Fish, B. (1976). Biological disorders in infants at risk for schizophrenia. In E. R. Ritvo (Ed.), *Autism: Diagnosis, current research and management.* New York: Spectrum.

Fish, B. (1977). Neurobiologic antecedents of schizophrenia in children: Evidence for an inherited congenital neurointegrative defect. *Archives of General Psychiatry, 34*, 1297–1313.

Folstein, S., & Rutter, M. (1977). Genetic influences and infantile autism: A genetic study of 21 twin pairs. *Journal of Child Psychology and Psychiatry, 18*, 297–321.

Foxx, R. M., & Azrin, N. H. (1973). The elimination of autistic self-stimulatory behavior by overcorrection. *Journal of Applied Behavior Analysis, 6*, 1–14.

Frankel, F., Simmons, J., Fichter, M., & Freeman, B. J. (1984). Stimulus overselectivity in autistic and mentally retarded children—A research note. *Journal of Child Psychology and Psychiatry, 25* (1), 147–155.

Freeman, B. J., Ritvo, E. R., Schroth, P. C., Tonick, I., Guthrie, D., & Wake, L. (1981). Behavioral characteristics of high- and low-IQ autistic children. *American Journal of Psychiatry, 138*, 25–29.

Frith, U. (1971). Spontaneous patterns produced by autistic, normal and subnormal children. In M. Rutter (Ed.), *Infantile autism: Concepts, characteristics and treatment* (pp. 113–131). Edinburgh: Churchill & Livingstone.

Frith, U., & Hermelin, B. (1969). The role of usual and motor cues for normal, subnormal and autistic children. *Journal of Child Psychology and Psychiatry, 10*, 153.

Frith, U., & Snowling, M. (1983). Reading for meaning and reading for sound in autistic and dyslexic children. *British Journal of Developmental Psychology, 1*, 329–342.

Fyffe, C., & Prior, M. (1978). Evidence for language recording in autistic, retarded and normal children: A re-examination. *British Journal of Psychology, 69*, 393–402.

Fulkerson, S. C., & Freeman, W. M. (1980). Perceptual-motor deficiency in autistic children. *Perceptual and Motor Skills, 50*, 331–336.

Garralda, M. E. (1983). Hallucinations in psychiatrically disordered children: Preliminary communication. *Journal of the Royal Society of Medicine, 75*, 181–185.

Geller, E., Ritvo, E. R., Freeman, B. J., & Yuwiler, A. (1982). Preliminary observations on the effect of fenfluramine on blood serotonin and symptoms in three autistic boys. *New England Journal of Medicine, 307*, 165–169.

Gillberg, C. (1984). Infantile autism and other childhood psychoses in a Swedish urban region. Epidemiological aspects. *Journal of Child Psychology and Psychiatry, 25*, 35–44.

Gillberg, C., & Schaumann, H. (1981). Infantile autism and puberty. *Journal of Autism and Developmental Disorders, 11*, 365–371.

Glish, M. A., Erlenmeyer-Kimling, L., & Watt, N. F. (1982). Parental assessment of the social and emotional adaptation of children at high risk for schizophrenia. In

D. B. Lahey & A. E. Kazdin (Eds.), *Advances in clinical child psychology* (Vol. 5). New York: Plenum.

Goldfarb, W. (1961). *Childhood schizophrenia*, Cambridge, MA: Harvard University Press.

Graham, P., & Rutter, M. (1976). Adolescent disorders. In M. Rutter & L. Hersov (Eds.), *Child psychiatry—Modern approaches*. Oxford: Blackwell.

Green, W., Campbell, M., Hardesty, A., Grega, D., Padron-Gayol, M., Shell, J., & Erlenmeyer-Kimling, L. (1984). A comparison of schizophrenic and autistic children. *Journal of the American Academy of Child Psychiatry, 23*, 399–409.

Group for the Advancement of Psychiatry (1966). *Psychopathological disorders in childhood: theoretical considerations and a proposed classification*. New York: Author.

Gualtieri, C. T., Adams, A., Shen, C. D., & Loiselle, D. (1982). Minor physical anomalies in alcoholic and schizophrenic adults and hyperactive and autistic children. *American Journal of Psychiatry, 139*, 640–643.

Hagen, J. W., Winsberg, G. B., & Wolff, P. (1969). Cognitive and linguistic deficits in psychotic children. *Child Development, 39*, 1103–1117.

Haier, R. V. (1980). The diagnosis of schizophrenia: A review of recent research. *Schizophrenia Bulletin, 6*, 417–428.

Harris, S. L. (1975). Teaching language to non-verbal children—with emphasis on problems of generalization. *Psychological Bulletin, 82*, 4, 565–580.

Hermelin, B. (1976). Coding and the sense modalities. In L. Wing (Ed.), *Early childhood autism*. New York: Pergamon.

Hermelin, B. (1982). Thoughts and feelings. *Australian Autism Review, 1*, 10–19.

Hermelin, B., & O'Connor, N. (1970). *Psychological Experiments with Autistic Children*. Oxford: Pergamon.

Hertzig, M., & Walker, H. (1975). Symptom formation as an expression of disordered information processing in schizophrenic children. *Journal of Autism and Developmental Disorders, 5*, 13–24.

Hewitt, F. M. (1965). Teaching speech to an autistic child through operant conditioning. *American Journal of Orthopsychiatry, 35*, 927–936.

Hobson, R. P. (1983). The autistic child's recognition of age-related features of people, animals and things. *British Journal of Developmental Psychology, 1*, 343–352.

Hoffmann, W., & Prior, M. (1982). Neuropsychological dimensions of autism in children. A test of the hemispheric dysfunction hypothesis. *Journal of Clinical Neuropsychology, 4*(1), 27–42.

Hoshino, Y., Kumashiro, H., Yashima, Y., Tachibana, R., & Watanabe, M. (1982). The epidemiological study of autism in Fukushima-Ken. *Folia Psychiatrica et Neurologica Japonica, 36*, 115–124.

Howells, J. G., & Guirguis, W. R. (1984). Childhood schizophrenia 20 years later. *Archives of General Psychiatry, 41*, 123–128.

Howlin, P. (1982). Echolalic and spontaneous phrase speech in autistic children. *Journal of Child Psychology and Psychiatry, 23*, 281–293.

James, A. L., & Barry, R. J. (1980). A review of psychophysiology in early onset psychosis. *Schizophrenia Bulletin, 6*, 506–525.

Jones, V., & Prior, M. (1985). Motor imitation abilities and neurological signs in autistic children. *Journal of Autism and Developmental Disorders, 15*, 1, 37–46.

Kanner, L. (1943). Autistic disturbances of affective contact. *Nervous Child, 2*, 217–250.

Kanner, L. (1954). General concept of schizophrenia at different ages. In R. McIntosh & C. Hare (Eds.), *Proceedings of the association for research in nervous and mental diseases. Neurology and psychiatry in childhood.* Baltimore: Williams & Wilkins.

Kanner, L. (1971). Childhood psychosis: A historical over-view. *Journal of Autism and Childhood Schizophrenia, 1*, 14–19.

Kanner, L. (1973). The birth of early infantile autism. *Journal of Autism and Childhood Schizophrenia, 3*, 93–95.

Kessler, S. (1980). Genetics of schizophrenia: A review. *Schizophrenia Bulletin, 6*, 404–416.

Klebanoff, L. (1959). Parental attitudes of mothers of schizophrenic brain-injured and retarded, and normal children. *American Journal of Orthopsychiatry, 29*, 445–454.

Knobloch, H., & Pasamanick, B. (1975). Some etiological and prognostic factors in early infantile autism and psychosis. *Pediatrics, 55*, 182–191.

Koegel, R. L., & Lovaas, O. I. (1978). Comments on autism and stimulus overselectivity. *Journal of Abnormal Psychology, 87*, 563–565.

Koegel, R. L., & Rincover, A. (1974). Treatment of psychotic children in a classroom environment: I. Learning in a large group. *Journal of Applied Behavior Analysis, 7*, 45–59.

Kolvin, I. (1971). Six studies in the childhood psychoses. I—Diagnostic criteria and classification. *British Journal of Psychiatry, 118*, 381–384.

Kolvin, I., Garside, R., & Kidd, J. (1971). Six studies in the childhood psychoses. IV. Parental personality and attitude in childhood psychoses. *British Journal of Psychiatry, 118*, 403–406.

Kolvin, I., Ounsted, C., Humphrey, N., & McNay, A. (1971). Six studies in the Childhood Psychoses. II—Phenomenology of childhood psychoses. *British Journal of Psychiatry, 118*, 385–395.

Kolvin, I., Ounsted, C., Richardson, I., & Garside, R. (1971). Six studies in the childhood psychoses. III. The family and social background in childhood psychoses. *British Journal of Psychiatry, 118*, 396–402.

Konstantareas, M. M., Webster, C. D., & Oxman, J. (1979). Manual language acquisition and its influence on other areas of functioning in four autistic-like children. *Journal of Child Psychology and Psychiatry, 20*, 337–350.

Kootz, J. P., Marinelli, B., & Cohen, D. J. (1981). Sensory receptor sensitivity in autistic children: Response times to proximal and distal stimulation. *Archives of General Psychiatry, 58*, 271–273.

Kydd, R. R., & Werry, J. S. (1982). Schizophrenia in children under sixteen years. *Journal of Autism and Developmental Disorders, 12*, 343–357.

Lennox, C., Callias, M., & Rutter, M. (1977). Cognitive characteristics of parents and autistic children. *Journal of Autism and Childhood Schizophrenia, 7*, 243–261.

Liem, J.H. (1980). Family studies of schizophrenia: An update and commentary. *Schizophrenia Bulletin, 6*, 429–455.

Lockyer, L., & Rutter, M. (1970). A five to fifteen year follow-up study of infantile psychosis: IV. Patterns of cognitive ability. *British Journal of Social and Clinical Psychology, 9*, 152–163.

Lotter, V. (1966). Epidemiology of autistic conditions in young children: I. Prevalence. *Social Psychiatry, 1*, 124–137.

Lotter, V. (1967). Epidemiology of autistic conditions in young children: II. Some characteristic of the parents' and children's. *Social Psychiatry, 1*, 163–173.

Lotter, V. (1974). Social adjustment and placement of autistic children in Middlesex: A follow-up study. *Journal of Child Psychology and Psychiatry, 19*, 231–244.

Lotter, V. (1978). Childhood autism in Africa. *Journal of Child Psychology and Psychiatry, 19*, 231–244.

Lovaas, O. I., & Butcher, B. D. (1974). *Perspectives in behavior modification with deviant children.* Englewood Cliffs, NJ: Prentice-Hall.

Loveland, K. A., & Landry, S. H. (1985). *Joint attention and language in autism and developmental language delay.*

Mahler, M. (1965). On early infantile psychosis. The symbiotic and autistic syndromes. *Journal of the American Academy of Psychiatry, 4*, 554–568.

Maurer, R. G., & Damasio, A. R. (1982). Childhood autism from the point of view of behavioral neurology. *Journal of Autism and Developmental Disorders, 12*, 195–206.

McCrimmon, D. J., Cleghorn, J. N., Arsanow, R. F., & Steffy, R. A. (1980). Children at risk for schizophrenia: Clinical and attentional characteristics. *Archives of General Psychiatry, 37*, 671–674.

Menyuk, P., & Wilbur, R. (1981). Preface to special issue on language. *Journal of Autism and Developmental Disorders, 11* (1), 1–13.

Najem, G. R., Lindenthal, J. J., Louria, D. S., & Thind, I. S. (1980). Epidemiology of schizophrenia. *Public Health Reviews, 9*, 113–137.

Ogdon, D., Bass, C., Thomas, E., & Lordi, W. (1968). Parents of autistic children. *American Journal of Orthopsychiatry, 38*, 653–658.

Ornitz, E., Guthrie, D., & Farley, A. (1978). The early symptoms of childhood autism. In G. Serban (Ed.), *Cognitive deficits in the development of mental illness.* New York: Brunner/Mazel.

Ornitz, E. M., & Ritvo, E. (1976). The syndrome of autism: A critical review. *American Journal of Psychiatry, 133*, 609–621.

Parker, G. (1982). Re-searching the schizophrenic mother. *Journal of Nervous and Mental Disease, 170*, 452–462.

Petty, L. K., Ornitz, E. M., Michelman, J. D., & Zimmerman, E. G. (1984). Autistic children who become schizophrenic. *Archives of General Psychiatry, 41*, 129–135.

Pierce, S., & Bartolucci, G. (1977). A syntactic investigation of verbal autistic, mentally retarded and normal children. *Journal of Autism and Childhood Schizophrenia, 7*, 121–134.

Piggot, L. R. (1979). Overview of selected basic research in autism. *Journal of Autism and Developmental Disorders, 9*, 199–217:

Pittfield, M., & Oppenheim, A. (1965). Child-rearing attitudes of mothers of psychotic children. *Journal of Child Psychology and Psychiatry, 5*, 51–57.

Porges, S. W. (1976). Peripheral and neurochemical parallels of psychopathology: A psychophysiological model relating autonomic imbalance to hyperactivity, psychopathy, and autism. *Advances in Child Development and Behavior, 11*, 35–65.

Potter, H. W. (1933). Schizophrenia in children. *American Journal of Psychiatry, 12*, 1253–1270.

Prior, M. R. (1977a). Conditional matching learning set in autistic children. *Journal of Child Psychology and Psychiatry, 18*, 183–189.

Prior, M. R. (1977b). Psycholinguistic disabilities of autistic and retarded children. *Journal of Mental Deficiency Research, 21*, 37–45.

Prior, M. R. (1979). Cognitive abilities and disabilities in infantile autism. A review. *Journal of Abnormal Child Psychology, 7*, 357–380.

Prior, M. R. (1984). Developing concepts of childhood autism: The influence of experimental cognitive research. *Journal of Consulting and Clinical Psychology, 52*, 4–16.

Prior, M. R. (1985). Biological factors in childhood autism: A review submitted for publication.

Prior, M., Boulton, D., Gajzago, C., & Perry, D. (1975). The classification of childhood psychoses by numerical taxonomy. *Journal of Child Psychology and Psychiatry, 16*, 321–330.

Prior, M. R., & Chen, C. S. (1975). Learning set acquisition in autistic children. *Journal of Abnormal Psychology, 84*, 701–708.

Prior, M. R., & Chen, C. S. (1976). Short-term and serial memory in autistic, retarded, and normal children. *Journal of Autism and Childhood Schizophrenia, 6*, 121–131.

Prior, M., Gazjago, C., & Knox, D. (1976). An epidemiological study of autistic and psychotic children in the four eastern states of Australia. *Australian & New Zealand Journal of Psychiatry, 10*, 173–184.

Prior, M., & McGillivray, J. (1980). The performance of autistic children on three learning set tasks. *Journal of Child Psychology and Psychiatry, 21*, 313–324.

Prior, M., & Sanson, A. (1978). A follow-up study of autistic children in Victoria. *Australian Autism Review, 1, 4*, 12–18.

Prior, M. R., Tress, B., Hoffmann, W., & Boldt, D. (1984). A computed tomographic study of children with classic autism. *Archives of Neurology, 41*, 482–484.

Prior, N., Perry, D., & Gajzago, C. (1975). Kanner's syndrome or early-onset psychosis: A taxonomic analysis of 142 cases. *Journal of Autism and Childhood Schizophrenia, 5*, 71–80.

Quay, H. C. (1985). A critical analysis of DSM III as a taxonomy of psychopathology in childhood and adolescence. In T. Miller & G. Klerman (Eds.), *Contemporary issues in psychopathology*, New York: Guilford.

Quay, H. C., & Peterson, D. R. (1983). *Interim manual for the revised behavior problem check list*. Authors, University of Miami.

Quitkin, F., Rifkin, A., & Klein, D. F. (1976). Neurologic soft signs in schizophrenia and character disorders. Organicity in schizophrenia with pre morbid asociality and emotionally unstable character disorders. *Archives of General Psychiatry, 33*, 845–953.

Rank, B. (1949). Adaptation of psychoanalytic technique for the treatment of young children with atypical development. *American Journal of Orthopsychiatry, 19*, 130–139.

Reiser, D. (1963). Psychosis of infancy and early childhood. *New England Journal of Medicine, 269*, 844–850.

Reiss, D., Feinstein, C., Weinberger, D. R., King, R., Wyatt, R. J., & Braillier, D. (1983). Ventricular enlargement in child psychiatric patients: A controlled study with planimetric measurements. *American Journal of Psychiatry, 140*, 453–456.

Richer, J. (1978). The partial noncommunication of culture to autistic children—An application of human ethology. In M. Rutter & E. Schopler (Eds.), *Autism: A reappraisal of concepts and treatment* (pp. 47–61). New York: Plenum.

Ricks, D. M., & Wing, L. (1975). Language, communication, and the use of symbols in normal and autistic children. *Journal of Autism and Childhood Schizophrenia, 5*, 191–221.

Rimland, B. (1964). *Infantile autism*. New York: Appleton-Century-Crofts.

Rimland, B. (1974). Infantile autism: Status and research. In A. Davids (Ed.), *Child personality & psychopathology: Current topics* (Vol. 1). New York: Wiley.

Rincover, A., & Koegel, R. L. (1975). Setting generality and stimulus control in autistic children. *Journal of Applied Behavior Analysis, 8*, 235–246.

Ritvo, E. R., & Freeman, B. J. (1978). Introduction: The National Society for Autistic Children's Definition of the Syndrome of Autism. *Journal of the American Academy of Child Psychiatry, 17*, 565–575.

Ritvo, E. R., Ritvo, E. C., & Brothers, A. M. (1982). Genetic and immunohematological factors in autism. *Journal of Autism and Developmental Disorders, 12*, 109–114.

Rothstein, A. (1981). Hallucinatory phenomena in childhood: A critique of the literature. *Journal of the American Academy of Child Psychiatry, 20*, 623–635.

Ruttenberg, B. A., Dratman, M. L., Franknoi, J., & Wencar, C. (1966). An instrument for evaluating autistic children. *Journal of the American Academy of Child Psychiatry, 5*, 453–478.

Rutter, M. (1972). Childhood schizophrenia reconsidered. *Journal of Autism—Childhood Schizophrenia, 2*, 315–337.

Rutter, M. (1974). The development of infantile autism. *Psychological Medicine, 4*, 147–163.

Rutter, M. (1978). Diagnosis and definition of childhood autism. *Journal of Autism and Childhood Schizophrenia, 8*, 139–161.

Rutter, M. (1983). Cognitive deficits in the pathogenesis of autism. *Journal of Child Psychology and Psychiatry, 24*(4), 513–532.

Rutter, M., & Garmezy, N. (1983). Developmental psychopathology. In P. H. Mussen (Ed.), *Handbook of child psychology* (4th ed., pp. 775–912). New York: Wiley.

Rutter, M., & Lockyer, L. (1967). A five-to-fifteen year follow-up study of infantile psychosis. I. Description of sample. *British Journal of Psychiatry, 113*, 1169–1182.

Schopler, E. (1966). Visual versus tactual receptor preferences in normal and schizophrenic children. *Journal of Abnormal and Social Psychology, 71*, 108–114.

Schopler, E. (1974). Changes in direction with psychotic children. In A. Davids (Ed.), *Child personality and psychopathology: Current topics* (Vol. I). New York: Wiley.

Schopler, E., Brehm, S. S., Kinsbourne, M., & Reichler, R. J. (1971). Effect of treatment structure on development in autistic children. *Archives of General Psychiatry, 24*, 415–421.

Schriebmann, L. (1975). Effects of within-stimulus and extra-stimulus prompting on discrimination learning in autistic children. *Journal of Applied Behavior Analysis, 1*, 91–112.

Shah, A., Holmes, N., & Wing, L. (1982). Prevalence of autism and related conditions in adults in a mental handicap hospital. *Applied Research in Mental Retardation, 3*, 303–317.

Shapiro, T., & Lucy, P. (1978). Echoing in autistic children: A chronometric study of semantic processing. *Journal of Child Psychology and Psychiatry, 19*, 373–378.

Sigman, M., & Ungerer, J. (1984). Cognitive and language skills in autistic, mentally retarded and normal children. *Developmental Psychology, 20*, 293–302.

Small, J. G. Cited in DeMyer, M. K., Hingtgen, N. N., & Jackson, R. K. (1981), Infantile autism reviewed: A decade of research. *Schizophrenia Bulletin, 7*, 388–451.

Spiker, D., & Ricks, M. (1984). Visual self-recognition in autistic children: Developmental relationships. *Child Development, 55*, 214–225.

Stevens-Long, J., & Lovaas, O. I. (1974). Research and treatment with autistic children in a program of behavior therapy. In A. Davids (Ed.), *Child personality and psychopathology*. New York: Wiley.

Stevens-Long, J., Schwartz, J. L., & Bliss, D. (1976). The acquisition and generalization of compound sentence structure in an autistic child. *Behavior Therapy, 7*(3), 397–404.

Student, M., & Sohmer, H. (1978). Evidence from auditory nerve and brainstem evoked responses for an organic brain lesion in children with autistic traits. *Journal of Autism and Childhood Schizophrenia, 8*, 13–20.

Szurek, S. (1956). Psychotic episodes and psychotic maldevelopment. *American Journal of Orthopsychiatry, 26*, 519–543.

Tager-Flusberg, H. (1981). On the nature of linguistic functioning in early infantile autism. *Journal of Autism and Developmental Disorders, 11*, 45–56.

Tanguay, P. E., & Edwards, R. M. (1982). Electrophysiological studies of autism: The whisper of the bang. *Journal of Autism and Developmental Disorders, 12*, 177–184.

Tinbergen, E. A., & Tinbergen, N. (1972). Early childhood autism: An ethological approach. *Beihefte zur Zeitschrift fur Tierpsychologie*, No. 10.

Torrey, E. F., Hersh, S. P., & McCabe, K. D. (1975). Early childhood psychosis and bleeding during pregnancy: A prospective study of gravid women and their offspring. *Journal of Autism and Childhood Schizophrenia, 5*, 287–297.

Treffert, D. A. (1970). Epidemiology of infantile autism. *Archives of General Psychiatry, 22*, 431–438.

Tymchuk, A. J., Simmons, J. Q., & Neafsey, S. (1977). Intellectual characteristics of adolescent childhood psychotics with high verbal ability. *Journal of Mental Deficiency Research, 21*, 133–138.

Ungerer, J., & Sigman, M. (1981). Symbolic play and language comprehension in autistic children. *Journal of the American Academy of Child Psychiatry, 20*, 319–337.

Vilensky, J. A., Damasio, A. R., & Maurer, R. G. (1981). Gait disturbances in patients with autistic behavior: A preliminary study. *Archives of Neurology, 38*, 646–649.

Vrono, M. S. H. (1974). Schizophrenia in childhood and adolescence: Clinical features in course. *International Journal of Mental Health, 2*, 8–113.

Walker, H. A., & Birch, H. G. (1974). Intellectual patterning in schizophrenic children. *Journal of Autism and Childhood Schizophrenia, 4*, 143–161.

Walker, H., & Bortner, M. (1975). Concept usage in schizophrenic children. *Journal of Autism and Childhood Schizophrenia, 5*, 155–167.

Waterhouse, L., & Fein, D. (1984). Developmental trends in cognitive skills for children diagnosed as autistic and schizophrenic. *Child Development, 55*, 236–248.

Weinberger, D., Wagner, R., & Wyatt, R. (1983). Neuropathological studies of schizophrenia: A selective review. *Schizophrenia Bulletin, 9*, 193–212.

Werry, J. S. (1979). The childhood psychoses. In H. C. Quay & J. S. Werry (Eds.), *Psychopathological disorders of childhood* (2nd ed.). New York: Wiley.

Werry, J. S., Carlielle, J., & Fitzpatrick, J. (1983). Rhythmic motor activities (Stereotypies) in children under five: Etiology and prevalence. *Journal of the American Academy of Child Psychiatry, 22*, 329–336.

Werry, J. S., Methven, R. J., Fitzpatrick, J., & Dixon, H. (1983). The inter diagnoser reliability of the DSM-III in children. *Journal of Abnormal Child Psychology, 11*, 341–354.

Wing, L. (1969). The handicap of autistic children—A comparative study. *Journal of Child Psychology and Psychiatry, 10*, 1–40.

Wing, L. (Ed.). (1976). *Early childhood autism: Clinical, educational and social aspects* (2nd ed.). Oxford: Pergamon.

Wing, L. (1980). Childhood autism and social class: A question of selection? *British Journal of Psychiatry, 137*, 410–417.

Wing, L. (1981). Sex ratios in early childhood autism and related conditions. *Psychiatry Research, 5*, 129–137.

Wing, L., & Gould, J. (1979). Severe impairments of social interaction and associated abnormalities in children: Epidemiology and classification. *Journal of Autism and Developmental Disorders, 9*, 11–29.

Wing, L., Gould, J., Yeates, S. R., & Brierley, L. M. (1977). Symbolic play in severely mentally retarded and in autistic children. *Journal of Child Psychology and Psychiatry, 18*, 167–178.

Wolff, S., & Chick, J. (1980). Schizoid personality in childhood. A controlled follow-up study. *Psychological Medicine, 10*, 85–100.

Wynne, L.C. (1981). Current concepts about schizophrenia and family relationships. *Journal of Nervous and Mental Disease, 169*, 82–89.

Young, J. G., Cavanagh, M. E., Anderson, G. M., Shaywitz, A., & Cohen, D. J. (1982). Clinical neurochemistry of autism and associated disorders. *Journal of Autism and Developmental Disorders, 12*, 177–186.

6 ORGANIC AND SUBSTANCE USE DISORDERS

JOHN S. WERRY

ORGANIC DISORDERS

Introduction

Because of the extent of the literature on putative organic factors in childhood psychopathology, the scope of this chapter is limited to those clinical syndromes in which there is an *obligatory requirement for the unequivocal presence of major brain disorder*. The majority of studies of brain disorders and behavior are eliminated because such studies have not been concerned in the main with the syndromes clearly classified as the organic disorders, but with "brain damage," with isolated behaviors such as hyperactivity, with discrete cognitive functions, or with disorders (such as attention deficit disorder) in which an organic etiology may be suspected but not as yet by any means proven. Also, many of these studies are not of brain damage in the established neurological sense, but with factors associated with an unknown (and probably low) risk of incurring it, such as a history of perinatal insults.

Put another way, this chapter considers those diagnostic entities in which neurological criteria *are* necessary, whereas most studies either take syndromes in which there is, as yet, no such diagnostic requirement or take brain damage as the independent variable and then examine the correlates of it. Those disorders in which organic factors are suspected but not proven are discussed in chapters on other disorders, while the role of brain damage and other biological factors in psychopathology is discussed in Chapter 8. Nevertheless, a few untidy areas remain, such as mental retardation, and these will be discussed as they arise.

Because the medical aspects of the organic syndromes predominate, they have attracted, as yet, little attention as empirical clinical entities from psychologists and other nonmedical mental health professionals, though neuropsychology has contributed significantly to the diagnosis and defining of impact of brain damage (Satz & Fletcher, 1981) as well as behavior modification and education to its management and rehabilitation. The mode of operation of neuropsychology, however, has been almost entirely within the predetermined medical/neurological model, not the empirical statistical, nosological one. In a useful overview of organic disorders, Lipowski (1978) pointed out that between 1950 and 1975, the medical specialty of psychiatry likewise showed almost no interest in these disorders. As a result, these syndromes, though accepted medically and of considerable face validity, will have little of the robust status, established correlates, and supporting validity that obtains with, say, conduct disorder seen in Chapter 2.

Nevertheless, the organic disorders are important in childhood psychopathology. First, they may present initially with behavioral or cognitive disturbances; second, they often have such problems as correlates; third, mental health professionals often "inherit" such patients as medical diagnosis and treatment are concluded. Finally, with the increasing involvement of the mental health professions in pediatrics, there is a need for some knowledge among such professions and a place for it in their training programs so that they may play a much more positive role in the diagnosis, management, and research into these disorders.

The DSM-III (American Psychiatric Association, 1980) lists nine types of organic disorders that are defined primarily on the basis of symptomatology. Two of these (intoxication and withdrawal) are substance-induced while the others are delirium, dementia, amnestic syndrome, organic hallucinosis, and affective and personality syndromes. These nine types are then subclassified by the specific etiology or pathology, if known. Only the nine major phenomenological syndromes will be discussed, however, and most only briefly since they are unstudied, rare in, or largely irrelevant to children. For a clearer presentation, intoxication and withdrawal are discussed later under substance use disorders, rather than with organic disorders where they belong in the DSM-III.

Lipowski (1978) has pointed out that there are two groupings of these clinical syndromes: *global* and *partial*. The global syndromes (delirium and dementia) are technically the organic psychoses and can be usefully thought of as acute and chronic "brain failure," respectively, affecting a wide range of brain functions, while the partial syndromes affect (predominantly) one major function—cognition, emotion, or social behavior—and presumably reflect more localized brain disease. The general problem of the global or "mass action" approach to brain damage and disorders is discussed in Chapter 8. But to summarize, while the concept is useful here in describing two of the clinical syndromes, in individuals with the same disease there will be variations in the amount and areas of the brain affected. As a result, clinical symptomatology will always vary somewhat within this basic global picture (see Albert, 1981).

All of these disorders, whether global or partial, require clear proof, or at least convincing suspicion, of a *major* physical disorder within the brain or alternatively of serious distortions of its function by alterations in body chemistry, blood gases, body temperature, and so on as a result of changes in other organs or systems. Conversely, however, organic brain disease alone cannot define an organic disorder. The requisite psychopathological symptoms must also be present. This issue is particularly important when such disease or disorder occurred pre- or perinatally and obfuscates much of the work with "brain damage" that is further unspecified (see Chapter 8; Rutter, 1981, 1982).

Before leaving this general discussion, something should be said of ways of assessing the *psychopathology* of brain disorders, though this is discussed in detail in Chapter 8. Because assessment is predominantly of cognitive and motor functions, it is largely the domain of neuropsychology, a field that is too rich, controversial, and expansive to be reviewed here, and good reviews are readily available (e.g., Feuerstein, Ward, & LeBaron, 1979; Fletcher & Satz, 1983; Heilman & Satz, 1982; Satz & Fletcher, 1981). These reviews provide abundant evidence that neuropsychological methods can, not only detect impaired brain function, but differentiate generalized from localized disorder. It will therefore be a disappointment to find how little neuropsychology has been applied to the organic disorders in children and, when it has, how poor those studies are. The more persistent problems seem to be poor definition or description of neurological status; mixing of subjects with congenital and acquired brain disease; heterogeneous types of organic disorders in which children with global, partial, and motor-only syndromes are intermixed and treated as if they were the same; failure to take account of the effect of IQ on other aspects of the neuropsychological test battery (Siedenberg, Giordani, Berent, & Boll, 1983); use of only one or two tests or of those in which a variety of discrete cognitive functions are hopelessly intermixed.

Generally speaking, though, the most consistent work and best validated battery of tests seems to be the extended Reitan Batteries (Feuerstein et al., 1979; Flor-Henry, 1982). The validity and particulars are described by Flor-Henry (1982) and for children by Feuerstein et al. (1979). The battery attempts to measure general intellect (WISC), abstract reasoning, cognitive flexibility, memory, attention and concentration, sensory perception and integration, and motor function. The one area that is missing and that is emphasized by Albert (1981) in her review of the geriatric area is language (particularly aphasia).

The promise of these tests as a way of systematizing and strengthening the traditional but poorly validated medical-neurological clinical examination and thus contributing to the study, diagnosis, and management of the organic disorders in children cannot be overemphasized. A good example of this can be seen in the lonely study by Prugh, Wagonfield, Metcalf, and Jordan (1980) of delirium in children, which is described in the next section, though even they fail to tap the full potential of neuropsychological tests available.

Delirium

This is the first of Lipowski's (1978) global syndromes. The critical DSM-III diagnostic elements are:

A. Clouding of consciousness
B. Two of: perceptual disturbances; incoherent speech; disturbances of sleep–wake cycle and/or changes in psychomotor activity levels
C. Disorientation and memory impairment
D. Acute onset and fluctuating diurnal course
E. Evidence of an organic etiology.

Clouding of consciousness is of central importance with emphasis on reduced awareness and attentional disturbances affecting shift, focus, and sustaining of attention. As so often in the DSM-III, however, how to measure these is not stated, opening up the possibility of diagnostic confusion, particularly with dementia (Lipowski, 1982, 1983).

In the pre-antibiotic era, delirium in children was both commonplace and expected in febrile illness. Though now less common, it still occurs, but not infrequently in mild forms and so is missed (see Prugh et al., 1980). It is caused by such events as systemic infections of a bacillary nature, infections of the brain and its covering (encephalitis and meningitis), head injury, metabolic disorders such as diabetes, liver and kidney disease, and cerebrovascular accidents. Increasingly, though, delirium is caused by the ingestion of deliriant or toxic substances, sometimes in the context of drug abuse, sometimes as in accidental poisoning of very young children but also, as in the elderly (Albert, 1981), as a result of overenthusiastic pharmacological treatment of physical disorders. Any drug that enters the brain and influences its function can, theoretically, produce delirium in susceptible persons especially at the extremes of life, if the dose is very high or if brain or bodily function is already impaired by other diseases. The drugs commonly implicated now in children are the psycho- and neurotropic drugs such as anticholinergics, anticonvulsants, antipsychotics, antidepressants, and sedatives (see also Chapter 12).

The only good study of delirium in children seems to be that of Prugh et al. (1980), who compared 33 children and early adolescents suffering from acute brain disorders with a matched, physically ill, similarly hospitalized group on a set of clinical, neurological, EEG, and neuropsychological variables. The first finding of importance was that many of the children did, in fact, have undetected disordered consciousness (i.e., delirium), which tended to be misinterpreted as "naughtiness." Second, of the 17 variables clearly differentiating the two groups, most confirmed what now are the DSM-III descriptors of delirium. Third, the usefulness of neuropsychological tests in the diagnosis of delirium was shown, as was that of the EEG. Many of the neurological and perceptual tests said to indicate "*minimal brain dysfunction*," however, did not differentiate the two groups! (See also Chapter 8.) Outcome depended on the cause, but in those who recovered there was a slow and variable improvement of cognitive function. These findings are rather similar to those in head injury reported by Rutter (1981).

Difficulties arise when the symptomatology suggests delirium but there is no clear evidence of physical illness. This is most likely to happen with drug-induced deliria and with dissociative (see Chapter 7) and schizophreniform disorders of fulminating onset. Careful examination of the patient's history and symptomatology (or behavior) and use of neuropsychological tests should clarify the diagnosis, since while confusion, disorientation, hallucinations, incoherence, inattention, and so on may be present in these nonorganic disorders, they take a characteristic form that differs from those seen in organic disorders. Prugh et al. (1980) offer useful suggestions for a multimeasure, multisource diagnostic battery based on their study.

The best developed literature in the assessment of delirium is in gerontology. The review of ways of evaluating level of consciousness and attention in the elderly by Albert (1981) suggests that most of these procedures could easily be modified for use with children.

The epidemiology of delirium has not been studied but would be expected to approximate that of the diseases or drugs that cause it. It would be no surprise, though, to find that delirium, like admissions to pediatric hospitals, would be commoner in males and those of less advantaged socioeconomic groups, since this appears to be the general pattern of serious pediatric illness. Outcome will also depend on the particular cause, but if survival is the result, recovery of at least some degree of function would be expected since much of the brain failure is caused not by irreversible, but by temporary disruption of brain function (e.g., by swelling, inflammatory processes, metabolic changes, etc.).

Dementia

In contrast to delirium, dementia, may present insidiously and in a situation of apparent reasonable health, mobility, and social function. In some cases, though, it may follow after delirium, or coma in, for example, encephalitis or head injury (Rutter, 1981). It should be noted that dementia carries no prognostic connotations, and recovery may in fact continue over a period of many months especially after acute time-limited brain disorders such as head injury (see Rutter, 1981). The essential DSM-III features of dementia are:

A. Loss of intellectual abilities
B. Memory impairment
C. At least one of—impairment of abstract thinking; impaired judgment; other disturbances of higher cortical function (aphasia, apraxia, agnosia); personality change.
D. Clouding of consciousness bars the diagnosis (though, as already noted, this item is poorly defined and could cause difficulties in some cases)
E. Evidence of or reasonable suspicion of an organic etiology.

Since the criterion for degree of loss of intellectual function is stated only as "sufficient to interfere with social or intellectual function" (p. 107), there are obviously degrees of dementia.

Lipowski (1982, 1983) has offered a useful, if unvalidated list of differential diagnostic pointers for discriminating dementia and delirium and Albert (1981) of neuropsychological aids to diagnosis in the elderly, which could be adapted to children.

The symptomatology is largely cognitive and shows the influence of American neuropsychology (see Flor-Henry, 1982), which, it will be remembered, began with the study of clearly and seriously brain-damaged adults who would have been expected to include a significant number of cases of dementia. It might therefore be thought that there would be a good literature describing how accurately to measure these symptoms and attesting to the validity of dementia as a disorder. While this applies somewhat to the senile dementias (Albert, 1981), most studies in children have been concerned with brain damage (localized, generalized, and motor intermixed), not dementia, and further most leave much to be desired methodologically (Feuerstein et al., 1979; see also Chapter 8).

It seems to be true, however, that, statistically, severe brain disorder is associated with intellectual impairment and other essential features of dementia (see Feuerstein et al., 1979; Flor-Henry, 1982; Rutter, 1981; Chapter 8) and thus, that such a disorder could be said to exist but not a great deal more. In fact dementia does not appear much in the pediatric literatures except when the degree is very severe. It could also be argued that mental retardation is actually lifelong dementia and, thus, the research in this area would be applicable; but the DSM-III criteria for dementia require a period of normal function, and it is uncertain how lifelong intellectual impairment would influence the resultant clinical picture and correlates.

A more serious problem is that dementia is a symptomatological phenotype that has no connotations of precise etiology, of epidemiology, of course, or of treatment. In fact Albert (1981) has argued against the concept in favor of etiologically based diseases because of specific neuropsychological patterns of diseases within the broad syndrome and the close relationship between specific diseases, treatment, and outcome. This may be true as a general proposition, but there would seem to be utility and hence increased need for the concept in childhood psychopathology at the level of initial examination and investigation since there it could lead to improved cognitive assessment to alert the clinician to the possibility of an organic disorder.

For example, in a study of 12 children with organic disorders who presented initially with behavioral symptoms, Rivinus, Jamison, and Graham (1975) found that of the six who proved to have dementia, deteriorating school performance was one of three helpful pointers.

Rutter has pointed out that EEG or other evidence of abnormal electrophysiological activity in the brain is an important correlate of cognitive changes after brain injury or damage and thus presumptively of dementia.

But Flor-Henry (1982) rates the "hit" rate of neuropsychological tests in adults much higher than that of the EEG, which would be expected to have better validity in delirium because of the high level of activity of the disease process here. Circumstantial proof of the potential diagnostic value of neuropsychological tests in dementia in children can be seen in the study by Selz and Reitan (1979) of normal, brain-damaged, and learning disabled children. Within the brain-damaged group there was a subgroup with major intellectual and cognitive impairment which was readily separated out by neuropsychological tests. Many of these children had had postnatal diseases and might thus qualify for the diagnosis of mild dementia. Similar results were obtained by Tsushima and Towne (1977).

In contrast to neuropsychological tests, however, other psychological variables beloved of clinicians may be misleading. Evans-Jones and Rosenbloom (1978) described 10 cases of onset around age two, most of whom had clear preceding psychosocial stressors underlining the need, as stressed in the DSM-III, to concentrate on the symptomatology in the child and not to be misled by putative psychological or ecological etiologies.

The ICD-9 has a category within the Psychoses with Origin Specific to Childhood section called disintegrative psychosis. In this, an apparently normal infant or young child (age limit unspecified) develops loss of social skills, speech, and, usually, intellectual function often with behavioral and relationship difficulties (see Noronha, 1974; Evans-Jones & Rosenbloom, 1978). Following Kolvin, Ounsted, and Roth (1971), who found most psychosis presenting between three and five was of the disintegrative type, the ICD-9 seems to imply that this picture begins only early in life (say, before age five). This is clearly wrong, as the study by Evans-Jones and Rosenbloom (1978) shows. Further, inasmuch as the core symptoms of disintegrative psychosis are usually similar to the DSM-III criteria for dementia but add other criteria such as stereotypies, relationship problems, and hyperactivity, it seems hard to justify this category, particularly since it threatens to blur the ever-delicate lines between dementia and autism.

Amnestic, Organic Delusional, Hallucinatory, Affective, and Personality Syndromes

While dementia and delirium are the two examples of Lipowski's (1978) global brain syndromes (or organic psychoses), all those listed in the heading are *partial* syndromes, that is, the symptomatology is centered primarily on specific functions such as memory or perception and thus, presumably, the disease is largely confined to discrete areas of the brain. Once again, clear evidence or strong suspicion of organic brain disease is necessary for these diagnoses.

Apart from isolated clinical studies (e.g., Waller & Rush 1983), none of these syndromes has yet been properly researched or in some cases been shown to occur in children. Hallucinations are neither uncommon nor diagnostically specific in children (Garralda, 1984a, 1984b) and have been discussed in the chapter on schizophrenia, but they probably seldom if ever reflect true organic hallucinatory disorders, which must occur in a state of *clear consciousness*. When caused by organic brain disease, hallucinations in children would, in all probability, be part of a toxic or other delirium and occur in a state of confusion.

The one possible exception in terms of relevance to children is the organic personality syndrome.

The DSM-III criteria for its diagnosis are:

A. A marked change in behavior or personality involving at least one of

    (i) emotional lability

    (ii) impairment in impulse control (poor social judgment, sexual indiscretions, shoplifting, etc.)

    (iii) apathy or indifference

    (iv) suspiciousness

B. No features of other organic disorders

C. Evidence of an organic etiology

D. This diagnosis is not to be given to a child or adolescent if the clinical picture has the features of attention deficit disorder (ADD).

While ADD (see Chapter 4) shares some of the basic symptomatology, organic personality syndrome is differentiated by the requirement for a marked change in behavior (though ADD may of course occasionally have a clear onset too), and the requirement for clear evidence or high suspicion of a *major* organic disease.

Though the literature does not as yet seem to have reported the diagnosis of organic personality syndrome in children, Rutter (1981) and his colleagues found that only socially disinhibited or inappropriate behavior (characterized by such behaviors as embarrassing outspokenness, disinhibited sexual behavior, overtalkativeness, forgetfulness, impulsiveness, carelessness about hygiene and dress) distinguished the children with severe head injuries from contrast groups at follow-up. The features outlined by Rutter constitute what used to be called "the frontal lobe syndrome" and are now embodied in the first criterion (A) for the organic personality syndrome in the DSM-III and are described in greater detail in the preamble to the disorder in the *Manual* (pp. 118–119). This and clinical wisdom suggest that this diagnostic label could be useful in brain-damaged non-mentally retarded children, though the insistence in the DSM-III on a *deterioration* in function seems to limit its usefulness unnecessarily, since much major brain damage in children occurs before, at, or shortly after birth. The wish to avoid confusion between ADD and mental retardation is understandable, but at the moment, a child who manifests the basic symptomatology of the organic personality syndrome including clear evidence of major brain damage, which, however, occurred pre- or perinatally, would probably have to be classified as ADD. This would add further diagnostic heterogeneity to this disorder since in the overwhelming majority of cases of ADD there is no such major organic evidence.

Summary

The subdivision of organic disorders into global (dementia, delirium, or the organic psychosis) and partial (e.g., organic personality syndrome) is both useful clinically and reinforces the need to eschew the simplistic views of brain function that have dominated child psychopathology until recently. Such a classification in children and adolescents, however, lacks the kind of study it deserves, given the probable frequency of the organic disorders. Further, there is good evidence to suggest that neuropsychological diagnostic tests could perform a very useful role at initial assessment (1) in raising the index of suspicion about an organic disorder when the symptomatology is primarily behavioral or cognitive rather than neurological or physical; (2) when organic brain disease is diagnosed, in assessing function and in assisting location and suggesting etiology in cases (such as encephalitis) not easily diagnosable by organ imaging or other medical techniques; (3) in treatment and rehabilitation; and (4) in upgrading the quality of research in this field.

Though well established in clinical pediatrics, the validity and utility of the organic disorders, requires considerably more study before their status can be made equal to those of the more traditional disorders in childhood psychopathology. The importance of social sciences in diagnosis, treatment and rehabilitation suggest that a much greater involvement by psychologists, social workers and similar non-medical disciplines in pediatrics is to be fostered.

SUBSTANCE DISORDERS

The term *substance* is a generic one covering any chemical, licit or otherwise, in whatever form and however taken that is used deliberately to induce body (mostly psychological) changes for other than therapeutic purposes.

As noted, the DSM-III (American Psychiatric Association, 1980) somewhat untidily divides these into two groups: the substance-related organic disorders and the substance-induced disorders. As with the organic disorders, the failure of psychologists so far to apply their nosological strategies and techniques in this area leaves no option but to accept *pro tem* the authoritative, but quite untested, medical classification.

Organic Disorders (Substance Related)

Here, the emphasis is on changes in brain and other function (behavioral, cognitive, motor, physiological) that are of an ''organic'' nature, though the distinction between these and substance use disorders (e.g., dependence) is rather blurred at times. As with other organic disorders, the general syndromes or symptomatological pictures are first defined and then particularized by etiology, in this case by the substance concerned. While a drug may induce other organic brain syndromes (e.g., delirium, dementia, or hallucinosis), two extra syndromes, intoxication and withdrawal, are invoked in DSM-III (American Psychiatric Association, 1980) so as to cover the full spectrum of organic disorders.

Intoxication—Diagnostic Criteria

A. Development of a substance-specific syndrome that follows the recent ingestion and presence in the body of a substance.

B. Maladaptive behavior during the waking state due to the effect of the substance on the central nervous system.

C. The clinical picture does not correspond to any of the specific organic brain syndromes such as delirium, etc.

Withdrawal—Diagnostic Criteria

A. Development of a substance-specific syndrome that follows the cessation of or reduction in intake of a substance that was previously regularly used by the individual to induce a state of intoxication.

B. The clinical picture does not correspond to any of the specific organic brain syndromes, such as delirium, etc.

Most withdrawal symptoms reflect so-called rebound phenomena since compensatory cellular mechanisms enhanced by the chronic action of the drug greatly exaggerate normal neurotransmitter or other effects when the drug is discontinued. Though these drugs are taken for brain-related effects, most also have peripheral neurotransmitter effects as well, which means that autonomic and visceral effects figure prominently in withdrawal and are often the most spectacular and distressing though rarely life-threatening except in neonates of dependent mothers. The common symptoms are vomiting, diarrhea, sweating, malaise, sleep disturbances (the above symptoms are common after alcohol, opiates, anticholinergics, antidepressants, and antipsychotics), convulsions (alcohol and other sedatives), depression (stimulants), and a compelling desire to take the substance (tobacco and most dependency-producing drugs). Withdrawal is the obverse of dependence and, thus, the time it takes to become vulnerable to either depends on the substance (opiates and stimulants are rapid), the dose and the length of time the substance has been taken (delirium tremens requires years of hard drinking), and the pharmacokinetics of the substance (most benzodiazepine anxiolytics are stored and slowly excreted so that withdrawal symptoms such as convulsions are infrequent).

Substance Use Disorders

Two of these are described, and because there are rather marked differences among substances, they are simply described in general rather than specific terms.

Abuse is characterized by:

A. Pattern of pathological use.

B. Impairment in social or occupational functioning due to substance use.

C. Minimal duration of disturbance of at least one month.

Dependence is characterized by:

A. Tolerance or withdrawal.

B. In the case of certain commonly used substances such as alcohol and cannabis where the development of tolerance is usual, evidence of impairment of function is also required.

Like the organic disorders such as dementia, both substance-related organic disorders and the substance-induced disorders are only general phenomenological syndromes and they must be further subsclassified by etiology, in this case by the substance involved. This is because each substance tends to have peculiarities of its own. For example, alcohol can produce every one of the organic syndromes from delirium and dementia to hallucinosis, while tobacco produces only dependence.

Substances and Their Syndromes

Only those that are relevant to children and younger adolescents will receive mention and then in accordance with their importance in these age-groups. Little will be said of the empirical validity of these syndromes since the pharmacological studies upon which they are based, though extensive, are established almost entirely only in adults. What is presented is a distillate of current pharmacological knowledge (see Gilman, Goodman, & Gilman, 1980), which is assumed to be true of children and adolescents.

Because most children and younger adolescents use substances only occasionally, dependence and other chronic syndromes are rare and most of this review will center on intoxication and abuse and most emphasis given to the commoner substances. Useful overviews of the nonmedical aspects of this area are those by Kandel (1982) and by Sutker (1982), the latter of which gives particular attention to contemporary persono-social theory.

ALCOHOL AND THE GENERAL BRAIN DEPRESSANTS (INCLUDING SOLVENTS)

The CNS depressant drugs, which include alcohol, anxiolytics, sedatives, and so on, are reviewed in Chapter 12. Of all self-administered substances, alcohol is generally the first experienced, the most widely used, and of greatest public health import (accidents) in younger age-groups. So general is its use that there is little need to describe the alcohol type of intoxication. What is less well known, though, is that alcohol is only one of a wide variety of intoxicants the action of which is essentially similar and which are widely sampled by older children and adolescents (see following discussion). Most common of these are the volatile organic substances such as solvents, glues, gasoline, and aerosols. Almost without exception, these substances are cyclic or aliphatic hydrocarbons with six carbon atoms or less, sometimes halogenated as well (e.g., chloroform, carbon tetrachloride) (Barnes, 1979; Press & Done, 1967). Similar substances (though gaseous forms are more convenient) are used medically in anesthesia, while solid forms (such as barbiturates) are widely used as sleep-inducing drugs, anxiolytics, or anticonvulsants.

The common action of this wide array of substances is presently unclear, but since early in the century, it has been posited to be related to their high lipid (fat) solubility. Unlike most neurotropic drugs, such as the opiates, most do not have specific neurotransmitter effects, but are thought to change the physicochemical characteristics of the neuronal and axonal membrane so as to lower its permeability to ions such as chloride and thus its excitability (Gilman et al., 1980, pp. 271–272). The fact that young persons use nonmedical substances and sniff them rather than ingest them has tended to obscure the fact that from a *pharmacological* point of view they are really little different (apart from reported but unproven weak hallucinogenic properties) from alcohol, sedatives, and anesthetic agents (Barnes, 1979); hallucinations are in any case nonspecific in children (Garralda, 1984a, 1984b) and also occur with any sedative (see later text). In fact, modern sniffing differs little pharmacologically (or socially) from the ether and nitrous oxide parties indulged in by Victorian and New England gentry.

The effect of these substances is progressively to depress all brain function from above down so that the finest, most complex, and most highly evolved brain areas (cortex, basal ganglia, and cerebellum) and their functions—inhibition of behavior, decorum, empathy, altruism, judgment, cognition, memory, and motor coordination—are first affected. If the substance continues to be administered (e.g., as in anesthesia or drug overdosage), gross impairment ending in unconsciousness, surgical anesthesia, coma, and even death may result, depending on dose and the potency of the substance used. Hallucinations may occur early in this phase.

Fortunately, however, most volatile solvents are taken only intermittently and by inhalation thus directly into the bloodstream and thence directly to the brain without first being filtered by the liver. This produces a "buzz," which quickly terminates sniffing because intoxication prevents further inhalation from the hand-held bag by impairing consciousness and motor coordination. This all usually occurs at low total dosage, and the high cerebral blood concentration causing the "buzz" is rapidly diluted throughout body fat and eliminated via the lungs, thus dissipating the effect unless sniffing is resumed to saturate body fat stores. Another factor probably mitigating against lethal dosages is the social situation of sniffing akin to that seen with cannabis of passing the "bag" round. Thus withdrawal and coma would be expected to be a most infrequent consequence of abuse of these substances. The ability of inhalation methods to produce quick effects and rapid dissipation is why they are preferred in anesthesia.

In solvent abuse, however, death most commonly results, not from any overdose coma, but from toxic effects and, less often, asphyxiation due to blockage of the airways with vomitus or from the plastic bags in which volatile solvents are often inhaled to increase their concentration (Garriott & Petty, 1980).

One must distinguish the dose-dependent sedative effects of solvents from true *toxic* effects peculiar to some of the substances used. Gasoline in many countries still contains high proportions of lead, which, because it is in an organic (tetraethyl) form, has a high solubility in, and affinity for, brain and other fatty tissues, producing lead encephalopathy, a kind of delirium, which may result in dementia of varying degrees, though such cases seem rare except in the chronically intoxicated (Coulehan et al., 1983). Some glues, nail polishes, and the like contain irritating solvents such as acetone, which may cause respiratory difficulties. Halogenated hydrocarbons, of which chloroform, dry-cleaning fluids, fire extinguishers, and certain aerosols are examples, may produce cardiac arrest; others are liver or kidney poisons (e.g., certain dry-cleaning fluids) (Gilman et al., 1980, pp. 568–569).

In a study of all inhalant deaths ($N = 34$) in Dallas County in the eight years from 1971 to 1978 by Garriott and Petty (1980), the overwhelming majority of deaths were due to sudden cardiac death almost entirely associated with use of halogenated hydrocarbons, particularly the "Freons" in aerosols. Toluene, the most ubiquitously sniffed solvent, was involved in only one death. The peak mortality was at 18 years of age and in the year 1974. The rapid decline in mortality after 1974 is believed to be related to two factors: public education of the dangers of use and the discarding of fluorinated hydrocarbons because of their purported impact on the ozone layer.

The wonder is that such toxic complications and death itself are rare (34 in Dallas in 8 years and 14 cases in New Zealand between 1978 and 1981[1]) and, apart from sudden death, found usually only in those few cases whose time is spent in a perpetual stupor (e.g., Coulehan et al., 1983) or who suffer unusual misadventure such as asphyxiation (Gilman et al., 1980, p. 568). As is characteristic, public concern greatly exaggerates the toxicity of these substances.

OPIATES

These drugs are only rarely abused by children or younger adolescents. Their pharmacological effects are respiratory depression, euphoria, sedation, and pain relief. They have the greatest dependency-producing potential of any drugs. They also have the highest mortality of any substance due partly to high potency and partly to unhygienic preparation and administration (see Gilman et al., 1980, pp. 544–549).

STIMULANTS AND CAFFEINE

The therapeutic effects of stimulants such as amphetamines in children are well described in Chapter 12. Similar effects would be expected in illicit use except that as higher doses are used, euphoria, excitement, insomnia, and increased activity, which may border on the manic, become likely (Gilman et al., 1980, pp. 553–557). In susceptible individuals, but in almost anyone in high enough doses, a toxic delirium or more often the so-called amphetamine psychosis, difficult to distinguish from a paranoid state, can occur. Apart from a local anesthetic action and a shorter duration of action, co-

[1]As analyzed by the author from data on all solvent/gasoline-related deaths in New Zealand during 1978–1981 supplied by the N.Z. Chief Health Statistician.

caine is identical in action to amphetamines (Gilman et al., 1980, pp. 554–556).

Caffeine produces a mild version of this stimulation syndrome and may cause unpleasant symptoms (caffeinism) such as headache and nervousness (Rumsey & Rapoport, 1983) but does not produce psychosis except in very toxic, life-threatening overdose. The importance of caffeine is that children may have easy access to a caffeine-containing substance, such as tea, coffee, or more importantly certain colas. The effects of caffeine have only recently begun to attract serious attention in children but would seem to be worthwhile to explore further (see review by Rumsey & Rapoport, 1983).

CANNABIS AND HALLUCINOGENS

Cannabis, LSD, mescaline, phenylcyclidine, and anticholinergics contained in many plants produce an intoxication akin to a toxic delirium of substance-specific type though, in lower dosage, the perceptual distortions that are an essential part of delirium may be mild and sought-after.

The toxicity of cannabis is still hotly debated, but earlier exaggerated claims covered almost everything from permanent brain damage to genetic effect. Current concern centers on impairment of driving skills and lung disease, the latter because of the similarity of tobacco and cannabis tars (see Kandel, 1982). Psychopathological sequelae such as amotivational states seem more of a cause than a result of cannabis use.

Hallucinogens such as LSD and mescaline are relatively nontoxic, with accidents or suicide probably the greatest risk to life. Bad trips, flashbacks and tolerance mean, however, that interest in these so called psychedelic drugs declines rapidly and continued use is rare (Gilman et al., 1980, p. 567). Further, use has declined since the 1960s and now is very low (see Kandel, 1982). Occasionally, rather more toxic substances such as PCP (phencyclidine, angel dust) appear, and are a cause for concern, but fortunately they seem infrequent and evanescent as fads among drug abusers change.

There has, however, been a near universal tendency grossly to overestimate the toxicity of all illicit drugs (except perhaps opiates), whatever the type. No doubt much of this is due to the fact that illicit substances are used by young persons, who have been always perceived as up to no good and generally less law-abiding than their elders were at a similar age!

Patterns of Drug Use   Studies of drug-use patterns in children and adolescents range from deviant groups to population surveys (Kandel, 1982). The former are of limited value and are valid only for the groups concerned, most of which not only have very high rates of use, but are also of substances that do not rank nearly so highly in the population as a whole. Since 1970 there has been an increasing tendency to look at sections of the population either regionally or nationally, using household or school surveys. Much of this was stimulated by concern about cannabis, though other drugs were included. Many of these studies are longitudinal.

As Kandel (1982) points out, the findings have a general consistency which may be summarized as follows:

1. The chronological or developmental sequence of substances used is characteristic. (i) Beer or wine, then (ii) Cigarettes or hard liquor (iii) Cannabis (iv) Other illicit drugs. Movement from illicit drugs initially to alcohol and smoking almost never occurs.
2. Apart from alcohol, and possibly tobacco and cannabis, *experimenting* is much commoner than continued use.
3. While there is an orderly developmental progression, the number passing from one phase to the next diminishes exponentially so that illicit drug use, other than cannabis, affects only a small minority of the population.
4. With the exception of solvents, age greatly influences frequency and, because of its correlation with phase, type of substance used.

There are few data on children under 12. In the United Kingdom regular smoking is around 5 percent at age 11 to 12, though about 40 percent have tried smoking (National Children's Bureau, 1980). In the age group 12 to 13 inclusive the U.S. figures for alcohol and smoking (in the past month) are probably around 10 percent each and 5 percent for cannabis; other substances are not only used by far fewer, but they are used only very occasionally. From age 14 through 15, use of everything at least doubles (cannabis triples), and this upward trend continues until social maturity, when illicit drug use declines sharply, though there is then an increase in licit, *medically* prescribed psychotropic substances such as sedatives. In the case of tobacco and alcohol there is often a long latency between the first taste and regular use (Casswell & Hood, 1977; National Children's Bureau, 1980; Scott, 1979).

There is, however, a conspicuous omission of the volatile organic substances from many of these studies since reporting of them dates only from 1970 (Barnes, 1979). There is some reason to believe from clinical samples that solvent sniffing may begin in childhood, though the Monitoring the Future Project (Bachman, Johnston, & O'Malley, 1981) showed a total (ever, past year, or current) use of only 17 percent. Since these data were collected in high school seniors, it is hard to know how accurate the "ever" figure really is for children since longitudinal studies of smoking show that after a few years adolescents tend to forget their earlier experimenting (Murray, Swan, Johnson, & Bewley, 1983). A survey of Indian children in two isolated Manitoba communities suggested a 50 to 100 percent "ever" use of gasoline in the children (Boeckx, Postl, & Coodin, 1977), while a survey by Coulehan et al. (1983) of 537 Navajo junior and senior high school students in a boarding school showed a frequency rather similar to that of the Monitoring the Future Study: 11.4 percent ever with 7.5 percent current. The Navajo study showed that the average age at which sniffing had begun was

12.9 years. For most, sniffing was once in a while and in a group situation. Alcohol and cannabis were much more commonly used. In his review, Barnes found varying prevalence figures (1–60%) depending on population, place, age, sex, ethnicity, and severity. Surveys of normal school populations suggest that trying "once" may be close to 20 percent with occasional use (within six months) between 1 and 3 percent. The average age of first sniffing is around 12 or 13 but declines markedly in later high school.

All of these data have been derived from self-reports. O'Malley, Bachman, and Johnston (1983) have looked at the reliability and validity of this method and conclude that in their Monitoring the Future Study at least, self-reports have proven robust both in consistency over time and in terms of their correlates.

Correlates of Substance Use

In their comprehensive reviews Kandel (1982) and Sutker (1982) again document the consistency of the studies here. Much of the data (apart from earlier peaking) are also true of solvent abuse not so well covered (Barnes, 1979). Older age of beginning use and female sex are negatively correlated with use, especially abuse and/or illicit substances. Race affects only the illicit drugs (except cannabis), while regional effects are slight though in the predicted direction (lower in the South). Users of illicit drugs are less conforming in every area: school attendance and performance, delinquency, traffic accidents, religious values. They tend to come from poor family backgrounds but particularly those characterized by alcohol and tobacco abuse, low educational aspirations for children, and an environment that is not emotionally nurturant. Similar correlates are to be found with regular adolescent drunkenness, early smoking, and heavy gasoline and solvent sniffing (Boeckx et al., 1977; National Children's Bureau, 1980). One of the strongest correlates of substance use, however, is with use among friends. Dysphoria and low self-esteem are also important in the personality area.

This catalog of correlates is of course remarkably similar to those of adolescent psychopathology in general.

Predictors

As Kandel (1982) has pointed out, correlates are not the same as predictors. The longitudinal studies as well as some of the clearly antecedent nature of some variables have resulted in attempts to find predictors. Kandel separated these into four domains: parental influences, peer influences, beliefs/values, and behaviors (such as delinquencies). The amount of variance predicted by these four areas was substance phase specific. With the exception of adolescent values in initiation to hard liquor, they all contributed at least 10 percent of the variance to all phases. The contribution of parental factors was highest (40%) in initiation to illicit drug use other than cannabis.

Causes

Bry (1983) has pointed out that it is the *number* of risk factors rather than the pattern that is the best predictor of drug abuse and has suggested a stress-theory model in which drug abuse is seen as a coping mechanism. Segal (1983) has drawn attention to the importance of motivational variables in substance use and in designing prevention programs. Some of these motivational factors are sociability, relieving negative mood states (all substances), expanded awareness (illicit drugs), sensation seeking, and need for insight. He points out that only when the substance use is deviant does the motivational pattern likewise become deviant or psychopathological. An additional important factor in solvent abuse is lack of spending money, suggesting that this is a substitute for high-cost substances such as alcohol or illicit drugs (Barnes, 1979).

Familial studies including those of adopted-away children of alcoholics have suggested some genetic predisposition, and while there are some theories as to what may constitute any such biological vulnerabilities or markers, they are as yet unvalidated (Behar et al., 1983).

In summary, substance use is a complexly determined behavior with situational, peer, family, and personal factors playing the major roles. The more deviant the individual and his world, the more likely the substance use will also be deviant.

Outcome

The overall tendency is for use to increase with age, though for illicit drug use the peak is in early adulthood (Kandel, 1982). It seems that solvent abuse peaks in mid-adolescence and presages the general movement away from illicit to licit substances. It is important to remember, however, that while experimentation with drugs is common, few children and young persons will go on to become regular users of any but alcohol, tobacco, and to a lesser degree, cannabis. Even with smoking a high proportion of those who try it never become regular smokers, a feature not true of alcohol. While dropout and the move away from illicit drugs may be seen by some as a cause for comfort, it still leaves a major public health problem. The highest cause of mortality and morbidity by far in children and adolescents is from traffic accidents in which alcohol is a factor, particularly in young male drivers. The longer term consequences of smoking and alcohol consumption are of course well known (see Gilman et al., 1980). Thus, there is a need for concern even about the relatively socially acceptable outcome of substance use in the majority.

The earlier the onset of regular substance use, the more likely is the abuse of alcohol, heavy smoking, and illicit drug use, meaning that regular substance use in childhood is a serious matter. In a recent mailed questionnaire study (Schuckit & Russell, 1983) of age of first drink in male university students in San Diego (mean age 23), it was found that splitting the group into terciles by age of first drink (< 14, 14–16, 17 +) defined a progression along a set of alcohol, drug-related problems, and illicit drug use other than cannabis. Thus, the relationships between early drinking and a poorer outcome held true even in a group with relatively good functioning. Warnings of late psychopathological consequences of illicit substance use such as amotivational states, brain damage, and psychoses such as schizophrenia are often mooted, but like the moral threat of eternal damnation for sin, which they resemble, are not only unavailing as a deterrent but largely unsubstantiated (Gilman et al., 1980, p. 567; Kandel, 1982).

Summary

Regular use and/or abuse of substances is uncommon in childhood and found only in a minority of adolescents under 15. Experimenting with and occasional use of substances, however, especially of alcohol, tobacco, cannabis, and volatile organic substances, is more common (in decreasing order of frequency). The younger the onset, the worse the outlook. Deviant use is also much more likely in those with social, family, and individual pathology. The greatest importance of substance use in young persons is a personal and public health risk—in the present and near future primarily for road accidents and in the long term for substantially reduced life expectancy. In this respect, alcohol, tobacco, and to a lesser extent cannabis are the drugs of most concern. While the role of cannabis with or without alcohol in road accidents seems clear (Kandel, 1982), the long-term health risks can only be inferred from similarity of its tars to those of tobacco. Unlike smoking tobacco, however, cannabis use is more clearly time limited so that one is left with the inescapable conclusion, that *alcohol and tobacco are, as ever, the real drug problem*. Since giving up the use of these substances is difficult and treatment programs are of unproven value, it seems wisest to concentrate on preventing children and young people from starting smoking and drinking not overtargeting the high-risk but numerically small group of illicit drug users.

In his review Scott (1979) concludes that young children (six years old) seem often to have valueless attitudes to alcohol but in middle childhood this changes to an active rejection of future drinking in about half—yet by age 16, 90 percent or more of the population will have had their first drink. In the majority of instances, the first drink is taken within the family (Routledge, 1979).

Smoking has a somewhat different course (Murray et al., 1983; National Children's Bureau, 1980). Many persons have their first cigarette before puberty. Few enjoy their first smoke (Murray et al., 1983), however, and there is usually a long latency between the first occasion and regular smoking. These facts about alcohol and tobacco suggest preventive possibilities with children and adolescents, though regrettably these are as yet largely unproven (McAllister, Perry, & Maccoby, 1979; National Children's Bureau, 1980). Nevertheless, the signposts for the future seem clear. What is needed is more systematic research into prevention with younger age groups—and a change in social values devaluing all substance use such as seems to be occurring with tobacco and, much too slowly, with alcohol.

REFERENCES

Albert, M. S. (1981). Geriatric neuropsychology. *Journal of Consulting & Clinical Psychology*, *49*, 835–850.

American Psychiatric Association. (1980). *Diagnostic and statistical manual of mental disorders* (3rd ed.). Washington, DC: Author.

Bachman, J. G., Johnson, L. D., & O'Malley, P. M. (1981). Smoking, drinking, and drug use among American high school students: Correlates and trends, 1975–1979. *American Journal of Public Health, 71*, 59–69.

Barnes, G. E. (1979). Solvent abuse: A review. *International Journal of the Addictions, 14*, 1–26.

Behar, D., Berg, C. J., Rapoport, J. L., Nelson, W., Linnoila, M., Cohen, M., Bozevich, C., & Marshall, T. (1983). Behavioral and physiological effects of ethanol in high risk and control children: A pilot study. *Alcoholism, Clinical and Experimental Research, 7*, 404–410.

Boeckx, R. L., Postl, B., & Coodin, F. J. (1977). Gasoline sniffing and tetraethyl lead poisoning in children. *Pediatrics, 60*, 140–145.

Bry, B. H. (1983). Predicting drug abuse: Review and reformulation. *International Journal of the Addictions, 18*, 223–233.

Casswell, S., & Hood, M. (1977). Recreational drug use among Auckland High School students. *New Zealand Medical Journal, 85*, 315–319.

Coulehan, J. L., Hirsch, W., Brillman, J., Sanandrai, J., Welty, T., Colaiaco, P., Koros, A., & Lober, A. (1983). Gasoline sniffing and lead toxicity in Navajo adolescents. *Pediatrics, 71*, 113–117.

Evans-Jones, L. G., & Rosenbloom, L. (1978). Disintegrative psychosis in childhood. *Developmental Medicine and Child Neurology, 20*, 462–470.

Feuerstein, M., Ward, M. M., & LeBaron, S. W. M. (1979). Neuropsychological and neurophysiological assessment of children with learning and behavior problems. In B. B. Lahey & A. E. Kazdin (Eds.), *Advances in clinical child psychology* (Vol. 2, pp. 241–278). New York: Plenum.

Fletcher, J. M., & Satz, P. (1983). Age, plasticity and equipotentiality: A reply to Smith. *Journal of Consulting and Clinical Psychology, 51*, 763–767.

Flor-Henry, P. (1982). Neuropsychological studies in patients with psychiatric disorders. In K. M. Heilman & P. Satz (Eds.), *Neuropsychology of human emotion* (pp. 193–220). New York: Guilford.

Garralda, M. E. (1984a). Hallucinations in children with conduct and emotional disorders: I. The clinical phenomena. *Psychological Medicine, 14*, 589–596.

Garralda, M. E. (1984b). Hallucinations in children with conduct and emotional disorders: II. The follow-up study. *Psychological Medicine, 14*, 597–604.

Garriott, J., & Petty, C. S. (1980). Death from inhalant abuse: Toxicological and pathological evaluation of 34 cases. *Clinical Toxicology, 16*, 305–315.

Gilman, A. G., Goodman, L. S., & Gilman, A. (1980). *The pharmacological basis of therapeutics* (6th ed., pp. 258–275, 271–272, 535–584, 544–549, 553–557, 554–556, 567, 568–569). New York: Macmillan.

Heilman, K. M., & Satz, P. (1982). *The neuropsychology of human emotion*. New York: Guilford.

Kandel, D. B. (1982). Epidemiological and psychosocial perspectives in adolescent drug use. *Journal of American Academy of Child Psychiatry, 21*, 328–347.

Kolvin, I., Ounsted, C., & Roth, M. (1971). Six studies in the childhood psychoses—cerebral dysfunction and childhood psychosis. *British Journal of Psychiatry, 118*, 407–414.

Lipowski, Z. J. (1978). Organic brain syndromes: A reformulation. *Comprehensive Psychiatry, 19*, 309–321.

Lipowski, Z. J. (1982). Differentiating dementia from delirium in the elderly. *Clinical Gerontology, 1*, 3–10.

Lipowski, Z. J. (1983). Transient confusional disorders (delirium, acute confusional states) in the elderly. *American Journal of Psychiatry, 140*, 1426–1436.

McAllister, A. L., Perry, C., & Maccoby, N. (1979). Adolescent smoking: Onset and prevention. *Pediatrics, 63*, 650–658.

Murray, M., Swan, A. V., Johnson, M. R. D., & Bewley, B. R. (1983). Some factors associated with increased risk of smoking by children. *Journal of Child Psychology & Psychiatry, 24*, 223–232.

National Children's Bureau. (1980). *Children and alcohol: A review of research*. Highlight No. 37. London: National Children's Bureau.

Noronha, M. J. (1974). Cerebral degenerative disorders of infancy and childhood. *Developmental Medicine and Child Neurology, 16*, 228–241.

O'Malley, P. M., Bachman, J. G., & Johnston, L. D. (1983). Reliability and consistency in self-reports of drug abuse. *International Journal of the Addictions, 18*, 805–824.

Press, E., & Done, A. K. (1967). Solvent sniffing. *Pediatrics, 39*, 451–461, 611–622.

Prugh, D. H., Wagonfield, S., Metcalf, D., & Jordan, K. (1980). A clinical study of delirium in children and adolescents. *Psychosomatic Medicine, 42* (1 Suppl), 177–195.

Rivinus, T. M., Jamison, D. L., & Graham, P. J. (1975). Childhood neurological disorder presenting as psychiatric disorder. *Archives of Disease in Childhood, 50*, 115–119.

Routledge, M. (1979). Young people and alcohol. Wellington, New Zealand: Council for Educational Research.

Rumsey, J. M., & Rapoport, J. L. (1983). In R. J. Wurtman & J. J. Wurtman (Eds.), *Nutrition and the brain* (Vol. 16). New York: Raven.

Rutter, M. (1981). Psychological sequelae of brain damage in children. *American Journal of Psychiatry, 138*, 1533–1544.

Rutter, M. (1982). Syndromes of minimal brain dysfunction in childhood. *American Journal of Psychiatry, 139*, 21–33.

Satz, P., & Fletcher, J. M. (1981). Emergent trends in neuropsychology: An overview. *Journal of Consulting and Clinical Psychology, 49*, 851–865.

Scott, A. (1979). Adolescent smoking. Highlight No. 38. London: National Children's Bureau.

Schuckit, M. A., & Russell, J. A. (1983). Clinical importance of the age at first drink in a group of young men. *American Journal of Psychiatry, 140,* 1221–1223.

Segal, B. (1983). Drug and youth: A review of the problem. *International Journal of the Addictions, 18,* 429–433.

Selz, M., & Reitan, R. M. (1979). Neuropsychological test performance of normal, learning-disabled and brain damaged older children. *Journal of Nervous and Mental Disease, 167,* 298–302.

Siedenberg, M., Giordani, B., Berent, S., & Boll, T. J. (1983). IQ level and performance on the Halstead-Reitan Neuropsychological Test Battery for older children. *Journal of Consulting and Clinical Psychology, 51,* 406–413.

Sutker, P. B. (1982). Adolescent drug use and alcohol behaviors. In T. M. Field, A. Huston, H. C. Quay, L. Troll, & G. E. Finley (Eds.), *Review of human development* (pp. 356–380). New York: Wiley.

Tsushima, W. T., & Towne, W. (1977). Neuropsychological abilities of young children with questionable brain disorders. *Journal of Consulting and Clinical Psychology, 45,* 757–762.

Waller, D. A., & Rush, A. J. (1983). Differentiating primary affective disease, organic affective syndromes and situational depression on a pediatric service. *Journal of the American Academy of Child Psychiatry, 22,* 52–58.

7

PHYSICAL ILLNESS, SYMPTOMS, AND ALLIED DISORDERS[1]

JOHN S. WERRY

INTRODUCTION

Here a wide spectrum of disorders not covered elsewhere will be reviewed. The predominant symptoms are usually physical, though in some disorders, the interpretation of "physical" has had to be rather broadly interpreted (e.g., memory loss). There are also brief reviews of the effects of physical illness or handicap upon psychological status of children (hospitalization is now covered in Chapter 17). Because of the large number of topics to be covered, discussion has often had to be brief and mainly to indicate where to find further reliable information (if such exists).

Terminology

Although the term *psychosomatic* (psychophysiologic) is now obsolete, its use is likely to continue. Strictly speaking, psychosomatic disorders are physical illnesses of proven or presumed psychogenic origin (American Psychiatric Association, 1968). The term *psychosomatic* is widely used, however, to imply a somatic symptom without apparent physical cause. Such symptoms (e.g., obscure stomachaches) are more properly called psychogenic or, usually more truthfully, of unknown etiology since to prove that a physical symptom is causally related to psychological stimuli is often difficult and seldom undertaken. More commonly, as in DSM-III, temporal proximity is assumed to be indicative of causality—a logical fallacy that allows the perpetuation of much of the error characterizing the whole "psychosomatic" area. Indeed, many of the erstwhile psychosomatic disorders

[1]The author would like to thank Dr. Alan Zametkin of U.S. National Institute of Mental Health for assistance with the bibliography.

such as asthma and ulcerative colitis are now considered to be of physical etiology.

The terms *conversion* and *dissociative symptoms* are best reserved, as in DSM-III, for neurological-type symptoms (such as paralyses, anesthesias, and amnesias) that do not conform to known patterns of nervous function or disease. What the lay person and too many professionals mean by "hysterical" is better called "histrionic," as in DSM-III.

Concepts of Psychosomatic Relationships

The brief historical review that follows is based on Bakal (1979), Engel (1962), and Lader (1972) amongst others.

Modern views of the idea that psychological factors can induce disease probably began with Cannon's studies of the sympathetic system (fight or flight), which fathered the nonspecific notion of *stress* as an undifferentiated response to a wide variety of threatening or stressful stimuli. This view was extended to include the endocrine system by Selye, in his General Adaptational Syndrome, and was modified by H. Wolff and Flanders Dunbar to allow for individual variation in response based on personality, constitution, or injury. Later, at the hands of psychophysiologists such as Lacey, came the concept of response specificity; the response, though nonspecific as far as differentiating among stressing stimuli, was specific to that individual (or in Dunbar's view, groups of similar individuals or personalities). The current view of the nonspecific concept of stress is best seen as a scale in which all stressors are given a severity weighting and then summed to yield a total stress score (see Bakal, 1979; Dohrenwend & Dohrenwend, 1974). A residual of response and/or personality specificity can be seen in the Types A and B personalities as varying in vulnerability to cardiovascular disease (see Bakal, 1979).

In contrast to the nonspecific view, psychoanalytic theory has argued the specific view that the physical symptom(s) symbolize or are characteristic of the conflict (or stress). Elaborations of this view by Alexander and others will be found in discussions of asthma and other disorders.

The work of Engel (1962) with gastrotomized patients suggests this compromise: there may be at least two types of response dictated by the emotion experienced—one fight or flight and one of conservation-withdrawal (e.g., depression).

Studies in Children

Most of the studies on "psychosomatic" disorders in childhood have concentrated on first attempting to show that psychological factors might be causal and, second, on describing the nature and source of the psychogenic agent. Techniques of demonstrating causality are mostly correlative ones. Sometimes the correlation is with specific events presumed to be traumatic (such as coercive toilet training) but, for the most part, focus has been on demonstrating the coexistence of psychopathology in the child (and/or parent) with physical disease. Problems of establishing a causal relationship between physical symptoms and psychological state will be discussed in more detail in Chapter 8; relationships between parental factors and childhood psychopathology are discussed in Chapter 9.

This chapter focuses on (1) an examination of whether correlation has been proven and, if so, (2) whether it is invariant as it should be if the condition is exclusively "psychosomatic." Experimental demonstrations of psychophysiological changes are rare. Since the studies of "psychosomatic" disorders and symptoms have certain repetitiousness of theoretical content, execution, and errors of logic and methodology, one or two conditions, such as asthma, have been examined in more detail.

Classification

In Table 7.1, an attempt has been made to classify all those disorders in DSM-III in which "physical" symptoms are predominant and in which psychological factors are considered important in etiology. There are three problems. The first lies in the variable nature of the role of psychological factors across and within the individual disorders. For example, eating disorders are probably nearly always psychogenic, whereas enuresis is so in only a minority of cases (though affected by psychological factors in many more). Second, the absence of any demonstrable abnormality of structure or function may reflect deficiencies of current knowledge rather than a psychogenic origin. Finally, what is involuntary and what voluntary (which distinguishes some disorders) is in many cases a problem of baffling complexity.

ICD-9 groups most of the disorders discussed here under a default major category "Special Symptoms or Syndromes not Elsewhere Classified,"

TABLE 7.1 *DSM-III Disorders Where Physical Symptoms Predominate and Psychological Factors Are Important*

	Involuntary	Voluntary
Physical disease	1. Psychological factors affecting physical conditions	1. Factitious disorders 2. Eating disorders (some)
Physical symptoms without disease[a]	1. Somatoform disorders 2. Dissociative disorders 3. Psychosexual disorders 4. Other disorders with physical manifestations 5. Stereotyped movement disorders 6. Developmental disorders	1. Malingering 2. Eating disorders (some)

[a]Limited, to some extent by current state of medical knowledge.

though the conservatism of the ICD-9 can be seen in the persistence of Hysteria (to cover Dissociative and Conversion Disorders) and of a true (i.e., etiological) psychosomatic category "Physiological Malfunction arising from Mental Factors."

PSYCHOLOGICAL FACTORS AFFECTING PHYSICAL CONDITIONS

The DSM-III diagnostic criteria are:

A. Psychologically meaningful environmental stimuli are temporally related to the initiation or exacerbation of a physical condition.
B. The physical condition has either demonstrable organic pathology or a known pathophysiological process (e.g., migraine headache, vomiting).
C. Not due to a somatoform disorder.

While the erstwhile psychosomatic disorders required both a physical disease *and* a psychological cause to be present, the DSM-III equivalent is considerably broader, allowing not only inclusion of temporary disturbances, but also any disorder where psychological factors are involved in initiation or excerbation, even where this role is neither exclusive nor primary.

Asthma

A comprehensive review of this disorder to be found in Bierman and Pearlman (1983); much of the medical data that follow are derived from that source.

DEFINITION AND EPIDEMIOLOGY

Asthma is an episodic disorder of the respiratory system marked by paroxysms of difficulty in breathing, particularly in expiration, resulting from spasm of the bronchioles (or penultimate fine airways in the lung). It is basically a localized overreaction of the parasympathetic nervous system and/or exaggerated antiinflammatory-type response. Hence it is treated (reasonably effectively) by adrenergic drugs, anticholinergics or antiinflammatory agents. It is the most frequent chronic disorder of childhood resulting in significant disability and accounts for 25 percent of school absences due to chronic illness (Steiner, Fritz, Hilliard, & Lewiston, 1982).

Asthma occurs with a frequency ranging from 2 percent in the child population in U.K. (Graham, Rutter, Yule, & Pless, 1967) to around 5 percent in the U.S. (Bierman & Pearlman, 1983). Parental surveys often underestimate the prevalence and may explain some of these discrepancies. There are said to be ethnic and regional variations. It is more common in children than adults (Purcell, 1975), and twice more so in boys than girls (Bierman & Pearlman, 1983; Graham et al., 1967; Purcell, 1965, 1975). The spontaneous remission rate at adolescence is in the region of 70 percent, though recurrences in adulthood are common. The mortality rate is 1.5 per 1000 asthmatics per year, death usually occurring in adult life, or in poorly treated children.

ETIOLOGY AND PSYCHOPATHOLOGY

Etiological factors may be thought of as primary, or those that initially create the condition, and secondary, or those precipitating attacks. There are four broad classes of potential primary and secondary etiological agents (Bierman & Pearlman, 1983): (1) allergens such as pollens; (2) infections of the respiratory tract; (3) irritants including, cold or dry air, dust; (4) and psychological variables. They have been assigned differing importance by different investigators and specialists and in different epochs.

Currently, it is held that the two major factors are allergy and a hypersensitivity of the bronchioles to biochemical substances such as histamines, which are ordinarily released as part of the normal reaction to inflammation, irritation, and so on. Both of these have some hereditary base but are independent of each other; they are commonly found together but by no means always. Further, the allergic component is often nonspecific and only partly related to individual attacks.

Psychological etiological theories have been summarized and critically reviewed by a number of investigators (Dubo et al., 1961; Herbert, 1965; Purcell, 1965, 1975; Purcell & Weiss, 1970). Specific theories posit (1) a personality type, most commonly (according to Herbert, 1965) the anxious-dependent personality characterized additionally by an inability to express emotions, especially aggression and grief; or (2) a specific conflict, most notably stated in the hypothesis of French and Alexander (1941) that asthma symbolizes a suppressed cry for help.

Nonspecific theories are represented by Rees (1964), who, like modern stress theorists (Bakal, 1979; Dohrenwend & Dohrenwend, 1974), sees all psychological variables reducible to incremental effects on arousal level. This, by some psychophysiological concomitant (e.g., histamine release), precipitates the asthmatic attack. Learning theory explanations of the pathogenesis of asthma (see Ullmann & Krasner, 1975) may be primary or secondary, classical or operant. Classical theorists (Franks & Leigh, 1959) see the link between the eliciting stimuli and asthma as accidental, as typified in the many anecdotal, but poorly documented, stories of attacks being precipitated by flowers and then pictures of flowers, whereas operant explanations (Purcell, Turnbull, & Bernstein, 1962) see stimulus and response functionally linked in an escape-avoidance situation.

There are derivatives of these etiological theories that should enable some empirical testing of their validity, at least in an indirect way. Thus, the specific personality theory posits that all asthmatics would have similar profiles and that these profiles should be more common in asthmatics than in controls. French and Alexander's conflict theory would predict that asthmatics would be less able to express grief or anxiety. The nonspecific theory of Rees should demonstrate the covariance of asthma and a state of arousal, independent of the cause. The learning theory explanations would predict that certain psychological stimuli peculiar to each individual asthmatic would precipitate attacks and that conditioning–extinction procedures could strengthen and weaken the power of eliciting stimuli and of the asthmatic response. Purcell (1965, 1975) and Purcell and Weiss (1970) have pointed out that there have been remarkably few systematic attempts to test these postulates, but we will now discuss briefly those that do exist.

While early studies (Miller & Baruch, 1950) found that the asthmatic children had more difficulty expressing hostility, later and better studies by Beech and Nace (1965), Gauthier et al. (1977), Graham et al. (1967), Steinhausen (1982), and Viney and Westbrook (1985) have found no such differences.

Graham et al. (1967) pointed out that the typical study of the asthmatic child samples only a highly selective portion of the total asthmatic population, which is biased toward overinclusion of the emotionally disturbed child. In their epidemiological investigation of the physical health and behavioral and educational adjustment of a large cohort of children, they found no difference between asthmatics and normals in the frequency of psychopathology or between physically handicapped and asthmatics in ability to express emotion. According to parents, any emotion, not just Alexander's anger or anxiety, was important in precipitation, an observation that is more in keeping with the nonspecific arousal view. There was some relationship between the severity of the emotional disorder and the asthma, a finding contradictory to that of Block (1968), Dubo et al., (1961), and Purcell (1965). Graham et al. (1967) concluded that previous studies finding an excess of emotional disturbance in asthmatic children resulted from faulty sampling and that, because of the similarities in findings to physically handicapped children, any disturbance that occurs is the *result* not the cause of the illness.

Neuhaus (1958) found no differences among asthmatics, symptomatic cardiacs, and sibs, all three groups differing from unrelated normals. [It also presaged later work demonstrating a pathogenic effect of physical illness on the healthy children in families and the unsuitability of sibs as normal controls (Breslau, 1983).] This illustrates Graham et al.'s point that children with physical disorders represent a more appropriate contrast group than normals, since then there is some control for both the effect of the illness on the child and the families, and for the sampling bias in children seen by doctors or professionals. This effect on family function is also seen in the tendency of parents to overestimate the degree of psychopathology in their asthmatic children (e.g., Graham et al., 1967; Purcell, 1975).

Block (1968; Block, Jennings, Harvey & Simpson, 1964) proposed a subcategorization of asthmatic children into two groups using an "allergic potential score" (APS). Although the asthmatic group as a whole was not significantly different from a physically disabled group, significant differences in emotional maturity emerged between the low APS group and the high APS and disability groups, which did not differ from each other. Since the severity of the asthma was similar in the two groups, Block argued that the psychopathology could not be reactive to the disease, as others have hypothesized.

In a well-controlled study, Rees (1964) found that multiple causation was the rule in asthma and infective, allergic, and psychological factors are of varying importance in different individuals and in different attacks in the same individual. Rees appears one of the few to draw a distinction between the primary and the secondary causes; he also felt that secondary causes were always heterogeneous, whatever the primary etiology. His results are consistent with Purcell's work and modern views (e.g., Bierman & Pearlman, 1983).

Purcell, Bernstein, and Burkantz (1961), like Block, subdivided asthmatics into two broad groups, but on a prognostic not allergic basis: the rapidly remitting type (RR) who became free of all attacks within three months of hospitalization without steroid therapy, and the steroid-dependent (SD) type who could not be maintained free of attacks without steroid therapy. However, no differences except subjective parent- or patient-derived differences were found. Both groups, however, tried to avoid states of excitement of any kind and certain responses associated with increased respiration, such as coughing, laughing, and crying (Purcell, 1963), which led Purcell et al. to hypothesize that if it were true that asthmatics suppress crying, this may be a learned mechanism for preventing attacks rather than one of psychopathological import!

Along with a number of others (e.g., Block, 1968; Herbert, 1965) Purcell (1965) concluded that studies of personality in asthma are not fruitful and suggested that attention should be focused on the individual asthmatic attack and immediately antecedent psychological events. In a study along these lines, Weiss (1966) investigated the mood states of SD children and found negative mood to be significantly more frequently associated with attacks than asthma-free periods, but that in both situations positive moods far overshadowed negative, suggesting that SD asthmatic children were far from anxious or unhappy.

In subsequent studies summarized by Purcell (1975), his group defined two subtypes of RR asthmatics: those with a high APS (Block, 1968), and those with low APS. The former showed little sign of psychopathology and were presumed to remit because of removal from allergens (or infective agents) in their normal environment. The low APS RR subgroup benefited from "parentectomy" and also, characteristically, develop asthma at a later age.

In summary, while asthmatic children probably do have an increased risk of psychopathology this is small, variable, and probably secondary to the illness, there may be subgroups in whom emotional factors are (relatively) important.

PSYCHOPHYSIOLOGICAL STUDIES

As pointed out by Herbert (1965) and Purcell (1975), studies that attempt to link closely antecedent events with attacks or respiratory function are more likely to be of value. Owen and Williams (1961) showed that abnormal respiratory responses in asthmatics could be related to the mother's voice, independent of content. Hahn (1966) showed that asthmatics have abnormal autonomic responses suggestive of homeostatic dysfunction and tend to overreact with negative mood to stress.

Purcell (1965) in reviewing the animal and human studies concluded that, although certain abnormal respiratory responses have been conditioned, particularly in animals, there is as yet no clear evidence of conditioning asthma in animal or human.

Purcell (1975) used telemetric monitoring of vocalization during free play rating of affective content, which was correlated with proximate checks of expiratory volume. In keeping with the indirect data of Graham et al. (1967) and Reese (1964), most of the boys showed an increase in vocal behavior and tended to decrease in expiratory volume. While only a minority showed correlations between emotions (anger particularly) and reduced expiration, these were substantial. This study deserves commendation, not only for its precision, but for its attempt to demonstrate functional relationships. It also serves to stress the heterogeneity of etiology in asthma.

Purcell (1975) has argued that emotional states immediately antecedent to an asthma attack rather than personality or conflict in child (or parent) are the critical psychogenic variables and discusses in detail possible psychophysiological mechanisms, most of which are still quite tenable.

PARENTS OF ASTHMATIC CHILDREN

As will be seen in Chapter 9, measuring parental factors and establishing relationships with psychopathology in the child is complex. Nevertheless, there are numerous studies of the parents of asthmatic children that attempt to demonstrate an increased disturbance in parents and in their child-rearing attitudes and, thus, (wrongly) presume to have proven a psychosomatic basis to asthma in children. Fitzelle (1959) found no differences in personality characteristics and child-rearing attitudes of parents of 100 asthmatic children seen in a hospital clinic and the parents of 100 physically disabled children. Dubo et al. (1961) found that of 71 variables, the only relationships that emerged were within the various measures of severity of the asthma and between the child's and the parent's level of adjustment.

Purcell's group found the rapidly remitting (RR) group to have more punitive and authoritarian parents (Purcell & Metz, 1962) than the steroid-dependent (SD) group, which did not differ from normals; the RR group viewed their fathers as weak and passive; the SD group did not differ in any way from a normal control group matched for sex, age, and school grade (Baraff & Cunningham, 1965; Purcell & Clifford, 1966). Mothers, however, were similarly regarded by all the children within a more passive-affectional role.

Block (1968; Block et al., 1964), using the APS as a diagnostic criterion, found that although there were no differences between mothers of asthmatic and physically handicapped children, there were significantly more indices of unhealthy attitudes (overprotection, ambivalence about motherhood) and more marital conflicts in the mothers of the low APS group as compared to the high APS and physically handicapped groups. In one of the few studies to use direct observation of mothers with their children, Gauthier et al. (1977) found them to function well. Studies of parents thus are conflicting, and there has been a failure to recognize how the child's illness may distort normal parenting.

TREATMENT

The cornerstone of therapy in asthma is medical, but if psychological factors such as anxiety are important in asthma, treatments that can relieve or mitigate them should be useful, too.

These studies have been reviewed by Purcell and Weiss (1970), who point out that practically every psychotherapeutic procedure from psychoanalysis to hypnosis has been claimed to be of value in asthma, but that such claims are based on studies replete with methodological errors. There are, in effect, no acceptable studies of the effect of psychotherapy on asthma in children. In a recent review Rainwater and Alexander (1983) concluded that effects of behavioral methods on respiratory function are minimal and their utility is in teaching compliance with treatment and in emotional problems secondary to having asthma.

Hospitalization or "parentectomy," itself, is claimed to be useful in cases refractory to outpatient care, particularly for the rapidly remitting (RR) asthmatic, with improvement persisting after discharge (Purcell & Weiss, 1970). A word of caution, though; for some reason the RR group seems to have disappeared (Creer, Ipacs, & Creer, 1983). This is probably due to better medical management, including newer drugs and more family-oriented pediatrics.

In spite of the fact that psychotropic drugs are frequently described as useful (Purcell & Weiss, 1970), evaluation of their worth is difficult, since good studies are lacking.

SUMMARY

There is no evidence that *all* asthmatic children have significant psychopathology or abnormal parenting. When all asthmatic children in the population are studied, differences from normal children become almost imperceptible and such as are found seem characteristic of physically handicapped children in general. Thus there is no good evidence that asthma is a "psychosomatic" disease, but as with all disabling, episodically life-threatening physical illness, asthma itself can create psychopathology in child, parents, and siblings. Parents of children with asthma may become more overprotective and anxious, overestimating their child's pathology and psychopathology. This has led to errors in studies that relied solely on parental reports of psychopathology or did not use appropriate (disabled) control groups. While modern reviews such as Bierman and Pearlman's (1983) dismiss emotional factors as important in primary etiology, the residues of past work suggest that they may play a role once asthma is well established, especially in precipitating or prolonging some attacks. The most robust are any that result in increased respiration, but others could be important. It also seems likely that the role of emotional factors will vary greatly from child to child and from attack to attack.

In view of the efficacy of modern medical methods and the high mortality associated with failure to utilize them efficiently, prevention of abnormal illness behavior, especially failure to comply with treatment, is now the most urgent line of research.

Ulcerative Colitis

Ulcerative colitis is a serious disease of the colon and rectum characterized by bloody diarrhea, ulceration of the bowel, and the absence of pathogenic microorganisms. The first two features differentiate it from simple nervous diarrhea and the latter two from infective kinds.

The onset is usually in adulthood with 10 percent of cases occurring in older children and adolescents. Onset is typically insidious, although in about 10 percent of children it is fulminating and life-threatening. There seem to be no discriminating sex or socioeconomic features, though good data are inevitably scant. In an exhaustive search Steinhausen and Kies (1982) could find only seven active cases in children and adolescents in West Berlin.

Even though the course of the disease in most instances is that of a low-grade chronicity with intermittent exacerbations, serious long-term complications, notably malignant disease of the bowel, are common and justify surgery in chronic cases (Broberger & Lagercrantz, 1966). With the rise in popularity of immunological theories of etiology and effective, if symptomatic, treatment, interest in this disorder in childhood psychopathology seem to have waned in the last decade (Steinhausen & Kies, 1982), though its historical role in psychosomatics is substantial.

Although the primary etiological importance of physical factors had been increasingly recognized, Feldman, Cantor, Soll, and Bachrach (1967) pointed out that many professionals then still discussed the condition as if it were a truly psychosomatic disease. Even when proponents admitted the importance of physical factors (Engel, 1962; Jackson & Yalom, 1966; Josselyn, Littner, & Spurlock, 1966; McDermott & Finch, 1967), there was still the belief that practically all ulcerative colitis patients (and their parents) had severe abnormality of personality, unconscious conflict, mood, or family interaction that long predated the onset of the illness.

In one of the few studies using normative and control data, Feldman et al. (1967) failed to find any importance or specificity of psychopathology in ulcerative colitis. In the only recent and acceptable study, Steinhausen and Kies (1982) found a marked increase in emotional (i.e., anxiety-withdrawal) disturbance in seven children with ulcerative colitis as compared with normal controls, but the results were similar in Crohn's disease—another serious and chronic but distinctive inflammatory disorder of the bowel. They suspected that this increase in psychopathology was due to the problem of chronic illness rather than causal, and indeed empirical studies of chronic illness support such a conclusion (see asthma and subsequent text). Interestingly too, locus-of-control measures contradicted psychoanalytic hypotheses. Neither did families differ.

The efficacy of psychotherapeutic techniques is unknown, except that there appears to be little correlation between psychological and physical improvement (Feldman et al., 1967; McDermott & Finch, 1967), casting further doubt on the functional relationship between psychological variables and ulcerative colitis. Sensibly, the role of psychotherapy in children appears to have shifted among its protagonists from a primary to a supportive role in the disease (McDermott & Finch, 1967; Steinhausen & Kies, 1982). This seems eminently defensible in view of the frequency of psychological complications of this serious, unpleasant disorder (Steinhausen & Kies, 1982).

STEREOTYPED MOVEMENT DISORDERS

DSM-III defines this group of disorders as being characterized by particular abnormalities (subsequently defined) of gross motor movement. As the name suggests, these are of a stereotyped or repetitious nature and are of two forms, tics and voluntary rhythmic movements. Interest in these disorders has increased markedly in recent years.

Tic Disorders (Including Tourette's)

DEFINITIONS AND CLASSIFICATION

Tics are defined in DSM-III as muscular movements that are sudden, repetitive, involuntary, apparently purposeless, and restricted to some circumscribed muscle group and that may result in noises or words. A useful detailed listing of their distinction from choreiform, dystonic, athetotic, and other abnormal movements such as tardive dyskinesia is also given in DSM-III (p. 73). Their most characteristic features are the relative invariability of their expression and their restriction, in most cases, to a small group of muscles innervated by the cranial (as opposed to spinal) nerves, most conspicuously muscles of the head, neck, and diaphragm.

Three types of tic disorder are listed:

1. **Transient tic disorder**   This requires:
   a. Onset before adulthood.
   b. Tics.
   c. Ability to suppress the tics voluntarily for at least "minutes."
   d. Variation in intensity over weeks.
   e. Duration of at least one month but less than one year.

2. **Chronic tic disorder** This differs from transient in unvarying intensity, duration of at least one year, and no specified age of onset and from Tourette's by the number of tics being less than four at a time, as well as other features.

3. **Tourette's disorder** Onset here is between 2 and 15 years of age; tics are both multiple and multiple vocal. Duration is over one year and variations with time required.

Some of the distinctions (e.g., one-year duration) are obviously arbitrary, and the lack of any variability over time in chronic tic disorder improbable. DSM-III does state, however, that whether any or all of these three are distinct or just a continuum of severity is unknown.

Measurement of tics by frequency counting techniques can be highly reliable though subject to marked sampling error because of high variability unless conditions are standardized (see Harcherik, Leckman, Detlor, & Cohen, 1984; Turner & Morrison, 1983). Harcherik et al. (1984) offer a multidimensional instrument for Tourette's (tics, motor restlessness, behavior and performance), which is a combination of frequency counting and rating techniques.

Earlier writing (e.g., Corbett, Mathews, Connell, & Shapiro, 1969; Kelman, 1965; Lucas, Kauffman, & Morris, 1967) claimed that, on the basis of sex distribution, age of onset, initial locus of symptoms in head and neck, prognosis, and lack of bona fide pathological signs in either, Tourette's was only a more severe form of tic disorder. Since the mid 1970s however, the distinctiveness of Tourette's has found increasing favor (Bruun et al., 1976; Cohen & Leckman, 1984; Fernando, 1976; Friedhoff & Chase, 1982; Woodrow, 1974).

OCCURRENCE

The few studies of children's tics in the general population show widely varying frequencies depending on definitional criteria (Lapouse & Monk, 1958, 1964; Torup, 1962). Lapouse and Monk (1958, 1964) found a frequency of 12 percent between the ages of 6 and 12 years, being slightly commoner in boys in the 9 to 12 age-group. Tourette's is said to have a prevalence of around 0.5/1000 in the general population (Bruun, 1984), but this is only an estimate.

Studies of pediatric (Torup, 1962) and psychiatric clinic populations (Kelman, 1965; Lucas et al., 1967; Mahler, 1949; Ritvo, 1945; Torup, 1962; Zausmer, 1954) show that, consistent with general intake patterns, males predominate and that tics are more severe and chronic than in the population as a whole. Both epidemiological and clinical studies suggest that, although the peak prevalence is between 9 and 12 years of age, many cases are of earlier onset and that the course is typically benign and/or flitting from one tic to another and are not seen by pediatricians and even less so by psychiatrists (Torup, 1962). In contrast, Tourette's disorder has an earlier mean age of onset, around 7 years (Fernando, 1976; Woodrow, 1974), males predominate (3:1), and the disorder is persistent if fluctuant in all but a minority of cases (Bruun, 1984).

The theory that tics reflect a brain disorder always had proponents, especially for Tourette's disorder (see Cohen & Leckman, 1984; Kelman, 1965). It is true that tics can occasionally be a symptom of serious brain disorders such as subarachnoid cysts, encephalitis, and so on, but these causes are rare while tics are common. Even psychoanalysts (e.g., Mahler, 1949) argued for a constitutional predisposition (motor urgency) and explained the preponderance of boys as a gender difference in the neuromuscular apparatus. This idea now has some support in the increased frequency of ADD with or as a precursor to and in families of Tourette's disorder (see Comings & Comings, 1984; Friedhoff & Chase, 1982). Most earlier work (e.g., Kelman, 1965; Lucas et al., 1967; Pasamanick & Kawi, 1956), however, concentrated on the usual minimal-brain-damage concept and its birth history, EEG, neurological, and psychometric variables. Unequivocal evidence for an organic etiology of tics, even in Tourette's disorder, was, and still is, elusive (Fernando, 1976; Kelman, 1965; Woodrow, 1974) and as with other psychopathological syndromes, is mostly "soft" and nonspecific, though there are some stronger leads in the biochemical area now (e.g., Cohen & Leckman, 1984; Sweet, Solomon, Wayne, Shapiro, & Shapiro, 1973; Woodrow, 1974). The efficacy of antipsychotics such as haloperidol or pimozide (see Chapter 12) in Tourette's disorder and, conversely, the production of movement disorders by L-dopa and recent biochemical research do, however, suggest that tics may be related to abnormalities of dopamine or other neurotransmitters, especially in Tourette's disorder (Cohen & Leckman, 1984; Friedhoff & Chase, 1982; Leckman et al., 1983); but again proof positive is still awaited. Genetic studies suggest that there is probably a hereditary basis to some cases of Tourette's and multiple tics and/or some relationship to ADD (Commings & Commings, 1984; Pauls, Kruger, Leckman, Cohen, & Kidd, 1984). This suggests a biological factor but does not indicate its nature.

In specific psychogenic theories, Mahler (1949) posited that tics symbolized the particular conflict or character organization of the child. Nonspecific psychological theories vary from a simple psychophysiological concomitant of anxiety (Bakwin & Bakwin, 1966; Kanner, 1957) to a learned behavior through imitation, conditioning of a reflex such as blinking (Bakwin & Bakwin, 1966) or one of the common rhythmic movements of childhood (Yates, 1970), the adventitious association of anxiety reduction with a tension symptom (Walton, 1961; Yates, 1958, 1970), or as an operant response (Turner & Morrison, 1983).

PSYCHOPATHOLOGICAL CORRELATES IN THE CHILD AND FAMILY

Children with tics seen in clinics are said to have an increased frequency of anxiety-type symptoms such as sensitivity, restlessness, irritability, and phobias (Lucas et al., 1967; Torup, 1962; Zausmer, 1954). Recent studies suggest that cases of Tourette's disorder have an increased rate of psychopathology of various kinds (Harcherik et al., 1984), though how much of this is due to the well-known secondary effects of the disorder and biased sampling (clinic populations) is as yet unclear.

Early studies found tics to be associated with anxiety, conflict, overprotection, overexpectation, suppression, and rigidity in parents (Lucas et al., 1967; Mahler, 1949; Torup, 1962; Zausmer, 1954), but these studies are of poor quality, and the findings are not specific to tics.

As noted, a variably increased rate of a positive family history of tics (Commings & Commings, 1984; Torup, 1962; Zausmer, 1954) and of ADD as well has been noted in more rigorous recent work with Tourette's (Pauls et al., 1984); but this does not mean that all children with tics or even Tourette's will have this associated family psychopathology.

Experimental Studies In spite of the fact that tics seem anxiety related, there are few psychophysiological studies of tics, which is all the more surprising in view of the ease with which tics can be measured. Connell, Corbett, Horne, and Mathews (1967), Feldman and Werry (1966), Walton (1961), and Yates (1958) did take systematic measures of tics in the course of treatment that seem to bear out the predicted close connection between frequency of *established* tics and anxiety in a quantitative way, but this, of course, has no necessary implications for etiology.

TREATMENT

There is no doubt that psychotherapy of various kinds is frequently given to children with tics, but there are no adequate studies by which to evaluate its effectiveness.

Although drugs are used in the treatment of tics, especially Tourette's, only one or two studies (e.g., Connell et al., 1967) are satisfactory since most lack double-blind controls or quantitative and reliable measures of the tics, and the effect of drugs is confounded with that of other treatments (e.g., Shapiro & Shapiro, 1984). However, the evidence is consistent now in suggesting a suppressant effect with high doses of dopamine blockers (neuroleptics or antipsychotics) like haloperidol (Bruun et al., 1976; Fernando, 1976) or pimozide (Shapiro & Shapiro, 1984); the alpha adrenergic drug clonidine also may be helpful (Leckman et al., 1983). None of these drugs is curative and side effects are troublesome, but the symptomatic relief is often much appreciated by patients. Pharmacotherapy is discussed further in Chapter 12.

Behavioral approaches are popular (see Turner & Morrison, 1983). The first of these was Dunlap's (1932) massed or negative practice (Clark, 1966; Feldman & Werry, 1966; Walton, 1961; Yates, 1958). Walton (1961) was the first to apply this technique in a child but, unfortunately, the treatment was confounded by simultaneous administrations of chlorpromazine and there was no experimental control. Children and younger adolescents are difficult to motivate for this treatment, which requires considerable homework, which, if they dislike it, may make their tics worse (e.g., Feldman & Werry, 1966). Other behavioral approaches to tics have been reviewed by Turner and Morrison (1983). They conclude that while modest success is evident in a variety of methods, no optimal one has been defined and, further, that Tourette's is resistent to massed practice and has yet to be shown to be helped by other behavioral techniques.

OUTCOME

In cases seen in clinics (which it must be remembered are mostly chronic tic disorder in DSM-III terms), follow-up and follow-back studies find a complete, or nearly so, spontaneous remission in almost all children with tics, this remission occurring after a few years and by puberty (Corbett et al., 1969; Torup, 1962; Zausmer, 1954). The prognosis in Tourette's disorder is quite different, however. While some (Fernando, 1976; Kelman, 1965; Lucas et al., 1967; Woodrow, 1974) conclude that long-term prognosis is not always poor, in by far the largest series ($N = 78$), Bruun et al. (1976) found only four patients to be symptom-free without continuing medication after a variable interval of follow-up (2–10 years). Even so, the statement that Tourette's is of lifelong duration (e.g., Leckman et al., 1983) seems true only for the vast majority, not the entirety, and follow-up into old age is still to be done.

SUMMARY

Tics are a common childhood problem, and only a small minority of cases—the chronic, the severe, and those complicated by psychopathology or other problems—find their way to clinics. The age of onset is most commonly between 6 and 12 years, with the peak prevalence between 9 and 12 years. There appears to be a spontaneous remission in most tics at or before puberty, though mild residuals in the face may persist. In clinics, boys with tics are seen more frequently than girls, but there is reason to suppose that this is no more so than for most psychopathological disorders. The separateness of Tourette's disorder as a clinical entity is unproven but seems well-established and heuristic. The exact origin and relationship of tics to common rhythmic, choreiform, and repetitive movements of childhood and to ADD remains unclear, but there is probably some interrelatedness. There is some clinical and empirical evidence that children with tics seen in clinics may have increased rates of anxiety-withdrawal disorder and of living in anxiogenic families, which, further, themselves exhibit an increased frequency of tics. Tourette's seems often to have some genetic basis, and this may also be true of tics in general (though less often). There is some genetic association between Tourette's and ADD. Drugs such as antipsychotics and clonidine can reduce tiquing, but in view of the high rate of spontaneous remission in simple tics, and the possibility of long-term neurological side effects, their use should ordinarily be restricted to Tourette's disorder. Of psychological interventions only behavior therapy has produced the data necessary to evaluate itself, where the results are only modestly encouraging except in Tourette's, where they seem ineffective.

Whether or not tics then are true organic disorders, psychogenic, psychophysiological concomitants, or phenotypic cannot yet be answered with any certainty, though the last seems most probable. Occasionally harbingers of serious neurological disease, in the majority of cases tics represent a complex and varying interaction between genetic, temperamental, and developmental vulnerability, anxiety-withdrawal, situational stress, and environmental contingencies. The somatic system involved seems dopaminergic, but this has no necessary *etiological* implications.

Atypical Stereotyped Movement Disorder (Stereotypies and Self-mutilation)

DEFINITION AND EPIDEMIOLOGY

While self-mutilation is by no means synonymous, it will be discussed here with stereotypies, because much self-mutilation actually results from stereotypies, perhaps the best example of this commonality being seen in headbanging (Green, 1967). Self-mutilation as a repetitive, tissue-damaging activity resulting from stereotyped behavior should be distinguished from the Deliberate Self-harm Syndrome described by Pattison and Kahan (1983), which is an episodic, tension-relieving, often lethal behavior of later adolescence. Stereotypies are repetitive, relatively invariant movements of head, body, and/or hands (Berkson, 1967; Kaufmann & Levitt, 1965) that, unlike most tics, involve at least a whole region of the body in an integrated, purposeful, and apparently voluntary movement, though their differentiation from some gross tics, as in Tourette's disorder, may be difficult at first glance. They take such forms as rhythmic movements of head or trunk, self-manipulations, flapping of the hands, posturing, and picking at or biting oneself (Berkson & Davenport, 1962). In a recent review Werry, Carlielle, and Fitzpatrick (1983) also include thumbsucking and attachment to blankets and other soft objects when this involves stroking or sucking or other rhythmic behavior.

Reviews of stereotypies may be found in Baumeister and Forehand (1973), Kravitz and Boehm (1971), Sallustro and Atwell (1978), and Werry, Carlielle, and Fitzpatrick (1983).

Stereotypies, notably headbanging and rocking, are common in normal infants, estimates of frequency ranging from around 10 to 90 percent, with the average around 15 to 20 percent in better studies (De Lissovoy, 1961; Kravitz & Boehm, 1971; Lourie, 1949; Sallustro & Atwell, 1978; Werry, Carlielle, & Fitzpatrick, 1983). Thumbsucking is by far the commonest stereotypy, being nearly universal at birth (Werry, Carlielle, & Fitzpatrick, 1983). These normal stereotypies have a rather narrow age spectrum of rapidly rising and then falling frequency. This age spectrum differs for different stereotypies and depends on motor development; thumbsucking is present at birth and decays exponentially thereafter, while rocking and headbanging, which require good postural control, do not peak until around one year. With the exception of headbanging and possibly rocking, stereotypies are equally distributed between the sexes. Such normal stereotypies are ordinarily short-lived, however, persisting beyond the age of two or three years only in a minority (De Lissovoy, 1961; Kravitz, Rosenthal, Teplitz, Murphy, & Lesser, 1960; Lourie, 1949; Werry, Carlielle, & Fitzpatrick, 1983). After this age, stereotypies normally are replaced by irregular, changing manipulations of the self, clothes, and environment (Hutt, Hutt, Lee, & Ounsted, 1965; Lebowitz, Colbert & Palmer, 1961).

Although most common overall, in normal infants and toddlers, stereotypies occur more often and persist longer in certain abnormal populations: retarded, blind, psychotic, and institutionalized children. Other differences are that, whereas in normal children the stereotypies occur in highly specific situations and states (such as in the crib, when fatigued or inactive), in abnormal populations they are often persistent and take exaggerated or bizarre forms, such as twirling, handflapping, plunging, and self-multilation. As a general rule, it seems that the less stimulation the child receives or can utilize (blind, profoundly retarded, psychotic, institutionalized), the more obstinate, the more exaggerated, and the more bizarre the stereotypy (Baumeister & Forehand, 1973; Berkson, 1968; De Lissovoy, 1962; Hutt et al., 1965; Ritvo, Ornitz, & La Franchi, 1968; Rutter & Lockyer, 1967; Sorosky, Ornitz, Brown, & Ritvo, 1968).

ETIOLOGY

Werry, Carlielle, & Fitzpatrick (1983) suggested five broad groups of etiological hypotheses for stereotypies:

1. They result from understimulation of the organism and represent an effort to restore an optimal level of arousal (see Berkson, 1968).
2. They are a consequence of overstimulation and are homeostatic in reducing responsiveness to stimuli (Hutt et al., 1965).
3. They are neurogenic; when normal they reflect a level of neuromuscular organization (Thelen, 1979) or when abnormal are the direct result of a neurological lesion (Ornitz & Ritvo, 1968; Ritvo et al., 1968).
4. They are behaviors that reward the organism either through internal proprioceptive stimulation or favorable response of the external environment (Green, 1968; Greenberg, 1964; Lovaas, Freitag, Gold, & Kassorla, 1965; Schaefer, 1970).
5. They are means of facilitating normal sensorimotor development (like fledglings flapping wings).

As in many other childhood psychopathological disorders, in looking at these etiological hypotheses, there are two rather separate but seldom discriminated questions: How do stereotypies arise? What keeps them going?

The results of studies in animals and humans are generally contradictory, suggesting that the etiological hypotheses are not mutually exclusive, nor valid in every case, nor at every point in time (Baumeister & Forehand, 1973; Berkson, 1965; Lovaas, Freitag, Gold, & Kassorla, 1965; Werry, Carlielle, & Fitzpatrick, 1983).

What does seem clear is that many steroetypies are influenced both by the level of stimulation *and* by contingencies. For example, Thelen (1979) found that those children who were stimulated (jiggled) more by caretakers had lower rates of stereotypies, while studies of institutionalized retardates show that stereotypies vary inversely with the amount of programmed activities (see Baumeister & Forehand, 1973) and in autistic children with vigorous exercise (Kern, Koegal, & Dunlap, 1984). Stereotypies normally rapidly disappear as normal infants improve their motor and cognitive skills and find more interesting things to do.

Conversely, stereotypies are common in animals reared in isolation (Berkson & Mason, 1964a, 1964b; Harlow, 1962; Mason & Sponholz, 1963), in children reared in institutions (Freud & Burlingham, 1944; Levy, 1944; Spitz & Wolf, 1946), and in multihandicapped children, all of whom are characterized by an impaired capacity to utilize normal environmental stimulation.

But contingencies also operate. Aversive stimulation stops self-mutilating stereotypies (Bailey, Pokrzywinski, & Bryant, 1983; Baroff & Tate, 1968), and shame as children grow older seems a highly probable terminator. Middle-class mothers in Milwaukee actively encouraged blanket stroking, while black mothers punished it, giving a rate of stereotypy in white children almost twice as high (Litt, 1981).

As Thelen (1979) and Werry, Carlielle, and Fitzpatrick (1983) argue, the ethological view seems highly probable—that is, *rhythmic behaviors* are inexorable during the first year or so of life reflecting specific levels of motor development, whereas their persistence (or *stereotypies*) are due to impeded development and/or are learned.

TREATMENT AND OUTCOME

Lourie (1949) claimed success in treating rhythmic stereotypies by setting a metronome to the periodicity, but De Lissovoy (1962) found it ineffective, except in modifying the basic rhythm in a few cases. The literature suggests that punishment can be deterrent and is probably widely used in mild forms (e.g., shame) by parents and peers. If we knew what causes the usual "spontaneous" decline, treatment could be rationalized. Werry, Carlielle, and Fitzpatrick (1983) suggested that in affluent societies the isolating of babies from maternal contact may promote stereotypies in children and that paying more attention to not allowing infants wakeful periods in stimulus-deprived environments (such as bare cribs in total darkness) and encouraging more carrying and jiggling of infants might prevent many "normal" persistent stereotypies.

In abnormal populations, environmental enrichment and activity can be effective in reducing stereotypies, especially in institutionalized populations (Berkson, 1968; Berkson & Mason, 1964a; Kern et al., 1984), but in *severely* emotionally, sensorily, and intellectually handicapped children, stereotypies can be highly resistant to modification, presumably because of either a very limited capacity to engage in higher level behaviors and/or the need to reduce persistent high anxiety. That is, stimuli and reinforcers are endogenous and powerful; to find alternatives is the nub of the problem. Medication has as yet no well-established role, though antipsychotics do seem to reduce stereotypies somewhat (Aman & Singh, 1983a). Self-mutilating behavior has been the subject of more study and appears to be amenable, at least in the short run, to aversive and, less commonly, to nonaversive operant procedures (Bailey et al., 1983; Hutt et al., 1965; Lovaas & Simmons, 1962; Lovaas, Freitag, Gold, & Kassorla, 1965; Lovaas, Schaeffer, & Simmons, 1965; Tate & Baroff, 1966; Winton, Singh, & Dawson, 1984).

While the original work (e.g., Lovaas & Simmons, 1962; Tate & Baroff, 1966) used ethically questionable (except possibly as life-saving measures) contingencies like electric shock, later studies have shown that relatively benign contingencies such as spraying the face with a fine cold water mist (Bailey et al., 1983) or visual occlusion (Winston et al., 1984) can be highly effective.

SUMMARY

In spite of the fact that the exact etiology of stereotypies and self-multilating behavior is unknown, there is good reason to suppose that they have their roots in certain transitory, largely neurodevelopmentally determined behaviors of early life that become indurated as a result of caretaker contingencies and/or deficiencies in the supply, reception, or utilization of complex environmental stimuli preventing the learning of higher, more rewarding patterns of behavior. There is little information on treatment in normals, though there is reason to believe that better attention to experimental control, particularly using the operant paradigm, could prove fruitful, as could a study of so-called spontaneous remission. In abnormal populations, stimulating and contingency factors have been shown to be powerful therapeutic variables.

EATING AND ALLIED DISORDERS
Pica

This is the repeated ingestion of nonnutritive substances such as paint, hair, pebbles, or, as in one of the author's cases, lead sinkers! Regular foods are also consumed, however, and in normal quantities. In his review Woolston (1983) points out that little is known about this disorder. The importance of pica lies primarily in its social unacceptability and, less commonly, in its health consequences when the substance ingested (e.g., old paint or poisons) is toxic. As far as etiology is concerned, Woolston concludes that pica can have a variety of etiologies ranging from abnormal development to abnormal environments.

Rumination Disorder (of Infancy)

In this disorder, the infant repeatedly regurgitates the contents of the stomach into the mouth with spilling and/or vomiting. Again little is known of this eating disorder (Winton & Singh, 1983; Woolston, 1983), which ordinarily begins between 3 and 12 months. It is commonly produced by tongue thrusting or placing the fingers in the throat and can occur in both normal and retarded children. In extreme cases it can result in serious nutritional or electrolyte disturbances and even death. There are psychodynamic theories of etiology, based on a disturbed mother–child dyad, while behavioral views concentrate on the natural contingencies applied to the behavior (Winton & Singh, 1983). The behavioral views, however, explain persistence, not origin. Woolston (1983) suggested that gastroesophogeal reflux of organic origin is the primary cause and that the reflux is then reinforced in various ways. A number of behavioral treatments appear to have been successful, but no study adequately determines what works or what works best or for how long (Winton & Singh, 1983). Woolston (1983) made much the same conclusions about medication and psychotherapy.

(Nonorganic) Failure to Thrive and Psychosocial Dwarfism

Some infants within the first two years of life show a deceleration in weight gain and slowing of development in the absence of physical or severe psychiatric disorder such as autism. This is referred to as Nonorganic Failure to Thrive (NFTT) and constitutes between 15 and 50 percent of all cases of failure to thrive, which, in turn, accounts for up to 5 percent of pediatric admissions (Woolston, 1983).

Psychosocial dwarfism is supposed to be quite distinct from NFTT in that it appears later (18 to 48 months), is consistently accompanied by low levels of growth hormone, by sleep disturbances, and by bizarre eating habits around acquisition of food and water such as gorging, stealing, and hoarding. All this occurs despite reputedly normal feeding practices, but the condition responds promptly to placing the child in a different environment (Green, Campbell, & David, 1984; Woolston, 1983).

Both NFTT (excluding that due to rumination) and psychosocial dwarfism are popularly said to be due to "maternal deprivation" or to be nonnutritional in nature (see Woolston, 1983). In a scathing critique of research in NFTT and psychosocial dwarfism, Woolston (1983) points out that the standard is abysmally poor, and he concludes, as do Green et al. (1984) and Kotelchuck and Neuberger (1983), that the extent to which NFTT is actually due to food deprivation or to maternal deprivation is quite unclear. There does, however, seem to be an increasing consensus that NFTT is an heterogeneous condition that may well include starved, stressed, deprived, and even oppositional, food-refusing infants in varying combinations. Also, families range all the way from grossly abusing or disorganized to apparently normal.

In one of the few properly controlled studies, Kotelchuck and Neuberger (1983) compared children with NFTT and those with acute short-term medical illnesses and found that only three of 44 variables predicted NFTT—the most important being a "sickly" child, with lesser contributions from social isolation of the family and marked discrepancy in the two parents' education. They concluded that maternal behavior in NFTT may often be secondary to having a sickly child, not primary.

Bulimia

This is a recently described disorder that literally means "ox-hunger" but has come to mean binge-eating in which guilt, conscious effort to undo the effects of binging, and only minor distortions of mean body weight occur. DSM-III sets out the following diagnostic criteria:

A. Recurrent episodes of binge-eating
B. At least three of: consumption of high-caloric food; inconspicuous eating; termination only by abdominal pain; self-induced vomiting; sleep or social interruption; repeated attempts to lose weight; frequent weight fluctuations due to binges and fasts
C. Awareness that the eating pattern is abnormal and fear of not being able to stop
D. Depressed mood and self-deprecating thoughts following eating binges
E. Not due to anorexia nervosa or any known physical disorder.

Not surprisingly in view of its recency, little is known about the validity of this disorder *qua* disorder, though a recent review has over 200 citations (Huon & Brown, 1984). It is said to be much commoner in females and has some association with anorexia nervosa (see later discussion). Palmer (1982) pointed out that bulimia (and anorexia) is an extreme manifestation of the restrained eating/body beautiful obsession typical of Western society that affects young females most extremely but also to a lesser extent males (see Halmi, 1983). It seems that periodic loss of control over the usual restrained eating is very common in affluent societies (Huon & Brown, 1984) but in bulimia, it is frequent, gross, and guilt inducing, and its potential weight increments are actively counteracted by the person concerned. In one study, using DSM-III criteria, Halmi (1983) found that 19 percent of female and 5 percent of male students in a U.S. liberal arts college reported all the necessary and sufficient features for the diagnosis of bulimia.

In their review, Maloney and Klykylo (1983) report that there may be occasional medical complications such as rectal bleeding (from purging), electrolyte disturbances (from vomiting and purging), parotid enlargement, and dental changes (from vomiting). Depression, with risk of suicide, is said also to be a complication, but the size of any such risk is unknown.

Anorexia Nervosa

DEFINITION AND EPIDEMIOLOGY
First described and named by the English physician Gull in 1878, this disorder attained its current level of notoriety only in the last decade (Palmer, 1982).

DSM-III sets out the following criteria:

A. Intense fear of becoming obese, which does not diminish as weight loss progresses.
B. Disturbances of body image—claiming to feel fat even when emaciated.
C. Weight loss of 25 percent.
D. Refusal to maintain body weight over a minimal normal weight.
E. No known physical illness. When, as not infrequently happens, bulemic symptoms are also present, both diagnoses are to be made.

Other definitions (e.g., the ICD-9) do not specify the amount of weight loss and give more prominence to features often associated such as amenorrhea, lanugo hair, and bulemia.

The disorder is much commoner—at least 9 to 10 times so—in females (Halmi, 1983; Maloney & Klykylo, 1983; Palmer, 1982). The exact prevalence of the disorder is unknown but may be around 1 percent at age 16 to 18, with the yearly incidence about one-third that (Maloney & Klykylo, 1983; Palmer, 1982). The reason the true frequency is unclear is because anorexics usually do not see themselves as sick and resist professional consultation. Only those in whom the disorder is extreme or life-threatening have a high probability of having specialized (particularly psychiatric) care.

If no weight criterion is applied, those with "anorexic" eating behaviors and attitudes may be as prevalent as 6 percent in the population. There are socioeconomic variations, but since most of the these data accrue from cooperative, captive, literate populations such as private schools and colleges, this makes the reputed excess of the disorder in higher socioeconomic groups difficult to evaluate. The disorder is also commoner in certain occupational groups such as dance students, models, and athletes for whom there is a particular need to control weight (Palmer, 1982).

It is widely held that the disorder is increasing in frequency. All comparative data are based on clinically defined populations, however, where the increased referral rates to psychiatric and all medical facilities is indisputably rising rapidly (Maloney & Klykylo, 1983; Palmer, 1982; Willi & Grossman, 1983). Whether this is an artifact of greater awareness (and hence higher referral rates), due to improvement in and acceptance of medical (including psychiatric) services, or due to a true increase in the disorder is unclear, though there is reason to believe that some of this increase is probably real and related to changing concepts of the ideal body form. In a remarkable study, Garner, Garfinkel, Schwartz, and Thompson (1980) were able to show, using "girlie" centerfolds, beauty queen contests, and similar idealized portrayals of the female form, that there has been a marked movement toward "thinness as beautiful" over the last 20 years. It should be noted, though, that to a lesser extent there has been a similar development in concepts of male beauty, which emphasize leanness and muscularity, particularly in later life. Nevertheless, only 5 percent of male college students had bulemic-type eating behavior as opposed to 19 percent of females, and very few had the anorexic-type eating attitudes found in 6 percent of females (Halmi, 1983; Palmer, 1982).

CORRELATES

Female sex, higher socioeconomic class, occupations requiring thinness, and bulemic symptoms have already been mentioned as positively correlated, though obviously none of these is specific to anorexia. There is also a raised familial risk, though this has not yet been proven to be genetic (Halmi, 1983; Palmer, 1982).

There are a host of biological correlates—amennorhea, endocrine disturbances, growth of fine hair on the body (lanugo), abnormal EEGs, cerebral atrophy on CT scans, slowed pulse rate, lowered blood pressure, and blood fat and electrolyte changes (Halmi, 1983; Lippe, 1983; Palmer, 1982). The blood sedimentation rate, however, is said to be normal, unlike in other wasting diseases, and this maybe of diagnostic value (Halmi, 1983). Controversy still exists as to whether these changes are secondary to starvation, psychologically induced, or causal. Most of these values revert to normal as normal weight is regained. The balance of opinion is that the majority are secondary to starvation. Along with the other endocrine changes, the dexamethasone suppression test appears to become abnormal in direct proportion to the amount of weight loss, thus invalidating this as a test for depression in anorexia (see Halmi, 1983).

While distortions in objectively measured body image (overestimating size) do occur, they have been shown not to be specific to anorexia but are common in normal young women (Palmer, 1982).

Psychological and personality correlates have been comprehensively and critically reviewed by Palmer (1982). Bruch (1974, 1982) saw the anorexic as having failed to develop a sense of autonomy, perceiving herself powerless in her sociofamilial environment. The anorexia develops because this is the one area in which autonomy and control of environment can be exerted. The data suggest, however, that there is no one personality or type of psychopathology in anorexia (Dally, 1969; Maloney & Klykylo, 1983; Palmer, 1982), although anorexics, especially those with bulemic symptoms, may have an increased risk of histrionic conduct disorder–type psychopathology (Halmi, 1983; Palmer, 1982).

Well-controlled data on family correlates are sparse. There is some evidence of an increase in affective illness in families, but other forms of serious psychopathology are also not uncommon (e.g., Harper, 1983; see also Palmer, 1982). Familial preoccupation with weight and its control is also positively, though again not inexorably, correlated. Family dynamic studies have suggested enmeshment, overprotectiveness, rigidity, lack of conflict resolution, and involvement of the child in unresolved marital conflicts (see Liebman, Sargent, & Silver, 1983), though Harper (1983) stresses the variety of family pathology seen. Adequate family studies are rare. The idea that, in a significant but unknown proportion of cases, anorexic symptomatology is *prolonged* by the consequences of parental behavior is also popular among behaviorists (Eckert, Goldberg, Halmi, Casper, & Davis, 1979; Werry & Bull, 1975) and forms the basis, in one guise or another, of many weight-restoration programs.

ETIOLOGY

Biogenic (including genetic) views suffer from their nonspecific (to anorexia) nature and the more probable view that they are secondary to the onset of starvation. Psychogenic, psychodynamic, and family views are likewise sharply divergent and are so lacking in good empirical studies as to prevent adequate evaluation (Harper, 1983; Palmer, 1982).

The one thing that seems to characterize most anorexics is that *for a variety of reasons*, they start dieting, but unlike most of their peers who also worry about their body image and practice some degree of eating restriction, they go about it with great tenacity, seriousness, and success.

As Palmer (1982) has pointed out, the correlates suggest that there are probably a number of *classes* of etiological variables—biological, psychological, family, and social—and that the admixture may vary. It is hard, however, to ignore the two central facts: first, it occurs primarily in adolescent females when both development of secondary sexual characteristics and "selling oneself" to the opposite sex are paramount, and second, its frequency is probably increasing when thinness, especially in females, has become more desirable in society at large (Garner et al., 1980). Thus, our culture plants the seed, but what it is that makes it grow to such monstrous proportions is presently unclear. Psychopathology in the patient (which may, however, be quite diverse) seems likely to prove the major factor responsible. When the disorder is fully evolved, the question changes to, What keeps the disorder going? These latter factors are not necessarily the same as those that cause the disorder initially.

TREATMENT AND OUTCOME

As Palmer (1982) has noted, there is a plethora of treatments, but they all seem to be united in two common aims. The first is alleviation of the state of starvation and any dangerous complications thereof, almost invariably in an inpatient setting, most commonly with bed rest at the beginning. All treatment methods seem to be reasonably successful at putting on weight, and there is nothing at the moment that indicates the superiority of any. Pharmacotherapy, in which antipsychotics (see Chapter 12) have figured prominently, are probably widely used to reduce motor activity and restlessness and, hence, like bed rest, encourage a positive energy balance and, thus, weight gain. The role of medication is unproven, however, and few programs seem to give it other than a peripheral role.

The second aim is to try to resolve the fundamental disorder that underlies anorexia and that, it is generally agreed, is seldom altered at all by the refeeding programs. It is here that psychotherapy of currently popular types is favored, though all admit to the difficulty of working with anorexics.

Long-term outcome studies (Halmi, 1983; Hsu, 1980; Palmer, 1982; Swift, 1982) suggest that while normalization of weight, of social function, and, slightly less commonly, of menstrual cycles are found in a variable majority, food restriction and psychopathology, especially obsessive and depressive symptoms, usually persist. There is a mortality of around 5 percent with death most usually occurring after several years of the illness. The causes are either illness related (and this may explain some of the decline recently) or suicide. Outcome has been derived mostly from hospitalized groups, and outpatients may well have a somewhat better prognosis.

Unfavorable predictors of outcome seem to be later age of onset, severe weight loss, and a marked degree of psychopathology. The role of associated bulimia is disputed (Halmi, 1983), and it is possible that unfavorable personality differences in bulemic patients may be the determinants rather than the bulimia per se.

Despite consensus on outcome among reviewers, most express concern about the inadequacies of the data. For example, Swift (1982), who reviewed studies of outcome in early-onset anorexics (age 15 or less), concluded that all studies had multiple methodological flaws, so that the contention, for example, that early onset is associated with a more favorable outcome as yet lacks sufficient confirmation.

SUMMARY

This group of disorders seems to have burst upon the Affluent Society in the last decade or so. In some cases, principally those occurring in infancy, they seem to be, at least in part, caused by poor parenting, but contributions from the child are also important. Those of late childhood and adolescence seem attributable to the concept of "thin is beautiful" in affluent societies at a time when abundance of food and decline in exercise make weight gain almost inevitable. Those who exhibit clinical disorders are casualities of popular distortions of body image and patterns of food restriction to control inexorable weight gain. They appear to be made vulnerable by preexisting psychopathology, which may take a variety of forms; there is no one personality, conflict, or family style associated with these disorders.

In general, symptomatic treatment is successful and long-term prognosis favorable in most cases, but a few may develop serious health impairment, become chronic, or suffer psychiatric disorders in later life. Overall, none is as serious or continuous a public health problem as less glamorous (to professionals) obesity (next topic).

Obesity

Obesity is recognized as the most common and important pediatric (and adult) nutritional disease of Western nations (Dietz, 1983; Lloyd, 1969). Although it is customary to stress the impact of obesity on ultimate physical health, it is likely that the psychological disability accompanying obesity is of equal importance (Mayer, 1966a, 1966b). By the age of five and consistently thereafter, obese children are ranked by peers even lower in popularity than those with physical handicaps (Dietz, 1983).

DEFINITION AND EPIDEMIOLOGY

The use of weight alone as a criterion of obesity may be inaccurate, since obesity implies an excess of adipose tissue, and the source of apparent excess weight may lie entirely in skeletal and muscular tissues (Dietz, 1983; Mayer, 1966b). This distinction is not trivial since it is likely that the mortality rates may be quite different in the two groups.

The most commonly used scales employ a two-dimensional index for the definition of obesity, that is, height and weight (sometimes with a crude estimate of the skeletal size). For children, the practice seems to be to relate the height and weight to age percentiles. Dissatisfaction with the height–weight method has led to efforts to measure adipose tissue directly by a variety of methods, of which the most popular, though not necessarily most reliable, is measurement of skin folds with calipers (Dietz, 1983; Foreyt & Goodrick, 1981).

When height–weight data are related to age tables, the prevalence of obesity is found to vary with age (Bruch, 1974; Rauh, Schumsky, & Witt, 1967).

Theory and empirical data suggest that there are three prognostically and etiologically different groups: developing, established, and remitting obesity (Asher, 1966; Bruch, 1974; Garrow, 1974; Grant, 1966; Heald, 1966). Yet most research in obesity has been and still is (e.g., Dietz 1983) of the chronically obese.

In children, the grossly obese, those with short stature and/or "buffulo"-type obesity, are those most likely to have pathological causes and to have seriously diminished life expectancy (Dietz, 1983).

Prevalence estimates of obesity in children and adolescents vary from 5 to 15 percent according to the definitions used (Dietz, 1983). Onset probably is uniform throughout childhood and increases only slightly in adolescence in females. It is influenced by gender, but in a complex way (Rauh et al., 1967), and by cultural, ethnic, and socioeconomic factors (Bruch, 1974; Wilkinson, Pearlson, Parkin, & Phillips, 1977). Demographic features are clearer in adulthood where socially and gender *advantaged* groups show higher prevalences of obesity, though immigrant groups tend to be obese for the first three generations (Dietz, 1983). In childhood, however, these ecological variables are sometimes reversed (Rauh et al., 1967). Somatotype is an important influence on obesity, at least in the adolescent and adult female (Mayer, 1966a). It is also more common in parents, twins, and sibs of obese children, but these associations are also true of adopted children (Dietz, 1983).

ETIOLOGY

To become obese, energy intake must exceed expenditure of energy—a small, scarcely detectable positive energy balance is capable of producing gross obesity in a few years (Garrow, 1974). There are numerous complexities in this deceptively simple equation, however, since environmental and biological influences on both intake and utilization of energy are myriad (Bruch, 1974; Deitz, 1983; Garrow, 1974; Mayer, 1966b). As Bruch (1974) points out, these complexities are seldom recognized and obesity is usually regarded, especially in psychiatric literature, as etiologically simple and homogeneous: due to overeating.

A further common error is to assume that original etiology must still be present. Experimental studies on animals show that obesity develops over a period of time, but that ultimately a steady (obese) state is achieved. The only departure from the normal in this new steady state may be the now greatly increased adipose tissue. An etiological study done at this phase could conceivably show no disturbance of either energy intake or output. Also, any metabolic distortions are more likely a result than a cause of the obesity (Dietz, 1983).

Garrow (1974), Mayer (1966b), and Dietz (1983) have reviewed the mechanisms that maintain the balance between energy intake and energy output, and the disturbances that may occur. For present purposes, it may be assumed that very few cases of obesity in children have demonstrable pathological causes. Dietz (1983) estimated these at only 1 percent in his obesity clinic and stated that they were readily detectable on careful history, examination, and height/weight ratios. This leaves three possible causes for the majority of cases: eating too much, too little motor activity, or too efficient conversion of food into fat (Dietz, 1983). In contradistinction to popular belief, reviews have revealed that obese children and adolescents seldom seem to eat more than or different food than their peers—if anything they eat less (Durnin, 1974)—suggesting either that studies are usually done in the etiologically deceptive steady state or that the cause lies in inadequate expenditure of energy. Mayer (1966b) claimed that the empirical data supported the latter, but more recent work suggests the more efficient utilization of food also remains a distinct possibility (Dietz, 1983). The etiological link between the observed somatotypic differences and obesity is not clear (American Academy of Pediatrics, 1967; "Management," 1966; Bruch, 1974; Mayer, 1966b; Wilkinson et al., 1977). Dietz (1983) suggested, however, that the balance of evidence, notably the family studies and other epidemiological correlates, suggest primarily an environmental or nonbiological origin.

It is apparent that social and psychological variables could operate causatively at one or many points—on feeding, appetite, satiety point, metabolism, and activity—so that their potential role is not in question. Their relative importance and locus of action, however, have not been established, despite the voluminous literature (Dietz, 1983; Garrow, 1974; Maloney & Klykylo, 1983; Silverstone, 1974).

As in so many other conditions, almost all studies in obesity are based on small numbers, or highly selected children biased toward overinclusion of disturbed children, and use poor diagnostic methods in poor experimental designs. The best known worker in this area, Hilde Bruch (1963a, 1963b, 1974), considers obesity to result from a hyperphagia that is embedded in a matrix of severe disturbance of body concept similar to schizophrenia, resulting from impaired communication within the family. But Bruch does make it clear that obesity is not always associated with severe psychopathology and, in many cases, is simply one's body type or is compatible with good adjustment.

Mayer (1966b) believes psychopathology is the consequence of obesity, principally due to rejection by peers and adults. Dietz (1983) cited studies of the prejudice and low esteem with which obese children are regarded by their peers. An epidemiological study (Wilkinson et al., 1977) of nonreferred obese children found little evidence of psychopathology, though there were signs that the children were more overindulged (e.g., only children, older parents).

The exact frequency and kinds of psychopathology associated with obesity in children appears to be unknown and, when present, any relationship to the etiology of the obesity is also unclear. It seems best to agree with Bruch (1974) that obesity is not etiologically a homogeneous entity.

TREATMENT AND OUTCOME

As a general rule, the earlier the onset, the more favorable the outcome, and most obese *children* do not become obese adults. But by adolescence, 80 percent of the obese will go on to become obese adults. Severity at any age, however, is correlated with poor outcome. For example, in Swedish boys studied for seven years (see Dietz, 1983), those who were 120 to 155 percent of their ideal weight had an even chance of remission, those 155 to 182 percent had one chance in four, and of those over 182 percent, none remitted. As Dietz (1983) pointed out, the reason for the power of severity is that for growth—which is probably a major cause of spontaneous remission—to neutralize the effect of a 20 percent excess, weight must be held constant for 18 months and then for a further 18 months for each extra 20 percent.

There are few controlled studies of treatment of obesity in children and none using psychotherapeutic methods (Maloney & Klykylo, 1983). Such studies as there are generally favor behavior modification, though addition of medication and exercise improve results (Brownell, Kelman, & Stunkard, 1983). Controlled studies, mostly behavioral methods or with anorectic drugs, suggest that while almost anything works to some extent in the short run, weight losses are small and long-term results disappointing (Brownell et al., 1983; Christakis et al., 1966; Dwyer & Mayer, 1974; Foreyt & Goodrick, 1981; Garrow, 1974; "Obesity," 1966; Lloyd, 1969; Lloyd, Wolff, & Whelen, 1961; Shutter & Garell, 1966). A general air of gloom pervades the professional literature, which may explain the popularity of diets and of lay groups like Weight Watchers. Pessimism about treatment and the high early mortality associated with *gross* obesity and with it treatment by highly restrictive diets has renewed interest in surgical techniques, including in adolescents (Dietz, 1983; Maloney & Klykylo, 1983), but this should be regarded as still experimental.

The best treatment for obesity would seem to lie in its prevention, which implies the need for much better studies of the eating habits and activity patterns of the *becoming* obese child at all ages. The treatment of established obesity, which involves the reduction of caloric intake to deplete fat stores and the development of greater physical activity, awaits the development of better motivational techniques.

SUMMARY

The American Academy of Pediatrics concluded in 1967 that despite much research little was known about obesity and not much seems to have changed in nearly 20 years. Very obese children and obese adolescents have such a poor ultimate prognosis that they deserve greater attention.

ELIMINATION DISORDERS

No such composite grouping occurs in DSM-III or ICD-9, but for reasons that will become apparent, there is much to commend such a nonpsychiatric entitlement to replace the existing DSM-III categories.

Enuresis

DEFINITION AND EPIDEMIOLOGY

DSM-III lists the following criteria, none of which is truly psychopathological:

A. Repeated, involuntary voiding of urine by day or night.
B. At least two such events per month for children between ages of five and six and at least once per month for older children.
C. Not due to physical disorder. It also called it Functional Enuresis, a vague term that usually implies psychogenic origin.

One of the best reviews of this disorder is still Kolvin, McKeith, and Meadow (1973), and of its history throughout the ages, Glicklich (1951).

OCCURRENCE

Acquisition of bladder control is part of an orderly sequence of control of elimination, proceeding from bowel at night to bowel by day, then bladder by day and, finally, after a period of several months, of bladder by night (Largo & Stultze, 1977a, 1977b; Stein & Susser, 1967). Nocturnal incontinence falls sharply between the ages of two and four years, and, apart from a slight rise (secondary enuresis) between five and seven years (McGee & Silva, 1982; Rutter, Yule, & Graham, 1973), there is a gradual flattening out of the gradient of decline from four through to adolescence. But continence is a parlous condition, nocturnally in 25 percent of children and diurnally in 10 percent (Oppel, Harper, & Rowland, 1968), with relapses having a median duration of 2.5 years and 1.2 years, respectively. The frequency of bedwetting is as high as 10 to 20 percent at the age of six, though 10 percent seems a more average figure (Largo & Stultze, 1977a; McGee & Silva, 1982; Oppel, Harper, & Rowland, 1968; Rutter et al., 1973). After the age of five, enuresis is more prevalent and severe in boys (McGee & Silva, 1982; Oppel, Harper, & Rowland, 1968; Rutter et al., 1973), in certain cultures (Stein & Susser, 1967), and in the neurologically handicapped and children of lower IQ (Oppel, Harper, & Rider, 1968). The relationship to social class is unclear (Blomfield & Douglas, 1956; Hallgren, 1956a, 1956b; McGee & Silva, 1982; Oppel, Harper, & Rowland, 1968; Rutter et al., 1973).

Family factors correlated with enuresis are a history of enuresis and indicators of social disorganization, such as broken homes, mother–child separations, or maternal incompetence (Bakwin, 1961; Hallgren, 1956a, 1956b, 1957; Oppel, Harper, & Rowland, 1968; Oppel, Harper, & Rider, 1968; Stein & Susser, 1966, 1967).

In spite of common and apparently authoritative statements to the contrary, the relationship of enuresis to toilet-training practice is unclear (Dimson, 1959; Klackenberg, 1955; McGraw, 1940). On the other hand, Dimson (1959) did find a relationship between enuresis and resistance to toileting by the child. Largo and Stultze (1977b) showed that toilet training may facilitate daytime continence somewhat but has no impact on nighttime wetting. This is consistent too with results of treatment (see later section).

ETIOLOGY

Psychodynamic theories consider enuresis necessarily to be the symptom of an underlying emotional disturbance (Sperling, 1965). Behavioral theories consider enuresis as a simple deficit in function, a failure to develop cortical control over the subcortical micturition reflex (Lovibond & Coote, 1969). In this latter case, enuresis can be due to failure of training or the disruptive influence of anxiety on learning.

Nor surprisingly, psychologists (Eysenck, 1959; Jones, 1960; Lovibond & Coote, 1969; Mowrer & Mowrer, 1938) have focused on learning, but physicians (Bakwin, 1961; "Enuresis," 1960; Broughton, 1968; Mahoney, 1971; Muellner, 1960; Stein & Susser, 1967) have emphasized physical abnormalities and dysfunctions, usually of the urinary tract or nervous system.

In the only controlled clinical study, however, Boyd (1960) was unable to demonstrate that enuretics were less rousable than normal children. In their review of 12 EEG studies plus their own, Mikkelsen and colleagues (1980) showed that enuresis occurs at any stage of sleep and there is no evidence of any abnormality in the EEG or in the pattern of sleep. Other physical theories suggest obstructive lesions and defects of the adrenergic mechanisms that cause bladder muscle inhibition and tightening of the internal sphincter (Mahoney, 1971), but these remain unproven.

Hallgren (1957), Lovibond and Coote (1969), and Muellner (1960) have shown that diurnal frequency, urgency, and reduced bladder capacity are very often correlated with enuresis, especially diurnal enuresis, and influence its prognosis. Muellner (1960) elaborated these findings into an "overactive bladder" etiological hypothesis updated in terms of α-adrenergic mechanisms by Mahoney (1971). As Berg, Fielding, and Meadow (1977) point out, however, there have been few studies that have looked at this in an objective way. They found that frequency, but not bladder capacity, differentiated diurnal enuretics from those who wet only at night.

PSYCHOPATHOLOGY AND THE ENURETIC CHILD

A large number of earlier studies claimed to show that enuretic children have a significantly increased prevalence of psychopathology, some claiming a practically invariant correlation between enuresis and psychopathology. Better controlled studies (Hallgren, 1957; Oppel, Harper, & Rider, 1968; Rutter et al., 1973; Shaffer, 1973; Stein, Susser, & Wilson, 1965; Werry & Cohrssen, 1965), while mostly confirming a somewhat higher frequency of psychopathology in enuretic children, especially girls, show that this correlation is by no means invariant or sizable. This means that the majority of enuretics do not have any emotional disturbance.

One cause of the earlier overestimation of psychopathology is biased sampling. Hallgren (1957), Rutter et al. (1973), and Shaffer (1973) found that enuretic children not seen had a lower frequency of psychopathology than those seen by a physician and, in fact, were only slightly distinguishable from normal children. In those that do have psychopathology, its causal relationship to the symptom of enuresis is unclear as yet and, in some cases at least, it may be either coincidental or secondary to the enuresis. Rutter et al. (1973) suggested that there are two types of nocturnal enuresis: a developmental disorder (night wetting only and commoner in boys) and another characterized by psychiatric disorder (concomitant diurnal wetting and commoner in girls). Berg et al. (1977) in a factor-analytic study found only weak support for this, and the outstanding feature of enuretics who also had daytime wetting was "an urinary urge syndrome," not psychopathology.

Also unestablished at this point is whether, when present, psychopathology is of specific kind. Although it is commonly assumed that enuresis is correlated with anxiety-withdrawal, most studies beginning with those by Michaels and Goodman (1934) and supported by Hallgren (1957), Oppel, Harper, and Rider (1968), and Stein and Susser (1966, 1967) suggested that it is associated at least equally frequently with conduct disorder. Shaffer (1973) concludes that, while the strongest association is with immaturity, overcompliance, and timidity, there is no consistent pattern.

TREATMENT AND OUTCOME

There is strong evidence to show that enuresis is often responsive to a wide variety of nonspecific, placebo procedures (see Werry & Cohrssen, 1965). No doubt, in some cases, particularly in younger age-groups, this is part of the normal spontaneous remission–relapse cycle (Forrester, Stein, & Susser, 1964; Oppel, Harper, & Rowland, 1968) instead of a true placebo response. Data do not support the effectiveness of psychotherapy over placebo (De Leon & Mandell, 1966; Doleys, 1977; Werry & Cohrssen, 1965).

With the exception of the antidepressant drugs, medication has not earned a significant place in the treatment of enuresis. Controlled studies have shown that the antidepressants (probably by affecting local and central bladder control mechanisms rather than by any antidepressant or sleep lightening action [Rapoport et al., 1980]) are superior to placebo, but this effect is almost always drug-dependent and children are seldom, if ever, definitely cured by this treatment (Blackwell & Currah, 1973). Side effects may be unpleasant and, rarely, dangerous (Blackwell & Currah, 1973; see also

Chapter 12). Antidepressants should be used only for temporary relief in socially vital situations; such stringent criteria can apply only to a small group of enuretics. Psychopathology in the child does not seem to influence response to antidepressant medication, further evidence in favor of a nonpsychotropic action (Rapoport et al., 1980).

Originally introduced by the German pediatrician Pfaundler in 1904, and rediscovered by Mowrer and Mowrer in 1938, the bed buzzer had undergone a rise in popularity parallel with that of behavior therapy. Reviews of the effectiveness and rationale of this conditioning apparatus may be found in Chapter 14 as well as in Lovibond and Coote (1969), Werry (1967), and Doleys (1977). There is now compelling evidence to show that it is superior to no treatment as well as to psychotherapy and to amphetamine, but that failures and relapses are common (Disch, Yule, Corbett, & Hand, 1983; Doleys, 1977). Various intensive supervision programs and adjunctive treatments such as bladder training may improve success rate. Failures of the behavioral treatment of enuresis seem to be related primarily to adverse family factors, with psychopathology in the child a weaker influence (Disch et al., 1983).

The bladder training method of Muellner (1960) is also basically a learning technique aimed at increasing the functional capacity of the bladder by fluid loading and postponing the act of micturition for increasing periods. However, while this certainly increases daytime bladder capacity, it has no effect on night wetting (Doleys, Ciminero, Tollison, Williams, & Wells, 1977; Harris & Purohit, 1977). Variations of this technique, notably by Azrin and co-workers, are reviewed in Chapter 14 and appear to increase the efficacy of the bed buzzer but are ineffective without it.

The prognosis for untreated enuresis is benign. By the age of 14, all but about 2 percent of enuretic children will have undergone spontaneous remission (Lovibond & Coote, 1969). Nevertheless, as Lovibond and Coote point out, the unpredictability of the time of spontaneous cure and the general inconvenience of the symptom suggest that a "nonheroic" trial of treatment in willing and suitable patients should be undertaken, probably beginning with a placebo and then using the conditioning treatment.

SUMMARY

Enuresis appears to be a multifactorially determined condition or, in short, a phenotype in which a multiplicity of physiological, psychological, and social factors can be etiological—either singly or in combination. In the majority of instances, however, enuresis is not a true psychiatric disorder, despite its classification in the DSM-III and ICD-9 as such. It is particularly unfortunate that though the DSM-III lists no *psychopathological* diagnostic criteria for enuresis, it allows the myth of enuresis as necessarily a psychiatric disorder to persist. The most effective treatment is the bed buzzer with dry bed training but, even with it, execution can be difficult, failures not uncommon, and relapses high.

Rutter (1973) points out that enuresis is a particularly rich area for research because of the wide range of physical, psychological, and social variables implicated in this disorder; some of this is well illustrated in recent biological studies (e.g., Mikkelsen et al., 1980; Rapoport et al., 1980) and in behavioral treatments, but other areas seem relatively unexplored.

Encopresis

Useful reviews are those by Doleys (1978), Fitts and Mann (1976), and Levine (1975).

DEFINITION AND EPIDEMIOLOGY

Encopresis has mostly been used to include any kind of fecal incontinence occurring after some normative age and in the absence of physical disease or abnormality. Most children acquire bowel control by the fourth birthday (Bellman, 1966; Largo & Stultze, 1977a; Stein & Susser, 1967). Stein and Susser (1967) found that bowel control was typically completely achieved before any bladder control, while Largo and Stultze (1977a) found that children in a large sample retained the same relative positions in acquiring bowel and bladder control (i.e., early or late). As with urinary continence, girls usually achieve bowel control earlier than boys.

DSM-III diagnostic criteria are:

A. Repeated voluntary or involuntary passage of feces of normal or near normal consistency in places not appropriate for that purpose in the individual's sociocultural setting.
B. At least once a month after age of four.
C. Not due to a physical disorder.

This definition has the virtue of delineating both age and severity, which in the past have differed from study to study (Fitts & Mann, 1976); the preamble also makes it clear that it includes retention with overflow or constipation-type (see subsequent discussion), whereas pediatric texts are wont to separate this off from encopresis.

Bellman (1966), in Sweden, found the prevalence of encopresis to decrease slowly as a function of age, reaching practically zero at 16. The prevalence in boys at 8 years was 2.3 percent against 0.7 percent for girls. This higher frequency in boys has been observed consistently (Anthony, 1957; Bellman, 1966; Berg & Jones, 1964; Levine, 1975).

CLINICAL FEATURES AND ETIOLOGICAL THEORIES

According to Levine (1975), encopresis typically occurs later in the day, with accidents during school unusual; in half his cases it was associated with excitement or stress, and with enuresis in about one-third. Abdominal pain and large stools are said by Levine to be associated, but many parents have no real knowledge of their children's toilet habits and give inaccurate, conventionalized answers. The commonest symptom, though, seems to be rectal insensitivity, that is, reports by the child that they do not feel the stools coming or if they do, that they cannot make it to the toilet in time.

It is important to distinguish between two kinds of encopretic children—nonretentive, who produce a fully formed, soft stool, and retentive, with constant leaking of fecal-stained fluid from the rectum. The retentive are found to have the rectum and, in severe cases, the colon, too, distended by hard feces, which ultimately weakens or extinguishes the normal defectory reflex. The retention could have a number of possible causes. Pediatricians have argued more for physical factors, notably constipation developing in late infancy causing pain on defecation (Coekin & Gairdner, 1960; Davidson, Kugler, & Bauer, 1963), while psychiatrists have emphasized distortion of the normal anal-rententive phase of psychosexual development or disturbance of parent–child relationships (Anthony, 1957; McTaggart & Scott, 1959).

In nonretentive encopresis, Anthony (1957) has suggested two etiological possibilities. In the first, because of coercive toilet training, the child may have developed anxiety surrounding the toileting situation that should be apparent from the child's refusal to sit on the toilet (pot phobia of Berg & Jones, 1964). In the second, the child has simply never learned or been taught the toileting sequence or received reward, actual or fantasied, from depositing feces in the toilet. Berg and Jones (1964) and Woodmansey (1967) added a third possibility marked by urgency, which may have a physiological basis.

There is, however, a serious disagreement in the literature about the frequency of the two main kinds (retentive and nonretentive). Bellman (1966) and Berg, Forsythe, Holt, and Watts (1983) claim that retention is uncommon, but a more careful diagnostic assessment by Levine (1975) revealed that 80 percent of his clinic cases showed it at the first visit.

The various etiological possibilities are discussed in more detail in Bellman (1966), Berg and Jones (1964), Doleys (1978), and Levine (1975), but the best that can be said is that the cause, especially the primary cause in retentive cases, is obscure.

PSYCHOPATHOLOGY AND ENCOPRESIS

Pediatricians, who see large numbers of unselected children (Bakwin & Bakwin, 1966; Coekin & Gairdner, 1960; Davidson et al., 1963), have argued that the majority of retentive encopretics have no associated psychopathology, whereas child psychiatrists argue that most, if not all, encopretics have significant psychopathology (e.g., McTaggart & Scott, 1959; Warson, Caldwell, Warinner, Kirk, & Jensen, 1954).

In a controlled study, Bellman (1966) found that clinic and hospital cases differed from normal controls in behavior suggestive of anxious-withdrawal disorder and in a more punitive family background. However, Bellman (1966) was unable to tell whether these features were primary or secondary to the encopresis, although she thought the balance of evidence suggested they were etiological. The picture is thus unclear; while encopretic children as a group are probably more disturbed than continent children, the possibility that this can be secondary to this extremely socially distressing condition and that its importance differs in the various kinds of encopresis should be borne in mind.

TREATMENT AND OUTCOME

Bellman (1966), in a two-year follow-up study, found that about 50 percent of the children had remitted spontaneously and practically all had remitted by the age of 16. In view of this and since controlled treatment trials are rare, it is difficult to evaluate the effectiveness of the various treatments available. Despite the popularity of enemas, laxatives, and other medications, their efficacy remains to be established (Doleys, 1978). In fact, a recent study by Berg et al. (1983) suggested that laxatives add little to behavioral programs. There appear to be no good studies of the effect of psychotherapy on encopresis, though success appears to be under 50 percent (Doleys, 1978) in what are probably highly selected samples, biased toward severity and, by Levine's (1975) criteria, poorer outcome. Behavior modification methods have been described and summarized by Seymour (1976) and Doleys (1978). They claim high success rates, though as Doleys (1978) points out, of 20 studies only four had an N of six or more and/or had control groups.

Outcome with combination medical-behavioral treatment was affected adversely by degree of associated psychopathology, learning difficulties, severity of incontinence, and poor compliance in a study of 127 clinic cases (Levine & Bakow, 1976; Levine, Mazonson, & Bakow, 1980). Symptom substitution following treatment has not been seen (Doleys, 1978; Levine et al., 1980).

SOMATOFORM, DISSOCIATIVE, AND ALLIED DISORDERS

Introduction

This group of disorders is characterized by physical and other symptoms suggestive of physical disease but for which there appears to be no physical explanation and, *where there is good reason to believe the symptoms are causally linked to psychological factors*. The importance of this latter, italicized requirement cannot be too strongly emphasized. Medical diagnostic techniques and knowledge are far from 100 percent accurate so that exact diagnosis often cannot be established. Operating from the premise that no demonstrable physical cause equals a psychogenic cause, proof of the role of psychological factors has often been found by diagnostic and measurement techniques of unestablished but probably low reliability and validity. But the worst error of all has been to accept these dubiously obtained signs of psychopathology in patient or environment as *causally* linked to the physical symptoms without ever having formally established this to be so. A good, if rare, example of how the etiological role of psychological variables in physical complaints may be demonstrated other than by correlation is seen in the case of a 10-year-old boy with paralysis of the legs reported by Delamater, Rosenbloom, Conners, and Hertweck (1983).

The somatoform disorders and allied disorders in DSM-III were born of years of dissatisfaction with the variously used global term of "hysteria," which diagnostic label, however, is continued in the ICD-9.

While the literature on this group of disorders in adults is large, the reviews by Delamater et al. (1983), Kolvin and Goodyer (1982), Goodyer (1981), and Procter (1958) show that studies relating to children and adolescents are sparse and, in the past, diagnostically vague and difficult to interpret in DSM-III terms.

DSM-III defines the discrete disorders in the somatoform and dissociative disorders by the major presenting physical or quasi-physical symptoms. As noted, these disorders plus Factitious Disorder and Malingering all required absence of genuine physical disease, and in those where physical symptoms predominate, good evidence of psychological origin is needed. With the exception of Factitious Disorder and Malingering, all also require the patient to be unaware of any psychological origin of the symptoms and for the symptoms to be beyond voluntary control—a point that is not always easy to establish.

Somatoform Disorders

In the only study reporting the frequency and reliability of this group of disorders in children, Werry, Methven, Fitzpatrick, and Dixon (1983) found a frequency of 5 percent in 200 successive inpatients to a child psychiatric unit in a pediatric hospital and only a modest degree of interdiagnoser reliability (Kappa = 0.49).

SOMATIZATION DISORDER (BRICQUET'S SYNDROME OR POLYSYMPTOMATIC HYSTERIA)

DSM-III requires multiple somatic symptoms of several years' duration. The disorder is said to have onset in adolescence, to be rare in males, and to be associated with similar disorder and/or antisocial disorder in close relatives. The only study of children found by Kolvin and Goodyer (1982) reported a small number of children in a psychiatric clinic with multiple somatic complaints. Kolvin and Goodyer also conclude that psychogenic pain disorders (see later section) in children may be a forerunner of somatization disorder in adult life.

CONVERSION DISORDER (ALSO KNOWN AS MONOSYMPTOMATIC HYSTERIA)

There are rather more data on this disorder in children (Delamater et al., 1983; Goodyer, 1981; Kolvin & Goodyer, 1982; Procter, 1958). Here, the defining symptomatology is quasi-neurological. Typical symptoms seen in children are paralyses, abnormal gait, impaired vision, and fits. In the majority of cases, especially in children, the tentative diagnosis can be made quickly and easily on a physical examination in that the abnormality differs from that seen in physical illness, usually (1) not following functional anatomy (2) taking a well-recognized, often shifting and bizarre form, and/or (3) occurring with objectively demonstrable normal function in the affected area (e.g., normal reflexes). This characteristic clinical picture, however, does not seem to deter medical investigations, which are usually extensive and prolonged (Goodyer, 1981). The frequency of conversion disorders in children is low, but constitute around 1 to 2 percent of clinic referrals outside the United States (Goodyer, 1981; Werry et al., 1983b), with higher frequencies (13%) in Proctor's U.S. study. Delamater et al. (1983) suggest variability in diagnostic criteria (and they might have added patient groups) as probably responsible for these wide variations.

The youngest age of onset is said by reviewers to be five years and the sexes are equal until adolescence when the predominance of females begins to rise, ultimately to match that seen in adults. Disturbances in family background are said to be characteristic, but no particular temperament or personality is associated. Such demographic and prevalence data need, however, to be recognized as largely based on isolated studies and small samples and to be biased by the referral patterns of the clinics concerned.

The effectiveness of treatment cannot be evaluated except in the case of behavioral therapy and then only for the single cases reported (Delamater et al., 1983), but outcome seems generally favorable at 12 months (Goodyer, 1981)—except that one of the more persistent findings in adult and children is that a significant minority are subsequently shown to have organic disorder related to the symptomatology. Whether these latter should really be described as a conversion disorder or whether they reflect the difficulty, outlined before, of deciding in some cases what the diagnosis is because of the deficiencies of medical investigations, is difficult to say; but such statistics certainly call for caution in the assignment of a diagnosis.

PSYCHOGENIC PAIN DISORDER

Here the presenting symptom is severe prolonged pain for which no *adequate* physical basis can be found (and which can be related to psychological factors). Unexplained chronic pain is the nemesis of medicine and as a result has become an area of great interest in adults (Zlutnick & Taylor, 1983). In contrast to those in adults, studies in children have centered largely on recurrent abdominal pain rather than backache and headache, though a few epidemiological studies of the latter in children do exist (see Feuerstein & Gainer, 1983). These reviewers suggest that there is a slow rise from around 2 to 3 percent at age 7 years to about 20 percent by 15 years of all types of recurrent headaches. Kolvin and Nicol (1979) have reviewed recurrent abdominal pain in children (sometimes called the periodic pain syndrome). The average in the population for pains several times in the past few months is about 5 to 10 percent. There is possibly an age effect on prevalence with two peaks, one around five years and the other toward puberty. It may be somewhat commoner in girls. Remembering that these studies are of *recurrent* abdominal pain (not acute attacks in a clearly physically ill child), less than 10 percent are found to reflect organic disease, with localized rather than diffuse abdominal pain being one good organic indicator (vomiting is not). Recurrent abdominal pain is associated significantly often with other pain, especially headache and limb pains. Other correlates are pain in parents (especially headache and stomachache) and with psychopathology in the child, but good studies are too few to enable conclusions to be made.

As far as etiology is concerned, in the majority, the role of physical factors, including the popular notions of abdominal migraine or epilepsy, has either not been established or has been shown to be nonexistent, but interestingly, neither has any psychogenic etiology been proven. Follow-up studies show that in about one-third of cases, abdominal pains in childhood predict abdominal pain and other vague symptoms into adulthood, though all studies leave much to be desired methodologically, particularly in the area of subject attrition. The evidence presented and reviewed by Kolvin and Nicol (1979) does not allow firm conclusions to be drawn about whether recurrent abdominal pain in children is psychogenic, though it is commonly assumed to be so. It seems likely, however, that an unknown percentage is and that it may well be this type that, like psychogenic pain disorder in adults, has a tendency to become chronic and to be associated with abnormal illness behavior in parents.

In passing it should be noted that abdominal and other pain is often associated with anxiety in children (see Chapter 3) but this is not psychogenic pain disorder but rather a disorder defined by the more predominant anxiety-withdrawal symptoms. Some of the methods of pain research in adults coupled with better ways of measuring psychological variables and establishing causal relationships (such as systematic manipulation of contingencies) could do much to improve the state of knowledge in this common pediatric problem.

DISSOCIATIVE DISORDERS
Dissociative disorders are defined by disturbances in consciousness or memory (psychogenic amnesia and psychogenic fugue) or identity (multiple personality). These disorders are all said to be rare, though the first two, according to DSM-III, typically occur in adolescent females. Apart from an occasional individual case report, no good studies of younger adolescents could be found, though Procter (1958) included them in his larger study of hysteria in children.

Factitious Disorder and Malingering

These two disorders differ from all of the foregoing in that the symptoms are under voluntary control. In the former, physical disorder or psychological symptoms (particularly simulated psychoses) are produced deliberately simply to assume the sick role. In malingering, the illness is faked with very clear beneficial results to the person such as to gain access to opiate drugs.

Both are said to occur in association with marked psychopathology such as conduct or antisocial personality disorder. While these two disorders fill a useful nosological role clinically and are seen from time to time in older children and adolescents, distinctions between the two and other validating characteristics remain to be defined.

CHRONIC ILLNESS AND DISABILITY

Approximately 10 percent of children suffer from some kind of chronic illness or disability (Steinhausen, 1981) of which the more common are asthma, sensory handicap, cystic fibrosis, malignant disease, and a group of neurological disorders such as epilepsy, cerebral palsy, and myelodysplasia (spina bifida). Four percent of children in the United States have serious physical restriction on their activities, and this percentage is rising with improving survival rates (Breslau, Staruch, & Mortimer, 1982).

While earlier studies showed that physically disabled children have markedly increased rates of emotional and other psychopathological disturbances (Pless & Pinkerton, 1975; Tavormina, Kastner, Slater, & Watt, 1976), later work has tempered these findings and shown this area of investigation to be rather complex (e.g., Breslau, 1985; Pless & Zvagulis, 1981). Earlier methodological shortcomings were absent or inappropriate contrast groups, poor measures, and failure to allow for different effects from different disorders.

A commonly used control group, siblings, is flawed by increased psychopathology (Breslau, 1983, 1985), no doubt due to the disruptions of family functioning associated with having a disabled child (Breslau et al., 1982; Markova, MacDonald, & Forbes, 1980).

The nature of the illness seems important, in particular whether or not it involves the brain and/or is physically obvious. The impact of brain-related disabilities seems clear: increased rates of psychopathology by a factor of two to three (Breslau, 1985; Rutter, 1981), not due solely to mental retardation, though this does increase risk in its own right (Breslau, 1985; Koocher, O'Malley, Gogan, & Foster, 1980; Wing & Gould, 1979). Further, the result of brain damage is specific: cognitive difficulties and social isolation (Breslau, 1985; Wing & Gould, 1979; see also Chapter 8). When the effects of mental retardation and brain disorder are controlled or excluded, effects of chronic illness or disability are considerably weaker and the effect of degree of disability is unclear (Breslau, 1985; Markova et al., 1980; Steinhausen, 1981; Tavormina et al., 1976; Viney & Westbrook, in press). In all studies, though, the majority of disabled children have no apparent psychopathology; the disagreement is regarding just how many do. There is general agreement that the nonbrain-related psychopathology is of the internalizing (anxious-withdrawn) type, though oppositional behavior to parents is sometimes claimed as well.

Some additional variables would be predicted and/or have been shown to have an effect in a single study: degree of threat to life (Koocher et al., 1980;

medical procedures; age of onset (Koocher et al., 1980); sensory handicaps (Tavormina et al., 1976); and parental reaction to the illness (Breslau et al., 1982; Minde, Whitelaw, Brown, & Fitz-Hardinge, 1983; Koocher et al., 1980).

In summary, chronic physical illness or handicap seems to have a complex effect upon risk of disturbance, the risk being enhanced by mental retardation, brain disorder, and less certainly, severity and visibility of handicap, sensory handicap, threat to life, medical procedures, and parental reaction to illness. Untangling this complex set of variables suggests why there is some conflict in findings. Siblings of disabled children are also secondarily made vulnerable, though to a lesser degree than the affected sib.

In spite of all this, a sizable majority of children with chronic illness or disability seem to be well adjusted, and many of those with psychopathology are affected to only a minor degree (Breslau, 1985; Tavormina et al., 1976; Steinhausen, 1981).

PSYCHOSEXUAL DISORDERS AND SEXUAL ABUSE

Psychosexual Disorders

The DSM-III presents three broad groupings: gender identity disorders, in which there is a mismatch between anatomical sex and gender identity (whether one sees oneself as a boy or a girl); paraphilias, with bizarre imagery or acts (including unusual or illegal objects of sexuality); and psychosexual dysfunctions, which are problems of sexual performance.

Rutter (1971, 1980) has reviewed psychosexual development and its anomalies in considerable detail. In brief, gender identity appears entirely due to nonbiological factors—namely, sex assignment at birth, which brings with it immediately and in perpetuity, a set of cues and learning experiences that reinforce male or female identity. The evidence for this is based significantly on mismatches between anatomical sex and assigned gender in the various congenital sexual anomalies such as pseudohermaphroditism. Gender identity is firmly established in the overwhelming majority of children by age three or four and is irrevocable unless there has been some continuing ambiguity about the infant/child's sex assignment.

Gender identity disorders are important in children because every clinic occasionally sees boys brought because they are effeminate and, less frequently, girls who are excessively tomboyish, though few of these would meet the rather extreme DSM-III criteria for this disorder in children:

A. Persistent desire to be, or statement that one is, of the opposite sex.
B. Persistent repudiation of sexual anatomy.
C. Onset before puberty.

The cause of these disorders, which are better called disturbances of sex-role behavior, is obscure, but it is thought to be related to rearing factors that allow or foster an opposite gender identity or behavior, though excess of androgens before birth may be a factor in a few cases of tomboyishness. Most of the clinical work in this area has been done by Green (1974) and most (understandably) with effeminate boys since this creates far more anxiety in parents than tomboyishness. The importance of these disturbances in children is what they forebode for adulthood—whether they presage homosexuality or identity disorders such as transexualism or paraphilias like transvestism. Green's and others' studies (Rutter, 1980) suggest that only some—perhaps around half—will go on to show psychosexual disorders in adulthood. Conversely, only about half of adults with psychosexual disturbances can recall gender-identity or behavior conflicts in childhood.

Disorders of sexual orientation, activity, and performance are only of minimal interest in children, since while sexual interest and activities such as genital stimulation and noncoital hetero- and homosexual play is common in childhood, for the vast majority of persons and societies, adult-type sexual behavior rarely begins in earnest until later adolescence/early adulthood. Also, it is quite clear that these early sexual behaviors may be quite different from adult sexual behaviors, this applying particularly to early homosexual activities, which tend to be opportunist rather than by choice.

A more important question in the age-group with which this chapter is concerned is to what extent childhood experiences prejudice normal gender identity, sexual orientation, and performance in adulthood. Precocious puberty (before 9 in girls, 11 in boys) seems to offer, in girls, a minor predisposition to sexual and general psychopathology, which effects are probably due to psychosocial factors such as being out of step in appearance with peers rather than biological factors per se (Ehrhardt et al., 1984). As Rutter (1980) points out, the evidence that psychosocial factors are primarily the determinants of gender identity, sexual preference, and performance is overwhelming. The precise nature of these variables is unclear, however, except that, like other aspects of development, they are probably influenced by a wide range of general variables (such as affection given, acceptance of the child, tolerance, and so on) so that psychosexual disturbances are likely to form part of more generalized psychopathology. Some specific variables are of particular interest, however.

One of these is being reared in a homosexual parenting partnership, which has been studied, among others (see Golombok, Spencer, & Rutter, 1983) by Golombok et al., who compared children from lesbian and single-parent households, and by Green (1978), who looked only at children of homosexual and transsexual parents. The results from all studies are consistent: gender identity, sex-role behavior, and sexual orientation were in almost every case consonant with anatomical sex. The majority of subjects had, however, been conceived and reared in infancy in heterosexual partnerships. An interesting feature of the study by Golombok et al. was that children in the lesbian households actually had far more continuing contact with adult males than did those living with solo mothers!

Sexual Abuse

The second variable of topical interest is that of sexual abuse. The size of this problem is just beginning to become apparent, as is our dearth of knowledge regarding long-term outcome. Mrazek (1980) and Green (1984) point out that studies are few and flawed, and it is impossible to disentangle the effects of commonly associated deprivation and disorganization, as well as what happens to the child when the offense is revealed, from any impact of sexual abuse itself. Particularly to be deplored are the uncontrolled, retrospective studies of biased, abnormal (e.g., psychiatric or criminal) populations that are frequently cited as evidence for a poor outcome. Good prospective studies, especially those in which sexual abuse was the *only* abnormality of rearing and/or in which the sexual abuse occurred with consent and collusion of the child are essential for establishing the impact of this regrettably common distortion of normal child rearing.

SLEEP DISORDERS

The function of sleep is unknown though long supposed to be necessary for repair and restoration of bodily and psychological function (Anders, 1982). Sleep follows a distinct pattern (or architecture) of recurring, roughly 90-minute cycles, which are subdivided into five electroencephalographically distinct subpatterns. Four are levels of diminishing arousal (stages I through IV) and one a qualitatively different phase, REM (rapid eye movement) sleep, during which much of dreaming occurs. REM sleep occurs near the end of a cycle and is followed by a rapid arousal to near or actual wakefulness and reentry into the next cycle.

Developmentally, there is a decrease in the REM/NREM ratio from birth through the first few months of life and an evolution of sleep throughout the life span toward reduction in total sleep time and amount of deep sleep.

Distortions of sleep architecture are produced by most neuro- and psychotropic drugs, by psychiatric disorders (e.g., Puig-Antich et al., 1982), by interruptions to sleep, and by extreme fatigue. In general, these disruptions are followed by rebound or compensatory changes once the disrupting influence is removed.

Sleep Walking and Night Terrors

These are the only two sleep disorders in the DSM-III, both within the child section and both usually mislabeled "Nightmares," which they are not. Though infrequent, especially with any regularity (about 2 percent between 5 and 20 years according to one study by Simonds & Parraga [1982]), they are of high visibility and, as a result, of concern. Because they are popularly attributed to anxiety (though without proof), they have a high referral rate to mental health facilities. They occur in Stage IV going into Stage III sleep, where they seem to be exaggerations of the high state of physiological arousal often occurring then. They are marked by motor activities (screaming, sitting up, walking, etc.), which attract attention and seem to indicate fear. Unlike in a nightmare, the child is actually deeply asleep, impossible to console or to wake, and there is complete amnesia the next day for the episode. By the time the children are seen by professionals, the parents have often unwittingly "taught" the child to say that a nightmare is responsible for their nocturnal activities.

The cause is unknown, and there seems to be no treatment beyond reassurance and securing the child's environment to prevent injury (Anders, 1982). Episodes are probably transient. Drug treatment, which in theory could be effective by suppressing Stage IV sleep, is too high a price to pay, especially since the episodes are irregular and infrequent, because drugs impair normal sleep and cause daytime sedation and dependence.

Simple Sleep Problems

These are common in children and have been reviewed by Anders (1979, 1982), Bax (1980), Dunn (1980), and Seymour, Bayfield, Brock, and During (1983). Most of the work has been done with infants and younger children (Anders, 1979; Beltramini & Hertzig, 1983; Bernal, 1973; Blurton-Jones, Rosetti-Fereira, Farquhar-Brown, & MacDonald, 1978; Carey, 1974; Jenkins, Bax, & Hart, 1980; Richman, 1981a, 1981b; Richman, Stevenson, & Graham, 1975). Studies are nearly all in agreement that the common problems are resisting going to bed, not settling to sleep, and nightwaking. Exact frequencies vary from study to study. Factors generally agreed to covary with frequency are: (1) Child based—age (maximal before two), perinatal complications, early adaptational styles of "temperament," other behavioral or developmental problems. (2) Caretaker—rapidity of response to crying, external stressors, stress symptoms, and psychiatric disorder. Richman (1981b) points out that relationships, especially with parental variables, have not been shown to be cause and effect, nor has their precise nature been established.

Not affecting sleep are child's sex, mother's social class, education, or age, and such factors as breast versus bottle feeding, night feeds, comforters, noise, light or darkness.

Unclear are the roles of ordinal position (only and higher order status may increase problems), physical illness and hospitalization in the children, length of time the child is nursed at feeding, and child-rearing practices.

Most seem to agree that sleep problems are often chronic or recurrent and date from birth in about 10 percent but can also arise at any age and result in considerable parental distress.

There are almost no studies of management by caretakers or professionals except that parents often take or allow the child in their bed (Bax, 1980; Richman, 1981a, 1981b; Werry & Carlielle, 1983), professional help is seldom sought, but when it is, medication is usually prescribed despite its unknown efficacy (Werry & Carlielle, 1983). In a summary of treatment, Seymour et al. (1983) point out that they all center on the controversial "letting the child cry" extinction approach. They describe their own comprehensive management program and claim widespread acceptance of this approach with proper parent support and preparation. While they achieved a high success rate, about 50 percent of cases relapsed during times of subsequent crisis or stress.

Studies of older children and adolescents are infrequent but have been summarized in Simonds and Parraga (1982). Sleep disorders of any regularity are uncommon and decrease with age. The most common complaints are restless sleep (27%), fear of the dark (10%), and occasional nightmares (16%). Excessive daytime somnolence is reported to be common in adolescence and may be attributable to pubertal hormonal changes or to the notoriously erratic sleep habits in this age-group (Anders, 1982). Rarely, this may be narcolepsy (brief irresistable REM sleep episodes often accompanied by muscle weakness and hallucinations), which is first seen at around age 15.

SUMMARY

Sleep disorders in children (mostly night waking and resisting going to bed) are common before age two, when they seem to be a result of an interaction between normal variations in sleep and the distancing of infant from primary caretaker. The risk of disturbance in sleep patterns is increased in abnormal children and caretakers. These minor sleep problems are most often handled successfully by parents without professional advice and largely by comforting and/or allowing children to sleep with them. Professionals, however, favor the "let them cry" approach. Doctors prescribe drugs (which are of unproven value). Sleep walking and night terrors are found later and have a higher prospect of referral but are poorly researched. In particular, their status as psychopathological in origin is unestablished.

DEVELOPMENTAL DISORDERS

Strictly speaking a developmental disorder is one in which the abnormality is chronological or one of *time* rather than of *type*. That is, if *positive*, the symptomatology is something(s) that would be normal at an earlier age but should have disappeared by now (e.g., bed-wetting, thumbsucking) or if *negative*, function(s) that has failed to emerge by the maximum normal age (e.g., aphasia, alexia). In this context, a large number of the disorders with origin specific to childhood such as elimination, sleep, attention deficit, stereotypies, and even mental retardation could be included under developmental disorders. Proof of the validity of such a grouping could be tested in empirical statistical studies. However, both ICD-9 and DSM-III restrict this category by affixing "Specific" to the title and including only those disorders where: (1) The developmental delay or sign is out of keeping with the general level of development expected from the child's IQ and sociocultural background. (2) The area of delay includes reading, arithmetic, language, speech (except stuttering, which is considered qualitatively not chronologically abnormal), or motor skills (not included in the DSM-III). (3) No other psychiatric or medical diagnosis such as Autism or Cerebral Palsy is also present that could encompass the symptomatology.

Apart from these three criteria, no assumptions as to etiology or prognosis (the latter is often wrongly assumed to be necessarily benign) are implied. In DSM-III developmental disorders are coded on a separate axis to emphasize their distinctiveness from true psychopathological disorders. Because of this they will be mentioned only briefly, though their common association with psychopathological disorders warrants inclusion here and recommendations for further reading.

Specific Learning Disorders

No attempt will be made to review this vast, poorly defined, contentious, and surprisingly poorly researched area. Good reviews among others are those by Aman and Singh (1983b), Barkley (1981), Feagans (1983), Feuerstein, Ward, and LeBaron (1979), and Rutter and Yule (1973, 1975) (dyslexia only). The summary here is a distillate of these reviews.

Methodological defects are numerous and substantial. The definition of these disorders usually varies too widely for good cross-study comparisons (even the usually meticulous DSM-III fails to define a severity criterion stating merely "significantly"); subjects are usually not adequately described, socioeconomically unrepresentative, of mild degree, or with prominent psychopathology (notably ADD); studies are rarely adequately controlled, and measures are often of unknown reliability and validity. Evidence suggests that the etiology is variable, with genetic, brain dysfunction, socioeconomic, family, school, and adventitious factors such as errors of technique all being posited and having their acolytes. As a group, children with learning disorders may well have more minor neuropsychological and attention deficit disorder–type symptoms than normal children and less so than unequivocally brain-damaged children. But the degree, frequency, and significance of these findings are all debatable. They do not confirm a biological origin (see Chapter 8) and, further, are not specific, being also found in other psychopathological groups such as ADD and conduct disorders (Feagans, 1983; Feuerstein et al., 1979; Halperin, Gittelman, Klein, & Rudel, 1984). Most serious, though, is that despite the popularity of remedial programs, the few outcome data available suggest that learning disorders (especially when of any severity) persist throughout school years and, so far, have not been shown to be influenced except in the short term by remedial education (Ackerman, Dykman, & Peters, 1977; Carroll, 1972; Feagans, 1983; Gittelman & Feingold, 1983) or by pharmacotherapy alone or in combination with remedial programs (Aman, 1980; Gittelman, Klein, & Feingold, 1983; see also Chapter 12). This unpalatable fact seems to have done little to dampen the enthusiasm of parents or professionals for remedial programs.

Speech and Language Disorder

An excellent discussion of the development of language and of the variables, normal and abnormal, influencing it is to be found in Howlin (1980). Though "speech" and "language" tend to be used interchangeably, they are quite distinct in that "language" refers to syntactical and semantic components while "speech" is simply the final motor act or the way that the muscles of phonation are coordinated. Both ICD-9 and DSM-III define certain speech disorders such as stuttering or elective mutism as psychopathological, but also have separate developmental language disorders. In DSM-III, language disorders are further subclassified neurologically into primarily understanding language (receptive) and primarily expressive. Both systems require that the language difficulty not be secondary to other disorders such as mental retardation, autism, or elective mutism.

Elective mutism is rare but distinctive (Kolvin & Fundudis, 1981) in that a child who has historically and currently clear evidence of normal language refuses to speak. In the majority of cases, after a period of relatively normal language and speech, the child simply stops talking (except, sometimes, in one or two very selective environments such as with peers) but understands and communicates with gestures. Far too often, however, elective mutism is misdiagnosed in preschool children when the disorder is a true delay in speaking due to mental retardation or a developmental language disorder, the latter of which probably has a frequency of at least around 1 percent (Howlin, 1980). Ordinarily, there is a significant but highly variable interval between the acquisition of receptive language and talking (Howlin, 1980). One unusual feature of elective mutism among childhood psychopathological disorders in general and language problems in particular is that girls probably outnumber boys (Kolvin & Fundudis, 1981). In one of the few controlled studies done, Kolvin and Fundudis found elective mutism to be associated with psychopathology, particularly that of the anxiety-withdrawal type, with family psychopathology and, somewhat interestingly, with a history of immaturity and speech difficulties that may thus dictate the "choice" of symptomatology.

The developmental language disorders encompass all degrees of severity from what is often called congenital asphasia, which has been studied most intensively and satisfactorily by Rutter and associates (see Bartak, Rutter, & Cox, 1975) and Cantwell and Baker (1977, 1978a, 1978b, 1980), through to minor delays. Despite the wide variation in the age in which normal children begin to talk, no effort has been made in either ICD-9 or DSM-III to set a minimal age criterion, thus opening the possibility to overenthusiastic diagnosis and treatment in a preschool group.

The importance of speech and language disorders for childhood psychopathology is that (1) they are common in child psychiatric populations (Gualtieri, Koriath, Van Bourgondien, & Saleby, 1983); (2) they can be a cardinal symptom of a wide range of psychiatric disorders of which mental retardation, pervasive developmental disorder, elective mutism, dementia, and schizophrenia are examples; and (3) studies have repeatedly shown that children with language problems have an increased risk of associated psychopathology (Cantwell & Baker, 1977; Cantwell, Baker & Mattison, 1979). The studies by Cantwell and Baker suggest that this risk is particularly increased if there are other problems such as academic failure.

SUMMARY

The study of speech and language disorders is a specialized area, and the other sources cited here should be consulted for further details. Suffice it to say that minor degrees are common, these disorders are often found in psychiatric populations, the etiology is variable and probably complex (Howlin, 1980) with biological, psychopathological, parental, and other ecological factors all interacting. As with learning disorders, remediation is enthusiastically endorsed and undertaken by professionals, but there is a conspicuous absence of controlled studies by which to assess its efficacy (Howlin, 1980).

SUMMARY

This chapter has covered a wide range of topics united only in that their defining characteristics are physical symptoms (except those stemming directly from true brain disorders). Some of the disorders are truly psychopathological while others may be so in some cases. Some are of physical origin with secondary psychological consequences and others are of unknown etiology often facilely assumed to be psychogenic, masking our real ignorance. Collectively, however, they are more common and affect more children than any other of the disorders covered in other chapters. They are also of prime importance in pediatrics where they are often poorly recognized and diagnosed largely by exclusion of mostly infrequent physical disorders and only after extensive, painful and costly investigations.

Representing as they do the psychobiological interface, they present a unique opportunity for those trained in the psychosocial sciences to make a real contribution to research in and the practice of pediatric and adolescent medicine.

REFERENCES

Ackerman, P. T., Dykman, R. A., & Peters, J. E. (1977). Teenage status of hyperactive and non hyperactive learning disabled boys. *American Journal of Orthopsychiatry, 47*, 577–596.

Aman, M. G. (1980). Psychotropic drugs and learning problems—a selective review. *Journal of Learning Disabilities, 13*, 36–46.

Aman, M. G., & Singh, N. N. (1983a). Pharmacological interventions. In J. L. Matson & J. A. Mulick (Eds.), *Handbook of mental retardation* (pp. 317–337). New York: Pergamon.

Aman, M. G., & Singh, N. N. (1983b). Specific reading disorders: Concepts of etiology reconsidered. In K. D. Gadow & I. Bialer (Eds.), *Advances in learning and behavioral disabilities* (Vol. 2, pp. 1–47). Greenwich, CT: JAI Press.

American Academy of Pediatrics. (1967). Obesity in childhood. *Pediatrics, 40*, 455–467.

American Psychiatric Association. (1968). *Diagnostic and statistical manual of mental disorders* (*DSM-II*) (2nd ed.). Washington, DC: Author.

American Psychiatric Association. (1980). *Diagnostic and statistical manual of mental disorders (DSM-III)* (3rd ed.). Washington, D.C.: Author.

Anders, T. F. (1979). Night-waking during the first year of life. *Pediatrics, 63*, 860–864.

Anders, T. F. (1982). Neurophysiological studies of sleep in infants and children. *Journal of Child Psychology and Psychiatry, 23*, 75–83.

Anthony, F. (1957). An experimental approach to the psychopathology of childhood—encopresis. *British Journal of Medical Psychology, 30*, 146–175.

Asher, P. (1966). Fat babies and fat children. The prognosis of obesity in the very young. *Archives of Diseases in Childhood, 41*, 672–673.

Bakal, D. A. (1979). *Psychology and medicine: Psychobiological dimensions of health and illness*. London: Tavistock.

Bailey, S. L., Pokrzywinski, J., & Bryant, L. E. (1983). Using water mist to reduce self injurious stereotypic behavior. *Applied Research in Mental Retardation, 4*, 229–242.

Bakwin, H. (1961). Enuresis in children. *Journal of Psychosomatic Research, 8*, 89–100.

Bakwin, H., & Bakwin, R. (1966). *Clinical management of behavior disorders in children*. Philadelphia: Saunders.

Baraff, A., & Cunningham, A. (1965). Asthmatic and normal children. *Journal of the American Medical Association, 192*, 99–101.

Baroff, S., & Tate, B. (1968). The use of aversive stimulation in the treatment of chronic self-injurious behavior. *Journal of the American Academy of Child Psychiatry, 7*, 454–470.

Barkley, R. A. (1981). Learning disabilities. In E. J. Mash & L. G. Terdal (Eds.), *Behavioral assessment of childhood disorders* (pp. 441–482). New York: Guilford.

Bartak, L., Rutter, M., & Cox, A. (1975). A comparative study of infantile autism and specific developmental receptive language disorder. *British Journal of Psychiatry, 126*, 127–145.

Baumeister, A. A., & Forehand, R. (1973). Stereotyped acts. In N.R. Ellis (Ed.), *International review of research in mental retardation* (Vol. 5, pp. 55–96). New York: Academic Press.

Bax, M. O. (1980). Sleep disturbance in the young child. *British Medical Journal, 1*, 1177–1179.

Beech, H., & Nace, E. (1965). Asthma and aggression: The investigation of a hypothetical relationship employing a new procedure. *British Journal of Social and Clinical Psychology, 4*, 124–130.

Bellman, M. (1966). Studies on encopresis. *Acta Paediatrica Scandinavica* (Supplement 170).

Beltramini, A. U., & Hertzig, M. E. (1983). Sleep and bedtime behavior in preschool aged children. *Pediatrics, 71*, 153–158.

Berg, I., Fielding, D., & Meadow, R. (1977). Psychiatric disturbance, urgency and bacteriuria in children with day and night wetting. *Archives of Disease in Childhood, 52*, 651–657.

Berg, I., Forsythe, I., Holt, P., & Watts, J. (1983). A controlled trial of "Senokot" in faecal soiling treated by behavioral methods. *Journal of Child Psychology and Psychiatry, 24*, 543–550.

Berg, I., & Jones, K. (1964). Functional faecal-incontinence in children. *Archives of Diseases in Childhood, 39*, 465–472.

Berkson, G. (1965). Stereotyped movements of mental defectives. VI. No effect of amphetamine or a barbiturate. *Perceptual Motor Skills, 21*, 698.

Berkson, G. (1967). Abnormal stereotyped motor acts. In J. Zubin & H. Hunt (Eds.), *Comparative psychopathology*. New York: Grune & Stratton.

Berkson, G. (1968). Development of abnormal stereotyped behaviors. *Developmental Psychology, 1*, 118–132.

Berkson, G., & Davenport, R. (1962). Stereotyped movements of mental defectives. I. Initial survey. *American Journal of Mental Deficiency, 66*, 849–852.

Berkson, G., & Mason, W. (1964a). Stereotyped movements of mental defectives. IV. The effects of toys and the character of the acts. *American Journal of Mental Deficiency, 68*, 511–524.

Berkson, G., & Mason, W. (1964b). Stereotyped behaviors of chimpanzees: Relation to general arousal and alternative activities. *Perceptual Motor Skills, 19*, 635–652.

Bernal, J. F. (1973). Night-waking in first 14 months. *Developmental Medicine and Child Neurology, 15*, 760–769.

Bierman, C. W., & Pearlman, D. S. (1983). Asthma. In Kendig, E. L., & Chernick, V. (Eds.), *Disorders of the respiratory tract in children* (4th ed., pp. 496–543). Philadelphia: Saunders.

Blackwell, B., & Currah, J. (1973). The psychopharmacology of nocturnal enuresis. In I. Kolvin, R. MacKeith, & S. Meadow (Eds.), *Bladder control in enuresis* (*Clinics in developmental medicine*, Nos. 48/49) (pp. 231–257). London: Heinemann.

Block, J. (1968). Further considerations of psychosomatic predisposing factors in allergy. *Psychosomatic Medicine, 30*, 202–208.

Block, J., Jennings, P., Harvey, E., & Simpson, E. (1964). Interaction between allergic potential and psychopathology in childhood. *Psychosomatic Medicine, 26*, 307–320.

Blomfield, J., & Douglas, J. (1956). Bedwetting prevalence among children aged 4–7 years. *Lancet, 1*, 850–852.

Blurton-Jones, N., Rosetti-Fereira, M. C., Farquhar-Brown, M., & MacDonald, L. (1978). The association between perinatal factors and later night-waking. *Developmental Medicine and Child Neurology, 20*, 420–434.

Boyd, M. (1960). The depth of sleep in enuretic school children and in nonenuretic controls. *Journal of Psychosomatic Research, 4*, 274–281.

Breslau, N. (1983). The psychological study of chronically ill and disabled children: Are healthy siblings appropriate controls? *Journal of Abnormal Child Psychology, 11*, 379–381.

Breslau, N. (1985). Psychiatric disorder in children with physical disabilities. *Journal of the American Academy of Child Psychiatry, 24*, 87–94.

Breslau, N., Staruch, K. S., & Mortimer, E. A. (1982). Psychological distress in mothers of disabled children. *American Journal of Diseases of Children, 136*, 682–686.

Broberger, O., & Lagercrantz, R. (1966). Ulcerative colitis in childhood and adolescence. *Advances in Pediatrics, 14*, 9–54.

Broughton, R. (1968). Sleep disorders: Disorders of arousal? *Science, 159*, 1070–1078.

Brownell, K. D., Kelman, J. H., & Stunkard, A. J. (1983). Treatment of obese children with and without their mothers: Changes in weight and blood pressure. *Pediatrics, 71*, 515–523.

Bruch, H. (1963a). Psychotherapeutic problems in eating disorders. *Psychoanalytic Review, 50*, 43–57.

Bruch, H. (1963b). Disturbed communication in eating disorders. *American Journal of Orthopsychiatry, 33*, 99–104.

Bruch, H. (1974). *Eating disorders: Obesity, anorexia nervosa, and the person within*. London: Routledge & Kegan Paul.

Bruch, H. (1982). Anorexia nervosa: Therapy & theory. *American Journal of Psychiatry, 139*, 1531–1538.

Bruun, R. D. (1984). Gilles de la Tourette's syndrome: An overview of clinical experience. *Journal of the American Academy of Child Psychiatry, 23*, 126–133.

Bruun, R., Shapiro, A., Shapiro, E., Sweet, R., Wayne, H., & Solomon, G. (1976). A follow-up of 78 patients with Gilles de la Tourette syndrome. *American Journal of Psychiatry, 133*, 944–947.

Cantwell, D. P., & Baker, L. (1977). Psychiatric disorder in children with speech and language retardation. *Archives of General Psychiatry, 34*, 583–591.

Cantwell, D. P., & Baker, L. (1978a). The language environment of autistic and dysphasic children. *Journal of the American Academy of Child Psychiatry, 17*, 604–613.

Cantwell, D. P., & Baker, L. (1978b). Imitations and echoes in autistic and dysphasic children. *Journal of the American Academy of Child Psychiatry, 1*, 614–624.

Cantwell, D. P., & Baker, L. (1980). Academic failures in children with communication disorders. *Journal of the American Academy of Child Psychiatry, 19*, 579–591.

Cantwell, D. P., Baker, L., & Mattison, R. E. (1979). The prevalence of psychiatric disorder in children with speech and language disorder. *Journal of the American Academy of Child Psychiatry, 18*, 450–461.

Carey, W. B. (1974). Night waking and temperament in infancy. *Journal of Pediatrics, 84*, 756–758.

Carroll, H. C. M. (1972). The remedial teaching of reading: An evaluation. *Remedial Education, 7*, 10–15.

Christakis, G., Sajecki, S., Hillman, R., Miller, E., Blumenthal, S., & Archer, M. (1966). Effect of a combined nutrition education and physical fitness program on the weight status of obese high school boys. *Federation Proceedings, 25*, 15–19.

Clark, D. (1966). Behaviour therapy of Gilles de la Tourette's syndrome. *British Journal of Psychiatry, 112*, 771–778.

Coekin, M., & Gairdner, D. (1960). Faecal incontinence in children. *British Medical Journal, 2*, 1175–1180.

Cohen, D. J., & Leckman, J. F. (1984). Introduction to special section on Tourette's syndrome. *Journal of the American Academy of Child Psychiatry, 23*, 123–125.

Comings, D. E., & Comings, B. G. (1984). Tourette's syndrome and Attention Deficit Disorder with Hyperactivity: Are they genetically related? *Journal of the American Academy of Child Psychiatry, 23*, 126–133.

Connell, P., Corbett, J., Horne, D., & Mathews, A. (1967). Drug treatment of adolescent tiquers. *British Journal of Psychiatry, 113*, 375–381.

Corbett, J., Mathews, A., Connell, P., & Shapiro, D. (1969). Tics and Gilles de la Tourette's syndrome: A follow-up study and critical review. *British Journal of Psychiatry, 115*, 1229–1241.

Creer, T. L., Ipacs, J., & Creer, P. P. (1983). Changing behavioral and social variables at a residential treatment facility for childhood asthma. *Journal of Asthma, 20*, 11–15.

Dally, P. (1969). *Anorexia nervosa*. London: Heinemann.

Davidson, M., Kugler, M., & Bauer, C. (1963). Diagnosis and management in childen with severe and protracted constipation and obstipation. *Journal of Pediatrics, 62*, 261–275.

Delamater, A. M., Rosenbloom, N., Conners, C. K., & Hertweck, L. (1983). The behavioral treatment of hysterical paralysis in a ten year old boy: A case study. *Journal of the American Academy of Child Psychiatry, 22*, 73–79.

De Leon, G., & Mandell, W. (1966). A comparison of conditioning and psychotherapy in the treatment of functional enuresis. *Journal of Clinical Psychology, 22*, 326–330.

De Lissovoy, V. (1961). Head banging in early childhood: A study of incidence. *Journal of Pediatrics, 58*, 803–805.

De Lissovoy, V. (1962). Head banging in early childhood. *Child Development, 33*, 43–56.

Dietz, W. H. (1983). Childhood obesity: Susceptibility, cause and management. *Journal of Pediatrics, 103*, 676–686.

Dimson, S. (1959). Toilet training and enuresis. *British Medical Journal, 2*, 666–670.

Disch, S., Yule, W., Corbett, J., & Hand, D. (1983). Outcome of treatment with the enuresis alarm. *Developmental Medicine & Child Neurology, 25*, 67–80.

Dohrenwend, B. S., & Dohrenwend, B. P. (1974). *Stressful life events: Their nature and effects*. New York: Wiley.

Doleys, D. M. (1977). Behavioral treatment for nocturnal enuresis in children: A review of the recent literature. *Psychological Bulletin, 84*, 30–54.

Doleys, D. M. (1978). Treatment of enuresis and encopresis. *Progress in Behavior Modification, 6*, 85–121.

Doleys, D. M., Ciminero, A. R., Tollison, J. W., Williams, C. L., & Wells, K. C. (1977). Dry-bed training and retention control training: A comparison. *Behavior Therapy, 8*, 541–548.

Dubo, S., McLean, J., Ching, A., Wright, H., Kauffman, P., & Sheldon, J. (1961). A study of relationships between family situation, bronchial asthma, and personal adjustment in children. *Journal of Pediatrics, 59*, 402–414.

Dunlap, K. (1932). *Habits, their making and unmaking*. New York: Liveright.

Dunn, J. (1980). Feeding and sleeping. In M. Rutter (Ed.), *The scientific foundations of developmental psychiatry* (pp. 101–109). London: Heinemann.

Durnin, J. (1974). Discussion of psychological and social factors in the pathogenesis of obesity by J. T. Silverstone. In W. Burland, P. Samuels, & J. Yudkin (Eds.), *Obesity: Proceedings of a Servier Research Institute symposium* (pp. 111–115). Edinburgh: Churchill, Livingstone.

Dwyer, J., & Mayer, J. (1974). A preventive programme for obesity control. In W. Burland, P. Samuel, & J. Yudkin (Ed.), *Obesity: Proceedings of a Servier Research Institute symposium* (pp. 253–270). Edinburgh: Churchill, Livingstone.

Eckert, E. D., Goldberg, S. C., Halmi, K. A., Casper, R. C., & Davis, J. M. (1979). Behaviour therapy in anorexia nervosa. *British Journal of Psychiatry, 134*, 55–59.

Ehrhardt, A. A., Meyer-Bahlburg, H. F., Bell, J. J., Cohen, S. F., Healey, J. M., Stiel, R., Feldman, J. F., Morishima, A., & New, M. I. (1984). Idiopathic precocious puberty in girls: Psychiatric follow-up in adolescence. *Journal of the American Academy of Child Psychiatry, 23,* 23–33.

Engel, G. (1962). *Psychological development in health and disease.* Philadelphia: Saunders.

Enuresis [Editorial]. (1960). *British Medical Journal, 1*, 1416–1417.

Eysenck, H. (1959). Learning theory and behaviour therapy. *Journal of Mental Science, 105*, 61–75.

Feagans, L. (1983). A current view of learning disabilities. *Journal of Pediatrics, 102*, 487–493.

Feldman, F., Cantor, D., Soll, S., & Bachrach, W. (1967). Psychiatric study of a consecutive series of 34 patients with ulcerative colitis. *British Medical Journal, 3*, 14–17.

Feldman, R., & Werry, J. S. (1966). An unsuccessful attempt to treat a tiquer by massed practice. *Behaviour Research and Therapy, 4*, 111–117.

Fernando, S. (1976). Six cases of Gilles de la Tourette's syndrome. *British Journal of Psychiatry, 128*, 436–441.

Feuerstein, M., Ward, M. M., & LeBaron, S. W. M. (1979). Neuropsychological and neurophysiological assessment of children with learning and behavior problems: A critical appraisal. In B. B. Lahey & A. E. Kazdin (Eds.), *Advances in clinical child psychology* (Vol. II, pp. 241–278). New York: Plenum.

Feuerstein, M., & Gainer, J. (1983). Chronic headache etiology and measurement in behavioral medicine: Assessment and treatment strategies. In D. M. Doleys, R. L. Meredith, & A. R. Ciminero (Eds.), *Behavioral medicine* (pp. 199–249). New York: Plenum.

Fitts, M. D., & Mann, R. A. (1976). Encopresis: An historical and behavioral perspective of definition. *Journal of Pediatric Psychology, 4*, 31–33.

Fitzelle, G. (1959). Personality factors and certain attitudes toward child rearing among parents of asthmatic children. *Psychosomatic Medicine, 21*, 208–217.

Foreyt, J. P., & Goodrick, G. K. (1981). Childhood obesity. In E.J. Mash & L.G. Terdal (Eds.), *Behavioral assessment of childhood disorders* (pp. 573–599). New York: Guilford.

Forrester, R., Stein, Z., & Susser, M. (1964). A trial of conditioning therapy in nocturnal enuresis. *Developmental Medicine and Child Neurology, 6*, 158–166.

Franks, C., & Leigh, D. (1959). The conditioned eyeblink response in asthmatic and non-asthmatic subjects. *Journal of Psychosomatic Research, 4*, 88–93.

French, T., & Alexander, F. (1941). Psychogenic factors in bronchial asthma. *Psychosomatic Medicine Mongraphs, 4* (1).

Freud, A., & Burlingham, D. (1944). *Infants without families.* New York: International Universities Press.

Friedhoff, A. J., & Chase, T. N. (Eds.) (1982). *Gilles de la Tourette syndrome, advances in neurology* (Vol. 35). New York: Raven.

Garner, D. M., Garfinkel, P. E., Schwartz, D., & Thompson, M. (1980). Cultural expectations of thinness in women. *Psychological Reports, 47*, 483–491.

Garrow, J. (1974). *Energy balance and obesity in man.* Amsterdam: North-Holland.

Gauthier, Y., Fortin, C., Drapeau, P., Breton, J. J., Gosselin, J., Quintal, L., Weisnagel, J., Tetreault, L., & Pinard, G. (1977). The mother–child relationship and the development of autonomy and self assertion in young (14–30 months) asthmatic children. *Journal of the American Academy of Child Psychiatry, 16,* 109–131.

Gittelman, R., & Feingold, I. (1983). Children with reading disorders. I. Efficacy of reading remediation. *Journal of Child Psychology and Psychiatry, 24,* 167–192.

Gittelman, R., Klein, D. F., & Feingold, I. (1983). Children with reading disorders. II. Effects of methylphenidate in combination with reading remediation. *Journal of Child Psychology and Psychiatry, 24,* 193–212.

Glicklich, L. (1951). An historical account of enuresis. *Journal of Pediatrics, 8,* 859–876.

Golombok, S., Spencer, A., & Rutter, M. (1983). Children in lesbian and single-parent households: Psychosexual and psychiatric appraisal. *Journal of Child Psychology and Psychiatry, 24,* 531–572.

Goodyer, Z. (1981). Hysterical conversion reactions in childhood. *Journal of Child Psychology and Psychiatry, 22,* 179–188.

Graham, P., Rutter, M., Yule, W., & Pless, I. (1967). Asthma—a psychosomatic disorder? Some epidemiological considerations. *British Journal of Preventive and Social Medicine, 21,* 78–85.

Grant, M. (1966). Juvenile obesity—chronic, progressive, and transient. *Medical Officer, 115,* 331–335.

Green, A. (1967). Self-mutilation in schizophrenic children. *Archives of General Psychiatry, 17,* 234–244.

Green, A. (1968). Self-destructive behavior in physically abused schizophrenic children. *Archives of General Psychiatry, 19,* 171–1879.

Green, A. H. (1984). Child maltreatment: Recent studies and future directions. *Journal of the American Academy of Child Psychiatry, 23,* 675–678.

Green, R. (1974). *Sexual identity conflict in children and adults.* New York: Basic Books.

Green, R. (1978). Sexual identity of 37 children raised by homosexual or transsexual parents. *American Journal of Psychiatry, 135,* 692–697.

Green, W. H., Campbell, M., & David, R. (1984). Psychosocial dwarfism: A critical review of the evidence. *Journal of the American Academy of Child Psychiatry, 23,* 39–48.

Greenberg, N. (1964). Origins of head-rolling (spasmus nutans) during early infancy. *Psychosomatic Medicine, 26,* 162–171.

Gualtieri, C. T., Koriath, U., Van Bourgondien, M., & Saleby, N. (1983). Language disorders in children referred for psychiatric services. *Journal of the American Academy of Child Psychiatry, 22,* 165–171.

Hahn, W. (1966). Autonomic responses of asthmatic children. *Psychosomatic Medicine, 28,* 323–332.

Hallgren, B. (1956a). Enuresis. I. A study with reference to the morbidity risk and symptomatology. *Acta Psychiatrica et Neurologica Scandinavica, 31,* 379–403.

Hallgren, B. (1956b). Enuresis. II. A study with reference to certain physical, mental, and social factors possibly associated with enuresis. *Acta Psychiatrica et Neurologica Scandinavica, 31*, 405–436.

Hallgren, B. (1957). Enuresis: A clinical and genetic study. *Acta Psychiatrica et Neurologica Scandinavica, 32* (Supplement No. 114).

Halmi, K. A. (1983). Anorexia nervosa and bulemia. *Psychosomatics, 24*, 111–129.

Halperin, J. M., Gittelman, R., Klein, D. F., & Rudel, R. G. (1984). Reading-disabled hyperactive children, a clinical subgroup of Attention Deficit Disorder? *Journal of Abnormal Child Psychology, 12*, 1–14.

Harcherik, D. F., Leckman, J. F., Detlor, J., & Cohen, D. J. (1984). A new instrument for clinical studies of Tourette's syndrome. *Journal of the American Academy of Child Psychiatry, 23*, 153–160.

Harlow, H. (1962). The heterosexual affectional system in monkeys. *American Psychologist, 17*, 1–9.

Harper, G. (1983). Varieties of parenting-failure in anorexia nervosa. *Journal of the American Academy of Child Psychiatry, 22*, 134–139.

Harris, L. S., & Purohit, A. P. (1977). Bladder training and enuresis: A controlled trial. *Behaviour Research & Therapy, 15*, 485–490.

Heald, F. (1966). Natural history and physiological basis of adolescent obesity. *Federation Proceedings, 25*, 1–3.

Herbert, M. (1965). Personality factors and bronchial asthma: A study of South African Indian children. *Journal of Psychosomatic Research, 8*, 353–364.

Howlin, P. (1980). Language. In M. Rutter (Ed.), *Scientific foundations of developmental psychiatry* (pp. 198–220). London: Heinemann.

Hsu, L. K. G. (1980). Outcome of anorexia nervosa. *Archives of General Psychiatry, 37*, 1041–1046.

Huon, G. F., & Brown, L. B. (1984). Bulimia: The emergence of the syndrome. *Australian & New Zealand Journal of Psychiatry, 24*, 113–126.

Hutt, S., Hutt, C., Lee, D., & Ounsted, C. (1965). A behavioral and electroencephalographic study of autistic children. *Journal of Psychiatric Research, 3*, 181–197.

Jackson, D., & Yalom, I. (1966). Family research on the problem of ulcerative colitis. *Archives of General Psychiatry, 15*, 410–418.

Jenkins, S., Bax, M. C. O., & Hart, H. (1980). Behaviour problems in preschool children. *Journal of Child Psychology and Psychiatry, 21*, 5–17.

Jones, H. (1960). The behavioural treatment of enuresis nocturna. In H. Eysenck (Ed.), *Behaviour therapy and the neuroses* (pp. 377–403). Oxford: Pergamon.

Josselyn, I., Littner, N., & Spurlock, J. (1966). Psychologic aspects of ulcerative colitis in children. *Journal of the American Medical Women's Association, 21*, 303–306.

Kanner, L. (1957). *Child psychiatry* (pp.422–423). Springfield, IL: Charles C. Thomas.

Kaufman, M., & Levitt, H. (1965). A study of three stereotyped behaviors in institutionalized mental defectives. *American Journal of Mental Deficiency, 69*, 467–473.

Kelman, D. (1965). Gilles de la Tourette's disease in children: A review of the literature. *Journal of Child Psychology and Psychiatry, 6,* 219–226.

Kern, L., Koegel, R. L., & Dunlop, G. (1984). The influence of vigorous versus mild exercise on autistic stereotyped behaviors. *Journal of Autism & Developmental Disorders, 14,* 57–67.

Klackenberg, G. (1955). Primary enuresis: When is a child dry at night? *Acta Paediatrica, 44,* 513–517.

Kolvin, I., & Fundudis, T. (1981). Elective mute children: Psychological development and background factors. *Journal of Child Psychology and Psychiatry, 22,* 219–232.

Kolvin, I., & Goodyer, I. (1982). Child psychiatry. In K. L. Granville-Grossman (Ed.), *Recent advances in clinical psychiatry* (Vol. 4, pp. 1–24). Edinburgh: Churchill, Livingstone.

Kolvin, I., McKeith, R., & Meadow, S. (Eds.). (1973). *Bladder control in enuresis (Clinics in developmental medicine,* Nos. 48/49). London: Heinemann.

Kolvin, I., & Nicol, A. R. (1979). Child psychiatry. In K. Granville-Grossman (Ed.), *Recent advances in clinical psychiatry* (Vol. 3, pp. 297–332). Edinburgh: Churchill, Livingstone.

Koocher, G. P., O'Malley, J. E., Gogan, J. L., & Foster, D. J. (1980). Psychological adjustment among pediatric cancer survivors. *Journal of Child Psychology and Psychiatry, 21,* 163–174.

Kotelchuk, M., & Neuberger, F. H. (1983). Failure to thrive: A controlled study of familial characteristics. *Journal of the American Academy of Child Psychiatry, 22,* 322–328.

Kravitz, H., & Boehm, J. J. (1971). Rhythmic habit patterns in infancy: Their sequence, age of onset and frequency. *Child Development, 42,* 399–413.

Kravitz, H., Rosenthal, V., Teplitz, Z., Murphy, J., & Lesser, R. (1960). A study of head-banging in infants and children. *Diseases of the Nervous System, 21,* 203–208.

Lader, M. (1972). *Psychophysiological research and psychosomatic medicine in psychology, emotion and psychiatric illness* (CIBA Foundation Sympoisum #8) (pp. 297–311). Amsterdam: Elsevier.

Lapouse, R., & Monk, M. (1958). An epidemiologic study of behavior characteristics in children. *American Journal of Public Health, 48,* 1134–1144.

Lapouse, R., & Monk, M. (1964). Behavior deviations in a representative sample of children: Variation by sex, age, race, social class, and family size. *American Journal of Orthpsychiatry, 34,* 436–446.

Largo, R. H., & Stultze, W. (1977a). Longitudinal study of bowel and bladder control by day and at night in the first six years of life. I: Epidemiology and interrelations between bowel and bladder control. *Developmental Medicine & Child Neurology, 19,* 598–606.

Largo, R. H., & Stultze, W. (1977b). Longitudinal study of bowel and bladder control by day and at night in the first six years of life. II: The role of potty training and the child's initiative. *Developmental Medicine & Child Neurology, 19,* 607–613.

Lebowitz, N., Colbert, F., & Palmer, J. (1961). Schizophrenia in children. *American Journal of Diseases of Children, 102*, 25–27.

Leckman, J. F., Detlor, J., Harcherik, D. F., Young, J. G., Anderson, G. M., Shaywitz, B. A., & Cohen, D. J. (1983). Acute and chronic clonidine treatment in Tourette's syndrome: A preliminary report on clinical response and effect on plasma and urinary catecholamine metabolites, growth hormone, and blood pressure. *Journal of the American Academy of Child Psychiatry, 22*, 433–440.

Levine, M. D. (1975). Children with encopresis: A descriptive analysis. *Pediatrics, 56*, 412–416.

Levine, M. D., & Bakow, H. (1976). Children with encopresis: A study of treatment outcome. *Pediatrics, 58*, 845–852.

Levine, M. D., Mazonson, P., & Bakow, H. (1980). Behavioral symptom substitution in children cured of encopresis. *American Journal of Diseases in Children, 134*, 663–667.

Levy, D. (1944). On the problem of movement restraint (tics, stereotyped movements, hyperactivity). *American Journal of Orthopsychiatry, 14*, 644–671.

Liebman, R., Sargent, J., & Silver, M. (1983). A family systems orientation to the treatment of anorexia nervosa. *Journal of the American Academy of Child Psychiatry, 22*, 128–133.

Lippe, B. M. (1983). The physiologic aspects of eating disorders. *Journal of the American Academy of Child Psychiatry, 22*, 108–113.

Litt, C. (1981). Children's attachment to transitional objects: A study of two pediatric populations. *American Journal of Orthopsychiatry, 49*, 131–139.

Lloyd, J. (1969). Obesity in childhood: Incidence, natural history and etiology. In I. Baird & A. Howard (Eds.), *Obesity: Medical and scientific aspects*. Edinburgh: Churchill Livingstone.

Lloyd, J., Wolff, O., & Whelen, W. (1961). Childhood obesity. A long term study of height and weight. *British Medical Journal, 2*, 145–148.

Lourie, R. (1949). The role of rhythmic patterns in childhood. *Archives of General Psychiatry, 105*, 653–660.

Lovaas, O., Freitag, G., Gold, V., & Kassorla, I. (1965). Experimental studies in childhood schizophrenia: Analysis of self-destructive behavior. *Journal of Experimental Child Psychology, 2*, 67–84.

Lovaas, O., Schaeffer, B., & Simmons, J. (1965). Building social behavior in autistic children by use of electric shock. *Journal of Experimental Research in Personality, 1*, 99–109.

Lovaas, O., & Simmons, J. (1962). Manipulation of self-destruction in three retarded children. *Journal of Applied Behavior Analysis, 2*, 143–157.

Lovibund, S., & Coote, M. (1969). Enuresis. In C. Costello (Ed.), *Symptoms of psychopathology* (pp. 373–396). New York: Wiley.

Lucas, A., Kauffman, P., & Morris, E. (1967). Gilles de la Tourette's disease: A clinical study of fifteen cases. *Journal of the American Academy of Child Psychiatry, 6*, 700–722.

Mahler, M. (1949). A psychoanalytic evaluation of tic in psychopathology of children. *Psychoanalytic Study of the Child, 3/4*, 279–310.

Mahoney, D. (1971). Studies of enuresis. I. Incidence of obstructive lesions and pathophysiology of enuresis. *Journal of Urology, 106*, 951–955.

Maloney, M. J., & Klykylo, W. M. (1983). An overview of anorexia nervosa, bulemia and obesity in children and adolescents. *Journal of the American Academy of Child Psychiatry, 22*, 99–107.

Management of the fat child [Editorial]. (1966). *British Medical Journal, 2*, 961–962.

Markova, I., MacDonald, K., & Forbes, C. (1980). Impact of haemophilia on child-rearing practices and parental cooperation. *Journal of Child Psychology and Psychiatry, 21*, 153–162.

Mason, W., & Sponholz, R. (1963). Behavior of Rhesus monkeys raised in isolation. *Journal of Psychiatric Research, 1*, 299–306.

Mayer, J. (1966a). Physical activity and anthropometric measurements of obese adolescents. *Federation Proceedings, 25*, 11–14.

Mayer, J. (1966b). Some aspects of the problem of regulation of food intake and obesity. *New England Journal of Medicine, 274*, 610–616, 662–673, 722–731.

McDermott, J., & Finch, S. (1967). Ulcerative colitis in children: Reassessment of a dilemma. *Journal of the American Academy of Child Psychiatry, 6*, 512–525.

McGee, R., & Silva, P. A. (1982). *A thousand New Zealand children: Their health and development from birth to seven* (pp. 58–59). Auckland, NZ: Medical Research Council.

McGraw, M. (1940). Neurological maturation as exemplified by the achievement of bladder control. *Journal of Pediatrics, 16*, 580–590.

McTaggart, A., & Scott, M. (1959). A review of twelve cases of encopresis. *Journal of Pediatrics, 54*, 762–768.

Michaels, J., & Goodman, S. (1934). Incidence and intercorrelations of enuresis and other neuropathic traits in so-called normal children. *American Journal of Orthopsychiatry, 4*, 79–106.

Mikkelsen, E. J., Rapoport, J. L., Nee, L., Greunau, C., Mendelson, W., & Gillin, J. (1980). Childhood enuresis. I. Sleep patterns and psychopathology. *Archives of General Psychiatry, 37*, 1139–1144.

Miller, H., & Baruch, D. (1950). A study of hostility in allergic children. *American Journal of Orthopsychiatry, 20*, 506–519.

Minde, K., Whitelaw, A., Brown, J., & Fitz-Hardinge, P. (1983). Effect of neonatal complications in premature infants on early parent–infant interactions. *Developmental Medicine & Child Neurology, 25*, 763–777.

Mowrer, O., & Mowrer, W. (1938). Enuresis: A method for its study and treatment. *American Journal of Orthopsychiatry, 8*, 436–447.

Mrazek, P. B. (1980). Sexual abuses of children. *Journal of Child Psychology and Psychiatry, 21*, 91–95.

Muellner, S. (1960). Development of urinary control in children: A new concept in cause, prevention and treatment of primary enuresis. *Journal of Urology, 84*, 714–716.

Neuhaus, E. C. (1958). A personality study of asthmatic and cardiac children. *Psychosomatic Medicine, 20*, 181–186.

Obesity in Childhood [Annotation]. (1966). *Lancet, 2*, 327.

Oppel, W., Harper, P., & Rowland, V. (1968). The age of attaining bladder control. *Journal of Pediatrics, 42,* 614–626.

Oppel, W., Harper, P., & Rider, R. (1968). Social, psychological, and neurological factors associated with nocturnal enuresis. *Journal of Pediatrics, 42,* 627–641.

Ornitz, E., & Ritvo, E. (1968). Perceptual inconstancy in early infantile autism. *Archives of General Psychiatry, 18,* 76–98.

Owen, F., & Williams G. (1961). Patterns of respiratory disturbance in asthmatic children evoked by the stimulus of the mother's voice. *American Journal of Diseases of Children, 102,* 133–134.

Palmer, R. C. (1982). Anorexia nervosa. In K. Granville-Grossman (Ed.), *Recent advances in clinical psychiatry* (Vol. 4, pp. 101–122). Edinburgh: Churchill, Livingstone.

Pasamanick, B., & Kawi, A. (1956). A study of the association of prenatal and paranatal factors with the development of tics in children: A preliminary investigation. *Journal of Pediatrics, 48,* 596–601.

Pattison, E. M., & Kahan, J. (1983). The deliberate self-harm syndrome. *American Journal of Psychiatry, 140,* 867–872.

Pauls, D. L., Kruger, S. D., Leckman, J. F., Cohen, D. J., & Kidd, K. K. (1984). The risk of Tourette's syndrome and chronic multiple tics among relatives of Tourette's syndrome patients obtained by direct interview. *Journal of the American Academy of Child Psychiatry, 23,* 134–137.

Pless, I. B., & Pinkerton, P. (1975). *Chronic childhood disorder & promoting patterns of adjustment.* Chicago: Year Book Medical.

Pless, I. B., & Zvagulis, I. (1981). The health of children with special needs. In *Research priorities in maternal and child health.* Washington, DC: Government Printing Office (USDHHS: Office for Maternal & Child Health). (Publication No. PHS 3M/2-82:185).

Procter, J. T. (1958). Hysteria in childhood. *American Journal of Orthopsychiatry, 28,* 394–407.

Puig-Antich, J., Goetz, R., Hanlon, C., Davies, M., Thompson, J., Chambers, W. J., Tabrizi, M. A., & Weitzman, E. D. (1982). Sleep architecture and REM sleep measures in prepubertal children with major depression: A controlled study. *Archives of General Psychiatry, 39,* 932–939.

Purcell, K. (1963). Distinctions between subgroups of asthmatic children: Children's perceptions of events associated with asthma. *Journal of Pediatrics, 31,* 486–494.

Purcell, K. (1965). Critical appraisal of psychosomatic studies of asthma. *New York State Journal of Medicine, 65,* 2103–2109.

Purcell, K. (1975). Childhood asthma, the role of family relationships, personality, and emotions. In A. Davids (Ed.), *Child personality and psychopathology: Current topics* (Vol. 2, pp. 101–136). New York: Wiley.

Purcell, K., Bernstein, L., & Bukantz, S. (1961). A preliminary comparison of rapidly remitting and persistently "steroid-dependent" asthmatic children. *Psychosomatic Medicine, 23,* 304–310.

Purcell, K., & Clifford, E. (1966). Binocular rivalry and the study of identification in asthmatic and nonasthmatic boys. *Journal of Consulting Psychology, 30,* 388–394.

Purcell, K., & Metz, J. (1962). Distinctions between subgroups of asthmatic children: Some parent attitude variables related to age of onset of asthma. *Journal of Psychosomatic Research, 6*, 251–258.

Purcell, K., Turnbull, J., & Bernstein, L. (1962). Distinctions between subgroups of asthmatic children: Psychological test and behavior rating comparisons. *Journal of Psychosomatic Research, 6*, 283–291.

Purcell, K., & Weiss, J. (1970). Asthma. In C. Costello (Eds.), *Symptoms of psychopathology* (pp. 597–623). New York: Wiley.

Rainwater, N., & Alexander, A. B. (1983). Respiratory disorders. In D. M. Doleys, R. L. Meredith, & A. R. Ciminero (Eds.), *Behavioral medicine: Assessment and treatment strategies* (pp. 435–446). New York: Plenum.

Rapoport, J. L., Mikkelsen, E. J., Zavadil, A., Nee, L., Greunau, C., Mendelson, W., & Gillin, C. (1980). Childhood enuresis: II. Psychopathology tricyclic concentration in plasma and antienuretic effect. *Archives of General Psychiatry, 37*, 1146–1152.

Rauh, J., Schumsky, D., & Witt, M. (1967). Heights, weights, and obesity in urban school children. *Child Development, 38*, 515–530.

Rees, L. (1964). The importance of psychological, allergic, and infective factors in childhood asthma. *Journal of Psychosomatic Research, 7*, 253–262.

Richman, N. (1981a). A community survey of characteristics of 1–2 year olds with sleep disruptions. *Journal of the American Academy of Child Psychiatry, 20*, 281–291.

Richman, N. (1981b). Sleep problems in young children. *Archives of Disease in Childhood, 56*, 491–493.

Richman, N., Stevenson, J. E., & Graham, P. (1975). Prevalence of behaviour problems in three-year-old children: An epidemiological study in a London Borough. *Journal of Child Psychology and Psychiatry, 16*, 277–287.

Ritvo, E., Ornitz, E., & La Franchi, S. (1968). Frequency of repetitive behaviors in early infantile autism and its variants. *Archives of General Psychiatry, 19*, 341–347.

Ritvo, S. (1945). Survey of the recent literature of tics in children. *Nervous Child, 4*, 308–312.

Rutter, M. (1971). Normal psychosexual development. *Journal of Child Psychology & Psychiatry, 11*, 259–283.

Rutter, M. (1973). Indications for research: III. In I. Kolvin, R. MacKeith, & S. Meadow (Eds.), *Bladder control in enuresis* (pp. 292–300). (*Clinics in developmental medicine*, Nos. 48/49). London: Heinemann.

Rutter, M. (1980). Psychosexual development. In M. Rutter (Ed.), *Scientific foundation of developmental psychiatry* (pp. 322–339). London: Heinemann.

Rutter, M. (1981). Psychological sequelae of brain damage in children. *American Journal of Psychiatry, 138*, 1533–1544.

Rutter, M., & Lockyer, L. (1967). A five to fifteen year follow-up study of infantile psychosis. I. Description of sample. *British Journal of Psychiatry, 113*, 1169–1182.

Rutter, M., & Yule, W. (1973). Specific reading retardation. In L. Mann & D. A. Sabatino. (Eds.), *The first review of special education* (Vol. II, pp. 1–50). Philadelphia: J. S. E. Press.

Rutter, M., & Yule, W. (1975). The concept of specific reading retardation. *Journal of Child Psychology and Psychiatry, 16*, 181–197.

Rutter, M., Yule, W., & Graham, P. (1973). Enuresis and behavioural deviance: Some epidemiological considerations. In I. Kolvin, R. MacKeith, & S. Meadow (Eds.), *Bladder control in enuresis* (pp. 137–150). (*Clinics in developmental medicine*, Nos. 48/49). London: Heinemann.

Sallustro, F., & Atwell, C. W. (1978). Bodyrocking, head banging and head rolling in normal children. *Journal of Pediatrics, 93*, 704–708.

Schaefer, H. (1970). Self-injurious behavior: Shaping "headbanging" in monkeys. *Journal of Applied Behavior Analysis, 3*, 111–116.

Seymour, F. (1976). The treatment of encopresis using behaviour modifications. *Australian Paediatric Journal, 12*, 326–329.

Seymour, F. W., Bayfield, G., Brock, P., & During, M. (1983). Management of night waking in young children. *Australian Journal of Family Therapy, 4*, 217–223.

Shaffer, D. (1973). The association between enuresis and emotional disorder: A review of the literature. In I. Kolvin, R. MacKeith, & S. Meadow (Eds.), *Bladder control in enuresis* (pp. 118–136). (*Clinics in developmental medicine*, Nos. 48/49). London: Heinemann.

Shapiro, A. K., & Shapiro, E. (1984). Controlled study of pimozide v placebo in Tourette's syndrome. *Journal of the American Academy of Child Psychiatry, 23*, 161–173.

Shutter, L., & Garell, D. (1966). Obesity in children and adolescents: A double-blind study with cross-over. *The Journal of School Health, 36*, 273–275.

Silverstone, J. (1974). Psychological and social factors in the pathogenesis of obesity. In W. Burland, P. Samuel, & J. Yudkin (Eds.), *Obesity: Proceedings of a Servier Research Institution symposium*. Edinburgh: Churchill, Livingstone.

Simonds, J. F., & Parraga, H. (1982). Sleep disorders and sleep behaviors. *Journal of the American Academy of Child Psychiatry, 21*, 383–388.

Sorosky, A., Ornitz, E., Brown, M., & Ritvo, E. (1968). Systematic observations of autistic behavior. *Archives of General Psychiatry, 18*, 439–449.

Sperling, M. (1965). Dynamic considerations and treatment of enuresis. *Journal of the American Academy of Child Psychiatry, 4*, 19–31.

Spitz, R., & Wolf, K. (1946). Anaclitic depression. *Psychoanalytic Study of Children, 2*, 313–342.

Stein, Z., & Susser, M. (1966). Nocturnal enuresis as a phenomenon of institutions. *Developmental Medicine and Child Neurology, 8*, 677–685.

Stein, Z., & Susser, M. (1967). Social factors in the development of sphincter control. *Developmental Medicine and Child Neurology, 9*, 692–706.

Stein, Z., Susser, M., & Wilson, A. (1965). Families of enuretic children. *Developmental Medicine and Child Neurology, 7*, 658–676.

Steiner, H., Fritz, G. K., Hilliard, J., & Lewiston, N. J. (1982). Psychosomatic appraisal to childhood asthma. *Journal of Asthma, 19*, 111–121.

Steinhausen, H. C. (1981). Chronically ill and handicapped children and adolescents: Personality studies in relation to disease. *Journal of Abnormal Child Psychology, 9*, 291–297.

Steinhausen, H. C. (1982). Locus of control among psychosomatically and chronically ill children and adolescents. *Journal of Abnormal Child Psychology, 10,* 609–618.

Steinhausen, H. C., & Kies, H. (1982). Comparative studies of ulcerative colitis and Crohn's disease in children and adolescents. *Journal of Child Psychology and Psychiatry, 23,* 33–42.

Sweet, R., Solomon, G., Wayne, H., Shapiro, E., & Shapiro, A. (1973). Neurological features of Gilles de la Tourette's syndrome. *Journal of Neurosurgery and Psychiatry, 36,* 109.

Swift, W. J. (1982). The long-term outcome of early onset anorexia nervosa: A critical review. *Journal of the American Academy of Child Psychiatry, 21,* 38–46.

Tate, B., & Baroff, G. (1966). Aversive control of self-injurious behaviour in a psychotic boy. *Behaviour Research and Therapy, 4,* 281–287.

Tavormina, J. B., Kastner, L. S., Slater, P. M., & Watt, S. L. (1976). Chronically ill children—a psychologically and emotionally deviant population. *Journal of Abnormal Child Psychology, 4,* 99–110.

Thelen, E. (1979). Rhythmical stereotypes in normal human infants. *Animal Behavior, 27,* 699–715.

Torup, E. (1962). A follow-up study of children with tics. *Acta Paediatrica, 51,* 261–268.

Turner, S. M., & Morrison, R. L. (1983). Movement disorders. In D. M. Doleys, R. C. Meredith & A. R. Ciminero (Eds.), *Behavioral medicine* (pp. 407–433.) New York: Plenum.

Ullmann, L., & Krasner, L. (1975). *A psychological approach to abnormal behavior* (2nd ed.). Englewood Cliffs, NJ: Prentice-Hall.

Viney, L. L., & Westbrook, M. T. (1985). Patterns of psychological reaction to asthma in children. *Journal of Abnormal Child Psychology, 13,* 477–484.

Walton, D. (1961). Experimental psychology and the treatment of a tiqueur. *Journal of Child Psychology and Psychiatry, 2,* 148–155.

Warson, S., Caldwell, M., Warinner, A., Kirk, A., & Jensen, R. (1954). The dynamics of encopresis. *American Journal of Orthopsychiatry, 24,* 402–415.

Weiss, J. S. (1966). Mood states associated with asthma in children. *Journal of Psychosomatic Research, 120,* 267–273.

Werry, J. S. (1967). Enuresis nocturna. *Medical Times, 95,* 985.

Werry, J. S., & Bull, D. (1975). Anorexia nervosa: A case study using behavior therapy. *Journal of the American Academy of Child Psychiatry, 14,* 646–651.

Werry, J. S., & Carlielle, J. (1983) The nuclear family, suburban neurosis and iatrogenesis in mothers of preschool children. *Journal of the American Academy of Child Psychiatry, 22,* 172–179.

Werry, J. S., Carlielle, J., & Fitzpatrick, J. (1983). Rhythmic motor activities in children under five: Etiology and prevalence. *Journal of the American Academy of Child Psychiatry, 22,* 329–336.

Werry, J. S., & Cohrssen, J. (1965). Enuresis—an etiologic and therapeutic study. *Journal of Pediatrics, 67,* 423–431.

Werry, J. S., Methven, R. J., Fitzpatrick, J., & Dixon, H. (1983). The interrater reliability of DSM-III in children. *Journal of Abnormal Child Psychology, 11*, 341–354.

Wilkinson, P., Pearlson, J., Parkin, J., & Phillips, P. (1977). Obesity in childhood: A community study in Newcastle on Tyne. *Lancet, 1*, 350–352.

Willi, J., & Grossman, S. (1983). Epidemiology of anorexia nervosa in a defined region of Switzerland. *American Journal of Psychiatry, 140*, 564–567.

Wing, L., & Gould, J. (1979). Severe impairments of social interaction and associated abnormalities in children: Epidemiology and classification. *Journal of Autism and Developmental Disorders, 9*, 11–29.

Winton, A. S. W., & Singh, N. N. (1983). Rumination in pediatric populations: A behavioral analysis. *Journal of the American Academy of Child Psychiatry, 22*, 269–275.

Winton, A. S. W., Singh, N. N., & Dawson, M. J. (1984). Effects of facial screening and blindfold on self-injurious behavior. *Applied Research in Mental Retardation, 5*, 29–42.

Woodmansey, A. (1967). Emotion and the motion: An inquiry into the causes and prevention of functional disorders of defecation. *British Journal of Medical Psychology, 40*, 207–223.

Woodrow, K. (1974). Gilles de la Tourette's disease—a review. *American Journal of Psychiatry, 131*, 1000–1003.

Woolston, J. L. (1983). Eating disorders in infancy and early childhood. *Journal of the American Academy of Child Psychiatry, 22*, 114–121.

Yates, A. (1958). The application of learning theory to the treatment of tics. *Journal of Abnormal and Social Psychology, 56*, 175–182.

Yates, A. (1970). Tics. In C. Costello (Ed.), *Symptoms of psychopathology* (pp. 320–335). New York: Wiley.

Zausmer, D. (1954). Treatment of tics in childhood. *Archives of Disease in Childhood, 29*, 537–542.

Zlutnick, S., & Taylor, C. B. (1983). Chronic pain. In R. M. Doleys, R. L. Meredith, & A. R. Ciminero (Eds.), *Behavioral medicine* (pp. 269–293). New York: Plenum.

8 BIOLOGICAL FACTORS

JOHN S. WERRY

INTRODUCTION

Major impairment of brain function ordinarily produces the organic brain disorders discussed in Chapter 6. However, especially when lesser in degrees or merely suspected, it is also widely posited to produce *nonorganic* psychopathological disorders and symptoms. It is the latter that are reviewed here.

Concern about the role of organic factors in the etiology of certain children's behavior symptoms and disorders has burgeoned since the 1970s, so that the literature in this area is now vast. Unfortunately, the quantity of studies is not matched by their quality and results are often contradictory. In spite of this, the better studies, some of which are now over 20 years old, have tended to produce consistent findings, though public and professional opinion seems, so far, to have been little influenced and swings between two extreme etiological poles—for and against biological factors.

ANATOMICAL, PHYSIOLOGICAL, PATHOLOGICAL, AND DEVELOPMENTAL CONSIDERATIONS

The brain is a semifluid mass of nervous (nerve cells or neurons and their processes or axons and dendrites), supporting (glial), and nutritional (blood vessels) tissue with a very high fat or lipid content. It is protected by a hydraulic suspension system (in cerebrospinal fluid) within a bony container, the skull. At birth, the brain is more or less fully formed (but far from differentiated) and has its life-complement of neurons, which cannot, at least at this writing, be replaced if they die. As a result, at birth and during early childhood, the head is large relative to the rest of the body and such growth as there is occurs in supporting, nutritional, dendritic, and axonal tissue. Neurons also increase in size but not in number. At birth, only those neurons vital to survival (e.g., respiration) are differentiated and functioning fully; this makes the neonatal brain *relatively* resistant to anoxia and trauma, though a few areas (such as the temporal lobe and parts of the motor system) appear more vulnerable than others.

The process of differentiation of the brain occurs at a negatively decelerating rate from conception until late adolescence. Differentiation is primarily in the increase in size and complexity of neurons and, most noticeably, the development of interconnections—dendrites for incoming stimuli and axons (or fibers) for outgoing.

Because neurons are highly specialized and highly evolved cells, they can function only in a very fixed physicochemical milieu and thus are profoundly affected by relatively small changes in temperature, in oxygen, glucose, and electrolyte concentrations, and by toxic substances. There are, however, elaborate mechanisms for protecting the milieu of the brain. While the brain cannot replace dead neurons as other organs can, there is abundant reserve capacity and duplication of function. Further, many acute pathological processes such as injury, cerebrovascular accidents (strokes), and infections cause much, but only temporary, disruption of function through swelling, metabolic changes, and release of toxic products of tissue damage. Together, these two facts mean that initial dysfunction is always, to a varying degree, much worse than the final state. In children too, though it may be slowed or distorted, normal brain development does not stop just because part of the brain is damaged or otherwise dysfunctional. These factors of reserve, duplication, temporary changes, and normal development allow for a surprising degree of spontaneous recovery.

The organization of the brain into regions, lobes, nuclei (collections of cells), and tracts (fiber pathways) is reflected in localization of function, which is often unilateral. Though function is generally localized, however, the brain works as an interdependent set of systems so that disorders in one area may have effects not only on brain function as a whole but also on sites quite remote from the lesion.

The study of brain disorders suggests that certain brain functions require the brain as a whole to be functioning (see Albert, 1981; Rutter, 1981, 1982a; Chapter 6) so that when damage or dysfunction is extensive, these functions are impeded. Of these, the prime examples are consciousness, general awareness, and ability to interpret the world within and without (i.e., intelligence). This means that dependent on its extensiveness, brain disorder should produce two distinct kinds of dysfunction, which Lipowski (1982) has described as global and partial.

It is widely held that brain disorder occurring early in life (e.g., damage to the dominant speech center in the brain) is less serious than that occurring in adulthood (e.g., Rutter, 1981). This notion is unsupported and probably contradicted by the facts, as the comprehensive and critical reviews by Satz and Fletcher (1981) and Fletcher and Satz (1983) show, despite challenges (e.g., Smith, 1983). The reason that this probable myth of age effects persists, as the reviews by Satz and Fletcher show, is due partly to the extraordinary methodological difficulties of this area of research detailed later, but above all, by the confounding of age and time after follow-up—for obvious reasons children are likely to be followed for much greater intervals of time than are adults.

CONCEPTS OF BRAIN–BEHAVIOR RELATIONSHIPS

In discussing the relationship between brain disorder and personality, Teuber (1960) described two predominating points of view: the "hard" and the "soft." In the hard, the lesion is seen as directly instrumental in producing the behavioral disorder, either a general brain-damage syndrome or a series of specific syndromes depending on the site or type of the lesion (e.g., Wender, 1971). In the soft view, cerebral status is a relatively minor variable, the behavioral effect of which is overriden and made quite unpredictable or unimportant by the individual personality or, particularly in children, by subsequent experience (e.g., Sameroff & Chandler, 1975).

Intermediate views (see Gorenstein & Newman, 1980; Rutter, 1981, 1982a; Rutter, Graham, & Yule, 1970) suggest that certain primary deficits, especially of cognitive, motivational, and motor function, may be direct results of cerebral pathology, but that the resultant behavioral disturbances are determined largely by the interaction of the now vulnerable child with his environment. The current interest in temperament as a predisposition toward certain behavioral styles is an extension of this concept (see Rutter, 1982b; Chapter 2).

In addition to hard/soft controversy, there is the quantitative/qualitative or nonspecific/specific controversy. The quantitative or nonspecific view sees brain disorder as a unitary variable producing a characteristic set of behaviors and cognitive deficits the nature of which is dependent on the *amount* of brain damage rather than the site or the etiology. This view is manifest in the notions of the continuum of reproductive casualty of Pasamanick (Pasamanick & Knobloch, 1960) and of minimal brain dysfunction (MBD) of Clements and Peters (1962). This nonspecific or quantitative view is still held by a substantial number of those who work with disturbed or learning-disabled children, particularly in the United States.

The opposing qualitative or specific view has been espoused especially by the British, who have been persistent in their denunciation of quantitative views like MBD as neurologically unsound (Rutter, 1981, 1982a; Shaffer, 1973), arguing that in view of the well-known localization of the function in the brain, with the possible exception of overall intelligence, the effects of brain damage are dependent primarily on the site of the lesion and the age at which it is incurred. This view is much more consistent with animal experiments (Schulman, Kaspar, & Throne, 1965) and with clinical facts (except age) in adults where some neuropsychologists working in medical settings have had a unique opportunity to validate their concepts and tests against subsequent localization of lesions by neurological and neurosurgical procedures (see McFie, 1975).

Nevertheless, most studies of children have been concerned with answering relatively simplistic questions, principally whether "brain damage" in children, independent of site, size, or age of onset: (1) has discernible effects on behavior or personality, and, if so, (2) whether it tends to produce specific types of psychopathology.

This chapter will consider only the relationship between abnormal structure (damage) or abnormal physical functioning (dysfunction) of the brain and abnormal behavior that is not commonly agreed to be a sign of an organic brain disorder (see Chapter 6). The term "brain disorder" will ordinarily include brain damage and dysfunction, whether the latter is due primarily to disease of the brain or of other organs.

INTERACTIVE EFFECTS

Both "brain damage," as customarily and rather inexactly defined, and psychopathology are relatively common conditions, so that in a significant number of cases their concurrence must be simply one of coincidence (e.g., EEG abnormalities and behavior disorders). It is often not possible to determine in an individual case whether this relationship is causal or casual (Pond, 1961). Even where the relationship between the brain damage and the behavior seems to be causal, brain damage has a psychological as well as a physical impact, and in some cases, brain damage is pathogenic because of its psychological rather than its physical consequences (Rutter, 1981, 1982a). The evidence that brain disorder increases, nonspecifically, vulnerability to psychopathology (Rutter, 1981) suggests that the interaction between biological and psychosocial variables is complex indeed and made even more so by the close association of brain damaging and psychosocially disadvantaging environments (Sameroff & Chandler, 1975; Rutter, 1981).

DIAGNOSIS OF BRAIN DISORDER

Deciding definitely whether there is a structural abnormality or physiological dysfunction in the brain is more difficult than may appear, and pinpointing its locus and extent is even more hazardous especially when, for example, after head injury, multiple loci, some quite remote from the injury, may be affected. Because of the delicacy, inaccessibility, and complexity of the brain, most of the diagnostic techniques are necessarily indirect and inferential, though modern techniques like CAT (Computerized Axial Tomography), PET (Positron Emission Tomography), and NMR (Nuclear Magnetic Resonance) scans are revolutionizing this area. Large sections of the brain are "silent"; that is, they seem to have no externally measurable functions, either input (sensory-perceptual) or output (motor-vocal-autonomic). Structural damage is easier to detect than functional (though this is changing). For example, a CAT scan is worthless in a purely biochemical disorder like early phenylketonuria, though PET and NMR scans, which are function oriented, may ultimately prove helpful. For these reasons, many diagnostic techniques may be negative in the presence of substantial brain damage (Flor-Henry, 1982; Rutter, 1981, 1982a). Conversely, particularly with tests of higher or more subtle function, positive results can occur in the absence of brain damage (see Reitan & Davison, 1974; Rutter et al., 1970).

Autopsy and Biopsy

Autopsy, the surest of all techniques, is available only in a tiny minority of cases, and then usually only where the diagnosis is already clear, so that its value in settling some of the controversies in this area has been negligible. Biopsy, usually done only when a major disease is established, does not eliminate the possibility of damage in areas other than those viewed at the time of surgery. Flor-Henry (1982) gave these methods a hit rate of 50 to 90 percent, being highest for obvious reasons in diffuse disease and those that result in structural changes.

Pre- and Perinatal History

This is one of the least useful, yet most often used of all diagnostic criteria. Wenar (1963) reviewed the literature on the reliability of mothers' development histories and found that, with the exception of the length of gestation and some global estimate of the difficulty of delivery and birthweight, most of the important details of pregnancy, delivery, and neonatal status could not be reliably recalled. Minde, Webb, and Sykes (1968) found similar discrepancies between mothers' histories and medical records. Even when medical birth records are used, there is usually an absence of data and what is recorded is often neither objective nor quantifiable. Furthermore, the probability of damage actually following most of the popularly perceived "traumatic events" during pregnancy and the perinatal period is unknown, but detectable consequences later in life seem infrequent (Sameroff & Chandler, 1975) and usually are revealed only by large samples such as the U.S. Perinatal Collaborative Study of 30,000 children (Nichols & Chen, 1981). The best indicator of brain damage is the neonatal symptom complex of *hypoxic-ischemic encephalopathy*. This diagnosis is based on careful, complex neonatal assessment of alertness, reflexes, heart rate, tone, pupil size, seizures, sucking, and EEG patterns graded into three levels of severity (see Finer, Robertson, Richards, Pinnell, & Peters, 1981). There is a poor correlation between outcome and the popularly recorded pre- and perinatal variables because etiology is less important than actual oxygen supply to the fetus, of which they are only indirect indicators (Finer et al., 1981). This subject is discussed in more detail subsequently.

Neurological Examination

This can detect major degrees of cerebral damage with a significant degree of accuracy when the lesion impinges on nonsilent areas of the brain. Unfortunately, in patients where other diagnostic aids have proved most ambiguous, the neurological examination is also often likewise. Children with psychiatric problems are prone to exhibit so-called equivocal or soft neurological signs, the significance of which is obscure (see Reeves & Werry, in press; Rutter, 1982a; Touwen & Sporrel, 1979).

The last decade or so has seen several commendable efforts in the standardization of neurological examination in populations of psychiatric children. Four deserve special comment because of attempts to establish their reliability and/or validity. The first is the Physical and Neurological Examination for Soft Signs (PANESS) (Close, 1973), developed for but adopted without trial by the U.S. National Institute of Mental Health as part of its package for psychopharmacological studies with children (*Psychopharmacology Bulletin*, 1973); the second, 80 possible signs collected by Peters, Dykman, Ackerman, and Romine (1974); the third, almost 100 signs collected by Werry et al. (1972); and the last by Rutter et al. (1970).

In spite of its official sanction, PANESS appears to have a large number of signs that do not occur, and it fails to discriminate between "brain-damaged" and normal populations (Camp, Bialer, Sverd, & Winsberg, 1978; Werry & Aman, 1976). An improved version had good interexaminer and test retest reliability, however, but only for the total score and those items reflecting sensorimotor coordination (Holden, Tarnowski, & Prinz, 1982). The examination of Peters et al. and Werry et al. also have a significant number of signs that do not occur, but do discriminate, albeit imperfectly, between minimally brain dysfunctioned, psychopathological, and normal samples. They have not won wide acceptance and their interpretation is difficult in topographical and diagnostic terms.

The best effort, in terms of conceptualization and establishment of reliability and validity, is that by Rutter et al. (1970). They delineate three types of signs: (1) those that, when clearly present, always denote abnormality. These comprise mostly the traditional or so-called hard neurological signs and, as would be expected, offered the greatest discriminative power between brain-damaged and normal groups. (2) Those sometimes indicative of cerebral pathology (e.g., nystagmus and ataxia). (3) Signs that are not abnormal in any qualitative sense but only in a chronological or developmental context, since they are found in normal children at younger ages (e.g., dyslexia, enuresis, or dyspraxia). Presumably these are the true "soft" signs in the sense that their significance is unclear and their etiology is almost certainly heterogeneous. Rutter et al. eschew the term "soft signs" pointing out that the only really "soft" signs are those whose "softness" is due to their unreliability or inconstancy, for example, minor degrees of reflex asymmetries. Their term *developmental signs* is clearly preferable to the term *soft*, but unlikely to displace it now.

Nichols and Chen (1981) in their prospective study of 30,000 U.S. children found that soft signs at age seven (mostly fine and gross motor incoordination) did show a weak and inefficient association with pre- and perinatal insults, but a little better with genetic factors. As this and nearly all of the studies mentioned show, neurological examinations of psychopathological samples tend to produce primarily abnormalities of sensorimotor coordination of uncertain significance.

Another popular quasi-neurological test, the Oseretsky motor-development scale (Sloan, 1975), has been revised by Sloan (1975)—called the Lincoln-Oseretsky Scale—by Rutter et al. (1970), and by Bialer, Doll, and Winsberg (1974). While the shortened versions appear reliable and valid in discriminating between brain-damaged and normal populations, it is important to realize that it is only a test of *motor development*. Although in Rutter's studies it correlated well with the neurological estimates of dyspraxia (impaired coordination), it offered no differentiation between different types of impaired coordination, for example, that due to cerebral palsy or simple tremor. Camp et al. (1978) also found a correlation with the PANESS, which as the study by Holden et al. (1982) showed, derives much of its substance from motor items.

Minor physical anomalies, originally described by Goldfarb in his studies of the childhood psychoses (see Waldrop, Pedersen, & Bell, 1968) and scored according to a method developed by Waldrop et al., are thought to reflect either genetic factors or minor distortions of intrauterine development during the first 12 weeks. While studies suggest that the frequency of these minor physical anomalies may be increased in psychiatric and other exceptional children (see Firestone & Prabhu, 1983; Krouse & Kauffman, 1982; Rapoport & Quinn, 1975), their etiology and significance is unclear. They may be genetic and nonspecific "high-risk" indicators for a variety of physical and psychopathological disorders (e.g., Firestone & Prabhu, 1983). There are also serious problems of reliability across investigators (Krouse & Kauffman, 1982).

The Electroencephalogram (EEG)

The problems of reliability and interpretation of EEG abnormalities in children are essentially similar to those of the neurological examination, namely, lack of agreement on criteria of abnormality—Freeman (1967) cites one of the few studies of the reliability of the EEG as showing an agreement of only 40 percent—and on the significance, in terms of damage or dysfunction, of many of these abnormalities, especially the more minor ones.

According to Millichap (1975), abnormalities in the EEG are ordinarily classified according to (1) wave form, (2) wave frequency, (3) rhythmicity or regularity of pattern, (4) distribution of abnormalities in the brain (diffuse or focal), and (5) degree of abnormality (grades I–III). There are two principal types of abnormalities. (1) *Arrhythmias*, in which the basic rhythm of the resting EEG for a particular age (in older children and adults this is the alpha rhythm of 8–14 CPS) is lacking, usually being replaced by slower waves of greater amplitude that are often indicative of significant disease or disorder within the brain. The normal development sequence from birth onward, however, is for these slow rhythms to increase gradually in frequency until the adult-type alpha is achieved somewhere between 6 and 12 years. Thus, the significance of arrhythmias in young children is often uncertain, being more in the nature of a developmental than a hard sign. (2) *Dysrhythmias* describes abnormalities in which the basic rhythmic pattern is interrupted or replaced by abnormal wave forms, like spikes found in epilepsy.

Ordinarily, the EEG is recorded in the resting state, often with the addition of special procedures—such as photic driving, hyperventilation, and, sometimes, sleep—that tend to exaggerate or uncover abnormalities. In the search to expand the usefulness of the EEG in psychiatric populations of children, recent developments have explored computer-based techniques of analysis, like power spectral analysis (e.g., Craggs, Wright, & Werry, 1980; Montagu, 1975; Satterfield, Cantwell, & Satterfield, 1974), and techniques of studying the brain in action, such as evoked potentials, that follow the administration of various kinds of sensory and psychological stimuli and give some objective measure of attentional processes (see Chiappa & Roper, 1982). While some of these techniques show promise (see later discussion), they must be regarded as still largely exploratory in childhood psychopathology and highly technical (see Chiappa & Roper, 1982; Feuerstein, Ward, & LeBaron, 1979; Rutter, 1982a).

Although children with psychiatric disorders often have abnormal EEGs (see Rutter, 1982a), as with neurological signs, most of these EEG abnormalities fall in a no-man's land between normality and undeniable pathology. There is a large overlap in frequency of abnormalities in child psychiatric disorders between those considered "organic" and those not; there is no specificity of abnormalities in individual disorders and no difference in behavioral or cognitive symptomatology between children with or without EEG changes; and there are inconsistent findings across studies and a poor correlation between EEG and birth history abnormalities in psychiatric disorders (Feuerstein et al., 1979; Harris, 1978; Rutter, 1982a; Werry, 1968). Further, as with many of the soft neurological signs, the frequency of these common EEG abnormalities tends to decrease with age (Ellingson, 1954; Wiener, Delano, & Klass, 1966; Wikler, Dixon, & Parker, 1970), which makes their significance even more obscure.

Organ-imaging Techniques

Skull x-rays, pneumoencephalograms (in which the cerebral ventricular system and the subarachnoid system are outlined radiologically by replacing the cerebrospinal fluid with air), cerebral angiograms (where blood vessels of the brain are outlined by injecting a radio-opaque substance intraarterially), brain scans (which outline brain tissue with radioactive substances), and other such radiological techniques require fairly gross distortions of the structure of the brain in order to show any abnormalities, and not surprisingly their hit rate is rather low (Flor-Henry, 1982). Since many of the behavior disturbances in children attributed to minimal brain damage are said to be spread diffusely throughout the brain, most of the above investigations would be useful in childhood psychopathology only in the true organic disorders (see Chapter 6).

New techniques such as CAT, PET, and NMR and radioimmune receptor assays do, however, offer exciting prospects in childhood psychopathology, especially in such disorders as the psychoses. Not only are these techniques more "fine-grained" than others, but PET and NMR can detect functional as well as structural changes. To date, however, CAT scans have been disappointing (see Chapter 5) and PET and NMR scans are as yet largely unresearched in childhood disorders.

Biochemical and Pharmacological Techniques

There has been a great increase in interest in biochemical aspects of psychiatry. Reflections of this, though in a somewhat lower key, can be seen in child psychiatry (e.g., Cohen & Young, 1977; Coleman, 1973; Lechman, 1983; Lechman et. al., 1980; Rapoport, Quinn, & Lamprecht, 1974; Rapoport, Quinn, Scribanau, & Murphy, 1974). In much of this work, biochemical analyses of blood, urine, or CSF for hormones, neurotransmitters, or their degraded products figure largely, but these analyses continue to be bedeviled by lack of sensitivity and/or specificity to any or even all psychiatric disorders. This is not too surprising when it is remembered (1) that such transmitter or metabolic substances are rarely if ever found *only* in the brain let alone only in that part of the brain suspected to be affected, and (2) that changes in their concentration can be due to exercise, diet, excitement, homeostastic diurnal variation, or poor measurement technique.

Newer developments are pharmacological probing as in the popular dexamethasone suppression test for depression, the radioimmune receptor analyses using haloperidol, and more crudely, classification by drug response. These areas along with PET or NMR are probably the New Frontier of biological psychiatry, but none has yet achieved the status of other than a research tool in children, and as with earlier biochemical work, there is still a distressing lack of replication of positive findings (Lechman, 1983; Ritvo, Freeman, Geller, & Yuwiler, 1983).

Psychodiagnostic Techniques

Although psychological tests have been used extensively in making diagnoses of brain damage and in localizing it (see Flor-Henry, 1982), their sensitivity and specificity is questionable. Herbert (1964), in a comprehensive review of early work in this area as it applied to children, pointed out that most of the studies aimed at ascertaining differences in performance on psychological tests between brain-damaged and normal groups relied on a neurological diagnosis, itself of limited validity, to delineate criterion groups. Other problems raised by Herbert include poor test construction, lack of standardization of tests, lack of cross-validation studies, preoccupation with mentally retarded criterion groups, lack of control for visual field defects or external stimulus variables, and, most serious of all, the considerable overlap in scores between brain-damaged and normal children.

The careful attempts of Reitan and his pupils to develop a neuropsychological diagnostic battery for children (see Reitan & Boll, 1973; Feuerstein et al., 1979) has improved the situation, although the absence of true norms and the severely neurologically abnormal validating populations presently limit their usefulness in psychiatric populations where the changes, if any, are small and the possibility of validation by neurodiagnostic means usually absent. As Rutter et al. (1970), Satz and Fletcher (1981), and Sprague (1973) have pointed out, the greatest usefulness of psychodiagnosis is, or should be, in the assessment of present function and in the formulation of management programs rather than in neurologizing about a remote etiology. Such a statement needs, however, to be tempered by the very real value of the neuropsychological tests in the true organic disorders (see Chapter 6) where the manifestations are often first or mostly cognitive (Albert, 1981; Flor-Henry, 1982). While these tests may provide some evidence suggestive of brain damage, they should never be used as the sole criterion for diagnosing cerebral pathology.

Summary of Diagnosis of Brain Disorder

Thus, the diagnosis of brain damage, unless gross, depends on a group of medical, historical, and psychological measures, most of which are of low or untested reliability, discriminate poorly between normal and *mildly* brain-damaged populations, and apparently measure a variety of unrelated functions instead of some homogeneous variable "brain damage." Under the circumstances, the diagnosis of brain damage or dysfunction in the majority of children with nonorganic psychopathology is no more than an enlightened guess. Even where the diagnosis can be firmly established, there is as yet usually no way of proving that the damage is *causally* related to the behavior observed. What makes establishing this connection even more difficult is the repeated demonstration of the close relationship between the causes of brain damage and a host of sociofamilial variables that are disadvantageous to social adjustment *and* to physical health (see also Chapters 9 and 10).

BIOLOGICAL FACTORS AND CHILDHOOD PSYCHOPATHOLOGY

For the purposes of orderly discussion, studies will be grouped in the following manner: (1) those in which brain disorder or insult is the means for selecting the abnormal group, or the independent variable; (2) those in which psychopathology further unspecified is the criterion; and (3) those concerned with specific brain-damage variables, such as site of the lesion. The role of biological factors in each specific psychopathological disorder has been discussed in Chapters 1 through 7.

Groups Selected for Brain Disorder or Insult

In this type of study, the starting point has been the selection of a group of children differentiated from normal children by the presence of proven or, more commonly, suspected brain damage or by a specific type of insult. Studies of this type are fewer than those that take psychopathology as the criterion, and the results in general differ. Most are remote with respect to time of brain disorder or insult, which antedates the investigations of behavioral status or other dependent variables by some years, but a few are truly prospective and hence more reliable about events in early life.

UNSPECIFIED BRAIN DAMAGE

Strauss and Lehtinen (1947) claimed that in a group of institutionalized, mildly retarded children, those designated by neurological examination or history as being "brain injured" or "exogenously" retarded displayed certain differences when compared with non-brain-injured or "endogeneous" retardates on behavior ratings made by teachers and by cottage parents. Characteristics of the brain-injured child were erratic, uncoordinated, uncontrolled, uninhibited, socially unacceptable, hyperactive, and stereotyped behaviors; they also exhibited catastrophic emotional reactions to frustrations, lack of fear or prudence, and sometimes, emotional shallowness, and bladder and bowel difficulties (Strauss & Lehtinen, 1947, p. 84). Sarason (1949, pp. 52-58) criticized Strauss and Lehtinen's method of diagnosing brain injury because of excessive reliance on history taken mostly from parents and psychological tests results, neither of which has a sufficient degree of reliability or validity to use in making such a diagnosis (see previous discussion). In an historic, but ignored and often rediscovered, statement (e.g., Rutter, 1982a), Sarason concluded that the behavioral abnormalities described by Strauss had not been demonstrated to be either the result of brain damage or, conversely, characteristic of every brain-damaged child. Gallagher (1957) also pointed out that Strauss and Lehtinen appear to have developed their behavior-rating scale by choosing items that seemed to discriminate between the two original groups and to have then validated the scale by testing it on the same two groups of children! One further point, long overlooked, is that Strauss and Lehtinen's group were all retarded and thus had *major* not minimal brain damage (see Chapter 6).

Ernhart, Graham, Eichman, Marshall, and Thurston (1963) compared a group of preschool children with independently established lesions in the cerebral hemispheres to a non-brain-damaged group on personality and cognitive measures. Some behavioral impairment as judged by reliable parent and examiner ratings was found in the brain-damaged group, though these differences were slight when compared with the differences in perceptual and cognitive functioning; the differences also covered a wide range of unfavorable personality characteristics—not just those described as typical of brain-injured behavior.

The findings of this study were later largely replicated in studies by Rutter and colleagues (see Rutter, 1981). In a well-designed epidemiological study, Graham and Rutter (1968; Rutter et al., 1970) found children with major neurological disease (epilepsy, cerebral palsy, etc.) to have a frequency of psychiatric disorder five times as high as that observed in the normal population and three times as high in children with other physical handicaps. No specific brain-damage–behavior syndrome was found. A subsequent study of carefully matched physically handicapped children (Seidel, Chadwick, & Rutter, 1975), with and without brain disease, showed that this increase was due to brain damage, not to handicap. Most of the disorder was of an anxiety-withdrawal nature, school related, and probably due to a marked increase in reading difficulties and mental retardation, making school adjustment difficult. Wing and Gould (1979) identified social isolation as a major disability in brain-damaged children, which was made worse by more severe intellectual impairment.

In a recent study, Breslau and Marshall (1985) showed that indisputably brain-damaged children were, and continued to be after five years, significantly more handicapped than physically disabled children in cognitive and social function (more isolated). While some of this risk was related to mental retardation, as shown by Wing and Gould (1979), there was a brain-damage component in its own right.

This group of studies suggest that brain damage increases the risk of psychopathology significantly, but with the possible exceptions of social isolation and disinhibition (see Rutter, 1981), there is little evidence of specificity. The risk rises with severity of handicap and/or mental retardation. In mildly damaged children the risk is probably low.

PRENATAL AND PERINATAL ABNORMALITY (EXCLUDING PREMATURITY/LOW BIRTHWEIGHT)

The idea that the fetus is highly vulnerable to noxious events and that its passage to the outside world using its head as a battering ram is the supreme risk in life is not new (Towbin, 1978). That the prime sequelae of pre- or perinatal brain damage are death, cerebral palsy, epilepsy, and mental retardation is well established. However, the concept of a continuum of reproductive casualty (Rogers, Lilienfield, & Pasamanick, 1955) in which mild (or minimal) degrees of pre- and perinatal damage might be manifest *only* in psychopathology, while more contentious, seems as profound in its impact as any idea in child development. Within a very short period, the idea of pregnancy and birth damage as an important etiological influence became part of the dogma of childhood psychopathology. Evidence from good studies by which to adjudge the role of pre- and perinatal insults was already available by 1972, when the first edition of this book was published (Werry, 1972). The subsequent 15 or so years since have in general merely consolidated what was apparent then and has been more or less restated at irregular but increasingly frequent intervals (e.g., Sameroff & Chandler, 1975; Rutter, 1981, 1982a). The important studies of the 1950s and 1960s that established this will be reviewed first, after which the successive literature will be only summarized.

Before so doing, a brief overview of what is now known about the pathological effects of pre/perinatal insults will be presented, largely from Towbin's (1978) review. The most important pathogenic influence in reproductive casualty, by far, is anoxia, with actual birth injury a poor, if nevertheless important, second, then other infrequent events such as maternal infections, toxins, ionizing radiations, drugs, genetic malformations, and so on. Fetal immaturity or true prematurity (see later text) greatly enhances risk, especially to anoxia, and results in deep damage that has a high likelihood of producing death, mental retardation, cerebral palsy, and/or epilepsy. Anoxia occurring in a full-term otherwise normal baby results primarily in cortical damage. Injury, interestingly, seems to affect primarily the brain stem and spinal cord, though it also can cause damage to the temporal lobes by forcing the poles (or tips) through the fibrous supporting membranes. This is an important cause of epilepsy (Griffiths & Laurence, 1974).

Pathological studies have shown that damage can be microscopic or visible to the naked eye, diffuse or focal. They also affirm that the effect of damage is necessarily more disruptive at its occurrence than several weeks/or months later, when acute swelling, tissue death, and reaction subside. Obstetrics and neonatal pediatrics have been concerned to define both risk factors and brain damage. Simple observational measures such as the Apgar scale have given way to multifactorial methods in composite, quantifiable "hypoxic-ischemic encephalopathy syndrome" (Finer et al., 1981; see the foregoing text). Emphasis has shifted from purportedly brain damaging events or "insults" to demonstrable brain dysfunction in the neonate because of the weak long-term predictive power of indirect indicators—the overwhelming majority of high-risk babies fail to evince any subsequent abnormality. *Insult is not damage, though in a few cases it may prove to be so.*

This last statement should be kept firmly in mind as we now move to look at studies of pre/perinatal insult and subsequent psychopathology. It also needs to be remembered that this review does not dispute the effect of major brain insult in causing death or motor, intellectual, or epileptic sequelae; here, however, we are concerned with psychopathology.

The first set of early methodologically adequate studies took high-risk babies and followed them for variable periods.

In a prospective study Graham, Ernhart, Thurston, and Craft (1962) investigated the effect of clearly established anoxia or other severe pre- or perinatal complications on later personality and cognitive development in preschool-age children and compared their findings with three other similar studies. In two of these three (Schacter & Apgar, 1959; Fraser & Wilks, 1959), the findings were similar to their own. The criterion groups showed evidence of slight but significant impairment of cognitive function, but no or very questionable differences in the frequency of psychopathology. A follow-up of Graham's group at seven years (Corah, Anthony, Painter, Stern, & Thurston, 1965) revealed slight but significant impairment in social competence, impulsivity, and distractibility. However, there was a negative correlation between degrees of anoxia and psychopathology!

A fourth study, by Prechtl and his group (Prechtl, 1960; Prechtl & Dijkstra, 1960), produced strikingly positive results. Highly influential, especially in Europe, this study is actually methodologically less rigorous and more vague than Graham's studies. Of 400 infants who had suffered pre- or perinatal complications, the frequency of symptoms such as short attention span, lability of mood, hyperactivity, anxiety, negativism, and disturbances in social interaction was found on reexamination between the ages of two and four years to be most frequent (70%) in the group that had both a history of complications and an abnormal neonatal neurological status; least frequent (12%) in the group that was normal in both these respects; while the group with only an abnormal history was intermediate (38%). The frequency of psychopathology is very high compared with most other studies and could be an artefact of methods of measurement or of the short period of follow-up since most longer term studies show attentuation of changes with age (see later text).

Ucko (1965) compared boys with a history of neonatal anoxia with controls matched for age, sex, social class, and birth order and matched approximately for maternal age. There was no difference in overall cognitive and behavioral development in the two groups, but the asphyxiated children were significantly more reactive temperamentally and were much more difficult to manage without actually being behaviorally abnormal. This reactivity was positively correlated with the severity of the asphyxia. Ucko pointed out that this temperamental reactivity had strong positive aspects as well as negative ones, as seen in the strong affectional expressions and enjoyment of pleasurable experiences some of the children exhibited.

Since these early studies mostly of high-risk (for brain damage) populations, the emphasis seems to have shifted to long-term prospective studies of birth cohorts. These studies are valuable in that they involve large, usually representative samples, begin in pregnancy and have recorded at the time in standardized ways the pre- and perinatal insults, and have mostly followed the impact of such insults over a period of many years, usually into late adolescence. They also have attempted to look at the interaction between these biological variables and psychosocial variables. Such studies are by Douglas (Douglas & Gear, 1976), the English Perinatal Study (Butler & Bonham, 1963; Davie, Butler, & Goldstein, 1972), the Kauai longitudinal study (Werner & Smith, 1979), the U.S. Collaborative Perinatal study (Nichols & Chen, 1981; Niswander & Gordon, 1972), and the Dunedin Multidisciplinary Child Development Study in New Zealand (McGee, Silva, & Williams, 1984). While the results vary somewhat, the common thread is that perinatal insults are weak in effect, any psychopathology associated is only slightly increased, it can take a number of forms, the effect is greatly influenced by adverse sociofamilial environments, and the size of any effect diminishes with time. In short, Pasamanick's continuum of reproductive casualty recedes and ultimately is subordinated to Sameroff and Chandler's continuum of caretaking casualty. A further interesting feature of many of these and similar studies is to show that disadvantaged children suffer more pre- and perinatal complications so that disentangling physical and psychosocial effects is very complex and a source of potential error (see also subsequent section, Prematurity).

These studies often have very low frequencies of or exclude children with major brain damage, however, so that the apparent contradiction here with good studies (e.g., Breslau & Marshall, 1985; Rutter, 1981) showing significant and durable risk of all forms of psychopathology from clear and obvious brain damage probably arises from differences between the effects of putative/minor and major damage.

LOW BIRTH WEIGHT (PREMATURITY)

Prematurity was once defined solely as a birth weight of less than 5 pounds or so. Though not necessarily followed by brain damage, it was generally regarded as one of its more important causes, especially where birth weight was under 3 pounds or 1500 grams (Drillien, 1964, 1972). Though the term *premature baby* is indelibly inculcated into the vernacular, the medical term is now more accurately *baby of low birth weight* (LBW)—2500 grams or less. Babies of 1500 grams or less are called "very low birth weight" (VLBW).

There are two types of LBW babies: those who are significantly *small for their gestational age* (SGA) and those whose weight is *appropriate* for their gestational age (AGA) but who are small because of premature birth. The SGA group is small because of primary fetal factors such as malformations and primary maternal factors such as the fetal alcohol syndrome, rubella, "toxemia" of pregnancy (now called hypertension-edema-proteinuria syndrome), and so on. The low weight of the AGA group seems to be largely caused by the onset of premature labor in apparently normal pregnancy. Like other pre- and perinatal complications, both forms of low birth weight are highly correlated with psychosocial disadvantage (Escalona, 1982). Prognosis of SGA babies seems to be closely related to size of the head (and hence of the brain) at birth: if normal for that age, the ultimate outlook is good though development is slower for the first few years of life. A small head suggests permanent, serious brain damage. An SGA baby may be premature but may not be. On the other hand, an AGA low-birth-weight baby is necessarily premature. In the last decade or so, most Western countries have established regional intensive care facilities for LBW babies and this coupled with greatly improved methods of detecting and dealing with the risks such as respiratory distress and Rh incompatability, has ensured the routine survival of babies at ever-diminishing gestational ages. For example, the survival of VLBW infants between 1000 and 1500 grams has increased to around 90 percent with most of the increase occurring in the 1970s (Vohr & Hack, 1982). Now, most interest centers on children under 1000 grams and as low as 500 grams (about 1 pound) where survival has risen to near 50 percent.

It now seems that unless there is clear evidence of perinatal problems or poor neonatal care, a baby of greater than 1500 grams is unlikely to have any special difficulties. If less than 1500 grams, survival is reduced to 58 percent and about 20 percent of survivors have serious handicaps, while if 800 grams or less, more than 50 percent are handicapped, though even here, prospects are improving (Levene & Dubowitz, 1982; Vohr & Hack, 1982). VLBW is only a minor contributor numerically, however, to the overall prevalence of handicap, the etiology of most cases being still unknown (Levene & Dubowitz, 1982).

The implication is that the probability of brain damage depends on the weight, the head size at birth, the year in which the child was born, and what sort of care was given. This makes much of the old literature merely of historical interest. Prematurity then was expected to cause brain damage significantly often, and so studies of "prematures" (then defined solely on birth weight) under five-and-a-half pounds were expected to show effects on behavior qualitatively similar to those purportedly resulting from brain damage. This seemed to be the case in eight studies reviewed by Wiener (1962) and subsequent investigations (Davie et al., 1972; Drillien, 1972). Wiener (1962) and Sameroff and Chandler (1975) have pointed out, however, that it was not clear whether associations were due to brain damage, to sensory and maternal deprivation accompanying the prolonged hospitalization of the early months, to the commonly associated physical handicaps, to parental labeling of the child as delicate, or to the social and economic disadvantage so highly correlated with prematurity.

Robinson and Robinson (1965, pp. 148–150) stated that much of the supposed cognitive and behavioral difference between LBW and full-term infants was attributable to this sociofamilial pathology and disadvantage. One of their own studies showed that, when corrections were made for differences in socioeconomic class, the slight excess of behavior problems in the LBW group disappeared.

More recent studies (Davies, 1976; Douglas & Gear, 1976; Drillien, Thomson, & Burgoyne, 1980; Vohr & Hack, 1982) suggest that there is little difference in long-term outcome for LBWs who are free of serious disease at birth. In those of greatest risk (under 1000 g), study of long-term psychopathological sequelae is hampered by small samples, long periods of sensory and maternal deprivation, sensory and physical handicaps, and psychosocial disadvantage. Escalona (1982) has concluded that whether or not babies of low birth weight are more vulnerable to factors productive of psychopathology still remains to be proven. It would seem though that as in other types of brain damage, the risk should increase with degree of brain damage (i.e., inversely with birth weight, head size, etc.).

ENCEPHALITIS AND MENINGITIS

Encephalitis or inflammation of the brain may be epidemic or sporadic and is most commonly due to viral infections such as measles and herpes, though most are unidentifiable (DeLong, Bean, & Brown, 1981). Meningitis (inflammation of brain coverings) is more usually bacterial (and treatable!). In theory, encephalitis, involving as it does brain tissue, should be more brain injurious than meningitis. During the acute phase, the psychopathological features are those of delirium and/or dementia (see Chapter 6), which may persist for several months (e.g., DeLong et al., 1981). Here only long-term psychopathological sequelae after apparent recovery are reviewed.

The epidemic of lethargic encephalitis at the end of World War I gave rise to a series of reports that permanent behavioral disturbances could result, particularly when the encephalitis occurred in childhood (Ebaugh, 1922; Kennedy, 1924; Strecker, 1929). These early studies had several defects: the diagnosis of encephalitis was often not adequately established; no attempt was made to separate social immaturity due to commonly coexistent mental deficiency from psychopathology; and all suffered from biased sampling, usually being studies only of children referred because of sequelae.

Gibbs, Gibbs, Spies, and Carpenter (1964) conducted a study of 250 children who had recovered from encephalitis of various kinds and found a 10 percent overall frequency of behavior disorders, established by unidentified means, at follow-up. In an all-too-common logical error, the authors attributed these disorders and the EEG abnormalities to the encephalitis, which seems unwarranted since there were no pre hoc measurements and a 10 percent prevalence of behavior disorders seems to be close to the level in the general population. Sabatino and Cramblett (1968) studied sequelae in children, seven months to two years after what appear to be serologically and clinically well-authenticated attacks of California viral encephalitis (Cramblett, Stegmiller, & Spencer, 1966). Although the authors concluded that a significant proportion of the children exhibited many symptoms of hyperkinetic syndrome, the degree of psychopathology as measured by a behavior checklist (Quay & Peterson, 1975) was slight and well below that observed in psychiatric populations. Furthermore, symptoms of anxiety were as much increased as those of conduct disorder. One study of the long-term effects of congenital rubella encephalitis that had not resulted in mental retardation (Desmond, et al., 1978) found that 48 percent of 29 children had persistent organic behavior disorder (i.e., ADD with hyperactivity), though only two were severe enough to require medication. Some children had other types of psychopathology. No diagnostic methods or criteria are described for ADD, however, and all the children with it were also profoundly hearing impaired.

The danger of uncontrolled studies is well illustrated (once again) in a careful study by Tejani, Dobias, and Sambursky, (1982) where those postencephalitic children with a low IQ were found to have similarly retarded sibling controls!

EPILEPSY

Interpretation of relationships between brain status and psychopathology are particularly difficult with epilepsy because, in addition to the association with physical and learning handicaps characteristic of all forms of brain damage, seizures are highly visible, poorly socially accepted, dangerous events treated with medications, all of which can have negative effects on behavior and learning quite independent of brain factors (Stores, 1975). In view of the prevalence of epilepsy and the frequency with which personality disorders are attributed to it, especially disorders related to the temporal lobe, it is somewhat surprising to find that there have been few adequate psychopathological studies in children with this disease, particularly as compared with normal controls (Hermann, 1982; Tizard, 1962).

Tizard (1962) concluded that (1) there was no evidence that all or most epileptics have a characteristic personality, and (2) the prevalence of psychopathology *might* be higher in epileptics or some types of epileptics (e.g., temporal lobe). Subsequent evidence, however, from studies of epileptic children and of behavior improvement reported to occur after surgery for epilepsy (Holdsworth & Whitmore, 1974; Rutter, 1981) suggest that there is a moderate (around 25%) increase in associated psychiatric disorder; but the problems are less in degree than those seen in children without epilepsy but diagnosed as ADD (Campbell, 1974). Less certainly, there may also be a site effect, implicating the temporal lobe particularly (Rutter, 1981); this now seems more doubtful (Hermann, 1982). Psychopathology (and cognitive disorder) are greatly increased if the epilepsy is active (Holdsworth & Whitmore, 1974; Rutter, 1981) and if damage is bilateral, extensive, and/or deep electrophysiologically or clinically (Hermann, 1982).

CEREBRAL PALSY

Good behavioral studies in cerebral palsy or early brain damage with motor involvement are about as infrequent as in epilepsy. Cruickshank and Bice (1966) cited several twin studies in which psychopathology was found to be equally common in the healthy twin and that the psychological impact of and the parents' reaction to the cerebral palsy is the more probable explanation of the psychopathology. This does not agree, however, with Rutter's (Rutter, 1981; Rutter et al., 1970; Seidel, Chadwick, & Rutter, 1975) and Breslau and Marshall's (1985) (both rather more carefully obtained) results that found some influence of environmental factors but that were able to show a distinctive neuropsychiatric effect of this disorder (over and above physical handicap, etc.).

HEAD INJURY

In recent work Shaffer et al. (1975) studied 98 children who had been treated for compound skull fractures several years previously. The frequency of psychiatric disorder was 63 percent as judged by a reliable and valid psychiatric history and examination and 35 percent (vs. 18% in controls) as rated by teachers. The degree of psychiatric handicap was not related to the age, site, or severity of injury but was to the degree of sociofamilial disadvantage, though not entirely. After reviewing previous studies and their own results, they concluded that head injury, like brain damage in general, does indeed increase the risk of psychiatric disorder, a risk that is substantially increased by environmental adversity. Subsequent studies (Rutter, 1977) suggested that head injury and environment operate additively, not interactively.

Rutter (1981) has detailed his two-year prospective studies of head injury, which divided children seen soon after head injury on the basis of posttraumatic amnesia (a good indicator of degree of damage). A matched contrast group of children who had suffered orthopedic injuries was also included. These studies showed that the risk of psychiatric disorder was increased threefold (to around 50%), and unlike Shaffer's study the more severe the head injury, the greater the risk. Further, this disorder was persistent throughout the entire two-and-a-quarter-year follow-up period, while cognitive changes tended to improve. Interestingly, children with mild head injuries had an increased rate of premorbid psychiatric disorder, suggesting that psychiatric disorder contributed to the risk of mild head injury, not vice versa. Most of the injury-induced disorder was nonspecific, but the risk of symptoms of disinhibited behavior, "frontal lobe syndrome," or in DSM-III terms Organic Personality Syndrome was evident in a subgroup.

LEAD AND OTHER HEAVY METALS

Lead is a ubiquitous substance in modern urban environments so that there is both a regular dietary and inhalatory intake (Klaasen, 1980). Little of this, around 0.3 mg/day, is absorbed in adults, but children take up about 40 percent of their intake. Unusually high intakes in children are attributable to peeling lead paints (now illegal) in deteriorated housing and excessive sniffing of leaded gasoline (see Chapter 6). Though initially distributed widely, lead ultimately is stored mostly in bone and such as remains in blood, within the red cells. Ordinarily a dynamic equilibrium between intake and excretion obtains, but once the intake exceeds 0.3 mg/day, a build-up in the store or "burden" occurs. The lead burden is estimated ordinarily from the blood level, and values of 40 μg/dl are considered nontoxic, while at twice that, clinical evidence of lead poisoning produces a dangerous and obvious encephalopathy in children (which includes delirium and dementia), most of the current concern in children is with so-called subclinical lead levels and whether or not these can result in cognitive and behavioral effects (Rutter, 1980a). The toxic action of lead is unclear, but it seems to be related to its interference with fundamental cell mechanisms (Niklowitz, 1977). Reducing the lead burden is difficult because it is stored in bone in insoluble forms. Chelating agents can "wrap" the lead with a soluble cover and thus facilitate excretion. Treatment with chelating agents and looking for associated behavioral change has also been used to see whether lead is an etiological agent in psychopathological disorders, but the more usual technique is to compare children with high and low lead burdens. Other poisonous heavy metals such as mercury, arsenic, and cadmium are equally ubiquitous and poisonous but seem so far to have attracted less attention (see later text).

A comparative study of hyperactive and normal inner-city children, which showed that the "hyperactive" children have raised lead levels in blood (David, Clark, & Voeller, 1972), was replicated in studies of the behavioral characteristics of children with asymptomatic but increased lead burden (Baloh, Sturm, Green, & Gleser, 1975; Needleman & Bellinger, 1981). David, Hoffman, Sverd, and Clerk (1977) and Needleman and Bellinger (1981) were able to show that any association of hyperactivity and lead is unlikely to be due to the hyperactivity increasing the lead intake (e.g., by pica). Ross and Ross (1982) have reviewed these and further studies of lead, cognition, and behavior. Though they conclude that lead and hyperactivity are linked, the difficulties of this kind of research (e.g., confounding of lead burden and social disadvantage; diagnostic difficulties) suggest caution. For example, an impeccable study by Gittelman and Eskenazi (1983) of hyperactive, learning-disabled, and control groups found at best only weak support for raised lead levels in hyperactivity.

More recent studies by Marlowe and associates have looked not only at lead but also other metals. Marlowe and his associates (Marlowe, Errera, Ballowe, & Jacobs, 1983; Marlow et al., 1985) have studied the relationship of low levels of toxic metals (determined by analyses of hair) to behavior disorder. In their first study (Marlowe et al., 1983) they found that lead levels alone were higher in a group of children classified by a public school as "emotionally disturbed" when compared to controls. Additionally, levels of arsenic ($r = .35$), cadmium ($r = .51$), and aluminum ($r = .47$) were significantly correlated (with SES partialled out) with teacher-rated behavior problems in the disturbed but not the control group.

In their second study (Marlowe et al., 1985), teacher ratings of problem behavior in randomly selected elementary-age children were obtained. Controlling for a variety of familial and sociodemographic variables, they found a number of significant correlations between metal levels and problem behavior. Both lead (.38) and cadmium (.42) were related to ratings of conduct disorder (levels of lead and aluminum were related to ratings of distractibility).

In summary, there is suggestive evidence of some link between psychopathology and toxic metals, but the link is strongest with impaired cognitive, not behavioral, function (Rutter, 1980a). Thus it would be predicted that any impact upon psychopathology should both cut across diagnostic groups *and* be most discernible in those disorders that have a more marked cognitive component (e.g., ADD).

CHROMOSOMAL GENETIC INFLUENCES AND TEMPERAMENT

Since they normally affect many genes, chromosomal variations such as Trisomy 21 (Down's syndrome) or XY anomalies result in morphological differences and, outside the XY chromosomes, often in gross congenital abnormalities. Chromosomal differences or abnormalities have been linked to certain personality features (e.g., Down's syndrome children were said to be placid; women emotional and men aggressive) or to psychopathological traits (e.g., criminal aggressiveness with XYY).

Studies in children detected to have chromosomal abnormalities of the XXY or XYY type in routine cytogenetic screening at birth do suggest a slight increase in risk of psychopathology. In the XXY child (Bancroft, Axworthy, & Ratcliffe, 1982) this conformed to a "feminoid" type, excess timidity (without, however, problems of gender identity), and teasing from male peers, but while XYY (Ratcliffe & Field, 1982) also appeared to produce a slightly increased rate of psychopathology, it did not take a "masculine" aggressive but was, again, predominantly emotional in type. Caution is needed here since numbers were understandably rather small, the studies were not blind, and physical anomalies of stature (both) and of gonadal development and testosterone levels (in XXY) are often associated, thus causing increasing self-consciousness and difficulties in adolescence. Moreover, the child was identified as abnormal from birth. Nevertheless, there does seem to be some evidence to suggest that testosterone levels may influence the amount of male-type behavior: girls who have congenitally raised levels often show an increase in tomboyish behavior. However, child-rearing and sociocultural variables are rather more powerful factors on behavior than hormones and, except rarely, are exclusively responsible for gender identity and, probably, sexual preference (Rutter, 1980b). This topic has been reviewed in greater detail in Chapter 7.

Genes, of course, are the fundamental codes or patterns that determine the syntheses of particular proteins and/or enzymes (or catalysts of metabolism) with, in general, one gene being responsible for one biochemical substance. The effect of an abnormal gene depends on many factors such as the criticalness to life of the biochemical process involved, effect of other genes (e.g., polygenic processes), and whether the gene on the paired chromosome is also abnormal or overpowered. Heterozygous individuals who have one normal gene may show abnormality only when the process affected is put under load, as is posited in some of the nutritional theories of psychopathology (see subsequent discussion).

There are two kinds of ultimate genetic effects: (1) *pathological,* which cause disease, and (2) *variation* within the normal distribution curve (often polygenic). About 50 percent of human genes seem to be capable of differing significantly and yet allowing life and some development, however brief, to occur or, in technical parlance, are polymorphic (Plomin, 1982). The role of pathological genes is obvious in some of the organic disorders such as dementia (Chapter 6) and very probable in some of the psychoses (Chapter 5) and Tourette's disorder (Chapter 7), but the role of varietal genes in childhood psychopathology is much more difficult to determine even though the face validity of such a concept seems high. Most of the work here relates to temperament or dimensions of personality (see Plomin, 1982) and in ADD (see McMahon, 1980; Chapter 4). Twin studies consistently show similarities in monozygous twins that cannot be attributed to a shared identity and/ or upbringing for certain *major* psychiatric disorders such as schizophrenia (Kendler, 1983). However, minor variations such as temperament and/or personality have so far failed to show the validity of genetic influences, with modern methods revealing that much of the positive earlier work was artefactual (Plomin, 1982). Several major studies of twins and adoptees are underway, but at the moment, the idea of varietal or nonpathological genetic influences in childhood psychopathology remains only an hypothesis (Bohman, 1981; Plomin, 1982). Some of the difficulties in this area are related to the elusiveness of temperament as an enduring behavioral style evident beyond early postnatal life since the test–retest reliability of such styles in the first few years of life is still unacceptably low (McNeil & Persson-Blennow, 1982; Rutter, 1982b). Also, differentiation of this from personality as an unpredictable, changing blend of nature and nurture is very complex (Rutter, 1982b).

DIETARY FACTORS

This area has been well reviewed by Conners (1980) and Rumsey and Rapoport (1983). The ascribing of critical roles in childhood psychopathology to dietary substances such as vitamins, amino acids, trace elements, sugars, fats, and so on is far from new but seems to have gained considerable momentum in the last few years. A typical example is the Feingold (1975) hypothesis about salicylates and food additives. In spite of popularization of this (and most other dietary views) as "food allergies," what the Feingold and most of the other dietary theories (including so-called orthomolecular psychiatry) propose is not a true hyperimmune response in which antibodies to the dietary substance are unexpectedly produced causing a true allergic reaction with histamine release and consequent tissue change. Rather, they propose in terms of biochemical kinetics, a *toxicity* due to unusual by-products or a deficiency of essential metabolites because of absolute or relative weaknesses in synthesizing systems. For example, Feingold originally proposed that naturally occurring salicylates in the diet inhibited the body enzymes systems that synthesize prostaglandins just as they do in laboratory experiments. While children with robust enzyme systems showed no effects, those whose enzyme systems were on the "weak" side then showed some significant impairment of synthesis—a sort of system overload. Since prostaglandins are essential neurotransmitters (the exact function of which is unclear), Feingold suggested that disordered brain function (principally MBD) could result. Such a model of ordinary substances proving "toxic" is, of course, well established in a number of what are called biochemical genetic diseases, of which phenylketonuria is a good example. The orthomolecular view is similar but a polar opposite: large doses of substances such as vitamins are seen as needed because the enzyme systems, existing in reduced amounts or being kinetically weak, need *increased* amounts of the dietary substance to maintain normal output.

In a scholarly, yet compassionate review, Conners (1980) tried both to pay tribute to Feingold's sincerity and farsightedness in attracting attention to diet and children's behavior in a time when food is more and more refined and chemically altered, yet also to explain why Feingold's hypothesis was unsustainable. The Feingold hypothesis had one substantial benefit: it brought to notice the defining of the parameters of an adequate trial for dietary factors in behavior (see Conners, 1980; Rumsey & Rapoport, 1983). Thus, in newer areas such as sugars, the use of (apparent) responders and double-blind "challenges" based on elimination or low concentration diets have appeared early (see Rapoport & Kruesi, 1983; Rumsey & Rapoport, 1983). The Feingold hypothesis seems on the wane, but its place has been taken by sugars (see Rapoport & Kruesi, 1983; Rumsey & Rapoport, 1983) with other substances (e.g., certain fats such as oil of primrose) knocking on the door.

In their comprehensive review Rapoport and Kruesi (1983) and Rumsey and Rapoport (1983) concluded that at the present time, there is no firm evidence of behavioral toxicity (such as hyperactivity or antisocial behavior) resulting from dietary substances (including sugar and caffeine) in normal children, though there is some evidence that children with different behavioral styles may self-select different diets—in short this may be effect not cause! They did, however, call for more studies including what they called the "benefit/risk" ratio of dietary manipulations.

SUMMARY OF BRAIN DISORDER/INSULT AS A SELECTION CRITERION
Although somewhat contradictory, studies of brain damage, or of noxious events likely to result in it, show that there is an increased risk of subsequent psychopathology but that this risk is ordinarily small and difficult to detect, rising as the degree of brain damage increases, especially if it results in major neurological and/or intellectual handicap. Any behavioral abnormality is not necessarily of a specific type, such as ADD or even MBD, though the evidence is weakly positive that social isolation and disinhibition are two of the possible and perhaps more common results. What emerges rather more strongly from the studies is the amazing recuperative power of the brain after injury, the adaptational power of the child, and the strong influence of the psychosocial environment, or what Sameroff and Chandler (1975) have called the continuum of caretaking casualty. The child's behavior is a complex, ever-changing distillate of past and present forces—biological, psychological, and social. In this melange of influences, unless accompanied by gross distortions such as physical or mental handicap or active epilepsy, most brain insults or disorder appear as only an "inefficient predictor" of later behavior (Nichols & Chen, 1981).

It is possible that ways of conceptualizing brain damage other than simplistically as a functionally and temporally homogeneous variable and of isolating primary rather than derived deficits—for example, cognitive disabilities, socialization deficits, or changes in temperamental factors, like reactivity, regularity, or reinforceability—may demonstrate relationships between brain damage and behavior somewhat more clearly (see below).

GROUPS SELECTED BY UNSPECIFIED PSYCHIATRIC DISORDER

Here (unspecified) *psychopathology* is the criterion by which children to be studied have been selected, rather than *brain damage* or *insult*, and attempts have been made to determine the frequency or significance of abnormal brain status in the etiology of the observed behavior disorders. Most of these studies are over two decades old, since interest now is in specific disorders (see Chapters 1 through 6); but both the conclusions and regrettably the errors in the early studies are still being reiterated today, giving them a continuing, if diminishing, pertinence (see Werry, 1972, for fuller review).

The most important are those of Pasamanick and his group (Pasamanick & Knobloch, 1960; Rogers et al., 1955), who studied about 500 children with "behavior disorders." Forty percent exhibited hyperactivity or confusion-disorganization, while the remainder exhibited conditions ranging from conduct disorder to anxiety. Through inspection of medical records, the frequency of pre- and perinatal complications was compared with a normal control group matched for race, sex, and birthplace. The deviant group had a statistically significant excess of low birth weight and abnormalities of pregnancy prone to cause chronic fetal anoxia, such as the hypertension-edema-proteinuria syndrome and antepartum bleeding. The behavioral syndrome of "hyperactivity-confusion" was found to be responsible for all of the statistically significant differences observed between the two groups in the case of white children.

This widely cited group of studies is generally accepted as evidence of the importance of brain injury in the genesis of psychopathology in children. Pond (1961) early criticized these studies on the ground that socioeconomic factors were not adequately controlled. For example, though control and criterion groups appeared similar on most social variables, as in other studies (Rutter et al., 1970; Sameroff & Chandler, 1975) there was a significant excess (57% vs. 36%) of socially disorganized families in the white behaviorally disturbed group. As noted above, what is also unclear is whether these complications are more validly indicative of brain damage (the frequency with which they actually cause brain damage is unknown) or of social pathology, which, as expected, was shown in Pasamanick's study to be highly correlated with the pre- and perinatal complications. It should also be pointed out that differences between the behaviorally disturbed and normal groups were quantitatively small. For example, the distribution of abnormalities of the pre- and perinatal period in the criterion and control groups was white children, 39 percent versus 31 percent; nonwhite children, 73 percent versus 54 percent (Rogers et al., 1955, p. 56). Thus, many normal children had complications and many behaviorally disturbed had none. Even in the most divergent hyperactive-confused-disorganized group, which was contributing all the excess of complications in the white psychopathological group, the difference between the behaviorally disturbed and control groups was only 42 percent versus 31 percent frequency of complications (p. 60). In view of the unknown, but likely low, probability with which these complications actually result in significant brain injury, it is apparent that brain damage could, at best, only be a minor determinant of the behavior disorders observed, and as repeatedly stated in other studies, weak or inefficient predictors (McGee et al., 1984; Nichols & Chen, 1981; Rutter, 1981, 1982a).

In contrast, most recently, McGee et al. (1984) in a prospective child development study of a total birth cohort ($N = 900$) compared children with and without stable "behavior problems" as defined by total scores on the Isle of Wight (or Rutter) Parent Scale. Of all the pre/perinatal insult variables only SGA (small for gestational age) emerged as predictive but was very weak compared with sociofamilial factors.

The notion of primary organic deficits interacting with the sociofamilial environment to produce secondary symptoms is elemental to more recent thinking about organic factors in childhood psychopathology (Cantwell, 1975; Paternite, Loney, & Langhorne, 1976; Rutter, 1981; Safer & Allen, 1976; Sameroff & Chandler, 1975). There is considerable disagreement, however, about what these primary deficits are, and there is some evidence that it may just be vulnerability to psychopathology (Rutter, 1981).

A wide variety of older studies (see Werry, 1972) purported to show an increased frequency of organic indicators in undifferentiated psychopathological groups (see Ellingson, 1954; Feuerstein et al., 1979; Holden et al., 1982; Krouse & Kauffman, 1982; Reeves & Werry, in press; Rutter et al., 1970; Wikler et al., 1970). These were also discussed under diagnostic techniques previously. Later work has questioned these earlier studies and/or shown that different disorders have differential rates, limiting their value.

SUMMARY OF PSYCHOPATHOLOGY AS SELECTION CRITERION

Studies of general psychiatric populations suggest that, as a group, emotionally disturbed children may exhibit an increased frequency of EEG abnormalities, "equivocal" or "soft" neurological signs, and minor physical anomalies. Any increase in the frequency of pre- and perinatal complications is more uncertain. There is evidence that any increase in these various abnormalities may result largely from certain psychopathological conditions, such as psychoses and attention or conduct disorders (see subsequent text). Very properly, interest in this type of study has declined in favor of those using specific diagnostic groups. Although suggestive of an organic etiology, these findings do not preclude adverse experience, psychophysiological effects, or normal variation as etiological factors, alone or in concert with physical factors. These findings are also common in nonpsychiatric disorders such as learning disorders (Feuerstein et al., 1979) and in association with social disadvantage. When the latter is controlled, most of the difference disappears (e.g., Nichols & Chen, 1981; Sameroff & Chandler, 1975).

**Minimal Brain
Dysfunction**

The role of biological factors in the accepted specific psychopathological disorders has been discussed earlier in this volume. However, this leaves the question as to whether there is a specific brain–behavior syndrome as originally proposed by Strauss and Lehtinen (1947) in which behavior is a true neurological symptom that clusters with other such symptoms in a lawful and predictable way. The notion of minimal cerebral dysfunction, as commonly used, is hopelessly vague and a clear derivative of the outdated nonspecific or quantitative view of brain action discussed earlier in this chapter.

In a pioneering study Schulman et al. (1965) examined the relationship between a number of cognitive, neurological, EEG, and behavioral measures in a group of 37 boys of IQ 55 to 57. They found a very low degree of interrelatedness between (and very often low reliability in) all variables. Hyperactivity, distractibility, inconsistency, and emotional lability did not intercorrelate to form a syndrome, and with the exception of distractibility, neither were they related to other indices of brain damage.

There have been several efforts to examine the relationship between behavioral, cognitive, and various organic indicators in the search for empirical confirmation of a minimal brain dysfunction syndrome through the use of multivariate statistical techniques. Jenkins (1964), using clinical records of 3000 children, isolated a dimension he called "brain injury," despite the fact that the only item in the cluster in any way indicative of brain injury was the "question of encephalitis." Furthermore, only in girls did this dimension have any features of the hyperkinetic syndrome. In recent years Langhorne and Loney (1976), Nichols and Chen (1981), Paine, Werry, and Quay (1968), Routh and Roberts (1972), and Werry (1968), using factor-analytic techniques, found behavioral, cognitive, neurological, and medical historical variables to emerge in discrete source (of data) factors, suggesting that certainly, as presently measured, the various components scarcely make up a neat, single, MBD syndrome.

The study by Nichols and Chen is particularly noteworthy since as part of the U.S. Perinatal Study, it was prospective, had a large sample size (29,000), provided a set of over 300 multisource variables collected from pregnancy through age seven, and was analyzed with the best in modern multivariate techniques. The separateness of attentional, neurological, and learning syndrome was confirmed not only empirically but also in terms of their correlates. While some "organic" predictors emerged for each group, they were in general weak, inefficient, and dwarfed by sociofamilial and other experimental variables.

Laudably, in research at least there has been some movement away from the simplistic notion of MBD in line with the suggestion of Clements (1966) to define subgroups, as follows:

1. **By grouping symptoms on the basis of localization of brain function** (see McFie, 1975). This is seen particularly in the multiaxial classification proposed by Rutter (Rutter, Shaffer, & Shepherd 1975) in such diag-

nostic terms as dyspraxia, dyslalia, dysphasia, dyslexia, and so on. The highly influential theory of Wender (1971), who viewed the primary deficits in minimal brain dysfunction as those of activity level and of response to reward and punishment, is also a brain localization theory. Wender's theory relates to functional systems defined by the neurotransmitter substances involved (dopaminergic, adrenergic). While the theory has unproven assumptions about the basic deficits in MBD and is reductionist, it has been surprisingly fruitful in its stimulation of research and other theory. For example, some elements of it can be seen in Gorenstein and Newman's (1980) notions about disinhibitory psychopathology and Gray's (1982) theory of anxiety, the latter of which is very much a localization theory.

2. **By empirically derived symptom clusters** (Cantwell, 1975; Langhorne & Loney, 1976; Nichols & Chen, 1981).

3. **By psychophysiological response patterns** (Conners, 1975; Feuerstein et al., 1979; Satterfield, 1975).

4. **By particular clinical features** such as minor physical anomalies (Rapoport & Quinn, 1975).

5. **By response to medication** —stimulants and various combinations of drugs (see Chapter 11).

6. **By biochemical studies** (e.g., Cohen & Young, 1977) and other modern medical techniques (Rutter, 1982a).

Although most of the above efforts are, as yet, only beginnings, mostly disappointing (see Rutter, 1982a), and have centered mostly on ADD, they do auger a desirable move away from the simplistic and neurologically untenable notion of MBD as a homogeneous entity. Hearteningly, these clinical studies also are being complemented by basic animal research that obviously offers far more scope for experimental intervention and for the accurate localization of damage or dysfunction (Corson, Corson, Arnold, & Knopp, 1976; Eastgate, Wright, & Werry, 1978; Shaywitz, Klopper, Yager, & Gordon, 1976; Shaywitz, Yager, & Klopper, 1976; Silbergeld & Goldberg, 1975).

Specific Brain-damage Variables

1. **Age of injury** Immaturity is said to increase the compensatory ability of the brain (McFie, 1975; Rutter, 1982a; Rutter et al., 1970; Shaffer, 1973; Towbin, 1978), but Satz and Fletcher (1981; Fletcher & Satz, 1983) dispute that this is so because studies confound *age* with *length of follow-up* and evidence for permanent disability (e.g., cerebral palsy, mental retardation) is as convincing. Unfortunately, the subject of early versus late injury and type of psychopathology has been little studied and by only one group. What data there are suggest little relationship (e.g., Rutter, 1981, 1982a; Shaffer et al., 1975).

2. **Site of lesion** Eisenberg (1957) and McFie (1975) have presented lucid and readable summaries of ideas on cerebral location of higher functions and possible clinical results. Maurer and Damasco (1982) have posited a

frontal-lobe focus for autism, and schizophrenia is held to be a disorder of dopaminergic systems (see Chapter 5). The actual evidence linking particular chronic psychopathological states to cerebral topography is, however, at best slender and mostly inferential. Further, the same regions have been posited as causing widely different psychopathology. The head injury literature is largely negative (see Shaffer et al., 1975; Rutter, 1982a) for site effects, though damage usually occurs in sites away from the injury as well.

On the other hand, there is good evidence to suggest that like motor functions, cognitive functions are affected by site (see Albert, 1981; Chapter 6).

The most recent arguments for site effects by Maurer and Damasco (1982) for autism and Gray (1982) for ADD, conduct disorder, or anxiety-withdrawal (see Chapter 1) have an elegance and testability lacking in previous such efforts. Further, the advances in pharmacological and organ imaging techniques such as PET and NMR scans offer rather more immediate investigative tools than in the past.

3. **Specific etiology**   As has already been discussed, despite attempts to relate specific types of psychopathology to specific etiological conditions, there is little evidence to support these contentions. In any case, it seems on a priori grounds that etiology effects should be more heuristically resolvable into site, speed, and associated effects (such as swelling) rather than the etiological nature of the lesion.

4. **Sex**   Most of the studies of disorders thought to have some biological base such as hyperactivity, autism, learning disorders, and so on report a significant excess of boys (e.g., Nichols & Chen, 1981; Ross & Ross, 1982; see also Chapters 1 through 6). While there is an apparently greater vulnerability of males to neonatal insults, as adjudged by perinatal mortality rates (Butler & Bonham, 1964, p. 133), it remains to be demonstrated that the excess of boys seen in some disorders such as with ADD reflects a brain damage instead of a cultural or biological sex effect of more pronounced aggressiveness in males leading to higher referral rates (Werry & Quay, 1971). It is of interest to note that in their population study, Graham and Rutter (1968) found rates of disturbance in neurologically impaired children to be equal in the two sexes, thus supporting some selectivity in referral.

SUMMARY

This review of the relationship between biological (i.e., brain) factors and childhood psychopathology has shown that while the idea of such a causal relationship has considerable face validity, the power and nature of any such relationship is difficult to demonstrate and to unravel.

When biological factors result in *major* brain disorder, the risk of psychopathological states is greatly increased, though by no means made inexorable. In general, consciousness, cognition, sensory and motor function, and seizure threshold are the functions most powerfully affected, and it is when these are impaired that psychopathology is most likely to be found. So far there is little evidence of any specific psychopathology due to brain damage outside that seen in the true organic disorders such as delirium and dementia, though possibilities seem strongest in the very severe disorders or psychoses such as autism and schizophrenia. Other possible exceptions are the symptoms of social isolation and behavioral disinhibition.

Much brain disorder in children probably occurs during the pre- and perinatal period but cannot be inferred accurately from a history of insults, which are highly inefficient predictors. Further, improvements in ante- and perinatal medicine have greatly reduced the ultimate impact of such events. The best indicators of significant brain disorder seem to be multidimensional measures of function in the neonate. It seems likely that much brain disorder in this period is trivial and when so, for reasons already outlined, is largely overridden by the more powerful and durable effect of the child's sociofamilial environment as life proceeds.

Thus, studies of psychopathological status that are remote in time from a brain injury and that use inefficient predictors of brain disorder, such as low birth weight and insults of pregnancy or delivery, would seem likely to reveal effects only in very large samples where, further, the strong effect of sociofamilial variables can be partialed out. And this seems to be so, though once the major handicapping disorders of cerebral palsy, mental retardation, and epilepsy are excluded, most such studies can detect only very weak effects by school age.

There are, however, strong theoretical reasons and residual empirical straws that allow survival of the hypothesis that some children may develop psychoses and disorders of learning or of inhibition or of socialization as a result of brain damage or disorder and that differences in symptomatology may in part be due to the region of the brain affected. However, current techniques of locating and assessing minor or nonobvious brain dysfunction as well as ways of measuring psychopathology do not yet really allow testing of such hypotheses adequately, though both it and a recognition of the methodological problems involved can still provide powerful stimuli to research in childhood psychopathology.

To this reviewer, it seems that current phenomenologically determined diagnostic categories in childhood psychopathology are too crude and heterogeneous readily to reveal a biological role in nonpsychotic disorder except possibly in large populations or very carefully defined subgroups. Also, until we can find indicators of disorder that lie closer to the functional system impaired and constitute less complex end results (unlike the overinclusive ADD or conduct disorders), not much progress can be made. Unfortunately, attempts to do this and define subgroups by laboratory studies of attention, cortical evoked potentials, biochemical metabolites, or response to pharmacotherapy in ADD show just how monumental and frustrating a task this is.

Some, like the radical behaviorists of the 1970s, might conclude from the foregoing that any notion of brain factors in psychopathology should be abandoned as elusive, distracting, or dangerously medicalizing to childhood psychopathology. To do so would be, however, not only to turn our backs on a large amount of past research and painfully gained knowledge in childhood psychopathology, but to cut ourselves off from the ineluctable fact that in the end all behavior is mediated through the brain. It appears certain that refinements in neuropharmacological technique in the future will greatly extend the possibility of changing behavior through changing brain status. The potential for relieving and changing the self-destructive behavior of extreme conduct disorder and the misery of such emotional disorders as autism, obsessive-compulsive disorder, or depression suggests that research into the biological aspects of childhood psychopathology must not be abandoned because of the difficulties it presents. As often pointed out, Science is both inexorable and value-free; we cannot resist its momentum but we can choose to use, humanely and wisely, what it reveals.

REFERENCES

Albert, M. S. (1981). Geriatric neuropsychology. *Journal of Consulting and Clinical Psychology, 49*, 835–850.

Baloh, R., Sturm, R., Green, B., & Gleser, G. (1975). Neuropsychological effects of asymptomatic increased lead absorption: A controlled study. *Archives of Neurology, 32*, 326–330.

Bancroft, J., Axworthy, D., & Ratcliffe, S. G. (1982). The personality and psychosexual development of boys with 47 XXY chromosome constitution. *Journal of Child Psychology and Psychiatry, 23*, 169–180.

Bialer, I., Doll, L., & Winsberg, B. G. (1974). A modified Lincoln-Oseretsky Motor Development Scale: Provisional standardization. *Perceptual and Motor Skills, 38*, 599–614.

Bohman, M. (1981). The interaction of heredity and childhood environment: Some adoption studies. *Journal of Child Psychology and Psychiatry, 22*, 195–200.

Breslau, N., & Marshall, I. A. (1985). Psychological disturbance in children with physical disabilities. *Journal of Abnormal Child Psychology, 13*, 199–216.

Butler, N., & Bonham, D. (1963). *Perinatal mortality*. Edinburgh: Livingstone.

Camp, J. A., Bialer, I., Sverd, J., & Winsberg, B. G. (1978). Clinical usefulness of the NIMH physical and neurological examination for soft signs. *American Journal of Psychiatry, 135*, 362–364.

Campbell, S. B. (1974). Cognitive styles and behavior problems of clinic boys: A comparison in epileptic, hyperactive, learning-disabled, and normal groups. *Journal of Abnormal Child Psychology, 2*, 307–312.

Cantwell, D. P. (1975). *The hyperactive child—diagnosis, management, current research*. New York: Spectrum.

Chiappa, K. H., & Roper, A. H. (1982). Evoked potentials in clinical medicine. *New England Journal of Medicine, 306*, 1140–1149, 1205–1211.

Clements, S. D. (1966). Minimal brain dysfunction in children. *NINDB Monograph No. 3*. Washington, DC: U.S. Public Health Service.

Clements, S. D., & Peters, J. E. (1962). Minimal brain dysfunction in the school-age child. *Archives of General Psychiatry, 6*, 185–187.

Close, J. (1973). Scored neurological examination. *Psychopharmacology Bulletin, Special Issue: Pharmacotherapy of Children*, 142–148.

Cohen, D. J., & Young, J. G. (1977). Neurochemistry and child psychiatry. *Journal of the American Academy of Child Psychiatry, 16*, 353–411.

Coleman, M. (1973). Serotonin and central nervous system syndromes of childhood: A review. *Journal of Autism and Childhood Schizophrenia, 3*, 27–35.

Conners, C. K. (1975). Minimal brain dysfunction in psychopathology in children. In A. Davids (Ed.), *Child personality and psychopathology: Current topics* (Vol. 2). New York: Wiley.

Conners, C. K. (1980). *Food additives and hyperactive children*. New York: Plenum.

Corah, N. L., Anthony, E. J., Painter, P., Stern, J., & Thurston, D. (1965). Effects of perinatal anoxia after seven years. *Psychological Monographs* (Vol. 3), *79*, 596.

Corson, S., Corson, E., Arnold, L., & Knopp, W. (1976). Animal models of violence and hyperkinesis: Interaction of psychopharmacologic and psychosocial therapy in behavior modification. In G. Serban & A. Kling (Eds.), *Animal models in human psychobiology*. New York: Plenum.

Craggs, M. D., Wright, J. J., & Werry, J. S. (1980). A pilot study of the effects of methylphenidate on the vigilance-related EEG in hyperactivity. *Electroencephalography and Clinical Neurophysiology, 48*, 34–42.

Cramblett, H. G., Stegmiller, H., & Spencer, C. (1966). California encephalitis virus infections in children. Clinical and laboratory studies. *Journal of the American Medical Association, 198*, 108–112.

Cruickshank, W., & Bice, H. (1966). In W. Cruickshank (Ed.), *Cerebral palsy: Its individual and community problems* (2nd ed.). Syracuse, NY: Syracuse University Press.

David, O. J., Clark, J., & Voeller, K. (1972). Lead and hyperactivity. *Lancet, 2*, 900–903.

David, O. J., Hoffman, S. P., Sverd, J., & Clark, J. (1977). Lead and hyperactivity: Lead levels among hyperactive children. *Journal of Abnormal Child Psychology, 5*, 405–416.

Davie, R., Butler, N., & Goldstein, H. (1972). *From birth to seven: A report of the National Child Development Study*. London: Longman.

Davies, P. A. (1976). Outlook for low birthweight children—then and now. *Archives of Diseases in Childhood, 51*, 817–819.

DeLong, G. R., Bean, S. C., & Brown, F. R. (1981). Acquired reversible autistic syndrome in acute encephalopathic illness in children. *Archives of Neurology, 38*, 191–194.

Desmond, M. M., Fisher, E. S., Vorderman, A. L., Schaffer, H. G., Andrew, L. P., Zion, T. E., & Catlin, F. I. (1978). The longitudinal course of congenital rubella encephalitis in nonretarded children. *Journal of Pediatrics, 93*, 584–591.

Douglas, J. W., & Gear, R. (1976). Children of low birthweight in the 1946 National cohort. Behaviour and educational achievement in adolescence. *Archives of Diseases in Childhood, 51*, 820–827.

Drillien, C. (1964). *The growth and development of the prematurely born infants.* Baltimore: Williams & Wilkins.

Drillien, C. (1972). Aetiology and outcome in low birth weight infants. *Developmental Medicine and Child Neurology, 14*, 563–584.

Drillien, C. M., Thomson, A. J. M., Burgoyne, K. (1980). Low-birth weight children at early school-age: A longitudinal study. *Developmental Medicine and Child Neurology, 22*, 26–47.

Eastgate, S. M., Wright, J. J., & Werry, J. S. (1978). Behavioral effects of methylphenidate in 6-hydroxydopamine treated neonatal rats. *Psychopharmacologia, 58*, 157–160.

Ebaugh, F. G. (1923). Neuropsychiatric sequelae of acute epidemic encephalitis in children. *American Journal of Diseases in Children, 25*, 89–97.

Eisenberg, L. (1957). Psychiatric implication of brain damage in children. *Psychiatric Quarterly, 31*, 72–92.

Ellingson, R. (1954). The incidence of EEG abnormality among patients with mental disorders of apparently nonorganic origin: A critical review. *American Journal of Psychiatry, 111*, 263–275.

Ernhart, C. B., Graham, F. K., Eichman, P. L., Marshall, J. M., & Thurston, D. (1963). Brain injury in the preschool child: Some developmental considerations. II. Comparison of brain injured and normal children. *Psychological Monographs, 77*, 17–33.

Escalona, S. K. (1982). Babies at double hazard: Early development of infants at biologic and social risk. *Pediatrics, 70*, 670–676.

Feingold, B. (1975). *Why your child is hyperactive.* New York: Random House.

Feuerstein, M., Ward, M. M., LeBaron, S. W. M. (1979). Neuropsychological and neurophysiological assessment of children with learning and behavior problems: A critical appraisal. In B. B. Lahey & A. E. Kazdin (Eds.), *Advances in clinical child psychology* (Vol. 2, pp. 241–278). New York: Plenum.

Finer, N. N., Robertson, C. M., Richards, R. T., Pinnell, L. E., & Peters, K. L. (1981). Hypoxic-ischemic encephalopathy in term neonates: Perinatal factors and outcome. *Journal of Pediatrics, 98*, 112–117.

Firestone, P., & Prabhu, A. N. (1983). Minor physical anomalies and obstetrical complications: Their relationship to hyperactive, psychoneurotic and normal children and their families. *Journal of Abnormal Child Psychology, 11*, 207–216.

Fletcher, J. M., & Satz, P. (1983). Age, plasticity and equipotentiality: A reply to Smith. *Journal of Consulting and Clinical Psychology, 51*, 763–767.

Flor-Henry, P. (1982). Neuropsychological studies in patients with psychiatric disorders. In K. M. Heilman & P. Satz (Eds.), *Neuropsychology of human emotion* (pp. 193–200). New York: Guilford.

Fraser, M. S., & Wilks, J. (1959). The residual effects of neonatal asphyxia. *Journal of Obstetrics and Gynecology of the British Empire, 66*, 748–752.

Freeman, R. D. (1967). Special education and the EEG: Marriage of convenience. *Journal of Special Education, 2*, 61–73.

Gallagher, J. J. (1957). A comparison of brain injured and non-brain injured mentally retarded children on severe psychological variables. *Society for Research in Child Development Monograph No. 65.*

Gibbs, F. A., Gibbs, E. L., Spies, H. W., & Carpenter, H. (1964). Common types of childhood encephalitis. *Archives of Neurology, 10*, 1–11.

Gittelman, R., & Eskenazi, B. (1983). Lead and hyperactivity revisited. *Archives of General Psychiatry, 40*, 827–833.

Gorenstein, E. E., & Newman, J. P. (1980). Disinhibitory psychopathology: A new perspective and a model for research. *Psychological Review, 87*, 301–315.

Graham, F. K., Ernhart, C. B., Thurston, D., & Craft, M. (1962). Development three years after perinatal anoxia and other potentially damaging newborn experiences. *Psychological Monographs, 76*, 1–53.

Graham, P., & Rutter, M. (1968). Organic brain dysfunction and child psychiatric disorder. *British Medical Journal, 3*, 695–700.

Gray, J. A. (1982). *The neuropsychology of anxiety*. Oxford: Oxford University Press.

Griffiths, A. D., & Laurence, K. M. (1974). The effect of hypoxia and hypoglycaemia on the brain of the newborn human infant. *Developmental Medicine and Child Neurology, 16*, 308–319.

Harris, R. (1978). Relationship between EEG abnormality and aggressive and antisocial behaviour: A critical appraisal. In L. A. Hersov, M. Berger, & D. Shaffer (Eds.), *Aggression and antisocial behavior in childhood and adolescence* (pp. 13–27). Oxford: Pergamon.

Herbert, M. (1964). The concept and testing of brain-damage in children: A review. *Journal of Child Psychology and Psychiatry, 5*, 197–216.

Hermann, B. P. (1982). Neuropsychological functioning and psychopathology in children with epilepsy. *Epilepsia, 23*, 545–554.

Holden, E. W., Tarnowski, K. J., & Prinz, R. J. (1982). Reliability of neurological soft signs in children: Reevaluation of the PANESS. *Journal of Abnormal Child Psychology, 10*, 163–172.

Holdsworth, L., & Whitmore, K. (1974). A study of children with epilepsy attending ordinary schools. I. Their seizure patterns, progress and behaviour in school. *Developmental Medicine and Child Neurology, 16*, 746–758.

Jenkins, R. L. (1964). Diagnoses, dynamics and treatment in child psychiatry. In R. Jenkins & J. Cole (Eds.), *Research Report No. 18*. Washington, DC: American Psychiatric Association.

Kendler, K. S. (1983). Overview: A current perspective on twin studies of schizophrenia. *American Journal of Psychiatry, 140*, 1413–1425.

Kennedy, R. L. J. (1924). The prognosis of sequelae of epidemic encephalitis in children. *American Journal of Diseases in Children, 28*, 158–172.

Klaasen, C. D. (1980). Heavy metals and heavy metal antagonists. In A. G. Gilman, L. G. Goodman, & A. Gilman (Eds.), *The pharmacological basis of therapeutics* (6th ed., pp. 1615–1637). New York: Macmillan.

Krouse, J. P., & Kauffman, J. (1982). Minor physical anomalies in exceptional children: A review and critique of research. *Journal of Abnormal Child Psychology, 10*, 247–266.

Langhorne, J. E., & Loney, J. (1976). Childhood hyperkinesis: A return to the source. *Journal of Abnormal Psychology, 85*, 201–209.

Lechman, J. F. (1983). The dexamethasone suppression test. *Journal of the American Academy of Child Psychiatry, 22*, 477–479.

Lechman, J. F., Cohen, D. J., Shaywitz, B. A., Caparulo, B. K., Heniger, G. R., & Bowers, M. B. (1980). CSF monoamine metabolites in child and adult psychiatric patients: A developmental perspective. *Archives of General Psychiatry, 37*, 677–681.

Levene, M. I., & Dubowitz, L. M. S. (1982). Low birth weight babies: Long term follow-up. *British Journal of Hospital Medicine, 28*, 487–493.

Lipowski, Z. J. (1982). Differentiating dementia from delirium in the elderly. *Clinical Gerontology, 1*, 3–10.

Marlowe, M., Errera, J., Ballowe, T., & Jacobs, J. (1983). Low metal levels in emotionally disturbed children. *Journal of Abnormal Psychology, 92*, 386–389.

Marlowe, M., Cossairt, A., Moon, C., Errera, J., MacNeel, A., Peak, R., Ray, J., & Schroeder, C. (1985). Main and interaction effects of metallic toxins on classroom behavior. *Journal of Abnormal Child Psychology, 13*, 185–198.

Maurer, R. G., & Damasco, A. R. (1982). Childhood autism from the point of view of behavioral neurology. *Journal of Autism and Developmental Disorders, 12*, 195–205.

McFie, J. (1975). *Assessment of organic intellectual impairment.* London: Academic Press.

McGee, R., Silva, P. A., & Williams, S. (1984). Perinatal, neurological, environmental and developmental characteristics of seven-year-old children with stable behaviour problems. *Journal of Child Psychology and Psychiatry, 25*, 573–586.

McMahon, R. C. (1980). Genetic etiology in the Hyperactive Child Syndrome: A critical review. *American Journal of Orthopsychiatry, 50*, 145–150.

McNeil, T. F., & Persson-Blennow, I. (1982). Temperament questionnaires in clinical research. In M. Rutter (Ed.), *Temperamental differences in infants and young children* (pp. 20–31). London: Pitman Books (CIBA Foundation Symposium No. 89).

Millichap, J. (1975). *The hyperactive child with minimal brain dysfunction: Questions and answers.* Chicago: Year Book Medical Publishers.

Minde, K., Webb, G., & Sykes, D. (1968). Studies on the hyperactive child. VI. Prenatal and paranatal factors associated with hyperactivity. *Developmental Medicine and Child Neurology, 10*, 355–363.

Montagu, J. (1975). The hyperkinetic child: A behavioral, electrodermal and EEG investigation. *Developmental Medicine and Child Neurology, 17*, 299–305.

Needleman, H. L., & Bellinger, D. C. (1981). The epidemiology of low-level lead exposure in childhood. *Journal of the American Academy of Child Psychiatry, 20*, 496–512.

Nichols, P. L., & Chen, T. C. (1981). *Minimal Brain Dysfunction: A prospective study.* Hillsdale, NJ: Earlbaum.

Niklowitz, W. J. (1977). Subcellular mechanisms in lead toxicity: Significance in childhood encephalopathy, neurological sequelae, and late dementias. In L. Roizin, H. Shiraki, & N. Grcevic (Eds.), *Neurotoxicology.* New York: Raven Press.

Niswander, K., & Gordon, M. (1972). *The collaborative perinatal study of the National Institute of Neurological Diseases and Stroke: The women and their pregnancies.* Philadelphia: Saunders.

Paine, R., Werry, J. S., & Quay, H. C. (1968). A study of "Minimal Cerebral Dysfunction." *Developmental Medicine and Child Neurology, 10*, 505–520.

Pasamanick, B., & Knobloch, H. (1960). Brain damage and reproductive casualty. *American Journal of Orthopsychiatry, 30*, 298–305.

Paternite, C. E., Loney, J., & Langhorne, J. E. (1976). Relationships between symptomatology and SES-related factors in hyperkinetic/MBD boys. *American Journal of Orthopsychiatry, 46*, 291–301.

Peters, J., Dykman, R., Ackerman, P., & Romine, J. (1974). The special neurological examination. In C. Conners (Ed.), *Clinical use of stimulant drugs in children.* Amsterdam: Excerpta Medica.

Plomin, R. (1982). Behavioural genetics and temperament. In M. Rutter (Ed.), *Temperamental differences in infants and young children* (pp. 155–167). London: Pitman Books (CIBA Foundation Symposium No. 89).

Pond, D. A. (1961). Psychiatric aspects of epileptic and brain-damaged children. *British Medical Journal, 2*, 1377–1382, 1454–1459.

Prechtl, H. F. R. (1960). The long term value of the neurological examination of the newborn infant. *Developmental Medicine and Child Neurology, 2*, 69–74.

Prechtl, H., & Dijkstra, J. (1960). Neurological diagnosis of cerebral injury in the newborn. In B. tenBerge (Ed.), *Prenatal care.* Groningen, Netherlands: Noordhoff.

Psychopharmacology Bulletin. (1973). Pharmacotherapy of Children (Special Issue).

Quay, H. C., & Peterson, D. R. (1975). *Manual for the Behavior Problem Checklist.* Unpublished.

Rapoport, J. L., & Kruesi, M. J. P. (1983). Behavior and nutrition: A mini review. *Contemporary Nutrition, 8*(10), 1–2.

Rapoport, J., & Quinn, P. (1975). Minor physical anomalies (stigmata) and early developmental deviation: A major biologic subgroup of hyperactive children. *International Journal of Mental Health, 4*, 29–44.

Rapoport, J., Quinn, P., & Lamprecht, F. (1974). Minor physical anomalies and plasma dopamine-hydroxylase activity in hyperactive boys. *American Journal of Psychiatry, 131*, 386–390.

Rapoport, J., Quinn, P., Scribanau, N., & Murphy, D. (1974). Platelet serotonin of hyperactive school age boys. *British Journal of Psychiatry, 125*, 138–140.

Ratcliffe, S. G., & Field, M. A. (1982). Emotional disorder in XYY children. *Journal of Clinical Psychology and Psychiatry, 23*, 401–406.

Reeves, J. C., & Werry, J. S. (In press). Soft signs in abnormality. II: Hyperactivity. In D. E. Tupper (Ed.), *Soft neurological signs: Manifestations, measurement, research and meaning.* New York: Grune & Stratton.

Reitan, R., & Boll, T. (1973). The neuropsychological correlates of minimal brain dysfunction. *Annals of the New York Academy of Sciences, 205*, 65–88.

Reitan, R., & Davison, L. (Eds.). (1974). *Clinical neuropsychology: Current status and applications.* New York: Winston-Wiley.

Ritvo, E. R., Freeman, B. J., Galler, E., & Yuwiler, A. (1983). Effects of fenfluramine on 14 outpatients with the syndrome of autism. *Journal of the American Academy of Child Psychiatry, 22*, 549–564.

Robinson, H., & Robinson, N. (1965). *The mentally retarded child*. New York: McGraw-Hill.

Rogers, M. E., Lilienfeld, A. M., & Pasamanick, B. (1955). Pre- and paranatal factors in the development of childhood behavior disorders. *Acta Neurologica et Psychiatrica Scandinavica, 56–66*, Suppl. 102.

Ross, D. M., & Ross, S. A. (1982). *Hyperactivity: Research, theory, action* (2nd ed.). New York: Wiley.

Routh, D., & Roberts, R. (1972). Minimal brain dysfunction in children: Failure to find evidence for a behavioral syndrome. *Psychological Reports, 31*, 307–314.

Rumsey, J. M., & Rapoport, J. L. (1983). Assessing behavioral and cognitive effects of diet in pediatric populations. In R. J. Wurtman & J. J. Wurtman (Eds.), *Nutrition and the brain* (Vol. 6, pp. 101–161). New York: Raven Press.

Rutter, M. (1977). Brain damage syndromes in children: Concepts and findings. *Journal of Child Psychology and Psychiatry, 18*, 1–21.

Rutter, M. (1980a). Raised lead levels and impaired cognitive/behavioural functioning: A review of the evidence. *Supplement to Developmental Medicine and Child Neurology, 22*.

Rutter, M. (1980b). Psychosexual development. In M. Rutter (Ed.), *The scientific foundations of developmental psychiatry* (pp. 322–339). London: Heinemann.

Rutter, M. (1981). Psychological sequelae of brain damage in children. *American Journal of Psychiatry, 138*, 1533–1544.

Rutter, M. (1982a). Syndromes attributed to "minimal brain dysfunction" in childhood. *American Journal of Psychiatry, 139*, 1–33.

Rutter, M. (1982b). Temperament: Concepts, issues and problems. In M. Rutter (Ed.), *Temperamental differences in infants and young children* (pp. 1–19). London: Pitman Books (CIBA Foundation Symposium No. 89).

Rutter, M., Graham, P., & Yule, W. (1970). A neuropsychiatric study in childhood. *Clinics in Developmental Medicine*, Nos. 35/36. London: Heinemann.

Rutter, M., Shaffer, D., & Shepherd, M. (1975). *A multi-axial classification of child psychiatric disorders: An evaluation of a proposal*. Geneva: World Health Organization.

Sabatino, D. A., & Cramblett, H. G. (1968). Behavioural sequelae of California encephalitis virus infection in children. *Developmental Medicine and Child Neurology, 10*, 331–337.

Safer, D., & Allen, P. (1976). *Hyperactive children: Diagnosis and management*. Baltimore: University Park Press.

Sameroff, A., & Chandler, M. (1975). Reproductive risk and the continuum of caretaking casualty. In F. Horowitz, M. Hetherington, S. Scarr-Salapatek, & G. Siegel (Eds.), *Review of child development research*. (Vol. 4). Chicago: University of Chicago Press.

Sarason, S. B. (1949). *Psychological problems in mental deficiency*. New York: Harper.

Satterfield, J. H. (1975). Psychophysiological studies. In D. P. Cantwell (Ed.), *The hyperactive child—diagnosis, management, current research*. New York: Spectrum.

Satterfield, J. H., Cantwell, D. P., & Satterfield, B. T. (1974). Pathophysiology of the hyperactive child syndrome. *Archives of General Psychiatry, 31*, 839–844.

Satz, P., & Fletcher, J. M. (1981). Emergent trends in neuropsychology: An overview. *Journal of Consulting and Clinical Psychology, 49*, 851–865.

Schachter, F., & Apgar, V. (1959). Perinatal asphyxia and psychological signs of brain damage in childhood. *Pediatrics, 24*, 1016–1025.

Schulman, J. L., Kaspar, J. C., & Throne, F. M. (1965). *Brain damage and behavior: A clinical-experimental study*. Springfield, IL: Charles C. Thomas.

Seidel, U. P., Chadwick, O. F., & Rutter, M. (1975). Psychological disorder in crippled children: A comparative study of children with and without brain damage. *Developmental Medicine and Child Neurology, 17*, 563–573.

Shaffer, D. (1973). Psychiatric aspects of brain injury in childhood: A review. *Developmental Medicine and Child Neurology, 15*, 211–220.

Shaffer, D., Chadwick, O. F., & Rutter, M. (1975). Psychiatric outcome of localized head injury in children. In *Outcome of severe damage to the central nervous system* (Ciba Foundation Symposium No. 34). Amsterdam: Excerpta Medica.

Shaywitz, B. A., Klopper, J. H., Yager, R. D., & Gordon, J. (1976). Paradoxical response to amphetamine in developing rats treated with 6-hydroxydopamine. *Nature, 261*, 153–155.

Shaywitz, B. A., Yager, R. D., & Klopper, J. H. (1976). Selective brain dopamine depletion in developing rats: An experimental model of minimal brain dysfunction. *Science, 191*, 305–308.

Silbergeld, E. K., & Goldberg, A. M. (1975). Pharmacological and neurochemical investigations of lead-induced hyperactivity. *Neuropharmacology, 14*, 431–444.

Sloan, W. (1975). The Lincoln-Oseretsky Motor Development Scale. *Genetic Psychology Monographs, 51*, 183–252.

Smith, A. (1983). Overview or "underview"? Comment on Satz and Fletcher's "Emergent trends in neuropsychology: An overview." *Journal of Consulting and Clinical Psychology, 51*, 768–775.

Sprague, R. L. (1973). Minimal brain dysfunction from a behavioral viewpoint. *Annals of the New York Academy of Sciences, 205*, 349–361.

Stores, G. (1975). Behavioral effects of anti-epileptic drugs. *Developmental Medicine and Child Neurology, 17*, 647–658.

Strauss, A., & Lehtinen, L. (1947). *Psychopathology and education of the brain-injured child*. New York: Grune & Stratton.

Strecker, E. A. (1929). Behavior problems in encephalitis. *Archives of Neurology and Psychiatry, 21*, 137–144.

Tejani, A., Dobias, B., & Sambursky, J. (1982). Long-term prognosis after *H. influenzae* meningitis: Prospective evaluation. *Developmental Medicine and Child Neurology, 24*, 338–343.

Teuber, H. L. (1960). The premorbid personality and reaction to brain damage. *American Journal of Orthopsychiatry, 30*, 322–327.

Tizard, B. (1962). The personality of epileptics: A discussion of the evidence. *Psychological Bulletin, 59*, 196–210.

Touwen, B. C., & Sporrel, T. (1979). Soft signs and MBD. *Developmental Medicine and Child Neurology, 21*, 528–530.

Towbin, A. (1978). Cerebral dysfunction related to perinatal organic damage: Clinical-neuropathologic correlations. *Journal of Abnormal Psychology, 87*, 617–635.

Ucko, L. E. (1965). A comparative study of asphyxiated and non-asphyxiated boys from birth to five years. *Developmental Medicine and Child Neurology, 7*, 643–657.

Vohr, B. R., & Hack, M. (1982). Developmental follow-up of low-birth-weight infants. *Pediatric Clinics of North America, 29*, 1441–1454.

Waldrop, M. F., Pedersen, F. A., & Bell, R. Q. (1968). Minor physical anomalies and behavior in preschool children. *Child Development, 39*, 391–400.

Wenar, C. (1963). The reliability of developmental histories: Summary and evaluation of evidence. *Psychosomatic Medicine, 25*, 505–509.

Wender, P. (1971). *Minimal brain dysfunction in children*. New York: Wiley.

Werner, E. E., & Smith, R. S. (1979). An epidemiologic perspective on some antecedents and consequences of childhood mental health problems and learning disabilities. A report from the Kauai Longitudinal Study. *Journal of the American Academy of Child Psychiatry, 18*, 292–306.

Werry, J. S. (1968). Studies of the hyperactive child. IV. An empirical analysis of the minimal brain dysfunction syndrome. *Archives of General Psychiatry, 19*, 9–16.

Werry, J. S. (1972). Organic factors in childhood psychopathology. In H. C. Quay & J. S. Werry (Eds.), *Psychopathological disorders of childhood* (1st ed., pp. 83–121). New York: Wiley.

Werry, J. S., & Aman, M. G. (1976). The reliability and diagnostic validity of the Physical and Neurological Examination for Soft Signs (PANESS). *Journal of Autism and Childhood Schizophrenia, 6*, 253–262.

Werry, J. S., Minde, K., Guzman, A., Weiss, G., Dogan, K., & Hoy, E. (1972). Studies on the hyperactive child. VII. Neurological status compared with neurotic and normal children. *American Journal of Orthopsychiatry, 42*, 441–451.

Werry, J. S., & Quay, H. C. (1971). The prevalence of behavior symptoms in younger elementary school children. *American Journal of Orthopsychiatry, 41*, 136–143.

Wiener, G. (1962). Psychologic correlates of premature birth: A review. *Journal of Nervous and Mental Disease, 134*, 129–144.

Wiener, J. M., Delano, J. G., & Klass, D. W. (1966). An EEG study of delinquent and nondelinquent adolescents. *Archives of General Psychiatry, 15*, 144–150.

Wikler, A., Dixon, J. F., & Parker, J. B., Jr. (1970). Brain function in problem children and controls: Psychometric, neurological and electroencephalographic comparisons. *American Journal of Psychiatry, 127*, 634–645.

Wing, L., & Gould, J. (1979). Severe impairments of social interaction and associated abnormalities in children: Epidemiology and classification. *Journal of Autism and Developmental Disorders, 9*, 11–19.

9 FAMILY FACTORS AND PSYCHOPATHOLOGY IN CHILDREN

E. MAVIS HETHERINGTON AND BARCLAY MARTIN

INTRODUCTION

Most theories of child development emphasize family interaction as an important factor contributing to the development of personality and psychopathology. Theories vary not so much in emphasizing the importance of the family system, but in the aspects and processes of the system that they regard as critical. Psychoanalytic theory has stressed the caretaking functions of the mother as they interact with psychosexual development and the role of parental behavior in the resolution of the Oedipus complex as basic. Behavior theory has focused on the parents as models and as sources of reinforcement, and role theory has emphasized the critical function of parents in communicating social roles and standards. Cognitive theory has elaborated on the effects of the family in the development of attributional style, interpersonal perception, communication, role-taking skills, and belief systems, which may mediate the performance of social behavior. Systems theory has emphasized the family as an interacting whole with psychopathology reflected as part of a dysfunctional system rather than as an attribute of an individual within the system.

Each of these views has a measure of validity. In this chapter we will make use of contributions from most of them, but we especially will emphasize a developmental-ecological perspective that focuses on the dynamics of change over time. These changes include changes in the individual, the family system, and the extrafamilial ecology as well as secular shifts in society.

Although a developmental approach to the study of the individual has a long tradition in psychology, the concept of the family as the unit of developmental study until recently has been advocated more by sociologists (e.g., Aldous, 1978; Duvall, 1971; Rodgers, 1964) than by developmental psychologists. These writers describe family stages or careers and various developmental tasks associated with different parts of the family life cycle.

The term *developmental tasks* has been used to refer both to the individual's development (e.g., the tasks of motor development, resolving dependence–independence issues, achieving sex-role identity, etc.) and to family development. From the family perspective there are a number of "tasks" to be dealt with, some of which are associated with particular stages in the life cycle and others that cut across several stages. Examples across time include the development and maintenance of a viable marital relationship, coping with pregnancy and childbirth, dealing with the tensions of adolescence, and coping with old age.

Although the concept of family development is useful, it must be kept in mind that the broader ecology that encompasses the family also is changing. The extent to which the social environment is supportive, stressful, or changing at various times in the course of individual and family development will modify family relations and the well-being of family members. To describe the development of psychopathology a dynamic perspective must be taken of a developing child and family with changing capacities, tasks, and resources functioning within a shifting sociocultural and historical context. Different patterns of family interaction may be adaptive or pathogenic in different phases of individual or family development in these diverse contexts. The parental protectiveness necessary for infants will be destructive in relations with adolescents. The patterns of parenting associated with adaptive or deviant behavior in children may differ in an inner-city environment, an affluent suburb, or an isolated Virginia mountain hollow, in times of war and peace, economic stability or depression.

Nonnormative events such as the death of a child, loss of a job, war, or severe illness that can drastically alter the trajectory of development may also be encountered. Some theorists view these transitions as nodes or crossroads in development when family functioning is destabilized and family members are particularly vulnerable to being deflected into deviant developmental pathways (Hetherington, 1984). The variation in the frequency, timing, and intensity of these nonnormative life events and differences in resources and coping styles for dealing with them contribute to the difficulty in making long-term predictions about the relation between family functioning and psychopathological disorders in children.

The American family is going through a period of rapid transition. Sex roles within the family are changing and a greater number of children are living in single-parent homes or in reconstituted families. There is an increase in the number of teenage parents, in fathers gaining custody of their children, and in single-parent adoptions. Alternatives to the traditional nuclear family are being actively sought (Eiduson & Weisner, 1976; Lamb, 1982). What impact this will have on the role of family interaction in the development of psychopathology is unknown. It may be that the results of the studies made in the 1960s have little relevance for today's changing families and that the findings of current studies will tell us little about American families in the 1990s.

Finally, it must be remembered that there are multiple pathways to the development of social and cognitive competence and of psychopathology in children. There is no environment, set of life experiences, or magically effective child-rearing formula that ensures the positive adjustment of children. The heady optimism of the early behaviorists who believed that the development of behavior could be systematically shaped through the application of reinforcement and punishment is waning. Parental practices must be adapted to the biological predispositions and needs of the individual child. Often very similar family situations are associated with divergent developmental patterns in different children. Some children seem vulnerable to minor life stresses, others seem to be relatively resilient or even developmentally enhanced by their encounters with adversity and stressful experiences. With these reservations in mind, let us move on to examine the relationship between the family and the development of psychopathology in children.

THE FAMILY SYSTEM

In spite of the fact that studies of socialization are basically correlational, most experimenters have interpreted their findings in terms of the attitudes and behaviors of the parents causing the behaviors in the child. Recent investigators propose a more truly interactional model of family dynamics whereby both the effects of parents on each other and on their child and the effects of the child on the parents are studied (Bell & Harper, 1977; Belsky, 1984; Hetherington, Cox, & Cox, 1982; Patterson, 1982). Even infants exert considerable control over the behavior of parents and, with age, it might be expected that the social skills used in shaping another's behavior would increase. Bell (1968) has argued that upper-limit controls, such as parental physical punishment, could as easily be considered a result as a cause of children's aggression or impulsivity. Similarly, lower-limit controls may be stimulated by passivity, inhibition, or lack of competence in the child. The frequently reported rejection by parents of delinquents may be a response to the child's antisocial behavior. The intrusiveness of the parents of withdrawn children may be an attempt to elicit behavior from a passive child.

Interaction in one family dyad, or subsystem, can be importantly influenced by the character of interactions in other subsystems. Parent–child interaction can be influenced by the relationship between parents, the marital relationship can be influenced by the behavior of a child, and there will be an interaction between mother–child and father–child relations. When there is more than one child, the complexity of the system increases at a rapid rate, and includes, or course, sibling interactions. A child's interaction with other family members may be influenced by the number and sex of other siblings, the ordinal position of the child in the sibling hierarchy, and the age-spacing between siblings.

Because of methodological limitations, researchers have tended to study individuals, dyads, or in rare cases the mother–father–child triad. Their attempts at studying the family system have involved giving a composite picture of the family by assessing the functioning of these subsystems. Many family theorists would argue, however, that the family system has an identity and characteristic style of functioning that is more than the sum of the subcomponents within it. In the past decade there has been an increase in studies investigating the whole family system (McCubbin & Patterson, 1981; Olson, McCubbin, & Associates, 1983; Olson, Sprenkle, & Russell, 1979; Reiss, 1981). Different dimensions of family functioning such as cohesiveness, adaptability, and communication have been identified. Investigators are just beginning to understand how the configurations of these dimensions may be related to pathological or constructive outcomes.

THE THINKING FAMILY

There also has been a renewed interest in self-report data that has been in part a reflection of increased concern with the role of cognition in social behavior, a concern in understanding how people process, interpret, and appraise social information (Maccoby & Martin, 1983). Self-reports are a fruitful source of information about family members' perceptions, values, expectations, attributions, and beliefs. These cognitions mediate responses to the behavior of other family members. Distressed couples perceive even the neutral and positively intended behaviors of their spouses more negatively than do nondistressed couples and reciprocate in kind (Gottman, 1979). As was discussed in Chapter 1, highly aggressive boys perceive the behavior of others as being more hostile. Parents' belief systems about the capabilities, motivation, and degree of deviancy of their children are related to discipline practices, teaching strategies, and child abuse (McGillicuddy-DeLisi, 1982). Moreover, parents' self-esteem and view of their effectiveness in coping with life events will affect their control strategies in attempting to modify their children's behavior (Hetherington et al., 1982; Patterson, 1982). Thus, perceptions, beliefs, and attributions about the self and other family members have a major impact on family interaction.

VULNERABILITY, STRESSES, AND RESOURCES

Some children because of genetic or biological factors, life experiences, or adverse environments seem particularly vulnerable to the development of psychopathology. However not all, or not even most of these at-risk children, become disordered. These better than expected outcomes have been attributed by Garmezy (1984), to three categories of potential protective factors: (1) personality dispositions of the child; (2) a supportive family milieu; and (3) an external support system that encourages and reinforces a child's coping efforts and strengthens them by inculcating positive values.

It is adaptation to inevitable stress rather than freedom from problems that is related to successful family functioning and the psychological adjustment of family members. It has been hypothesized that the most desirable circumstance to promote the development of adaptive coping strategies is exposure to a series of graduated but negotiable life challenges; massing or accumulation of unresolved problems contributes to the development of psychopathology in children. Successful management makes families more resilient and able to resolve future problems (Garmezy, 1984).

As we have noted, the management of stress will be modified both by the characteristics of families and their members and the resources available to them. Ease of adjustment to stress in both males and females is related to high self-esteem, feelings of internal control, low anxiety, open mindedness, and tolerance for change (Hetherington, 1984). For females independence and nontraditional sex roles also facilitate coping (Hetherington, 1984). In addition, family characteristics such as adaptability, cohesion, communication, and problem-solving skills play an important role. The way in which individuals and families approach and interpret problems is directly related to the effects these stressful life events will have. Active problem-solving strategies associated with rationally redefining the situation to make the problem more manageable rather than avoiding the problem are associated with positive outcomes (Olson et al., 1983).

Some of the resources available are external to the immediate family and may involve such social supports as nonresidential kin, friends, neighbors, the work place, school, church, or social and community agencies. It is not only the availability of such resources but the use made of them under various circumstances that is related to successful coping. For example, Garbarino and Sherman (1980) found that families in neighborhoods with a high incidence of child abuse in contrast to those with low rates of child abuse used the supports available to them less effectively. They were less likely to use preventive resources but more likely to resort to treatment services when a family crisis arose. However, they usually waited until their problems had advanced to a desperate situation before using community resources.

Although extreme social isolation exacerbates family problems, there is considerable disagreement about how support from others moderates the effects of stressful life events. Different individuals dealing with different types of problems may find different kinds of support networks useful. Moreover, some kinds of support may give immediate relief but not be useful in the long run. In addition, support from others sometimes involves certain concomitant obligations that families may find aversive. For example, economic support from in-laws may involve greater intrusion by the in-laws in family decision making involving finances. In competent families self-reliance is more effective than help seeking in dealing with family relationship problems (Pearlin & Schooler, 1978); however, for most individuals confronting stress, social support that involves emotional concern from others has a positive influence in coping (House, 1981). Wives are more likely to value and use help from social networks across all family stages than are husbands. This pattern seems to be sex related, since a parallel pattern holds in adolescent daughters and sons (McCubbin & Patterson, 1981).

Although there has been considerable research on the role of extrafamilial supports in the adjustment of adults to crises, less is known about their effects on the mental health of children. There is evidence that the peer group and school may play particularly important roles in the adjustment of children undergoing stress (Hartup, 1983; Hetherington, 1984; Hetherington et al., 1982; Patterson, 1982; Rutter, 1983). The validation of competence, personal control, and self-worth is an important role of peers, teachers, and the school. Children attending different schools have been found to vary markedly in rates of absenteeism, behavior problems, and the ability to cope with high-risk environments or stressful life transitions such as divorce. Salutary schools have relatively structured predictable environments, regular schedules with high expectations for responsible behavior on the part of children, and clearly stated and consistently enforced rules. However, the social milieu of the school is also characterized by warmth, attentiveness, supportiveness, and rewards for good performance by the school staff (Hetherington et al., 1982; Rutter, 1983). It may be that a structured, predictable, supportive environment is particularly important for children going through stressful or turbulent life experiences.

THE DEVELOPMENT OF THE FAMILY SYSTEM

The Marital Relationship

The first family developmental task is the establishment of the husband–wife relationship. Two individuals with different biological predispositions, personalities, experiences, family histories, beliefs and expectations, needs and resources marry. These characteristics will shape and be modified by the ensuing family system. As soon as two or more individuals begin to interact, their behavioral dispositions begin to be affected, sometimes to a minor or trivial extent, sometimes to a profound degree. The relationship between husbands and wives and their marital satisfaction have impact not only on their own psychological well-being but on their children's well-being. Mates who are chosen because they offer an escape from an unhappy family of origin, because of an unplanned pregnancy, or for any number of hidden emotional agendas are fraught with potential for future marital strain.

THE MENTAL HEALTH OF MARRIED COUPLES

Clinicians (e.g., Bowen, 1978; Satir, 1964), without any systematic data, have proposed that individuals tend to select mates whose general level of mental health is about the same as their own. Empirical research is not entirely clear on this point. There is evidence that indicates that when one spouse has a psychological disorder, the other spouse has an increased likelihood of also having some kind of psychological disorder (see Merikangas, 1982, for a review of this research). This above-chance concordance could result because prospective mates with equal vulnerabilities to psychopathology select each other, as Bowen and Satir suggest (the assortative mating hypothesis), or it could result from the interactive dynamics of the marriage. Some researchers have found an increasing concordance for psychological disorders (usually anxiety-type disorders) as a function of the duration of the marriage (Hagnell & Kreitman, 1974; Hare & Shaw, 1965; Kreitman, 1964; Kreitman, Collins, Nelson, & Troop, 1970; Ovenstone, 1973), implying that marital interaction is the source of the concordance. Other investigators have not found an increase in similarity as a function of marriage duration (Agulnik, 1970; Slater & Woodside, 1951), a finding more consistent with assortative mating. Perhaps both factors contribute to the obtained concordances.

Family conflict, separation, and divorce are associated with emotional problems in married couples. Unipolar depression, anxiety, aggression, anger, low self-esteem, and sleep, eating, sexual, drug, and alcohol problems are common in the first few years following separation and divorce (Barrett, 1973; Hetherington et al., 1982; Wallerstein & Kelly, 1980). These tend to diminish as the divorced spouses cope with their new life situations (Spivey & Scherman, 1980). Divorced and separated people are, however, overrepresented in samples of psychiatric patients, while married adults are underrepresented (Bloom, Asher, & White, 1978). Divorced people more often attempt suicide, are physically ill, and are involved in automobile accidents, accidental falls, fires and explosions, homicide, and violence than are nondivorced adults (Bloom et al., 1978; Briscoe, Smith, Robins, Marten, & Gaskin, 1973). Since such studies have been performed on couples who are in the process of divorcing or are already divorced, these problems could be either a cause or an effect of the divorce.

The mental health of husbands and wives is important because psychopathology in parents is associated with psychopathology in children, not only due to possible shared genetic factors but also because such parents model aberrant behavior and because psychological disorders in parents are related to disruptions in parenting practices.

THE MARITAL RELATIONSHIP AND PARENTING

Marital satisfaction has been defined as the subjective "feelings of happiness, satisfaction and pleasure experienced by a spouse when considering all current aspects of his marriage" (Hawkins, 1968, p. 164). More behaviorally oriented investigators have operationalized marital satisfaction as the ratio of positive, pleasing to negative, displeasing affectional interchanges between husband and wife (Patterson, 1982). Marital satisfaction is highly correlated with both family satisfaction and life satisfaction (Olson et al., 1983). Marital dissatisfaction is related to family conflict and, as we will see later, discord is associated with conduct disorders in children. Although it is frequently cited that women are more dissatisfied than men in their marital relationship, this may be to some extent associated with general family dissatisfaction and the parenting role of women. Women receive more aversive responses and fewer pleasurable responses from their children than do fathers, and mothers spend more time actively involved in parenting (Patterson, 1982).

The birth of an infant affects the marital relationship, and the quality of the marriage affects the way parents respond to their infant. The way parents respond to their infant can modify infant characteristics, which in turn can affect the marital relationship. A recent review of the literature on this topic concludes that these effects have been demonstrated over a wide range of developmental periods and are not confined to parent–infant relations (Belsky, 1984).

Pregnancy and the birth of the first child is a major transition in the family life cycle. There is some evidence that couples' satisfaction with their marital relationship decreases somewhat after the birth of their first-born (Olson et al., 1983) and may decrease even further after the birth of their second-born (Feldman, 1971; Ryder, 1973). When marital dissatisfaction or conflict becomes extreme, there is evidence that maternal attitudes and behaviors toward the infant are likely to be more negative. Thus, mothers who experience little emotional support from their husbands are more likely to have negative attitudes toward their infants and poor postpartum adjustment (Shereshefsky & Yarrow, 1973; Wandersman, Wandersman, & Kahn, 1980).

Moreover, competency and involvement in the parenting of infants by both mothers and fathers have been related to marital quality and to supportiveness and positive regard by the spouse (Belsky, Gilstrap, & Rovine, 1984; Cowan & Cowan, 1983; Crnic, Ragozin, Greenberg, Robinson, & Basham, 1983; Pederson, 1982; Wandersman et al., 1980). In families of elementary-school age (Johnson & Lobitz, 1974) and adolescent children (Olweus, 1980), the quality of the marital relationship also has been found to be related to parental negativeness to children, which in turn has been associated with the development of aggressiveness in sons.

Even in divorced families emotional support of custodial mothers by noncustodial fathers results in more positive mother–child relations and fewer behavior disorders in children (Hetherington et al., 1982; Wallerstein & Kelly, 1980). Belsky (1984) cautions, however, that there may be circumstances under which families of origin or social networks are more influential sources of support than is the marital relationship.

Under circumstances such as single parenthood and teenage parenthood, social networks will presumably serve as the principal source of support. . . . The same may be true for traditional blue-collar marriages, in which husband and wife roles typically serve more instrumental than intimate functions and in which neither friendship nor romance, and thus emotional support, are the principal reasons for the relationship. (p. 90)

DIVORCE: AN OUTCOME OF MARITAL DISSATISFACTION

Divorce has become an increasingly common solution to marital dissatisfaction. The divorce rate has doubled in the past two decades and 40 percent of American children will experience their parents divorce before they reach the age of 18. About 90 percent of these children will find themselves in the custody of their mother in a single-parent household in which they see their father irregularly or not at all. Moreover, 75 percent of divorcing adults will remarry and 55 percent of these remarriages will end in a divorce. Thus, a significant number of children will experience a series of stressful transitions and reorganizations of their families and households. The point at which the investigator taps into these transitions will shape his or her view of their effects on the adjustment of children. Most children manifest some disturbances—often a combination of anger, anxiety, depression, dependency, and noncompliance—in the immediate aftermath of divorce; however, most children and adults also recover and adjust to their new life situation by about three years after divorce. (For recent reviews of the effects of divorce on family functioning and the adjustment of children, see Emery, Hetherington, & Fisher, 1984; Hetherington, 1981; Hetherington & Camara, 1984). Both the short- and long-term effects of divorce on children vary with the social and cognitive competencies and resources available to children of different types (Wallerstein & Kelly, 1980). If the marriage was particularly conflict ridden or the noncustodial parent deviant and disruptive, in the long run divorce followed by a well-functioning one-parent household may be a relief to both parents and children and may enhance social and cognitive development of the children. Weiss (1979) has commented on the unusual maturity and responsibility of some children who have successfully negotiated the separation and divorce of their parents. However, most children view their parents' divorce as an undesired and stressful life event, and divorced and one-parent families are exposed to a cluster of experiences that make maintaining a cohesive family and raising children difficult.

Mothers in one-parent households frequently suffer from economic duress, from an overburden of occupational, child-care, and household tasks that are regarded as a full-time job for two adults in a nondivorced family, from social isolation and a lack of social, emotional, and financial support. It might be thought that the presence of children would attenuate the sense of loneliness frequently reported by divorced adults; however, recent studies (Hetherington et al., 1982; Weiss, 1979) suggest that the presence of children may actually make mothers feel more unhappy, frustrated, helpless, anxious, and incompetent. This is particularly true of divorced mothers with young, noncompliant, acting-out sons. In two-parent homes, another parent can ease some of the stresses of parenthood.

Single-parent families also differ from nondivorced families in that the single-parent family has only one parental figure to serve as the agent of socialization and is likely to become more salient in the development of the child. Furthermore, there is not a spouse to serve as a buffer between parent and child in a single-parent family. As we noted earlier, in nuclear families the presence of a loving, competent, or well-adjusted parent can help counteract the effects of a rejecting, incompetent, emotionally unstable parent.

The single mother may confront specific problems of authority in discipline. In intact families, children exhibit less noncompliant and deviant behavior toward their fathers than their mothers and, when undesirable behavior occurs, the father can terminate it more readily than the mother can (Hetherington et al., 1982). Even in divorced families custodial fathers report fewer problems with discipline than do custodial mothers.

This is not meant to be a panegyric to the nuclear family. The rising divorce rate is just one manifestation of lack of marital satisfaction and dissension in the nuclear family. Research findings are consistent in showing that children reared in conflict-ridden, nuclear families are more poorly adjusted than children in well-functioning single-parent homes (Hetherington, et al., 1982; McCord, McCord, & Thurber, 1962; Nye, 1957; Sill, 1984). The point that must be emphasized is that in single-parent, mother-headed households, the mother is confronted by many stresses that threaten her social and psychological well-being. The way in which she copes and adapts to these stresses may be determinative in shaping the development of her children. The adjustment of children following divorce is associated with the adjustment of the custodial parent, continuing family conflict, and the number of environmental changes including changes in family relations encountered by the child.

Families with Infants

WHAT THE INFANT BRINGS TO THE RELATIONSHIP

Infants manifest marked differences in temperament and in sensorimotor, cognitive, and social competencies. Some of these are due to genetic factors, some to pre- and perinatal factors. (See Chapter 8 for a more detailed review of this topic.)

Temperament Temperamentally difficult infants have been described as irritable and difficult to soothe, slow to adapt to change, generally negative in mood states, and irregular in sleep, feeding, and biological cycles. When parents view their children as being temperamentally difficult, they are less positively responsive and more negative, critical, and punitive toward them (Campbell, 1979; Dunn, 1980; Kelly, 1976; Milliones, 1978; Rutter, 1978). Temperamentally difficult children not only are more likely to be the elicitors and targets of parental irritability, frustration, and adverse behaviors but also are less likely to be able to cope with negative parental behavior when it occurs. Rutter (1983) proposed that a child's temperament may put the child at risk or protect the child through its effect on parent–child interaction.

Pre- and Perinatal Factors   Infants may be at risk because of a wide range of prenatal and perinatal factors. As already noted (see Chapter 8), many of these children who appear to be at risk and who show short-term deficits rapidly move on to function normally, whereas others show steadily increasing levels of social and cognitive impairment. What contributes to these divergent long-term outcomes? Family relations and socioeconomic status consistently are found to play major roles in modifying developmental outcomes for high-risk infants.

An example of infants who would seem to carry some increased risk for interactional difficulties are those of very low birth weight (often prematurely born), and they illustrate how complex this infant–family–ecology interaction is. Such infants spend their early weeks relatively isolated in an incubator at a time when parent–child interaction would ordinarily be facilitating bonds of attachment. Both the social and sensory stimulation available to low-birth-weight infants is limited because of their existence in an isolette. Low-birth-weight infants are small and fragile and have an unattractive wizened appearance with little of the baby fat that makes most infants appear cuddly and appealing. Moreover, they have a high-pitched, noxious cry that most adults find annoying and disturbing (Frodi et al., 1978). It is not surprising that many parents are apprehensive or avoid contact with their-low-birth-weight infants. The stress associated with having a low-birth-weight baby affects the entire family system. A possibly positive outcome is that many fathers spend more time in child care with a low-birth-weight or premature infant than with a full-term infant because of the greater demands placed upon the caretakers. However, the divorce rate is higher among couples having a prematurely born child, suggesting that coping with a preterm infant interferes with gratifying marital relations (Liederman, 1983).

In the early weeks of life premature infants are less responsive, less vocal, and more fretful than nonpremature infants, and mothers show less face-to-face interaction, physical contact, cuddling, and smiling to premature than to full-term babies (DiVitto & Goldberg, 1979; Klaus & Kennell, 1970; Leifer, Liederman, Barnett, & Williams, 1972). This may be associated with the low sense of self-esteem and feelings of incompetence in their maternal role experienced by mothers of premature infants (Liederman, 1983). Around four to six months of age, mothers of premature babies are more vocal and attentive than mothers of nonpremature infants, apparently in an attempt to stimulate their infants.

Evidence is not consistent on the extent to which these difficulties in interaction between mothers and their premature infants continue as the children grow older; however, as with milder degrees of brain damage (see Chapter 8), the findings strongly suggest that in middle-class families differences in maternal behavior and in child development in pre- and full-term babies have largely disappeared by the end of the second year, although they continue to increase in economically deprived families (Crawford, 1982; Crnic et al., 1983; Field, Dempsey, & Schuman, 1981; Goldberg, Brachfeld, & DiVitto, 1980; Werner & Smith 1977, 1982).

In conclusion, individual differences in infants, whether resulting from genetic differences or prenatal and perinatal difficulties, may be associated with some increased risk for disturbed early parent–child relationships, which in most cases may not be long lasting. For some parents and children, however, because of multiple stressors and limited resources, these difficulties do not go away and, instead, escalate to more troublesome behavior problems at a later age, and it is in these children and their families that we have a special interest.

WHAT THE PARENT BRINGS TO THE RELATIONSHIP

Parent and child characteristics interact to produce deviant, maladaptive behavior in children. Variations in parental responses to the same degree of difficult child behavior based on differences in parents' personalities, expectations, and appraisals play an important role in the emergence of psychopathology in some children and not in others. For example, Hunter, Kilstrom, Kraybill, and Loda (1978) prospectively studied 225 infants who were either premature or ill at birth. Ten subsequently were reported as victims of child abuse during the first year of life. In contrast to the nonabusive parents, the abusive parents were more socially isolated, apathetic, and dependent and had serious marital problems, inadequate child-care arrangements, and less spacing between children. These abusive parents thus brought different personality characteristics, response dispositions, and resources to the relationship than were found in the other parents.

Other researchers have assessed maternal characteristics before birth and found correlations between these measures and maternal and infant characteristics after birth (Heinicke, Diskin, Ramsey-Klee, & Given, 1983; Moss, 1967; Robson, Pedersen, & Moss, 1969; Shereshefsky & Yarrow, 1973). Moss (1967), for example, found that mothers' acceptance of the nurturing role and general positive evaluation of babies measured 2 years before birth predicted actual responsiveness to their infants at age 3 months. Heinicke et al. (1983) found that mothers' responsiveness to infants' needs at 1, 3, 6, and 12 months was predicted by a cluster of maternal variables obtained before birth: adaptation-competence, ego strength, and basic trust. Characteristics of the maternal personality also have been found to be associated with various perinatal problems. Werner and Smith (1982) found for middle-class but not for lower-class women, that negative feelings about their pregnancy, psychological trauma experienced during the pregnancy, and anxiety shown during a prenatal interview significantly predicted such perinatal risk factors as prematurity, difficult delivery, and poor condition of the newborn (e.g., respiratory distress and convulsions). Such findings raise the possibility that maternal characteristics have already begun to have their impact on the fetus before birth.

Some parents experience psychopathological disorders of their own that interfere with adequate care of their children. Although there are findings that indicate that severity of psychopathology may be more important than type of psychopathology (Harder, Kokes, Fisher, & Strauss, 1980; Sameroff, Seifer, & Zax, 1982), some evidence is accumulating that parental depression may have a particularly adverse effect on children.

Depressed mothers are less stimulating and more hostile and rejecting to their children than are normal mothers, and this tends to disrupt child development (Orvaschel, Weissman, & Kidd, 1980). Sameroff et al. (1982) found that dysthymic mothers, relative to normal or schizophrenic mothers, are less spontaneous, vocal, and close to their child during home observations. Family environments in which there is a depressed parent are characterized by fewer shared recreational activities, less emphasis on independence of family members, less cohesion and control, and more conflict than families with normal parents (Billings & Moos, 1983). The effects of parental depression are discussed further in the section on childhood depression.

In contrast to the studies of depressed mothers, observational studies have not found striking differences between the parenting behaviors of mothers with and without a history of schizophrenia (Sameroff, Barocas, & Seifer, 1980; Schachter, Elmer, Ragins, Wimberly, & Lachin, 1977), although some trends have been found for schizophrenic mothers to be less spontaneous and less expressive. Several studies suggest, however, that separation from a schizophrenic mother during childhood is related to reduced symptomatology in these high-risk children in adolescence or young adulthood (Rieder & Nichols, 1979; Sobel, 1961; Walker, Cudeck, Mednick, & Schulsinger, 1981).

These results may seem inconsistent with some adoption studies in which rates of schizophrenia were found to be as high in children of one schizophrenic parent who were put out for adoption as in those reared by their schizophrenic parent (Gottesman & Shields, 1982). There are data, however, that suggest that the more severe the parental pathology, the more likely a child is to be placed for adoption (Sameroff & Zax, 1978). If there is a substantial genetic component to schizophrenia, this selection factor would bias adoptees toward schizophrenia relative to those children reared by their biological mothers, and thus possibly cancel out any advantage gained by being separated from a schizophrenic mother.

The general point to be made here is that before the birth of the child, parents already have behavioral dispositions, in some instances to a psychopathological degree, that can affect their subsequent interactions with their children. These interactions and their impact on children will be modified to a large degree by the stresses encountered and resources available to the family.

THE ATTACHMENT PROCESS

Infants of many species show attachment to a specific adult, usually the mother, manifested by tendencies to seek physical contact or proximity, maintain visual or auditory contact, and show distress at forced separation. Although it has long been theorized that the quality of these early attachment relationships serve as a foundation for the later social relationships and adaptive behavior of children, it is only in the past decade that a systematic body of research has been developed that examines these long-term outcomes.

The human infant develops an attachment to its mother sometime between 5 and 14 months of age with a wide range of individual differences in age of onset (Ainsworth, Blehar, Waters, & Wall, 1978). Ainsworth and her associates have developed a standardized procedure called the strange situation for measuring attachment that relies heavily on the behavior of infants when their mother departs and when they are reunited with their mother after a period of separation. Infants' attachment behaviors are classified as *secure*, *insecure-avoidant*, or *insecure-ambivalent* on the basis, respectively, of proximity-seeking, avoidant, or angry-resistant responses to reunion. Classifications of infants of middle-class parents into these categories have been found to be stable between 12 and 18 months of age (D. B. Connell, as reported in Ainsworth et al., 1978; Waters, 1978). The style of interaction between mothers and their infants during the first few months of life have been found to be related to these attachment categories assessed at one year of age. Thus, mothers of securely attached infants were more responsive to their infants' cries, held their babies more tenderly and carefully, paced the interaction more contingently during face-to-face interaction, and exhibited greater sensitivity in initiating and terminating feeding (Ainsworth et al., 1978).

According to Ainsworth and her colleagues, securely attached infants can use the mother as a base from which to explore, manipulate the environment, and thus develop confidence in their competencies. The insecurely (or anxiously) attached infants would seem to be at some risk for future adjustment difficulties. Several studies support this possibility. Securely attached infants have been demonstrated to be better adjusted over at least the first five years of life. They are more enthusiastic, positive in mood, and cooperative in their relations with others in the home, in the school, and in the peer group and are more persistent, flexible, and resourceful in problem solving (Arend, Gove, & Sroufe, 1979; Matas, Arend, & Sroufe, 1978; Waters, Wippman, & Sroufe, 1979).

The finding that disruptions in attachment are related to disruptions in later extrafamilial relationships may be particularly important in understanding the development of psychopathology in children. Children's peer interactions and play not only provide a critical opportunity in which to acquire social competencies but also have been found to play an important role in working through or modifying problem behavior (Hartup, 1983). In addition, age-inappropriate play, disruptions in play, and unpopularity with peers consistently have been found to be related to stress, anxiety, and emotional disturbance in children (Hartup, 1983). These findings suggest that the pattern of early attachment to the mother develops attitudes, affect, sensitivity, security, and social skills that enhance or impede the later development of social relationships.

Most infants form attachments to more than one member of the family, and with increasing age the spectrum of people to whom the child is attached may expand. Even in infancy the mother is not the primary object of attachment for all children. A systems view would naturally make us curious about attachment to father. Studies in which the same infant's attachment to both parents has been assessed find no consistency (Main & Weston, 1981) or a very small degree of consistency (Lamb, 1978) between the attachment patterns to mothers and to fathers. This differential tendency to attach to father and to mother suggests that attachment amounts to more than individual differences in infant characteristics and is to a substantial extent an interactional outcome between the infant and each parent.

It has been found that attachment to the father enhances the quality of mother–child interactions (Easterbrooks & Goldberg, 1984). Paternal involvement, behavioral sensitivity, and attitudes appear to be strongly related to children's affect, frustration, attentiveness, and persistence in problem-solving tasks (Easterbrooks & Goldberg, 1984). Main and Weston (1981) also found that the positive correlates of secure attachment, as measured by social competence in another situation, were enhanced if the infant was securely attached to both parents; or, conversely, the negative correlates of insecure attachment to one parent were reduced if the infant was securely attached to the other parent.

We have already suggested that both infant and maternal characteristics present at birth contribute to the quality of mother–infant interaction in the early months, and by extrapolation one might expect these same variables to play a role in the later development of attachment. Indeed, there is evidence that infants who are temperamentally difficult in the first few months have a higher likelihood of being classified as insecure-ambivalent in their attachment at one year, although there is not yet evidence of a relationship between early temperament and the insecure-avoidant category (Ainsworth et al., 1978; Waters, Vaughn, & Egeland, 1980). In considering these results along with the relative lack of consistency of attachment behavior to mother and to father, it would seem that, although infant temperament contributes something to the attachment process, much of the variance must be explained in terms of the interactional histories of each parent–child dyad.

Again we must emphasize that family interaction can be understood only in relation to the larger social setting in which it occurs. Crockenberg (1981) brought together infant temperament, parenting, and ecological variables in one study. Measures of infant irritability in the first 10 days, maternal responsiveness in mother–infant interaction at 3 months, and social support assessed by interview at 3 months were all related to infant attachment at one year. Social support, which included support from the father as well as relatives and other people, served as an important moderator variable. High infant irritability in the first 10 days was associated with insecure attachment only within the low-social-support group. It is possible that mothers who had irritable infants but who also had strong social supports may have been able to interact with their infants in ways that prevented the development of insecure attachment. Just how social support mediates this beneficial effect or how lack of social support mediates the more disturbed outcome remains to be studied. It might be suggested that a mother who is enjoying supportive relationships would get some relief time and assistance which would make it easier to be relaxed and attentive to her infant and not so easily frustrated by a "difficult" infant. Recall that Crnic et al. (1983) also found that social support from spouse or lover was associated with more positive mother–infant interaction at 4 months.

Other studies have found that when shifts in attachment categories occur, they seem to be related to changes in parenting, stresses, and social support. A decrease in life stresses and an increase in social supports and caretaking competence is associated with a shift toward secure attachment in the second year of life and the reverse experiences are related to shifts from initial secure attachment to later insecure attachment (Egeland & Farber, 1984; Vaughn, Egeland, & Sroufe, 1979). Overall, then, research suggests the likelihood that, in addition to infant temperament and individual parental characteristics, security of infant attachment is influenced by the stressfulness of life circumstances and by the social supports available to the parents.

Families with School Aged Children and Adolescents

THE INTERACTIONAL DYNAMICS OF RESPONSIVENESS AND CONTROL

In attempts to describe parent–child interaction, two dimensions of parenting behavior consistently emerge. The first is a dimension dealing with the emotional relationship with the child and ranges from warm, responsive, child-centered behavior to rejecting, unresponsive behavior. The second dimension is a demandingness/control dimension, which ranges from restrictive demands and control strategies based on the greater power of the parent to parenting behavior that is undemanding, permissive, and low in control attempts. The interaction of these two dimensions produces a fourfold pattern of parenting (Table 9.1). It is not the effect of a single parenting attribute but the interaction among them that leads to different outcomes for children.

In any interaction there is some mutual influence, and therefore each person is, in a sense, exerting some control over the other. Issues of control, however, become more salient when one person is trying to get the other to do something that the other is not particularly inclined to do, as is fre-

TABLE 9.1 *A Two-dimensional Classification of Parenting*

	Accepting, Responsive, Child-centered	Rejecting, Unresponsive Parent-centered
Demanding, Controlling	Authoritative-reciprocal, high in bidirectional communication	Authoritarian power-assertive
Undemanding, Low in Control Attempts	Indulgent	Neglecting, ignoring, indifferent, uninvolved

Source: From Maccoby and Martin (1983, p. 39).

quently the case in the socialization process. Depending on the types of controlling strategies used and the affectional relationship, difficulties in interaction or symptomatic behavior may develop.

Let us consider the classic longitudinal study by Baumrind (1967, 1971) to illustrate some developmental correlates of both the warmth/responsiveness and control domains. On the basis of observer ratings, Baumrind (1967) identified three groups of children from a larger group of three- to four-year-old nursery school children. Baumrind's Group I (the energetic, friendly group) was composed of children rated higher than either of the other two groups on each of the following: self-reliance; approach to novel or stressful situations with interest and curiosity; confidence; self-control in situations requiring some appropriate restraint; high energy level; achievement orientation; cheerful mood; and friendly peer relations—clearly a psychologically healthy set of youngsters. Group II children (the conflicted-irritable group) when compared to Group III children (the impulsive-aggressive group) were more passively hostile, guileful, unhappy in mood, and vulnerable to stress, but they did more careful work. Group III children were more purely impulsive and lacking in self-discipline but also more cheerful; they also recovered from expressions of annoyance more quickly than did Group II children.

Parent behavior was assessed by a 3-hour unstructured home observation, a 40-minute structured, laboratory observation of mother–child interaction, and an interview. Parents of the friendly resilient children in Group I, relative to parents in both other groups, exerted more general control over the child's behavior and did not succumb to the child's coercion and nagging; made more demands for mature, age-appropriate behavior; engaged in more open communication with the child in which reasons were given; more often solicited the child's opinion; occasionally retracted a demand on the basis of the child's experience; and used more open rather than disguised means of influence. They were also more responsive and nurturant as indicated by a greater use of positive reinforcement and lesser use of punishment. Thus we have an *authoritative* parent who is loving and responsive to the child's needs, and explains things to the child but is willing to impose clearly communicated restrictions when they are deemed appropriate. In contrast the parents of the unhappy, withdrawn, conflicted children in Group II were somewhat less demanding but more rigid in their control attempts, as well as intrusive and lacking in sensitivity and nurturance. They seldom considered their children's needs and feelings, did not communicate the reasons for their demands, and were willing to use hostile power-assertive forms of discipline such as physical punishment in order to control their children's behavior. Finally, parents of the impulsive, immature, aggressive children in Group III had reasonably affectionate relationships with their children but were reluctant to exert control, particularly in the face of the child's opposition. Their lax, inconsistent discipline was associated with the development of uncontrolled impulsive behavior in their children.

Baumrind (as reported in Maccoby & Martin, 1983) reassessed the families when the children were eight to nine years old and found that authoritative parenting continued to be associated with positive outcomes for children and that responsive, firm parent–child relationships were especially important in the development of competence in sons. Baumrind's work has been extremely important in countering the permissive child-rearing movement that was rampant in the 1950s and 1960s. Her emphasis on the importance of firm, consistent parental control in a context of nurturance and sensitivity to the child's needs as precursors of the development of social and cognitive effectance in children, however, is not accepted by all psychologists.

WHAT IS THE OPTIMUM LEVEL OF CONTROL?
Stayton, Hogan, and Ainsworth (1971) argue that parental tactics of control are not so important and suggest that human infants are genetically disposed to acquire self-restraints and to comply with adult demands if provided with an ordinary, predictable social environment, and that no specialized training procedures are required. Their finding that young children's internalized controls were correlated with maternal sensitivity to the child's needs but not to frequency of verbal commands or physical interventions was taken as support for this view. Lewis (1981) likewise suggests that Baumrind (1967) has gone too far in emphasizing firm control and that such a view is counter to a body of experimental research on attribution theory. Attribution research finds that strong external controls seem to produce a reduction in internalization of standards, whereas the least degree of external control sufficient to elicit compliance is associated with the greatest internalization. Attribution theory, in other words, would suggest that the least degree of external parental control needed to obtain compliance rather than strict disciplinary practices would be associated with more self-control and responsibility in children.

Lewis (1981) reevaluated Baumrind's (1967) results and concluded that the measures of parental control in that study could have reflected an absence of parent–child conflict or the child's willingness to obey rather than the parents' willingness to exercise control. Baumrind (1983) concedes that extreme degrees of parental control, especially when not accompanied by those characteristics subsumed under warmth, may well be associated with noncompliance in children, particularly in adolescence. Perhaps Baumrind has overstated to some extent the importance of firm control, but Lewis (1981) and Stayton et al. (1971) may have gone too far in the opposite direction in playing down the importance of parental control. Empirical data cannot clearly resolve the issue at this time, although two studies should be mentioned that would seem to suggest that maternal sensitivity is at least as important as maternal control as a correlate of child compliance. In one study Lytton (1977, 1980) found that harmonious mother–child relationships are likely to exist when 30-month-old boys complied with maternal requests *and* the mothers complied with their boys' requests. In a second study, Schaffer and Crook (1980) studied child compliance and maternal control techniques at even earlier ages, 15 and 24 months, and found that mothers' success in obtaining compliance to requests was greatly facilitated by the mothers' sensitivity to the child's attentional state at the time of the request:

> . . . *a request for action coming out of the blue has little chance of suc-ceeding; such a request must be part of a sequential strategy, the first step of which is to ensure that the child is appropriately oriented. . . . Thus even the imposition of controls by an adult or a child represents a dyadic process, in the sense that both the behavior of the adult and the outcome are a function of the child's initial state. By successfully manipulating this state, the parent can avoid the clash-of-wills that is so often portrayed as typical of all socialization efforts, whereby compliance is supposedly ex-tracted from an invariably reluctant child. (p. 60)*

It should be noted that these results are compatible with Baumrind's position, which emphasizes the importance of both responsiveness and control.

What would seem to be left out of this controversy, although not entirely by Lewis (1981), are individual differences in the infant or child. As most parents of more than one child know, some children are easier to deal with than others. The principle derived from attribution theory has a key qualification; namely, internalization is maximum when the *minimum* control necessary to produce compliance is used. Some infants probably require higher minimum levels of control to gain compliance in the first place. Does that mean that these infants will develop less internalization of parental requests? Possibly. The harmonious mother–child interaction described in these studies is reminiscent of the kind of early infancy interaction that predicts secure attachment at 12 months of age, which also was found by Crockenberg (1981) to be affected by infant temperament. One might speculate, for example, that Baumrind's Group I children would have shown secure attachments to one or both parents at one year of age, and possibly had malleable temperaments in the first months of life.

It can be seen that the Baumrind tripartite parenting typology does not deal with the fourth parenting style falling in the lower right-hand quadrant of Table 9.1. These parents are detached, neglecting, uninvolved parents who focus on their own needs rather than the needs of the child. Responsible parenting is too much trouble for them, and they wish to spend as little time and effort involved with the child as possible (Maccoby & Martin, 1983). Such parenting is sometimes found in depressed parents (Egeland & Sroufe, 1981) or in parents undergoing severe stress such as marital discord or divorce when parents are focused on solving their own problems rather than those of the child (Hetherington et al., 1982).

In infants, lack of parental involvement is associated with disruptions in attachment (Egeland & Sroufe, 1981); in older children it is associated with aggression, noncompliance, impulsivity, moodiness, and low self-esteem (Block, 1971). When parents abdicate their parenting responsibilities, their adolescent and young adult offspring tend to have problems with delinquency (Patterson, 1982), alcohol, precocious sexuality, encounters with the law, truancy, and undesirable companions (Pulkkinen, 1982). Such children, who are alienated from their families, have problems that flood over into a broad range of social and cognitive areas.

In conclusion, the processes involved in responsiveness and control are most profitably viewed in interactive terms. Harmonious interactions between parent and child are more likely to result when parental control efforts are sensitive and moderated by the infant's or child's state, in other words, accompanied by many of the qualities we have summarized as responsiveness and warmth. When parental control efforts are insensitive to the child's state or at the other extreme when little or no effort at control is made, there is again a mutual control process but with results not so harmonious. Characteristics and experiences that both parent and child bring to their relationship will influence the future course of the interaction.

The Sibling System

The two aspects of the sibling system that have been investigated most frequently in relation to the development of psychopathology in children are family size and birth order. A few enterprising investigators have also attempted to consider sex of the siblings and age spacing between siblings. When all of the possible combinations of these four significant factors are considered, some of the complexity in studying the sibling system can be seen.

In conceptualizing the impact of family size and sibling configuration on the adjustment of the child, one must consider the effect of these factors both on parent–child relations and on sibling relations.

FAMILY SIZE

In large families discipline tends to become more authoritarian and severe, with roles and responsibilities more precisely assigned (Bossard & Boll, 1960). There is more use of restrictive, hostile maternal control, particularly toward daughters in large families (Nuttall & Nuttall, 1971). It is not surprising that as the task overload that accompanies multiple children increases, there is less parental warmth, attention, and supervision toward children and more assignment of caretaking, teaching, and disciplinary roles to older siblings, especially older girls (Cicirelli, 1982). With this configuration of family relationships, the finding that children from large families are more independent, lower in academic achievement, but more aggressive and antisocial than children from smaller families is not unexpected (Burgess, Kimball, & Burgess, 1978; Rutter, Tizard, & Whitmore, 1970).

In small families, anxiety-withdrawal disorders are more prevalent (Riess, 1976; Rosenberg & Sutton-Smith, 1964; Rutter & Graham, 1970). However, differences in socioeconomic status and intelligence levels have not been well controlled in most of the research on family size. It is plausible to think that family size might have some direct association with aggression in that parents would have less time to monitor the behavior of any individual child, and sibling interaction would have a greater influence on child behavior. Conversely, in small families there is greater opportunity for the parents to be overly intrusive and controlling with their children, a common correlate of anxiety-withdrawal disorders. As we will discuss in the section on conduct disorders, Patterson (1982) provides data suggesting that sibling interactions are also especially influential in the development of aggressive behavior.

THE SIBLING CONFIGURATION

With family size and socioeconomic level controlled, research has not shown strong tendencies for adult psychopathology to be related to sibling position (Wagner, Schubert, & Schubert, 1979). With respect to children, however, there is some suggestive evidence that firstborns, especially males, and perhaps middle-borns are more vulnerable to psychological difficulties than are siblings in other positions.

Being Firstborn: Help or Hindrance? Four studies with children indicate that, with family size controlled, firstborn males are more likely to have psychological problems than are later-born males (Fishbein, 1981; Lahey, Hammer, Crumrine, & Forehand, 1980; Tuckman & Regan, 1967). In only two of these studies did firstborn girls show greater frequencies of problem behavior. One other study, which included boys and girls not analyzed separately, also found firstborns to have more problems (Shrader & Leventhal, 1968). Lahey et al. (1980) reported two studies, and in their second study firstborn boys showed more symptoms of an acting-out, aggressive behavior as well as of more internalizing, anxious behavior. Since these behaviors were rated by teachers, the results cannot be explained in terms of parents reporting more symptomatic behavior because of more anxious involvement with firstborns.

There is one important discordant finding in the literature. Werner and Smith (1982) found more firstborn males among children who were resilient in the face of being low birth weight and living in poverty. This finding suggests that the firstborn effect may be moderated by severe poverty where the additional attention provided to firstborns outweighs other factors. The severely impoverished, however, would represent a very small proportion of families attending most child guidance clinics.

What factors in family relations might facilitate the unusual combination of competencies and vulnerabilities of firstborns? The most obvious factor is the individual attention given to firstborns in the first year or two of life. Although the birth of a second child causes the mother to become more negative (Lasko, 1954), these effects are further amplified if the firstborn is male or has a difficult temperament and if the mother is depressed (Dunn & Kendrick, 1981; Nadelman & Begun, 1982). However, greater participation in the care of the firstborn by the father following the birth of a second child may counter the child's feeling of displacement and jealousy (Lamb, 1979).

The age spacing between firstborns and second-borns may be an important factor. Lasko (1954) reported that both first- and second-borns were more distressed by the birth of a younger sibling for intermediate age spacings (2 to 3 years) than for either shorter or longer spacings. For male adolescent firstborns (excluding only children), Kidwell (1981) also found a curvilinear relationship between spacing of the next younger sibling and perceived parental support. Parents were perceived as least supportive if the next younger sibling was two to four years different in age and most supportive is the next younger sibling was either one year or five years different in age. Kidwell suggests that the two- to four-year spacing accentuates the feeling of having to share the parents' time and other resources. For a one-year spacing the child has had only a short period of time in which parental attention was unshared; for the five-year spacing he or she has had a long period of unshared attention.

In spite of the disruptive effects of the birth of a sibling, there seems to be a special relation between firstborns and their parents both in infancy and childhood. Parents tend to be more stimulating, affectionate, and attentive with the firstborn than second-born infants, especially if the second-born is a female (Jacobs & Moss, 1976). As firstborn children grow older, parents continue to have higher expectations and make greater demands for achievement of firstborns, especially firstborn boys (Cushna, 1966; Hilton, 1967; Rothbart, 1971) and they use more power-assertive forms of discipline such as physical punishment to enforce their demands. This is associated with the greater disciplinary friction found between parents and their firstborn children.

The unique role of the firstborn child, who has more responsibility and power in relation to his or her less mature siblings, leads to both more antagonistic, aggressive bullying behavior and more nurturant, prosocial behavior toward their younger siblings (Abramovitch, Pepler, & Corter, 1982). Although much research has focused on sibling rivalry and the negative aspects of sibling relationships, siblings, particularly as they grow older, often have extremely close supportive relationships that serve as a major resource in times of stress (Bank & Kahn, 1982).

Middle-borns   There is evidence that aggressive children more often fall in the middle ordinal position (Anderson, 1969; Rutter et al., 1970). Patterson (1982) speculates that the ideal situation in which aggression can be learned is one in which an older sibling or parent serves as an occasional aggressive model and there is an abundant supply of younger siblings to be victims. Although some studies have found lower self-esteem in middle-borns than either first- or later-borns, overall the results are inconsistent (see Nystul, 1974, and Schooler, 1972, for reviews). Kidwell (1982), however, has shown that with family size controlled, the age spacing of the siblings is an important moderator variable. In her study of adolescent males, middle-born subjects reported lower self-esteem than either firstborns or later-borns, an effect that was greatly accentuated when the average age spacing to the nearest older and younger sibling was two years. At smaller or larger average age differences, the middle-borns were only slightly lower in self-esteem. Achieving status, affection, and recognition from parents may be more difficult for middle-borns, especially with age spacings of about two years. Kidwell (1981) also found that male adolescents, all sibling positions combined, perceived their parents as more punitive the fewer the number of years between the subject and his closest sibling. In addition, with all sibling positions combined, males perceived greater parental punitiveness when the closest sibling was a female, with the perceived punitiveness being a curvilinear function of nearness in age—a spacing of two to three years showing the most perceived punitiveness.

The overwhelming majority of children in any one position in the sibling configuration do not, however, develop psychological disorders. The observed trends suggest that when certain other family interactional dispositions are present, being in a particular sibling position can increase the probability that symptoms will develop.

THE RELATION OF FAMILY INTERACTION AND CHILDHOOD PSYCHOPATHOLOGY

The question of interest to many investigators is whether different patterns of family relations are associated with specific types of childhood psychopathology. It can be seen from our previous discussion that this is a very difficult question to answer because of the many individual, experiential, developmental, and ecological factors that modify that relationship.

Since familial correlates of attention deficit disorder, autism, schizophrenia, substance abuse, and psychosomatic disorders have been reviewed earlier (Chapters 4, 5, 6, and 7), this section will focus on two categories of childhood disorders: those behaviors that lead to disruption and suffering for others (conduct disorders) and those disorders that result largely in discomfort and suffering for the child (anxiety-withdrawal and dysphoric disorders).

Perhaps because of their greater negative social impact, more research has focused on conduct disorders, particularly in the form of excessive aggression or juvenile delinquency, than on other disorders.

Conduct Disorders

As was noted in Chapters 1 and 2, conduct disorder comprises an extremely heterogeneous group of behaviors including temper tantrums, excessive quarreling, fighting, stealing, disobedience, truancy, firesetting, and assault, but can be profitably viewed as two dimensional: undersocialized and socialized. Patterson (1982) has argued that children of both dimensions share a common attribute of noncompliance. Both the argumentative, teasing, violent, boastful behavior of the undersocialized and the stealing, truancy, vandalism, loitering, and consorting with bad companions of the socialized group are associated with parents who permit children to disobey and who allow their children to be out of control. Patterson (1982) proposes that the drift toward continued psychopathology in adulthood occurs when this early excessively coercive, noncompliant behavior is combined with a lack of social and academic skills. When the coercive child fails to learn social skills and simple work skills in the home, the child has later difficulty in relations with peers, in forming intimate relations, and in acquiring academic and occupational competencies. The competencies of the socially or academically skilled child serve as moderating factors and make the child less likely to be labeled as deviant as well as providing outlets for personal gratification and success experiences. There is a substantial body of research literature demonstrating that conduct-disordered adolescents frequently are lacking in interpersonal, academic, and work skills (Dishion, Loeber, Stouthamer-Loeber, & Patterson, 1984). Thus, in Patterson's view it is not early excessive noncompliance or the lack of social and work skills alone, but the combination of these factors that leads to long-term deviant outcomes.

PARENTAL CHARACTERISTICS AND CONDUCT DISORDERS

A survey of the research literature suggests that deviant parents have deviant children (Rutter, 1966). Social learning theorists have emphasized imitation of an antisocial, aggressive or criminal model as one of the important factors in the development of antisocial behavior in children (Bandura & Walters, 1963; Berkowitz, 1962). Parents of children with conduct disorders have been found to be maladjusted, inconsistent, arbitrary, and given to explosive expressions of anger. Mothers are often depressed, tense, angry, and nonconforming (Goodstein & Rowley, 1961; Wolking, Dunteman, & Bailery, 1967; Patterson, 1982), while fathers of children with conduct disorders are inadequate and emotionally distant, and have been reported to score high on the clinical scales of the MMPI (Johnson & Lobitz, 1974). Maternal irritability and depression have been found to play particularly important roles in the development of aggressive behavior in children (Hetherington et al., 1982; Patterson, 1982). Depressed, irritable, negativistic, socially isolated mothers are not only more likely to perceive their children's behavior more negatively (Forehand, Wells, & Griest, 1980; Olweus, 1980) but also may respond more aversively to their behavior (Wahler, 1979). Although irritability in fathers also is correlated with conduct disorders in children, it seems to be less important because fathers in these families often participate minimally in child rearing (Patterson, 1982). It has been suggested that the depression, low self-esteem, and irritability of mothers of children with conduct disorders may in part be a secondary reaction to their failure in parental control and to the chronic high level of coercive behaviors they experience from their children. This possibility is supported by findings from several recent studies (Hetherington et al., 1982; Patterson, 1982; Forehand et al., 1980) that found that maternal depression decreased and feeling of self-esteem and efficacy increased after successful treatment or reduction of antisocial or oppositional behavior in children.

These findings parallel those of studies of parents of delinquents that show a high frequency of deviant or criminal behavior and less mature moral judgments in families of delinquents. Mothers of delinquents show a lower level of moral judgment on Kohlberg's structured moral dilemmas than do mothers of nondelinquents (Hudgins & Prentice, 1973). These differences between parents of delinquents and nondelinquents are not confined to ethical judgments but extend to antisocial behavior. Glueck and Glueck (1950) found that 84 percent of the delinquents in Massachusetts reformatories had families that included criminals. McCord and McCord (1958) found that a criminal father and cold mother in combination presented the combination of parental characteristics most likely to lead to delinquency, particularly if the father was also cruel and neglecting. Where mothers were lacking in affection and served as a deviant model, delinquency was also frequent. However, consistent discipline or affection from one parent could partially counteract the effects of a criminal role model. This effect of a good relationship with one parent partially buffering the adverse effects of a poor relationship or negative attribute of the other parent has been demonstrated in a number of studies (Hetherington & Frankie, 1967; Hetherington et al., 1982; O'Leary, 1984; Rutter, 1983). In a long-term follow-up of these boys, who had been studied first when they were between 5 and 13 years old, McCord (1979) found that parent aggressiveness, paternal alcoholism and criminality, and lack of maternal self-control were associated with the number of serious crimes later committed by their adult sons.

It could be argued that the relationship between negative parental characteristics and conduct disorders is genetic, and certainly biological factors are important in this relationship (see Chapter 2). However, cross-fostering studies show that criminality in sons is more common when both the biolog-ical and adoptive fathers have criminal records than when criminality oc-curs only in one of the fathers (Hutchings & Mednick, 1974). Thus there seems to be an interaction between genetic susceptibility and adverse family factors in precipitating antisocial behavior in children.

PARENT–CHILD INTERACTION AND CONDUCT DISORDERS

Studies using interviews and questionnaires have documented certain pat-terns of family relations in families in which there is an antisocial or delin-quent child (for reviews of this literature see Maccoby & Martin, 1983; Mar-tin, 1975; Parke & Slaby, 1983; Patterson, 1982). Parents in these families have been found to be rejecting, to use harsh, power-assertive punishment, to model aggressive or criminal behavior and to be erratically permissive and inconsistent in enforcing rules. However, it is not just whether parents are permissive or restricting in attempting to control their child that is asso-ciated with conduct disorders in children, but also the type of reinforce-ments and punishments they use and the manner in which they are adminis-tered as well as the children's behaviors targeted by parents for their control attempts. Not all parents find the same behaviors equally objectionable; some parents may tolerate aggression but respond aversively to lying or theft, others may ignore stealing but ruthlessly suppress disobedience. Ob-servational studies and studies examining configurations of family relation-ships have allowed us to examine and clarify some of the interactive pro-cesses underlying the correlations found among relatively global interview and questionnaire measures. Moreover, some recent studies suggest that not only may we be able to discriminate between families of nondeviant children and those with conduct disorders but also that we may be able to differenti-ate between patterns of family interaction associated with the development of antisocial aggression and with stealing.

Studies involving direct observations of behavior have confirmed that parents of aggressive or clinic-referred children show more rejection toward their children (Bugental, Love, Kaswan, & April, 1971; Oleinick, Bahn, Eisenberg, & Lilienfeld, 1966; Patterson, 1982; Schulman, Shoemaker, & Moelis, 1962). It is the way in which they express this disapproval, however, that distinguishes them most markedly from parents of nondeviant children. They issue more commands (Terdal, Jackson, & Garner, 1976) and punish deviant behavior more frequently (Sallows, 1973), but the proportion of de-viant behaviors punished does not differ from that in nonclinic populations (Patterson, 1976). Their children are just emitting a higher frequency and rate of deviant behaviors. In addition, parents of aggressive children are more likely to actually respond positively to deviant child behavior (Sal-lows, 1973; Wahler, 1968) and aversively to nondeviant behavior (Lobitz & Johnson, 1975; Patterson, 1982). Parents of aggressive children are responding to their children's behavior—but in a noncontingent manner. Perhaps it is because of a history of these inappropriate reinforcement contingencies that aggressive children are less responsive to rewards and punishments that are dispensed by adults and parents, particularly by mothers (Patterson, 1982). Whereas parental punishment may inhibit responses in nondeviant children, it accelerates coercive behavior in aggressive children. Punishment, in other words, has its intended effect for normal children but has the opposite effect with antisocial children of increasing the behavior it is supposed to decrease.

Patterson (1982) suggested that this effect may result from the fact that although parents, especially mothers, of antisocial children engage in much scolding, threatening, and other aversive responses, they do not enforce their threats with firm, consistent consequences. Furthermore, the parent gives in to the accelerating coerciveness on the part of the child on enough occasions to achieve an effective partial reinforcement schedule. Mothers in these families are especially vulnerable to falling into the "reinforcement trap," that is, yielding to and thus reinforcing their child's coercive behavior in order to gain immediate relief at the expense of even more coercive behavior in the future. Because of their poor parenting skills, mothers of aggressive children create a situation where family members accelerate their coercive behaviors. These mothers get trapped in a coercive cycle of their own making. Their inept skills make them more likely to be the instigators and the targets of coercive behavior by their children and less able to terminate chains of coercive behavior. This leads to feelings of helplessness in the mother that intensify her ineptness as a parent.

Quay has suggested that this coercive cycle may initially have been, at least partly, set in motion by a physiologically based combination of stimulus-seeking and resistance to the effects of both physical and social punishments (Quay, 1977; see also Chapter 1). Such a noxious combination of child attributes could contribute to parental frustration and the triggering of a coercive cycle. However, Patterson emphasizes not only the critical role played in temperamental predispositions to be irritable in family members but also the roles of the daily hassles and life stresses that increase the probability of irascible responses.

Several studies have found that boys are more likely to get involved in coercive cycles and are less likely to comply to parental commands than are girls (Hetherington et al., 1982; Lytton & Zwirner, 1975). In addition, patterns of parental punishment associated with compliance and aggression differ for boys and girls.

In summary, the parenting pattern for the development of undersocialized conduct disorders appears to be one where family members are irritable and enmeshed. The parent responds coercively to a wide array of child behaviors but is inept in carrying through threats and punishing the child for noncompliant behavior. Escalating cycles of coercive behavior, particularly between mothers and sons, are likely to be found in such families.

How does this pattern differ from that found in families of children who have socialized conduct disorders; who commit crimes against property, vandalize, or steal? We might call the parents of such children parent centered rather than child centered. They are focused on gratification of their own needs and are more distant and unfriendly although less coercive than parents of undersocialized aggressive children (Patterson, 1982). They are uninvolved in the role of caretaker but they are sufficiently skilled in managing their children to suppress overt coercive behavior toward themselves or among siblings. Their disengagement extends to a lack of monitoring of their children's activities outside of the home.

In addition to their lack of parental involvement, these parents show a remarkable lack of concern with property violations and interpret such acts by their children so as to make them seem acceptable, and hence such behavior goes unpunished. When their children steal, these parents do not recognize that a serious problem exists. This may in part be because these parents view themselves as being rebellious and nonconforming and probably also mislabel their own antisocial behavior. This combination of an antisocial role model and systematic misclassification of crimes against property may be related to the finding that many delinquents believe that their antisocial acts are justifiable.

Following our earlier discussion of the importance of parental involvment, monitoring, and control, it is not surprising to find that these parent-centered families are more likely to produce adolescents and young adults who are truant, have drinking problems, are precociously sexually active, have a record of arrests, and spend time on the streets with friends who are disliked by the parents (Pulkkinen, 1982). Moreover, as would be predicted by Patterson, their delinquency often is associated with a wide array of social and cognitive incompetencies, in relations with peers and adults, in achievement and school performance, and in the world of work (Patterson, 1982; Pulkkinen, 1982).

FAMILY CONFLICT AND THE DEVELOPMENT OF CONDUCT DISORDERS

Family conflict has been associated with both anxiety-withdrawal (Gassner & Murray, 1969) and conduct disorders (Block, Block, & Morrison, 1981; Chawla & Gupt, 1979; Emery & O'Leary, 1982; Hetherington et al., 1982; Oltmanns, Broderick, & O'Leary, 1977; Porter & O'Leary, 1980; Rutter, 1971; Whitehead, 1979). However, family conflict seems to be more closely related to the development of conduct disorders than anxiety disorders. Moreover, this relationship more often is found in boys than in girls and is somewhat stronger in clinic than nonclinic populations (see Emery, 1982, for a review). Rutter (1971), for example, studied a sample of London families in which one or both parents had been under psychiatric care. When marriages were rated as "good," and there was little marital conflict, none of the boys showed antisocial behavior, compared with 22 percent when the marriage was "fair," and 39 percent when the marriage was "very poor." The quality of the marriage would seem to have outweighed the effect of having one parent who had experienced a psychiatric disorder. In addition, Rutter found that the association between marital conflict and the son's antisocial behavior was strongly affected by whether or not the son had a good relationship with one or both parents. When the marital relationship was "very poor" and the son had a good relationship with one or both parents, 38 percent were antisocial; when the son had a poor relationship with both parents and the marital relationship was "very poor," almost 90 percent were antisocial. Research has also shown that the relationship between marital conflict and antisocial behavior in sons is stronger when the conflict is overt than when it is more covert or the marriage is characterized by apathy (Hetherington et al., 1982; Porter & O'Leary, 1980).

One can advance a number of explanations for the obtained association between severity of marital conflict and conduct disorders in boys. Parents who engage in overt conflict with each other may also be the kind of people who engage in more harsh and punitive disciplinary practices with their children, a well established correlate of antisocial behavior in children (Martin, 1975). In addition, these parents are providing clear models of aggressive behavior. Furthermore, if parents who engage in more dramatic displays of overt conflict tend also to be generally more impulsive and erratic in their behavior, they might well be more inconsistent in their disciplinary tactics than parents who show less overt conflict. As we have noted, inconsistency of discipline also has been found to characterize parents of antisocial children. However, perhaps causality works the other way. It may be that an aggressive, acting-out child produces tensions between the parents, but one bit of data does not support this interpretation of cause and effect. Oltmanns et al., (1977) found that marital satisfaction did not increase after problem behavior in children had been successfully decreased by a therapeutic intervention. Another possibility, suggested largely by family therapists (e.g., Minuchin & Fishman, 1981), is that children may develop behavior problems in order to draw attention to themselves and distract the parents from their conflicts. Of course, if this were successful, then we should not find a strong association between child problems and overt marital conflict. Yet another possibility is that a parent who is dissatisfied with the marriage may substitute a child for the spouse and the resulting over-involvement may engender behavior problems. There is no clear empirical support for either of these explanations.

Emery, Weintraub, and Neale (1982) examined the relationship between marital conflict and problem behaviors at school for children who had a parent diagnosed as schizophrenic, unipolar depression, bipolar depression, or with both parents normal. Children with a schizophrenic or affectively disordered parent were rated by both teachers and peers as more aggressive and as more withdrawn than children of normal parents. However, the investigators found significant correlations between marital dissatisfaction and teacher ratings of disruptiveness and inattention and peer ratings of aggression only for the children of a unipolar or a bipolar depressed parent but not for children of a schizophrenic or normal parent. In addition, partial correlation analyses indicated that the relationship between having an affectively disordered parent and children's disturbed behavior in school was largely accounted for by the degree of marital discord. When there was no marital discord in families with an affectively disordered parent, the children's school behavior was not rated differently than those with normal parents. The authors suggest that the effect of an affectively disturbed parent is largely transmitted environmentally via a disturbed marriage, whereas the effect of a schizophrenic parent may occur primarily through genetic transmission. Given the consistent sex differences found in most other studies it is unfortunate that the authors did not analyze their data by sex or at least report the sex composition of their samples.

It is of considerable interest that the relationship between marital conflict and conduct disorders is so much stronger for boys than for girls. One explanation is that boys respond to marital conflict with antisocial behavior, which is easily observed and is noxious to other people, whereas girls react to marital conflict in a more internalizing way with anxiety and withdrawal and are less likely to be referred to clinicians. Two studies of nonclinic samples (Block et al., 1981; Whitehead, 1979) did find that marital conflict was related to aggressive, acting-out behavior in boys and, to a lesser degree, to more anxious, withdrawn behavior in girls. Studies of clinical samples have not found that either conduct disorders or anxiety-withdrawal disorders were associated with marital conflict in girls (Emery & O'Leary, 1982; Gassner & Murray, 1969; Porter & O'Leary, 1980; Rutter, 1971). Another explanation is that parents are more likely to expose their sons than their daughters to conflict and to other stressors and that boys receive less support and protection during stressful life events than do girls (Hetherington et al., 1982). This seems to be the case during such stressful transitions as divorce (Hetherington et al., 1982) or birth of a younger sibling (Dunn & Kendrick, 1981). Finally, it has been proposed that males may be biologically predisposed to experience stresses such as family conflict more aversively and hence be more vulnerable to the effects of difficult life situations. Recent evidence (Gottman, 1984) suggests that differences in responses of the autonomic nervous system of males and females may underly the tendency of husbands to withdraw or stonewall and of wives to nag and persist in the face of marital disagreements.

Whatever the underlying causal factors may be, males have been found to be more vulnerable to a wide range of stressors including family conflict to such an extent that some authors refer to females as "the buffered sex." In the longitudinal study of children on the island of Kauai (see Chapter 8), it is notable that substantially more high-risk girls than boys were resilient and recovered rapidly in the face of adverse pre- and perinatal factors and poor family environments. The investigators put forth a provocative suggestion, however, that boys may be relatively more vulnerable to problems of aggression in the first decade of life, whereas girls may develop personality problems, particularly excessive dependency, in response to the sexual expectations and social pressures of adolescence (Werner & Smith, 1982). Thus, although boys seems to be more vulnerable than girls to adversity, the timing and types of stresses and response to them varies for the two sexes.

THE SIBLING SYSTEM AND THE DEVELOPMENT OF CONDUCT DISORDERS

Siblings play an important role in precipitating and sustaining each other's aggressive behavior. Conduct disorders tend to run in families, with similarities in antisocial behavior being found not only between parent and child but between siblings (Patterson, 1982; Shaw & McKay, 1942). Children with early histories of violence or coercive behavior toward their siblings are more violent to people outside the family (Dengerink & Covery, 1981). It should be noted that just as there is specificity in the antisocial behaviors trained by parents, siblings' interactions appear to facilitate particular kinds of conduct disorders. Comparative studies of children who are identified as being either social aggressors or delinquents involved in crimes against property find that there is a significant likelihood that their siblings will be labeled in the same way (Loeber, Weissman, & Reid, 1983; Patterson, 1984; Wadsworth, 1979; West & Farrington, 1973). Loeber et al. (1983) found that 64 percent of mothers whose sons later became assaultive reported sibling fighting as a problem, whereas this was a problem in only 20 percent of sons who later became thieves.

Although physical aggression among siblings decreases with age, it remains a common way of resolving conflict, particularly for boys throughout adolescence (Straus, Gelles, & Steinmetz, 1980). Aggression is most common in families with all male siblings and least common in families with all female siblings, and this difference increases with age. The rate of physical aggression among siblings is much higher than the rate of husband–wife violence or aggression directed toward children by parents (Straus et al., 1980). Moreover, siblings are more likely than parents to respond positively to socially aggressive behavior (Patterson, 1982). Siblings of aggressive children are more likely to initiate aggressive encounters and to sustain and escalate aggressive interchanges (Patterson, 1984). In sibling interchanges in families of aggressive boys (Patterson, 1984) or abused children (Reid, Patterson, & Loeber, 1982), high-amplitude aggression increases with the duration of coercive interchanges. Coercive interchanges are longer in families of aggressive children, and both siblings and the mother play a critical role in moving these children in a progression from high rates of noncompliance to high rates of nonphysical coercive behaviors such as teasing or yelling and finally to physical aggression (Patterson, 1984). Although interactions among siblings of families with a child who has a conduct disorder are more coercive than those in families with a nondeviant child, the aggressive child is more likely than the normal child to initiate hostile exchanges with his mother than with any other family member. Mothers appear to be the prime targets of coercive behavior for aggressive children (Patterson, 1982). It should be noted that observational studies have found that although siblings of these problem children are more aggressive with each other, they do not exhibit more coercive behavior toward their mother than do nondeviant children. Only the problem child is permitted to be out of control in interacting with parents (Patterson, 1984).

If both parents and siblings play important roles in training the socially aggressive child, then it might be expected that fewer only children would be found in samples of children with antisocial behavior, and this seems to be the case. Highly aggressive children tend to be found more often in middle positions than only- or youngest-child positions (Anderson, 1969; Patterson, 1984; Rutter et al., 1970).

Of considerable interest is the finding that intervention programs that have been oriented toward improving parenting practices or training families of delinquents or acting-out children in effective problem solving and coping techniques decrease antisocial behavior and recidivism rates not only in the target child but also in their untreated siblings (Alexander, 1974; Arnold, Levine, & Patterson, 1975; Klein, Alexander, & Parsons, 1977; Malouf & Alexander, 1974). This lends some credence to the notion that children with conduct disorders are part of a larger dysfunctional family system.

CONDUCT DISORDERS IN CHILDREN FOLLOWING DIVORCE

Boys in mother-headed divorced families in comparison to those in non-divorced families have been found to be more frequently delinquent, aggressive, antisocial, impulsive, noncompliant, and rebellious against adult authority figures. Moreover, they have less well internalized standards of moral judgment, are less controlled and less able to delay immediate gratification, and are less able to deal flexibly and adaptively with stressful problems. Many of the early studies on which these findings were based have been criticized for methodological shortcomings, particularly lack of control for socioeconomic status, age of the child at the time of separation, the reason for separation of the parents, and time since separation and divorce. In addition, characteristics of the child such as sex, age at testing, race, and birth order were seldom considered in early studies. However, studies using more rigorous methodology (Hetherington et al., 1982; Patterson, 1982; Santrock & Warshak, 1979) and large-scale surveys (Guidubaldi, Perry, & Cleminshaw, 1983; Zill, 1984) have confirmed these findings. Although the support for cognitive deficits for boys in mother-headed families are not as well substantiated as those for conduct disorders, there is evidence of problems in school achievement and problem solving in boys from divorced families (see Guidubaldi et al., 1983; Hetherington, Camera, & Featherman, 1983, for a review of this literature). In addition, even when controls for maternal education and income are included, boys from divorced families manifest a broad array of antisocial behavior and problems in achievement and relations at school (Guidubaldi et al., 1983; Peterson & Zill, 1983).

Family Interaction and Divorce   The immediate aftermath of divorce is accompanied by a period of diminished parenting. Although noncustodial parents sometimes are more indulgent and involved immediately following divorce, they rapidly become less available to their children and divorced spouses. Custodial mothers, because of their additional stresses and responsibilities, may also become less psychologically and physically available to their children. In addition, custodial mothers, particularly mothers of sons, frequently find themselves involved in coercive cycles with their sons. Their low self-esteem, anxiety, depression, and feelings of external control are associated with inconsistent, punitive discipline where many rules are set but not systematically enforced, and sons are allowed to successfully use coercive strategies. This leads to an escalation in the noncompliant, demanding, coercive behavior of the boys, which in turn increases the feelings of helplessness and low self-esteem in mothers and further diminishes their effectiveness in parenting (Hetherington et al., 1982; Patterson, 1982). In view of our previous discussion of the role of such coercive cycles in the development of conduct disorders, it is not surprising to find that divorce is associated with extreme forms of antisocial behavior in boys. Patterson (1982) found that in a sample of out-of-control families, those with absent fathers had observed rates of coercive behaviors twice as high as those in two-parent households; moreover, these families were more difficult to treat than were intact families. Patterson attributes this to the mutual support and buffering provided by two parents.

In addition, mothers in one-parent households are less likely to identify stealing in their young sons than are parents in two-parent families (Loeber, Schmaling, & Reid, 1981). Moreover, the longer the parents have been separated, the more likely is the divorced mother to fail to identify that her son is stealing. In families with mothers who have been single for a long period, the disruption of the mother's monitoring of the child's activities is more marked than when the mother has been alone for a short time.

It would be tempting but misleading and overly simplistic to relate the increased incidence of conduct disorders and delinquency in mother-headed households solely to father absence. An impressive amount of evidence has been rallied to show that this relationship is more strongly related

> *not primarily to father's absence but rather to stress and conflict within the home, inability of the mother to exercise adequate supervision, depressed income and living conditions (including exposure to unfavorable, neighborhood influences), the mother's psychological and behavioral reaction to separation from her spouse as well as to the social and economic difficulties of her situation as a sole parent, and community attitudes toward the boy and family. (Herzog & Sudia, 1973, p. 154)*

Further evidence that the effects are not attributable simply to unavailability of a father is found in a longitudinal study of divorce in which the fathers maintained visitation rights and had some contact with their children (Hetherington et al., 1982). When there was agreement in childrearing, a positive attitude toward the spouse, and low conflict between parents and when the father was emotionally stable, frequent visitation by the father was associated with more positive adjustment and self-control in the child. When there was disagreement and inconsistency in attitudes toward the child or when the father was poorly adjusted, frequent contact with the child was associated with poor mother–child functioning and with disruptions in the children's behavior. Again we see that it is not a simple matter of father availability and amount of contact, but that the quality of the contact is the significant factor. In addition, supportive figures other than father, such as grandparents, have been found to attenuate the adverse effects of one-parent households. It has been argued that "aloneness" rather than lack of a father may be the critical factor in the disruption of family functioning in mother-headed households (Kellam, Ensminger, & Turner, 1977).

The Effects of Sex of the Child and Cause of Parental Loss on Adjustment of the Children There are two noteworthy findings in the literature on divorce that have not yet been adequately accounted for. The first is that differences in self-control and acting-out behavior between the children in nuclear and single-parent families are less marked or are not obtained for girls in comparison to boys (Guidubaldi et al., 1983; Gurin, Veroff, & Feld, 1960; Hetherington et al., 1982; Hoffman, 1970; Langner & Michael, 1963; Nye, 1957; Rosenberg, 1965; Santrock, 1975). The second is that, when differences in conduct disorders occur between children in single-parent and nuclear homes, they are most likely to be found in children whose parents have been divorced rather than those in which the father has died.

Studies of both clinic and nonclinic samples of children have shown that children from divorced parents are more likely to manifest their disturbance in conduct-disorder behavior. The research showing that children whose fathers have died are more likely to show depression, anxiety, or habit disturbances is less consistent and compelling (Felner, Farber, Ginter, Bioke, & Cowen, 1980; Felner, Stolberg, & Cowen, 1975; Hetherington, 1972; Santrock, 1975; Tuckman & Regan, 1966). In addition, girls are less likely to respond in an antisocial, aggressive manner to marital disruption or to their parents' divorce than are boys (Hetherington et al., 1982; Rutter, 1971; Tuckman & Reagan, 1966). Why should children, boys especially, respond with conduct problems to divorce more often than to the death of the father? It has been suggested that children adopt the predominant behavior exhibited by their parents during a crisis and that this becomes a guiding framework for later behavior and coping. For example, in the case of divorce—particularly in one that has been preceded by considerable acrimony and conflict—anger, aggression, and hostility are the behaviors displayed by the parents and adopted by the child. Rutter (1974) has emphasized that it is conflict and multiple stressors rather than separation that is the critical factor that leads to conduct disorders in children in such families. In the case of death, it is the parent's mourning, depression, and withdrawal that is exhibited to the child (Felner et al., 1975).

In addition to acrimony and conflict (which are likely to accompany divorce but not the death of a father), the greater social stigma associated with divorce, anger at being abandoned by the father, and the more negative image of the father, perhaps communicated by the mother, may all contribute to greater stress and resentment in the divorced family. Divorcees are also likely to be younger than widows and to have younger children. Young children have been shown to create more stress in mothers than do older children. Moreover, children with divorced or separated parents have been found to experience greater economic stress, and family problems as well as greater parental rejection than those from homes broken by parental death or those from intact homes (Felner et al., 1980). Finally, widows seem to have more extensive support systems, particularly from the spouse's family, than are available to divorcees (Hetherington, 1972). These factors may all contribute to greater duress and frustration in divorced families and also contribute to acting-out behavior in children.

Why do boys respond to divorce with more antisocial, aggressive, uncontrolled behavior than do girls? Evidence is accumulating that the same-sex parent may be particularly salient in the development of social competence in children. Although boys are more severely affected by family conflict and divorce, children in the custody of the same-sex parent show fewer behavior disorders following divorce than do those with opposite-sex custodial parents (Peterson & Zill, 1983; Warshak & Santrock, 1983). Moreover, remarriage of a divorced mother is associated with increased levels of behavior problems in girls but a decreased level of both antisocial and depressed/withdrawn behavior in boys (Peterson & Zill, 1983; Santrock, Warshak, Lindberg, & Meadows, 1982). This may be because girls form a close relationship with their divorced mothers, whereas the acrimonious relationship found between divorced mothers and sons may be diminished by the introduction of a competent, involved, supportive stepfather (Hetherington et al., 1982).

It also may be that the greater aggressiveness frequently observed in boys and the greater assertiveness in the culturally proscribed male role necessitates the use of firmer, more consistent discipline practices in the control of boys than of girls. Boys in nuclear families are less compliant than girls, children are less compliant to mothers than fathers, and as we have seen children are notably less compliant to divorced than nondivorced mothers. It could be argued that it is more essential for boys to have a male model whom they could imitate and who exhibits self-controlled, ethical behavior. It also could be argued that the image of greater power and authority vested in the father is more critical in controlling boys, who are culturally predisposed to be more aggressive. In addition, the support of a warm, involved husband may be particularly important in sustaining good maternal parenting practices when mothers are dealing with sons, who seem to have more difficulty in coping with a variety of stressful life events and who are more prone than daughters to respond with a noxious combination of demandingness and noncompliance (Hetherington et al., 1982). Finally, as was discussed earlier, boys receive less support from family, peers, and teachers during parental separation and divorce than do girls.

Although it has been emphasized that the effects of conflict and marital separation are greater in the development of conduct disorders in boys than in girls, there is some suggestion that girls may respond with more subtle disorders such as withdrawal and depression and that adverse effects may be delayed for girls. In older studies of delinquency (Monahan, 1957, 1960; Toby, 1957) it was found that broken homes were more frequent among female than male delinquents. At that time female delinquents were arrested or referred to the courts as being incorrigible or being involved in acting-out sexual behavior. It may be that the effects of being raised in a mother-headed, single-parent home do not appear in girls until adolescence, and then, rather than being manifested in aggressive acting-out behavior, it is found in disruptions in heterosexual relationships.

Early interactions of daughters with a loving, attentive father may be an effective and nonstressful way of acquiring the attitudes, skills, and confidence that facilitate successful heterosexual relations. In nuclear families, women who have had close, warm relationships with their fathers are more likely than women with aloof, unaffectionate fathers to have happy marriages and a high rate of orgasmic satisfaction (Biller, 1976; Fisher, 1973; Johnson, 1975).

Women from mother-headed families or families in which there were frequent early separations from the father are more likely to have unsatisfactory sexual relationships (Fisher, 1973; Jacobson & Ryder, 1969). In addition, there seems to be a modest generational transmission effect of marital instability where both the male and female children from single parents are, themselves, more likely to divorce. This does not seem to be attributable solely to having only one parent, since it is more likely to occur if the child has lived with a single mother instead of a single father and in families where separation has been caused by divorce rather than death. It may be that greater stresses are associated with being a single mother than being a single father, or with being divorced than being widowed (Mueller & Pope, 1977; Pope & Mueller, 1976).

One study (Hetherington, 1972) has examined in detail some of the differences in the heterosexual behavior among adolescent, white, lower- and lower-middle-class girls from divorced, widowed, or nuclear families. It was found that girls from the three types of families exhibited very different patterns of behavior in relating to male peers or adults. Many of the differences in the girls' responses to men were found to be attributable to the attitudes toward the father conveyed by the mother.

In girls from mother-headed homes, a disruption in relationships with males appeared either as excessive sexual anxiety, shyness, and discomfort around males or as sexually precocious and inappropriately assertive behavior with male peers and adults. The former syndrome was more common when separation had occurred because of the father's death; the latter occurred when separation was a result of divorce. These behaviors did not occur in interacting with females.

In addition, daughters of divorced parents were more likely to have negative attitudes toward men, to marry unstable, abusive men, and to be pregnant at the time of marriage. This pattern of disruptions in adolescent and young adult sexual and affectional relations following parental divorce also has been reported in a longitudinal follow-up of the Wallerstein and Kelly (1980) study. They also report high rates of depression in adolescent girls from divorced families; however, since they have no nondivorced comparison group and since depression increases in adolescent girls, it is difficult to interpret this finding.

In summary, in considering the effects upon children of a marital disruption or of being raised in a single-parent home, the complex network of stresses and support systems that accrue to these experiences must be considered. In mother-headed, single-parent families, the support systems available to the mother and the responses of the mother in coping with the demands of her situation may play a particularly critical role in the development of social and intellectual competence or of psychopathology in children.

Family Interaction and Anxiety-Withdrawal Disorders in Children

Anxiety disorders tend to run in families (e.g., Crowe, Noyes, Pauls, & Slymen, 1983; Harris, Noyes, Crowe, & Chaudhyr, 1983; Noyes, Clancy, Crowe, Hoenk, & Slymen, 1978), a fact that is consistent with both genetic and family interactional determinants. Direct observation of family interaction in families with anxious-withdrawn children has not kept pace with the studies of antisocial children, possibly because the relevant interaction in these families is more subtle and of lower base rate than is the case for the more dramatic displays of families of antisocial children.

For the child showing separation anxiety or school phobias, there is reasonably good evidence that an over involved parent and overdependent child system has developed (Coolidge & Brodie, 1974; Eisenberg, 1958; Hersov, 1960; Waldron, Shrier, Stone, & Tobin, 1975). Overprotective parental behavior may also be related to social phobias, agoraphobias, and generalized anxiety disorders (Jenkins, 1973; Parker, 1983; Solyom, Silberfeld, & Solyom, 1976). Overprotection is usually manifested in several ways: restrictive control of the child's behavior, intrusion into the child's psychological and physical privacy, active encouragement of dependency, and the exclusion of outside influences. There is also evidence that parental hostility and nonaccepting attitudes often accompany the overprotection. Waldron et al. (1975), for example, compared ratings of family characteristics made from case history files of 35 school-phobic children with families of 35 children showing other internalizing symptoms. Mothers of school-phobic children were rated more frequently as having difficulty separating from their child (74% vs. 32%); both parents of school-phobic children were rated more often as resenting the child's demands (73% vs. 47%) and scapegoating the child (65% vs. 38%); and the mother of school-phobic children more often indicated that their child was more important to them than was their husband (38% vs. 9%).

Parker (1983) has developed a questionnaire to measure children's perceptions of parental caring (what we have called warmth–hostility or responsiveness) as well as parental overprotection. He found that mothers *and* fathers were perceived as being more overprotective and less caring in a group of social phobic adults and in a group of adults with generalized anxiety than in a matched normal control group. An agoraphobic group was not different from the normal group on these measures.

Parker (1983) provided some evidence for the validity of these retrospective reports by adult offspring, namely, that ratings of overprotectiveness based on interviews with the mothers were significantly associated with the offsprings' questionnaire measures. Interestingly, Parker (1983) did not find his two scales of these dimensions to be orthogonal; they correlated negatively in the − .25 to − .45 range. Children perceive overprotective parents as also being hostile or rejecting, a finding consistent with the psychodynamic interpretation of the parental overprotection as reflecting, in part, guilt about rejecting feelings and behaviors.

Parker (1983) also found that both fathers and mothers who were high on protection and low on caring had the highest trait anxiety scores. This finding is consistent with research reported at the beginning of this section that showed that anxiety disorders tend to run in families, a finding that suggests the possibility of a genetic component. To evaluate the contribution of a genetic factor, Parker (1982) performed a study with adoptees and found the adopted children's trait anxiety scores to be significantly correlated with their adoptive mothers' overprotection and caring, but not with either of these variables for the adoptive fathers. Thus genetic transmission, at least for maternal anxiety, would not seem to be a complete explanation for the relationships found in Parker's and others' studies.

The origins of the overprotective parent and overdependent child system have not been traced by prospective longitudinal research, but the attachment research may give us a clue. Ainsworth, Bell, and Stayton (1971) directly observed 23 mothers interacting with their infants every 3 weeks from birth until the infants were 54 weeks old. At 12 months of age infants who were securely attached to their mothers were found to have experienced mothers who had responded sensitively to the infants' signals during feeding time, as well as in other situations. Infants who showed signs of excessive attachment—crying when separated, difficult to control when reunited with mother, and low levels of exploratory behavior—had mothers who had displayed a mixture of positive and negative behaviors. These mothers interacted playfully and affectionately on occasion, but at many other times either highly interfered with the baby's exploration or grossly ignored it. These infants at 12 months showed the insecure-ambivalent pattern of attachment. Their actual interaction with their mothers was frequently accompanied by both clinging and whining and by angry, contact-resisting behavior. Perhaps mothers and infants who show this form of ambivalent attachment are at risk for developing the overprotective mother and overdependent child pattern associated with separation and other forms of anxiety.

Several investigators have reported that a substantial number of children who refuse to go to school express fears of harm befalling their mothers when separated from them (e.g., Garvey & Hegrenes, 1966; Hersov, 1960). The psychodynamic hypothesis that this fear derives from intense hostile feelings toward the mother has not been convincingly demonstrated, but it is consistent with the Ainsworth et al. (1971) finding of a mixture of separation anxiety and angry behavior on the part of the overattached infant.

As Sroufe (1983) has pointed out, however, the relationships between early forms of attachment and specific types of later maladjustment have not been clearly demonstrated, and, in fact, may never be shown with any high degree of specificity since the interactional dynamics between the young child and others is constantly subject to changing circumstances. Nevertheless, there is growing evidence that persisting insecure attachment (whether avoidant or ambivalent at 12 to 18 months) is associated with adjustment problems at 3 to 5 years of age, and many of these difficulties are characterized by anxiety, avoidance, and poor social skills. Sroufe (1983), for example, found 4-year-olds who had been classified as insecurely attached to have lower self-esteem, to be less ego-resilient, to be more dependent, to show more negative and less positive affect, and to be less popular with friends.

Various circumstances in the mother's life may contribute to her overprotective tendencies. Eisenberg (1958), for example, found that the child may have been a late arrival after many sterile years; the child may have been seen in terms of the mother's own unhappy childhood with the result that she wished to protect the child from similar experiences; or a bad marriage may have caused the mother to turn to her child for a secure relationship. Parker's (1983) finding of higher levels of trait anxiety in his high-protection and low-caring mothers and fathers suggests that these parents may have a long standing personality tendency to be anxious about many things in life in addition to parenting. Osofsky and Connors (1979) report that high maternal anxiety interferes with the development of synchronous mother–infant interaction by reducing the mother's sensitivity to the infant's signals.

Thus anxious mothers may facilitate the development of anxious attachment patterns in their infants, which in turn may be forerunners of later separation anxieties or other types of anxiety reactions. At older ages parental modeling of anxious behavior, cognitive warnings about potential dangers, and the lack of opportunity for overly restricted children to learn to master their own fears might all contribute to the development of anxiety disorders.

Life stresses involving family members may play a role in the precipitation of school phobias. Waldron et al. (1975) found that 46 percent of families with a school-phobic child reported stresses in the past year such as a serious physical illness or injury to another family member, absence of a parent, or depression in a parent compared with 17 percent of the control families. Also with respect to school phobic-children, especially older children, traumatic experiences at school can contribute to the development of the phobia (Smith, 1970; Yates, 1970).

Anxiety is usually considered to be an important component in obsessive-compulsive disorders. Adams (1973) reports a clinical investigation of 49 obsessional children and their families that though lacking in terms of measures for interrater reliability and a comparison group of nonobsessive children, is useful as a starting point in understanding the family interaction correlates of these children. These children were characterized as profoundly unhappy, humorless, lacking in zest, given to pedantic verbosity, and showing a variety of obsessive and compulsive rituals. Their families were largely urban, affluent, and middle class. Descriptions of the family environments suggest modeling and reinforcement of obsessive styles by the parents. These families tended to be highly verbal, and emotions were ignored or talked away. The parents did not prize warm interpersonal relationships, had few close friends, and did not encourage their children to seek outside friendships. A number of parents showed some tendency toward hoarding, devoting much time to saving, spending, and accounting, as if they lived amidst scarcity instead of in their actual affluence.

These parents also behaved in ways likely to induce strong conflicts centering around the expression of unacceptable behaviors, especially aggression. Thus, they emphasized the importance of "correctness" in thought and behavior, usually, but not always, reflecting conventional social values. Most parents stressed cleanliness of the body as well as of the mind; rigid, punitive, or prolonged bowel training was reported to have occurred in 41 percent of the families.

PARENTAL DOMINANCE AND CONFLICT AND ANXIETY-WITHDRAWAL DISORDERS

As we have seen, marital conflict has been shown to be strongly associated with the development of conduct disorders in boys. The relationship of this variable by itself to anxiety-withdrawal disorders has not been so clearly demonstrated. As reported previously, there are two studies of nonclinic samples (Block et al., 1981; Whitehead, 1979) in which marital conflict was found to be related to aggressive, acting-out behavior in boys and, to a lesser degree, to more anxious-withdrawn behavior in girls. However, studies of clinic samples have not found anxiety-withdrawal disorders to be associated with marital conflict for either boys or girls (Emery & O'Leary, 1982; Gassner & Murray, 1969; Porter & O'Leary, 1980; Rutter, 1971).

On the other hand, there is evidence that when marital conflict is accompanied by opposite sex parent dominance, children of both sexes are at risk for developing the more internalizing type of disorders (Gassner & Murray, 1969; Hetherington, Stouwie, & Ridberg, 1971; Klein, Plutchik, & Conte, 1973; Schwarz & Getter, 1980). Let us consider some theoretical background for this "triple interaction hypothesis," as Schwarz and Getter (1980) refer to it, that involves marital conflict, parent dominance, and sex of child. Under normal circumstances in our culture children show a relative tendency to model their behavior on, and thereby identify with, the same-sex parent. This tendency can be complicated and perhaps thwarted under certain circumstances. Thus, in addition to imitating the same-sex parent there is a tendency, especially for boys, to imitate the more dominant parent, particularly when the dominant parent is rated high on warmth (Hetherington, 1965; Hetherington & Frankie, 1967). Mixed identification tendencies might result from having a warm, opposite-sex parent who is dominant, but these tendencies do not necessarily increase the risk for psychopathology. However, children may also identify with a dominant parent, even when this parent is also low on warmth and parental conflict is high. This was found by Hetherington and Frankie (1967), who interpreted their results as supporting the psychodynamically derived concept of identification with the aggressor. Does such an identification with the aggressor increase the risk for psychopathology regardless of whether the parent is the same or opposite sex? This has not yet been determined by empirical research. When the dominant parent is of the opposite sex and there is high marital conflict, however, the child may be placed in an especially difficult position with respect to modeling and imitative tendencies. Thus, a son whose dominant father is in overt conflict with a weak, passive aggressive wife can follow the expected tendency to identify with his father, both because the father is the same sex parent and because he is dominant. By contrast, a daughter in the same situation may tend to identify with her mother because she is the same sex; but the daughter may also have a conflicting tendency to identify with the father because of his dominance and power. Overt marital conflict is an important feature in this line of reasoning. The father's disparagement of the mother and possibly disparagement of the daughter if she behaves like the mother may make it hard for the daughter to identify with the mother. Conflict within the daughter may then develop over whether to be like the mother or the father. This conflict as well as the partial identification with a weak, disparaged mother might then be accompanied by anxiety, low self-esteem, depression and other neurotic symptoms.

The previously listed studies provide support for this line of thinking. For example, Gassner and Murray (1969) found internalizing children of both sexes seen at a child guidance clinic to come more often from families in which marital conflict was high and the opposite sex parent was dominant (both assessed by the revealed-differences technique) than were normal children. Schwarz and Getter (1980) used self-report questionnaires to measure all variables on college subjects and found the predicted triple interaction effect with neuroticism as the dependent variable. Klein, Plutchik et al., (1973) studied families coming for family therapy and found that sons had more behavior problems (of all kinds) when their mother was dominant and their father was passive, and the opposite held for the girls. Marital conflict was not measured in this study.

Finally, research by Hetherington et al. (1971) further confirms the importance of parent dominance and marital conflict, at least for males. In this study adolescent delinquents were segregated into three types: internalizing delinquents who showed signs of conflict, anxiety, or guilt about their antisocial behavior; socialized-aggressive delinquents; and conduct-disordered delinquents (or undersocialized delinquents). Mother dominance and marital conflict, as measured by the revealed-differences technique (a family problem-solving task), was high for the internalizing male delinquents, and father dominance with relatively low marital conflict was characteristic of the socialized-aggressive delinquents. However, the triple interaction was not supported by the finding that internalizing female delinquents were also found in families with high maternal dominance but low marital conflict. This latter finding should warn us that the high marital conflict and opposite-sex parent dominance pattern is not associated with all forms of child deviance.

Dysphoria in Children

Although childhood dysphoria has become the focus of considerable research (see Chapter 3) in recent years, there have been few studies of its family interactional correlates. We should also keep in mind that depressive symptoms rarely occur alone and are frequently mixed with anxiety, withdrawal, and less often with conduct problems. Two types of evidence bear at least indirectly on the question of how family variables are related to depression symptoms in childhood: the effects of loss due to death or separation and the correlates of certain kinds of parent–child interactions.

Crook and Eliot (1980) and Tennant, Bebbington, and Hurry (1980) after extensive reviews of the literature concluded that when groups of *adult* depressed patients are matched with comparison groups on age and socioeconomic level, there is no consistent evidence that adult depression or any subtype of adult depression is related to parental death during childhood or any particular period during childhood. The studies reviewed used adult subjects, and it is possible that parental deaths may be related to childhood dysphoria but not to major adult depression. In those rare studies that have found a relationship between parental loss and adult depression, a complex and difficult-to-explain interaction between type of separation, type of adult symptom, and age of the child at separation emerges (Tennant, Hurry, & Bebbington, 1982). It is likely that the effect of a parental death on a child is so moderated by other factors such as the nature of the relationships with both the deceased and surviving parent, the availability of a replacement parent, and the multitude of experiences that happen between the childhood loss and the possible development of adult depression that the parental death per se does not have a clear and consistent long-term effect.

Research findings suggest at least a short-term relationship between parental death and shyness and anxiety in children (Felner et al., 1980). A study by McConville, Boag, and Purohit (1973) of a sample of inpatient dysphoric children suggests that a more fine-grained focus on types of depressive symptoms in children may yield more consistent relationships to parental death. They found children having strong guilt reactions, feelings of being wicked or hated, and wishes to be dead were more likely to have experienced the recent bereavement of a parent.

Separation from parents for reasons other than death may also contribute to dysphoria in children, but the evidence for this is by no means strong. Freud and Burlingham's (1943) early study of children separated from their parents in wartime London showed rather convincingly that temporary depressive symptoms occurred but most of the children recovered after several weeks.

The nature of the relationships with the parents may contribute more importantly to childhood feelings of depression than the occurrence of separations due to death or other causes. As we have indicated earlier, there is considerable evidence that children who have a parent (or parents) with an affective disorder are at risk for psychological disorders, including depressive disorders (see Beardslee, Bemporad, Keller, & Klerman, 1983, for a review). Although genetic factors no doubt contribute to this risk, affectively disordered parents interact with their children in ways that further add to the risk. The long-term emotional nonavailability, withdrawal, and disorganization of the depressed mother is especially detrimental to normal child development (Davenport, Zahn-Waxler, Adland, & Mayfield, 1984; Sameroff et al., 1982). It has been associated with avoidant patterns of attachment (Gaensbauer, Harmon, Cytryn, & McKnew, 1984), depression, attention deficit, separation anxiety, conduct disorders, and lack of competence in school and in peer interactions in the child (Baldwin, Cole, & Baldwin, 1982; Weissman et al., 1984).

Nonresponsiveness seems to be especially prominent in depressed mothers. Several experimental studies have documented the adverse effects of even a brief period of maternal nonresponsiveness on normal infants (Carpenter, Tecce, Stechler, & Friedman, 1970; Cohn & Tronick, 1983; Tronick, Als, Adamson, Wise, & Brazelton, 1978). Cohn and Tronick (1983), for example, found that normal infants reacted to three minutes of maternal "depression" (face relatively expressionless and speaking in flat uninteresting monotone) with repetitive episodes of protest, wariness, and looking away. The negative reactions of the infants continued for some time after mothers switched from depressed to normal interaction. If such a brief period of maternal "depression" can produce such a marked change in infant responding, it is easy to imagine that the effect of a chronically depressed mother might be severe and long lasting.

Another strategy in the study of family interactional variables related to depression relies on retrospective reports by depressed adults on parent–child relationships. A number of studies have found depressed adults compared with nondepressed adults to remember their parents as rejecting, depriving, and, in many cases, overcontrolling (Jacobson, Sasman, DiMascio, 1975; Lamont, Fishcoff & Gottlieb, 1976; Parker, 1983; Raskin, Boothe, Reatig, Schulterbrandt, & Odle, 1971). Parker (1983) reports four studies, two with clinical samples of depressed patients and two with samples of nonpatient subjects, in which the more depressed patients or subjects perceived both their mothers and their fathers as being high on protection and low on caring—the same parental characteristics he found to be associated with phobic and generalized anxiety disorders. Lamont et al. (1976), however, found parents of those with dysphoric disorders to be higher on this pattern than parents of anxiety neurotics. Nevertheless, it would not seem that this pattern of parental characteristics is associated in a highly specific way with a particular type of offspring psychopathology. We should not forget in this regard that many individuals show a mixed pattern of depression and anxiety. Perhaps at this time we can only conclude that a rather broad spectrum of more internalizing types of disorders involving anxiety and depression are associated with this parental pattern.

Parker (1983) did not find that individuals with bipolar affective disorders differed from normals on these measures, a finding similar to an earlier one reported by Abrahams and Whitlock (1969). This lack of evidence for parent–child interactional correlates for the bipolar disorder is consistent with a more genetic causation; however, the results of Gaensbauer et al. (1984) indicated fairly clear disturbances in the directly observed early mother–child interactions for families with a bipolar parent. At this point the relative contributions of genetic and family interactional styles to the development of bipolar disorders remains unclear.

Retrospective reports may not accurately reflect actual parental behavior and, especially in the case of depressed individuals, may be colored by their current depressed outlook. Parker (1981) has provided some data that bear on these criticisms. He showed that his questionnaire measures of perceived parental caring and overprotection were not affected by changes in depression level by administering the questionnaire on two occasions to the same individuals, who had undergone substantial changes in severity of depression. He also showed that measures obtained from siblings and from the mothers themselves were substantially correlated with the target subjects' reports.

Schwartz and Zuroff (1979) provide a tie between research suggesting that high protection and low caring are related to anxiety-depressive disorders and research that has suggested that marital conflict and opposite sex parent dominance is related to anxiety-withdrawal symptoms. These authors found that depression was highest in female college students who reported high marital conflict, high father dominance, and high inconsistency in their fathers' expressions of love.

The theme that runs through all of the studies reviewed in this section—from infancy to retrospective reports by adults—is that childhood dysphoria is associated with unresponsive, uncaring parenting combined with some degree of parental overprotection. This would be consistent with psychoanalytic speculations, which have hypothesized a strongly ambivalent attitude toward one or both parents. The long-term inability to obtain positive, responsive parental attention could lead to the feelings of despair and to the cognitive attitudes of hopelessness, helplessness, and low self-esteem associated with depression. The accompanying levels of parental control and protectiveness might make it more difficult to engage in outright defiance and rebellion as in the conduct disorders. It is still not clear why this parental pattern leads to depression in some instances and anxiety disorders in others. Some genetic predisposition may increase the likelihood of anxiety disorders (e.g., Scarr, 1969), but it is also probable that a more fine-grained analysis of the family interaction will yield additional discriminating characteristics.

SUMMARY

In this chapter we have discussed familial correlates of childhood psychopathology. There appear to be multiple paths to the development of psychopathology in children, and the same family factors may contribute to the development of different forms of psychopathology in different children. The development of more complex conceptual perspectives and more sophisticated research methods in the past decade stirs hope that the network of factors modifying and mediating the relation between family processes and children's adjustment is beginning to be understood.

REFERENCES

Abraham, M. J., & Whitlock, F. A. (1969). Childhood experience and depression. *British Journal of Psychiatry, 115,* 883–888.

Abramovitch, R., Pepler, D., & Corter, C. (1982). Patterns of sibling interaction among preschool-age children. In M. E. Lamb & B. Sutton-Smith (Eds.), *Sibling relationships.* Hillsdale, NJ: Erlbaum.

Adams, P. L. (1973). *Obsessive children*. New York: Brunner/Mazel.

Agulnik, P. L. (1970). The spouse of the phobic patient. *British Journal of Psychiatry, 117*, 59–67.

Ainsworth, M. D. S., Bell, S. M., & Stayton, D. J. (1971). Individual differences in strange-situation behavior of one-year olds. In H. R. Schaffer (Ed.), *The origins of human social relations* (pp. 17–57). New York: Academic Press.

Ainsworth, M., Blehar, M., Waters, E., & Wall, S. (1978). *Patterns of attachment*. Hillsdale, NJ: Erlbaum.

Aldous, J. (1978). *Developmental change in families*. New York: Wiley.

Alexander, J. F. (1974). *Behavior modification in rehabilitation settings*. Springfield, IL: Charles C. Thomas.

Anderson, L. M. (1969). Personality characteristics of parents of neurotic, aggressive, and normal preadolescent boys. *Journal of Consulting and Clinical Psychology, 33*, 575–581.

Arend, R., Gove, F. L., & Stroufe, L. A. (1979). Continuity of individual adaptation from infancy to kindergarten: A predictive study of ego-resiliency and curiosity in preschoolers. *Child Development, 50*, 950–959.

Arnold, J. E., Levine, A. G., & Patterson, G. R. (1975). Changes in sibling behavior following family intervention. *Journal of Consulting and Clinical Psychology, 43*, 683–688.

Baldwin, A. L., Cole, R. E., & Baldwin, C. P. (1982). Parental pathology, family interaction, and the competence of the child in school. *Monographs of the Society for Research in Child Development, 47* (5, Serial No. 197).

Bandura, A., & Walters, R. H. (1963). *Social learning and personality development*. New York: Holt, Rinehart & Winston.

Bank, S. P., & Kahn, M. D. (1982). *The sibling bond*. New York: Basic Books.

Barrett, R. K. (1973). *The relationship of emotional disorders to marital adjustment and disruption*. Unpublished dissertation. Kent State University, Kent State, OH.

Baumrind, D. (1967). Child care practices anteceding three patterns of preschool behavior. *Genetic Psychology Monographs, 75*, 43–83.

Baumrind, D. H. (1971). Harmonious parents and their preschool children. *Developmental Psychology, 4*, 99–102.

Baumrind, D. (1983). Rejoinder to Lewis's reinterpretation of parental firm control effects: Are authoritative families really harmonious? *Psychological Bulletin, 94*, 132–142.

Beardslee, W. R., Bemporad, J., Keller, M. B., & Klerman, G. L. (1983). Children of parents with major affective disorder: A review. *American Journal of Psychiatry, 140*, 825–831.

Bell, R. Q. (1968). A reinterpretation of the direction of effects in studies of socialization. *Psychological Review, 75*, 81–95.

Bell, R. Q., & Harper, L. V. (1977). *Child effects on adults*. Hillsdale, NJ: Erlbaum.

Belsky, J. (1984). The determinants of parenting: A process model. *Child Development, 55*, 83–96.

Belsky, J., Gilstrap, B., & Rovine, M. (1984). Stability and change in mother–infant and father–infant interaction in a family setting: One, three and nine months. *Child Development, 55*, 692–705.

Berkowitz, L. (1962). *Aggression: A social psychological analysis.* New York: Mc-Graw-Hill.

Biller, H. B. (1976). The father and personality development: Paternal deprivation and sex-role development. In M. E. Lamb (Ed.), *The role of the father in child development* (pp. 89–156). New York: Wiley.

Billings, A. G., & Moos, R. H. (1983). Comparisons of children of depressed and nondepressed parents: A social-environmental perspective. *Journal of Abnormal Child Psychology, 11*, 463–486.

Block, J. (1971). *Lives through time.* Berkeley: Bancroft Books.

Block, J. H., Block, J., & Morrison, A. (1981). Parental agreement–disagreement on child-rearing orientations and gender-related personality correlates in children. *Child Development, 52*, 965–974.

Bloom, B. L., Asher, S. J., & White, S. W. (1978). Marital disruption as a stressor: A review and analysis. *Psychological Bulletin, 85*, 867–894.

Bossard, J. H. S., & Boll, E. (1960). *The sociology of child development.* New York: Harper & Row.

Bowen, M. (1978). *Family therapy in clinical practice.* New York: Jason Aronson.

Briscoe, C. W., Smith, J. B., Robins, E., Marten, S., & Gaskin, F. (1973). Divorce and psychiatric disease. *Archives of General Psychiatry, 29*, 119–125.

Bugental, D. B., Love, L. R., Kaswan, J. J., & April, C. (1971). Verbal–nonverbal conflict in parental messages to normal and disturbed children. *Journal of Abnormal Psychology, 77*, 6–10.

Burgess, J. M., Kimball, W. H., & Burgess, R. L. (1978). *Family interaction as a function of family size.* Paper presented at the Southeastern Conference on Human Development. (Also reported in Patterson, 1982.)

Campbell, S. (1979). Mother–infant interaction as a function of maternal ratings of temperament. *Child Psychiatry and Human Development, 10*, 67–76.

Carpenter, G. C., Tecce, J. J., Stechler, G., & Friedman, S. (1970). Differential visual behavior to human and humanoid faces in early infancy. *Merrill-Palmer Quarterly of Behavior and Development, 16*, 91–108.

Chawla, P. L., & Gupt, K. (1979). A comparative study of parents of emotionally disturbed and normal children. *British Journal of Psychiatry, 134*, 406–411.

Circirelli, V. G. (1982). Sibling influence throughout the life-span. In M. E. Lamb & B. Sutton-Smith (Eds.), *Sibling relationships* (pp. 267–284). Hillsdale, NJ: Erlbaum.

Cohn, J. F., & Tronick, E. Z. (1983). Three-month-old infants' reaction to simulated maternal depression. *Child Development, 54*, 185–193.

Coolidge, J. C., & Brodie, R. D. (1974). Observations of mothers of 49 school phobic children. *Journal of the American Academy of Child Psychiatry, 13*, 275–285.

Cowan, F. P., & Cowan, P. (1983, April). *A preventive intervention for couples during family formation.* Paper presented at the meetings for the Society for Research in Child Development, Detroit.

Crawford, J. W. (1982). Mother–infant interaction in premature and full-term infants. *Child Development, 53*, 957–962.

Crnic, K. A., Ragozin, A. S., Greenberg, M. T., Robinson, N. M., & Basham, R. B. (1983). Social interaction and developmental competence of preterm and full-term infants during the first year of life. *Child Development, 54*, 1199–1210.

Crockenberg, S. B. (1981). Infant irritability, mother responsiveness, and social support influences on the security of infant–mother attachment. *Child Development, 52*, 857–865.

Crook, T., & Eliot, J. (1980). Parental death during childhood and adult depression: A critical review of the literature. *Psychological Bulletin, 87*, 252–259.

Crowe, R. R., Noyes, R., Pauls, D. L., & Slymen, D. (1983). A family study of panic disorder. *Archives of General Psychiatry, 40*, 1065–1069.

Cushna, B. (1966, Sept.). *Agency and birth order differences in very early childhood*. Paper presented at the meeting of the American Psychological Association, New York.

Davenport, Y. B., Zahn-Waxler, C., Adland, M. L., & Mayfield, A. (1984). Early child-rearing practices in families with a manic-depressive parent. *American Journal of Psychiatry, 141*, 230–235.

Dengerink, H. A., & Covery, M. (1981). Implications of an escape-avoidance theory of aggressive responses to attack. In R. Green & D. Stern (Eds.), *Aggression: Theoretical and empirical reviews*. New York: Academic Press.

Dishion, T. J., Loeber, R., Stouthamer-Loeber, M., & Patterson, G. R. (1984). Skill deficits and male adolescent delinquency. *Journal of Abnormal Child Psychiatry, 12*, 37–54.

DiVitto, B., & Goldberg, S. (1979). The development of early parent-infant interaction as a function of newborn medical status. In T. Field, A. Sostek, S. Goldberg, & H. H. Shuman (Eds.), *Infants born at risk*, *Behavior & Development* (pp. 311–332). Holliswood, New York: Spectrum.

Dunn, J. (1980). Individual differences in temperament. In M. Rutter (Ed.), *Scientific foundations of developmental psychiatry* (pp. 101–109). London: Heinemann.

Dunn, J., & Kendrick, C. (1981). Interaction between young siblings: Association with the interaction between mother and first-born. *Developmental Psychology, 17*, 336–343.

Dunn, J., & Kendrick, C. (1982). Siblings and their mothers: developing relationships within the family. In M. E. Lamb & B. Sutton-Smith (Eds.), *Sibling relationships* (pp. 39–60). Hillsdale, NJ: Erlbaum.

Duvall, E. M. (1971). *Family development*. Philadelphia: J. B. Lippincott.

Easterbrooks, A. M., & Goldberg, W. A. (1984). Toddler development in the family. Impact of father involvement and parenting characteristics. *Child Development, 55*, 740–752.

Egeland, B., & Farber, E. A. (1984). Infant-mother attachment: Factors related to its development and changes over time. *Child Development, 55*, 753–771.

Egeland, B., & Sroufe, L. A. (1981). Attachment and early maltreatment. *Child Development, 52*, 44–52.

Eiduson, B. T., & Weisner, T. S. (1976, April). *Alternative socialization settings for infants and young children*. Paper presented at Western Meeting of the Society for Research in Child Development, Emeryville, CA.

Eisenberg, L. (1958). School phobia: A study in the communication of anxiety. *American Journal of Psychiatry, 114*, 712–718.

Emery, R. E. (1982). Interparental conflict and the children of discord and divorce. *Psychological Bulletin, 92*, 310–330.

Emery, R. E., Hetherington, E. M., & Fisher, L. (1984). Divorce, children and social policy. In H. Stevenson, & A. Siegal (Eds.), *Social policy and children* (pp. 189–266). Chicago: University of Chicago Press.

Emery, R. E., & O'Leary, K. D. (1982). Children's perceptions of marital discord and behavior problems of boys and girls. *Journal of Abnormal Child Psychology, 10*, 11–24.

Emery, R. E., Weintraub, S., & Neale, J. M. (1982). Effects of marital discord on the school behavior of children of schizophrenic, affectively disordered, and normal parents. *Journal of Abnormal Child Psychology, 10*, 215–228.

Feldman, H. (1971). The effects of children on the family. In A. Michel (Ed.), *Family issues of employed women in Europe and America* (pp. 104–125). Leiden: E. J. Brill.

Felner, R., Farber, S., Gintner, M., Bioke, M., & Cowen, E. (1980). Family stress and organization following parental divorce or death. *Journal of Divorce, 4*, 67–76.

Felner, R. D., Stolberg, A., & Cowen, E. L. (1975). Crisis events and school mental health referral patterns of young children. *Journal of Consulting and Clinical Psychology, 43*, 305–310.

Field, T., Dempsey, J., & Shuman, H. (1981). Developmental follow-up of pre- and postterm infants. In S. L. Friedman & M. Sigman (Eds.), *Preterm birth and psychological development* (pp. 299–312). New York: Academic Press.

Fishbein, H. D. (1981). Sibling set configuration and family dysfunction. *Family Process, 20*, 311–318.

Fisher, S. F. (1973). *The female orgasm: Psychology, physiology, fantasy*. New York: Basic Books.

Forehand, R., Wells, K., & Griest, D. (1980). An examination of the social validity of a parent training program. *Behavior Therapy, 11*, 488–507.

Freud, A., & Burlingham, D. T. (1943). *War and children*. New York: Willard.

Frodi, A. M., Lamb, M. E., Leavitt, L. A., Donovan, W. L., Neff, C., & Sherry, D. (1978). Fathers' and mothers' responses to the faces and cries of normal and premature infants. *Developmental Psychology, 14*, 490–498.

Gaensbauer, T. J., Harmon, R. J., Cytryn, L., & McKnew, D. H. (1984). Social and affective development in infants with a manic-depressive parent. *American Journal of Psychiatry, 141*, 223–229.

Garbarino, J., & Sherman, D. (1980). High-risk neighborhoods and high-risk families: The human ecology of child maltreatment. *Child Development, 51*, 188–198.

Garmezy, N. (1984). Stress-resistant children: The search for protective factors. In J. E. Stevenson (Ed.), *Recent research in developmental psychopathology. Journal of Child Psychology and Psychiatry*. Book supplement, No. 4. Oxford: Pergamon Press.

Garvey, W. P., & Hegrenes, J. R. (1966). Desensitization techniques in the treatment of school phobia. *American Journal of Orthopsychiatry, 36*, 147–152.

Gassner, S., & Murray, E. J. (1969). Dominance and conflict in the interactions between parents of normal and neurotic children. *Journal of Abnormal and Social Psychology, 74*, 33–41.

Glueck, S., & Glueck, E. T. (1950). *Unraveling juvenile delinquency*. New York: Commonwealth Fund.

Goldberg, S., Brachfeld, S., & DiVitto, B. (1980). Feeding, fussing, and play: Parent-infant interaction in the first year as a function of prematurity and perinatal medical problems. In T. M. Field, S. Goldberg, D. Stern, & A. M. Sostek (Eds.), *High-risk infants and children* (pp. 133–153). New York: Academic Press.

Goodstein, L. D., & Rowley, V. N. (1961). A further study of MMPI differences between parents of disturbed and nondisturbed children. *Journal of Consulting Psychology, 25*, 460–464.

Gottesman, I., & Shields, J. (1982). *Schizophrenia the epigenetic puzzle.* Cambridge: Cambridge University Press.

Gottman, J. M. (1979). *Marital interaction: Experimental investigations.* New York: Academic Press.

Gottman, J. M. (1984, Aug.). *Sex differences in emotions.* Paper presented at the American Psychological Association Convention, Toronto, Canada.

Guidubaldi, J., Perry, J. D., & Cleminshaw, H. K. (1983, Summer). The legacy of parental divorce. *School Psychology Review.*

Gurin, G., Veroff, J., & Feld, S. (1960). *Americans view their mental health.* New York: Basic Books.

Hagnell, O., & Kreitman, N. (1974). Mental illness in married pairs in a total population. *British Journal of Psychiatry, 125*, 293–302.

Hare, E. H., & Shaw, G. K. (1965). The patients' spouse and concordance on neuroticism. *British Journal of Psychiatry, 111*, 102–103.

Harder, D., Kokes, R., Fisher, L., & Strauss, J. (1980). Child competence and psychiatric risk. *Journal of Nervous and Mental Disease, 168*, 343–347.

Harris, E. L., Noyes, R., Crowe, R. R., & Chaudhry, D. R. (1983). Family study of agoraphobia. *Archives of General Psychiatry, 40*, 1061.

Hartup, W. W. (1983). Peer relations. In E. M. Hetherington (Ed.), *Socialization, personality and social development. Volume IV. Handbook of Child Psychology* (pp. 103–196). New York: Wiley.

Hawkins, J. L. (1968). *A measure of marital cohesion.* Unpublished Manuscript. University of Minnesota.

Heinicke, C. M., Diskin, S. D., Ramsey-Klee, D. M., & Given, K. (1983). Pre-birth parent characteristics and family development in the first year of life. *Child Development, 54*, 194–208.

Hersov, L. A. (1960). Persistent non-attendance at school. *Journal of Child Psychology and Psychiatry, 1*, 130–136.

Herzog, E., & Sudia, E. C. (1973). Children in fatherless families. In B. Caldwell & H. Ricciuti (Eds.), *Review of child development research* (Vol 3, pp. 141–232). Chicago: University of Chicago Press.

Hetherington, E. M. (1965). A developmental study of the effects of sex of the dominant parent on sex-role preference, identification, and imitation in children. *Journal of Personality and Social Psychology, 2*, 188–194.

Hetherington, E. M. (1972). Effects of paternal absence on personality development in adolescent daughters. *Developmental Psychology, 7*, 313–326.

Hetherington, E. M. (1981). Children and divorce. In R. Henderson (Ed.), *Parent–child interaction. Theory, research and prospect* (pp. 33–58). Academic Press: New York.

Hetherington, E. M. (1984). Stress and coping in children and families. In A. Doyle, D. Gold, & Moskowitz (Eds.), *Children in families under stress* (pp. 7–34). Washington, DC: Jossey Bass.

Hetherington, E. M., & Camara, K. A. (1984). Families in transition: The process of dissolution and reconstitution. In R. D. Parke (Ed.), *Review of child development research: The family* (Vol. VI, pp. 398–439).

Hetherington, E. M., Camara, K. A., & Featherman, D. L. (1983). Achievement and intellectual functioning of children from one parent households. In J. Spence (Ed.), *Achievement and achievement motives* (pp. 204–284). San Francisco: Freeman.

Hetherington, E. M., Cox, M., & Cox, C. R. (1982). Effects of divorce on parents and children. In M. Lamb (Ed.), *Nontraditional families* (pp. 223–288). Hillsdale, NJ: Erlbaum.

Hetherington, E. M., & Frankie, G. (1967). Effects of parental dominance, warmth, and conflict on imitation in children. *Journal of Personality and Social Psychology, 6,* 119–125.

Hetherington, E. M., Stouwie, R., & Ridberg, E. H. (1971). Patterns of family interaction and child rearing attitudes related to three dimensions of juvenile delinquency. *Journal of Abnormal Psychology, 77,* 160–176.

Hilton, I. (1967). Differences in the behavior of mothers toward first and later born children. *Journal of Personality and Social Psychology, 7,* 282–290.

Hoffman, L. W. (1970). Moral development. In P. Mussen (Ed.), *Handbook of child psychology* (pp. 261–359). New York: Wiley.

House, J. (1981). *Work stress and social support.* Reading, MA: Addison-Wesley.

Hudgins, W., & Prentice, N. M. (1973). Moral judgment in delinquent and nondelinquent adolescents and their mothers. *Journal of Abnormal Psychology, 82,* 145–152.

Hunter, R. S., Kilstrom, N., Kraybill, E. N., & Loda, F. (1978). Antecedents of child abuse and neglect in premature infants: A prospective study in a newborn intensive care unit. *Pediatrics, 61,* 629–635.

Hutchings, B., & Mednick, S. A. (1974). Registered criminality in the adoptive and biological parents of registered male adoptees. In S. A. Mednick, F. Schulsinger, B. Bell, P. H. Venables, & K. O. Christiansen (Eds.), *Genetics, environment and psychopathology* (pp. 215–230). Amsterdam: North-Holland/American Elsevier.

Jacobs, B. S., & Moss, H. A. (1976). Birth order and sex of sibling as determinants of mother–infant interaction. *Child Development, 47,* 315–322.

Jacobson, G., & Ryder, R. G. (1969). Parental loss and some characteristics of the early marriage relationship. *American Journal of Orthopsychiatry, 39,* 799–787.

Jacobson, S., Sasman, J., & DiMascio, A. (1975). Deprivation in the childhood of depressed women. *Journal of Nervous and Mental Disease, 160,* 5–14.

Jenkins, R. L. (1973). *Behavior disorders of childhood and adolescence.* Springfield, IL: Charles C. Thomas.

Johnson, M. M. (1975). Fathers, mothers and sex typing. *Sociological Inquiry, 45,* 15–26.

Johnson, S. M., & Lobitz, G. R. (1974). The personal and marital status of parents as related to observed child deviance and parenting behaviors. *Journal of Abnormal Child Psychology, 3,* 193–208.

Kellam, S. G., Ensminger, M. A., & Turner, J. T. (1977). Family structure and the mental health of children. *Archives of General Psychiatry, 34*, 1012–1022.

Kelly, P. (1976). The relation of infants' temperament and mother's psychopathology to interactions in early infancy. In K. F. Riegel & J. A. Meacham (Eds.), *The developing individual in a changing world* (Vol. II, pp. 664–675). Chicago: Aldine.

Kidwell, J. S. (1981). Number of siblings, sibling spacing, sex, and birth order: Their effects on perceived parent–adolescent relationships. *Journal of Marriage and the Family, 43*, 315–332.

Kidwell, J. S. (1982). The neglected birth order: Middleborns. *Journal of Marriage and the Family, 44*, 225–235.

Klein, M. M., Plutchik, R., & Conte, H. R. (1973). Parental dominance-passivity and behavior problems of children. *Journal of Consulting and Clinical Psychology, 40*, 416–419.

Klein, N. C., Alexander, J. F., & Parsons, B. V. (1977). Impact of family systems intervention on recidivism, and sibling delinquency: A model of primary prevention and program evaluation. *Journal of Consulting and Clinical Psychology, 45*, 469–474.

Klaus, M. H., & Kennell, J. H. (1970). Mothers separated from their newborn infants. *Pediatric Clinics of North America, 17*, 1015–1037.

Kreitman, N. (1964). The patient's spouse. *British Journal of Psychiatry, 110*, 159–173.

Kreitman, N., Collins, J., Nelson, B., & Troop, J. (1970). Neurosis and marital interaction: I. Personality and symptoms. *British Journal of Psychiatry, 117*, 33–46.

Lahey, B. B., Hammer, D., Crumrine, P. L., & Forehand, R. L. (1980). Birth order × sex interactions in child behavior problems. *Developmental Psychology, 6*, 608–615.

Lamb, M. E. (1978). Qualitative aspects of mother and father infant attachments. *Infant Behavior and Development, 1*, 265–275.

Lamb, M. E. (1979). Influence of the child on marital quality and family interaction during the prenatal, perinatal and infancy period. In R. M. Lerner & G. D. Spanier (Eds.), *Child Influences on Marital and Family Interaction: A life-span perspective* (pp. 137–164). New York: Academic Press.

Lamb, M. E. (Ed.); (1982). *Nontraditional families: Parenting and childrearing.* Hillsdale, NJ: Earlbaum.

Lamont, J., Fischoff, S., & Gottlieb, H. (1976). Recall of parental behaviors in female neurotic depressives. *Journal of Clinical Psychology, 32*, 762–764.

Langner, G. S., & Michael, S. T. (1963). *Life stresses and mental health.* New York: Free Press.

Lasko, J. K. (1954). Parent behavior toward first and second children. *Genetic Psychology Monographs, 49*, 96–137.

Leifer, A. D., Liederman, P. H., Barnett, C. R., & Williams, J. A. (1972). Effects of mother-infant separation on maternal attachment behavior. *Child Development, 43*, 1203–1218.

Lewis, C. C. (1981). The effects of parental firm control: A reinterpretation of findings. *Psychological Bulletin, 90*, 547–563.

Liederman, P. H. (1983). Social ecology and childbirth: The newborn nursery as environmental stressor. In N. Garmezy, & M. Rutter (Eds.), *Stress, coping and development in children* (pp. 133–160). New York: McGraw-Hill.

Lobitz, G. R., & Johnson, S. M. (1975). Normal versus deviant children: A multimethod comparison. *Journal of Abnormal Psychology, 3*, 353–374.

Loeber, R., Schmaling, K., & Reid, J. (1981). *The identification of boys who steal.* NIMH Site Visit Report.

Loeber, R., Weissman, W., & Reid, J. B. (1983). Family interactions of assaultive adolescents, stealers and nondelinquents. *Journal of Abnormal Child Psychology, 11*, 1–14.

Lytton, H. (1977). Correlates of compliance and the rudiments of conscience in 2-year-old boys. *Canadian Journal of Behavioral Sciences, 9*, 242–251.

Lytton, H. (1980). *Parent–child interaction: The socialization process observed in twin and singleton families.* New York: Plenum.

Lytton, H., & Zwirner, W. (1975). Compliance and its controlling stimuli observed in a natural setting. *Developmental Psychology, 11*, 769–779.

Maccoby, E. E., & Martin, J. A. (1983). Socialization in the context of the family: Parent–child interaction. In E. M. Hetherington (Ed.), *Socialization, personality and social development. Vol. IV. Handbook of child psychology* (pp. 1–102). New York: Wiley.

Main, M., & Weston, D. R. (1981). The quality of the toddler's relationship to mother and to father: Related to conflict behavior and the readiness to establish new relationships. *Child Development, 52*, 932–940.

Malouf, R., & Alexander, J. (1974). Family crisis intervention. A model and technique of training. In R. E. Hardy & J. C. Cull (Eds.), *Therapeutic needs of the family* (pp. 47–55). Springfield, IL: Charles C. Thomas.

Martin, B. (1975). Parent–child relations. In F. D. Horowitz (Ed.), *Review of child development research* (Vol 4, pp. 463–540). Chicago: University of Chicago Press.

Matas, L., Arend, R. A., & Sroufe, L. A. (1978). Continuity of adaptation in the second year: The relationship between quality of attachment and later competence. *Child Development, 49*, 547–556.

McConville, B. J., Boag, L. C., & Purohit, A. P. (1973). Three types of childhood depression. *Canadian Psychiatric Association Journal, 18*, 133–137.

McCord, J. (1979). Some child-rearing antecedents of criminal behavior in adult men. *Journal of Personality and Social Psychology, 37*, 1477–1486.

McCord, J., & McCord, W. (1958). The effects of parental role model of criminality. *Journal of Social Issues, 14*, 66–75.

McCord, W., McCord, J., & Thurber, E. (1962). Some effects of parental absence on male children. *Journal of Abnormal and Social Psychology, 64*, 361–369.

McCubbin, H. I., & Patterson, J. M. (1981, October). Family stress and adaptation to crises: A double ABCX model of family behavior. Paper presented at the annual meeting of the National Council on Family Relations, Milwaukee.

McGillicuddy-DeLisi, A. V. (1982). Parental beliefs about developmental processes. *Human Development, 25*, 192–200.

Merikangas, K. R. (1982). Assortative mating for psychiatric disorders and psychological traits. *Archives of General Psychiatry, 39*, 1173–1180.

Milliones, J. (1978). Relationship between perceived child temperament and maternal behavior. *Child Development, 49*, 1255–1257.

Minuchin, S., & Fishman, H. C. (1981). *Family therapy techniques.* Cambridge, MA: Harvard University Press.

Monahan, T. F. (1957). Family status and the delinquent child: A reappraisal and some new findings. *Social Forces, 35*, 250–258.

Monahan, T. F. (1960). Broken homes by age of delinquent children. *Journal of Social Psychology, 51*, 387–395.

Moss, H. A. (1967). Sex, age, and state as determinants of mother-infant interaction. *Merrill-Palmer Quarterly, 13*, 19–36.

Mueller, C. W., & Pope, H. (1977). Marital instability: A study of its transmission between generations. *Journal of Marriage and the Family, 39*, 83–93.

Nadelman, L., & Begun, A. (1982). The effect of the newborn on the older sibling: Mothers' questionnaires. In M. E. Lamb & B. Sutton-Smith (Eds.), *Sibling relationships* (pp. 13–38). Hillsdale, NJ: Erlbaum.

Noyes, R., Clancy, J., Crowe, R., Hoenk, P. R., & Slymen, D. J. (1978). The family prevalence of anxiety neurosis. *Archives of General Psychiatry, 35*, 1057–1059.

Nuttall, E., & Nuttall, R. (1971). The effects of size of family on parent–child relationships. *Proceedings of the American Psychological Association, 6*, 267–268.

Nye, F. I. (1957). Child adjustment in broken and in unhappy homes. *Marriage and Family Living, 19*, 356–360.

Nystul, M. S. (1974). The effects of birth order and sex on self-concept. *Journal of Individual Psychology, 30*, 211–214.

O'Leary, K. D. (1984). Marital discord and children: Problems, strategies, methodologies and results. In A. Doyle, D. Gold, & D. S. Moskowitz (Eds.), *Children in families under stress* (pp. 35–46). New Directions for Child Development, No. 24. San Francisco: Jossey-Bass.

Oleinick, M. S., Bahn, A. K., Eisenberg, L., & Lilienfeld, A. M. (1966). Early socialization experiences and intrafamilial environment. *Archives of General Psychiatry, 15*, 344–353.

Olson, D. H., McCubbin, H. I., & Associates (1983). *Families: What makes them work.* Beverly Hills: Sage.

Olson, D. H., Sprenkle, D. H., & Russell, C. S. (1979). Circumplex model of marital and family systems: Cohesion and adaptability dimensions, family types and clinical applications. *Family Process, 18*, 3–28.

Oltmanns, T. F., Broderick, J. E., & O'Leary, K. D. (1977). Marital adjustment and efficacy of behavior therapy with children. *Journal of Consulting and Clinical Psychology, 45*, 724–729.

Olweus, D. (1980). Familial and temperamental determinants of aggressive behavior in adolescent boys: A causal analysis. *Developmental Psychology, 16*, 644–660.

Orvaschel, H., Weissman, M., & Kidd, K. K. (1980). Children and depression: The children of depressed parents, the childhood of depressed patients, depression in children. *Journal of Affective Disorders, 2*, 1–16.

Osofsky, J. D., & Connors, K. (1979). Mother-infant interaction: An integrative view of a complex system. In J. D. Osofsky (Ed.), *Handbook of infant development* (pp. 519–548). New York: Wiley.

Ovenstone, I. M. K. (1973). The development of neurosis in the wives of neurotic men: II. Marital role functions and marital tension. *British Journal of Psychiatry, 122*, 711–717.

Parke, R. D., & Slaby, R. G. (1983). The development of aggression. In E. M. Hetherington (Ed.), *Socialization, personality and social development. Vol. IV. Handbook of child psychology* (pp. 549–642). New York: Wiley.

Parker, G. (1981). Parental reports of depressives. *Journal of Affective Disorders, 3*, 131–140.

Parker, G. (1982). Parental representations and affective disorders: Examination for an hereditary link. *British Journal of Medical Psychology, 55*, 57–61.

Parker, G. (1983). *Parental overprotection: A risk factor in psychosocial development*. New York: Grune & Stratton.

Patterson, G. R. (1976). The aggressive child: Victim and architect of a coercive system. In E. Mash, L. Hamerlynck, & L. Handy (Eds.), *Behavior modification in families. I. Theory and research* (pp. 267–316). New York: Brunner/Mazel.

Patterson, G. R. (1982). *Coercive family process*. Eugene, OR: Castalia.

Patterson, G. R. (1984). The contribution of siblings to training for fighting: A microsocial analysis. In J. Block, D. Olweus, & M. Radke-Yarrow (Eds.), *Development and antisocial and prosocial behavior*. New York: Academic Press.

Pearlin, L., & Schooler, C. (1978). The structure of coping. *Journal of Health and Social Behavior, 19*, 2–21.

Pedersen, F. (1982). Mother, father and infants as an interactive system. In J. Belsky (Ed.), *In the beginning: Readings on infancy* (pp. 216–226). New York: Columbia University Press.

Peterson, J. L., & Zill, N. (1983, April). *Marital disruption, parent/child relationships and behavioral problems in children*. Paper presented at the meetings of the Society for Research in Child Development, Detroit, MI.

Pope, H., & Mueller, C. W. (1976). The intergenerational transmission of marital instability: Comparisons by race and sex. *The Journal of Social Issues, 321*, 149–166.

Porter, B., & O'Leary, K. D. (1980). Marital discord and childhood behavior problems. *Journal of Abnormal Child Psychology, 8*, 287–295.

Pulkkinen, L. (1982). Self-control and continuity from childhood to adolescence. In P. B. Baltes & O. G. Brim (Eds.), *Life-span development and behavior* (Vol. 4, pp. 63–105). New York: Academic Press.

Quay, H. C. (1977). Psychopathic behavior: Reflections on its nature, origins and treatment. In I. Uzgiris & F. Weizmann (Eds.), *The structuring of experience* (pp. 371–384). New York: Plenum.

Raskin, A., Boothe, H. H., Reatig, N. A., Schulterbrandt, J. G., & Odle, D. (1971). Factor analyses of normal and depressed patients' memories of parental behavior. *Psychological Reports, 29*, 871–879.

Reid, J. B., Patterson, G. R., & Loeber, R. (1982). The abused child: Victim, instigator or innocent bystander. In D. Bernstein (Ed.), *Response, structure and organization*. Lincoln: University of Nebraska Press.

Reiss, D. (1981). *The families' construction of reality*. Cambridge, MA: Harvard University Press.

Rieder, R., & Nichols, P. (1979). Offspring of schizophrenics: III. Hyperactivity and neurological soft signs. *Archives of General Psychiatry, 36*, 665–674.

Riess, B. F. (1976, Dec.). *Character disorder and sibling constellation.* Paper presented at XVI Interamerican Congress of Psychology, Miami Beach.

Robson, K. S., Pederson, F. A., & Moss, H. A. (1969). Developmental observations of diadic gazing in relation to the fear of strangers and social approach behavior. *Child Development, 40*, 619–627.

Rodgers, R. (1964). Toward a theory of family development. *Journal of Marriage and the Family, 26*, 262–270.

Rosenberg, B. G., & Sutton-Smith, B. (1964). Ordinal position and sex-role identification. *Genetic Psychology Monographs, 109*, 271–279.

Rosenberg, M. (1965). *Society and the adolescent self-image.* Princeton, NJ: Princeton University Press.

Rothbart, M. K. (1971). Birth order and mother–child interaction in an achievement situation. *Journal of Personality and Social Psychology, 17*, 113–120.

Rutter, M. (1966). *Children of sick parents: An environmental and psychiatric study.* London: Oxford University Press.

Rutter, M. (1971). Parent-child separation: Psychological effects on the children. *Journal of Child Psychology and Psychiatry, 12*, 233–256.

Rutter, M. (1977). Separation, loss and family relationships. In M. Rutter & L. Hersov (Eds.), *Child psychiatry.* London: Blackwell Scientific.

Rutter, M. (1978). Early sources of security and competence. In J. S. Bruner & A. Garton (Eds.), *Human growth and development.* London: Oxford University Press.

Rutter, M. (1983). Stress, coping and development: Some issues and some questions. In N. Garmezy & M. Rutter (Eds.), *Stress, coping and development in children* (pp. 1–42). New York: McGraw-Hill.

Rutter, M., & Graham, P. (1970). Social circumstances of children with psychiatric disorder. In M. Rutter, J. Tizard, & K. Whitmore (Eds.), *Education, health, and behavior: Psychological and medical study of childhood development* (pp. 256–262). New York: Wiley.

Rutter, M., Tizard, J., & Whitmore, K. (1970). *Education, health and behavior.* New York: Wiley.

Ryder, R. G. (1973). Longitudinal data relating marriage satisfaction and having a child. *Journal of Marriage and the Family, 35*, 604–606.

Sallows, G. (1973, May). *Responsiveness of deviant and normal children to naturally occurring parental consequences.* Paper presented at the Midwestern Psychological Association Convention, Chicago, IL.

Sameroff, A. J., Barocas, R., & Seifer, R. (1980, March). *Rochester longitudinal study progress report.* Paper presented at Risk Research Consortium Conference, San Juan, Puerto Rico.

Sameroff, A. J., Seifer, R., & Zax, M. (1982). Early development of children at risk for emotional disorder. *Monographs of the Society for Research in Child Development, 47*, No. 199.

Sameroff, A. J., & Zax, M. (1978). In search of schizophrenia: Young offspring of schizophrenic women. In L. C. Wynne, R. L. Cromwell, & S. Mathysse (Eds.),

The nature of schizophrenia: New approaches to research and treatment (pp. 430–441). New York: Wiley.

Santrock, J. W. (1975). Father absence, perceived maternal behavior, and moral development in boys. *Child Development, 46*, 753–757.

Santrock, J. W., & Warshak, R. A. (1979). Father custody and social development in boys and girls. *Journal of Social Issues, 35*, 112–125.

Santrock, J. W., Warshak, R., Lindbergh, C., & Meadows, L. (1982). Children's and parents' observed social behavior in stepfather families. *Child Development, 53*, 472–480.

Satir, V. (1964). *Conjoint family therapy*. Palo Alto, CA: Science and Behavior Books.

Scarr, S. (1969). Social introversion-extroversion as a heritable response. *Child Development, 40*, 823–832.

Schachter, J., Elmer, E., Ragins, N., Wimberly, F., & Lachin, J. M. (1977). Assessment of mother–infant interaction: Schizophrenic and nonschizophrenic mothers. *Merril-Palmer Quarterly, 23*, 193–206.

Schaffer, H. R., & Crook, C. K. (1980). Child compliance and maternal control techniques. *Developmental Psychology, 16*, 54–61.

Schooler, C. (1972). Birth order effects: Not here, not now! *Psychological Bulletin, 78*, 161–175.

Schulman, F. R., Shoemaker, D. J., & Moelis, I. (1962). Laboratory measurements of parental behavior. *Journal of Consulting Psychology, 26*, 109–114.

Schwarz, J. C., & Getter, H. (1980). Parental conflict and dominance in late adolescent maladjustment: A triple interaction model. *Journal of Abnormal Psychology, 89*, 573–580.

Schwarz, J. C., & Zuroff, D. C. (1979). Family structure and depression in female college students: Effects of parental conflict, decision-working power, and inconsistency of love. *Journal of Abnormal Psychology, 88*, 398–406.

Shaw, C. R., & McKay, H. D. (1942). *Juvenile delinquency and urban areas*. Chicago: University of Chicago Press.

Shereshefsky, P. M., & Yarrow, L. J. (1973). *Psychological aspects of a first pregnancy and early postnatal adaptation*. New York: Raven.

Shrader, W. K., & Leventhal, T. (1968). Birth order of children and parental report of problems. *Child Development, 39*, 1165–1175.

Slater, E., & Woodside, M. (1951). *Patterns of marriage*. London: Cassell Ltd.

Smith, S. L. (1970). School refusal with anxiety: A reivew of sixty-three cases. *Canadian Psychological Association Journal, 15*, 257–264.

Sobel, D. E. (1961). Children of schizophrenic patients: Preliminary observations on early development. *American Journal of Psychiatry, 118*, 512–517.

Solyom, L., Silberfeld, M., & Solyom, C. (1976). Maternal overprotection in the aetiology of agoraphobia. *Canadian Psychiatric Association Journal, 21*, 109–113.

Spivey, P. B., & Scherman, A. (1980, Fall). The effect of time lapse on personality characteristics and stress on divorced women. *Journal of Divorce, 4*, 49–59.

Sroufe, L. A. (1983). Infant-caregiver attachment and patterns of adaptation in preschool: The roots of maladaptation and competence. In M. Perlmutter (Ed.), *The*

Minnesota symposium on child development (Vol 16, pp. 41–84). Hillsdale, NJ: Erlbaum.

Stayton, D. J., Hogan, R., & Ainsworth, M. D. S. (1971). Infant obedience and maternal behavior: The origin of socialization reconsidered. *Child Development, 42*, 1057–1069.

Straus, M. A., Gelles, R., & Steinmetz, S. (1980). *Behind closed doors*. New York: Doubleday.

Tennant, C., Bebbington, P., & Hurry, J. (1980). Parental death in childhood and risk of adult depressive disorders: A review. *Psychological Medicine, 10*, 289–299.

Tennant, C., Hurry, J., & Bebbington, P. (1982). The relation of childhood separation experiences to adult depressive and anxiety states. *British Journal of Psychiatry, 141*, 475–482.

Terdal, L., Jackson, R., & Garner, A. (1976). Mother–child interactions: A comparison between normal and developmentally delayed groups. In E. Mash, L. Hamerlynck, & L. Handy (Eds.), *Behavior modification in families. I. Theory and research* (pp. 249–264). New York: Brunner/Mazel.

Toby, J. (1957). The differential impact of family disorganization. *American Sociological Review, 22*, 505–512.

Tronick, E., Als, H., Adamson, L., Wise, S., & Brazelton, T. B. (1978). The infant's response to entrapment between contradictory messages in face-to-face interaction. *Journal of American Academy of Child Psychiatry, 17*, 1–13.

Tuckman, J., & Regan, R. A. (1966). Intactness of the home and behavioral problems in children. *Journal of Child Psychology and Psychiatry, 7*, 225–233.

Tuckman, J., & Regan, R. A. (1967). Ordinal position and behavior problems in children. *Journal of Health and Social Behavior, 8*, 32–39.

Vaughn, B., Egeland, B., & Sroufe, L. A. (1979). Individual differences in infant–mother attachment at twelve and eighteen months: Stability and change in families under stress. *Child Development, 50*, 971–975.

Wadsworth, M. E. J. (1979). *Roots of delinquency and crime*. Oxford: Robertson.

Wagner, M. E., Schubert, H. J. P., & Schubert, D. S. P. (1979). Sibship-constellation effects on psychosocial development, creativity, and health. In H. W. Reese & L. P. Lipsitt (Eds.), *Advances in child development and behavior* (Vol. 14, pp. 58–148). New York: Academic Press.

Wahler, R. G. (1968). Oppositional children: A quest for parental reinforcement control. *Journal of Applied Behavior Analysis, 3*, 159–170.

Wahler, R. G. (1979). *The insular mother: Her problems in parent–child treatment*. Unpublished manuscript.

Waldron, S., Shrier, D. K., Stone, B., & Tobin, F. (1975). School phobia and other childhood neuroses: A systematic study of the children and their families. *American Journal of Psychiatry, 132*, 802–808.

Walker, E., Cudeck, B., Mednick, S., & Schulsinger, F. (1981). The effects of parental absence and institutionalization on the development of clinical symptoms in high risk children. *Acta Psychiatrica Scandinavica, 63*, 95–109.

Wallerstein, J. S., & Kelly, J. B. (1980). *Surviving the breakup: How children and parents cope with divorce*. New York: Basic Books.

Wandersman, L., Wandersman, A., & Kahn, S. (1980). Social support in the transition to parenthood. *Journal of Community Psychology, 8*, 332–342.

Warshak, R. A., & Santrock, J. W. (1983). The impact of divorce in father-custody and mother-custody homes: The child's perspective. In L. A. Kurdek (Ed.), *Children and divorce* (pp. 29–46). New Directions for Child Development, No. 19. San Francisco: Jossey-Bass.

Waters, E. (1978). The reliability and stability of individual differences in infant–mother attachment. *Child Development, 49*, 483–494.

Waters, E., Vaughn, B. E., & Egeland, B. R. (1980). Individual differences in infant–mother attachment relationships at age one: Antecedents in neonatal behavior in an urban, economically disadvantaged sample. *Child Development, 51*, 208–216.

Waters, E., Wippman, J., & Sroufe, L. A. (1979). Attachment, positive affect, and competence in the peer group: Two studies in construct validation. *Child Development, 50*, 821–829.

Weiss, R. S. (1979). *Going it alone*. New York: Basic Books.

Weissman, M. M., Prusoff, B. A., Gammon, G. D., Merikangas, K. R., Leckman, J. F., & Kidd, K. K. (1984). Psychopathology in the children (ages 6–18) of depressed and normal parents. *Journal of the American Academy of Child Psychiatry, 23*, 78–84.

Werner, E. E., & Smith, R. S. (1977). *Kauai's children come of age*. Honolulu: University Press of Hawaii.

Werner, E. E., & Smith, R. S. (1982). *Vulnerable but invincible*. New York: McGraw-Hill.

West, D. J., & Farrington, D. P. (1973). *Who becomes delinquent?* London: Heinemann.

Whitehead, L. (1979). Sex differences in children's responses to family stress: A reevaluation. *Journal of Child Psychology and Psychiatry and Allied Disciplines, 20*, 247–254.

Wolking, W. D., Dunteman, G. H., & Bailery, J. P. (1967). Multivariate analyses of parents' MMPI based on psychiatric diagnosis of their children. *Journal of Consulting Psychology, 31*, 521–524.

Yates, A. J. (1970). *Behavior Therapy*. New York: Wiley.

Zill, N. (1984). *Happy, healthy and insecure*. New York: Doubleday.

10 THE SOCIOCULTURAL CONTEXT OF CHILDHOOD DISORDERS

DAVID P. FARRINGTON

INTRODUCTION

The aim of this chapter is to review the relationship between childhood disorder and four sociocultural factors: social class, ethnic origin, the peer group, and the neighborhood. The major type of childhood disorder reviewed is conduct disorder, both socialized and undersocialized, especially that which is dealt with by the juvenile justice system as delinquency (see Chapter 1). Most of the quoted research has been carried out in North America or Great Britain, although a few studies have been conducted in other Northern European countries such as Sweden, Denmark, Norway, and West Germany.

The major problem in drawing conclusions about sociocultural factors in childhood psychopathology is that most possible predisposing factors tend to be interrelated. Children who live in deprived inner-city areas (at least in North America and Great Britain) tend to be from ethnic minorities, tend to have parents with low status, low-paid jobs, or no job at all, and tend to have friends who commit deviant acts. Furthermore, sociocultural factors tend to be related to individual characteristics and to family influences, both of which are reviewed elsewhere (see Chapter 9). Children from low-income families tend to have many siblings, which may make peer influence more important relative to parental influence, tend to receive poor nutrition and medical care from conception onwards, and tend to be exposed to lax and erratic child-management practices and to parental conflict, violence, and alcohol abuse. However, this chapter aims to review only evidence on the four categories of factors outlined above. One other sociocultural factor—the school—is not included here because it is the focus of Chapter

16. In general, the four types of factors will be treated one by one, but their interrelationship will be returned to at intervals.

As noted above, the emphasis in this chapter will be on juvenile delinquency, which is a legal concept rather than a psychopathological disorder. Delinquency is associated with conduct disorder (Chapter 2), however, which has a prime symptomatology of stealing, lying, aggression, truancy, and destructiveness, with disorders subsuming inattentiveness, impulsiveness, restlessness, and hyperactivity (Chapter 4), and with abuse of substances such as drugs, alcohol, and solvents (Chapter 6). Loeber (1982) and Loeber and Dishion (1983) have reviewed the extent to which many of these behaviors predict delinquency. Other disorders, such as those of anxiety-withdrawal and dysphoria, childhood schizophrenia, and autism, will be discussed less, partly because they are less clearly correlated with juvenile delinquency and partly because there has been far less research on their sociocultural correlates (as can be seen in Walker & Roberts, 1983). Juvenile delinquency has probably attracted most attention because of its high and conspicuous nuisance value. One consequence of concentrating on delinquency is that most of the research is concerned with boys only.

As an example of the complex interrelationships among some disorders, West (1969) found that a rating of nervous disturbance of boys at age eight to nine years, based on mothers' reports of such items as fears, enuresis, tics, and sleep disturbance, was significantly correlated with teachers' ratings of bad behavior in class at the same age. In the same London longitudinal survey of over 400 boys, however, West and Farrington (1973) discovered that, not only was nervous disturbance uncorrelated with later juvenile delinquency, but a combined rating of nervous-withdrawn at age eight to nine was *negatively* related to delinquency after controlling for poor (erratic or harsh) parental child-rearing behavior. Boys receiving poor parental behavior were more likely to be nervous-withdrawn and more likely to be juvenile delinquents, but at each level of parental behavior the nervous-withdrawn boys were less likely to be delinquents than the remainder.

Juvenile delinquency is a heterogeneous category, covering acts as diverse as theft, vandalism, violence against the person, drug use, and various kinds of heterosexual and homosexual indecency. In North America, traditionally, the category of delinquency has included not only these acts (which would be prohibited for adults) but also status offenses such as drinking alcohol and violating curfew. In England, the juvenile court has had both civil and criminal jurisdiction since its inception, and the term *delinquency* is usually restricted to acts such as theft, which are dealt with under its criminal jurisdiction. Behavior dealt with under its civil jurisdiction, such as truancy and being beyond parental control, is not usually considered delinquent in England. The recent tendency in North America to eliminate status offenses from the category of delinquency (National Council on Crime and Delinquency, 1975) should result in more comparability between Great Britain and North America in the definition of delinquency.

As with psychopathological disorders, an important question is the extent to which there are different dimensions of delinquent behavior. Because of the emphasis in this chapter on sociocultural factors, this question cannot be discussed in detail here. It seems clear, however, that there is a great deal of versatility in juvenile offending. In their prospective longitudinal survey, West and Farrington (1977) found little evidence of specialization in offending, since most youths convicted of aggressive crimes, damaging property, or drug use had also been convicted of crimes of dishonesty. Also, when Wolfgang, Figlio, and Sellin (1972) divided juvenile offenses in their Philadelphia cohort of nearly 10,000 boys into five broad types (non-index, injury, theft, damage, and combination), they discovered that the type of offense committed on any arrest was *unrelated* to the type committed on the previous arrest. It is less common to find a complete lack of specialization, however, than some specialization superimposed on a high degree of versatility (Bursik, 1980; Rojek & Erickson, 1982). Interestingly, Wolfgang (1980) found that there was specialization in his adult data. The most extensive review of versatility versus specialization in juvenile delinquency has been provided by Klein (1984), who concluded that delinquency was predominantly versatile. There is probably enough specialization to justify some typologies, however, such as the overt versus covert (aggression vs. dishonesty) distinction of Loeber (1982), which may have a parallel in the undersocialized–socialized dimension of conduct disorder.

The major methods of measuring child disorders, of course, are by means of interviews with (or questionnaires completed by) parents, teachers, children, and sometimes peers, systematic observation, and psychometric testing (see Chapter 11). In contrast, juvenile delinquency is almost always measured using either official records collected by the police and other criminal justice agencies or self-reports by children (Farrington, 1984). Peer reports of offending have been used (Gold, 1970), but only rarely, and the same is true of systematic observation (Buckle and Farrington, 1984). A recent development is the use of victim reports of the characteristics of offenders (Hindelang, 1981). The major problem with the dominant method of official records of delinquency is that they reflect not only childhood behavior but also reactions of official agencies. In other words, factors related to official delinquency may be associated not with offending but with the likelihood of selection for processing by the police and the courts. The problem of disentangling delinquent behavior and selection biases will be discussed later.

The emphasis throughout this chapter will be on relatively large-scale surveys (in the hundreds at least) of representative samples in the community, rather than on more specialized, small-scale studies of clinic or hospital samples. Particular emphasis will be given to prospective longitudinal surveys, and it will be argued in the Summary that these are especially useful. A large part of our knowledge about the natural history and causes of juvenile delinquency and adult crime comes from longitudinal surveys of crime and delinquency, and many of these have been reviewed by Farrington (1979b).

Child problem behavior is predictive not only of juvenile delinquency but of adult crimes as well, and some of the most interesting demonstrations of the continuity between child problem behavior and adult crime have been completed by Robins (1979, 1983; see also Chapter 2). In a longitudinal survey of over 200 black males in St. Louis, Robins and Wish (1977) distinguished between quantitative developmental processes, where the likelihood of committing an untried deviant act depended principally on the number of other types of acts already tried, and qualitative processes, where certain specific acts tended to be stepping stones to others. They studied 13 acts of childhood deviance, including elementary school failure and truancy, dropping out of high school before graduation, juvenile arrests, precocious sexual experience, drinking, and drug use. In general, all the acts tended to be related to each other, reflecting the versatility of problem behavior. The acts committed at about the same age tended to be most closely related. Few significant relationships between an act and a later one held independently of the number of acts committed before the first one. This suggested that the developmental process was primarily quantitative (versatile) rather than qualitative (specialized). There were, however, some qualitative relationships that were plausible theoretically. For example, drinking led to marijuana and amphetamine use, truancy led to dropping out of school, and (in the only reciprocal relationship) truancy led to school failure and school failure led to truancy.

Robins and Ratcliff (1980) then investigated the relationship between nine types of childhood deviance and five types of adult arrests. In general, the probability of an adult arrest increased with the number of different types of childhood deviance. They went on to study whether specific types of childhood acts predicted specific types of adult arrests, controlling both for the number of childhood acts and for the number of adult arrests. The only significant relationship was in drug use. For sex, the relationship was opposite to the expected one, since those with early sex experience were less likely to commit rape than the remainder. Robins has consistently argued that, since the major relationships in her research are quantitative rather than qualitative (the overall level of childhood deviance predicting the overall level of adult deviance), there is a single syndrome made up of a broad variety of antisocial acts arising in childhood and continuing into adulthood (but see Chapter 2). This chapter is concerned with sociocultural influences on this broad-band externalizing syndrome, with special reference to legally defined juvenile delinquency and other conduct problems.

SOCIAL CLASS

Definition and Measurement

In many projects, a disordered group of children is matched with a control group on demographic factors such as age, sex, race, and social class. This reflects the widespread belief in the importance of these factors, but of course prevents this importance from being tested. Historically, social class, or socioeconomic status, has been an important variable because of the belief of sociologists that human behavior could be explained by reference to societal variables. Borrowing freely from geology, their model of society was somewhat analogous to the earth, characterized as it was by a series of strata. Each person's behavior was thought to be determined to some extent by his or her position in strata of wealth, power, or prestige. Generally, the social class of a family has been measured primarily according to rankings by sociologists of the occupational prestige of the family breadwinner. Persons with professional or managerial jobs were ranked in the highest class, while those with unskilled manual jobs were ranked in the lowest.

Over the years, many other measures of social class have become popular, including family income, educational levels of parents, type of housing, overcrowding in the house, possessions, dependence on welfare benefits, and even general lifestyle. Sometimes, a number of these measures have been combined to form a scale of social class, but the extent to which these different operational definitions reflect the same underlying theoretical construct is not clear. Nor is it clear what that construct is, although there is the obvious assumption that the social class of the family will impinge in some way on the child. More seriously, the social class of a child is sometimes defined not according to the circumstances of his or her parents but according to the characteristics of the area of residence (e.g., Wolfgang et al., 1972) or school (Roff & Wirt, 1984). As will be pointed out in the later section on The Neighborhood, characteristics of individuals cannot necessarily be inferred from characteristics of areas.

Just as there are problems in defining social class, there are difficulties in measuring it. Children may not know enough about the occupations of parents to permit them to be categorized on a scale of occupational prestige, or may provide misleading information. Mothers may not know a father's earnings exactly, or may be unwilling to speak about such a sensitive topic as family income. In general, the occupational prestige scales date from many years ago, when it was more common for the father to be the family breadwinner and for the mother to be a housewife. Because of this, it may be difficult to derive a realistic measure of socioeconomic status for a family with a single parent or with two working parents (Mueller & Parcel, 1981).

| **Relation with Juvenile Delinquency** | The relation between social class and juvenile delinquency in the United States is a matter of some dispute. As Thornberry and Farnworth (1982) pointed out: |

In the literature on criminal behavior no variable occupies a more central role than social class. Despite that centrality, no variable is subject to more controversy concerning its relationship to crime. We have been informed, at one time or another, that social class has a strong, moderate, and weak inverse relationship to criminal behavior; that the two variables

are unrelated; and even that the expected inverse relationship is reversed.
(p. 505)

There *is* a great deal of inconsistency in the literature. Perhaps rather surprisingly, however, the majority of American researchers who have carried out major community surveys have found very little relationship between social class (usually measured by parental occupation) and juvenile delinquency (whether measured by official records or by self-reports). This was the result obtained by Thornberry and Farnworth (1982) in the Philadelphia cohort study, for example. In the first major comparison of self-reported and official delinquency in a nationally representative sample of over 800 American adolescents, Williams and Gold (1972) came to the same conclusion. Beginning with the pioneering self-report research of Short and Nye (1957), it was common to argue that low social class was related to official delinquency but not to self-reported delinquency, and hence that the official processing of offenders was biased against lower-class youth. In their careful review of the literature, however, Hindelang, Hirschi, and Weis (1981) found that the belief that low social class was related to official delinquency was entirely based on ecological (area) correlations. Studies based on individuals showed no discrepancy between official and self-report measures and no relation with social class.

The major argument against this conclusion derives from the important longitudinal survey of a national sample of over 1700 adolescents directed by Elliott (Elliott & Ageton, 1980; Elliott & Huizinga, 1983). Elliott found that, while there was little relation between social class and self-reported delinquency prevalence rates (meaning the number of persons committing acts), there was a considerable relation between low social class and incidence rates (meaning the number of acts committed). In other words, lower-social-class youth differed not in their likelihood of committing any offense but in the numbers of offenses they committed. It may be that previous surveys had not been sufficiently sensitive to detect class differences that occurred mainly at the frequent, serious end of the spectrum of offending.

British surveys have usually found a relation between class and delinquency. In their national longitudinal survey of over 5000 children born in 1946, Douglas, Ross, Hammond, and Mulligan (1966) reported a variation in the prevalence of official (male) delinquency from 3 percent to 19 percent between the top and bottom ranks of a four-point scale of social class. Their scale was based not only on the father's occupation, however, but also on the educational status and social class background of both parents. Using the father's occupation only, May (1981), with Scottish boys, and Ouston (1984), with London boys and girls, obtained similar relationships between social class and official delinquency. Regarding self-reports of offending, Belson (1975) found that these varied inversely with occupational prestige in his large-scale survey of over 1400 London boys.

European studies have also generally found a relation between social class and delinquency. In major Swedish longitudinal surveys, Jansen (1983) reported that official delinquency varied inversely with occupational prestige, and Magnusson, Stattin, and Duner (1983) showed that it varied inversely with parental education. A similar inverse relationship between occupational prestige and official delinquency was obtained in Denmark by Hogh and Wolf (1983), while in West Germany Remschmidt, Hohner, Merschmann, and Walter (1977) showed that low occupational prestige was correlated with high self-reported offending for boys. The research of Van Dusen, Mednick, Gabrielli, and Hutchings (1983) with adopted children in Denmark is especially interesting in showing a relation between official delinquency and the occupational prestige of both biological and adoptive parents.

The inconsistent American results may reflect the unsatisfactoriness of occupational prestige measures. In England, West and Farrington (1973) found that official delinquency was related to low family income, unsatisfactory housing, neglected accommodation, support by social agencies, physical neglect by parents, and an erratic paternal work record—but not to occupational prestige. They concluded that their measure of occupational prestige did not adequately reflect differences between their families in socioeconomic conditions, and that their best measure of social class (or economic disadvantage) was family income. Interestingly, somewhat similar results were obtained in the major American self-report survey by Hirschi (1969) of over 4000 children in California. While delinquency was not related to paternal occupation or education, it was related to paternal unemployment and to the welfare status of the family. Similarly, in her American longitudinal surveys, Robins (1979) found that occupational prestige did not predict official delinquency but that poverty did.

It is implausible to argue that economic disadvantage, as reflected by such measures as low income, slum housing, and unemployed parents, is not related to delinquency. Beginning with the pioneering work of Burt (1925) in England and Glueck and Glueck (1950) in the United States, this result has been obtained consistently. The failure of some American studies to demonstrate relationships between occupational prestige and delinquency probably reflects the fact that occupational prestige does not accurately measure a theoretical construct that influences delinquency in the United States. Social class, as commonly measured in some studies, may not be related to delinquency, but economic disadvantage probably is.

Relation with Other Disorders

There is little compelling evidence pointing to a relation between social class and other child disorders. In studies with children aged 3, Richman, Stevenson, and Graham (1975) in England and Earls (1980) in the United States enquired about such symptoms as eating and sleeping problems, encopresis, overactivity, poor concentration, unhappiness, worries, temper tantrums, and difficulties in relationships with siblings or peers. Both found no relationship between the total number of problems and occupational prestige, although Richman et al. reported that the total score was related to the type of housing. Similarly, in the large-scale American study of 1300 Washington, D.C., children aged 4 to 16 by Achenbach and Edelbrock (1981), and in the smaller project on nearly 500 Buffalo children aged six to twelve by Lapouse and Monk (1964), there were very few significant relationships between behavior symptoms and occupational prestige.

Results in large-scale British studies also show that most relationships with social class are not statistically significant. In his national longitudinal survey, Douglas (1964) found that there was little relation at age 11 between social class and emotional (anxiety-withdrawal) symptoms such as bedwetting, nightmares, and nailbiting, except that lower-class girls were more likely to wet their beds. In the same survey, Douglas, Ross, and Simpson (1968) reported that aggressiveness and nervousness had little relation with social class at age 15 after controlling for school type. There was a tendency, however, for lower-class boys to be rated as more aggressive than middle-class boys. In their Isle of Wight study of over 3400 children, Rutter, Tizard, and Whitmore (1970) found no significant relation between occupational prestige and either neurotic or antisocial disorder at ages 9 to 12, although again lower-class children tended to be more disordered. However, Davie, Butler, and Goldstein (1972), in their national longitudinal survey of over 15,000 children born in 1958, found many significant relationships with occupational prestige. Lower-class children at age 7 showed more withdrawal, depression, restlessness, hostility, destructiveness, aggression, irritability, and disobedience.

Studies of other types of disorder do not show consistently that they are more common among lower-class children. For example, in her careful review of prospective longitudinal studies of drug use, Kandel (1980) concluded that social class did not predict initiation into marijuana use. In a large-scale study of over 9000 children in Michigan, Bosco and Robin (1980) found no relation between occupational prestige and hyperkinesis. In smaller-scale British studies, however, Kolvin, Ounsted, Richardson, and Garside (1971) reported that infantile psychosis of early onset (especially autism) tended to be commoner in *upper*-class children, while psychosis of later onset (especially childhood schizophrenia) tended to be commoner in lower-class children. The upper-class preponderance of autistic children has also been noted by other researchers (Cox, Rutter, Newman, & Bartak, 1975), but this result is now disputed (Dawson & Mesibov, 1983; DeMyer, Hingtgen, & Jackson, 1981).

Interpreting the Results

There are basically four problems in interpreting the relation between social class and childhood disorder. The first is whether the two measures are related at all. As the above review indicates, the literature is full of inconsistencies and contradictions. Where social class does seem to be related to childhood disorder, the second problem is whether this result is caused artefactually by social-class biases in the detection or measurement of disorder.

Are disordered children who are also lower class more likely to come to the attention of researchers than other disordered children?

Assuming that the relation is not entirely due to some kind of bias, the third problem is whether it holds independently of other variables. If a theoretical construct that causes a disorder is also correlated with social class, this might create an illusory correlation between social class and the disorder—illusory in the sense that there is no causal link between social class and the disorder. Finally, if the relation between social class and childhood disorder holds independently of other measured variables, the fourth problem is to understand what this means. What are the important theoretical constructs being measured by social class, and what are the causal linkages between these constructs and the theoretical constructs underlying the measure of disorder?

These problems will be illustrated by reference to juvenile delinquency. The above review shows that some studies (especially the British and European ones) have reported a correlation between low social class and delinquency, while others have not. Very few of these studies have investigated the problem of whether the correlation reflects social-class bias. The most obvious way in which this might occur is if lower-class children who commit offenses are more likely to appear in an official record than other children who commit offenses, and indeed Elliott and Voss (1974) found that lower-class children had many more police contacts per 100 self-reported offenses than middle-class children. It is also possible that lower-class children who commit offenses are more likely to admit them than other children.

There is some evidence of lower-class bias in police processing of offenders. For example, Farrington and Bennett (1981) showed that children of manual workers who were arrested were more likely to be prosecuted in court than other arrested children. Several American researchers (Cohen and Kluegel, 1978; Terry, 1967) in carefully controlled studies have found, however, no evidence of class biases in official processing. Class biases do not invariably tend to magnify the number of lower-class children in official records; for example, Shepherd, Oppenheim, and Mitchell (1966) in England found that children of *higher*-class parents were more likely to attend child guidance clinics, because their mothers worried more about their problems. Also, Wing (1980) showed that autistic children in the community tended to be representative of all social classes, but that those with higher-class parents were more likely to be seen in clinics.

One way of investigating how far the characteristics of official delinquents reflect class biases in police processing is to compare official and self-reported delinquents. It might be assumed that self-reports reflect delinquent behavior, while official records reflect both delinquent behavior and selection biases. If so, the partial correlation between class and official delinquency, controlling for self-reported delinquency, is a measure of the extent to which class is related to official processing independently of delinquent behavior. These kinds of analyses were completed by Farrington

(1979a) in the London longitudinal survey. As pointed out earlier, occupational prestige did not predict juvenile delinquency in this study, but low family income did. Farrington found that income was related to official delinquency independently of self-reported delinquency, suggesting that some part of the relation between income and official delinquency reflected processing biases.

The third problem is whether the relation between social class and delinquency holds independently of other possible predisposing factors. In the London longitudinal survey, West and Farrington (1973) used matching analyses to investigate the independent contributions of different factors to official delinquency, and concluded that five factors were independently predictive: low family income, large family size, poor parental child-rearing behavior, convicted parents, and low intelligence. It was noticeable, however, that low family income did not predict delinquency independently of low intelligence, whereas low intelligence did predict delinquency independently of low family income. Therefore, it is possible that poverty was related to delinquency partly because of the tendency of poorer parents to have less intelligent children.

Henggeler, Urey, and Borduin (1982) also argued that intelligence was an important mediator between social class and behavior-problem children, because lower-class mothers used simpler language and were less verbal in interacting with their preschool children. These ideas also figure prominently in Cohen's (1955) delinquent subculture theory, discussed in the later section on sociocultural theories. Further discussion of the theoretical interpretation of any relationship between social class and delinquency will be postponed until then, but the conclusions reached by Wolkind and Rutter (1985) seem quite plausible: "It appears that the characteristics of the parents (e.g. whether or not they are criminal), of the family (e.g. in terms of discord), and of the home living conditions (as with overcrowding or run-down dilapidated housing) matter much more than parental occupation" (p. 88).

ETHNIC ORIGIN

Relation with Juvenile Delinquency

Fortunately, there is far less disagreement about the relation between race and juvenile delinquency than about the relation involving social class. It is clear that blacks in the United States are far more likely to become official delinquents than whites. For example, in the major Philadelphia cohort study of Wolfgang et al. (1972), 50 percent of the black males were arrested before age 18, in comparison with 29 percent of the white males. The careful review of the literature on the prevalence of delinquency by Gordon (1976) shows consistent black–white differences in official delinquency, while a summary table prepared by Hindelang et al. (1981, p. 158) demonstrates ratios of the order of 3:1 for both males and females.

It has been argued that these consistently high ratios reflect discrimination in official processing rather than differences in delinquent behavior.

For example, Williams and Gold (1972), in their national survey, found that black–white ratios for official delinquency were much greater than corresponding ratios for self-reported delinquency. However, other explanations have been put forward for the discrepancy between official and self-report measures. Hindelang et al. (1981) argued that the black–white ratio was greatest for the most serious offenses, and that this ratio was diluted in most self-report questionnaires by the overrepresentation of trivial offenses. They also found that black males were especially likely to underreport their offending, and therefore concluded that the questionnaires were differentially valid by race.

Elliott and Ageton (1980), in their national longitudinal survey, argued that previous questionnaires had not been sufficiently sensitive to detect black–white differences that occurred, especially in the number of acts committed. They showed that truncating the data at an extreme category of three or more offenses, as many previous researchers had done, greatly reduced black–white differences that appeared when adolescents could record 200 or more offenses in the previous year. Bearing in mind the high black–white ratios also found in victim reports of offender characteristics (Hindelang, 1981), it seems clear that black juveniles commit more offenses than white juveniles in the United States. On both official and self-reported delinquency measures, however, Oriental juveniles seem to commit fewer offenses than whites (Elliott & Voss, 1974).

The relation between ethnic origin and delinquency has rarely been studied in Great Britain. Two studies in Bradford, however, a city with a large Asian population (originating in India, Pakistan, and Bangladesh), showed that Asian juveniles had a *lower* official delinquency rate than whites (Batta, McCulloch, & Smith, 1975; Mawby, McCulloch, & Batta, 1979). Blacks (mainly originating in the West Indies), on the other hand, had a higher official delinquency rate than whites in two London studies (Ouston, 1984; Stevens & Willis, 1979). Systematic comparisons of black, Asian, and white juveniles on self-reported and official delinquency in Great Britain have not yet been published.

Relation with Other Disorders

Tuddenham, Brooks, and Milkovich (1974) have probably carried out the most detailed study of ethnicity and childhood disorder in the United States. In a sample of over 3000 California children aged 9 to 11, they found that white and Oriental mothers made the most positive reports about their children's behavior. Blacks were said to be restless, untruthful, unaffectionate, and prone to stuttering. Orientals were said to be shy, not daredevils, not nailbiters, and not involved in fights. Chicanos were more likely to stay away from home without permission, and the boys tended to be bullies. Whites were more truthful than blacks and less shy than Orientals. In contrast, Achenbach and Edelbrock (1981) found very few racial differences.

British projects have often documented a greater frequency of behavior problems among West Indians than among whites. In the Inner London study of Rutter et al. (1974), for example, conduct disorder was more prevalent at age 10 among West Indian boys and girls than among white boys and girls, although there were no differences in emotional (anxiety-withdrawal) disorder. The black boys and girls were especially high on restlessness, fighting, disobedience, aggressiveness, bullying, destructiveness, lying, stealing, apathy, and irritability, while the black girls (only) were notably solitary and tearful. Interestingly, these results did not vary according to whether the children were born in England or in the West Indies.

In smaller-scale Inner London studies, Graham and Meadows (1967) and Nicol (1971) also showed that West Indian children had a higher rate of conduct disorder than white controls, while there was a tendency in the Graham and Meadows project for the West Indian children to have a low rate of neurotic disorder. Wing (1980) reported higher rates of autism among blacks and Asians in Inner London than among whites. However, Richman et al. (1975) found little difference in behavior problems between black and white three-year-olds in an Outer London borough.

Interpreting the Results

Some part of the difference between blacks and whites in official delinquency is probably attributable to discrimination in processing. In the Philadelphia cohort study, Thornberry (1973) found that, even after allowing for important factors such as the seriousness of the offense and the prior juvenile record, black youths were more likely to be taken to court and given institutional sentences than whites. Similarly, in London, Landau (1981) discovered that black youths were more likely to be taken to court than whites. Also, Elliott and Voss (1974), in their survey of over 2600 California children, showed that blacks had far more police contacts per 100 self-reported offenses than whites.

Black–white differences may not hold independently of other predisposing factors. Rutter, Yule, Morton, and Bagley (1975) outlined some of the deprivations suffered by their black families, especially in regard to lower-status jobs and poorer-quality housing. Ouston (1984) was able to show that her black–white differences in official delinquency did not hold independently of differences in social class or teachers' ratings of attainment. Similarly, Cochrane (1979) found few differences in conduct disorder or in emotional (anxiety-withdrawal) disorder between black, Asian, and white children attending the same deprived inner-city schools in Birmingham. In the United States, Gordon (1976) argued that black–white differences in official delinquency could be explained by reference to black–white differences in intelligence and to the known relation between intelligence and delinquency (Hirschi & Hindelang, 1977).

If ethnic differences in delinquency do hold independently of other factors, they might be explained by reference to some of the subcultural theories described below. Brake (1980) has argued that blacks and Asians in Great Britain belong to different subcultures with different sets of values from the dominant white culture. Batta et al. (1975) and Mawby et al. (1979) explained the low delinquency rate of Asians in their studies by reference to the close-knit, highly controlling Asian subculture. It is not clear, however, that ethnic differences in delinquency do hold independently of differences in other individual, family, and social factors.

THE PEER GROUP

As pointed out in Chapter 1, the third edition of the *Diagnostic and Statistical Manual* of the American Psychiatric Association (1980) classifies conduct disorder as aggressive or nonaggressive and as socialized or undersocialized. Generally, the socialized-aggressive adolescents are those who commit delinquent acts with others, who are loyal to delinquent friends, or who belong to a delinquent gang. The emphasis on socialized aggression as a distinct category (sometimes called subcultural delinquency) dates from the work of Hewitt and Jenkins (1946). The use of this category recognizes the role of the peer group in conduct disorder (see Chapter 2).

The review by Zimring (1981) shows that, at least for the last 60 years, most American adolescents have committed their delinquent acts in small groups (of two or three people, usually) rather than alone. Similar results have been obtained in England by West and Farrington (1973) and in Norway by Sveri (1965). Generally, the frequency of group offending decreases with age, although some researchers (Craig & Budd, 1967) have found that it is more common at ages 14 to 16 than at younger ages.

Most analyses are based on offenders rather than offenses. The frequency of group offenders will always be greater than the frequency of group offenses, because of the multiple counting of offenders. To take an example from Sveri (1965, Table 1), at ages 13–14, only 16.6 percent of offenders were alone, 28.8 percent were in a group of two, 17.1 percent were in a group of three, and 37.5 percent were in a group of four or more. Assuming an average group size of six for those in a group of four or more, it follows that 38.6 percent of *offenses* were committed by lone offenders, 33.5 percent by groups of two, 13.3 percent by groups of three, and 14.6 percent by groups of four or more.

The above figures refer to official delinquents. If people committing offenses in groups are more likely to be apprehended than those acting alone, it is possible that official figures could overestimate the true prevalence of group offending. In agreement with this suggestion, Hindelang (1976) found that offenders in groups were more likely to be picked up by the police than those acting alone, even after controlling for the frequency and seriousness of offending. Self-reported delinquency surveys rarely provide detailed information about group offending. If they enquire about this at all, they often ask whether each act was committed usually alone or usually with others, rather than trying to obtain precise quantitative estimates of numbers of acts committed and numbers of persons involved.

Using the self-report method, Hindelang (1971) in the United States found that only 2 out of 18 acts (drinking alcohol and using marijuana) were more often committed with others than alone. Interestingly, group offenders did not usually commit acts more often than individual offenders. Hindelang (1976) concluded, however, that fighting and carrying a weapon (more characteristic of undersocialized conduct disorder) were often committed alone, while taking cars, destroying property, getting drunk, using pot or pills, and burglary (more characteristic of socialized conduct disorder) were often committed with others.

In a British self-report survey based on a small sample of 54 boys aged 11 to 14, Shapland (1978) reported that 60 percent of acts were committed with peers, 10 percent with adults, and 30 percent alone. It was significant that no boy said that he committed any offense with girls. One of the most useful studies is the systematic comparison of group offending in official records and self-reports by Eynon and Reckless (1961) in Ohio. They found that both methods indicated that about three-quarters of institutionalized male delinquents had been with companions when they had committed their *first* delinquent act at an average age of about 13.

While group offending is very common, delinquent gangs are not. Probably the major study of gangs was carried out in Chicago by Short and Strodtbeck (1965). They could not find any delinquent gangs whose primary activities were crimes of dishonesty or drug use, nor any middle-class delinquent gangs. They studied 16 gangs, totaling nearly 600 boys, which were the most notorious in Chicago in 1960 (using detached workers), but these were primarily black gangs oriented toward violence. Surprisingly, the gang members were little different from non-gang members or even from middle-class boys in their evaluation of middle-class values in a semantic differential.

Later studies disagree about the extent to which gang membership is an important factor in the totality of delinquency. Miller (1975) carried out a national survey of several of the largest American cities, questioning police and other agencies. He reported that about one-third of all juveniles arrested for violence were gang members, and that gang members accounted for about one-quarter of all juvenile homicides. O'Hagan (1976), in a small survey of 60 institutionalized Scottish delinquents, found that 80 percent claimed to be members of juvenile gangs that engaged in theft, vandalism, or violence.

Morash (1983) studied over 500 youths in Boston, however, and found that there was a negligible association between being a member of a stereotypical gang and committing delinquent acts. Similarly, West and Farrington (1977) reported that, while 85 percent of their London boys went around in a group of four or more males, only 5 percent were members of a gang with a recognizable identity, a leadership structure, and some kind of uniform. These mostly centered round a particular club or cafe. While official delinquency was associated with going round in a group, fewer of the gang boys were official delinquents than of the remainder. These large-scale surveys of youths seem likely to provide the most reliable information about gangs.

The major problem of interpretation is whether adolescents are more likely to commit offenses while they are in groups than while they are alone, or whether the high prevalence of group offending merely reflects the fact that, when adolescents go out, they tend to go out in groups. Do peers tend to encourage and facilitate offending, or is it just that most kinds of activities out of the home (both delinquent and nondelinquent) tend to be done in groups? Another possibility is that the commission of delinquent acts encourages an association with other delinquents, perhaps because "birds of a feather flock together" or because of the stigmatizing and isolating effects of court appearances and institutionalization. It is surprisingly difficult to decide among these various possibilities, although most researchers argue that peer influence is an important factor.

There is clearly a close relationship between the delinquent activities of an adolescent and those of his or her friends. Both in the United States (Hirschi, 1969) and in Great Britain (West & Farrington, 1973), it has been found that a boy's reports of his own offending are significantly correlated with his reports of his friends' delinquency. Similarly, Hardt and Peterson (1968) showed that the official delinquency records of a boy's friends were significantly related to his own official and self-reported offending. In the major national survey of Elliott, Huizinga, and Ageton (1985), having delinquent peers was the best predictor of self-reported delinquency in a multivariate analysis. None of the existing studies, however, has demonstrated unambiguously that associating with delinquent peers precedes or causes a boy's own delinquency. As the review by Campbell (1981) shows, even less is known about the role of the peer group in female delinquency.

It might be expected that the more closely a boy was attached to his peers, the greater would be their influence. A number of studies have related peer attachment to delinquency, but with inconsistent results. For example, Hirschi (1969) found that low attachment to peers was correlated with high self-reported delinquency, while Hindelang (1973) reported that high attachment to peers was correlated with high self-reported delinquency. Presumably, it is necessary to distinguish between attachment to delinquent peers and attachment to nondelinquent peers, as these might be expected to have different effects. Delinquent peers are likely to be most influential where they have the highest status within the peer group and are the most popular. Studies both in the United States (Roff & Wirt, 1984) and in Great Britain (West & Farrington, 1973) show, however, that delinquents are usually unpopular with their peers.

The importance of peer influence has also been identified in other kinds of problem behavior. For example, in a study of over 400 high school students in Colorado, Jessor and Jessor (1977) found that adolescents' reports of problem drinking, marijuana use, and sexual experience were significantly related to the extent to which their friends approved of and provided models for these acts. In another project on over 1000 adolescent–parent–best friend triads in New York state, Kandel, Treiman, Faust, and Single (1976) showed that the best predictor of an adolescent's marijuana use was his or her best friend's marijuana use. On the other hand, the review by Gorsuch and Butler (1976) suggests two other possible reasons for this correlation. Drug use can lead to the selection of drug-using peers as friends, and also youths with a high potential for drug use may choose friends with a similarly high potential.

If indeed delinquent peers facilitate delinquency, it should be possible to reduce delinquency either by reducing the delinquency of peers or by exposing adolescents to prosocial peers. Generally, programs that have been targeted on group delinquency have not been very successful. Klein (1969), for example, evaluated a detached worker program in Los Angeles that aimed to prevent delinquency in black gangs by transforming the gangs into social clubs and encouraging their participation in legal activities. He found that the detached workers had made the gangs more cohesive, but that the increased cohesiveness was correlated with increased group delinquency!

The experiment in St. Louis by Feldman, Caplinger, and Wodarski (1983) is more encouraging. They studied over 400 boys who were referred because of antisocial behavior and randomly assigned them to two kinds of activity groups, each comprising about 10 to 12 adolescents. The groups either consisted entirely of referred youths or consisted of one or two referred youths and about 10 nonreferred (prosocial) peers. Feldman et al. found that, on the basis of systematic observation, self-reports by the youths, and ratings by the group leaders, the antisocial behavior of the referred youths in mixed groups (with prosocial peers) decreased relative to that of the referred youths in unmixed groups. This result is in conformity with other experimental attempts to reduce delinquency in peer groups using prosocial models (Sarason, 1978). While the correlational studies are not entirely convincing, these intervention experiments suggest that the peer group can have an important role in producing, maintaining, and reducing delinquency.

THE NEIGHBORHOOD

Relation with Juvenile Delinquency

Studies of the importance of the area of residence can be divided into two broad categories. First, there are the "ecological" studies, which follow the pioneering work of Shaw and McKay (1969) in Chicago and five other cities. These show the correlations, over small areas of a city, between rates of official juvenile delinquency and other rates—for example, of population density, racial composition, owner occupation, poor housing, infant mortality, alcoholism, mental illness, and suicide. Second, there are the comparisons of much larger areas—for example, comparisons of inner city, suburban, and rural areas.

Shaw and McKay (1969) found that the distribution of juvenile delinquency (defined according to where delinquents lived rather than where they committed their offenses) followed patterns of physical structure and social organization in cities. Generally, delinquents were concentrated in areas of physical deterioration and neighborhood disorganization. A large proportion of offenders came from a small proportion of areas in Chicago. Furthermore, the distribution of delinquency was surprisingly consistent over time. Shaw and McKay concluded that variations in delinquency reflected variations in the social values and norms to which children were exposed, which tended to be consistent over time in any given area. Since delinquency was caused by social disorganization, they argued that it could be prevented by community organization. This idea led to the Chicago Area Project, which aimed to coordinate community resources to increase the educational, recreational, and occupational opportunities for young people. However, the success of this project in reducing delinquency has never been rigorously demonstrated.

Later work has tended to cast doubt on the consistency of delinquency rates over time. Bursik and Webb (1982) tested Shaw and McKay's cultural-transmission hypothesis using more recent data in Chicago and more sophisticated quantitative methods. They concluded that the distribution of delinquency was not stable after 1950, but reflected demographic changes. Variations in delinquency rates in different areas were significantly correlated with variations in the percentage of nonwhites, the percentage of foreign-born whites, and the percentage of overcrowded households. The greatest increase in delinquency in an area occurred when blacks moved from the minority to the majority. These results suggest that Shaw and McKay's ideas about community values that persist despite successive waves of immigration and emigration need revising.

Similar ecological studies have been carried out in Great Britain (for a review, see Baldwin, 1979). Wallis and Maliphant (1967) in London showed that official delinquency rates correlated with rates of local authority renting, percentage of land used industrially or commercially, population density, and with the proportion of the population under age 21. Delinquency rates were negatively related to suicide and unemployment rates, however, and were not related to illegitimacy or mental-illness rates. Power, Benn, and Morris (1972) carried out a similar study in one working-class London borough and found that official delinquency rates varied with rates of overcrowding and fertility and with the social class and type of housing of an area.

Comparisons of larger areas have usually revealed high delinquency rates in inner-city areas and low rates in rural areas. In general, delinquency rates have varied more reliably with the social class of areas than with the social class of individuals. For example, Clark and Wenninger (1962) compared four areas in Illinois and concluded that self-reported offending rates were greatest in the inner city, less in a lower-class urban area, less still in an upper-middle-class urban area, and lowest of all in a rural farm area. While there were considerable differences between areas, there was little relationship between social class and self-reported delinquency for individuals within areas. Gold and Reimer (1975), in their national self-report survey, also found that male delinquency was highest in the city centers and lowest in the rural areas.

Relation with Other Disorders

An interesting ecological study of over 1000 children referred to a child guidance clinic in an Outer London borough was completed by Gath, Cooper, Gattoni, and Rockett (1977). Most of the referrals were for conduct disorder or neurosis. Gath et al. found that the highest rates of child guidance cases (and also of delinquency) were in the densely populated areas of the borough, which were lower-class areas with high rates of local authority renting and low owner occupation rates. While referral rates were correlated with social class (occupational prestige) for area, they were not correlated for individuals. Gath et al. found, however, that middle-class children were likely to be referred by medical agencies for neurotic symptoms, while lower-class children were likely to be referred by schools and social agencies for conduct disorder.

One of the most significant studies of urban versus rural areas is the comparison by Rutter, Cox, Tupling, Berger, and Yule (1975) of 10-year-old children in Inner London and in the Isle of Wight. They found a much higher incidence of conduct disorder and neurosis in their Inner London sample. Rutter, Yule, Quinton, Rowlands, Yule, and Berger (1975) investigated factors that might explain this urban–rural difference. They found that four sets of variables—family discord, parental deviance, social disadvantage, and school characteristics—correlated with conduct disorder in each area and that the higher rates of disorder in Inner London were at least partly due to the higher incidence of these four adverse factors.

Studies in other countries also tend to show systematic urban–rural differences. For example, Johnston, Bachman, and O'Malley (1980), in a national American survey, reported that drug use was highest in the largest metropolitan areas and lowest in the nonmetropolitan areas. Lavik (1977) compared Oslo with a rural area of Norway and found more behavior problems, delinquency, truancy, alcohol, and drug abuse in 16-year-olds in Oslo. Kastrup (1977), however, found little difference in disorders of 6-year-olds between the two Danish communities of Aarhus (population 250,000) and Samso (population 5000). It may be that the prevalence of childhood disorder is especially high in the largest cities, and that Aarhus was not a large enough city for this pattern to show.

Interpreting the Results

Ecological studies have many problems of interpretation, because it is not possible to draw conclusions about individuals from correlations based on areas. This is the "ecological fallacy" identified many years ago by Robinson (1950). To give an example, Wallis and Maliphant (1967) found that delinquency rates in areas were negatively correlated with divorce rates in areas, but that the individual delinquents in their study were more likely to have divorced parents than a representative sample of boys. In order to draw conclusions about individuals, it is necessary to carry out research based on individuals. It may be, however, that some variables based on areas are more important than the same variables based on individuals. For example, Clark and Wenninger's (1962) research suggests that an individual's delinquency rate is more closely correlated with the social class of the area than with the social class of the family.

The results quoted in this section are compatible with the hypothesis that some aspects of the inner-city environment tend to produce delinquency and childhood disorder. However, a number of methodological problems with the researches should be noted. First of all, it might be argued that disordered behavior is more likely to be recorded in cities, perhaps because there is more police activity or better psychiatric service. The fact that the urban–rural differences hold up in self-reported delinquency studies suggests, however, that this cannot be the complete explanation. A second problem is the difficulty of defining a community. In most projects, areas are defined according to census or electoral districts, which may not reflect real community boundaries. Hence, real differences between neighborhoods may be blurred.

A third problem is that delinquency rates are almost always calculated according to the areas of residence of offenders, which may be different from the areas in which offenses are committed. Any theory of environmental influences on offending must take account of this distinction. Finally, the fact that delinquency is greater in certain areas does not necessarily mean that the areas have some causal influence. It could be that deprived people tend to congregate in deprived inner-city areas, perhaps because it is only in these areas that they can afford to pay the rents. Also, in many parts of Great Britain it is the local authority's housing policy to allocate the worst accommodation in the worst areas to those who are perceived as the worst families (Gill, 1977). Therefore, it may be that the problem people cause the problem areas rather than the reverse.

In favor of the proposition that inner-city living causes delinquency, Osborn (1980) found that moving out of London was associated with a significant decrease in offending. Also, Rutter (1981) showed that the differences between Inner London and the Isle of Wight held even when the analyses were restricted to children reared in the same area by parents reared in the same area. This result demonstrates that the movement of problem families into problem areas cannot be the whole explanation of area differences in disorder. Differences in family and school factors may be part of the explanation. Indeed, Wolkind and Rutter (1985) concluded that inner-city living had little direct impact on childhood disorder but had indirect effects mediated by family discord and parental deviance. It may be, however, that some aspect of the neighborhood is conducive to delinquency, perhaps because the inner city leads to a breakdown of community ties or neighborhood patterns of mutual support, or perhaps because the high population density produces tension, frustration, or anonymity. The next section will discuss more detailed theories about why these sociocultural factors might be important.

SOCIOCULTURAL THEORIES OF DELINQUENCY

Social Learning Theories

Most sociocultural theories of delinquency were designed to explain the presumed high delinquency rates of lower-class young males living in inner-city areas. The earlier theories all emphasized the importance of the peer group, especially in relation to gangs or subcultures, which were the focus of a great deal of criminological research in the 1950s and 1960s, when city gangs were perceived as an important social problem in the United States.

One of the first postwar sociocultural theories to attract wide attention was the differential association theory of Sutherland (Sutherland & Cressey, 1969). This was essentially a social learning theory, proposing that delinquent attitudes, motives, rationalizations, and techniques of committing crimes are learned during interaction with others in intimate personal groups. Whether people become delinquents depends primarily on whether they are exposed differentially more to delinquent than to law-abiding attitudes. Hence, children from criminal families and from criminal areas and those with delinquent peers will be most likely to commit delinquent acts.

As an alternative to the idea that specifically delinquent attitudes are learned, Miller (1958) suggested that lower-class attitudes in general are conducive to delinquency. He argued that, when children are learning to conform to the standards of the lower-class culture, they are effectively learning to commit delinquent acts. According to Miller, certain characteristics are greatly valued among the lower-classes—notably being tough, taking risks, seeking excitement, and making easy money. Children can obtain status among their peers by displaying these characteristics and, in turn, these characteristics are likely to lead to delinquent behavior. This theory was based on Miller's experiences with delinquent street corner groups.

A third social learning theory with an emphasis on sociocultural factors was proposed by Trasler (1962). He suggested that children learn to refrain from delinquency as a result of punishment imposed by their parents. Each time a child is punished for committing an act, the pain and fear aroused tend to become conditioned to the act in the child's mind. A child who has been punished several times for the same act feels fear when he or she next contemplates it, and this fear tends to block the commission of the act. According to Trasler's social learning theory, conscience is a conditioned fear response. Whether a child commits delinquent acts depends primarily on the strength of the conscience, which in turn depends on the styles of punishment applied by a child's parents.

Trasler argued that lower-class children are more likely to commit delinquent acts because of deficiencies in the techniques of training used by their parents. Whereas love-oriented discipline is used by middle-class parents, lower-class parents use object-oriented discipline based on rewards and punishments. Lower-class children spend more time with peers and less time with parents, and hence are more susceptible to peer influence and can turn to peers for solace after being punished by their parents. Middle-class children are closely supervised by their parents, so that they are very lonely if they incur parental disapproval. Middle-class parents are more consistent and more concerned to build up general principles of conduct, and hence they are more successful socializers.

Strain Theories

The social learning theories were opposed by strain theories in the late 1950s and 1960s. These suggested that lower-class youths commit delinquent acts because of the discrepancy between their aspirations and their ability to achieve goals of status or material success. According to Cohen (1955), lower-class boys compete with middle-class boys in school according to middle-class standards. Lower-class boys are handicapped in this competition, because their parents are less likely to have taught them abstract reasoning, middle-class manners, the avoidance of aggression, and the postponement of immediate gratification in favor of long-term goals. Consequently, they are likely to antagonize their teachers and to perform badly in school. Faced with the problem that they cannot achieve status according to the middle-class standards of the school, these boys solve this problem by joining a delinquent subculture in which they can achieve status. They live their lives according to values that are in opposition to those of the larger society. Behaviors such as aggression and theft, which are wrong by middle-class standards, are right by the standards of the delinquent subculture and convey status.

Cloward and Ohlin (1960) argued that Western society encourages everyone to strive for material wealth but makes it very difficult for lower-class youths who fail within the educational system to achieve wealth by legitimate methods. These youths are therefore driven to use illegitimate methods to achieve their goals. They can adopt illegitimate methods and join delinquent subcultures, however, only if they have the example of successful adult criminals in their neighborhood. There are three types of subcultures: criminal (where delinquent behavior is used to achieve success goals), conflict (based on toughness and fighting), and retreatist (based on drug use).

Control Theory

The social learning and strain theories of delinquency were largely supplanted by control and labeling theories in the 1970s. Labeling theory (Lemert, 1972) will not be discussed here, because it is concerned with social reaction to delinquency rather than with any of the four sociocultural factors that are the focus of this chapter. Control theory (Hirschi, 1969) is based on the assumption that people do not commit delinquent acts if they have a strong bond to society. The bond has four elements: attachment, commitment, involvement, and belief. Attachment refers to the extent to which people care about and internalize the wishes and expectations of others, especially parents, teachers, and peers. Commitment refers to the rational element in crime, suggesting that people weigh the benefits against the costs. Involvement draws attention to the fact that many people are so busy doing conventional activities that they have little time or opportunity for delinquency, and belief refers to the extent to which people believe in the rules of society. To a considerable extent, Hirschi's theory is a summary of the relationships in his correlational data, and it is symptomatic of the tendency for theories and data to be increasingly closely linked.

Integrative Theories

The trend in the 1980s is toward more complex integrative theories. Elliott et al. (1985) attempted to combine strain, control, and social learning theories. One of their key ideas is that delinquency results from differential bonding to conventional and delinquent groups. There are three alternative paths to delinquency. The strain theory path occurs when conventional bonding (produced by effective early childhood socialization) is attenuated by poor school performance and limited opportunities for achieving goals. Delinquency acts as an alternative method of achieving material success. The control theory path occurs when childhood socialization is ineffective, producing weak internal and external controls over delinquency. Essentially, strain theory explains why pressures toward delinquency arise, while control theory explains why these pressures are not kept in check. The third, social learning path occurs when delinquency is reinforced by an individual's interpersonal network. In the socialization process, conventional or delinquent behavior can be reinforced, and the primary reinforcer for delinquent behavior is the peer group. It follows that delinquency is most serious when strain, weak conventional bonding, and strong bonding to a delinquent peer group occur together. This theory guided the design of Elliott's national longitudinal survey.

Another integrative theory of delinquency was proposed by Farrington (1986). He suggested that delinquent acts are the end product of a four-stage process. In the first stage, motivation arises. The main desires that ultimately produce delinquent acts are for material goods, status among intimates, and excitement. These desires are greater among children from poorer families. In the second stage, a legal or illegal method of satisfying the desire is chosen. Children from poorer families are less able to satisfy their desires by legal methods, and so they tend to choose illegal methods. The relative inability of poorer children to achieve goals by legitimate methods is partly because they tend to fail in school and hence tend to have erratic, low-status employment histories. School failure in turn is often a consequence of the unstimulating intellectual environment that low-income parents tend to provide for their children, and the lack of emphasis on abstract concepts.

In the third stage, a motivation to commit a delinquent act is magnified or opposed by internalized beliefs and attitudes about lawbreaking that have been built up in a learning process as a result of a history of rewards and punishments. The belief that delinquency is wrong, or a strong conscience, tends to be built up if parents are in favor of legal norms, if they exercise close supervision over their children, and if they punish socially disapproved behavior using love-oriented discipline. The belief that delinquency is legitimate, and antiestablishment attitudes generally, tend to be built up if children have been exposed to attitudes and behavior favoring delinquency, especially by members of their family and their friends. The fourth stage is a decision process in a particular situation and is affected by immediate situational factors. Whether the tendency to commit a delinquent act becomes the actuality depends on the costs, benefits, and probabilities of the outcomes (e.g., the material goods that can be stolen, peer approval, being caught by the police). In general, people are hedonistic and make rational decisions.

The latest theories largely fit the known facts about delinquency and attempt to explain the role not only of sociocultural factors but of other factors as well. As theories become more complex, however, they also become more difficult to disprove. It may be that the further development of theories should be halted until careful empirical research of the type described in the next section has demonstrated causal relationships more securely.

SUMMARY

There is clearly a correlation between sociocultural factors such as economic disadvantage, ethnic origin, having delinquent peers, and living in an inner-city neighborhood, and childhood behavior such as delinquency, conduct disorder, attention deficit disorder, and substance abuse. However, these types of childhood behaviors are also related to biological factors and individual factors (discussed in Chapter 2), family factors (discussed in Chapter 9), and school factors such as classroom reinforcements (Rutter, Maughan, Mortimore, Ouston, & Smith, 1979). It is not clear that any of the sociocultural factors discussed here has a direct effect on childhood disorder independently of other factors.

The major problem of interpretation, as indicated at the beginning of this chapter, is that all predisposing factors tend to be interrelated. We need to know how many distinctively different theoretical constructs underlie these predisposing factors, how many underlie the measures of childhood behavior, and how one set of theoretical constructs is related to the others. We need to know which theoretical constructs cause, and which are merely correlated with, delinquency and conduct disorder. We need to know how theoretical constructs interact to produce delinquency and conduct disorder, and how conduct disorder itself may affect apparently predisposing (e.g., family and school) factors.

In principle, the best way of demonstrating a causal effect of one factor on another is to carry out a randomized experiment. An example is the experiment by Feldman et al. (1983) in St. Louis reviewed before. Antisocial boys were randomly assigned to either antisocial or prosocial peer groups, and the antisocial behavior of those in the prosocial peer groups was less than that of those in the antisocial peer groups. The clear implication of this result is that changes in the peer group caused changes in antisocial behavior. The great advantage of randomized experiments is that both the independent variable (the peer group, here) and all extraneous variables are controlled (Farrington, 1983). Experimentation is clearly a useful way of disentangling causes and effects from the mass of interrelated variables.

Unfortunately, randomized experiments are not possible with all variables. In practice, it would be difficult to change economic disadvantage or inner-city residence, and virtually impossible to change ethnic origin. Of the sociocultural factors reviewed here, having delinquent peers is probably the most susceptible to experimentation, although it would be difficult to imagine an experiment in which children were deliberately exposed to delinquent peers to see whether their own delinquency would increase as a result. Prevention or treatment experiments are more justifiable and feasible.

Where randomized experiments cannot be carried out, some other method of controlling variables must be found. Nowadays, it is common to control variables statistically rather than experimentally, using a method such as path analysis (Elliott et al., 1985). The problem with this, however, is that it is still essentially a correlational method. It can demonstrate that variations between children in one factor are correlated with variations in a second factor, independently of variations in other factors. It cannot, however, show that changes in one factor will cause changes in a second, because this refers to changes within children.

One of the best ways of showing the effect of changes in one factor on changes in another is to carry out a longitudinal survey and analyze it as a quasi-experiment. If a longitudinal survey has repeated measurement of association with delinquent peers and of delinquent behavior, for example, it should be possible to pinpoint when changes in delinquent peers occur and to relate these to changes in delinquent behavior. If there is a causal link between delinquent peers and delinquent behavior, changes in delinquent peers should be followed (with some measurable probability and within some measurable time interval) by changes in delinquent behavior. Equally, if there is a causal link between delinquent behavior and delinquent peers, changes in delinquent behavior should be followed by changes in delinquent peers. The point of the quasi-experimental analysis is to eliminate alternative plausible explanations of any observed relationships, such as maturation, history, testing, instrumentation, mortality, regression, and selection effects (Cook & Campbell, 1979).

This kind of analysis has many advantages. It is better able to establish causal relationships than a multivariate technique such as path analysis because it is a within-subjects analysis, where each person acts as his or her own control, and because it enables a careful specification of time ordering. It is better than a randomized experiment because it is naturalistic as opposed to artificial and because it enables all variables to be studied simultaneously. Randomized experiments are often limited, in that they study the effects of only one or two independent variables and hence cannot study interactions between larger numbers of variables or conditional relationships that hold only within a specified range of values of extraneous variables (boundary conditions).

Unfortunately, longitudinal studies of childhood disorder, with frequent collection of data on a wide variety of variables, and analyzed quasi-experimentally, are rare. As an example of what could be done, Farrington (1977) showed that convictions were followed by an increase in delinquent behavior, and that this effect held independently of extraneous variables and could not be explained away by a variety of plausible hypotheses. Similarly, Farrington (1978) reported data that suggested that newly emerging marital disharmony in a family was followed by newly emerging child aggressiveness, although in this case he did not do explicit quasi-experimental analyses. In order to draw conclusions about causal effects, experimental or quasi-experimental longitudinal studies are needed. Other advantages of longitudinal studies, especially in documenting the natural history of delinquency and crime, have been reviewed by Farrington (1979b).

In principle, the causal effects of economic disadvantage, delinquent peers, and inner-city residence could be investigated in longitudinal surveys, because each of these factors could be expected to vary over time in some children. The effects of ethnic origin could not be studied in this way, however, because this factor varies only between children. It may be that ethnic origin should be regarded as a boundary condition or as a factor that interacts with causes rather than as a causal factor itself. The discovery of causes should have implications (at least in principle) for prevention, but prevention efforts must be limited to factors that can vary within children.

To conclude, we need to go beyond correlations between sociocultural factors and childhood disorder to establish causal relationships. The best methods of establishing causal relationships are to carry out longitudinal surveys analyzed quasi-experimentally and to carry out prevention or treatment experiments. These methods would advance our knowledge about the role of sociocultural—and other—factors in the genesis of child disorder and would help to develop theories that were more firmly grounded in empirical data.

This review of the sociocultural context of childhood disorders has been limited by the difficulty of bringing together two largely separate bodies of knowledge. On the one hand, there is research on childhood psychopathology, which concentrates predominantly on individual and family factors and which often reports results for total psychiatric disorder rather than for specific behaviors. On the other hand, there is research on sociocultural factors, which concentrates predominantly on juvenile delinquency, a phenomenon that may or may not reflect psychopathology in any given case. The lack of contact between these two bodies of literature has sharply restricted our present understanding of the role of sociocultural variables in childhood psychopathology. What is needed in the future is much more integration of the two research traditions and more collaboration between researchers from different disciplines. Hopefully, this should lead to a more complete appreciation of all of the different kinds of factors that interact to produce all of the different kinds of childhood disorders.

REFERENCES

Achenbach, T. M., & Edelbrock, C. S. (1981). Behavior problems and competencies reported by parents of normal and disturbed children aged 4 through 16. *Monographs of the Society for Research in Child Development, 46* (1, Serial No. 188).

American Psychiatric Association. (1980). *Diagnostic and statistical manual of mental disorders* (3rd ed.). Washington, DC: American Psychiatric Association.

Baldwin, J. (1979). Ecological and areal studies in Great Britain and the United States. In N. Morris & M. Tonry (Eds.), *Crime and justice* (Vol. 1, pp. 29–66). Chicago: University of Chicago Press.

Batta, I. D., McCulloch, J. W., & Smith, N. J. (1975). A study of juvenile delinquency amongst Asians and half-Asians. *British Journal of Criminology, 15*, 32–42.

Belson, W. A. (1975). *Juvenile theft.* London: Harper & Row.

Bosco, J. J., & Robin, S. S. (1980). Hyperkinesis: Prevention and treatment. In C. K. Whalen & B. Henker (Eds.), *Hyperactive children* (pp. 173–187). New York: Academic Press.

Brake, M. (1980). *The sociology of youth culture and youth subcultures.* London: Routledge & Kegan Paul.

Buckle, A., & Farrington, D. P. (1984). An observational study of shoplifting. *British Journal of Criminology, 24*, 63–73.

Bursik, R. J. (1980). The dynamics of specialization in juvenile offenses. *Social Forces, 58*, 851–864.

Bursik, R. J., & Webb, J. (1982). Community change and patterns of delinquency. *American Journal of Sociology, 88*, 24–42.

Burt, C. (1925). *The young delinquent.* London: University of London Press.

Campbell, A. (1981). *Girl delinquents.* Oxford: Blackwell.

Clark, J. P., & Wenninger, E. P. (1962). Socio-economic class and area as correlates of illegal behavior among juveniles. *American Sociological Review, 27*, 826–834.

Cloward, R. A., & Ohlin, L. E. (1960). *Delinquency and opportunity.* New York: Free Press.

Cochrane, R. (1979). Psychological and behavioral disturbance in West Indians, Indians, and Pakistanis in Britain: A comparison of rates among children and adults. *British Journal of Psychiatry, 134*, 201–210.

Cohen, A. K. (1955). *Delinquent boys.* Glencoe, IL: Free Press.

Cohen, L. E., & Kluegel, J. R. (1978). Determinants of juvenile court dispositions: Ascriptive and achieved factors in two metropolitan courts. *American Sociological Review, 43*, 162–176.

Cook, T. D., & Campbell, D. T. (1979). *Quasi-experimentation.* Chicago: Rand McNally.

Cox, A., Rutter, M., Newman, S., & Bartak, L. (1975). A comparative study of infantile autism and specific developmental receptive language disorder: II. Parental characteristics. *British Journal of Psychiatry, 126*, 146–159.

Craig, M. M., & Budd, L. A. (1967). The juvenile offender: Recidivism and companions. *Crime and Delinquency, 13*, 344–351.

Davie, R., Butler, N., & Goldstein, H. (1972). *From birth to seven.* London: Longman.

Dawson, G., & Mesibov, G. B. (1983). Childhood psychoses. In C. E. Walker & M. C. Roberts (Eds.), *Handbook of clinical child psychology* (pp. 543–572). New York: Wiley.

DeMyer, M. K., Hingtgen, J. N., & Jackson, R. K. (1981). Infantile autism reviewed: A decade of research. *Schizophrenia Bulletin, 7*, 388–451.

Douglas, J. W. B. (1964). *The home and the school.* London: MacGibbon & Kee.

Douglas, J. W. B., Ross, J. M., & Simpson, H. R. (1968). *All our future.* London: Peter Davies.

Douglas, J. W. B., Ross, J. M., Hammond, W. A., & Mulligan, D. G. (1966). Delinquency and social class. *British Journal of Criminology, 6*, 294–302.

Earls, F. (1980). Prevalence of behavior problems in 3-year-old children. *Archives of General Psychiatry, 37*, 1153–1157.

Elliott, D. S., & Ageton, S. S. (1980). Reconciling race and class differences in self-reported and official estimates of delinquency. *American Sociological Review, 45*, 95–110.

Elliott, D. S., & Huizinga, D. (1983). Social class and delinquent behavior in a national youth panel: 1976–1980. *Criminology, 21*, 149–177.

Elliott, D. S., Huizinga, D., & Ageton, S. S. (1985). *Explaining delinquency and drug use.* Beverly Hills, CA: Sage.

Elliott, D. S., & Voss, H. L. (1974). *Delinquency and dropout.* Lexington, MA: Heath.

Eynon, T. G., & Reckless, W. C. (1961). Companionship at delinquency onset. *British Journal of Criminology, 2*, 162–170.

Farrington, D. P. (1977). The effects of public labelling. *British Journal of Criminology, 17*, 112–125.

Farrington, D. P. (1978). The family backgrounds of aggressive youths. In L. Hersov, M. Berger, & D. Shaffer (Eds.), *Aggression and antisocial behavior in childhood and adolescence* (pp. 73–93). Oxford: Pergamon.

Farrington, D. P. (1979a). Environmental stress, delinquent behavior, and convictions. In I. G. Sarason & C. D. Spielberger (Eds.), *Stress and anxiety* (Vol. 6, pp. 93–107). Washington, DC: Hemisphere.

Farrington, D. P. (1979b). Longitudinal research on crime and delinquency. In N. Morris & M. Tonry (Eds.), *Crime and justice* (Vol. 1, pp. 289–348). Chicago: University of Chicago Press.

Farrington, D. P. (1983). Randomized experiments on crime and justice. In M. Tonry & N. Morris (Eds.), *Crime and justice* (Vol. 4, pp. 257–308). Chicago: University of Chicago Press.

Farrington, D. P. (1984). Measuring the natural history of delinquency and crime. In R. A. Glow (Ed.), *Advances in the behavioral measurement of children* (Vol. 1, pp. 217–263). Greenwich, CT: JAI Press.

Farrington, D. P. (1986). Stepping stones to adult criminal careers. In D. Olweus, J. Block, & M. R. Yarrow (Eds.), *Development of antisocial and prosocial behavior* (pp. 359–384). New York: Academic Press.

Farrington, D. P., & Bennett, T. (1981). Police cautioning of juveniles in London. *British Journal of Criminology, 21*, 123–135.

Feldman, R. A., Caplinger, T. E., & Wodarski, J. S. (1983). *The St. Louis conundrum.* Englewood Cliffs, NJ: Prentice-Hall.

Gath, D., Cooper, B., Gattoni, F., & Rockett, D. (1977). *Child guidance and delinquency in a London borough.* Oxford: Oxford University Press.

Gill, O. (1977). *Luke Street.* London: Macmillan.

Glueck, S., & Glueck, E. T. (1950). *Unraveling juvenile delinquency.* Cambridge, MA: Harvard University Press.

Gold, M. (1970). *Delinquent behavior in an American city.* Belmont, CA: Brooks/Cole.

Gold, M., & Reimer, D. J. (1975). Changing patterns of delinquent behavior among Americans 13 through 16 years old: 1967–72. *Crime and Delinquency Literature, 7*, 483–517.

Gordon, R. A. (1976). Prevalence: The rare datum in delinquency measurement and its implications for the theory of delinquency. In M. W. Klein (Ed.), *The juvenile justice system* (pp. 201–284). Beverly Hills: Sage.

Gorsuch, R. L., & Butler, M. C. (1976). Initial drug use: A review of predisposing social psychological factors. *Psychological Bulletin, 83*, 120–137.

Graham, P. J., & Meadows, C. E. (1967). Psychiatric disorder in the children of West Indian immigrants. *Journal of Child Psychology and Psychiatry, 8*, 105–116.

Hardt, R. H., & Peterson, S. J. (1968). Arrests of self and friends as indicators of delinquency involvement. *Journal of Research in Crime and Delinquency, 5*, 44–51.

Henggeler, S. W., Urey, J. R., & Borduin, C. M. (1982). Social class, psychopathology, and family interaction. In S. W. Henggeler (Ed.), *Delinquency and adolescent psychopathology* (pp. 99–115). Boston: John Wright.

Hewitt, L. E., & Jenkins, R. L. (1946). *Fundamental patterns of maladjustment.* Springfield: State of Illinois.

Hindelang, M. J. (1971). The social versus solitary nature of delinquent involvements. *British Journal of Criminology, 11*, 167–175.

Hindelang, M. J. (1973). Causes of delinquency: A partial replication and extension. *Social Problems, 20*, 471–487.

Hindelang, M. J. (1976). With a little help from their friends: Group participation in reported delinquent behavior. *British Journal of Criminology, 16*, 109–125.

Hindelang, M. J. (1981). Variations in sex-race-age-specific incidence rates of offending. *American Sociological Review, 46*, 461–474.

Hindelang, M. J., Hirschi, T., & Weis, J. G. (1981). *Measuring delinquency.* Beverly Hills: Sage.

Hirschi, T. (1969). *Causes of delinquency.* Berkeley: University of California Press.

Hirschi, T., & Hindelang, M. J. (1977). Intelligence and delinquency: A revisionist review. *American Sociological Review, 42*, 571–587.

Hogh, E., & Wolf, P. (1983). Violent crime in a birth cohort: Copenhagen 1953–1977. In K. T. Van Dusen & S. A. Mednick (Eds.), *Prospective studies of crime and delinquency* (pp. 249–267). Boston: Kluwer-Nijhoff.

Janson, C. G. (1983). Delinquency among metropolitan boys: A progress report. In K. T. Van Dusen & S. A. Mednick (Eds.), *Prospective studies of crime and delinquency* (pp. 147–180). Boston: Kluwer-Nijhoff.

Jessor, R., & Jessor, S. L. (1977). *Problem behavior and psychosocial development.* New York: Academic Press.

Johnston, L. D., Bachman, J. G., & O'Malley, P. M. (1980). Drug use among American high school students. In L. Brill & C. Winick (Eds.), *The yearbook of substance use and abuse* (pp. 297–322). New York: Human Sciences Press.

Kandel, D. B. (1980). Convergences in prospective longitudinal surveys of drug use in normal populations. In S. B. Sells, R. Crandall, M. Roff, J. S. Strauss, & W. Pollin (Eds.), *Human functioning in longitudinal perspective* (pp. 181–209). Baltimore: Williams & Wilkins.

Kandel, D. B., Treiman, D., Faust, R., & Single, E. (1976). Adolescent involvement in legal and illegal drug use: A multiple classification analysis. *Social Forces, 55*, 438–458.

Kastrup, M. (1977). Urban–rural differences in 6-year-olds. In P. J. Graham (Ed.), *Epidemiological approaches in psychiatry* (pp. 181–194). London: Academic Press.

Klein, M. W. (1969). Gang cohesiveness, delinquency, and a street-work program. *Journal of Research in Crime and Delinquency, 6*, 135–166.

Klein, M. W. (1984). Offense specialization and versatility among juveniles. *British Journal of Criminology, 24*, 185–194.

Kolvin, I., Ounsted, C., Richardson, L. M., & Garside, R. F. (1971). The family and social background in childhood psychoses. *British Journal of Psychiatry, 118*, 396–402.

Landau, S. (1981). Juveniles and the police. *British Journal of Criminology, 21*, 27–46.

Lapouse, R., & Monk, M. A. (1964). Behavior deviations in a representative sample of children: Variation by sex, age, race, social class, and family size. *American Journal of Orthopsychiatry, 34*, 436–446.

Lavik, N. J. (1977). Urban–rural differences in rates of disorder: A comparative psychiatric population study of Norwegian adolescents. In P. J. Graham (Ed.),

Epidemiological approaches in child psychiatry (pp. 223–251). London: Academic Press.

Lemert, E. M. (1972). *Human deviance, social problems, and social control* (2nd ed.). Englewood Cliffs, NJ: Prentice-Hall.

Loeber, R. (1982). The stability of antisocial and delinquent child behavior: A review. *Child Development, 53*, 1431–1446.

Loeber, R., & Dishion, T. (1983). Early predictors of male delinquency: A review. *Psychological Bulletin, 94*, 68–99.

Magnusson, D., Stattin, H., & Duner, A. (1983). Aggression and criminality in a longitudinal perspective. In K. T. Van Dusen & S. A. Mednick (Eds.), *Prospective studies of crime and delinquency* (pp. 277–301). Boston: Kluwer-Nijhoff.

Mawby, R. I., McCulloch, J. W., & Batta, I. D. (1979). Crime amongst Asian juveniles in Bradford. *International Journal of the Sociology of Law, 7*, 297–306.

May, D. R. (1981). The Aberdeen delinquency study. In S. A. Mednick & A. E. Baert (Eds.), *Prospective longitudinal research* (pp. 69–76). Oxford: Oxford University Press.

Miller, W. B. (1958). Lower class culture as a generating milieu of gang delinquency. *Journal of Social Issues, 14*, 5–19.

Miller, W. B. (1975). *Violence by youth gangs and youth groups as a crime problem in major American cities.* Washington, DC: National Institute of Juvenile Justice and Delinquency Prevention.

Morash, M. (1983). Gangs, groups, and delinquency. *British Journal of Criminology, 23*, 309–331.

Mueller, C. W., & Parcel, T. L. (1981). Measures of socioeconomic status: Alternatives and recommendations. *Child Development, 52*, 13–30.

National Council on Crime and Delinquency (1975). Jurisdiction over status offenses should be removed from the juvenile court: A policy statement. *Crime and Delinquency, 21*, 97–99.

Nicol, A. R. (1971). Psychiatric disorder in the children of Caribbean immigrants. *Journal of Child Psychology and Psychiatry, 12*, 273–287.

O'Hagan, F. J. (1976). Gang characteristics: An empirical study. *Journal of Child Psychology and Psychiatry, 17*, 305–314.

Osborn, S. G. (1980). Moving home, leaving London, and delinquent trends. *British Journal of Criminology, 20*, 54–61.

Ouston, J. (1984). Delinquency, family background, and educational attainment. *British Journal of Criminology, 24*, 2–26.

Power, M. J., Benn, R. T., & Morris, J. N. (1972). Neighborhood, school, and juveniles before the courts. *British Journal of Criminology, 12*, 111–132.

Remschmidt, H., Hohner, G., Merschmann, W., & Walter, R. (1977). Epidemiology of delinquent behavior in children. In P. J. Graham (Ed.), *Epidemiological approaches in child psychiatry* (pp. 253–274). London: Academic Press.

Richman, N., Stevenson, J. E., & Graham, P. J. (1975). Prevalence of behavior problems in 3-year-old children: An epidemiological study in a London borough. *Journal of Child Psychology and Psychiatry, 16*, 277–287.

Robins, L. N. (1979). Sturdy childhood predictors of adult outcomes: Replications from longitudinal studies. In J. E.Barrett, R. M. Rose, & G. L. Klerman (Eds.), *Stress and mental disorder* (pp. 219–235). New York: Raven Press.

Robins, L. N. (1983). Continuities and discontinuities in the psychiatric disorders of children. In D. E. Mechanic (Ed.), *Handbook of health, health care, and the health professions* (pp. 195–219). New York: Free Press.

Robins, L. N., & Ratcliff, K. S. (1980). Childhood conduct disorders and later arrest. In L. N. Robins, P. J. Clayton, & J. K. Wing (Eds.), *The social consequences of psychiatric illness* (pp. 248–263). New York: Brunner/Mazel.

Robins, L. N., & Wish, E. (1977). Childhood deviance as a developmental process: A study of 223 urban black men from birth to 18. *Social Forces, 56,* 448–473.

Robinson, W. S. (1950). Ecological correlations and the behavior of individuals. *American Sociological Review, 15,* 351–357.

Roff, J. D., & Wirt, R. D. (1984). Childhood aggression and social adjustment as antecedents of delinquency. *Journal of Abnormal Child Psychology, 12,* 111–126.

Rojek, D. G., & Erickson, M. L. (1982). Delinquent careers. *Criminology, 20,* 5–28.

Rutter, M. (1981). The city and the child. *American Journal of Orthopsychiatry, 51,* 610–625.

Rutter, M., Cox, A., Tupling, C., Berger, M., & Yule, W. (1975). Attainment and adjustment in two geographical areas: I. The prevalence of psychiatric disorder. *British Journal of Psychiatry, 126,* 493–509.

Rutter, M., Maughan, B., Mortimore, P., Ouston, J., & Smith, A. (1979). *Fifteen thousand hours.* London: Open Books.

Rutter, M., Tizard, J., & Whitmore, K. (1970). *Education, health, and behavior.* London: Longman.

Rutter, M., Yule, B., Morton, J., & Bagley, C. (1975). Children of West Indian immigrants: III. Home circumstances and family patterns. *Journal of Child Psychology and Psychiatry, 16,* 105–123.

Rutter, M., Yule, B., Quinton, D., Rowlands, O., Yule, W., & Berger, M. (1975). Attainment and adjustment in two geographical areas: III. Some factors accounting for area differences. *British Journal of Psychiatry, 126,* 520–533.

Rutter, M., Yule, W., Berger, M., Yule, B., Morton, J., & Bagley, C. (1974). Children of West Indian immigrants: I. Rates of behavioral deviance and of psychiatric disorder. *Journal of Child Psychology and Psychiatry, 15,* 241–262.

Sarason, I. G. (1978). A cognitive social learning approach to juvenile delinquency. In R. D. Hare & D. Schalling (Eds.), *Psychopathic behavior* (pp. 299–317). Chichester: Wiley.

Shapland, J. M. (1978). Self-reported delinquency in boys aged 11 to 14. *British Journal of Criminology, 18,* 255–266.

Shaw, C. R., & McKay, H. D. (1969). *Juvenile delinquency and urban areas* (rev. ed.). Chicago: University of Chicago Press.

Shepherd, M., Oppenheim, A. N., & Mitchell, S. (1966). Childhood behavior disorders and the child guidance clinic: An epidemiological study. *Journal of Child Psychology and Psychiatry, 7,* 39–52.

Short, J. F., & Nye, F. I. (1957). Reported behavior as a criterion of deviant behavior. *Social Problems, 5,* 207–213.

Short, J. F., & Strodtbeck, F. L. (1965). *Group process and gang delinquency.* Chicago: University of Chicago Press.

Stevens, P., & Willis, C. F. (1979). *Race, crime, and arrests.* London: Her Majesty's Stationery Office.

Sutherland, E. H., & Cressey, D. R. (1969). A sociological theory of criminal behavior. In D. R. Cressey & D. A. Ward (Eds.), *Delinquency, crime, and social process* (pp. 426–432). New York: Harper & Row.

Sveri, K. (1965). Group activity. In K. O. Christiansen (Ed.), *Scandinavian studies in criminology* (Vol. 1, pp. 173–185). London: Tavistock.

Terry, R. M. (1967). The screening of juvenile offenders. *Journal of Criminal Law, Criminology, and Police Science, 58*, 173–181.

Thornberry, T. P. (1973). Race, socioeconomic status, and sentencing in the juvenile justice system. *Journal of Criminal Law and Criminology, 64*, 90–98.

Thornberry, T. P., & Farnworth, M. (1982). Social correlates of criminal involvement: Further evidence on the relationship between social status and criminal behavior. *American Sociological Review, 47*, 505–518.

Trasler, G. B. (1962). *The explanation of criminality.* London: Routledge & Kegan Paul.

Tuddenham, R. D., Brooks, J., & Milkovich, L. (1974). Mothers' reports of behavior of 10-year-olds: Relationships with sex, ethnicity, and mother's education. *Developmental Psychology, 10*, 95–995.

Van Dusen, K. T., Mednick, S. A., Gabrielli, W. F., & Hutchings, B. (1983). Social class and crime in an adoption cohort. *Journal of Criminal Law and Criminology, 74*, 249–269.

Walker, C. E., & Roberts, M. C. (Eds.). (1983). *Handbook of clinical child psychology.* New York: Wiley.

Wallis, C. P., & Maliphant, R. (1967). Delinquent areas in the county of London: Ecological factors. *British Journal of Criminology, 7*, 250–284.

West, D. J. (1969). *Present conduct and future delinquency.* London: Heinemann.

West, D. J., & Farrington, D. P. (1973). *Who becomes delinquent?* London: Heinemann.

West, D. J., & Farrington, D. P. (1977). *The delinquent way of life.* London: Heinemann.

Williams, J. R., & Gold, M. (1972). From delinquent behavior to official delinquency. *Social Problems, 20*, 209–229.

Wing, L. (1980). Childhood autism and social class: A question of selection? *British Journal of Psychiatry, 137*, 410–417.

Wolfgang, M. E. (1980). Some new findings from the longitudinal study of crime. *Australian Journal of Forensic Sciences, 13*, 12–29.

Wolfgang, M. E., Figlio, R. M., & Sellin, T. (1972). *Delinquency in a birth cohort.* Chicago: University of Chicago Press.

Wolkind, S., & Rutter, M. (1985). Sociocultural factors. In M. Rutter & L. Hersov (Eds.), *Child and adolescent psychiatry* (2nd ed., pp. 82–100). Oxford: Blackwell.

Zimring, F. E. (1981). Kids, groups, and crime: Some implications of a well-known secret. *Journal of Criminal Law and Criminology, 72*, 867–885.

11 ASSESSMENT AND ASSESSMENT OF CHANGE

K. DANIEL O'LEARY AND SUZANNE B. JOHNSON

INTRODUCTION

From the 1930s to the 1960s assessment was often viewed as a waste of time because differential treatments were not dictated or suggested by assessment results. However, assessment has once again begun to play a prominent and respectable role in both academic and clinical settings. It is now believed that differential treatments can be indicated by findings from appropriately applied assessment methods. The revision of the American Psychiatric Association's *Diagnostic and Statistical Manual* (DSM-III, 1980), already discussed at length in Chapter 1, is a prime example of the resurgence of concern for reliable and valid classification and diagnosis.

Our previous review on assessment of children's social and emotional problems was organized around the major assessment methods: interviews, projective methods, rating scales, and observational procedures (O'Leary & Johnson, 1979). This organizational approach had the advantage of giving the reader a review of the relative strengths and weaknesses of the assessment method. It had the disadvantage, however, of offering little information about what specific tools were available for the specific psychopathological disorders of childhood. Consequently, we have now chosen to focus on assessment issues relevant to each of six major categories of childhood disorders: conduct disorders, attention deficit disorders, anxiety, depression, pervasive developmental disorders, and psychosomatic disorders.

Of course, no assessment chapter is devoid of theoretical bias. A treatise on child assessment might vary greatly depending on whether the chapter was written from a family systems, psychodynamic, ecological, or social learning perspective. We have approached the area from a broad social learning perspective (O'Leary & Wilson, 1975), and assessment methods were selected based on both frequency of use and psychometric adequacy.

CONDUCT DISORDERS

As has been discussed in Chapters 1 and 2, conduct disorder subsumes problems of noncompliance, aggression, and antisocial behavior and, in its various forms, is the most prevalent disorder. The most common assessment methods for conduct disorders include behavioral checklists completed by the teacher, parent, or other informant procedures by which the youngster's behavior is directly observed and recorded using a specific observational code. Self-report and psychophysiological measures have been used much less frequently than other techniques.

Behavioral Checklists

Several behavioral checklists or rating scales are available for the assessment of conduct problems. The youngster's parent and/or teacher is typically asked to complete the checklist concerning the child's behavior.

TEACHER RATINGS

The most common assessment devices for evaluating conduct problems of elementary school children include

- The Behavior Problem Checklist (BPC) and the more recent Revised Behavior Problem Checklist (RBPC) (see Quay, 1977, 1983; Quay & Peterson, 1975, 1983)
- The Conners' (1969) Teacher Rating Scale (TRS)
- The Louisville School Behavior Checklist (SBC—Miller, 1972)

All have been shown to have adequate test–retest reliability and adequate internal consistency (see Boyle & Jones, 1985, for a review) and can be easily scored. The RBPC has 22 items to assess conduct problems, the TRC has 15 items and the SBC has 23 items.

The conduct problem scales of all of these instruments have demonstrated sensitivity to treatment changes of a behavioral or pharmacological nature. The original BPC has been used most frequently in psychological studies (see Quay & Peterson, 1983), whereas the Conners' TRS has been used most frequently in pharmacological investigations (Guy, 1976).

PARENT RATINGS

In addition to the BPC other parental rating scales include the Child Behavior Checklist (CBC) (Achenbach & Edelbrock, 1983) and a parent version of the Conners' Rating Scale (Goyette, Conners, & Ulrich, 1978).

As mentioned previously, the RBPC has 22 items assessing conduct problems, while the CBC's conduct problem scale consists of 23 items for boys and 25 items for girls (Achenbach & Edelbrock, 1983). Conners' Parent Questionnaire has 7 items on the conduct problem factor (Guy, 1976). The CBC is the only instrument that contains scales with different items for boys and girls, recognizing that somewhat different behaviors may be related to conduct disorders for boys than for girls.

Mother–Father Agreement

In some of the original work on the BPC, Peterson (1961) found that interparent agreement on the conduct problem factor was .77 in a sample of kindergarten children ($N = 126$). Agreements on the BPC conduct problem factor were .54 for a "disturbed" sample ($N = 58$) and .62 for a normal sample ($N = 38$). Overall agreement for the full combined sample was .73 (see Quay & Peterson, 1975). Mothers have been found to endorse more items on the conduct problem scale than fathers for both the "disturbed" and normal samples (Jacob, Grounds, & Haley, 1982). Agreement between father and mother ratings on the conduct problem factor (aggression) of the CBC ranged between .72 and .80 for varied ages of boys and between .33 and .68 for varied ages of girls. Interestingly, for an age range most often assessed in previous research, namely for girls between 6 and 11 years of age, parents had an agreement coefficient of only .33 (Achenbach & Edelbrock, 1983). Further, it appears that parents agree less about girls' than about boys' behavior problems. Whether this lesser agreement is due to more time spent by fathers with boys than with girls is not clear, but such time might influence the ratings. Although the overall *mean* difference between mothers' and fathers' ratings was small, mothers' ratings of conduct problems were higher than fathers' ratings (Achenbach & Edelbrock, 1983) as was the case in the Jacob et al. (1982) study.

Parent–Teacher Agreement

As might be expected, agreement between parent and teacher ratings is less than agreement between fathers and mothers. Peterson (1961) found parent–teacher agreement of .41 for the conduct disorder factor. Quay, Sprague, Schulman, and Miller (1966) found that mother–teacher and father–teacher correlations for the conduct disorder factor were .33 and .23, respectively. The authors are not aware of similar published reports regarding parent–teacher agreement for the CBC or the Conners' Parent and Teacher conduct problem scales.

One may ask whether it is likely that a child with conduct problems will display more deviant behavior at school than at home. Certainly, many problems of children become manifest only when they attend school and have to face the more formal and structured aspects of a classroom. A comparison of the extent to which children display conduct problems in one place or another necessitates having an assessment device that assesses comparable behaviors at home and school. The BPC (and the RBPC) enables one to make such an assessment. Emery and O'Leary (1984) examined BPCs from the parents and teachers of 132 children in an elementary school in a suburban Long Island community. Girls were more likely to show conduct disorders at home (mean = 5.3) than at school (mean = 3.3), while the boys did not display significantly different levels of conduct problems in both settings. (home = 5.9; school = 6.9). Parents often feel their child's behavior is within normal limits even though school personnel may see the child as quite deviant. Given different tolerance levels for certain types of behavior, it is of course possible that teacher–parent differences that exist may reflect tolerance differences, not behavioral differences in children.

Self-reports

Children with conduct disorders often have significant reading problems, and this reading deficiency may be one reason why self-reports of conduct problems are used much less frequently than teacher and parent reports. When self-reports by children regarding conduct problems are necessary, one may have to read items on a scale to children at least between the first and sixth grades. As indicated in a chapter on self-report instruments (Finch & Rogers, 1984), the paucity of self-report instruments may be due in part to the skepticism of behaviorally oriented psychologists about self-report measurements and their emphasis on direct observation. As they stated, "In no area was this more evident than in behavioral assessment of children for whom target behaviors were more easily quantifiable and with whom use of self-report was considered questionable due to limited verbal development. If adults were poor reporters, could children be anything but worse?" (p. 106). Fortunately, child behavioral researchers have become much more accepting of diverse assessment methods and numerous behavioral researchers in the child area (e.g., Hartmann, 1983; O'Leary, 1979; Patterson, 1982; Wolf, 1978) have clearly advocated multimethod assessment. One of the few measures of self-reports of conduct problems for children is that of Nelson and Finch (1978), who developed the children's Inventory of Anger, which was designed to have a fourth-grade reading level. Drawings of faces with happy to mad faces were used as aids to provide visual images for the anchor points on the scale. The measurement device has good test–retest reliability when read to children individually ($r = .82$), but the concurrent validity of the test appears questionable. Scores on the test were either not significantly correlated with teacher ratings or were minimally correlated with them, depending upon the study (Finch & Rogers, 1984).

A child version of the CBC has been developed that is called the Youth Self-Report. It is designed for ages 11 to 18 years and requires a minimum of fifth-grade reading skill. As with similar instruments, it can be read aloud to the children. At this writing, there were insufficient research reports to allow specific statements to be made regarding the various factors of the youth version of the instrument. Given the similarity of items, however, especially in the behavior problem area (Achenbach & Edelbrock, 1983, pp. 162–166), it seems reasonable to assume that there would be a conduct problem factor of the Youth Self-Report. Further, total behavior problem scores from the youth and mother ratings correlated significantly at intake ($r = .37$) and follow-up ($r = .56$). Initial work with this instrument suggests that it is a promising measure.

Herjanic and Reich (1982) assessed the reliability of children's reporting, by comparing mothers' reports with those of their children, who ranged in age from 6 to 16. Though the investigators were not specifically interested in conduct problems or aggression, their analyses of a topical area, "Relationships with Peers," revealed that there was little agreement between mothers and their children as determined by Kappas. On the other hand, analyses of 10 of the items from a topical area, "Social Adjustment," revealed "middle range" (.30–49) to high ($\geq$ .50) Kappas for 7 items. In general, questions of children and their mothers that yielded reasonably high agreement were objective and concrete (e.g., Have you been suspended or expelled from school?), factual (e.g., Have you been in trouble with the police or a juvenile officer?), and unambiguous and not easily misinterpreted (e.g., Have you had an accident so that you went to the emergency room?). In summary, research on self-reports of aggression by children has just begun to receive serious attention.

Behavioral Observations

There are several observational schemes that have been used to measure the behavior of aggressive children in the classroom. O'Leary, Romanczyk, Kass, Dietz, and Santogrossi (1979) developed a coding system for measuring classroom behavior of aggressive boys that has sufficient reliability and validity to distinguish target conduct-problem children from randomly selected same-sex peers. The codes were designed to enable classroom observers to note the presence or absence of discrete behaviors. The observational coding system was an outgrowth of earlier observational schedules used at the Universities of Washington and Illinois by Bijou and Becker and their colleagues. When boys were selected for extreme aggression scores on the Louisville School Behavior Checklist, the particular behavioral codes that differentiated aggressive boys from randomly selected boys were interference with others, noncompliance, aggression, off-task, vocalization, and solicitation of teacher attention (Kent & O'Leary, 1976). A second coding system was developed for use in both formal and informal classrooms (Kent, Miner, Kay, & O'Leary, 1979) and has been used primarily in assessing children with conduct problems. Methodological issues with these codes such as presence of observer, frequency of observer checking, and observer drift (changing observational criteria across time) have been investigated by O'Leary and his colleagues and summarized by Kent and Foster (1977) and Patterson (1982). Fortunately, reactivity to the presence of observers in the classroom does not appear to be a problem if there is an initial adaptation period for three to five days before actual data are obtained. Reliabilities decrease if occasional reliability checks are not made and if the observer knows when he or she is to be checked. Finally, changes in observational criteria occur across time if restandardization of the observers does not occur periodically (O'Leary, 1981).

Patterson and colleagues have been assessing the behavior of aggressive children longer than almost any other child clinical psychologists. They have focused on the interactional nature of aggressive children and their parents in accord with their coercion hypothesis (Patterson, 1982, already discussed in Chapter 9). Patterson and colleagues assess the probability of a given parent behavior when a certain child behavior has been displayed, and vice versa. While such observations are not the type that can be made routinely by clinicians, systems like those devised by Patterson and associates are clearly necessary to study interactional patterns. While much has been written on the interactional nature of parent–child, child–parent, teacher–child, child–teacher sequences, there is relatively little empirical work regarding their interactions other than the research of Patterson and colleagues. Interactional sequences require sophisticated data analytic procedures involving many conditional probabilities and many lagged conditional probabilities (i.e., given that a certain behavior occurred and two specific other behaviors followed, what is the probability that another specific behavior occurred?). While such data analytic procedures are not now used by practicing clinicians, observational recording devices with computers are available to allow researchers to determine the conditional probabilities of many behaviors.

ATTENTION DEFICIT DISORDERS WITH HYPERACTIVITY (ADDH)

Behavioral checklists or ratings are the most commonly used assessment methods to evaluate ADDH. Direct observational procedures have been used widely in research evaluating children with ADDH, though such observational procedures are rarely used by clinicians. Self-report measures have rarely been used with children with the problems discussed in this section, but laboratory measures of attention and activity level have been employed on research bases.

Teacher Ratings

The TRS already discussed was developed to assess changes in children's behavior as a function of pharmacological intervention, especially psychostimulant medication for hyperactive children. A 10-item abbreviated TRS (ATRS) was later developed and has become used routinely to assess ADDH in a number of studies regarding the prevelance of this disorder (see Arias & O'Leary, 1984, for review). The TRS has become even more widely used as a measure of treatment outcome (see Abikoff, 1979, for review). The use of the ATRS was unfortunate because it became known as a measure of hyperactivity despite the fact that it contained an amalgam of heterogeneous items that loaded on the hyperactivity, conduct problem, inattention, and hyperactivity factors of the original TRS. As noted by Guy (1976), however, the abbreviated scale "is not so much an independent scale as it is a device which reduces-by-abbreviation the burden of repeated assessments for teachers" (p. 301).

The 10-item ATRS contains 4 items that a priori are not seen as critical to a diagnosis of ADDH: cries often and easily, demands must be met immediately, temper outbursts, and disturbs other children. The item "cries often and easily'' consistently loads on a depression or affective problem factor (Glow, 1981; O'Leary, Vivian, & Nisi, 1985; Trites, Blouin, & Laprade, 1982). The other 3 items have not loaded consistently on any other factor (Arias & O'Leary, 1984). In brief, the ATRS is more heterogeneous as a measure of hyperactivity than would be desired from a theoretical standpoint.

Another teacher rating method is a checklist developed by Ullmann, Sleator, and Sprague (1984) for the specific purpose of assessing ADDH. This scale has four factors: attention, hyperactivity, social skills, and opposition. Five items comprise the hyperactivity factor, all of which seem theoretically relevant to the hyperactivity dimension. Some of the items have clear overlap with the Conners TRS. Children's scores on the hyperactivity factor correlated .69 with a factor labeled oppositional (Ullmann et al., 1984).

A third rating method is a scale that straightforwardly lists the ADDH criteria of the DSM-III (American Psychiatric Association, 1980) for teachers to evaluate (Pelham & Bender, 1982). This method did not provide higher reliability or validity coefficients than obtained with previous scales. Consequently, Atkins, Pelham, and Licht (1985) have argued with empirical data that a multivariate assessment of the construct of ADD is necessary, and that such multimodal assessment should include academic evaluation, direct observation of classroom behavior, and assessment of organizational skills (neatness and preparedness).

Parent Ratings

There are two parent rating devices that have been used frequently to assess ADDH. However, both were developed before the current focus on attentional factors in ADD. These are the Conners' Parent Rating Scale (Conners, 1970) and the Werry, Weiss, and Peters Activity Scale (Werry & Sprague, 1970).

The Conners' Parent Rating Scale (also called Parent Symptom Questionnaire) contains 48 items that, when factor analyzed, yield five factors: conduct problems, inattention, psychosomatic, impulsivity-hyperactivity, and anxiety. Only 4 items load on the hyperactivity factor although 10 are used to calculate a child's score on the hyperactivity index. Boys tend to be rated higher on the hyperactivity index, and mean scores decline with age. As with other scales mentioned earlier, mothers rate boys as more hyperactive than do fathers (Barkley, 1981; Goyette et al., 1978). Barkley (1981) found that children's scores on the hyperactivity factor did not correlate significantly with objective measures of attention or hyperactivity but did correlate with objective measures of noncompliance. Unfortunately, a 4-item scale is generally not sufficient to meet most psychometric standards of reliability and validity, and assessment research on hyperactivity in the home is clearly needed.

Another rating scale used to assess children's behavior in the home is the Werry-Weiss-Peters Activity Scale. The questionnaire has 22 items involving behavior in seven areas such as meals, television, homework, and sleep. Norms have been provided by Routh, Schroeder, and O'Tuama (1974), and there is a decided drop in mean activity level across an age range of three to nine years. This scale effectively discriminates hyperactive and nonhyperactive children, and it is sensitive to changes associated with drug treatment and parent training (Barkley, 1981). However, it does not correlate significantly with objective measures of activity, but it does correlate with objective measures of noncompliance (Barkley, 1981).

Behavioral Observations

Abikoff, Gittelman-Klein, and Klein (1977) demonstrated that a revision of the Stony Brook codes used by Kent and O'Leary (1976) was able to differentiate significantly ADDH children from their same-sex counterparts reported to be average by their teachers. The particular behaviors that differentiated ADDH children from other children were interference, solicitation, off-task, minor motor movement, gross motor activity, noncompliance, out of chair, aggression to teacher, and aggression to children. There was very adequate interobserver agreement, but the authors pointed out that single-category criteria were poor discriminators between the groups (i.e., using each of the individual codes, discrimination between the groups was very poor). Interference and off-task (an inattention measure) were the best two code discriminators between the groups. Using a combination of categories, correct classification of ADDH and non-ADDH was possible in 80 percent of the cases. Interestingly, there was some evidence that minor motor movements and off-task behavior decreased with age in ADDH children.

Whalen, Henker, Collins, Finck, and Dotemoto (1979) found relations of only "moderate strength" when they correlated 20 classroom behavioral categories with daily teacher ratings that reflected overall problems of ADDH children. The highest single correlation (.78) was between "on-task" behavior and ATRS. Eleven of the 20 correlations were significant; the average significant correlation between the disruptive behavior categories and the teacher ratings was .41, with a range of .25 to .55. Daily teacher ratings were made at the end of each morning, and classroom observations of each child were made during 40 30-second observations intervals (20 minutes/child).

Several investigators have not found observational coding systems to differentiate ADDH from non-ADDH children (e.g., Blunden, Spring, & Greenberg, 1974) despite the highly significant differentiation of such children in these studies with teacher ratings. However, the relationship between teacher ratings and classroom observations is undoubtedly influenced by the temporal interval used. Only two studies (Jacob, O'Leary, & Rosenblad, 1978; Kent, O'Leary, Colletti, & Drabman, 1976) have data that reflect children's behavior ratings and observation for the same time period (O'Leary, 1981). Interestingly, the correlations between teacher ratings and overall problem behavior (.69 and .60, respectively) in these studies are the highest reflected in the literature. The lack of congruence between temporal intervals for teacher ratings and observations may well explain the often low to moderate correlations found between teacher ratings and classroom observations of hyperactivity.

Observational systems exist that can be used to assess children with ADDH. As noted elsewhere (O'Leary, 1981), there are clear advantages of collecting data from direct observations so that the data are comparatively immune to demand characteristics. Collecting observational data is costly and time consuming, however, and with older youngsters there can be reactivity effects when the observers are known to the children.

Self-reports

Self-ratings of attentional problems and hyperactivity have not been used with any regularity. Whalen and Henker (1980) used structured interviews of ADDH children in their research on causal attributions, and the children often referred to their attentional and/or motoric problems. However, the interviews were not designed to assess attentional problems or hyperactivity per se. It would be interesting to assess children's feelings and self-ratings of their own activity level and attentional problems. Such assessments, however, would probably be less reliable than the self-reports of anger and conduct problems like hitting, kicking, swearing, and other manifestations of conduct problems, since these are much more specific and discrete than difficulty concentrating, problems attending, and high activity level.

Laboratory Assessments

ELECTROENCEPHALOGRAM (EEG)

Minimal Brain Dysfunction (MBD) was seen by many professionals as the cause of hyperactivity and related attentional problems. The MBD concept led to frequent use of the EEG, but the clinical utility of the EEG with children with problems of hyperactivity and attentional problems has been questioned by many experts. The EEG has not proven to be a reliable predictor of response to psychostimulant treatment (Cantwell, 1975), and, as Werry (1978) concluded, the EEG is useful only as an assessment instrument for serious neurological disorders like epilepsy.

ACTIVITY MEASURES

Activity measures of children have been obtained with electromechanical devices used to measure movement directly. These measures have yielded significant correlations with teacher ratings of hyperactivity, but at present, such devices are used almost solely for research purposes.

ATTENTIONAL MEASURES

According to Loney (1980), the most useful laboratory measure of attention and/or vigilance is the Continuous Performance Test (CPT). Sequences of letters or figures are presented and the child indicates whenever a particular stimulus appears. Scores on the CPT reliably differentiate ADDH from non-ADDH children (Safer &Allen, 1976).

ANXIETY

Anxiety has played a central role in the development of abnormal behavior since Freud's classic case of Little Hans in 1909, which established the beginnings of child psychoanalysis, and since the Watson and Rayner case in 1920 of Little Albert in which a childhood fear was purportedly conditioned. (See also Chapter 3.) It has become useful to distinguish anxiety and fears: The latter are considered as reactions to relatively specific stimuli; anxieties are considered more diffuse reactions to stimuli. Fears and anxieties are considered to be clinically significant when they are age inappropriate, persistent, and maladaptive. Both fears and phobias are characterized by feelings of panic and/or tension. Often a child will have increased rapid heart beat and breathing as well as sweating. These affective and physiological responses may be accompanied by behavioral responses such as crying, demanding assistance, and attempting to run away from the stimulus(i) that causes the fear or anxiety.

Anxiety is a complex construct involving cognitive, motor, and physiological components (Lang, 1968). It may be experienced under very specific conditions, but generally it is experienced in multiple settings. In its more generalized form, the source of anxiety is often unclear to the child or adult.

Since the cognitive, motor, and physiological components of anxiety rarely vary in a consistent fashion, assessment of more than one component is recommended. Nevertheless, self-report measures are the most common methods used.

Self-report Measures

A variety of self-report measures are available. Some focus on anxiety as a generalized trait. Others measure specific fears. Some of the more commonly used measures are described below.

CHILDREN'S MANIFEST ANXIETY SCALE (CMAS)

This scale, developed by Casteneda, McCandless, and Palmero (1956), consists of 42 anxiety items and 11 additional items that constitute a Lie Scale. It is assumed to measure the child's tendency to experience a general or chronic state of anxiety across a variety of situations. Test–retest reliability estimates have been generally adequate, with correlations ranging from .70 to .94 (Casteneda et al., 1956; Holloway, 1958). CMAS scores show low to moderate correlations with other self-report anxiety measurements (Johnson & Melamed, 1979).

Factor analytic studies have suggested that the CMAS is comprised of two or three factors with the first factor consisting of items focusing on worry or oversensitivity. Items involving somatic concerns or items focusing on cognitive components such as concentration and decision making comprise the remaining factor(s) (Finch, Kendall, & Montgomery, 1974a; Scherer & Nakamura, 1968).

STATE-TRAIT ANXIETY INVENTORY FOR CHILDREN (STAIC)
This instrument consists of two 20-item scales developed by Speilberger (1973). One scale measures transitory anxiety that varies over time and across situations (A-State). The other is designed to measure anxiety as a relatively stable trait (A-Trait). Both scales have shown evidence of internal consistency ($r = .88$ to .89; Finch, Montgomery, & Deardorff, 1974). Estimates of test–retest reliability have been variable (e.g., correlations ranging from .44 to .94 for A-Trait; Finch et al., 1974b; Bedell & Roitzsch, 1976). Correlations with other instruments designed to measure state or trait anxiety have not consistently supported the state–trait distinction. However, A-State scores do seem to be more sensitive to experimentally induced situational stress than are A-Trait scores (Johnson & Melamed, 1979). Norms are available in the test manual.

Factor analytic studies of A-Trait items have resulted in findings similar to factor analytic studies of CMAS items. Items cluster into three groupings: worry, indecisiveness, and somatic complaints. In contrast, factor analysis of the A-State items result in a single bipolar factor with feelings of tension, nervousness, and worry at one pole, and sensations of pleasantness, relaxation, and happiness at the other pole (Finch, Kendall, & Montgomery, 1976).

FEAR SURVEY FOR CHILDREN (FSS-FC) AND THE LOUISVILLE FEAR SURVEY (LFSC)
Modeled after Wolpe and Lang's (1964) Fear Survey Schedule for Adults, the FFS-FC consists of 80 specific fears related to the following categories: school, home, social, physical, animal, travel, classical phobia, and miscellaneous (Scherer & Nakamura, 1968). No norms are available. The authors reported the scale's split-half reliability ($r = .94$) but no data on its test–retest reliability. Although this measure may be sensitive to therapeutic effects, in most studies FSS-FC changes have not been statistically significant (Johnson & Melamed, 1979).

The total number of fear items checked on the FSS-FC is sometimes used as a measure of chronic anxiety. In fact, FSS-FC scores correlate moderately with CMAS scores ($r = .49$; Scherer & Nakamura, 1968).

The LFSC (Miller, 1967) is similar to the FSS-FC, consisting of 81 potentially fearful items. Ratings are made on a three-point scale: no fear, normal or rational fear, or unrealistic fear. Factor analytic studies of both of these instruments have suggested that children's fear may be categorized into (1) fear of physical injury and personal loss; (2) fear of natural and supernatural danger; and (3) fear related to phychologically stressful situations such as school, doctor, tests, and so on (Miller, Barrett, Hampe, & Noble, 1971; Scherer & Nakamura, 1968). While the CMAS and STAIC focus on the child's experience of anxiety, the FSS-FC and the LFSC focus on the objects of the child's anxiety. Consequently, factor analyses of the CMAS and STAIC responses have yielded similar results that are quite different from factor analytic solutions derived from the FSS-FC and LFSC.

Behavioral Measures

Behavioral measures of children's fears fall into four categories: behavioral avoidance tests, observational codes, behavioral checklists, and global behavioral ratings.

BEHAVIORAL AVOIDANCE TEST (BAT)

This assessment method is used with very specific fears such as snake, dog, or water phobias. The child is asked to perform the same graded series of approach behaviors toward the phobic objects both before and after treatment (e.g., Bandura, Grusec, & Menlove, 1967). Since the BAT is administered in a standard, carefully controlled fashion, scoring of the child's approach behavior is relatively straightforward. The BAT appears to be sensitive to treatment effects but does not always correlate with children's self-report measures of fear and may be highly sensitive to experimental demand characteristics (Johnson & Melamed, 1979).

OBSERVATIONAL CODES

A number of observational codes have been developed to measure behavior presumably associated with anxiety. Using a time-sampling procedure, an observer records the presence or absence of each behavior during each observation interval. The behaviors selected for observation are those that are presumed to be characteristic of anxiety in a given setting. For example, the Observer Rating Scale of anxiety (ORSA) is an observational code that includes "crying," "trembling hands," "stuttering," "talking about being afraid." It was developed by Melamed and Siegel (1975) to study anxiety in children facing surgery. Similar codes have been designed to assess anxiety in children facing dental procedures (Melamed, Hawes, Heiby, & Glick, 1975) and to assess anxiety behaviors in diabetic children learning to self-inject insulin (Gilbert et al., 1982). Interobserver agreement estimates are usually above 85 percent. Although behavioral observational data do not consistently correlate with children's self-reports of anxiety, they do seem to be sensitive to treatment effects (Johnson & Melamed, 1979).

BEHAVIORAL CHECKLISTS

Behavioral checklists involve a standard set of specific behaviors that are rated by someone who knows the child well (e.g., parent or teacher). Usually each behavior is checked as occurring or not occurring, or it is rated on a scale ranging from low to high frequency. Most behavior checklists do not measure anxiety per se, but do estimate more global dimensions of behavior that include anxiety and withdrawal. For example, as already discussed in relation to conduct disorder, the RBPC (Quay & Peterson, 1983) provides an estimate of the severity of the youngster's anxious, withdrawn behaviors through the scoring of its Anxiety-Withdrawal Scale.

The Personality Inventory for Children (PIC) is one of the few checklist-type instruments that offer separate anxiety, withdrawal, and depression scales. The child's primary caretaker completes this 600-item, true-false instrument, designed for children 3 to 16 years of age. A total of 12 clinical scales are scored. Supportive reliability and validity data are provided by the authors as well as normative data (Lachar & Gdowski, 1979a, 1979b; Wirt, Lachar, Klinedinst, & Seat, 1977). However, the instrument is very long, taking 1½ to 2 hours to complete. Recent research suggests that the anxiety scale may not be valid for preschool children (DeMoor-Peal & Handal, 1983). Future studies need to address not only the validity of the PIC Scales but the utility of the instrument in view of the length of time required for completion.

Space limitations prevent us from discussing all of the behavioral checklists relevant to the measurement of anxiety or withdrawal. Others that the reader may wish to explore include the Preschool Behavior Questionnaire (Behar & Stringfield, 1974); the Devereux Elementary School Behavior Rating Scale (Spivack & Swift, 1967); the Louisville Behavior Checklist (Miller, Barrett, Hampe, & Noble, 1971); and the already discussed TRS.

GLOBAL BEHAVIORAL RATINGS

Observers or other persons present in an anxiety-arousing situation (e.g., dentist, nurse, physician) are sometimes asked to make a global rating of the youngster's fear-related behaviors. Interrater reliabilities of such ratings are usually above $r = .75$ and such measures are often sensitive to treatment effects (Johnson & Melamed, 1979; Gilbert et al., 1982). Nevertheless, such ratings should not be used in isolation, as a number of investigators have found them to be especially susceptible to observer bias (Kent, O'Leary, Diament, & Dietz, 1974; Shuller & McNamara, 1976).

DEPRESSION

Childhood depression has attracted significant attention in the past decade. As noted in Chapter 3, however, although there is controversy about whether there is a childhood counterpart to adult depression, there is little question about whether children can experience dysphoria.

Since the assessment of childhood depression is a relatively recent area of investigation, the available assessment methodologies are new and offer only preliminary evidence of reliability and validity. Efforts have been directed primarily at self-report scales and interviews, not surprising in view of the internal nature of the diagnostic criteria (i.e., feelings of dysphoria and loss of interest or pleasure). The more commonly used self-report and interview methods are described next. In addition, other approaches to the assessment of this problem will be mentioned briefly.

Self-report Measures

Both self-report and interview measures of childhood depression are often based on instruments developed to measure adult affective disorders, a reasonable point of departure provided that there is some recognition of differences in symptomatology between adults and children. For example, somatic complaints and school refusal may be signs of depression more frequently seen in children, while psychomotor retardation or disturbances of thinking may be more characteristic of adult rather than childhood depression (Kazdin & Petti, 1982).

CHILD DEPRESSION INVENTORY (CDI)

This 27-item instrument was developed by Kovacs and Beck (1977) for youngsters 7 to 17 years old. It is derived from the Beck Depression Inventory, an instrument widely used with adults. The youngster responds to each item on a three-point scale, reflecting the presence, absence, and frequency of the symptom. Normative data are available with cutoff scores for varying degrees of depression (Kovacs, 1981). Data supportive of both the instrument's internal consistency and test–retest reliability are also available (Helsel & Matson, 1984; Kazdin & Petti, 1982). Several studies have found CDI scores to discriminate between depressed youngsters and those with other psychiatric diagnoses (Kazdin, Esveldt-Dawson, Unis, & Rancurello, 1983; Kazdin, French, & Unis, 1983). CDI scores also correlate well with other self-report or interview measures of depression completed by the child (Kazdin & Heidish, 1984). However, although mothers and fathers often agree on the severity of the child's depression, parent–child reports are often in disagreement (Kazdin, Esveldt-Dawson, Unis, & Rancurello, 1983; Kazdin, French, & Unis, 1983; Reynolds, Anderson, & Bactrel, 1985). In the two studies by Kazdin and colleagues, mother–father CDI correlations ranged from .61 to .74, while parent–child CDI correlations ranged from .01 to .40. Typically, the child reports his depression to be less severe than his parents (particularly his mother) perceive it to be (see also Leon, Kendall, & Garber, 1980).

A shorter version of the CDI is available (Carlson & Cantwell, 1979). There are, however, fewer psychometric data on this abbreviated instrument.

CHILDREN'S DEPRESSION SCALE (CDS)

Developed by Lang and Tisher (1978), the CDS uses a novel format. Each of the 66 items is presented on a card that the child sorts into one of five boxes ranging from "very wrong" (or uncharacteristic of the child) to "very right" (or very characteristic of the child). Most of the items focus on depressive symptoms but some items describe positive experiences. Sometimes, people who know the child well (e.g., parents, teachers, siblings) are asked to rate the child's depression using this method. Kazdin (1981) reported that the internal consistency of the CDS is very high ($r = .96$) and it has been used to distinguish normal from clinically depressed samples. However, the CDS has not enjoyed as widespread use as the CDI.

Interview Measures

A number of investigators have attempted quantitative assessment of depression through the use of structured interviews. Published methods of this type vary somewhat in the number and content of the ratings to be completed during or after the interview. The Bellvue Index of Depression (BID) (Petti, 1978), for example, consists of 40 items to be rated for both severity and duration. In contrast, the Child's Affective Rating Scale (McKnew & Cytryn, 1979) requires only three relatively global ratings. Many of these procedures encourage the interviewer to obtain information from sources other than the child before completing ratings. Clear guidelines for combining data from a variety of informants, however, are not always available (Kazdin, 1981).

BELLEVUE INDEX OF DEPRESSION (BID)
Petti (1978) devised this scale based on earlier work by Weinberg and colleagues (Ling, Oftedal, & Weinberg, 1970; Weinberg, Rutman, Sullivan, Penick, & Dietz, 1973). The interviewer asks the child to respond to each of 40 items and then rates the item for both absence or severity of the symptom and duration. The interviewer is encouraged to obtain data from sources other than the child before making his or her final BID ratings. Criteria for diagnosis of depression are provided. Petti (1978) reported that diagnosis using BID scores showed good agreement with an independent clinician's diagnosis of depression. In two interesting studies, Kazdin and his colleagues explored the relationship between information obtained from different informants (Kazdin, Esveldt-Dawson, Unis, & Rancurello, 1983; Kazdin, French, & Unis, 1983). Mothers, fathers, and children (6–13 years of age) were interviewed independently concerning the youngster's possible depression. Whereas BID scores obtained from mother and father interviews showed good agreement ($r = .66$ to $.69$), parents and children often failed to agree ($r = .27$ to $.41$), with children typically receiving lower BID scores. BID scores, however, whether obtained from parents or children, significantly discriminated between depressed and nondepressed groups (see also Kazdin & Heidish, 1984).

INTERVIEW SCHEDULE FOR CHILDREN (ISC)
Kovacs (1978), who developed the CDI, designed this structured interview, which requires ratings on 37 items of symptoms or symptom clusters. In addition to emotional, cognitive and motivational components of depression,

ratings are made on symptoms presumed to "mask" depression, (see Chapter 1.) Both mother and child are interviewed separately and clinical judgment is used to resolve discrepancies. The author has reported adequate interjudge agreement using the ISC (Kovacs, Feinberg, Crouse-Novak, Paulauskas, & Finkelstein, 1984), although additional reliability and validity research is needed.

CHILDREN'S DEPRESSION RATING SCALE (CDRS)

This 16-item scale was designed to be used in the same way as the adult-oriented Hamilton Depression Rating Scale (Pozanski, Cook, & Carrol, 1979). Ratings are completed after interviewing the child and other relevant informants. Good agreement has been documented between independent raters who participated in or observed the same interview. Agreement between independent raters conducting independent interviews has not been reported, nor are clear criteria for a diagnosis of depression specified (Kazdin & Petti, 1982).

KIDDIE-SADS (K-SADS)

Based on the Schedule for Affective Disorders and Schizophrenia for Adults (Endicott & Spitzer, 1978), this interview was developed for 6 to 16-year-olds. Like the ISC, the K-SADS involves ratings relevant to other diagnostic categories in addition to ratings of depressive symptoms. The authors, Chambers and Puig-Antich, report good interrater reliability ($r = .65$ to $.90$; Kazdin, 1981) and provide evidence that the measure is sensitive to drug treatment effects (Puig-Antich et al. 1979). When children and mothers are interviewed separately, moderate levels of diagnostic agreement result (e.g., 76%, Orvaschel, Weissman, Padian, & Lowe, 1981). Consequently, information from both parent and child sources should be considered.

CHILDREN'S AFFECTIVE RATING SCALE (CARS)

This measure comes the closest to a global rating of depression because only three items are scored—depressive mood and behavior, verbal expression, and fantasy—each on a 10-point scale. Ratings are to be completed after a structured interview with the child. The authors report good agreement between independent raters who completed the CARS after observing the same interview ($r = .71$ to $.95$). CARS scores also agreed with diagnostic decisions made by an independent clinician. Test–retest reliability estimates over a four-month interval were adequate for boys ($r = .64$), but inadequate for girls ($r = -.43$). However, the test–retest interval may have been too long (McKnew, Cytryn, Efron, Gershon, & Bunney, 1979). Clear criteria for a diagnosis of depression are not provided.

Other Assessment Methods

Self-report inventories and interviews are clearly the most common methods for assessing depression. Little attention has been given to behavioral or physiological assessment strategies, although there are a few exceptions in this regard. The PIC, mentioned previously, has a Depression Scale. PIC Depression Scale scores show low but significant correlations with CDI scores (Leon et al., 1980; Reynolds et al., 1985). Achenbach's CBC is also completed by the parent and offers a Depression Scale score. CBC Depression Scale scores have discriminated between disturbed and normal samples (Achenbach, 1978b; Achenbach & Edelbrock, 1983). In an effort to utilize information from peers, Lefkowitz and Tesiny (1980) developed the Peer Nomination Inventory of Depression (PNID), providing extensive data on the psychometric properties of the instrument. They and others have found that PNID scores correlate at statistically significant, low to moderate levels with both self-report measures of depression and teacher ratings of depression (Jacobson, Lahey, & Strauss, 1983).

Almost no studies have utilized direct observational methods. Chiles, Hiller, and Cox (1980) reported that the Behavior Inventory for Depressed Adolescents, consisting of 27 observer-rated items, was able to discriminate depressed from nondepressed inpatients. However, few details are given about the measure or its psychometric characteristics.

Biological theories of depression postulate that hypothalamic-pituitary-adrenal (HPA) axis and cortisol hypersecretion may be involved in affective disorders. In normals, cortisol secretion ceases in the evening and early morning. Depressed patients continue to secrete cortisol during these times, showing an increased number of secretory episodes and a higher total amount of cortisol excretion in 24 hours. The dexamethasone suppression test has been used to monitor the activity of the HPA axis. In normals, exogenous dexamethasone administration two hours after the nadir of cortisol secretion suppresses further cortisol excretion for 24 hours. This response is not observed in some depressed patients. Although most of this work has been done with adults, it can serve as a basis for the identification of possible biochemical correlates of depression in childhood (Kashani & Cantwell, 1983). However, the clinical use of the dexamethasone suppression test with children or adolescents is premature at this time (Ha, Kaplan, & Foley, 1984).

PERVASIVE DEVELOPMENTAL DISORDERS

Some of the most severe problems of young children have been variously labeled childhood schizophrenia, autism, and childhood psychoses. Children with these problems are now often given the label Infantile Autism or Childhood Onset Pervasive Developmental Disorder. One of the main reasons for the elimination of the term *childhood schizophrenia* from the American Psychiatric Association's *Diagnostic and Statistical Manual* (1980) is that there are generally not differential treatment implications that result from the labels "autism" and "childhood" schizophrenia. In addition, the major journal in the area was changed from the *Journal of Autism and Childhood Schizophrenia* to *Journal of Autism and Developmental Disabilities* in 1977. Its editor, Schopler, argued that the name change reflected a desire to integrate research from various developmental areas with the research on severe childhood psychopathology. Nonetheless, for clinical and research purposes, the term Infantile Autism is used as a subcategory of developmental disorders. (See Chapter 5.)

As already discussed in Chapter 5, the causes of pervasive developmental disorder are unclear. Some investigators such as DesLauriers (1978) hold that autism is a disorder of affect (i.e., an inability to relate to others in an emotional sense). More recently, investigators have hypothesized that faulty perception is a prominent core defect of children with autism, and this has become an often accepted though controversial view (Wicks-Nelson & Israel, 1984). A third view is that autistic children have severe selective attention problems (Lovaas, Young, & Newsom, 1978). More specifically, autistic children are said to respond to only *one* component of a stimulus complex, whereas retarded children responded to *some* components and normal children respond to *all* of the components in the stimulus complex (Lovaas et al., 1978). Interestingly, overselectivity or responding to one component of the stimulus configuration is not due to specific sensory defects, since such children can learn to respond to components of the stimulus complex they initially ignored. Finally, Rutter (1978) has suggested a fourth view: the core defect of autism is a language deficit. Rutter holds that language deficits in autistic children are severe and that they represent a true cognitive incapacity, not simply a disturbance in social relationships.

It would be expected that one's view regarding the etiology of autism would influence the types of assessment used. For example, one might expect that affect defects, perceptual problems, stimulus overselectivity, and language defects would be foci of assessments of autistic children. As will be illustrated here, there is some evidence that such targets are sometimes the focus of assessments, but with the exception of language evaluation, clinical assessments of children with pervasive developmental disorders typically are done with clinical interviews and behavioral checklists designed to provide an overall assessment of the child, not an in-depth focus on a particular function of the child or a hypothesized deficit.

Checklists

One of the best-known checklists is Rimland's Diagnostic Checklist for Disturbed Children (1964). This checklist was developed to differentiate children with Kanner's syndrome or Early Infantile Autism from children with other developmental disabilities. The checklist consists of 80 items (250 items in the 1974 version) that are completed by parents or guardians; the items address questions about birth, early development, and current capabilities. An autism score is obtained, and a cutoff score of 20 is said to yield a diagnosis of autism. The scores obtained on this checklist correlate reasonably well with diagnoses made by Kanner (Rimland, 1971).

The Vineland Social Maturity Scale (Doll, 1965) is used to assess the behavioral functions of individuals (dressing, eating, socializing); the 117 items on the scale are arranged in a chronological fashion according to the age at which they would be expected to appear in a normal sample. This chronological sequencing makes the administration of the scale very easy and a social age can be readily calculated. The ease of administration is a clear advantage of this scale, but the scale does not lead to differential diagnoses of mental retardation or developmental disability.

The Adaptive Behavior Scale (ABS) consists of 10 areas of positive or competent behaviors (e.g., language development and socialization) and 14 areas of maladaptive behavior (withdrawal and violent behavior). The ABS (Grossman, 1977) has been advocated widely by the American Association on Mental Deficiency, and it is used in conjunction with IQ tests to assess a child's social and intellectual functioning. Adaptive behavior is categorized from mild to profound impairment, but the scales are not precise enough to yield classifications as reliable as those obtained with intelligence tests.

The original BPC (Quay & Peterson, 1975), has been used with adolescent schizophrenics and such individuals have received high scores on the immaturity factor, but misclassification of individuals into schizophrenic versus nonschizophrenic category has been found to be 30 percent (Herr, Eaves, & Algozzine, 1977). The RBPC has a six-item psychotic behavior scale derived from factor analysis, but this scale has not yet been adequately studied (Quay & Peterson, 1983). This paucity of studies may be due in part to the small number of items that relate to the features of infantile autism and pervasive developmental disorders described earlier.

Similarly, the CBC has few items relevant to children with pervasive developmental disorders, but a schizoid scale is contained in the CBC. The authors note that the schizoid scale is not equivalent to any clinical diagnosis, and a number of items on the schizoid scale suggest anxiety rather than schizoid features (Achenbach & Edelbrock, 1983).

Behavioral Observations

Use of the target behavior approach has led behavior therapists to concentrate on the particular behaviors to be changed. (See Chapter 14.) Observational methodology in which very specific behaviors are frequently observed *in vivo*, like the observational methodology described with conduct-disorder children and ADDH children, has also been used with children with severe developmental disorder. For example, Lovaas, Koegel, Simmons, and Long (1973) observed self-stimulation, echolalia, appropriate verbal, social nonverbal, and appropriate play behavior before and after treatment to assess treatment efficacy. The methodological problems discussed earlier in this chapter are as germane to the problems of assessing children with severe developmental disorder as they are to the problems of assessing children with ADDH or conduct disorder. Fortunately, target behavior observations can be executed with high reliability, with minimal reactivity, and with minimal observer drift if an adaptation period is used, if there is periodic reliability retraining, and if there is intermittent reliability checking of observers.

Clinical Interviews

As Newsom and Rincover (1981) noted, global, "whole-child" assessments are conducted routinely in every community setting whenever a child with a pervasive developmental disorder is admitted to a facility. Important screening information is obtained initially from a clinical interview and from informal observations of the child in a classroom or in the home. A summary of the areas that are felt useful to cover in a screening interview was provided by Newsom and Rincover (1981). They suggest that one assess activity level, responsiveness to external stimuli, preoccupation with self-stimulatory behavior, amount and quality of speech, independence in self-care, responsiveness to requests and punishment, responsiveness to praise and phsyical affection, dietary restrictions, history of medication use, unusual strengths, and topography and rate of self-injurious behavior.

In addition to these issues, it is important to know the types of parent management techniques that have been tried, and the types of reinforcers and punishers that have been used. The interviewer should also try to assess the parent's ability and/or willingness to implement teaching and parental management procedures in the home. Whatever one's etiological or treatment views, teaching a child with pervasive developmental disorders is the *sine qua non* of intervention. Dietary regimens and psychopharmacological therapy may be necessary in some instances, but these interventions do not bring about changes in the critical social skills necessary for progress in these children. Some clinical assessment of the various psychological, social, and medical stresses on the parents is also necessary, as such stresses may deter or prevent the parents from teaching the child on a systematic bases. Severe financial stresses, a chronic medical condition, and/or severe marital discord can critically limit parents' teaching of a child with pervasive developmental disorders.

PSYCHOSOMATIC DISORDERS

Hippocrates is credited with drawing an association between human temperaments and physical conditions. Persons with different personality types— melancholic, phlegmatic, sanguine, and choleric—had different physical symptoms (see Hawkins, 1982). Later, the term *psychosomatic* or *psychophysiologic* began to be used to describe physical disorders caused by psychological factors. Early attempts to define symptoms as purely physical or purely psychological are an example of mind–body dualism first proposed by René Descartes in the 17th century. Descartes believed that the mind and body were distinct entities with different laws of causality. This strongly influenced Western thinking. Hence, attempts were made to classify illness as psychosomatic, somatoform, or organic (Bakal, 1979). From the 1930s to the 1950s, various personality types were specified as etiologically involved with certain diseases (Dunbar, 1955). While the theory that specific personality types cause specific diseases has not received strong empirical support (Latimer, 1979), the term *psychosomatic* has enjoyed widespread use. Unfortunately, the term is often used to describe any somatic symptom that has no proven physical cause. Such use is quite at variance with the original meaning of the term. Some have argued that the term be abandoned altogether since it encourages mind–body dualism (Latimer, 1979). In fact, it is no longer used in DSM-III. (See Chapter 7.)

Today's movement away from mind–body dualism recognizes both psychological and physiological components of health and disease. This comes at a time when the pattern of disease has changed in industrialized societies. As infectious diseases have been conquered, chronic illnesses and conditions that result from accidents, poisonings, or violence have emerged as the primary focus of health care. Most of these are strongly influenced by behavioral factors. For example, in 1980, the Center of Disease Control of the U.S. Public Health Service estimated that 50 percent of the mortality from the 10 leading causes of death in the United States can be attributed to lifestyles (e.g., smoking, diet, alcohol abuse; Miller, 1983).

Among children, 7 to 10 percent suffer from a serious chronic disease. Yet these patients constitute 50 percent of pediatric practice (Magrab & Calcagno, 1978). There is little doubt that psychological factors influence most or all of these conditions. The role of stress has received particular emphasis.

In the diathesis–stress model of illness, the patient has a biological vulnerability that is a necessary but not sufficient condition for disease onset. It is the interaction between the patient's "predisposition" and stress that leads to the actual display of the disorder. Or in the patient with a known physical condition (e.g., asthma, juvenile diabetes), the disease may be exacerbated by stress onset. In diabetes, for example, emotional upset may lead to an increase in the stress hormones, which, in turn, may result in an increase in glucose and free fatty acids, placing the child in poor metabolic control (Tarnow & Silverman, 1981–1982). Neuroendocrine mechanisms are thought to be responsible for airway obstruction that results when some asthmatic patients are faced with stress.

While stress is considered an important precursor to physical dysfunction, methods of assessing stress in childhood populations have been given little attention. The clinical interview remains the primary method of acquiring relevant information. Unlike the area of depression, there are no well-researched, structured interviews available to assess stress effects (Purcell's Precipitant Interview for Asthmatic Patients is a possible exception; Purcell & Weiss, 1970). Self-report questionnaires and checklists have been or are being developed, but reliability and validity data are minimal. Psychophysiological studies are rare and have never been used as a standard assessment method. Behavioral methods are notable by their absence.

Self-report Measures

Self-report measures vary from checklists of stressful events, to diaries of daily events.

Holmes and Rahe (1967) were the first to quantify life stress by developing a life-event scale. Adult respondents were to check all events listed that they had experienced during a specified time period (e.g., six months). Coddington's (1972) Social Readjustment Rating Scale for Children (SRRS-C) was the first to be developed for childhood populations. This was followed by Johnson and McCutcheon's (1980) Life Events Checklist (LEC). Although there are far fewer data available on the SRRS-C or the LEC than on life-event checklists developed for adults (see Zimmerman, 1983, for a review), both measures have shown significant relationships to children's health status (Bedell, Giordani, Amour, Tavormina, & Boll, 1977; Brand, Johnson, & Johnson, 1984; Chase & Jackson, 1981; Coddington, 1972; Gad & Johnson, 1980). However, although many of the correlations reported are of statistical significance, they are often only low to moderate in strength.

Checklists offer the advantage of standardization. They may, however, miss an event that may be stressful for an individual. Or an individual may check off an item that he or she experienced but did not find particularly stressful. The available instruments are also descriptive of events that occur over several months' time and may not accurately estimate day-to-day stresses.

Sometimes a diary of daily events can be useful for identifying emotional situations that elicit illness episodes. Hinkle and Wolf's (1949) case report of a juvenile diabetic with recurrent acidosis is an example. The adolescent's diary offered clear evidence of the relationship between emotional arousal and ketone production in this young girl.

Recently, there has been an interest in developing a more standardized means of assessing daily stressful experiences. The Hassles Scale (Kanner, Coyne, Schaefer, & Lazarus, 1981) offers 117 daily "hassles" or irritating demands that the respondent checks off as occurring or not occurring. Test–retest reliability averaged $r = .79$ in a sample of older adults. This measure needs to be modified for use with children or adolescents.

Psychophysiological Measures

Monitoring psychophysiological reactions to a laboratory stressor is sometimes used as an assessment method. The youngster is usually assessed before, during, and after the stress manipulation with psychophysiological measures relevant to the youngster's physical disorder. Tal and Miklich (1976), for example, had asthmatic youngsters imagine a neutral or relaxing scene, a fearful scene, and an anger scene. Heart rate and pulmonary functioning were evaluated. Heart rate increased and pulmonary function decreased to both the anger and fearful scenes. Pulmonary function improved during relaxation and heart rate decreased. Patients with histories of emotionally triggered asthma showed the greatest differential response to the three conditions.

Psychophysiological assessment of laboratory-induced stress, however, has never been used as a standard assessment method. The procedure typically requires expensive equipment, the child must usually sit passively while the stress is induced, and even the selection and control of the "stress" to be manipulated presents methodological problems. Obviously, the child's reaction to a laboratory-induced stress experience may or may not be representative of his response to more naturally occurring stresses in the real world.

SUMMARY

Considerably more concern for psychometric issues in the assessment of childhood problems exists now than was the case when the first volume of this book was published in 1972. The increased concern for assessment is well exemplified by the formation of the journal *Behavioral Assessment* in 1979 by the Association for the Advancement of Behavior Therapy. The journal was initiated in order to highlight some interesting developments in the assessment area and to foster assessment research.

The phenomenon of childhood depression has been questioned by some, but with the increase in adolescent suicides in the United States, it is likely that childhood and adolescent depression will be accepted as a legitimate area of inquiry. It is apparent that significant discrepancies exist between maternal and child reports of depression, and that children typically report fewer symptoms. It is unclear whether mothers overemphasize their children's difficulties or whether children underestimate them.

Assessment methods commonly used in the area of childhood psychopathology include self-report instruments, interviews, and behavioral checklists or observations. However, the assessment method most frequently employed and the focus of assessment methodological research differs somewhat across the major categories of childhood disorders. Behavioral checklists completed by parent and teacher or direct behavioral observations are the most common and most methodologically rigorous methods used for conduct disorder, ADDH, and pervasive developmental disorder. In contrast, self-report instruments are the primary measurement method used for anxiety, depression, and psychosomatic disorders. In other words, childhood disorders that are characterized by problematic overt behavior utilize behavioral checklists and direct observation. On the other hand, childhood disorders characterized by dysphoric internal states rely more heavily on self-report instruments. The assessment of anxiety comes the closest to utilizing a multidimensional approach. Anxiety is frequently measured by different but equally reliable methods including self-report, behavioral observation, and psychophysiological recording.

Interviews, of course, are used when assessing all types of childhood psychopathology. They differ, however, in their methodological rigor. The area of childhood depression has yielded the most reliable interview methodology, despite the remaining controversy about depression as a true *disorder* of childhood. Here, the emphasis has been on the reliable measurement of multiple *informants'* estimates of the child's internal state. This contrasts somewhat with the assessment of anxiety, which has emphasized the use of multiple methods (i.e., self-report, behavioral, and psychophysiological).

The influence of family therapy and systems theory led researchers to begin dealing with nonlinear models of parent–child interaction. The work of Patterson (1982) illustrates the use of conditional probabilities to investigate the role of parent–child and child–parent influences, and it is expected that this trend to explore bidirectional influences will increase markedly in the next decade. In the same vein, it is expected that more system variables will be explored for their moderating influence on parent–child effects. For example, the role of marital discord, overt marital hostility, insularity, and influence of positive and negative contacts with significant others have been explored recently (O'Leary, 1984; Wahler, 1980). Maternal and depression health status clearly have a significant role in parent–child interactions (Griest, Wells, & Forehand, 1979; Wolfe, Jaffe, Wilson, & Zak, 1984).

REFERENCES

Abikoff, H. (1979). Cognitive training interventions in children: Review of a new approach. *Journal of Learning Disabilities, 12,* 65–77.

Abikoff, H., Gittelman-Klein, R., & Klein, D. F. (1977). Validation of a classroom observation code for hyperactive children. *Journal of Consulting and Clinical Psychology, 45,* 772–783.

Achenbach, T. M. (1978a). The child behavior profile: I. Boys aged 6–11. *Journal of Consulting and Clinical Psychology, 46*(3), 478–488.

Achenbach, T. M. (1978b). The child behavior profile: II. Boys aged 12–16 and girls aged 6–11 and 12–16. *Journal of Consulting and Clinical Psychology, 47*(2), 223–233.

Achenbach, T. M., & Edelbrock, C. (1983). *Manual for the Child Behavior Checklist and Revised Child Behavior Profile.* Burlington, VT: University Associates in Psychiatry.

American Psychiatric Association. (1980). *Diagnostic and statistical manual* (3rd ed.). Washington, DC: American Psychiatric Association.

Arias, I., & O'Leary, K. D. (1984). *Prevalence rates of hyperactivity across cultures.* Unpublished manuscript, State University of New York at Stony Brook, Department of Psychology, Stony Brook.

Atkins, M. S., Pelham, W. E., & Licht, M. H. (1985). A comparison of objective classroom measures and teacher ratings of attention deficit disorder. *Journal of Abnormal Child Psychology, 13.*

Bakal, D. A. (1979). *Psychology and medicine: Psychobiological dimensions of health and illness.* New York: Springer.

Bandura, A., Grusec, J., & Menlove, F. (1967). Vicarious extinction of avoidance behavior. *Journal of Personality and Social Psychology, 5,* 16–23.

Barkley, R. A. (1981). *Hyperactive children: A handbook for diagnosis and treatment.* New York: Guilford.

Bedell, J., & Roitzsch, J. (1976). The effects of stress on state and trait anxiety in emotionally disturbed, normal, and delinquent children. *Journal of Abnormal Child Psychology, 4*, 173–177.

Bedell, J. R., Giordani, B., Amour, J. L., Tavormina, J., & Boll, T. (1977). Life stress and the psychological and medical adjustment of chronically ill children. *Journal of Psychosomatic Research, 21*, 237–242.

Behar, L. B., & Stringfield, S. (1974). *Manual for the Preschool Behavior Questionnaire*. Durham, NC: Author.

Blunden, D., Spring, C., & Greenberg, I. M. (1974). Validation of the classroom behavior Inventory. *Journal of Consulting Clinical Psychology, 42*, 84–88.

Boyle, M. H., & Jones, S. C. (1985). Selecting measures of emotional and behavioral disorders of childhood for use in general populations. *Journal of Child Psychology and Psychiatry, 26*, 137–159.

Brand, A. H., Johnson, J. H., & Johnson, S. B. (1984). *Life stress and diabetic control in children and adolescents with insulin dependent diabetes mellitus.* Unpublished manuscript, University of Florida, Gainesville.

Cantwell, D. P. (1975). *The hyperactive child.* New York: Spectrum.

Carlson, G. A., & Cantwell, D. P. (1979). A survey of depressive symptoms in child and adolescent psychiatric population. *Journal of the American Academy of Child Psychiatry, 18*, 587–599.

Castaneda, A., McCandless, B., & Palmero, D. (1956). The children's form of the Manifest Anxiety Scale. *Child Development, 27*, 217–326.

Chase, H. P., & Jackson, G. G. (1981). Stress and sugar control in children with insulin dependent diabetes mellitus. *Journal of Pediatrics, 98*(6), 1011–1013.

Chiles, J. A., Miller, M. L., & Cox, G. B. (1980). Depression in an adolescent delinquent population. *Archives of General Psychiatry, 37*, 1179–1184.

Coddington, R. D. (1972). The significance of life events as etiologic factors in the diseases of children—II: A study of a normal population. *Journal of Psychosomatic Research, 16*, 205–213.

Conners, C. K. (1969). A teacher rating scale for use in drug studies with children. *American Journal of Psychiatry, 126*, 884–888.

Conners, C. K. (1970). Symptom patterns in hyperkinetic, neurotic, and normal children. *Child Development, 41*, 667–682.

DeMoor-Peal, R., & Handal, P. J. (1983). Validity of the Personality Inventory for Children with four-year old males and females: A caution. *Journal of Pediatric Psychology, 8*, 261–270.

DesLauriers, A. M. (1978). The cognitive-affective dilemma in early infantile autism: The case of Clarence. *Journal of Autism and Child Schizophrenia, 8*, 219–229.

Doll, E. A. (1965). *Vineland Social Maturity Scale* (1965 ed.) Circle Pines, MN: American Guidance Service.

Dunbar, H. F. (1955). Emotions and bodily changes: A survey of literature on psychosomatic interrelationships—1910–1953. In E. T. Carlson (Ed.), *Classics in psychiatry.* New York: Arno Press.

Emery, R. E., & O'Leary, K. D. (1984). Marital discord and child behavior problems in a nonclinic sample. *Journal of Abnormal Child Psychology, 12*, 411–420.

Endicott, J., & Spitzer, R. L. (1978). A diagnostic interview. *Archives of General Psychiatry, 35*, 837–844.

Finch, A., Montgomery, L., & Deardorff, P. (1974). Reliability of state-trait anxiety with emotionally disturbed children. *Journal of Abnormal Child Psychology, 2,* 67–69.

Finch, A., Jr., Kendall, P., & Montgomery, L. (1974a). Multidimensionality of anxiety in children: Factor structure of the Children's Manifest Anxiety Scale. *Journal of Abnormal Child Psychology, 2,* 331–335.

Finch, A., Jr., Kendall, P., & Montgomery, L. (1974b). Reliability of state–trait anxiety with emotionally disturbed children. *Journal of Abnormal Child Psychology, 2,* 67–69.

Finch, A., Jr., Kendall, P., & Montgomery, L. (1976). Qualitative differences in the experience of state–trait anxiety in emotionally disturbed and normal children. *Journal of Personality Assessment, 40,* 522–530.

Finch, A. J., & Rogers, T. R. (1984). Self-report instruments. In T. H. Ollendick & M. Hersen (Eds.), *Child behavioral assessment* (pp. 106–124). New York: Pergamon Press.

Gad, M. T., & Johnson, J. H. (1980). Correlates of adolescent life stress as related to race, SES, and levels of perceived social support. *Journal of Clinical Child Psychology, Spring, 9,* 13–16.

Gilbert, B. O., Johnson, S. B., Spillar, R., McCallum, M., Silverstein, J. H., & Rosenbloom, A. (1982). The effects of peer-molding film on children learning to self-inject insulin. *Behavior Therapy, 13,* 186–193.

Glow, R. A. (1981). Cross validity and normative data on the revised Conners Parent and Teacher Rating Scale. In K. D. Gadow & J. Loney (Eds.), *Psychosocial aspects of drug treatment for hyperactivity* (pp. 107–150). Boulder, CO: Westview Press.

Goyette, C. H., Conners, C. K., & Ulrich, R. F. (1978). Normative data on Revised Conners Parent and Teacher Rating Scales. *Journal of Abnormal Child Psychology, 6,* 221–236.

Griest, D. L., Wells, K. C., & Forehand, R. (1979). An examination of predictors of maternal perceptions of maladjustment in clinic-referred children. *Journal of Abnormal Psychology, 88,* 277–281.

Grossman, H. J. (Ed.). (1977). *Manual on terminology and classification in mental retardation.* Washington, DC: American Association on Mental Deficiency.

Guy, W. (1976). *ECDEU assessment manual for psychopharmacology.* Rockville, MD: U.S. Department of Health, Education and Welfare.

Ha, H., Kaplan, S., & Foley, C. (1984). The dexamethasone suppression test in adolescent psychiatric patients. *American Journal of Psychiatry, 141,* 421–423.

Hartmann, D. P. (1983). Editorial. *Behavioral Assessment, 5,* 1–3.

Hawkins, D. R. (1982). Specificity revisited: Personality profiles and behavioral issues. *Psychotherapy and Psychosomatics, 38,* 54–63.

Helsel, W. J., & Matson, J. L. (1984). The assessment of depression in children: The internal structure of the Child Depression Inventory (CDI). *Behavior Research Therapy, 22,* 289–298.

Herjanic, B., & Reich, W. (1982). Development of a structured psychiatric interview for children: Agreement between child and parent on individual symptoms. *Journal of Abnormal Child Psychology, 10*, 307–324.

Herr, D., Eaves, R. C., & Algozzine, B. (1977). Use of the Behavior Problem Checklist with psychotic adolescents. *Journal of Consulting and Clinical Psychology, 45*, 1176–1177.

Hinkle, L. E., Jr., & Wolf, S. (1949). Experimental study of life situations, emotions, and the occurrence of acidosis in a juvenile diabetic. *American Journal of Medical Sciences, 217*, 130–135.

Holloway, H. (1958). Reliability of the Children's Manifest Anxiety Scale at the rural third grade level. *Journal of Educational Psychology, 49*, 193–196.

Holmes, T. H., & Rahe, R. H. (1967). The social readjustment rating scale. *Journal of Psychomatic Research, 11*, 213–218.

Jacob, T., Grounds, L., & Haley, R. (1982). Correspondence between parents' reports on the Behavior Problem Checklist. *Journal of Abnormal Child Psychology, 10*, 593–608.

Jacob, R. G., O'Leary, K. D., & Rosenblad, C. (1978). Formal and informal classroom settings: Effect on hyperactivity. *Journal of Abnormal Child Psychology, 6*, 47–59.

Jacobsen, R. H., Lahey, B. B., & Strauss, C. C. (1983). Correlates of depressed mood in normal children. *Journal of Abnormal Child Psychology, 11*, 29–40.

Johnson, J. H., & McCutcheon, S. (1980). Assessing life stress in older children and adolescents: Development of the Life Events Checklist. In I. G. Sarason & C. D. Speilberger (Eds.), *Stress and anxiety* (Vol. 7). Washington, DC: Hemisphere.

Johnson, S. B., & Melamed, B. (1979). The assessment and treatment of children's fears. In B. Lahey & A. Kazdin (Eds.), *Advances in clinical child psychology* (Vol. II, pp. 107–139). New York: Plenum Press.

Kanner, A. D., Coyne, J. C., Schaefer, C., & Lazarus, R. S. (1981). Comparison of two modes of stress measurement: Daily hassles and uplifts versus major life events. *Journal of Behavioral Medicine, 4*, 1–39.

Kashani, J. H., & Cantwell, D. P. (1983). Etiology and treatment of childhood depression: A biopsycho-social perspective. *Comprehensive Psychiatry, 24*, 476–486.

Kazdin, A. E. (1981). Assessment techniques for childhood depression. *American Academy of Child Psychiatry, 20*, 358–375.

Kazdin, A. E., Esveldt-Dawson, K., Unis, A. S., & Rancurello, M. D. (1983). Child and parent evaluations of depression and aggression in psychiatric inpatient children. *Journal of Abnormal Child Psychology, 11*, 401–413.

Kazdin, A. E., & Petti, T. A. (1982). Self-report and interview measures of childhood and adolescent depression. *Journal of Child Psychology & Psychiatry & Allied Disciplines, 23*, 437–457.

Kazdin, A. E., French, N. H., & Unis, A. S. (1983). Child, mother, and father evaluations of depression in psychiatric inpatient children. *Journal of Abnormal Child Psychology, 11*, 167–179.

Kazdin, A. E., & Heidish, I. E. (1984). Convergence of clinically derived diagnoses and parent checklists among inpatient children. *Journal of Abnormal Child Psychology, 12*, 421–436.

Kent, R. N., & Foster, S. L. (1977). Direct observation procedures: Methodological issues in naturalistic settings. In A. R. Ciminero, K. S. Calhoun, & H. E. Adams (Eds.), *Handbook of behavioral assessment.* New York: Wiley–Interscience.

Kent, R. N., Miner, G., Kay, W., & O'Leary, K. D. (1979). *Stony Brook observer manual.* Unpublished manuscript. Stony Brook: State University of New York at Stony Brook.

Kent, R. N., & O'Leary, K. D. (1976). A controlled evaluation of behavior modification with conduct problem children. *Journal of Consulting and Clinical Psychology, 44,* 586–596.

Kent, R. N., O'Leary, K. D., Colletti, G., & Drabman, R. S. (1976). *Increasing the validity of observational recording procedures.* Unpublished manuscript. Stony Brook: State University of New York at Stony Brook.

Kent, R., O'Leary, K. D., Diament, C., & Dietz, A. (1974). Expectation bias in observational evaluation of therapeutic change. *Journal of Consulting and Clinical Psychology, 42,* 774–780.

Kovacs, M., & Beck, A.T. (1977). An empirical-clinical approach toward a definition of childhood depression. In J. G. Schulterbrandt & A. Raskin (Eds.), *Depression in childhood: Diagnosis, treatment, and conceptual models* (pp. 1–25). New York: Raven Press.

Kovacs, M. (1978). Interview Schedule for Children (ISC). Pittsburgh: University of Pittsburgh School of Medicine.

Kovacs, M. (1981). Rating scales to assess depression in school aged children. *Acta Paedopsychiatrica, 46,* 305–315.

Kovacs, M., Feinberg, T. L., Crouse-Novak, M. A., Paulauskas, S. L., & Finkelstein, R. (1984). Depressive disorders in childhood: I. A longitudinal prospective study of characteristics and recovery. *Archives of General Psychiatry, 41,* 229–237.

Lachar, D., & Gdowski, C. L. (1979a). Problem behavior factor correlates of Personality Inventory for Children Profile scores. *Journal of Consulting and Clinical Psychology, 47,* 39–48.

Lachar, D., & Gdowski, C. L. (1979b). *Actuarial assessment of child and adolescent personality: An interpretive guide for the Personality Inventory for Children Profile.* Los Angeles: Western Psychological Services.

Lang, M., & Tisher, M. (1978). *Children's Depression Scale.* Victoria, Australia: The Australian Council for Educational Research.

Lang, P. (1968). Fear reduction and fear behavior: Problems in treating a construct. In J. M. Schlien (Ed.), *Research in psychotherapy* (pp. 93–103). Washington, DC.: American Psychological Association.

Latimer, P. (1979). Psychophysiologic disorders: A critical appraisal of concept and theory illustrated with reference to the irritable bowel syndrome (IBS). *Psychological Medicine, 9,* 71–80.

Lefkowitz, M. M., & Tesiny, E. P. (1980). Assessment of childhood depression. *Journal of Consulting Clinical Psychology, 48,* 43–50.

Leon, G. R., Kendall, P. C., & Garber, J. (1980). Depression in children: Parent, teacher, and child perspectives *Journal of Abnormal Child Psychology, 8,* 221–235.

Ling, W., Oftedal, G., & Weinberg, W. (1970). Depressive illness in childhood presenting as severe headache. *American Journal of the Diseases in Childhood, 120*, 122–124.

Loney, J. (1980). Childhood hyperactivity. In R. H. Woody (Ed.), *Encyclopedia of clinical assessment* (pp. 265–285). San Francisco: Jossey-Bass.

Lovaas, O. I., Koegel, R. L., Simmons, J. Q., & Long, J. S. (1973). Some generalization and follow-up measures of autistic children in behavior therapy. *Journal of Applied Behavior Analysis, 6*, 131–165.

Lovaas, O. I., Young, D. G., & Newsom, C. D. (1978). Childhood psychosis: Behavioral treatment. In B. B. Wolman (Ed.), *Handbook of treatment of mental disorders in childhood and adolescence* (pp. 385–420). Englewood Cliffs, NJ: Prentice-Hall.

Magrab, P., & Calcagno, P. (1978). Psychological impact of chronic pediatric conditions. In P. R. Magrab (Ed.), *Psychological management of pediatric problems* (pp. 3–14). Baltimore: University Park Press.

McKnew, D. H., & Cytryn, L. (1979). Urinary metabolites in chronically depressed children. *American Academy of Child Psychiatry, 18*, 608–615.

McKnew, D. H., Cytryn, L., Efron, A. M., Gershon, E. S., & Bunney, W. E., Jr. (1979). Offspring of patients with affective disorders. *British Journal of Psychiatry, 134*, 148–152.

Melamed, B., Hawes, R., Heiby, E., & Glick, J. (1975). Use of filmed modeling to reduce uncooperative behavior of children during dental treatment. *Journal of Dental Research, 54*, 797–801.

Melamed, B., & Siegel, L. (1975). Reduction of anxiety in children facing hospitalization and surgery by use of filmed modeling. *Journal of Consulting and Clinical Psychology, 43*, 511–521.

Miller, L. C. (1967). Louisville Behavior Checklist for males, 6–12 years of age. *Psychological Reports, 21*, 885–896.

Miller, L. C. (1972). School Behavior Checklist: An inventory of deviant behavior for elementary school children. *Journal of Consulting and Clinical Psychology, 38*, 138–144.

Miller, L. C., Barrett, C. L., Hampe, E. I., & Noble, H. (1971). Revised anxiety scales for the Louisville Behavior Checklist. *Psychological Reports, 29*, 503–511.

Miller, N. E. (1983). Behavioral medicine: Symbiosis between laboratory and clinic. *Annual Review of Psychology, 34*, 1–34.

Montgomery, L. E., Nelson, W. M., III, & Finch, A. J., Jr. (1979). *Anger in children: Preliminary investigations of anger-evoking stimuli in children.* Paper presented at the 25th meeting of the Southeastern Psychological Association, New Orleans.

Nelson, W. M., III, & Finch, A. J. (1978). *The Children's Inventory of Anger.* Unpublished manuscript, Xavier University.

Newsom, C., & Rincover, A. (1981). Autism. In E. J. Mash & L. G. Terdal (Eds.), *Behavioral assessment of children's disorders.* New York: Guilford Press.

O'Leary, K. D. (1979). Behavioral assessment. *Behavioral Assessment, 1*, 31–36.

O'Leary, K. D. (1981). Assessment of hyperactivity: Observational and rating methodologies. In S. A. Miller (Ed.), *Nutrition and behavior* (pp. 291–298). Philadelphia: Franklin Institute Press.

O'Leary, K. D. (1984). Marital discord and children: Problems, strategies, methodologies, and results. In A. Doyle, D. Godd, & D. S. Moskowitz (Eds.), *Children in families under stress*. San Francisco: Jossey-Bass.

O'Leary, K. D., & Johnson, S. B. (1979). Psychological assessment. In H. C. Quay & J. S. Werry (Eds.), *Psychopathological disorders of childhood* (2nd Ed.). New York: Wiley.

O'Leary, K. D., Romanczyk, R. G., Kass, R. E., Dietz, A., & Santogrossi, D. (1979). *Procedures for classroom observation of teachers and children*. Unpublished manuscript. Stony Brook: State University of New York at Stony Brook.

O'Leary, K. D., Vivian, D., & Nisi, A. (1985). Hyperactivity in Italy. *Journal of Abnormal Child Psychology, 13*, 485–500.

O'Leary, K. D., & Wilson, G. T. (1975). *Behavior therapy: Applications and outcome*. Englewood Cliffs, NJ: Prentice-Hall.

Orvaschel, H., Weissman, M. M., Padian, N., & Lowe, T. L. (1981). Assessing psychopathology in children of psychiatrically disturbed parents. *Journal of the American Academy of Child Psychiatry, 20*, 167–183.

Patterson, G. R. (1982). *A social learning approach* (*Vol. 3*): *Coercive family process*. Eugene, OR: Castalia.

Pelham, W. E., & Bender, M. E. (1982). Peer relationships in hyperactive children: Description and treatment. In K. D. Gadow & I. Bialer (Eds.), *Advances in learning and behavioral disabilities* (Vol. 1, pp. 365–436). Greenwich, CT: Jai.

Peterson, D. R. (1961). Behavior problems of middle childhood. *Journal of Consulting Psychology, 42*, 205–209.

Petti, T. A. (1978). Depression in hospitalized child psychiatry patients. Approaches to measuring depression. *Journal of the American Academy of Child Psychiatry, 17*, 49–59.

Pozanski, E. O., Cook, S. C., & Carroll, B. J. (1979). A depression rating scale for children. *Pediatrics, 64*, 442–450.

Puig-Antich, J., Perel, J. M., Lupatkin, W., Chambers, W. J., Shea, C., Tabrizi, M. A., & Stiller, R. L. (1979). Plasma levels of imipramine (IMI) and desmethylimipramine (DMI) and clinical response in prepubertal major depressive disorder. *Journal of the American Academy of Child Psychiatry, 18*, 616–627.

Purcell, L., & Weiss, J. H. (1970). Asthma. In C. G. Costello (Ed.), *Symptoms of psychopathology: A handbook* (pp. 597–623). New York: Wiley.

Quay, H. C. (1977). Measuring dimensions of deviant behavior. The Behavior Problem Checklist. *Journal of Abnormal Child Psychology, 5*, 277–287.

Quay, H. C. (1983). A dimensional approach to behavior disorder. The Revised Behavior Problem Checklist. *School Psychology Review, 12*, 244–249.

Quay, H. C., & Peterson, D. R. (1975). *Manual for the Behavior Problem Checklist*. Mimeographed.

Quay, H. C., & Peterson, D. R. (1983). Interim manual for the *Revised Behavior Problem Checklist*. Box 248074, University of Miami, Coral Gables, FL 33124.

Quay, H. C., Sprague, R. L., Shulman, H. C., & Miller, A. L. (1966). Some correlates of personality disorder and conduct disorder in a child guidance sample. *Psychology in the Schools, 3*, 44–47.

Reynolds, W. M., Anderson, G., & Bactrel, N. (1985). Measuring depression in children: A multimethod assessment investigation. *Journal of Abnormal Child Psychology, 13*, 513–526.

Rimland, B. (1964). *Infantile autism.* New York: Appleton-Century-Crofts.

Rimland, B. (1971). The differentiation of childhood psychoses: An analysis of checklists for 2,218 psychotic children. *Journal of Autism and Childhood Schizophrenia, 1*, 161–174.

Routh, D. K., Schroeder, C. S., & O'Tuama, L. S. (1974). Development of activity level in children. *Developmental Psychology, 10*, 163–168.

Rutter, M. (1978). Language disorder and infantile autism. In M. Rutter & E. Schopler (Eds.), *Autism: A reappraisal of concepts and treatment* (pp. 85–104). New York: Plenum.

Safer, D. J., & Allen, R. P. (1976). *Hyperactive children: Diagnosis and management.* Baltimore, MD: University Park Press.

Scherer, M., & Nakamura, C. (1968). A fear survey schedule for children (FSS-FC): A factor analytic comparison with manifest anxiety (CMAS). *Behavior Research and Therapy, 6*, 173–182.

Shuller, D., & McNamara, J. (1976). Expectancy factors in behavioral observation. *Behavior Therapy, 1*, 519–527.

Speilberger, C. (1973). *Manual for the state-trait inventory for children.* Palo Alto, CA: Consulting Psychologists Press.

Spivak, G., & Swift, M. (1967). *Devereux elementary school behavior rating scale.* Deven, PA: Devereux Foundation.

Tal, A., & Miklich, D. R. (1976). Emotionally induced decreases in pulmonary flow rates in asthmatic children. *Psychosomatic Medicine, 38*, 190–200.

Tarnow, J., & Silverman, S. (1981–1982). The psychophysiologic effects of stress in juvenile diabetes mellitus. *Psychiatry in Medicine, 11*, 25–44.

Trites, R., Blouin, A. G., & Laprade, K. (1982). Factor analysis of the Conners Teacher Rating Scale based on a large normative sample. *Journal of Consulting and Clinical Psychology, 50*, 615–623.

Ullmann, R. K., Sleator, E. K., & Sprague, R. L. (1984). A new rating scale for diagnosis and monitoring for ADD children. *Psychopharmacology Bulletin, 20*, 160–164.

Wahler, R. G. (1980). The insular mother: Her problems in parent–child treatment. *Journal of Applied Behavior Analysis, 13*, 207–219.

Weinberg, W. A., Rutman, J., Sullivan, L., Penick, E. C., & Dietz, S. G. (1973). Depression in children referred to an educational diagnostic center: Diagnosis and treatment. *Behavioral Pediatrics, 83*, 1065–1072.

Werry, J. S. (1978). Measures in pediatric psychopharmacology. In J. S. Werry (Ed.), *Pediatric psychopharmacology* (pp. 29–78). New York: Brunner/Mazel.

Werry, J., & Sprague, R. (1970). Hyperactivity. In G. Costello (Ed.), *Symptoms of psychopathology* (pp. 397–417). New York: Wiley.

Werry, J. S., Sprague, R. L., & Cohen, M. N. (1975). Conners Teacher Rating Scale for use in drug studies with children: An empirical study. *Journal of Abnormal Child Psychology, 3*, 217–229.

Whalen, C. K., & Henker, B. (Eds.). (1980). *Hyperactive children the social ecology of identification and treatment.* New York: Academic Press.

Whalen, C. K., Henker, B., Collins, B. E., Finck, D., & Dotemoto, S. (1979). A social ecology of hyperactive boys: Medication effects in structured classroom environments. *Journal of Applied Behavior Analysis, 12*, 65–81.

Wicks-Nelson, R., & Israel, A. C. (1984). *Behavior disorders of childhood.* Englewood Cliffs, NJ: Prentice-Hall.

Wirt, R. D., Lachar, D., Klinedinst, J. K., & Seat, P. D. (1977). *Multi-dimensional description of child personality: A manual for the Personality Inventory for Children.* Los Angeles: Western Psychological Services.

Wolf, M. M. (1978). Social validity: The case for subjective measurement or how applied behavior analysis is finding its heart. *Journal of Applied Behavior Analysis, 11*, 203–214.

Wolfe, D., Jaffe, P., Wilson, S., & Zak, L. (1984). *Predicting children's adjustment to family violence: Beyond univariate analyses.* Paper presented at the Second Family Violence Research Conference, University of New Hampshire.

Wolpe, J., & Lang, P. (1964). A fear survey schedule for use in behavior therapy. *Behavior Research and Therapy, 2*, 27–30.

Zimmerman, M. (1983). Methodological issues in the assessment of life events: A review of issues and research. *Clinical Psychology Review, 3*, 339–370.

12 PSYCHO-PHARMACO-THERAPY

RACHEL GITTELMAN AND ANDRES KANNER

INTRODUCTION

Most psychopharmacological research has dealt with adult psychiatric disorders; the relative success of pharmacological treatments in adult patients (such as shortening the length of stay of psychiatric patients in institutions, inducing more effective, and rapid relief of symptomatology) has served as a model in the development of pharmacologic treatments for various psychopathological conditions of childhood. As a consequence, the role of pharmacotherapy as a treatment modality in child psychiatry has gained increasing if belated importance in the last decade.

Originally, medication was prescribed mostly for the relief of symptoms rather than for the treatment of overall psychiatric disorders; for example, antihistamine sedatives were prescribed for small children with sleep disturbances or neuroleptics for aggression in institutionalized children. Now, the aim is to develop a pharmacotherapy that yields a comprehensive therapeutic effect rather than symptomatic relief, such as treating major depressive disorders of childhood with antidepressants or phobic and compulsive disorders with clomipramine. Such developments will generate a greater understanding of each psychiatric condition, its malleability with treatment, its biological features, and perhaps its psychobiological correlates.

In this chapter we review current knowledge regarding the drug treatment of several major psychiatric disorders of childhood; we summarize briefly the overall clinical characteristics of each condition and present the different pharmacotherapeutic strategies for the treatment of these disorders. We first summarize some basic pharmacological principles that apply to the use of psychotherapeutic drugs.

PHARMACOLOGICAL PRINCIPLES

From a rigorous scientific approach, one would expect that the development of efficacious drug treatments comes from an understanding of the physiological dysfunctions specific to each disorder. However, this is not the case for a surprising number of drugs in medicine and especially so for drugs that affect behavior (psychoactive or psychotropic drugs). In all instances, the effects of the latter were discovered accidentally, and not through a logical sequence starting from well-established information of pathological physiology on to the development of therapeutics. The knowledge necessary for this most desirable strategy is still wanting for all the disorders we shall discuss, though, as can be seen in Chapters 2 through 8, there are at last some promising leads.

Because the psychoactive drugs *are* effective in modifying behavior, however, the specific ways in which they influence the brain, its chemistry, and its physical and physiological properties become of great scientific interest, since these actions provide important clues as to what may have gone wrong in those afflicted. For example, since all drugs effective in schizophrenia have been found to have one property in common (dopamine blockade), the so-called dopaminergic hypothesis of schizophrenia is currently popular (see Chapter 5). Therefore, the pharmacological properties of psychotherapeutic drugs have become a thriving scientific pursuit.

In spite of the very rich findings that have emerged recently in adults, the pharmacological aspects of psychoactive drugs are not yet helpful to the clinician who treats children. At this point, the formal characteristics of the drugs we discuss are not relevant guides for prescription. In spite of this, we summarize several important aspects of drug properties so that the approaches used to identify possible mechanisms associated with psychopathological disorders may be appreciated. This is particularly so since it is very likely that this field of study will continue to yield important information about the nature of brain function, and that, eventually, it will become pertinent in the day-to-day clinical management of psychiatric patients. A more detailed discussion of the basic principles of drug action can be found in Werry (1978) or in any standard text on pharmacology such as Gilman, Goodman, and Gilman (1980).

PHARMACOKINETICS

The term *pharmacokinetics* refers to how a drug is absorbed, distributed across different tissues and organs, metabolized into an inactive compound, and finally excreted from the body.

All the psychoactive agents used for the treatment of children at present are administered orally, except in emergencies. Following the ingestion of a drug, it is absorbed through the stomach or the small intestine and enters the gut bloodstream. The drug must then pass through the liver, which is a kind of complex filter containing many enzymes that often modify the original compound into a variety of other compounds, leaving only a certain percentage of the drug intact and potentially active. This is called the "first pass" effect, and since it seems to vary in size from one individual to the next, it is thought to explain some of the wide variations in therapeutic dosage levels seen with some drugs. Most drugs are transformed into one or more chemicals, referred to as drug *metabolites*. One or several may account for the clinical effect of the drug, but the majority of metabolites are pharmacologically inactive.

When the drug leaves the liver and enters the general circulation, it is transported in the blood in two forms, which exist in a dynamic equilibrium: a larger fraction of the drug travels bound to a plasma protein such as albumin or globulin, and a smaller percentage is transported in free form. Only unbound drug molecules are available for pharmacological effects, for passage across membranes (e.g., into saliva), or for elimination.

As a drug travels through the general circulation, it is distributed through the different tissues following certain physicochemical laws; these include the fat (lipid) solubility of the drug, the thickness of the membranes the drug has to cross, the molecular size of the medication, and the ionization state of the medication. The greater the lipid solubility, the more readily the drug will dissolve in a cell membrane and the faster a transfer will occur, all other factors being favorable. Since the brain is a very "fatty" organ, most psychoactive substances must be highly lipid soluble to be differentially effective on the CNS (central nervous system).

The degree of ionization also has very important effects on the transfer of the drug across cell membranes, especially in the brain, which has an extra protective membrane around it called the "blood–brain barrier." Thus, in general, un-ionized molecules are lipid (fat) soluble and cross the membrane easily, but ionized molecules are not, and thus ordinarily do not pass into the brain at all.

The length of time a drug stays in the body varies from compound to compound and is reflected in the *half-life* of the drug. The half-life is defined as the time required for the elimination of 50 percent of the drug from the body. The half-life of a drug will affect the number of dosages that have to be administered in order to maintain a stable drug level in the body. A word of warning, however—with most psychoactive drugs half-life is ordinarily measured only indirectly in blood (serum) or, increasingly in children, in saliva. As with diazepam (Valium), for example, the drug is stored and changed in tissues such as the gut wall, and the serum half-life bears little resemblance to the real state of the stored drug. We thus must distinguish between *serum* level and the (bio)availability of the drug.

The process of elimination from the body occurs through the continuing activation of the drug as it is constantly circulated by the liver, and excretion of the inactive as well as active metabolites through the kidney into the urine or the bile into the feces. A few drugs (e.g., lithium) are excreted unchanged, thereby raising problems if they are very toxic and the kidneys are not functioning well.

MECHANISM OF DRUG ACTION

Most psychoactive drugs exert their therapeutic effects by modifying brain functions through an interaction with specific biochemical substances in the brain, called *neurotransmitters*. These are released by nerve impulses in minute quantities into the synapse (or connections between nerve cells or neurons), where they interact with specific *receptors* on the next neuron, whereafter they are inactivated on the spot. The better known neurotransmitters include noradrenaline (NA), dopamine (DA), serotonin, (5HT), GABA (gamma aminobutyric acid), and acetylcholine (ACH). Only about 10 percent of neurotransmission is accounted for. New neurotransmitters are constantly being identified (neuropeptides, endorphins, etc.). It is a great oversimplification to state that better understanding of the interaction among neurotransmitters is needed before determining the potential effect of drugs on neurotransmitters. Certain drugs may act on a variety of neurotransmitters, whereas others may affect one neurotransmitter alone. The ways they affect these neurotransmitters vary: some (e.g., antidepressants) prevent their inactivation; some (e.g., neuroleptics) "sit" in the receptors and block them; and others (e.g., stimulants) release stored neurotransmitters. A few, such as lithium, alcohol, anticonvulsants, barbiturates, and glue, do not act on neurotramsmitters but on the cell membrane, depressing its excitability in general.

CLASSIFICATION OF DRUGS
What's in a Name?

Drugs available commercially have two names: one (the generic) that refers to the chemical compound itself, like acetaminophen, for example, and a brand name, in this instance Tylenol, a common pain killer. The generic name usually indicates some aspects of the chemical structure. The brand name is selected for strictly commercial reasons, on occasion to create some expected state, such as Halcion, an antianxiety agent, which is pronounced like the word "halcyon," and therefore evokes a calm, happy state. (Since no English word can be trademarked, slight changes in spelling may be introduced in common names.) Trade or brand names are always capitalized whereas generic are not.

Classification

There is no single classificatory principle for psychoactive drugs. They can be grouped according to their chemical structure, such as "tricyclic," "benzodiazepine," or "phenothiazine," or according to their effect on brain chemistry; for example, some antidepressants are called "monoamine oxidase inhibitors" because of their action on the monoamine oxidase enzyme. Drugs are identified also according to their effects on brain function, such as the "psychostimulants" or "neuroleptics." To complicate matters further, drugs are also described according to their mode of clinical action: antidepressants, antianxiety agents, antipsychotic agents, and so on. Drugs called antidepressants may belong to the family of the tricyclics or to the monoamine oxidase inhibitors; the term *tricyclic* refers to the chemical structure of the compound, while the term *monoamine oxidase inhibitor* describes the mode of chemical action, but both are antidepressants.

Sometimes the terms are combined, so that we may find references to "tricyclic antidepressants." It is important to note that the term describing the clinical action of a drug, like antidepressant, does not exhaust its potential usefulness and does not reflect the limits of its activity. The clinical term reflects the first major application of the drug. As the drug becomes better known, it is put to new uses, yet the old appellation often remains. As an example, a tricyclic, imipramine, was the first antidepressant discovered. In subsequent years, it has been found to have "antipanic" activity in adults suffering from spontaneous panic attacks and to be effective in suppressing enuresis. Yet the term *antidepressant* is the only one used, and "antipanic" or "antienuretic" do not exist in our current jargon. Because of this potential confusion, recent drugs have not been given names that describe their clinical effect.

The main psychoactive drugs used for the treatment of children with emotional and behavioral problems include the psychostimulants, the antidepressants, the anxiolytics, and the antipsychotics. Note that the first term pertains to the action of the drug group on the brain, but the last three describe the drugs' clinical effects. If we wanted to classify all four groups by the same criterion, we would have to substitute the term "antihyperactivity" agents for that of psychostimulants since the psychostimulants are the drugs of choice for the treatment of attention deficit disorder with hyperactivity (ADDH). (See Chapter 4.) Unfortunately, that term would be misleading, since the psychostimulants are also used for other purposes, and they are antihyperactivity drugs only in some disorders and not others. This example illustrates the confusing aspects of the terminology.

DRUGS USED IN CHILD PHARMACOTHERAPY AND MAJOR SIDE EFFECTS

All drugs have side effects. These may be classified in various ways: one is by *time*—those that occur as treatment begins, short-term effects; those that emerge as treatment is extended, long-term effects; finally, those effects that develop when medication is stopped, withdrawal side effects.

A few general rules apply to an understanding of side effects. Most side effects reflect an integral part of the spectrum of the activity of the drug and are not "side" at all but dose dependent. A few are quite idiosyncratic and based on hereditary sensitivities or the development of allergies to the drug. Higher doses are regularly associated with greater severity of side effects. There is enormous individual variation in susceptibility to untoward effects so that the same dose may be innocuous for some and intolerable for others. On the whole, short-term side effects are more marked at the beginning of treatment, if we assume there has been no change in dosage. (A full discussion of side effects is presented in Klein, Gittelman, Quitkin, & Rifkin, 1980.)

Psychostimulants

The psychostimulants (also called stimulants) are a group of drugs that, as their principal action, induce an excitation of the central nervous system that acts to improve the efficiency of the organism, especially in fatigue or other impaired states (Cantwell & Carlson, 1978; Weiss & Laties, 1962). Those commonly used include dextroamphetamine (Dexedrine), methylphenidate (Ritalin), and magnesium pemoline (Cylert). The chemical structure of these agents is similar to that of the endogenous or naturally occurring "stimulant" neurotransmitters known as catecholamines (dopamine, noradrenaline), and it has been suggested that their action is due to an enhancement of the effect of the catecholamines in the brain (Wender, 1971). Magnesium pemoline is the newest of these drugs and the least understood but seems to have a longer duration of action.

SIDE EFFECTS

The common short-term side effects of stimulants include delayed onset of sleep and poor appetite or anorexia. More rarely, abdominal pain and headaches occur. Also infrequently, children appear tearful, sad, or even apathetic.

The long-term effects include some reduction in growth velocity in height and weight (Mattes & Gittelman, 1983). It appears that this phenomenon is dose dependent, reversible upon discontinuation of the drugs so that the treated children's final height does not appear compromised (Gittelman, 1982; Roche, Lipman, Overall, & Hung, 1979). Of the psychostimulants, dextroamphetamine seems to have a greater growth-inhibiting effect than methylphenidate (Safer & Allen, 1973), or magnesium pemoline, but this may be because it is overall a much more potent drug than the other two and the exact milligram dose equivalence of the three drugs is unknown, not 2:1 as usually stated. The mechanism of this side effect is unclear.

Antidepressants

The antidepressants include drugs that have been used since the 1950s to treat, as their name implies, depressive disorders in adults. The antidepressants have been divided into two large chemical subgroups: the tricyclic antidepressants (TCA), and the monoamine oxidase inhibitors (MAOI) (Gilman et al., 1980). Recently, other types of antidepressants have been synthesized, but their application in child pharmacotherapy is still awaited. Therefore, they will not be discussed in this chapter.

Despite the long existence of the TCAs and MAOIs, their clinical effectiveness in pediatric psychopharmacotherapy has received very little attention except in enuresis. Three tricyclics have been investigated: imipramine (Tofranil), amitryptiline (Elavil), and clomipramine (not marketed in the United States). In part, this may be a reflection of the fact that clinical depression was not recognized in child psychiatry until recently and its drug responsivity remains to be established. (For a discussion of this issue, see Chapter 3.) Only one MAOI has been reported on in children, phenelzine (Nardil) (Frommer, 1967, 1968a, 1968b, 1972).

SIDE EFFECTS

The commonest side effects are due to blockage of acetylcholine or the atropine syndrome: dry mouth, sweating, and constipation. Tremor, sweating, tension, tearfulness, and mild weight loss have been reported in children (Rapoport & Mikkelson, 1978), and these are probably adrenergic. Complex or unexplained are changes in cardiac function that may occur. These can be detected on electrocardiograms (EKG) but become troublesome only in high doses. Therefore, the use of EKGs is recommended if the dosage (5 mg/kg) warrants it.

The MAOIs have the undesirable property of raising blood pressure if combined with tyramine, a compound that occurs in fermented foodstuffs (such as pickles, cheese, etc.) Therefore, special dietary precautions are needed.

There are so far no long-term side effects associated with the use of antidepressants in children, but this does not mean that caution should not be exercised.

Anxiolytics, Sedatives, and Anticonvulsants

The anxiolytic drugs include agents whose primary function is to relieve anxiety. In addition, these agents are hypnotics (sleep-inducing drugs), anticonvulsants, intoxicants, and general anesthetics, since these are all stages on a continuum of sedation. They all have in common a depressant effect on the excitability of all cells but affect the sensitive brain cells most, in a reversal of evolution that is from cortex down. In child psychopharmacotherapy, agents from the family of the benzodiazepines have been most commonly used. The benzodiazepines are the most widely prescribed compounds for adults today, and among these, diazepam (Valium) and chlordiazepoxide (Librium) are the best known. Newer types of benzodiazepines have been synthesized in recent years, and their effectiveness has been tested in adults, but not in children.

The use of benzodiazepines and barbiturates in pediatric psychiatry has not been based on systematic studies. The lack of pharmacological research in childhood anxiety disorders may be in part due to the view that anxiety in children often responds to minor interventions. As stated by Eisenberg and associates: ". . . of all psychiatric symptoms, anxiety in children responds the best to placebo" (Eisenberg et al., 1963).

The greatest importance of this group of drugs in child psychopathology is in drug, alcohol, and solvent abuse, discussed at length in Chapter 6.

The anticonvulsants were first developed during the early twentieth century to control seizures (convulsions) (Stores, 1978). Because some behavior problems were believed to be related to brain damage, anticonvulsants enjoyed a vogue in the 1940s for the treatment of various childhood conduct problems, especially those involving temper outbursts and other difficult behaviors. Interest in the anticonvulsants dwindled, probably because of the consistently disappointing results associated with their use. The development of carbamazepine (Tegretol) in the 1960s has changed the picture somewhat; it has been reported to have beneficial effects in some adult psychiatric disorders, notably manic states. These observations are sparking new interest in the possible usefulness of this drug in children with behavior disorders, though for all practical purposes their psychoactive action seems undistinguishable from the sedatives and anxiolytics (see previous discussion). Work with epileptic children (Stores, 1978) suggests that these drugs make children irritable and impair cognition. (See also Chapter 6.)

SIDE EFFECTS
The principal side effects of benzodiazepines are sedation, motor incoordination, slowing of reaction time, disinhibition, and impaired cognition. Anxiolytics are not known to cause long-term side effects in children.

Antihistamines and Anticholinergics

Once popular for the use of behavior problems in children, these drugs are now the most commonly used drugs to sedate infants and small children with irritability and sleep disturbances. The sedation produced by this type of drug (seen as an annoying side effect when they are used in allergies) is poorly understood and studied. It is thought, however, to be derived not from the antihistamine action but from the commonly associated anticholinergic action (see later text under Antipsychotics). This type of sedation is unpleasant and can, if doses are very high, result in a toxic delirium. (See Chapter 6 for features of delirium.) It also impairs cognition, especially memory storage (see review by Werry, 1980). Despite their widespread use, there are only a few controlled studies of the use of these drugs, two in small children with sleep disturbances and one in ADDH (Zametkin, Reeves, Webster, & Werry, in press), none of which supports the usefulness or indeed the acceptability of these drugs, so they will not be discussed further.

Antipsychotics (or Neuroleptics)

The neuroleptics constitute a large family of drugs that is subdivided into several chemical groups (Klein et al., 1980). Aside from their different chemical structures, they vary in potency and side effects. Of the different neuroleptics available, the most commonly used in pediatric psychiatry have included the phenothiazines (above all, CPZ or chlorpromazine [Thorazine], thioridazine [Mellaril], and a butyrophenone [haloperidol—Haldol]).

The site and mode of action of these drugs is said to involve a blockage of the postsynaptic receptor cells for dopamine, noradrenalin, and often acetylcholine, so that less is available in the brain. The effectiveness of these agents in the treatment of psychosis, ADDH, and aggressive behavior has been investigated in a number of studies (see subsequent text).

SIDE EFFECTS
These (mostly) derive logically from the drug's actions. Blockage of acetylcholine (strongest with CPZ and thioridazine, least with haloperidol and pi-

mozide) brings sedation and the atropenic syndrome described for antidepressants. Blockage of dopamine may bring apathy. The short-term side effects and dysregulation of the extrapyramidal system that may lead to (1) involuntary tetanus-like but harmless spasms of the head, eyes, neck, or extremities called dystonias, which occur early; (2) Parkinsonian tremor and rigidity; and (3) akathisia or restless legs, which are usually mistaken for agitation and are very uncomfortable.

Long-term side effects include tardive dyskinesia and withdrawal dyskinesias. Both consist of involuntary movements of the fingers, legs, trunk, or facial muscles (Campbell, Grega, Green, & Bennett, 1983; Gualtieri, Barnhill, McGimsey & Schell, 1980). Tardive dyskinesia, unusual in children, increases with age, dose, and length of medication. The difference from withdrawal dyskinesias is that it can begin during the course of treatment and last for an extended time, whereas withdrawal dyskinesias begin when the drug is stopped and usually remit within three months.

Lithium

Lithium is a light metal allied to sodium and potassium whose original use in psychiatry was for the treatment of adult manic disorders. It is not a common treatment in children. Lithium is the only psychoactive drug (except anticonvulsants) for which the level in the blood regularly and reliably indicates whether an adequate and safe dose is being used (Rapoport, Mikkelsen, & Werry, 1978).

At high doses and in dehydration, lithium is a toxic, dangerous drug with no antidote; but because its concentration in the blood can be measured accurately, it can be used safely if carefully.

There are a variety of side effects associated with the use of lithium. Some examples are nausea, vomiting, tremor, diarrhea, sedation, and ultimately confusion.

CLINICAL EFFICACY

How do we know whether a drug is effective for treating a specific psychiatric disorder? Those concerned with the merit of the evidence for drug efficacy should be familiar with some basic principles of treatment evaluation. (For a simple but excellent discussion of treatment evaluation, see Conners, 1980.)

1. Studies examining the effects of a given compound should include a group of patients that is as homogeneous as possible. If various disorders are combined, the results will be uninterpretable since, regardless of what is found, it will not be possible to know whether the findings apply to all the patient types studied, or only to some.
2. The studies must be carried out in controlled fashion. Treatment controls usually consist of placebos, but they may also be other drugs, if one is interested in knowing whether a new drug is as effective as one whose effi-

cacy is already well established. In either case, the assessment of patients must be double blind, so that neither the patient nor the assessing clinician knows what treatment the patient is receiving. Uncontrolled studies as a group grossly overestimate the value of psychoactive drugs in children, and such studies are no longer acceptable except in the very preliminary study of new drugs, or new applications of old drugs. It is very important that the assignment of patients to each treatment be done randomly. This means that the decision as to what treatment the patient receives is made by chance alone.

3. In addition, the groups must be sufficiently large to permit the detection of drug effects. It is possible to study efficacious treatments, but miss their value by failing to have large enough samples. The size of the groups will depend on size of drug effect relative to placebo. Sometimes this can be estimated. However, size of sample goes beyond detecting a drug effect at a statistical level. The larger the sample, the more likely it will be representative.

4. Before concluding that a drug is effective in the treatment of a disorder, positive findings should be replicated in studies carried out by different research groups. (There can be exceptions in cases where a single study is very large, but on the whole, the caution holds true.)

Unfortunately, until a decade ago, adherence to these principles was the exception rather than the rule. This phenomenon can be attributed to the fact that psychiatric disorders were poorly defined, thus preventing the identification of similar patients for study. The situation has improved with the advent of objective standards for identifying certain disorders, and of DSM-III. (These issues are reviewed in Chapter 1.)

The rest of our discussion concerns the effect of drug treatment in a number of childhood disorders. The number of conditions is much smaller than those discussed in Chapters 2 through 7. This apparent neglect reflects the fact that there is no known appropriate pharmacotherapy for most of the childhood psychological disorders.

ATTENTION DEFICIT DISORDER WITH HYPERACTIVITY

Attention deficit disorder with hyperactivity (ADDH) is one of the best studied childhood disorders and is described in detail in Chapter 4. It refers to what is commonly known as hyperactivity. The key symptoms consist of attention deficits, excessive motor activity, and impulsivity.

The pharmacological treatment of ADDH includes the use of psychostimulants, neuroleptics, and tricyclic antidepressants.

This section is the longest, because of the extensive literature that exists concerning a number of important issues in the pharmacotherapy of children with ADDH.

Psychostimulants

The first use of stimulant drugs in children was empirical and followed clinical observations. In the 1930s Bradley gave hospitalized children a stimulant to enhance their school performance, following reports of such a drug effect in normal adults. Serendipitously, he found that the behavior of some youngsters improved (Bradley, 1937). Subsequently, systematic research was undertaken.

Several dozen placebo-controlled investigations of the stimulants have been conducted in children with ADDH. Except for studies of caffeine, it is striking that almost all have reported clinical improvement associated with drug treatment in school-age children in spite of the diagnostic imprecision that often characterizes the studies. This literature spans the past 25 years and has been summarized in several reviews (e.g., Barkley, 1977a; Klein et al., 1980, Ch. 19); therefore, we emphasize more recent aspects of research concerning stimulant effects in children.

DEXTROAMPHETAMINE (DEXEDRINE)

A large number of studies have reported improvement with dextroamphetamine on teacher and parent behavior ratings (Arnold, Christopher, Huestis, & Smeltzer, 1978; Arnold, Huestis, Smeltzer, Scheib, Wemmer, & Colner, 1976; Comly, 1971; Conners, Eisenberg, & Barcai, 1967; Conners, Rothschild, Eisenberg, Schwartz, & Robinson, 1969; Conners, Taylor, Meo, Kurtz, & Fournier, 1972; Epstein, Lasagna, Conners, & Rodriquez, 1968; Finnerty, Soltys & Cole, 1971; Rapoport, Abramson, Alexander, & Lott, 1971; Weiss, Werry, Minde, Douglas, & Sykes, 1968). The dosages used have ranged from 10 to 25 mg/day. Consequently, even low to moderate dosages of dextroamphetamine induce significant improvement in a variety of behaviors. This effect is very reliable since it is detected even in studies that include few children.

METHYLPHENIDATE (RITALIN)

The results with methylphenidate are extremely consistent in indicating significant improvement in a broad range of behaviors; notably, reduced motor activity, enhanced attention, and better social behavior have been reported (Conners, 1975a; Conners, Taylor, & Dooling, 1980; Dykman, McGrew, Harris, Peters, & Ackerman, 1976; Firestone, Davey, Goodman, & Peters, 1978; Gittelman-Klein, Klein, Katz, Saraf, & Pollack, 1976; Greenberg, Yellin, Spring, & Metcalf, 1975; Henker, Whalen & Collins, 1979; Rapoport et al., 1971; Schain & Reynard, 1975; Weiss, Minde, Douglas, Werry, & Sykes, 1971; Werry & Aman, 1975; Werry, Aman & Lapen, 1976; Werry & Sprague, 1974).

The effect of both methylphenidate and dextroamphetamine is very rapid, often apparent within minutes of ingestion and, if the dose is sufficiently high, the change in the child's behavior can be dramatic.

The clinical efficacy of methylphenidate and dextroamphetamine appears equivalent (Arnold et al., 1976; Conner et al., 1972, 1980; Dykman et al., 1976; Winsberg, Press, Bialer, & Kupietz, 1974), but the amphetamine is a more potent agent per weight unit of drug.

The duration of action varies from 4 to 12 hours (Brown, Ebert, Mikkelsèn, & Hunt, 1979) so that the need for more than a single dose per day varies.

MAGNESIUM PEMOLINE (CYLERT)

Magnesium pemoline, though a relatively new compound, has been well studied in hyperactive children. Its main advantage is that it is relatively long-acting, and therefore, may not require multiple dosages per day (Conners et al., 1972; Dykman et al., 1976; Page, Bernstein, Janicki, & Michelli, 1974, Page, Janicki, Bernstein, Curren, & Michelli, 1974a, 1974b).

The overall impression is that the effects of pemoline are not as regularly dramatic as those of other effective stimulants, and that more than a once-daily dose may be required.

CAFFEINE

In 1973, a clinical report suggested a clearly beneficial effect of caffeine in the treatment of hyperactive children (Schnackenberg, 1973). Since then, a number of studies have compared caffeine with a placebo or with other stimulants (Arnold et al., 1978; Conners, 1975b; 1979; Firestone, Davey, Goodman, & Peters, 1978; Firestone, Poitras-Wright, & Douglas, 1978; Garfinkel, Webster & Sloman, 1975; Gross, 1975; Harvey & Marsh, 1978).

Seven controlled studies of caffeine in hyperactive children have been conducted. Five of them failed to detect a significant advantage for caffeine over a placebo; two report significant improvement among hyperactive children treated with caffeine. It is conceivable that caffeine has only a weak effect, so that most studies are unlikely to detect it unless large samples are used.

SPECIFIC BEHAVIORAL EFFECTS OF STIMULANTS

In addition to the symptoms included in behavioral scales obtained from teachers and parents, the effects of stimulants on other behaviors also have been studied.

Social Behavior   There has been much argument that psychostimulants are used by overzealous physicians responding to pressure from teachers or parents, because the medications control the children, who then can be manipulated easily by "repressive" adults (Grinspoon & Singer, 1973; Schrag & Divoky, 1975).

The results of studies of the social behavior of children receiving methylphenidate offer a rational view of the effects of medication on the interpersonal functions of children with ADDH. In studies by Gittelman-Klein, Klein, Abikoff, Katz, Gloisten, and Kates (1976) and Gittelman, Abikoff, Pollack, Klein, Katz, and Mattes (1980) of ADDH children treated with moderately high doses of methylphenidate, the drug did not inhibit spontaneous social contact from the child to his teacher, even though the drug markedly reduced inattention, motor activity, and impulsiveness in the classroom. These benefits did not require the cost of excessive passivity. Bugental and co-workers also reported that stimulant treatment did not interfere with the children's ability to apply cognitive strategies relying on self-control (Bugental, Whalen, & Henker, 1977).

In a study of classroom behavior, the social behavior of ADDH children treated with methylphenidate was no longer distinguishable from the behavior of normal peers (Whalen, Collins, Henker, Alkus, Adams, & Stapp, 1978; Whalen & Henker, 1976). On the drug, however, the children were found to have more negative affect, but no impairment in communicative efficiency. The results of this careful work are consistent with the view that methylphenidate makes the behavior of hyperactive children indistinguishable from that of normal children. This effect is, of course, most striking in the setting in which the hyperactive children are most different from their normal peers.

Children with ADDH have been found to differ in their mother–child interaction from normal children (Campbell, 1973, 1975; Campbell, Schleifer, Weiss, & Perlman, 1977; and see Chapter 9). In an interesting series of studies by Cunningham and Barkley (Barkley & Cunningham, 1979, 1980; Cunningham & Barkley, 1978), the mothers of hyperactive and normal children were observed during free play and during structured tasks. Mothers of hyperactive children responded less often to their children, were more negative and more controlling, and gave more commands than the mothers of normal children; in turn, the hyperactive children were less compliant than normals. A number of changes in the mother–child interaction were observed when the children were treated (Barkley & Cunningham, 1979). While the children were on methylphenidate, as compared to a placebo, the mothers interacted more with their children, gave fewer commands, and were more responsive. As for the children, they were more compliant while on methylphenidate, but not more so than normal children. Therefore, even though the stimulant increased compliance, it did not do so beyond the bounds of normal behavior. In another placebo-controlled study (Humphries, Kinsbourne, & Swanson, 1978), mother and child performed better together while the child was on medication. When treated, the children displayed more behavior directed toward their mother, who behaved in a less controlling fashion.

Similar findings have been found regarding teacher–child relationships. Teachers showed an increase in positive, and a decrease in negative, attention toward the treated children, and a normalization of teacher–pupil interaction was seen (Whalen, Henker & Dotemoto, 1980, 1981; Whalen, Henker, & Finck, 1981).

As is evident, the objective data on the social behavior of hyperactive children are not consistent with the view that stimulant treatments are chemical straightjackets.

Other Behavioral Effects The effect of stimulants on speech production, motor movement, and handwriting has been investigated. In a study by Rapoport and colleagues (Rapoport, Buchsbaum, Weingartner, Zahn, Ludlow, & Mikkelson, 1980), a single dose of dextroamphetamine decreased the rate of speech in hyperactive children, whereas it increased it in normal children and adults.

A good deal of research has evaluated the effects of stimulants on motor movement. Several single-dose studies have reported decreases in specific counts of motor activity in a variety of settings (Barkley, 1977b; Ellis, Witt, Reynolds & Sprague, 1974; Rapoport et al., 1971; Rapoport, Tepsic, Grice, Johnson, & Langer, 1980; Sprague, Barnes, & Werry, 1970).

Methylphenidate has been reported also to improve fine motor coordination on graphomotor tasks (Lerer, Lerer, & Artner, 1977) and to reduce eye movements of hyperactive children (Bala et al., 1981). The eye movements may reflect activity level or, more likely, some aspect of attentional function.

Effects on Cognitive Performance   Stimulants improve a variety of cognitive functions in hyperactive children such as vigilance, rate of learning, or impulsive responding. Performance on many psychometric tests have been found to improve with short-term stimulant treatment (Cohen, Douglas, & Morgenstern, 1971; Conners, 1971; Conners, Eisenberg, & Sharpe, 1964; Gittelman-Klein & Klein, 1975; Knights, 1974; Sykes, Douglas, & Morgenstern, 1973; Sykes, Douglas, Weiss, & Minde, 1971). In addition, performance on tests of reading and arithmetic, on measures of reaction time, on motor and sensory tests, as well as on handwriting, all improved by stimulant treatment (Butter & Lapierre, 1974; Cohen et al., 1971; Lerer et al., 1977; Spring, Greenberg, Scott, & Hopwood, 1973; Wade, 1976).

Though an overall positive stimulant effect has been demonstrated on cognitive function, studies have not obtained identical drug effects on psychometric tasks, so that no single measure has been consistently improved by stimulants. Therefore, it is generally believed that the observed improvement in test performance following stimulant treatment is due to enhanced vigilance or concentration, and not to the amelioration of a specific skill, such as memory.

Using different experimental paradigms, recent studies indicating that stimulants increase vigilance by narrowing the children's attentional focus and by decreasing the degree to which extraneous stimuli interfere with concentration (Fisher, 1978; Sostek, Buchsbaum, & Rapoport, 1980; Thurston, Sobol, Swanson, & Kinsbourne, 1979) have been influential in the formulation of psychological theories of the hyperkinetic syndrome. It has been proposed (Douglas, 1972, 1983; see also Chapter 4) that attentional dysregulation is the central problem in hyperactive children. In a series of reports comparing normal or non-ADDH groups with ADDH children who received a single dose of stimulants, it was found that attention improved in both groups (Rapoport, Buchsbaum, Weingartner, Zahn, Ludlow, & Mikkelson, 1980; Werry & Aman, 1984). Therefore, better attention induced by psychostimulants is not specific to ADDH. Consequently, the formulation of a theory for the disorder is not easily derived from the pattern of stimulant activity on behavior or cognitive function.

If the theory is correct that attentional improvement is the foundation for social and motor improvement, then improvement on attentional and clinical measures should be highly associated. However, this has not been found to be so (Gittelman-Klein & Klein, 1975; Sprague & Sleator, 1977). Furthermore, caffeine has been reported to have significant positive effects on attention, while not affecting, or even *increasing*, motor activity (Conners, 1979; Elkins et al., 1981). In addition, hyperactive children have been found to have more movement than normals during sleep (Porrino et al., 1983); this motor dysregulation cannot be the result of impaired attentional mechanisms.

In 1976 Swanson and Kinsbourne (1976) reported state-dependent effects on a visual memory task in hyperactive children treated with stimulants. State-dependent effects occur if learning that takes place in one state (such as drug treatment) is impaired in another state (such as off-drug). For treated hyperactive children, this would mean that tasks learned while the children were on medication would not be performed as well when off-drug as they would if they had never been on the medication. Understandably, this possibility generated a great deal of concern. Some argued that stimulants should be avoided to prevent children from being at a disadvantage when treatment ceased. Subsequent investigations have examined state-dependent learning in hyperactive children using a variety of cogent strategies (Becker-Mattes, Mattes, Abikoff, & Brandt, 1985; Rapoport, 1983; Stenhausen & Kreuzer, 1981; Weingartner, Langer, Grice, & Rapoport, 1982). Only one (Shea, 1982) has found such an effect. Even when found, these effects do not appear to be of such magnitude as to attribute them clinical significance (Gittelman, 1983).

PREDICTION OF STIMULANT EFFECTS

The ability to identify predictors of stimulant effects in hyperactive children would have substantial scientific merit. Reliable predictors would point the way to testable models of etiology, possibly pathophysiology, and would facilitate the development of new and better treatments.

The contention that medications have a selective effect on hyperactive children with organic features has received considerable attention, with mixed results (Burk, 1964; Conners, 1966; Epstein et al., 1968; Satterfield, Cantwell, Lesser, & Podosin, 1972; Satterfield, Lesser, Saul, & Cantwell, 1973; Schain & Reynard, 1975; Steinberg, Troshinsky, & Steinberg, 1971; Weiss et al., 1968). It is clear that ADDH children do not need to have brain damage in order to obtain a very positive therapeutic stimulant effect.

The relationships between psychophysiological measures of brain function and drug effect have also been studied (see Hastings & Barkley, 1978). Central measures have included auditory and visual evoked response. In addition, peripheral autonomic system functions, such as skin conductance as measured by galvanic skin responses, heart rate, and respiration rate, have been correlated with stimulant drug effects. Several investigators have reported that stimulants normalize the auditory evoked responses of hyperactive children (Buchsbaum & Wender, 1973; Halliday, Rosenthal, Naylor, & Callaway, 1976; Prichep, Sutton, & Hakerem, 1976) and that low arousal, as well as variability in arousal, predict a good response to stimulants (Buchsbaum & Wender, 1973; Satterfield et al., 1972; Shouse & Lubar, 1978; Weber & Sulzbacher, 1975). Others (Halliday et al., 1976) have been unable to corroborate these findings.

Conflicting results are even more the rule in studies that have used peripheral autonomic indices for arousal than in studies of cortical measures of arousal. Several issues complicate research in neurophysiology with children. Patterns of evoked responses may change with age. Consequently, studies using samples with different age ranges will fail to produce similar findings. Furthermore, physiological functions, and their response to stimulants, may differ depending on the task a child is involved in. Some contexts have been noted to affect drug activity on neurophysiological measures. Whether a child has to perform a task or sit passively, whether the task is difficult or not, and whether the child received positive or negative feedback have all been found to lead to different patterns of drug effect. Since investigators have not used children of identical ages and applied similar conditions, it is difficult to ascertain the significance of the findings. We conclude that the research concerning stimulant effects on psychophysiological measures has not generated sufficiently consistent data to enable a straightforward interpretation of drug effects.

Barkley (1977a) has suggested that, since the evidence points to an energizing or activating effect of the stimulants, these drugs probably stimulate inhibitory systems. This view was originally proposed by Bradley (Bradley, 1937, 1950) and has much in common with that derived from Gray's behavioral inhibition system and theory for conduct disorders described in Chapter 2. With stimulants, the better functioning inhibitory systems are postulated to enable the child to ignore irrelevant, distracting stimuli.

SUMMARY

The effectiveness of stimulants for the treatment of ADDH is very well documented for school-age children. Emerging evidence suggests that adolescents also respond positively (Varly, 1983). Following drug administration, one observes a decrease in motor activity, better social interaction, better response to discipline, and better self-application in school and elsewhere. The effect of the stimulants is quite marked, and treated children may even become "normalized," so that their behavior cannot be distinguished from normals' (Abikoff & Gittelman, 1985). Aspects of children's interaction with adults are also improved.

The stimulants enhance cognitive performance on a variety of psychological tests, but no one specific ability seems affected and so far there is no evidence of true learning or the acquisition of new skills. There is no clear evidence for state-dependent drug effects on learning. Studies concerning drug effects on brain function have not yielded consistent findings.

Neuroleptics (Antipsychotics)

The neuroleptics have been studied for the treatment of ADDH because they were believed to be "tranquilizers," and children with ADDH can certainly be viewed as in need of tranquilizing.

A number of studies by Werry and his colleagues were the first to show that neuroleptics ameliorate the behavioral problems of children with ADDH (Werry & Aman, 1975; Werry et al. 1976; Werry & Sprague, 1974). Others have also reported similar results (Rapoport et al., 1971; Gittelman-Klein, Klein, Katz, Saraf, & Pollack, 1976).

There appears to be no distinction in clinical efficacy among the several neuroleptics that have been studied. Improvement has been reported on motor activity, disruptive behavior, concentration, and social behavior, but the beneficial effect was not nearly as great as with a stimulant (Gittelman-Klein, Klein, Katz, Saraff, & Pollack, 1976).

Besides the relatively less adequate clinical effects of the neuroleptics compared with the stimulants, these drugs can at times lead to long-lasting neurological side effects (see previous discussion). Therefore, this class of drugs is generally avoided when other treatments are available.

NEUROLEPTIC EFFECTS ON COGNITIVE PERFORMANCE

Unlike the stimulants, the expectation for the neuroleptics is that they would interfere with cognitive performance. The weight of the evidence indicates, however, that these drugs do not induce a real decrement in children's ability to perform on psychometric tasks. Many studies of treated children have not shown that children obtain worse scores while on neuroleptics (Freibergs, Douglas, & Weiss, 1968; Sprague et al., 1970; Werry & Aman, 1975; Werry, Weiss, Douglas & Martin, 1966). In one study of a very mixed group of institutionalized children, performance on one out of six tasks was impaired by a neuroleptic (Helper, Wilcott, & Garfield, 1963). Therefore, in some cases, it is possible for some disadvantage to occur, but it is not the usual case. There is no doubt, however, that with regard to effects on cognitive performance, the neuroleptics have a much less desirable outcome than the stimulants do.

Tricyclics/ Antidepressants

The use of antidepressants in ADDH is unrelated to this particular clinical use of the drug and has been tried empirically without clear rationale. They have been the least studied of the pharmacological agents used in the treatment of ADDH. The antidepressant most commonly used is imipramine. Several studies, both open and placebo controlled, have reported positive effects of imipramine on the symptoms of ADDH, but these effects are less than impressive (Greenberg et al., 1975; Huessey & Wright, 1969; Rapoport, Quinn, Bradbard, Riddle, & Brooks, 1974; Waizer, Hoffman, Polizos, & Englehardt, 1974; Winsberg, Bialer, Kupietz, & Tobias, 1972; Yepes, Balka, Winsberg, & Bialer, 1977); in addition, Gittelman-Klein (1974), on the one hand, and Quinn & Rapoport (1975), on the other, suggest that, even in cases where imipramine has provided a favorable effect, these effects tend to disappear or decrease after a short time. Therefore, these drugs are not considered part of the standard management of ADDH but may be a backup.

CONDUCT DISORDERS

The characteristics of children with conduct disorders are discussed in Chapter 2. Conduct disorder can occur alone or in association with other disorders. Attention deficit disorders are the most common other concurrent conditions and distinguishing conduct disorder from ADDH can be difficult. (See Chapter 4.) Conduct disorders can be associated also with neurological disorders, such as a seizure disorder (epilepsy), to cite the most frequent one (see Chapter 8.) Because we are concerned with pharmacotherapy, the overlap between conduct disorder and ADDH is critical, since, as we have noted, very effective medications exist for the treatment of ADDH. The occasional co-occurrence of seizure disorder with conduct disorders is also important for pharmacotherapy, since treatment of the seizure disorder may influence the behavioral disturbance.

Recently, it has been claimed that a depressive syndrome may accompany a conduct disorder, and that in such cases, the use of antidepressant medication is indicated (Puig-Antich, 1982). More will be said about this issue.

From the foregoing and the discussion in Chapters 1, 2, and 4, it is apparent that conduct disorders do not always occur in isolation and conduct-type symptoms can occur in any disorder. This complicates evaluation of pharmacotherapy, since the exact nature of the children's difficulties is not reported in the published studies.

Psychostimulants, neuroleptics, lithium, tricyclic antidepressants, and anticonvulsants have all been used in the treatment of children with conduct disorders, though good studies are few. Eisenberg and co-workers (1963) found that dextroamphetamine improved the behavior of aggressive institutionalized delinquents. A subsequent study of brief methylphenidate treatment failed to yield positive results in a similar group (Conners, Kramer, Rothschild, Schwartz, & Stone, 1964).

Only one placebo-controlled study of stimulant treatment in an outpatient group of conduct disorders has appeared (Maletzky, 1974). The author reported significant clinical improvement.

In these studies the diagnostic characteristics of the youngsters did not preclude the presence of ADDH symptoms; as a matter of fact, the presence of hyperactivity was required in the last study (Maletzky, 1974). Therefore, it is not clear to what extent the positive stimulant effects reported were due to the amelioration of symptoms associated with the hyperactivity syndrome, such as impulsivity. It is also possible that stimulants are effective in pure conduct disorders. However, the information collected so far does not provide this information.

Several early reports (Alderton & Hoddinott, 1969; Cunningham, Pillai, & Blachford Rogers, 1968) claimed that neuroleptics were helpful in reducing aggressive behavior of severe conduct disorders. These studies were unsatisfactory, however, and therefore inconclusive.

Recently, Campbell and associates (Campbell et al., 1984) reported a placebo-controlled trial of haloperidol and lithium in hospitalized children carefully diagnosed as aggressive conduct disorders. They found both medications to be superior to placebo; lithium and haloperidol had similar levels of efficacy.

Lithium has been reported to improve aggressivity in children of normal intelligence as well as in mentally retarded and autistic children (Campbell, Fish, Korein, Shapiro, Collins, & Koh, 1972; Campbell, Schulman, & Rapoport, 1978; Gram & Rafaelsen, 1972; Platt, Campbell, Green, & Grega, 1984). Unfortunately, the number of studies reporting on the effectiveness of lithium is small, and experience with lithium in children is scant.

At one time, the impulsive nature of some forms of aggression were viewed by some as the result of seizure-like disorders. Consequently, anticonvulsant drugs enjoyed a certain vogue. Experience with the older anticonvulsants has not been encouraging (Stores, 1978; Trimble & Reynolds, 1976). Diphenylhydantoin (Dilantin) has not been shown to be more effective than placebo in improving the behavior of delinquents or children with conduct disorders or temper tantrums (Conners, Kramer, Rothschild, Schwartz & Stone, 1971; Lefkowitz, 1969; Looker & Conners, 1970). More recently, a newer anticonvulsant, carbamazepine (Tegretol) has been claimed to decrease the severity and frequency of outbursts of rage and aggressivity in adults and youngsters with conduct disorders (Post & Uhde, 1983). Carbamazepine is the anticonvulsant of choice for the treatment of most childhood epilepsy except petit mal. Much epilepsy derives from injury to the temporal lobe at birth. Seizures emanating from this area in the brain are believed to be more associated with violent behavior and conduct disorders than is the case in other types of seizures (Dalby, 1975). It is held that for children with seizures who also present irritability, outbursts of rage, and other behavioral problems, carbamazepine can result in marked improvement, but this has not been put to the test yet despite its 10 or more year history. All that can be affirmed is that anticonvulsants are not useful in unselected cases of conduct disorders.

A clinical report has claimed that tricyclic antidepressants reduce the conduct problems of children who have a conduct disorder and a concurrent major depressive disorder (Puig-Antich, 1982). In this case as well, this observation awaits confirmation from systematic studies.

Finally, Williams, Mehl, Yudofsky, Adams, and Roseman (1982) have reported clinical observations that high doses of propranolol (Inderal) (an adrenergic blocker drug commonly used for the treatment of hypertension) are effective in reducing rage outbursts in children. This claim, too, requires proper testing.

In summary, there is no well-established pharmacotherapy of conduct disorders except for the single satisfactory study of lithium by Campbell and co-workers (1984). Further research is required to provide clear estimates of drug efficacy in children with pure conduct disorders and in those who also suffer from ADDH or from depression.

ANXIETY DISORDERS

Anxiety and fears in children may reflect normal developmental variations, or it may be the expression of a psychological disorder. The anxiety disorders of childhood have been subclassified into three psychopathologic entities in the DSM-III classification: separation anxiety disorder, overanxiety disorder, and avoidant disorder of childhood. These are discussed in detail in Chapters 1 and 3, where it was noted that their distinctiveness lacks reliability. Children can sometimes also have adult-type disorders, however, such as obsessive compulsive and phobic disorder.

PHARMACOTHERAPY OF ANXIETY DISORDERS

In contrast to the abundant research available on the pharmacotherapy of anxiety disorders in adults, there is little known for childhood anxiety disorders. The pharmacological agents most commonly used for the treatment of anxiety disorders in adults are all benzodiazepines. More recently, the tricyclic and other antidepressants have gained importance in the treatment of adult anxiety states (Klein et al., 1980).

Among the benzodiazepines, diazepam (Valium) and chlordiazepoxide (Librium) are the best known. These agents have been shown to relieve symptoms of anxiety in adults (Klein et al., 1980). In contrast, their effectiveness in children has not been well investigated (Gittelman-Klein, 1978).

Antianxiety agents have been used in a wide variety of childhood conditions because of the assumption that anxiety is at the root of many different behavioral problems such as conduct problems, hyperactivity, temper outbursts, and others. In spite of a host of clinical reports endorsing the effectiveness of antianxiety agents, notably the benzodiazepines, no systematic study of their effect has been undertaken (Kraft, Ardali, Duffy, Hart, & Pearch, 1965; Lucas & Pasley, 1969; Molling, Lockner, Sauls, & Eisenberg, 1962; Signorato & Lutati, 1967; Simonelli, 1975; Skynner, 1961).

The only controlled pharmacological studies done in childhood anxiety disorders focused on children suffering from school phobia. It is generally agreed that "school phobia" is a misnomer. Most children with school phobia, though not all, suffer from separation anxiety. Gittelman-Klein and Klein (1973, 1980) conducted a placebo-controlled study with imipramine in school-phobic children, most of whom had separation anxiety; the authors found imipramine to be superior to placebo in improving the symptoms of school phobia and separation anxiety.

A second study (Berney et al. 1980) did not find a different tricyclic antidepressant, clorimipramine, to be more effective than placebo in the treatment of school-phobic children. (The different results obtained by the two studies may stem from the fact that Berney et al. used much lower doses than Gittelman-Klein and Klein [1973].)

The mechanisms through which imipramine may act to improve symptoms of separation anxiety disorder are not understood. Since only one controlled study has found an antidepressant useful in treating school-phobic children, further work is needed before one can consider this type of drug effective for the management of school phobia and separation anxiety disorder.

Pharmacological treatment for the other forms of childhood anxiety disorder—overanxiety and avoidant disorders—has not been studied.

In summary, the pharmacotherapy of anxiety disorders in children and adolescents is very limited, so that little is known. This lack of knowledge parallels the little information we have about the natural history, psychobiological, genetic, and epidemiological correlates of these disorders.

Obsessive-compulsive Disorder

As noted in Chapter 3, obsessive-compulsive disorder is uncommon in children. It is observed in about 1 percent of the children seen in psychiatric treatment centers (Rapoport, 1985). It can appear as an isolated condition, or it may be associated with other entities such as depressive disorders, schizophrenia, or Tourette's disorder. Though obsessive-compulsive disorder is grouped with the anxiety disorders, the reasons for doing so are not compelling. Its place in the classification awaits further research.

Recent research has suggested an association between obsessive-compulsive disorder and organic abnormalities such as enlarged ventricles and abnormal neuropsychological function that suggests abnormalities in the bifrontal and temporal areas of the brain (Behar et al., 1984; Flor-Henry, Yeudell, Koles, & Howarth, 1979). Tricyclic antidepressants (Ananth, 1976; Ananth, Solyom, Bryntwick, & Krishnappa, 1979; Marshall, 1971; Thoren, Asberg, Cronholm, Jorestedt, & Traskman, 1980; Yaruria-Tobias, Nezuroglu, & Berman, 1976) have been reported to relieve the symptoms of the disorder.

The only controlled study in young people (Flament et al., 1985) found clomipramine to be superior to placebo in 19 obsessive-compulsive children and adolescents. Because this compound belongs to the antidepressant class of drugs, it has been claimed that its anticompulsive effects were due to the improvement in depression. In this study, however, the effects on obsessive-compulsive symptoms were not related to the presence of depression. This finding indicates that the drug has specific "anti-obsessive-compulsive" effect. In addition, the authors observed a relapse of obsessional symptoms upon discontinuation of clomipramine. Unfortunately, clomipramine is not available in the United States, though it is elsewhere. Alternatives to clomipramine would be other tricyclic antidepressants such as amytriptyline.

The pharmacotherapy of obsessive-compulsive disorder is promising. More research is necessary to determine the effectiveness of clomipramine and other antidepressants.

DEPRESSION

The diagnosis of major depressive disorder in childhood has been a subject of great controversy. (See Chapter 3.) Its existence and the manifestation of its symptoms have been widely debated. Today, the acceptance of major depressive disorder in childhood is reflected in its integration into the DSM-III classification, but recognition by a panel of experts does not establish diagnostic validity. Most critical here is not whether depression occurs in children but whether a drug-sensitive form similar to that seen in adults does.

Pharmacotherapy of Childhood Depression

We mention briefly the pharmacological treatment of major depressive disorders in adults, since it has served as a model for the treatment of childhood depression. Two types of antidepressants are used in adults: the antidepressants belonging to the tricyclic antidepressant group, and those belonging to the MAO inhibitors. (Some have claimed that lithium may also be useful, but this is a controversial issue; see Klein et al., 1980.) Recently, it has been reported that different types of adult major depressive disorders may respond differently to each type of drug (Liebowitz, et al., 1984). So far, no attempt has been made to refine the broad diagnostic group of major depressive disorder in children or adolescents in the manner it is done in adults.

In children, tricyclic antidepressants, mainly imipramine, have been tried, and several clinical reports claim that they are useful. In the first controlled study of imipramine in the treatment of major depressive disorders in children, Puig-Antich and his team (Puig-Antich, 1978; Puig-Antich, Blau, Marx, Greenhill, & Chambers, 1978, Puig-Antich et al. 1979) found no difference between the drug and a placebo after five weeks of treatment. Both treatment groups had high rates of remission.

The same group of investigators conducted an open (uncontrolled) trial of imipramine in adolescents suffering from major depressive disorder and found that few adolescents responded to the antidepressant.

In a small study of nine children who received a similar antidepressant (amitriptyline) and a placebo, each for four weeks, the drug was not superior to the placebo (Kashani, Shekim, & Reid, 1984). The number of children was small, and as we note in the discussion of drug trials design, insufficient sample sizes provide equivocal results.

No conclusions can be reached at this time on the effectiveness of tricyclic antidepressants in the treatment of depressive disorders in children or adolescents. This is an area where there is much ongoing activity and where further information is likely to be forthcoming.

PERVASIVE DEVELOPMENTAL DISORDERS

The pervasive developmental disorders in the DSM-III classification encompass a group of psychotic disorders whose main characteristics involve the absence of adequate social and emotional responsivity manifested in the form of severe asociality, lack of appropriate emotional reciprocity, lack of empathy, impairment in language skills, as well as dysfunction in several psychological functions including attention, perception, reality testing, and motor activity. These are discussed more fully in Chapter 5.

Pharmacotherapy of Pervasive Developmental (Autistic) Disorders (PDD)

The pharmacotherapy of PDD has relied mostly on the use of neuroleptics. Several have been studied; as is the case for most other disorders, the literature antedates the diagnostic classification of DSM-III, so that most studies have not made the now current clinical distinctions. PDD includes infantile autism and childhood onset Pervasive Developmental Disorders (see Chapter 5). Only one study has specifically focused on children with infantile autism. Campbell and associates (Campbell, Anderson, Meier, Cohen, Small, Samit, & Sachar, 1978) examined the effects of a neuroleptic (haloperidol) in combination with training in word acquisition. The drug induced a significant improvement in word acquisition, but the absolute magnitude of the effect was slight. In addition, several aspects of behavior were improved with the drug compared with the placebo (Anderson et al, 1984).

Only one other well-executed placebo-controlled study of a neuroleptic in PDD has been reported. Marked effects for the drug were found on a number of symptoms such as activity level, concentration, eating, sleeping, and mood. However, the drug did not affect language skills (Engelhardt, Polizos, & Margolis, 1970).

A number of clinical reports, some more careful than others, have reported from mild to marked improvement with neuroleptics in children with autism and other PDD disorders (Campbell, Fish, Shapiro, & Floyd, 1971b, 1972; Campbell et al., 1972; Engelhardt, Polizos, Waizer, & Hoffman, 1973; Faretra, Dooher, & Dowling, 1970; Fish, Campbell, Shapiro, & Floyd, 1969; Fish, Campbell, Shapiro, & Weinstein, 1969; Saletu, Saletu, Simeon, Viamontes, & Itil, 1975; Waizer, Polizos, Hoffman, Engelhardt, & Margolis, 1972; Wolpert, Hagamen, & Merlis, 1967).

The conclusion we draw from these results and our clinical experience is that neuroleptics do not modify the primary clinical feature of this class of disorders; even when children respond, they continue to display severely deviant behavior, such as social indifference and markedly impaired communication skills. What most reports show is that specific symptoms—motor hyperactivity, rage outbursts, excitability, and sleeplessness—that are often present in these children are ameliorated. This drug effect results in a much more manageable child, but one who is seriously ill, nevertheless.

Other drugs have been studied in children with PDD; they include L-dopa (a drug used for treatment of Parkinson's disease—a neurological disorder of adult life) (Campbell et al., 1976), serotonin (a neurotransmitter) (Sverd, Kupietz, Winsberg, Hurwie, & Becker, 1978), thyroid replacement drugs (Campbell, 1973; Campbell et al., 1973; Campbell, Small, Hollander, Korein, Cohen, Kalmign, & Ferris, 1978), stimulants (Campbell et al., 1976; Campbell et al., 1972), antidepressants (Campbell, Fish, Shapiro, & Floyd, 1971a; Kurtis, 1966), antihistamines (Campbell, 1977; Engelhardt et al., 1970), lithium (Campbell, Fish, Korein, Shapiro, Collins, & Koh, 1972; Gram & Rafaelsen, 1972), and megavitamins (Rimland, 1973; Rimland, Callaway, & Dreyfus, 1978; Roukema & Emery, 1970). None of these has produced encouraging results, and amphetamines caused a worsening of symptoms. The use of megavitamins has generated a controversial debate since some parent groups have expressed the firm belief that they are worthwhile treatments. However, the evidence to support this hope is not encouraging. The PDDs include the most severely handicapped children and those with the grimmest prognosis. Therefore, it is understandable that many therapeutic agents will be tried, even without very good reason to do so, since the amelioration of this debilitating condition would be a major accomplishment. At the same time, parents of such children understandably may develop enthusiasm for a treatment, though its efficacy is still questionable. These factors have led to the trial of drugs for which there was little, if any, rationale.

Unfortunately, pharmacotherapy has little to offer for the treatment of PDD, except for the increased ease in daily living that the neuroleptics afford to the child and family.

CHILDHOOD SCHIZOPHRENIA

The onset of schizophrenia occurs typically in adolescence or young adulthood; though it has been observed in childhood, its occurrence then is very rare. One would expect the drug treatment of children and adults with schizophrenia to be similar. Therefore, all established neuroleptics (and there are many) would be expected to be effective in children with schizophrenia. The literature documenting the efficacy of neuroleptics in schizophrenia is vast (for a review, see Klein et al., 1980), but strikingly, there has not been a single study, or even clinical report, of the use of neuroleptics in groups of children with schizophrenia.

The problems of differential diagnoses between schizophrenia and other psychotic disorders of childhood are discussed in Chapter 5. The issue of treatment of childhood schizophrenia is complicated by the fact that there is confusion about the limits of the disorder (Cantor, Evans, Pearce, & Pezzor-Pierce, 1982). As our review indicates, neuroleptics affect secondary symptoms of infantile autism (such as hyperactivity), whereas they ameliorate the principal psychotic symptoms of schizophrenia (i.e., thought disorder, delusions). It is easy to see how studies that include an admixture of these disorders would lead to a confused picture of the drug treatment effects.

Though the expectation that schizophrenia in childhood responds to neuroleptics in the same fashion as the adult form is reasonable, it is not based on data obtained in studies of children but is assumed from the rich literature on adults (see Klein et al., 1980). Therefore, no definite judgment is possible with regard to the use of pharmacological treatments in childhood schizophrenia.

Campbell, a specialist in the drug treatment of psychotic children, reports that, from her clinical experience, children with schizophrenia respond less well than adults (Campbell, 1985). The same reservations do not apply to the care of adolescents, where neuroleptics are the treatment of choice.

Interestingly, these drugs are effective in both withdrawn, retarded, perplexed, uncommunicative schizophrenic adolescents and in those who are agitated, excited, and overactive. Therefore, they are not "tranquilizers," as was originally believed, but they seem to affect an underlying defect that is probably common to withdrawn as well as excited patients.

As is the case in other disorders we discuss, theories of brain dysfunction have been generated as a result of the marked effect of the neuroleptics on schizophrenic patients. Because these drugs, to put it simply, reduce the level of dopamine in the brain, dysregulation in the functions associated with this neurotransmitter has been viewed as a leading cause of schizophrenia. Much contrary evidence has been generated, and the status of the "dopamine hypothesis" in schizophrenia is still unresolved.

The use of neuroleptics in schizophrenia usually stretches over extended time periods since the disorder is one of the most persistent and debilitating of all psychiatric disorders. A serious complicating aspect of treatment is the emergence of tardive dyskinesia among a substantial proportion of patients who receive long-term treatment (see Klein et al., 1980, for a full review of these issues).

STEREOTYPED MOVEMENT DISORDERS

This class of psychopathology includes tic disorders; they are discussed in Chapter 7. The simple motor tics, diagnosed as transient or chronic motor tic disorders, are not usually treated with medication. There have been no reports of drug trial in these relatively benign conditions. Tourette's disorder, on the other hand, can be very disabling, and pharmacotherapy plays an important role in its management (Cohen, Leckman, & Shaywitz, 1985; Shapiro & Shapiro, 1981).

Tourette's Disorder

This disorder was first described by a French neurologist, Gilles de la Tourette, in the late nineteenth century. It is characterized by multiple tics associated with sniffing, snorting, involuntary vocalization, and at times aggressive and sexual impulses that the person finds troublesome. It constitutes the most severe tic syndrome. The association of ADDH with Tourette's deficit disorder (62% of a series of 250 consecutive unselected Tourette's patients [Comings & Comings, 1984]) is of clinical and pharmacological significance since the use of psychostimulants for the relief of symptoms of ADDH can worsen the symptoms of Tourette's disorder.

Neuroleptics such as haloperidol (Haldol) have been used since the late 1960s and, to date, remain the most effective treatment available. A new neuroleptic, pimozide, has been introduced recently as an alternative for the treatment of Tourette's syndrome. Ross and Moldofsky (1978), following a double-blind crossover study comparing haloperidol to pimozide, found both drugs to be effective in reducing tics; nevertheless, pimozide had significantly fewer side effects. Shapiro and Shapiro (1984) confirmed these findings in a double-blind crossover prospective study in 20 patients. In addition, they report similar but milder and more easily managed side effects with pimozide, leading to better patient acceptance. Pimozide may have fewer side effects, but some of the putative clinical advantages may prove to be due to the use of relatively lower doses or to enthusiasm for a new drug.

Clonidine, a noradrenalin blocker, although used primarily for the treatment of hypertension, is also used to relieve the withdrawal symptoms of opiate dependence and has been claimed to be helpful in Tourette's disorder (Bruun, 1984; Cohen, Detlor, Young, & Shaywitz, 1980). The clinical experience with clonidine for the treatment of Tourette's syndrome has been relatively short. In Bruun's (1984) experience, the use of clonidine was effective in 50 percent of 72 patients. An interesting observation was that in 11 cases the combination of clonidine with haloperidol enabled a reduction in the dose of haloperidol by an average of 72 percent. Some clinicians have suggested that clonidine may be more effective than haloperidol (Bruun, 1984; Leckman et al., 1982), but there is no unanimity on this point.

Finally, it has been suggested that one of the benzodiazepines used as an anticonvulsant, clonazepam, may be helpful (Bruun, 1984), but it has not been formally tested.

A complicating factor in the pharmacotherapy of Tourette's disorder is the marked variability in drug sensitivity. Some patients require small doses, others very high ones. Moreover, the dosage requirement for any one child may change radically over time. Nevertheless, the advent of pharmacotherapy has provided the first glimpse of hope for this otherwise very refractory and disabling illness, though the effects are symptomatic not curative and lifelong medication seems necessary in about 75 percent (Bruun, 1984).

Enuresis This condition is discussed in Chapter 7. Those interested in issues of drug treatment, not presented in this chapter, are referred to a recent review by Shaffer (1985).

SUMMARY From this chapter it should be apparent that one cannot have a single opinion regarding the merits of pharmacotherapy in childhood disorders. While we as yet lack any instance in which drugs can cure definitively any childhood psychopathological disorder (Werry, 1982), in some disorders there is abundant evidence that they are extremely helpful, as is the case for ADDH, where the stimulants tend to normalize many aspects of the children's behavior. In other disorders, the effect may be real, but not sufficient to affect the most important clinical features of the disorder; a case in point is the pharmacotherapy of infantile autism.

In other cases, such as Tourette's syndrome, the symptoms of the disorder can be modified by drug treatment, but unpredictably, and the management of patients is difficult. Finally, in several childhood conditions the role of pharmacotherapy is still in question and awaits further work; such is the case for conduct disorders, anxiety disorders, and depression.

The other two important classes of childhood disorders, mental retardation and specific developmental disorders (i.e., reading retardation, language impairment), are not significantly ameliorated by pharmacotherapy (Aman, 1984; Gittelman, Klein, & Feingold, 1983; Gittelman-Klein & Klein, 1976), though some of the disturbed behavior associated with these disorders (e.g., aggression, hyperactivity) may be reduced with pharmacotherapy. These conditions fall largely outside the limits of this text but are referred to briefly in Chapters 6 and 7.

From this chapter the reader will not have a full, or nearly full, appreciation of the positive aspects of pharmacotherapy, nor of the management problems associated with it. However, it is important to be informed about a growing field that, with the explosion of knowledge in the neurosciences, is likely to continue to arouse increasing scientific interest, as well as, regrettably, passion, which, by definition, is unreasoned. It is the goal of science to replace prejudice with informed opinion. This chapter aims to be a small step in this direction.

REFERENCES
Abikoff, H., & Gittelman, R. (1985). The normalizing effects of methylphenidate on the classroom behavior of ADDH children. *Journal of Abnormal Child Psychology*, *13*, 33–44.

Alderton, H., & Hoddinott, B. A. (1969). A controlled study of the use of thiorida-zine in the treatment of hyperactive and aggressive children in a children's psychiatric hospital. *Canadian Psychiatric Association Journal, 9*, 239–247.

Aman, M. G. (1984). Drugs and learning in mentally retarded persons. In G. D. Burrows & J. S. Werry (Eds.), *Advances in human psychopharmacology* (Vol. 3, pp. 121–163). Greenwich, CT: JAI Press.

Ananth, J. (1976). Treatment of obsessive-compulsive neurosis: A pharmacologic approach. *Psychosomatics, 17*, 180–184.

Ananth, J., Solyom, L., Bryntwick, S., & Krishnappa, U. (1979). Chlorimipramine therapy for obsessive-compulsive neurosis. *American Journal of Psychiatry, 136*, 700–701.

Anderson, L. T., Campbell, M., Grega, D. M., Perry, R., Small, A. M., & Green, W. H. (1984). Haloperidol in the treatment of infantile autism: Effects on learning and behavioral symptoms. *American Journal of Psychiatry, 141*, 1195–1202.

Arnold, L. F., Christopher, J., Huestis, R., & Smeltzer, D. J. (1978). Methylpheni-date vs. dextroamphetamine vs. caffeine in minimal brain dysfunction: Controlled comparison by placebo washout design with Bayes analysis. *Archives of General Psychiatry, 35*, 463–473.

Arnold, L., Huestis, R., Smeltzer, D., Scheib, J., Wemmer, D., & Colner, G. (1976). Levoamphetamine vs. dextroamphetamine in minimal brain dysfunction. *Archives of General Psychiatry, 33*, 292–301.

Bala, S. P., Cohen, B., Morris, A. G., Atkin, A., Gittelman, R., & Kates, W. (1981). Saccades of hyperactive and normal boys during occular pursuit. *Developmental Medicine and Child Neurology, 23*, 323–336.

Barkley, R. A. (1977a). Review of stimulant drug research with hyperactive children. *Journal of Child Psychology and Psychiatry, 18*, 147–166.

Barkley, R. A. (1977b). The effects of methylphenidate on various types of activity level and attention in hyperkinetic children. *Journal of Abnormal Child Psychology, 5*, 351–369.

Barkley, R. A., & Cunningham, C. E. (1979). The effects of methylphenidate on the mother–child interaction of hyperactive children. *Archives of General Psychiatry, 36*, 101–108.

Barkley, R. A., & Cunningham, C. E. (1980). The parent–child interactions of hyperactive children and their modification by stimulant drugs. In R. M. Knights & D. Bakker (Eds.), *Treatment of Hyperactive and Learning Disordered Children* (pp. 219–236). Baltimore: University Park Press.

Becker-Mattes, A., Mattes, J., Abikoff, H., & Brandt, L. (1985). State dependent learning in hyperactive children on methylphenidate. *American Journal of Psychiatry, 142*, 455–459.

Behar, D., Rapoport, J. L., Berg, C. J., Denckla, M. B., Mann, L., Cox, C., Fedio, P., Fahn, T., & Wolfman, M. G. (1984). Computerized tomography and neuro-psychological test measures in adolescents with obsessive compulsive disorder. *American Journal of Psychiatry, 141*, 363–369.

Berney, T., Kolvin, I., Bhate, S. R., Garside, R. F., Jeans, J., Kay, B., & Scarth, L. (1980). School phobia: A therapeutic trial with clomipramine and short-term outcome. *British Journal of Psychiatry, 138*, 110–118.

Bradley, C. (1937). The behavior of children receiving Benzedrine. *American Journal of Psychiatry*, *94*, 577–585.

Bradley, C. (1950). Benzedrine and Dexedrine in the treatment of children's behavior disorders. *Pediatrics*, *5*, 24–37.

Brown, G. L., Ebert, M. H., Mikkelsen, E. J., & Hunt, R. D. (1979). Clinical pharmacology of D-amphetamine in hyperactive children. In L. A. Gottschalk (Ed.), *Pharmacokinetics of psychoactive drugs* (pp. 137–153). New York: Spectrum.

Bruun, R. (1984). Gilles de la Tourette's syndrome: An overview of clinical experience. *Journal of the American Academy of Child Psychiatry*, *23*, 126–133.

Buchsbaum, M., & Wender, P. (1973). Average evoked responses in normal and minimally brain dysfunctioned children treated with amphetamine: A preliminary report. *Archives of General Psychiatry*, *29*, 764–769.

Bugental, D. B., Whalen, C. K., & Henker, B. (1977). Causal attributions of hyperactive children and motivational assumptions of two behavior change approaches: Evidence for an interactivist position. *Child Development*, *48*, 874–884.

Burk, H. P. (1964). Effects of amphetamine therapy on hyperkinetic children. *Archives of General Psychiatry*, *11*, 604–609.

Butter, H. J., & Lapierre, Y. D. (1974). The effect of methylphenidate on sensory perception and integration in hyperactive children. *International Pharmacopsychiatry*, *9*, 235–244.

Campbell, M. (1977). Treatment of childhood and adolescent schizophrenia. In J. M. Wiener (Ed.), *Psychopharmacology in childhood and adolescence*. (pp 101–118). New York: Basic Books.

Campbell, M. (1985). On the use of neuroleptics in children and adolescents. *Psychiatric Annals*, *15*, 101–107.

Campbell, M., Anderson, L. T., Meier, M., Cohen, I. L., Small, A. M., Samit, C., & Sachar, E. J. (1978). A comparison of haloperidol and behavior therapy and the interaction of both in autistic children. *Journal of the American Academy of Child Psychiatry*, *17*, 640–655.

Campbell, M., Fish, B., David, R., Shapiro, T., Collins, P., & Koh, C. (1973). Liothyronine treatment in psychotic and non-psychotic children under 6 years. *Archives of General Psychiatry*, *29*, 602–608.

Campbell, M., Fish, B., Korein, J., Shapiro, T., Collins, P., & Koh, C. (1972). Lithium and chlorpromazine: A controlled crossover study of hyperactive severely disturbed young children. *Journal of Autism and Childhood Schizophrenia*, 2, 234–263.

Campbell, M., Fish, B., Shapiro, T., & Floyd, A., Jr. (1970). Thiothixene in young disturbed preschool children: A pilot study. *Archives of General Psychiatry*, *23*, 70–72.

Campbell, M., Fish, B., Shapiro, T., & Floyd, A., Jr. (1971a). Imipramine in preschool autistic and schizophrenic children. *Journal of Autism and Childhood Schizophrenia*, *1*, 267–282.

Campbell, M., Fish, B., Shapiro, T., & Floyd, A., Jr. (1971b). A study of molindone in disturbed preschool children. *Current Therapeutics Research*, *13*, 28–33.

Campbell, M., Fish, B., Shapiro, T., & Floyd, A., Jr. (1972). Acute responses of schizophrenic children to a sedative and "stimulating" neuroleptic: A pharmacologic yardstick. *Current Therapeutics Research, 14*, 759–766.

Campbell, M., Grega, D. M., Green, W. H., & Bennett, W. G. (1983). Neuroleptic-induced dyskinesias in children. *Clinical Neuropharmacology. 6*, 207–222.

Campbell, M., Small, A. M., Collins, P. J., Friedman, E., David, R., & Genieser, N. B. (1976). Levodopa and levoamphetamine: A crossover study in schizophrenic children. *Current Therapeutics Research, 19*, 70–86.

Campbell, M., Schulman, D., & Rapoport, J. (1978). The current status of lithium therapy in child and adolescent psychiatry. A report of the Committee of Biological Aspects of Child Psychiatry of the American Academy of Child Psychiatry. *Journal of the American Academy of Child Psychiatry, 21*, 3–9.

Campbell, M., Small, A. M., Hollander, C. S., Korein, J., Cohen, I. L., Kalmign, M., & Ferris, S. (1978). A controlled crossover study of triidothyronine in young psychotic children. *Journal of Autism and Childhood Schizophrenia, 8*, 371–381.

Campbell, M., Small, A. M., Green, W. H., Jennings, S. J., Perry, R., Bennett, W. G., & Anderson, L. (1984). Behavioral efficacy of haloperidol and lithium carbonate: A comparison in hospitalized aggressive children with conduct disorder. *Archives of General Psychiatry, 120*, 650–656.

Campbell, S. B. (1973). Mother–child interactions in reflective, impulsive, and hyperactive children. *Developmental Psychology, 8*, 341–347.

Campbell, S. B. (1975). Mother–child interactions: A comparison of hyperactive, learning disabled, and normal boys. *American Journal of Orthopsychiatry, 45*, 51–57.

Campbell, S. B., Schleifer, M., Weiss, G., & Perlman, T. (1977). A two year follow-up of hyperactive preschoolers. *American Journal of Orthopsychiatry, 47*, 149–162.

Cantor, S., Evans, J., Pearce, J., & Pezzot-Pearce, T. (1982). Childhood schizophrenia: Present but not accounted for. *American Journal of Psychiatry, 139*, 758–762.

Cantwell, D. P., & Carlson, G. A. (1978). In J. S. Werry (Ed.), *Pediatric psychopharmacology: The use of behavior modification drugs in children* (pp. 171–207). New York: Brunner/Mazel.

Cohen, D. J., Detlor, J., Young, G., & Shaywitz, B. A. (1980). Clonidine ameliorates Gilles de la Tourette syndrome. *Archives of General Psychiatry, 37*, 1350–1357.

Cohen, D. J., Leckman, J. F., & Shaywitz, B. A. (1985). The Tourette syndrome and other tics. In D. Shaffer, A. A. Ehrhardt, & L. L. Greenhill (Eds.), *The clinical guide to child psychiatry* (pp. 3–28). New York: Free Press.

Cohen, N. J., Douglas, V. I., & Morgenstern, G. (1971). The effect of methylphenidate on attentive behavior and autonomic activity in hyperactive children. *Psychopharmacologia, 22*, 282–294.

Comings, D. E., & Comings, B. G. (1984). Tourette's syndrome and attention deficit with hyperactivity: Are they genetically related? *Journal of the American Academy of Child Psychiatry, 23*, 138–146.

Comly, H. H. (1971). Cerebral stimulants for children with learning disorders. *Journal of Learning Disabilities, 4*, 484–490.

Conners, C. K. (1966). The effect of Dexedrine on rapid discrimination and motor control of hyperkinetic children under mild stress. *Journal of Nervous and Mental Disorders, 142*, 429–433.

Conners, C. K. (1971). The effect of stimulant drugs on human figure drawings in children with minimal brain dysfunction. *Psychopharmacologia, 19*, 329–333.

Conners, C. K. (1975a). Controlled trial of methylphenidate in preschool children with minimal brain dysfunction. In R. Gittelman-Klein (Ed.), *Recent advances in child psychopharmacology* (pp. 64–78). New York: Human Sciences Press.

Conners, C. K. (1975b). A placebo-crossover study of caffeine treatment of hyperkinetic children. In R. Gittelman-Klein (Ed.), *Recent advances in child psychopharmacology* (pp. 136–137). New York: Human Sciences Press.

Conners, C. K. (1979). The acute effects of caffeine on evoked response, vigilance, and activity level in hyperkinetic children. *Journal of Abnormal Child Psychiatry, 7*, 145–151.

Conners, C. K. (1980). *Food additives and hyperactive children.* New York: Plenum Press.

Conners, C. K., Eisenberg, L., & Barcai, A. (1967). Effect of dextroamphetamine on children. *Archives of General Psychiatry, 17*, 478–485.

Conners, C. K., Eisenberg, L., & Sharpe, L. (1964). Effects of methylphenidate (Ritalin) on paired-associate learning and Porteus maze performance in emotionally disturbed children. *Journal of Consulting Psychology, 28*, 14–22.

Conners, C. K., Kramer, R., Rothschild, G. H., Schwartz, L., & Stone, A. (1964). Treatment of young delinquent boys with diphenylhydantoin sodium and methylphenidate. *Archives of General Psychiatry, 24*, 156–160.

Conners, C. K., Kramer, R., Rothchild, G. H., Schwartz, L., & Stone, A. (1971). Treatment of young delinquent boys with diphenylhydantoin sodium and methylphenidate. *Archives of General Psychiatry, 24*, 156–160.

Conners, C., Rothschild, G., Eisenberg, L., Schwartz, L. S., & Robinson, E. (1969). Dextroamphetamine sulfate in children with learning disorders: Effects on perception, learning, achievement. *Archives of General Psychiatry*, *21*, 182–190.

Conners, C. K., Taylor, E., & Dooling, E. (1980). Pemoline, methylphenidate and placebo in children with minimal brain dysfunction. *Archives of General Psychiatry*, *37*, 922–930.

Conners, C. K., Taylor, E., Meo, G., Kurtz, M. A., & Fournier, M. (1972). Magnesium pemoline and dextroamphetamine: A controlled study in children with minimal brain dysfunction. *Psychopharmacologia, 26*, 321–336.

Cunningham, C. E., & Barkley, R. A. (1978). The interactions of hyperactive and normal children with their mothers in free play and structured task. *Child Development*, *50*, 217–224.

Cunningham, M. A., Pillai, V., & Blachford Rogers, W. J. (1968). Haloperidol in the treatment of children with severe behaviour disorders. *British Journal of Psychiatry*, *114*, 845–854.

Dalby, M. A. (1975). Behavioral effects of carbamazepine. In J. R. Penry & D. D. Daly (Eds.), *Complex partial seizures and their treatment* (*Advances in Neurology*, Vol. 11, pp. 331–344). New York: Raven Press.

Douglas, V. I. (1983). Attentional and cognitive problems. In M. Rutter (Ed.), *Developmental neuropsychiatry* (pp. 280–329). New York: Guilford Press.

Douglas, V. I. (1972). Stop, look and listen: The problem of sustained attention and impulse control in hyperactive and normal children. *Canadian Journal of Behavioral Science, 4,* 259–282.

Dykman, R. A., McGrew, J., Harris, T. S., Peters, J. F., & Ackerman, P. T. (1976). Two blinded studies of the effects of stimulant drugs on children: Pemoline, methylphenidate, and placebo. In R. P. Anderson & C. G. Halcomb (Eds.), *Learning disability minimal brain dysfunction syndrome* (pp. 1–11). Springfield, IL: Charles C. Thomas.

Eisenberg, L., Lachman, R., Molling, P. A., Lockner, A., Mizelle, J. D., & Conners, C. K. (1963). A psychopharmacologic experiment in a training school for delinquent boys. *American Journal of Orthopsychiatry, 33,* 431–447.

Elkins, R. H., Rapoport, J. L., Zahn, T. P., Buchsbaum, M. S., Weingartner, H., Kopin, I. J., Langes, D., & Johnson, C. (1981). Acute effects of caffeine in normal prepubertal boys. *American Journal of Psychiatry, 138,* 178–183.

Ellis, M. J., Witt, P. A., Reynolds, R., & Sprague, R. L. (1974). Methylphenidate and the activity of hyperactives in the informal setting. *Child Development, 45,* 217–220.

Engelhardt, D. M., Polizos, P., & Margolis, R. A. (1970, March). *Psychological syndromes responsive to pharmacotherapy. Autism and schizophrenic behavior.* Presented at the Symposium on Psychopharmacology in Children. State of Massachusetts, Department of Mental Health, Cushing Hospital, Framingham, MA.

Engelhardt, D., Polizos, P., Waizer, J., & Hoffman, S. (1973). A double blind comparison of fluphenazine and haloperidol. *Journal of Autism and Childhood Schizophrenia, 3,* 128–137.

Epstein, L. C., Lasagna, L., Conners, C. K., & Rodriguez, A. (1968). Correlation of dextroamphetamine excretion and drug response in hyperactive children. *Journal of Nervous and Mental Disorders, 146,* 136–146.

Faretra, G., Dooher, L., & Dowling, J. (1970). Comparison of haloperidol and fluphenazine in disturbed children. *American Journal of Psychiatry, 126,* 1670–1673.

Finnerty, R. J., Soltys, J. J., & Cole, J. O. (1971). The use of *d*-amphetamine with hyperkinetic children. *Psychopharmacologia, 21,* 302–308.

Firestone, P., Davey, J., Goodman, J. T., & Peters, S. (1978). The effects of caffeine and methylphenidate on hyperactive children. *Journal of American Academy of Child Psychiatry, 17,* 455–456.

Firestone, P., Poitras-Wright, H., & Douglas, V. I. (1978). The effects of caffeine on hyperactive children. *Journal of Learning Disabilities, 11,* 133–142.

Fish, B., Campbell, M., Shapiro, T., & Floyd, A., Jr. (1969). Comparison of trifluperidol, trifluoperazine and chlorpromazine in preschool schizophrenic children: The value of less sedative antipsychotic agents. *Current Therapeutics Research, 11,* 589–595.

Fish, B., Campbell, M., Shapiro, T., & Weinstein, J. (1969). Preliminary findings on thiothixene compared to other drugs in psychotic children under five years. In H. Lehman & T. Ban (Eds.), *The thioxanthenes: Modern problems of pharmacopsychiatry* (pp. 90–99). Basel: Karger.

Fisher, M. A. (1978). Dextroamphetamine and placebo practive effects on selective attention in hyperactive children. *Journal of Abnormal Child Psychology*, *6*, 25–32.

Flament, M. F., Rapoport, J. L., Berg, C. J., Sceery, W., Kilts, C., Mellström, B., & Linnoila, M. (1985). Clomipramine treatment of childhood obsessive compulsive disorder: A double blind controlled study. *Archives of General Psychiatry*, *42*, 977–983.

Flor-Henry, Y., Yeudell, L. T., Koles, F. J., & Howarth, B. G. (1979). Neuropsychological and power spectral EEG investigations of the obsessive-compulsive syndrome. *Biological Psychiatry*, *14*, 119–130.

Friebergs, V., Douglas, V. I., & Weiss, G. (1968). The effect of chlorpromazine on concept learning in hyperactive children under two conditions of reinforcement. *Psychopharmacologia*, *13*, 299–310.

Frommer, E. A. (1967). Treatment of childhood depression with antidepressant drugs. *British Medical Journal*, *1*, 729–732.

Frommer, E. A. (1968a). Depressive illness in childhood. *British Journal of Psychiatry (Special Bulletin)*, *2*, 117–136.

Frommer, E. A. (1968b). Depressive illness in childhood. In A. Coppen & A. Walk (Eds.), *Recent developments in affective disorders* (pp. 117–136). London: Headley.

Frommer, E. A. (1972). Indications for antidepressant treatment with special reference to depressed preschool children. In A. L. Annell (Ed.), *Depressive states in childhood and adolescence* (pp. 449–454). New York: Wiley.

Garfinkel, B., Webster, C., & Sloman, L. (1975). Methylphenidate and caffeine in the treatment of children with minimal brain dysfunction. *American Journal of Psychiatry*, *132*, 723–728.

Gilman, A. G., Goodman, L. S., & Gilman, A. (1980). *Goodman and Gilman's The pharmacological basis of therapeutics* (6th ed.) New York: Macmillan.

Gittelman, R. (1982, Dec.). *Final height of stimulant treated hyperactive children*. Paper presented at the annual meeting of the American College of Neuropsychopharmacology, San Juan, Puerto Rico.

Gittelman, R. (1983). Hyperkinetic syndrome: Treatment issues and principles. In M. Rutter (Ed.), *Developmental neuropsychiatry* (pp. 437–449). New York: Guilford Press.

Gittelman, R., Abikoff, H., Pollack, E., Klein, D. F., Katz, S., & Mattes, J. (1980). A controlled trial of behavior modification and methylphenidate in hyperactive children. In C. K. Whalen & B. Henker (Eds.), *Hyperactive children: The social ecology of identification and treatment* (pp. 221–243). New York: Academic Press.

Gittelman, R., Klein, D. F., & Feingold, I. (1983). Children with reading disorders. II. Effects of methylphenidate in combination with reading instruction. *Journal of Child Psychology and Psychiatry*, *24*, 193–212.

Gittelman-Klein, R. (1974). Pilot clinical trial of imipramine in hyperkinetic children. In C. K. Conners (Ed.), *Clinical use of stimulant drugs in children* (pp. 192–201). The Hague: Excerpta Medica.

Gittelman-Klein, R. (1978). Psychopharmacological treatment of anxiety disorders, mood disorders and Tourette's disorder in children. In M. A. Lipton, A. DiMascio, & K. F. Killam (Eds.), *Psychopharmacology: A generation of progress* (pp. 1471–1480). New York: Raven Press.

Gittelman-Klein, R., & Klein D. F. (1973). School phobia: Diagnostic consideration in the light of imipramine effects. *Journal of Nervous and Mental Disorders, 156,* 199–215.

Gittelman-Klein, R., & Klein, D. F. (1975). Are behavioral and psychometric changes related in methylphenidate-treated, hyperactive children? *International Journal of Mental Health, 4,* 182–198.

Gittelman-Klein, R., & Klein, D. F. (1976). Methylphenidate effects in learning disabilities. *Archives of General Psychiatry, 33,* 655–664.

Gittelman-Klein, R., & Klein, D. F. (1980). Separation anxiety in school refusal: Its treatment with drugs. In L. Hersov & I. Berg (Eds.), *Out of school* (pp. 221–243). New York: Wiley.

Gittelman-Klein, R., Klein, D. F., Abikoff, H., Katz, S., Gloisten, A., & Kates, W. (1976). Relative efficacy of methylphenidate and behavior modification in hyperkinetic children: An interim report. *Journal of Abnormal Child Psychology, 4,* 361–380.

Gittelman-Klein, R., Klein, D. F., Katz, S., Saraf, K., & Pollack, E. (1976). Comparative effects of methylphenidate and thioridazine in hyperkinetic children. *Archives of General Psychiatry, 33,* 1217–1231.

Greenberg, L. M., Yellin, A. M., Spring, C., & Metcalf, M. (1975). Clinical effects of imipramine and methylphenidate in hyperactive children. In R. Gittelman-Klein (Ed.), *Recent advances in child psychopharmacology* (pp. 148–159). New York: Human Sciences Press.

Gram, L., & Rafaelsen, J. (1972). Lithium treatment of psychotic children and adolescents. *Acta Psychiatrica Scandinavica, 48,* 253–260.

Grinspoon, L., & Singer, S. B. (1973). Amphetamine in the treatment of hyperkinetic children. *Harvard Educational Research, 43,* 515–554.

Gross, M. (1975). Caffeine in the treatment of children with minimal brain dsyfunction of hyperkinetic syndrome. *Psychosomatics, 16,* 26–27.

Gualtieri, C., Barnhill, J., McGimsey, J., & Schell, D. (1980). Tardive dyskinesia and other movement disorders in children treated with psychotropic drugs. *Journal of the American Academy of Child Psychiatry, 19,* 491–510.

Halliday, R., Rosenthal, J. H., Naylor, H., & Callaway, E. (1976). Average evoked potential predictors of clinical improvement in hyperactive children treated with methylphenidate: An initial study and replication. *Psychophysiology, 13,* 429–439.

Harvey, D. H. P., & Marsh, R. W. (1978). The effects of decaffeinated coffee versus whole coffee on hyperactive children. *Developmental Medicine and Child Neurology, 20,* 81–86.

Hastings, J. E., & Barkley, R. A. (1978). A review of psychophysiological research with hyperkinetic children. *Journal of Abnormal Child Psychology, 6,* 413–447.

Helper, M. M., Wilcott, R. C., & Garfield, S. L. (1963). Effects of chlorpromazine on learning and related processes in emotionally disturbed children. *Journal of Consulting Psychology, 27,* 1–9.

Henker, B., Whalen, C. K., & Collins, B. E. (1979). Double-blind and triple-blind assessments of medication and placebo responses in hyperactive children. *Journal of Abnormal Child Psychology*, 7, 1–13.

Huessey, H. R., & Wright, A. L. (1969). Graded imipramine regimen favored in hyperkinetic children. *Journal of the American Medical Association*, *208*, 1613–1614.

Humphries, T., Kinsbourne, M., & Swanson, J. (1978). Stimulant effects on cooperation and social interaction between hyperactive children and their mothers. *Journal of Child Psychology and Psychiatry*, *19*, 13–22.

Kashani, J. H., Shekim, W. O., Reid, J. (1984). Amitriptyline in children with major depressive disorder: A double blind crossover pilot study. *Journal of the American Academy of Child Psychiatry*, *23*, 348–351.

Klein, D. F., Gittelman, R., Quitkin, F. M., & Rifkin. A. (1980). *Diagnosis and drug treatment of psychiatric disorders: Adults and children* (2nd ed.). Baltimore: Williams & Wilkins.

Knights, R. M. (1974). Psychometric assessment of stimulant-induced behavior change. In C. K. Conners (Ed.), *Clinical use of stimulant drugs in children* (pp. 221–231). The Hague: Excerpta Medica.

Kraft, I. A., Ardali, C., Duffy, J. H., Hart, J. T., & Pearch, P. (1965). A clinical study of chlordiazepoxide used in psychiatric disorders of children. *International Journal of Neuropsychiatry*, *1*, 433–437.

Kurtis, L. B. (1966). Clinical study of the response to nortriptyline on autistic children. *International Journal of Neuropsychiatry*, *2*, 298–301.

Leckman, J. F., Cohen, D. J., Detlor, J., Young, J. G., Harcherik, D., & Shaywitz, B. A. (1982). Clonidine in the treatment of Tourette syndrome. *Advances in Neurology*, *35*, 391–401.

Lefkowitz, M. (1969). Effects of diphenylhydantoin on disruptive behavior: Study of male delinquents. *Archives of General Psychiatry*, *20*, 643–651.

Lerer, R. J., Lerer, M. P., & Artner, J. (1977). The effects of methylphenidate on the handwriting of children with minimal brain dysfunction. *Journal of Pediatrics*, *91*, 127–132.

Liebowitz, M. R., Quitkin, F. M., Stewart, J. W., McGrath, P. J., Harrison, W., Rabkin, J., Tricano, E., Markowitz, J. S., & Klein, D. F. (1984). Phenelzine vs. imipramine in atypical depression. *Archives of General Psychiatry*, *41*, 669–677.

Looker, A., & Conners, C. K. (1970). Diphenylhydantoin in children with severe temper tantrums. *Archives of General Psychiatry*, *23*, 80–89.

Lucas, A. R., & Pasley, F. C. (1969). Psychoactive drugs in the treatment of emotionally disturbed children: Haloperidol and diazepam. *Comprehensive Psychiatry*, *10*, 376–386.

Maletzky, B. M. (1974). *d*-Amphetamine and delinquency: Hyperkinesis persisting? *Diseases of the Nervous System*, *35*, 543–547.

Marshall, W. K. (1971). Treatment of obsessional illness and phobic anxiety states with chlorimipramine. *British Journal of Psychiatry*, *119*, 467–471.

Mattes, J., & Gittelman, R. (1983). Growth of hyperactive children on maintenance regimen of methylphenidate. *Archives of General Psychiatry*, *38*, 714–718.

Molling, P. A., Lockner, A. W., Sauls, R. J., & Eisenberg, L. (1962). Committed delinquent boys. *Archives of General Psychiatry*, *7*, 70–76.

Page, J. G., Bernstein, J. E., Janicki, R. S. & Michelli, F. A. (1974a). A multi-clinic trial of pemoline in childhood hyperkinesis. In C. K. Conners (Ed.), *Clinical use of stimulant drugs in children* (pp. 98–124). The Hague: Excerpta Medica.

Page, J. G., Janicki, R. S., Bernstein, J. E., Curran, C. F., & Michelli, P. A. (1974b). Pemoline (Cylert) in the treatment of childhood hyperkinesis. *Journal of Learning Disabilities, 7,* 498–503.

Platt, J. E., Campbell, M., Green, W. H., & Grega, D. M. (1984). Cognitive effects of lithium carbonate and haloperidol in treatment resistant aggressive children. *Archives of General Psychiatry, 41,* 657–662.

Porrino, L. J., Rapoport, J. L., Behar, D., Ismond, D. R., Sceery, W., & Bunney, W. E., Jr. (1983). A naturalistic assessment of the motor activity of hyperactive boys. II. Stimulant drug effect. *Archives of General Psychiatry, 40,* 688–693.

Post, R. M., & Uhde, T. W. (1983). Treatment of mood disorders with antiepileptic medications: Clinical and theoretical implications. *Epilepsia, 24* (suppl. 2), 97–108.

Puig-Antich, J. (1978, Dec.). *Imipramine side effects and blood levels of metabolites in depressed children.* Presented at The American College of Neuropsychopharmacology, Maui, HA.

Puig-Antich, J. (1982). Major depression and conduct disorder in prepuberty. *Journal of the American Academy of Child Psychiatry, 21,* 118–128.

Puig-Antich, J., Blau, S., Marx, N., Greenhill, L. L., & Chambers, W. (1978). Prepubertal major depressive disorder. A pilot study. *Journal of the American Academy of Child Psychiatry, 17,* 695–707.

Puig-Antich, J., Perel, J. M., Lupatkin, W., Chambers, W. J., Shea, C., Tabrizi, M. A., & Stiller, R. L. (1979). Plasma levels of imipramine (IMI) and desmethylimipramine (DMI) and clinical response in prepubertal major depressive disorder. *Journal of the American Academy of Child Psychiatry, 18,* 616–627.

Prichep, L. S., Sutton, S., & Hakerem, G. (1976). Evoked potentials in hyperkinetic and normal children under certainty and uncertainty: A placebo and methylphenidate study. *Psychophysiology, 13,* 419–428.

Quinn, P. O., & Rapoport, J. L. (1975). One year follow-up of hyperactive boys treated with imipramine or methylphenidate. *American Journal of Psychiatry, 132,* 241–245.

Rapoport, J. (1983). Stimulant drug treatment of hyperactivity: An update. In S. Guze (Ed.), *Child psychiatry—new directions* (pp. 189–199). New York: Raven Press.

Rapoport, J. L. (1985). Childhood obsessive compulsive disorder. In D. Shaffer, A. A. Ehrhardt, & L. L. Greenhill (Eds.), *The clinical guide to child psychiatry* (pp. 208–218). New York: Free Press.

Rapoport, J. L., Abramson, A., Alexander, D., & Lott, I. (1971). Playroom observations of hyperactive children on medication. *American Academy of Child Psychiatry, 10,* 524–534.

Rapoport, J. L., Buchsbaum, M., Weingartner, H., Zahn, T., Ludlow, C., & Mikkelsen, E. J. (1980). Dextroamphetamine: Cognitive and behavioral effects in normal and hyperactive children and normal adults. *Archives General Psychiatry, 37,* 933–943.

Rapoport, J. L., & Mikkelsen, E. J. (1978). Antidepressants. In J. S. Werry (Ed.), *Pediatric psychopharmacology: The use of behavior modifying drugs in children* (pp. 208–233). New York: Brunner/Mazel.

Rapoport, J. L., Mikkelsen, E. J., & Werry, J. S. (1978). Antimanic, antianxiety, hallucinogenic and miscellaneous drugs. In J. S. Werry (Ed.), *Pediatric psychopharmacology: The use of behavior modifying in children* (pp. 316–355). New York: Brunner/Mazel.

Rapoport, J. L., Quinn, P. O., Bradbard, G., Riddle, D., & Brooks, E. (1974). Imipramine and methylphenidate treatments of hyperactive boys. *Archives of General Psychiatry, 30*, 789–793.

Rapoport, J. L., Tepsic, P. H., Grice, J., Johnson, C., & Langer, D. (1980). Decreased motor activity of hyperactive children on dextroamphetamine during active gym program. *Psychiatry Research, 2*, 225–229.

Rimland, B. (1973). High-dosage levels of certain vitamins in the treatment of children with severe mental disorders. In D. Hawkins & L. Pauling (Eds.), *Orthomolecular psychiatry: Treatment of schizophrenia* (pp. 513–539). San Francisco: Freeman.

Rimland, B., Callaway, E., & Dreyfus, P. (1978). The effect of high doses of vitamin B_6 on autistic children: A double-blind crossover study. *American Journal of Psychiatry, 135*, 472–475.

Roche, A. F., Lipman, R. S., Overall, J. E., & Hung, W. (1979). The effects of stimulant medication on the growth of hyperkinetic children. *Pediatrics, 63*, 847–850.

Ross, M. S., & Moldofsky, H. (1978). A comparison of pimozide and haloperidol in the treatment of Gilles de la Tourette's syndrome. *American Journal of Psychiatry, 135*, 585–587.

Roukema, R. W., & Emery, L. (1970). Megavitamin therapy with severely disturbed children. *American Journal of Psychiatry, 127*, 167.

Safer, D., & Allen, R. (1973). Single daily dose methylphenidate in hyperactive children. *Diseases of the Nervous System, 34*, 325–328.

Safer, D. J., Allen, R. P., & Barr, E. (1975). Growth rebound after termination of stimulant drugs. *Journal of Pediatrics, 8*, 113–116.

Saletu, B., Saletu, M., Simeon, J., Viamontes, G., & Itil, T. M. (1975). Comparative symptomatological and evoked potential studies with *d*-amphetamine, thioridazine, and placebo in hyperkinetic children. *Biological Psychiatry, 10*, 255–275.

Satterfield, J. H., Cantwell, D. P., Lesser, L. I., & Podosin, R. L. (1972). Physiological studies of the hyperkinetic child. *American Journal of Psychiatry, 128*, 1418–1424.

Satterfield, J. H., Lesser, L. I., Saul, R. E., & Cantwell, D. P. (1973). EEG aspects in the diagnosis and treatment of minimal brain dysfunction. *Annals of the New York Academy of Sciences, 205*, 274–282.

Schain, R. J., & Reynard, C. L. (1975). Observations on effects of a central stimulant drug (methylphenidate) in children with hyperactive behavior. *Journal of Pediatrics, 55*, 709–716.

Schnackenberg, R. C. (1973). Caffeine as a substitute for schedule II stimulants in hyperactive children. *American Journal of Psychiatry, 130*, 796–800.

Schrag, P., & Divoky, D. (1975). *The myth of the hyperactive child and other means of child control.* New York: Pantheon.

Shaffer, D. (1985). Nocturnal enuresis: Its investigation and treatment. In D. Shaffer, A. A. Ehrhardt, & L. L. Greenhill (Eds.), *The clinical guide to child psychiatry* (pp. 29–47). New York: Free Press.

Shapiro, A. K., & Shapiro, E. (1981). The treatment and etiology of tics and Tourette syndrome. *Comprehensive Psychiatry*, *22*, 193–205.

Shapiro, A. K., & Shapiro, E. (1984). Controlled study of pimozide vs. placebo in Tourette's syndrome. *Journal of the American Academy of Child Psychiatry*, *23*, 161–173.

Shea, V. T. (1982). State-dependent learning in children receiving methylphenidate. *Journal of Psychopharmacology*, *78*, 266–270.

Shouse, M. N., & Lubar, J. F. (1978). Physiological basis of hyperkinesis treated with methylphenidate. *Journal of Pediatrics*, *62*, 343–351.

Signorato, V., & Lutati, U. V. (1967). Il diazepam nel trattamento dell'impulsivita patologica "epilettorida" del l'infanzia. *Minerva Pediatrics*, *19*, 372–374.

Simonelli, V. M. (1975). Evaluation of the efficacy of a new preparation containing benzodiazepine under forms of drops in subjects suffering from anxiety and erethistic syndrome in pediatric age. *Pediatria (Napoli)*, *83*, 762–772.

Skynner, A. C. R. (1961). Effects of chlordiazepoxide (letter). *Lancet*, *1*, 1110.

Sostek, A. J., Buchsbaum, M. S., & Rapoport, J. L. (1980). Effects of amphetamine on vigilance performance in normal and hyperactive children. *Journal of Abnormal Child Psychology*, *8*, 491–500.

Sprague, R. L., Barnes, K. R., & Werry, J. S. (1970). Methylphenidate and thioridazine: Learning, reaction time, activity, and classroom behavior in disturbed children. *American Journal of Orthopsychiatry*, *40*, 615–628.

Sprague, R. L., & Sleator, E. K. (1977). Methylphenidate in hyperkinetic children: Differences in dose effects in learning and social behavior. *Science*, *198*, 1274–1276.

Spring, C., Greenberg, L., Scott, J., & Hopwood, J. (1973). Reaction time and effect of Ritalin on children with learning problems. *Perceptual and Motor Skills*, *36*, 75–82.

Steinberg, G. G., Troshinsky, C., & Steinberg, H. R. (1971). Dextroamphetamine-responsive behavior disorder in school children. *American Journal of Psychiatry*, *128*, 174–179.

Stenhausen, H., & Kreuzer, E. (1981). Learning in hyperactive children: Are there stimulant-related and state-dependent effects? *Journal of Psychopharmacology*, *74*, 384–390.

Stores, G. (1978). Antiepileptics (anticonvulsants). In J. S. Werry (Ed.), *Pediatric psychopharmacology: The use of behavior modifying drugs in children* (pp. 274–315). New York: Brunner/Mazel.

Sverd, J., Kupietz, S. S., Winsberg, B. G., Hurwic, M. J., & Becker, L. (1978). Effects of *L*-5-Hydroxytryptophan in autistic children. *Journal of Autism and Childhood Schizophrenia*, *8*, 171–180.

Swanson, J. M., & Kinsbourne, M. (1976). Stimulant-related state-dependent learning in hyperactive children. *Science*, *192*, 1354–1357.

Sykes, D. H., Douglas, V. I., & Morgenstern, G. (1973). Sustained attention in hyperactive children. *Journal of Child Psychology and Psychiatry, 4*, 213–220.

Sykes, D. H., Douglas, V. I., Weiss, G., & Minde, K. K. (1971). Attention in hyperactive children and the effect of methylphenidate (Ritalin). *Journal of Child Psychology and Psychiatry, 12*, 129–139.

Thoren, P., Asberg, M., Cronholm, B., Jorestedt, L., & Traskman, L. (1980). Clomipramine treatment of obsessive-compulsive disorder. I. A controlled clinical trial. *Archives of General Psychiatry, 37*, 1281–1285.

Thurston, C. M., Sobol, M. P., Swanson, J., & Kinsbourne, M. (1979). Effects of methylphenidate (Ritalin) on selective attention in hyperactive children. *Journal of Abnormal Child Psychology, 7*, 471–481.

Trimble, M., & Reynolds, E. (1976). Anticonvulsant drugs and mental symptoms. *Psychological Medicine, 6*, 169–178.

Varly, C. (1983). Effects of methylphenidate in adolescents with attention deficit disorder. *Journal of the American Academy of Child Psychiatry, 22*, 351–354.

Wade, M. G. (1976). Effects of methylphenidate on motor skill acquisition of hyperactive children. *Journal of Learning Disabilities, 9*, 443–447.

Waizer, J., Hoffman, S., Polizos, R., & Engelhardt, D. (1974). Outpatient treatment of hyperactive school children with imipramine. *American Journal of Psychiatry, 131*, 587–591.

Waizer, J., Polizos, P., Hoffman, S., Engelhardt, D., & Margolis, R. (1972). A single blind evaluation of thiothixene with outpatient schizophrenic children. *Journal of Autism and Childhood Schizophrenia, 2*, 378–386.

Weber, B. A., & Sulzbacher, S. I. (1975). Use of CNS stimulant medication in averaged electroencephalic audiometry with children with MBD. *Journal of Learning Disabilities, 8*, 300–313.

Weingartner, H., Langer, D., Grice, J., & Rapoport, J. (1982). Acquisition and retrieval of information in amphetamine treated hyperactive children. *Journal of Psychiatric Research, 6*, 21–29.

Weiss, B., & Laties, V. (1962). Enhancement of human performance by caffeine and the amphetamines. *Pharmacological Review, 14*, 1–36.

Weiss, G., Minde, K., Douglas, V., Werry, J., & Sykes, D. (1971). Comparison of the effects of chlorpromazine, dextroamphetamine and methylphenidate on the behavior and intellectual functioning of hyperactive children. *Canadian Medical Association Journal, 104*, 20–25.

Weiss, G., Werry, J. S., Minde, K., Douglas, V., & Sykes, D. (1968). Studies on the hyperactive child. V: The effects of dextroamphetamine and chlorpromazine on behavior and intellectual functioning. *Journal of Child Psychology and Psychiatry, 9*, 145–156.

Wender, P. (1971). *Minimal brain dysfunction in children*. New York: Wiley.

Werry, J. S. (Ed.). (1978). *Pediatric psychopharmacology: The use of behavior modifying drugs in children*. New York: Brunner/Mazel.

Werry, J. S. (1982). An overview of pediatric psychopharmacology. *Journal of the American Academy of Child Psychiatry, 21*, 3–9.

Werry, J. S., & Aman, M. G. (1975). Methylphenidate and haloperidol in children: Effects on attention, memory, and activity. *Archives of General Psychiatry, 32,* 790–795.

Werry, J. S., & Aman, M. G. (1984). Methylphenidate in hyperactive and enuretic children. In L. L. Greenhill & B. Shopsin (Eds.), *The psychobiology of childhood: A profile of current issues* (pp. 183–196). New York: SP Medical & Scientific Books.

Werry, J. S., Aman, M., & Lampen, E. (1976). Haloperidol and methylphenidate in hyperactive children. *Acta Paedopsychiatry, 42,* 26–40.

Werry, J. S., & Sprague, R. L. (1974). Methylphenidate in children. Effects of dosage. *Australian and New Zealand Journal of Psychiatry, 8,* 9–19.

Werry, J. S., Weiss, G., Douglas, V., & Martin, J. (1966). Studies on the hyperactive child. III. The effect of chlorpromazine upon behavior and learning ability. *Journal of the American Academy of Child Psychiatry, 5,* 292–312.

Whalen, C. K., Collins, B. E., Henker, B., Alkus, S. R., Adams, D., & Stapp, J. (1978). Behavior observations of hyperactive children and methylphenidate effects in systematically structured classroom environments: Now you see them, now you don't. *Journal of Pediatric Psychology, 3,* 177–187.

Whalen, C. K., & Henker, B. (1976). Psychostimulants and children: A review and analysis. *Psychological Bulletin, 83,* 1113–1130.

Whalen, C. K., Henker, B., & Dotemoto, S. (1980). Methylphenidate and hyperactivity: Effects on teacher behaviors. *Science, 208,* 1280–1282.

Whalen, C. K., Henker, B., & Dotemoto, S. (1981). Teacher response to the methylphenidate (Ritalin) versus placebo status of hyperactive boys in the classroom. *Child Development, 52,* 1005–1014.

Whalen, C. K., Henker, B., & Finck, D. (1981). Medication effects in the classroom: Three naturalistic indicators. *Journal of Abnormal Child Psychology, 9,* 419–433.

Williams, D., Mehl, R., Yudofsky, S., Adams, D., & Roseman, D. (1982). The effects of propranolol on uncontrolled rage outbursts in children and adolescents with organic brain dysfunction. *Journal of the American Academy of Child Psychiatry, 21,* 129–135.

Winsberg, B. G., Bialer, I., Kupietz, S., & Tobias, J. (1972). Effects of imipramine and dextroamphetamine on behavior of neuropsychiatrically impaired children. *American Journal of Psychiatry, 128,* 109–115.

Winsberg, B., Press, M., Bialer, I., & Kupietz, S. L. (1974). Dextroamphetamine and methylphenidate in the treatment of hyperactive/aggressive children. *Journal of Pediatrics, 53,* 236–241.

Wolpert, A., Hagamen, M., & Merlis, S. (1967). A comparison study of thiothixene and trifluoperazine in childhood schizophrenia. *Current Therapy Research, 9,* 482–485.

Yaryuria-Tobias, J. A., Nezuroglu, F. A., & Berman, L. (1976). Chlorimipramine for obsessive-compulsive neurosis. *Current Therapeutic Research, 20,* 541–548.

Yepes, L. E., Balka, E. B., Winsberg, B. G., & Bialer, I. (1977). Amitriptyline and methylphenidate treatment of behaviorally disordered children. *Journal of Child Psychology and Psychiatry, 18,* 39–52.

13 THE TRADITIONAL PSYCHOTHERAPIES

MARIA KOVACS AND STANA PAULAUSKAS

INTRODUCTION

As has been pointed out in earlier chapters, about 12 to 15 percent of children have some type of psychopathological disorder. If the utilization of mental health services among troubled adults is any indication (Shapiro et al., 1984), only a portion of these youngsters receive professional help.

It is safe to say, however, that when the behavior of a child becomes sufficiently disturbing to others, a referral for help is very likely to follow. At that point, one of several things may happen. The professional who evaluates the child may conclude that the youngster does not require treatment. On the other hand, if intervention is indicated, the first decision concerns whether or not the young patient needs hospitalization or residential care. If the nature of the problem suggests that the child can be treated as an outpatient, then in a clinic the case would be assigned to a therapist; in a private practice setting, the practitioner would commence with the treatment.

The treatment may involve a particular form of psychotherapy, behavior therapy, family therapy, or pharmacotherapy, or any combination of the foregoing. Moreover, some psychotherapies and behavioral interventions may be delivered in an individual format—"one-on-one"—or in a group context, and with or without the participation of family members. In theory, treatment options are limited only by the resources and the imagination of the professionals who are involved with the young patient. From a practical standpoint, however, the choice of therapy is probably determined to a considerable extent by the theoretical and experiential background of the therapist *and* the financial status of the child's family.

Notwithstanding the development and proliferation of "newer" interventions over the past 20 years, some type of traditional psychotherapy is probably the most commonly used method with children (Dulcan, 1984; Tuma & Sobotka, 1983). Along with Tuma and Sobotka (1983), by "traditional psychotherapy" or "psychologic therapy" we mean the psychoanalytic, psychodynamically-oriented, relationship, or client-centered therapies and their derivatives.

These therapies have several characteristics in common. They focus on the young patients themselves as persons and are typically delivered in a one-on-one format; they derive from theories that emphasize the developmental, intraindividual, dynamic, and relationship basis of psychopathology as opposed, for example, to principles of learning or social modeling (see Chapter 14); and the quality of the interaction between the young patient and the therapist is an integral aspect of the treatment (Dulcan, 1984; Tuma & Sobotka, 1983). In the broadest sense, then, all of these therapies involve an identified patient and a trained professional, the latter of whom relies on certain interpersonal processes to bring about alterations in the patient's maladaptive or deviant feelings, attitudes, cognitions, or behaviors (Strupp, 1978; Sullivan, 1954).

From the standard clinical perspective, the overall goal of psychotherapy is to ameliorate, resolve, or prevent psychopathological conditions or their manifestations in order to enhance the patient's adaptive functioning. From a social and economic viewpoint, psychotherapy is merely one example of a professional service that is provided to the public for a fee. Therefore, it is important to investigate the effectiveness of these interventions not only because of clinical and scientific considerations but also for the benefit of the consumers of these services.

In light of the foregoing, the present chapter was initially conceptualized as a summary and critique of the studies of traditional psychotherapies that have appeared since the publication of the last major review of this area (Barrett, Hampe, & Miller, 1978). We were particularly interested in the progress that has been made with outpatient populations because they represent the bulk of children who receive mental health care. In order to delimit the scope of the chapter, we decided to focus on school-aged youngsters. And, as commonly accepted, we were going to include a publication in our review only if it met certain minimal scientific criteria, namely: the demographic characteristics, source, presenting problem, or diagnostic makeup of the subject samples were defined; the effectiveness of the traditional therapy was assessed with respect to a comparison treatment or control group; and outcome was measured in a manner that was quantifiable, reliable, and replicable. Then, we conducted a computerized search of the literature by means of the Psychological Abstracts and Index Medicus, starting with the 1977 volumes. Journals of family therapy were perused separately to locate studies that may have compared various interventions with one another. However, we were unable to find even a handful of articles that reported on the effectiveness of some type of traditional psychotherapy in accordance with the criteria that were just outlined.

Because progress in this area has been disappointing and insubstantial, it seemed appropriate to ask "how come?" Are there certain factors or issues that may account for the apparent demise of experimental studies on the outcome of traditional psychotherapies with school-aged children? To approach this issue, we first provide an overview of the evolution of research on child psychotherapy. Then, we address a number of areas that may have been sufficiently problematic to have hindered progress in the field, namely: patient availability, the nature of traditional psychotherapies, developmental considerations in the treatment of children, and the nature of psychiatric diagnosis.

HISTORICAL TRENDS IN RESEARCH ON CHILD PSYCHOTHERAPY

The major review articles of child psychotherapy over the past three decades clearly reveal the changes that have occurred in the field. There has been a growing emphasis on empiricism and scientific rigor in the assessment of treatment outcome. "New" interventions that became legitimized have gradually replaced the traditional therapies. And finally, among the experts, optimism that psychotherapy can ameliorate certain emotional and behavior problems has waxed and waned depending on the evidence that was available at different times and on the persuasiveness of the advocates of the various approaches.

The questions that have been posed by reviewers over the years and the resultant conclusions are probably the best examples of how research in this area has evolved. In earlier evaluations of the available evidence, the basic issue was "Does psychotherapy work?"—and the answer was sobering and unfavorable (Levitt, 1957, 1963). Eventually, however, the question was redefined in a more focused manner, namely, "*what* treatment, by *whom*, is most effective for *this* individual with *that* specific problem, and under *which* set of circumstances?" (Paul, 1967). Thereby, three points became obvious: first, that methodologically inadequate studies cannot provide useful answers about the outcome of psychotherapy; second, that certain basic variables must be operationally defined and measured in order to improve the quality of research; and third, that notwithstanding the difficulties of evaluating treatment results, it is possible to make progress in this area (Hartmann, Roper, & Gelfand, 1977; Paul, 1967).

A Review of Reviews

Levitt's (1957) review was one of the earliest and most influential in the field because it cast doubt on the belief that psychotherapy made a difference in recovery from neurotic disorders. More specifically, he reported that the rate of improvement among youngsters who received psychotherapy (from 67% to 78%) was comparable to the rate of baseline improvement (73%). The latter concept referred to the percentage of cases who improved without treatment or in spite of having terminated their clinic contacts. For his data base, Levitt (1957) used the results of over two dozen studies that were published between 1929 and 1955. The samples were heterogeneous with respect to age (preschoolers to 21-year-olds) and presenting problem ("neuroses"), although reports on "delinquents, mental defectives, and psychotics" were excluded. Outcome was categorized as improved or unimproved based on the evaluation by the therapists at the end of treatment or at follow-up. For his baseline-improvement data, Levitt (1957) relied on figures from two studies.

Not surprisingly, the above conclusion raised much controversy, and a series of "counter" reviews followed. There were several points of contention: (1) the manner in which Levitt (1957) summarized the available data, (2) the generality of the question he posed, and (3) the appropriateness of the control groups from whom the figures of baseline improvement were derived. As Hood-Williams (1960) pointed out, averaging success rates across studies assumes that the studies were similar to one another on variables that may have affected the results. To demonstrate that Levitt's (1957) data base did not meet this assumption, Hood-Williams (1960) reanalyzed some of the figures. He reported that when the studies were categorized as "high success" or "low success," it was evident that they were conducted at different points in time. "High success" projects were generally done prior to the year of 1940, whereas studies that reported "low success" were conducted after 1940. There was, therefore, an apparent cohort effect that may have reflected shifts in the severities of the disorders in the clinical population. And the original publications contained scant information about the lengths of treatment, the background of the therapists, and the severity of the children's presenting problems, each of which may have influenced treatment success. Additionally, Hood-Williams (1960) highlighted that control cases must be selected with greater care because if they differ from the treated cases on salient dimensions (e.g., severity of illness), the interpretation of the results is distorted. It was argued that because Levitt (1957) did not take into account such between-group differences, his method of averaging treatment outcomes had led to an unwarranted conclusion.

Heinicke and Goldman (1960) specifically illustrated that, if the selection of articles were guided by methodological considerations, the psychotherapy literature revealed a more positive trend than Levitt (1957) suggested. They found an 80 percent treatment success rate across 17 studies (conducted between 1933 and 1956) that not only utilized comparable forms of eclectic psychotherapy but also relied on multiple criteria to determine the status of the patients at follow-up. Based on the two best studies that were available, it was also demonstrated that the ratio of fully improved to partly improved cases was much higher in the treated samples than among the "untreated" controls. Then, Heinicke and Goldman (1960) called attention to additional variables that must be considered in the evaluation of outcome research: the diagnoses of the patients, the point in time when treatment effects are assessed, the criteria for improvement, and the characteristics of the young patients' families. And in concluding their review, the authors underscored that the most fruitful question in this field is not whether psychotherapy "works" but rather, "what changes can we observe in a certain kind of child or family which can be attributed to involvement in a certain kind of therapeutic interaction?''

The interaction between psychiatric diagnosis and treatment outcome was the primary focus for Eisenberg and Gruenberg (1961). They noted, for example, that it was comparatively easy to achieve "total or almost total" psychological recovery among children whose "psychogenic disorders" were due to maternal deprivation, if they were provided with adequate substitute objects. It also appeared that, whereas young children with separation anxiety or school phobia were likely to be treatment successes, the outcome of psychotherapy was far less favorable if the youngsters manifested delinquent, hyperkinetic, and sociopathic behaviors. Therefore, if the results of studies are summarized without taking into account diagnostic issues, treatment successes will be masked by the failures that are due to certain disorders.

Notwithstanding the sentiment that failure to detect a positive psychotherapy effect reflected shortcomings in the analytic methods of the reviewer, Levitt's (1963) second article again raised doubts about the viability of these interventions with children. He tallied the results from 22 publications that appeared between 1954 and 1961 and that included an evaluation of outcome at the end of treatment or at follow-up. In response to previous criticisms, he computed separate success rates for five diagnostic or problem groups, namely: psychosis, conduct disorders or aggressive behavior, neurosis, special symptoms such as tics and enuresis, and mixed or unclassified presentations. Once again, however, he reported that, across the various diagnostic groups, the rates of improvement due to treatment (from 55% to 77%) were comparable to the extent of positive outcome (73%) among untreated cases ("baseline" improvement).

More than a decade later, Heinicke and Strassmann (1975) published a detailed rebuttal; they reemphasized that Levitt's (1957, 1963) reviews suffered from analytic flaws because he failed to take into account that the characteristics of both the patients *and* the therapists may have influenced treatment success. Heinicke and Strassmann (1975) specifically underscored that the developmental stage of the child and the attributes of the parents are important variables. They pointed out, for example, that according to at least six studies (published between 1959 and 1968), the availability, support, and mental health of the parents may be prognosticators of good treatment response among the children. Finally, these reviewers were among the first, not only to lament the scant progress in "well-designed and implemented studies" as well as the vague published descriptions of the therapies, but to recommend systematic, standardized research tools to evaluate treatment results.

In subsequent years, the increasing frustration with the quality of the psychotherapy outcome literature led to a new class of review articles that provided guidelines for methodologically sound investigations. In their extensive chapter, Hartmann et al. (1977), for example, allocated only a few pages to reviewing the status of various interventions. Instead, they focused on the major measurement and design issues that treatment researchers must face. Aside from discussing in detail the importance of variables already mentioned (e.g., proper control groups, the background of the therapists, psychometrically sound measures), they emphasized the need for the following: patient selection according to inclusionary and exclusionary criteria, random assignment to treatment, a focus on limited target behaviors in setting treatment goals, and the use of measures that assess various areas of functioning. Moreover, they recommended that the proper application of data-analytic techniques be balanced by an awareness that statistically significant results and clinically relevant findings do not necessarily go hand in hand.

Although Barrett et al. (1978) concurred that not much was to be gained from reworking old data on the outcomes of traditional interventions, they did examine the evidence in support of play therapy. Based on articles published between 1945 and 1972, it did appear that, with children of various ages and difficulties, play therapy was associated with improved skills or social adjustment. Barrett et al. (1978) also illustrated that even a methodologically sound investigation does not yield readily interpretable results: in their own study of phobic children, the effects of the treatments varied depending on the source of the outcome ratings that were analyzed (parents vs. researcher) and as a function of the ages of the young patients. In closing, these reviewers reiterated the importance of many of the methodological issues that were discussed by Hartmann et al. (1977); underscored the salience of chronological age in regard to outcome; and noted that the long-term effects of psychological interventions must be also examined.

With the passage of time, the "newer" therapies—family, group, and the cognitive-behavior therapies—became accepted and their impact became evident. The reviews focused more and more on specific interventions, and outcome was linked increasingly to particular diagnoses or presenting problems. Wells and Dezen (1978), for example, were concerned solely with the literature on the nonbehavioral family therapies, published between 1971 and 1976. They noted that the clinical (uncontrolled) evidence in favor of these interventions was strongest with children and adolescents who had psychosomatic reactions or moderate degrees of disturbance. According to controlled studies, however, the family therapies, alternate treatments, or no "formal" treatment all had similar outcomes. Not surprisingly, these reviewers also concluded their article with a discussion of research problems that have beset the field of family therapy.

From the late 1970s onward, the legacy of Hartmann et al. (1977), namely, sophisticated criticism and attention to methodological concerns, became a standard part of the evaluative literature. The hard-nosed empiricism also reflected the fact that improved research methods and tools had become available. Although, once again, many experts became optimistic about the effects of psychological interventions with children, much of this sentiment derived from the study of nontraditional therapies and their applications in controlled environments (e.g., inpatient units or school settings). For example, for his conclusion that, with children and adolescents aged 12 to 18, psychotherapy was superior to "no therapy" (75% vs. 39% median success rates, respectively), Tramontana (1980) relied on 33 studies that were published between 1967 and 1977. In the clinical, uncontrolled studies, group psychotherapy was used most often, and the cases were outpatients as well as institutionalized or noninstitutionalized delinquents. Most of the experimental investigations reported on the use of group therapy with delinquent boys; however, individual therapy, behavior modification, and transactional analysis were also represented. Although only five studies met the author's criteria for scientific rigor, he noted that outcome was apparently influenced by diagnosis. Neurotic youngsters seemed to do well with or without therapy; patients with psychotic or personality disturbances did poorly or unpredictably; and treatment response was typically unfavorable among children whose disorders started early or insidiously.

Shortly thereafter, Rutter (1982) concurred that "*some* psychological therapies can and do influence children's maladaptive behavior in beneficial ways" (p. 733). Along with Tramontana (1980), he based his conclusions mostly on studies that used the "newer" therapies to ameliorate particular complaints. He noted that, for children who were deviant as compared to their peers, school-based group therapy and behavior modification offered greater benefits than no treatment; that the medical condition of youngsters with asthma improved as a consequence of family psychotherapy; and that, compared to standard clinical services, the families of autistic children clearly profited from a home-based behaviorally targeted program. Rutter (1982) also underscored some negative trends. Long-term, unfocused psychotherapy or counseling, for example, has not been effective with delinquent and conduct disordered children. Likewise, there has been scant evidence in favor of supportive therapy for enuresis or insight-oriented psychotherapy with young, autistic children.

Without belaboring the point, we close this section by noting that the emphases on specific types of patients, particular classes of therapies, and methodological concerns continue to be hallmarks of recent evaluative reviews. Urbain and Kendall's (1980) article, for example, focused on social-cognitive and self-control skills training with various populations but for specific target behaviors such as impulsivity, aggressiveness, or social isolation. Putallaz and Gottman (1983) evaluated the usefulness of direct instruction or "coaching" to ameliorate deficits in social skills. Dulcan (1984) focused her entire article on the effectiveness of brief psychotherapy. Inevitably, the conclusions have been cautiously optimistic and qualified; for instance, whereas brief psychotherapy appears to be beneficial, such an effect is most likely if the young patient is motivated and generally well-integrated (Dulcan, 1984). And finally, although psychotherapy research with children supposedly has unique problems because of the developmental stage and socially dependent nature of its target population (Heinicke & Strassmann, 1975; Rutter, 1982), it is curious that one of the most recent reviews (Shaffer, 1984) was organized along methodological considerations that have emerged almost exclusively from research on the treatment of disturbed *adults*.

An Integrated Perspective

As viewed through the eyes of experts in the field, the historical trends in child psychotherapy research permit a number of conclusions. All in all, it is quite obvious that, although the call to arms was sounded close to 20 years ago, we still do not have sufficient information about what psychotherapy works best for certain children under particular circumstances (see also Chapter 15).

First, the effectiveness of the various psychological interventions as compared to one another is one of the most poorly understood areas. The evidence has not been convincing that Therapy A is substantially better than Therapy B or Therapy C for the treatment of outpatients of school age. There has been particularly strong disagreement in regard to the efficacy of traditional psychotherapies. Although critical re-reviews, partial reviews, or selective reviews of this area have alleged that by "cutting the pie" in a different fashion, positive treatment effects are discerned more readily, this has really not been the case. Instead, the latter body of literature has primarily documented that, as an interpersonal process, psychotherapy takes place in the context of the child's social and familial environment, aspects of which have impact on the likelihood of clinical improvement. Consequently, such variables must be taken into account in treatment outcome research.

On the other hand, the evidence is reasonably impressive that the nature of the child's disorder plays a role in the response to treatment. That is, youngsters with certain disorders are not likely to manifest significant changes in their behavior as a consequence of psychotherapy. Taken together with the natural history and phenomenology of some psychopathological conditions, such a trend is not surprising. For example, longitudinal follow-up studies of youngsters have documented that conduct disorders are likely to persist over time and are often associated with poor outcome in adulthood (see Chapter 2). Likewise, the diagnosis of attention deficit disorder among children typically signals continued significant problems in adolescence and in adulthood (see Chapter 4). Additionally, because children who are psychotic or autistic manifest a profound impairment in their ability to perceive the world as others do and to act in accordance with age-appropriate and socially accepted norms, it could be posited, a priori, that their response to psychotherapy would be poor, if any. Therefore, whereas traditional Therapy A may not be any more effective than Therapy B or Therapy C, it does appear that children with Condition X and those with Condition Y should be differentiated from one another in the assessment of treatment outcome.

The circumstances under which certain children may or may not respond to psychotherapy represents another area that has not been well understood or thoroughly investigated. This state of affairs may reflect that the word *circumstance* or *condition* refers to a multitude of social, familial, environmental, or illness-related variables, many of which cannot be measured adequately or controlled experimentally. Attention has been paid to one type of circumstance, however, namely, the treatment setting. Unfortunately, the impact of the latter on treatment response cannot be interpreted easily. This is because the setting in which the child is treated is usually confounded by the nature and severity of the child's disorder. Nonetheless, the inclination to conduct research in schools (Chapter 16), inpatient units, or residential institutions (Chapter 15) could suggest that (1) the settings have been purposefully chosen to control environmental variables or (2) the investigators have found it expedient to work with captive populations under circumstances that allow some control over patient compliance to a protocol.

Our overview of the literature has also revealed that as soon as experts in the field agreed that methodologically sound studies were needed, their task became twofold: to outline and illustrate the characteristics of a good investigation and to encourage researchers to implement such designs. We have found no recent evidence, however, of substantial activity in the investigation of traditional psychotherapies with children. Our impression of an overall lack of research progress is not new; similar sentiments were expressed by Heinicke and Strassmann in 1975 and by Barrett et al. in 1978. This situation contrasts sharply with continued developments regarding the behavioral interventions (Chapter 14), their cognitive-therapy derivatives, and the group and family therapies.

Clinical, practical, social, and economic considerations have probably all contributed to the stagnation of research on the traditional therapies. For example, there have been gradual but clear shifts in concepts of child psychopathology and in professional views concerning the goals of treatment (Rutter, 1982). Economic factors have encouraged a move toward brief or crisis-oriented therapies (Dulcan, 1984). Because it is beyond the scope of the present chapter to discuss this area in its entirety, however, in the following sections we focus on a few issues that may have been particularly problematic.

WHY DON'T WE KNOW MORE ABOUT THE EFFECTIVENESS OF THE TRADITIONAL PSYCHOTHERAPIES?

We do not know enough about the effectiveness of the traditional therapies with children because there has not been a sufficiently large volume of well-designed studies. In our opinion, the following four issues may have had a particularly negative impact on the field: (1) the demands for very complex and sophisticated treatment protocols, (2) the apparently elusive nature of some traditional psychotherapies, (3) the developmental characteristics of the subject populations, and (4) disagreements and uncertainties in regard to psychiatric diagnosis.

The Research Design and the Problem of Subject Availability

In his historic article on strategies of outcome research in psychotherapy, Paul (1967) delineated the salient issues and noted that every investigation must control, describe, or measure the critical variables. Hartmann et al. (1977), who specifically addressed the field of child psychotherapy, advised, however, that researchers should not be intimidated by the existing methodological problems.

Nonetheless, in view of the labor-intensive nature of psychotherapy and the number of factors that must be controlled or manipulated in a study, it is no wonder that investigators have not risen to the challenge! For example, sample sizes are of utmost importance because conclusions about the interventions are based on the responses of subject *groups*. Therefore, the samples have to be sufficiently large to accommodate attrition or "drop-outs" (about one-third, Levitt, 1957). In other words, there must be enough cases at the end of the study (from 15 to 20 for each intervention) in order to draw valid conclusions.

The samples should be homogeneous, or similar to one another, with respect to variables that may affect the outcome of the study. For example, the children's chronological age is important because it may influence psychological accessibility to an intervention. The "experimental" group and the control or comparison group should be equivalent on pertinent clinical variables. In the latter category, the severity of the presenting problems and their durations may be particularly critical.

Decisions must be made about which therapy will be tested and about how to assure that the therapists do what they are supposed to do. The therapists should be similar to one another with respect to professional degrees and clinical experience. The number of treatment contacts and their frequencies have to be standardized. The duration of the interventions must be sufficient to allow one to detect treatment effects, but short enough so as not to be confounded by developmental changes that normally characterize juveniles.

Issues of measurement are no less important. At which time should treatment effects be assessed? Although, at the very least, it is necessary to determine the subjects' status at baseline and at the end of treatment, follow-up evaluations are also advisable. What areas of functioning should be monitored and how? Are there standardized, psychometric instruments that are pertinent to the goals of the study? In addition, outcome should be examined from several perspectives. Thus, clinical staff who conduct the evaluations must be blind to the nature of the therapy the subjects are receiving. It is a good idea to get ratings from the children's parents as well, but which parent—the mother, the father, or both? And if it is possible to gather evaluations from teachers, which teachers should be asked?

The major methodological issues have been discussed in detail in Chapter 11 and by others, and the reader may refer to them for further information (for example, Barrett et al., 1978; Hartmann et al., 1977). It is notable, however, that the range of general problems in research with children does not differ substantially from the concerns that have beset treatment outcome studies with adults (Gottman & Markman, 1978; Paul, 1967). And yet research with adults has continued to flourish. We propose, therefore, that with juvenile populations, *specific* variables (such as *lack of patients*) are most likely to account for the absence of progress.

Although reliable data on the prevalence of psychopathological disorders among school-aged youngsters are just beginning to accumulate, there is considerable clinical consensus in two regards: psychiatric illness is probably not as frequent among children as it is among adults, and distressed juveniles are less likely to be referred for ambulatory care than their adult counterparts. Therefore, mental health clinics may not have a sufficiently large population of children to support continuous research endeavors. Because psychotherapy outcome studies have been traditionally conducted in *clinics*, and because there is no reason to believe that the prevalence of and treatment-seeking for child psychopathologies have significantly changed, this problem is likely to continue.

Lack of patient availability is compounded by the referral patterns that have been observed in child guidance and child psychiatric clinics. Such agencies have predominantly male clientele; boys outnumber girls by a ratio of three to one. Moreover, boys are typically brought for treatment because of their conduct, whereas girls are more often referred for emotional problems. And as we have seen in Chapter 3, certain disorders—for instance, obsessive compulsive disorder—are infrequent. Such factors further reduce the likelihood of finding sufficiently large and diagnostically homogeneous samples for outpatient psychotherapy research.

The increasing utilization of nonclinic recruitment sites appears to support the thesis that the outpatient pool of youngsters is smaller than desirable. In contrast, schools, inpatient units, or residential institutions provide researchers with sizable samples. A school, for example, allows immediate access to a large cohort. And subject selection is facilitated by teachers who can pinpoint children for a particular study (see, for example, Kendall & Zupan, 1981). In any case, although the foregoing settings may be better sources of subjects than clinics, clinic and nonclinic samples are probably not comparable to one another.

But lack of subjects cannot explain entirely the shortfall of psychotherapy research with children. We can only speculate about other factors that may have contributed. For example, interest in the psychological welfare of children was first formalized through the Child Guidance movement of the 1920s (Sears, 1975); thus, the field is relatively new and "immature." Furthermore, the success of the behavioral interventions with children in recent decades may have shunted manpower and research interest away from the more traditional therapies. Additionally, the clinics wherein traditional therapies were favored probably did not provide a climate conducive to research. Finally, the *nature* of the traditional therapies themselves may have played a role in discouraging their empiric study, as we now discuss.

The Traditional Psychotherapies

According to Tuma and Sobotka (1983), psychoanalysis, psychoanalytically oriented psychotherapy, relationship therapy, structured play therapy, and client-centered therapy represent the traditional interventions for children. Their theoretical foundations and clinical approaches also qualify transactional analysis and modifications of Beck's (1976) cognitive therapy for use with children (DiGiuseppe, 1981), among others, as traditional therapies.

To examine the efficacy of psychotherapy, the researcher has a two-fold task: to define the treatment as precisely as possible, and to make sure that the therapists do their work in a uniform fashion. However, to an empirically oriented investigator, the traditional therapies and their goals were probably too diffuse and esoteric. Therefore, these interventions may have been bypassed for study because they did not readily lend themselves to systematic description and standard application. The following selective overview underscores the methodological issues in this regard.

Tuma and Sobotka (1983) consider *psychoanalysis* to be the prototype of the traditional therapies that are currently used with children. Within this framework, the patient's problems are traced back to early, unconscious, developmental issues that have not been resolved. In the context of the analytic relationship, including "transference," the child is expected to achieve insight into and work through his or her conflicts and thereby reach a new level of psychic functioning. The analyst facilitates this process by establishing proper communication with the youngster and by using techniques such as reflection, labeling, and, most of all, interpretation of play productions, daydreams, or nightdreams. Because it is taken for granted that children do not readily acknowledge their problems and may be unmotivated to change, much energy and time are expended to build a therapeutic alliance.

In his case report of a six-year-old girl who was enuretic and "babyish," Feigelson (1977) underscored the essential characteristics of child analysis. Over the period of the first one-and-a-half years, the young patient was seen four to five times per week. During the sessions, the analyst interpreted her defenses and resistance, did not gratify her transference wishes, but attended to and respected the child's developmental stage. Play was used as the natural medium of communication. The youngster's initial willingness to deal with her symptoms and defenses, and then, to move on to "Oedipal and primal scene themes" were cited as examples of the process that is necessary to achieve a "higher level of psychic organization."

Sherick, Kearney, Buxton, and Stevens (1978) reported that with children who had deficient egos, traditional, interpretive methods had detrimental results. They described, therefore, the use of adjunctive "ego-strengthening techniques" with four cases. The children were treated for variable lengths of time; at least one was in analysis for three-and-a-half years. The case histories served to buttress the thesis that, if a child has impaired reality testing, poor impulse control, and insufficient secondary process thinking, the techniques in question are useful adjuncts in analysis; they support the healthy aspects of the self and temper the potentially negative effects of interpretation. With one child, various techniques were used to discourage his excessive supernatural and aggressive fantasies and to foster his "allegiance to reality" instead. For example, the youngster was provided with cutout drawings of monsters—their imaginary qualities were reemphasized; then they were confined to a locker to be let out only at the proper time, that is, at Halloween.

An intervention that has been labeled *short-term psychodynamic psychotherapy*, time-limited or elective brief psychotherapy, or focused dynamic psychotherapy (among others) is another type of traditional psychotherapy (Dulcan, 1984; Tuma & Sobotka, 1983). Because all forms of this intervention derive from the analytic schools, it is presumed that the young patient is not conscious of the nature of his or her problems. Therefore, the salient therapeutic techniques are interpretation and clarification of symptoms and defenses, in accordance with a psychodynamic understanding of the patient. However, these targeted therapies have several features that distinguish them from their predecessors. Early on, the therapist focuses on one problem or symptom; the number of sessions is limited; treatment length rarely exceeds several months; the therapist is fairly active; and the goals are directed toward specific symptoms or ego functions rather than toward reworking the entire personality.

Turecki (1982) reported on the use and efficacy of elective brief psychotherapy with seven children who were 10 to 17 years old. The sessions were limited (from 6 to 14) and the therapists, who were child psychiatric fellows, apparently followed certain guidelines. The latter included the use of a psychodynamic formulation to select a focus for treatment, staying with the focus, establishing a positive relationship, and being particularly alert to issues of termination. "Beyond this the therapists were given carte blanche as to how to conduct the therapy" (Turecki, 1982). For example, a 12-year-old boy's chronic disruptiveness and defiance were formulated to be the expressions of unresolved, traumatic losses that occurred when he was five years old, among which the death of his mother was the most painful. Therefore, the focus of the therapy was to help the child to deal with his feelings in that regard. This goal was apparently achieved "through the process of affective remembering." The author stated that, at the end of treatment, all seven patients were rated by their therapists as "symptomatically improved." Four children were reinterviewed two-and-a-half years later. Based on their own and their parents' accounts, three of them were judged to have maintained their improvements, whereas one youngster had again deteriorated.

Tuma and Sobotka (1983) described three other traditional psychotherapies: client-centered or nondirective therapy, relationship therapy, and structured play therapy. There is no convincing evidence, however, that structured play therapy is a distinct treatment with a corresponding theory of psychopathology. Rather, structured or unstructured play is a *technique* that serves various purposes. For example, in child analysis, the young patient's play activities during the sessions are viewed as symbolic expressions of his or her conflicts. The analyst therefore interprets the play productions accordingly (Feigelson, 1977). Because youngsters "resist" direct discussion of their problems, play may be also used in brief psychotherapy. The child *and* the therapist interact in a structured fashion by means of a series of drawing games; thereby, both communication and problem resolution are facilitated (Claman, 1980). Play activities, including drawing pictures, modeling with clay or putty, and making up tales or stories, seem to be used most commonly, however, with children who are unable to express their feelings and concerns because they lack the needed skills or are unwilling to do so for fear of the consequences (Elitzur, 1978; Ramon & Baharav, 1978; Remotigue-Ano, 1980; Wenger, 1982).

Our computer search did not yield any recent articles that described the efficacy of relationship therapy (Tuma & Sobotka, 1983) with children. And we found only one study in which client-centered or *nondirective therapy* was used, but it was the treatment control condition (Michelson, et al. 1983)! Because it served to control for "therapist contact, nonspecific treatment factors, history and maturational effects," the investigators evidently believed that nondirective therapy was not a highly viable intervention.

It is not surprising, therefore, that Michelson et al. (1983) gave a very scant description of nondirective therapy. According to the article, its goal was "to promote the open expression of feelings." In order to achieve that, the therapists scheduled weekly activities in the context of which they employed the techniques of reflection, clarification, and interpretation. Eight-to 12-year-old boys who were referred to a child psychiatric clinic because of "social adjustment disorders" were randomly assigned to the control condition or to one of two experimental treatments. The cases were seen for 12 weekly one-hour sessions using a group therapy format. Interestingly, post-treatment and follow-up comparisons on paper-and-pencil scales and observational measures did not find significant between-group differences. According to some analyses, however, there were a few areas in which the controls did not do as well as the other children.

The great majority of clinicians probably view themselves as *eclectic* in their theoretic and treatment approaches. Such a stance can refer to any combination of philosophies and strategies. Although none of the recent reviewers of the field have mentioned eclecticism as a form of traditional psychotherapy (Dulcan, 1984; Shaffer, 1984; Tuma & Sobotka, 1983), there are numerous examples of it in the literature. But because eclecticism has always gotten "bad press" from researchers and reviewers alike, it is notable that this label does not appear in the articles. Only upon reading the description of the therapy does its eclectic nature become evident.

The work of Rosenheim and Ichilov (1979) exemplifies this approach. They studied short-term (three- to four-month), goal-oriented psychotherapy with the children of fatally ill parents. The treatment sought to provide the youngsters with "an open opportunity for catharsis"—a goal derived from psychodynamic formulations. The children were also helped to evaluate their inner and outer realities in a more realistic fashion and to formulate alternative actions in regard to problems; the latter goals therefore combined approaches from the targeted brief psychotherapies and the non-traditional social-problem-solving interventions. The use of "occasional environmental manipulation" exemplified a combination of social case work and behavior modification. Children were accepted into the study if they were 10 to 14 years old, had no history of psychopathology, and were aware of the gravity of their parent's condition. The 24 cases were randomly assigned to the experimental treatment or to a control condition (which was not described). The therapy involved 10 to 12 individual weekly sessions in each child's home by a therapist who was a psychology graduate student. Standardized assessments of levels of anxiety and of social and scholastic functioning revealed that the treated cases did significantly better than the controls.

Verbal and experiential psychotherapy, as described by Lockwood (1981), is another example of an eclectic approach. Her assumptions, that intrapsychic needs and existential interactions are equally important in the therapy process and that children can borrow "ego strength" from others, reflect the tenets of psychodynamic and relationship therapy. Her use of role-playing, psychodrama, and actual interactions to teach problem-solving strategies mirror a merger of techniques and philosophies from the social-behavioral and psychodynamic schools of thought. And the author's expectations that youngsters have certain cognitive abilities and can label affective experiences derive from the experimental literature on child development.

To document the effects of verbal experiential psychotherapy on the symptoms and overall adjustment of moderately to severely disturbed outpatients, a post hoc follow-up study was conducted. A sample of 25 children, 9 to 13 years old, were treated over a period of 2 to 24 months; the therapy was delivered in group sessions each of which lasted one-and-a-half hours. Six months after the end of treatment, various informants were interviewed to obtain their assessments of the children's status. Composite ratings revealed that over three-fourths of the cases were judged improved (Lockwood, 1981).

During our overview of the literature, we found a predominance of case presentations, clinical descriptions, and quasi-experimental studies. And even when the authors attempted to present treatment outcome in a scientific fashion, it was difficult to interpret the results because the behavior of the therapists was not standardized. For example, Turecki (1982) provided his clinicians only with general guidelines concerning the conduct of brief, psychodynamic psychotherapy—then they were given "carte blanche." Therefore, there was no compelling evidence that the successes resulted from the application of *that* intervention rather than from the use of whatever strategies the therapists may have devised on their own. Likewise, there did not appear to be rules about ways to manage issues of termination. Therefore, the results could neither prove nor disprove the author's claim that the one failure he described was due, in fact, to the therapist's inability to handle the patient's potential conflicts about termination (Turecki, 1982).

Furthermore, the extant reports do not include sufficient details about the traditional interventions to allow replications. Rosenheim and Ichilov (1979), for example, provided scant information about their goal-oriented psychotherapy, the techniques that were used, and the topical areas that were permissible. Nor did they describe how salient goals were accomplished—what did the therapist do to provide "an open opportunity for catharsis," for instance? Because Lockwood's (1981) article conveyed a similar lack of specificity, one can readily imagine that no other study could deliver the verbal experiential therapy in the manner that she and her therapists did.

It is clear from the foregoing that the "hard core" empirically oriented investigators have not been interested in the traditional therapies. This may reflect a change in professional views about what psychopathology is and what ought to be done about it—just as Rutter (1982) has proposed. In our opinion, however, pragmatic issues have also contributed to the somewhat restricted research emphasis of recent years. Namely, those interventions received the greatest attention that were brief and circumscribed, or readily lent themselves to the construction of treatment manuals.

The use of treatment manuals has, in fact, become one of the hallmarks of an empirically sound study. They have been pioneered by researchers in the field of adult psychiatry in order to facilitate the study of psychotherapy outcome (Beck, Rush, Shaw, & Emery, 1979; Klerman & Weissman, 1982). A treatment manual consists of a detailed exposition of the nature of a therapy and its goals. It provides guidelines as to what the therapist must do in order to achieve those goals. It also specifies the intervention strategies that are permissible, the conditions under which they are applied, and how they are tailored to target symptoms or particular complaints. Because a manual basically provides an operational description of an intervention to which clinicians must adhere, its use in research maximizes the likelihood that the therapy is delivered in a standardized fashion and allows others to replicate a study.

Such manuals have not been developed for the traditional therapies with children, however. Perhaps researchers were intimidated by the broad conceptual schemas and the often complex techniques that characterize the traditional interventions. Perhaps the practical problems in trying to operationalize these therapies seemed excessive. In any case, the lack of treatment manuals has clearly undermined progress in the field.

Developmental Considerations in the Use of the Traditional Therapies

The study of the traditional therapies also may have been hindered because it is difficult to translate some of their aspects into *developmentally* suitable terms. This methodological concern is readily illustrated by the concept that psychotherapy is a special case of interpersonal dialogue (Strupp, 1978;

Sullivan, 1954). The distinguishing features of this dialogue not only define the therapeutic relationship but are also presumed to facilitate the process of change. More specifically, psychotherapy entails (1) a patient who is troubled, distressed, or otherwise impaired psychologically, interpersonally, or socially, who therefore desires relief and is willing to change on some level and to some extent, and (2) the therapist, who is a trained expert, whose job it is to help the patient to resolve his or her problems and to provide relief thereby. The uniqueness of the relationship allows the patient to trust and have confidence in the therapist; this is necessary for self-disclosure, *and* it enables the patient to persist in the search for recovery.

Based on their clinical experiences, therapists have long recognized, however, that children may have trouble perceiving the foregoing "adult-like" but necessary features of psychotherapy; therefore, they are less likely to play their roles in the expected fashion. For example, it is commonly known that youngsters rarely self-identify as patients. In fact, because they do not typically initiate their own treatment referrals, they probably experience the process as coercive and anxiety-producing. Moreover, as a rule, children are unwilling to acknowledge that they have a problem. It is particularly difficult to establish a trusting relationship with them because they do not readily recognize the special nature of the therapeutic situation and its distinctiveness from other adult–child hierarchical relationships (Claman, 1980; Cramer, 1980; Feigelson, 1977; Simmons, 1981; Tuma & Sobotka, 1983).

Therefore, clinicians have long sought to raise the awareness of young patients to an "adult-like" appreciation of the therapeutic alliance. To achieve this goal, various direct or indirect techniques have been proposed. For example, according to Cramer (1980), the child must be told in advance that the clinician is a person who is "sincerely interested in helping." Furthermore, the young patient must be also reassured that "the danger of trusting other adults does not exist with him [the clinician]." In a similar spirit, Claman (1980) described several strategies that can be used by the therapist in order to overcome the "resistance" of youngsters when they are expected to discuss directly their problems and concerns.

There is no compelling evidence, however, that the foregoing strategies are successful in achieving the stated goals. In fact, the available research findings indicate that a child's stage of cognitive and social development will be the limiting factor on his or her ability to acknowledge personal problems, to trust the therapist, and to view the therapist as a competent and professional helping agent. Therefore, children may differ qualitatively in their perceptions of salient therapeutic constructs because of the developmental progression of pertinent capacities.

For example, in order to operationalize the unique, distinguishing features of psychotherapy, it would have to be taken into account that the recognition of psychopathology unfolds gradually with age. There is a substantial body of research that bears on this issue. One group of investigators found that, when fourth- and sixth-grade students were presented with vignettes of imaginary peers, the older children were the ones who were more likely to detect the presence of emotional disturbance (Marsden & Kalter, 1976; Marsden, Kalter, Plunkett, & Barr-Grossman, 1977). Coie and Pennington (1976) reported that when first, fourth, seventh, and eleventh graders were compared to one another, the youngest ones had the greatest difficulty in seeing psychopathology for what it was—namely, deviant behavior. Only the oldest subjects recognized that deviance reflected a person's failure to fulfill prevailing social definitions of psychological stability.

Children's perception of the *causes* of deviance is subject to a developmental progression as well. For example, it has been reported that 9- to 13-year-olds generally attributed psychological and behavioral problems to environmental and social factors such as watching too much TV or people being mean (Roberts, Beidleman, & Wurtele, 1981). Children and adolescents who attended outpatient clinics also felt that their problems were due mostly to external causes, and they made such attributions to a greater extent than did their parents (Compas, Friedland-Bandes, Bastien, & Adelman, 1981). Likewise, in a study of fifth through twelfth graders, Dollinger, Thelen, and Walsh (1980) found that all their subjects conceptualized psychological problems *primarily* from a social perspective, that is, as arising from familial, marital, or interpersonal conflicts. With increasing age, however, the subjects were more and more likely to define problems in terms of "internal" dimensions such as one's feelings, moods, and cognitions.

Furthermore, it is questionable whether younger children view trust in the way adults do, or whether they recognize its role in the therapeutic situation. The evidence indicates that notions of trust progress developmentally from physicalistic, to behavioral, to interpersonal, and finally to psychological-interpersonal definitions (Selman, Jaquette, & Redman-Lavin, 1977). Therefore, probably only adolescent and older patients are able to acknowledge that trust, as a *psychological* construct, is a salient aspect of psychotherapy. It has been reported, for example, that adolescents who viewed their outpatient experience as having been helpful did note that trust was an integral part of it (Meyer & Zegans, 1975). Chassin, Young, and Light (1980) found that both delinquent institutionalized adolescents and similarly aged psychiatrically disturbed inpatients preferred warm and trusting therapeutic relationships (see also Chapter 15). And the latter youngsters were particularly likely to endorse "traditional" notions of therapy.

Children's concepts of help and of a helping agent also suggest that their perceptions and the expectations of therapists may be at odds. For the younger ones, "being helped" probably denotes some form of direct action. And only with increasing age do youngsters recognize that indirect methods, such as giving advice or discussing problems, are potent and appropriate ways to assist (Barnett, Darcie, Holland, & Kobasigawa, 1982; Roberts et al., 1981). For example, Barnett et al. (1982) found that six-year-olds cited global traits ("nice," "kind") and specific behaviors ("plays with me," "buys us stuff") as the characteristics of good helpers. References to competence (knows what to do) began to appear among the third graders. But the sixth graders were the most likely to recognize that willingness to help and empathic ability were necessary attributes of a good helper.

As this overview suggests, there are developmental constraints on the ability to perceive presumably salient aspects of psychotherapy and to fulfill one's "role" accordingly. Likewise, there are probably qualitative differences among young patients with respect to their understanding of and compliance with *specific* traditional therapeutic strategies. Therefore, the operational description of a therapy would have to include age-appropriate definitions of salient constructs and developmentally suitable therapeutic techniques. In light of the difficulties inherent in such an undertaking, the lack of treatment manuals is not surprising.

Diagnostic Considerations

As we already noted, by the late 1970s there was considerable evidence that treatment response was influenced by the nature of the children's psychopathology or diagnosis. Since that time, however, there has not been much progress in regard to how different *types* of juvenile patients respond to the traditional psychotherapies. Unfortunately, researchers may have been discouraged from using diagnosis as a subject selection criterion for a psychotherapy study. This situation may have arisen because of disagreements about the role of diagnosis, the appropriateness of the official nomenclature—the DSM-III (APA, 1980)—and the problems of trying to standardize the diagnostic process already discussed in Chapter 1.

Instead, in most of the recent articles on the traditional therapies, the authors used presenting problems and clinical (as opposed to diagnostic) constructs to describe their patients. And even when the relevant information was provided, there were rarely any details as to how and by whom the diagnoses were ascertained. For example, in his report, Feigelson (1977) mentioned only that his patient was referred for analysis because of "enuresis" and "babyish" behavior toward her mother. The youngsters who were treated by Sherick et al. (1978) were referred for a variety of reasons including "aggressive" or "self-injurious" behavior as well as "solitariness and crying episodes," but all of them allegedly had "deficient" ego structures. In describing the children in her study, Lockwood (1981) stated that they had "moderate to severe" psychopathology. Although the author also noted that there was high interrater agreement on "specific diagnosis," she did not report which disorders were present or how the diagnoses were derived.

Turecki (1982) noted that elective brief psychotherapy was particularly appropriate for children who had reactive disorders or those who had suffered an object loss, but he failed to provide diagnostic data on his patients. Instead, he stated that his sample was referred for a variety of problems including "chronic disruptiveness and defiance," as well as "incestuous activity." Michelson et al. (1983) did note that their cases were diagnosed by a clinical assessment team as manifesting "social-adjustment disorders with chief complaints of dysfunctional peer relations, social-skill deficits and social rejection" and that children with "psychosis, organic brain syndrome, mental retardation or severe antisocial tendencies" were excluded. Whereas their exclusionary criteria, therefore, did involve diagnoses, the inclusionary criteria were *not* stated in current nosologic terms.

There have been recent articles that did refer to specific psychiatric diagnostic entities. As a rule, however, these publications were either case reports or studies of some nontraditional therapy. For example, Elitzur (1978) described a short-term treatment for young patients who suffered from phobic disorders. In their study of a nontraditional intervention, Hinshaw, Whalen, and Henker (1984) selected their subjects based on physicians' diagnoses of "hyperactivity, hyperkinesis, or attention deficit disorder with hyperactivity," and pertinent anamnestic data. Finally, Schoettle (1980) chose an 11-year-old hospitalized boy "with the diagnosis of anorexia nervosa with associated depression" in order to illustrate the use of guided imagery as a therapeutic technique.

It is notable, however, that the better empirical studies of the past few years bypassed psychiatric diagnosis as a subject selection criterion. Instead, there has been a growing tendency to define patient *types* by means of specific symptoms or in accordance with cutoff scores on standardized psychometric scales. Whereas the foregoing selection approaches are methodologically sound, they unfortunately provide scant information about the nature of the patients' disorders. In recent controlled investigations, most of which utilized the nontraditional therapies, subjects were selected, for instance, if they manifested behaviors such as lack of self-control that interfered with their functioning in the classroom (Kendall & Zupan, 1981); observable conduct problems (Bell, Mundy, & Quay, 1983); aggressivity (Garrison & Stolberg, 1983); social withdrawal (Edleson & Rose, 1981); or other overt examples of social dysfunction (Michelson et al., 1983).

The psychopathological condition from which a child suffers cannot be inferred automatically, however, from one or more target behaviors or from the complaint with which the family presents for treatment. For instance, whereas behaviors such as disobedience, temper tantrums, or impulsivity are primarily associated with conduct disorder, they *can* be observed among children who have various diagnoses including major depressive disorder, attention deficit disorder, or developmental delay (APA, 1980; Kovacs & Beck, 1977; Puig-Antich, 1982). Indeed, Kendall and Zupan's (1981) sample, which was homogeneous with respect to problems of self-control, did include various clinical-diagnostic pictures, namely, "acting-out, aggressive hyperactive, and conduct problem type children." Therefore, insofar as the basic disorder dominates treatment response and long-term outcome, rather than particular symptoms (Rutter, 1982), studies that ignore diagnoses yield meager information about what type of treatment works best for what kind of patient.

SUMMARY

Since the 1970s, the study of the traditional psychotherapies with outpatient juveniles has been on the decline. Concomitantly, there has been scant progress in regard to which therapy works best for what type of child under what circumstances. In the present chapter, we focused on a number of issues that may have been particularly responsible for the lack of empirical data on these interventions.

Notwithstanding such a state of affairs, it is our opinion that the traditional therapies are here to stay—if not in their original, unadulterated forms, then in some modified versions. These systems of psychotherapy will continue to attract laymen and professionals alike, and they will remain the choice of intervention for many clinicians. The staying power of the traditional therapies reflect, in part, their overall appeal; they seem to do justice to the complexity of human nature to a greater extent than many newer or behaviorally oriented interventions. Furthermore, their explanations of the causes of psychopathology and their emphasis on the devastating personal impact of psychiatric illness are familiar because they are mirrored in other aspects of our culture: in the arts, in literature, in existential philosophy, and in some religious systems.

If we take for granted that, as far as the clinical community is concerned, the traditional therapies are here to stay, it is clear that if they continue to claim to be a professional, predictable, and transmissible technology, they must be investigated in ways that are scientifically acceptable. In order to do that, some or all of these interventions must be operationalized. Recall that this process accomplishes two important research functions: it provides a fairly precise definition of the therapy, and it states what the clinician must do in order to deliver the treatment in a standard fashion. The former step is necessary because systems of psychotherapy vary in their explanations of psychopathology, symptomatic foci, and goals. The latter precaution is needed because professionals of the same orientation can differ markedly in their personal styles and therapeutic techniques.

In light of the current standards in psychotherapy research, it is notable that no manuals have been constructed for the traditional interventions with children. This is not to say, however, that juveniles cannot be treated in accordance with operational and specific criteria. In fact, the better empirical studies of the past few years have used manuals to standardize their protocols. However, these investigations were concerned with nontraditional interventions such as cognitive-behavioral training procedures (Bell et al., 1983; Kendall & Zupan, 1981) or affective imagery techniques (Garrison & Stolberg, 1983).

Why, then, have empirically oriented investigators chosen to bypass the traditional therapies, in terms of both the construction of treatment manuals and the study of their effectiveness? In our opinion, one of the reasons may be that the nature and assumptions of these systems present too many practical and technical problems. Child psychoanalysis is a case in point. Its emphasis on the analytic *process*, its reliance on interpretation as the salient therapeutic strategy (which can be highly individualized and creative, at best), and its focus on the unconscious all militate against an operational description. And it is unlikely that the analytic community would endorse such an undertaking. In any case, because psychoanalysis takes years, it is a particularly poor candidate for a controlled study: it is not clear what intervention could serve as a comparison, it is unlikely that the required sample sizes could be kept intact for such time periods, and it is not clear how treatment effects could be differentiated from salient maturational and developmental changes that occur among school-aged children.

The focused, brief, dynamic psychotherapies, the existential or relationship therapies, and their derivatives, also appear to have numerous ambiguous and esoteric components. Is it possible, for instance, to describe explicitly what is meant by "self-awareness" of one's symptoms or the strategies that are used to achieve that goal? Exactly how does a therapist help a child "to focus" on a symptom or problem? What are the components of a "psychodynamic formulation" and how does one arrive at it? The availability of manuals for similar therapies with *adults* suggest that it is possible to operationalize such concepts. Interpersonal psychotherapy and cognitive therapy, which have been used in the treatment of depressed adults, are cases in point. Although both were derived from traditional interventions, they have been operationalized by the professionals who developed them (Beck et al., 1979; Klerman & Weissman, 1982), and both have been and continue to be tested in clinical trials.

It is possible that similar manuals have not been developed for children because the traditional therapies have had no influential, research-oriented advocate in the pediatric arena. In other words, because these therapies are neither conceptually simple nor clinically easy to apply, one has to have an overriding personal commitment to their study. In this day and age when researchers are under increasing pressure to produce and to publish, the time and energy required for such an endeavor may be an insurmountable roadblock to most investigators.

Our discussion of developmental issues in the delivery of the traditional therapies may have created the impression that they represent further insurmountable roadblocks to research. This is not the case, however. According to Kendall, Lerner, and Craighead (1984), for instance, it is possible to assure a correspondence between a child's stage of intellectual or emotional development and nontraditional intervention techniques. They noted, as one example, that self-instructional training would have limited success with a three-year-old because the requisite "mediational thinking" has not yet developed. With respect to the traditional therapies, however, the basic question is not only whether their tenets and strategies can be operationalized in developmentally suitable fashions, but also whether all their presumably important features *are* indeed important with juveniles.

In this regard, it must be remembered that all systems of psychotherapy originated with the need to understand and to ameliorate psychopathology among *adults*. It is possible, therefore, that certain features or assumptions are neither relevant nor helpful to the therapeutic process with children. Perhaps notions of trust and confidence, in the manner that adults define them, are of little consequence to juvenile patients. If that were demonstrated to be the case, the assumptive basis of the traditional therapies could be simplified; they would thereby be easier to operationalize for use with youngsters. Toward this aim, it might be best to suspend temporarily comparisons of various treatments; instead, researchers could focus on trying to understand better the process of change in therapy (Garfield, 1983) and how this learning experience occurs among children.

In our overview of the field, we also emphasized the need to focus on diagnostically homogeneous samples in order to understand better the interface between patient "type" and treatment outcome. The study of how these two variables are intertwined is made easier by recent methodological developments, including semistructured clinical interviews that facilitate the process of psychiatric diagnosis (Kovacs, 1986). There has been also increasing evidence that the operational criteria of the DSM-III (APA, 1980) can be used with school-aged cohorts. Therefore, diagnostic issues no longer need to be passed over in the study of treatment outcome with child patients.

Of course, the foregoing methodological advances do not address other dilemmas such as the rarity of certain disorders among outpatient, juvenile cohorts. Additionally, the more prevalent disorders, namely, disorders of conduct, tend to have poor short- and long-term prognoses in spite of treatment (Chapter 2); therefore, a researcher may be wary of focusing on them. But there may be ways to resolve these problems. First, innovative small-sample designs could be developed that do permit reliable and valid conclusions about the effects of therapy. It also may be advisable to conduct multicenter, collaborative trials wherein the results of an intervention could be "summed" and examined cumulatively over the various research sites.

Finally, a comment is in order about our definition of a traditional therapy and the fact that we did not review the effectiveness of family interventions. From the start, our domain of interest was the nonbehavior therapies. In terms of their historic development, theoretical underpinnings, and treatment targets, there is a natural dividing line between the behavior and the nonbehavior therapies, also reflected in their separation in this book. Furthermore, many of the family interventions with children are behavioral (see Chapter 14). And as we perused the family therapy literature for studies of traditional interventions, it became evident that coverage of that field was beyond the scope of the present chapter.

Family therapy, as an overall label, refers to a range of philosophies and treatment techniques. There is Minuchin's structural family therapy (Liebman, Minuchin, & Baker, 1974); there are interventions that represent a more traditional "systems approach" (Lask & Matthew, 1979); there are those that derive from psychodynamic views of the family (Sigal, Barrs, & Doubilet, 1976); and there are the more pragmatically oriented, interactional approaches (Eyberg & Robinson, 1982), among others. An overview of this body of literature would have raised numerous methodological issues, in addition to those that we have already discussed, and would have also doubled the length of this chapter. Finally, the fact that the family therapies rarely focus on the child as the patient presented a theoretical and conceptual dilemma that could not be resolved within the limits that we have set for ourselves. However, interested readers will find the referenced studies to be a good introduction to research in this area. Suffice it to say that many of the problems to which we already alluded are equally true of the family therapy field where enthusiasm has outstripped hard-nosed empiricism and skepticism.

REFERENCES

American Psychiatric Association (1980). *Diagnostic and statistical manual of mental disorders* (3rd ed.). Washington, DC: APA.

Barnett, K., Darcie, G., Holland, C. J., & Kobasigawa, A. (1982). Children's cognitions about effective helping. *Developmental Psychology*, *18*, 267–277.

Barrett, C. L., Hampe, I. E., & Miller, L. C. (1978). Research on child psychotherapy. In S. L. Garfield & A. E. Bergin (Eds.), *Handbook of psychotherapy and behavior change: An empirical analysis* (2nd ed., pp. 411–435). New York: Wiley.

Beck, A. T. (1976). *Cognitive therapy and the emotional disorders*. New York: International Universities Press.

Beck, A. T., Rush, A. J., Shaw, B. F., & Emery, G. (1979). *Cognitive therapy of depression*. New York: Guilford Press.

Bell, C. R., Mundy, P., & Quay, H. C. (1983). Modifying impulsive responding in conduct-disordered institutionalized boys. *Psychological Reports*, *52*, 307–310.

Chassin, L., Young, R. D., & Light, R. (1980). Evaluations of treatment techniques by delinquent and disturbed adolescents. *Journal of Clinical Child Psychology*, *9*, 220–223.

Claman, L. (1980). The squiggle-drawing game in child psychotherapy. *American Journal of Psychotherapy*, *34*, 414–425.

Coie, J. D., & Pennington, B. F. (1976). Children's perceptions of deviance and disorder. *Child Development*, *47*, 407–413.

Compas, B. E., Friedland-Bandes, R., Bastien, R., & Adelman, H. S. (1981). Parent and causal attributions related to the child's clinical picture. *Journal of Abnormal Child Psychology*, *9*, 389–397.

Cramer, J. B. (1980). Psychiatric examination of the child. In H. I. Kaplan, A. M. Freedman, & B. J. Sadock (Eds.), *Comprehensive textbook of psychiatry* (3rd ed., pp. 2453–2461). Baltimore: Williams & Wilkins.

DiGiuseppe, R. A. (1981). Cognitive therapy with children. In G. Emery, S. D. Hollon, & R. C. Bedrosian (Eds.), *New directions in cognitive therapy* (pp. 50–67). New York: Guilford Press.

Dollinger, S. J., Thelen, M. H., & Walsh, M. L. (1980). Children's conceptions of psychologic problems. *Journal of Clinical Child Psychology*, *9*, 191–194.

Dulcan, M. K. (1984). Brief psychotherapy with children and their families: The state of the art. *Journal of the American Academy of Child Psychiatry*, *23*, 544–551.

Edleson, J. L., & Rose, S. D. (1981). Investigations into the efficacy of short-term group social skills training for socially isolated children. *Child Behavior Therapy*, *3*, 1–16.

Eisenberg, L., & Gruenberg, E. M. (1961). The current status of secondary prevention in child psychiatry. *American Journal of Orthopsychiatry*, *31*, 355–367.

Elitzur, B. (1978). In and out of Pandora's box. *Journal of Contemporary Psychotherapy*, *9*, 151–154.

Eyberg, S. M., & Robinson, E. A. (1982). Parent–child interaction training: Effects on family functioning. *Journal of Clinical Child Psychology*, *11*, 130–137.

Feigelson, C. I. (1977). On the essential characteristics of child analysis. *Psychoanalytic Study of the Child*, *32*, 353–361.

Garfield, S. L. (1983). Effectiveness of psychotherapy: The perennial controversy. *Professional Psychology: Research and Practice*, *14*, 35–43.

Gottman, J., & Markman, H. J. (1978). Experimental designs in psychotherapy research. In S. L. Garfield & A. E. Bergin (Eds.), *Handbook of psychotherapy and behavior change: An empirical analysis* (2nd ed., pp. 23–62). New York: Wiley.

Garrison, S. R., & Stolberg, A. L. (1983). Modification of anger in children by affective imagery training. *Journal of Abnormal Child Psychology*, *11*, 115–129.

Hartmann, D. P., Roper, B. L., & Gelfand, D. M. (1977). An evaluation of alternative modes of child psychotherapy. In B. B. Lahey & A. E. Kazdin (Eds.), *Advances in clinical child psychology* (Vol. 1, pp. 1–46). New York: Plenum Press.

Heinicke, C. M., & Goldman, A. (1960). Research on psychotherapy with children: A review and suggestions for further study. *American Journal of Orthopsychiatry*, *30*, 483–494.

Heinicke, C. M., & Strassmann, L. H. (1975). Toward more effective research on child psychotherapy. *Journal of the American Academy of Child Psychiatry*, *14*, 561–588.

Hinshaw, S. P., Whalen, C. K., & Henker, B. (1984). Cognitive-behavioral and pharmacologic interventions for hyperactive boys: Comparative and combined effects. *Journal of Consulting and Clinical Psychology*, *52*, 739–749.

Hood-Williams, J. (1960). The results of psychotherapy with children: A reevaluation. *Journal of Consulting Psychology*, *24*, 84–88.

Kendall, P. C., Lerner, R. M., & Craighead, W. E. (1984). Human development and intervention in child psychopathology. *Child Development*, *55*, 71–82.

Kendall, P. C., & Zupan, B. A. (1981). Individual versus group application of cognitive-behavioral self-control procedures with children. *Behavior Therapy*, *12*, 344–359.

Klerman, G. L., & Weissman, M. M. (1982). Interpersonal psychotherapy: Theory and research. In A. J. Rush (Ed.), *Short-term psychotherapies for depression. Behavioral, interpersonal, cognitive, and psychodynamic approaches* (pp. 88–106). New York: Guilford Press.

Kovacs, M. (1986). A developmental perspective on methods and measures in the assessment of depressive disorders: The clinical interview. In M. Rutter, C. E. Izard,

& P. B. Read (Eds.), *Depression in young people: Developmental and clinical perspectives* (pp. 435–465). New York: Guilford Press.

Kovacs, M., & Beck, A. T. (1977). An empirical-clinical approach toward a definition of childhood depression. In J. G. Schulterbrandt & A. Raskin (Eds.), *Depression in childhood: Diagnosis, treatment, and conceptual models* (pp. 1–25). New York: Raven Press.

Lask, B., & Matthew, D. (1979). Childhood asthma. A controlled trial of family psychotherapy. *Archives of Disease in Childhood*, *54*, 116–119.

Levitt, E. E. (1957). The results of psychotherapy with children: An evaluation. *Journal of Consulting Psychology*, *21*, 189–196.

Levitt, E. E. (1963). Psychotherapy with children: A further evaluation. *Behavior Research and Therapy*, *1*, 45–51.

Liebman, R., Minuchin, S., & Baker, L. (1974). The use of structural family therapy in the treatment of intractable asthma. *American Journal of Psychiatry*, *131*, 535–540.

Lockwood, J. L. (1981). Treatment of disturbed children in verbal and experiential group psychotherapy. *International Journal of Group Psychotherapy*, *31*, 355–366.

Marsden, G., & Kalter, N. (1976). Children's understanding of their emotionally disturbed peers: I. The concept of emotional disturbance. *Psychiatry*, *39*, 227–238.

Marsden, G., Kalter, N., Plunkett, J. W., & Barr-Grossman, T. (1977). Children's social judgments concerning emotionally disturbed peers. *Journal of Consulting and Clinical Psychology*, *45*, 948.

Meyer, J. H., & Zegans, L. S. (1975). Adolescents perceive their psychotherapy. *Psychiatry*, *38*, 11–22.

Michelson, L., Mannarino, A. P., Marchione, K. E., Stern, M., Figueroa, J., & Beck, S. (1983). A comparative outcome study of behavioral social-skills training, interpersonal-problem-solving and non-directive control treatments with child psychiatric outpatients. *Behavior Research and Therapy*, *21*, 545–556.

Paul, G. L. (1967). Strategy of outcome research in psychotherapy. *Journal of Consulting Psychology*, *31*, 109–118.

Puig-Antich, J. (1982). Major depression and conduct disorder in prepuberty. *Journal of the American Academy of Child Psychiatry*, *21*, 118–128.

Putallaz, M., & Gottman, J. (1983). Social relationship problems in children: An approach to intervention. In B. B. Lahey & A. E. Kazdin (Eds.), *Advances in clinical child psychology* (Vol. 6, pp. 1–43). New York: Plenum Press.

Ramon, E., & Baharav, Y. (1978). A new approach to creative psychotherapy by integration of folk legends, drama and clay modelling. *Confinia Psychiatrica*, *21*, 133–139.

Remotigue-Ano, N. (1980). The hidden agenda of story-making therapy. *American Journal of Psychotherapy*, *34*, 261–268.

Roberts, M. C., Beidleman, W. B., & Wurtele, S. K. (1981). Children's perceptions of medical and psychological disorders in their peers. *Journal of Clinical Child Psychology*, *10*, 76–78.

Rosenheim, E., & Ichilov, Y. (1979). Short-term preventive therapy with children of fatally-ill parents. *Israel Annals of Psychiatry*, *17*, 67–73.

Rutter, M. (1982). Psychological therapies in child psychiatry: Issues and prospects. *Psychological Medicine, 12*, 723–740.

Schoettle, U. C. (1980). Guided imagery—A tool in child psychotherapy. *American Journal of Psychotherapy, 34*, 220–227.

Sears, R. R. (1975). Your ancients revisited: A history of child development. In E. M. Hetherington (Ed.), *Review of child development research* (Vol. 5, pp. 1–73). Chicago: University of Chicago Press.

Selman, R. L., Jaquette, D., & Redman-Lavin, D. (1977). Interpersonal awareness in children: Toward an integration of developmental and clinical child psychology. *American Journal of Orthopsychiatry, 47*, 264–274.

Shaffer, D. (1984). Notes on psychotherapy research among children and adolescents. *Journal of the American Academy of Child Psychiatry, 23*, 552–561.

Shapiro, S., Skinner, E. A., Kessler, L. G., Von Korff, M., German, P. S., Tischler, G. L., Leaf, P. J., Benham, L., Cottler, L., & Regier, D. A. (1984). Utilization of health and mental health services: Three epidemiologic catchment area sites. *Archives of General Psychiatry, 41*, 971–978.

Sherick, I., Kearney, C., Buxton, M., & Stevens, B. (1978). Ego strengthening psychotherapy with children having primary ego deficiencies. *Journal of Child Psychotherapy, 4*, 51–68.

Sigal, J. J., Barrs, C. B., & Doubilet, A. L. (1976). Problems in measuring the success of family therapy in a common clinical setting: Impasse and solutions. *Family Process, 15*, 225–233.

Simmons, J. S. (1981). *Psychiatric examination of children* (3rd ed.). Philadelphia: Lea & Febiger.

Strupp, H. H. (1978). Psychotherapy research and practice: An overview. In S. L. Garfield & A. E. Bergin (Eds.), *Handbook of psychotherapy and behavior change: An empirical analysis* (2nd ed., pp. 3–22). New York: Wiley.

Sullivan, H. S. (1954). The psychiatric interview. (H. S. Perry & M. L. Gawel, Eds.). New York: W. W. Norton.

Tramontana, M. G. (1980). Critical review of research on psychotherapy outcome with adolescents: 1967–1977. *Psychological Bulletin, 88*, 429–450.

Tuma, J. M., & Sobotka, K. R. (1983). Traditional therapies with children. In T. H. Ollendick & M. Hersen (Eds.), *Handbook of child psychopathology* (pp. 391–426). New York: Plenum Press.

Turecki, S. (1982). Elective brief psychotherapy with children. *American Journal of Psychotherapy, 36*, 479–488.

Urbain, E. S., & Kendall, P. C. (1980). Review of social-cognitive problem-solving interventions with children. *Psychological Bulletin, 88*, 109–143.

Wells, R. A., & Dezen, A. E. (1978). The results of family therapy revisited: The nonbehavioral methods. *Family Process, 17*, 251–274.

Wenger, C. (1982). The suitcase story: A therapeutic technique for children in out-of-home placement. *American Journal of Orthopsychiatry, 52*, 353–355.

14 BEHAVIORAL APPROACHES TO TREATMENT

JEANNE DEVANY AND ROSEMERY O. NELSON

INTRODUCTION

Behavior therapy as a field encompasses diverse techniques and outlooks (cf. Ross, 1981); broadly speaking, behavior therapy is an approach that draws heavily on empirical research findings, focuses primarily on current behavior and the factors contributing to its maintenance, and emphasizes consistent and objective assessment of change. In other words, behavior therapy is an *approach* to therapy, an empirical approach, rather than simply a set of techniques, as some mistakenly believe.

A behavior therapist accepts as the appropriate focus of intervention the child's present behavior while recognizing that past events and circumstances as well as organic and genetic processes have played a role in the development of current behavior. Past circumstances and genetic endowment, however, cannot be changed; only the current environment and state of the organism can be altered to facilitate the learning and performance of more appropriate and more adaptive behavior. The role of the behavior therapist is to teach more adaptive behavior and to assist in altering the environment so that more adaptive behavior will "pay off" for the child and, so, will be maintained. Behavior therapists frequently take an openly educative role with parents and children. Direct instruction is often used. This emphasis on learning and on the "here and now" of behavior reflects the origins of behavior therapy and behavior modification in the experimental analysis of behavior within the field of psychology (Baer, Wolf, & Risley, 1968; Skinner, 1953).

In this chapter, we present an illustrative overview of the field of behavior therapy with children. Basic principles of learning are presented, and some fundamental behavior techniques are described. This coverage is not designed to be comprehensive; there are far too many published reports and experiments covering a wide array of clinical problems to present each area

523

in adequate detail. A number of comprehensive texts are available for those who wish to learn more (e.g., Ollendick & Cerny, 1981; Ross, 1981).

PRINCIPLES OF LEARNING

Three learning paradigms are extensively used in behavior therapy. The first is *classical (respondent or Pavlovian) conditioning*, which is the type of learning that occurs when we form associations between environmental events and bodily reactions such as anxiety or the secretion of digestive juices. An innate response (such as fear) that is automatically elicited by a stimulus (say an accident in a particular car) eventually will come to be elicited by another stimulus (such as any car) that, prior to the learning, did not elicit the response. Classical conditioning can be thought of as a kind of stimulus substitution where one stimulus (the conditioned stimulus) comes to serve the same function as the original unconditioned stimulus. It is also known as respondent conditioning since the organism responds automatically to the stimulus. Some abnormal behaviors (like some phobias) appear to be learned through classical conditioning, and procedures derived from it are often used in the treatment of phobias and other anxiety problems.

In *operant conditioning*, the person engages in activity ("operates on" the environment), and these acts result in some change in the environment. Simply put, operant conditioning is the type of learning that occurs as a result of the association of behaviors with their consequences. A behavior can result in the presentation of some new event in the environment, the removal of stimuli in the environment, or in no change at all. When positive (roughly speaking, rewarding) events occur as a result of some action, the behavior will increase in frequency; this is known as positive reinforcement. For example, if a withdrawn child haltingly requests permission to join her classmates in a recess game and is warmly welcomed, in the future she probably will ask more often. If aversive stimulation or a negative event follows a behavior, the behavior often decreases in frequency and may be suppressed altogether. When this occurs, this is called punishment. (Frequently, it is referred to as positive punishment, the contingent application of negative consequences producing a reduction in behavior, to distinguish it from negative punishment, where a behavior decreases because its emission results in the *loss* of a reinforcing event. The term "punishment" technically refers to both.) For example, a child is made to wipe the entire floor clean whenever he throws milk on the floor; this behavior decreases in frequency and is eventually eliminated. In this case, the floor-cleaning requirement punished the behavior of throwing milk on the floor.

Physical punishment, which lay persons generally think of as "punishment," involving slapping, spanking, or electric shock, is generally not recommended by behavior therapists. Many oppose physical punishment on humane or philosophical grounds (e.g., Maurer, 1983); for others, it is a matter of practicality. The use of slapping and spanking to control behavior is a practice that can easily be abused; and when it is, the danger of harm to a child is real. In addition, the use of physical force to solve interpersonal disputes or other problems sets an example (or *models*) a behavior that many parents and therapists would prefer that children not learn. That is, when parents or therapists use physical punishment, children may learn that the use of force is an acceptable method of solving problems. Certainly, this is a side effect of the use of punishment that is of some concern. Finally, the use of physical punishment is problematic because its effectiveness is often limited. The undesired behavior may be suppressed only in the presence of the punishing parent (or therapist; Lovaas & Simmons, 1969), or the effect may be limited only to the places (such as home) that physical punishment has actually been administered. In other cases, the effects of punishment may generalize well beyond the behavior or situation and produce anxious reactions or withdrawal.

Sometimes, physical punishment may be an appropriate intervention. When an extremely maladaptive behavior, such as severe head-banging or eye-gouging, threatens to lead to permanent physical impairment or extensive tissue damage, physical punishment may rapidly eliminate the behavior. However, it is important to note that punishment procedures must be carefully applied in order to be effective and that negative side effects (Mayhew & Harris, 1978) as well as positive side effects (Risley, 1968) may occur. The assistance of a qualified professional is essential in planning a punishment program for severe behavior problems.

Some behaviors result in the removal or termination of environmental stimulation. If the child's behavior results in the termination of an aversive event, then the behavior producing the termination will increase in frequency; this is called negative (taking away) reinforcement. For example, a child's persistent whining is stilled when a parent "gives in" and buys the requested candy at the grocery store. In this case, on the one hand, the parent is negatively reinforced for buying the candy by the cessation of the whining; the child's whining and obnoxious behavior, on the other hand, are positively reinforced by the candy presentation. This pattern has been called the "negative reinforcement trap" (cf. Patterson, 1971; Wahler, 1969) and can lead to progressively more coercive interactions between the child and the parents.

When a behavior was formerly followed by reinforcing consequences and these are no longer forthcoming, the behavior will temporarily increase and then eventually decrease in frequency. This process is known as *extinction*.

Although several examples were given in the foregoing discussion, it is essential to remember that consequences must be defined functionally (that is, based on the effect they actually have) rather than statically or topographically (based on the effect it seems they *should* have). For some children, food delivery does not act as a reward even if the children seem as though they should be hungry. For other children, parental or teacher reprimands or even physical restraint (Favell, McGimsey, Jones, & Cannon, 1981) may increase the very misbehaviors they are designed to decrease. We can designate a particular event as a reinforcer or punisher only after observing its effect on behavior. Whether or not a stimulus acts as a reinforcer or punisher depends on the child's previous experiences, her or his current skills and developmental level, the current environmental context, and the child's present physiological state.

The third learning paradigm could be called *mediational learning*. One type of mediational learning is modeling (Bandura, 1969). For example, new behavior can be acquired through the observation of another person (the model) engaging in that behavior. Most of us have seen training films designed to teach us to floss our teeth or operate our cars; through viewing them, we have learned skills that would have been difficult to teach through operant methods. It appears, though, that reinforcement is necessary for the reliable emission of the newly learned behavior (Hayes, Rincover, & Volosin, 1980). That is, if the new behavior brings no payoff in the natural environment, the child will not continue to engage in it. Some factors that enhance the effectiveness of observational learning are the delivery of rewards to the model (in view of the observer) and the use of models who are similar to the child in some respects but are of slightly higher status than the child. Other mediational approaches employ instructions and other verbal interventions. Some of these interventions are designed to change a child's negative thinking patterns (e.g., "I'm a failure") (Ellis & Bernard, 1983), while others are more explicitly designed to improve a child's problem-solving or self-control skills (e.g., Meichenbaum & Goodman, 1971; Snyder & White, 1979).

SPECIFIC TECHNIQUES
Shaping

Often, the desired behavior is not in the child's repertoire. In this case, the therapist must gradually build the skill. One method is called *shaping*, wherein the therapist temporarily accepts the child's current skill level/performance and uses it as a base from which to build more appropriate behavior through rewarding successive approximations to the final desired goal. For example, in language training with mute children, the child by definition does not produce intelligible words. The therapist may prompt (facilitate) the child's vocalizations through gentle tickling or mild horseplay and generously reward every vocal sound the child makes. After the child is vocalizing at a fairly high rate, the therapist selects a language sound ("aah," "ma") that is similar to the vocalization emitted by the child. The therapist instructs the child "say 'aah' " and if the child responds, the child is rewarded. Initially, very gross approximations to the "aah" sound may be accepted, but the therapist rewards the child on succeeding trials only for vocalizations that are as good as or better than the child's "best" production. This requires careful attention on the therapist's part. Incorrect or sloppy responses are ignored. Eventually, the child learns to say "aah" when given the instruction, "say aah." Then training on another vowel or consonant sound will begin. Once the child has learned several sounds, they will be combined into words (e.g., "momma") that then will be taught (cf. Lovaas, 1977).

Chaining

Another method of building new behaviors is *chaining*. Here a large task is broken down into smaller component parts (the chain), and these are sequentially taught. The last part of the chain is usually taught first, then the second to last, and so forth. For example, in teaching psychotic children to dress themselves, the therapist may break down the job of "putting on pants" into components: puts right foot in pant leg, puts left foot in pants leg, pulls up pants to knees, pulls up pants to waist, fastens pants. The child is first taught to fasten the pants (assuming that the physical skills required here are in the child's repertoire) when told "put on your pants." Successful performance is rewarded; once the child is reliably fastening the pants when instructed, the next step is taught. As the child masters that step, the next step back in the chain is taught until the child successfully completes the entire sequence. Often the therapist will employ physical or verbal guidance (prompting) to help the child learn the response, but this assistance must be gradually removed (*faded*) as soon as possible. Shaping, chaining, prompting, and fading are all used extensively, alone or combination, in child behavior therapy.

Reinforcement Procedures

The success of shaping, chaining, prompting, and fading is dependent on the potency of the rewards used. The "payoff" for engaging in the target behavior must be great enough to motivate the child to change. Considerable ingenuity is often needed to find effective reinforcers. Fortunately, most children find parental or teacher attention and affection powerful reinforcers (although there are exceptions, see Chapter 2). The therapist can teach the parents, or significant others, to attend to the child, praise the child, or otherwise be affectionate when the child is behaving appropriately and to withhold attention when the child is behaving inappropriately. The rearrangement of the consequences of a behavior is referred to as *contingency management*. Many contingency management programs combine techniques to increase appropriate behavior and to decrease inappropriate behavior.

For some purposes, parental attention may not be a sufficient or appropriate reward. For example, a child may complete her weekly chores when her mother stands by encouraging her. However, this may create problems for the mother and prevent the child from learning independent work skills. A more appropriate reward for completed chores might be telephone or television privileges or the opportunity to go to the movies. Many "naturally occurring" activities may function as effective reinforcers. In fact, as children approach adolescence, the opportunity to engage in activities with peers may be more powerful than parental approval. Also, for some children, family interactions have become so tension-filled and aversive that parental reward value is quite low. For these children as well, the use of activities and spending money as reinforcers can be highly effective.

Severely impaired children, such as some retarded and autistic children, may be completely unresponsive to the naturally occurring social events that shape and maintain the repertoires of normal children. Since these children are socially unresponsive and generally lack play skills, the activities that would interest a normally developing child do not interest them. Primitive or primary reward systems often involving food must be developed in order to teach more appropriate language, social, and self-care behaviors and to ensure that the child continues to engage in these behaviors once they have been learned. Generally, a primary reward such as food is paired with praise and smiling in the hope that these social stimuli will take on secondary rewarding properties (Lovaas, Frietag, Kinder, Rubenstein, Schaeffer, & Simmons, 1966). As the child acquires play, social, and language skills, games and other activities and parental affection may become more powerful rewards, and reliance on food rewards can be decreased. Sensory reinforcement, through the contingent provision of toys or events providing visual, tactile, and auditory stimulation, has also proven to be useful in the treatment of severely developmentally handicapped children (Devany & Rincover, 1982).

School children may also benefit from the use of *token* reinforcement systems. In these systems, appropriate behavior is immediately rewarded with a token (e.g., a poker chip, a marble, a hatch mark on a card); these tokens may later be cashed in for privileges, activities, or special treats (back-up reinforcers). Tokens provide symbolic rewards that can reinforce appropriate behavior immediately without disrupting ongoing activities. They also allow the child to save up enough tokens to purchase preferred treats or activities. Although token systems are most often used in classrooms (Kazdin, 1977b; see also Chapter 16), they may be profitably used by parents to shape and maintain adaptive behavior at home as well.

Modeling

Modeling procedures are based on the principles of mediational learning (Kirkland & Thelen, 1977). Three variations of modeling have been used: *symbolic modeling*, in which the child watches a film or videotape of the desired performance; *vicarious modeling*, in which the child observes a live model; and *participant modeling*, in which the child joins in making the desired response (or successive approximations to it). Symbolic modeling has been useful in reducing children's anxiety over upcoming surgery or dental work (Adelson, Liebert, Poulos, & Herskovitz, 1972; Melamed & Siegel, 1975). Participant modeling has been found to be effective in reducing debilitating fears in adults (e.g., Lassen & McConnell, 1977) and appears to be effective with children as well (Matson, 1981). In this procedure, the child participates in the activity along with the models and is rewarded for gradually increasing the level of participation. Also, in therapy sessions, the therapist may demonstrate an appropriate behavior and have the child practice it.

Self-control and Cognitive Interventions

Self-control packages, designed to increase a child's ability to modulate attention and behavior, have become popular in the last 10 years. In particular, these procedures have been used with hyperactive and impulsive children, who frequently perform poorly in academic tasks because of poor attention or erratic response strategies (cf. Kendall & Finch, 1978). Typically, the child is taught a series of self-statements. Once the self-statements (e.g., ''I must stop and look,'' ''What is my task?'') are mastered, the child in encouraged to rehearse them covertly (subaudibly) and to employ them in appropriate situations. Although these interventions have reportedly been successful in altering children's responses on a variety of tasks, such as matching figures, the general practical utility of these procedures remains to be established (Hobbs, Moquin, Tyroler, & Lahey, 1980; Urbain & Kendall, 1980).

Other interventions are also designed to change the child's self-verbalizations or thoughts. Some rely on the use of the child's imagination; for example, a fearful child might be encouraged to imagine how a favorite superhero or pop star might behave in problematic situations (Lazarus & Abramovitz, 1962). Other procedures are based on cognitive interventions found successful with adults, such as Ellis's rational emotive therapy (Bernard & Joyce, 1984; Ellis & Bernard, 1983). In general, these techniques (modified for use with children) appear promising, but more systematic evaluation of their effectiveness is needed before firm statements about their utility can be made.

Comments on Punishment

The techniques discussed previously are designed to increase adaptive behaviors. A number of behavioral techniques have been designed to decrease or eliminate undesirable behaviors. One principle, positive punishment, has already been described. It is important to bear in mind the difference between the *theoretical* principle of punishment (any event of whatever form that follows a behavior, thereby decreasing the future probability of that behavior) and the colloquial much more restricted use of the word ''punishment'' (physical slaps, spankings, reprimands, etc.). Harsh words and spankings may inadvertently cause unwanted behaviors to increase because they give attention to the child, who may find attention to be positively reinforcing. Both punishment procedures and reinforcement procedures must be functionally defined. That is, behavior therapists define procedures based on the *effect* the procedure has on behavior rather than what we think beforehand the procedure should do.

Time-out

In time-out procedures, the child is removed from a rewarding situation (e.g., TV room) to a less rewarding situation (such as a chair facing the wall). The loss of reinforcement or the opportunity to obtain reinforcement while in the time-out setting punishes the inappropriate behavior. Again, it must be stressed that the effectiveness of time-out cannot be a priori presumed and must be evaluated as part of treatment. In some cases, time-out can result in an *increase* in the undesired target behavior (Solnick, Rincover, & Petersen, 1977); this appears to occur when time-out releases the child from an unpleasant or overly demanding situation or allows the child to engage in a highly preferred behavior such as self-stimulation. Since the time-out procedure usually produces a loss of reinforcement, however, it is classed as a type of negative punishment. Putting a child in isolation is sometimes euphemistically called "time-out" when it is actually (positive) punishment because seclusion may in fact be strongly aversive itself. Such euphemisms do little credit to behavior therapy as they suggest the therapist is insensitive to the highly unpleasant aspects of seclusion.

Response Cost

Particularly with older children, time-out may be inappropriate or ineffective. The loss of privileges (or tokens or money earned) may be an effective punishment instead. When parents arrange to "dock" a child's allowance for failure to complete household chores or for instances of intersibling conflict, response cost is being used. In response cost procedures, the behavior(s) to be decreased and the consequences of the behavior(s) are clearly specified a priori with the help of the therapist. Response cost is frequently used in conjunction with reinforcement procedures in which the performance of appropriate behaviors earns points, privileges, or other rewards.

Extinction

In extinction, the consequences that had reinforced the occurrence of a particular behavior are withheld; the behavior no longer "pays off" for the child. For a example, a child's whining and crying may cause her parents to delay bedtime and to sit by the bed until she falls asleep. The bedtime delay and the parental attention presumably reinforces the inappropriate behavior. Firm insistence on the predetermined bedtime and parental ignoring of the wailing would eventually eliminate these behaviors, and the child would go to bed peaceably at the regular time.

In extinction, the behavior that is extinguished typically increases in frequency and intensity before dropping off to very low or nonexistent levels. When extinction is used, parents should be forwarned of this typical pattern and see it as a first sign of success. Because of the temporary increase in behavior, extinction is not a suitable procedure with behaviors that could result in serious physical or emotional distress to the child.

BEHAVIORAL ASSESSMENT

Since behavioral assessment is covered in detail in Chapter 11, this section presents only some of its major terms and assumptions. Behavior in and of itself is neither normal nor abnormal. These evaluative labels are applied to behavior, in part, depending on the frequency with which it occurs within a particular environmental setting. Some behaviors are "abnormal" because they occur at a much greater frequency than is usual for the context. An example of this is hyperactive behavior, in which the child's overall motor activity is much higher than in peers. These we call *behavioral excesses*, and techniques designed to decrease the frequency of the behaviors are applied. Other behaviors are termed "abnormal" because their rate of occurrence is much lower than average or optimal levels; these are called *behavioral deficits*. An example would be a 14-year-old who lacks communicative speech and is not able to dress without assistance.

Other behavior is deemed abnormal because it occurs in an *inappropriate* setting (e.g., nudity in the street) or because the behavior is *developmentally* inconsistent (a six-year-old who still uses baby talk to communicate). The tolerance level and expectancies of signficant others in the child's life also exert powerful influence on what behavior is labeled abnormal. An educationally deprived parent may say of a retarded son, "There's nothing wrong with him—he just can't read or write." A mother whose own energy level is very low may describe her child as hyperactive when in fact the child's activity level is well within normal limits. Whenever a child is brought into treatment, the therapist must evaluate the presence and extent of behavioral excesses and deficits, note the age of the child, and identify environmental characteristics that support inappropriate behavior or may facilitate more adaptive responding. The treatment plan is based on this behavioral analysis of the problem, rather than on diagnosis alone.

BEHAVIOR THERAPY WITH CHILDHOOD DISORDERS

Hyperactivity and Attention Deficit Disorder

As noted in Chapter 4, motoric overactivity is of much less clinical significance than attentional deficits, poor academic performance, or noncompliance. Thus, behavior therapy for children diagnosed as "hyperactive" or "attention deficit disordered" (ADD) has usually focused on improving the child's academic or other appropriate behavior rather than reducing activity rate. (Comprehensive reviews of the literature may be found in Barkley, 1981; Lahey, 1979; Ross & Ross, 1976.)

Sometimes behavioral interventions are conducted in the classroom to improve on-task behavior or academic improvement. In such cases, the teacher may reward a child with praise, stars, hugs, or individual attention for completing clearly specified tasks, such as correctly completing 80 percent of a group of arithmetic problems.

Other interventions require coordination between home and school. For example, in one project (O'Leary, Pelham, Rosenbaum, & Price, 1976), nine hyperactive children received a behavioral 10-week treatment. The program involved a home-based reward system. Under this, individual daily academic goals were identified for each child. At the end of the day, the teacher evaluated whether the child had met these preset goals and noted the result on a daily report card, which the child took home. If the child had successfully met the daily goals, the parents provided a reward. The reward list was individually tailored to each family's circumstances and the preferences of the individual children, and included activities such as extra television time or playing a game with a parent. If the child succeeded in meeting the daily goals on four of the five school days in a week, then a "weekly" reward such as a trip to a fast-food restaurant or a fishing expedition was earned. At the end of the program, the children were reevaluated by the treatment planners. The children who participated in the treatment program received significantly lower scores on problem-behavior rating scales than did a group of children who did not get any treatment. That is, compared to the children's own behavior at the beginning of the project and compared to the behavior of other children of the same grade and sex who did not receive treatment, the behavior of the children who participated in the program improved.

This program and others similar to it are attractive because the effort required to implement it is not very substantial once the program is in place. The rewards are events controlled by the parents and could include the earning of privileges or special treats without much financial outlay. The monitoring of the child's performance by the teacher, once learned, may actually facilitate better teaching as it ensures that the teacher is sensitive to the child's actual performance on a daily basis. The program does require consistent rewarding by the parents and may not be effective when children are living in chaotic home conditions.

A comprehensive individual intervention program for a hyperactive child was reported by Kendall and Urbain (1981) and illustrates the use of cognitive-behavioral interventions as well as contingency management procedures. The child was a seven-year-old who had been adopted by her foster parents. She was of normal intelligence and was described as likable but disruptive, distractible, and having a short attention span. She was prescribed medication for the control of her "hyperactivity." Her foster parents were also concerned with her noncompliant behavior and occasional stealing.

The therapists decided to focus their intervention on helping the child to improve her self-control skills. She was seen on a weekly basis for about 12 months and trained in the use of self-instructions. The therapist demonstrated the task (for example, copying a geometric form) and verbally described the steps needed to successfully complete the task. Typically, the therapist would identify the problem (e.g., "What do I need to do? I need to copy this figure"), describe an approach to the problem (e.g., "If I start at the top and work downward like this, I can follow the design and not miss any parts"), make a statement focusing the child's attention ("I need to look carefully at the problem, at the whole picture, and think of what I need to do''), and give a congratulatory statement following successful task completion.

In the first phase of treatment, the child and the therapist practiced the appropriate use of self-instructions on a variety of tasks (such as puzzles). In the next phase of treatment, a contingency management procedure was introduced so that tokens could be earned by correct performance. Tokens were lost for incorrect task performance or for failing to use the self-instructions. She could re-earn the lost tokens by performing the task correctly or by using the self-instructions.

In the third phase of treatment, the use of self-instructions, the token rewards, and response cost were continued, and a new procedure was introduced. Self-instructional cue cards, emphasizing the skills needed to solve interpersonal problems, were introduced. The therapist role-played the use of cue cards to teach the child to apply these steps in social situations. After the child became familiar with the correct use of the cards, the discussions were expanded to include the rehearsal of more reflective responses to situations, the use of the self-instructions to develop a more appropriate strategy, and rehearsal of the more reflective approach. After several weeks of practice in the office, she was encouraged to begin using the "stop and think" approach in day-to-day life between sessions. She was able to earn additional tokens and gold stars by reporting the use of self-instructions in extratherapy situations. In later sessions, her mother was included to learn about the "stop and think" system, and some modifications in the system were made for use at home.

The therapist kept consistent records of the child's behavior to monitor improvement. The data collected showed that her inappropriate behavior did not decrease appreciably until the response cost procedure was added. That is, the self-instructional component was only minimally successful in decreasing her inappropriate behavior.

The results of this case study are consistent with the available evidence regarding the effectiveness of cognitive and self-instructional procedures. While enthusiasm for these techniques remains fairly high, it has not been demonstrated that the procedures in and of themselves have substantial impact on real-life behavior problems without the concurrent use of more powerful interventions (such as the response cost procedure). Considerable research work continues to be done in this area, so more sophisticated and powerful cognitive interventions may yet be developed for use in children.

This case study is noteworthy because it demonstrates the utility of ongoing assessment of the child's behavior as a means of monitoring improvement. It would have been more difficult to determine that her behavior was not improving with self-instructions if her therapist had not been keeping objective records of her behavior. While it would have been useful to have additional data on the extent to which behavioral improvement generalized to school and home, for practical reasons, this is frequently impossible to do in outpatient settings. Anecdotal reports from the mother, however, indicated that her behavior at home had improved considerably.

Hyperactivity (and ADD) is one of the few areas in which we have some evidence on the effectiveness of behavioral interventions relative to medication and the interactions between behavioral and pharmacological interventions. In one well-designed study (Gittelman-Klein et al., 1976) using severely hyperactive children, individualized contingency management programs were compared with medication alone and a combined medication-contingency package. Although the behavior of some children in each group improved, no significant difference between the medication-alone group and the medication–contingency-management group was found. That is, the use of the combined medication–contingency-management procedure did not produce any greater improvement than the use of the medication. Similarly, there does not appear to be an interaction when medication is combined with cognitive behavior therapy (Brown, Wynne, & Medenis, 1985) on measures of attention span and academic performance. A combined cognitive-behavior treatment and medication program proved significantly more effective than either treatment alone in improving social interactions. It is also important to note that contingency management programs alone can be effective in reducing hyperactivity without medication (Lahey, 1979). In fact, medication alone may decrease hyperactive behavior but fail to produce desirable change in academic behavior, whereas contingency management procedures may produce changes in both areas (Ayllon, Layman, & Kandel, 1975).

Disorders of Anxiety and Dysphoria

Modeling procedures have been used extensively in the treatment of *anxiety disorders* in children. Participant modeling in particular has been effective; in participant modeling, both the child and the model encounter the feared situation or stimulus in a series of graded steps (Bandura, Blanchard, & Ritter, 1969). In one evaluation of the effectiveness of participant modeling (Lewis, 1974), a group of children attending a summer camp were treated for fear of water. The combined use of symbolic modeling (through film) and gradual participation with a model produced the greatest decrement in the children's fear. In another study of participant modeling (Matson, 1981), three mentally retarded girls were treated for long-standing fears of unfamiliar adults. This excessive shyness or "stranger phobia" was a problem for their families as it limited the activities in which they could engage. For obvious reasons, the therapist was reluctant to eliminate completely the girls' fear of strange adults; the compromise was to reduce the children's fear and avoidance of adults with whom their parents requested that they interact. The mother was asked to model appropriate interaction with a stranger for the child and the child practiced the interaction. Between sessions, the child and mother practiced at home. After the child was adequately performing this task, the mother and child interacted with unfamiliar adults.

Initially, the mother walked up to the other adult while holding the child's hand, and the child was prompted to make an appropriate greeting. Success was rewarded with food and tokens. Over time, as the child improved, the mother gradually decreased the assistance and her physical proximity to the child until she could successfully instruct the child to interact with the adult as she stood six feet away. The treatment provided measurably effective for all three girls in increasing the number of words spoken to the unfamiliar adult, in decreasing the distance between the child and the adult to a distance comparable to that kept by children of the same age and mental condition who did not show excessive fear, and in decreasing the girls' self-rating of fear experienced in the interaction. When the children were reevaluated after six months, it was found that behavioral improvement and the fear reduction had continued.

With another child (Luiselli, 1978) the modeling component appeared less important, and the emphasis was on rewarding gradual improvements in performance. A seven-year-old autistic child intensely feared riding his school bus. Placing him on the bus precipitated episodes of hyperventilation, screaming, and tantruming. Treatment consisted of *successive approximations* (shaping) to the desired goal—riding the bus without distress. At first, the bus was parked next to his home, and he was generously rewarded with praise and snacks for quietly sitting in the parked bus with the therapist for a brief period. He was rewarded for gradually increasing the amount of time spent in the bus. By the fifth day of treatment, he rode the entire way to school on the bus with his therapist without incident. By the seventh day, he was able to ride alone to school without assistance.

Another approach has been the use of more comprehensive treatment packages designed to reward appropriate approach behavior and to decrease inappropriate avoidance behavior. For example, a contingency-management program using a home-based motivational system was used to treat the school phobia of an eight-year-old girl (Ayllon, Smith, & Rogers, 1970). Interestingly, although the use of stars and other rewards did produce some improvements in the child's behavior, she did not begin attending school voluntarily until her mother punished her noncompliant "phobic" behavior by spanking her one day.

Systematic desensitization, in which feelings of relaxation are paired with mental images of the feared stimuli or situations, has also been useful in the treatment of children's fears. For example, systematic desensitization was used to treat a boy who was afraid of blood, heights, and taking tests (Van Hasselt, Hersen, Bellack, Rosenblum, & Lamparski, 1979). In systematic desensitization, the child is exposed to a feared situation in graded doses either in real life (in vivo desensitization) or in imagination (imaginal desensitization). Although the underlying mechanism in systematic desensitization has not been determined, the technique is based on the notion that pairing the feared stimulus (for example, heights) with incompatible feelings (of relaxation) will produce a decrease in the fear response to the stimulus. Typically, the therapist develops with the child a hierarchy of situations or scenes involving the feared stimulus that are graded from minimally stressful to intensely stressful. After the child has mastered relaxation skills, the therapist exposes the relaxed child to the least feared stimulus scene for a brief period. The child is instructed to remain relaxed and to indicate to the therapist when anxiety is felt. The therapist discontinues the scene (or when in vivo, removes the child from the feared situation), and the child is instructed to relax again. When the child can tolerate the presence of the least stressful scene for some time without experiencing anxiety, the next scene is introduced, and the procedure is repeated. The child and therapist gradually move up the hierarchy in this manner until the child is able to imagine the most stressful/fear-producing situation while remaining free of anxiety. (Morris & Kratochwill [1983] have recently reviewed the literature on the use of systematic desensitization with children.) While other, more rapid, methods such as implosion therapy or exposure are often used with adults, the use of less intrusive procedures (such as systematic desensitization) is ethically desirable when children are seen in treatment (Johnson & Melamed, 1979).

The behavioral literature in the treatment of syndromal *depression* in children is sparse. A number of case studies (Petti, 1981; Petti & Wells, 1980) have been published describing the utility of behavioral methods combined with other modalities for treating depressed children. However, the specific contribution of behavior therapy to the child's improvement is difficult to evaluate from these reports. In one study (Frame, Matson, Sonis, Fialkov, & Kazdin, 1982), several specific depressive behaviors of a 10-year-old boy were modified through social-skills training. The behaviors targeted for change often have been associated with the syndrome of depression: inaudible voice volume, lack of eye contact, bland affect, and inappropriate posture. During treatment, appropriate behavior was modeled, he was directed to practice it, and he was praised for appropriate behavior and corrected for inappropriate behavior. Skills training was sequentially introduced; first posture was targeted, then eye contact, then inaudible speech, and, finally, bland affect. (This kind of sequential treatment is known as a *multiple baseline design*. When a particular behavior changes when and only when the behavior is treated, it allows the therapist to be more confident that it is the treatment package and not other factors that is producing the desired behavior change.) In this case, the introduction of skills training produced immediate improvement in each treated behavior. Unfortunately, it is not clear whether the skills training had any effect on the other symptoms associated with depression, such as the child's mood, appetite, or enjoyment and interest in pleasurable activities. Thus, while this report remains one of the methodologically most sophisticated published to date on a treatment for depressive symptoms in childhood, it is clear that further evaluation is necessary before we can draw conclusions about the utility of behavioral techniques with depressed children.

**Social Isolation and
Withdrawal**

Shyness and social isolation have been increasingly studied in recent years. Although many shy and withdrawn children appear to "grow out of it," becoming more socially involved as they grow older, some extremely withdrawn and isolated children may miss many learning experiences provided by peers and so many remain socially isolated as adults. This has implications not only for the child's present and future quality of life but also for the child's future mental health, as some research indicates that isolated individuals run a greater risk of mental illness than persons with adequate social support (see Chapter 3).

Modeling of appropriate social behavior on film (symbolic modeling) has been effective in increasing the social interaction of withdrawn children. In a classic study, O'Connor (1969) treated socially withdrawn preschoolers. Half of the children viewed a film portraying peer models in progressively more active social interactions, while half of the children saw a "control" film on the behavior of dolphins. Following treatment, the children who saw the modeling film interacted with their peers to the same extent as their socially normal classmates. The behavior of the children who viewed the control film, however, was unchanged. In a later study (O'Connor, 1972), it was shown that these gains were maintained at a follow-up three weeks later. Not all evaluations of symbolic modeling have reported such success, however (Morris & Kratochwill, 1983).

Contingency management has also been used to treat isolate behavior. In one study (Allen, Hart, Buell, Harris, & Wolf, 1964), a four-year-old girl's interactions with her classmates were markedly increased by instructing her teachers to provide social approval and attention when she approached and interacted with the other children. Behavior that was directed solely toward the teacher no longer received praise and attention, unless appropriate. In a similar study, an isolate child was taught to use various pieces of outdoor play equipment through physical prompting (lifting her onto the play equipment) and through social approval and attention from her teachers (Buell, Stoddard, Harris, & Baer, 1968). Eventually, physical prompting became unnecessary. As her use of the play equipment increased, she also began to talk more to the other children, touch them, and engage in cooperative play with them. In other words, her appropriate social interactions with her classmates increased as she acquired a common childhood skill (play) that facilitated social interaction. Socialization itself was never directly targeted in treatment. This clever procedure may also be applied to older children or adolescents; the child may be taught a valued skill, such as playing the guitar, that will facilitate contact with other children. Once the child has made contact with a peer group, in some cases exposure to the "natural communities of reinforcement" (Baer & Wolf, 1970) will shape and maintain appropriate social behavior without further intervention.

In other cases, additional treatment is needed. Some children may lack the skills needed to interact appropriately when they are with their peers. Social-skills training may be useful in providing the child with skills needed for effective interaction. Although a variety of social-skills training programs have been developed (Cartledge & Milburn, 1980), they share many features in common. Typically, the therapist first identifies a set of social skills that appear necessary for successful interaction within a particular age-group, for example, inviting another child to join a game. Once the targets are identified, the child may role-play the situation with the therapist to determine whether the skills are in the child's repertoire. Following the assessment, the therapist or an aide models the appropriate skill and directs the child to engage in the behavior. The child is rewarded with praise (and, perhaps, tokens) for approximating the desired behavior. As the child's performance improves, the therapist differentially rewards performances that are closer and closer approximations to the target. Successful results using this type of program, which combines modeling with reinforcement, have been obtained with elementary school children (Cooke & Apolloni, 1967; Ladd, 1981), learning-disabled children (LaGreca & Santogrossi, 1980), emotionally disturbed children (Matson et al., 1980), and children with assertiveness problems (Bornstein, Bellack, & Hersen, 1977).

Although these interventions have frequently succeeded in producing dramatic changes in children's behavior on role-plays or on within-session measures, the extent to which these changes generalize into the natural environment is not clear. In evaluating the utility of a treatment, it may not be sufficient to determine whether the treatment had an effect only in changing the child's scores on a psychometric or behavioral assessment device. The extent to which the change is meaningful (clinically significant) often must be assessed as well. For example, in the literature on social-skills training with children, numerous articles describing effective treatment procedures aimed at increasing specific skill components have been published. In very few instances have the effects of these skills on the child's social standing, personal satisfaction, peer adjustment, or parent/teacher satisfaction been made. In other words, in the area of social-skills training, the extent to which the changes produced in the clinic "make a difference" in the child's functioning at home or school has not been determined. Thus, many skills-training packages lack "social validity" (Kazdin, 1977a; Wolf, 1978). Further research is needed to evaluate the impact of skills training in enhancing the child's ability to deal effectively with other children and adults in day-to-day situations outside of therapy.

Conduct Disorders, Aggression, and Delinquency

In Chapter 2, the failure of the literature to discriminate between unsocialized and socialized conduct problems was noted. The same deficiency is found in the behavioral literature, although there are empirical and theoretical reasons for suggesting that different responses to behavioral interventions may be found in the two groups. Behavior therapists generally view conduct-type problems as "skills deficits"; the child has failed to learn to delay gratification or has not acquired the skills needed to obtain gratification appropriately. From this point of view, effective treatment would require the development of new, more socially appropriate, behavioral repertoires, as well as the elimination of the norm-violating behavior.

One difficulty facing behavior therapists who work with conduct problem children is that much of the behavior provides immediate reinforcement in the form of consumption, excitement, or peer approval. The therapist's social approval for improvements in self-control and for other appropriate behavior pales in comparison to these immediate consequences. Thus, shaping more adaptive behavior (here defined as behavior more conforming to society's standards) is often difficult.

Behavioral interventions with conduct disordered subjects have been conducted in institutions, in residential community settings (group homes), and in the home. Institutional settings are chronically plagued with problems of understaffing, overcrowding, and insufficient funds; these problems make implementation of behavior management programs difficult. In many cases behavior management programs may be implemented in order to reduce disruptive behavior and thereby facilitate the smooth operation of the facility (cf. Burchard & Tyler, 1965). Interventions aimed at providing the children with needed academic, vocational, and social skills appear to be less common, although some programs have been developed. Residential programs are discussed in Chapter 15.

In some cases, intervention can be made in the family setting. *Behavioral contracting* is one technique that has been used successfully in behavioral family therapy (Stuart, Jayaratne, & Tripodi, 1976). This is an explicit (usually written) mutual agreement between parties specifying the rights and responsibilities of each party in which the parents and the delinquent child negotiate the allocation of specific privileges in exchange for clearly specified behaviors. For example, the parents of a 13-year-old may agree to provide an allowance (to be spent as their daughter wishes) if she agrees to return home by dinnertime everyday. A "clause" can be written in the contract for failure to perform the behavior; the allowance may be docked a specified sum for each 10-minute infraction of the rule.

Behavioral contracting is obviously not a panacea for the problems of conduct disordered youth. If parents do not or cannot exert control over the behavior or do not control any rewards the child finds attractive (as in the case of families where the child finds the approval of peers extremely potent), then the contract will be ineffective. Contracts are, however, useful in defusing hostile nonproductive situations (Ross, 1981). Since the expectations of all parties are mutually negotiated and agreed upon, as well as put explicitly in writing, many arguments and misunderstandings are avoided, and the parents and child may begin to interact in a more positive manner overall (Tharp & Wetzel, 1969). More complete programs have proven successful in modifying disruptive and antisocial behavior by teaching the parents to differentially reward or ignore aspects of their child's behavior (Fleishman, 1981; Patterson, 1971).

Management of Physical Symptoms

CHRONIC PAIN

Though pain primarily functions to provide information that something physical is wrong and requires attention, research work with adults has suggested that environmental factors (such as warmth and sympathy) may *in some cases* lead to the actual experience of pain even without a physiological cause or with a minimal physiological cause. If a child (or an adult for that matter) receives warmth and affection from others for saying that a wound hurts, for grimacing in pain, or for actually experiencing pain, the chances are great that these behaviors will increase in frequency and, possibly, intensity. The goal of behavioral pain management is to rearrange the environment to reduce behaviors that interfere with the child's rehabilitation and to increase the child's ability to lead a rich and varied life. Of course, the goal of the treatment is not to eliminate expressions of concern and caring by adults in the child's environment but to ensure that affection and empathy do not inadvertently hinder the child's progress toward health (Varni, 1983).

The field of pain management with children is still in its infancy but initial results look promising. In one case, a three-year-old girl who had apparently been the victim of child abuse was in the hospital for 10 months for treatment of second- and third-degree burns over the lower half of her body (Varni, Bessman, Russo, & Cataldo, 1980). There were several medical complications in addition to the burns. At the beginning of the treatment, the girl engaged in sobbing and screaming, grimaces, and other nonverbal gestures, signaling the presence of discomfort, and made many statements indicating that she was in pain (e.g., "My legs hurts."). These behaviors appeared to be increasing both in frequency and intensity, and significantly interfered with her rehabilitation program. Systematic observation showed that these "pain" behaviors reliably occurred at a high rate when adults were present and occurred much less frequently when the child was alone, did not know that she was being observed, or was engaged in interesting activities with warm, approving adults. This strongly suggested that adult attention and approval were factors maintaining these behaviors, and that they were not solely elicited and maintained by internal painful stimulation.

Based on this analysis, the child's caretakers were taught to praise the child for smiling, talking about things besides pain, helping with the rehabilitation procedures, and any behaviors other than the targeted "pain behaviors." Technically, this procedure is known as *differential reinforcement of other* (nontarget) *behavior* or *DRO*. The environment is purposely set up to support (reward) adaptive behaviors of many types and topographies, while the maladaptive behavior (the target) is no longer reinforced. The procedure accomplishes two goals simultaneously: adaptive behaviors are increased in frequency and strength, while inappropriate behaviors are weakened and eventually are no longer used. In this particular treatment procedure, the young girl was also rewarded with ice cream and other preferred foods for increasingly extended periods of time without engaging in the target behaviors. These procedures were effective in reducing the pain behaviors and complaints to low levels. The child began to take a more active role in her rehabilitation and was able to participate in social activities with other children, which her previous behavior had made impractical. The child's own psychological outlook was "brighter," and she no longer appeared in intense distress as she had before treatment.

As discussed in Chapter 7, headaches are a frequent complaint among children (Deubner, 1977), and social-environmental factors are believed to play a major role in their genesis (Brown, 1977). Headaches can significantly interfere with a child's ability to attend or to succeed in school. One method used to reduce the frequency and intensity of headaches has been relaxation training combined with biofeedback. In biofeedback training, the child is given mechanical feedback about increases in hand temperature when a circulation problem is believed to be the cause (as in migraine headaches) or decreases in muscle tension when muscle tension is believed to be the cause (tension headaches). Autonomic and voluntary responses to produce the desired physiological response can be differentially rewarded and shaped through the feedback from the monitoring device.

The successful modification of pediatric migraine headache pain was recently reported by Labbe and Williamson (1984). One of the children studied was a nine-and-a-half-year-old girl who had been suffering from migraines for two years. Her headaches lasted about four hours apiece and occurred four to eight times per month. A self-monitoring procedure whereby she recorded the number and intensity of her headaches four times per day was used. After a baseline period, 10 treatment sessions were given. She was taught to warm her hands through biofeedback to produce increased hand temperature and hence, hopefully, general vasodilation to prevent the spasm of migraine. Relaxation exercises were paired with imaginal scenes designed to produce warm feelings without the biofeedback equipment. Between sessions, she practiced hand-warming at home for 5 to 10 minutes per day. The treatment was successful in reducing the number and intensity of her headaches as well as the headaches of two other children who participated in the project. One month following treatment all three children were still doing well. These results are consistent with reports from other researchers (Andrasik, Blanchard, Edlund, & Rosenblum, 1982).

In some instances, contingency management procedures may also need to be used when the headaches are related to contingent sympathy and attention from parents or teachers and when report of headache results in excuse from school or from unpleasant assignments. In such cases, marked reduction in the headaches complaints can be achieved by changing the consequences (Ramsden, Friedman, & Williamson, 1983).

SEIZURES

In most cases, seizures are best and effectively controlled through the use of anticonvulsant medications. In some cases, however, medication is only partially effective or may produce undesirable side effects, such as sedation or poor coordination that interfere with the child's social and academic functioning. It is also not at all uncommon to find admixtures of true seizures and pseudoseizures in epileptic children. In other cases the differentiation of true from pseudoseizures can be quite difficult. Behavioral interventions to help in seizure control have used relaxation training and contingency management to eliminate seizures. They may also help in differentiating pseudo from true seizures.

Systematic desensitization was used successfully to treat the anxiety associated with seizures in a 12-year-old boy (Ince, 1976) who suffered petit mal and grand mal seizures, frequently requiring visits to the school infirmary. He was reluctant to attend school as he was shunned and teased by the other students; medication had not been effective in controlling the seizures.

In this case several anxiety hierarchies were constructed: being ridiculed by other children, having seizures in public places, and receiving a new drug for seizure control. The child was taught relaxation skills and was given a tape with which to practice relaxation at home. After relaxation skills were mastered, the hierarchy scenes were described, and he imagined each situation while remaining relaxed. When he was able to imagine a lower scene without experiencing anxiety, the next higher item was presented. By the end of the third session, he reported feeling much less anxious and, by the fifth session, was reportedly no longer troubled by anxiety in any of the problem situations.

At this point, his relaxation skills were used to help control his seizures. Since his seizures were preceded by an aura (an idiosyncratic sensory preseizure experience), he was instructed to repeat to himself the word "relax" whenever he experienced an aura. (Previously, "relax" had been paired with the experience of relaxation). Before treatment, he was suffering 9 or 10 grand mal seizures and 25 petit mal seizures per week. No reduction in seizure frequency occurred when the systematic desensitization was used; but when the relaxation procedure for seizure control was begun, there was an immediate reduction in both types of seizures. Grand mal seizures were eliminated and petit mal seizures reportedly occcurred only 3 or 4 times per week. When the occurrence of seizures began to increase slightly after several weeks, the parents brought him back for a "booster session" in which he was repeatedly relaxed and the cue word ("relax") was paired with his relaxed state. Following this booster session, he reportedly did not experience any further grand mal or petit mal seizures several months posttreatment. The results of this case study are particularly interesting because this child's seizures had previously been uncontrolled even when very powerful medications were used.

One hypothesis about the reasons for the procedure's effectiveness is that he was able to interrupt the chain of events leading to a full-blown seizure through the relaxation response.[1] In a similar vein, seizure frequency was

[1]Since seizures typically occur in low states of arousal, the effect of relaxation and the failure of medication suggest that these may have been (mostly) pseudoseizures in this case. It also explains why the shaking (or arousing) procedures in the next cases were effective.—Eds.

greatly reduced in several children when their preseizure chain was disrupted. Each of the children engaged in an idiosyncratic preseizure behavior (e.g., arm raising) that indicated that a seizure was about to occur. When this was observed, the child was shaken vigorously (Zlutnick, Mayville, & Moffat, 1975), greatly reducing the incidence of seizures.

Other treatment techniques have included differential reinforcement, that is, ignoring seizure activity and rewarding nonseizure activity, when no organic basis could be found (pseudoseizures). When no medical reason can be identified, one may reasonably hypothesize that there is an environmental "payoff" for the seizure behavior; ignoring the seizures reduces or eliminates these. Even when an organic basis for the seizures exist, reinforcement for seizure-free periods can be effective in reducing the overall frequency of seizures to a considerable extent since it is not at all uncommon for seizures and pseudoseizures to coexist (Balaschak, 1976). In a recent case (Dollinger, 1983), a teenager suffered from "blackouts" that had no apparent organic basis but were thought to reflect intrafamilial and psychosexual problems. She was experiencing the problem in virtually all settings and at all hours of the day. A contingency management plan was worked out between the mother and daughter. Driving practice in empty parking lots and other safe areas in increasing amounts was used as a reward for seizure reduction. This procedure was effective in reducing the reported number of blackouts to zero in 15 weeks. This improvement was maintained at follow-up three years later.

Behavior therapy also has been applied to bedwetting (Doleys, 1977, 1983) and fecal soiling (Doleys, 1983; Doleys & Arnold, 1975) and to the management of asthma in children (Creer, Renne, & Chai, 1982).

BEHAVIOR THERAPY WITH PSYCHOTIC AND SEVERELY AND PROFOUNDLY RETARDED CHILDREN

In working with children who are labeled severely or profounded retarded or psychotic, behavior therapists have found it most productive to identify classes of behaviors that need to be decreased in frequency or intensity (behavioral excesses) and need to be increased (behavioral deficits) rather than targeting presumed underlying organic or emotional pathology. Since we are currently quite limited in our ability to define and locate, let alone repair, damage to the central nervous system (see Chapter 5) and since efforts to correct hypothesized intrapsychic problems are labor intensive and of unknown effectiveness (see Chapter 13), this behavioral approach appears to be the most practical approach in dealing with the complex behavior problems of these children.

Typically, children who receive diagnoses of psychosis or severe/profound retardation lack basic self-care and language skills and may show aberrant interpersonal behavior, such as avoidance of social contact. Therapy is aimed at increasing the child's behavior in these areas. Frequently, before therapy can progress, behaviors that are incompatible with learning, such as excessive tantruming, self-stimulation, and self-injurious behavior, must be eliminated or controlled.

Decreasing Undesirable Behavior

TANTRUMS

Tantrums obviously occur in normal children of various ages, as well as in diagnostic groups. A tantrum may be defined as an angry noncompliant outburst, often with screaming, crying, and aggressive behavior, such as thrashing, kicking, or throwing toys. Time-out (or more truthfully in some cases, seclusion) is often effective in reducing or eliminating tantrums. Time-out may not always be effective since it may give the child the opportunity to engage in other behaviors that are highly rewarding, such as self-stimulation (Solnick et al., 1977). When this is the case, the use of "time-out" may actually increase the unwanted behavior it consequates. Another example of a "paradoxical" effect of time-out is the situation in which engaging in aggressive or tantrumous behavior enables the child to escape from an unpleasant or difficult situation. If the tantrum succeeds in removing the child from the aversive situation (for example, having to perform some chore or complete a training exercise), the child will be negatively reinforced for engaging in the behavior, and the rate of tantrums, in similar situations, will increase.

When tantrums (and other behaviors such as self-injury or aggressive behavior) serve the function of allowing the child to escape demands, the treatment should focus on the task or situation demands to be sure that the child is capable of performing the required behavior and, if necessary, changing the task demands to be within the child's capabilities. Once this is done, the tantrum behavior (or aggression, etc.) may be put on *extinction*. In other words, the tantrum no longer produces escape; it is no longer reinforced (cf. Carr, Newsom, & Binkhoff, 1976). The therapist may, for example, present a training task and allow the child to tantrum without removing him from the situation and without removing the therapeutic demand for compliance and an appropriate response. Typically, the tantrums increase in frequency and severity briefly (extinction burst) and then decrease. Eventually the child may no longer engage in tantrums at all.

SELF-INJURIOUS BEHAVIOR

Self-injurious behavior is one of the most disturbing behaviors engaged in by the developmentally disabled. The head may be repetitively banged against the wall or floors or fingers chewed through to the bone. The risk of infection and permanent injury is real, and the occurrence of self-injury interferes with efforts to teach the child more adaptive behaviors.

The etiology and motivation of self-injury is a very complex topic; several motivational bases of the problem have been identified (Carr, 1977). Some forms of self-injury appear to be maintained by negative reinforcement, that is, as discussed with tantrums, the child may escape difficult task demands through headbanging or other self-injurious activities. In those cases, extinction procedures may be used after the task demands have been reassessed and the child has been fitted with protective clothing to minimize injury during the extinction periods. In other cases, self-injury appears to be maintained by positive reinforcement—the love and affection expressed by parents and caretakers whenever the child slams his head into the floor or gouges an eye. It is a natural human reaction to attempt to comfort a child in pain or distress, as these children appear to be as they mutilate themselves. However, caresses and attention that occur when the child hits may serve to increase the frequency of these behaviors. When this is the case, extinction may be used to eliminate the self-injury while (simultaneously) the child is generously provided with love and attention contingent upon more appropriate behaviors. Extinction frequently is not a feasible option, however, since increases in the frequency and intensity of self-injury during an extinction burst may result in considerable damage. In such cases and in other cases where the maintaining conditions are unknown or are difficult to alter, physical punishment may be used to suppress the self-injury. Sometimes spankings are effective (Lovaas, Berberich, Perloff, & Schaeffer, 1966); in other cases, aversive stimuli such as lemon juice squirted in the child's mouth (Sajwaj, Libet, & Agras, 1974), aromatic ammonia (Tanner & Zeiler, 1975), or, in some severe cases, electric shock (Lovaas & Simmons, 1969) delivered contingently upon the self-injury, have been successfully used. Less intrusive (and, therefore, ethically more acceptable) procedures such as briefly screening the child's face (Winton, Singh, & Dawson, 1984) or masking the sensory (i.e., tactile, kinesthetic) consequences of the behavior (Rincover & Devany, 1982) have also been shown effective in some cases.

Communication training was shown to be an effective treatment for children's behavior problems, which included self-injury, tantrums, and aggression (Carr & Durand, 1985). Behavioral assessment divided the children into those whose behavior problems occurred in difficult task situations versus those whose occurred during sparse adult attention. This assessment was functionally validated through treatment outcome. The former group's behavior improved when taught to say "Help me," but not "Am I doing good work?" Conversely, the latter group's behavior improved when taught to say "Am I doing good work?" but not "Help me."

Sometimes self-injury is said to be done due to an organic or biological defect, as in the case of Lesch-Nyhan syndrome. Lesch-Nyhan syndrome is an inherited disorder of purine metabolism that results in severe mental retardation and compulsive self-injury, particularly biting of the lips and fingers. Although the cause of this self-injury is reportedly organic, in some cases self-injury due to Lesch-Nyhan disease is amenable to treatment with behavioral methods. In one report (Nidiffer, Iwata, Kelly, & Ward-Zimmerman, 1983), a five-year-old Lesch-Nyhan sufferer was observed to bite his fingers more than 250 times during a 15-minute observation period. The treatment consisted of rewarding the boy for engaging in behaviors that were *incompatible* with the finger-biting. He was rewarded with a small amount of food for every 30-second interval that he spent engaged in incompatible behaviors. Thus, the range of behaviors for which he could obtain a food reward was very broad and could (appropriately) vary from situation to situation throughout the day. The procedure was effective in reducing the child's finger-biting and head-banging to less than 5 percent of the pretreatment levels. In addition, the child's adaptive, appropriate behavior increased dramatically in both the hospital environment and at home. The use of positive reinforcement for alternative, adaptive responses increased the child's overall skills and enhanced his ability to interact effectively with the environment while at the same time nearly eliminating the troublesome behavior. Similar procedures have been used successfully with children whose self-injury is not obviously biologically based (Harris & Ersner-Hershfield, 1978).

SELF-STIMULATION

Self-stimulation (a form of stereotypy discussed in Chapter 7) can be defined as repetitive body movements that have no apparent effect on the environment. They appear to be intrinsically reinforcing. Self-stimulation has been notoriously difficult to eliminate in handicapped children, although the suppression of self-stimulation is important if the child is to progress in treatment (Lovaas & Newsom, 1976) because self-stimulation interferes with the acquisition of new behavior (Koegel & Covert, 1972). Punishment, as described earlier for self-injury, has been used to achieve suppression of self-stimulation (Bucher & Lovaas, 1968). Differential reinforcement of other behavior (DRO), in which the child is rewarded for periods without self-stimulation, has also been used (Dietz & Repp, 1973), although DRO procedures have not been shown to be as effective as other procedures (Foxx & Azrin, 1973).

Since self-stimulation is so persistent, some investigators have suggested that it is maintained by extremely potent sensory consequences. If so, perhaps by masking or removing the sensory consequences, the behavior can be suppressed. In several cases (Rincover, Cook, Peoples, & Packard, 1979), very durable, high-rate, self-stimulatory behavior has been eliminated when the (presumed) sensory consequences of the behavior were eliminated. For example, one child repetitively flipped plates on the hard tabletops of the residential center where he lived. A *sensory extinction* procedure to eliminate the auditory consequences of the plate spinning was introduced: the table tops were carpeted. Plate-spinning dramatically decreased to near zero levels and remained there. When the visual consequences were removed, by temporarily blindfolding the child, no reduction in self-stimulation was obtained. Since the child was no longer plate-spinning constantly, treatment staff were able to concentrate on building more adaptive skills into his repertoire. The success of the auditory sensory extinction procedure suggested that auditory consequences were powerful reinforcers for the child. He was therefore systematically taught to play the autoharp, an age-appropriate activity that eventually supplanted his self-stimulation and appeared to increase his socialization with peers. In fact, this appears to be one of the major benefits of the use of sensory extinction procedures: while the procedure is in place, a therapeutic "window" is created in which the child is no longer engaging in the self-stimulation, and, in addition, a class of powerful sensory consequences for use in rewarding more appropriate behaviors has been identified.

Self-stimulatory behavior has also been treated using *overcorrection* (Foxx & Azrin, 1973). In this procedure, the body part(s) that are involved in the self-stimulatory behavior are *manually guided* through a series of incompatible motions. For example, a child who repetitively claps his hands as a form of self-stimulation was manually guided through a series of arm exercises each time he engaged in clapping. The manual guidance was faded out, and the child performed the exercises when verbally instructed. Eventually, the teachers were able to stop the self-stimulation with a verbal warning (backed up with the overcorrection procedure if the warning was ineffective). Similar success has been reported by other researchers (Doke & Epstein, 1975; Wells, Forehand, Hickey, & Green, 1975). In some variations of the procedure, the child may be required to engage in more adaptive activity that is incompatible with the self-stimulation. For example, a child who puts nonedible items in her mouth may be required to brush her mouth and teeth with a weak Listerine solution. Overall, based on current experimental evidence, overcorrection procedures appear to be a highly effective procedure in suppressing self-stimulation. They have also been effective in decreasing self-injurious behavior (Conley & Wolery, 1980).

As noted in Chapter 7, most infants and toddlers (and to a lesser extent, older children) engage in self-stimulatory behavior. Intervention is rarely warranted in these populations because the self-stimulation does not usually impair the child's ability to behave adaptively nor is it socially stigmatizing.

In some instances, a child may self-stimulate because the environment is grossly understimulating. This can often occur in large institutions. Or the environment may contain an adequate array of toys and play equipment, but the child may lack the skills needed to interact with them in a rewarding manner. Thus, in some cases, environmental enrichment or the teaching of specific skills may be efficient methods of reducing or eliminating self-stimulation.

Increasing Desirable Behavior

Self-care skills (that is, toothbrushing, hair combing, dressing, toileting, bathing, etc.) generally must be specifically taught to the developmentally disabled. Since teaching these skills is greatly facilitated when the child is able to copy the behavior of a model, nonverbal imitation training is frequently conducted if the child lacks these nonverbal imitation skills. Once the child has learned to imitate the actions of others, the child may be rewarded for progressive improvements in executing the modeled self-care behaviors. Other behaviors may be taught through chaining and shaping.

Generally, the initial phases of a treatment program are aimed at eliminating grossly disruptive behavior, teaching compliance to instructions, and teaching language skills. Most children receive speech training; if this is not successful, training in sign language, using essentially the same procedure, may be instituted. Language is heavily emphasized because the prognosis for children who have some language skills before the age of five is considerably brighter than for children who do not (Baltaxe & Simmons, 1975). Disruptive and maladaptive behavior may also serve a communicative function for a child may bang her head as a way of expressing frustration and indicating "This task is too hard for me" (Carr, 1977). It is wise to teach the child to express such needs and wants verbally or manually (with signs) at the same time that self-injurious of disruptive behavior is eliminated (Carr & Durand, 1985).

Language training is aimed at teaching the child words (or signs) and the appropriate use of those words within sentences (grammatically) and in the natural environment (pragmatically). In the program developed at UCLA (Devany, Rincover, & Lovaas, 1981; Lovaas, 1977), for example, the language training program is divided into steps. Briefly, the child first is taught to verbally imitate the therapist's productions. For example, the therapist may say, "Say 'oo'" and the child is rewarded if she says, "oo." With mute children, this may take considerable time as the child's grunts and cries must often carefully be shaped into closer and closer approximations of the therapist's speech. Once the child is reliably imitating the therapist's vocalizations, the child is taught to label objects and events. This training includes teaching the child to respond appropriately to the speech of others (understanding) and to produce intelligible appropriate labels (production). For example, the child would be taught through shaping and fading to respond appropriately to the instructions "Pour the milk" and "Drink the milk" and to say "Milk" when presented with a glass of milk. Once the child has mastered several nouns and verbs, the therapist and parents may require that the child combine them to form grammatically correct two-word phrases (e.g., "Want milk") in order to obtain reinforcement. Once the child has mastered a basic labeling vocabulary, more abstract terms such as adverbs and adjectives, prepositions, pronouns, "yes" and "no," and time-related words are taught. After the child has acquired a relatively large vocabulary and several terms to express relationships between events, the therapist may teach the child to ask and answer simple social questions (such as "How are you?"), to request information and provide information on request. Once these simple conversational skills are mastered, training may shift to the recall and description of past events and training to improve the quality and spontaneity of the child's speech. Throughout the training, the child is encouraged to use newly acquired skills for communication during time outside the therapy session. Parents, siblings, and teachers who are kept up to date on the child's progress can prompt the child to use new skills in the natural environment, facilitating the transfer of the new skills. and also reward the child for her or his success. As training progresses, the child is taught to use language to develop a sense of identity and to foster appropriate social interactions with families (conversations) and with other children (play).

For most developmentally delayed children, especially the severely handicapped, most tasks/skills must be taught in this fashion. Tasks are broken down into small components and these are taught to the child one at a time, with a new step added as an old one is mastered. Not only are the children deficient in many areas, but they are often motivated by only a limited array of experiences (such as food), which greatly hampers this learning. This forces the therapist, teachers, and parents to rely on artificial reward systems with the eventual hope that toys and social approval will acquire reward value as the child acquires play skills and social skills.

Behavior therapy programs for the developmentally disabled have been successful in eliminating grossly stigmatizing and maladaptive behaviors in many children and in providing functional communication skills to children who previously could not speak or sign. Self-care skills have improved the quality of life and enhanced the personal dignity of many who were formerly completely cared for by others. In a few cases, autistic children reportedly have overcome their tremendous deficits and become "normal," virtually indistinguishable from their peers (Lovaas, 1980).

Although these gains represent tremendous advances in the teaching and care of retarded, autistic, and psychotic children, there are limitations to the effectiveness of our current behavioral techniques. Because these children so often are not responsive to the natural social events that shape and maintain the behavior of normal children, artificial motivational systems employing food and other rewards must be employed. While these may be effective in maintaining high levels of appropriate behavior while the child is in treatment, once the child returns to the natural environment, these gains are often lost (Lovaas, Koegel, Simmons, & Long, 1973). In Lovaas's now classic follow-up of 20 children who had passed through his program, the children who were discharged from treatment to homes where parents had been trained to implement the same training and motivational procedures maintained the behavior changes they had made, while children who did not return to such homes lost the gains they had made over the course of treatment. In other words, the children's behavior changes were not *maintained* over time unless their parents had received special training. Another limitation of behavioral training has been that improvements in behavior may be confined only to the setting in which treatment occurs or to highly similar settings. That is, behavior change may fail to *generalize* to new environments. While this problem can be overcome to some degree by training-for-generalization (e.g., using multiple therapists; cf. Stokes & Baer, 1977), it continues to pose a problem to the practical success of behavior modification (behavior therapy) programs.

Finally, the question of functional utility must be addressed. Some children have made remarkable gains in treatment, and there have been reports of substantial behavioral improvements when intensive behavior therapy begins with very young autistic children (Lovaas, 1980). Older children, unresponsive children, or those with serious central nervous system impairment may not make such advances, however. Lovaas and his colleagues (1973) in their follow-up study, noted that for many of the autistic/schizophrenic children they treated, the behavior gains achieved after hour upon hour of intensive individualized treatment were equivalent to moving 10 steps up a 100-step ladder. While no one can deny that these children in many cases enjoy richer, more comfortable lives, it is also undeniable that new techniques and treatment methods will be necessary if the majority of these children will be able to live "normal" lives, if in fact such a goal is realizable (for the severely and profoundly retarded, it may not).

SUMMARY

This chapter has illustrated behavior therapy techniques and principles applied to various clinical problems seen in children. Although there is considerable evidence of the utility of behavior therapy with children, considerably more research needs to be done, and several problems remain. Programs are often effective while the program is in place or for the short term; ensuring that gains are maintained over time continues to be problematic. More effective interventions with many serious disorders, such as substance abuse and conduct disorders, must be developed and the generality and efficiency of behavioral treatments (relative to others) remains to be established.

Some of this information may be acquired through rigorously conducted treatment studies involving large numbers of randomly assigned children. Only a few such studies have been done with children. Most of the literature cited here consists of reports of case studies or experimental analyses of behavior change in one or a few children. Nevertheless, when properly conducted, such single-subject research can illuminate the maintaining variables of problem behaviors through a more intensive examination of environmental and motivational factors than would be possible when studying large groups of children. For example, our current knowledge about the multiple determinants of self-injurious behavior could not have been obtained through the evaluation of treatment impact on *groups* of children.

Some (e.g., Smith & Glass, 1977) have argued that behavior therapy is no more effective than other types of intervention. It is important to remember, however, that meta-analysis and other treatment comparisons generally rely on studies that indicate the effects of a standard behavior technique or treatment package on the behavior of a group of children. Given the great variability we see even among children who carry the same diagnostic label, it is not surprising that a particular behavioral technique (for example, contingency management) may be found to be no more effective than another intervention technique (for example, medication) along some dimensions. In such studies, no individualized analysis has been made of a child's behavioral strengths and weaknesses and the context in which the problem behaviors occur. Well-designed group studies employing individualized treatment (e.g., Gittelman-Klein et al., 1976) can provide useful information about the relative success rates of various treatments in a population of children with similar problems, the relative costs of different treatments, and relative success in maintaining long-term behavior change. Nevertheless, they do not tell us whether a particular treatment will be effective (or the degree to which it will be effective) with a specific child. This problem, identifying effective treatments for the needs of unique children, remains a challenge for clinical researchers (Barlow, Hayes, & Nelson, 1984) regardless of theoretical orientation.

These problems aside, in the 25 years since behavioral techniques have been introduced, substantial improvements in children with a variety of presenting problems have been documented. The optimism expressed now about the future of behavior therapy with children is an optimism tempered by encountering real limitations and pitfalls, rather than the "blind faith" optimism of the past. Systematic application of therapeutic components, careful analysis of the context of behavior, and regular assessment of behavior have been responsible for these therapeutic advances. It is to be expected that continued application of this approach to clinical problems will enhance our abilities as therapists to intervene successfully.

REFERENCES

Adelson, R., Liebert, R. M., Poulos, R. W., & Herskovitz, A. (1972). A modeling film to reduce children's fear of dental treatment. *International Association for Dental Research Abstracts*, 114.

Allen, K. E., Hart, B. M., Buell, J., Harris, F., & Wolf, M. (1964). Effects of social reinforcement on isolate behavior of a nursery school child. *Child Development, 35*, 511–518.

Andrasik, F., Blanchard, B., Edlund, S. R. & Rosenblum, E. L. (1982). Autogenic feedback in the treatment of two children with migraine headache. *Child & Family Behavior Therapy, 4*, 13–23.

Ayllon, T., Layman, D., & Kandel, H. J. (1975). A behavioral-educational alternative to drug control of hyperactive children. *Journal of Applied Behavior Analysis, 8*, 137–146.

Ayllon, T., Smith, D., & Rogers, M. (1970). Behavioral management of school phobia. *Journal of Behavior Therapy and Experimental Psychiatry, 1*, 125–138.

Baer, D. M., & Wolf, M. (1970). The entry into natural communities of reinforcement. In R. Ulrich, T. Stachnik, & R. Mabry (Eds.), *Control of human behavior* (Vol. 2, pp. 319–324). New York: Scott, Foresman.

Baer, D. M., Wolf, M., & Risley, T. (1968). Some current dimensions of applied behavior analysis. *Journal of Applied Behavior Analysis, 1*, 91–97.

Balaschak, B. (1976). Teacher implemented behavior modification in a case of organically based epilepsy. *Journal of Consulting and Clinical Psychology, 44*, 218–223.

Baltaxe, C., & Simmons, J. Q. (1975). Language in childhood psychosis: A review. *Journal of Speech and Hearing Disorders, 40*, 439–458.

Bandura, A. (1969). *Principles of behavior modification.* New York: Holt, Rinehart, & Winston.

Bandura, A., Blanchard, E. B., & Ritter, B. (1969). Relative efficacy of desensitization and modeling approaches for inducing behavioral, affective, and attitudinal changes. *Journal of Personality and Social Psychology, 13*, 173–199.

Barkley, R. A. (1981). *Hyperactive children: A handbook for diagnosis and treatment.* New York: Guilford Press.

Barlow, D. H., Hayes, S. C., & Nelson, R. O. (1984). *The scientist-practitioner.* New York: Pergamon.

Bernard, M. E., & Joyce, M. R. (1984). *Rational-emotive therapy with children and adolescents.* New York: Wiley.

Bornstein, M. R., Bellack, A. A., & Hersen, M. (1977). Social skills training for unassertive children: A multiple baseline analysis. *Journal of Applied Behavior Analysis, 10*, 183–195.

Brown, J. K. (1977). Migraine and migraine equivalents in children. *Developmental Medicine and Child Neurology, 19*, 683–692.

Brown, R. T., Wynne, M. E., & Medenis, R. (1985). Methylphenidate and cognitive therapy: A comparison of treatment approaches. *Journal of Abnormal Child Psychology, 13(1)*, 69–87.

Bucher, B., & Lovaas, O. I. (1968). Use of aversive stimulation in behavior modification. In M. R. Jones (Ed.), *Miami symposium on prediction of behavior 1967: Aversive stimulation* (pp. 77–145). Coral Gables, FL: University of Miami Press.

Buell, J., Stoddard, P. Harris, F., & Baer, D. (1968). Collateral social development accompanying reinforcement of outdoor play in a preschool child. *Journal of Applied Behavior Analysis, 1*, 167–173.

Burchard, J., & Tyler, V. (1965). The modification of delinquent behavior through operant conditioning. *Behaviour Research and Therapy, 2*, 245–250.

Carr, E. G. (1977). The motivation of self-injurious behavior: A review of some hypotheses. *Psychological Bulletin, 84*, 800–816.

Carr, E. G., & Durand, V. M. (1985). The social-communicative basis of severe behavior problems in children. In S. Reiss & R. Bootzin (Eds.), *Theoretical issues in behavior therapy.* New York: Academic Press.

Carr, E. G., Newsom, C. D., & Binkhoff, J. (1976). Stimulus control of self destructive behavior in a psychotic child. *Journal of Abnormal Child Psychology, 4*, 139–153.

Cartledge, G., & Milburn, J. (1980). *Teaching social skills to children: Innovative approaches*. New York: Pergamon.

Cooke, T. P., & Apolloni, T. (1976). Developing positive social-emotional behaviors: A study of training and generalization effects. *Journal of Applied Behavior Analysis, 9*, 65–78.

Conley, O. S., & Wolery, M. (1980). Treatment of overcorrection of self-injurious eye-gouging in preschool blind children. *Journal of Behavior Therapy and Experimental Psychiatry, 11*, 121–125.

Creer, T. L., Renne, C. M., & Chai, H. (1982). The application of behavioral techniques to childhood asthma. In D. C. Russo & J. W. Varni (Eds.), *Behavioral pediatrics: Research and practice* (pp. 27–66). New York: Plenum Press.

Deubner, D. C. (1977). An epidemiologic study of migraine and headache in 10–20 year olds. *Headache, 17*, 173–180.

Devany, J. M., & Rincover, A. (1982). Self-stimulatory behavior and sensory reinforcement. In R. Koegel, A. Rincover, & A. Egel (Eds.), *Educating and understanding autistic children* (pp. 127–141). San Diego: College Hill Press.

Devany, J. M., Rincover, A., & Lovaas, O. I. (1981). Teaching speech to nonverbal children. In J. M. Kauffman & D. P. Hallahan (Eds.) *Handbook of special education*. Englewood Cliffs, NJ: Prentice-Hall.

Dietz, S., & Repp, A. (1973). Decreasing classroom misbehavior through the use of DRL schedules of reinforcement. *Journal of Applied Behavior Analysis, 6*, 457–463.

Doke, L., & Epstein, L. (1975). Oral overcorrection: Side effects and extended applications. *Journal of Experimental Child Psychology, 20*, 496–511.

Doleys, D. (1977). Behavioral treatments for nocturnal enuresis in children: A review of the recent literature. *Psychological Bulletin, 84*, 30–54.

Doleys, D. (1983). Enuresis and encopresis. In T. H. Ollendrick & M. Hersen (Eds.), *Handbook of child psychopathology* (pp. 201–226). New York: Plenum Press.

Doleys, D., & Arnold, S. (1975). Treatment of childhood encopresis: Full cleanliness training. *Mental retardation, 13*, 14–16.

Dollinger, L. (1983). A case report of dissociative neurosis (depersonalization disorder) in an adolescent treated with family therapy and behavior modification. *Journal of Consulting and Clinical Psychology, 51*, 479–484.

Ellis, A., & Bernard, M. E. (Eds.) (1983). *Rational-emotive approaches to the problems of childhood*. New York: Plenum Press.

Favell, J. E., McGimsey, J. F., Jones, M. L., & Cannon, P. R. (1981). Physical restraint as positive reinforcement. *American Journal of Mental Deficiency, 85*, 425–432.

Fleischman, M. J. (1981). A replication of Patterson's "Intervention for boys with conduct problems." *Journal of Consulting and Clinical Psychology, 49*, 342–351.

Frame, C., Matson, J. L., Sonis, W. A., Fialkov, M. J., & Kazdin, A. (1982). Behavioral treatment of depression in a prepubertal child. *Journal of Behavior Therapy and Experimental Psychiatry, 13*, 239–243.

Foxx, R. M., & Azrin, N. H. (1973). The elimination of autistic self-stimulatory behavior by overcorrection. *Journal of Applied Behavior Analysis, 6*, 1–14.

Gittelman-Klein, R., Klein, D., Abikoff, H., Katz, S., Gloisten, A., & Kates, W. (1976). Relative efficacy of methylphenidate and behavior modification in hyperactive children: An interim report. *Journal of Abnormal Child Psychology*, *4*, 361–379.

Harris, S., & Ersner-Hershfield, R. (1978). Behavioral suppression of seriously disruptive behavior in psychotic and retarded patients: A review of punishment and its alternatives. *Psychological Bulletin*, *85*, 1352–1375.

Hayes, S. C., Rincover, A., & Volosin, D. (1980). Variables influencing the acquisition and maintenance of aggressive behavior. *Journal of Abnormal Psychology*, *89*, 254–262.

Hobbs, S. A., Moquin, L. E., Tyroler, M. & Lahey, B. B. (1980). Cognitive behavior therapy with children: Has clinical utility been demonstrated? *Psychological Bulletin*, *87*, 147–165.

Ince, L. (1976). The use of relaxation training and a conditioned stimulus in the elimination of epileptic seizures in a child. *Journal of Behavior Therapy and Experimental Psychiatry*, *7*, 39–42.

Johnson, S. B., & Melamed, B. G. (1979). The assessment and treatment of children's fear. In B. B. Lahey & A. E. Kazdin (Eds.), *Advances in clinical child psychology* (Vol. 2, pp. 172–184). New York: Plenum Press.

Kazdin, A. (1977a). Assessing the clinical or applied importance of behavior change through social validation. *Behavior Modification*, *1*, 427–452.

Kazdin, A. (1977b). *The token economy*. New York: Plenum Press.

Kendall, P., & Finch, A. J. (1978). A cognitive behavioral treatment for impulsivity: A group comparison study. *Journal of Consulting and Clinical Psychology*, *46*, 110–118.

Kendall, P. C., & Urbain, E. S. (1981). Cognitive-behavioral intervention with a hyperactive girl: Evaluation via behavioral observations and cognitive performance. *Behavioral Assessment*, *3*, 345–357.

Kirkland, K. D., & Thelen, M. H. (1977). Uses of modeling in child treatment. In B. B. Lahey & A. E. Kazdin (Eds.) *Advances in Clinical Child Psychology* (Vol. 1, pp. 307–328). New York: Plenum Press.

Koegel, R. L., & Covert A. (1972). The relationship of self-stimulation to learning in autistic children. *Journal of Applied Behavior Analysis*, *5*, 381–387.

Labbe, E., & Williamson, D. (1984). Temperature biofeedback in the treatment of children with migraine headache. *Journal of Consulting and Clinical Psychology*, *52*, 968–976.

Ladd, G. (1981). Effectiveness of a social learning method for enhancing children's social interaction and peer acceptance. *Child Development*, *52*, 171–178.

LaGreca, A. M., & Santogrossi, D. (1980). Social skills training with elementary school students: A behavioral group approach. *Journal of Consulting and Clinical Psychology*, *48*, 220–227.

Lahey, B. (1979). *Behavior therapy with hyperactive and learning disabled children*. New York: Oxford University Press.

Lassen, M. E., & McConnell, S. C. (1977). Treatment of a severe bird phobia by participant modeling. *Journal of Behavior Therapy and Experimental Psychiatry*, *8*, 165–168.

Lazarus, A., & Abramovitz, A. (1962). The use of "emotive imagery" in the treatment of children's phobias. *Journal of Mental Science, 108*, 191–195.

Lewis, S. (1974). A comparison of behavior therapy techniques in the reduction of fearful avoidance behavior. *Behavior Therapy, 5*, 648–655.

Lovaas, O. I. (1977). *The autistic child.* New York: Irvington.

Lovaas, O. I. (1980). *Report of the results of the UCLA Early Intervention Project.* Paper presented at the Annual Convention of the American Psychological Association, Washington, DC.

Lovaas, O. I., Berberich, J. P., Perloff, B. F., & Schaeffer, B. (1966). Acquisition of imitative speech in schizophrenic children. *Science, 151*, 705–707.

Lovaas, O. I., Frietag, G., Kinder, M. I., Rubenstein, B. D., Schaefer, B., & Simmons, J. Q. (1966). Establishment of social reinforcers in two schizophrenic children on the basis of food. *Journal of Experimental Child Psychology, 4*, 109–125.

Lovaas, O. I., Koegel, R., Simmons, J. Q., & Long, J. S. (1973). Some generalization and follow-up measures on autistic children in behavior therapy. *Journal of Applied Behavior Analysis, 6*, 131–166.

Lovaas, O. I., & Newsom, C. D. (1976). Behavior modification with psychotic children. In H. Leitenberg (Ed.), *Handbook of behavior modification and behavior therapy* (pp. 303–360). Englewood Cliffs, NJ: Prentice-Hall.

Lovaas, O. I., & Simmons, J. Q. (1969). Manipulation of self-destruction in three retarded children. *Journal of Applied Behavior Analysis, 3*, 143–157.

Luiselli, J. D. (1978). Treatment of an autistic child's fear of riding a school bus through exposure and reinforcement. *Journal of Behavior Therapy and Experimental Psychiatry, 9*, 169–172.

Matson, J. (1981). Assessment and treatment of clinical phobias in mentally retarded children. *Journal of Applied Behavior Analysis, 14*, 145–152.

Matson, J. L., Esveldt-Dawson, K., Andrasik, F., Ollendick, T. H., Petti, T., & Hersen, M. (1980). Direct, observational, and generalization effects of social skills training with emotionally disturbed children. *Behavior Therapy, 11*, 522–531.

Maurer, A. (1983). The shock rod controversy. *Journal of Clinical Child Psychology, 12*, 272–278.

Mayhew, G., & Harris, F. C. (1978). Some negative side effects of a punishment procedure for stereotyped behavior. *Journal of Behavior Therapy and Experimental Psychiatry, 9*, 245–251.

Meichenbaum, D. & Goodman, J. (1971). Training impulsive children to talk to themselves: A means of developing self-control. *Journal of Abnormal Psychology, 77*, 115–126.

Melamed, B., & Siegel, L. (1975). Reduction of anxiety in children facing hospitalization and surgery by use of filmed modeling. *Journal of Consulting and Clinical Psychology, 43*, 511–521.

Morris, R. J., & Kratochwill, T. R. (1983). *The practice of child therapy.* New York: Pergamon Press.

Nidiffer, F. D., Iwata, B., Kelly, T. E., & Ward-Zimmerman, B. (1983). *Biochemical and behavioral assessment during the reduction of self-mutilation in a Lesch-Nyhan syndrome child.* Unpublished paper.

O'Conner, R. D. (1969). Modification of social withdrawal through symbolic modeling. *Journal of Applied Behavior Analysis*, *2*, 15–22.

O'Connor, R. D. (172). Relative efficacy of modeling, shaping, and the combined procedures for modification of social withdrawal. *Journal of Abnormal Psychology*, *79*, 327–334.

O'Leary, K. D., Pelham, W. E., Rosenbaum, A., & Price, G. H. (1976). Behavioral treatment of hyperkinetic children. *Clinical Pediatrics*, *15*, 510–515.

Ollendick, T. H., & Cerny, J. A. (1981). *Clinical behavior therapy with children*. New York: Plenum Press.

Patterson, G. (1971). *Families: Applications of social learning to family life*. Champaign, IL: Research Press.

Petti, T. A. (1981). Active treatment of childhood depression. In J. F. Clarkin & H. Glaser (Eds.). *Depression: Behavioral and directive intervention strategies* (pp. 311–343). New York: Garland Press.

Petti, T. A., & Wells, K. (1980). Crisis treatment of a preadolescent who accidentally killed his twin. *American Journal of Psychotherapy*, *34*, 434–443.

Ramsden, R., Friedman, B. & Williamson, D. A. (1983). Treatment of childhood headache reports with contingency management procedures. *Journal of Clinical Child Psychology*, *12*, 202–206.

Rincover, A., & Devany, J. (1982). The application of sensory extinction procedures to self-injury. *Analysis and Intervention in Developmental Disabilities*, *2*, 67–81.

Rincover, A., Cook, A. R., Peoples, A., & Packard, D. (1979). Sensory extinction and sensory reinforcement principles for programming multiple adaptive behavior change. *Journal of Applied Behavior Analysis*, *12*, 221–233.

Risley, T. (1968). The effects and side-effects of punishing the autistic behaviors of a deviant child. *Journal of Applied Behavior Analysis*, *1*, 21–34.

Ross, A. O. (1981). *Child behavior therapy*. New York: Wiley.

Ross, D. M., & Ross, S. A. (1976). *Hyperactivity: Research, theory and action*. New York: Wiley.

Sajwaj, T., Libet, J., & Agras, S. (1974). Lemon juice therapy: The control of life-threatening rumination in a six-month-old infant. *Journal of Applied Behavior Analysis*, *7*, 557–563.

Skinner, B. F. (1953). *Science and human behavior*. New York: Macmillan.

Smith, M. L., & Glass, G. V. (1977). Meta-analysis of psychotherapy outcome studies. *American Psychologist*, *32*, 752–760.

Snyder, J. J., & White, M. H. (1979). The use of cognitive self-instruction in the treatment of behaviorally disturbed adolescents. *Behavior Therapy*, *10*, 227–235.

Solnick, J., Rincover, A., & Petersen, C. R. (1977). Some determinants of the reinforcing and punishing effects of time-out. *Journal of Applied Behavior Analysis*, *10*, 415–424.

Stokes, T., & Baer, D. M. (1977). An implicit technology of generalization. *Journal of Applied Behavior Analysis*, *10*, 349–367.

Stuart, R. B., Jayaratne, S., & Tripodi, T. (1976). Changing adolescent deviant behavior through reprogramming the behavior of parents and teachers. *Canadian Journal of Behavioral Science*, *8*, 132–144.

Tanner, B. A., & Zeiler, M. (1975). Punishment of self-injurious behavior using aromatic ammonia as the aversive stimulus. *Journal of Applied Behavior Analysis*, *8,*53–57.

Tharp, R. G., & Wetzel, R. J. (1969). *Behavior modification in the natural environment*. New York: Academic Press.

Urbain, E. S., & Kendall, P. C. (1980). Review of social-cognitive problem-solving interventions with children. *Psychological Bulletin, 88*, 109–143.

Van Hasselt, V. B., Hersen, M., Bellack, A. S., Rosenblum, N. D., & Lamparski, D. (1979). Tripartite assessment of the effects of systematic desensitization in a multi-phobic child: An experimental analysis. *Journal of Behavior Therapy and Experimental Psychiatry, 10*, 51–55.

Varni, J. (1983). *Clinical behavioral pediatrics*. New York: Pergamon Press.

Varni, J., Bessman, C., Russo, D., & Cataldo, M. (1980). Behavioral management of chronic pain in children: A case study. *Archives of Physical Medicine and Rehabilitation, 61*, 375–379.

Wahler, R. G. (1969). Oppositional children: A quest for parental reinforcement control. *Journal of Applied Behavior Analysis, 2*, 159–170.

Wells, K., Forehand, R., Hickey, K., & Green, K. (1975). Effects of a procedure derived from the overcorrection principle on manipulated and nonmanipulated behaviors. *Journal of Applied Behavior Analysis, 10*, 679–687.

Winton, A. S. W., Singh, N., & Dawson, M. J. (1984). Effects of facial screening and blindfold on self-injurious behavior. *Applied Research in Mental Retardation, 5*, 29–42.

Wolf, M. M. (1978). Social validity: The case of objective measurement. *Journal of Applied Behavior Analysis, 11*, 203–214.

Zlutnick, S., Mayville, W. J., & Moffat, S. (1975). Modification of seizure disorders: The interruption of behavioral chains. *Journal of Applied Behavior Analysis, 8*, 1–12.

15 RESIDENTIAL TREATMENT

HERBERT C. QUAY

INTRODUCTION

It is unfortunate that progress in the conceptualization, implementation, and especially the evaluation of residential treatment has not kept pace with progress in other aspects of child and adolescent psychopathology—progress that has been attested to in many of the earlier chapters in this book. There are likely a number of reasons for this lack of progress. The movement toward education and treatment in the "least restrictive environment" (see also Chapters 16 and 17) has led to a deemphasis on residential treatment for children by both the mental health and legal-correctional systems. At the same time there has been diminished financial support for behavioral research in general, no doubt discouraging the necessarily expensive evaluation of residential programs. Then too, the rehabilitative, psychologically minded program philosophy that characterized most of the better correctional institutions in the 1960s and 1970s has given way to a more punitive approach in the face of budgetary strictures and influence of a "nothing works" philosophy. Furthermore, medically-psychiatrically oriented facilities seem no more desirous of operationalizing and rigorously evaluating the effectiveness of their programs than in previous years.

Despite the current emphasis on deinstitutionalization, a United States government report indicated that there were 15,423 admissions to residential treatment centers in 1979 (a rate of 24 admissions per 100,000 population under age 18) and that there were a total of 18,276 persons in residence in these facilities at the end of 1979. In 1980 there were 368 residential treatment centers in the United States with slightly over 20,000 beds available (Redick & Witkin, 1983). Furthermore, as some authors have noted (e.g., Barker, 1982; Martin, Pozdnjakoff & Wilding, 1976), residential treatment may be the best, if not the only, alternative available in a number of situations. (See also Chapter 17.)

EVALUATION DESIGN

Despite these factors, recent evaulations *have* appeared, but there has been (a now outmoded) reliance on very weak designs employing pre–post measurement without contrast groups (e.g., Fineberg, Kettlewell, & Sowards, 1982; Gossett, Barnhart, Lewis, & Phillips, 1977; Lewis, Lewis, Shanock, Klatskin, & Osborne, 1980; Munson & Blincoe, 1984; Schain, Gardella, & Pon, 1982; Winsberg, Bialer, Kupietz, Botti, & Balka, 1980). In review papers, the degree of concern with an evaluation of the studies reviewed is reflected in the conclusions about the effectiveness of residential treatment (e.g., see Fineberg, Sowards, & Kettlewell, 1980, in contrast to Blotcky, Dimpiero, & Gossett, 1984). While many of these more recent uncontrolled studies report short-term positive changes of one sort or another (e.g., Fineberg et al., 1982; Munson & Blincoe, 1984; Winsberg et al., 1980), others assessing children over longer follow-up periods find little evidence for lasting effects (e.g., Gossett et al., 1977; Lewis et al., 1980; Schain et al., 1982).

PROGRAM DESCRIPTIONS AND TREATMENT PRESCRIPTIONS

Despite the lack of progress in evaluation, prescriptions for and description of programs arising from a variety of theoretical perspectives are not lacking (e.g., Agee, 1979; Brendtro & Ness, 1982; Gossett, Lewis, & Barnhart, 1983; Kennedy, 1985; Raubolt, 1983; Whitaker, 1980). As might be expected, prescriptions often run counter to one another.

PROGRAM INTEGRITY

On the positive side, there has been a welcome increase in concern for the problem of the integrity of the treatment, referred to earlier by this writer (Quay, 1977) as the "third face" of evaluation. Sechrest and his colleagues (Sechrest, West, Phillips, Redner, & Yeaton, 1979) have called attention to the problems involved and have suggested guidelines, as have Gendreau and Ross (1979), Rutter and Giller (1984), and Tremblay (1983). Scheirer and Rezmovic (1983) reviewed 74 studies that included some measure of degree of implementation and concluded that the measures used were inadequate to establish the validity of the construct of implementation; they suggested that a more careful analysis of program elements is needed. Salend (1984) considered threats to integrity in behaviorally oriented research, and at a very practical level, both Colyar (1983) and Uranich (1983–84) identified factors that can undermine a planned intervention. In an insightful paper, Johnson (1981) documented the drift of a program away from its intended objectives.

This emphasis on program integrity is a healthy one since it is impossible, no matter how sophisticated the experimental design, to evaluate a treatment without being able to specify what it was and whether or not it was delivered. Furthermore, such concern should lead to further specification as to exactly what *is* the treatment in residential treatment.

REVIEW OF STUDIES

Despite the passage of considerable time, our knowledge about the effects of residential treatment remains based on the studies reviewed in the original version of this chapter (Quay, 1979) with only occasional updates of or additions to earlier works. Our emphasis in the chapter is still on a description and discussion of those studies in which there have been research designs of sufficient rigor to permit some conclusions to be drawn as to the efficacy of the treatment.

Treatment in the Hospital and Mental Health Setting

THE BALDERTON HOSPITAL STUDY

Craft, Stephenson, and Granger (1964) studied the effects of two different treatment regimes on two groups of randomly assigned cases from a pool of adolescent males who had either been placed on probation, with the condition that they receive treatment, or had been sent for treatment from a correctional institution. The two groups were housed separately and exposed either to a self-governing group therapy program or a program emphasizing control on an "enlightened and sympathetic but authoritarian basis" (p. 546). Both units received merit money on the basis of performance on a work detail, a measure of a helpful attitude, and personal neatness and cleanliness. According to the investigators, both groups were severely delinquent with a high previous conviction rate, had highly maladjusted scores on the MMPI, and had a high performance in excess of verbal IQ; all of these features led to a diagnosis of psychopathy in all cases.

Results were based on a sample of cases who remained in treatment at least three months; there were 21 in group therapy and 23 under the authoritarian regime. In terms of entry versus discharge measures, the authoritarian group showed a slight, but statistically significant, increase in IQ and a significant decrease in Porteus maze "Q" score—an error measure related to impulsivity. Scores on the Bristol Social Adjustment scales and on the MMPI were essentially unchanged in both groups.

Follow-up data were obtained by means of a questionnaire completed by after-care personnel, and 38 cases were personally interviewed by their therapists about 15 months after discharge. The number of offenses committed since discharge was significantly less in the group subjected to the authoritarian regime; 11 of the authoritarian boys had committed a total of 14 offenses, while 14 of the group-therapy boys had committed a total of 27 offenses. One-quarter of the authoritarian group and more than one-half of the therapy boys were judged as still in need of institutional care.

As the authors themselves pointed out, the lack of an untreated comparison group makes it difficult to determine whether either treatment made the boys better or worse. At the same time, the conclusion that group psychotherapy in a permissive setting was inferior to a more structured regime was difficult to refute.

It is interesting that the results of this study are in accord with the results of those experimental studies discussed in Chapter 2, which suggested a lack of responsiveness on the part of individuals manifesting extreme conduct disorder to verbally oriented methods of behavior change.

The University of Illinois-Adler Center Project

This study, reported by Monkman (1972), was carried out jointly by researchers including child psychiatrists, psychologists, and social workers at the University of Illinois and practitioners in a facility of the Illinois Department of Mental Health. The evaluation was based on a group of 30 children who were residents over a 27-month period. The children were between the ages of 7 and 13, and ranged in intelligence from trainable to gifted; none were severely overtly psychotic, though a number demonstrated "bizarre behavior." The treatment approach involved the entire milieu and was conceptualized as having five dimensions.

The first dimension of the milieu was a progressive movement system from admission to discharge, then back into the community. In order to accomplish this objective, the system was constructed so that each child was required to engage increasingly in behavior that was appropriate for living in the community. Operationally, there were an orientation level and three treatment levels, each with increasing expectations for appropriate behavior.

The second dimension involved daily routines and the minimum appropriate self-care behaviors expected of each child. These minimum behaviors were itemized on a daily checklist that permitted continuous assessment of the performance rate of the child on these behaviors.

A third dimension consisted of categories of expected social functioning and appropriate social behaviors. These categories were not discrete, as was the case for the minimum appropriate behaviors, but represented areas of development for the child's functioning. The categories were operationalized and served as guidelines in developing the programs for the individual children. For each child, both the quality and quantity of expected behavior varied. Of concern here were such behaviors as cooperation, sharing, helping, participation, interaction, and self-directed activities aimed at individual betterment.

The fourth dimension of the program was a system of feedback and reinforcement. Reinforcers varied between children and varied with the individual child at different times. Various symbols of social approval and such tangible reinforcers as candy, toys, recreational activities, and home visits were used.

The fifth dimension was a system for punishing undesirable behavior and involved two procedures: time-out from reinforcement was used to remove the child from the ongoing situation, and a response-cost procedure was used, which took the form of fines to be paid from the reinforcing checkmarks normally earned by each child. A comparison of these two types of punishment was undertaken as a part of the overall research effort.

The basic philosophy of the project was that individual children were learners and were thus able to change their behavior in interaction with their environment over a period of time. The orientation of the entire program was based on social learning and reinforcement theory.

Both initial and continuous staff training was an integral part of the project. Training centered around the foregoing dimensions of the milieu, cottage management, recreation and arts and crafts activities, school and cottage coordination, physical health and drugs, observation and recording, and individual child care.

Four instruments were used for program monitoring and evaluation. A daily checklist was completed by cottage staff for each child every day that the child was in the cottage. This checklist assessed the presence or absence of the minimum appropriate behaviors that constituted the second dimension of the milieu. Reliability checks indicated that there was greater than 80 percent agreement on all of the items on the checklist.

A second instrument, called a mark sheet, was prepared by cottage staff and carried daily by each child. This sheet indicate the child's target behaviors for his or her program and the number of checkmarks that a child could earn in a day by exhibiting these target behaviors. The mark sheet was an immediately available reminder to the child and staff of the target behaviors and provided a continuous record of the child's progress. The third evaluation instrument was a special behavior report from that was filled out each time the staff invoked a punishment contingency. This form was particularly relevant to the study comparing time-out with response-cost in the suppression of deviant behavior.

A fourth evaluative variable was independent observations made by non-cottage staff who were hired and trained to observe children and to record their observations on a prepared form. Observations were made continuously over the course of participation in the program while children were in class, during free periods, and in the cottage. The percentage of agreement between independent raters across all children was close to 90 percent for both cottage and school setting.

Evaluative data of two types have been presented by Monkman (1972). In Appendix E of the report, descriptions of the programs and data with regard to in-program performance of 27 children are presented. These data are, unfortunately, not summarized, and it is clearly difficult for a reviewer to do so. The overall impression is that most subjects manifested less deviant and more pro-social behaviors with increasing time in the program, but a rigorous test of this hypothesis is not possible.

Postprogram results were obtained on 18 cases for whom information was obtained at an average of 8.8 months after discharge. The average length of residence in the experimental program for these children was 8.3 months with a range of 3 to 12 months. Information was obtained by means of a follow-up questionnaire, the contents of which were subsequently rated by graduate students in clinical psychology who had not been previously exposed to the children.

According to Monkman (1972, p. 132), "The data showed that those problems classified as home were rated 55 percent as improved, and 27 percent as improved to a degree that they were considered indistinguishable from problems of normal children." For problems occurring primarily in school, 53 percent were classified as improved and 7 percent were rated as improved to a degree that they were considered no different from the problems of normal children.

On a subject-by-subject basis, 2 children were rated as functioning normally in the home setting, 9 children were rated as improved in the home setting, 2 children fell into the questionable improvement range, and 1 child was rated unimproved. Within the school setting, 10 children were rated improved, and 8 children were rated as questionably improved.

With respect to the extent to which the problems occurring at the time of the postdischarge assessment were different from the presenting problems, 4 children were considered to need outpatient services of a long-term nature, 11 children were considered to need short-term outpatient services, and 2 children were seen as needing limited consultative services with parents or teachers. Apparently, in none of these cases was reinstitutionalization judged to be required.

As noted before, this project also provided data on a formal comparison of time-out from reinforcement and response-cost procedure as punishment. Results suggested that both techniques were effective in suppressing targeted deviant behavior but that, overall, time-out produced a greater effect on undesirable behavior than did the response-cost procedures.

Despite a multitude of objective data obtained on a day-to-day basis for facets of the in-program performance, no conclusions can be drawn about the lasting effects of the program due to the absence of a contrast group. The small number of subjects and their very mixed nature, with respect to both intelligence and behavior, clearly precludes any conclusions about the interaction between the various factors of this treatment approach and the characteristics of its subjects.

TREATMENT IN THE GROUP-HOME SETTING

The two major efforts to be reviewed here arose out of a disaffection with the medical model of treatment and the medical aura of either the hospital or the mental health center. While the specific techniques differ, both projects emphasized social learning rather than intrapsychic change.

Project Re-Ed

PROGRAM DESCRIPTION

Project Re-Ed (Bower, Lourie, Strother, & Sutherland, 1969; Hobbs, 1966; Weinstein, 1969, 1974), the most ambitious undertaking yet reported in providing and evaluating residential care, was designed to provide a short-term residential program to reeducate children "too disturbed or disturbing" to be maintained in their own homes or schools.

The setting for the project was a number of residential schools in which the staff responsible for designing and implementing the program for the children were specially trained teachers. Mental health specialists and representatives of other disciplines served as consultants rather than as direct providers of service. The Re-Ed staff worked with the children but also dealt with families, schools, and other community agencies in an attempt to help specific aspects of the child's ecology more effectively meet her or his needs. A team of two teacher-counselors was responsible for a group of eight children for 24 hours. In addition, specialized teaching personnel were employed, and aides were used to cover the bedtime hours. A third member of the team, called a liaison-teacher, worked primarily with others in the child's social system. Children went home for weekends and vacations, and visits by parents and teachers were encouraged in order to keep the child involved in a natural social system.

The goals, the theoretical orientation, and some of the operations of the project have been succinctly stated by Weinstein:

> *Re-Ed is quite explicit as to what its goals are and what they are not. No claim is made that deep personality change is effected in the brief length of stay at Re-Ed. . . . Rather, Re-Ed aims at improving the "fit" between the child and others in his social system so that they—his family, school, peers and others in his social world, can provide him with the supports and instruction he needs for appropriate further development. Almost always this means changing the attitudes and behavior of the child, to make him more acceptable to others in his social system, more tolerable and manageable, more able to win their support, affection and commitment, more willing to learn from them and adapt to their needs, expectations and requirements. Usually, it also involves changing the expectations and behaviors of others in his social system, making their expectations more realistic in terms of his abilities, interests and values, and making their behaviors more likely to elicit and maintain the behaviors they want him to display. . . . And Re-Ed's goal is to increase concordance between his behavior and their expectations—by whatever means necessary—above a minimal threshold, to a level where they can provide for his needs for socialization and affection and he can benefit from their efforts. (Weinstein, 1974, p. 3)*

While there were, and still are, a number of Re-Ed schools, the formal evaluation to date (see Weinstein, 1974, from whom all evaluative data have been taken) is limited to a sample of 122 white boys who had attended one of the schools over a five-year period. The criteria for admission were that the child be between 6 and 12 years of age, that he be too disturbed to be treated on an outpatient basis, but that he not require hospitalization or continued surveillance as a result of lack of sufficient contact and control, and that the basic problem not be that of brain damage or mental retardation. The average length of stay was 8.1 months with a standard deviation of 2.8 months.

A comparison group of "untreated disturbed" children was constructed from the nominations by principals of schools from which many experimental children had come. An additional sample of non-problem children was also obtained by the same procedures. Each of the comparison groups consisted of 128 children.

Data on the experimental children were collected at four points: prior to entry, just prior to discharge, and at 6 and 18 months after discharge. Data on the two comparison groups were collected at approximately the same time intervals.

Initial analyses of the data indicated that there were no significant pre-existing differences among the groups on age (about 10 years), intelligence (IQ about 100), or socioeconomic status (most parents were high school graduates in skilled-labor or white-collar occupations). Comparison of the groups on a host of other variables suggested that the Re-Ed children were seen as somewhat more severely disturbed in terms of internal stress than were the untreated disturbed children—a variable subsequently shown, however, to be unrelated to behavior change over time.

Results at the Time of Discharge Although comparable data were obviously not available for the two comparison groups, a variety of ratings were made on the experimental group at the time of discharge by Re-Ed staff and referring agencies. With regard to overall change, the liaison teacher rated 94 percent of all cases as either moderately or much improved; only 6 percent were rated as slightly improved, and none was rated as the same or worse. The referring agencies, who supplied time-of-discharge ratings in only 60 cases of the total sample, judged 88 percent of the children as moderately or much improved, 12 percent as slightly improved, and none as the same or worse.

It is of interest to note that there was some disagreement about exactly which cases were slightly, moderately, or much improved, as the correlations between the two sets of rating was only .39. The findings for overall major to moderate improvement, as judged by Re-Ed staff, generally held for the more specific categories of social behavior, attitudes toward and motivation for learning, and academic skill acquisition. Similar degrees of disagreement about specific children were also manifested in these ratings with interrater reliabilities: .28 for behavioral improvement and .21 for attitude change; judgments about academic skills were made more reliably ($r = .62$).

Predictions by staff as to future adjustment were generally optimistic, though not to the degree of blind faith in the future ability of all discharged children to cope. In keeping with the ecological conceptual framework of the project, ratings were also made of changes in various factors in the child's social systems; changes for the better were noted, but not to the levels to which the children, themselves, were rated as changed.

At discharge, measures on a variety of psychological variables were also obtained. In these instances comparisons could be made with the pretest scores of the experimental group and of the two contrast groups, and with the posttest scores of the latter two groups.

Furthermore, although the project did not utilize any formal classification scheme, either for admission or for treatment prescriptions, "in assigning children to groups, Re-Ed staff spontaneously used the labels 'acting out' and 'withdrawn'" (Weinstein, 1974, p. 69). While this dichotomous diagnostic classification did not influence treatment, it was used, post hoc, to group the project children for the analysis of pre–post changes. Eighty-eight of the group were classified as acting-out, while 34 were classified as withdrawn.

The analysis of a number of measures of psychological functioning revealed that significant gains were made by the experimental children in the reduction of discrepancies between the perceived self and the ideal self, particularly in the case of the withdrawn children, who were more discrepant initially than either the acting-out experimental children or the normals. The effect of the treatment was to increase significantly the degree of internal locus of control in both experimental subgroups—a variable on which the withdrawn group was initially more external than either the acting-outs or the normals.

On two separate measures of impulsivity, the total experimental group was not initially different from the normal comparison group or, as might be expected, from the untreated disturbed group; but at the posttest the total Re-Ed group was less impulsive than the untreated controls. When the project children were dichotomized, however, the acting-out group was initially more impulsive than both the withdrawn group and the normals. At posttest this group was found not to differ from either the withdrawn or the normal comparison groups.

On a measure of social schema, related to emotional disturbance (see Weinstein, 1968), the experimental groups reduced their degree of deviance at posttest, with the greatest gains enjoyed by the withdrawn children.

In summary, the at-discharge data suggested that the project led to a more positive self-concept, more internal locus of control, decreased motor and cognitive impulsivity, and more constructive family relationships as perceived by the child. Over the same time period, there was no significant improvement in these areas among the untreated disturbed group.

Postdischarge School Adjustment For the project staff, the focus of much effort was the reintegration of these children into the school system. School adjustment was considered to be an important outcome variable, and judgments about various facets of it were made on the basis of a form filled out by teachers prior to program entry and at 6 months and 18 months postdischarge. In 98 percent of the cases, three different teachers provided this information. The information contained in the teacher rating form was then rated on a number of dimensions by research staff; all reliability checks indicated good interrater agreement, with correlations generally ranging from .8 to .9 and above. In addition, these ratings were generally stable over time for both the normals and the untreated disturbed group.

An analysis of the global ratings of school behavior revealed that (1) both the project and untreated disturbed children improved significantly between the entry rating and the 6-month rating, and between the 6-month and the 18-month rating; however, the improvements were greater for the Re-Ed group; (2) there were no changes between the 6-month and 18-month ratings, but at 18 months Re-Ed children were rated as less deviant than the untreated group; (3) the greater improvement of the project cases was not a function of their initially higher level of deviance. When the data were considered in terms of percentages of children who improved, it was found that 92 percent of project children were rated as having fairly severe or very severe problems at entry; 44 percent at 6 months postdischarge and 51 percent at 18 months postdischarge were also so rated. Of the untreated group, the initial percentage was 91; subsequent percentages were 65 and 67.

In spite of the significant differences between Re-Ed and the untreated cases, it is of interest that 18 months after the program ended, one-half of the treated group was still seen as having fairly severe or very severe problems. It is also important to note that, in the untreated disturbed group, those who improved over time numbered about one-third of the total, a figure that is well below the 66 percent frequently cited in the "spontaneous recovery" literature. (See Chapter 13.) Other findings of interest were that, although both the withdrawn and acting-out groups improved, at 18 months the acting-out group was still rated as having more severe problems, and that although the Re-Ed children improved significantly, the amount of improvement was not sufficient to make them indistinguishable from the normal controls or from a sample of randomly selected public school children. Additional analyses indicated that project children significantly improved with regard to classroom disruptiveness and increased in the use of their own learning potential.

In terms of academic performance, a number of findings emerged. Of those children with academic difficulties at entry (68 percent of Re-Ed children and 63 percent of the untreated disturbed), the Re-Ed children were seen as having fewer academic problems at both the 6-month and 18-month ratings. Both groups showed improved performance between the initial and the 6-month rating, and between the initial and the 18-month rating, with Re-Ed children showing significantly greater improvements at both times. When all the children (not just those with initial academic difficulties) were considered, improvement in academic status between entry and the 6-month assessment and between entry and the 18-month assessment was significant for the Re-Ed children but not for the untreated children. Although the Re-Ed children received significantly better ratings than the untreated children at 6 months, however, the difference was no longer significant at 18 months.

At all three assessments, both the Re-Ed and untreated children were viewed as less academically adequate than the normal children. Among the Re-Ed children, the acting-out and withdrawn groups did not differ significantly at any of the testing periods.

Some interesting additional analyses were undertaken with regard to the relationship between academic performance and behavior. These analyses suggested that those children who were academically able to cope maintained their behavioral gains, while those who were experiencing academic difficulties deteriorated behaviorally. A correlation of .48 was obtained between the global academic rating that the child received at 6 months and the difference between the global behavior ratings he or she received at 6 and 18 months. On the other hand, the correlation between the child's behavioral status at 6 months and the amount of change in his or her academic status between 6 and 18 months was only .11. As Weinstein (1974, p. 158) pointed out, "These results highlight the importance of academic adequacy to the behavioral adjustment of school children. They suggest that it is a worthwhile investment for treatment agencies to bring the academic skills of the disturbed child up near grade level before returning him to school; otherwise, the behavioral gains made during treatment may be endangered."

Further evidence for the importance of academic competence was the finding that in the untreated disturbed group, 51 percent of the children without initial academic problems improved in their school behavior between the 6-month and 18-month ratings as compared to only 24 percent of the children with initial academic problems. Furthermore, in the 2-year interval between the entry and 18-month testing, 59 percent of the untreated children without initial academic problems improved behaviorally, while only 21 percent of the children with initial academic problems improved. For the Re-Ed children, however, improvement of school behavior was independent of initial academic success.

Some confirmation of the findings on academic ratings was subsequently found in the analysis of actual academic achievement. The data suggested that untreated disturbed children get farther behind grade norms the longer they remain in school and that the Re-Ed intervention successfully arrested this increase in disparity between these children and their classmates. In terms of rates of learning, those Re-Ed children improved who were initially in need of such improvement—increasing their rate of learning in both reading and arithmetic over their pre-Re-Ed rate. During the same interval, the learning rate of the untreated children remained unchanged. After the Re-Ed experience, more treated than untreated children were learning at the normal expected rate in both reading and arithmetic.

A final approach to the measurement of classroom behavior involved sociometric ratings. Initially, neither the Re-Ed group nor the untreated disturbed group differed from one another in terms of sociometric acceptance or rejection. Neither were there any significant changes in either of the groups among the various time periods. The failure of the project to develop greater peer acceptance was seen as somewhat disappointing, and it was suggested that the future development of the Re-Ed program might focus more on this aspect.

Overall, there is little doubt that the treatment afforded in project Re-Ed favorably affected both the behavioral and academic functioning of those children who were exposed to it. Although there was some erosion of effect over time, by and large, project children were doing better than the untreated controls at 18 months postdischarge. This is not to say that the effect of the treatment was to make normal children out of a group that was clearly severely disturbed at the outset. As was noted, at the 18-month evaluation, one-half of the treated children were still judged to be either severely or very severely disturbed.

The findings of the influence of academic competence on behavior should serve to dispel the frequently held notion that, when the behavior is brought under control, academic achievement will follow and everything will then proceed satisfactorily. The results of this project make it amply clear that, if children in academic difficulties are going to be returned to an academic setting, one aspect of a residential program will have to be academic remediation.

In terms of the care, thoughtfulness, and effort that went into the evaluation, this project might well serve as a model for the evaluation of residential treatment. With the wisdom that comes from hindsight, one could only wish that more direct observation of behavior had been built into the design so that there might have been less dependence on more global measures of change.

The findings with respect to the comparison of the acting-out and withdrawn children are of interest in further establishing the validity of these two groupings.

Achievement Place

In this treatment model a trained child-care couple, called teaching-parents, live with a small group (generally about 6) of young people, ages 10 to 16, who have usually had repeated contacts with juvenile authorities. The range of intelligence has been from dull to superior, but most have been labeled by the schools as slow learners. Thirty percent have been in special educational programs and more than half have failed one or more grades. Most have been truant, and about two-thirds have been suspended prior to entering Achievement Place. A wide variety of diagnostic labels have been used by professionals to describe their psychopathology (Wolf et al., 1976).

The program is based on the principles of behavior modification (see Chapter 14) and involves "teaching, self-government, motivational, relationship-development and advocacy procedures" (Braukmann, Kirigin, & Wolf, 1976). When children enter an Achievement Place, they are introduced to a point system and given a point card on which their behavior and the number of points they earn and lose is recorded. Initially, points are exchanged for privileges every day; subsequently, exchanges are made on a weekly basis. As soon as possible, an attempt is made to phase out the point system, and the child goes on a merit system in which no points are given or taken away and all privileges are free. The merit system is the last step each child must attain prior to returning home. Points reinforce a variety of behaviors, including performance in the public school that the children continue to attend. A more complete description of the program may be found in Phillips, Phillips, Fixsen, and Wolf (1973) and in Wolf et al. (1976).

The teaching parents are trained over a one-year period by means of workshops, supervised practicum experiences, and consultations. The teaching parents are also provided feedback from schools and community agencies with which they are in continuous contact, as well as from parents and the children themselves.

A variety of in-program effects have been carefully documented in a series of published studies. Positive effects have been recorded for social behaviors, cleanliness, punctuality, school work, conversational skills, and conflict negotiation. (See Kifer, Lewis, Green, & Phillips, 1974; Minkin et al., 1976; Phillips, 1968; Phillips, Phillips, Fixsen, & Wolf, 1971.)

Postprogram evaluation has involved comparing treated cases in terms of pre- and postprogram rates of offenses and comparing Achievement Place cases with similar cases treated in other group homes. Braukman et al. (1976) reported that the 28 cases in the original Achievement Place had averaged 3.4 offenses per year prior to treatment; the average during the treatment year dropped to .9 offenses per case. Sixteen comparison cases had averaged 3.4 offenses prior to treatment but increased to an average of 7.3 while in treatment. A similar drop in in-program offenses occurred for 45 cases treated in five later replications of the original Achievement Place.

In terms of insitutionalization, either during the program or within one year following, the rates were 14 percent for the original setting, 31 percent for the three comparison homes, and 18 percent for the later replications. Finally, offenses occurring during the year following treatment were compared. The original Achievement Place cases and the comparison cases were no different; each averaged about two offenses per child. The later replications seemed to be doing slightly better, averaging just over one offense per case.

The postprogram offense rates were clearly disappointing, and Braukmann et al. (1976) suggested that both after-care and longer periods of treatment might be helpful. Hoefler and Bornstein (1975) pointed out that, while Achievement Place has been genuinely successful in changing in-program behavior, more attention needed to be given to generalization and maintenance and to a more precise analysis of the influence of multiple factors in producing in-program change.

Further evidence for in-program but not postprogram success has been provided by Kirigin, Braukmann, Atwater, and Wolf (1982), who compared

13 Achievement Place homes with 9 comparison group homes; 102 boys and 38 girls were in the experimental group, whereas 22 boys and 30 girls were in the comparison homes. The number of cases involved in recorded offenses was obtained for three time periods: one year pretreatment, during treatment, and one year posttreatment. For boys there were no differences between the Achievement Place group and those in comparison homes in pretreatment involvement (94% vs. 91%), a significant reduction during treatment (56% vs. 86%), but no differences post-treatment (57% vs. 73%). For girls, the pattern was the same: no pretreatment differences (95% vs. 73%), significant in-treatment differences (41% vs. 80%), and no post-treatment differences (27% vs. 47%). There were similar findings for number of offenses per case; significant differences in favor of the experimental group during, but not following, treatment.

From the original site, the program, now referred to as the Teaching Family Model (TFM), expanded into a large network of group homes. Weinrott, Jones, and Howard (1982) conducted an extensive and complex longitudinal summative evaluation of 26 TFM and 25 comparison group home programs and have provided an effectiveness analysis. They concluded that the TFM houses outperformed the comparison programs in cost-effectiveness only on measures of educational progress; there were no differences in reduced deviant behavior, occupational status or social/personality adjustment. As Weinrott et al. (1982, p. 146) pointed out, however, "although the average youth (or program) outcome did not favor the TFM over the comparison group (or vice versa), the beneficial pre-to-post changes for youth in both groups may mean that the TFM and comparison treatment programs were equally effective." They also noted that not all youth benefited equally from the TFM programs, but attributed the differences primarily to differences in quality of the programs and demographic characteristics of the youth served. The possible contribution of different dimensions of disorder might be equally well addressed.

Finally, in a rather sobering conclusion to their work, they noted,

One thing is abundantly clear. Community based residential treatment of the type described herein is very, very expensive in light of the following results: First, only 45% of youths in both samples completed all phases of their programs. The remaining 55% failed to function adequately (13%), ran away and never returned (10%), were removed by the court for serious and repeated offenses (9%), or left for reasons unrelated to progress in treatment (23%). Second, there were very few differences between program completers and dropouts on outcome measures obtained during the second and third years following discharge. (p. 197)

Although there is now good evidence for positive in-program changes, the problem of generalization and maintenance (not unique to the TFM model) remains unsolved.

STUDIES OF INSTITUTIONALIZED DELINQUENTS

Controlled studies of the effect of treatment on institutionalized delinquents have most often grown out of research aimed at testing the value of a differential classification approach to the prescription of treatment. Despite the fact that all of the studies to be discussed below were carried out in the context of a correctional rather than a mental health or an educational system, they have frequently been the most sophisticated in their approach to both treatment and evaluation.

The Preston Typology Study

This study (Jesness, 1971) was the first to use the California I-level classification system (see Sullivan, Grant, & Grant, 1957; Warren, 1969) as a basis for the application of differing treatment strategies to delinquents in a residential setting. The study took place in a large (900 beds) institution for male delinquents, ages 16 to 20, operated by the California Youth Authority.

Subjects were assigned randomly either to the experimental or the control group. The 518 control boys were assigned to living units on the basis of the institution's preexisting criteria, which did not involve personality classification. The 655 experimental subjects were assigned to a living unit based on their delinquent subtype.

Classification of all subjects involved integration of data from three sources: an interview, a personality inventory, and a sentence-completion test. According to Jesness, "The interviewer's impressions agreed with the final staff diagnosis in 56 percent of the cases, the sentence completion test diagnosis agreed in 35 percent of the cases, and the inventory classification in 49 percent of the cases. Agreement among independent interviews occurred in 55 percent of the cases, while agreement between independent staffing teams was 60 percent" (Jesness, 1971, p. 42).

This study is unusual in that the reliability of diagnosis is reported. The fact that staffing teams, who apparently made the diagnosis leading to program assignment, agreed in only 60 percent of the cases reflects the persistent problems of reliability with all clinically derived classification systems. (See Chapter 1.) The extent to which subjects are misdiagnosed and, thus, misplaced can, of course, lead to a dilution of the results.

Space does not permit a description of the characteristics of the six experimental living units; treatment prescriptions for the differing subtypes may be found in Jesness (1971) and in Warren (1966). Program monitoring was accomplished by means of questionnaires administered to both staff and inmates with supplemental ratings by experts.

Results were reported in terms of both in-program and postprogram criteria. According to Jesness, "Data on the immediate impact of the experimental program on the institution indicated fairly consistently that the introduction of the I-level system tended to decrease unit management problems. During the operational phase of the study, significantly fewer reports of serious rule infractions and peer problems were reported in the experimental units'' (Jesness, 1971, p. 447). One cannot, of course, rule out differential staff responses to the inmates' behavior rather than actual changes in the behavior itself when accounting for these results. Additional in-program data with regard to changes on psychometric instruments were also reported, with some subtypes showing greater changes in self-report measures and other showing greater improvement in behavioral criteria.

Postprogram effects were measured by parole violations at both 15 months and 24 months postrelease. An overall comparison of the experimental and control cases revealed no differences in parole violations. Fifty-four percent of both groups had made violations on or before 15 months, while 64 percent of both groups had made violations on or before 24 months. Neither were there any differences in outcome between any of the subtypes in either the experimental or the control group.

The results of this study were clearly disappointing in terms of effects on postprogram rates of law violations. However, the decrease in conflict within the institution and the increase staff professionalism and morale reported, though not related to a reduction in recidivism, could clearly have longer term effects for subsequent treatment in the Preston Institution. An overall evaluation of this pioneering study must also take into account its influence in encouraging other research studies in the use of rationally derived differential treatment strategies for delinquents subclassified according to psychological and behavioral characteristics.

The California Community Treatment Project (CTP)

This effort, a landmark in the treatment of delinquent youth, was begun in 1961 and was established to avoid the need for institutional placement for certain kinds of delinquents. A review of the entire program is provided by Palmer (1974). (See also Chapter 17.)

The emphasis of this project has been on nonresidential treatment, but in 1969, based on the earlier recognition that ''the difficulties and delinquent orientation of 25 to 35 percent were hardly being influenced by the intensive CTP program'' (Palmer, 1974, p. 7), a residential component was added to serve some youths in the initial stages of their career in the California Youth Authority.

The initial step in selecting clientele for the residential component involved a staff decision as to whether institutionalization should be the initial step (followed by community treatment), or whether direct placement should be made to the community component for a given case. After this decision was made, assignment to the two conditions was then made randomly. The same staff, it should be noted, served both the community and the residential components.

The method of case assignment provided for four groups: (1) those deemed in need of initial institutional placement and, being so were placed in a facility, (2) those deemed in need of initial institutionalization but placed directly in the community program, (3) those not seen as needing institutional experience but receiving it, and (4) those seen as amenable to direct placement in a community and being so placed. Thus, the research design permits the comparison of judged amenables versus nonamenables to the two treatment conditions. Furthermore, the design also permits comparisons among youths of the differing subtypes of the California I-level system.

The residential facility normally housed about 25 youths at one time. Staffed by carefully selected "youth counselors" and "group supervisors" (Palmer, 1974, p. 9), it was continually accessible to all other personnel in the project.

Program features (see Palmer & Werner, 1972) included three to four visits per week by the parole agent, individualized counseling averaging 2.6 hours per week by the parole agent, group counseling for about one hour per week, school attendance for 87 percent of the youths, athletics, arts and crafts, and out-of-dorm activities such as musical events and other cultural activities.

The major outcome measure was rearrest during the first 18 months on parole. Results for the initial 106 cases indicated that of those judged as needing initial residential placement and actually receiving it, 58 percent were rearrested; of those judged in need but not receiving needed residential placement, 94 percent were rearrested. The mean number of offenses for the two groups was .96 versus 1.56; for each month on parole the mean rates were .066 versus .140. According to Palmer (1974) these differences were significant when background variables such as age, IQ, socioeconomic status, race, delinquent subtype, and levels of parole risks were controlled.

As regards the group judged amenable to direct community placement, there were few substantial differences between those first institutionalized and those placed appropriately according to need. Overall, looking at those appropriately placed against those inappropriately placed, the mean rate of offending per month was .067 for the former and .107 for the latter, a difference Palmer reports as significant.

With regard to the results Palmer concludes, "The various findings which have been presented here seem to suggest the obvious: delinquent behavior can probably be reduced in connection with community and residential programs *alike* by means of careful diagnosis and subsequent placement of individuals into appropriate rather than inappropriate or less-than-optimal settings and programs" (Palmer, 1974, p. 10).

The size of the samples on which these results were obtained clearly did not suffice for much in the way of analyses of the performance on nine different delinquent subtypes. Palmer (1974) suggested, however, that the initial residential placement in the special facility was helpful in the case of neurotic youths with aggressive tendencies, whereas it did not seem to be helpful in the case of subtypes Palmer refers to as "power oriented"—those seemingly akin to the conduct-disorder and socialized-aggressive groups described in Chapter 2.

These results, which can be considered preliminary, suggest strongly that initial residential placement is helpful for those deemed, on the basis of clinical judgment, as needing it. The results also suggest that the determination of those who should receive institutional placement might be made on the basis of a classification system with a very limited number of categories.

The Close–Holton Study

This study (Jesness, 1975) compared the effects of behavior modification and transactional analysis on a variety of outcome criteria. The setting for the experiment was two newly opened institutions, the O. H. Close School and the Karl Holton School of the California Youth Authority, each housing about 400 youths in 50-bed living units.

Experimental subjects were between 15 and 17 years old and were assigned randomly to either of the two experimental programs. The median age was 16.6; 33 percent had had a prior commitment to the youth authority; 56 percent were white, 28 percent black, 13 percent Mexican-American, and 2 percent other. At admission, each youth was classified into one of the nine delinquent subtypes of the California I-level system.

In order to implement the treatment modalities, training in both techniques was carried out both prior to the implementation of the research design and continuously throughout the experiment. Program details may be found in Jesness and DeRisi (1973) and Jesness (1975). Boys at the Close School averaged a 30-week stay and participated in an average of 40 transactional-analysis-group sessions. Boys at Holton stayed 35 weeks on the average and negotiated an average of 19 written contracts related to critical behavior deficiencies.

As to the extent to which the "ideals" of the two programs were actually implemented, Jesness noted: "Counselors at Close were expected to conduct at least two transactional analysis sessions with their clients each week. In addition to the academic contracting, Holton counselors were expected to negotiate at least one behavioral contingency contract each week with their clients. Staff at Close fulfilled two-thirds of their expected quota, Holton staff one-half of theirs" (Jesness, 1975, p. 764). It should be noted that this study is unusual in that it provided a quantified estimate as to the actual degree of implementation of the treatment program.

A variety of outcome measures were obtained upon completion of the program, including opinion scales, achievement tests, a personality inventory, staff ratings of behavior, and a measure of ego development. Particular attention was given to a measure of "positive regard" as an index of the overall quality of the relationship between the boy and the staff, as perceived by the boy on leaving the program. In addition, reconviction data were obtained for follow-up periods of 6, 12, 18, and 24 months.

The outcome variables were analyzed with respect to the efforts of each program separately, differences between the two programs, and the interaction of the programs with comparisons of the various delinquent subtypes. Here these results can only be summarized.

Boys in both programs made academic gains beyond those projected. The contingency management program, contrary to expectation, enjoyed an advantage with higher maturity subjects, while the Close classrooms were more effective with lower maturity subjects.

Boys in both programs obtained more favorable scores on the personality inventory (the Jesness scales), with the transactional analysis subjects more frequently improving to a greater extent. There were also some differential effects of the two programs on the delinquent subtypes, with the manipulators seeming to benefit most from the transactional analysis experience.

On the staff ratings of behavior, there were some differences between the programs and some differential effects—the behavior modification program apparently enjoying the greatest success with the acting-out neurotics, while the transactional analysis program produced the greatest changes in the cultural conformists. Overall, behavior ratings were slightly, but significantly, more affected by the behavior modification program.

Positive regard was generally higher for the transactional analysis program, with about 65 percent of Close subjects indicating high positive regard as contrasted with only about 45 percent at Holton.

The parole follow-up data were not revealing of any differences between the programs at any of the parole exposure periods. By 24 months, slightly more than 47 percent of boys at each institution had violated parole and had been returned to an institution. The rates of parole violation at one year for both schools, however, were lower than they had been at the two institutions in the two years prior to the implementation of the experiment. Rates of violation for both Close and Holton were also lower than for two other California institutions serving boys of approximately the same age. With respect to differential effects on the nine delinquent subtypes, the only signficant finding was that the transactional analysis program was more successful in reducing subsequent violations among the manipulators.

A final analysis of the outcome criteria used the measure of positive regard. When high and low positive regard groups were compared, those in the higher regard group generally showed more improvement, a finding that was true in regard to parole outcome as well as to the behavior rating and self-report measures. In fact, positive regard accounted for as much of a variance of the outcome measures as did the two treatments, about 15 percent in each case.

The Close–Holton study is the most elaborate evaluation of specified treatment modalities in an institutional setting undertaken to date. The basic conclusions that can be drawn are (1) that neither treatment was implemented to preset standards, (2) that neither was superior to the other overall, (3) that both were superior to no specified treatment in reducing parole violations at 12 months, (4) that self-report measures were more positively affected by the transactional analysis approach while rated behavior was more affected by behavior modification, (5) that different subtypes of the California I-level system were differentially affected to some degree, and (6) that the boys' positive regard for their experiences was a significant factor in all outcome variables.

For a postscript on this program in terms of current concern in correctional philosophy, the interested reader should see Jesness (1980).

The Robert F. Kennedy Youth Center (KYC) Study

This study, analyzing the differential treatment of delinquent males with an average of 17 years, used a classification method that arose out of multivariate statistical research, which has been discussed at length in Chapter 1.

An attempt was made to conceptualize differential psychological interventions for inmates classified into one of the four groups and to implement these methods by means of living units composed of homogenous groups (Gerard, 1970). For the conduct-disorder cases, behavior modification was used; for the anxiety-withdrawal group, a program of both individual and group counseling was implemented; and for the socialized-aggressive group, the treatment method was reality therapy. There was considerable difficulty in conceptualizing and implementing a treatment approach for the immaturity cases; however, an intervention based on the principles of transactional analysis was finally implemented well into the study period.

In addition to the subtype-specific treatments, the entire institution had an overriding token economy and used an innovative decentralized approach to the organization of a correctional institution (see Levinson & Gerard, 1973). In addition, academic and vocational education, recreation, religious programs, and self-enlightenment programs were available to all inmates. The setting of the program was a newly constructed, architecturally innovative, open institution with a generally treatment-oriented and experimentally minded staff.

Although it was possible to specify the nature of the formal subtype-specific treatments reasonably well and attempts were made by institution management to monitor them, this study illustrates all too well the problem of separating out any effects these might have had from the effects of the institution-wide token economy, the innovative management organization, and the physical setting itself.

Although a variety of measures of in-program performance have been reported, including academic skill, gains-reduced disciplinary problems, and positive behavior changes (see Thomas, 1974; Johnson, 1977), the formal evaluation rested on recidivism, defined as a return to any state or federal prison for at least 60 days over a three-year period following release.

The experimental design as reported by Cavior and Schmidt (1978) involved a comparison of the four subgroups (total $n = 281$) of experimentals with four similar subgroups who were incarcerated in a more typical institution (total $n = 405$). Unfortunately, it was not possible to randomly assign youths to the two institutions from a pool of eligibles. Because of its openness and lack of security, KYC was not assigned cases whose histories included physical violence; the control institution cases were also of a higher mean age (19.8 vs. 17.8). On a basis of an actuarial prediction formula, however, the KYC sample was predicted, a priori, to do worse on parole.

Results indicated that the KYC group did not significantly better on parole than did the control cases either before or after being equated for a priori risk. There were suggestive differences with regard to the effect of both institutions on certain subgroups; for example, the KYC success rate for the psychopathic (undersocialized conduct disorder) group was 64.5 percent compared to 56.0 percent for the controls. However, none of the differences between the subgroups was statistically significant.

It is interesting to note that by the end of the three-year follow-up, 58 percent of both groups had been in prison for at least 60 days sometime during that period, despite both traditional and highly innovative correctional programs.

While many elements of the KYC program have now been widely emulated and the style of management has been widely accepted in the field of corrections, the failure of the program to differentially reduce recidivism was clearly disappointing. The close-to-significant difference in the parole performance of the psychopathic group who had been subject to a treatment modality with a great deal of structure and clear expectations, rewards, and punishments suggests, as was the case in the Balderton Hospital Study (Craft et al., 1964), that children and adolescents with severe conduct disorders may benefit more from the less verbally oriented approaches.

SUMMARY

Although there is ample evidence for the effectiveness of residential treatment to bring about in-program behavior change, there is very little, if any, evidence for lasting change deriving from any of the differing intervention modalities that have been studied. Progress, if any, in the last six to eight years is almost nonexistent. Yet residential placement, if not treatment, is clearly here to stay, if only for the limited number of children and adolescents who are clearly dangerous to themselves or, more likely, to others.

That certain type of residential interventions may work better with some disorders than with others is clear from extant research and has been more recently reiterated (e.g., Palmer, 1984; Rutter, 1982; Tramontana, 1980), but recent studies of differential treatment are seriously lacking. As was the case in a number of earlier studies reviewed herein, some more recent follow-up studies of treated children suggest that (undersocialized) conduct disorder symptoms, especially when they are pervasive and severe, are less amenable to change than are symptoms of anxiety, withdrawal, and dysphoria (e.g., Blotcky et al., 1984; Gossett et al., 1977; Nielson, Young, & Latham, 1982). Since cases of conduct disorder predominate, especially in correctional institutions and even elsewhere (e.g., Schain, Bushi, Gardella, & Guthrie, 1980), research into institutional treatment for this troublesome group should be given a high priority.

REFERENCES

Agee, V. L. (1979). *Treatment of the violent incorrigible adolescent.* Lexington, MA: Lexington Books.

Barker, P. (1982). Residential treatment for disturbed children: Its place in the '80's. *Canadian Journal of Psychiatry, 27,* 634–639.

Blotcky, M. J., Dimpiero, T. C., & Gossett, J. T. (1984). Follow-up of children treated in psychiatric hospitals: A review of studies. *American Journal of Psychiatry, 141,* 1499–1507.

Bower, E. M., Lourie, R. S., Strother, C. R., & Sutherland, R. L. (1969). *Project Re-Ed: Evaluation by a panel of visitors.* Nashville, TN: George Peabody College for Teachers.

Braukmann, C. J., Kirigin, K. A., & Wolf, M. W. (1976). *Achievement Place: The researcher's perspective.* Paper presented at the meeting of the American Psychological Association, Washington, DC.

Brendtro, C. K., & Ness, A. E. (1982). Perspectives on peer group treatment: The use and abuse of guided group interaction/positive peer culture. *Children and Youth Services Review, 4,* 307–324.

Cavior, H. E., & Schmidt, A. A. (1978). Test of the effectiveness of a differential treatment strategy at the Robert F. Kennedy Center. *Criminal Justice and Behavior, 5,* 131–139.

Colyar, D. E. (1983). Ten laws of residential treatment: What can go wrong when you're not looking. *Child Care Quarterly, 12,* 136–143.

Craft, M., Stephenson, G., & Granger, C. (1964). A controlled trial of authoritarian and self-governing regimen with adolescent psychopaths. *American Journal of Orthopsychiatry, 34,* 543–554.

Fineberg, B. L., Kettlewell, P. W., & Sowards, S. K. (1982). An evaluation of adolescent inpatient services. *American Journal of Orthopsychiatry, 52,* 337–345.

Fineberg, B. L., Sowards, S. K., & Kettlewell, P. W. (1980). Adolescent inpatient treatment: A literature review. *Adolescence, 15,* 913–925.

Gendreau, P., & Ross, R. R. (1979). Effective correctional treatment: Bibliotherapy for cynics. *Crime and Delinquency, 25,* 463–489.

Gerard, R. E. (1970). Institutional innovations in juvenile corrections. *Federal Probation, 36,* 37–44.

Gossett, J. T., Barnhart, D., Lewis, J. M., & Phillips, V. A. (1977). Follow-up of adolescents treated in a psychiatric hospital. Predictors of outcome. *Archives of General Psychiatry, 34,* 1037–1042.

Gossett, J. T., Lewis, J. M., & Barnhart, F. D. (1983). *To find a way: The outcome of hospital treatment of disturbed adolescents.* New York: Brunner/Mazel.

Hobbs, N. (1966). Helping disturbed children: Ecological and psychological strategies. *American Psychologist, 21,* 1105-1115.

Hoefler, S. A., & Bornstein, P. H. (1975). Achievement Place: An evaluative review. *Criminal Justice and Behavior, 2,* 146–168.

Jesness, C. F. (1971). The Preston Typology Study. An experiment with differential treatment in an institution. *Journal of Research in Crime and Delinquency, 8,* 38–52.

Jesness, C. F. (1975). Comparative effectiveness of behavior modification and transactional analysis programs for delinquents. *Journal of Consulting and Clinical Psychology, 43*, 758–779.

Jesness, C. F. (1980). Was the Close–Holton project a "bummer"? In R. R. Ross & P. Gendreau (Eds.), *Effective correctional treatment* (pp. 361–366). Toronto: Butterworths.

Jesness, C. F., DeRisi, W. (1973). Some variations in techniques of contingency management in a school for delinquents. In J. S. Stumphauzer (Ed.), *Behavior therapy with delinquents*. Springfield, IL: Charles C. Thomas.

Johnson, V. S. (1977). An environment for treating youthful offenders: The Robert F. Kennedy Youth Center. *Offender Rehabilitation, 2*, 159–171.

Johnson, V. S. (1981). Staff drift: A problem in program integrity. *Criminal Justice and Behavior, 8*, 223–231.

Kennedy, B. (1985). Residential treatment of adolescents: A treatment model. *Canadian Journal of Psychiatry, 30*, 18–21.

Kifer, R. E., Lewis, M. A., Green, D. R., & Phillips, E. C. (1974). Training predelinquent youths and their parents to negotiate conflict situations. *Journal of Applied Behavior Analysis, 7*, 357–364.

Kirigin, K. A., Braukmann, C. J., Atwater, J. D., & Wolf, M. M. (1982). An evaluation of teaching-family (Achievement Place) group houses for juvenile offenders. *Journal of Applied Behavior Analysis, 15*, 1–16.

Levinson, R. B., & Gerard, R. E. (1973). Functional units: A different correctional approach. *Federal Probation, 39*, 8–16.

Lewis, M., Lewis, D. O., Shanock, S. S., Klatskin, E., & Osborne, J. R. (1980). The undoing of residential treatment. A follow-up study of 51 adolescents. *Journal of The American Academy of Child Psychiatry, 19*, 160–171.

Martin, L. H., Pozdnjakoff, I., & Wilding, J. (1976). The uses of residential care. *Child Welfare, 55*, 269–278.

Minkin, N., Braukmann, C. J., Minkin, B. L., Timbers, G. D., Timbers, B. I., Fixsen, D. L., Phillips, E. L., & Wolf, M. M. (1976). The social validation and training of conversation skills. *Journal of Applied Behavior Analysis, 9*, 126–139.

Monkman, M. M. (1972). *A milieu therapy program for behaviorally disturbed children*. Springfield, IL: Charles C. Thomas.

Munson, R. F., & Blincoe, M. M. (1984). Evaluation of a residential treatment center for emotionally disturbed adolescents. *Adolescence, 19*, 253–260.

Nielson, G., Young, D., & Latham, S. (1982). Multiply acting out adolescents: Developmental correlates and response to secure treatment. *International Journal of Offender Therapy and Comparative Criminology, 26*, 195–207.

Palmer, T. (1974). The Youth Authority's Community Treatment Project. *Federal Probation, 38*, 3–14.

Palmer, T. (1984). Treatment and the role of classification: A review of basics. *Crime and Delinquency, 30*, 245–267.

Palmer T., & Werner, E. (1972). *California's Community Treatment Project, Research Report #12. The Phase III Experiment: Progress to date*. Sacramento: California Youth Authority.

Phillips, E. L. (1968). Achievement Place: Token reinforcement procedures in a home-style rehabilitation setting for "pre-delinquent" boys. *Journal of Applied Behavior Analysis, 1,* 213–223.

Phillips, E. L., Phillips, E. A., Fixsen, D. L., & Wolf, M. M. (1971). Achievement Place: Modification of the behaviors of predelinquent boys within a token economy. *Journal of Applied Behavior Analysis, 4,* 45–59.

Phillips, E. L., Phillips, E. A., Fixsen, D. L., & Wolf, M. (1973, June). Achievement Place. Behavior shaping works for delinquents. *Psychology Today, 7,* 75–79.

Quay, H. C. (1977). The three faces of evaluation: What can be expected to work. *Criminal Justice and Behavior, 4,* 341–354.

Quay, H. C. (1979). Residential treatment. In H. C. Quay & J. S. Werry (Eds.), *Psychopathological disorders of childhood* (2d ed., pp. 387–410). New York: Wiley.

Raubolt, R. R. (1983). Treating children in residential group psychotherapy. *Child Welfare, 62,* 147–155.

Redick, R. W., & Witkin, M. J. (1983) *Residential treatment centers for emotionally disturbed children, United States, 1977–78 and 1978–79.* Mental Health Statistical Note No. 162. Washington, DC: USDHEW, PHS, ADAMHA, NIH, Division of Biometry and Epidemiology.

Rutter, M. (1982). Psychological therapies in child psychiatry: Issues and prospects. *Psychological Medicine, 12,* 723–740.

Rutter, M., & Giller, H. (1984). *Juvenile delinquency: Trends and perspectives.* New York: Guilford Press.

Salend, S. J. (1984). Therapy outcome research: Threats to treatment integrity. *Behavior Modification, 8,* 211–222.

Schain, R. J., Bushi, S., Gardella, D., & Guthrie, D. (1980). Characteristics of children admitted to a state mental hospital. *Hospital and Community Psychiatry, 31* 49–51.

Schain, R. J., Gardella, D., & Pon, J. (1982). Five year outcome of children admitted to a state hospital. *Hospital and Community Psychiatry, 33,* 847–848.

Scheirer, M. H., & Rezmovic, E. L. (1983). Measuring the degree of program implementation. *Evaluation Review, 7,* 599–633.

Sechrest, L., West, S. G., Phillips, M. A., Redner, R., & Yeaton, W. (1979). Some neglected problems in evaluation research: Strength and integrity of treatments. In L. Sechrest and associates (Eds.), *Evaluation studies review manual* (Vol. 4, pp. 15–35). Beverly Hills: Sage.

Sullivan, C., Grant, M. Q., & Grant, J. D. (1957). The development of interpersonal maturity: Applications to delinquency. *Psychiatry, 20,* 373–385.

Thomas, P. R. (1974). *Effects of contingent–noncontingent structural environments on selected behaviors of Federal youth offenders.* Doctoral dissertation, West Virginia University.

Tramontana, M. G. (1980). Critical review of research on psychotherapy outcome with adolescents: 1967–1977. *Psychological Bulletin, 88,* 429–450.

Tremblay, R. E. (1983). Characteristics of training centers that have a positive influence. In R. R. Corrodo, M. Le Blanc, & J. Trepanier. (Eds.), *Current issues in criminal justice* (pp. 249–386). Toronto: Butterworths.

Uranich, W. B. (1983–84). Administration as an opposing force to rehabilitation: A case in point. *Juvenile and Family Court Journal*, Winter, 11–20.

Warren, M. Q. (1966). *Interpersonal maturity level classification: Juveniles: diagnosis and treatment of low, middle and high maturity delinquent*. Sacramento: California Youth Authority.

Warren, M. Q. (1969). The case for differential treatment of delinquents. *Annals of the American Academy of Political and Social Science, 381*, 47–59.

Weinrott, M. R., Jones, R. R., & Howard, J. R. (1982). Cost-effectiveness of teaching family programs for delinquents: Results of a national evaluation. *Evaluation Review, 6,* 173–201.

Weinstein, L. (1968). The mother–child schema, anxiety and academic achievement in elementary school boys. *Child Development, 39*, 257–264.

Weinstein, L. (1969). Project Re-Ed schools for emotionally disturbed children: Effectiveness as viewed by referring agencies, parents and teachers. *Exceptional Children, 35*, 703–711.

Weinstein, L. (1974, Dec.). *Evaluation of a program for re-educating disturbed children: A follow-up comparison with untreated children*. Final Report to the Bureau for the Education of the Handicapped, OE, USDHEW. Project Nos. 6-2974 and 552023.

Whitaker, J. K. (1980). *Caring for troubled children*. San Francisco: Jossey-Bass.

Winsberg, B. G., Bialer, I., Kupietz, S., Botti, E., & Balka, E. B. (1980). Home vs. hospital care of children with behavior disorders: A controlled investigation. *Archives of General Psychiatry, 37*, 412–418.

Wolf, M. M., Phillips, E. L., Fixsen, D. L., Braukmann, C. J., Kirigin, K. A., Willner, A. G., & Schumaker, J. (1976). Achievement Place: The teaching family model. *Child Care Quarterly, 5*, 92–103.

16 EDUCATIONAL INTERVENTION

DONALD L. MACMILLAN AND KENNETH A. KAVALE

INTRODUCTION

Educators are confronted with some children whose behavior deviates so markedly from the norm that it necessitates "special" interventions. The norm for judging classroom behavior as acceptable is imprecise and clearly differs from one classroom to another. Thus, it is crucial to realize that behavior is deviant in the context of the social systems, in this case the classroom, in which that determination is to be made. An extended discussion of issues concerning the definition and labeling of deviance as it relates to psychopathology are provided by Cromwell, Blashfield, and Strauss (1975), Phillips, Draguns, and Bartlett (1975), Prugh, Engel, and Morse (1975), and Quay (1975).

Furthermore, it is important to realize that from an educational perspective the terms *psychopathology* does not have a precise equivalent. Psychopathology or behavior disorder is defined and classified in different ways in different school systems. Thus, there are special educational categories, and services provided, for children labeled as emotionally disturbed (ED), behaviorally disordered (BD), with minimal brain dysfunction (MBD), and educationally handicapped (EH). Under each of these educational rubrics some number of children are placed and served who exhibit the disorders discussed earlier in this volume. Yet each of these categories contain children who would not strictly qualify as having a particular disorder. As a result, the educational research literature seldom contains a study wherein subjects are described in terms of specific disorders but instead are described as being found in an educational program the nature of which depends on the designations employed in the various states and school systems.

While the field of special education continues to advocate "noncategorical" approaches to meet the needs of handicapped children, the apparent hope is that the vast range of individual differences evident in the popula-

583

tion of handicapped learners will be accommodated instructionally through the individualized educational program (IEP) now required for each child designated as handicapped. For example, in California special educational services are now guided by the *California Master Plan for Special Education* (1973). Previously, classes existed for educable mentally retarded (EMR) and for the educationally handicapped (EH), the latter being a category encompassing children who in other states would have been classified as emotionally disturbed (ED), learning disabled (LD), and with minimal brain dysfunction (MBD). Under this new plan, EMR and EH children have been combined into a new categorical group, the learning handicapped (LH). One consequence of this action is that the heterogeneity within a given LH class is greater than was evident with the older EMR and EH classes. Another consequence of the increased heterogeneity is that a given approach is less likely to be successful with a sizable segment of the children in the LH class. This creation of educational categories by administrative edict, rather than by research designed to discover behavioral–psychological–learning style homogeneities of children further separates research from application and creates categories of children with dissimilar educational needs. The intent of categorization is to reduce the degree of within-group variation on some dimension of educational significance, which has been summarily ignored when new categorization schemes are introduced that ignore extant research evidence.

HETEROGENEITY OF POPULATIONS

There have been responses to the heterogeneity problem consisting of efforts to group children into more homogenous subgroups within the more global categories of behavior disorders or learning disabled. In Chapter 1 a multivariate statistical approach was described that has differentiated deviant children into behaviorally homogeneous subgroups. There have been other approaches in the LD field aimed at reducing heterogeneity. Examples include the work of Keogh and her colleagues (Keogh, Major, Reid, Gandara, & Omori, 1978; Keogh, Major-Kingsley, Omori-Gordon, & Reid, 1982) in developing a set of sample descriptors or "markers" useful in characterizing subjects.

Torgesen (1982) utilized "rationally defined subgroups" to reduce sample variance by selecting subjects according to very stringent criteria: controls on chronological age (CA), IQ, degree of school failure, and (for purposes of his research) deficiencies in short-term memory.

Employing cluster analysis Satz and Morris (1981) and McKinney and Fisher (1982) have been able to define various subgroups of LD children, the meaningfulness of which remains to be demonstrated.

What appears paradoxical is that in the schools the apparent trend is toward more global categories with the hope that individualization will occur as a result of the IEP, while the research community continues to search for ways to identify more homogeneous subgroups within categories. Only by reducing the heterogeneity in groups of children is the likelihood of identifying aptitude × treatment interactions going to increase.

PREVALENCE

Estimates of the prevalence of disorders in school-age children are fraught with definitional problems and subjectivity of clinical criteria. Thus, Kauffman (1981) reported estimates of behavior disorders ranging from .5 percent of the school population to 20 percent or more. For a long time, the Bureau of Education for the Handicapped (BEH, now the Office of Special Education, or OSE) estimated prevalence arbitrarily at 2 percent for behavior disorders. OSE does not use specific disorders so one must consider the percentage of school children designated as MR, ED, or LD. Table 16.1 contains the child counts reported for the school years 1978–1979 and 1981–1982 to the OSE. Along with the national average several "extreme" states are included to show the variability in prevalence rates between states. In addition to the lack of uniformity across states, another factor appears to be operative. In states where the prevalence of MR was high (Alabama, Arkansas, Mississippi), the prevalence of ED and LD appears to be rather low (Alabama's ED percentage and Arkansas' LD percentage are exceptions). In other states (e.g., Maryland and Rhode Island) with low MR rates, the LD rates are extremely high. No parsimonious explanation regarding the precision in differential diagnosis or reasons for real differences to exist between the states comes to mind. However, one is tempted to speculate about states in which MR labeling is avoided and that the same children are being labeled and served as LD.

Forness (1985) recently examined changes in the numbers of handicapped children served between school years 1976–1977 and 1981–1982 in three categories: MR, LD, and ED (see Table 16.2). Nationally, Forness noted a slight decrease in MR accompanied by a dramatic increase in LD and a more modest increase in ED. California reported a more dramatic decrease in MR and

TABLE 16.1 *Percent of School Age Children Served Under Three Categories for Two School Years: National and Selected State Figures*

	1978–79			1981–82		
	MR	**ED**	**LD**	**MR**	**ED**	**LD**
National	**1.60**	**0.53**	**2.28**	**1.52**	**0.64**	**2.98**
Alabama	3.89	0.29	1.45	4.00	0.43	2.12
Arkansas	3.09	0.06	2.14	2.97	0.09	3.28
Mississippi	2.91	0.02	0.98	2.96	0.05	1.87
Maryland	1.05	0.26	4.41	1.10	0.26	5.58
Rhode Island	0.88	0.44	3.34	0.84	0.59	5.48

an incredible increase in LD, while showing a 58 percent loss of ED (while nationally ED had increased). One reason for the California decrease is that Senate Bill 1870 included the term "behaviorally disordered" (generally meaning a milder form of ED) and severely emotionally disturbed (SED), the former being traditionally placed in classrooms for the educationally handicapped. Forness (1985) speculated that among the factors that might explain the decline in ED enrollments in California were ramifications of implementing the *California Master Plan for Special Education* (1973). That is, autism was subsumed under the Physically Handicapped category in California, and difficulties have arisen over documenting children as SED given the clinical criteria for such a diagnosis.

The point to be emphasized here, however, is the considerable variability between states in certifying children as ED or BD and the apparent "shifting of cases" between categories. There is recognition that a child needs special education, but there is an apparent desire to certify the child into the "least objectionable category."

DEVELOPMENTS AFFECTING EDUCATIONAL TREATMENT

Special education has undergone dramatic changes over the past 15 years as a result of court cases and legislation. The changes were frequently not by choice but rather were mandated by the courts or legislation. Although much of the concern arose in the context of mental retardation (see MacMillan, 1982) the principles have extended to other classifications of children, including educational programs for ED, LD, and MBD. Concerns over labeling, due process, segregation, and the like have been addressed in the formulation of PL 94-142, or The Education for All Handicapped Children Act. There are two guiding principles that have dramatically altered the educational service delivery system: (1) placement in an educational setting that is the least restrictive environment (LRE)—designed to prevent unneces-

TABLE 16.2 *Changes in Numbers of Handicapped School Children Served in a Five-Year Period*[a]

	United States			California		
	1976–77	**1981–82**	**Difference**	**1976–77**	**1981–82**	**Difference**
MR	970,00	802,00	17% loss	42,900	29,900	30% loss
LD	797,000	1,627,000	104% gain	74,400	190,700	156% gain
ED	283,000	342,000	21% gain	22,000	9,200	58% loss

[a]Numbers have been rounded to nearest thousand (U.S.) or hundred (California).
Source: From S.R. Forness, Effects of public policy at the state level: California's impact on MR, LD, and ED categories, *Remedial and Special Education 6*, 32–43.

sary segregated education; and (2) individualized educational plans (IEP)—designed to ensure accountability by those responsible for the education of the handicapped learner through a specific plan of treatment tailored to meet individual needs.

The importance of LRE and IEP for the educational treatment of children with psychopathological disorders is considerable. In the past one could design, implement, or evaluate a "program" for children classified as LD, ED, or BD. Usually, the educational program had goals and objectives that were to be achieved through a treatment program. Traditionally, these programs were carried out in a self-contained special class with a rather low pupil/teacher ratio. Following passage of PL 94-142 we find these same children served in a "continuum" of placements—special schools, special classes, resource rooms, and regular classes. The LRE component prefers regular class placement whenever feasible, with the special education being provided in the regular class or in a resource room. Since each child must have an IEP, there are individualized long-term and short-term goals specified, which vary from child to child. As a result, there is not a "BD program" or a "LD program" with common goals and activities prescribed for all students enrolled. Rather, there are a variety of goals and activities specified for students.

Previously, it was possible to evaluate a given program by measuring a common set of outcomes (e.g., achievement, attitudes, adjustment) consistent with program goals in an effort to ascertain whether the program was successful. Currently, that is not possible given the individuality of goals and activities (specified in the IEP) and the setting (consistent with LRE) in which educational services are provided. Hence, the types of program evaluations provided by Vacc (1968, 1972) are no longer feasible. Today, the within-group (e.g., BD) variability in terms of treatments is too great to permit between-group comparisons. Instead, research and evaluation efforts are going to have to account for this within-group variability as it explains variance on the outcomes of interest.

INTERVENTION APPROACHES

Regardless of *where* psychopathologically disordered children are serviced, the question of *what* is done for and with such children is most important. Intervention approaches have as their goal the alteration of behavior by reducing disturbance while increasing appropriate behavior and positive mental health. The field of education of children with behavior disorders has been marked by particular intervention approaches dictated largely by the etiological or conceptual approach to psychopathology, each claiming to be "the" approach for the educational treatment of psychopathology. Observation reveals, however, that no single intervention strategy is universally accepted as the "truth" (Rich, 1978).

THEORETICAL MODELS

Rhodes and Tracy (1974) outlined the five basic models of psychopathology/intervention in behaviorally disordered (BD) children: biophysical, behavioral, psychodynamic, sociological, and ecological.

The biophysical model is characterized by the assumption that psychopathology is caused by CNS dysfunction (genetic, biochemical, etc.). It is a model that emphasizes that the problem resides within the individual rather than within the external environmental conditions.

Behavioral theory assumes that maladaptive behaviors are either defects of learning or are learned, and follow one of the behavioral theories of which the operant paradigm is the most popular. In the case of maladaptive behavior, it may be assumed that psychodynamic theory views the causes of maladaptive behavior as the result of a dynamic equilibrium of opposing internal psychological processes. It encompasses several viewpoints, ranging from classical psychoanalytic theory as presented by Freud (largely unconscious, endoorganismic and limited to the first few years of life) to the more environmental, self-directed, and lifelong processes of Erickson, Hartman, and others.

Sociological theory seeks to explain emotional disturbance as the breaking of social norms. These paradigms (see Rhodes & Tracy, 1974, for a review) emphasize the social milieu and a focus on group behavior in determining interpersonal relationships. Disturbed behavior, therefore, is not a function of the individual behavior itself but rather the result of a labeling process by those who enforce social rules.

Ecological or systems theory emphasizes the interrelationships of individuals and their environments. Each individual resides within an ecosystem and disturbance arises when there is a mismatch between the individual and major features of the ecosystem (Rhodes, 1967). The disturbance is viewed as a property of the ecosystem as a whole—not the individual's behavior, the behavior of others, or any other single aspect of the ecosystem. Ecological theory can incorporate the explanations of psychopathology provided by the other theories but transcends them to include the interface between the person and the environmental components.

Countertheory was also identified by Rhodes and Tracy (1974) as a movement that includes current notions of reform and dissent about the goals, values, and methods of education. It is marked by diversity of position (e.g., Kozol, Illich, Goodman, Neill) with themes suggesting that labeling individuals is a dehumanizing process and that no behavioral standards are more desirable than another since self-determination is of paramount value.

CLASSIFICATION OF INTERVENTION

Rhodes and Tracy (1974) suggested that intervention strategies are best classified by anchoring them in the theoretical models used to describe the nature of child deviance. Much of the popular literature describing the education of disturbed students has subsequently used the Rhodes and Tracy framework to organize and describe intervention strategies (e.g., Apter & Conoley, 1984; Cullinan, Epstein & Lloyd, 1983; McDowell, Adamson & Wood, 1983; Morse & Smith, 1980; Newcomer, 1980; Reinert, 1980; Shea, 1978).

There were, however, earlier attempts to classify the educational interventions used with disturbed children. One of the earliest was by Hollister and Godston (1962), who identified 12 criteria that represented fundamental differences among intervention practices regarding administrative procedures, student selection, classroom methodology, and supportive operations. Classroom methodology was dealt with by six criteria involving:

- The extent to which the teacher established a climate of emotional trust, understanding, and support;
- The extent to which a teacher guides students toward realizing their potential;
- The extent to which a teacher formulates an educational program to overcome perceptual distortions that interfere with learning;
- The extent to which a teacher structures the environment and guides the student to control maladaptive behavior;
- The extent to which the teacher provides corrective learning experiences wherein inappropriate behavior is unlearned while appropriate behaviors are maximized; and
- The extent to which the teacher provides an individualized curriculum of academic skills that enable the child to cope with and to solve problems.

These criteria could be evaluated in any classroom and placed on a continuum from "no demonstration" to "frequent demonstration."

Morse, Cutler, and Fink (1964) further subclassified ED classes into seven approaches. Three types (naturalistic, chaotic, and primitive) are not included here because they operated on an inconsistent philosophical foundation that resulted in unorganized and loosely defined designs. The remaining four methodological types were more consistent with respect to both theoretical and pragmatic designs. These are now described.

1. **Psychiatric Dynamic Design.** Major emphasis was on dynamic therapy and pupil acceptance, with educational aspects played down. Individual therapy was expected or required; parental therapy was stressed, with heavy psychiatric involvement in diagnosis, decision making, treatment processes, consultation, and evaluation. Emphasis was on acceptance, use of interpersonal relationship, and overall tone.

2. **Psychoeducational Design.** Psychiatric and educational emphasis were balanced with joint planning. Educational decisions were made with a consideration of underlying and unconscious motivation. Educational aspects stressed creative, project-type work, individual differences, and a benign but not permissive atmosphere. Clinical participation was apparent, but not omnipresent or decisive in day-to-day actions.

3. **Psychological Behavioral Design.** This was based on systematic psychology of learning theory, with emphasis on diagnosis and learning one's potential capacities and relationship to specific remediation techniques. It involved the use of associative learning and formal habit. It contained a nonpunitive structure with emphasis on changing symptomatic responses through specific techniques on a planned ego level.

4. **Educational Design.** The emphasis was on formalized, accepted educational procedures, inhibition of symptomatic behavior, and attention to skill training and drill. There was little use of group processes. Emphasis was on control, with restrictive handling seen as corrective in a nonhostile atmosphere. There was reliance on extensions of traditional procedures without much systematic attention to the theoretical design.

PREVALENCE OF INTERVENTION APPROACHES

Analysis of interventions suggest that educational methods for ED students vary greatly. With the advent of mainstreaming (Pappanikou & Paul, 1977), the greater number of teachers responsible for the education of ED students in the "least restrictive environment" makes it very difficult to obtain reliable estimates regarding the prevalence of intervention approaches. Consequently, prevalence estimates of the different intervention strategies can be made reliably only from special classes for the ED.

Morse, et al. (1964) found that 14 percent of ED classes were psychodynamically oriented, 4 percent were behavioral, and a majority of the classes (29 percent) were described as "educational." In later surveys, Fink, Glass, and Guskin (1975) found that behavioral classes had risen to 36 percent, whereas the psychodynamically oriented classes decreased by one-half (7 percent), but Kavale and Hirshoren (1980) found 62 percent and 13 percent, respectively. The latter figures were about equal to the percentages found by Morse, et al. (1964). The ecological classification was included only in the Kavale and Hirshoren (1980) survey and accounted for a mere 6 percent of the programs.

These data suggest that there is a trend in educational management of ED children away from the psychological treatments toward more behavioral interventions. Although these surveys focused on the behavioral, psychodynamic, and ecological models as the major categories derived from conceptual positions, two other classifications emerged empirically as more popular: psychoeducational and "others." Psychoeducational interventions are a broadening of primarily psychodynamic approaches to incorporate aspects of behavioral, sociological, and ecological theories; thus, they intervene at the level of the negative psychological conditions (e.g., feelings, emotions, self-concept) and attempt to promote positive mental health in the form of improved academic performance, appropriate social behavior, and the like. The "other" category is comprised primarily of eclectic interventions that amalgamate components of the different theoretical models, but in which no one predominates.

The large percentage of programs that fall within an eclectic (including psychoeducational) classification suggests that educational programs for ED students more often than not do not fall clearly within the parameters defined by any single theoretical model. The theoretically "pure" program is represented in only a minority of programs. But even in these presumably "pure" programs, there is a lack of theoretical purity, as demonstrated in the Kavale and Hirshoren (1980) survey. Besides asking respondents to classify the theoretical foundation of their programs, they were also asked to check from a series of statements those which were considered to reflect major assumptions of their programs. Although approximately two-thirds of the respondents checked four or five statements in accord with their theoretical view, about one-third checked no more than three statements in accord with their stated theoretical model and almost two-thirds checked four or five statements reflecting other theoretical viewpoints. Chi-square tests revealed that no significantly greater proportion of statements were checked that reflected the particular aspects of any program type. Consequently, it appears that school programs for ED students may maintain a particular theoretical bias but in practice such programs are far from homogeneous.

THEORETICALLY "PURE" INTERVENTION APPROACHES

The primary conclusion from surveys of school programs is the suggestion that educational programs do not adhere rigidly to the tenets of theoretical models but rather take a more pragmatic approach based upon an eclectic combination of intervention strategies derived from the theoretical models. There are, however, a few examples of intervention approaches that seem to derive from theoretical models. Although derivatives of these programs are widely practiced, all derive from single efforts by charismatic individuals before 1970. Few, if any, have derived their continued popularity on proof of efficacy or cost benefit.

BIOPHYSICAL APPROACHES

These models emphasize structure in educational settings and are based on the work of Strauss and Lehtinen (1947) as articulated by Cruickshank, Bentzen, Ratzeburg, and Tannhauser (1961) in what is known as the Montgomery County Project.

They hypothesized that learning problems present because of certain specific characteristics of brain damage that include (1) distractibility, (2) motor disinhibition, (3) dissociation, (4) figure–ground disturbance, (5) preseveration, and (6) impaired body image. The teaching method was based upon an acceptance that the defect resides within the student, that a normal learning environment was not appropriate, and that a different learning environment had to be created that taught to the disability.

To accomplish this goal, four primary elements were included in the environmental design:

1. **Reduced Environmental Stimuli.** The structured classroom designed by Cruickshank et al. (1961) minimized extraneous stimuli exemplified by making windows opaque, coloring walls, floors, and furniture in a neutral color, sound proofing, etc.
2. **Reduced Space.** Each student was provided with a cubicle just large enough for a desk and chair, which were placed so the student's back is to the classroom.
3. **Structured School Program.** This was accomplished through a stable teacher-controlled predictable routine.
4. **Stimulus Value of Materials.** The stimulus value of teaching materials was enhanced to reduce distractibility and minimize perseveration. Materials were free of extraneous illustrations and important features were highlighted (using color or size). Only a single project was allowed on the desk at a time.

This approach was studied over a two-year period with two classes rigidly adhering to the experimental program while two maintained a more traditional program. There were no significant differences between the two program types; children in all four classes gained in achievement, perception, and social behavior. Subsequent studies investigating the effects of cubicles on performance have found no superiority in functioning in a stimulus control condition (Cruse, 1962). Although increased attention span is observed with the use of cubicles, there appears to be no resulting increase in reading achievement while working in a cubicle (Haubrich & Shores, 1976; Shores & Haubrich, 1969).

BEHAVIORAL PROGRAMS

The principles and techniques of behavior therapy have been discussed in Chapter 14. Among the first behavioral programs developed was the Children's Rehabilitation Unit at the University of Kansas (Whelan, 1966). The program emphasized token reinforcement methods to increase adaptive behaviors. Additionally, academic tasks were delivered on the basis of the Premack Principle. Thus, the program intervened at the level of the whole child and used behavioral principles to build a total curriculum.

A special class later converted to a resource-room model for improving attending skills, academic skills, and social behavior was developed by Quay and associates (Glavin, Quay, Annesley, & Werry, 1971; Glavin, Quay & Werry, 1971; Quay, Glavin, Annesley, & Werry, 1972; Quay, Sprague, Werry, & McQueen, 1967; Quay, Werry, McQueen, & Sprague, 1966). In the resource model, for example, the resource period was divided into four 15-

minute segments. At the beginning of each of the first three segments, students were required to work on academic tasks wherein beginning, continuing, and completing tasks were reinforced with tokens as originally developed by Hewett (see following discussion of his work). During the final segment, students could either use the tokens to enter a free-time area or work to earn additional tokens. After the period ended, students counted, reported, and recorded earnings, which could be used immediately or accumulated for later use. When evaluated, the results indicated that although the program was successful in improving achievement and behavior in both the special class and resource rooms, the gains did not generalize to the students' regular class performance.

The Center at the University of Oregon for Research in Behavioral Education of the Handicapped has developed intervention packages. These packages include: (1) Contingencies for Learning Academic and Social Skills (CLASS), designed to allow regular class teachers to control aggressive and disruptive student behaviors; (2) Program for Academic Survival Skills (PASS), designed to enhance educational readiness skills; (3) Procedures for Establishing Effective Relationship Skills (PEERS), designed to encourage socially withdrawn pupils to interact with classmates; and (4) Reprogramming Environmental Contingencies for Effective Social Skills (RECESS), designed to correct aggressive school and playground behavior. Generally, these programs have been shown to be successful. The CLASS program (Hops, Beickel, & Walker, 1976) has been shown to normalize the behavior of conduct disordered students (Hops & Beickel, 1975; Hops, Walker, & Fleischman, 1976).

Behavioral remediation approaches emphasize assessment of specific skills and the structuring of instruction to promote their acquisition and maintenance. One method is academic behavior modification characterized by direct, daily, continuous, and reliable measurement of academic behavior (see Lovitt, 1975). After measurement, the teacher selects procedures that emphasize either (1) antecedent techniques (i.e., aids that assist students in emitting correct academic responses) or (2) consequent techniques (i.e., teacher-managed events that follow responses in order to increase, decrease, or maintain correct responding (see Axelrod, 1977; Rose, Koorland, & Epstein, 1982). Also possible is precision teaching (Lindsley 1964, 1971; White & Haring, 1980), which is a specialized behavioral measurement and intervention system that places responsibility for carrying out the program on the student whose academic behaviors are to be modified.

Engelman and associates (Becker, Engelman, & Thomas, 1975a, 1975b; Carnine & Gilbert, 1979; Engelman, 1969) developed ''direct instruction'' whereby students are taught a general case strategy for attacking and solving problems (Lloyd, Epstein, & Cullinan, 1981). For each problem type, the student learns a set of preskills and a rule for sequencing these preskills so that any problem type may be solved (e.g., read, compute). Direct instruction is highly structured and teaching behaviors are clearly specified, even scripted, so exact techniques are available for prompting, reinforcing, pacing, and correcting. Direct Teaching practices, as well as academic behavior modification, were used by Epstein and Cullinan (1981) in Project ExCEL with good outcomes in terms of mastery as the primary criterion.

PSYCHODYNAMIC PROGRAMS

Among the first to apply Freudian psychoanalytic principles to the education of emotionally disturbed children was Aichhorn (1965), in the 1920s, who viewed disturbed behavior as the result of conflicts between the children and one or both of their parents. Because of these conflicts, the children developed "strong hate reactions" and never had their needs for affection satisfied. The method of treatment was based on the statement, "As far as possible, let the boys alone" (Aichhorn, 1965, p. 172).

The atmosphere provided a consistently friendly and accepting atmosphere that allowed for discussion and play opportunities. Gradually, greater demands were placed upon the children. Initially aggressive behavior increased to great intensity, but eventually it diminished. Soon after, strong bonds developed between children and staff, and growth and development followed. This bond was an example of transference, a patient's transferring of emotional feelings normally felt for a parent or loved one to the therapist. Aichhorn stressed the importance of the child identifying with the teacher: "The source of traits needed to be taken over by the child is in the worker. It is the tender feeling for the teacher that gives the pupil the incentive to do what is prescribed and not to do what is forbidden" (p. 211).

Bettelheim (1950, 1955) described the program at the Sonia Shankman Orthogenic School at the University of Chicago where milieu therapy was directed at satisfying the emotional needs of children (the majority of whom were autistic). Milieu therapy demands an ordered, controlled environment while at the same time stressing permissiveness. This permissiveness allows for assertive action on the child's part that is needed to avoid the danger of a passive, automatic, robot-like adjustment to institutional regulation, which is termed "psychological institutionalism" (Bettelheim & Sylvester, 1948). The atmosphere is one of structured permissiveness that results in a warm, trusting personal interaction between child and counselor. This one-to-one relationship with an understanding and flexible adult is the goal rather than having the child becoming integrated in a peer social group (Henry, 1957).

Although formal schooling is considered an integral part of the milieu therapy, a majority of time is spent dealing with the child's emotional problems. Less attention is devoted to a child's academic accomplishment, and classroom activities are more concerned with fostering a relaxed atmosphere. It is assumed that once the emotional problems have been resolved, the child will then be willing to reverse the "decision to fail" (Bettelheim, 1961). At this point, individualized instruction can be initiated and educational progress achieved (Bettelheim, 1970).

The psychodynamic model continues to influence educational programs (Berkowitz & Rothman, 1960, 1967; Hirschberg, 1953; LaVietes, 1962; Rothman, 1970; Trieschman, Whittaker, & Brendtro, 1969) by emphasizing permissiveness in an effort to work through problems. Although widely accepted as true, there is surprisingly little empirical support to suggest that permissiveness based on the catharsis theory is either necessary or desirable (Bandura, 1973; Berkowitz, 1973).

Besides the form of the environmental structure, Anna Freud (1954) discussed the relationship between psychoanalysis and education, and suggested that psychoanalysis allows the teacher to gain greater insight into the nature of teacher–child relationships. In the early 1960s, emphasis was placed in psychiatric day treatment (Cohen, 1965; LaVietes, Hulse, & Blau, 1960; Moller, 1964) that incorporated techniques such as neutralization, wherein nonconflictual activities are emphasized (Jacobson & Faegre, 1959; Newman, 1961), psychoanalytically based discipline (Sperling, 1951), and therapeutically oriented tutoring to improve academic functioning (Brendtro & Stern, 1967; Prentice & Sperry, 1965).

As is the case with psychotherapy (see Chapter 13), there is limited empirical evidence to support the continuing, if limited, popularity of psychodynamically oriented educational programs. Most of the evaluations are of the clinical, anecdotal variety that makes it difficult to evaluate effectiveness in terms of school-related variables like achievement.

ECOLOGICAL PROGRAMS

The ecological or systems model is based on several assumptions about the nature of child and environment interaction:

1. The child is an integral part of a social system.
2. Disturbance is not inherent in the child but rather is a discordance in the system.
3. This discordance is the result of a disparity between a child's needs and environmental expectations, which results in a mismatch.
4. The goal of intervention is to bring a balance back to the system.

Although these general principles are agreed on, the ecological perspective has revealed diversity with respect to specifics and how an ecological model applies to understanding disturbance (e.g., Feagans, 1972; Hobbs, 1966, 1982; Rhodes, 1967; Swap, 1974, 1978). Rhodes (1970) offered an ecological definition that states that (1) some characteristic of a child's behavior agitates an ecosystem, (2) the ecosystem responds in ways that result in further agitation in the child, and (3) a reciprocally disturbing set of interactions is set in motion. Behavior disorders arise when there is a mismatch between a child and major features of the ecosystem.

Swap, Prieto, and Harth (1982) suggested that ecological interventions are eclectic in the sense that they borrow techniques from many theoretical models. There is no ecological "master plan," but rather specific procedures differ depending on whether the intervention is directed at changing the child, changing the environment, or changing the interface of child–environment interaction. The goal of ecological intervention is not a particular state of being or behavior pattern but instead an increased concordance between child and environment. The best known example of an educational program based on ecological principles is Project Re-Ed (Re-education of emotionally disturbed children) (Hobbs, 1965, 1968). Though the emphasis was on reeducation, the program is residential in nature and has been discussed in Chapter 15.

ECLECTIC INTERVENTIONS

As noted earlier, most educational programming for disturbed children is eclectic in the sense of combining features derived from various theoretical models. Eclectic approaches are often criticized as soft-headed mixtures blended together with little rhyme or reason. To the contrary, eclectic approaches may offer strengths that make the whole greater than the parts, but only when there is a careful synthesis of assorted theoretical components that meets the diverse pragmatic demands of educational programs for disturbed students.

In an extension of the structured approach of Cruickshank et al. (1961), Haring and Phillips (1962) developed the Arlington Project in Virginia where, to the emphasis on a structured predictable learning environment, they added rewarding consequences for appropriate behavior and accomplishments. Thus, this project was a pioneering application of the behavioral model in terms of consequences for performance that were applied in a structured and consistent environment.

Haring and Phillips (1962) believed that inappropriate or maladaptive behavior should be replaced with behaviors that will result in more successful adjustment at school and at home. Additionally, academic achievement is considered important since they see a reciprocal relation between behavior and achievement because "Proper self discipline promotes achievement, and achievement develops self-discipline" (Haring & Phillips, 1962, p. 181).

Classroom structure was established by the following elements: individualized instruction, seating limits, play limits, conduct limits, movement privileges, and parent involvement. Haring and Phillips (1962) (see also Phillips & Haring, 1959) compared the effectiveness of their structural approach with both a permissive approach and an approach using typical classroom procedures. Their structured approach proved superior and revealed an increase in both academic achievement and behavioral adjustment. They concluded that a structured classroom wherein there is clear direction, firm expectation, and consistent follow-through produces positive benefits for disturbed students in both behavior and achievement.

The engineered classroom (Hewett, 1967, 1968; Hewett & Taylor, 1980) combined a structured approach with systematically applied behavior modification. Within Hewett's framework, emotional disturbance is viewed as the result of failure of students to attain certain levels of learning competence. This learning competence is conceptualized in a developmental hierarchy that encompasses the essential skills that all children require to be successful in school: (1) attention—attend to stimulation; (2) response—reaction to stimuli; (3) order—organizational factors; (4) exploratory—active participation in learning; (5) social—development of relationships and self-concept; (6) mastery—achieving skills that permit independent functioning; and (7) achievement—self-motivation in learning.

Failure to achieve competence at any one of these levels leads to the label "emotionally disturbed." Hewett and Taylor (1980) outlined the typical behaviors displayed by students who have not achieved a given level of competence and these are summarized in Table 16.3. The classroom program was designed to enable students to achieve appropriate levels of competence through careful choice of curriculum (task), conditions (structure), and consequences (rewards).

Curriculum (task) was chosen on the basis of assessed deficiency in the student and began at the level of competence. The curriculum tasks were based upon the developmental sequence of educational goals and took a "thimbleful" approach wherein small forward steps were programmed and small gains rewarded. Specific curriculum areas are described in detail by Hewett and Taylor (1980).

Learning took place under a specified set of conditions and represented the structure inherent in the engineered classroom. The conditions reflected the degree of teacher control and represent the "when, how, how long, how much, and how well" (Hewett & Taylor, 1980, p. 109). Specific teacher behaviors that were needed at each level were set forth.

Consequences were the positive and negative experiences provided for appropriate and inappropriate behavior. Hewett and Forness (1984) identified six types of positive consequences: (1) acquisition of knowledge and skill, (2) knowledge of results, (3) social approval, (4) multisensory stimulation and activity, (5) task completion, and (6) tangible rewards.

By including all components of the learning triangle, the outcome was what Hewett and Taylor (1980) term the "orchestration of success." To evaluate the Santa Monica Project (Hewett, Taylor, & Artuso, 1969), six classes of disturbed students equated on the basis of IQ, age, and achievement level were studied under varying conditions. The experimental classes followed the "engineered classroom" model while the control classes could follow any programming except that they could not use a check-mark system of rewards. Thus, the system of check marks for appropriate behavior became the independent variable. The dependent measures included task attention, reading achievement, and arithmetic achievement.

TABLE 16.3 *Summary of the Developmental Sequence of Educational Goals*

Level	Attention	Response	Order	Exploratory	Social	Mastery	Achievement
Child's Problem	Inattention due to with-drawal or resistance	Lack of involvement and unwill-ingness to respond in learning	Inability to follow directions	Incomplete or inaccurate knowledge of environment	Failure to value social approval or disapproval	Deficits in basic adaptive and school skills not in keeping with IQ	Lack of self motivation for learning
Educational Task	Get child to pay attention to teacher and task	Get child to respond to tasks he likes and which offer promise of success	Get child to complete tasks with specific starting points and steps leading to a conclusion	Increase child's efficiency as an explorer and get him involved in multisensory exploration of his environ-ment	Get child to work for teacher and peer group approval and to avoid their disapproval	Remediation of basic skill deficiencies	Development of interest in acquiring knowledge
Learner Reward	Provided by tangible rewards (e.g., food, money, tokens)	Provided by gaining social attention	Provided through task completion	Provided by sensory stimulation	Provided by social approval	Provided through task accuracy	Provided through intellectual task success
Teacher Structure	Minimal	Still limited	Emphasized	Emphasized	Based on standards of social appro-priateness	Minimal	

Source: From Hewett, 1967.

TABLE 16.4 *Design of Hewett's Santa Monica Project*

Class	Fall Semester	Spring Semester
1 (E)	Experimental	Experimental
2 (C)	Control	Control
3 & 4 (CE)	Control	Experimental
5 & 6 (EC)	Experimental	Control

Over the course of the school year, the experimental condition resulted in superior task attention (except in the case of the class that was experimental in the fall and then became control in the spring, which actually improved on task attention without a check-mark system). The experimental condition produced progress in arithmetic but not reading. It was suggested that the systematic application of a check-mark system of reinforcement in the fall semester allowed teachers to become effective with social reinforcers that could be used to motivate and manage students.

Although the evaluation of the Santa Monica Project employed a between-subjects design, controlled teacher behavior, and used a variety of dependent measures, O'Leary and Drabman (1971) questioned whether too much attention was paid to the token system instead of academic work. For example, it is possible that the verbal praise paired with check marks became the reinforcing agent. It may also be the case that the check-mark system may simply force teachers to interact with students more frequently and more positively. Thus, the check-mark system may not be as important a component for students as for teachers since it contributes to systematizing teacher behavior.

PSYCHO-EDUCATIONAL MODEL

The psychoeducational approach to the education of disturbed students possesses perhaps the longest history and most diverse set of interventions.

Rezmerski (1982) and Knoblock (1973) have discussed the theoretical and historical foundations of the psychoeducational model and demonstrated how the model has fluctuated between emphasis on therapy and on education. For example, in early psychoeducational programs there was an emphasis on an expression of feelings (e.g., Berkowitz & Rothman, 1960), but this was replaced by increased attention on educational interventions and increased structure in the environment (Fenichel, 1966). Thus, there was greater recognition of the educational component wherein the educational process is an integral part of the psychological understanding necessary to provide therapeutic support. This suggests that an understanding of the child's basic needs is necessary to chart the course of educational events.

Consequently, even though the emphasis is on education, a psychoeducational program also results in something therapeutic in the sense of promoting constructive affective experiences. The psychoeducational approach can then be considered as a "restorative curriculum that capitalizes on the latent self-corrective capacities of the disturbed child to enhance emotional growth and mental health (Cheney & Morse, 1976, p. 318).

Long, Morse, and Newman (1980) have described the assumptions inherent in the psychoeducational model:

1. Cognitive and affective processes are in continuous interaction.
2. Attention must be directed toward the student's interaction with teachers and peers to develop a supportive educational milieu.
3. The psychoeducational process requires the creation of an environment in which the disturbed student can function successfully.
4. Each student must believe that he or she possesses the capacity and resources to function appropriately and successfully.
5. The learning process becomes invested with interest, meaning, and purpose when it is based on the recognition of feelings and emotions.
6. Learning style is individual to each student.
7. Crises are optimal times for both students and teachers to learn.
8. Behavioral limits can be a form of love.
9. Students learn through a process of unconscious identification with significant adults in their lives.
10. Teaching students social and academic skills enhances their capacity to cope with stress in the environment.

PSYCHO-EDUCATIONAL TECHNIQUES

Two highly charismatic figures from the 1950s, Redl and Bettelheim, primarily represent this position. Programs of this type, however, are characterized largely by belief, assertion, and wordy elaborations of technique rather than by careful empirical evaluation. Redl (1959a) suggested that psychoeducational processes take place in a therapeutic milieu. Whereas Bettelheim (1950) viewed the milieu as only exposure to a total environment designed specifically for treatment, Redl (1959a) felt that the milieu could include part of the child's natural environment. Within the milieu, Redl (1966) believed that group psychological factors are the primary influences in producing classroom difficulties rather than individual teacher–student interactions alone. Because the focus is upon the group, the teacher must base intervention strategies on their effect on both the individual student and the group. Redl (1966) offered a solution in terms of the "law of marginal antisepsis," which states that a given technique that is appropriate for the individual must be at least harmless to the growth of the group and vice versa. The optimal techniques for reacting to classroom dynamics are reflected in several different classroom activities (see Long, Alpher, Butt, & Cully, 1976).

Redl and Wattenberg (1959) have described techniques that can be divided in four categories: (1) techniques supporting self-control, (2) techniques involving task assistance, (3) techniques of reality and value appraisals, and (4) techniques using the pleasure-group principle. In a similar analysis of techniques to be used to deal with "surface" behavior problems produced by emotional conflicts, Long and Newman (1976) conceptualized four strategies. In *permitting*, the teacher identifies behaviors that can and cannot be performed in school. Consequently, expectations are defined clearly and the student does not have to test limits. *Tolerating* is a strategy useful where new behaviors have not been fully established. The teacher neither approves nor permits the behavior but will tolerate it until the student can improve further. Adjustment and evaluation of ongoing activities (e.g., schedules, physical structure, seating arrangements) to affect surface behavior is termed *preventive planning*. When these techniques are not effective, *interfering strategies* are used to reduce surface behavior problems on a short-term basis called "emotional first aid" (see Long & Newman, 1976; Redl & Wineman, 1952).

Specifically, Redl and Wineman (1951) suggested that behavior should be interfered with when the following criteria are present: (1) reality dangers, (2) psychological protection, (3) protection against too much excitement, (4) protection of property, (5) protection of an ongoing program, (6) protection against negative contagion, (7) highlighting school policy, (8) avoiding conflict with the outside world, and (9) protecting a teacher's inner comfort.

Within the psychoeducational framework, surface management techniques (including antiseptic bouncing and physical restraint) are not considered punishment. The concept of punishment within this theoretical framework is discussed at length in Redl and Wattenberg (1959).

Redl (1959b) suggested that the major tool for providing disturbed students with self-awareness is the life-space interview (LSI). The LSI is based upon an immediate crisis in the student's life. A particular incident serves as the focus of the interview, which is held immediately after the incident. In most cases, the interview is held by a person who is part of the child's milieu and who has directly observed, or even participated in, the event precipitating the crisis. It is not a moralistic approach but a dynamic one based on the interviewer's empathic relationship with the child (Newman, 1963). Redl (1959b) outlined the major goals of the LSI and the therapeutic techniques associated with each.

Morse (1963) suggested that the LSI can be used by teachers not only in crisis incidents but also in less emotionally charged situations. To be successful, Morse (1963) suggested that teachers must (1) understand that the school is an integral part of the child's milieu, (2) be sensitive to the child's behavior as a reflection of a life-space, and (3) be able to place themselves in the child's position and understand how the child expresses feelings in the milieu. While Redl (1959b) provided a theoretical framework for the LSI, Morse (1971c) and Brenner (1963) provided practical, if untested, guidelines for the LSI.

Morse (1971a) developed the concept of crisis intervention to perform the same function as the LSI but in nonresidential settings. Traditionally, within school settings, a student experiencing an emotional crisis was typically sent to the principal. But this procedure was usually removed from the situation where the crisis occurred and was sometimes hours later. The traditional approach focused on the immediate behavior but delegated the real corrective therapy to an individual who would see the child at a later date. In crisis intervention both steps are combined: the surface behavior is managed while the deeper significance of incident is also considered.

Morse (1962, 1971b) outlined the responsibilities of the crisis (or helping) teacher who works with both a student's emotional and academic problems. These often occur together, and many crises are perpetuated by a student's frustration over academic failure. Even though a student may not be teachable in the immediate crisis situation, the student needs to know immediately how to cope with the stressful situation. The crisis teacher was, in essence, an early version of the resource teacher. In a similar view, Newman (1967) described an interdisciplinary psychoeducational consultation model for assisting teachers to understand, explore, and cope with the demands of teaching and interactions with disturbed students. By building a relationship with the teacher, the consultant encourages the teacher to share feelings about students and offers psychoeducational interpretations about patterns of behavior to bridge the gap between educational principles and mental health principles (Newman et al., 1971).

As with most ED program interventions, research has been done in the efficacy of the crisis intervention approach. The few available studies suggest that the technique aids students in increasing self-esteem and motivation and in establishing social relationships (see Morse, 1971b).

Reality therapy (Glaser, 1965) is another methodology that can be viewed within a psychoeducational framework. It is not highly theoretical and avoids the "whys" of emotional disturbance. Thus, the position is closely allied with the behaviorists in the sense of focusing on overt behavior. But reality therapy provides a rationale for behavior change that involves feelings of responsibility. Responsibility is a central concept since it leads to happiness, which is a state based on one's own decisions, not one's present condition.

Glaser (1965) has outlined a 10-step approach that is based on the assumption that a child is capable of making conscious decisions regarding behavior. The approach includes many parallels to life-space intervening and crisis intervention.

In *Schools without Failure*, Glaser (1969) described the use of class meetings led by the teacher to solve behavioral and educational problems.

Although like Bettelheim and Redl, Glaser has received widespread attention, relatively little formal, systematic evaluation of his approach has been done. The few studies conducted to date, however, have failed generally to demonstrate the effectiveness of reality therapy (Elardo & Elardo, 1976:

Shearn & Randolph, 1978). For example, Welch and Dolly (1980) did not find any signficant teacher or student behavior change resulting from training in reality therapy and class meeting techniques.

Carl Fenichel (1966, 1970, 1976) described a psychoeducational model developed at the League School for Seriously Disturbed Children. As a response against the permissiveness of the classical psychoanalytic approach, the League School was founded to provide a structured, day-school program wherein learning evolves from and revolves around the teacher, who is the basis for all behavioral and academic change (Fenichel, Freedman, & Klapper, 1960).

Hillcrest Children's Center is a psychoeducational residential and day school treatment facility for disturbed students. The program provides both emotional and academic intervention. The academic component is eclectic and stresses individualized instruction. The emotional intervention, psychoeducationally based, relies on the teaching of self-control (Fagen & Long, 1976, 1979). A Self-Control Curriculum (Fagen, Long, & Stevens, 1975) was developed because it was felt that learning is improved when the students possess positive feelings about their being, the teacher, and the material.

Laneve (1979) described the psychoeducational oriented day-school program at the Mark Twain School. The student is first assigned a teacher-advisor who coordinates the program and is the leader of a therapeutic team that designs an individually tailored program. The team assesses academic, emotional, and social strengths and weaknesses to provide educational treatment objectives that are implemented in individual, small-group, and classroom activities.

Fagen (1979) suggested that the common element among the students is a failure to identify that must be replaced by success in three primary areas: academic proficiency, adult and peer relationships, and personal growth and development.

The Treatment and Education of Autistic and Related Communications Handicapped Children (TEACCH) program is a psychoeducationally based program for severely disturbed (psychotic) young children involving schools and parents (Lansing & Schopler, 1978; Reichler & Schopler, 1976; Schopler, Reichler, & Lansing, 1980) adopted statewide in North Carolina. Upon referral, the child is assessed with the *Psychoeducational Profile* (Schopler & Reichler, 1979) to provide an inventory of the child's skills (e.g., Imitation, Perception, Fine Motor, Gross Motor, Eye–Hand Integration, Cognitive Performance, and Cognitive Verbal Skills) for formulating educational goals and strategies. Besides special education interventions in school, parents are trained as the primary therapists and provide an important link between home and school intervention. Although the program has been operating for some time, there are no controlled evaluations of the effectiveness of the total program.

The Rutland Center is a psychoeducational program called Developmental Therapy, initiated by Wood (1972, 1975b), which uses a team approach to maintain children in public schools. Wood (1975b) identified five behavioral stages corresponding to four curriculum areas—Behavior, Communication, Socialization, and Academic (Wood, 1975a; Wood & Swan, 1978; Wood, Swan, & Newman, 1982)—for which a variety of teacher-made and commercial materials exist that are interesting to children, are appropriate to the child's developmental level, and encourage exploration and pleasurable outcomes (Wood, 1981).

Although some evaluation of Developmental Therapy has been attempted (Huberty, Quirk, & Swan, 1973), there has been no summative evaluation to differentiate the effects of the program from the effects of maturation. Although this system represents a hierarchical theory of development, there is no empirical evidence to suggest that these stages are either necessary or desirable (Kavale, 1978).

Humanistic "open classroom" education has its roots in the psychoeducational model, and Dupont (1975) suggested that its philosophical roots are found in humanistic psychology emphasizing individuality, acceptance, and equality (Maslow, 1968; Rogers, 1969). Knoblock (1973) provided guidelines for the application of the open classroom model by specifying both child behaviors and teacher behaviors.

Because of the humanistic philosophy, there is little formal evaluation and little structure. Consequently, implementation may reveal wide variability and usually reflects the particular talents and interests of the teachers and students involved.

COUNTERTHEORY MODEL

None of the models reviewed previously is considered satisfactory by countertheorists. Although encompassing a variety of viewpoints, the common thread is a belief that traditional approaches to the education of disturbed students have been characterized by:

1. The dehumanizing effect of institutions developed to provide service to children.
2. The tendency of service delivery systems to exclude youngsters believed to be "deviant."
3. The concept of "deviance" itself, as well as the concept of "normality."
4. The nature of the helping contract, which seems to reinforce the notion that the helper is, in some unspoken ways, superior to the client. Such a notion can only increase the client's dependency and powerlessness.
5. The tendency of institutions to perpetuate themselves by contributing to the identification of a steady flow of "deviant" children.
6. The self-fulfilling prophecy, so frequently set in motion by society's need to categorize and label even minor "differences" in its population.

7. A model of education that seems to approximate a production line, modeling and shaping the great diversity among children into standardized models.
8. The idea that education consists of a known set of information and skills that must be passed on to and mastered by each generation.
9. The belief that the teacher's role is to dispense bits of truth to students and its implication of irrelevance and exploitation.
10. The potential use of the concept of literacy for political exploitation (Gibbins & Tracy, 1978).

The response of countertheorists to these perceived difficulties is to advocate major and radical reforms in the concept of school as it is now known or the abolition of schooling entirely. Generally, countertheorists support holistic views of the child rather than a fragmented view. An example is found in Summerhill (Neill, 1960) whose goal is to produce happy adults, which is achieved by the following principles:

1. There is a firm faith in the goodness of the child.
2. The aim of education is to achieve happiness.
3. Education is both cognitive and affective.
4. Eduction must be individualized and geared to the child's capacities.
5. Discipline should be avoided.
6. Freedom is important and must be based on mutual respect.
7. The child must be told the truth by teachers.
8. Guilt feelings impede growth toward independence.

Other countertheorists have ranged across a wide spectrum. Holt (1964, 1969, 1972) has questioned the effects of modern schools on children; Kozol (1967), Kohl (1967) and Reimer (1967) have decried what they see as the dehumanization of children in inner-city school situations; Jones (1968) has criticized the neglect of affective variables in education; Fantini and Weinstein (1968) described the benefits of a humanistic education curriculum; Dennison (1969) criticized the isolation of schools from the greater social community; Postman and Weingartner (1969) described what they assessed as the subversive aspects of schooling; Goodman (1964) and Hentoff (1977) objected to the goal of education being the preservation of normalcy; and Silberman (1970) described the crisis in the classroom and its negative effects upon the child. Advocates of the movement to "deschool" society (Freire, 1972; Illich, 1971; Melton, 1975) have suggested that children will be free to learn only when institutionalized education is ended.

Despite its wide dissemination, countertheory has had relatively little impact on the education of disturbed students. Countertheory provides a sounding board for radical views but is of little practical value. The strident polemical nature of the countertheory literature has diminished its influence and, by its very nature, is difficult to evaluate critically. Consequently, countertheory remains on a theoretical level, and as a political force until it is implemented in a less radical form, it will possess little pragmatic value for educating disturbed students.

ADJUNCT INTERVENTION

Psychodynamic Therapies

Psychodynamic therapy covers a wide variety of methodological approaches that serve to support educational interventions (see also Chapter 13). At one end is individual psychotherapy (Baruch, 1952; Ginott, 1959) whereas the other end is marked by group therapy (Bion, 1962; Newman, 1971). Although the relationship between educators and psychoanalysts should be a mutually collaborative one, past experience has shown the relationship to be one of suspicion and mistrust.

The psychodynamic model has also served as the theoretical basis of expressive therapies whose goal is to permit students to express themselves in a nonthreatening manner. The expressive mediums include play (Axline, 1947), drama (Greenberg, 1974), puppetry (Woltman, 1951), art (Kramer, 1971), music (Michel, 1976), and dance (Chace, 1958). It should be noted that expressive therapies need not be limited to clinical settings and may be used as vehicles of communication in the classroom.

Biophysical Interventions

Historically and legally, biophysical interventions have been the exclusive responsibility of the medical profession, but educators do have responsibility for observing, monitoring, and evaluating the performance of students (Morse & Smith, 1980).

Kavale and Nye (1984) synthesized statistically the findings from 70 studies using the techniques of meta-analysis (Glass, McGaw, & Smith, 1981). The basic statistic is the "effect size" (ES) defined by $ES = X_e - X_c/SD_c$, which transforms findings into a common metric (standard deviation units). An ES may be interpreted as a z-score where an ES of $+1.00$ indicates that a subject at the 50th percentile of the control group would be expected to rise to the 84th percentile of the control group after drug treatment and, thus, be better off than 84 percent of subjects not being treated with drugs, while only 16 percent of the control group would be better off at the end than the average drug-treated child.

The ES (average effect size) was .302 based on 401 comparisons of which 33 percent were negative (thus favoring the control group). This indicates a 67 percent positive response to drug intervention where the average drug-treated subject moves from the 50th percentile to the 62nd percentile. This 12 percentile rank gain suggests that drug-treated subjects would be expected to be better off than 62 percent of untreated subjects.

A single index of drug efficacy (i.e., .302) may mask important relationships so the ES measurements were aggregated into three major outcome classes: behavioral, cognitive, and physiological outcomes whose ES's were .277, .739, and .157, respectively. These ES's were not significantly different and translate in 9, 27, and 6 percentile rank increases for the behavioral, cognitive, and physiological classes, respectively. Further insight can be achieved by aggregating ES measurements into more specific outcome categories associated with the outcome classes. These findings are shown in Table 16.5.

The treatment of hyperactive children with stimulant drugs is among the most emotionally loaded issues in the educational field.

Kavale (1982) found 135 studies assessing the effectiveness of stimulant drug treatment for hyperactivity. The studies sampled represented approximately 5300 subjects averaging 8.75 years of age with an average IQ of 102 who received medication for an average of 10 weeks. The ES across 984 ES measurements was .578, which suggests that an average drug-treated child would be expected to be better off than 72 percent of untreated control children.

Three major outcome classes were again identified (behavioral, cognitive, and physiological); the findings are illustrated in Figure 16.1 in the form of normal distributions comparing hypothetical drug-treated and control populations. This more refined analysis revealed substantial positive effects on behavioral and cognitive outcomes. The negative effect for physiological outcomes indicated that drug intervention produced some negative consequences. (The physiological findings are generally difficult to interpret and are outside the scope of this chapter.)

Further refinement of the data in each outcome class is presented in Table 16.6. Note the impressive gains (with the exception of anxiety) on behavioral

TABLE 16.5 *Average Effect Sizes for Outcome Categories*

Outcome Category	Mean Effect Size	Percentile Status
Behavior		
Improvement Ratings	.487	69
Self-Help	.389	65
Socialization	− .053	48
School Behavior	.155	56
Cognitive		
Attention/Concentration	.455	67
Intelligence	.965	83
Achievement	.114	54
Paired Associate Learning	.760	78
Verbalization	.378	65
Perception	.333	63
Physiological		
Neurological	.383	65
Biophysical	− .695	24

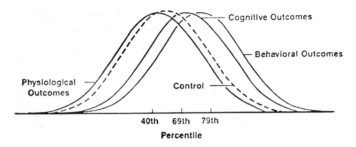

Behavioral ES = 0.804
Cognitive ES = 0.491
Physiological ES = -0.246

FIGURE 16.1. Effect of stimulant drug therapy on behavioral, cognitive, and physiological outcome classes.

outcomes. Substantial benefits were found on ratings of behavioral functioning, lowered activity levels, and improved attending skills. Although not of the same magnitude as behavioral improvements, cognitive functioning also exhibited improvement.

TABLE 16.6 *Average Effect Sizes for Outcome Categories*

	Mean Effect Size	No. of Effect Sizes
Behavioral		
Global Improvement Ratings	.886	192
Rating Scales & Checklists	.837	113
Activity Level	.846	127
Attention & Concentration	.782	119
Behavior (Social & Classroom)	.634	92
Anxiety	.118	12
Cognitive		
Intelligence	.391	54
Achievement	.383	47
Drawing & Copying	.467	38
Perceptual, Memory, & Motor	.412	91
Learning Characteristics	.367	41
Physiological		
Biochemical	.558	7
Psychophysiological	-.275	51

Diet treatment has been suggested as an intervention for behavior problems, specifically hyperactivity (Feingold, 1975, 1976).

Kavale and Forness (1983) examined 23 studies assessing the efficacy of the Feingold K-P diet in treating hyperactivity. The 23 studies produces 125 ES measurements and yielded an ES of .118. The average subject was 8.3 years of age, had an IQ of 99, and remained on the Feingold K-P diet for 39 weeks. In relative terms, the .118 ES indicates that a child no better off than average (i.e., at the 50th percentile) would rise to the 55th percentile as a result of the Feingold K-P diet. When compared to the 22 percentile ranks gain for stimulant drug treatment, the 5 percentile rank improvement for diet intervention is less than one-fourth as large. Although the average ages and IQs were similar for drug-treated and diet-treated subjects, the average duration of treatment differed: 39 versus 10 weeks. In relation to ES (.118 vs. .587), these comparisons suggest that drug treatment is approximately five times as effective in about one-fourth the time when compared to Feingold K-P diet treatment.

The ES data were next aggregated into descriptive outcome categories. The findings are shown in Table 16.7. The only obvious effect of diet treatment is upon overt behavior—specifically, a reduction in hyperactivity—with little influence upon more cognitive aspects of behavior. This conclusion, however, must be tempered. Global ratings of improvement possess two major problems: objectively defining improvement, and psychometric deficiencies (reliability and validity). These problems influence the "reactivity" or subjectivity of outcome measures. The correlation of ES and ratings of reactivity was significant ($r = .181$), suggesting that larger treatment effects were slightly associated with more reactive measures. Additionally, aggregations of reactive versus nonreactive measures found ES's of .179 and .001, respectively, suggesting that in instances in which instruments paralleled the valued outcomes of observers, there was a tendency to view more improvement as revealed in larger treatment effects.

TABLE 16.7 *Average Effect Size for Outcome Categories*

Category	Mean Effect Size	No. of Effect Sizes
Conners Scale—Parents	.156	26
Conners Scale—Teachers	.268	9
Global Improvement	.128	23
Hyperkinesis Rating	.293	15
Attention	.015	36
Disruptive Behavior	.052	6
Impulsivity	.153	5
Learning Ability	− .055	10

SUMMARY

Educational programming for behaviorally disordered students takes a variety of forms. Although theoretical models have defined fairly discrete parameters for viewing behavior disorders, the interventions based on these theoretical models have not shown the same discreteness. Some programs may be recognized as stemming mainly from one theoretical orientation, but it is far more likely that an educational intervention will reveal an eclectic orientation that combines features associated with several models.

Cullinan et al. (1983) have defined criteria for judging the value of interventions based on theoretical models. These criteria include:

1. **Replicability**—the degree to which an intervention method can be communicated to and used by others more or less as it was originally employed.
2. **Efficiency**—the extent to which the intervention can be delivered effectually in terms of length of intervention required, group versus individual administration, and length of training needed.
3. **Breadth**—the variety of behavior disorders with which the model is concerned.
4. **Effectiveness**—the extent to which an individual will benefit from the intervention (e.g., behavioral change, attitude change, achievement), which is defined in two ways:
   a. Restricted effectiveness refers to whether an intervention can cause the beneficial changes claimed by those who use it.
   b. Extended effectiveness is concerned with the power of an intervention to produce beneficial changes (in addition to the kind involved in restricted effectiveness) in terms of (i) durability (long-term outcomes), (ii) ability to produce response generalization, and (iii) ability to produce situation generalization.

Given these criteria, it is possible to rate the psychoeducational (as a broader application of the psychodynamic model), behavioral, and ecological models displayed in Table 16.8.

This analysis shows that the behavioral model rates highly on all criteria except extended effectiveness. But the extent to which an intervention approach generalizes as well as its effectiveness over time is an important con-

TABLE 16.8 *Intervention Features*

Feature	Psychoeducational	Behavioral	Ecological
Replicability	Medium	High	Low
Efficiency	Low	High	Low
Breadth	High	High	Low
Restricted Effectiveness	Medium	High	Medium
Extended Effectiveness	Medium	Low	Medium

sideration in the treatment of disturbed students. The low rating on this criterion may account for the fact that the behavioral model has been included in a majority of educational programs but rarely as a total program. Because behavioral interventions receive high ratings on all criteria except providing extended effectiveness, they are preferred in educational settings. Nevertheless, the limitation imposed by poor extended effectiveness suggests that behavioral interventions must be incorporated in another model for maximum effectiveness (i.e., extended effectiveness). Consequently, behavioral interventions are often the major means of behavior management in a total intervention system that takes an eclectic approach.

The problems in implementing the ecological model in a practical program suggests that while the model is appealing in theory, it is difficult to put into practice, as evidenced by the low ratings on three criteria. This explains why individuals who state their programs to be ecological do not support this view when asked to report on the goals and methods used in their programs (see Kavale & Hirshoren, 1980).

The psychoeducational model generally rates between the behavioral and ecological models but fails on the criterion of efficiency. It is difficult to implement and maintain but, when accomplished, the results are generally favorable. Generally, psychoeducational interventions must be applied over a long period of time and require considerable training on the part of the personnel involved.

Thus, the educational programming based on the different models possess strengths and weaknesses. Most are attributable to charismatic individuals and predate the 1970s but all suffer from the lack of good evaluation. Without good evaluation, it is possible for useless techniques to continue and for valuable techniques to be disregarded. Educational programming for disturbed students is especially prone to those problems and special educators must insist on scientific evaluations of techniques, curricula, and programs and be less swayed by popularity as a criterion.

Although behavioral interventions are amply evaluated (e.g., Kazdin & Wilson, 1978), the evaluations focus on circumscribed efforts that allow for judgments about restricted effectiveness but not extended effectiveness. The psychoeducational model and ecological model are often evaluated through case studies and clinical reports that are interesting but lack the rigor and objectivity evidenced in scientific evaluation. However, evaluating real-world educational programs for disturbed students is a difficult process because (1) all relevant characteristics of a student cannot be examined, (2) it is usually not possible to include all the necessary and desirable aspects of an evaluation design, (3) a single study often cannot provide answers to all relevant questions, (4) outcomes are usually not clear-cut and are difficult to interpret unequivocally, and (5) the educational systems are apathetic toward evaluation.

Yet it is clear that educational programs for disturbed students can improve only if they are evaluated in a more scientific manner. A major outcome of such evaluations will not only be information on particular programs but also information that will lead to more and better questions about educational programs. These questions may then lead to a better articulation between theory and practice in the education of disturbed children. In this way, the quest to identify *the* teacher operating *the* intervention approach that is most effective for disturbed students may not be the appropriate task. Under the likely assumption that no single intervention model is clearly superior, and the knowledge that teacher behavior reveals considerable variability and disturbed students represent a heterogeneous group, educational programming must present a synthesis. This synthesis will direct a search which seeks to determine *which* teacher, implementing *which* intervention, will be most effective for *which* disturbed student. The synthesis required must transcend the present intuitive eclectic approaches which simply combine elements of different programs and replace them with functional relationships which represent the congruence among factors. In this way, educational programming will be based upon an optimal interaction that produces the most effective and efficient combination to serve the educational needs of disturbed students.

REFERENCES

Aichhorn, A. (1965). *Wayward youth*. New York: Viking Press. (Originally published in 1925.)

A master plan for special education in California (1973). Sacramento: California State Department of Education.

Apter, S. (1977). Applications of ecological theory. Toward a community special education model. *Exceptional Children, 43*, 366–373.

Apter, S. J., & Conoley, J. C. (1984). *Childhood behavior disorders and emotional disturbance*. Englewood Cliffs, NJ: Prentice-Hall.

Axelrod, S. (1977). *Behavior modification for the classroom teacher*. New York: McGraw-Hill.

Axline, V. (1947). *Play therapy*. Boston: Houghton Mifflin.

Bandura, A. (1973). *Aggression: A social learning analysis*. Englewood Cliffs, NJ: Prentice-Hall.

Baruch, D. (1952). *One little boy*. New York: Julian Press.

Becker, W. C., Engelman, S., & Thomas, D. R. (1975a). *Teaching 1: Classroom management*. Chicago: Science Research Associates.

Becker, W. C., Engelman, S., & Thomas, D. R. (1975b). *Teaching 2: Cognitive learning and instruction*. Chicago: Science Research Associates.

Berkowitz, L. (1973). Control of aggression. In B. Caldwell & H. Ricciuti (Eds.), *Child development research* (Vol. 3, pp. 95–140). Chicago: University of Chicago Press.

Berkowitz, P. H., & Rothman, E. P. (1960). *The disturbed child: Recognition and psychoeducational therapy in the classroom*. New York: New York University Press.

Berkowitz, P. H., & Rothman, E. P. (Eds.). (1967). *Public education for disturbed children in New York City*. Springfield, IL: Charles C. Thomas.

Bettelheim, B. (1950). *Love is not enough*. Glencoe, IL: Free Press.

Bettelheim, B. (1955). *Truants from life*. Glencoe, IL: Free Press.

Bettelheim, B. (1961). The decision to fail. *The School Review, 69*, 389–412.

Bettelheim, B. (1970). Listening to children. In P. Gallagher & L. Edwards (Eds.), *Educating the emotionally disturbed: Theory to practice* (pp. 77–89). Lawrence, KS: University of Kansas Press.

Bettelheim, B., & Sylvester, E. A. (1948). A therapeutic milieu. *American Journal of Orthopsychiatry, 18*, 191–206.

Bion, W. (1962). *Experience in groups*. New York: Basic Books.

Brendtro, L. K., & Stern, P. R. (1967). A modification in the sequential tutoring of emotionally disturbed children. *Exceptional Children, 33*, 517–521.

Brenner, M. B. (1963). Life space interview in the school setting. *American Journal of Orthopsychiatry, 33*, 717–719.

Carnine, D., & Gilbert, J. (1979). *Direct instruction reading*. Columbus, OH: Merrill.

Chace, M. (1958). Dance in growth or treatment settings. *Music Therapy, 1*, 119–122.

Cheney, C., & Morse, W. (1976). Psychodynamic interventions. In N. Long, W. Morse, & R. Newman (Eds.), *Conflict in the classroom* (3rd ed., pp. 240–245). Belmont, CA: Wadsworth.

Cohen, R. S. (1965). Therapeutic education and day treatment: A new professional liaison. *Exceptional Children, 32*, 23–28.

Cromwell, R. L., Blashfield, R. K., & Strauss, J. S. (1975). Criteria for classification systems. In N. Hobbs (Ed.), *Issues in the classification of children*, Vol. 1 (pp.4–25). San Francisco: Jossey-Bass.

Cruickshank, W., Bentzen, F., Ratzeburg, F., & Tannhauser, M. A. (1961). *A teaching method for brain-injured and hyperactive children*. Syracuse, NY: Syracuse University Press.

Cruse, D. (1962). The effect of distraction upon the performance of brain-injured and familial retarded children. In E. Trapp & P. Himmelstein (Eds.), *Readings on the exceptional child* (pp. 492–500). New York: Appleton-Century-Crofts.

Cullinan, D., Epstein, M. H., & Lloyd, J. W. (1983). *Behavior disorders of children and adolescents*. Englewood Cliffs, NJ: Prentice-Hall.

Dennison, G. (1969). *The lives of children: The story of the First Street School*. New York: Random House.

Dupont, H. (1975).The humanistic open-education model. In H. Dupont (Ed.), *Educating emotionally disturbed children: Readings* (2nd ed., pp. 448–449). New York: Holt, Rinehart & Winston.

Elardo, P., & Elardo, R. (1976). A critical analysis of social development programs in elementary education. *Journal of School Psychology, 14*, 118–130.

Engelman, S. (1969). *Preventing failure in the primary grades*. Chicago: Science Research Associates.

Epstein, M. H., & Cullinan, D. (1981). Project ExCEL: A behaviorally-oriented educational program for learning disabled pupils. *Education and Treatment of Children, 4*, 357–373.

Fagen, S. A. (1979). Psychoeducational management and self-control. In D. Cullinan & M. Epstein (Eds.), *Special education for adolescents* (pp. 235–271). Columbus, OH: Merrill.

Fagen, S. A., & Long, N. J. (1976). Teaching children self-control: A new responsibility for teachers. *Focus on Exceptional Children, 7* (Whole #8).

Fagen, S. A., & Long, N. J. (1979). A psychoeducational curriculum approach to teaching self-control. *Behavioral Disorders, 4*, 68–82.

Fagen, S. A., Long, N. J., & Stevens, D. J. (1975). Teaching children self-control. Columbus, OH: Merrill.

Fantini, M., & Weinstein, G. (1968). *Disadvantaged children: Challenge to education*. New York: Harper & Row.

Feagans, L. (1972). Ecological theory as a model for constructing a theory of emotional disturbance. In W. Rhodes & M. Tracy (Eds.), *A study of child variance: Conceptual models* (Vol. 1, pp. 323–389). Ann Arbor: University of Michigan Press.

Feingold, B. F. (1975). *Why is your child hyperactive?* New York: Random House.

Feingold, B. F. (1976). Hyperkinesis and learning disabilities linked to the ingestion of artificial food colors and flavors. *Journal of Learning Disabilities, 9*, 551–559.

Fenichel, C. (1966). Psychoeducational approaches for seriously disturbed children in the classroom. In P. Knoblock (Ed.), *Intervention approaches in educating emotionally disturbed children* (pp. 5–18). Syracuse, NY: Syracuse University Press.

Fenichel, C. (1970). Education as therapy for the seriously disturbed. In *Crisis in child mental health. Report of the Joint Commission on mental health of children* (pp. 143–159). New York: Harper & Row.

Fenichel, C. (1976). Socializing the severely disturbed child. In E. Schopler & R. Reichler (Eds.), *Psychopathology and child development: Research and treatment* (pp. 219–227). New York: Plenum.

Fenichel, C., Freedman, A. M., & Klapper, Z. (1960). A day school for schizophrenic children. *American Journal of Orthopsychiatry, 30*, 130–143.

Fink, A. H., Glass, R. M., & Guskin, S. L. (1975). An analysis of teacher education programs in behavior disorders. *Exceptional Children, 42*, 47–48.

Forness, S. R. (1985). Effects of public policy at the state level: California's impact on MR, LD, and ED categories. *Remedial and Special Education, 6*, 32–43.

Freire, P. (1972). *Pedagogy of the oppressed*. New York: Herter & Herter.

Freud, A. (1954). *Psychoanalysis for teachers and parents*. New York: Emerson Books.

Gibbons, S., & Tracy, M. (1978). Counter-theoretical views and approaches. In W. Rhodes & J. Paul (Eds.), *Emotionally disturbed and deviant children: New views and approaches* (pp. 227–255). Englewood Cliffs, NJ: Prentice-Hall.

Ginott, H. G. (1959). The theory and practice of "therapeutic intervention" in child treatment. *Journal of Consulting Psychology, 23*, 160–166.

Glass, G. V., McGaw, B., & Smith, M. L. (1981). *Meta-analysis in social research*. Beverly Hills: Sage.

Glasser, W. (1965). *Reality therapy*. New York: Harper & Row.

Glasser, W. (1969). *Schools without failure*. New York: Harper & Row.

Glavin, J. P., Quay, H. C., Annesley, F. R., & Werry, J. S. (1971). An experimental resource room for behavior problem children. *Exceptional Children, 38*, 131–137.

Glavin, J. P., Quay, H. C., & Werry, J. S. (1971). Behavioral and academic gains of conduct problem children in different classroom settings. *Exceptional Children, 37*, 441–446.

Goodman, P. (1964). *Compulsory miseducation and the community of scholars*. New York: Vintage Books.

Greenberg, I. (1974). *Psychodrama: Theory and therapy*. New York: Behavioral Publications.

Haring, N. G., & Phillips, E. L. (1962). *Educating emotionally disturbed children*. New York: McGraw-Hill.

Haubrich, P. A., & Shores, R. E. (1976). Attending behavior and academic performance of emotionally disturbed children. *Exceptional Children, 42*, 337–338.

Henry, J. (1957). The culture of interpersonal relations in a therapeutic institution for emotionally disturbed children. *American Journal of Orthopsychiatry. 27*, 426–435.

Hentoff, N. (1977). *Does anyone give a damn?* Westminster, MD: Namar.

Hewett, F. M. (1967). Educational engineering with emotionally disturbed children. *Exceptional Children, 33*, 459–467.

Hewett, F. M. (1968). *The emotionally disturbed child in the classroom*. Boston: Allyn & Bacon.

Hewett, F. M., & Forness, S. R. (1984). *Education of exceptional learners* (3rd ed.). Boston: Allyn & Bacon.

Hewett, F. M., & Taylor, F. D. (1980). *The emotionally disturbed child in the classroom* (2nd ed.). Boston: Allyn & Bacon.

Hewett, F. M., Taylor, F. D., & Artuso, A. A. (1969). The Santa Monica project: Evaluation of an engineered classroom design with emotionally disturbed children. *Exceptional Children, 35*, 523–529.

Hirschberg, J. C. (1953). The role of education in the treatment of emotionally disturbed children through planned ego development. *American Journal of Orthopsychiatry, 23*, 684–690.

Hobbs, N. (1965). How the Re-Ed plan developed. In N. Long, W. Morse, & R. Newman (Eds.), *Conflict in the classroom* (pp. 286–294). Belmont, CA: Wadsworth.

Hobbs, N. (1966). Helping disturbed children: Psychological and ecological strategies. *American Psychologist, 35*, 523–529.

Hobbs, N. (1968). Re-education, reality, and responsibility. In J. Carter (Ed.), *Research contributions from psychology to community mental health* (pp. 7–18). New York: Behavioral Publications.

Hobbs, N. (1982). *The troubled and troubling child*. San Francisco: Jossey-Bass.

Hollister, W. G., & Godston, S. E. (1962). Psychoeducational processes in classes for emotionally handicapped children. *Exceptional Children, 28*, 351–356.

Holt, J. (1964). *How children fail*. New York: Pitman.

Holt, J. (1969). *How children learn*. New York: Pitman.

Holt, J. (1972). *Freedom and beyond*. New York: Dutton.

Hops, H., & Beickel, S. (1975). *CLASS: A standardized in-class program for acting-out children. I: Preliminary investigations* (Report B). Eugene: University of Oregon, Center at Oregon for Research in the Behavioral Education of the Handicapped.

Hops, H., Beickel, S., & Walker, H. (1976). *Contingencies for learning academic and social skills: Programs for acting-out children*. Eugene: University of Oregon, Center at Oregon for Research in the Behavioral Education of the Handicapped.

Hops, H., Walker, H., & Fleischman, D. (1976). *CLASS: A standardized in-class program for acting-out children. II: Field test evaluations* (Report No. 22). Eugene: University of Oregon, Center at Oregon for Research in the Behavioral Education of the Handicapped.

Huberty, C. J., Quirk, J., & Swan, W. W. (1973). An evaluation system for a psychoeducational treatment program for emotionally disturbed children. *Educational Technology, 13*, 73–80.

Illich, I. (1971). *Deschooling society*. New York: Harper & Row.

Jacobson, S., & Faegre, C. (1959). Neutralization: A tool for the teacher of the disturbed children. *Exceptional Children, 25*, 243–246.

Jones, R. (1968). *Fantasy and feeling in education*. New York: New York University Press.

Kauffman, J. M. (1981). *Characteristics of children's behavior disorders* (2nd ed.). Columbus, OH: Merrill.

Kavale, K. A. (1978). Review of "Developmental therapy: A textbook for teachers as therapists for emotionally disturbed young children" by M. M. Wood (Ed.). *Behavioral Disorders, 3*, 328–331.

Kavale, K. A. (1982). The efficacy of stimulant drug treatment for hyperactivity: A meta-analysis. *Journal of Learning Disabilities, 75*, 280–289.

Kavale, K., & Hirshoren, A. (1980). Public school and university teacher training programs for behaviorally disordered children: Are they compatible? *Behavioral Disorders, 5*, 151–155.

Kavale, K. A., & Forness, S. R. (1983). Hyperactivity and diet treatment: A meta-analysis of the Feingold hypothesis. *Journal of Learning Disabilities, 16*, 324–330.

Kavale, K. A., & Nye, C. (1984). The effectiveness of drug treatment for severe behavior disorders: A meta-analysis. *Behavioral Disorders, 9*, 117–130.

Kazdin, A. E. & Wilson, G. T. (1978). *Evaluation of behavior therapy: Issues, evidence, and research strategies*. Cambridge, MA: Ballinger.

Keogh, B., Major-Kingsley, S., Omori-Gordon, H., & Reid, H. P. (1982). *A system of marker variables for the field of learning disabilities*. Syracuse, NY: Syracuse University Press.

Keogh, B. K., Major, S. M., Reid, H. P., Gandara, P., & Omori, H. (1978). Marker variables: A search for comparability and generalizability in the field of learning disabilities. *Learning Disabilities Quarterly, 1*, 5–11.

Knoblock, P. (1973). Open education for emotionally disturbed children. *Exceptional Children, 39*, 358–365.

Kohl, H. (1967). *Thirty-six children*. New York: World Publications.

Kozol, J. (1967). *Death at an early age: The destruction of the hearts and minds of Negro children in the Boston public schools*. Boston: Houghton Mifflin.

Kramer, E. (1971). *Art as therapy with children*. New York: Schocken.

Laneve, R. S. (1979). Mark Twain School: A therapeutic educational environment for emotionally disturbed students. *Behavioral Disorders, 4*, 183–192.

Lansing, M. D., & Schopler, E. (1978). Individualized education: A public school model. In M. Rutter & E. Schopler (Eds.), *Autism: A reappraisal of concepts and treatment* (pp. 439–452). New York: Plenum.

LaVietes, R. (1962). The teacher's role in the education of emotionally disturbed children. *American Journal of Orthopsychiatry, 32*, 854–862.

LaVietes, R. L., Hulse, W. C., & Blau, A. (1960). A psychiatric day treatment center and school for young children and their parents. *American Journal of Orthopsychiatry, 30*, 468–482.

Lindsley, O. (1964). Direct measurement and prosthesis of retarded behavior. *Journal of Education, 147*, 62–81.

Lindsley, O. (1971). Precision teaching perspective: An interview with Ogden R. Lindsley. *Teaching Exceptional Children, 3*, 111–119.

Lloyd, J., Epstein, M., & Cullinan, D. (1981). Direct teaching for learning disabilities. In J. Gottlieb & S. Strichart (Eds.), *Developmental theory and research in learning disabilities* (pp. 278–309). Baltimore: University Park Press.

Long, N., Alpher, R., Butt, F., & Cully, M. (1976). Helping children cope with feelings. In N. Long, W. Morse, & R. Newman (Eds.), *Conflict in the classroom: The education of children with problems* (3rd ed., pp. 297–301). Belmont, CA: Wadsworth.

Long, N. J., Morse, W. C., & Newman, R. G. (1980). *Conflict in the classroom: Education of emotionally disturbed children* (4th ed.). Belmont, CA: Wadsworth.

Long, N., & Newman, R. (1976). Managing surface behavior of children in school. In N. Long, W. Morse, & R. Newman (Eds.), *Conflict in the classroom: The education of children with problems* (3rd ed., pp. 308–316). Belmont, CA: Wadsworth.

Lovitt, T. C. (1975). Applied behavior analysis and learning disabilities. Part II. Specific research recommendations and suggestions for practitioners. *Journal of Learning Disabilities, 8*, 504–518.

MacMillan, D. L. (1982). *Mental retardation in school and society* (2nd ed.). Boston: Little, Brown.

Maslow, A. (1968). Some educational implications of the humanistic psychologies. *Harvard Educational Review, 38*, 385–396.

McDowell, R. L., Adamson, G. W., & Wood, F. H. (Eds.). (1983). *Teaching emotionally disturbed children*. Boston: Little, Brown.

McKinney, J. D., & Fisher, L. (1982, April). *The search for subtypes of specific learning disability*. Paper read at the Gatlin Conference on Research in Mental Retardation/Developmental Disabilities, Gatlinburg, TN.

Melton, D. (1975). *Burn the schools—Save the children*. New York: Crowell.

Michel, D. E. (1976). *Music therapy: An introduction to therapy and special education through music*. Springfield, IL: Charles C. Thomas.

Moller, H. (1964). The treatment of childhood schizophrenia in a public school system. *Psychology in the Schools, 1*, 297–304.

Morse, W. C. (1962). The crisis teacher: Public school provision for the disturbed pupil. *The University of Michigan School of Education Bulletin, 37*, 101–104.

Morse, W. C. (1963). Training teachers in life space interviewing. In R. Newman & M. Keith (Eds.), *The school-centered life space interview* (pp. 61–67). Washington, DC: Washington School of Psychiatry.

Morse, W. C. (1971a). Crisis intervention in school mental health and special classes for the disturbed. In N. Long, W. Morse, & R. Newman (Eds.), *Conflict in the classroom: Education of children with problems.* (2nd ed., pp. 459–465). Belmont, CA: Wadsworth.

Morse, W. C. (1971b). The crisis or helping teacher. In N. Long, W. Morse, & R. Newman (Eds.), *Conflict in the classroom: Education of children with problems* (2nd ed., pp. 294–305). Belmont, CA: Wadsworth.

Morse, W. C. (1971c). Worksheet on life space interviewing for teachers. In N. Long, W. Morse, & R. Newman (Eds.), *Conflict in the classroom: Education of children with problems* (2nd ed., pp. 485–490). Belmont, CA: Wadsworth.

Morse, W. C., Cutler, R. L., & Fink, A. H. (1964). *Public school classes for the emotionally handicapped: A research analysis.* Washington, DC: Council for Exceptional Children.

Morse, W. C., & Smith, J. M. (1980). *Understanding child variance.* Reston, VA: Council for Exceptional Children.

Neill, A. (1960). *Summerhill: A radical approach to child rearing.* New York: Hart.

Newcomer, P. L. (1980). *Understanding and teaching emotionally disturbed children.* Boston: Allyn & Bacon.

Newman, R. G. (1961). Conveying essential messages to the emotionally disturbed child at school. *Exceptional Children, 28*, 199–204.

Newman, R. G. (1963). The school-centered life span interview. In R. Newman & M. Keith (Eds.), *The school-centered life space interview* (pp. 13–34). Washington, DC: Washington School of Psychiatry.

Newman, R. G. (1967). *Psychological consultation in the schools: A catalyst for learning.* New York: Basic Books.

Newman, R. G. (1971). Groups: How they grew and what they're all about. In N. Long, W. Morse, & R. Newman (Eds.), *Conflict in the classroom: Education of children with problems* (2nd ed., pp. 231–235). Belmont, CA: Wadsworth.

Newman, R. G., Bloomberg, C., Emerson, P., Keith, M., Kitchner, H., & Redl, F. (1971). Psychoeducational consultation. In N. Long, W. Morse, & R. Newman (Eds.), *Conflict in the classroom: Education of children with problems* (2nd ed., pp. 275–286). Belmont, CA: Wadsworth.

O'Leary, K. D., & Drabman, R. (1971). Token reinforcement programs in the classroom: A review. *Psychological Bulletin, 75*, 379–398.

Pappanikou, A. J., & Paul, J. L. (Eds.) (1977). *Mainstreaming emotionally disturbed children.* Syracuse: Syracuse University Press.

Phillips, E. L., & Haring, N. G. (1959). Results from special techniques for teaching emotionally disturbed children. *Exceptional Children, 26*, 64–67.

Phillips, L., Draguns, J. G., & Bartlett, D. P. (1975). Classification of behavior disorders. In N. Hobbs (Ed.), *Issues in the classification of children*, Vol. 1. (pp. 26–55). San Francisco: Jossey-Bass.

Postman, N., & Weingartner, C. (1969). *Teaching as a subversive activity*. New York: Dell.

Prentice, N. M., & Sperry, B. M. (1965). Therapeutically oriented tutoring of children with primary neurotic learning inhibitions. *American Journal of Orthopsychiatry, 35*, 521–530.

Prugh, D. G., Engel, M., & Morse, W. C. (1975). Emotional disturbance in children. In N. Hobbs (Ed.) *Issues in the classification of children*, Vol. 1. (pp. 261–299). San Francisco: Jossey-Bass.

Quay, H. C., Glavin, J. P., Annesley, F. R., & Werry, J. S. (1972). The modification of problem behavior and academic achievement in a resource room. *Journal of School Psychology, 10*, 187–198.

Quay, H. C., Sprague, R. L., Werry, J. S., & McQueen, M. M. (1967). Conditioning visual orientation of conduct problem children in the classroom. *Journal of Experimental Child Psychology, 5*, 512–517.

Quay, H. C., Werry, J. S., McQueen, M. M., & Sprague, R. L. (1966). Remediation of the conduct problem child in the special class setting. *Exceptional Children, 32*, 509–515.

Redl, F. (1959a). The concept of a therapeutic milieu. *American Journal of Orthopsychiatry, 29*, 721–734.

Redl, F. (1959b). The concept of the life space interview. *American Journal of Orthopsychiatry, 29*, 1–18.

Redl, F. (1966). *When we deal with children*. New York: Free Press.

Redl, F., & Wattenberg, W. (1959). *Mental hygiene in teaching*. New York: Harcourt Brace Jovanovich.

Redl, F., & Wineman, D. (1951). *Children who hate*. New York: Free Press.

Redl, F., & Wineman, D. (1952). *Controls from within*. New York: Free Press.

Reichler, R. J., & Schopler, E. (1976). Developmental therapy: A program model for providing individualized services in the community. In E. Schopler & R. Reichler (Eds.), *Psychopathology and child development* (pp. 347–372). New York: Plenum.

Reimer, E. (1967). *Unusual ideas in education*. Garden City, NY: Doubleday.

Reinert, H. R. (1980). *Children in conflict: Educational strategies for the emotionally disturbed and behaviorally disordered* (2nd ed.). St. Louis: Mosby.

Rezmierski, V. E. (1982). The psychoeducational model: Theory and historical perspective. In R. McDowell, G. Adamson, & F. Wood (Eds.), *Teaching emotionally disturbed children* (pp. 47–69). Boston: Little, Brown.

Rhodes, W. C. (1967). The disturbing child: A problem of ecological management. *Exceptional Children, 33*, 449–455.

Rhodes, W. C. (1970). A community participation analysis of emotional disturbance. *Exceptional Children, 36*, 309–314.

Rhodes, W. C., & Tracy, M. (Eds.). (1974). *A study of child variance: Interventions* (Vol. 2). Ann Arbor: University of Michigan Press.

Rich, H. L. (1978). A model for educating the emotionally disturbed and behaviorally disordered. *Focus on Exceptional Children, 10* (Whole #3).

Rogers, C. (1969). *Freedom to learn*. Columbus, OH: Merrill.

Rose, T. L., Koorland, M. A., & Epstein, M. H. (1982). A review of applied behavior analysis interventions with learning disabled children. *Education and Treatment of Children. 5*, 41–58.

Rothman, E. P. (1970). *The angel inside went sour*. New York: David McKay.

Satz, P., & Morris, R. (1981). Learning disability subtypes: A review. In F. J. Pirozzolo & M. C. Wittrock (Eds.), *Neuropsychological and cognitive processes in reading* (pp. 109–141). New York: Academic Press.

Schopler, E., & Reichler, R. J. (1979). *Individualized assessment and treatment for autistic and developmentally disabled children* (Vol. 1). Baltimore: University Park Press.

Schopler, E., Reichler, R. J., & Lansing, M. (1980). *Individualized assessment and treatment for autistic and developmentally disabled children* (Vol. 2). Baltimore: University Park Press.

Shea, T. M. (1978). *Teaching children and youth with behavior disorders*. St. Louis: Mosby.

Shearn, D., & Randolph, D. (1978). Effects of reality therapy methods applied in the classroom. *Psychology in the Schools, 15*, 79–83.

Shores, R. E., & Haubrich, P. A. (1969). Effect of cubicles in educating emotionally disturbed children. *Exceptional Children, 36*, 21–24.

Silberman, C. (1970). *Crisis in the classroom*. New York: Random House.

Sperling, M. (1951). Psychoanalytic aspects of discipline. *The Nervous Child, 9*, 174–185.

Strauss, A. A., & Lehtinen, L. E. (1947), *Psychopathology and education of the brain-injured child*. New York: Grune & Stratton.

Swap, S. (1974). Disturbing classroom behaviors: A developmental and ecological view. *Exceptional Children, 41*, 163–172.

Swap, S. (1978). The ecological model of emotional disturbance in children: A status report and proposed synthesis. *Behavioral Disorders, 3*, 186–196.

Swap, S., Prieto, A., & Harth, R. (1982). Ecological perspectives of the emotionally disturbed child. In R. McDowell, G. Adamson, & F. Woods (Eds.), *Teaching emotionally disturbed children* (pp. 70–98). Boston: Little, Brown.

Torgesen, J. (1982). The use of rationally defined subgroups in research on learning disabilities. In J. P. Das, R. F. Mulcahy, & A. E. Wall (Eds.), *Theory and research in learning disabilities* (pp. 111–131). New York: Plenum.

Trieschman, A. E., Whittaker, J. K., & Brendtro, L. K. (1969). *The other 23 hours*. Chicago: Aldine.

Vacc, N. A. (1968). A study of emotionally disturbed children in regular and special classes. *Exceptional Children, 35*, 197–206.

Vacc, N. A. (1972). Long term effects of special class intervention for emotionally disturbed children. *Exceptional Children, 39*, 15–22.

Welch, F., & Dolly, J. (1980). A systematic evaluation of Glasser's techniques. *Psychology in the Schools, 17*, 385–389.

Whelan, R. J. (1966). The relevance of behavior modification procedures for teachers of emotionally disturbed children. In P. Knoblock (Ed.), *Intervention approaches in educating emotionally disturbed children* (pp. 35–73). Syracuse, NY: Syracuse University Press.

White, O. R., & Haring, N. G. (1980). *Exceptional teaching* (2nd ed.). Columbus, OH: Merrill.

Woltmann, A. (1951). The use of puppetry as a projective method in therapy. In H. Anderson & G. Anderson (Eds.), *An introduction to projective techniques* (pp. 606–638). Englewood Cliffs, NJ: Prentice-Hall.

Wood, M. M. (Ed.). (1972). *The Rutland Center model for treating emotionally disturbed children.* Athens, GA: Technical Assistance Office to the Georgia Psychoeducational Center Network.

Wood, M. M. (1975a). A developmental curriculum for social and emotional growth. In D. Lillie (Ed.), *Early childhood education: An individualized approach to developmental instruction* (pp. 163–182). Chicago: SRA.

Wood, M. M. (Ed.). (1975b). *Developmental therapy.* Baltimore: University Park Press.

Wood, M. M. (Ed.). (1981). *Developmental therapy sourcebook* (Vols. 1 and 2). Baltimore: University Park Press.

Wood, M. M., & Swan, W. W. (1978). A developmental approach to educating the disturbed young child. *Behavioral Disorders, 3,* 197–209.

Wood, M. M., Swan, W. W., & Newman, V. S. (1982). Developmental therapy for the severely emotionally disturbed and autistic. In R. McDowell, G. Adamson, & F. Wood (Eds.), *Teaching emotionally disturbed children* (pp. 264–299). Boston: Little, Brown.

17 COMMUNITY INTERVENTION AND PREVENTION

LIZETTE PETERSON AND MICHAEL C. ROBERTS

INTRODUCTION

Community interventions share with traditional clinical interventions the goal of delimiting and remediating psychopathology in children. The methods and focus of community interventions differ, however, from those of traditional interventions in many ways (e.g., Bloom, 1973; Cowen, 1971, 1973; Zax & Specter, 1974). First, community interventions are more likely to be organized at a systems level, intervening with existing social groups instead of intervening at the individual level. Second, community interventionists view mental health problems more broadly than do traditional interventionists, encompassing programs that seek to improve social and physical well-being, as well as emotional well-being, in the belief that all of these factors are interrelated. Also, community interventions tend to focus on the enhancement of competency and adaptive responding rather than being oriented toward pathology alone. Finally, community interventions tend to be more proactive than traditional clinical interventions; they seek out the child rather than waiting for the child or the parents to seek out their services.

Perhaps one of the most important differences between traditional clinical and community interventions is the focus of community orientations upon prevention. Preventive interventions can seek to treat an existing disorder through tertiary prevention, to delimit a disorder before it has become debilitating through secondary prevention, or to block a disorder from appearing at all through primary prevention (Caplan, 1964). Recently, some investigators (e.g., Cowen, 1980) have suggested that the term *prevention* should be reserved for primary preventive interventions that occur before any problem is noted, to clearly delineate such interventions from more traditional clinical endeavors in which therapeutic interventions take place only after the problems are noted. We will adopt this terminology in the present discussion.

Preventing rather than remediating disorders clearly characterizes community interventions. In order to prevent disorders, competencies such as social abilities, cognitive skills, and emotional self-control must be enhanced rather than pathology (which does not yet exist) being attacked. In addition, interventions with groups of children rather than individuals are typically used. If prevention is to be proven effective, it may be necessary to treat many individuals who are at risk for developing the disorder in the future in order to demonstrate that intervention diminishes the rate of the disorder. Finally, preventive interventions of necessity rely more on a developmental orientation than do traditional interventions. If a disorder is to be prevented, knowledge of what constitutes normal development is necessary, as is an understanding of what developmental stages are at greatest risk for problems (Gelfand & Peterson, 1985; Roberts, Maddux, & Wright, 1984). Thus, preventive interventions and the current impetus toward combining traditional clinical and developmental psychology in a new scientific orientation—developmental psychopathology (e.g., Rolf & Read, 1984)—are uniquely suited to one another.

Prevention is, in fact, more appropriate in childhood than at any other time or to say this another way, childhood is the best time for prevention (Roberts & Peterson, 1984a). Primary prevention implies intervention before the onset of any problem. Because both internalizing and externalizing psychopathology (see Chapter 1) and physical problems that may be related to psychopathology (see Chapters 6 and 7) all begin in childhood, effective prevention must precede them. Also, a tactic that focuses on competency enhancement is likely to be most effective when applied during the time of greatest competency acquisition, which is during childhood for many skills such as language, social abilities, or self-efficacy beliefs.

Not all community interventions involve prevention, as the subsequent discussion will demonstrate, and not all prevention involves children. Child psychopathology, community interventions, and prevention are interwoven concepts, however, and we will attempt to provide a description of their combined character. This discussion will provide an illustration of some of the best known community interventions as opposed to a comprehensive review of all such interventions. The discussion will be organized by the different intervention modes that have been used to deliver treatments, including intervention through institutions like schools and hospitals, intracommunity interventions through social service agencies and community mental health centers, and interventions through the courts, the media, and the ecological setting.

Within each of these differing intervention modes, three different tactics of contact will be described. First, population-wide interventions seek to contact whole communities at one time; media-based interventions often fall into this category. Second, milestone interventions attempt to influence children at crucial developmental milestones; orientation programs before entering elementary school and birth control instruction prior to puberty exemplify this approach. Third, high-risk group interventions are focused upon those individuals judged to be at special risk; children of schizophrenic parents or premature infants fall within this approach.

Different interventions such as educational, affective, and environmental treatments will be evident in our discussion. For example, early substance-abuse prevention programs as well as peer tutoring programs and *Sesame Street* use an educational approach. Affective interventions that focus on enhancing self-esteem and social competence are exemplified by school-based affective education programs. Environmental interventions include altering elementary school class size and structure.

These modes, tactics, and treatments are not mutually exclusive but rather tend to overlap. Programs targeted toward preventing substance abuse, for example, have relied on school, community agency, and media modes using educational, affective, and environmental interventions.

Thus, this illustrative review will select from among these modes, tactics, and treatments to best characterize recent community interventions. This review can probably best be described as optimistic, as it will focus on the most successful preventive interventions and on the forms of physical and psychological dysfunction that best lend themselves to prevention. We should acknowledge at the outset, however, that there is a more negative side to prevention. Some disorders such as the psychoses or severe mental retardation will probably never be totally prevented, and early success with less severe disorders may not translate into prevention later in life. It can only do the area of prevention a disservice to overestimate what can reasonably be expected of our current technology (Rutter, 1982).

Furthermore, research in this area is only beginning to test the limitations of preventive endeavors. Although community interventions have been discussed for 20 years as the "third mental health revolution" (e.g., Hobbs, 1964), much of the early community intervention research involved more rhetoric than substance (Bower, 1973). A few programs will be discussed that have been in place, creating both sound research and community service, for many years (e.g., Cowen, Gesten, & Wilson, 1979). Most others, however, are relatively recent programs. More tend to be university "demonstration projects" than actual independently funded and community-controlled endeavors. We will not discuss the issue of implementation and program integrity in depth as it has been discussed in Chapter 15 (see also Stolz, 1984, for a detailed discussion), but we do acknowledge it as a serious concern for community endeavors. Undergraduate and graduate level training in community interventions (Jason, 1984), concern for cost effectiveness (Peterson & Mori, 1985), demonstrations of social validity (Kazdin, 1977), and attempts to involve community members in the planning and conducting of interventions (Glenwick & Jason, 1984) are all recently focused concerns. Attention to such issues may assist in the widespread implementation of prevention programs through the intervention modes described below to all children who might profit from such interventions.

MODES OF INTERVENTION

Institutional Intervention

SCHOOLS

Next to the influence of the family, the school may be the most widespread and powerful socializing agent (Rickel, Dyhdalo, & Smith, 1984). School is considered to be the source of most formal education and is acknowledged by many as the primary vehicle for social-skill acquisition as well. School can be an important source of problem prevention, identification, or remediation, or it can ignore, enhance, or even create psychopathology (see also Chapter 16). Unaddressed school maladaptation has been linked to later psychological and educational problems (Zax, Cowen, Rappaport, Beach, & Laird, 1968).

The concept that education could be used to solve social and emotional problems as well as intellectual difficulties has been reiterated historically by individuals from Rousseau and Montessori to Pestalozzi (Fowler, 1968). The 1920s and 1930s brought research evidence of the detrimental effects of deprived environments on children on barges (Gordon, 1923) and in poor mountain villages (Asher, 1935). These reports were followed by the suggestion that successful rehabilitation was possible (Rheingold & Bayley, 1964; Skodak & Skeels, 1945). The 1960s produced a variety of social-action projects, and one of the visions of the Great Society was Project Head Start, which marked the first widespread preschool preventive intervention for low-income children.

Traditional Preschool Intervention Initially, the Head Start programs involved very short-term interventions, often only an eight-week summer session. They typically involved the tactic of selecting high-risk children believed to be "culturally disadvantaged" and applying a variety of educational interventions. The programs' goals were to provide early social as well as educational experiences, with the belief that such supplemental intervention would allow children from low-income families to begin school with the same skills and background as their middle-class peers. The first evaluations of these programs were not well conceived, and they typically concluded that there were no long-term cognitive or affective gains to such programs (e.g., Cicirelli, 1969). These results may have been due to inadequacy of research design, including factors such as weak measurement, a lack of comparable control groups, and absence of follow-up data (Barnow & Cain, 1977; Campbell & Erlebacher, 1975). The effects of these programs also may have been limited by ineffective intervention techniques and by programs that were far too brief. The disappointing results led some investigators to conclude, however, that early intervention would always be ineffective because intelligence was set by genetic factors (Jensen, 1969).

The last two decades have seen continued controversy on the utility of preschool intervention. In fact, there have now been over 100 studies evaluating Head Start (Brown, 1978). Recently, the Consortium for Longitudinal Studies has reported long-term findings on 11 projects begun in 1963–1969 (Lazar & Darlington, 1982). These projects were similar to Head Start projects in terms of the children they served and in the types of methods used but were conceptualized as research projects from their inception. Two of the projects, Gordon and Jester's Parent Education Program in Florida and Levenstein's Mother–Child Home Program of Long Island, New York, employed the mother as the change agent and brought educational materials and toys into the homes of children less than four years of age. Three projects utilized an approach that involved home visits with both parent and child, but also employed a preschool experience for three- and four-year-olds. Those included Gray's Early Training Project in Tennessee, Miller's Experimental Variation of Head Start in Kentucky, and Weikart's Perry Preschool Project in Michigan. Finally, the majority of the programs involved nursery school programs that utilized either small groups or one-adult-to-one-child groupings. These programs included Beller's Philadelphia Project of Pennsylvania, Deutsch's Institute for Developmental Studies in New York, Karnes's Curriculum Comparison Study of Illinois, Palmer's Harlem Training Project in New York, Woolman's Micro-Social Learning System in New Jersey, and Zigler's New Haven Follow-Through Study of Connecticut.

It is not possible to detail all of the findings from these studies here. However, Lazar and Darlington (1982) summarize the findings extremely well:

> *The consortium results indicate that early education affected low-income children in ways that were both statistically and educationally significant. The consortium programs represented relatively small inputs into the children's lives. Most operated for only a few hours daily over the course of a year or two at most. Although parental influence was recognized to be important, there were no massive efforts to retrain parents or restructure home environments. When programs ended there were generally no extensive follow-through programs to support and maintain the children's gains. Nevertheless, the programs clearly had long-term effects. (p. 58)*

One of the most significant findings was that children assigned to these special preschool experiences were less likely to be referred to Special Education classes in high school than were comparison children. Some of the projects found affective gains as well, ranging from children's better attitudes toward school to parents' increased aspirations for their children. The degree to which these positive findings from such specialized research projects may represent the typical gains in preschool programs is unclear, however. It seems likely that such results represent the optimal rather than the average gains children experience in early education programs.

Expanded Preschool Interventions   Since the 1960s, there have been large gains in the sophistication of preschool prevention. Recent programs have focused their attention on skills that children may not possess at first assessment in preschool and that are necessary to elementary school success. Risley (1972), for example, has referred to such behaviors as "survival skills," and his training techniques help children acquire these skills such as telling time, obeying rules, enjoying teacher praise, and producing spontaneous, appropriate speech (Risley, Reynolds, & Hart, 1970).

Another of the better known recent preschool approaches has been conducted by Spivack and Shure (1974) and focuses on teaching children a graded set of lessons with the goal of producing the ability to solve social dilemmas. This program, entitled Interpersonal Problem Solving, begins by teaching children appropriate language ("if, then" thinking, for example, to understand consequences of behavior) and leads children to develop the ability to assertively but not aggressively deal with social issues. Spivack and Shure reported that improvements in children's ability to generate alternative solutions and to recognize consequences are reflected in teachers' ratings of improved behavioral adjustment (e.g., Spivack, Platt, & Shure, 1976). Other researchers have failed to replicate this finding with problem-solving training (e.g., Durlak, 1983b; Rickel, Eshelman, & Loigman, 1983; Sharp, 1981), however, so the final conclusions regarding the general impact of interpersonal problem-solving techniques remain unclear at this time.

In contrast to these techniques, which focus almost exclusively on at-risk children, some other recent programs attempt to treat both parents and their at-risk preschoolers. Jason, DeAmicis, and Carter (1978), for example, describe a successful program for high-risk preschoolers who were identified by routine pediatric exam to show social and behavioral (but not physiological or neurological) problems. These children and their parents experienced both home and school intervention sessions with goals ranging from increasing self-esteem and prosocial behavior to improving language skills.

The tactic of improving maintenance of intervention through parental involvement is shared by other programs as well. For example, the Early Intervention Program (EIP) for Preschoolers and Parents attempts to prevent problems by teaching parents more effective child-management techniques (Reisinger & Lavigne, 1980). Similarly, the Preschool Mental Health Project selects high-risk children from preschool classrooms on the basis of the presence of potentially problematic behavior such as extreme shyness or aggressiveness. Then, an in-school intervention is combined with a five-week intensive parent-training program (Rickel et al., 1984).

These programs have all demonstrated the possibility of long-term improvements in children's social and behavioral adjustment. They are organized more broadly than the initial Head Start interventions and are focused on more than remediating academic problems. Although these and similar programs are based on the belief that very early intervention is preferable, it is clear that even later intervention can be successful. In fact, Rickel et al.'s (1984) Preschool Mental Health Project is based in part on a long-term intervention oriented toward elementary school children, Cowen's Primary Mental Health Project, which will be discussed next.

Elementary School Treatment   Cowen's Primary Mental Health Project (PMHP) has been in continuous operation since 1957 and as such qualifies as one of the oldest and best known school-based intervention programs. It is also one of the most widely researched. Cowen and colleagues (1975) summarized 15 individual evaluations of the program conducted between 1957 and 1974 and Weissberg, Cowen, Lotyczewski, and Gesten (1983) summarized seven consecutive cohort evaluations from 1974 to 1981. In the first decade of the program, children from a single Rochester, New York, elementary school were screened using data from group personality and intellectual assessments, interviews with mothers, teachers' reports, and direct classroom observation. About 30 percent of the elementary school children so evaluated were identified as needing intervention. This figure is higher than might be expected because children were included in the program not only if they were already manifesting difficulties but also if they were judged to be at risk for developing problems. Follow-up of these children confirmed them to be less well accepted by peers, judged more maladjusted by teachers, experiencing poorer health, and achieving lower test scores and grades. Initially, the PMHP program's full-time school psychologist and social worker engaged each of the children in a meaningful relationship, provided educational assistance, and helped to establish goals. Later, paraprofessionals assisted in these roles. Results suggested that children receiving such intervention had fewer nurse referrals, higher grades and achievement test scores, better teacher-rated adjustment, and lower self-rated anxiety.

Currently, PMHP is located in more than 20 Rochester area schools, and similar programs can be found in over 300 schools nationwide (Cowen, Spinell, Wright, & Weissberg, 1983). The most recent outcome evaluation suggests that the program results in improvement in teacher ratings of assertiveness, sociability, and frustration tolerance (Weissberg et al., 1983).

The term "Primary" in the Primary Mental Health Project refers to the primary or elementary school basis of the program rather than to primary prevention. In fact the project involves both primary and secondary prevention. Some project interventions target children merely at risk but not yet experiencing problems, while other components serve children who are already experiencing problems with the goal of delimiting the problems. The combined difficulty of identifying elementary school age children who are at high risk but not yet experiencing problems and of needing to intervene early to stop further problems in children already beginning to manifest emotional or cognitive maladaptation is a common dilemma, which was also experienced by PMHP. Consequently, most of the intervention programs within elementary schools have involved both primary and secondary prevention.

Durlak's Social Skills Program (Durlak, 1983a) is a good example of such interventions. It has been applied in two states in the United States and in Germany, targeting both conduct disordered and anxious-withdrawn children. Pairs of group leaders see children in small groups of five to eight children for about one hour a week outside of the school setting, with the primary goal of shaping and reinforcing positive social behavior that is incompatible with their particular dysfunction. Thus, conduct disordered children are encouraged to listen to others and follow directions, while anxious-withdrawn children receive token rewards for speaking up, being a part of group discussions, and being appropriately assertive.

There are other well-known programs, too numerous to detail here, that have involved individual behavior treatment (e.g., Allen, Chinsky, Larcen, Lochman, & Selinger, 1976), group role-playing and cognitive restructuring (e.g., Butler, Miezitis, Friedman, & Cole, 1980), structured group sessions plus teacher consultation (e.g., Kirschenbaum, 1979, 1983), or group problem-solving training (e.g., Mannarino, Durlak, Christy, & Magnussen, 1982). They target children from first to sixth grade, typically using students or paraprofessionals as change agents. Most of these programs have documented decreased behavioral problems and improved social and individual behavior. Thus, these secondary prevention programs with high-risk children offer much promise for reducing maladaptation in elementary school age individuals.

Some very recent approaches are beginning to bridge the gap between secondary and primary prevention by identifying children thought to be at risk for future maladaptation through the use of readily available classroom outcome measures that would not normally be thought to signify pathology. For example, LaDouceur and Armstrong (1983) used poor first exam scores to identify children at risk for academic problems in the coming year. The at-risk group then received an intensive behavioral study skills intervention for 10 weeks that resulted in significant improvements in grade-point average. Similarly, Blechman and her colleagues (Blechman, Taylor, & Schrader, 1981; Blechman, Kotanchik, & Taylor, 1981) identified at-risk children who had highly inconsistent accuracy in completing classroom assignments. A home-based reinforcement system and a family problem-solving intervention were then applied, and both academic and behavioral gains were reported. These programs approximate primary prevention in school children and underline again the potential promise of such interventions.

A third method of intervention for elementary school children has attempted true primary prevention by treating whole classrooms of children and focusing upon competency enhancement rather than pathology. These programs typically have been labeled "affective education." There have been three major types of affective education programs. Some have focused upon interpersonal goals such as improving children's self-esteem and their attitudes toward school. Others have established cognitive goals such as increased perspective taking or problem-solving skills, and still others have sought behavioral changes such as reduced classroom management problems and peer conflicts, and improved communication skills (Baskin & Hess, 1980). Dinkmeyer's (1970) Development of Understanding of Self and Others (DUSO) is perhaps the best known program and serves as a good prototype of affective education. Children ages 5 to 10 years participate in daily 20-minute teacher-conducted sessions throughout the school year. Each session is a semistructured unit; it consists of a story that presents a problem situation. Then, children are asked to resolve the situation through discussion, role-playing, and puppet drama. There are eight general goals, which include the child's understanding of topics such as feelings, goals and purposive behaviors, and choices and categories. Unfortunately, DUSO and other affective education programs have not been well researched to date. Durlak and Jason (1984) summarized several of the best known affective education programs, including Gordon's (1976) Teacher Effectiveness Training, Bessell and Palomares's (1970) Human Development Program, Glasser's (1969) School Without Failure, and Ojemann's (1958) Causal Approach. They concluded that although the majority of studies on affective education have shown positive results, experimental designs that lack random assignment, control groups, and reliable and valid measurement devices have predominated. Most important, the long-term follow-up necessary to demonstrate the preventive properties of the programs has not yet been conducted.

These classroom-wide primary prevention methods will require more research to determine whether they reach their interpersonal, cognitive, and behavioral goals. Few of these goals, it must be recalled, deal directly with academic or school-related difficulty. Instead, the school is used as a "captive" setting in which children are present and as an opportunity to enhance many types of children's skills at coping not only with academic tasks but with life in general. There have been many other such programs that have been school-based but oriented not toward remediating academic deficits but instead toward the prevention or remediation of a variety of differing kinds of pathology, from poor health to substance abuse, and from negative reactions to school transition to depression or conduct problems resulting from parental divorce. The following sections will briefly outline some examples of these programs.

Health Enhancement There are a variety of health education interventions that have sought either to increase positive health behaviors such as exercise and tooth brushing or to reduce negative behaviors such as smoking and drinking (Albino, 1984). It is generally agreed that both the physical and the psychological costs of serious illness can be reduced by the early adoption of a more healthful lifestyle (Knowles, 1977; Matarazzo, 1980), and programs that intervene with children seem most likely to promote such lifelong habits (Peterson, Hartmann, & Gelfand, 1980).

Behavioral techniques tend to predominate in these health-oriented programs. In one school-based study, Botvin, Cantlon, Carter, and Williams (1979) demonstrated that nutrition education coupled with exercise and behavior modification of eating habits resulted in successful weight loss in obese children. Other programs with elementary school age children have increased appropriate nutrition rather than focusing on weight loss per se, using a variety of procedures such as contracting, feedback rewards, and family involvement (e.g., Coates, Jeffrey, & Slinkard, 1981). Similarly, Martens, Frazier, Hirt, Meskin, and Proshek (1973) rewarded reductions in dental plaque rather than simply teaching children how to brush their teeth. Even six months after the completion of the program, experimental subjects still had reduced plaque when compared to control children. These procedures have been successfully extended to over 1000 adolescent subjects (e.g., Albino, Juliano, & Slakter, 1977; Albino, Tedesco, & Lee, 1980), as well as to first and second graders (Swain, Allard, & Holborn, 1982). Thus, behavioral techniques show clear ability to increase health-enhancing behaviors.

Decreasing health debilitating behaviors is also an important goal, but the techniques used in such programs have been more complex (Thompson, 1978). As noted earlier, substance-abuse prevention programs have involved school, community, and media-based interventions, but we will focus on school-based interventions here. Such interventions have typically attempted to decrease smoking onset through the use of peer models who describe the immediate as well as long-term advantages of not smoking, and who demonstrate ways of dealing with peer pressure to smoke and with parental smoking (e.g., Evans, Rozelle, Mittelmark, Hansen, Bane, & Havis, 1978; Thompson, 1978).

The use of live peer group leaders and group problem solving to effect psychological "innoculation" against smoking has characterized the school-based Stanford University Heart Disease Prevention Program (e.g., Coates & Perry, 1981; McAlister, Perry, & Maccoby, 1979). Botvin's prevention programs have also utilized peer leaders but have tended to focus on competence enhancement and on increasing self-esteem and self-confidence to help cope with social anxiety, without the use of cigarettes (Botvin & Eng, 1980). Similar programs have attempted to modify adolescents' attitudes toward drinking (e.g., Stainback & Rogers, 1983) and to widen the circle of friends who do not use marijuana (e.g., Smith, 1983). Schinke and Gilchrist (1985) note that in recent years, a great deal of progress has been made in primary prevention of substance abuse, but these programs are best seen as "hopeful, incremental beginnings." A better understanding of smoking onset and maintenance, as well as improved ability to influence children prior to onset is necessary for extended success in this area.

Life Changes In addition to studies that focus on health enhancement, programs to help children deal with specific life crises have emerged. Some all-too-common crises faced by children include school transition, parental divorce, and hospitalization. These life events have been found to result in social, academic, and emotional difficulties (Felner, 1984). Recently, some of the first efforts to prevent distress due to school transition have begun. In one such study, the role of the homeroom teacher was extended to that of counselor, and the homeroom teachers also served as explicit links to the rest of the school. Parental involvement in their child's education was encouraged, again through the homeroom teacher. In addition, the program limited the number of new social encounters with other students by ensuring that the same students attended classes together rather than each different course involving a new group of unknown peers. The results from this project suggested that distress due to school transition can be prevented. Children who were changing schools and who were not included in the program decreased in their academic adjustment, self-concept, and ratings of school climate, whereas children in transition receiving the preventive treatment did not show such decreases. Further, treated children had higher G.P.A.s (Felner, Ginter, & Primavera, 1982).

Other attempts to deal with transition in the elementary school have sought to improve children's coping skills and their understanding of the experience of changing schools (e.g., Bogat, Jones, & Jason, 1980). Dealing successfully with school transition is an important challenge for prevention researchers; in this mobile society, larger numbers of children each year must cope with school changes. Additionally, there are milestones at kindergarten, seventh, and ninth grade typically associated with school changes that all children must pass. Thus, this is a new area of prevention worthy of continued intervention and investigation.

Similarly, nearly half of all new marriages end in divorce (Hetherington, 1979) and 60 percent of these divorces involve children (see Chapter 9). A large literature exists on the negative impact of divorce upon children (e.g., Kalter, 1977; Felner, Farber, & Primavera, 1983). Wallerstein and Kelly's 10-year longitudinal study concluded that the majority of children still experience some affective and behavior problems five years after the divorce (Wallerstein & Kelly, 1980). Initial programs to prevent such problems have shown some success. Felner, Norton, Cowen, and Farber (1981), for example, demonstrated that preventive intervention for children who had experienced parental divorce, separation, or death resulted in improved behavioral teacher ratings and decreased self-reported anxiety. Stolberg and his colleagues (Stolberg & Anker, 1984; Stolberg, Cullen, & Garrison, 1982) recently reported on the development of the Divorce Adjustment Project (DAP), which utilizes supportive group therapy for both parents and children. The children's group emphasizes building greater anger control, increased ability to relax, and enhanced communication skills. Curiously, the children receiving the group intervention whose parents were not involved in a parent group showed the largest improvements in self-concept, and these improvements were maintained at follow-up.

Pedro-Carroll and Cowen (1985) recently reported on a similar school-based intervention, the Children of Divorce Intervention Program (CODIP). Groups of fourth- to sixth-grade children experienced a 10-week supportive group program in which feelings were shared, a sense of isolation was reduced, and coping competencies such as problem solving, communication, and anger control were taught. Pedro-Carroll and Cowen report that treated children improved in a variety of ways, including decreased teacher-rated problem behaviors, improved parent-rated adjustment, and decreased self-reported anxiety. These preliminary projects demonstrate both the potential success for widespread, preventive intervention and the need for additional study in this area. Perhaps someday, such programs will be routinely available for children undergoing family changes such as divorce.

Finally, statistics suggest that increasing numbers of children experience emergency room medical intervention and a large proportion of children will experience elective hospitalization (Peterson & Mori, in press). For example, some 45 percent of children in England have been hospitalized once by age seven and the percentage of preschool children being admitted is rising (National Children's Bureau, 1976). Only a brief overview of hospitalization can be presented here, and fuller details can be found in Davenport and Werry (1970), Douglas (1975), Ferguson (1979), Peterson and Mori (in press), Vernon, Foley, and Schulman (1965), Wolfer and Visintainer (1979), and in Chapter 17.

There are three distinct possible periods when the consequences of hospitalization may occur: (1) during hospitalization, (2) immediately after return from the hospital, or (3) over the long-term. Problems are thought to stem from parental separation, exposure to an unfamiliar environment, and physical discomfort from both the medical problem itself and from diagnostic and treatment procedures. Longitudinal data from children hospitalized prior to the use of current medical and visitation procedures suggested that there might be long-term negative outgrowths of hospitalization, including learning disabilities and delinquency (Douglas, 1975). Presently, many children may return from modern, caring pediatric hospitalization without negative and perhaps with positive consequences. Inadequate preparation, separation from parents, repeated painful medical procedures, or preexisting behavioral problems may all put the child at risk for a variety of emotional disturbances, however, ranging from withdrawal and depression to acting out (Prugh & Jordan, 1975). It thus seems important to reduce the risk of hospital-related problems by ensuring continued parental and family support, reducing unnecessary hospitalization, shortening length of stay, improving hospital procedures with an eye toward minimizing injections, blood drawing, and other invasive procedures, and detecting vulnerable children and implementing special intervention programs for them (see Chapter 17). In addition, preventive programs that focus on the psychological preparation of children may reduce the risk of a negative hospital experience. There have been a few school-based programs that have attempted primary prevention by preparing whole classrooms of well children for the possibility of hospitalization using modeling films (Klinzing & Klinzing, 1977; Roberts, Wurtele, Boone, Ginther, & Elkins, 1981), lectures and inclass demonstrations of medical equipment (Peterson & Ridley-Johnson, 1984), and simulated hospital tours (Elkins & Roberts, 1984). These studies have typically demonstrated increased hospital-relevant information and decreased fearfulness regarding hospitalization.

The majority of programs that have successfully prepared children for hospitalization, however, have relied upon actual in-hospital preparation. The present discussion has attempted to underline the important role that schools as institutions have served as a prevention and treatment medium. It is not possible to outline in similar detail the many other institutions that serve children and that have housed community intervention programs, but one such institution deserves brief mention.

HOSPITAL-BASED INTERVENTIONS

While no other institution has such extensive and extended access to children as do schools, hospitals also house community interventions that serve children. For example, both university-based (e.g., Melamed & Siegel, 1975) and private (e.g., Peterson & Shigetomi, 1981) hospitals routinely offer preventive preparation for prospective child patients, and such preparation has been shown to eliminate fearful, withdrawn behavior as well as aggressive, uncooperative responding in child patients. Hospitals have also instituted programs that encourage parent and child contact following birth. For high-risk mothers, decreased child maltreatment has been linked to such practices (e.g., O'Connor et al., 1982). Similarly, hospitals are increasingly utilizing preventive services that involve increased stimulation for high-risk infants. Research suggests that such stimulation can ameliorate the effects of low birth weight or prematurity, reducing the risk of learning disability, attentional deficits, and other types of pathology linked to early birth (Field, Sostek, Goldberg, & Shuman, 1979). Routine screening by hospitals for metabolic disorders such as PKU and hypothyroidism, which can cause severe mental retardation, is yet another type of preventive service offered routinely by hospitals (Magrab, Sostek, & Powell, 1984).

This initial portion of the chapter has focused on schools and hospitals as institutions that serve as sites for community interventions. It is important to reiterate that both institutions have as a primary charge the education of or the medical treatment of children. Preventive or remediative interventions for psychopathology may sometimes more properly be construed as the responsibility of community social service agencies and these "intracommunity" intervention sites will be considered next.

Intracommunity Interventions

Social service agencies and Community Mental Health Centers (CMHCs) comprise two of the largest community-oriented preventive systems, and as such will be the primary focus of the following sections. Prior to beginning that discussion, however, it should be recognized that other systems also provide prevention-related services in the community, although these systems are not solely established for such services (Jason, Durlak, & Holton-Walker, 1984). For example, religious institutions frequently develop service programs that contain preventive components or emphases. Many local churches and religious organizations (e.g., the Salvation Army) run soup kitchens, shelters for the homeless, child runaway counseling services, and day-care centers for low-income children. Additionally, many civic groups within a community are an underrecognized and often underutilized resource for preventive programming. Because of their commitment to service to the community, such groups as Rotary Clubs, Lions Clubs, and Shriners, among others, provide meaningful projects such as lending car safety seats, protecting children's sight, preventing fires and burns, encouraging reading, and detecting early visual and dental problems.

These largely volunteer, community-based groups fill a critical need for services, often when other institutions and agencies are unable to provide them. Under present federal policies, an emphasis has been placed on community volunteerism for fulfilling service needs. More such services are going to be required as agencies charged with community preventive missions receive reduced financial support. This reduction in funding unfortunately occurs just as many community agencies and community centers are developing more demonstrably effective programming.

A description of programs within officially sanctioned social service agencies and CMHCs can provide a good illustration of the types of programs available in this variety of community settings. For example, because of the intertwining of both mental health and physical health, prevention-oriented programs through social service agencies and CMHCs as well as through volunteer organizations often aim at and have impact on both mental and physical health. The following discussion focuses on the ways community-based systems provide primary and secondary prevention services within social service agencies.

SOCIAL SERVICE AGENCIES

Over the years, various governmental levels (local, state, federal) have responded to the needs of the population by developing units responsible for providing preventive services. Often in response to federal initiatives and funding, states have organized public health departments, maternal and child health sections, and public welfare agencies. These agencies are charged with promoting the health and welfare of the population, each unit usually taking a particular emphasis. Each state and locale has organized and labeled such agencies differently, but there are characteristics common to all. For example, every state has an agency mechanism for responding to child abuse and attempting to prevent it. All states have systems for providing aid to dependent children to provide for basic needs of housing, clothing, and nutrition. States have public health departments for overseeing child health issues such as disease immunization and public food preparation. There are agencies for monitoring (and sometimes licensing) child-care facilities to ensure that a minimal standard of care is provided. Such governmental systems vary greatly in meeting needs, as they also vary greatly in governmental financial support and political philosophy. All of these have impact on the quality of life experienced by developing children.

Nutritional Service Programs Deficiencies in nutrition have adverse consequences for children's physical and mental health. Prenatal malnutrition, based on the mother's nutritional status, has impact on such child outcomes as growth retardation and low birth weight, preterm birth, and infant mortality. These all relate to risk factors for intellectual and health impairment (Wachs & Weizmann, 1983). Poor nutrition during the child's early years as well as during the school years relates to concurrent and subsequent difficulties in school performance and health maintenance. Arising from concerns over the increased risk for children owing to malnutrition, a federally funded program was enacted entitled Supplemental Food Program for Women, Infants, and Children. In common parlance, the program is known as WIC. First authorized in 1973, WIC is administered at the federal level by the Department of Agriculture with state and local social service agencies implementing the actual program. WIC provides food coupons or the foods themselves to populations at risk for developing health and development problems. WIC is mandated to ensure nutritious food supplements to low-income pregnant and lactating women, their infants, and young children up to age four years. These categories were designed to include those susceptible to or exhibiting detrimental conditions. Food items include iron-fortified formula, cereals, fruit juices, cheese, milk, and eggs. WIC has been occasionally involved in political controversy over continued financing, and unfortunately it has not been well evaluated to support a position pro or con. Early studies, mostly poorly designed, found positive effects for WIC interventions on birth weight, children's weight and height acceleration, and anemia (Edozien, Switzer, & Bryan, 1979). More recent studies, which are better designed but still lack some controls, which may be impossible to obtain, find benefits for specific components of WIC. For example, enrollment in the WIC Program appears related to prevention of iron depletion in young children, thereby preventing deleterious effects on cognitive performance resulting from iron deficiency and anemia (Miller, Swaney, & Deinard, 1985). Other studies also report positive effects on cognition and behavior (e.g., Hicks, Langham, & Takenaka, 1982). Controversy remains over the research methodologies as well as the findings of these and other studies (Rush, 1982). Nonetheless, WIC remains in place and clearly demonstrates the provision of social service service agency–based efforts for nutrition and development in young children.

Protective and Preventive Service Programs Specific state agencies have been designated to protect the well-being of children. Usually this has been construed to mean investigating child-abuse charges and, when abuse is determined, providing alternative care while working with a family through counseling and support to prevent future episodes. Recently, some social service agencies have expanded their orientation beyond secondary and tertiary responses to existing or threatened child abuse to include primary prevention. Similarly, an expanded interpretation of child protective services has recently included services for children who are at home without direct adult supervision, the "latchkey children." These children are so named because they come home after school and let themselves into their residences with a latchkey, often worn around their necks to prevent loss during the day. Latchkey children form a growing at-risk population because they are more susceptible to injurious situations and increased stress. Community agencies have slowly recognized that these children require social services. In some cases, community centers have developed broad training programs to prepare children for latchkey experiences; however, these have been unevaluated (e.g., Swan, Biggs, & Kelso, 1982). In other cases, civic groups have become involved. For example, the Boy Scouts of America distribute a "Prepared for Today" manual through its scout troops to schools and civic groups. This manual relies on an adult (parent) discussing with the child certain topics, such as being alone, how to answer a phone safely, and fixing food. Peterson (1984a) has also developed a "Safe at Home" program that utilizes behavioral techniques and intensive training interventions on how to (1) react to emergencies (fire, cut hand, tornado), (2) respond to strangers who come to the door or call on the telephone, and (3) select nutritious, safe snacks and optimal after-school activities, all aimed at successful training in home safety behavior. In a comparative evaluation, Peterson (1984b) served latchkey children from a community agency, assigning some children to a program that employed the Boy Scout "Prepared for Today" manual, the remainder to a program using her "Safe at Home" manual. She found that the "Safe at Home" format resulted in greater increases in home safety behavior than did the "Prepared for Today" manual, which in turn was preferable to no training. This evaluation demonstrated a cost-effective way of working with latchkey children that is adaptable to social service agency programming.

Another way agencies respond to the latchkey situation is through a telephone call-in service. Guerney and Moore (1982) described the PhoneFriend in State College, Pennsylvania, available after school to children who are home alone. The service provided a resource of social contact that was supportive and instructive when the child might need it. Trained volunteers answered the phone-in service and were prepared to give both affective and instrumental responses to the child callers on issues of first aid, power failure, fears and boredom, strange noises, prowlers, and help in finding somebody or some program. The preliminary analysis of this community program supported the telephone method for serving latchkey children.

Injury-prevention Programs Other state agencies, usually within departments of public health, target the prevention of unintentional injuries in childhood. Injuries are the leading cause of death in childhood, and nonfatal injuries have adverse impact on children and families at a higher rate than any psychological disorder. Health education programs and special projects provide information to teachers, parents, and children about hazards and preventive actions. For example, these agencies distribute poison-prevention films, brochures, coloring books, and other media to help children identify and avoid hazardous substances and to encourage parents to safely prepare the child's environment. Other agency programs attempt to prevent injury and death by encouraging child safety seat usage (Decker, Dewey, Hutcheson, & Schaffner, 1984; Roberts & Turner, 1984), and by removing fire hazards (McLoughlin, Vince, & Crawford, 1982). The State-wide Child Injury Prevention Project (SCIPP) in Massachusetts represents one of the more ambitious injury-prevention programs. SCIPP is a federally funded demonstration program housed in the Massachusetts Department of Public Health (Department of Health and Human Services, 1983; Gallagher et al., 1982). The program mandates state and local agencies, community members, and hospitals to gather information on childhood injuries and to develop ways to prevent accidental death and injury. Within this program, workers established a surveillance system to collect data on the epidemiology of childhood fatal and nonfatal injuries (Gallagher, Finison, Guyer, & Goodenough, 1984). These data helped guide the development of prevention projects comprising SCIPP. These projects cover poison control, burn prevention, child passenger safety, pediatric accident prevention, and home health hazard prevention. These state agency projects involve such interventions as developing a school curriculum and workshop program on burns and fire hazards for teachers then to transmit to their pupils. Materials include audiovisual media, posters, brochures, and games. The home hazard project includes two levels of intervention. One intervention educates parents about ways to change home hazards, for example, through proper storage of hazardous substances, safety plugs for electrical outlets, and toddler gates on stairs. The second level of intervention seeks to enforce existing housing code regulations by having home inspectors examine lighting, electrical wiring, hot water heaters, and other items in the housing standards. The child passenger safety component of SCIPP worked for passage of the state's mandatory safety seat law for children. Additionally, this component drafted educational programs on the benefits of safety seats for parents of newborns while in the hospital. Programs to lend car seats to parents also are in place. These various components of SCIPP illustrate how state and local agencies, in this case, public health departments and community liaisons, target the prevention of childhood injuries.

These three agency-based interventions in communities for nutrition, latchkey children, and safety represent ways children and their families can be helped to achieve safer and healthier environments—ways conducive to positive development of children. Other such programs conducted by social service agencies include child sexual-abuse prevention projects, programs for both preventing and responding to adolescent pregnancies, and drug- and alcohol-abuse prevention programs. These typically involve educational curricula, teacher, parent, and child education, and counseling by social service workers. Since they have a mission to assist developing children, these agencies are often approached first for preventive programming. Such programming must surmount many difficulties, including resistant targeted problems, an absence of a clearly identified service provider, and financial constraints. As will be seen next, community mental health centers face similar barriers to successful treatment and prevention.

COMPREHENSIVE COMMUNITY MENTAL HEALTH CENTERS

Concern about the prevention of psychological disorders had a significant role in the movement to pass the Community Mental Health Center Act of 1963. The resulting community mental health centers (CMHCs), constructed and funded with federal money, were charged with the prevention of emotional problems through consultation and education services as one of their primary obligations. These services were to include public information about mental health, publicity about available services, and a variety of prevention efforts to promote mental health such as self-help groups, stress management training, parent training, and mass media campaigns. CMHCs were to be a source of prevention efforts within each local community rather than just another provider of clinical services to those already experiencing psychological difficulties. With a few exceptions, however, CMHCs appear to have neglected prevention programming, with less than 5 percent of funds ultimately expended for prevention. The current decrease in federal support has exacerbated the lack of prevention work in CMHCs because CMHCs must survive by bringing in money from other sources (such as insurance reimbursement), which authorize payment only for therapeutic treatment of existing disorders and not for prevention of potential problems (Roberts & Peterson, 1984b). Despite the overall trend for CMHCs to neglect prevention services to the community, several exemplary programs demonstrate the worth of such services. In this section, we will examine a few of these CMHC-based programs.

Self-help Groups CMHCs frequently foster the organization of groups whose members aid one another in a variety of ways, ranging from reducing the stress of adverse circumstances to improving skills and personal competence. Self-help groups most often are comprised of individuals in the community who are at risk for, or are showing early signs of, psychological difficulties. For example, the Ravenswood Community Mental Health Center in Chicago supports several self-help groups that are directed at a variety of potentially problematic child-related situations such as being a single parent, a new mother, or a youth with anorexia nervosa/bulimia (Chutis, 1983). These groups begin with CMHC professional staff assistance, but gradually the group members themselves assume authority roles, decision making, and self-reliance, with an aim to developing problem-solving and social skills in their members. At many CMHCs across the country, other self-help groups accommodate children of divorcing parents to help them deal effectively with the developmental tasks of divorce. For example, in one program (Kalter, Pickar, & Lesowitz, 1984), small groups of children met one hour a week over a two-month period with two adult facilitators. The children used these group sessions to disclose their fears and hopes about the divorce experience and to gain peer support. Additionally, with the aid of the adult facilitators, the children role-played difficult situations associated with divorce such as parents' dating, custody, and visitation arrangements.

Other CMHCs are establishing groups for children and youth in the community who have handicaps or chronic illnesses as well as additional groups for their parents and families. For example, the Staten Island Children's Community Mental Health Center conducts a group for parents who have recently moved into the catchment area and whose children might be undergoing some stress associated with the relocation (Heller, 1975). The parents meet once a week over a 10-week period to discuss their children's difficulties and ways to help improve their adjustment.

Crisis Intervention Due to their proximity and established relationship to a community, CMHCs are in an optimal position to provide services to people who are undergoing crises and heightened stress. Such people may not be manifesting psychological symptoms at the time of the crisis, but they are at risk for developing problems at some later point. Preventive interventions can forestall later reactions to emergencies or potential emergencies, natural and man-made disasters such as floods, tornadoes, earthquakes, nuclear power plant accidents, factory shutdowns, and toxic waste exposure. For example, one mental health center responded impressively to crises associated with the phased court-ordered desegregation of the Boston Public Schools in 1975 (Cromer & Burns, 1982). Opposition to bussing led to rumors of violence, seeking to prevent the desegregation in a Charlestown neighborhood. In advance of the bussing date, the center staff began efforts to defuse the tension and to encourage a peaceful resolution for groups and individuals. These efforts included holding group discussions, encouraging recognition of various points of view and of concerns for the safety of all schoolchildren, developing a rumor-control hotline, and providing alternative ways for expressing grievances. The Center also provided therapeutic services for families coping inadequately with the increased stress and for children reporting psychosomatic complaints of headaches and stomachaches. The utility of community crisis intervention was also demonstrated when an Israeli border town was attacked by terrorists who, after penetrating a well-defended border, killed several people including a child (Klingman & Ben Eli, 1981). The day after the attack, primary and secondary psychological services were implemented. Extreme stress reactions were observed in the children and their parents—for example, reactions to noises and increases in aggression, anger, anxiety, and specific fears. In the primary prevention stage, professionals consulted with schoolteachers to help them understand their pupils' reactions and to promote coping through discussion, providing factual information, and cathartic play in the classroom immediately after the traumatic event. In the secondary prevention stage, special teachers screened children to identify those showing signs of poor psychological adjustment. These children were then provided short-term goal-oriented treatment through group counseling.

Similar psychological interventions in crises are required when children have been subjected to unusual stress, as in the Chowchilla, California, case when a school bus load of children was held hostage for ransom. These children and their families were at risk for trauma-related emotional impairment (Terr, 1979, 1981). In the case of natural disasters, CMHCs provide crisis intervention to help enhance positive adjustment and to prevent maladaptive reactions from becoming engrained. For example, children in California have received special programs following particularly strong earthquakes, and other victims of floods, hurricanes, and tornadoes have been targeted (Howard & Goldman, 1972; Kliman, 1975; Zarle, Hartsough, & Ottinger, 1974). Crisis intervention frequently relies on existing social support networks involving both formal and informal helpgivers. Since CMHCs are established units within communities, their facilities and staff provide a ready basis should crises develop requiring psychological prevention and treatment.

Social Network Interventions Even outside crisis situations, CMHCs develop community programs to enhance the social networks available to people. Very simply, social networks are the variety of people to whom those under stress can turn for support (e.g., relatives, neighbors, and friends). Social networks, social support, and relationship systems provide children and parents with corrective information, role models, ways of ventilating frustration or anxiety, and emotional, and sometimes financial, assistance. Social networks influence child-rearing in particular (Masterpasqua & Swift, 1984), and negative child-rearing tactics such as child abuse may be prevented through enhancement of isolated parents' social support. Masterpasqua (1982; Masterpasqua, Shuman, O'Shea, & Gonzalez, 1980) describes a CMHC-based program developed to strengthen the relationships of pregnant adolescents with various caregivers. Childbirth classes provided instruction, anticipatory guidance about potential problems, and an ongoing support base with peers and professional health care providers. Following birth, parent–infant support groups foster social networks between parents in similar situations. Lois Wandersman (1983) has suggested that "Ultimately, supportive behaviors and family interaction will help new parents grow in confidence, improve their parenting behaviors, and facilitate their children's development" (p. 102). Social network interventions may be particularly important for parents who are poor, young, or having their first child, and for parents of premature, ill, or handicapped infants. Other social support programs through CMHCs have begun for children who have been abused (through Parents' Anonymous) and whose parents are alcoholics (ALANON, ALATEEN).

This section has summarized only a few of the types of programs provided through CMHCs; many more exist. Additionally, many more community interventions could be effectively implemented utilizing CMHC structures. As noted before, however, current trends in financing, political ideology, and professional training impede full development of community intervention (Roberts & Peterson, 1984b). Although not all aspects of CMHC-based intervention have been evaluated, Masterpasqua and Swift (1984) have cogently argued that an adequate research base exists to continue and expand community programming.

We turn now toward interventions applied to entire populations but focused on effecting change within the community. Like the programs that have developed within the CMHC system, these society-wide interventions are influenced both by political climate and by current clinical intervention theories.

Society-wide Interventions

This section will describe community interventions organized at a society-wide level that contact children through legislated or court-directed action, through the media, or through ecological changes in the environment. We will begin by discussing an example of legally mandated action in the prevention and treatment of juvenile delinquency.

COURT OR POLICE-REFERRED INTERVENTION

In addition to the reforms within preschool and elementary schools discussed earlier that began with the Great Society movement in the 1960s, general dissatisfaction with the practices of incarcerating juvenile offenders at this time led to the instituting of "diversion" practices. The basic concept of these programs was to divert children and early adolescents who had not yet been involved in serious offenses from further legal involvement. Large-scale government funding in the 1970s was instrumental in establishing exemplary diversion projects (Kobrin & Klein, 1983).

Juvenile Diversion The term *juvenile diversion project* is no more specific than the term *intervention*, as a large variety of treatment techniques have come under the rubric of diversion. In a description of one of the earliest programs (now over 50 years old) that might be termed "juvenile diversion," Schlossman, Zellman, and Shavelson (1984) outlined the development of the Chicago Area Project. There have been a number of individual programs under this general heading, but all typify diversion projects by relying on the establishment of an important interpersonal relationship and the use of broadly specified ancillary techniques such as providing recreational opportunities and the establishing of "curbside counseling" in the community.

The best documented programs have been evaluated carefully and give meticulous descriptions of their subject selection, control matching, and measurement procedures. Their descriptions of treatment procedures, however, like that of the Chicago Area Project, are often more abbreviated and generic, yet include multiple approaches. For example, Collingwood, Douds, and Williams's (1976) Youth Services Program (YSP) utilized interpersonal counseling based on Carkuff's (1971) Human Resource Development model, in addition to teaching problem solving, interpersonal skills, and academic abilities, and to improving physical fitness with resulting increases in self-esteem. Parents' skills at setting limits at home and responding appropriately to school attendance and grades were also targeted. Similarly, the Juvenile Services Program evaluated by Quay and Love (1977) utilized a variety of interventions, including vocational, personal, and social counseling in addition to academic tutoring and training job placement skills.

Some juvenile diversion programs, such as the Diagnostic Program (Cox, Carmichael, & Dightman, 1977), have focused on intensive prescriptive evaluations, using medical, educational, psychological, peer, parent, and other community sources of information to formulate an individualized program for juveniles. This individualized "prescription" is then filled by assigning the individual to various packages of community resources such as counseling facilities, foster homes, or day schools. Still other programs (e.g., Ostrom, Steel, Rosenblood, & Mirels, 1971) have been founded on social psychological principles and have employed leaders recruited from similar neighborhoods, also with police records. These leaders demonstrate through role-play in a group-therapy format more acceptable ways of "beating the system" than breaking the law. Although such programs have relied upon monetary reinforcement for group attendance, change is anticipated to result from group processes and social learning rather than through monetary reward.

Relationship Building and Reinforcement This pattern of utilizing reinforcement as a means to an end, but relying on relationship building as the active change agent, is common to many diversion projects. For example, Lee and Haynes (1980) reviewed four studies that evaluated the project CREST (Clinical Research Support Teams). A graduate student leader with paraprofessional volunteers administered a gamut of techniques including one-on-one counseling, using either client-centered therapy or gestalt techniques. While this program utilized positive reinforcement at times, it eschewed "behavior modification" as being inappropriate for this relationship-oriented program.

Other programs have emphasized both relationship building and positive rewards. The Buddy System (O'Donnell, Lydgate, & Fo, 1979) relied upon a one-to-one intensive relationship and $10 worth of reinforcers each month, used judiciously to reward appropriate responding such as school attendance. Other researchers have demonstrated the utility of both behavioral contracting and relationship building child-advocacy techniques (Seidman, Rappaport, & Davidson, 1980).

Behavioral techniques have most frequently been used in programs that have a specifically focused goal. Walter and Mills (1979), for example, describe a Behavioral-Employment Intervention in which juveniles were rewarded for self-monitoring appropriate and inappropriate on-the-job behaviors and employers were shaped through attention and positive reinforcement to give positive feedback to their predelinquent employees. Such methods can show long-range success. Shore and Massimo (1979) were able to follow up on a small number of subjects and reported that over a decade after their behavioral vocational intervention had ceased, treated individuals showed more continued education, better job histories, and more stable family lives. Behavioral techniques are also valuable in academic settings, with similar documentation of long-term effects. The Kentsfield Rehabilitation Program (Davidson & Robinson, 1975) used a highly structured contingency system in which appropriate behaviors at morning public works projects and in afternoon classroom sessions were rewarded with points and progress through the system, from being a lowly "June-bug" to an "Ace." The points were exchanged for money, candy and other merchandise, and recreational opportunities. Long-term follow-up of the Kentsfield program suggests that its influence persists a decade later (Blakely, Davidson, Saylor, & Robinson, 1980).

Family Interventions Behavioral techniques have often been combined with systems-oriented interventions for the entire family. Alexander and Parsons (1973) provided one of the first demonstrations of short-term behavioral family intervention. Drawing on their earlier work, which assessed differences between delinquent and normal families, they established goals of enhancing communication, social reinforcements, and negotiation. After Wade and Morton trained with Alexander, Wade, Morton, Lind, and Ferris (1977) utilized very similar techniques in their Intensive Intervention Project in Honolulu. They focused on the family by enhancing expression of feelings, coping methods, interpersonal problem solving, and behavioral contracting, and demonstrated positive effects not only for the targeted delinquents but for their siblings as well.

Henggeler et al. (1986) have described a "multisystemic" family approach within the Memphis–Metro Youth Diversion Project in which an ecological orientation was taken toward the problems of delinquents and their families. Therapists chose from numerous family, social-learning, or cognitive-behavioral interventions applied during weekly home or clinic visits. Extrafamilial systems such as peers or school personnel were also targeted, and individual counseling was utilized as well. The authors compared this approach to routine referral to other existing agencies and found that the multisystems approach resulted in larger decreases in conduct problems, anxious-withdrawn behavior, and association with delinquent peers, as well as in increases in mother–adolescent warmth.

Conclusions Regarding Juvenile Diversion   Overall, the diversion projects have provided community intervention to individuals referred through the courts or police departments. Almost without exception, these demonstration projects have reported gains on the most important variable: the number of subsequent arrests is much lower among treated than control adolescents. Further, some treatments show additional positive benefit such as better performance in schools, more positive responses to the family, and so on. Thus, it seems clear that some juvenile diversion projects have important positive secondary prevention effects on children and adolescents, inhibiting future illegal activities and enhancing competencies. Some may even have primary preventive effects.

How well do such demonstration projects describe general juvenile diversion? That question has been the subject of ongoing controversy. Some individuals have suggested that such positive effects are not typical and that negative labeling of being involved in a court-referred project combined with the absence of the deterrent of sentencing is problematic (e.g., Rausch, 1983). Other investigators have reported that some individuals referred to diversion projects fail to receive any services at all (Dunford, 1977; Elliott, 1978). Still others argue that the potential "net widening" effects of juvenile diversion projects in which the "net" of the juvenile justice system expands to contact individuals who would not otherwise be contacted is unfortunate (e.g., Blomberg, 1983). Thus, it is not clear whether the success of the demonstration projects described here is likely to typify most juvenile diversion projects or whether there are not costs as well as benefits to such programs.

What is clear is that positive effects are possible and that the support for such programs is likely to continue in the future, making this an important area for additional investigation. There have been similar programs for less serious adolescent offenders, and these projects have been grouped under the heading of DSO Experiments (Deinstitutionalizing of Status Offenders; Kobrin & Klein, 1983). These studies show similar early promise for this type of intervention.

The society-wide nature of juvenile diversion projects is a function of the legal system applying equally to all individuals. In practice, however, only those individuals highly at risk or already demonstrating problems are actually contacted. In contrast, other society-wide interventions are applied to individuals at all levels of risk, although as will be seen in the next section on media-based interventions, they still tend to be targeted toward individuals at certain vulnerable stages of life.

MEDIA

Numerous mechanisms exist for delivering information to a large number of people, usually lumped together in the label "media." These include radio, television, newspaper, and magazines (and now audio- and videocassettes). Mental health and education professionals have been slow to fully utilize the unique capability of the media to have impact on individuals within society.

However, recent efforts and evaluations demonstrate the potential for positive benefit. Community mental health promotion can occur in a variety of ways including "daily, weekly, and suburban newspapers (editorials, features, columns, news); television (commercial and educational segments for news, features, public service announcements; community affairs programming; special coverage; talk shows); radio (news prepared tape interviews, and public service announcements); and others (minority press, business publications, billboards, placards, newsletters of community organizations)" (Brawley & Martinez-Brawley, 1984, p. 319). Not all media-based programs show positive results, but enough has been found to encourage expansion and continued evaluation. The media can deliver messages to a wide audience designed to (1) help viewers, readers, and listeners decide whether mental health services are required, while informing them of where community services may be obtained; and (2) provide information influencing positive beliefs and behavior without requiring direct contact with professionals. In this section, both aspects of media interventions will be discussed with target problems of preventing child abuse and enhancing educational performances.

Child Abuse As a prime example of media programming, the National Committee for Prevention of Child Abuse conducted a national public awareness campaign beginning in 1976. This campaign relied upon volunteers and donated public service advertising (into the millions of dollars). A variety of media sources were used, including television, radio, newspapers, magazines, and billboards (Cohn, 1982). A sequence of yearly themes was developed: "Child Abuse Hurts Everybody," "It Shouldn't Hurt To Be a Child," "Help Destroy a Family Tradition," "Neglect Can Kill, Too. It Just Takes a Little Longer," "Sexual Abuse of Children. Not Talking About It Won't Make It Go Away." The impact of these messages is difficult to assess definitely. Public attitude surveys indicate that recognition of child abuse as a serious social problem has increased over the years (Cohn, 1982). Requests for information or help also increased. One specific evaluation, conducted by Ratcliffe and Wittman (1983), reported on a paid media parenting campaign in Canada. Four television messages, 30 seconds in length, were broadcast, each portraying child-rearing situations such as toilet training, nighttime waking, sibling rivalry, and parent affection toward their children. Each message contained information on where to obtain material and helpful information on being a parent. Public opinion surveys indicated positive shifts in attitudes following the campaign. The application of media programming to the child-abuse problem demonstrates one use of media to help people learn about the existence of a problem, how to recognize the problem in their own community, and where preventive services can be obtained.

Educational Programming *Sesame Street* programs are the foremost example of the television medium serving an educational function. When first broadcast, the programs were targeted at disadvantaged children, but it rapidly became apparent that middle-class children comprised a large segment of the viewers. Instructional goals of *Sesame Street* included enhancement of the child viewers' (1) recognition of symbols (letters and numbers), (2) cognitive processes (visual and auditory discrimination), (3) conception of the physical environment (natural and man-made surroundings), and (4) knowledge of their social environment (names, relationships in family, and roles) (Lesser, 1974). The format and content of the program is well known, including prominent human and puppet characters, film clips, music, cartoons, and drill sequences. Each character portrays a specified role, for example, Big Bird depicts the concept that mistake-making is not a disaster. Nowicki and Bolick (1983) summarized the research literature on children's television viewing. Evaluation of *Sesame Street* and other children's programs (*Electric Company, Mr. Rogers' Neighborhood*) generally support the positive impact of these society-wide interventions on prosocial attitudes, behaviors, and cognitive variables, although the results of a few studies are equivocal. Apparently, no studies have found any negative effects (Nowicki & Bolick, 1983). As society-wide interventions, televised educational programs such as *Sesame Street* not only can influence the cognitive or intellectual performance of children but can improve social and coping skills as well. These potential attainments constitute preventive interventions available to all.

Not all media-based preventive interventions have demonstrated positive effects. Robertson (1983) labeled a failure the widespread media campaigns to increase the use of seat belts to prevent injury and death of passengers. Similarly, some researchers found that antismoking messages were effective only in increasing the amount of knowledge about the smoking and health relationship, but they were not effective in deterring youth from starting to smoke (Albino, 1984). Adequate evaluation of specific media campaigns remains a major problem in determining whether these society-wide interventions are effective. Since the inception of television, many writers have described the immense potential of television for being a positive influence. In some instances, the medium has been shown to have such beneficial effects. In many cases, television still remains a potential tool for prevention efforts.

ECOLOGICAL INTERVENTIONS

A final society-wide intervention is exemplified by improving the circumstances or surroundings of children and families so that the environment is more conducive to development (Jason et al., 1984). While many mental health interventions focus on the individual, ecological interventions focus on making the environment safer and healthier for the person within it. Abraham Wandersman and his colleagues (1983) described the overall environmental impact on mental and physical health as comprised of the physical environment (e.g., air pollution, noise, and toxic materials) and the human-built environment (e.g., houses, school buildings, lighting, and temperature). Although there is recent growth of work in ecological interventions, we will outline only a few as examples here.

Noise Research data indicate that noise has a detrimental effect on children's motivational, cognitive, and physiological functions. Glass and Singer (1972) studied children attending schools along the air flight pattern around Los Angeles airport. They found that, as compared to children in schools outside the patterns, these children were exposed to high levels of noise and had higher blood pressure, gave up on tasks faster, and were more distractible with increasing numbers of years exposed to the noise. Cohen, Glass, and Singer (1973) found that children living on apartment floors closer to highway noise had poorer auditory discrimination and poorer reading scores than those living even a few floors above. Other researchers obtained similar results for children living near railroads (Bronzaft & McCarthy, 1975). Noise levels particularly adversely affect the behavior and performance of children with attention deficit behavior (Whalen, Henker, Collins, Finck, & Dotemoto, 1979). Given these detrimental influences of high noise levels, primary prevention efforts can include modifications of the environment to make children's surroundings less conducive to noise pollution. For example, schools should be built away from locations with excessive noise. Structural design can improve noise conditions within schools and residences and other techniques such as insulation and soundproofing can help to reduce noise levels.

School Ecology The built environment consists of structures humans have erected for work, education, shelter, and recreation. These include the designs for houses, factories, playgrounds, and schools. Only recently has it been recognized that the physical design of a school and the use of its space have impact on the children within it. For example, studies show that smaller schools or small class units lead to more pupil involvement in activities, more attention to academic problems of the children, and more competency-building experiences (Glass & Smith, 1978). Jason et al. (1984) asserted that mental health professionals might implement these findings to develop smaller school divisions within large schools or to redesign school systems to reduce the size of each school. They further suggest that such ecological interventions could be preventive by enhancing schoolchildren's adjustment and competency.

Passive Prevention Prevention interventions can be conceptualized as ranging on a continuum from those that require active efforts by individuals who are to be protected to those that require minimal or no action by the individual, but that rely on environmental changes. Active prevention in mental health is exemplified by teaching children coping skills and training parents in child management. For physical health, active prevention includes maintaining a nutritious diet, exercising regularly, and buckling into a seat belt. Research has repeatedly demonstrated the difficulty of motivating positive behavior changes by individuals. In contrast, passive prevention is increasingly considered more effective because such environmental interventions can be implemented and protection gained without the individual having to take any action. For example, fluoride in drinking water attains dental cavity prevention even without tooth brushing or flossing (although such actions can add to the benefit). Other examples of effective passive prevention for safety include child-proof poison containers, flame-retardent children's sleepwear, and controls on hot water heater temperatures to prevent scalding burns. Additional prevention gains are noted through regulatory actions such as the 55-mile-per-hour speed limit, child passenger safety seat laws, drunk driving laws, and motorcycle helmet regulations. All of these efforts have demonstrated efficacy by reducing the rates of injury and deaths of children. The proposed implementation of airbags and automatic seat belts in cars is one important, but repeatedly delayed, passive prevention with potentially positive impact on a society-wide basis (Roberts & Turner, 1984; Robertson, 1983). Other passive prevention benefits could be realized through environmental improvements such as improved design and construction in playgrounds, highways, and car interiors, sanitation and disease-vector control, and air-quality standards (Roberts, Elkins, & Royal, 1984).

Although these passive prevention efforts describe physical health and safety actions, many society-wide interventions for mental health can also be conceptualized in this way. Indeed, the changes in noise levels or school physical design have impact on psychological and educational functioning. Similarly, mental health professionals' attention to other ecological/environmental conditions can improve the emotional welfare of children. For example, attention to temperature levels in schools, availability of educational materials, seating patterns, and the physical safety of inhabitants can improve psychological functioning. These require little individual active effort by the children and can be properly viewed as ecologically based passive prevention with society-wide effects.

SUMMARY

This chapter can only begin to introduce the reader to the wide variety of community interventions for children that exist. Within some areas such as preschool and school-based programs, there is a lengthy history of successful interventions and a host of evaluative studies have been conducted. In other areas such as the programs sponsored through social service agencies and Community Mental Health Centers, the interventions have a lengthy history but the role of mental health professionals in both evaluating current programs and planning future techniques remains underutilized. For still other programs such as the legally mandated juvenile diversion projects, the benefits and costs of intervention are still being debated, although research continues to suggest the effectiveness of systems and behavioral strategies. Media and ecologically based interventions have only begun to be

Future research may reveal their contributions to the treatment and prevention of physical and mental disability in children. Finally, in most instances the issue of differential effectiveness in preventing or reducing the seriousness of different forms of childhood psychopathology has yet to be explored. In this respect, these preventive intervention efforts are less sophisticated than those treatments targeted at individual children (Chapter 14) and many of those carried out in residential settings (Chapter 15).

All of these programs characterize community intervention with their focus on systems rather than individuals, on competency enhancement as well as treatment of pathology, and on proactive and preventive strategies. All show promise and yet all can benefit from improvements in methods of both intervention and evaluation. Most of all, these areas all show only limited implementation of existing treatment and prevention strategies. This absence of widespread use underlines the pressing need within the next decade to study methods of enhancing the adoption of community interventions that have been shown to be successful.

Rutter (1982) argues against the overenthusiastic expectation that primary prevention can be expected to easily or completely eliminate psychopathology in children and adults. As he pointed out and as we have seen throughout the chapter, many prevention programs remain underevaluated, some appear to be relatively ineffective, and still others may actually be damaging. Simply providing individuals with information does not always lead to preventive action, and the most successful prevention programs may be those that deal simultaneously with multiple risk factors and etiologies of psychopathology rather than with one primary cause of dysfunction. We strongly concur with Rutter's conclusion, however, that while acknowledging that there is no quick and easy road to success, we should pursue primary prevention in the future.

We have noted periodically throughout the chapter the central role that governmental funding and political climate have played in shaping community interventions. The successful study of program implementation will demand new and creative strategies not only for dissemination of successful techniques but also for creating new funding opportunities. Successful lobbying for governmental resources, the use of volunteer agencies where applicable, and even the marshalling of assistance from private industry may be necessary to ensure community interventions for all children who could benefit from such strategies. The 1980s may determine the degree to which physical and mental disorders in children can be prevented or can receive early intervention within the community.

REFERENCES

Albino, J. E. (1984). Prevention by acquiring health-enhancing habits. In M. C. Roberts & L. Peterson (Eds.) *Prevention of problems in childhood: Psychological research and applications* (pp. 200–231). New York: Wiley–Interscience.

Albino, J. E., Juliano, D. B., & Slakter, M. J. (1977). Effects of an instructional-motivational program on plaque and gingivitis in adolescents. *Journal of Public Health Dentistry, 5*, 4–10.

Albino, J. E., Tedesco, L. A., & Lee, C. Z. (1980). Peer leadership and health status: Factors moderating response to a children's dental health program. *Journal of Clinical Preventive Dentistry, 2*, 18–20.

Alexander, J. F., & Parsons, B. V. (1973). Short-term intervention with delinquent families: Impact on family process and recidivism. *Journal of Abnormal Psychology, 81*, 219–225.

Allen, G. J., Chinsky, J. M., Larcen, S. W., Lochman, J. E., & Selinger, H. V. (1976). *Community psychology and the schools. A behaviorally oriented multilevel preventive approach.* Hillsdale, NJ: Erlbaum.

Asher, E. J. (1935). The inadequacy of current intelligence tests for testing Kentucky mountain children. *Journal of Genetic Psychology, 16*, 480–486.

Barnow, B. S., & Cain, C. (1977). A reanalysis of the effect of Head Start on cognitive development: Methodology and empirical findings. *Journal of Human Resources, 12*, 177–197.

Baskin, E. J., & Hess, R. D. (1980). Does affective education work? A review of seven programs. *Journal of School Psychology, 18*, 40–50.

Bessell, H., & Palomares, U. (1970). *Methods in human development: Theory manual and curriculum activity guide.* San Diego: Human Development Training Institute.

Blakely, C. H., Davidson, W. S., Saylor, C. A., & Robinson, M. J. (1980). Kentfield rehabilitation program: Ten years later. In R. R. Ross & P. Gendreau (Eds.), *Effective correctional treatment* (pp. 321–326). Toronto: Butterworths.

Blechman, E. A., Kotanchik, N. L., & Taylor, C. J. (1981). Families and schools together: Early behavioral intervention with high risk children. *Behavior Therapy, 12*, 308–319.

Blechman, E. A., Taylor, C. J., & Schrader, S. M. (1981). Family problem solving versus home notes as early intervention for high-risk children. *Journal of Consulting and Clinical Psychology, 49*, 919–926.

Blomberg, T. C. (1983). Diversions, disparate results, and unresolved questions: An integrative evaluation perspective. *Journal of Research in Crime and Delinquency, 4*, 24–38.

Bloom, B. L. (1973). The domain of community psychology. *American Journal of Community Psychology, 1*, 8–11.

Bogat, G. A., Jones, J. W., & Jason, L. A. (1980). School transitions: Preventive intervention following an elementary school closing. *Journal of Community Psychology, 8*, 343–352.

Botvin, G. J., Cantlon, A., Carter, B. J., & Williams, C. L. (1979). Reducing adolescent obesity through a school-health program. *Journal of Pediatrics, 95*, 1060–1062.

Botvin, G. J., & Eng., A. A. (1980). A comprehensive school-based smoking prevention program. *The Journal of School Health, 50*, 209–213.

Bower, E. M. (1973). Community psychology and community schools. In W. L. Claiborn & R. Cohen (Eds.), *School intervention* (pp. 61–94). New York: Behavioral Publication.

Brawley, E. A., & Martinez-Brawley, E. E. (1984). Using community news media to broaden mental health center prevention efforts. *American Journal of Orthopsychiatry, 54*, 318–321.

Bronzaft, A. L., & McCarthy, D. P. (1975). The effect of elevated train noise on reading ability. *Environment and Behavior, 7*, 517–528.

Brown, B. (1978). *Found: Long-term gains from early intervention*. Boulder, CO: Westview.

Butler, L., Miezitis, S., Friedman, R., & Cole, E. (1980). The effect of two school-based intervention programs on depressive symptoms in preadolescents. *American Educational Research Journal, 17*, 111–119.

Campbell, D. T., & Erlebacher, A. (1975). How regression artifacts in quasi-experimental evaluations can mistakenly make compensatory education look harmful. In E. L. Struening & M. Guttentag (Eds.), *Handbook of evaluation research* (pp. 597–617). Beverly Hills: Sage.

Caplan, G. (1964). *Principles of preventive psychiatry*. New York: Basic Books.

Carkuff, R. R. (1971). *The development of human resources*. New York: Holt, Rinehart & Winston.

Chutis, L. (1983). Special roles of mental health professionals in self-help group development. In R. Hess & J. Hermalin (Eds.), *Innovations in prevention* (pp. 65–73). New York: Haworth-Press.

Cicirelli, V. (1969). *The impact of Head Start: An evaluation of Head Start on children's cognitive and affective development*. Report presented to the Office of Economic Opportunity, pursuant to Contract B89-4536 (Report No. PB184328). Westinghouse Learning Corporation for Federal Scientific and Technical Information, U.S. Institute for Applied Technology.

Coates, T. J., Jeffrey, R. W., & Slinkard, L. A. (1981). Heart, healthy eating and exercise: Introducing and maintaining changes in health behaviors. *American Journal of Public Health, 71*, 15–23.

Coates, T. J., & Perry, C. (1981). Multifactor risk reduction with children and adolescents taking care of the heart in behavior group therapy. In D. Upper & S. Ross (Eds.), *Behavior group therapy: An annual review* (pp. 181–217). Champaign, IL: Research Press.

Cohen, S., Glass, D., & Singer, J. (1973). Apartment noise, auditory discriminations, and reading ability in children. *Journal of Experimental Social Psychology, 9*, 407–422.

Cohn, A. H. (1982). The role of media campaigns in preventing child abuse. In K. Oates (Ed.), *Child abuse: A community concern* (pp. 215–230). New York: Brunner/Mazel.

Collingwood, T. R., Douds, A., & Williams, H. W. (1976). Juvenile diversion: The Dallas Police Department Youth Services Program. *Federal Probation, 40*, 23–27.

Cowen, E. L. (1971). Emergent directions in school mental health. *American Scientist, 59*, 723–733.

Cowen, E. L. (1973). Social and community interventions. *Annual Review of Psychology, 24*, 423–472.

Cowen, E. L. (1980). The wooing of primary prevention. *American Journal of Community Psychology, 8*, 258–284.

Cowen, E. L., Gesten, E. L., & Wilson, A. B. (1979). The Primary Mental Health Project (PMHP): Evaluation of current program effectiveness. *American Journal of Community Psychology, 7*, 293–303.

Cowen, E. L., Spinell, A., Wright, S., & Weissberg, R. P. (1983). Continuing dissemination of a school-based mental health program. *Professional Psychology, 13*, 118–127.

Cowen, E. L., Trost, M. A., Lorion, R. P., Dorr, D., Izzo, L. D., & Isaacson, R. V. (1975). *New ways in school mental health: Early detection and prevention of school maladaptation.* New York: Human Sciences Press.

Cox, G. B., Carmichael, S. J., & Dightman, C. (1977). An evaluation of a community based diagnostic program for juvenile offenders. *Juvenile Justice, 28*, 33–41.

Cromer, W. J., & Burns, B. J. (1982). A health center response to community crisis: Some principles of prevention and intervention. *Journal of Primary Prevention, 3*, 35–47.

Davenport, H., & Werry, J. (1970). The effect of general anesthesia, surgery, and hospitalization upon the behavior of children. *American Journal of Orthopsychiatry, 40*, 806–824.

Davidson, W. S., & Robinson, M. J. (1975). Community psychology and behavior modification: A community based program for the prevention of delinquency. *Journal of Corrective Psychiatry and Behavior Therapy, 21*, 1–12.

Decker, M. D., Dewey, M. J., Hutcheson, R. H., & Schaffner, W. (1984). The use and efficacy of child restraint devices: The Tennessee experience, 1982 and 1983. *Journal of the American Medical Association, 252*, 2571–2575.

Department of Health and Human Services (1983). *Developing childhood injury prevention programs: An administrative guide for state maternal and child health (Title V) Programs.* Washington, DC: Birch & Davis Associates.

Dinkmeyer, D. (1970). *Developing understanding of self and others.* Circle Pines, MN: American Guidance Service.

Douglas, J. W. B. (1975). Early hospital admission and later disturbances of behavior and learning. *Developmental Medicine and Child Neurology, 17*, 456–480.

Dunford, F. W. (1977). Police diversion: An illusion? *Criminology, 15*, 335–352.

Durlak, J. A. (1983a). Social problem-solving as a primary prevention strategy. In R. D. Felner, L. A. Jason, J. N. Moritsugu, & S. S. Farber (Eds.), *Prevention psychology: Theory, research and practice* (pp. 31–48). New York: Pergamon Press.

Durlak, J. A. (1983b). Providing mental health services to elementary school children. In C. E. Walker & M. C. Roberts (Eds.), *Handbook of clinical child psychology* (pp. 660–679). New York: Wiley–Interscience.

Durlak, J. A., & Jason, L. A. (1984). Preventive programs for school-aged children and adolescents. In M. C. Roberts & L. Peterson (Eds.), *Prevention of problems in childhood: Psychological research and applications* (pp. 103–132). New York: Wiley–Interscience.

Edozien, J. C., Switzer, B. R., & Bryan, R. B. (1979). Medical evaluation of the special supplemental food program for women, infants, and children. *American Journal of Clinical Nutrition, 32*, 677–692.

Elkins, P. D., & Roberts, M. C. (1984). A preliminary evaluation of hospital preparation for nonpatient children: Primary prevention in a "Let's Pretend Hospital." *Children's Health Care, 13,* 31–36.

Elliott, D. S. (1978). *Diversion: A study of alternative processing practices.* Final report to the Center for Studies of Crime and Delinquency, NIMH, Behavioral Research Institute, Boulder, CO.

Evans, R. I., Rozelle, R. M., Mittelmark, M. B., Hansen, W. B., Bane, A. L., & Havis, J. (1978). Deterring the onset of smoking in children: Knowledge of immediate physiological effects and coping with peer pressure, media pressure, and parent modeling. *Journal of Applied Social Psychology, 8,* 126–135.

Felner, R. D. (1984). Vulnerability in childhood: A preventive framework for understanding children's efforts to cope with life stress and transitions. In M. C. Roberts & L. Peterson (Eds.), *Prevention of problems in childhood: Psychological research and applications* (pp. 133–169). New York: Wiley–Interscience.

Felner, R. D., Farber, S. S., & Primavera, J. (1983). Transitions and stressful life events. A model for primary prevention. In R. D. Felner, L. A. Jason, J. N. Moritsugu, & S. S. Farber (Eds.), *Preventive psychology: Theory, research and practice* (pp. 199–215). New York: Pergamon Press.

Felner, R. D., Ginter, M. A., & Primavera, J. (1982). Primary prevention during school transitions: Social support and environmental structure. *American Journal of Community Psychology, 10,* 227–290.

Felner, R. D., Norton, P., Cowen, E. L., & Farber, S. S. (1981). A prevention program for children experiencing life crisis. *Professional Psychology, 12,* 446–452.

Ferguson, B. F. (1979). Preparing young children: A comparison of two methods. *Pediatrics, 64,* 656–664.

Field, T. M., Sostek, A., Goldberg, S., & Shuman, H. H. (Eds.). (1979). *Infants born at risk: Behavior and development.* New York: SP Medical and Scientific Books.

Fowler, W. (1968). The effect of early stimulation in the emergence of cognitive processes. In R. D. Hess & R. M. Bear (Eds.), *Early education: Current theory, research, and action* (pp. 111–146). Chicago: Aldine.

Gallagher, S. S., Finison, K., Guyer, B., & Goodenough, S. (1984). The incidence of injuries among 87,000 Massachusetts children and adolescents: Results of the 1980–1981 Statewide Childhood Injury Prevention Program surveillance system. *American Journal of Public Health, 74,* 1340–1346.

Gallagher, S. S., Guyer, B., Kotelchuk, M., Bass, J., Lovejoy, F. H., McLoughlin, E., & Mehta, K. (1982). A strategy for the reduction of injuries in Massachusetts: SCIPP. *New England Journal of Medicine, 307,* 1015–1019.

Gelfand, D. M., & Peterson, L. (1985). *Developmental psychology and child psychopathology.* Beverly Hills: Sage.

Glass, D., & Singer, J. (1972). *Urban stress.* New York: Academic Press.

Glass, G. V., & Smith, M. L. (1978). *Meta-analysis of research as the relationship of class size and achievement.* Boulder, CO: Laboratory of Educational Research, University of Colorado.

Glasser, W. (1969). *Schools without failure.* New York: Harper & Row.

Glenwick, D. S., & Jason, L. A. (1984). Behavioral community psychology: An introduction to the special issue. *Journal of Community Psychology, 12*, 103–112.

Gordon, H. (1923). *Mental and scholastic tests among retarded children: An inquiry into the effects of schooling on various tests.* Educational Pamphlets, No. 44. London: Board of Education.

Gordon, T. (1976). *P.E.T. in action.* New York: Wyden Book.

Guerney, L., & Moore, L. (1982, Aug.). *A prevention-oriented community service for latchkey children: An after-school telephone line.* Paper presented at the Annual Convention of the American Psychological Association, Washington, DC.

Heller, M. (1975). Preventive mental health services for families new to the community. *Hospital and Community Psychiatry, 26*, 493–494.

Henggeler, S. W., Rodick, J. D., Borduin, C. M., Hansen, C. L., Watson, S. M., & Urey, J. R. (1986). Multisystemic treatment of juvenile offenders: Effects on adolescent behavior and family interaction. *Developmental Psychology, 22*, 132–141.

Hetherington, E. M. (1979). Effects of father absence on personality development in adolescent daughters. *Developmental Psychology, 7*, 313–326.

Hicks, L. E., Langham, R. A., & Takenaka, J. (1982). Cognitive and health measures following early nutritional supplementation: A sibling study. *American Journal of Public Health, 72*, 1110–1118.

Hobbs, N. (1964). Mental health's third revolution. *American Journal of Orthopsychiatry, 34*, 1–20.

Howard, S. J., & Goldman, N. S. (1972). *Final progress report: Mental health intervention in a major disaster.* Van Nuys, CA: San Fernando Valley Child Guidance Clinic (Small Research Grant, MH21649-01).

Jason, L. A. (1984). Developing undergraduates' skills in behavioral interventions. *Journal of Community Psychology, 12*, 130–139.

Jason, L. A., DeAmicis, L., & Carter, B. (1978). Preventive intervention programs for disadvantaged children. *Community Mental Health Journal, 14*, 272–278.

Jason, L. A., Durlak, J. A., & Holton-Walker, E. (1984). Prevention of child problems in the schools. In M. C. Roberts & L. Peterson (Eds.), *Prevention of problems in childhood: Psychological research and applications* (pp. 311–341). New York: Wiley–Interscience.

Jensen, A. R. (1969). How much can we boost IQ and scholastic achievement? *Harvard Educational Review*, reprint series No. 2, 1–123.

Kalter, N. (1977). Children of divorce in an outpatient psychiatric population. *American Journal of Orthopsychiatry, 47*, 40–51.

Kalter, N., Pickar, J., & Lesowitz, M. (1984). School-based developmental facilitation groups for children of divorce: A preventive intervention. *American Journal of Orthopsychiatry, 54*, 613–623.

Kazdin, A. E. (1977). Assessing the clinical or applied importance of behavior change through social validation. *Behavior Modification, 1*, 427–452.

Kirschenbaum, D. S. (1979). Social competence intervention and evaluation in the inner city: Cincinnati's Social Skills Development Program. *Journal of Consulting and Clinical Psychology, 47*, 778–780.

Kirschenbaum, D. S. (1983). Toward more behavioral early intervention programs: A rationale. *Professional Psychology, 14*, 159–169.

Kliman, A. S. (1975). The Corning flood project: Psychological first aid following a natural disaster. In H. J. Howard, H.L.P. Resnik, & L. G. Parad (Eds.), *Emergency and disaster management: A mental health sourcebook* (pp. 325–335). Bowie, MD: Charles Press.

Klingman, A., & Ben Eli, Z. (1981). A school community in disaster: Primary and secondary prevention in situational crisis. *Professional Psychology, 12*, 523–533.

Klinzing, D. R., & Klinzing, D. G. (1977). Communicating with young children about hospitalization. *Communication Education, 26*, 307–313.

Knowles, J. H. (1977). *Doing better and feeling worse: Health in the United States.* New York: Norton.

Kobrin, S., & Klein, M. W. (1983). *Community treatment of juvenile offenders: The DSO Experiments.* Beverly Hills: Sage.

LaDouceur, R., & Armstrong, J. (1983). Evaluation of a behavioral program for the improvement of grades among high school students. *Journal of Counseling Psychology, 30*, 100–103.

Lazar, I., & Darlington, R. (1982). Lasting effects of early education: A report from the consortium for longitudinal studies. *Monographs of the Society for Research in Child Development*, Vol. 47, Nos. 2–3.

Lee, R., & Haynes, N. M. (1980). Project CREST and the dual treatment approach to delinquency: Method and research summarized. In R. R. Ross & P. Gendreau (Eds.), *Effective correctional treatment* (pp. 171–184). Toronto: Butterworths.

Lesser, G. S. (1974). *Children and television: Lessons from Sesame Street.* New York: Vintage.

Magrab, P. R., Sostek, A., & Powell, B. A. (1984). Prevention in the perinatal period. In M. C. Roberts & L. Peterson (Eds.), *Prevention of problems in childhood: Psychological research and applications* (pp. 43–73). New York: Wiley–Interscience.

Mannarino, A. P., Durlak, J. A., Christy, M., & Magnussen, M. G. (1982). Evaluation of social competence training in the schools. *Journal of School Psychology, 20*, 11–19.

Martens, L. W., Frazier, P. J., Hirt, K. J., Meskin, L. H., & Proshek, J. (1973). Developing brushing performance in second graders through behavior modification. *Health Services Reports, 88*, 818–823.

Masterpasqua, F. (1982). The effectiveness of childbirth education as an early intervention technique. *Hospital and Community Psychiatry, 33*, 56–58.

Masterpasqua, F., Shuman, B. J., O'Shea, L., & Gonzalez, R. (1980). Integrating early intervention into neighborhood health clinics: An ecological intervention. *Infant Mental Health, 1*, 108–115.

Masterpasqua, F., & Swift, M. (1984). Prevention of problems in childhood on a community-wide basis. In M. C. Roberts & L. Peterson (Eds.), *Prevention of problems in childhood: Psychological research and applications* (pp. 369–388). New York: Wiley–Interscience.

Matarazzo, J. D. (1980). Behavioral health and behavioral medicine: Frontiers for a new health psychology. *American Psychologist, 35*, 807–817.

McAlister, A. L., Perry, C., & Maccoby, N. (1979). Adolescent smoking: Onset and prevention. *Pediatrics, 63*, 650–658.

McLoughlin, E., Vince, C. J., & Crawford, J. P. (1982). Project burn prevention: Outcome and implications. *American Journal of Public Health, 72*, 241–247.

Melamed, B. G., & Siegel, L. J. (1975). Reduction of anxiety in children facing hospitalization and surgery by use of filmed modeling. *Journal of Consulting and Clinical Psychology, 43*, 511–521.

Miller, V., Swaney, S., & Deinard, A. (1985). Impact of the WIC program on the iron status of infants. *Pediatrics, 75*, 100–105.

National Children's Bureau. (1976). *Children in hospital—An abstract of research findings.* London: National Children's Bureau Information Service (Highlight No. 19).

Nowicki, S., & Bolick, T. (1983). Television viewing in children. In C. E. Walker & M. C. Roberts (Eds.), *Handbook of clinical child psychology* (pp. 1198–1218). New York: Wiley-Interscience.

O'Connor, S., Vietze, P., Sherrod, K., Sandler, H. M., Gerrity, S., & Altemeier, W. A. (1982). Mother–infant interaction and child development after rooming-in: Comparison of high-risk and low-risk mothers. *Prevention in Human Services, 1*, 25–43.

O'Donnell, C. R., Lydgate, T., & Fo, W. S. O. (1979). The Buddy System: Review and follow-up. *Child Behavior Therapy, 1*, 161–169.

Ojemann, R. H. (1958). The human relations program at the State University of Iowa. *Personnel and Guidance Journal, 37*, 199–206.

Ostrom, T. M., Steel, C. M., Rosenblood, L. K., & Mirels, H. L. (1971). Modification of delinquent behavior. *Journal of Applied Social Psychology, 1*, 118–136.

Pedro-Carroll, J. L., & Cowen, E. L. (1985). The children of divorce intervention project: An investigation of the efficacy of a school-based prevention program. *Journal of Consulting and Clinical Psychology, 53*, 603–611.

Peterson, L. (1984a). The "Safe-at-Home" game: Training comprehensive safety skills in latch-key children. *Behavior Modification, 18*, 474–494.

Peterson, L. (1984b). Teaching home safety and survival skills to latch-key children: A comparison of two manuals and methods. *Journal of Applied Behavior Analysis, 17*, 279–293.

Peterson, L., Hartmann, D. P., & Gelfand, D. M. (1980). Prevention of child behavior disorders: A lifestyle change for child psychologists. In P. Davidson & S. Davidson (Eds.), *Behavior medicine: Changing health lifestyle* (pp. 195–221). New York: Brunner/Mazel.

Peterson, L., & Mori, L. (1985). Prevention of child injury: An overview of targets, methods, and tactics for psychologists. *Journal of Consulting and Clinical Psychology, 53*, 586–595.

Peterson, L., & Mori, L. (In press). Preparation for hospitalization. In D. Routh (Ed.), *Handbook of pediatric psychology.* New York: Guilford Press.

Peterson, L., & Ridley-Johnson, R. (1984). Preparation of well children in the classroom: An unexpected contrast between the academic lecture and filmed modeling methods. *Journal of Pediatric Psychology, 9*, 349–361.

Peterson, L., & Shigetomi, C. (1981). The use of coping techniques to minimize anxiety in hospitalized children. *Behavior Therapy, 12*, 1–14.

Prugh, D. G., & Jordan, K. (1975). Physical illness or injury: The hospital as a source of emotional disturbances in child and family. In I. N. Berlin (Ed.), *Advocacy for child mental health* (pp. 208–249). New York: Brunner/Mazel.

Quay, H. C., & Love, C. T. (1977). The effect of a juvenile diversion program on rearrests. *Criminal Justice and Behavior, 4*, 377–396.

Ratcliffe, W. D., & Wittman, W. P. (1983). Parenting education: Test-market evaluation of a media campaign. In R. Hess & J. Hermalin (Eds.), *Innovations in prevention* (pp. 97–109). New York: Haworth Press.

Rausch, S. (1983). Court processing versus diversion of status offenders: A test of deterrence and labeling theories. *Journal of Research in Crime and Delinquency, 4*, 39–54.

Reisinger, J. J., & Lavigne, J. V. (1980). An early intervention model for pediatric settings. *Professional Psychology, 11*, 582–590.

Rheingold, H. L., & Bayley, N. (1964). The later effects of an experimental modification of mothering. In Y. Brackbill & G. G. Thompson (Eds.), *Behavior in infancy and early childhood* (pp. 515–524). New York: Free Press.

Rickel, A. U., Dyhdalo, L. L., & Smith, R. L. (1984). Prevention with preschoolers. In M. C. Roberts & L. Peterson (Eds.), *Prevention of problems in childhood: Psychological research and applications* (pp. 74–102). New York: Wiley–Interscience.

Rickel, A. U., Eshelman, A. K., & Loigman, G. A. (1983). Social problem solving training: A follow-up study of cognitive and behavioral effects. *American Journal of Community Psychology, 11*, 15–28.

Risley, T. (1972). Spontaneous language and the preschool environment. In J. C. Stanley (Ed.), *Preschool programs for the disadvantaged: Five experimental approaches to early childhood education* (pp. 92–110). Baltimore, MD: Johns Hopkins University Press.

Risley, T., Reynolds, N., & Hart, B. (1970). The disadvantaged: Behavior modification with disadvantaged preschool children. In R. H. Bradfield (Ed.), *Behavior modification: The human effort* (pp. 123–157). San Rafael, CA: Dimensions Publishing.

Roberts, M. C., Elkins, P. D., & Royal, G. P. (1984). Psychological applications to the prevention of accidents and illness. In M. C. Roberts & L. Peterson (Eds.), *Prevention of problems in childhood: Psychological research and applications* (pp. 173–199). New York: Wiley–Interscience.

Roberts, M. C., Maddux, J. E., & Wright, L. (1984). The developmental perspective in behavioral health. In J. D. Matarazzo, N. E. Miller, S. M. Weiss, J. A. Herd, & S. M. Weiss (Eds.), *Behavioral health: A handbook of health enhancement and disease prevention* (pp. 56–68). New York: Wiley.

Roberts, M. C., & Peterson, L. (Eds.). (1984a). *Prevention of problems in childhood: Psychological research and applications*. New York: Wiley–Interscience.

Roberts, M. C., & Peterson, L. (1984b). Prevention models: Theoretical and practical implications. In M. C. Roberts & L. Peterson (Eds.), *Prevention of problems in childhood: Psychological research and applications* (pp. 1–39). New York: Wiley–Interscience.

Roberts, M. C., & Turner, D. S. (1984). Preventing death and injury in childhood: A synthesis of child safety seat efforts. *Health Education Quarterly, 11*, 181–193.

Roberts, M. C., Wurtele, S. K., Boone, R. R., Ginther, L., & Elkins, P. (1981). Reduction of medical fears by use of modeling: A preventive application in a general population of children. *Journal of Pediatric Psychology, 6*, 293–300.

Robertson, L. S. (1983). *Injuries: Causes, control strategies, and public policy.* Lexington, MA: Lexington Books.

Rolf, J., & Read, P. B. (1984). Programs advancing developmental psychopathology. *Child Development, 55,* 8–16.

Rush, D. (1982). Is WIC worthwhile? *American Journal of Public Health, 72,* 1101–1103.

Rutter, M. (1982). Prevention of children's psychosocial disorders: Myth and substance. *Pediatrics, 70,* 883–894.

Schinke, S. P., & Gilchrist, L. D. (1985). Preventing substance abuse with children and youth. *Journal of Consulting and Clinical Psychology, 53,* 596–602.

Schlossman, S., Zellman, G., & Shavelson, R. (1984). *Delinquency prevention in South Chicago: A fifty-year assessment of the Chicago Area Project.* Santa Monica, CA: Rand.

Seidman, E., Rappaport, J., & Davidson, W. S. (1980). Adolescents in legal jeopardy: Initial success and replication of an alternative to the criminal justice system. In R. R. Ross & P. Gendreau (Eds.), *Effective correctional treatment* (pp. 103–123). Toronto: Butterworths.

Sharp, K. C. (1981). Impact of interpersonal problem-solving training on preschoolers' social competence. *Journal of Applied Developmental Psychology, 2,* 129–143.

Shore, M. F., & Massimo, J. L. (1979). Fifteen years after treatment: A follow-up study of comprehensive vocationally-oriented psychotherapy. *American Journal of Orthopsychiatry, 49,* 240–245.

Skodak, M., & Skeels, H. M. (1945). A follow-up study of children in adoptive homes. *Journal of Genetic Psychology, 66,* 21–58.

Smith, T. E. (1983). Reducing adolescents' marijuana abuse. *Social Work in Health Care, 9,* 33–44.

Spivack, G., Platt, J. J., & Shure, M. B. (1976). *The problem solving approach to adjustment.* San Francisco: Jossey-Bass.

Spivack, G., & Shure, M. B. (1974). *Social adjustment in young children.* San Francisco: Jossey-Bass.

Stainback, R. D., & Rogers, R. W. (1983). Identifying effective components of alcohol abuse prevention programs. *International Journal of the Addictions, 18,* 393–405.

Stolberg, A. L., & Anker, J. M. (1984). Cognitive and behavioral changes in children resulting from parental divorce and consequent environmental changes. *Journal of Divorce, 7,* 23–41.

Stolberg, A. L., Cullen, P. M., & Garrison, K. M. (1982). The Divorce Adjustment Project: Preventive programming for children of divorce. *Journal of Preventive Psychiatry, 1,* 365–368.

Stolz, S. B. (1984). Preventive models: Implications for a technology of practice. In M. C. Roberts & L. Peterson (Eds.), *Prevention of problems in childhood: Psychological research and applications* (pp. 391–413). New York: Wiley–Interscience.

Swain, J. J., Allard, G. B., & Holborn, S. W. (1982). The Good Toothbrushing Game: A school-based dental hygiene program for increasing the toothbrushing effectiveness of children. *Journal of Applied Behavior Analysis, 15,* 171–176.

Swan, H., Biggs, S. M., & Kelso, M. (1982). *I'm in charge: A self-care course for parents and children*. Olathe, KS: Johnson County Mental Health Center.

Terr, L. C. (1979). Children of Chowchilla: A study of psychic trauma. *Psychoanalytic Study of Children, 34*, 552–623.

Terr, L. C. (1981). Psychic trauma in children: Observations following the Chowchilla school-bus kidnapping. *American Journal of Psychiatry, 138*, 14–19.

Thompson, E. L. (1978). Smoking education programs, 1960–1976. *American Journal of Public Health, 68*, 250–257.

Vernon, D. T. A., Foley, J. M., & Schulman, J. L. (1967). Effect of mother–child separation and birth order on young children's responses to two potentially stressful experiences. *Journal of Personality and Social Psychology, 5*, 162–174.

Wachs, T. D., & Weizmann, F. (1983). Prenatal and genetic influences upon behavior and development. In C. E. Walker & M. C. Roberts (Eds.), *Handbook of clinical child psychology* (pp. 251–279). New York: Wiley-Interscience.

Wade, T. C., Morton, T. L., Lind, J. E., & Ferris, N. R. (1977). A family crisis intervention approach to diversion from the juvenile justice system. *Juvenile Justice Journal, 28*, 43–51.

Wallerstein, J. S., & Kelly, J. B. (1980). *Surviving the breakup: How children and parents cope with divorce*. New York: Basic Books.

Walter, T. L., & Mills, C. M. (1979). A behavioral-employment intervention program for reducing juvenile delinquency. In J. S. Stumpenhauzer (Ed.), *Progress in behavior therapy with delinquents* (pp. 141–161). Springfield, IL: Charles C. Thomas.

Wandersman, A., Andrews, A., Riddle, D., & Fancett, C. (1983). Environmental psychology and prevention. In R. D. Felner, L. A. Jason, J. N. Moritsugu, & S. S. Farber (Eds.), *Preventive psychology: Theory, research and practice* (pp. 104–127). New York: Pergamon Press.

Wandersman, L. P. (1983). An analysis of the effectiveness of parent–infant support groups. *Journal of Primary Prevention, 3*, 99–115.

Weissberg, R. P., Cowen, E. L., Lotyczewski, B. S., & Gesten, E. L. (1983). The Primary Mental Health Project: Seven consecutive years of program outcome research. *Journal of Consulting and Clinical Psychology, 51*, 100–107.

Whalen, C. K., Henker, B., Collins, B. E., Finck, D., & Dotemoto, S. (1979). A social ecology of hyperactive boys: Medication effects in structural classroom environments. *Journal of Applied Behavior Analysis, 12*, 65–81.

Wolfer, J. A., & Visintainer, M. A. (1979). Prehospital psychological preparation for tonsillectomy patients: Effects on children's and parent's adjustment. *Pediatrics, 64*, 646–655.

Zarle, T. H., Hartsough, D. M., & Ottinger, D. R. (1974). Tornado recovery: The development of a professional-paraprofessional response to a disaster. *Journal of Community Psychology, 2*, 311–320.

Zax, M., Cowen, E. L., Rappaport, J., Beach, D. R., & Laird, J. D. (1968). Follow-up study of children identified early as emotionally disturbed. *Journal of Consulting and Clinical Psychology, 32*, 369–374.

Zax, M., & Specter, G. A. (1974). *An introduction to community psychology*. New York: Wiley-Interscience.

AUTHOR INDEX

Abikoff, H., 122, 123, 135, 428, 430, 466, 469, 470
Abraham, M. J., 378
Abramovitch, R., 353
Abramovitz, A., 529
Abramson, A., 465
Abramson, L. Y., 79
Achenbach, T. M., 4, 10, 11, 13, 14, 17, 26, 57, 75, 76, 98, 187, 398, 401, 424–426, 439, 441
Ackerman, P., 121, 123, 126, 127, 129, 134, 137, 276, 299, 465
Ackerson, L., 8
Adams, A., 138, 175
Adams, D., 467, 473
Adams, P. L., 371
Adamson, G. W., 589
Adamson, L., 374
Adelman, H. S., 513
Adelson, R., 528
Adland, M. L., 374
Agee, V. L., 559
Ageton, S. S., 396, 401, 402
Agras, S., 545
Agrawal, K. C., 98
Agulnik, P. L., 338
Aichhorn, A., 594
Ainsworth, M., 345, 349, 369, 370
Akamatsu, T. J., 43
Albert, J., 39, 121
Albert, M. S., 212–216, 295, 303, 321
Albino, J. E., 630, 637, 647
Alderton, H., 473
Aldous, J., 332
Alexander, A. B., 240
Alexander, D., 465
Alexander, F., 236
Alexander, J. F., 363, 644
Algozzine, B., 441
Alkus, S. R., 467
Allard, G. B., 631
Allen, G. J., 629
Allen, K. E., 537
Allen, P., 318

Allen, R., 432, 460
Allen, T. W., 116–119, 131, 132
Alpher, R., 600
Als, H., 374
Aman, M., 17, 18, 74, 113, 115, 125, 138, 140, 142, 143, 250, 276, 299, 465, 468, 471, 481
Amour, J. L., 444
Amrung, S. A., 50
Ananth, J., 475
Anders, T. F., 273–275
Anderson, G., 175, 436
Anderson, J., 41, 93, 94, 96
Anderson, L. M., 354, 363
Anderson, L. T., 477
Andrasik, F., 541
Anku, J. M., 632
Annel, L. A., 182, 185, 194, 195
Annesley, F. R., 592
Anthony, E. J., 157, 158, 177, 182, 306
Anthony, F., 264, 265
Aoki, B., 89
Apgar, V., 306
Apolloni, T., 538
April, C., 357
Apter, S., 589, 595
Ardali, C., 474
Arend, R., 345
Arias, I., 428, 429
Armstrong, J., 629
Arnold, J. E., 363
Arnold, L., 320, 465, 466
Arnold, S., 543
Arsanow, R. F., 190, 191, 197
Artner, J., 468
Artuso, A., 597
Asarnow, R. G., 79, 89
Asberg, M., 475
Asher, P., 257
Asher, S. J., 338
Asher, S. R., 77, 84, 86
Atkins, M. S., 429
Atwater, J. D., 570
Atwell, C. W., 247

August, G. J., 57, 168
Ault, R., 121
Axelrod, S., 593
Axline, V., 606
Axworthy, D., 314
Ayllon, T., 535
Azrin, N. H., 171, 546, 547

Bachman, J. G., 225, 226
Bachrach, W., 241
Backman, J. G., 408
Bactrel, N., 436
Baer, D. M., 523, 537, 550
Bagley, C., 402
Baharav, Y., 509
Bahn, A. K., 357
Bailery, J. P., 355
Bailey, L. S., 249, 250
Bakal, D. A., 233, 236, 442
Baker, L., 277, 518
Bakow, H., 266
Bakwin, H., 244, 261, 265
Bakwin, R., 244, 265
Bala, S. P., 468
Balaschak, B., 543
Baldwin, A. L., 374
Baldwin, C. P., 374
Baldwin, J., 407
Balka, E. B., 472, 559
Ball, D. W., 119
Ballanger, J. C., 50
Ballowe, T., 313
Baloh, R., 313
Baltaxe, C., 165, 548
Bancroft, J., 314
Bandura, A., 355, 434, 526, 534, 595
Bane, A. L., 631
Bank, S. P., 354
Baraff, A., 239
Barcai, A., 465
Barden, R. C., 80
Bardwell, R., 62
Barenboim, C., 88
Barker, P., 558
Barlow, D. H., 551

Barnes, G. E., 221, 222, 225–227
Barnes, K. R., 468
Barnett, C. R., 372
Barnett, K., 513
Barnhart, D., 559
Barnhill, J., 463
Barnow, B. S., 625
Barocas, R., 344
Baroff, G., 250
Baroff, S., 249
Barrett, C. L., 434, 438, 497, 501,
    504, 505
Barrett, R. K., 338
Barr-Grossman, T., 513
Barrios, B. A., 76
Barrs, C. B., 518
Barry, R. J., 171, 172
Bartak, L., 162, 163, 165, 171, 177,
    277, 398
Bartlett, D. P., 583
Bartolucci, G., 165
Barton, S., 170
Baruch, D., 237, 606
Basham, R. B., 339
Baskin, E. J., 629
Bass, C., 176
Bastien, R., 513
Batta, I. D., 401, 403
Battle, E. S., 117
Bauer, C., 265
Baumeister, A. A., 247–249
Baumrind, D., 348–350
Bax, M., 54
Bax, M. C. O., 274
Bax, M. O., 274
Baxley, G. B., 137
Bayfield, G., 274
Bayley, N., 625
Beach, D. R., 625
Bean, S. C., 310
Bear, G. C., 39
Beardslee, W. R., 92, 374
Beaumont, G., 46
Bebbington, P., 373, 374
Beck, A. T., 436, 507, 511, 515, 517
Beck, S. J., 82
Becker, L., 478
Becker, W. C., 593
Becker-Mattes, A., 469
Bedell, J. R., 433, 444
Beech, H., 237
Begun, A., 353
Behar, D., 35, 227, 474
Behar, L. B., 436

Beickel, S., 593
Beidleman, W. B., 513
Beitchmann, J. H., 37
Bell, C. R., 515, 516
Bell, R. Q., 300, 334
Bell, S. M., 369
Bellack, A. A., 538
Bellack, A. S., 535
Bellinger, D. C., 313
Bellman, M., 264–266
Belsky, J., 334, 339
Belson, W. A., 396
Beltramini, A. U., 274
Bemporad, J., 82, 374
Bender, L., 158, 182, 185, 191, 194
Bender, M. E., 122, 133, 136–138,
    429
Ben Eli, Z., 640
Benezra, E., 126, 128
Benn, R., 124, 407
Bennett, T., 399
Bennett, W. G., 463
Bentzen, F., 591
Berberich, J. P., 545
Berent, S., 213
Berg, I., 261, 262, 264–266
Berger, M., 52, 93, 408
Bergman, L. R., 18
Berkowitz, L., 355, 595
Berkowitz, P. H., 595, 599
Berkson, G., 247–250
Berman, L., 475
Bernal, J. F., 274
Bernard, M. E., 526, 529
Berney, T., 475
Bernfeld, G., 143
Berstein, J. E., 466
Bernstein, L., 236, 238
Bernstein, P. H., 570
Bessell, H., 630
Bessman, C., 540
Bettelheim, B., 176, 594, 600, 602
Bewley, B. R., 225
Bialer, I., 299, 300, 495, 559
Bice, H., 311
Bierman, C. W., 235, 236, 238, 240
Biggs, S. M., 637
Biller, H. B., 367
Billings, A. G., 344
Binkoff, J., 166, 544
Bioke, M., 365
Bion, W., 606
Birch, H. G., 189
Blackford Rogers, W. J., 473
Blackwell, B., 262

Blakely, C. H., 644
Blanchard, B., 541
Blanchard, E. B., 534
Bland, R. C., 195, 196
Blashfield, R. K., 1, 2, 583
Blau, A., 595
Blau, S., 476
Blechman, E. A., 629
Blehar, M., 345
Blincoe, M. M., 559
Bliss, D., 166
Block, H. J., 121
Block, J., 121, 237–239, 351, 359
Block, J. H., 359, 372
Blomberg, T. C., 645
Blomfield, J., 260
Bloom, B. L., 338, 622
Blotcky, M. J., 559, 578
Blouin, A., 95, 429
Blunden, D., 430
Blurton-Jones, N., 244
Boag, L. C., 374
Boeck, R. L., 225, 226
Boehm, J. J., 247
Bogat, G. A., 632
Bohman, M., 48, 92, 315
Boldt, D., 176
Bolick, T., 647
Boll, E., 351
Boll, T., 213, 303, 444
Bond, L. A., 140
Bonham, D., 307, 321
Boone, R. R., 633
Boothe, H. H., 375
Bordwin, C. M., 400
Borkovec, T. D., 46
Bornstein, M. R., 538
Bornstein, P. H., 570
Bortner, M., 189
Bosco, J. J., 141, 398
Bossard, J. H. S., 351
Botti, E., 559
Botvin, G. A., 630, 631
Boucher, J., 167
Boulton, D., 16, 158, 161
Bowen, M., 181, 337, 338
Bower, E. M., 563, 624
Bowers, M. B., 192
Bowman, P. H., 82
Boyd, M., 261
Boyle, M. H., 424
Brachfeld, S., 343
Bradbard, G., 472
Bradley, C., 181, 464, 465

Brake, M., 403
Brand, A. H., 444
Brandon, S., 46
Brandt, L., 469
Brask, B. H., 177
Braswell, L., 39
Brauch, J. D., 98
Braukmann, C. J., 569, 570
Brawley, E. A., 646
Brazelton, T. B., 374
Breaux, A. M., 115, 122, 134
Brehm, S. S., 171
Bremer, D. A., 127
Brendtro, C. K., 559
Brendtro, L. K., 595
Brenner, M. B., 601
Breslau, N., 237, 270, 271, 305, 308, 311
Breslow, L., 190, 192
Bridger, W. H., 47
Brierley, L. M., 160
Briscoe, C. W., 338
Broberger, O., 241
Brock, P., 274
Broderick, J. E., 359
Brodie, R. D., 368
Bronzaft, A. L., 648
Brooks, E., 472
Brooks, J., 401
Broughton, R., 261
Brown, A. L., 127
Brown, B., 625
Brown, G. L., 50, 51, 465
Brown, J., 271
Brown, J. K., 541
Brown, J. L., 180
Brown, L. B., 252
Brown, M., 248
Brown, R. T., 534
Brown, S. C., 310
Brownwell, K. D., 259
Bruch, H., 254, 257–259
Bruun, R., 243–246, 480
Bry, G. H., 227
Bryan, J. H., 41
Bryan, R. B., 636
Bryant, L. E., 240
Bryntwick, S., 475
Bryson, C. Q., 167
Bucher, B., 546
Buchsbaum, M., 467, 468, 470
Buckle, A., 393
Budd, L. A., 403
Buell, J., 537

Bugental, D. B., 357, 467
Bugenthal, D. B., 137
Bukantz, S., 238
Bull, D., 254
Butcher, B. D., 171, 174
Butler, L., 629
Butler, M. C., 406
Butler, N., 307, 321, 398
Butt, F., 600
Butter, H. J., 468
Bunney, W. E., Jr., 438
Burchard, J., 539
Burgess, J. M., 352
Burgess, R. L., 352
Burgoyne, K., 309
Burk, H. P., 469
Burlingham, D., 249, 374
Burns, B. J., 640
Bursik, R. J., 393, 407
Burt, C., 397
Burton, N., 74
Bushi, S., 578
Buxton, M., 507

Cain, C., 625
Calcagno, P., 443
Caldwell, M., 265
Callaway, E., 470, 478
Callias, M., 177, 193
Camara, K. A., 340, 363
Cameron, C., 17
Camp, B. W., 39
Camp, J. A., 299, 300
Campagna, A. F., 39
Campbell, A., 405
Campbell, D. T., 415, 625
Campbell, M., 115, 176, 180, 251, 463, 473, 474, 477–479
Campbell, S. B., 82, 115, 120, 121, 127, 133–135, 137, 142, 143, 311, 341, 467
Campbell, W., 76
Cannon, P. R., 233, 525
Cantlon, A., 630
Cantor, D., 241
Cantor, S., 186, 187, 190, 193, 194, 479
Cantwell, D. P., 21, 24, 95, 114, 125, 131, 143, 277, 301, 318, 320, 431, 436, 460, 469
Caplan, G., 622
Caplan, J., 189
Caplinger, T. E., 406
Carey, W. B., 274

Carkuff, R. R., 643
Carlielle, J., 173, 247–249, 274
Carlson, G., 21, 94, 95, 436, 460
Carlstrom, G., 138
Carmichael, S. J., 643
Carnine, D., 593
Carpenter, G. C., 374
Carpenter, H., 310
Carr, A. G., 544, 545, 548
Carr, E. G., 165, 166
Carrol, S. C., 438
Carroll, H. C., 276
Carter, B., 627, 630
Cartledge, G., 538
Cartwright, D. S., 45
Casper, R. C., 254
Casswell, S., 225
Casteneda, A., 432
Cataldo, M., 540
Cavanagh, M. E., 175
Cavior, H. E., 577
Cederblad, M., 92
Cerny, J. A., 524
Cerreto, M. C., 53, 94, 95, 97
Chace, M., 606
Chadwick, O. F., 305, 311
Chai, H., 543
Chamberlain, P., 61
Chambers, W., 476
Chandler, M., 88, 140, 296–298, 305, 309, 316–318
Chapel, J. L., 139
Chase, D., 243
Chase, H. P., 444
Chase, T. N., 244
Chassin, L., 78, 81, 513
Chaudhry, D. R., 368
Chawla, P. L., 359
Chen, C. S., 167, 168
Chen, T. C., 139, 298, 299, 307, 316, 318, 319–321
Cheney, C., 600
Chess, S., 99, 175
Chiappa, K. H., 301
Chick, J., 184, 187
Chiles, J. A., 439
Chinsky, J. M., 629
Christakis, G., 259
Christiansen, K. O., 48
Christopher, J., 465
Christy, M., 629
Churchill, D. W., 162, 164, 171
Chutis, L., 639
Cicirelli, V., 352, 625

Ciminero, A. R., 263
Claman, L., 509, 512
Clancy, J., 368
Clark, D., 245
Clark, J., 313, 408
Clark, M. L., 84, 85, 88
Clark, P., 170, 174
Clarke, C., 91
Cleghorn, J. M., 197
Clements, S. D., 112, 123, 296
Cleminshaw, H. K., 363
Clifford, E., 239
Cloninger, C. R., 48, 92
Close, J., 299
Cloward, R. A., 411
Cluss, P., 120, 133, 135
Coates, T. J., 631
Cochrane, R., 402
Coddington, R. D., 444
Coekin, M., 265
Cohen, A. K., 400, 411
Cohen, D. J. 139, 161, 170, 175, 243, 244, 302, 320, 478, 480
Cohen, I. L., 115, 477, 478
Cohen, J., 20
Cohen, L. E., 399
Cohen, M. N., 141
Cohen, N., 121, 124, 130, 134, 468
Cohen, R. S., 595
Cohen, S., 648
Cohn, A. H., 646
Cohn, J. F., 374
Cohrssen, J., 262
Coie, J. D., 84, 513
Colbert, F., 248
Cole, E., 629
Cole, J. O., 465
Cole, R. E., 374
Coleman, M., 139, 180, 302
Colletti, G., 430
Collingwood, T. R., 643
Collins, B. E., 430, 465, 467, 648
Collins, J., 338
Collins, L. F., 17
Collins, P. J., 473, 478
Colner, G., 465
Colyar, D. E., 559
Comings, B. G., 244, 245, 480
Comings, D. E., 244, 245, 480
Comly, H. H., 465
Compas, B. E., 513
Conboy, J., 57
Conley, O., 547
Connell, D. B., 345
Connell, P., 243, 245

Conners, C. K., 90, 95, 114, 267, 315, 316, 320, 424, 429, 463, 465, 466, 468, 469, 472, 473
Connor, P. A., 35, 116, 136
Connors, K., 370
Conoley, J. C., 589
Consalvi, C., 45
Conte, H. R., 372
Coodin, F. J., 225
Cook, A. R., 546
Cook, S. C., 438
Cook, T. D., 415
Cooke, T. P., 86, 538
Coolidge, J. C., 368
Cooper, B., 192, 194, 408
Coote, M., 261, 263
Coppotelli, H., 84
Corah, N. L., 306
Corbett, J., 157, 243, 245, 246, 263
Corson, E., 320
Corson, S., 320
Corter, C., 353
Costello, A. J., 76, 115
Coulehan, J. L., 223, 225
Covert, A., 546
Covery, M., 362
Cowan, F. P., 339
Cowan, P., 190, 192, 339
Cowen, E. L., 365, 622, 624, 625, 628, 632
Coyne, J. C., 444
Cox, A., 52, 93, 162, 177, 277, 398, 408
Cox, C. R., 334
Cox, G. B., 439, 643
Cox, M., 334
Craft, M., 306, 560, 578
Craig, M. M., 403
Craighead, W. E., 517
Cramblett, H. G., 310
Cramer, J. B., 512
Crawford, J. P., 638
Crawford, J. W., 343
Creak, M., 157, 177
Creer, P. P., 240
Creer, T. L., 240, 543
Cress, J. N., 17
Cressey, D. R., 410
Crnic, K. A., 339, 343, 347
Crockenberg, S. B., 346, 350
Cromer, W. J., 640
Cromwell, R. L., 583
Cronholm, B., 478
Crook, C. K., 350

Crook, T., 373
Crouse-Novak, M. A., 73, 99, 438
Crowe, R. R., 368
Crowther, J. K., 140
Cruickshank, W., 311, 591, 592, 596
Crumrine, P. L., 352
Cruse, D., 592
Cudeck, B., 344
Cullinan, D., 589, 593, 594, 610
Cully, M., 600
Cummings, C., 35, 115
Cummings, L., 56, 98
Cunningham, A., 239
Cunningham, C. E., 118, 125, 129, 133, 134, 467
Cunningham, M. A., 473
Currah, J., 262
Curran, C. F., 466
Cushna, B., 353
Cutler, R. L., 589
Cymbalisty, B. Y., 45
Cytryn, L., 76, 374, 437, 438

Dalby, J. T., 126, 128
Dalby, M. A., 473
Dalby, P., 254
Damasco, A. R., 320, 321
Damasio, A. R., 173, 175, 176
Dandes, S. K., 86
Darcic, G., 513
Darlington, R., 626
Davenfort, Y. B., 374
Davenport, H., 633
Davenport, R., 247
Davey, J., 465, 466
David, O. J., 313
David, R., 251
Davids, A., 171
Davidson, M., 265
Davidson, W. S., 644
Davie, R., 307, 309, 398
Davis, P. A., 309
Davis, J. M., 254
Davison, L., 298
Dawson, G., 164, 398
Dawson, M. J., 250, 545
Day, D., 39, 121
De Amicis, L., 627
Deardorff, P., 433
de Blois, C. S., 35, 115
Decker, M. D., 638
DeFries, J. C., 48
Dehrenwend, B., 52
Deinard, A., 636

Dekirmenjian, H., 139
Delameter, A. H., 90
Delameter, A. M., 46, 123, 134, 267, 268
Delano, J. G., 301
de la Tourette, G., 480
De Leon, G., 262
De Lissovoy, V., 247–249
De Long, G. R., 310
Deluty, R. H., 39, 77
De Moor-Peal, R., 435
Dempsey, J., 343
De Myer, M. K., 158, 159, 161–163, 170–175, 177, 179–181, 398
DeMyer-Gapin, S., 44
Dengerink, H. A., 362
Denhoff, E., 111, 131
Dennison, G., 605
De Paulo, B. M., 38
DeRisi, W., 575
Des Lauriers, A. M., 440
Desmond, M. M., 310
Dettor, J., 243, 480
Deubner, D. C., 541
Deutsch, F., 86
Devany, J. M., 528, 545, 548
Devies, R. K., 46
Dewey, M. J., 638
Dezen, A. E., 501
Diament, C., 438
Dibble, E., 92
Dietrich, C., 42
Dietz, A., 427, 435
Dietz, S., 437, 546
Dietz, W. H., 256–259
Dightman, C., 643
Di Giuseppe, R. A., 507
Dijkstra, J., 307
DiMascio, A., 375
Dimpiero, T. C., 559
Dimson, S., 261
Dinkmeyer, D., 629
Disch, S., 263
Dishion, T., 355, 392
Diskin, S. D., 343
Di Vitto, B., 342, 343
Divoky, D., 112, 466
Dixon, H., 23, 53, 94, 185, 267, 301
Dobias, B., 310
Docter, R. F., 39
Dodge, K. A., 39, 84, 89, 137
Dohrenwend, B. P., 233, 236
Dohrenwend, B. S., 233, 236
Doke, L., 547

Doleys, D., 262, 263–266, 543
Doll, E. A., 440
Doll, L., 300
Dollinger, L., 543
Dollinger, S. J., 513
Dolly, J., 603
Done, A. K., 221
Dooher, L., 477
Dooling, E., 465
Dotemoto, S., 430, 467, 648
Doubilet, A. L., 518
Douds, A., 643
Douglas, J., 260
Douglas, J. W., 307, 309
Douglas, J. W. B., 396, 398, 633
Douglas, V. I., 465, 466, 468, 471
Dowling, J., 477
Downey, K., 92
Drabman, R., 430, 599
Draguns, J. G., 583
Drake, L., 123
Dratman, M. L., 162
Dreger, R. M., 11
Dreyfus, P., 478
Drillien, C., 308, 309
Dubeck, J. A., 45
Dubo, S., 236, 237, 239
Dubowitz, L. M., 309
Duffy, J. H., 474
Dugas, E., 140
Dulcan, M. K., 76, 496, 497, 502, 504, 508, 509
Dunbar, F., 233
Dunbar, H. F., 442
Duncan, S. W., 80
Duner, A., 397
Dunford, F. W., 645
Dunlap, K., 249
Dunn, J., 274, 341, 353, 361
Dunteman, G. H., 355
Dupont, H., 604
Durand, V. M., 545, 548
During, M., 274
Durlak, J. A., 627–630, 634
Durnin, J., 258
Dusek, J. B., 81, 82
Duvall, E. M., 332
Dweck, C. S., 80–82
Dwivedi, K. N., 46
Dwyer, J., 259
Dyhdalo, L. L., 625
Dykman, R., 276, 299, 465, 466

Earls, F., 53, 397
Easterbrooks, A. M., 346

Eastgate, S. M., 320
Eaves, R. C., 441
Ebaugh, F. G., 310
Ebert, M. H., 465
Eckert, E. D., 254
Eddy, M., 166
Edelbrock, C. S., 10, 11, 17, 26, 57, 75, 76, 98, 115, 398, 401, 424–426, 439, 441
Edleson, J. L., 515
Edlund, S. R., 541
Edozien, J. C., 636
Edwards, R. M., 175
Efron, A. M., 438
Egan, J., 95
Egeland, B., 346, 347, 351
Ehrhardt, A. A., 272
Eichman, P. L., 304
Eiduson, B. T., 333
Eisenberg, L., 176, 320, 357, 368, 370, 461, 465, 468, 472, 474, 500
Elardo, P., 123, 602
Elardo, R., 602
Eliot, J., 373
Elitzur, B., 509, 515
Elkins, P. D., 633, 649
Elkins, R., 75, 469
Ellingson, R., 301, 318
Elliot, E. S., 80–82
Elliott, D. S., 396, 399, 401, 402, 405, 412, 414, 645
Ellis, A., 526, 529
Ellis, M. J., 468
Ellis, P. L., 39
Elmer, E., 344
Eme, R. F., 17
Emery, G., 511
Emery, L., 478
Emery, R. E., 340, 359–361, 372, 425
Endicott, J., 438
Endman, M., 143
Eng, A. A., 631
Engel, G., 233, 241
Engel, M., 583
Engelmann, S., 593
Englehardt, D., 472, 477, 478
Ensminger, M. A., 365
Ensminger, M. E., 98
Epstein, L. C., 465, 469, 547
Epstein, M. H., 589, 593, 594
Erikson, M. L., 393
Erikson, R. V., 39
Erlebacher, A., 625
Erlenmyer-Kimling, L., 188
Ernhart, C. B., 304, 306

Eron, L. D., 54, 59
Errera, J., 313
Ersner-Hershfield, R., 546
Escalona, S. K., 208, 309
Eshelman, A. K., 627
Eskenazi, B., 313
Esman, A., 176
Esveldt-Dawson, K., 436, 437
Evans, J., 186, 479
Evans, R. I., 631
Evans-Jones, L. G., 217
Ewing, L. J., 115, 134
Eyberg, S. M., 519
Eynon, T. G., 404
Eysenck, H., 92, 261

Faegre, C., 595
Fagen, S. A., 603
Fagot, B. I., 54, 55
Fantini, M., 605
Farber, E. A., 347
Farber, S., 365, 632
Faretra, G., 477
Farley, A., 172
Farnworth, M., 395, 396
Farquhar-Brown, M., 274
Farrington, D. P., 57, 58, 64, 362,
    392, 393, 397, 399, 400, 403–405,
    412, 414, 415
Farudi, P. A., 43
Faust, R., 406
Favell, J. E., 525
Feagans, L., 276, 595
Featherman, D. L., 363
Feigelson, C. I., 507, 509, 512, 514
Fein, D., 164, 180, 189, 191, 192
Feinberg, T. L., 73, 99, 438
Feingold, B., 315, 609
Feingold, I., 276, 481
Feinstein, C., 95
Feiring, C., 98
Feld, S., 365
Feldman, F., 241, 242
Feldman, H., 339
Feldman, R., 245, 246, 406, 414
Felleman, E. S., 80
Felner, R., 365, 366, 374, 631, 632
Fencil-Morse, E., 79
Fenichel, C., 599, 603
Fenton, W. S., 185, 188
Ferguson, B., 47, 633
Ferguson, H. B., 116, 131–133,
    138–140
Fernando, S., 243–246
Ferrari, M., 170

Ferris, S., 478, 644
Feuerstein, M., 213, 216, 268, 276,
    301, 303, 318, 320
Fialkov, M. J., 536
Fichter, M., 169
Field, M. A., 314
Field, T., 343, 634
Fielding, D., 261
Figlio, R. M., 393
Finch, A., 426, 433, 529
Finch, S., 241, 242
Finck, D., 430, 467, 648
Fineberg, B. L., 559
Finer, N. N., 298, 306
Finison, K., 638
Fink, A. H., 589, 590
Finkelstein, J., 124
Finkelstein, R., 73, 99, 438
Finnerty, R. J., 467
Firestone, P., 115, 121, 123, 130, 139,
    300, 465, 466
Fischer, M., 56, 98, 99
Fischoff, S., 375
Fish, B., 157, 158, 190, 191, 473,
    476–478
Fishbein, H. D., 352
Fisher, B., 83
Fisher, L., 340, 344, 584
Fisher, M. A., 468
Fisher, S. F., 367
Fishman, H. C., 360
Fitts, M. D., 264
Fitzelle, G., 239
Fitz-Hardinge, P., 271
Fitzpatrick, J., 17, 23, 53, 94, 173,
    185, 247–249, 267
Fixsen, D. L., 570
Flament, M. F., 478
Fleischman, D., 593
Fleishman, M. J., 539
Fletcher, J. M., 211, 213, 295, 303,
    320
Flor-Henry, P., 213, 216, 217, 298,
    301–303
Flor-Henry, Y., 475
Floyd, A., Jr., 477, 478
Flynn, S., 77
Fo, U. S. O., 643
Fobes, J. C., 51
Foch, T., 49, 91
Foggitt, R. H., 46
Foley, C., 439
Foley, J. M., 633
Folstein, S., 168, 175
Forbes, C., 270

Ford, M. E., 80
Forchand, R., 86, 135, 247–249, 352,
    356, 446, 547
Foreyt, J. P., 257, 259
Forman, J. B. W., 20
Forness, S. R., 585, 586, 597, 609
Forrester, R., 262
Forsythe, I., 265
Foster, D. J., 270
Foster, S. L., 77, 86, 427
Fournier, M., 465
Fowles, D. C., 47, 90, 91
Fowles, W., 625
Foxx, R. M., 171, 546, 547
Frame, C., 16, 39, 114, 137, 536
Frankel, F., 169
Frankie, G., 356, 372
Franknoi, J., 162
Franks, C., 236
Fraser, M. S., 306
Frazier, P. J., 631
Freedman, A. M., 603
Freeman, B. J., 161, 163, 169, 175
Freeman, R. D., 300, 302
Freeman, W. M., 173
Freibergs, V., 129
Freire, P., 605
Freitag, G., 248–250
French, N. H., 436, 437
French, T., 236
Freud, A., 249, 374, 595
Friebergs, V., 471
Friedhoff, A., 243, 244
Friedland-Bandes, R., 513
Friedman, B., 541
Friedman, R., 80, 629
Friedman, S., 374
Frietag, G., 528
Frith, U., 166, 169
Fritz, G. K., 235
Frodi, A. M., 342
Frommer, E. A., 460
Fulkerson, S. C., 173
Fundudis, T., 277
Fyffe, C., 167

Gabrielli, W. F., 48, 397
Gad, M. T., 444
Gaensbauer, T. J., 374, 375
Gainer, J., 268
Gairdner, D., 265
Gajzago, C., 16, 158, 161, 169
Gallagher, J. J., 304
Gallagher, S. S., 638
Galler, E., 302

Gallimore, R., 17
Gammon, G. D., 92
Gandara, P., 584
Garbarino, J., 336
Garber, J., 80, 436
Garcia, R., 45
Garcia-Coll, C., 90, 91, 98
Gardella, D., 559, 578
Garell, D., 259
Garfield, S. L., 471, 518
Garfinkel, B., 466
Garfinkel, P. E., 253
Garmezy, N., 4, 77, 78, 192, 335, 336
Garner, A., 357
Garner, D. M., 253, 255
Garralda, M. E., 186, 190, 192, 194, 217, 222
Garriott, J., 222, 223
Garrison, K. M., 632
Garrison, S. R., 515, 516
Garrow, J., 257–259
Garside, R., 177, 186, 398
Garvey, W. P., 370
Gaskin, F., 338
Gastner, S., 359, 361, 372, 373
Gath, A., 53
Gath, D., 408
Gattoni, F., 408
Gauthier, Y., 237, 240
Gdowski, C. L., 435
Gear, R., 307, 309
Gelfand, B., 37
Gelfand, D. M., 498, 623, 630
Geller, E., 175
Gelles, R., 362
Gendreau, P., 559
Geraci, R., 86
Gerard, R. E., 574
Gershon, E. S., 92, 438
Gesten, E. L., 624, 628
Getter, H., 372, 373
Gibbs, E. L., 310
Gibbs, F. A., 310
Gibbons, S., 605
Gilbert, B. O., 434, 435
Gilbert, J., 593
Gilchrist, L. D., 631
Gilkey, K. M., 162
Gill, O., 409
Gilberg, C., 138–141, 177, 180
Giller, H., 559
Gilman, A., 221, 456
Gilman, A. G., 221–224, 227, 228, 456, 460
Gilstrap, B., 339

Ginott, H. G., 606
Ginter, M., 365, 632
Ginther, L., 633
Giordoni, B., 213, 444
Gittelman, R., 119, 129, 136, 276, 313, 459, 460, 466, 469, 470, 481
Gittelman-Klein, R., 122, 430, 465, 466, 468, 469, 471, 472, 474, 475, 481, 534, 551
Given, K., 343
Glass, D., 648
Glass, G. V., 550, 606, 648
Glass, R. M., 590
Glasser, W., 602
Glavin, J. P., 592
Glennon, B., 77
Glenwick, D. S., 624
Gleser, G., 313
Glick, J., 434
Glicklich, L., 260
Glish, M. A., 188, 196, 197
Gloisten, A., 466
Glow, P. H., 55, 99
Glow, R. A., 17, 18, 55, 93, 96, 99, 141, 429
Glueck, E., 40, 356, 397
Glueck, S., 40, 356, 397
Gluck, D. S., 115
Godston, S. E., 589
Gogan, J. L., 270
Goildberg, S. C., 254
Gold, M., 40, 393, 396, 401, 408
Gold, V., 248–250
Goldberg, A. M., 320
Goldberg, S., 342, 343, 634
Goldberg, W. A., 346
Golden, C. J., 79
Goldfarb, W., 158, 191
Goldman, A., 499
Goldman, N. S., 641
Goldstein, H., 307, 398
Golombok, S., 272
Gonso, J., 86
Gonzales, R., 641
Goodenough, S., 638
Goodman, J., 465, 466, 526
Goodman, L. S., 221, 456
Goodman, P., 588, 605
Goodman, S., 262
Goodrick, G. K., 257, 259
Goodstein, L. D., 355
Goodwin, F. K., 50
Goodyer, Z., 267, 268
Gordon, G. P., 17
Gordon, H., 628

Gordon, M., 122, 128, 307, 320
Gordon, N. H., 78
Gordon, R. A., 400, 402
Gorenstein, E., 116, 117, 120, 121, 130, 131, 296, 320
Gorsuch, R. L., 406
Gossett, J. T., 559, 578
Gotlib, I. H., 79, 89
Gottesman, I., 344
Gottlieb, H., 375
Gottman, J., 86, 335, 361, 502, 506
Gould, J., 157, 160–162, 174, 175, 178–180, 270, 305
Gould, M. S., 25, 52
Gove, F. L., 345
Goyette, C. H., 114, 429
Graham, F. K., 304, 306
Graham, P., 52, 53, 73, 77, 81, 83, 96, 135, 194, 216, 235, 237, 239, 260, 274, 304, 321, 352, 397, 402
Gram, L., 473, 478
Granger, C., 560
Grant, J. D., 8
Grant, M., 8, 257, 572
Gray, J. A., 47, 51, 75, 90, 320, 321
Green, A., 247, 248, 251, 273
Green, B., 313
Green, C., 45
Green, D. R., 570
Green, J., 21
Green, K., 82, 94, 547
Green, R., 271, 272
Green, W., 181, 184–187, 189, 192–194, 251, 463, 473
Greenberg, A., 139
Greenberg, I., 430, 606
Greenberg, L., 465, 468, 471
Greenberg, M. T., 339
Greenberg, N., 248
Greenhill, L. L., 476
Greenspan, S., 88
Greenwald, W. E., 137
Grega, D. M., 463, 473
Greist, D. L., 135
Grice, J., 468, 469
Griest, D. L., 356, 446
Griffiths, A. D., 306
Grinspoon, L., 112
Groff, M., 37
Gross, M., 466
Grossman, H. J., 441
Grossman, L., 75
Grossman, S., 253
Grounds, L., 425
Gruenberg, E. M., 500

Grusec, J., 434
Gualtieri, C., 138, 175, 277, 463
Guerney, L., 637
Guidubaldi, J., 363–365
Guirguis, W. R., 196
Gupt, K., 359
Gurin, G., 365
Guroff, J. J., 92
Guskin, S. L., 590
Guthrie, D., 578
Guy, W., 424, 428
Guyer, B., 638

Ha, H., 439
Hack, M., 308, 309
Haefele, W. F., 61
Hagamen, M., 477
Hagen, J. W., 167
Hagnell, O., 338
Hahn, W., 239
Haier, R. V., 184, 185, 188, 193
Hakerem, G., 470
Hale, R. L., 37
Haley, R., 425
Hallahan, D. P., 119
Hallgren, B., 260–262
Halliday, R. A., 470
Halmi, K. A., 252–256
Halperin, J. M., 276
Hammer, D., 47, 352
Hammond, W. A., 396
Hamovit, J., 92
Hampe, E. I., 435
Hampe, I. E., 497
Hand, D., 263
Handal, P. J., 435
Handol, P. J., 95
Hansen, W. B., 631
Hanson, C. L., 61
Harcherik, D. F., 243, 245
Harder, D., 344
Hardt, R. H., 405
Hare, E. H., 338
Hare, R. D., 43, 47
Haring, N. G., 593, 596
Harlow, H., 249
Harmon, R. J., 374
Harper, G., 254, 255
Harper, L. V., 334
Harper, P., 262
Harrington, D. M., 121
Harris, E. L., 368
Harris, F., 525, 537
Harris, L. S., 263

Harris, R., 301
Harris, S., 157, 166, 171, 546
Harris, T. S., 465
Harris, W. R., 50
Hart, B., 537, 627
Hart, J. T., 474
Hart, H., 54, 274
Harter, S., 39
Harth, R., 595
Hartig, M., 121
Hartmann, D., 121
Hartmann, D. B., 76
Hartmann, D. P., 426, 498, 500, 501, 505, 630
Hartsough, D. M., 641
Hartup, W., 84, 337, 346
Harvey, D. H. P., 466
Harvey, E., 237
Hasazi, J. E., 56, 98
Hassibi, M., 99
Hastings, J. E., 131, 132, 139, 469
Haubrich, P. A., 592
Havighurst, R. J., 82
Havis, J., 631
Hawes, R., 434
Hawkins, J. L., 336
Hawkins, R. R., 442
Hayashi, K., 18
Hayden, B., 38
Hayes, S. C., 526, 551
Haynes , N. M., 643
Heald, F., 257
Hecht, I. H., 37
Hechtman, L., 114, 124, 139
Hegrenes, J. R., 370
Heiby, E., 434
Heidish, I. E., 436, 437
Heilman, K. M., 213
Heinicke, C. M., 343, 499, 500, 503, 504
Heller, M., 640
Helper, M. M., 471
Helsel, W. J., 436
Henggeler, S. W., 44, 61, 85, 86, 400, 644
Henker, B., 115, 117, 120, 122, 123, 127, 133–137, 430, 431, 465, 467, 515, 648
Henn, F. A., 62, 63
Henry, J., 594
Hentoff, N., 605
Herbert, G. W., 17
Herbert, M., 236, 238, 302
Herjanic, B., 62, 76, 426

Herman, S., 39
Hermann, B. P., 311
Hermelin, B., 165, 167–170, 174, 175
Hernandez, J. M., 50
Herr, D., 441
Hersen, M., 535, 538
Hersh, S. P., 178
Herskovitz, A., 528
Hersov, L. A., 368, 370
Hertweck, L., 267
Hertzig, M., 189, 190, 274
Herzog, E., 364
Hess, R. D., 629
Hetherington, E. M., 333–341, 351, 356, 358–361, 363–367, 372, 373, 632
Hewett, F. M., 593, 597
Hewitt, F. M., 171
Hewitt, L. E., 8, 9, 403
Hickey, K., 547
Hicks, L. E., 636
Hierowski, E., 53
Hill, K. T., 78, 81
Hilliard, J., 235
Hilton, I., 353
Hindelang, M. J., 393, 396, 400–405
Hingtgen, J. N., 158, 398
Hinkle, L. E., Jr., 444
Hinshaw, S. P., 515
Hirschberg, J. C., 595
Hirschi, T., 396, 397, 405, 412
Hirshoren, A., 590, 591, 611
Hirt, K. J., 631
Hobbes, G., 116
Hobbs, N., 563, 595, 596, 624
Hobbs, S. A., 529
Hobson, R. P., 175
Hoddinott, B. A., 473
Hodges, K., 76, 79
Hoefler, S. A., 570
Hoenk, P. R., 368
Hoffman, L. W., 365
Hoffman, S., 313, 472, 477
Hoffmann, W., 163, 164, 176
Hogan, A. E., 37–39, 78
Hogan, R., 349
Hogh, E., 397
Hohner, G., 397
Holborn, S. W., 631
Holdworth, L., 311
Holden, E. W., 299, 300, 318
Holland, C. J., 513
Hollander, C. S., 478
Hollingsworth, C. E., 75, 99

Hollister, W. G., 589
Holloway, H., 432
Holmes, C. S., 57
Holmes, N., 161
Holmes, T. H., 443
Holt, J., 605
Holt, P., 265
Holton-Walker, E., 634
Homatidis, S., 45
Hong, G. K., 94
Hood, M., 225
Hood-Williams, J., 499
Hook, B., 92
Hoppe, C. M., 142
Hops, H., 593
Hopwood, J., 468
Horne, D., 245
Hoshino, Y., 177, 179
House, J., 337
Howard, K. I., 45
Howard, S. J., 641
Howarth, B. G., 475
Howells, J. G., 196
Howlin, P., 165, 276–278
Hoy, E., 124–126
Hsu, L. K. G., 255
Hubble, L. M., 37
Huberty, C. J., 604
Hudgins, W., 356
Huesmann, L. R., 54, 59
Huessey, H. R., 471
Huestis, R., 465
Huizinga, D., 296, 408
Hulse, W. C., 595
Humes, M., 164
Humphrey, N., 158, 172, 186
Humphries, T., 133, 134, 467
Hung, W., 460
Hunt, R. D., 466
Hunter, R. S., 343
Huon, G. F., 252
Hurry, J., 373, 374
Hurvic, M. J., 478
Hutcheson, R. H., 638
Hutchings, B., 357, 397
Hutt, C., 248
Hutt, S., 248, 250
Hymel, S., 77, 84, 86

Ichilov, Y., 509, 511
Illich, I., 588, 605
Ince, L., 542
Ingram, G., 45
Ini, S., 177

Ipacs, J., 240
Ismond, D. R., 139
Israel, A. C., 440
Itil, T. M., 477
Iwata, B., 545

Jackson, D., 241
Jackson, G. G., 444
Jackson, R., 158, 357, 398
Jacob, R. G., 430
Jacob, T., 425
Jacobs, B. S., 353
Jacobs, J. S., 313
Jacobsen, R., 78, 83, 87, 439
Jacobson, G., 367
Jacobson, S., 375, 595
Jaffe, P., 446
James, A. L., 171, 172
Jamison, D. L., 216
Janicki, R. S., 466
Janson, C. G., 396
Jaskir, J., 98
Jason, L. A., 624, 627, 630, 632, 634, 647, 648
Jaquette, D., 513
Jayaratne, S., 539
Jeffrey, R. W., 631
Jenkins, R. L., 8, 9, 62, 319, 368, 403
Jenkins, S., 54, 274
Jennings, K. D., 86
Jennings, P., 237
Jensen, A. R., 625
Jensen, R., 265
Jesness, C. F., 572, 573, 575, 577
Jessor, R., 405
Jessor, S. L., 405
Joffe, W., 77
Johns, J. H., 41
Johnson, C., 468
Johnson, J. H., 444
Johnson, M., 39
Johnson, M. M., 367
Johnson, M. R. D., 225
Johnson, S. B., 423, 432–435, 444, 536
Johnson, S. M., 339, 356, 357
Johnson, V. S., 559, 577
Johnston, C., 133–135
Johnston, L. D., 225, 226, 408
Jones, F. H., 86
Jones, H., 264, 265
Jones, J. W., 632
Jones, M. L., 525
Jones, R., 605

Jones, S. C., 424
Jones, V., 170, 173
Jordan, K., 213, 633
Jorestedt, L., 475
Josselyn, I., 241
Joyce, M. R., 529
Judd, L. J., 75
Juliano, D., 127, 631
Jurkovic, G. J., 37, 39

Kagan, J., 39, 90, 91, 98, 121
Kahan, J., 247
Kahn, M., 176, 354
Kahn, S., 339
Kalas, R., 76
Kalmign, M., 478
Kalter, N., 513, 632, 640
Kandel, D. B., 221, 224–228, 398, 406
Kandel, H. J., 534
Kanfer, F. H., 121
Kanner, A. D., 444
Kanner, L., 157, 159, 176, 177, 181, 182, 244
Kapche, R., 41
Kaplan, E., 164
Kaplan, S., 94, 439
Kashanik, J. H., 94, 95, 439, 476
Kaslow, N. J., 79, 80
Kaspar, J. C., 296
Kass, R. E., 427
Kassorla, I., 248–250
Kastner, L. S., 270
Kastrup, M., 408
Kaswan, J. J., 357
Kates, W., 466
Katz, S., 465, 466, 471
Kauffman, J. M., 119, 139, 300, 318, 585
Kauffman, P., 243
Kaufman, A. S., 37
Kaufmann, M., 247
Kavale, K. A., 590, 591, 604, 607, 609, 611
Kawi, A., 244
Kay, W., 427
Kazkin, A. E., 76, 436–438, 536, 538, 624, 611
Kearney, C., 507
Kellam, S. G., 98, 365
Keller, M. B., 92, 374
Kelly, J. B., 338–340, 368, 632
Kelly, P., 341
Kelly, T. E., 548

Kelman, D., 243, 244, 246
Kelman, J. H., 259
Kelso, M., 637
Kendler, K. S., 315
Kendall, P., 39, 127, 433, 436, 502, 506, 515–517, 529, 532
Kendrick, C., 353, 361
Kennard, M., 138
Kennedy, B., 559
Kennedy, R. L., 310
Kennell, J. H., 342
Kent, R. N., 427, 430, 435
Keogh, B. K., 584
Kermis, M. D., 81
Kern, L., 249, 250
Kessler, M., 76, 115
Kessler, S., 197
Kettlewell, K. W., 559
Kidd, J., 177, 186
Kidd, K. K., 92, 244, 344
Kidwell, J. S., 353, 354
Kies, H., 241, 242
Kifer, R. E., 570
Kilby, G., 137
Kilstrom, N., 343
Kimball, W. H., 352
Kinder, M. I., 528
King, C., 114, 137
Kinsbourne, M., 116, 117, 133, 171, 467–469
Kirrigin, K. A., 569, 570
Kirk, A., 265
Kirkland, C., 139
Kirkland, K. D., 528
Kirschenbaum, D. S., 629
Klaasen, C. D., 312
Klackenberg, G., 261
Klapper, Z., 603
Klario, S. H., 76
Klass, D. W., 311
Klatskin, E., 559
Klaus, M. H., 342
Klebanoff, L., 177
Klein, A. R., 120, 122, 128, 135, 137
Klein, D. C., 79
Klein, D. F., 192, 276, 430, 459, 462, 465, 466, 468, 469, 471, 474–476, 478, 479, 481
Klein, M. M., 372, 373
Klein, M. W., 393, 406, 642, 645
Klein, N. C., 363
Klerman, G. L., 92, 374, 511, 577
Kliman, A. S., 641
Kline, J., 76

Klinedinst, J. K., 435
Klingman, A., 640
Klinzing, D. G., 633
Klinzing, D. R., 633
Klopper, J. H., 320
Kluegel, J. R., 399
Klykylo, W. M., 252–254, 258, 259
Knights, R. M., 139, 468
Knobloch, H., 179, 180, 296, 317
Knoblock, P., 599, 604
Knopp, W., 320
Knowles, J. H., 630
Knox, D., 169
Kobasigawa, A., 513
Kobayashi, S., 18
Kobrin, S., 642, 645
Koegel, R., 166, 169, 171, 249, 441, 546, 549
Koh, C., 473, 478
Kohl, H., 605
Kohn, M., 82, 86, 98
Kokes, R., 344
Koles, F. J., 475
Kologinsky, E., 166
Kolvin, I., 157, 158, 162, 172, 177, 182, 186, 187, 192–194, 217, 260, 267–269, 277, 398
Koorland, M. A., 593
Kootz, J. P., 170
Konstantareas, M. M., 45, 166
Korein, J., 473, 478
Koriath, U., 277
Koscher, G. P., 270, 271
Kosier, T., 57
Kotanchik, N. J., 629
Kotelchuck, M., 251
Kotsopoulos, S., 53, 94
Kovacs, M., 73, 99, 100, 436–438, 515, 518
Kozol, J., 588, 605
Kraft, I. A., 474
Krakenbuhl, V., 99
Kramer, E., 606
Kramer, J., 120, 121
Kramer, R., 472, 473
Krantz, M., 86
Krasner, L., 236
Kratochwill, T. R., 536, 537
Kravitz, H., 247, 248
Kraybill, E. N., 343
Kreitman, N., 338
Kreuzer, E., 469
Krishnappa, U., 475
Krouse, J. P., 139, 300, 318

Kruesi, M. P. J., 316
Kruger, S. D., 244
Kugler, M., 265
Kukla, A., 82
Kumashiro, I. H., 177
Kupietz, S., 465, 472, 478, 559
Kurtis, L. B., 478
Kurtz, M. A., 465
Kydd, R. R., 185, 192, 194–196

Labbe, E., 541
Lachar, D., 435
Lachin, J. M., 344
Lacey, B., 117
Ladd, G., 538
Lader, M., 233
LaDouceur, R., 629
La Franchi, S., 248
Lagercrantz, R., 241
La Greca, A. M., 77, 84–86, 141, 538
Lahey, B. B., 16, 46, 78, 83, 90, 114, 123, 352, 439, 529, 531, 534
Laird, J. D., 625
Lamb, M. E., 333, 346, 353
Lambert, N. M., 123, 124, 141
Lamont, J., 375
Lamparski, D., 535
Lampen, E., 465
Lamprecht, F., 139, 302
Landau, S., 87, 115, 116, 120, 123, 133, 135–138, 144, 402
Landino, S. A., 37
Landry, S. H., 165
Laneve, R. S., 603
Lang, M., 436
Lang, P., 432, 433
Langer, D., 468, 469
Langham, R. A., 636
Langhorne, J., 115, 318–320
Langner, G. S., 365
Lansing, M. D., 603
Lapierre, Y. D., 468
Lapouse, R., 53, 97, 243, 398
Laprade, K., 115, 141, 429
Larcen, S. W., 629
Largo, R. H., 260, 261, 264
Lasagna, L., 465
Lask, B., 518
Lasko, J. K., 353
Lassen, M. E., 528
Latham, S., 578
Laties, V., 460
Latimer, P., 442, 443

Laufer, M. W., 111, 131
Laurence, K. M., 306
La Vietes, R. L., 595
Lavigne, J. V., 627
Lavik, N. J., 408
Layman, D., 534
Lazar, I., 626
Lazarus, A., 529
Lazarus, P. J., 79, 83
Lazarus, R. S., 444
LeBaron, S. W. M., 213, 276, 301
Lebowitz, N., 248
Lechman, J. F., 302
Leckman, J. F., 92, 243–246, 479, 480
Ledingham, J., 40, 83, 87, 98
Lee, C. Z., 631
Lee, D., 248
Lee, R., 643
Lefkowitz, M., 54, 59, 74, 78, 83, 87, 99, 439, 473
Lehtinen, L., 111, 304, 319, 591
Leifer, A. D., 342
Leigh, D., 236
Lemert, E. M., 411
Lennox, C., 177, 193
Leon, G. R., 436, 439
Lerer, M. P., 468
Lerer, R. J., 468
Lerner, R. M., 517
Lesowitz, M., 640
Lesser, G. S., 647
Lesser, L. I., 469
Lesser, R., 248
Levene, M. I., 309
Leventhal, T., 352
Levin, G. R., 42
Levine, A. G., 363
Levine, M. D., 264–266
Levinson, R. B., 37, 45, 577
Levitt, E., 498–500, 505
Levy, D., 249
Levy, F., 116
Lewis, C. C., 349, 350
Lewis, D. O., 559
Lewis, J. M., 559
Lewis, M., 98, 559, 570
Lewis, S., 534
Lewiston, N. J., 235
Lewitt, H., 247
Libet, J., 545
Licht, M. H., 429
Liddle, G. P., 82
Liebert, D. E., 87

Liebert, R. M., 528
Liebman, R., 254, 518
Liebowitz, M. R., 476
Liederman, P. H., 342
Liem, J. H., 193
Light, R., 513
Lilienfeld, A. M., 305, 357
Lindbergh, C., 366
Lindenthal, J. J., 194
Lindgren, S. D., 58
Lindholm, B. W., 17
Lindsay, R., 80
Lindsley, O., 593
Ling, W., 437
Links, P. S., 17, 53
Lipman, R. S., 460
Lippe, B. M., 254
Lipowski, Z. J., 212, 214, 216, 217, 295
Lipsky, A., 75
Littner, N., 241
Lloyd, J., 256, 259, 589, 593
Lobitz, G. R., 339, 356, 357
Lobovits, D. A., 95
Lochman, J. E., 629
Lockner, A. W., 474
Lockwood, J. L., 510, 511, 514
Lockyer, L., 163, 177, 180, 181, 248
Loda, F., 343
Loeber, R., 13, 35, 353, 362, 364, 393, 492
Loigman, J. V., 627
Loiselle, D., 138, 175
Loney, J., 57, 112–116, 123–125, 129, 135, 136, 138, 142–144, 318, 319, 320, 431
Long, J. S., 441, 549
Long, N., 600, 601, 603
Looker, A., 473
Lordi, W., 176
Lorr, M., 2
Lott, I., 465
Lotter, V., 160, 163, 177, 178, 181
Lotyczewski, B. S., 628
Louria, D. S., 194
Lourie, R., 248, 249, 563
Lovaas, O. I., 165, 169, 171, 174, 248–250, 440, 441, 525, 527, 528, 545, 546, 548–550
Love, C. T., 46, 643
Love, L. R., 357
Loveland, K. A., 165
Lovibund, S., 261, 263
Lovitt, T. C., 593

Lowe, M., 17
Lowe, T. L., 438
Lubar, J. F., 470
Lucas, A., 243–246, 474
Lucci, D., 164
Lucy, P., 165
Ludlow, C., 467, 468
Ludwig, R. P., 78, 79, 83
Luiselli, J. D., 535
Lundbing, U., 92
Lutati, U., 474
Lynch, G., 140
Lyons, A. E., 121
Lydgate, T., 643
Lytton, H., 350, 358

Maccoby, E. E., 348, 349, 351, 357
Maccoby, M., 335, 346
Maccoby, N., 228, 631
MacDonald, K., 270
MacDonald, L., 274
Macedo, C. A., 50
Machabanski, H., 17
Mack, J. L., 45
MacMillan, D. L., 586
Maddux, J. E., 623
Magnussen, M. G., 629
Magnusson, D., 18, 397
Magrat, P., 443, 634
Mahler, M., 176, 243–245
Mahoney, D., 261
Major, S. M., 584
Major-Kingsley, S., 584
Maletzky, B. M., 472
Maliphant, R., 407, 409
Maloney, M. J., 252–254, 258, 259
Malouf, R., 363
Mandell, W., 262
Mann, D., 40
Mann, R. A., 264
Mannarino, A. P., 629
Margolis, R., 477
Marinelli, B., 170
Markell, R. A., 77
Markman, H. J., 506
Markova, I., 270
Marlowe, M., 313
Marsden, G., 513
Marsh, R. W., 466
Marshall, I. A., 305, 308, 311
Marshall, J. M., 304
Marshall, W. K., 475
Marten, S., 338
Martens, L. W., 631

Martin, B., 335, 357, 360
Martin, J., 471
Martin, J. A., 348, 349, 351, 357
Martin, J. E., 115, 121, 123
Martin, L. H., 558
Martinez-Brawley, E. E., 646
Marx, N., 476
Mash, E. J., 133–135
Massimo, J. L., 644
Masterpasqua, F., 641, 642
Masters, J. C., 80
Maslow, A., 604
Mason, W., 241, 249, 250
Matarazzo, J. D., 630
Matas, L., 345
Mathews, A., 243, 245
Matson, J. L., 436, 529, 534, 536, 538
Mattes, J., 460, 466, 469
Matthew, D., 518
Matthews, C. V., 82
Matthews, W., 170, 185
Mattison, R., 21, 24, 277
Maughan, B., 413
Maurer, A., 524
Maurer, R. G., 173, 175, 176, 320, 321
Mawby, R. I., 401, 403
Maxwell, A. E., 17
May, D. R., 396
Mayer, J., 256–259
Mayfield, A., 374
Mayhew, G., 525
Mayville, W. J., 543
Mazonson, P., 266
McAllister, A. L., 228, 631
McCabe, K. D., 178
McCandless, B., 432
McCarthy, D. P., 648
McCaulay, M., 89
McConnell, S. C., 528
McConville, B. J., 374
McCord, J., 341, 356
McCord, W., 341, 356
McCray, D. S., 121, 123, 129
McCrimmon, D. J., 197
McCubbin, H. I., 335, 337
McCulloch, J. W., 401
McCutcheon, S., 444
McDermott, J., 241, 242
McDowell, R. L., 589
McFie, J., 296, 319, 320
McGaw, B., 606
McGee, R., 18, 37, 38, 41, 93, 115, 124, 125, 135, 141, 142, 260, 307, 318

McGillicuddy-DeLisi, A. V., 335
McGillivray, J., 168, 169, 189
McGimsey, J., 463, 525
McGraw, M., 261
McGrew, J., 465
McGuffog, C., 98
McKay, H. D., 362, 406, 407
McKeith, R., 260
McKinney, J. D., 584
McKnew, D., 76, 374, 437, 438
McLonghlin, E., 638
McMahon, R. C., 116, 135, 314
McNamara, J., 438
McNeil, T. F., 315
McNay, A., 158, 172, 186
McQueen, M. M., 592
McTaggart, A., 265
Meadow, R., 261
Meadow, S., 260
Meadows, C. E., 402
Meadows, L., 366
Medenis, R., 534
Mednick, S., 48, 344, 357, 397
Mehl, R., 473
Meichenbaum, D., 526
Meier, M., 477
Melamed, B., 432–435, 528, 536
Melamed, E., 634
Melton, D., 605
Menlove, F., 434
Menywk, P., 165
Meo, G., 465
Mergler, N. L., 81
Merikangas, K. R., 92, 338
Merlis, S., 477
Merschmann, W., 397
Mesibov, G. B., 398
Meskin, L. H., 631
Metcalf, D., 213
Metcalf, M., 465
Methven, R. J., 23, 53, 94, 185, 267
Metz, J., 239
Meyer, J. H., 513
Michael, C. M., 87
Michael, S. T., 365
Michaels, J., 262
Michel, D. E., 606
Michelli, F. A., 466
Michelman, J. D., 185
Michelson, L., 77, 509, 514, 515
Miezitis, S., 629
Mikkelsen, E. J., 261, 264, 461, 463, 465, 468
Miklich, D. R., 444
Milburn, J., 538

Milich, R., 87, 115, 116, 120, 121, 123, 133, 135–138, 142–144
Milkovich, L., 401
Miller, A. L., 425
Miller, H., 237
Miller, L. C., 424, 433–435, 497
Miller, M. L., 439
Miller, N. E., 443
Miller, V., 636
Miller, W. B., 404, 410
Millichap, J., 300
Milliones, J., 341
Millon, T., 4
Mills, C. M., 644
Minde, K., 121, 124, 134, 271, 298, 465, 468
Miner, G., 427
Minichiello, M. D., 50
Minkin, N., 570
Minty, G., 37
Minuchin, S., 360, 518
Mirels, H. L., 643
Mischel, H. N., 121
Mischel, W., 121
Mitchel, C., 121
Mitchele, E. L., 50
Mitchell, S., 59, 61, 399
Mittelmark, M. B., 631
Mizushima, K., 18
Moelis, I., 357
Moffat, S., 543
Moldofsky, H., 480
Moller, H., 595
Molling, P. A., 474
Monahan, T. F., 367
Monk, M. A., 53, 97, 243, 398
Monkman, M. M., 561–563
Montagu, J., 301
Montgomery, L., 433
Moore, D. R., 61
Moore, J., 45
Moore, L., 637
Moos, R. H., 344
Moquin, L. E., 529
Morash, M., 404
Morgenstern, G., 118, 121, 468
Mori, L., 624, 633
Morris, D. P., 87
Morris, E., 243
Morris, J. N., 407
Morris, R. J., 536, 537, 584
Morrison, A., 359
Morrison, R. L., 243–246
Morse, W. C., 583, 589, 590, 600–602, 606

Mortimer, E. A., 270
Mortimore, P., 413
Morton, J., 402
Mosher, L. R., 185
Moses, J. A., 42
Moss, H. A., 91, 343, 353
Mowrer, O., 261, 263
Mowrer, W., 261, 263
Mrazek, P. B., 273
Muelkler, C. W., 395
Mueller, C. W., 367
Mueller, H. F., 47
Muellner, S., 261, 263
Mukai, L. H., 61
Mulligan, D. G., 396
Mullins, L. L., 79, 89
Mundy, P., 515
Munson, R. F., 559
Murphy, D., 302
Murphy, J., 248
Murray, E. J., 359, 361, 372, 373
Murray, M., 225, 228

Nace, E., 237
Nadelman, L., 353
Najem, G. R., 194
Nakamura, C., 433, 434
Nandy, S., 53, 94
Narrol, H., 80
Nasby, W., 38
Nathan, P. E., 4
Naylor, H., 470
Neale, J. M., 87, 360
Neafsey, S., 163
Nee, J., 20
Needleman, H. L., 313
Neill, A., 588, 605
Nelson, B., 338
Nelson, R. O., 551
Nelson, W. M., 426
Ness, A. E., 559
Neuberger, F. H., 251
Neuhaus, E. C., 237
Newcomer, P. L., 589
Newman, J., 39, 116, 117, 120, 121, 130, 131, 296, 320
Newman, R. G., 595, 600–602, 606
Newman, S., 177, 398
Newman, V. S., 604
Newsom, C., 440, 442, 544, 546
Nezuroglu, F. A., 478
Nicholls, J. G., 81
Nichols, P., 139, 298, 299, 307, 316, 318–321, 344
Nicol, A. R., 46, 268, 269, 402

Nidiffer, F. D., 545
Nielson, G., 578
Niklowitz, W. J., 312
Nisi, A., 18, 429
Niswander, K., 307
Noble, H., 434, 435
Norton, J., 178
Norton, P., 632
North-Jones, M., 129
Norwood, R., 79
Nottelmann, E. D., 78, 81
Nowicki, S., 647
Noyes, R., 368
Nucci, L. P., 39
Nuttall, E., 352
Nuttall, R., 352
Nye, F. I., 341, 365, 396
Nyman, L., 176
Nystul, M. S., 354

O'Connor, M., 49, 92
O'Connor, N., 165, 167, 168, 170
O'Connor, R. D., 537
O'Connor, S., 634
Odle, D., 375
O'Donnell, C. R., 643
O'Donnell, J. P., 17, 18
Offord, D. R., 40
Oftedal, G., 437
Ogdow, D., 176
Oglesby, D. M., 123, 126, 127, 129
O'Hagan, F. J., 404
Ohlin, L. E., 411
Ojemann, R. H., 630
O'Leary, K. D., 18, 356, 359–361, 372, 423, 425–431, 435, 446, 531, 599
Olds, M. E., 51
Oleinick, M. S., 357
Ollendick, T. H., 76, 82, 524
Olson, D. H., 335, 336, 338, 339
Oltmanns, T. F., 359, 360
Olweus, D., 54, 55, 339, 356
O'Malley, J. E., 270
O'Malley, P. M., 225, 226, 408
Omori, H., 584
Omori-Gordon, H., 584
Oppel, W., 260–262
Oppenheim, A., 177, 399
Ornitz, E., 157, 158, 162, 169, 172, 175, 178, 185, 248
Orris, J. B., 43, 44
Orvaschel, H., 344, 438
Osborn, S. G., 409
Osborne, J. R., 559

O'Shea, L., 641
Osofsky, J. D., 370
Ostrom, T. M., 643
Ottinger, D. R., 641
O'Tuama, L. S., 430
Ounsted, C., 158, 172, 177, 186, 217, 248, 398
Ouston, J., 396, 401, 402, 413
Ovenstone, I. M. K., 338
Overall, J. E., 460
Owen, C., 54
Owen, F., 238
Oxman, J., 166

Pabst, P., 75
Packard, D., 546
Padian, N., 438
Page, J. G., 466
Paine, R., 319
Painter, P., 316
Palkes, H., 124
Palmer, J., 248
Palmer, R. C., 252–255
Palmer, T., 573, 574, 578
Palmero, D., 432
Palomares, U., 630
Panella, D., 44, 85, 86
Pappanikou, A. J., 590
Pappas, B. A., 116, 131–133, 138, 139
Parcel, T. L., 395
Pareskevopoulos, I. V., 17, 18
Parke, R. D., 357
Parker, J. B., 86
Parker, J. B., Jr., 301
Parker, G., 193, 368–370, 375
Parkin, J., 257
Parraga, H., 273, 275
Parry, P., 126, 128–130
Parsons, B. V., 363, 644
Pasamanick, B., 179, 180, 244, 296, 305, 317
Pasley, F. C., 474
Paternite, C., 115, 135, 138, 142, 318
Patterson, G. R., 334, 335, 337, 339, 351, 352, 354–359, 362–364, 426–428, 446, 539, 585
Patterson, J. M., 335, 337
Patterson, P., 37
Pattison, E. M., 247
Paul, G. L., 498, 505, 506
Paul, J. L., 590
Paulauskas, S. L., 73, 99, 120, 133, 135, 137, 438
Pauls, D. L., 92, 244, 245, 368

Paulsen, K. A., 39
Pearce, J., 186, 479
Pearch, P., 474
Pearlin, L., 337
Pearlman, D. S., 235, 236, 238, 240
Pearlson, J., 257
Pedersen, F., 300, 339
Pederson, F. A., 343
Pedro-Carroll, J. L., 632
Pekarik, E. G., 87
Pelham, W., 122, 133, 136–138, 429, 531
Penick, E. C., 437
Pennington, B. F., 513
Peoples, A., 546
Pepler, D., 353
Perlman, T., 467
Perloff, B. F., 545
Perry, C., 228, 631
Perry, D., 16, 158, 161
Perry, J. D., 363
Perry, R., 176
Persson-Blennow, I., 318
Peters, J., 112, 296, 299
Peters, J. E., 276
Peters, J. F., 465
Peters, K. L., 298
Peters, K. W., 117–121, 123–128
Peters, S., 139, 465, 466
Petersen, C. R., 530
Peterson, C., 79
Peterson, D. R., 9, 17, 26, 41, 45, 187, 310, 424, 425, 435, 441
Peterson, J. L., 360, 364
Peterson, L., 623, 624, 630, 633, 634, 637, 639, 642
Peterson, S. J., 405
Petti, T. A., 76, 436–438, 536
Petty, C. S., 222, 223
Petty, L. K., 185
Pezzott-Pearce, T., 186, 479
Pfadt, A., 122
Phillips, E. A., 570
Phillips, E. C., 570
Phillips, E. L., 570, 596
Phillips, L., 583, 596
Phillips, M. A., 559
Phillips, P., 257
Phillips, V. A., 559
Phillips, W., 39
Pickar, J., 640
Pierce, E. W., 134
Pierce, J. V., 82
Pierce, S., 165

Piggot, L. R., 175
Pilkonis, P., 79
Pillai, V., 473
Pinkerton, P., 270
Pinnell, L. E., 298
Pittfield, M., 177
Platt, J. E., 473
Platt, J. J., 627
Pless, I. B., 235, 270
Plomin, R., 48, 49, 91, 92, 314, 315
Plunkett, J. W., 513
Plutchik, R., 372, 373
Podosin, R. L., 469
Poitras-Wright, H., 466
Pokrzywinsky, J., 249
Polizos, P., 472, 477
Pollack, E., 465, 466, 471
Pollock, M., 99
Pon, J., 559
Pond, D. A., 297, 317
Pontius, W., 162
Pope, H., 367
Porges, S. W., 116, 117, 131, 132, 170
Porrino, C. J., 122
Porrino, L. J., 469
Porter, B., 359–361, 372
Post, R. M., 473
Postl, B., 225
Postman, N., 605
Potter, H. W., 181
Poulos, R. W., 528
Poushinsky, M. F., 40
Powell, B. A., 634
Power, M. J., 407
Pozanski, E. O., 438
Pozdnjakoff, I., 558
Poznanski, E. O., 77, 99
Prabhu, A. N., 139, 300
Prechtl, H., 307
Prell, D. B., 92
Prentice, N. M., 39, 356, 595
Press, E., 221
Press, M., 465
Price, C. H., 531
Price, K. P., 79
Prieto, A., 595
Prinz, R. J., 35, 77, 116, 136, 299
Prichep, L. S., 470
Primavera, J., 632
Prior, M., 16, 158, 161–165, 167–171, 173, 174, 176, 179–181, 189, 191
Prior, N., 161
Procter, J. T., 267, 269

Proshek, J., 631
Prugh, D. G., 583, 633
Prugh, D. H., 213–215
Prusoff, B. A., 92
Puig-Antich, J., 273, 438, 472, 473, 476, 515
Pulkkinen, L., 351, 359
Purcell, K., 235–240
Purcell, L., 443
Purohit, A. P., 263, 374
Putallaz, M., 502

Quay, H. C., 11, 13, 17, 18, 26, 36–39, 41, 43, 45–47, 51, 53, 78, 90, 96, 97, 112, 115, 140, 141, 160, 162, 187, 310, 319, 321, 358, 424, 425, 435, 441, 515, 559, 560, 583, 592, 643
Quinn, P., 139, 300, 302, 320, 472
Quinton, D., 408
Quirk, J., 604
Quitkin, F., 192, 459

Radosh, A., 119
Rafaelsen, J., 473, 478
Raging, N., 344
Ragozin, A. S., 339
Rahe, R. H., 443
Raine, A., 46
Rainwater, N., 240
Ramon, E., 509
Ramsden, R., 541
Ramsey-Klee, D. M., 343
Rancurello, M. D., 436, 437
Randolph, D., 603
Rank, B., 157, 176
Rapoport, J., 75, 115, 124, 125, 131, 138–140, 224, 262–264, 300, 302, 315, 316, 320, 461, 463, 465, 467–469, 471, 473, 475
Rappaport, J., 625, 644
Raps, C. S., 79
Raskin, A., 375
Rasmussen, B., 86
Rasmussen, P., 138
Ratcliff, K. S., 394
Ratcliffe, S. G., 314
Ratcliffe, W. D., 646
Ratzeburg, F., 591
Raubolt, R. R., 559
Rauh, J., 257
Rausch, A., 645
Ray, J. S., 95
Read, P. B., 623

Reatig, N. A., 375
Reckless, W. C., 404
Redick, R. W., 558
Redl, F., 600–602
Redman-Lavin, D., 513
Redner, R., 559
Rees, L., 236, 237, 239
Reese, R. R., 84
Reeves, J. C., 138, 140, 299, 318, 462
Regan, R. A., 352, 365
Rehm, L. P., 79
Reich, W., 76, 426
Reichler, R. J., 171, 603
Reid, H. P., 584
Reid, J., 362, 364, 476
Reimer, D. J., 408
Reimer, E., 605
Reimhera, F. W., 142
Reinert, H. R., 589
Reiser, D., 176
Reisinger, J. J., 627
Reiss, D., 192, 335
Reitan, R., 217, 298, 303
Remotigne-Ano, N., 509
Remschmidt, H., 25, 397
Renne, C. M., 543
Repp, A., 547
Reuterman, N. A., 45
Reynard, C. L., 465, 469
Reynolds, E., 473
Reynolds, N., 627
Reynolds, R., 468
Reynolds, W. M., 436, 439
Rezmerski, V. E., 599
Rezmovic, E. L., 559
Reznick, J. S., 90, 91
Rheingold, H. L., 625
Rhodes, W. C., 588, 595
Rich, H. L., 587
Richard, B. A., 89
Richard, H. C., 39
Richard, K., 86
Richards, R. T., 298
Richardson, I., 177, 186
Richardson, L. M., 398
Richer, J., 174
Richman, L. C., 38
Richman, N., 53, 55, 56, 135, 138,
  140, 142, 143, 274, 397, 402
Rickel, A. U., 625, 627
Ricks, D. M., 165, 168
Ricks, M., 170
Ridberg, E. H., 372
Riddle, D., 472

Riddle, K., 124, 125
Rider, R., 260, 262
Ridley-Johnson, R., 633
Rie, H. E., 123
Rieder, R., 344
Riess, B. F., 352
Rifkin, A., 192, 459
Rimland, B., 160, 162, 177, 179, 440,
  478
Rinconer, A., 166, 171, 442, 526, 528,
  530, 545, 546, 548
Risher, M., 436
Risley, T., 523, 525, 627
Ritchey, W. G., 77
Ritchey, W. L., 86
Ritter, B., 534
Ritvo, E., 157, 158, 161, 162, 169,
  175, 178, 248, 302
Ritvo, S., 243
Rivier, M., 139
Rivinus, T. M., 216
Roberts, A. H., 39
Roberts, M. C., 392, 513, 623, 633,
  638, 639, 642, 649
Roberts, R., 319
Robertson, C. M., 298
Robertson, L. S., 647, 649
Robin, S. S., 141, 398
Robins, C. N., 61, 62, 64, 100
Robins, E., 338
Robins, L., 87, 394, 397
Robinson, E., 468
Robinson, E. A., 519
Robinson, E. J., 123
Robinson, H., 309
Robinson, N., 309
Robinson, M. J., 644
Robinson, N. M., 339
Robinson, W. S., 409
Robson, K. S., 343
Roche, A. F., 460
Rockett, D., 408
Rodgers, R., 332
Rodick, J. D., 61
Rodriguez, A., 465
Roff, J. D., 58, 395, 405
Rogeness, G. A., 50, 51
Rogers, C., 604
Rogers, M. A., 305, 317, 535
Rogers, R. W., 631
Rogers, T. R., 426
Roitzsch, J., 433
Rojek, D. G., 393
Rolf, J., 56, 84, 98, 140, 623

Romanczyk, R. G., 427
Romine, J., 299
Roper, A. H., 301
Roper, B. L., 498
Rose, S. D., 515
Rose, T. L., 593
Rosenbaum, A., 531
Rosenblad, C., 430
Rosenblood, L. K., 643
Rosenbloom, L., 217
Rosenbloom, N., 267
Rosenbloom, S., 176
Rosenblum, E. L., 541
Rosenblum, N. D., 535
Rosenheim, E., 509, 511
Rosenthal, J. H., 470
Rosenthal, R. H., 116–119, 131, 132
Rosenthal, V., 248
Roseman, D., 473
Rosenberg, B. G., 352
Rosenberg, M., 365
Rosetti-Fereira, M. C., 274
Rosman, B., 39, 82, 86, 121
Ross, A. O., 524, 539
Ross, D. M., 111, 112, 114, 117, 118,
  122, 125, 130, 133, 140, 142, 143,
  313, 321, 531
Ross, J. M., 396, 398
Ross, M. S., 480
Ross, R. R., 559
Ross, S. A., 111, 112, 114, 117, 118,
  122, 125, 130, 133, 140, 142, 143,
  313, 321, 531
Roth, M., 217
Rothbart, M. K., 353
Rothman, E. P., 595, 599
Rothschild, G. H., 465, 472, 473
Rothstein, A., 186
Roukema, R. W., 478
Routh, D., 116, 319, 430
Routledge, M., 228
Rovine, M., 339
Rowland, V., 260–262
Rowlands, O., 408
Rowley, V. N., 355
Royal, G. P., 649
Rozelle, R. M., 631
Rubenstein, B. D., 528
Rubin, K. H., 84, 85, 88
Rudel, R. G., 276
Rump, E. E., 55, 99
Rumsey, J. M., 224, 315, 316
Rush, A. J., 217, 511
Rush, D., 636

Russell, A. T., 21
Russell, C. S., 335
Russell, J. A., 227
Russo, D., 540
Rutman, J., 437
Rutter, M., 4, 6, 25, 37, 40, 49, 52, 77,
    78, 93, 96, 112, 115, 138–141, 157,
    158, 162–164, 168, 170, 171, 174,
    175, 177, 180–182, 192–194, 213,
    215, 218, 235, 248, 260, 262, 264,
    270–272, 276, 277, 295–301,
    303–305, 308, 311–315, 317–321,
    337, 341, 352, 354–356, 359, 361,
    363, 365, 366, 372, 397, 398, 400,
    402, 408–410, 413, 440, 502–504,
    511, 515, 559, 578, 624, 650
Ruttenberg, B., 162
Ryder, R. G., 339, 367

Sabatino, D. A., 310
Sachar, E. J., 477
Safer, D., 318, 432, 460
Sajwaj, T., 545
Salend, S. J., 559
Saletu, B., 477
Saletu, M., 477
Sallows, G., 357
Sallustro, F., 247
Sambursky, J., 310
Sameroff, A., 140, 296–298, 305,
    309, 316–318, 344, 374
Samit, C., 477
Sandberg, S. T., 35, 115, 123, 135,
    138
Sandler, J., 77
Sandoval, J., 123, 124, 141
Sanson, A., 180
Santogrossi, D., 427, 538
Santrock, J. W., 363, 365, 366
Saraf, K., 465, 471
Sarason, I. G., 406
Sarason, S. B., 78, 81, 304
Sargent, J., 254
Sasman, J., 375
Sassone, D., 141
Satterfield, J. H., 125
Satterfield, B. T., 131, 301
Satterfield, H. H., 142, 144
Satterfield, J. H., 131, 301, 320, 469,
    470
Satir, V., 337, 338
Sattler, J. M., 37
Satz, P., 211, 213, 295, 303, 320, 584
Saul, R. E., 469
Sauls, R. J., 474

Saylor, C. A., 644
Scarr, S., 376
Schacher, R., 112, 115, 116, 138, 140,
    142
Schachter, J., 344
Schact, T., 4
Schacter, F., 306
Schaefer, C., 444
Schaefer, H., 248, 250
Schaeffer, B., 528, 545
Schaffer, H. R., 350
Schaffner, W., 638
Schain, R. J., 465, 469, 559, 578
Schaughency, B. S., 16
Schaughency, E. A., 114
Schaumann, H., 180
Scheib, J., 465
Scheirer, M. H., 559
Schell, A. M., 142
Schell, D., 463
Scherer, M., 433, 434
Scherman, A., 338
Schinke, S. P., 631
Schleifer, M., 121, 135, 143, 467
Schlossman, S., 642
Schmaling, K., 13, 35, 364
Schmeltzer, D. J., 465
Schmidt, A. A., 577
Schmidt, K., 47
Schoettle, U. C., 515
Scholten, C. A., 118
Schooler, C., 337, 354
Schopler, E., 170, 171, 177, 603
Schrader, S. M., 629
Schrag, P., 112, 466
Schrager, J. B., 121
Schribanau, N., 302
Schriebmann, L., 165, 171
Schroeder, C. S., 430
Schubert, D. S. P., 352
Schubert, H. J., 352
Schuck, S., 45
Schuckit, M. A., 227
Schulman, D., 473
Schulman, F. R., 357
Schulman, H. C., 425
Schulman, J. L., 296, 319, 633
Schulsinger, F., 344
Schulterbrandt, J. G., 375
Schuman, H., 343
Schumsky, D., 257
Schwartz, D., 253
Schwartz, J. L., 166
Schwartz, L., 468, 472, 473
Schwartz, M., 80

Schwartzman, A. E., 40, 83, 87, 98
Schwarz, J. C., 121, 372, 373, 376
Scott, A., 225, 228
Scott, J., 468
Scott, M., 265
Scott, T. J., 44
Sears, R. R., 506
Seat, P. D., 435
Sechrest, L., 559
Segal, B., 227
Seidel, U. P., 305, 311
Seidman, E., 644
Seifer, R., 344
Seligman, M. E. P., 79
Selinger, H. V., 629
Sellin, T., 393
Selman, R. L., 513
Selz, M., 217
Serbin, L., 87
Sergeant, J. A., 118
Seymour, F., 266, 274
Shaffer, D., 4, 25, 35, 112, 114, 262,
    296, 311, 319–321, 481, 503, 509
Shah, A., 161, 179–181
Shamsie, S. J., 47
Shanock, S. S., 559
Shantz, C. U., 88
Shapiro, A., 244, 245, 479, 480
Shapiro, D., 243
Shapiro, E., 244, 245, 479, 480
Shapiro, S., 496
Shapiro, T., 165, 473, 477, 478
Shapland, J. M., 404
Share, D., 41
Sharp, K. C., 627
Sharpe, L., 468
Shavelson, R., 642
Shaw, B. F., 511
Shaw, C. R., 362, 406, 407
Shaw, G. K., 338
Shaw, K., 86
Shaywitz, A., 175
Shaywitz, B. A., 139, 320, 479, 480
Shaywitz, C., 175
Shaywitz, S. E., 139
Shea, T. M., 589
Shea, V. T., 469
Shearn, D., 603
Shekim, W. O., 139, 476
Shen, C. D., 138, 175
Shepherd, M., 4, 399
Shereshefsky, P. M., 339, 343
Sheriek, I., 507, 514
Sherman, D., 336
Sherman, T., 190, 191

Sherry, T., 49, 92
Shields, J., 344
Shigetomi, C., 76, 634
Shinohara, M., 18
Shoemaker, D. J., 357
Shore, M. F., 644
Shores, R. E., 592
Short, J. F., 396, 404
Shouse, M. N., 470
Shrader, W. K., 352
Shrier, D. K., 368
Shuller, D., 435
Shuman, B. J., 641
Shuman, H. H., 634
Shure, M. B., 627
Shutter, L., 259
Siddle, D. A. T., 46
Siedenberg, M., 213
Siegel, A. W., 79
Siegel, L., 79, 434, 528, 634
Sigal, J. J., 518
Sigman, M., 166, 168
Signorato, V., 474
Sigvardsson, S., 48, 92
Silberfeld, M., 368
Silbergeld, E. K., 320
Silberman, C., 605
Silva, P., 18, 37, 38, 41, 93, 115, 139, 260, 307
Silver, M., 254
Silverman, S., 443
Silvern, L., 89
Silverstone, J., 258
Simeon, J., 477
Simonds, J. F., 94, 273, 275
Simmons, J., 250
Simmons, J. J., 42
Simmons, J. Q., 525, 528, 545, 548, 549
Simmons, J. S., 512
Simonelli, V. M., 474
Simpson, A., 139
Simpson, E., 237
Simpson, H. R., 398
Singer, J., 648
Singer, S., 35, 112, 466
Singh, N. N., 250, 251, 276, 545
Single, E., 406
Skeels, H. M., 625
Skinner, B. F., 524
Skodak, M., 625
Skrzypek, G. J., 43
Skynner, A. C., 474
Slaby, R. G., 354
Slakter, M. J., 631

Slater, E., 338
Slater, P. M., 270
Sleator, E. K., 429, 469
Slinkard, L. A., 631
Sloan, W., 300
Sloman, L., 466
Slymen, D., 368
Small, A. M., 115, 477, 478
Small, J. G., 171
Smith, A., 112, 295, 413
Smith, D., 535
Smith, G., 307
Smith, J. B., 338
Smith, J. M., 589, 606
Smith, K. M., 116, 117, 131, 132
Smith, M. L., 550, 606, 648
Smith, N. J., 401
Smith, R. L., 625
Smith, R. S., 343, 353, 362
Smith, S. L., 371
Smith, T. E., 631
Smyth, R. A., 45
Snidman, N., 91
Snowling, M., 166
Sobel, D. E., 344
Sobesky, W., 89
Sobol, M., 126, 468
Sobotka, K. R., 496, 497, 507–509, 512
Sohmer, H., 170
Solanto, M. V., 47
Soll, S., 241
Solnick, J., 530, 544
Solomon, G., 244
Solomons, G., 131
Soltys, J. J., 465
Solyom, C., 368
Solyom, L., 368, 475
Sonis, W. A., 536
Soroker, E., 87
Sorosky, A., 248
Sostek, A. J., 468, 634
Sowards, S. K., 559
Specter, G. A., 622
Speilberger, C. D., 81
Spencer, A., 272
Spencer, C., 310
Sperling, M., 261, 595
Sperry, B. M., 595
Spics, H. W., 310
Spiker, D., 170
Spinell, A., 628
Spitz, R., 249
Spitzer, R. L., 20, 438
Spivack, G., 435, 627

Spivey, P. B., 338
Sponholz, R., 249
Sporrel, T., 299
Sprague, R. L., 141, 303, 425, 429, 465, 468, 469, 471, 592
Sprenkle, D. H., 335
Spring, C., 430, 465, 468
Spurlock, J., 241
Sroufe, L. A., 345, 347, 351, 370
Stainback, R. D., 631
Stapp, J., 467
Staruch, K. S., 270
Stattin, H., 397
Stayton, D. J., 349, 350, 369
Stechler, G., 374
Steel, C. M., 643
Steffy, R. A., 197
Steg, J. P., 139
Stegmiller, H., 310
Stein, M. A., 17, 18
Stein, Z., 260–262
Steinberg, G. G., 469
Steinberg, H. R., 469
Steinhausen, H. C., 241, 242, 270, 271
Steinmetz, S., 362
Stempniak, M., 123
Stenhausen, H., 469
Stephenson, G., 560
Stepherd, M., 319
Stern, J., 127, 129, 306
Stern, L., 76
Stern, P. R., 595
Stevens, B., 507
Stevens, D. J., 603
Stevens, P., 401
Stevens-Long, J., 166, 169
Stevenson, J., 53, 135, 274, 397
Stewart, D. J., 42
Stewart, I. A., 139
Stewart, M. A., 35, 36, 53, 57, 115, 117, 124, 168
Stoddard, P., 537
Stokes, T., 550
Stolberg, A., 365, 515, 516, 632
Stolz, S. B., 624
Stone, A., 472, 473
Stone, B., 368
Stone, W. L., 84
Stores, G., 311, 461, 462, 473
Stork, P., 77, 84, 85
Stouthamer-Loeber, M., 355
Stouwie, R., 372
Strain, P. S., 86
Strassmann, L. H., 500, 503, 504

Straus, M. A., 362
Strauss, A., 111, 114, 304, 319, 591
Strauss, C. C., 16, 78, 83, 439
Strauss, J., 344, 583
Strecker, E. A., 310
Stringfield, S., 435
Strober, M., 21, 94, 97
Strodtbeck, F. L., 404
Strother, C. R., 563
Strupp, H. H., 497, 511
Stuart, R. B., 539
Student, M., 170
Stultze, W., 260, 261, 264
Stunkard, A. J., 259
Sturm, R., 313
Sudia, E. C., 364
Sullivan, C., 8, 572
Sullivan, H. S., 497, 512
Sullivan, K., 40
Sullivan, L., 437
Sulzbacher, S. I., 470
Susser, M., 260–262, 264
Sutherland, E. H., 410
Sutherland, R. L., 563
Sutker, P. B., 221, 226
Sutton, S., 470
Sutton-Smith, B., 352
Sverd, J., 299, 313, 478
Sveri, K., 403
Swain, J. J., 631
Swan, A. V., 225
Swan, H., 637
Swan, W. W., 604
Swaney, S., 636
Swanson, J., 116, 117, 126, 133,
    467–469
Swap, S., 595
Sweet, R., 244
Swift, M., 435, 641, 642
Swift, W. J., 255, 256
Switzer, B. R., 636
Sykes, D. H., 118, 298, 465, 468
Sylvester, E. A., 594
Synder, J. J., 526
Szumowski, E. K., 115, 134
Szurek, S., 176

Tachibana, R., 177
Tager-Flusberg, H., 166
Takenaka, J., 636
Tal, A., 444
Tallmadge, J., 134
Tanguay, P. E., 75, 175
Tannebaum, R. L., 79

Tanner, B. A., 545
Tannhauser, M. A., 591
Tant, J. L., 123, 126, 128
Tarnow, J., 443
Tarnowski, K. J., 299
Tate, B., 249, 250
Tavarmina, J., 444
Taylor, C. B., 268
Taylor, C. J., 629
Taylor, E., 115, 157, 465
Taylor, F. D., 597
Tecce, J. J., 374
Tedesco, L. A., 631
Tejani, A., 310
Tennant, C., 373, 374
Tennes, K., 92
Teplitz, Z., 248
Tepsic, P. H., 468
Terdal, L., 357
Terr, L. C., 641
Terry, R. M., 399
Tesiny, E. P., 78, 83, 87, 99, 439
Teuber, H. L., 296
Tharp, R. G., 539
Thelen, E., 248, 249
Thelen, M. H., 513, 528
Thind, I. S., 194
Thomas, A., 99
Thomas, D. R., 593
Thomas, E., 176
Thomas, P. R., 577
Thompson, E. L., 631
Thompson, M., 253
Thompson, W. B., 92
Thomson, A. J. M., 309
Thoren, P., 475
Thornberry, T. P., 395, 396, 402
Thurber, E., 341
Thurston, C. M., 468
Thurston, D., 304, 306
Tinbergen, E. A., 174
Tinsley, B. R., 86
Tizard, B., 311
Tizard, J., 40, 93, 140, 352, 397
Tobias, J., 472
Tobin, F., 368
Toby, J., 367
Tollison, J. W., 263
Torgesen, J., 584
Torrey, E. F., 178
Torup, E., 243, 245, 246
Touliatos J., 17
Touwen, B. C., 299
Towbin, A., 305, 306, 320

Towne, W., 217
Toyama, B., 18
Tracy, M., 588, 605
Tramontana, M. G., 502, 578
Traskman, L., 475
Trasler, G. B., 410
Treffert, D. A., 177, 178
Treiman, D., 406
Tremblay, R. E., 559
Tress, B., 176
Trieschman, A. E., 595
Trimble, M., 157, 473
Tripodi, T., 539
Trites, R. L., 115, 140, 141, 429
Tronick, E., 374
Troop, J., 338
Troshinsky, C., 469
Tryon, W. W., 79
Tsai, L., 168
Tsushima, W. T., 217
Tuckman, J., 352, 365
Tuddenham, R. D., 401
Tuma, J. M., 53, 94, 95, 97, 496, 497,
    507–509, 512
Tupling, C., 52, 93, 408
Turecki, S., 508, 510, 511, 514
Turnbull, J., 236
Turner, D. S., 638, 649
Turner, J. T., 365
Turner, P. F., 137
Turner, S. M., 243–245
Tyler, V., 539
Tymchuk, A. J., 163
Tyroler, M. J., 123, 529
Tyron, W., 122

Uhde, T. W., 473
Ullman, D. G., 123
Ullman, L., 236
Ullmann, R. K., 429
Ulrich, R. F., 114
Ungerer, J., 165, 166, 168
Unis, A. S., 436, 437
Uranich, W. B., 559
Urbain, E. S., 127, 502, 529, 532
Urey, J. R., 400

Vacc, N. A., 587
Van Bourgondien, M., 277
Van Dusen, K. T., 397
Van Hasselt, V. B., 535
Varly, C., 470
Varni, J., 540
Vaughn, B., 346, 347

Venables, P. H., 18, 46
Varnadekis, A., 92
Vernon, D. T. A., 633
Veroff, J., 365
Viamontes, G., 477
Vigil, D., 45
Vilensky, J. A., 173
Viney, L. L., 270
Vince, C. J., 638
Visintainer, M. A., 633
Vivian, D., 18, 429
Vliestra, A. G., 128
Voeller, K., 313
Vohr, B. R., 308, 309
Volotin, D., 526
Von Knorring, A.-L., 48, 92
Voss, H. L., 399, 401, 402
Vrono, M. S. H., 185
Vosk, B., 82, 86, 87

Wade, M. G., 468
Wade, T. C., 644
Wadsworth, M. E. J., 362
Wagner, M. E., 352
Wagner, R., 192
Wagonfield, S., 213
Wahler, R. G., 356, 357, 446, 525
Waizer, J., 472, 477
Walder, L., O., 54, 59
Waldron, S., 368, 369, 371
Waldrop, M. F., 300
Walker, C. E., 392
Walker, E., 344
Walker, H. A., 139, 189, 593
Wall, S., 345
Waller, D. A., 217
Wallerstein, J. S., 338–340, 368, 632
Wallis, C. P., 407, 409
Walsh, M. L., 513
Walter, R., 397
Walter, T. L., 644
Walters, R. H., 355
Walton, D., 245
Wandersman, A., 339, 647
Wandersman, L., 339, 641
Wanlass, R. L., 77
Ward, M. M., 213, 276, 301
Ward-Zimmerman, B., 545
Warinner, A., 265
Warren, M. Q., 8, 572
Warrington, E. K., 167
Warshak, R. A., 363, 366
Watanabe, M., 177

Waterhouse, L., 164, 180, 189, 191, 192
Waterman, J., 89
Waters, E., 345, 346
Waters, J., 17
Watt, N. F., 188, 270
Wattenberg, W., 601
Watts, J., 265
Wayne, H., 244
Webb, G., 298
Webb, J., 407
Weber, B. A., 470
Webster, C., 166, 466
Webster, L., 462
Wechsler, D., 124
Weinberg, W., 437
Weinberger, D., 192
Weiner, B., 82
Weingartner, C., 605
Weingartner, H., 126, 128, 467–469
Weinhold, C., 94
Weinrott, M. R., 571
Weinstein, G., 605
Weinstein, J., 477
Weinstein, L., 39, 563, 564, 566, 568
Weintraub, S., 87, 360
Weisner, T. S., 333
Weiss, B., 460
Weiss, G., 114, 121, 124, 139, 142–144, 465, 467–469, 471
Weiss, J., 236–238, 240
Weiss, J. G., 396
Weiss, J. H., 443
Weiss, R. S., 340
Weissberg, R. P., 628
Weissman, M., 92, 344, 362, 374, 438, 511, 517
Weisz, J. R., 77
Welch, F., 603
Wells, K., 135, 263, 356, 446, 536, 547
Wells, R. A., 501
Wemmer, D., 465
Wenar, C., 298
Wencar, C., 162
Wender, P., 112, 116, 131, 142, 296, 320, 460, 470
Wener, A., 124
Wenger, C., 509
Wenninger, E. P., 408, 409
Werner, E., 307, 343, 353, 362, 574
Werry, J. S., 8, 17, 23, 24, 53, 74, 94, 96, 97, 115, 122, 138, 140, 141, 173, 179, 185, 192, 194–196,

245–249, 254, 262, 263, 267, 268, 274, 299, 301, 305, 317–321, 429, 431, 456, 462, 463, 465, 468, 471, 481, 592, 633
West, D. J., 362, 392, 393, 397, 400, 403–405
West, P. A., 62
West, S. G., 559
Westbook, M. T., 270
Weston, D. R., 346
Wetzel, R. J., 539
Whalen, C. K., 115, 117, 120, 122, 123, 127, 133–137, 430, 465, 467, 515, 648
Whalen, K., 431
Whaley-Klahn, M. A., 592
Whelen, W., 259
Whitaker, J. K., 559
White, M. H., 526
White, O. R., 593
White, S. W., 338
Whitehead, L., 359, 361, 372
Whitehill, M., 44
Whitelaw, A., 271
Whitlock, F. A., 375
Whitmore, K., 40, 93, 140, 311, 352, 397
Whittaker, J. K., 595
Whitten, P., 137
Wiener, G., 309
Wiener, J. M., 301
Wieselberg, M., 35, 115
Wicks-Nelson, R., 440
Wikler, A., 301, 318
Wilbur, R., 165
Wilcott, R. C., 471
Wilding, J., 558
Wilkinson, P., 257–259
Wilks, J., 306
Will, L., 21
Willi, J., 253
Williams, C. L., 263, 630
Williams, D., 473
Williams, G., 238
Williams, H. W., 643
Williams, J. A., 342
Williams, J. R., 396, 401
Williams, S., 18, 37, 38, 41, 93, 115, 139, 307
Williamson, D., 541
Willis, C. F., 401
Wilson, A., 262, 624
Wilson, C. C., 35, 116, 136
Wilson, G. T., 423, 611

Wilson, S., 446
Wimberly, F., 344
Winder, C. L., 39
Wine, J., 78, 81
Wineman, D., 601
Wing, J. K., 195
Wing, L., 157, 160–162, 165, 168, 169, 172, 174, 175, 177–180, 184, 185, 270, 305, 399, 402
Winsberg, B. G., 299, 300, 465, 472, 478, 559
Winsberg, G. B., 167
Winton, A. S. W., 250, 251, 545
Wippman, J., 345
Wirt, R. D., 58, 395, 405, 435
Wise, S., 374
Wish, E., 394
Witkin, M. J., 558
Witt, J., 257
Witt, P. A., 468
Wittman, W. P., 646
Wodarski, J. S., 406
Wolery, M., 547
Wolf, K., 249
Wolf, M. M., 426, 523, 536, 537, 569, 570
Wolf, M. W., 569
Wolf, P., 397
Wolf, S., 444
Wolfe, D., 446
Wolfer, J. A., 633
Wolff, H., 233
Wolff, O., 259
Wolff, P., 167
Wolff, S., 184, 187
Wolfgang, M. E., 393, 395, 400
Wolkind, S., 400, 410

Wolking, W. D., 355
Wolpe, J., 433
Wolpert, A., 477
Woltmann, A., 606
Wood, D., 142
Wood, F. H., 589
Wood, M. M., 603, 604
Wood, R., 77
Woodmansey, A., 265
Woodrow, K., 243, 244, 246
Woodside, M., 338
Woolston, J. L., 250, 251
Worland, J., 115, 129, 130
Wright, A. L., 471
Wright, J. C., 128
Wright, J. J., 301, 320
Wright, L., 623
Wright, S., 628
Wunsch-Hitzig, R., 52
Wurtele, S. K., 633
Wyatt, R., 192
Wynne, L. C., 193
Wynne, M. E., 534

Yager, R. D., 320
Yalom, I., 241
Yang, K.-S., 18
Yarrow, L. J., 339, 343
Yaryuria-Tobias, J. A., 475
Yashima, Y., 177
Yates, A., 244, 245, 371
Yeates, S. R., 160
Yeaton, W., 559
Yellin, A. M., 465
Yepes, L. E., 472
Yeudell, L. T., 475
Young, D., 440, 578

Young, G., 480
Young, J. G., 302
Young, R. D., 114, 120, 128, 135, 137, 513
Yudofsky, S., 473
Yule, B., 402, 408
Yule, W., 52, 93, 235, 260, 263, 276, 408
Yung, J. G., 175
Yuwiler, A., 175, 302

Zahn, T., 467, 468
Zahn-Waxler, C., 374
Zak, L., 446
Zametkin, A., 232, 462
Zarle, T. H., 641
Zatz, S., 78, 81
Zausmer, D., 243, 245, 246
Zax, M., 344, 622, 625
Zegans, L. S., 513
Zeiler, M., 545
Zellman, G., 642
Zentall, S. S., 116, 117, 131
Zentall, T. R., 116, 117, 131
Zill, N., 363, 364, 366
Zimbardo, P. G., 79
Zimmerman, E. G., 185
Zimmerman, M., 444
Zimring, F. E., 403
Zlutnick, S., 268, 543
Zrull, J. P., 77, 99
Zubin, J., 4
Zupan, B. A., 39, 506
Zuroff, D. C., 376
Zvagulis, I., 270
Zweben, R. B., 47, 72
Zwirner, W., 358

SUBJECT INDEX

Abnormal psychology, *see names of
specific disorders*
Academic performance:
attention deficit disorder, 118,
124–125
autism and, 170–171
conduct disorders and, 40–41
divorce and, 364
family size and, 352
internalizing disorders and, 81–83
residential treatment outcomes and,
566–569
Achievement Place (group home),
569–571
Activity level, 122–123
Activity measures, 431
ADD, *see* Attention deficit disorder
(ADD)
Adolescents:
family system and, 347–351
peer group and, 404–405
Adults:
asthma and, 239
depression and, 73
Affect:
childhood depression and, 80
schizophrenia and, 190–191
Affective syndromes, 217–218
Age at onset:
anorexia nervosa, 255
attention deficit disorder, 113, 114
autism, 178
conversion disorder, 268
obesity, 259
psychosis, 157, 158
rumination disorder, 251
schizophrenia, 157, 181, 185, 186,
194
tic disorders, 244
Age level:
attachment process, 346
attention deficit disorder, 113, 114,
121–122, 134, 140, 142
atypical stereotyped movement
disorder, 247–248

autism, 178–179
brain damage, 320
childhood depression, 95
classification systems, 16, 17
cognition, 38
developmental disorders, 275
encopresis, 264
enuresis, 263
heart rate, 90–91
psychogenic pain disorder, 268–269
psychosexual disorder, 272
schizophrenia, 182, 186
substance disorders, 225–226,
227–228
Aggression:
attention deficit disorder, 116, 136
behavioral observation assessment,
427
behavior therapy for, 538–539
conduct disorders, 35
divorce, 366–367
family size, 352
mothers, 363
outcome and, 54–57
parenting and, 356, 360, 372
peer relations, 87
prediction of crime, 57–64
siblings, 362
socioeconomic class and, 398
Alcohol abuse:
genetics, 227
substance disorders, 221–223
see also Substance disorders
Amnestic syndrome, 217–218
Amphetamines, 224
Animal studies, 249
Anorexia nervosa, 252–256
correlates of, 254
defined, 252–253
epidemiology of, 253
etiology of, 255
outcome, 255–256
treatment, 255
Anticholinergics, 462
Anticonvulsants, 461–462

Antidepressants, 460–461, 471–472
Antihistamines, 462
Antipsychotics (neuroleptics),
462–463, 471
Anxiety:
asthma and, 240
cognitive functioning and, 78
conduct disorders and, 42
electroencephalography and, 47–48
encopresis and, 265
family size and, 352
peer relations and, 85–86
psychogenic pain disorder and, 269
sleep disorders and, 273
social withdrawal and, 78
stimulation seeking and, 43–44
tic disorders and, 244–245
see also Anxiety disorders; Anxiety-
withdrawal-dysphoria;
Internalizing disorders
Anxiety disorders:
academic performance and, 81–82
assessment of, 76–77, 432–435
behavior therapy for, 534–536
epidemiology and, 96–97
heart rate and, 90
internalizing disorders and, 74–75
psychopharmacotherapy for,
474–475
social cognition and, 88–89
see also Anxiety; Anxiety-
withdrawal-dysphoria;
Internalizing disorders
Anxiety-withdrawal-dysphoria:
attention deficit disorder and, 138
classification systems and, 15
cross-cultural generality and, 17
family factors and, 368–373
socioeconomic class and, 397, 398
Anxiolytics, 461–462
Arousal:
attention deficit disorder, 131–133
enuresis and, 261
Assessment, 423–454
anxiety, 432–435

Assessment (*Continued*)
attention deficit disorder, 114–115, 428–432
behavior therapy, 531
conduct disorders, 36, 424–428
depression, 435–439
distractability, 121
importance of, 423
internalizing disorders, 75–78
pervasive developmental disorders, 439–442
psychosomatic disorders, 442–445
see also Tests and testing
Asthma, 235–241
behavior therapy for, 543
defined, 235
epidemiology of, 235
etiology of, 236–238
family and, 239–240
psychopathology of, 238
psychophysiological studies in, 238–239
treatment of, 240
Attachment process:
dependency and, 370–371
family system and, 345–347
Attention:
anxiety disorders and, 81–82
autism and, 165, 169–170
conduct disorders and, 43–44
schizophrenia and, 191
Attention deficit disorder (ADD), 111–155
academic performance and, 40
assessment of, 114–115, 428–432
behavior therapy for, 531–534
classification systems and, 13–14
cognition and, 123–128
core features of, 117–123
cross-cultural generality and, 18
diagnostic criteria, 113–114
empirical validation, 115–116
epidemiology of, 52, 140–142
etiology of, 115, 116–117
history of, 111–112
interest in, 111
learning disorders, 276
motivation/reinforcement effects, 129–131
motor functioning and, 140
neurology and, 138–140
organic disorders and, 218
outcome, 142–144
psychopharmacotherapy for, 464–472

psychophysiological correlates, 46, 131–133
social behavior/cognition, 133–138
tic disorders and, 244
see also Hyperactivity
Attention measures, 431–432
Attributional style, 82
Atypical stereotyped movement disorder, 242–250
behavior therapy for, 546–547
defined, 247
epidemiology of, 247–248
etiology of, 248–249
outcome, 250
psychopharmacotherapy for, 479–481
tic disorders and, 242–247
treatment, 249–250
Autism:
attention deficit disorder and, 139
behavior therapy and, 549
characteristics of, 159
cognition and, 162–171
epidemiology of, 177–179
family correlates, 176–177
motor development/perceptuomotor skills and, 172–173
neurological pathological correlates of, 175–176
outcome, 179–181
psychopharmacotherapy for, 477–478
psychophysiological factors in, 171–172
schizophrenia differentiated from, 158, 186, 187
social behavior, 174–175
socioeconomic class and, 398
stereotypies and, 173–174
validity of syndrome, 160–162
views of, 160
Autopsy, 298
Avoidant disorder, 74

Balderton Hospital study, 560–561
Behavior:
academic performance and, 125
attention deficit disorder and, 116, 120, 122, 133–138, 142, 143–144
autism and, 168, 171, 173–174
brain and, 296–297
classification systems and, 9
conduct disorders and, 49–50

statistical classification systems and, 10, 11
Behavioral checklists, 424
Behavioral contracting, 539
Behavioral measures, 434–435
Behavioral observation:
attention deficit disorders, 430–431
conduct disorders, 427–428
pervasive developmental disorders, 441
Behavior disorders, *see* Conduct disorders
Behavior modification, *see* Behavior therapy
Behavior problems:
genetics and, 92
see also Behavior; Conduct disorders
Behavior therapy, 523–557
anxiety/dysphoria, 534–536
attention deficit disorder, 130, 531–534
behavioral assessment, 531
chaining in, 527
conduct disorders, 538–539
diversity in, 523
educational intervention, 592–594
extinction, 530
family factors and, 332
group-home setting, 569–571
learning paradigms in, 524–526
modeling in, 528–529
pain (chronic), 540–541
psychosis/profound retardation, 543–550
punishment and, 529
reinforcement procedures in, 527–528
response cost procedures in, 530
self-control/cognitive interventions, 529
shaping in, 526–527
social withdrawal, 537–538
time-out procedures in, 530
Bellevue Index of Depression (BID), 437
Bias, 10
Biochemistry:
attention deficit disorders and, 139
autism and, 175
brain disorders and, 302
conduct disorders and, 50–52
internalizing disorders and, 92

Biology:
    attention deficit disorder and, 139
    autism and, 168
Biophysical interventions, 606–609
Biopsy, 298
Birth order, 352–354
Bowel, 241–242
Brain:
    pharmacokinetics and, 457
    see also Brain damage; Brain
        disorders
Brain damage:
    attention deficit disorder and, 111
    autism and, 176
    behavior and, 296–297
    brain disorders and, 304–305
    organic disorders and, 211
    specific variables in, 320–321
Brain disorders, 211–219, 294–331
    anatomy and, 294–295
    brain-behavior relationships,
        296–297
    brain damage, 211, 304–305
    brain-damage variables (specific),
        320–321
    cerebral palsy, 311
    chromosomal influences, 313–315
    delirium, 214–215
    dementia, 215–217
    developmental considerations, 295
    diagnosis of, 297–303
    dietary factors in, 315–316
    DSM-III and, 212
    encephalitis/meningitis, 309–310
    epilepsy, 310–311
    head injury, 311–312
    heavy metals, 312–313
    interactive effects, 297
    low birth weight babies, 308–309
    minimal brain dysfunction,
        319–320
    neuropsychology and, 211–212, 213
    partial syndromes, 217–218
    psychopathology and, 317–318
    research in, 294
    tic disorders and, 244
    see also Brain damage
Bricquet's syndrome, 267
Bulemia, 252

Caffeine, 466
California Community Treatment
    Project (CTP), 573–575
Cannabis, 224
Categorical classification systems, 2

Central nervous system:
    alcohol abuse and, 221–222
    attention deficit disorder and, 125
    autism and, 171
    pharmacokinetics and, 457
    see also Brain damage; Brain
        disorders
Cerebral palsy, 311
Chaining, 527
Checklists, 439–442
Child abuse, 646
Child Depression Inventory (CDI),
    436
Childhood depressive disorder:
    academic performance and, 83
    assessment of, 77–78, 435–439
    childhood and, 73–74
    cognition and, 79–81
    epidemiology of, 94–96
    family system and, 344
    parental death and, 373–374
    peer relations and, 87–88
    psychopharmacotherapy for,
        476–477
    skepticism on, 73–74
    social cognition and, 89
    social withdrawal and, 78
Childhood psychosis, see Psychosis
Childhood schizophrenia, see
    Schizophrenia
Children's Affective Rating Scales
    (CARS), 438
Children's Depression Rating Scale
    (CDRS), 438
Children's Depression Scale (CDS),
    436–437
Children's Manifest Anxiety Scale
    (CMAS), 432–433
Chromosomes, 313–315. See also
    Genetics
Chronic illness disorder, 270–271
Classical (respondent) conditioning,
    524
Classification systems, 1–34
    clinically derived systems, 3–8
    clinical/statistical approaches
        compared, 18–20
    criteria for evaluation of, 2–3
    cross-cultural generality and, 17–18
    multivariate statistical approaches to,
        8–17
    pharmacology and, 458–459
    physical illness, 234–235
    psychosis, 157–158
    purposes of, 1–2

reliability and, 20–27
tic disorders, 242–243
Classroom, see Academic performance;
    Educational intervention
Clinical interview, 442
Clinically derived classification
    systems, 3–8
    autism and, 161
    comparisons of, 7–8
    DSM-III, 3–4
    ICD-9, 6–7
    schizophrenia, 188
    statistical approaches compared, 10,
        18–20
    WHO system, 4, 6
Close–Holton study, 575–577
Cocaine, 223–224
Cognition:
    attention deficit disorder, 123–128
    autism, 162–171
    conduct disorders, 37–39
    dementia, 216
    family factors and, 335
    internalizing disorders, 78–81
    neuroleptics, 471
    schizophrenia, 189–190
    stimulants and, 468–469
    see also Intelligence; Social cognition
Cognitive therapy:
    behavior therapy, 529
    family factors and, 332
Colitis (ulcerative), 241–242
Community intervention/prevention,
    622–660
    comprehensive community mental
        health centers, 639–642
    criminal justice system in,
        642–645
    ecological interventions, 647–649
    hospital-based, 634
    media and, 645–647
    preventive emphasis, 623
    school-based, 625–634
    social service agencies, 634,
        635–639
    uniqueness of, 622
Community mental health centers,
    639–642
Computed tomography:
    attention deficit disorder, 139
    autism, 176
    brain disorders, 297, 302
Conduct disorders, 35–72
    academic performance and, 40–41
    assessment of, 36, 424–428

Conduct disorders (*Continued*)
  attention deficit disorder and, 115, 117, 131, 138, 144
  behavior therapy for, 538–539
  biochemical factors in, 50–52
  central features of, 36
  cognitive functioning and, 37–39
  depression and, 74
  differentiation among, 35
  divorce and, 363, 368
  epidemiology and, 52–53
  family conflict and, 359–362
  family factors and, 355–368
  genetic factors in, 48–50
  instrumental learning and, 41–43
  invention programs and, 45–46
  outcome in, 53–64
  peer relations and, 44–45
  pharmacology and, 51, 472–474
  psychophysiological correlates in, 46–48
  sibling system and, 362–363
  stimulation seeking and, 43–44
  see also Socialized aggressive conduct disorder; Undersocialized aggressive conduct disorder
Consciousness:
  hallucination and, 218
  organic disorders and, 214
Contingency management, 527, 537
Control, 347–351
Control theory (juvenile delinquency), 411–412
Conversion disorder, 267–268
Countertheory model (educational intervention), 604–606
Criminality, juvenile delinquency and, 394. *See also* Juvenile delinquency
Criminal justice system:
  community intervention, 642–645
  ethnicity and, 402
  police departments, 399–400
Crohn's Disease, 241–242
Cross-cultural generality:
  attention deficit disorder, 141
  classification systems and, 17–18
  see also Epidemiology
Cultural factors, *see* Sociocultural context
Cylert (magnesium pemoline), 466

Data collection, 10
Delay of gratification, 121–122
Deinstitutionalization, 558

Delinquency, *see* Juvenile delinquency
Delirium:
  organic disorders, 214–215
  substance abuse, 222–223, 224
Delusional syndrome, 217–218
Dementia:
  organic disorders, 215–217
  substance abuse, 223
Dependency, 368–370
Depressive disorder, *see* Childhood depressive disorder; Dysphoria
Desensitization, *see* Systematic desensitization
Developmental disorders:
  behavior therapy and, 549
  criteria in, 275–276
  learning disorders, 276
  physical illness, 275–278
  speech/language disorders, 276–277
  see also Pervasive development disorders
Dexedrine (destroamphetamine), 465
Diagnostic and Statistical Manual, *see* DSM-III
Diet, *see* Nutrition
Disability disorder, 270–271
Discipline:
  conduct disorders and, 357–358
  family size and, 351–352
  family system and, 349–351
Disintegrative psychosis, 157
Dissociative disorders, 267, 269–270
Distractability:
  assessment of, 121
  attention deficit disorder, 118, 119
Divorce:
  conduct disorders and, 363–368
  family system and, 338
  marital dissatisfaction and, 340–341
  see also Family factors
Domestic conflict, *see* Family factors; Marital conflict
Down's syndrome, 313, 314
Drug abuse, *see* Substance disorders
DSM-III:
  anorexia nervosa, 252–253
  assessment and, 423
  attention deficit disorder, 112, 113–114, 122
  autism, 161, 162, 164, 178, 180
  bulimia, 252
  classification systems, 3–4
  comparisons of, 8, 18–20

  conduct disorders and, 36
  delirium, 214
  dementia, 215–217
  developmental disorders, 275
  dissociative disorders, 269
  enuresis, 260
  hallucination, 218
  histrionic disorders, 233
  infantile autism, 159
  internalizing disorders, 73, 93
  major categories, 5
  organic disorders, 212
  physical illness, 234
  psychosexual disorders, 271
  psychosis, 156
  psychosomatic disorders, 232
  reliability of, 20–25
  schizophrenia, 182, 184–185, 186, 187, 189, 194, 195, 196
  sleep disorders, 273
  somatization disorder, 267
  somatoform disorders, 267
  speech/language disorders, 277
  substance disorders, 219
  tic disorders, 242, 243
  WHO syste compared, 6
Dysphoria:
  behavior therapy for, 534–536
  family factors and, 373–376
  see also Childhood depressive disorder; Internalizing disorders

Eating disorders, 250–260
  anorexia nervosa, 252–256
  bulimia, 252
  failure to thrive, 251–252
  obesity, 256–260
  pica, 250
  rumination disorder, 251
Echolalia, 165
Ecological intervention:
  community-wide, 647–649
  educational intervention, 595–596
Ecological studies, *see* Neighborhood
Educational intervention, 583–621
  adjunct intervention in, 606–609
  approaches to, 587
  behavioral programs, 592–594
  biophysical approaches, 591–592
  classification and, 588–590
  countertheory model in, 604–606
  definitions and, 583–584
  eclectic interventions, 596–599
  ecological programs, 595–596

effectiveness summarized, 610–612
epidemiology and, 585–586
heterogeneity of population and, 584–585
prevalence of, 590–591
psychodynamic programs, 594–595
psychoeducational model in, 599–600
psychoeducational techniques in, 600–604
"pure" approaches in, 591
sociocultural developments and, 586–687
theory and, 588
Elderly, 215
Electrodermal responding (GSR):
attention deficit disorder, 131–132
autism, 172
conduct disorders, 46–47
internalizing disorders, 90
Electroencephalography (EEG):
attention deficit disorder, 132, 139, 431
autism, 171
brain disorders, 297, 300–301
conduct disorders, 47–48
dementia, 216–217
enuresis, 261
Elementary school treatment, 628–630
Elimination disorders, 260–266
encopresis, 264–266
enuresis, 260–264
Empathy, 39
Encephalitis, 309–310
Encopresis, 264–266
behavior therapy for, 543
defined, 264
epidemiology of, 264
etiology, 264–265
outcome in, 266
psychopathology and, 265–266
treatment of, 266
Enuresis:
behavior therapy for, 543
defined, 260
epidemiology of, 260
etiology of, 261
occurrence, 260–261
outcome in, 263
psychopathology and, 261–262
psychopharmacotherapy for, 481
treatment of, 262–263
Environmental toxins, *see* Toxins

Epidemiology:
anorexia nervosa, 253
asthma, 235
attention deficit disorder, 140–142
atypical stereotyped movement disorders, 247–248
autism, 177–179
brain disorders, 299–300
conduct disorders, 52–53
educational interventions and, 585–586
encopresis, 264
enuresis, 260
internalizing disorders, 93–97
obesity, 257
schizophrenia, 194
sleep disorders, 273
tic disorders, 243–244
Epilepsy, 310–311
Ethnicity:
assessment of impact of, 402–403
juvenile delinquency and, 400–401
psychological disorders and, 401–402
see also Race differences
Evoked potentials, 171–172
Extinction, 525, 530

Factitious disorder:
described, 269–270
DSM-III, 267
Factor analysis:
criticism of, 10
statistical classification systems and, 9
Failure to thrive, 251–252
Family conflict, *see* Divorce; Marital conflict
Family discipline, *see* Discipline
Family factors, 332–390
anorexia nervosa and, 254
anxiety-withdrawal disorder and, 368–373
asthma and, 239–240
at-risk children and, 335–336
attention deficit disorder, 134–135
autism and, 176–177
cognition and, 335
community intervention and, 644
conduct disorders and, 355–368
developmental approach and, 332–333
dysphoria and, 373–376
enuresis and, 261

family system and, 334–335, 337–354
psychosexual disorders and, 272
schizophrenia and, 193
sleep disorders and, 274
substance disorders and, 226
theory and, 332
tic disorders and, 244–245
vulnerability and, 335–337
Family size, 351–352
Family system, 337–354
adolescents and, 347–351
infants and, 341–347
marital relationship, 337–341
siblings in, 351–354
Fathers:
attachment process and, 346
attention deficit disorder and, 134
Fear Survey for Children (FSS-FC), 433–434
Frontal lobe syndrome, 218

Gender identity, 271–272
General intelligence, *see* Cognition; Intelligence
Genetics:
anorexia nervosa, 255
attention deficit disorder and, 116–117
biochemistry and, 50
brain disorders and, 300, 313–315
conduct disorders and, 48–50
discipline and, 349
infants and, 341
internalizing disorders and, 91–92
schizophrenia and, 193
substance disorders and, 227
Gestures, 165, 168, 175
Gratification delay, 121–122
Group-home treatment, 563–571
Achievement Place, 569–571
Project Re-Ed, 563–569

Hallucination, 217–218
Hallucinogens, 224
Headache, *see* Migraine headache
Head injury, 311–312
Head Start program, 625–626
Health education interventions, 630–631
Heart rate:
attention deficit disorders, 131–132
autism and, 172

Heart rate (*Continued*)
conduct disorders and, 46
internalizing disorders and, 90–91
Heavy metal:
brain disorders, 312–313
see also Toxins
Heredity, *see* Genetics
History, *see* Patient history
Histrionic disorders, 233
Homosexuality, 272
Hospital-based interventions, 634
Hyperactivity:
behavior therapy for, 531–534
psychopharmacotherapy for,
464–472
socioeconomic class and, 398
see also Attention deficit disorder
Hyperkinesis, *see* Attention deficit
disorder; Hyperactivity
Hypoxic-ischemic encephalopathy,
298
Hysterical disorders, 267

Illinois-Adler Center Project,
561–563
Impulsivity, 120–122, 123
Inattention, 117–120. *See also*
Attention deficit disorder
Individualized education program
(IEP), 584
Infantile autism, *see* Autism
Infants:
attachment process and, 345–347
dependency and, 369–370
family system and, 341–347
Infection, 309–310
Inhalants, 221–223
Injury-prevention programs, 637–639
Instrumental learning, 41–43
Intelligence:
attention deficit disorder, 124, 138
autism, 162–164, 175, 180–181
conduct disorders, 37–38
dementia, 216
family size studies, 352
internalizing disorders, 78
schizophrenia, 189
socioeconomic class, 400
see also Cognition
Internalizing disorders:
academic performance, 81–83
assessment of, 75–78
biochemical factors in, 92
cognition and, 78–81

diagnostic methods in, 73
epidemiology of, 93–97
heredity and, 91–92
intelligence and, 78
motivation/reinforcement effects,
83
outcome in, 97–101
peer relations, 84–88
psychophysiological correlates,
90–91
social cognition and, 88–89
subtypes of, 73–75
International Classification of Diseases
(ICD-8), 182
International Classification of Diseases
(ICD-9), 6–7
anorexia nervosa, 253
attention deficit disorder, 114
comparison of, 8, 18–20
dementia, 217
developmental disorders, 275
hysterical disorders, 267
internalizing disorders and, 73
physical illness and, 234–235
psychosis and, 156, 157
reliability of, 25
schizophrenia, 183, 184
speech disorders, 277
Intervention programs:
conduct disorders and, 45–46
family system and, 363
see also Behavior therapy;
Community intervention/
prevention; Psychotherapies
Interview measures, 437–438
Interview Schedule for Children (ISC),
437–438
Intoxication, 220
Isolation, *see* Social withdrawal

Juvenile delinquency:
academic performance and, 40
adult criminality and, 394
attention deficit disorder and, 143
behavior therapy for, 538–539
community intervention in, 642–645
conduct disorders and, 36, 45
divorce and, 364
empathy and, 39
ethnicity and, 400–401
intervention programs and, 45–46
neighborhood and, 406–408, 409
parenting and, 356–357
peer groups and, 403–406

prediction of, 57–64
sociocultural factors and, 392–393
socioeconomic class and, 395–397,
399
theories of, 410–413
Juvenile diversion project, 642–643

Kiddie-Sads (K-SADS), 438

Language:
attention deficit disorders, 126
autism and, 164–167, 180–181
behavior therapy and, 548
conduct disorders and, 39
developmental disorders and,
276–277
schizophrenia and, 190–191
Lead, 312–313
Learning:
autism and, 170–171
schizophrenia and, 192
see also Cognition; Intelligence
Learning disorders:
developmental disorders, 276
educational intervention, 584
Least restrictive environment
requirement, 586–587
Lithium, 463
Louisville Fear Survey (LFSC),
433–434
Low birth weight babies, 308–309
LSD, 224

Magnesium pemoline (Cylert), 466
Malingering disorder:
described, 269–270
DSM-III and, 267
Marital conflict:
anxiety-withdrawal disorders and,
371–373
conduct disorders and, 359–362
see also Family factors
Media, 645–647
Mediational learning, 526
Memory:
attention deficit disorder and,
125–126
autism and, 167–168
Meningitis, 309–310
Mental retardation:
attention deficit disorder and,
139
autism and, 163, 166
behavior therapy and, 543–550

brain damage and, 304
conduct disorders and, 41
Mescaline, 224
Metacognition, 127–128
Methylphenidate (Ritalin), 465–466
Migraine headache, 541
Minimal brain dysfunction:
    attention deficit disorder and, 123
    brain disorders, 319–320
    EEG assessment of, 431
    see also Attention deficit disorder
Modeling:
    anxiety disorders and, 534
    behavior therapy and, 528–529
    social withdrawal and, 537
Monosymptomatic hysteria, 267–268
Moral reasoning, 39
Mothers:
    aggression and, 363
    attention deficit disorder and, 133
    see also Family factors
Motivation:
    substance disorders and, 227
    tic disorders and, 246
Motivational set, 82
Motivation/reinforcement effects:
    attention deficit disorder, 129–131
    internalizing disorders and, 83
Motor development and functioning:
    attention deficit disorder, 140
    autism, 172–173
    schizophrenia, 192
Motor overactivity:
    classification systems and, 17
    undersocialized conduct disorder
        and, 35–36
    see also Attention deficit disorder;
        Hyperactivity
Movement disorders, *see* Atypical
    stereotyped movement disorders
Multivariate statistics, *see* Statistical
    classification systems

Neighborhood, 406–410
    assessment of impact of, 409–410
    juvenile delinquency and, 406–408
    psychological disorders and, 408
Neuroleptics (antipsychotics),
    462–463, 471
Neurology:
    attention deficit disorder, 111, 116,
        138–140
    autism and, 172–173, 175–176
    brain disorders, 298–300

schizophrenia, 192–193
tic disorders, 244
Neuropsychology:
    brain disorders, 302–303
    dementia, 216
    organic disorders, 211–212, 213
Neurotransmitters, 457–458
Night walking, 273, 274
Nonorganic failure to thrive, 251–252
Nuclear magnetic resonance, 297, 302
Nutrition, 315–316
Nutritional service programs, 636

Obesity, 256–260
    defined, 256–257
    epidemiology of, 257–259
    outcome in, 259
    treatment of, 259
Observation, *see* Behavioral observation
Obsessive-compulsive disorder:
    family factors and, 371
    internalizing disorders and, 75
    psychopharmacotherapy for,
        475–476
Obstetrics, 139
Operant conditioning:
    autism and, 171
    behavior therapy and, 524–526
Opiates, 223
Organic disorders, *see* Brain disorders
Outcome:
    anorexia nervosa, 255–256
    attention deficit disorder, 142–144
    atypical stereotyped movement
        disorder, 249
    autism, 179–181
    encopresis, 266
    enuresis, 263
    internalizing disorders, 97–101
    obesity, 259
    psychotherapies and, 500
    residential treatment programs,
        572–578
    schizophrenia, 194–196
    substance disorders, 227–228
    tic disorders, 246
Overanxious disorder, 74

Pain disorder (psychogenic), 268–269,
    540–541
Paranoia, 184
Parent-child relationships:
    attention deficit disorder, 133–135
    conduct disorders, 355–359

family system and, 338–340
    see also Family factors; Fathers;
        Mothers
Parent ratings:
    attention deficit disorders, 429–430
    conduct disorders, 424
Participant modeling, 528, 534
Patient history, 298
Peer relations:
    attention deficit disorder, 135–136,
        137–138
    childhood depression and, 78
    conduct disorders and, 43, 44–45
    internalizing disorders and, 84–88
    psychological disorders and,
        403–406
    social withdrawal and, 77
    substance disorders and, 226
Perception:
    autism and, 169–170
    schizophrenia and, 191
Perceptuomotor skills, 192
Perinatal factors:
    brain disorders, 298, 305–308
    infants and, 342–343
Personality, 296–297
Personality syndrome, 217–218
Pervasive developmental disorders:
    assessment of, 439–442
    categories of, 159–160
    infantile autism, 159
    psychopharmacotherapy for,
        477–478
    see also Developmental disorders
PET, *see* Positron emission tomography
Pharmacokinetics, 456–457. *See also*
    Psychopharmacotherapy
Pharmacology, *see*
    Psychopharmacotherapy
Phenylketonuria, 175
Physical illness, 232–293
    asthma, 235–241
    atypical stereotyped movement
        disorder, 247–250
    behavior therapy for, 540–543
    childhood studies in, 233–234
    chronic illness/disability, 270–271
    classification of, 234–235
    developmental disorders, 275–278
    dissociative disorders, 269–270
    eating disorders, 250–260
    elimination disorders, 260–266
    psychosexual disorders, 271–272
    psychosomatic concepts, 233

Physical illness (*Continued*)
  sexual abuse, 272–273
  sleep disorders, 273–275
  somatoform disorders, 266–269
  terminology in, 232–233
  tic disorders, 242–247
  ulcerative colitis, 241–242
Pica, 250
Play behavior, 122, 134, 135, 138
Play therapy, 508–509
Police departments, 399–400. *See also*
    Criminal justice system
Polysymptomatic hysteria, 267
Positron emission tomography (PET),
    297, 302
Prediction:
  autism and, 180–181
  classifications systems and, 2
  delinquency/criminality, 57–64,
    394
  internalizing disorders, 100–101
  stimulant effects, 469–470
  substance disorders, 226
Pregnancy:
  brain disorders, 298
  family system, 339
  see also Perinatal factors; Prenatal
    factors
Premature infants:
  brain disorders, 308–309
  family system and, 342
Prenatal factors:
  brain disorders, 298, 305–308
  infants and, 342–343
Preston Typology Study, 572–573
Primary Mental Health Project
    (PMHP), 628
Problem-solving skills, 126–128
Project Re-Ed, 563–569
Protective/preventive service
    programs, 636–637
Psychedelic drugs, 224
Psychoanalysis:
  educational intervention and, 589
  family factors and, 332
  psychotherapies and, 507
  stress and, 233
  see also Psychotherapies
Psychoeducational model, 599–600
Psychoeducational techniques,
    600–604
Psychogenic pain disorder, 268–269
Psychopharmacotherapy, 455–495
  anticholinergics, 462

anticonvulsants, 461–462
antidepressants, 460–461
antihistamines, 462
antipsychotics (neuroleptics),
    462–463
anxiety disorders and, 474–475
anxiolytics, 461–462
asthma and, 238, 240
attention deficit disorders and, 112,
    115, 118, 132, 133, 135–136,
    137, 464–472
atypical stereotyped movement
    disorder and, 250
brain disorders and, 302
childhood schizophrenia and,
    478–479
classification of drugs in, 458–459
clinical efficacy of, 463–464
conduct disorders and, 51, 472–474
delirium and, 214
depression and, 78, 476–477
educational intervention and,
    606–609
enuresis and, 262–263
lithium, 463
mechanism of action of, 457–458
obsessive-compulsive disorders and,
    477–478
pharmacokinetics and, 456–457
pharmacological principles in,
    455–456
psychostimulants, 459–460
sedatives, 461–462
sleep disorders and, 274
stereotyped movement disorders and,
    479–481
substance disorders and, 222, 225
tic disorders and, 244, 245–246
Psychophysiology:
  asthma, 238–239
  attention deficit disorder, 131–133
  autism, 171–172
  conduct disorders, 46–48
  internalizing disorders, 90–91
  psychosomatic disorders assessment,
    444–445
  schizophrenia, 191
Psychosexual disorders, 271–272
Psychosis:
  history of, 157–159
  term of, 156
  see also Autism; Pervasive
    development disorders;
    Schizophrenia

Psychosocial dwarfism, 251–252
Psychosomatic disorders:
  assessment of, 442–445
  concepts in, 233
  terminology and, 233
  see also Physical illness
Psychostimulants, 459–460
  attention deficit disorder and,
    464–472
  cognition and, 468–469
  prediction of effects of, 469–470
  substance disorders and,
    223–224
Psychotherapies, 496–522
  defined, 496–497
  developmental considerations in,
    511–514
  diagnostic considerations in,
    514–515
  educational interventions and,
    594–595, 606
  effectiveness evaluation problems in,
    504
  historical trends in research in,
    498–504
  research design problems in,
    505–506
  traditional forms, 507–511
  see also Psychoanalysis
Psychotic disorder, 16
Public health departments, 637
Punishment (behavior therapy),
    524–525, 529

Quantitative classification systems, 2.
    See also Statistical classification
    systems

Race differences:
  intelligence tests and, 37
  substance disorders and, 226
  see also Ethnicity
Radiology:
  brain disorders, 301–302
  see also Computed tomography
Rating scales, *see* Tests and testing
Reading ability, 166–167
Reality therapy, 602
Reinforcement procedures:
  behavior therapy, 527–528
  conduct disorders and, 41–43
  family system and, 358
  see also Motivation/reinforcement
    effects

Reliability:
classification systems, 2–3
DSM-III and, 20–25
schizophrenia and, 185
Repetition, 173–174
Residential treatment, 558–582
evaluation design in, 559
group-home setting, 563–571
outcomes of, 572–578
program descriptions/treatment in, 559
program integrity in, 559
progress in, 558
review of studies of, 560–563
Respondent (classical) conditioning, 524
Response cost procedures, 530
Retardation, see Mental retardation
Ritalin (methylphenidate), 465–466
Robert F. Kennedy Youth Center (KYC), 577–578
Rubella, 175
Rumination disorder, 251

Sampling techniques, 9
Schizoid-unresponsive, 15
Schizophrenia, 181–197
affect and, 191–192
age at onset and, 181
at-risk children for, 182, 188, 196–197
autism differentiated from, 158
cognitive processing and, 189–190
epidemiology of, 194
family correlates in, 193
family system and, 344
history of, 157–158, 181–182
intelligence and, 189
language and, 190–191
learning and, 192
motor development and, 192
neuropathology of, 192–193
outcome in, 194–196
parents and, 360–361
perception/attention in, 191
principal characteristics of, 182–185
psychopharmacotherapy for, 478–479
psychophysiological factors in, 191
validity of disorder, 185–188
School-based intervention, 625–634, 648. See also Educational intervention
Sedatives, 461–462

Seizures:
autism and, 175
behavior therapy for, 541–543
see also Epilepsy
Self-care skills, 547–548
Self-control techniques, 529
Self-help groups, 639–640
Self-injurious behavior, 544–546
Self-mutilation, 247–250
Self-report measures:
anxiety, 432–434
attention deficit disorders, 431
conduct disorders, 426–427
depression, 436–437
psychosomatic disorders, 443–444
Self-stimulation, 546–547
Sensorimotor ability, 166, 172–173
Sensory handicaps, 139
Separation (marital), 338. See also Divorce; Family factors
Separation anxiety disorder, 74
Sex differences:
anorexia nervosa, 253
asthma, 235
attention deficit disorder, 140, 141
autism, 178
brain damage and, 321
classification systems and, 17
conduct disorders and, 359–360
divorce and, 365–368
encopresis, 264
internalizing disorders and, 93–94, 96
marital conflicts and, 339, 361
prediction of crime and, 59
psychogenic pain disorder and, 269
schizophrenia and, 194
substance disorders and, 226
tic disorders, 244
Sexual abuse, 272–273
Sexuality:
peer groups and, 406
psychosexual disorders, 271–272
Shaping:
anxiety disorders, 535
behavior therapy and, 526–527
Shyness, see Social withdrawal
Siblings:
conduct disorders and, 362–363
family system and, 351–354
Single-parent families, see Divorce; Family factors
Situation:
attention deficit disorder, 136

statistical classification systems and, 11
Skills training, 547–550
Skin conductance tests, see Electrodermal responding (GSR)
Sleep disorders:
simple problems in, 274–275
sleep walking/night terrors, 273–274
Social cognition:
attention deficit disorder, 133–138
autism, 174–175
internalizing disorders, 88–89
see also Cognition; Intelligence
Social ineptness, 16
Social isolation, see Social withdrawal
Socialized aggressive conduct disorder:
central features of, 36
classification system and, 13
cross-cultural generality and, 18
differentiation of, 35, 37
peer relations and, 44, 45, 403
prediction and, 61
see also Conduct disorders; Undersocialized conduct disorder
Social learning theory, 410–411
Social network interventions, 641–642
Social reinforcement, 41–43
Social service-based interventions, 634, 635–639
Social-skills training, 537–538
Social withdrawal:
academic performance and, 82–83
assessment of, 77
behavior therapy for, 537–538
cognitive functioning and, 78–79
family size and, 352
peer relations and, 84, 86–87
social cognition and, 89
Sociocultural context, 391–422
delinquency theory and, 410–413
educational intervention and, 586–587
ethnicity and, 400–403
factors in, 391
family factors and, 346–347
interrelationships, 391–393
neighborhood, 406–410
peer groups, 403–406
socioeconomic class, 394–400
Socioeconomic class:
assessment of impact of, 398–400
attention deficit disorder and, 142
definition/measurement of, 394–395

Socioeconomic class (*Continued*)
   family size studies and, 352
   intelligence tests and, 37
   juvenile delinquency and, 395–397
   neighborhood and, 406–408
   prediction of crime and, 58–59
   psychological disorders and,
     397–398
Solvents, *see* Inhalants
Somatization disorder, 267
Somatoform disorder, 266–269
Special education, *see* Educational
    intervention
Speech disorders, 276–277
State-Trait Anxiety Inventory for
    Children (STAIC), 433
Statistical classification systems, 8–17
   autism and, 161
   clinical classification compared,
    18–20
   delinquency and, 36
   internalizing disorders and, 73
   reliability of, 26–27
   schizophrenia and, 185
Stereotypies, *see* Atypical stereotyped
    movement disorder
Stimulants, 459–460
   attention deficit disorder and,
    464–472
   cognition and, 468–469
   prediction of effects of, 469–470
   substance disorders and, 223–224
Stimulation seeking, 43–44
Strain theory (juvenile delinquency),
    411
Stress:
   family conflict and, 361–362
   family factors in, 335–337
   psychosomatic relationships and, 233
   substance disorders, 227
Substance disorders, 219–229
   alcohol (and solvents), 221–223
   cannabis/hallucinogens, 224
   correlates of, 226
   delirium and, 214
   drug use patterns, 224–226
   DSM-III and, 219
   etiology, 227

   malingering disorder, 269
   opiates, 223
   outcome in, 227–228
   peer group and, 404, 406
   predictors of, 226
   socioeconomic class and, 398
   stimulants/caffeine, 223–224
   substance-related, 219–220
   substance-use, 220–221
Symbolic modeling, 528
Systematic desensitization:
   anxiety disorders, 535
   seizure management, 542
Systems theory, 332

Tantrums, 544
Teacher ratings:
   attention deficit disorders, 428–429
   conduct disorders, 424
Temperament:
   conduct disorders and, 49
   family system and, 358
   infants and, 341–342
   internalizing disorder and, 91–92
Temptation resistance, 121–122
Tests and testing:
   anxiety disorders, 76–77, 78, 81, 82
   attention deficit disorder, 114–115,
    118, 122–123, 124
   autism, 162, 164
   brain disorders, 299, 302–303
   childhood depression, 77–78,
    79–80, 83, 87–88, 95–96
   conduct disorders, 424
   impulsivity, 120–121
   intelligence, 162–163
   internalizing disorders, 76
   organic disorders, 213
   peer relations and, 84, 85, 87
   social withdrawal, 77, 79
   see also Assessment
Tic disorders, 242–247
   classification of, 242–243
   defined, 242
   occurrence of, 243–244
   outcome in, 246
   psychopathological correlates of,
    244–245

   treatment of, 245–246
Time-out procedures, 530
Tobacco use, 227
Toilet training, 261, 265
Tourette's disorder, 243–247, 480
Toxins:
   attention deficit disorder and, 140
   brain disorders, 312–313
   dietary factors and, 315
Treatment and Education of Autistic
    and Related Communications
    Handicapped Children
    (TEACCH) program, 603
Tricyclics/antidepressants,
    471–472
Tuberous sclerosis, 175
Twin studies:
   behavior problems and, 92
   conduct disorders and, 49–50
   see also Genetics

Ulcerative colitis, 241–242
Undersocialized aggressive conduct
    disorder:
   central features of, 36
   classification system and, 11–13
   cross-cultural generality and, 17
   differentiation of, 35, 37
   peer relations and, 44–45
   prediction and, 61
   stimulation seeking and, 43
   see also Conduct disorder;
    Socialized aggressive conduct
    disorder

Validity, 3
Verbal reinforcement, 41–43
Vicarious modeling, 528
Violence, 57–64
Vomiting, 251
Vulnerability, 335

Withdrawal, *see* Internalizing
    disorders; Social withdrawal
Withdrawal (drug), 220
World Health Organization (WHO)
    classification system, 4, 6, 8,
    18–20